Fodor's 06

AUSTRALIA

Where to Stay and Eat
for All Budgets

Must-See Sights
and Local Secrets

Ratings You Can Trust

Fodor's Travel Publications   New York, Toronto, London, Sydney, Auckland
www.fodors.com

FODOR'S AUSTRALIA 2006
Editor: Sarah Gold

Editorial Production: Tom Holton
Editorial Contributors: Felice Aarons, Roger Allnutt, Melanie Ball, Emily Burg, Caroline Gladstone, Graham Hodgson, Liza Power, Sarah Sper, Shamara Williams
Maps: David Lindroth Inc., Mapping Specialists, *cartographers;* Rebecca Baer and Robert Blake, *map editors*
Design: Fabrizio La Rocca, *creative director;* Guido Caroti, *art director;* Melanie Marin, *senior picture editor*
Cover Design: Moon Sun Kim
Production/Manufacturing: Angela L. McLean
Cover Photo (Camel ride, Cable Beach, Broome): Steven David Miller/Nature Picture Library

ISBN 1–4000–1549–9

ISSN 1095–2675

SPECIAL SALES
This book is available for special discounts for bulk purchases for sales promotions or premiums. Special editions, including personalized covers, excerpts of existing books, and corporate imprints, can be created in large quantities for special needs. For more information, write to Special Markets/Premium Sales, 1745 Broadway, MD 6-2, New York, NY 10019, or e-mail specialmarkets@randomhouse.com.

AN IMPORTANT TIP & AN INVITATION
Although all prices, opening times, and other details in this book are based on information supplied to us at this writing, changes occur all the time in the travel world, and Fodor's cannot accept responsibility for facts that become outdated or for inadvertent errors or omissions. So **always confirm information when it matters,** especially if you're making a detour to visit a specific place. Your experiences—positive and negative—matter to us. If we have missed or misstated something, **please write to us.** We follow up on all suggestions. Contact the Australia editors at editors@fodors.com or c/o Fodor's at 1745 Broadway, New York, NY 10019.

Be a Fodor's Correspondent

Your opinion matters. It matters to us. It matters to your fellow Fodor's travelers, too. And we'd like to hear it. In fact, we *need* to hear it.

When you share your experiences and opinions, you become an active member of the Fodor's community. That means we'll not only use your feedback to make our books better, but we'll publish your names and comments whenever possible. Throughout our guides, look for "Word of Mouth," excerpts of your unvarnished feedback.

Here's how you can help improve Fodor's for all of us.

Tell us when we're right. We rely on local writers to give you an insider's perspective. But our writers and staff editors—who are the best in the business—depend on you. Your positive feedback is a vote to renew our recommendations for the next edition.

Tell us when we're wrong. We're proud that we update most of our guides every year. But we're not perfect. Things change. Hotels cut services. Museums change hours. Charming cafés lose charm. If our writer didn't quite capture the essence of a place, tell us how you'd do it differently. If any of our descriptions are inaccurate or inadequate, we'll incorporate your changes in the next edition and will correct factual errors at fodors.com *immediately*.

Tell us what to include. You probably have had fantastic travel experiences that aren't yet in Fodor's. Why not share them with a community of like-minded travelers? Maybe you chanced upon a beach or bistro or B&B that you don't want to keep to yourself. Tell us why we should include it. And share your discoveries and experiences with everyone directly at fodors.com. Your input may lead us to add a new listing or highlight a place we cover with a "Highly Recommended" star or with our highest rating, "Fodor's Choice."

Give us your opinion instantly at our feedback center at www.fodors.com/feedback. You may also e-mail editors@fodors.com with the subject line "Australia Editor." Or send your nominations, comments, and complaints by mail to Australia Editor, Fodor's, 1745 Broadway, New York, NY 10019.

You and travelers like you are the heart of the Fodor's community. Make our community richer by sharing your experiences. Be a Fodor's correspondent.

Happy traveling!

Tim Jarrell, Publisher

CONTENTS

Maps

CloseUps

ABOUT OUR WRITERS

Roger Allnutt, a freelance writer based in Canberra, is a member of the Australian Society of Travel Writers. His work is published regularly in newspapers and magazines in Australia, New Zealand, the United States, and the United Kingdom. In addition to traveling he enjoys food and wine, classical music, and tennis. Roger updated the Canberra and the A. C.T., Tasmania, and Smart Travel Tips chapters.

Melanie Ball began her career in freelance travel writing and photography somewhere between London and Johannesburg on an overland expedition truck in 1986. Her search for all things colorful, edible, unusual, and simply enjoyable has since taken her from Ethiopia to England and around Australia, and descriptions of her adventures appear in Australian newspapers and magazines. Melanie updated the New South Wales chapter, the Adelaide & South Australia chapter, and part of the Sydney chapter.

A native New Yorker, **Emily Burg** was a financial journalist reporting from Wall Street before she moved Down Under. The now-Sydneysider (and Harbour Bridge climber) encountered some of Australia's most amazing creatures while updating the chapters on tropical north Queensland, the Great Barrier Reef and Sydney—including baby crocodiles, leopard sharks, and even the elusive blue-necked Cassowary. Emily travels frequently between the hemispheres, testing out the efficacy of insect repellents and improving her left-hand-side driving skills.

As a journalist and travel writer for the past 15 years, **Caroline Gladstone** has been across Australia, the world, and the high seas. She was cruise editor of the Australian magazine *Traveltrade* for many years, during which time she cruised on some 25 ships. Caroline, who updated the southern coastal and Outback areas of the Queensland chapter, as well as the Red Centre chapter, is now a freelance travel and feature writer whose articles have appeared in *The Australian* and the *Sunday Telegraph* newspapers, and such magazines as *Holidays for Couples* and *Vacations & Travel*.

A fourth-generation Western Australian, **Graham Hodgson** has spent most of his life in the state's beautiful South West region. His 35-year career spans stints in newspaper journalism, government and corporate communications, regional tourism planning, and regional economic development. He has written about travel in Australia, New Zealand, Indonesia, Malaysia, Singapore, Zimbabwe, Thailand, France, and Italy for numerous newspapers, magazines, and online publications. He lives on a small, 5-acre holding (an escape from the 21st century), alternating his work commitments with tending to fruit trees, vegetables, chickens, hens, four pet sheep, and two cats. He updated the chapters on Perth & Western Australia, and Darwin, the Top End & the Kimberley.

Liza Power, who updated the Melbourne, Victoria, and Adventure Vacations chapters, kicked off her travel-writing career when she trotted off to South America at the age of 19. Numerous months later, she returned to Australia with a serious case of wanderlust. Since then, she has traveled from the Dogon lands of Mali to the steppes of Mongolia, as well as to Bogotá, Libya, Patagonia, and West Papua. Between her overseas jaunts and weekly adventure travel columns for Melbourne's *Age* newspaper, she explores her home state of Victoria.

ABOUT THIS BOOK

Our Ratings

Sometimes you find terrific travel experiences and sometimes they just find you. But usually it's up to you to select the right combination of experiences. That's where our ratings come in.

As travelers we've all discovered a place so wonderful that its worthiness is obvious. And sometimes that place is so experiential that superlatives don't do it justice: you just have to be there to know. These sights, properties, and experiences get our highest rating, **Fodor's Choice**, indicated by orange stars throughout this book.

Black stars highlight sights and properties we deem **Highly Recommended**, places that our writers, editors, and readers praise again and again for consistency and excellence.

By default, there's another category: any place we include in this book is by definition worth your time, unless we say otherwise. And we will.

Disagree with any of our choices? Care to nominate a place or suggest that we rate one more highly? Visit our feedback center at www.fodors.com/feedback.

Budget Well

Hotel and restaurant price categories from ¢ to $$$$ are defined in the opening pages of each chapter. For attractions, we always give standard adult admission fees; reductions are usually available for children, students, and senior citizens. Want to pay with plastic? **AE, DC, MC, V** following restaurant and hotel listings indicate if American Express, Diner's Club, MasterCard, and Visa are accepted.

Restaurants

Unless we state otherwise, restaurants are open for lunch and dinner daily. We mention dress only when there's a specific requirement and reservations only when they're essential or not accepted—it's always best to book ahead.

Hotels

Hotels have private bath, phone, TV, and air-conditioning and operate on the European Plan (a.k.a. EP, meaning without meals), unless we specify that they use the Continental Plan (CP, with a Continental breakfast), Breakfast Plan (BP, with a full breakfast), or Modified American Plan (MAP, with breakfast and dinner) or are all-inclusive (including all meals and most activities). We always

list facilities but not whether you'll be charged an extra fee to use them, so when pricing accommodations, find out what's included.

Many Listings
- ★ Fodor's Choice
- ★ Highly recommended
- ⊠ Physical address
- ⊕ Directions
- ⌂ Mailing address
- ☎ Telephone
- 🖷 Fax
- ⊕ On the Web
- ✉ E-mail
- 🖃 Admission fee
- ☉ Open/closed times
- ▶ Start of walk/itinerary
- Ⓜ Metro stations
- ⊟ Credit cards

Hotels & Restaurants
- 🏨 Hotel
- ⤴ Number of rooms
- ⚲ Facilities
- ⊠ Meal plans
- ✕ Restaurant
- ⚲ Reservations
- 🏛 Dress code
- 🚭 Smoking
- 🅱🆈 BYOB
- ✕🏨 Hotel with restaurant that warrants a visit

Outdoors
- 🏌 Golf
- ⛺ Camping

Other
- 🅒 Family-friendly
- 🔋 Contact information
- ⇨ See also
- ⊠ Branch address
- ☞ Take note

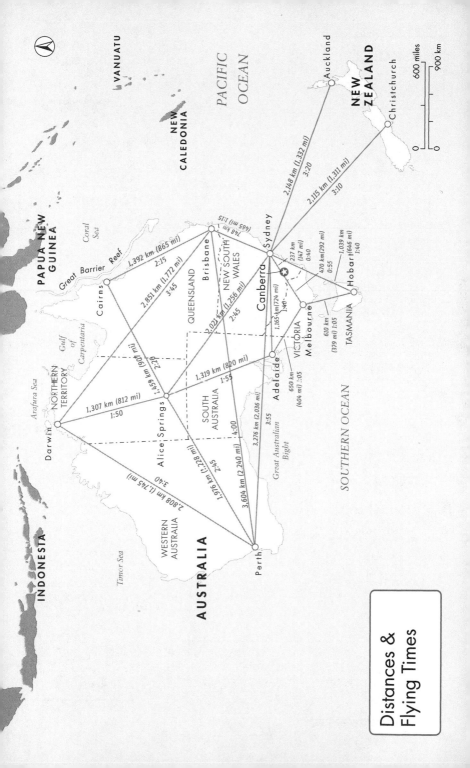

Distances &
Flying Times

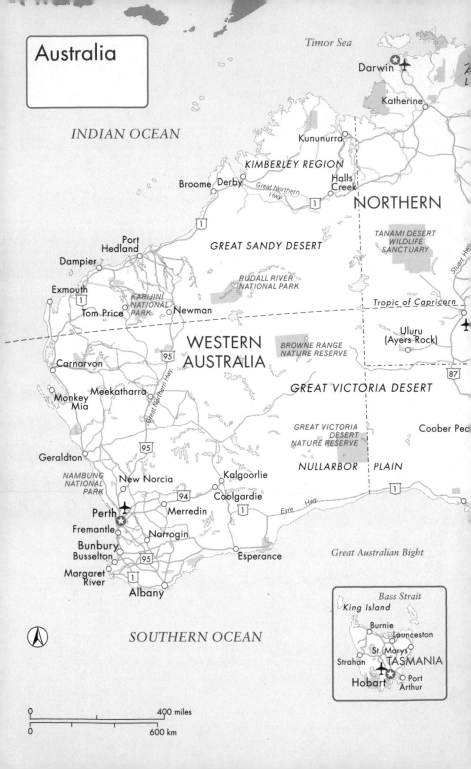

Arafura Sea
KAKADU NATIONAL PARK
Gulf of Carpentaria
PAPUA NEW GUINEA
NHEM
ND
Weipa
CAPE YORK PENINSULA
Coral Sea
Laura
Cooktown
Port Douglas
Mareeba
Cairns
Coral Sea Islands
Burketown
Normanton
Innisfail
GREAT
TERRITORY
Georgetown
Ingham
BARRIER
ennant
Creek
Mt. Isa
Cloncurry
QUEENSLAND
Townsville
Ayr
REEF
66
Hughenden
DIVIDING
Mackay
ice Springs
Bedourie
Longreach
66
Emerald
Blackwater
Rockhampton
Birdsville
Windorah
71
Gladstone
Charleville
54
RANGE
1
Oodnadatta
Lake Eyre
Rama
Kingaroy
Dalby
Nambour
71
Cunnamulla
Toowoomba
Brisbane
SOUTH
Marree
Goondiwindi
Warwick
AUSTRALIA
Lake Torrens
FLINDERS RANGES NATIONAL PARK
Bourke
Moree
Lismore
Pacific Hwy.
eduna
Port Augusta
Walgett
Armidale
Grafton
NEW
71
Nyngan
Coffs Harbour
Port Pirie
32
Broken Hill
SOUTH
Dubbo
Kempsey
Port Macquarie
WALES
1
Renmark
Mildura
Orange
Bathurst
Cowra
Young
Newcastle
Port
ncoln
Adelaide
Hay
Sydney
Kangaroo Island
Bordertown
VICTORIA
Shepparton
Bendigo
Albury
Canberra
Wollongong
Mt. Gambier
Ballarat
Seymour
Cooma
1
Portland
Colac
Melbourne
Bega
EYRE PENINSULA
Warrnambool
Wonthaggi
Geelong
Sale
Bairnsdale
Orbost
King Island
Bass Strait
Flinders Island
TASMANIA
(SEE INSET)
Murray R.
Sturt Hwy.
Mitchell Hwy.
Bruce Hwy.
GREAT DIVIDING RANGE

Australia is an ancient land. Originally part of the Gondwanaland super-continent that included present-day South America, Africa, Antarctica, India, and New Zealand, the island continent began to migrate to its current position around 100 million years ago. The eastern seaboard is backed by the Great Dividing Range, which parallels the coastline from northern Queensland all the way south into western Victoria. Watered by swift rivers, this littoral region is clothed with rolling pasturelands and lush rain forests. Off the coast of Queensland, the Great Barrier Reef runs from Cape York 2,000 km (1,250 mi) southward. Inland, beyond the Great Dividing Range, semiarid plains cover much of Queensland, New South Wales, Victoria, and South Australia. Deserts cover much of the rest of the country, including most of Western Australia and the Red Centre. Tasmania floats south of the mainland, looking on maps like it's plunging toward the Antarctic.

If you're coming from the Northern Hemisphere, remember that the compass is turned upside down: the farther north you go *toward* the equator, the hotter it gets. Australia is bisected by the Tropic of Capricorn—meaning that overall the continent is rather close to the equator—while the United States and Europe lie well above the Tropic of Cancer.

① Sydney

The vibrant, cosmopolitan gateway to Australia covers the waterfront with audacious Aussie attitude, sprawl, and pop culture. On the southeast coast of Australia and the state of New South Wales, Sydney is a city surrounded by beaches. And it's a city that whips up some of the most astonishing food on the current world scene, a Eurasian cornucopia overflowing with seafood and exotic flavors. You're bound to spend at least a couple of days here—take hold of them with both hands.

② New South Wales

Although Sydney may be the ultimate urban experience south of Hong Kong, southeastern Australia displays virtually all of the continent's rural and coastal variations: historic towns, mountain ranges, seductive sands, subtropical rain forest, and extensive vineyards. All of these variations make for great outdoor activities: hiking, scuba diving, fishing, skiing, trail riding, cave exploring, and rafting.

③ Canberra & the A. C. T.

The nation's spacious and immaculately landscaped capital city, Canberra sits between Sydney and Melbourne in the Australian Capital Territory (A.C.T.), in the midst of mountain ranges and rivers. Canberra has interesting architecture and museums and is the closest city to some of Australia's greatest national parks.

④ ⑤ Melbourne & Victoria

Melbourne, on the southern coast of Australia and the state of Victoria, is the urbane, cultivated sister of brassy Sydney. Outside the city you can watch fairy penguins on Phillip Island, marvel at the sculpted South Ocean coastline, sample excellent wines, or explore splendid national parks.

6 Tasmania

From Freycinet Peninsula to the wilds of Southwest National Park, Tasmania is a place of intoxicating natural beauty. The island, separated from the southeast coast of Australia by the Bass Strait, is a hiker's dream, rich with wilderness still unexplored. Remnants of the island's volatile days as a penal colony are in numerous small museums and historic sites.

7 8 Queensland & the Great Barrier Reef

A fusion of Florida, Las Vegas, and the Caribbean Islands, Queensland and the Great Barrier Reef draw crowd lovers and escapists alike. Name your outdoor pleasure and you'll probably find it here, whether you wish to explore marine wonders, stroll from cabana to casino, pose in front of the monumental kitsch of the Gold Coast, or cruise rivers and rain forests with fascinating tropical creatures.

9 Adelaide & South Australia

Come to park-enveloped Adelaide for its biennial Festival of the Arts or simply for a calmer-than-Sydney urban experience. Elsewhere in the state, you can step back in time on Kangaroo Island, explore Australia's celebrated wineries of the Barossa Region, or unwind on a Murray River cruise. South Australia also provides a chance to take in Australian wildlife and to trek through Flinders Ranges National Park.

10 The Red Centre

For tens of thousands of years, this vast desert territory, named for the deep color of its soil, has been occupied by Aboriginal people. Uluṟu, also known as Ayers Rock, is a great symbol in Aboriginal traditions, as are many sacred sites among Red Centre's mountain ranges, gorges, dry riverbeds, and spinifex plains. At the center lies Alice Springs, Australia's only desert city.

11 Darwin, the Top End & the Kimberley

From Darwin Harbor to the rocky domes and towers of Purnululu National Park, the Top End and the Kimberley's landforms are stunning and diverse. Besides being breathtakingly beautiful, this area of northern Australia holds many examples of ancient Aboriginal rock art. Darwin and Broome—both far closer to Asia than to any Australian cities—host the most racially diverse populations of the nation.

12 Perth & Western Australia

Those who make it to the "undiscovered country" of Australia's largest state are stunned by its sheer diversity. Relax on beautiful beaches, wonder at coastal formations in Nambung National Park, or swim with dolphins at Monkey Mia or Ningaloo Reef Marine Park. Explore the goldfields east of Perth or the historic towns, wineries, and seaside parks of the South West.

GREAT ITINERARIES

Highlights of Australia
16 or 17 days

This tour surveys the misty heights of Tasmania's Cradle Mountain, the steamy wetlands of Kakadu, the central deserts, and the northern rain forests. It finishes in Port Douglas, where you may want to linger if time permits.

SYDNEY

2 or 3 days. Spend a day cruising the harbor and exploring the Rocks. Take an evening stroll past the Opera House to the Royal Botanic Gardens. The next day take a Sydney Explorer bus tour and visit Darling Harbour, followed by dinner at Cockle Bay Wharf or Chinatown. Day 3 could be spent in Paddington, with a trip to Bondi Beach. ⇨ *Exploring Sydney and Beaches in Chapter 1.*

BLUE MOUNTAINS

1 day. Stop at Wentworth Falls for a view across the Jamison Valley and the National Pass trail. Pause for refreshments at Leura; then continue along Cliff Drive to Blackheath, with its great hiking and antiques shops. ⇨ *The Blue Mountains in Chapter 2.*

TASMANIA

6 days. Spend the first afternoon strolling Hobart's waterfront. The following day, drive to Port Arthur and explore Australia's convict past. On Day 3, head for Freycinet National Park and hike to Wineglass Bay; then overnight in Launceston. Finish off with two days of hiking in Cradle Mountain–Lake St. Clair National Park before driving back to Hobart for your final night. ⇨ *Hobart, Port Arthur, Freycinet National Park & East-Coast Resorts, and Launceston in Chapter 6.*

ULURU

2 days. Fly into Alice Springs to experience Uluru (Ayers Rock), a monolith that resonates with mystical force. Explore its base the first day, spend the night in town, and visit the vast Kata Tjuta (the Olgas) on Day 2. ⇨ *Uluru and Kata Tjuta in Chapter 10.*

KAKADU

2 days. Fly into Darwin and head for Kakadu National Park, with its escarpments, wetlands, and ancient Aboriginal rock art. ⇨ *Kakadu National Park in Chapter 11.*

Darwin — 256 km — Kakadu NP

GULF OF CARPENTARIA

3 hrs 45 min

NORTHERN TERRITORY

2 hrs

2 hrs

Western MacDonnell Ranges — Finke Gorge NP — **Alice Springs**

Kings Canyon — 450 km

Ayers Rock/ Uluru NP/ Olgas/Kata Tjuta Domes — 440 km

4 hrs

Flinders Ranges NP

St. Mary's Peak — Wilpena Pound

2 hrs

Port Augusta — 460 km

Barossa Valley

Adelaide — 70 km

MAP KEY
Highlights of Australia
Into the Outback

Cape
Tribulation
Port
Douglas
Cairns

PORT DOUGLAS

3 days. From Cairns drive north to small, glamorous Port Douglas, where catamarans and sloops cruise to the Great Barrier Reef. Take one day to explore the surrounding rain forest and another for a four-wheel-drive tour to Cape Tribulation. ⇨ *North from Cairns in Chapter 7.*

By Public Transportation

Daily flights depart from Sydney to Hobart (2 hours), from Hobart to Alice Springs via Melbourne (4 hours), from Alice Springs to Darwin (2 hours), and from Darwin to Cairns (3 hours, 45 minutes). From each hub you can rent a car or join a tour to get around.

Into the Outback
11 to 14 days

In the raw, brooding Outback, with a little imagination you can go back to a time when Earth was created by the giant ancestral beings from whom the Aboriginal people trace their lineage.

ADELAIDE

2 days. Begin the day with a visit to the Central Market area and a tour of the historic buildings along North Terrace. Stroll through the Botanic Gardens before catching a Pop-Eye launch back to the city center. Later head for the cafés in Rundle Mall. Spend the next day touring the wineries of the Barossa Region. ⇨ *Adelaide and Barossa Region in Chapter 9.*

FLINDERS RANGES NATIONAL PARK

3 days. From Adelaide, drive or join a four-wheel-drive tour via Port Augusta to Flinders Ranges and its towering crimson hills. Take time to ascend St. Mary's Peak at Wilpena Pound, an 80-square-km (31-square-mi) bowl ringed by quartzite hills. ⇨ *The Outback in Chapter 9.*

ALICE SPRINGS

2 days. Spend the afternoon viewing Aboriginal art in the galleries or on an excursion into the West MacDonnell Ranges. The next day head out from Alice Springs on the scenic Mereenie Loop, which also links Kings Canyon and Finke Gorge National Park, to visit Uluru (Ayers Rock). ⇨ *Alice Springs and Side Trips from Alice Springs in Chapter 10.*

ULURU

2 to 4 days. Take time to wonder at the magnificent Uluru (Ayers Rock) and then head out to visit Kata Tjuta (the Olgas) and hike through the Valley of the Winds. Spend one or more days on an Aboriginal guided tour learning about indigenous culture and lifestyle. ⇨ *Uluru and Kata Tjuta in Chapter 10.*

KAKADU

2 or 3 days. Kick back and enjoy the warm climate, abundant wildlife, and sandstone caves. When Aborigines camped here aeons ago they daubed the walls with ocher, clay, and charcoal. ⇨ *Kakadu National Park in Chapter 11.*

By Public Transportation

Flights depart daily from Adelaide to Alice Springs (2 hours), Alice Springs to Darwin (2 hours), and Darwin back to Adelaide (4½ hours). Use these cities as bases—either rent a car or take day tours of the sights mentioned.

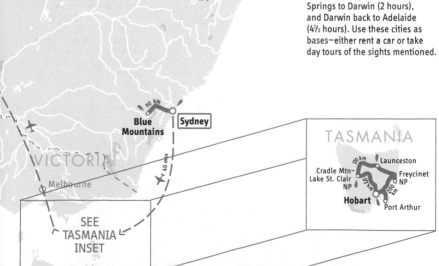

Blue Mountains | **Sydney**

90 km

VICTORIA

Melbourne

140 min

SEE TASMANIA INSET

TASMANIA

Cradle Mtn–Lake St. Clair NP
110 km
Launceston
Freycinet NP
175 km
Hobart
200 km
Port Arthur

Wines & Scenery of the Southeast
10 days

The continent's southeast corner holds serenity, grace, and some wonderful wines along with quiet country towns, Victorian architecture, and a rugged coastline.

RUTHERGLEN
1 day. Rutherglen's vineyards produce Australia's finest fortified wines. A half-day tour introduces you to Tokays, muscats, and ports underpinned with subtle layers of fruit. ⇨ *Murray River Region in Chapter 5.*

BENDIGO
2 days. At the northern extremity of Victoria's goldfields region, Bendigo prospered most from the gold rush of the 1850s and has a rich legacy of Victorian architecture. Ballarat, another gold-rush settlement, hosts reenactments of prosperous days. Between Bendigo and Ballarat lies Maldon, also well preserved. Down the road the Hepburn Springs Spa Resort has flotation tanks, saunas, a relaxation pool, and hot tubs. ⇨ *Gold Country in Chapter 5.*

MELBOURNE
2 days. In Australia's serene and gracious second-largest city spend a day exploring the riverside Southgate complex and the parks and gardens to the east. Then head for the bay-side suburb of St. Kilda for a walk along the Esplanade. Next day tour the Dandenongs, driving through the cool, moist hills of Belgrave and Sherbrooke. ⇨ *Victoria in Chapter 5.*

GREAT OCEAN ROAD
2 days. Pause at the charming village of Lorne; then circle rainforested Otway National Park and head for Port Campbell National Park, where you can see the Twelve Apostles, and other huge, beautiful limestone formations rising out fo the sea. Overnight in Port Fairy, take the Shipwreck Walk along the coast the nxt morning, and then drive across the South Australian border. ⇨ *West-Coast Region in Chapter 5.*

ADELAIDE
3 days. Devote a day to walking along the North Terrace to the Botanic Gardens and zoo, and another in the Adelaide Hills. The village of Hahndorf, founded by German settlers during the 19th century, is full of stone and timber structures. In the evening visit Warrawong Earth Sanctuary for wildlife-watching. Spend another day seeing the Barossa Region's wineries, fine restaurants, and historic inns. ⇨ *Adelaide, the Adelaide Hills, and the Barossa Region in Chapter 9.*

By Public Transportation
A rental car is the best means of transportation.

Tropical Wonders
13 or 14 days

The east coast's riotous greenery, tropical islands, and year-round warmth, not to mention the spectacular Great Barrier Reef, are difficult to resist.

BRISBANE
1 day. Explore the Queensland capital's city center and the South Bank Parklands. In the evening head for one of the riverside restaurants at Eagle Street Pier. ⇨ *Brisbane in Chapter 7.*

THE SUNSHINE COAST
2 days. Drive an hour north to stylish Noosa Heads, with its balmy climate, scenic beaches, and boutiques, cafés, and restaurants. ⇨ *Sunshine Coast & Airlie Beach in Chapter 7.*

FRASER ISLAND
2 days. Fly to Hervey Bay and take a ferry to Fraser Island to join a four-wheel-drive tour of rocky headlands, the rusting wreck of the *Maheno*, and towering sand dunes. In the interior are paperbark swamps, freshwater lakes, and forests of brush box trees. ⇨ *Fraser Island in Chapter 7.*

HERON ISLAND
2 days. Back at Hervey Bay, fly to Gladstone and then head on to this Great Barrier Reef island, where you can spend your time diving or bird-watching. ⇨ *Mackay–Capricorn Islands in Chapter 8.*

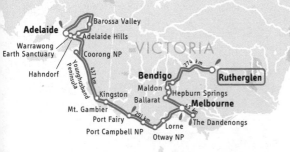

PORT DOUGLAS

3 days. Fly from Gladstone to Cairns, drive to Port Douglas, and spend the first day exploring this relaxed town. Devote another day to hiking the Mossman Gorge trails or cruising the Great Barrier Reef. If the weather sours, head toward Cairns and take the train through the rain forest to Kuranda. Return to Cairns via the Skyrail Rainforest Cableway. ⇨ *Cairns and North from Cairns in Chapter 7.*

CAPE TRIBULATION

2 days. Keep driving north from Port Douglas to this area of untamed beaches and rain forests. As the spirit moves you, stop for hiking, horseback riding, and beach combing on half-deserted strands. ⇨ *North from Cairns in Chapter 7.*

COOKTOWN

1 or 2 days. North from Cape Tribulation, the rough Bloomfield Track and numerous river crossings make the four-wheel-drive journey to Cooktown an adventure. Stop along the way at the spectacular Mossman Gorge, and have a pint and a meal at Ironbar in Port Douglas. ⇨ *North from Cairns in Chapter 7.*

By Public Transportation

Fly from Brisbane to Hervey Bay (one hour), where car ferries chug to Fraser Island from River Heads and Inskip Point. Daily flights connect Hervey Bay with Gladstone (one hour), and it's a two-hour boat trip or 25-minute helicopter ride from there to Heron Island. Daily flights link Gladstone to Cairns (one hour), where you can rent a car to tour Port Douglas and the north. In each region, the best way to get around is to rent a four-wheel-drive vehicle or join a tour.

°C	°F
100	212
40	105
37	98.6
30	90
25	80
20	70
15	60
10	50
5	40
0	32
-5	20
-10	10
-15	0
-20	

Australia is in the Southern Hemisphere, so the seasons are reversed. It's winter Down Under during the American and European summer.

The ideal time to visit the north, particularly the Northern Territory's Kakadu National Park, is early in the dry season (around May). Birdlife remains profuse on the drying floodplains, and waterfalls are still spectacular and accessible. The Dry (April–October) is also a good time to visit northern Queensland's beaches and rain forests. You can swim off the coast without fear of dangerous stinging box jellyfish, which infest ocean waters between November and March. In rain forests, heat and humidity are lower than later in the year, and crocodile viewing is at its prime, as the creatures tend to bask on riverbanks rather than submerge in the colder water.

During school holidays, Australians take to the roads in droves. Accommodations and attractions are crowded and hotel rooms and rental cars are unlikely to be discounted during these periods. The busiest period is mid-December to the end of January, which is the equivalent of the U.S. and British summer break. The dates of other school vacations vary from state to state, but generally fall around Easter, mid-June to July, and late September to mid-October.

Climate

Australia's climate is temperate in southern states, such as Victoria and Tasmania, particularly in coastal areas, and tropical in Australia's far north. The Australian summer north of the Tropic of Capricorn is a steam bath. Remember that by comparison no parts of North America or Europe are anywhere near as close to the equator. From September through November (the Australian spring), or from February through April (late summer–autumn), southern regions are generally sunny and warm, with only occasional rain in Sydney, Melbourne, and Adelaide. Perth and the south of Western Australia are at their finest in springtime, when wildflowers blanket the land. Some people would say that spring and fall are the best times to travel to Australia, unless you're dying to get away from a northern winter.

The following are average daily maximum and minimum temperatures for some major Australian cities.

🎬 Forecasts **Weather Channel Connection** ☎ 900/932-8437 95¢ per min from a Touch-Tone phone ⊕ www.weather.com.

SYDNEY

Jan.	79F	26C	May	67F	19C	Sept.	67F	17C
	65	18		52	11		52	11
Feb.	79F	26C	June	61F	16C	Oct.	72F	22C
	65	18		49	9		56	13
Mar.	76F	24C	July	61F	16C	Nov.	74F	23C
	63	17		49	9		61	16
Apr.	72F	22C	Aug.	63F	17C	Dec.	77F	25C
	58	14		49	9		63	17

MELBOURNE

Jan.	79F	26C	May	63F	17C	Sept.	63F	17C
	58	14		47	8		47	8
Feb.	79F	26C	June	58F	14C	Oct.	67F	19C
	58	14		45	7		49	9
Mar.	76F	24C	July	56F	13C	Nov.	72F	22C
	56	13		43	6		52	11
Apr.	68F	20C	Aug.	59F	15C	Dec.	76F	24C
	52	11		43	6		54	12

HOBART

Jan.	72F	22C	May	58F	14C	Sept.	59F	15C
	54	12		45	7		43	6
Feb.	72F	22C	June	54F	12C	Oct.	63F	17C
	54	12		41	5		47	8
Mar.	68F	20C	July	52F	11C	Nov.	67F	19C
	52	11		40	4		49	9
Apr.	63F	17C	Aug.	56F	13C	Dec.	70F	21C
	49	9		41	5		52	11

CAIRNS

Jan.	90F	32C	May	81F	27C	Sept.	83F	28C
	74	23		67	19		65	18
Feb.	90F	32C	June	79F	26C	Oct.	86F	30C
	74	23		65	18		68	20
Mar.	88F	31C	July	79F	26C	Nov.	88F	31C
	74	23		61	16		70	21
Apr.	85F	29C	Aug.	81F	27C	Dec.	90F	32C
	70	21		63	17		74	23

ALICE SPRINGS

Jan.	97F	36C	May	74F	23C	Sept.	81F	27C
	70	21		47	8		49	9
Feb.	95F	35C	June	67F	19C	Oct.	88F	31C
	70	21		41	5		58	14
Mar.	90F	32C	July	67F	19C	Nov.	94F	34C
	63	17		40	4		65	18
Apr.	81F	27C	Aug.	74F	23C	Dec.	97F	36C
	54	12		43	6		68	20

DARWIN

Jan.	90F	32C	May	92F	33C	Sept.	92F	33C
	77	25		74	23		74	23
Feb.	90F	32C	June	88F	31C	Oct.	94F	34C
	77	25		70	21		77	25
Mar.	92F	33C	July	88F	31C	Nov.	94F	34C
	77	25		67	19		79	26
Apr.	92F	33C	Aug.	90F	32C	Dec.	92F	33C
	76	24		70	21		79	26

PERTH

Jan.	85F	29C	May	69F	20C	Sept.	70F	21C
	63	17		53	12		50	10
Feb.	85F	29C	June	64F	18C	Oct.	76F	24C
	63	17		50	10		53	12
Mar.	81F	27C	July	63F	17C	Nov.	81F	27C
	61	16		48	9		57	14
Apr.	76F	24C	Aug.	67F	19C	Dec.	83F	28C
	57	14		48	9		61	16

CANBERRA

Jan.	85F	29C	May	61F	16C	Sept.	61F	16C
	58	14		49	4		49	4
Feb.	85F	29C	June	54F	12C	Oct.	68F	20C
	58	14		36	2		45	7
Mar.	77F	25C	July	54F	12C	Nov.	76F	24C
	54	12		32	0		50	10
Apr.	68F	20C	Aug.	58F	14C	Dec.	79F	26C
	45	7		34	1		54	12

Annual and biennial events include international cultural festivals, sporting matches, and uniquely Australian celebrations with a distinctly tongue-in-cheek flavor. With performing arts centers in most capital cities, arts festivals are major events on the calendar.

For more information about those festivals listed below without contact numbers, get in touch with the tourist office of the host city or region. Information about local tourist offices is listed in the A to Z section of each chapter.

SUMMER

January	**New Year's Day** is observed as a holiday nationwide.
January	**Sydney Festival,** which begins with harborside fireworks on New Year's Eve, is a monthlong, multicultural celebration with concerts, circuses, arts workshops, ferryboat races, and theater events.
January 26	**Australia Day** celebrates the founding of the nation with ferry races and other colorful boating activities on Sydney Harbour and fireworks at night at Darling Harbour.
February & March	**Sydney Gay and Lesbian Mardi Gras** fetes lesbian and gay life with a month of theater, performances, and art and photography exhibitions, culminating in a spectacular parade.
	Adelaide Festival of the Arts, Australia's monthlong feast of arts and culture, takes place every even-numbered year.
	WOMAdelaide Festival of world music is staged in Adelaide during odd-numbered years.
	Melbourne Formula 1 Grand Prix, held at Albert Park on the outskirts of the city, is Australia's premier motoring event.

AUTUMN

March	**Canberra Multicultural Festival** is the national capital's major annual event, lasting for 10 days, with a colorful hot-air balloon fiesta, music, concerts, and a street parade.
2nd or 3rd wk in March	**Melbourne Moomba Waterfest** is Melbourne's lighthearted end-of-summer celebration.
March or April	**Easter** holiday is observed Good Friday through Easter Monday.
March or April	The East Coast Blues and Roots Festival is Australia's premier blues music event, held under three big tents at Easter in Byron Bay. The likes of James Brown and Bo Diddley have entertained the music-loving crowd that return to this fantastic five-day event year after year.

March & April	**Barossa Vintage Festival,** the best-known wine-region harvest celebration, bears the stamp of the valley's Germanic heritage and highlights the joys of wine, food, music, and culture. The festival takes place around Easter every odd-numbered year.
April 25	**Anzac Day** honors fallen members of Australia's armed forces.
WINTER	
2nd Mon. in June	**Queen's Birthday** is observed in every state but Western Australia, which celebrates it in September or October.
July	**Camel Cup Races** in Alice Springs have to be seen to be believed, as do the carnival's concurrent camel polo matches.
August	**Darwin Cup** is the premier horse race of northern Australia, bringing a colorful brigade to Darwin from the cattle stations, Aboriginal communities, and islands across the Top End.
	Beer Can Regatta in Darwin shows a fine sensitivity to recycling: the sailing craft are constructed from used beer cans!
	Festival of Darwin celebrates the dry season.
SPRING	
September & October	**Warana Festival,** usually held over a 10-day period, celebrates Brisbane in spring blossom with arts, entertainment, and a series of gala events, including a festive parade.
	The **Birdsville Races** bring station owners and cattle musterers to Birdsville, Queensland, on the edge of the Simpson Desert, for a weekend of horse racing, socializing, and hard drinking.
	Floriade, in Canberra, is the largest floral show in Australia.
	Henley-On-Todd Regatta in Alice Springs is a boat race held in a dry riverbed. Crews "wear" the boats, and leg power replaces rowing.
	Fun in the Sun Festival in Cairns highlights the city's tropical setting with a grand parade, entertainment, exhibitions, and a yacht race.
November	**Mango Festival** in Broome, in Western Australia, is a rollicking big beach party with music and a mango cook-off.
	Melbourne International Festival of the Arts schedules Australia's top performing artists, along with outstanding international productions, at the Victorian Arts Centre and venues around Melbourne.
1st Tues. in November	**Melbourne Cup** is one of Australia's most famous sporting events— a horse race that brings the nation to a virtual standstill.
December	**Sydney to Hobart Yacht Race,** one of the world's classic blue-water races, runs from Sydney to Hobart, Tasmania, in two to three days.
December 25 & 26	**Christmas Day** and **Boxing Day** are holidays in all states.

PLEASURES & PASTIMES

Beautiful Beaches Australia is renowned for its beaches. Along its coastline are miles and miles of pristine sand where you can sunbathe in solitary splendor. Sydney has nearly 40 ocean beaches and many calm-water harbor beaches, while Queensland's Gold Coast is a 70-km (43-mi) stretch of clean sand washed by warm, moderate surf. Whitehaven—a beautiful near-deserted arc of a beach in the Whitsunday Islands—has some of the whitest, most powdery sand on earth. Fringing the Indian Ocean between Perth and South Fremantle are 19 wide beaches with good breaks.

Bushwalking With so much birdlife, flora, and fauna to admire, hiking—Aussies call it "bushwalking"—is a pleasurable and popular pastime. Get yourself out into one of the country's parks—the Australian bush is a national treasure. Australia has dozens of national parks, all with picnic areas and well-marked trails, and many with designated camping areas.

Country Vineyards Australian wines are among the best in the world, a judgment that international wine shows consistently reinforce. Established wine-growing areas include the Hunter Valley in New South Wales, South Australia's Barossa and Clare valleys, Margaret River in Western Australia, and the Yarra Valley and Mornington Peninsula regions of Victoria. Despite the differences in climate, Tasmania and southeastern Queensland have also emerged over the past decade as vineyard regions. Although many varietals are grown in these regions, Australia is particularly renowned for its excellent chardonnay and shiraz.

Dining in Oz Contemporary Australian cuisine emphasizes fresh ingredients, such as seasonal vegetables and fish. Each state has its own specialties, particularly seafood. "Bush tucker," the food native to Australia, which includes berries, herbs, and fruits, is found in many fashionable restaurants. "Mod-Oz" (Modern Australian) cuisine blends Mediterranean and Asian techniques and spices with uniquely Australian ingredients.

Underwater Australia With 36,735 km (22,776 mi) of coast bordering two oceans and four seas, Australians spend a good deal of their time in and on the water. Opportunities abound for scuba diving, snorkeling, surfing, waterskiing, and windsurfing. Prime diving season is September–December and mid-March–May.

FODOR'S CHOICE

The sights, restaurants, hotels, and other travel experiences on these pages are our editors' top picks—our Fodor's Choices. They're the best of their type in the area covered by the book—not to be missed and always worth your time. In the destination chapters that follow, you will find all the details.

LODGING

$$$$	**Bedarra Island Resort, Great Barrier Reef, Queensland.** World-famous faces jet to this all-inclusive resort, which provides the ultimate in tropical pampering.
$$$$	**Boroka Downs, Halls Gap, Victoria.** Sumptuous boutique suites have up-close views of local wildlife and the Grampians.
$$$$	**Cape Lodge, Margaret River, Western Australia.** Settled into neat vineyards and overlooking a private lake, this opulent Cape Dutch bed-and-breakfast brings a taste of South Africa to the region.
$$$$	**Lizard Island Lodge, Great Barrier Reef, Queensland.** The reef's most idyllic island retreat is the perfect tropical getaway.
$$$$	**Longitude 131°, Ayers Rock Resort, Red Centre.** Watch the sun rise and set over Uluru from your very, very comfortable bed.
$$$	**Observatory Hotel, Sydney.** Four stories of antiques and mahogany furnishings evoke the cozy opulence of a country estate.
$$$$	**Palazzo Versace, Main Beach, Queensland.** Billed as the only six-star hotel in Australia, this Gold Coast resort is all gold, marble, silk, and satin (and full of platinum guests.)
$$$$	**Park Hyatt, Sydney.** Spacious, elegant rooms all have balconies, sparkling views of the Opera House, and personal butler service.
$$$$	**Peppers Convent, Pokolbin, New South Wales.** This luxurious Hunter Valley home is a former convent surrounded by vineyards.
$$$$	**Rae's on Watego's, Byron Bay, New South Wales.** If high design is your cup of tea, check out this luxurious Mediterranean-style villa, where suites are decorated with an exotic collection of antiques and Indonesian art.
$$$$	**Seven Spirit Bay Wilderness Lodge, Gurig National Park, Northern Territory.** At this remote resort, accessible only by plane, nature walks and four-wheel-drive safaris let you see dingoes, wallabies, crocodiles, buffalo, and Timorese ponies in the wild.
$$$$	**Sheraton Mirage, Main Beach, Queensland.** Gaze over the breakers of the Pacific Ocean from your room and the white swans gliding on the resort's serene lagoon.

$$$$	**Silky Oaks Lodge and Restaurant, Mossman, Queensland.** Villas on stilts sit amid national parkland and verdant rain forest.
$$$–$$$$	**Henry Jones Art Hotel, Hobart, Tasmania.** Right on the Hobart waterfront, this row of historic warehouses has been transformed into a sensational, chic, art-theme hotel.
$$$–$$$$	**Hyatt Hotel Canberra.** This elegant hotel, which occupies a 1924 National Heritage building, has opulent marble bathtubs perfect for soaking.
$$$–$$$$	**Kingfisher Bay Resort and Village, Fraser Island, Queensland.** The perfect retreat after a day exploring glorious Fraser Island's sand dunes, wild beaches, and inland lakes and rain forests.
$$$–$$$$	**Park Hyatt, Melbourne.** This elegant, boutique-style hotel is perfectly set between Fitzroy Gardens and opulent Victorian buildings.
$$$–$$$$	**Villa Gusto, Victoria, Alpine National Park, Victoria.** Cast-iron fountains, 17th-century antiques, and exquisite tapestries add Italianate authenticity to the suites and the restaurant here.
$$–$$$$	**Freycinet Lodge, Freycinet National Park, Tasmania.** These 60 plush cabins are scattered among the densely wooded forest above Great Oyster Bay.
$$–$$$$	**Queenscliff Hotel, Victoria.** Gloriously restored to its original, 19th-century state, with pressed-metal ceilings, stained-glass windows, and elegant firelit sitting rooms.
$–$$$$	**Kings Canyon Resort, Red Centre.** View amazing landscapes from your whirlpool bath or while sipping champagne on the deck.
$$$	**Abbotsford Country House, South Australia.** A magnificent country house on 50 acres of vineyards has views of the Barossa Valley.
$$$	**Surfers Paradise Marriott Resort, Queensland.** This hotel on the Gold Coast has the ultimate "pool with a view," where brightly colored fish share the lagoon waters with real coral.
$$–$$$	**Hatherley House, Launceston, Tasmania.** This exquisite 1830s mansion in lush gardens is now a trendsetting hotel.
$$–$$$	**Rydges Capital Hill, Canberra.** Close to Parliament House, this hotel and its bar are a hub for parliamentary staff and members of the press.
$$	**Vineyard Cottages and Café, Queensland.** Dine in an early-20th-century church, sipping Granite Belt wines, then walk to your cozy cottage for the night.
$–$$	**Brickendon, Longford, Tasmania.** Children are welcome at this 1824 colonial village and farm surrounded by historic buildings.

$–$$	**Larkrise House, Foster, Victoria.** Forty acres of rolling farmland with glorious sea views—and lovely picture windows through which to enjoy them.
$–$$	**Matilda's of Ranelagh, Huon Valley, Tasmania** The official greeters at this delightful, 1850 Heritage-listed B&B are five golden retrievers.
$	**Whitsunday Moorings Bed and Breakfast, Airlie Beach, Queensland.** Views of the Whitsunday Islands are to die for, as you sip coffee or cocktails at this laid-back resort.

DINING

$$$$	**e'cco, Brisbane.** This intimate restaurant serves arguably the best Mod-Oz food in Brisbane.
$$$$	**Loose Box, Perth.** Owner-chef Alain Fabregues has received France's highest culinary honor, the Meilleur Ouvrier de France, as well as a French knighthood for his contribution to French culture and cuisine.
$$$$	**Robert's at Pepper Tree, Pokolbin, New South Wales.** In this airy, country-style dining room, you can try char-grilled quail or basil-and-pine-nut-crusted John Dory fillet.
$$$–$$$$	**Rockpool, Sydney.** This seductive chrome-and-glass restaurant fuses Mediterranean, Middle Eastern, Chinese, and Thai flavors.
$$$	**Kuniya Restaurant, Ayers Rock Resort, Red Centre.** Aboriginal mythology adorns the walls as you explore Australia with dishes from each state.
$$$	**Oyster Bay Meads, Mosman Bay, Perth.** Views of yachts and pelicans plus superb seafood make this Perth restaurant irresistible.
$$–$$$	**Café di Stasio, Melbourne.** A sleek marble bar and modishly ravaged walls contribute to the sense that you've stepped into a scene from *La Dolce Vita*.
$$–$$$	**Fee and Me, Launceston, Tasmania.** Tasmania's top dining spot focuses on succulent seafood and dressed-up home-style meals.
$$–$$$	**Steam Packet, Hobart, Tasmania.** Feast on local seafood, beef, and game while enjoying the alfresco scene on Hunter Street's Old Wharf.
$$	**Anise, Canberra.** The banana-and-frangipani tart, served with rum ice cream, is a superb way to finish your meal.
$$	**Chairman and Yip, Canberra.** Against a backdrop of artifacts from Maoist China, enjoy duck pancakes, and steamed barramundi with kumquats, ginger, and shallots.
$$	**Spirit House, Yandina, Queensland.** Savor delicious Thai- and Indonesian-inspired delicacies while gazing over ornamental ponds and Buddhas.

$$	**Vulcan's, Blackheath, New South Wales.** Amazing slow-roasted dishes with Asian or Middle Eastern spices are followed by luscious checkerboard ice cream.
$–$$	**Hanuman Thai, Alice Springs, Red Centre.** Those who scorn seafood will become converts after sampling the Hanuman oysters (grilled and seasoned with lemongrass and lime).
$–$$	**Hanuman Thai and Nonya Restaurant, Darwin.** Thai-Malaysian flavors have made this dazzling restaurant the city's Asian sensation.
$–$$	**Icebergs Dining Room and Bar, Bondi Beach, Sydney.** A chic poolside setting and a beachside backdrop draw Sydney's sophisticated crowd.
$–$$	**Kelleys, Hobart, Tasmania.** Some of Hobart's best seafood is served up in this 200-year-old sailmaker's cottage, where an open fireplace glows on chilly nights.
$–$$	**Melbourne Wine Room Restaurant, Melbourne.** Serene, romantic, and modestly glamorous, this is the perfect place to try wines by the glass, paired with stylish Italian cooking.
$–$$	**Monalto Vineyard & Olive Grove, Red Hill, Victoria.** Overlooking vineyards and rolling green hills, this eatery serves French-inspired food with the finest local ingredients.
$–$$	**Oyster Bar Meads Mosman Bay, Perth.** Visitors here argue about what's more spectacular: the delicious seafood or the gorgeous setting on the Swan River.

AMAZING WILDLIFE

Cradle Mountain–Lake St. Clair National Park, Tasmania. Keep an eye out for Tasmanian wildlife as you hike through this alpine park.

Heron Island, Great Barrier Reef, Queensland. The national park and bird sanctuary is part of the reef and a popular migration and breeding spot for loggerhead turtles and birds.

Kakadu National Park, the Top End. The billabongs (water holes) at Yellow Water, South Alligator River, and Magella Creek attract more than 280 species of birds.

Lady Elliot Island, Great Barrier Reef, Queensland. This 100-acre coral cay is a breeding ground for birds, turtles, and tropical fish.

Lone Pine Koala Sanctuary, Brisbane, Queensland. Pet the animals at this fauna park outside Brisbane—and have your picture taken while cuddling a koala.

Monkey Mia, Western Australia. Dolphins show up in Shark Bay to be hand-fed by the rangers, who will share the job with you.

Ningaloo Reef, Western Australia. Giant whale sharks, humpback whales, and turtles abound in the waters off Exmouth Peninsula.

Phillip Island, Victoria. The twilight return of the fairy penguins is a spectacular sight.

Sea Acres Rainforest Centre, New South Wales. An elevated boardwalk takes you above lush coastal rain forest filled with more than 170 plant species, native mammals, and prolific birdlife.

Seal Bay Conservation Park, Kangaroo Island, South Australia. Seal Bay's sea lion colony relaxes on the beach between fishing trips.

NATURAL WONDERS

Leeuwin–Naturaliste National Park, Western Australia. Human and animal relics, as well as more than 360 caves, are part of the rugged coastal scenery here.

Franklin-Gordon Wild Rivers National Park, Strahan, Tasmania. This section of the Tasmanian Wilderness World Heritage Area has rugged mountain peaks, areas of untouched rain forest, and deep gorges carved by the wild river valleys.

Freycinet National Park, Tasmania. Gorgeous turquoise bays and soft, sugar-white beaches meet with granite bluffs and thick forests in this park along the island's east coast.

Gariwerd National Park, Victoria. Formerly known as the Grampians, this territory of rugged peaks, towering trees, and waterfalls make it a haven for bushwalkers and nature lovers.

Great Barrier Reef, Queensland. The world's richest marine area supports wondrous undersea life, making for extraordinary diving and snorkeling.

Port Campbell National Park, Victoria. Rugged cliffs and columns of resilient rock stand in the roiling bays that fringe this dramatic section of coastline.

Purnululu (Bungle Bungle) National Park, The Kimberley. Great beehive-shape rock domes, striped in orange and black, seem to bubble up from the landscape here.

Snowy Mountains, New South Wales. Part of Kosciuszko National Park, this area is Australia's largest alpine region.

Three Sisters, New South Wales. These soaring sandstone pillars in the Blue Mountains recall an Aboriginal legend of sisters saved from a monster.

Uluru (Ayers Rock) and Kata Tjuta (the Olgas), the Red Centre. These massive rock formations, which together make up a World Heritage Site, are breathtaking and unforgettable.

THE REAL OZ

Australian War Memorial, Canberra. This nationally important shrine and museum commemorate more than a century of Australian military involvement.

Barossa Valley Wineries, South Australia. An hour's drive from Adelaide are world-renowned wineries with free tours and tastings.

Bondi Beach, Sydney. Follow the lead of Sydneysiders on Australia's most famous beach: shed your clothes, dive into the surf, work on your tan, grab a skateboard—or take in the whole scene from the promenade.

Chapel Street, Melbourne. Some of the city's ritziest boutique shops, cafés, art galleries, and restaurants are here in South Yarra.

Clare Valley Wineries, South Australia. Historic settlements and snug valleys surround the small family vineyards where Australia's finest Rieslings are produced.

Dreamworld, Coomera, Queensland. A theme park that combines adrenaline rides, cuddly Aussie animals, and a chance to meet Big Brother "celebrities."

El Questro Wilderness Park, Top End. This rugged, million-acre spread offers the chance to jump into life on a working Outback ranch.

Eumundi Markets, Queensland. This sleepy little Sunshine Coast town becomes a thriving metropolis on Wednesday and Saturday when these bustling markets, selling yummy food and crafts, take place.

Harbour Ferry Ride, Sydney. The journey to Manly captures stunning, breezy views of the city.

Hepburn Spa Resort, Hepburn Springs, Victoria. Mineral-rich underground springs feed communal spa pools, private aerospa baths, float tanks, and saunas at this spa oasis.

Lizard Island, Great Barrier Reef, Queensland. The boat crew feed the giant potato cod and the Maori wrasse at Cod Hole, off the outer reef of this island.

Mail Run Tour, South Australia. Join former miner Peter Rowe on his twice-weekly 12-hour, 600-km (372-mi) journey delivering mail and supplies to remote cattle stations and Outback towns.

Mornington Peninsula Wineries, Victoria. Set amid the state's prime vineyards, local wineries produce fine, cool-climate labels to go with the region's exceptional cuisine.

National Museum of Australia, Canberra. Exhibits here highlight the key people, events, and issues that shaped and influenced the nation.

Parliament House, Canberra. Much of this vast futuristic structure is submerged, covered by a domed glass roof that follows the contours of Capital Hill.

Port Arthur Historic Site, Tasmania. The restored penal settlement includes the original church, prison, hospital, and asylum.

Salamanca Place, Hobart, Tasmania. One of this city's liveliest gathering spots showcases the island's best crafts and antiques.

Skyrail Rainforest Cableway, Kuranda, Queensland. The journey takes you 7½ km (5 mi) over rain-forest canopy to Kuranda, near Cairns.

Western Australian Maritime Museum, Fremantle, Western Australia. Boat-lovers adore this upside-down-boat-shape spot at the edge of Fremantle Harbour.

Zig Zag Railway, Mount Victoria, New South Wales. Riding this vintage steam engine along cliff-side precipices through the Blue Mountains is thrilling.

SMART TRAVEL TIPS

Finding out about your destination before you leave home means you won't squander time organizing everyday minutiae once you've arrived. You'll be more streetwise when you hit the ground as well, better prepared to explore the aspects of Australia that drew you here in the first place. The organizations in this section can provide information to supplement this guide; contact them for up-to-the-minute details, and consult the A to Z sections in each chapter for facts on the various topics as they relate to the country's many regions. Happy landings!

AIR TRAVEL

The major gateways to Australia include Sydney, Melbourne, Perth, Brisbane, and Cairns. Flights depart from Los Angeles, San Francisco, Honolulu, New York, Toronto, and Vancouver, as well as from London, Frankfurt, and Rome. Depending on your airline, you may be allowed to stop over in Honolulu, Fiji, Tahiti, or Auckland from the United States, or Singapore, Hong Kong, Mauritius, Johannesburg, Tokyo, Kuala Lumpur, or Bangkok from Europe. You can fly nonstop to Sydney from Los Angeles, San Francisco, and Honolulu.

Your ticket price will be influenced by timing (when you buy as well as when you want to go) and the route you take (where you stop, if at all). Remember that Australia is a long-haul destination: a stopover may be preferable to being airborne for 15 hours straight.

Australia's major domestic carriers are Qantas (its subsidiaries include Airlink, Eastern, Southern, and Jetstar, a budget line) and Virgin Blue. Regional Express (Rex) flies between some eastern states; several smaller lines operate between the more far-flung regional centers. Australian Airlines, a cut-price overseas subsidiary of Qantas, connects Sydney, Melbourne, and Cairns to Bali, Indonesia; Sabah, Malaysia; and points in northern Asia.

BOOKING

When you book, look for nonstop flights and remember that "direct" flights stop at least once. Try to avoid connecting flights, which require a change of plane. Two airlines may operate a connecting flight jointly, so ask whether your airline operates every segment of the trip; you may find that the carrier you prefer flies you only part of the way. To find more booking tips and to check prices and make online flight reservations, log on to www. fodors.com.

CARRIERS

To & From Australia Air Canada ☎ 800/426-7000 in U.S., 800/665-1177 in Canada, 0871/220-1111 in U.K., 1300/655767 in Australia, 09/379-3371 in New Zealand ⊕ www.aircanada.com. **Air New Zealand** ☎ 800/262-1234 in U.S., 800/663-5494 in Canada, 0181/741-2299 in U.K., 13-2476 in Australia, 0800/737-000 in New Zealand ⊕ www.airnz.com. au. **British Airways** ☎ 800/247-9297 in U.S. and Canada, 20/8741-2299 in U.K., 1300/767177 in Australia, 09/356-8690 in New Zealand ⊕ www. britishairways.com. **Cathay Pacific** ☎ 800/233-2742 in U.S., 800/268-6868 in Canada, 0171/747-8888 in U.K., 13-1747 in Australia, 09/379-0861 in New Zealand ⊕ www.cathaypacific.com. **Emirates** ☎ 212/758-3944 in U.S., 870/243-2222 in U.K., 1300/303777 in Australia, 09/968-2200 in New Zealand ⊕ www.emirates.com. **Gulf Air** ☎ 888/359-4853 in U.S., 870/777-1717 in U.K., 1300/366337 in Australia ⊕ www.gulfair.com.au. **Japan Airlines** ☎ 800/525-3663 in U.S., 800/525-3663 in Canada, 0171/408-1000 in U.K., 02/9272-1111 in Australia, 09/379-3202 in New Zealand ⊕ www.japanair.com. **Malaysia Airlines** ☎ 800/552-9264 in U.S., 870/607-9090 in U.K., 13-2627 in Australia, 0800/777-747 in New Zealand ⊕ www.malaysiaairlines.com. **Qantas** ☎ 800/227-4500 in U.S. and Canada, 0845/774-7767 in U.K., 0800/808-767 in New Zealand ⊕ www.qantas.com. **Singapore Airlines** ☎ 800/742-3333 in U.S., 800/387-0038 in Canada, 0181/747-0007 in U.K., 13-1011 in Australia, 0800/808-909 in New Zealand ⊕ www.singaporeairlines.com. **United** ☎ 800/538-2929 in U.S., 800/241-6522 in Canada, 0845/844-4777 in U.K., 13-1777 in Australia, 0800/508-648 in New Zealand ⊕ www.united.com. **Within Australia Australian Airlines** ☎ 1300/799798. **Jetstar** ☎ 13-1538. **Qantas** ☎ 13-1313. **Regional Express** ☎ 13-1713. **Virgin Blue** ☎ 13-6789.

CHECK-IN & BOARDING

Always **find out your carrier's check-in policy.** Plan to arrive at the airport about 2 hours before your scheduled departure

time for domestic flights and 2½ to 3 hours before international flights. You may need to arrive earlier if you're flying from one of the busier airports or during peak air-traffic times.

Airlines routinely overbook planes. If there aren't enough volunteers, the airlines starts bumping passengers who checked in late and those flying on discounted tickets, so get to the gate and check in as early as possible, especially during peak periods.

Always **bring a government-issued photo ID** to the airport; even when it's not required, a passport is best.

CUTTING COSTS

The least-expensive airfares to Australia are priced for round-trip travel and must usually be purchased in advance. Airlines generally allow you to change your return date for a fee; most low-fare tickets, however, are nonrefundable.

Call a number of airlines and check the Internet; when you're quoted a good price, book it on the spot—the same fare may not be available the next day, or even the next hour. Always check different routings and look into using alternate airports. Most flights from the United States go over the Pacific, but in some instances it may be cheaper (albeit considerably longer) to fly over the Atlantic and Europe. Off-peak and red-eye flights may be significantly less expensive. Travel agents, especially low-fare specialists (⇨ Discounts & Deals), are helpful.

Consolidators are another good source. They buy tickets for scheduled flights at reduced rates from the airlines, then sell them at prices that beat the best fare available directly from the airlines. (Many also offer reduced car-rental and hotel rates.) Sometimes you can even get your money back if you need to return the ticket. Carefully read the fine print detailing penalties for changes and cancellations, purchase the ticket with a credit card, and confirm your consolidator reservation with the airline.

Many airlines, singly or in collaboration, offer discount air passes that allow foreigners to travel economically in a particular

Relax with personal screens in every seat.

Qantas is the only airline flying non-stop from the US to Australia and New Zealand with personal entertainment screens in every seat. And with so many audio, video and game channels to choose from, there's bound to be something to keep everyone amused. What's more, you'll also earn frequent flyer mileage on Alaska Airlines, American Airlines, Continental Airlines or US Airways. Just some of the reasons why you can relax when you're flying Qantas. The Spirit of Australia.
QantasUSA.com

country or region. These visitor passes usually must be reserved and purchased before you leave home. Information about passes often can be found on most airlines' international Web pages, which tend to be aimed at travelers from outside the carrier's home country. Also, try typing the name of the pass into a search engine, or search for "pass" within the carrier's Web site.

If you plan to travel within Australia, **book a Qantas OzPass (a.k.a. Boomerang Pass) before you leave home.** This pass is valid for 2 to 10 regions of economy-class air travel; the price depends on the number of regions you select. It's only available outside Australia, and with the purchase of an international ticket on Qantas or one of its One World network partners.

Consolidators AirlineConsolidator.com ☎ 888/468-5385 ⊕ www.airlineconsolidator.com; for international tickets. **Best Fares** ☎ 800/880-1234 ⊕ www.bestfares.com; $59.90 annual membership. **Cheap Tickets** ☎ 800/377-1000 or 800/652-4327 ⊕ www.cheaptickets.com. **Expedia** ☎ 800/397-3342 or 404/728-8787 ⊕ www.expedia.com. **Hotwire** ☎ 866/468-9473 or 920/330-9418 ⊕ www.hotwire.com. **Now Voyager Travel** ✉ 45 W. 21st St., Suite 5A, New York, NY 10010 ☎ 212/459-1616 ☎ 212/243-2711 ⊕ www.nowvoyagertravel.com. **Onetravel.com** ⊕ www.onetravel.com. **Orbitz** ☎ 888/656-4546 ⊕ www.orbitz.com. **Priceline.com** ⊕ www.priceline.com. **Travelocity** ☎ 888/709-5983, 877/282-2925 in Canada, 0870/111-7061 in U.K. ⊕ www.travelocity.com.

Discount Passes OzPass/Boomerang Pass Qantas ☎ 800/227-4500, 0845/774-7767 in U.K., 13-1313 in Australia, 0800/808-767 in New Zealand ⊕ www.qantas.com. **Pacific Explorer Airpass** Hideaway Holidays ☎ 02/9743-0253 in Australia ☎ 02/9743-3568 in Australia, 530/325-4069 in U.S. ⊕ www.hideawayholidays.com.au. **Polypass** Polynesian Airlines ☎ 800/264-0823 or 808/842-7659, 020/8846-0519 in U.K., 1300/653737 in Australia, 0800/800-993 in New Zealand ⊕ www.polynesianairlines.com. **Qantas** ☎ 800/227-4500 in U.S. and Canada, 0845/774-7767 in U.K., 13-1313 in Australia, 0800/808-767 in New Zealand ⊕ www.qantas.com. **SAS Air Passes** Scandinavian Airlines ☎ 800/221-2350, 0845/6072-7727 in U.K., 1300/727707 in Australia ⊕ www.scandinavian.net.

ENJOYING THE FLIGHT

State your seat preference when purchasing your ticket, and then repeat it when you confirm and when you check in. For more legroom, you can request one of the few emergency-aisle seats at check-in, if you're capable of moving obstacles comparable in weight to an airplane exit door (usually 35–60 pounds)—a Federal Aviation Administration requirement of passengers in these seats. Seats behind a bulkhead also offer more legroom, but they don't have under-seat storage. Don't sit in the row in front of the emergency aisle or in front of a bulkhead, where seats may not recline. SeatGuru.com has more information about specific seat configurations, which vary by aircraft. If sleeping well over a long flight is important to you, long-haul airlines like Qantas, British Airways, and United have **first-class and business-class sleeper seats,** which fully recline.

All flights from the United States and Europe to Australia are no-smoking, as are all flights within Australia. Ask the airline whether a snack or meal is served on the flight. If you have dietary concerns, request special meals when booking.

FLYING TIMES

Flying time approximations are as follows: 21 hours from New York to Sydney (via Los Angeles); 19 hours from Chicago to Sydney (via Los Angeles); 14 hours from Los Angeles to Sydney (nonstop); 16 hours from Los Angeles to Melbourne (via Auckland); 17 hours from Vancouver to Sydney (via Honolulu); 20 hours from Toronto to Sydney (via Los Angeles); and 20½ hours from London to Sydney or Melbourne (via Singapore or Bangkok).

Since Pacific-route flights from the United States to Australia cross the International Date Line, you lose a day, but regain it on the journey home.

HOW TO COMPLAIN

If your baggage goes astray or your flight goes awry, complain right away. Most carriers require that you **file a claim immediately.** The Aviation Consumer Protection Division of the Department of Transportation publishes *Fly-Rights,* which discusses airlines and consumer issues and is available online. You can also find articles and information on mytravelrights.com, the Web site of the nonprofit Consumer Travel Rights Center.

⚑ Airline Complaints Aviation Consumer Protection Division ✉ U.S. Department of Transportation, Office of Aviation Enforcement and Proceedings, C-75, Room 4107, 400 7th St. SW, Washington, DC 20590 ☎ 202/366-2220 ⊕ airconsumer.ost.dot.gov. **Federal Aviation Administration Consumer Hotline** ✉ For inquiries: FAA, 800 Independence Ave. SW, Washington, DC 20591 ☎ 800/322-7873 ⊕ www.faa.gov.

RECONFIRMING
Check the status of your flight before you leave for the airport. You can do this on your carrier's Web site, by linking to a flight-status checker (many Web booking services offer these), or by calling your carrier or travel agent. Always confirm international flights at least 72 hours ahead of the scheduled departure time.

AIRPORTS
From North America and Europe, it's usually cheapest to fly into Sydney's Kingsford-Smith Airport, which is Australia's main airport. It's on the east coast, where the other major airports are Brisbane International, Cairns, and Melbourne. Perth International Airport is the west coast's principal international entry point, Darwin is the northern gateway, and Alice Springs is the Red Centre's hub.

From the international hubs, it's relatively easy to get into town. Taxis and buses are pretty common. Sydney, however, doesn't have buses connecting the airport to the city, though it (along with Brisbane) does have an efficient train service. The highway to Melbourne's airport, which is rather removed from the city, is prone to rush-hour traffic.

⚑ Airport Information Adelaide Airport ☎ 08/8308-9211. **Alice Springs Airport** ☎ 08/8951-1211. **Brisbane International Airport** ☎ 07/3406-3190. **Cairns Airport** ☎ 07/4052-9703. **Darwin International Airport** ☎ 08/8945-5944. **Kingsford-Smith International Airport** ☎ 02/9667-9111. **Melbourne Airport** ☎ 03/9297-1600. **Perth International Airport** ☎ 08/9478-8888.

DUTY-FREE SHOPPING
In Australia there's no limit on what you can purchase, just the limitations imposed by your home country.

BOAT & FERRY TRAVEL
Many tour-boat operators make day trips to the Great Barrier Reef from the mainland. The central points of departure are Mackay, Airlie Beach, Townsville, Cairns, and Port Douglas. Boats also run between the Whitsunday Islands.

The daily *Spirit of Tasmania I* and *II* ferries take 10 hours to connect Melbourne with Devonport on Tasmania's north coast. The *Spirit of Tasmania III* sails 21 hours between Sydney and Devonport. Journeys depart from Sydney on Tuesday, Friday, and Sunday, and from Devonport on Monday, Thursday, and Saturday. The ship sails only twice weekly June through August. Make reservations as early as possible, particularly during the busy December and January school holidays.

The Sealink Ferry transports passengers and vehicles between Cape Jervis on the South Australian coastline and Penneshaw on Kangaroo Island.

FARES & SCHEDULES
You can pick up ferry and cruise schedules at most state tourism offices, as well as from the individual companies. All of the operators accept major credit cards and cash; some take traveler's checks.

⚑ Boat & Ferry Information Sealink Ferries ☎ 13-1301. *Spirit of Tasmania* ☎ 13-2010.

BUS TRAVEL
An excellent way to see the vast Australian continent, which is covered by a network of routes, is by bus. Buses have air-conditioning, toilets, and, in some cases, attendants and video systems. All are required by law to provide seat belts.

Travel times and (at this writing) approximate one-way prices are as follows: Sydney–Melbourne (15 hours, A$65); Sydney–Adelaide (23 hours, A$144); Sydney–Brisbane (15 hours, A$102); Brisbane–Cairns (30 hours, A$205); Melbourne–Adelaide (10 hours, A$65); Adelaide–Perth (39 hours, A$297);

Adelaide–Alice Springs (20 hours, A$216); Alice Springs–Uluru (Ayers Rock; 6 hours, A$76); Alice Springs–Darwin (20 hours, A$242); Cairns–Darwin (39 hours, A$449); Broome–Darwin (27 hours, A$308); Perth–Broome (34 hours, A$319). These are the maximum rates, but there are often specials and discounts. If you're planning to travel Australia by bus, with stops along the way, look into a bus pass.

CUTTING COSTS
Greyhound Australia offers several passes. Some cost 10%–15% less when purchased outside Australia. YHA members, VIP and ISIC Backpacker cardholders, and International Student Card holders also receive a 10% discount.

Distance passes remain valid for up to a year or until the maximum amount of kilometers has been reached. A 2,000-km (1,240-mi) pass costs A$321; a 10,000-km (6,200-mi) pass costs A$1,231. Many passes include discounts for accommodations and sightseeing, and are available in the United States and Canada through ATS Tours and in Canada through Goway Travel.

Use an OZ Experience bus pass to get off the beaten track. The company's routes link the cities with Australia's top attractions and adventure destinations, and the 12-month passes have unlimited stopovers in one direction. Several passes are available, including the Matey pass from Melbourne to Sydney, which visits Phillip Island, Lakes Entrance, the Snowy Mountains, and Canberra (A$215).

Many passes also provide discounts for accommodation and sightseeing, and are available in the United States and Canada through ATS Tours and in Canada through Goway Travel. Discount passes are also sold in Australia through STA Travel.

🛈 Discount Passes ATS Tours ☎ 800/423–2880 🖷 310/643–0032. **Goway Travel** ☎ 800/387–8850. **STA Travel** ☎ 1300/360960.

FARES & SCHEDULES
Bus schedules, fare information, and tickets are available from bus companies, tourist offices, and most travel agents. The Greyhound Australia Web site is a good resource, and it's possible to make online reservations.

PAYING
You can pay for bus fares with traveler's checks or major credit cards. Smaller bus lines may not accept American Express and Diners Club.

RESERVATIONS
You're guaranteed a seat if you book in advance—although it's still first come, first served.

SMOKING
Smoking isn't permitted. The penalty is a fine (and perhaps a sharp word from the driver).

🛈 Bus Information Greyhound Australia ☎ 13-1499 ⊕ www.greyhound.com.au.

CAR RENTAL
Rates in Sydney begin at A$50 a day for an economy car with air-conditioning, manual transmission, and 100 free km (62 free mi). Most companies also offer rates with unlimited mileage starting at around A$55–A$60 a day.

Larger agencies such as Avis, Budget, Thrifty, and Hertz have rental desks at airport terminals. Since a surcharge is commonly added to rentals picked up at airports, though, it's more economical to pick up a car at a city depot. Rates are similar for all the major cities, although you'll pay more if you rent in a remote location.

Only four-wheel-drive vehicles may travel on unpaved roads. Insurance generally doesn't cover damage to other types of cars traveling such roads.

A popular way to see Australia is to rent a camper van, which can hold up to eight. Smaller vans for two can be rented for around A$100 daily with unlimited mileage (there's usually a five-day minimum). Britz and Maui have offices around Australia, so one-way camper van and car rentals can be arranged.

🛈 Major Agencies Alamo ☎ 800/522–9696 ⊕ www.alamo.com. **Avis** ☎ 800/331–1084, 800/879–2847 in Canada, 0870/606–0100 in U.K., 02/9353–9000 in Australia, 09/526–2847 in New

Zealand ⊕ www.avis.com. **Budget** ☎ 800/527-0700 ⊕ www.budget.com. **Dollar** ☎ 800/800-6000, 0800/085-4578 in U.K. ⊕ www.dollar.com. **Hertz** ☎ 800/654-3001, 800/263-0600 in Canada, 0870/844-8844 in U.K., 02/9669-2444 in Australia, 09/256-8690 in New Zealand ⊕ www.hertz.com. **National Car Rental** ☎ 800/227-7368 ⊕ www.nationalcar.com. **Thrifty** ☎ 1300/367227 ⊕ www.thrifty.com.au.

🔁 **Local Agencies Bartrak** ☎ 03/9769-9970 **Britz** ☎ 1800/331454 ⊕ www.britz.com.au. **Kea Campers** ☎ 1800/252525. **Maui** ☎ 1300/363800 ⊕ www.maui.com.au.

CUTTING COSTS

Most major transport stations have details on discount car rentals. In other areas, check in the Yellow Pages under "Car Hire." Note that discount agency vehicles are usually two or three years old, and vehicles usually must be returned to where they were rented.

Join an automobile club to receive substantial discounts on car rentals, both in your home country and internationally. For a good deal, book through a travel agent who will shop around. Major car-rental agencies occasionally offer discounts if you book a vehicle via their Web sites.

🔁 **Auto Clubs** In Australia: **Australian Automobile Association** ☎ 02/6247-7311 ⊕ www.aaa.asn.au. In Canada: **Canadian Automobile Association** (CAA) ☎ 613/247-0117 ⊕ www.caa.ca. In New Zealand: **New Zealand Automobile Association** ☎ 0800/500-444 or 09/377-4660 ⊕ www.aa.co.nz. In the United Kingdom: **Automobile Association** (AA) ☎ 0990/500-600; **Royal Automobile Club** (RAC) ☎ 0990/722-722 for membership, 0345/121345 for insurance ⊕ www.rac.co.uk. In the United States: **American Automobile Association** ☎ 800/564-6222 ⊕ www.aaa.com.

INSURANCE

When driving a rented car you're generally responsible for any damage to or loss of the vehicle. You also may be liable for any property damage or personal injury that you may cause while driving. Before you rent, see what coverage you already have under the terms of your personal auto-insurance policy and credit cards.

Although insurance is included with standard rental vehicles in Australia, you're still responsible for an "excess" fee—a maximum amount that you'll have to pay if damage occurs. Fines can be incurred for accidents like a cracked windshield, which is a common occurrence on Australian roads. The amount of this "excess" is generally A$2,000–A$2,750 for a car, and can be much higher for a four-wheel-drive vehicle or camper van, but you can have this figure reduced by paying a daily fee.

REQUIREMENTS & RESTRICTIONS

In Australia you must be 21 to rent a car, and rates may be higher if you're under 25. There is no upper age limit for rental so long as you have a valid driver's license.

SURCHARGES

Before you pick up a car in one city and leave it in another, ask about drop-off charges or one-way service fees, which can be substantial. Also inquire about early-return policies; some rental agencies charge extra if you return the car before the time specified in your contract, while others give you a refund for the days not used. Most agencies note the tank's fuel level on your contract; to avoid a hefty refueling fee, return the car with the same tank level. If the tank was full, refill it just before you turn in the car, but be aware that gas stations near the rental outlet may overcharge. It's almost never a deal to buy a tank of gas with the car when you rent it; the understanding is that you'll return it empty, but some fuel usually remains.

Rental companies have varying policies and charges for unusual trips, such as lengthy cross-state expeditions around the Top End and Western Australia. Ask about additional mileage, fuel, and insurance charges if you're planning to cover a lot of ground. Also find out if the company charges for each additional driver, and if there's a car seat rental fee if you're traveling with children.

CAR TRAVEL

In Australia your own driver's license is accepted at most rental companies, provided that the information on the license is clear. An International Driver's Permit is required at others (but they'll still want to see your regular license). The international permit is available from the American or Canadian automobile association, and in the United Kingdom, from the Automobile Association or Royal Automobile Club.

Driving is easy in Australia, once you adjust to traveling on the left side of the road. When you're preparing a driving itinerary, it's vital to **bear in mind the huge distances involved.** Brisbane, Queensland's capital, is 1,032 km (640 mi) by road from Sydney, 1,718 km (1,065 mi) from Melbourne, and almost the same distance from Cairns. The journey from Sydney to Alice Springs, the gateway to Uluru (Ayers Rock), is 2½ hours by jet and a grueling 52 hours by road. Between major cities, flying is usually advised.

EMERGENCY SERVICES

If you have an emergency requiring an ambulance, the fire department, or the police, dial **000.** Many major highways now have telephones for breakdown assistance. Otherwise, flag down and ask a passing motorist to call the nearest motoring service organization for you. Most Australian drivers will be happy to assist, particularly in country areas.

Each state has its own motoring organization that provides assistance for vehicle breakdowns. When you rent a vehicle, you are entitled to assistance from the relevant motoring organization, free of charge. A toll-free, nationwide number is available for roadside assistance.

🚗 **Motoring Organization Hotline** ☎ 13–1111.

GASOLINE

Self-service stations are plentiful near major cities. The cost of gasoline ("petrol") varies from about A$1 per liter in Sydney to about A$1.25 per liter in the Outback. American Express, MasterCard, and Visa are accepted at most service stations. Pumps are similar to those in North America and Europe.

ROAD CONDITIONS

Except for some expressways in and around the major cities, most highways are two-lane roads with frequent passing lanes. Main roads are usually paved and well maintained, though lanes are narrower than in the United States.

Take precautions when you drive through the Outback. Road trains (i.e., truck convoys) can get up to 50 yards long, and passing them at that length becomes a matter of great caution, especially on two-lane roads in the bush. Many desert roads are unpaved, traffic is very light, and temperatures can be extreme. **Carry plenty of water and always tell someone your schedule.** Flash floods from sudden rain showers can occur on low-lying roads. Don't try to outdrive them. **Get to higher ground immediately when it rains.**

ROAD MAPS

Road maps are available at most gas stations and bookstores in the major cities. If you're planning an extensive road journey, pick up a comprehensive road atlas—such as the annual, widely available *Explore Australia* atlas published by Viking.

RULES OF THE ROAD

Speed limits are 50–60 kilometers per hour (kph) in populated areas, and 100–110 kph on open roads—the equivalent of 31–37 and 62–68 mph, respectively. Many towns have introduced uniform 50-kph (31-mph) limits in suburban areas. There are no speed limits on the open road in the Northern Territory. Limits in school areas are usually around 40 kph (25 mph). Surveillance of speeders and "drink-driving" (the legal limit is .05% blood-alcohol level) is thorough, and penalties are high. Seat belts are mandatory nationwide. Children must be restrained in a seat appropriate to their size. Car-rental agencies can install these for about A$30 per week, with 24 hours notice.

Traffic circles are widely used at intersections; cars that have already entered the circle have the right-of-way. At designated intersections in Melbourne's central business district you must get into the left lane to make a right-hand turn. Watch for the sign RIGHT-HAND TURN FROM LEFT LANE ONLY. Everywhere, **watch for sudden changes in speed limits.**

The Australian Automobile Association has a branch in each state, known as the National Roads and Motorists Association (NRMA) in New South Wales and Canberra, the Automobile Association in the

Northern Territory (AANT), and the Royal Automobile Club (RAC) in all other states. It's affiliated with AAA worldwide and offers reciprocal services to American, Canadian, and British members, including emergency road service, road maps, copies of each state and territory's Highway Code, and discounts on car rental and accommodations.

COMPUTERS ON THE ROAD

If you're traveling with a laptop, carry a spare battery and adapter. If you're going to use dial-up, get a telephone cord that's compatible with an Australian phone jack. Many hotels are equipped with phone jacks so that computers can be easily connected or have business centers with appropriate facilities. Never plug your computer into any socket before asking about surge protection. Some hotels don't have built-in current stabilizers, and extreme electrical fluctuations and surges can short your adapter or even destroy your computer. Before connecting your computer to a phone line, you may want to test the line as well. IBM sells a pen-size modem tester that plugs into a telephone jack to check whether it's safe to use.

Australia also has an extensive range of cafés, shops, and public libraries with Internet access.

CUSTOMS & DUTIES

When shopping abroad, keep receipts for all purchases. Upon reentering the country, **be ready to show customs officials what you've bought.** Pack purchases together in an easily accessible place. If you think a duty is incorrect, appeal the assessment. Take note of the inspector's badge number, and ask to see a supervisor. If the problem isn't resolved, write to the appropriate authorities, beginning with the port director at your point of entry.

IN AUSTRALIA

Australia has strict laws prohibiting or restricting the import of weapons and firearms. Antidrug laws are strictly enforced, and penalties are severe. All animals are subject to quarantine. Most canned or preserved food may be imported, but fresh fruit, vegetables, and all food served on aircraft coming from other countries is forbidden. All food, seeds, and wooden artifacts must be declared on your customs statement; you'll risk penalties if you don't declare an item and it's later discovered. If you have any doubts about a particular item, declare it on your statement; in most cases the item will be checked and passed.

Nonresidents over 18 may bring in 250 cigarettes, or 250 grams of cigars or tobacco, and 2 liters of liquor, provided this is carried with you. Other taxable goods to the value of A$400 for adults and A$200 for children may be included in personal baggage duty-free.

Australian Customs Service ᗉ Regional Director, Box 8, Sydney, NSW 2001 ☎ 1300/363263, 02/9213-2000, 1800/020504 or 02/8334-7444 quarantine-inquiry line ᕈ 02/9213-4043 ⊕ www.customs. gov.au.

IN CANADA

Canadian residents who have been out of Canada for at least seven days may bring in C$750 worth of goods duty-free. If you've been away fewer than seven days but more than 48 hours, the duty-free allowance drops to C$200. If your trip lasts 24 to 48 hours, the allowance is C$50. You may not pool allowances with family members. Goods claimed under the C$750 exemption may follow you by mail; those claimed under the lesser exemptions must accompany you. Alcohol and tobacco products may be included in the seven-day and 48-hour exemptions but not in the 24-hour exemption. If you meet the age requirements of the province or territory through which you reenter Canada, you may bring in, duty-free, 1.5 liters of wine *or* 1.14 liters (40 imperial ounces) of liquor *or* 24 12-ounce cans or bottles of beer or ale. Also, if you meet the local age requirement for tobacco products, you may bring in, duty-free, 200 cigarettes, 50 cigars or cigarillos, and 200 grams of tobacco. You may have to pay a minimum duty on tobacco products, regardless of whether or not you exceed your personal exemption. Check ahead of time with the Canada Customs and Revenue Agency or the Department of Agriculture for policies regarding meat products, seeds, plants, and fruits.

You may send an unlimited number of gifts (only one gift per recipient, however) worth up to C$60 each duty-free to Canada. Label the package UNSOLICITED GIFT—VALUE UNDER $60. Alcohol and tobacco are excluded.

🚩 **Canada Border Services Agency** ✉ Customs Information Services, 191 Laurier Ave. W, 15th fl., Ottawa, Ontario K1A 0L5 ☎ 800/461-9999 in Canada, 204/983-3500, 506/636-5064 ⊕ www.cbsa.gc.ca.

IN NEW ZEALAND

All homeward-bound residents may bring back NZ$700 worth of souvenirs and gifts; passengers may not pool their allowances, and children can claim only the concession on goods intended for their own use. For those 17 or older, the duty-free allowance also includes 4.5 liters of wine or beer; one 1,125-milliliter bottle of spirits; and either 200 cigarettes, 250 grams of tobacco, 50 cigars, or a combination of the three up to 250 grams. Meat products, seeds, plants, and fruits must be declared upon arrival to the Agricultural Services Department.

🚩 **New Zealand Customs** ✉ Head office: The Customhouse, 17–21 Whitmore St., Box 2218, Wellington ☎ 0800/428-786 or 09/300-5399 ⊕ www.customs. govt.nz.

IN THE U.K.

From countries outside the European Union, including Australia, you may bring home, duty-free, 200 cigarettes, 50 cigars, 100 cigarillos, or 250 grams of tobacco; 1 liter of spirits or 2 liters of fortified or sparkling wine or liqueurs; 2 liters of still table wine; 60 milliliters of perfume; 250 milliliters of toilet water; plus £145 worth of other goods, including gifts and souvenirs. Prohibited items include meat and dairy products, seeds, plants, and fruits.

🚩 **HM Customs and Excise** ✉ Portcullis House, 21 Cowbridge Rd. E, Cardiff CF11 9SS ☎ 0845/ 010-9000 or 0208/929-0152 advice service, 0208/ 929-6731 or 0208/910-3602 complaints ⊕ www. hmce.gov.uk.

IN THE U.S.

U.S. residents who have been out of the country for at least 48 hours may bring home, for personal use, $800 worth of foreign goods duty-free, as long as they haven't used the $800 allowance or any part of it in the past 30 days. This exemption may include 1 liter of alcohol (for travelers 21 and older), 200 cigarettes, and 100 non-Cuban cigars. Family members from the same household who are traveling together may pool their $800 personal exemptions. For fewer than 48 hours, the duty-free allowance drops to $200, which may include 50 cigarettes, 10 non-Cuban cigars, and 150 milliliters of alcohol (or 150 milliliters of perfume containing alcohol). The $200 allowance cannot be combined with other individuals' exemptions, and if you exceed it, the full value of all the goods will be taxed. Antiques, which U.S. Customs and Border Protection defines as objects more than 100 years old, enter duty-free, as do original works of art done entirely by hand, including paintings, drawings, and sculptures. This doesn't apply to folk art or handicrafts, which are in general dutiable.

You may also send packages home duty-free, with a limit of one parcel per addressee per day (except alcohol or tobacco products or perfume worth more than $5). You can mail up to $200 worth of goods for personal use; label the package PERSONAL USE and attach a list of its contents and their retail value. If the package contains your used personal belongings, mark it AMERICAN GOODS RETURNED to avoid paying duties. You may send up to $100 worth of goods as a gift; mark the package UNSOLICITED GIFT. Mailed items do not affect your duty-free allowance on your return.

To avoid paying duty on foreign-made high-ticket items you already own and will take on your trip, register them with a local customs office before you leave the country. Consider filing a Certificate of Registration for laptops, cameras, watches, and other digital devices identified with serial numbers or other permanent markings; you can keep the certificate for other trips. Otherwise, bring a sales receipt to show that you owned the item before you left the United States.

For more about duties, restricted items, and other information about international travel, check out U.S. Customs and Border Protection's online brochure, *Know Before You Go*.

🚹 **U.S. Customs and Border Protection** ✉ For inquiries: 1300 Pennsylvania Ave. NW, Washington, DC 20229 ⊕ www.cbp.gov ☎ 877/287-8667 or 202/354-1000 ✉ For complaints: Customer Satisfaction Unit, 1300 Pennsylvania Ave. NW, Room 5.4D, Washington, DC 20229.

DISABILITIES & ACCESSIBILITY

Since 1989, legislation has required that all new accommodations in Australia include provisions for travelers with disabilities. Conditions for travelers with disabilities are generally on par with those in North America. The National Information Communication Awareness Network (NICAN) has a free information service about activities, travel, and accommodations for travelers with disabilities.

🚹 **Local Resources National Information Communication Awareness Network (NICAN)** 📫 Box 407, Curtin, ACT 2607 ☎ 1800/806769 ✍ nican@spirit.com.au ⊕ www.nican.com.au.

LODGING

The National Roads and Motorists Association (NRMA) publishes an *Accommodation Directory* (A$7.70 members, A$15.95 nonmembers), indicating which properties have independent wheelchair access and which provide wheelchair access with assistance. Major international hotel chains usually have rooms with facilities for people with disabilities.

If you have a hearing impairment, check whether the hotel has devices to visually alert you if the phone or fire alarm rings or if someone knocks. Some hotels provide these devices without charge. Discuss your needs with hotel personnel if this equipment isn't available, so that a staff member can personally alert you in an emergency. If you're bringing a guide dog, get authorization ahead of time and write down the name of the person with whom you spoke.

🚹 **National Roads and Motorists Association (NRMA)** ✉ 151 Clarence St., Sydney, NSW 2000 ☎ 13-2132.

SIGHTS & ATTRACTIONS

Major urban attractions, such as the Sydney Opera House and the Australian Parliament, have provisions for travelers with disabilities. Many natural attractions are also accessible, including the Blue Mountains, Uluru (Ayers Rock), and the Great Barrier Reef.

TRANSPORTATION

Major car-rental companies, including Avis, Hertz, Budget, and Thrifty, can outfit vehicles with handheld controls (give at least a day's notice). Such vehicles are only available in the major cities. Wheelchair-accessible taxis are available in all state capitals.

Train passengers can request collapsible wheelchairs to negotiate narrow interior corridors. Compact toilet areas and platform access problems, however, can make long-distance train travel troublesome. Countrylink (in New South Wales) issues informational brochures about accessibility on their trains. Countrylink's Xplorer and XPT trains have specially designed wheelchair-access toilets as well as ramps for boarding and disembarking.

🚹 **Complaints Aviation Consumer Protection Division** (⇨ Air Travel) for airline-related problems. **Departmental Office of Civil Rights** ✉ For general inquiries: U.S. Department of Transportation, S-30, 400 7th St. SW, Room 10215, Washington, DC 20590 ☎ 202/366-4648 🖷 202/366-9371 ⊕ www.dotcr.ost.dot.gov. **Disability Rights Section** ✉ NYAV, U.S. Department of Justice, Civil Rights Division, 950 Pennsylvania Ave. NW, Washington, DC 20530 ☎ 800/514-0301, 202/514-0301 ADA information line, 800/514-0383 TTY, 202/514-0383 TTY ⊕ www.ada.gov. **U.S. Department of Transportation Hotline** ☎ for disability-related air-travel problems, 800/778-4838 or 800/455-9880 TTY.

DISCOUNTS & DEALS

Be a smart shopper and compare all your options before making decisions. A plane ticket bought with a promotional coupon from travel clubs, coupon books, and direct-mail offers or purchased on the Internet may not be cheaper than the least-expensive fare from a discount ticket agency. And always keep in mind that what you get is just as important as what you save.

DISCOUNT RESERVATIONS

To save money, look into discount reservations services with Web sites and toll-free numbers, which use their buying power to get a better price on hotels, airline tickets(⇨ Air Travel), even car rentals. When booking a room, always **call the hotel's local toll-free number** (if one is available) rather than the central reservations number—you'll often get a better price. Always ask about special packages or corporate rates.

When shopping for the best deal on hotels and car rentals, look for guaranteed exchange rates, which protect you against a falling dollar. With your rate locked in, you won't pay more, even if the price goes up in the local currency.

⌗ Hotel Rooms Accommodations Express ☎ 800/444-7666 or 800/277-1064. **Hotels.com** ☎ 800/246-8357 ⊕ www.hotels.com. **Steigenberger Reservation Service** ☎ 800/223-5652 ⊕ www.srs-worldhotels.com. **Turbotrip.com** ☎ 800/473-7829 ⊕ w3.turbotrip.com.

PACKAGE DEALS

Don't confuse packages and guided tours. When you buy a package, you travel on your own, just as though you had planned the trip yourself. Fly/drive packages, which combine airfare and car rental, are often a good deal. In cities, ask the local visitor's bureau about hotel and local transportation packages that include tickets to major museum exhibits or other special events.

EATING & DRINKING

Down Under, entrée means appetizer and main courses are American entrées. You'll also encounter the term "silver service," which indicates upscale dining. "Bistro" generally refers to a relatively inexpensive place. French fries are called chips, and if you want ketchup, ask for tomato sauce.

Many Australian restaurants serve prix-fixe dinners, but the majority are à la carte. The restaurants we list are the best in each price category. Properties indicated by an ✕⊡ are hotels with restaurants that deserve a special trip.

MEALTIMES

Breakfast is usually 7–10, lunch 11:30–2:30, and dinner begins around 6:30. In the cities, dining options are available at all hours, but the choices are far more restricted in the countryside. Unless otherwise noted, the restaurants listed in this guide are open daily for lunch and dinner.

RESERVATIONS & DRESS

Reservations are always a good idea; we mention them only when they're essential or not accepted. Book as far ahead as you can, and reconfirm as soon as you arrive. (Large parties should always call ahead to check the reservations policy.) We mention dress only when men are required to wear a jacket or a jacket and tie.

WINE, BEER & SPIRITS

Australia is the world's 10th-largest wine producer, and Australian wine has become something of a phenomenon. Take a walk through the aisles of your local wine shop and you'll come across Australian labels such as Rosemount and Lindemans. For more on Australian wine, *see* Pleasures and Pastimes *in* Chapter 1.

There's also a considerable cast of Australian beers, from the well-known Fosters to the products of smaller breweries. Traditional beer is strong and similar to Danish and German beers; it's typically served ice cold from the tap, with a little head.

Most restaurants serve liquor. In some states, cafés also serve alcohol. Bottle shops, which sell beer, wine, and spirits for consumption off the premises, can be found in most shopping centers.

In Australia the legal drinking age is 18. Bars usually close around 11 PM during the week, but close later on weekends. BYOB (Bring Your Own Bottle—usually limited to wine) restaurants are growing in popularity throughout Australia. These usually have corkage charges.

ELECTRICITY

The electrical current in Australia is 240 volts, 50 cycles alternating current (AC). Wall outlets take slanted three-prong plugs (but not the U.K. three-prong) and plugs with two flat prongs set in a V. To use electric-powered equipment purchased in the United States or Canada, **bring a converter and adapter.**

If your appliances are dual-voltage, you'll need only an adapter. Don't use 110-volt outlets marked FOR SHAVERS ONLY for high-wattage appliances such as blow-dryers. Most laptops operate equally well on 110 and 220 volts and require only an adapter.

EMBASSIES

Embassies and consulates in Australia provide assistance to their nationals in case of lost or stolen passports and documents, major medical problems, and other travel emergencies.

🇨🇦 **Canada Canadian High Commission** ✉ Commonwealth Ave., Yarralumla ACT 2600 2600 ☎ 02/6270-4000. **Consulate General** ✉ Quay West 111, Level 5, Harrington St., Sydney NSW 2000 ☎ 03/9364-3050. **Honorary Consulate General** ✉ 267 St. George's Terr., 3rd fl., Perth WA 6000 ☎ 08/9322-7930.

🇳🇿 **New Zealand Consulate General** ✉ Level 10, 55 Hunter St., Sydney NSW 2000 ☎ 02/8256-2000. **New Zealand High Commission** ✉ Commonwealth Ave., Yarralumla ACT 2600 ☎ 02/6270-4211.

🇬🇧 **U.K. British Consulate General** ✉ Gateway Bldg., Level 16, 1 Macquarie Pl., Sydney NSW 2000 ☎ 02/9247-7521. **British High Commission** ✉ Commonwealth Ave., Yarralumla ACT 2600 ☎ 02/6270-6666. **British High Commission, Consular Section** ✉ 39 Brindabella Circuit, Brindabella Business Park, Canberra Airport, Canberra ACT 2600 ☎ 1902/941555. **Consulate General** ✉ Grenfell Centre, Level 22, 25 Grenfell St., Adelaide SA 5000 ☎ 08/8212-7280 ✉ Waterfront Pl., Level 26, 1 Eagle St., Brisbane QLD 4000 ☎ 07/3236-2575 ✉ 90 Collins St., 17th fl., Melbourne VIC 3000 ☎ 03/9650-3699 ✉ Allendale Sq., Level 26, 77 St. George's Terr., Perth WA 6000 ☎ 08/9221-5400. **Honorary Consul** ✉ Trust Bank Tasmania, 39 Murray St., Hobart TAS 7000 ☎ 03/6230-3647.

🇺🇸 **U.S. Consulate General** ✉ Level 6, 553 St. Kilda Rd., Melbourne VIC 3000 ☎ 03/9526-5900 ✉ 16 St. George's Terr., 13th fl., Perth WA 6000 ☎ 08/9231-9400 ✉ MLC Centre, Level 59, 19-29 Martin Pl., Sydney NSW 2000 ☎ 02/9373-9200. **U.S. Embassy** ✉ Moonah Pl., Yarralumla ACT 2600 ☎ 02/6214-5600.

EMERGENCIES

Dial **000** for fire, police, or an ambulance.

For theft, wallet loss, small road accidents, and minor emergencies, contact the nearest police station. In a medical or dental emergency, your hotel staff will have information on and directions to the nearest hospital or clinic.

Pack a basic first-aid kit, especially if you're venturing into more remote areas. If you'll be carrying any medication, bring your doctor's contact information and prescription authorizations.

ETIQUETTE & BEHAVIOR

Australians are typically relaxed and informal in their social relationships, and visitors from other cultures will have little trouble fitting in. Social behavior broadly follows the same patterns as those in North America and the British Isles. Upon introduction, men will shake hands, but this will not usually be repeated on later encounters. A kiss on the cheek is a common greeting and farewell between the sexes, but only once the relationship has moved to a comfortable level of familiarity.

GAY & LESBIAN TRAVEL

Politically and socially, Australia is one of the gay-friendliest countries in the world, ranking right up there with the Netherlands, Denmark, and Canada. Gay tourism associations, often associated with a state tourism board, are well established and have plenty to offer lesbian and gay tourists.

Many publications detailing gay and lesbian activities are available. Most major cities—including Sydney, Brisbane, Melbourne, Perth, and Adelaide—publish gay and lesbian newspapers. The *Sydney Star Observer* has the largest circulation. Local independent travel magazines like the *Gay Australia Guide* (www.gayaustraliaguide. bigstep.com) also dispense advice.

HEALTH

You may take a four weeks' supply of prescribed medication into Australia (more with a doctor's certificate). Medical professionals are highly trained and hospitals are well equipped. Hygiene standards are high and well monitored, so don't worry about drinking the water or eating fresh produce. The primary health hazard is sunburn or sunstroke. Even if you're not normally bothered by strong sun you should **cover up with a long-sleeve shirt, a hat, and pants or a beach wrap.** Keep in mind that you'll burn more easily at higher altitudes and in the water. **Apply sunscreen liberally** before you go out—even for a half hour—and wear a visored cap and sunglasses.

Apply a reliable insect repellent to protect yourself from mosquito bites in summer months (particularly in the north). Although Australia is free of malaria, several cases of Ross River fever have been reported in recent years. Dengue fever has been reported in Northern Queensland. The mosquitoes that transmit these viruses are active in daylight hours.

Dehydration is a serious danger that can be easily avoided, so be sure to **carry water and drink often.** Above all, **limit the amount of time you spend in the sun** for the first few days until you are acclimatized, and **avoid sunbathing in the middle of the day.**

DIVERS' ALERT
Do not fly within 24 hours of scuba diving.

MEDICAL PLANS
No one plans to get sick while traveling, but it happens, so consider signing up with a medical-assistance company. Members get doctor referrals, emergency evacuation or repatriation, hotlines for medical consultation, cash for emergencies, and other assistance.

⑦ Medical-Assistance Companies International SOS Assistance ⊕ www.internationalsos.com ✉ 3600 Horizon Blvd., Suite 300, Trevose, PA 19053 ☎ 800/523-6586 or 215/245-4707 🖷 215/354-2338 ✉ Challis House, Level 5, 4 Martin Pl., Sydney 2000 Australia ☎ 03/9372-2400 🖷 03/9372-2408 ✉ Landmark House, Hammersmith Bridge Rd., 6th fl., London England W6 9DP ☎ 20/8762-8008 🖷 20/8748-7744 ✉ 12 Chemin Riantbosson, 1217 Meyrin 1, Geneva Switzerland ☎ 22/785-6464 🖷 22/785-6424 ✉ 331 N. Bridge Rd., 17-00, Odeon Towers, 188720 Singapore ☎ 6338-7800 🖷 6338-7611.

OVER-THE-COUNTER REMEDIES
Familiar brands of nonprescription medications are available in pharmacies (commonly called chemists).

PESTS & OTHER HAZARDS
No rural scene is complete without bush flies, a major annoyance. These tiny pests, found throughout Australia, are especially attracted to the eyes and mouth, in search of the fluids that are secreted there. Some travelers resort to wearing a face net, which can be suspended from a hat with a drawstring device.

SHOTS & MEDICATIONS
Unless you're arriving from an area that has been infected with yellow fever, typhoid, or cholera, you don't need any shots before entering Australia.

⑦ Health Warnings National Centers for Disease Control and Prevention (CDC) ✉ Office of Health Communication, National Center for Infectious Diseases, Division of Quarantine, Travelers' Health, 1600 Clifton Rd. NE, Atlanta, GA 30333 ☎ 877/394-8747 travelers' health line, 800/311-3435 other inquiries, 404/498-1600 Division of Quarantine 🖷 888/232-3299 ⊕ www.cdc.gov/travel. **Travel Health Online** ⊕ tripprep.com. **World Health Organization (WHO)** ⊕ www.who.int.

HOLIDAYS
New Year's Day, January 1; **Australia Day,** January 26; **Good Friday,** April 14, 2006 and April 6, 2007; **Easter,** April 16, 2006 and April 8, 2007; **Easter Monday,** April 17, 2006 and April 9, 2007; **Anzac Day,** April 25; **Christmas,** December 25; **Boxing Day,** December 26. There are also some state- and territory-specific public holidays.

HOURS OF OPERATION
Businesses and post offices open 9–5 on weekdays. In the Northern Territory, government departments are commonly open 8–4:40. When a holiday falls on a weekend, businesses are usually closed the following Monday.

GAS STATIONS
Gas stations in urban areas and along major highways open 24 hours. In rural areas, gas stations are open 8–6.

PHARMACIES
Pharmacies normally open weekdays 9–5:30, Saturday 9–12:30. Most 24-hour pharmacies are in the nightlife district.

SHOPS

Typically, shops open weekdays 8:30–5:30, and close at 9 PM on either Thursday or Friday. On Saturday, shops are open from 8:30 to sometime between noon and 4. Some stores, particularly those in touristy areas, may be open a few hours on Sunday.

INSURANCE

The most useful travel-insurance plan is a comprehensive policy that includes coverage for trip cancellation and interruption, default, trip delay, and medical expenses (with a waiver for preexisting conditions).

Without insurance you'll lose all or most of your money if you cancel your trip, regardless of the reason. Default insurance covers you if your tour operator, airline, or cruise line goes out of business—the chances of which have been increasing. Trip-delay covers expenses that arise because of bad weather or mechanical delays. Study the fine print when comparing policies.

If you're traveling internationally, a key component of travel insurance is coverage for medical bills incurred if you get sick on the road. Such expenses aren't generally covered by Medicare or private policies. U.K. residents can buy a travel-insurance policy valid for most vacations taken during the year in which it's purchased (but check preexisting-condition coverage). British citizens need extra medical coverage when traveling abroad.

Always **buy travel policies directly from the insurance company**; if you buy them from a cruise line, airline, or tour operator that goes out of business you probably won't be covered for the agency or operator's default, a major risk. Before making any purchase, review your existing health and home-owner's policies to find what they cover away from home.

🔀 Travel Insurers In the United States: **Access America** ✉ 2805 N. Parham Rd., Richmond, VA 23294 ☎ 800/284-8300 🖷 800/346-9265 or 804/673-1491 ⊕ www.accessamerica.com. **Travel Guard International** ✉ 1145 Clark St., Stevens Point, WI 54481 ☎ 800/826-1300 or 715/345-1041 🖷 800/955-8785 ⊕ www.travelguard.com.
🔀 In the United Kingdom: **Association of British Insurers** ✉ 51 Gresham St., London EC2V 7HQ ☎ 020/7600-3333 🖷 020/7696-8999 ⊕ www.abi.org.uk. In Canada: **RBC Insurance** ✉ 6880 Financial Dr., Mississauga, Ontario L5N 7Y5 ☎ 800/668-4342 or 905/816-2559 🖷 905/813-4704 ⊕ www.rbcinsurance.com. In Australia: **Insurance Council of Australia** ✉ Insurance Enquiries and Complaints: Collins St. W, Box 561, Melbourne, VIC 8007 ☎ 1300/780808 or 03/9629-4109 🖷 03/9621-2060 ⊕ www.iecltd.com.au. In New Zealand: **Insurance Council of New Zealand** ✉ Level 7, 111-115 Customhouse Quay, Box 474, Wellington ☎ 04/472-5230 🖷 04/473-3011 ⊕ www.icnz.org.nz.

LODGING

We list the best lodgings for each price category. The available facilities are specified, but we don't indicate whether they cost extra. Always ask about additional costs when pricing your hotel room.

A ✕🏠 icon indicates that a lodging establishment has a restaurant warranting a special trip. Except for designated B&Bs and farm stays, the listed prices are for room only, unless we specify that hotels use the **Continental Plan** (CP, with a Continental breakfast), **Breakfast Plan** (BP, with a full breakfast), **Modified American Plan** (MAP, with breakfast and dinner), **Full American Plan** (FAP, with all meals), or **All-Inclusive** (AI, including all meals and most activities). Surcharges sometimes apply during weekends, long weekends, and holiday seasons.

APARTMENT & VILLA RENTALS

For a home base that's roomy enough for a family and comes with cooking facilities, consider a furnished rental. These can save you money, especially if you're traveling with a group. Home-exchange directories sometimes list rentals as well as exchanges. Look online or check with each state's tourism office for more information.

🔀 International Agents Hideaways International ✉ 767 Islington St., Portsmouth, NH 03801 ☎ 800/843-4433 or 603/430-4433 🖷 603/430-4444 ⊕ www.hideaways.com, annual membership $185. **Villas International** ✉ 4340 Redwood Hwy., Suite D309, San Rafael, CA 94903 ☎ 800/221-2260 or 415/499-9490 🖷 415/499-9491 ⊕ www.villasintl.com.
🔀 Local Agents Australian Villas ✉ 187 Carlisle St., Balaclava, VIC 3183 ☎ 03/9537-7569.

BED & BREAKFASTS

B&Bs are popular in the cities as well as in country areas. They're welcoming and moderately priced alternatives to hotel accommodations. Prices range from A$80 to A$200 nightly for two. The bountiful breakfasts usually consist of fruit juice, cereal, toast, eggs and bacon, and tea or coffee. The word "boutique" in conjunction with a B&B implies a higher level of luxury and facilities—but at a higher price.

🔲 **Reservation Services Bed and Breakfast Australia** ⌂ Box 448, Homebush South, NSW 2140 ☎ 02/9763-5833 ᕵ 02/9763-1677 ⊕ www. bedandbreakfast.com.au. **Bed & Breakfast Farmstay Association of New South Wales** ⌂ Box R1372, Royal Exchange, NSW 1225 ☎ 02/4365-3028 or 1300/888862 ⊕ www.bedandbreakfast.org.au. **Oz Bed and Breakfast** ✉ 21 Cluden St, Holland Park West, QLD 4121 ☎ 0412/753910 ⊕ www. ozbedandbreakfast.com.

CAMPING

For a small nightly fee you can stay in a national park campground—some have hot showers and barbecue areas. Even at a remote campsite, a park ranger will check in every few days.

Australia also has hundreds of convenient caravan parks where for around A$15–A$20 per night for two you get a powered site and use of facilities like showers, laundry, and grills. Caravan parks often have small kiosks with basic provisions, as well as swimming pools and playgrounds, and are a great place to meet fellow travelers. Many designated campgrounds and caravan parks also have onsite cabins, some with kitchen facilities, for A$40–A$50 nightly.

In less-traveled parts of the Outback you can camp freely, but remember that you'll be on someone's property—despite the absence of fences or signs of human habitation. Keep away from livestock. Camp away from water supplies, and don't use soap or detergents that may contaminate drinking water. Leave gates as you find them. Bring your own cooking fuel. **Carry water if you travel into isolated areas,** including national parks. Take a *minimum* of 20 liters per person,

which will last a week even in the hottest conditions.

These are the unbreakable rules of Outback travel: 1) If you plan to go off the beaten track, let someone know your route and when you expect to return. 2) If you break down, don't leave your car for any reason. From a search-and-rescue plane it's far easier to spot a car than a person in the wild. 3) Protect and respect Aboriginal relics, paintings, carvings, and sacred sites, as well as pioneer markers and heritage buildings. 4) Don't sleep under trees; many shed their limbs.

In addition to its *Accommodation Directory,* the National Roads and Motorists Association (NRMA) also publishes a *Caravan and Camping Directory* (A$5.50 members, A$12.95 nonmembers). Members of overseas automobile organizations have reciprocal membership rights. Local newsstands have caravan and camping magazines with information on caravan parks.

🔲 **NRMA** ✉ 151 Clarence St., Sydney, NSW 2000 ☎ 13-2132.

HOME EXCHANGES

If you'd like to exchange your home for someone else's, join a home-exchange organization, which will send you its updated listings of available exchanges for a year and will include your own listing in at least one of them. It's up to you to make specific arrangements.

🔲 **Exchange Clubs HomeLink International** ⌂ Box 47747, Tampa, FL 33647 ☎ 800/638-3841 or 813/975-9825 ᕵ 813/910-8144 ⊕ www.homelink. org; $110 yearly for a listing, online access, and catalog; $75 without catalog. **Intervac U.S.** ✉ 30 Corte San Fernando, Tiburon, CA 94920 ☎ 800/756-4663 ᕵ 415/435-7440 ⊕ www.intervacus.com; $125 yearly for a listing, online access, and a catalog, $65 without catalog.

HOME & FARM STAYS

Most home and farm stays operate on a B&B basis, though some also include an evening meal. Farm accommodations vary from modest shearers' cabins to elegant homesteads. You can join in farm activities or explore the countryside. Some hosts run day trips, as well as horseback riding, hiking, and fishing trips. For two people the cost varies from A$100 to A$250 nightly, including all meals and some or all farm activities.

Reservation Services Australian Farm Host and Farm Holidays ☎ 800/551-2012, represented by ATS Tours. **Australian Home Accommodation** ☎ 800/423-2880, represented by ATS Tours. **Bed & Breakfast Australia** ⬚ Box 448, Homebush South, NSW 2140 ☎ 02/9763-5833 🖷 02/9763-1677 ⊕ www.bedandbreakfast.com.au. **Pacific Destination Center** ☎ 800/227-5317. **Royal Automobile Club of Queensland (RACQ) Travel Service** ⬚ Box 537, Fortitude Valley, QLD 4006 ☎ 07/3361-2802 🖷 07/3257-1504.

HOSTELS

No matter what your age, you can save on lodging costs by staying at hostels. In some 4,500 locations in more than 70 countries around the world, Hostelling International (HI), the umbrella group for a number of national youth-hostel associations, offers single-sex, dorm-style beds and, at many hostels, rooms for couples and family accommodations. Membership in any HI national hostel association, open to travelers of all ages, allows you to stay in HI-affiliated hostels at member rates; one-year membership is about $28 for adults (C$35 for a two-year minimum membership in Canada, £14 in the United Kingdom, A$52 in Australia, and NZ$40 in New Zealand); hostels charge about $10–$30 per night. Members have priority if the hostel is full; they're also eligible for discounts around the world, even on rail and bus travel in some countries.

Australian youth hostels are usually comfortable, well equipped, and family friendly. Travelers from all walks of life take advantage of these low-cost accommodations, which usually have dormitory and private rooms sharing a common area, kitchen, and laundry. Backpacker hostels, also widely available throughout Australia, can be less expensive, but aren't affiliated with HI. To find these, ask other travelers, or look for ads on bulletin boards at bus and train stations, grocery stores, and cafés.

Organizations Hostelling International–USA ⬚ 8401 Colesville Rd., Suite 600, Silver Spring, MD

20910 ☎ 301/495-1240 🖷 301/495-6697 ⊕ www. hiusa.org. **Hostelling International–Canada** ⬚ 205 Catherine St., Suite 400, Ottawa, Ontario K2P 1C3 ☎ 800/663-5777 or 613/237-7884 🖷 613/237-7868 ⊕ www.hihostels.ca. **YHA England and Wales** ⬚ Trevelyan House, Dimple Rd., Matlock, Derbyshire DE4 3YH U.K. ☎ 0870/870-8808, 0870/770-8868, or 0162/959-2600 🖷 0870/770-6127 ⊕ www.yha.org.uk. **YHA Australia** ⬚ 422 Kent St., Sydney, NSW 2001 ☎ 02/9261-1111 🖷 02/9261-1969 ⊕ www.yha.com.au. **YHA New Zealand** ⬚ Moorhouse City, Level 1, 166 Moorhouse Ave., Box 436, Christchurch ☎ 0800/278-299 or 03/379-9970 🖷 03/365-4476 ⊕ www.yha.org.nz.

HOTELS & MOTELS

All hotels listed have private bath unless otherwise noted. Hotel and motel rooms generally have private bathrooms with a combined shower-tub—called "en suites"; B&B hotels and hostels occasionally require guests to share bathrooms. Coffeemakers and refrigerators are found in virtually all motels; stocked minibars are the norm in deluxe hotels. You can expect a swimming pool, health club, tennis courts, and hot tubs in many resort hotels, some of which also have private golf courses. Motel chains such as Flag International are usually reliable and much less expensive than hotels. You often can check into a motel without booking ahead, but reservations are required for weekends and holidays. If you'd like to book a smaller hotel or B&B, and you'll be traveling with children, check that the facilities are appropriate for young ones—and make sure that they're welcome to stay.

Toll-Free Numbers Best Western ☎ 800/528-1234 ⊕ www.bestwestern.com. **Choice** ☎ 800/424-6423 ⊕ www.choicehotels.com. **Clarion** ☎ 800/424-6423 ⊕ www.choicehotels.com. **Comfort Inn** ☎ 800/424-6423 ⊕ www.choicehotels.com. **Four Seasons** ☎ 800/332-3442 ⊕ www.fourseasons.com. **Hilton** ☎ 800/445-8667 ⊕ www.hilton.com. **Holiday Inn** ☎ 800/465-4329 ⊕ www.ichotelsgroup.com. **Hyatt Hotels & Resorts** ☎ 800/233-1234 ⊕ www.hyatt.com. **Inter-Continental** ☎ 800/327-0200 ⊕ www.ichotelsgroup.com. **Le Meridien** ☎ 800/543-4300 ⊕ www.lemeridien.com. **Marriott** ☎ 800/228-9290 ⊕ www.marriott.com. **Quality Inn** ☎ 800/424-6423 ⊕ www.choicehotels.com. **Radisson** ☎ 800/333-3333 www.radisson.com. **Ramada** ☎ 800/228-2828, 800/854-7854 international reservations ⊕ www. ramada.com or www.ramadahotels.com. **Renaissance Hotels & Resorts** ☎ 800/468-3571 ⊕ www. marriott.com. **Sheraton** ☎ 800/325-3535 ⊕ www. starwood.com/sheraton. **Westin Hotels & Resorts** ☎ 800/228-3000 ⊕ www.starwood.com/westin.

MAIL & SHIPPING

Mail service in Australia is efficient. Allow a week for letters and postcards to reach the United States and the United Kingdom. Letters to New Zealand generally take four to five days.

OVERNIGHT SERVICES

Both DHL and Federal Express operate fast, reliable express courier services from Australia. Rates are around A$76 for a 1-kilogram (2-pound) parcel to the United States and around A$85 to Europe, including door-to-door service. Delivery time between Sydney and New York is approximately three days.

⎘ Major Services DHL Worldwide Express ☎ 13-1406. **Federal Express** ☎ 13-2610.

POSTAL RATES

Postage rates are A50¢ for domestic letters, A$1.65 per 50-gram (28.35 grams = 1 ounce) airmail letter, and A$1 for airmail postcards to North America and the United Kingdom. Overseas fax service at a post office costs A$7.50 for the first page, plus A$3 for the second page and A$1 for any additional pages.

RECEIVING MAIL

You can receive mail care of General Delivery (known as Poste Restante in Australia) at the General Post Office or any branch post office. The service is free and mail is held for one month. It's a good idea to **know the Australian postal code (zip code) of the area you are visiting.** These are available from the Australian Consulate General, and will allow you to receive General Delivery mail. You'll need identification to pick up mail. American Express also offers free mail collection at its main city offices for its cardholders.

SHIPPING PARCELS

Rates for large parcels shipped from Australia depend on their weight and shape.

Some companies provide boxes, and any materials you can fit inside weighing up to 25 kilograms (about 55 pounds) will cost about A$215, excluding any U.S. import charges. You can also consult your airline to find the rates for unaccompanied luggage. Overnight courier services like DHL and Federal Express will deliver packages of any size—for a price.

If you're shipping items in excess of 50 kilograms (110 pounds), it's less expensive to send goods by sea via a shipping agent. Shipping time to the United States and Europe is 10–12 weeks.

MEDIA

The Australian Broadcasting Commission (ABC) operates nationwide commercial-free radio and television, though commercial stations are also available. Even the smallest country towns have their own newspapers.

NEWSPAPERS & MAGAZINES

The *Australian* is the only national paper. Each major city has its own daily. The *Sydney Morning Herald* is the city's most authoritative source for such news. The *Melbourne Age,* a sister publication, is another reliable paper. Two tabloids, Sydney's *Daily Telegraph* and Melbourne's *Herald Sun,* focus on local affairs. Turn to the *Financial Review* for in-depth analyses of daily financial matters and international and Australian politics. *HQ* magazine is respected for its thoughtful, incisive, and often irreverent approach to social issues and the arts. The *Bulletin* is the only Australian magazine with news coverage along the lines of *Time* or *Newsweek.*

MONEY MATTERS

Prices for goods and services can be volatile at times. A 10% Goods and Services Tax (or GST—similar to V.A.T. in other countries) applies to most activities and goods, though some unprocessed foods are exempt.

These are some examples of the costs you may face in Australia (at least at this writing): A$2.50–A$4 for a cup of coffee; A$3–A$6 for a beer; A$3.50–A$8 for a take-out sandwich or meat pie; A$4–A$9 for a hamburger in a café; A$12–A$15 for a sandwich ordered through hotel room service; A$10 for a 2-km (1-mi) taxi ride.

Prices throughout this guide are given for adults. Substantially reduced fees are almost always available for children, students, and senior citizens. For information on taxes, *see* Taxes.

ATMS

You'll be able to find an ATM pretty much anywhere in Australia; you can withdraw money with a debit or credit card. Cards linked to the Cirrus network are widely accepted, but cards that don't use a four-digit PIN aren't universally accepted.

CREDIT CARDS

Most Australian establishments take credit cards: Visa and MasterCard are the most widely accepted, American Express and Diners Club aren't always accepted outside the cities. Just in case, bring enough cash to cover your expenses if you're visiting a national park or a remote area.

Throughout this guide, the following abbreviations are used: **AE**, American Express; **DC**, Diners Club; **MC**, MasterCard; and **V**, Visa.

🗷 Reporting Lost Cards **American Express** ☎ 1300/132639. **Diners Club** ☎ 1300/360060. **MasterCard** ☎ 1800/120113. **Visa** ☎ 1800/805341.

CURRENCY

All prices are quoted in Australian dollars. Australia's currency operates on a decimal system, with the dollar (A$) as the basic unit and 100 cents (¢) equaling $1. Bills, differentiated by color and size, come in $100, $50, $20, $10, and $5 denominations, and are made of plastic rather than paper. Coins are minted in $2, $1, 50¢, 20¢, 10¢, and 5¢ denominations.

CURRENCY EXCHANGE

At this writing, the exchange rate was about A$1.28 to the U.S. dollar, A$1.04 to the Canadian dollar, A$2.28 to the pound sterling, and A93¢ to the New Zealand dollar.

For the most favorable rates, **change money through banks.** Although ATM transaction fees may be higher abroad than at home, ATM rates are excellent because they're based on wholesale rates offered only by major banks. You won't do as well at exchange booths in airports, rail and bus stations, hotels, restaurants, or stores. To avoid lines at airport exchange booths, get a bit of local currency before you leave home.

🗷 **Exchange Services International Currency Express** ✉ 427 N. Camden Dr., Suite F, Beverly Hills, CA 90210 ☎ 888/278-6628 orders ⊟ 310/278-6410 ⊕ www.foreignmoney.com. **Travel Ex Currency Services** ☎ 800/287-7362 orders and retail locations ⊕ www.travelex.com.

TRAVELER'S CHECKS

If you'll be in rural areas or small towns, take cash; traveler's checks are best for cities. Lost or stolen checks can usually be replaced within 24 hours. To ensure a speedy refund, buy your own traveler's checks—don't let someone else pay for them: irregularities like this can cause delays. The person who bought the checks should make the call to request a refund.

PACKING

Wear layered outfits when you're Down Under, as the weather can turn on a dime. A light sweater or jacket, a raincoat, and an umbrella are valuable accessories, as is a hat with a brim. Carry insect repellent and **avoid lotions or perfume** in the tropics, as they attract mosquitoes and other insects.

Dress codes in the city are generally casual. Pack nicer duds—a cocktail dress for women or a jacket and tie for men—if you plan to partake of some fine dining. A light sweater or jacket will keep you comfy in autumn, but winter demands a heavier coat—ideally a raincoat with a zip-out wool lining. **Wear comfortable walking shoes:** you should pack sturdy walking boots, as well as running shoes or sneakers.

In your carry-on luggage pack an extra pair of eyeglasses or contact lenses and enough of any medication you take to last a few days longer than the entire trip. You may also ask your doctor to write a spare prescription using the drug's generic name, as brand names may vary from country to country. In luggage to be checked, **never pack prescription drugs, valuables, or undeveloped film.** And don't forget to carry with you the addresses of offices that handle refunds of lost traveler's checks. Check *Fodor's How to Pack* (available at online retailers and bookstores everywhere) for more tips.

To avoid customs and security delays, carry medications in their original packaging. Don't pack any sharp objects in your carry-on luggage, including knives of any size or material, scissors, nail clippers, and corkscrews, or anything else that might arouse suspicion.

To avoid having your checked luggage chosen for hand inspection, don't cram bags full. The U.S. Transportation Security Administration suggests packing shoes on top and placing personal items you don't want touched in clear plastic bags.

CHECKING LUGGAGE

You're allowed to carry aboard one bag and one personal article, such as a purse or a laptop computer. Make sure what you carry on fits under your seat or in the overhead bin. Get to the gate early, so you can board as soon as possible, before the overhead bins fill up.

Baggage allowances vary by carrier, destination, and ticket class. On international flights, you're usually allowed to check two bags weighing up to 70 pounds (32 kilograms) each, although a few airlines allow checked bags of up to 88 pounds (40 kilograms) in first class. Some international carriers don't allow more than 66 pounds (30 kilograms) per bag in business class and 44 pounds (20 kilograms) in economy. If you're flying to or through the United Kingdom, your luggage cannot exceed 70 pounds (32 kilograms) per bag. On domestic flights, the limit is usually 50 to 70 pounds (23 to 32 kilograms) per bag. In general, carry-on bags shouldn't exceed 40 pounds (18 kilograms). Most airlines won't accept bags that weigh more than 100 pounds (45 kilograms) on domestic or international flights. Expect to pay a fee for baggage that exceeds weight limits. Check baggage restrictions with your carrier before you pack.

Airline liability for baggage is limited to $2,500 per person on flights within the United States. On international flights it amounts to $9.07 per pound or $20 per kilogram for checked baggage (roughly $640 per 70-pound bag), with a maximum of $634.90 per piece, and $400 per passenger for unchecked baggage. You can buy additional coverage at check-in for about $10 per $1,000 of coverage, but it often excludes a rather extensive list of items, shown on your airline ticket.

Before departure, itemize your bags' contents and their worth, and label the bags with your name, address, and phone number. (If you use your home address, cover it so potential thieves can't see it readily.) Include a label inside each bag and **pack a copy of your itinerary.** At check-in, make sure each bag is correctly tagged with the destination airport's three-letter code. Because some checked bags will be opened for hand inspection, the U.S. Transportation Security Administration recommends that you leave luggage unlocked or use the plastic locks offered at check-in. TSA screeners place an inspection notice inside searched bags, which are resealed with a special lock.

If your bag has been searched and contents are missing or damaged, file a claim with the U.S. Transportation Security Administration's (TSA's) Consumer Response Center as soon as possible. If your bags arrive damaged or fail to arrive at all, file a written report with the airline before leaving the airport.

⛄ Complaints U.S. Transportation Security Administration Contact Center ☎ 866/289-9673 ⊕ www.tsa.gov.

PASSPORTS & VISAS

When traveling internationally, carry your passport even if you don't need one (it's always the best form of ID) and **make two photocopies of the data page** (one for someone at home and another for you, carried separately from your passport). If you lose your passport, promptly call the nearest embassy or consulate and the local police.

U.S. passport applications for children under age 14 require consent from both parents or legal guardians; both parents must appear together to sign the application. If only one parent appears, he or she must submit a written statement from the other parent authorizing passport issuance for the child. A parent with sole authority must present evidence of it when applying; acceptable documentation includes the child's certified birth certificate listing only the applying parent, a court order specifically permitting this parent's travel with the child, or a death certificate for the nonapplying parent. Application forms and instructions are available on the Web site of the U.S. State Department's Bureau of Consular Affairs (⊕ travel.state.gov).

ENTERING AUSTRALIA

A valid passport is necessary to enter Australia for stays of up to 90 days. Additionally, all foreign travelers to Australia, except for citizens of New Zealand, require a visa or an Electronic Travel Authority (ETA). The free ETA, an electronically stored travel permit, replaces the visa label or stamp in a passport, and enables passengers to be processed more quickly upon arriving in Australia. ETAs are available through travel agencies and airlines. To obtain an ETA for Australia you must: 1) hold an ETA-eligible passport; 2) visit Australia for tourism, family, or business; 3) stay less than three months; 4) be in good health; and 5) have no criminal convictions. If you're planning on getting a tourist ETA or visa, no work in the country is allowed. People who don't meet these requirements should contact their nearest Australian diplomatic office. If you plan to stay longer than three months you must obtain a visa (there's a $65 fee). If you travel to Australia on an under-three-month ETA and later decide to extend your visit, then you must apply for a visa at the nearest Australian Immigration regional office (there's a A$195 fee).

Passengers of Qantas can obtain an Australian visa from the airline. Otherwise, application forms are available from one of the offices listed below. Children traveling on a parent's passport don't need a separate application form, but should be included under Item 16 on a parent's form. For more information on entry requirements, visit the Department of Immigration and Multicultural and Indigenous Affairs Web site at ⊕ www.immi.gov.au.

PASSPORT OFFICES

The best time to apply for a passport or to renew is in fall and winter. Before any trip, check your passport's expiration date, and, if necessary, renew it as soon as possible.

⊿ Canadian Citizens Passport Office ⊠ To mail in applications: 70 Cremazie St., Gatineau, Québec J8Y 3P2 ☎ 800/567-6868 or 819/994-3500 ⊕ www. ppt.gc.ca.

⊿ New Zealand Citizens New Zealand Passports Office ☎ 0800/225-050 or 04/474-8100 ⊕ www. passports.govt.nz.

⊿ U.K. Citizens U.K. Passport Service ☎ 0870/ 521-0410 ⊕ www.passport.gov.uk.

⊿ U.S. Citizens National Passport Information Center ☎ 877/487-2778, 888/874-7793 TDD/TTY ⊕ travel.state.gov.

SAFETY

Don't wear a money belt or a waist pack, both of which peg you as a tourist. Distribute your cash and any valuables (including your credit cards and passport) between a deep front pocket, an inside jacket or vest pocket, and a hidden money pouch. Do not reach for the money pouch once you're in public.

Given Australia's relaxed lifestyle, it's easy to be seduced into believing that crime is nonexistent. In fact, Australia has its share of poverty, drugs, and crime. Although crime rates aren't high by world standards, you should be wary, especially of theft. In major tourist areas such as Sydney's Bondi or Queensland's Gold Coast, the risk increases. When you park your vehicle, hide any valuables. Don't leave anything of value on the beach when you go for a swim. Under no conditions should you hitchhike.

Always be cautious with your money and documents. Be particularly careful when withdrawing money from an ATM—do so during daylight hours, in the company of family or friends, and in a safe location.

WOMEN TRAVELERS

Traveling in Australia is generally safe for women, provided you follow a few common-sense precautions. **Avoid isolated** areas such as empty beaches. At night, avoid quiet streets. You'll probably receive attention if you enter pubs or clubs alone. Cafés are a safer bet. Look confident and purposeful.

If you carry a purse, choose one with a zipper and a thick strap that you can drape across your body; adjust the length so that the purse sits in front of you at or above hip level. (Don't wear a money belt or a waist pack.) Store only enough money in the purse to cover casual spending. Distribute the rest of your cash and any valuables between deep front pockets, inside jacket or vest pockets, and a concealed money pouch.

SHOPPING

It's relatively easy to find a bargain in Australia, though you might not have the time it takes to look for them. The quality's good and the prices are competitive, particularly for clothing. Bargain seekers can join a shopping tour in Melbourne or Sydney, which visit one or two factory outlets. Check with your concierge or the state tourist office for more information.

A 10% Goods and Services Tax (GST) is levied on all goods and services, except for some unprocessed foods. However, you can claim a GST refund on goods that you carry as hand luggage when you depart from Australia. These items must be inspected by customs officials. The refund is paid on goods costing at least A$300 that come from the same store and were purchased within 30 days prior to your departure. You can buy goods from several stores, provided that each store's tax invoice totals at least A$300. The refund is paid when you leave the country.

KEY DESTINATIONS

Sydney has the best one-stop shopping for distinctive Australian souvenirs like opals, Aboriginal art and artifacts, and bush apparel, particularly at the Rocks and Darling Harbour. Alice Springs, Ayers Rock Resort, and Darwin have stores specializing in Aboriginal art.

SMART SOUVENIRS

The didgeridoo, a traditional Northern Territory Aboriginal instrument, is a popular souvenir. Unpainted examples start at around A$70, while more spectacular versions will cost at least A$200. These instruments, however, aren't very portable. More transportable alternatives include a pair of Aboriginal clapping sticks, which run A$10–A$20, or a vividly colored wooden boomerang.

Tea tree oil, from the melaleuca tree's leaves, is a traditional bushman's salve. It also smells really good, and is usually available from airport stores selling "Australiana" products. Typically, a 50-milliliter bottle will cost A$7. There's a thriving industry of products made from local wood; Tasmania, in particular, is known for its Huon pine, sassafras, and blackwood creations. Nationwide, specialty shops sell top-grade prepacked beef and salmon. Of course, you can always take home a few bottles of superb Australian wine.

WATCH OUT

Australia has strict laws prohibiting the export of native animals and plants. It's also illegal to take or send out of the country without a permit objects that are deemed important to Australia's cultural heritage.

SPORTS & THE OUTDOORS

BEACHES

Australia is blessed with fine beaches, and many of them are near major cities. Swim only at designated areas where lifeguards are on duty. The surf is often rough, and many beaches have a treacherous undertow. Volunteer lifesavers monitor almost all metropolitan and town beaches in spring and summer.

On many Australian beaches women sunbathe topless; some beaches, like Sydney's Lady Jane and Perth's Swanbourne, are for those who prefer sunning and swimming au naturel.

BICYCLING

Biking is popular within Australia, where the flat terrain is perfect for long-distance cycling, but be aware of the large distances between the country's popular destinations. Local biking organizations can provide maps and advice.

Although major tourist areas have bike-rental agencies, you should bring your own if you'd like to do most of your exploring astride a bike seat. Most airlines accommodate bikes as luggage, provided they're dismantled and boxed; check with individual airlines about packing requirements. Some airlines sell bike boxes, which are often free at bike shops, for about A$15 (bike bags can be considerably more expensive). International travelers can often substitute a bike for a piece of checked luggage at no charge; otherwise, the cost is about A$100. U.S. and Canadian airlines charge A$40–A$80 each way.

🚴 **Bicycle Federation of Australia** ⊕ www.bfa. asn.au. **Breakaway Bicycle Club** ☎ 1877/829-8899 ⊕ www.breakawaybicycleclub.org.

BOATING & SAILING

Australians love messing about in boats, as you can plainly see on a warm afternoon in Sydney Harbour. The Whitsunday Islands, off Queensland's coast, afford tranquillity, warmth, and idyllic anchorages.

🚤 **Australian Yachting Federation** ✉ 33 Peel St., Kirribilli, NSW 2061 ☎ 02/9922-4333 🖷 02/ 9923-2883.

CRICKET

The nation unites in its obsession with this summer sport. Played between teams of 11 players, this slow and often incomprehensible game can take place over the course of a day. Test matches (full-scale international games) can last for five days. The faster-paced one-day games are gaining popularity. Cricket season runs from October through March.

DIVING

The Great Barrier Reef is one of the world's leading dive destinations, and there are many dive operators along the coast who can introduce you to its wonders. Scuba divers frequent the Ningaloo Reef in Western Australia. Even Sydney has several good underwater sites. If you're a novice, consider a resort dive. Once you've passed a brief safety lesson with a dive master in shallow water, you can make a 30-minute dive to a maximum depth of about 33 feet.

🤿 **Australian Underwater Federation** ✉ 42 Toyer Ave., Sans Souci, NSW 2219 ☎ 02/9529-6496.

FISHING

Record-breaking marlin are frequently caught on the east coast: the region around Cairns and Lizard Island has garnered world acclaim for its giant black marlin catches. Black and blue marlin, mackerel, tuna, barracuda, and sailfish are found all along the east coast. September through November is the best time for catching marlin off Cairns; the end of November through May is best in Bermagui on New South Wales' south coast.

Barramundi, jack, tarpon, and mackerel attract anglers to the waters of the Northern Territory's Top End, around Darwin and Bathurst Island. June through November is a good time for barramundi. Rainbow and brown trout thrive in the lake-fed streams of Tasmania, the rivers of the Australian Alps in Victoria and New South Wales, and in the Onkaparinga River on the outskirts of Adelaide. Fishing seasons vary by region, but are generally December–May.

FOOTBALL

Australia embraces four football codes: soccer, rugby union, rugby league, and the unique Australian Rules Football. If you're traveling between March and September, try to watch an Australian Rules match for an exhilarating spectacle.

GOLF

Australia has more than 1,400 golf courses. Some private clubs extend reciprocal rights to overseas club members on proof of membership. You can always arrange a round on a municipal course, though you may have to contend with kangaroos watching your form.

Golf clubs can usually be rented, but you'll need your own shoes. Greens fees at public courses start at A$30 for 18 holes.

⛳ **Classic Australian Golf Tours** ☎ 800/426-3610. **ITC Golf Tours** ☎ 800/257-4981. **Swain Australia Tours** ☎ 800/227-9246.

HIKING

For information on park trails in the state you'll be visiting, contact its National Parks and Wildlife Service department. Hiking tours can be arranged through the bushwalking clubs listed in each capital city's telephone directory.

Temperatures vary widely from day into night. **Bring warm clothing** for hiking and camping, along with **wet-weather gear.** Conditions can quickly do a 180-degree turn any time of year. If you're not dressed warmly enough, hypothermia can set in. You'll progress through the following symptoms when your body temperature dips below 35°C (95°F): chills, fatigue, then uncontrollable shivering and irrational behavior—victims may not recognize that they're cold. Someone who's suffering from any of these symptoms should immediately be wrapped in blankets and/or a sleeping bag and kept awake. Hydrating the person with warm liquids also helps.

Never drink from streams or lakes, no matter how clear they may seem. Giardia organisms, which cause nausea and diarrhea, can be a real problem. The easiest way to purify water is by dissolving a purification tablet in it, or by drawing it through a purification pump. Boiling water for 15 minutes is always reliable, if time- and fuel-consuming. For information on camping, *see* Lodging.

HORSE & CAMEL RIDING

With Australia's wide-open landscape and its history of rowdy stockmen, it's not surprising that horseback riding ranks among its most popular activities. Stables around the country organize trail rides ranging in length from a couple of hours to a week. The Blue Mountains near Sydney and the Snowy Mountains in southern New South Wales are ideal destinations for horseback adventures.

You can ride camels around Alice Springs and Uluru. Be aware that they can get quite cantankerous, and the ride may be bumpy.

SKIING

The season runs from late June through September. Admittedly, Australian ski resorts don't quite compare with those in the United States and Europe—the snowfall is less significant and there's less vertical rise—but they retain an appealing bushland character. The Snowy Mountains region of New South Wales and Victoria's High Country have the major downhill areas, though Tasmania also has snowfields. Cross-country skiing is more rewarding thanks to Australia's vast snowfields and curious flora and fauna. The principal cross-country areas are in Kosciuszko National Park in New South Wales, and in Victoria's Alps. Snowboarding is becoming more popular, and equipment is available at the ski resorts.

TENNIS

Australia has been spawning champion tennis players for a century. Most hotels and resorts have courts for guests.

TAXES

Everyone leaving Australia pays a A$38 departure tax, a.k.a. Passenger Movement Charge. It's included in your airline ticket price. There's also a 10% Goods and Services Tax (GST), which doesn't apply to certain foods.

TELEPHONES

The phone system is efficient and reliable. Australian regular numbers have eight digits. Get around hotel surcharges by calling from a public phone, or by charging to a local account (contact your local telephone service for details). Australia's cellular phones operate on either a GSM (Global System for Mobiles) or CDMA (Code Division Multiple Access) system. Some of your cell phone's functions won't work outside your home country. Check whether your phone is cleared for international access. In some of Australia's more remote parts cell phone reception is patchy. Your pager won't work in Australia.

AREA & COUNTRY CODES

The country code for Australia is 61. When dialing an Australian number from abroad, drop the initial "0" from the local area code. From the United States, dial 011, then 61, then the local area code. From the United Kingdom, dial 00, then 61.

Area codes for the major cities are 02 for Sydney and Canberra; 03 for Melbourne and Hobart; 07 for Brisbane and Cairns;

08 for Adelaide, Alice Springs, Ayers Rock Resort, Darwin, and Perth.

DIRECTORY & OPERATOR ASSISTANCE

For local directory assistance, dial 1223. For international directory assistance, dial 1225. For information on international call costs, dial 1300/362162.

INTERNATIONAL CALLS

To call overseas from Australia, dial 0011 or 0018, then the country code and the number. Kiosks and groceries in major cities sell international calling cards. You can also use credit cards on public phones.

LOCAL CALLS

A local call costs A40¢. Australian numbers with a "13" or "1300" prefix can be dialed countrywide for the cost of a local call. For example, dialing a 13 number for a company in Melbourne when you're in Sydney will be billed as a local call. Toll-free numbers in Australia have an 1800 prefix. Unless otherwise noted, toll-free numbers in this book are accessible only within Australia.

LONG-DISTANCE CALLS

Long-distance calls can be dialed directly using the city code or area code. Rates are divided into two time periods: Day (weekdays 7 AM–7 PM) and Economy (weekdays 7 PM–7 AM and Friday 7 PM–Monday 7 AM). Area codes are listed in the white pages of local telephone directories.

All regular telephone numbers in Australia have eight digits. When you're calling long-distance within Australia, remember to include the area code, even when you're calling from a number with the same area code. For example, when calling Canberra from Sydney, both of which have an 02 prefix, you still need to include the area code when you dial.

LONG-DISTANCE SERVICES

AT&T, MCI, and Sprint access codes make calling long-distance relatively convenient, but you may find the local access number blocked in many hotel rooms. First ask the hotel operator to connect you. If the hotel operator balks, ask for an international operator, or dial the interna-

tional operator yourself. One way to improve your odds of getting connected to your long-distance carrier is to travel with more than one company's calling card (a hotel may block Sprint, for example, but not MCI). If all else fails, use a credit card or call from a pay phone.

7 **Access Codes AT&T Direct** ☎ 800/435-0812. **MCI WorldCom** ☎ 800/444-4141. **Sprint International Access** ☎ 800/877-4646.

PHONE CARDS

Even if you plan on making just a few calls, phone cards will likely save you money. They may be purchased from post offices or news agencies. They're available in units of A$5, A$10, A$20, and A$50. Most public phones accept phone cards, and some—especially those in hotels and airports—also accept credit cards.

PUBLIC PHONES

Public phones are in shopping areas, on suburban streets, at train stations, and outside rural post offices—basically, they're everywhere.

Local calls cost A40¢ and are untimed. Long-distance calls, however, are timed. Rates vary depending on the distance between caller and recipient. If coins are used a warning beep is given to indicate that more money should be inserted. Phone cards are better for long-distance calls since you'll know how much money you've got left.

TIME

Without daylight saving time, Sydney is 14 hours ahead of New York and Toronto; 15 hours ahead of Chicago and Dallas; 17 hours ahead (or count back 7 hours and add a day) from Los Angeles, Seattle, and Vancouver; and 10 hours ahead of London. Around the Pacific Rim, Sydney is 2 hours behind Auckland, 1 hour ahead of Tokyo, and 2 hours ahead of Singapore.

Australia has three major time zones. Eastern Standard Time (EST) applies in Tasmania, Victoria, New South Wales, and Queensland; Central Standard Time applies in South Australia and the Northern Territory; and Western Standard Time applies in Western Australia. Central Standard Time is ½ hour behind EST, and Western Standard Time is 2 hours behind EST.

Within the EST zone, each state chooses a slightly different date on which to commence or end daylight saving from its neighboring state—except for Queensland, where the powerful farm lobby has prevented the state from introducing daylight saving, since it would make the cows wake up an hour earlier. Western Australia and the Northern Territory also decline to recognize daylight saving, which means that at certain times of the year Australia can have as many as six different time zones.

TIPPING

Hotels and restaurants don't add service charges. It's a widely accepted practice to tip a waiter 10%–12% for good service. Room service and housemaids aren't tipped except for special service. Taxi drivers don't expect a tip, but you may want to leave any small change. Guides, tour bus drivers, and chauffeurs don't expect tips either, though they're grateful if someone in the group takes up a collection for them. No tipping is necessary in hair salons or for theater ushers.

TOURS & PACKAGES

Because everything is prearranged on a prepackaged tour or independent vacation, you spend less time planning—and often get it all at a good price.

BOOKING WITH AN AGENT

Travel agents are excellent resources. But it's a good idea to collect brochures from several agencies, as some agents' suggestions may be influenced by relationships with tour and package firms that reward them for volume sales. If you have a special interest, find an agent with expertise in that area. The American Society of Travel Agents (ASTA) has a database of specialists worldwide; you can log on to the group's Web site to find one near you.

Make sure your travel agent knows the accommodations and other services of the place being recommended. Ask about the hotel's location, room size, beds, and whether it has a pool, room service, or programs for children, if you care about these. Has your agent been there in person or sent others whom you can contact?

Do some homework on your own, too: local tourism boards can provide information about lesser-known and small-niche operators, some of which may sell only direct.

BUYER BEWARE

Each year, consumers are stranded or lose their money when tour operators—even large ones with excellent reputations—go out of business. So check out the operator. Ask several travel agents about its reputation, and try to **book with a company that has a consumer-protection program.** (Look for information in the company's brochure.) In the United States, members of the United States Tour Operators Association are required to set aside funds (up to $1 million) to help eligible customers cover payments and travel arrangements in the event that the company defaults. It's also a good idea to choose a company that participates in the American Society of Travel Agents' Tour Operator Program; ASTA will act as mediator in any disputes between you and your tour operator.

Remember that the more your package or tour includes, the better you can predict the ultimate cost of your vacation. Make sure you know exactly what is covered, and beware of hidden costs. Are taxes, tips, and transfers included? Entertainment and excursions? These can add up.

🔁 Tour-Operator Recommendations American Society of Travel Agents (⇨ Travel Agencies). **Backroads International** ✉ 810 Cedar St., Berkeley, CA 94710 ☎ 800/462-2848 or 510/527-1555 🖷 510/527-1444 ⊕ www.backroads.com. **Earthwatch** ✉ 3 Clock Tower Pl., Suite 100, Maynard, MA 01754 ☎ 800/766-0188 or 978/461-0081 🖷 978/461-2332 ⊕ www.earthwatch.org. **Grand Circle** ☎ 800/959-0405 ⊕ www.gct.com. **Journeys International** ✉ 107 Aprill Dr., Suite 3, Ann Arbor, MI 48103 ☎ 800/255-8735 or 734/665-4407 🖷 734/665-2945 ⊕ www.journeys-itl.com. **National Tour Association (NTA)** ✉ 546 E. Main St., Lexington, KY 40508 ☎ 800/682-8886 or 859/226-4444 🖷 859/226-4404 ⊕ www.ntaonline.com. **United States Tour Operators Association (USTOA)** ✉ 275 Madison Ave., Suite 2014, New York, NY 10016 ☎ 212/599-6599 🖷 212/599-6744 ⊕ www.ustoa.com.

TRAIN TRAVEL

Australia has a network trains providing first- and economy-class service. The major interstate trains are the *Indian-Pacific* from Sydney to Perth via Adelaide (26 hours Sydney–Adelaide, 38 hours Adelaide–Perth); the *Ghan* from Adelaide via Alice Springs to Darwin (44½ hours); the *Overland* (night service) and *Daylink* from Melbourne to Adelaide (12 hours); and the *XPT* (Express Passenger Train) from Sydney to Brisbane (15 hours). Service between Melbourne and Sydney is on the daytime or overnight *XPT* (10½ hours). Within Queensland you can take several interesting train journeys: the *Queenslander* and *Sunlander,* which run along the coast; and the historic *Gulflander* and *Savannahlander,* which travel through Outback regions.

Book early whenever possible, especially for the *Indian-Pacific* and the *Ghan* during peak times (June–October and Christmas holidays). For more information on the train network or to make reservations or purchase discount passes, contact Rail Australia.

CLASSES

Apart from suburban commuter services, Australia's trains have first and second classes. Both are comfortable, but far from luxurious. Most people prefer to travel in their own vehicles. As a result, Australia's railways have received far less funding than highways, and the standards on Australia's train network fall far short of those found in Europe and the United States. Except on long-distance trains such as the *Ghan* or the *Indian-Pacific,* dining amenities are minimal. First class costs approximately 50% more than economy.

DISCOUNTS & PASSES

Advance purchase fares, which afford a 10%–40% discount between some major cities, are best bought before you arrive in Australia. **Make all rail reservations well in advance,** particularly during peak tourist seasons.

You need a passport to purchase an Australian rail pass. Passes must be presented to the ticket office before you embark on your journey; they don't include sleeping berths or meals.

The Austrail Flexi Pass allows a set number of nonconsecutive travel days on the national rail network. Because the value of the pass does not ebb away on days when you're not traveling, the Flexi Pass can be very cost-effective. Two passes are available, for 15 or 22 days. The 15-day pass allows 15 days of economy-class travel in a six-month period and costs A$862.40. The 22-day pass allows 22 days of travel in the same period and costs A$1,210.

The East Coast Discovery Pass allows economy-class travel between any two points from Melbourne to Cairns, with unlimited stops along the way. The pass is valid for six months, and for travel in one direction only. The cost of the pass is A$312.40 from Sydney to Cairns, A$393.80 from Melbourne to Cairns.

🚂 **Train Information Rail Australia** ⏏ Box 445, Marleston Business Centre, Marleston, SA 5033 ✉ Box 2430, Hollywood, CA 90078 ☎ 310/643–0044 ATS Tours in U.S. and Canada, 800/633–3404 Austravel Inc. in U.S., 800/387–8850 Goway Travel in Canada, 0171/828–4111 in U.K., 13–4592 in Australia ⊕ www.railaustralia.com.au.

FARES & SCHEDULES

Rail Australia provides information and booking services for all major train systems, including the *Ghan,* the *Indian-Pacific,* and the *Overland.*

PAYING

Almost all train companies accept credit cards, some even take traveler's checks.

RESERVATIONS

It's a good idea to **make advance reservations.** You should book (and pay for) your tickets as early as possible to secure choice seats during high season and holiday periods.

TRAVEL AGENCIES

A good travel agent puts your needs first. Look for an agency that has been in business at least five years, emphasizes customer service, and has someone on staff who specializes in your destination. In addition, **make sure the agency belongs to a professional trade organization.** The

American Society of Travel Agents (ASTA) has more than 10,000 members in some 140 countries, enforces a strict code of ethics, and will step in to mediate agent-client disputes involving ASTA members. ASTA also maintains a directory of agents on its Web site. If a travel agency is also acting as your tour operator, *see* Buyer Beware *in* Tours & Packages.

⚡ Local Agent Referrals American Society of Travel Agents (ASTA) ✉ 1101 King St., Suite 200, Alexandria, VA 22314 ☎ 800/965-2782 24-hr hotline, 703/739-2782 📠 703/684-8319 ⊕ www.astanet.com. **Association of British Travel Agents** ✉ 68-71 Newman St., London W1T 3AH ☎ 020/7637-2444 📠 020/7637-0713 ⊕ www.abta.com. **Association of Canadian Travel Agencies** ✉ 130 Albert St., Suite 1705, Ottawa, Ontario K1P 5G4 ☎ 613/237-3657 📠 613/237-7052 ⊕ www.acta.ca. **Australian Federation of Travel Agents** ✉ Level 3, 309 Pitt St., Sydney, NSW 2000 ☎ 02/9264-3299 or 1300/363416 📠 02/9264-1085 ⊕ www.afta.com.au. **Travel Agents' Association of New Zealand** ✉ Tourism and Travel House, Level 5, 79 Boulcott St., Box 1888, Wellington 6001 ☎ 04/499-0104 📠 04/499-0786 ⊕ www.taanz.org.nz.

VISITOR INFORMATION

Learn more about foreign destinations by checking government-issued travel advisories and country information. For a broader picture, consider information from more than one country.

For general information contact the tourism offices below and call for the free information-packed booklet "Destination Australia" (in the United States). The Australian Tourist Commission's Aussie Help Line, available from 8 AM to 7 PM Central Standard Time, can answer specific questions about planning your trip. Before you go, contact Friends Overseas—Australia to be put in touch with Australians who share your interests. Membership is A$25.

⚡ Countrywide Information Australian Tourist Commission ✉ U.S.: 2049 Century Park E, Los Angeles, CA 90067 ☎ 310/229-4870 📠 310/552-1215 ✉ U.K.: Gemini House, 10-18 Putney Hill, London SW15 6AA ☎ 0990/022-000 for information, 0990/561-434 for brochure line 📠 0181/940-5221 ✉ New Zealand: Level 13, 44-48 Emily Pl., Box 1666, Auckland 1 ☎ 0800/650-303. **"Destination Australia" booklet** ☎ 800/333-0262. **Friends Overseas—Aus-**tralia ✉ 68-01 Dartmouth St., Forest Hills, NY 11375 ☎ 718/261-0534.

⚡ Regional Information Australian Travel Headquarters ✉ 1600 Dove St., Suite 215, Newport Beach, CA 92660 ☎ 800/546-2155 or 714/852-2270 📠 714/852-2277 for South Australia. **Australia's Northern Territory** ✉ 3601 Aviation Blvd., Suite 2100, Manhattan Beach, CA 90266 ☎ 310/643-2636 📠 310/643-2637. **Queensland Tourist & Travel Corporation** ✉ 1800 Century Park E, Suite 330, Los Angeles, CA 90067 ☎ 310/788-0997.

⚡ Government Advisories U.S. Department of State ✉ Bureau of Consular Affairs, Overseas Citizens Services Office, 2201 C St. NW, Washington, DC 20520 ☎ 202/647-5225, 888/407-4747 or 317/472-2328 for interactive hotline ⊕ travel.state.gov. **Consular Affairs Bureau of Canada** ☎ 800/267-6788 or 613/944-6788 ⊕ www.voyage.gc.ca. **U.K. Foreign and Commonwealth Office** ✉ Travel Advice Unit, Consular Directorate, Old Admiralty Bldg., London SW1A 2PA ☎ 0870/606-0290 or 020/7008-1500 ⊕ www.fco.gov.uk/travel. **New Zealand Ministry of Foreign Affairs and Trade** ☎ 04/439-8000 ⊕ www.mft.govt.nz.

WEB SITES

Do check out the World Wide Web when planning your trip. You'll find everything from weather forecasts to virtual tours of famous cities. Be sure to visit Fodors.com (⊕ www.fodors.com), a complete travel-planning site. You can research prices and book plane tickets, hotel rooms, rental cars, vacation packages, and more. In addition, you can post your pressing questions in the Travel Talk section. Other planning tools include a currency converter and weather reports, and there are loads of links to travel resources.

The Australian Tourist Commission Web site (⊕ www.australia.com) is a good planning resource. For more specific information, contact the individual states' Web sites: Australian Capital Territory (⊕ www.visitcanberra.com.au); New South Wales (⊕ www.visitnsw.com.au); Northern Territory (⊕ www.ntholidays.com); Queensland (⊕ www.queenslandholidays.com.au or www.queenslandtravel.com.au); South Australia (⊕ www.southaustralia.com); Tasmania (⊕ www.discovertasmania.com.au); Victoria (⊕ www.visitvictoria.com); Western Australia (⊕ www.westernaustralia.com).

Sydney

WORD OF MOUTH

"If I can manage the Sydney Harbour Bridge climb, virtually anyone can. It is done at a very leisurely pace. The total experience lasts about three and half hours, of which you are only climbing up for about 30 minutes with plenty of breaks. Seriously, if you can walk a mile you will have no trouble with the bridge climb. It's worth every penny—but you'll needs lots of them, because it's not cheap."

—Walter_Walltotti

2

Updated by
Emily Burg and
Melanie Ball

SYDNEY BELONGS TO THE EXCLUSIVE CLUB OF WORLD CITIES that generate a sense of excitement from the air. Even at the end of a marathon flight across the Pacific, there's renewed vitality in the cabin as the plane circles the city, crossing the branching fingers of the harbor, where thousands of yachts are suspended on the dark water and the sails of the Opera House glisten in the distance. Endowed with dazzling beaches and a sunny Mediterranean climate, its setting alone guarantees Sydney a place among the most beautiful cities on the planet.

At 4 million people, Sydney is the biggest and most cosmopolitan city in Australia. Take a taxi from Sydney Airport and chances are that the driver won't say "G'day" with the accent you might expect. A wave of immigration in the 1950s has seen the Anglo-Irish immigrants who made up the city's original population enriched by Italians, Greeks, Turks, Lebanese, Chinese, Vietnamese, Thais, and Indonesians. This intermingling has created a cultural vibrancy and energy—and a culinary repertoire—that was missing only a generation ago.

Sydneysiders, as locals are known, embrace their harbor with a passion. Indented with numerous bays and beaches, Sydney Harbour is the presiding icon for the city, and for urban Australia. Captain Arthur Phillip, commander of the 11-ship First Fleet, wrote in his diary when he first set eyes on the harbor on January 26, 1788: "We had the satisfaction of finding the finest harbor in the world, in which a thousand ships of the line may ride in the most perfect security." It was not an easy beginning, however. Pushing inland, Australia's first settlers were confronted with harsh, foreign terrain that few of them possessed skills to navigate. They were the first round of wretched inmates (roughly 800) flushed from overcrowded jails in England and sent halfway around the globe to serve their sentences.

Sydney has long since outgrown the stigma of its convict origins, but the passage of time has not tamed its rebellious spirit. Sydney's panache and appetite for life are unchallenged in the Australian context. A walk among the scantily clad sunbathers at Bondi Beach or through the buzzing nightlife districts of Kings Cross and Oxford Street provides ample evidence.

Although a visit to Sydney is an essential part of an Australian experience, the city is no more representative of Australia than Los Angeles is of the United States. Sydney has joined the ranks of the great cities whose characters are essentially international. What Sydney offers are style, sophistication, and good—no, great—looks; an exhilarating prelude to the continent at its back door.

EXPLORING SYDNEY

Sydney is a giant, stretching nearly 97 km (60 mi) from top to bottom and about 55 km (34 mi) across. The harbor divides the city into northern and southern halves, with most of the headline attractions on the south shore. Most tourists spend their time on the harbor's south side, within an area bounded by Chinatown in the south, Harbour Bridge in the north, Darling Harbour to the west, and the beaches and coastline

GREAT ITINERARIES

You really need 3 days in Sydney to see the essential city center, while 6 days would give you time to explore the beaches and inner suburbs. A stay of 10 days would allow trips outside the city and give you time to explore a few of Sydney's lesser-known delights.

If you have 3 days

Start with an afternoon Sydney Harbour Explorer cruise for some of the best views of the city. Follow with a tour of the Rocks, the nation's birthplace, and take a sunset walk up onto the **Sydney Harbour Bridge** ㉔. The following day, take a Sydney Explorer tour to the famous **Sydney Opera House** ㊿ and relax at sunset in the **Royal Botanic Gardens** (51), **Domain South** ㊽, and **Domain North** (54) parks. On the third day, explore the city center, with another spectacular panorama from the **Sydney Tower** (63). Include a walk around Macquarie Street, a living reminder of Sydney's colonial history, and the contrasting experience of futuristic Darling Harbour, with its museums, aquarium, cafés, and lively shops.

If you have 6 days

Follow the three-day itinerary above, then visit Kings Cross, Darlinghurst, and Paddington on the fourth day. You could continue to **Bondi** (98), Australia's most famous beach. The next day, catch the ferry to **Manly** (92) to visit its beach and the historic Quarantine Station. From here, take an afternoon bus tour to the northern beaches, or return to the city to shop or visit museums and galleries. Options for the last day include a trip to a wildlife or national park, **Taronga Zoo** ⑬, or the **Sydney Olympic Park** (83) west of the city.

If you have 10 days

Follow the six-day itinerary above, and then travel beyond the city by rental car or with an organized tour. Take day trips to the Blue Mountains, Hunter Valley, **Ku-ring-gai Chase National Park** (79), the Hawkesbury River, or the historic city of Parramatta to Sydney's west. Or travel on the Bondi Explorer bus to **Vaucluse** ❻ or the charming harborside village of **Watsons Bay** ❼. You could take a boat tour to the historic harbor island of **Fort Denison** ⑭, play a round of golf, or just shop or relax on the beach.

---

to the east. North of Harbour Bridge lie the important commercial center of North Sydney and leafy but bland suburbs. Ocean beaches, Taronga Zoo, and Ku-ring-gai Chase National Park are the most likely reasons to venture north of the harbor.

Within a few hours' drive of Sydney are the World Heritage–listed Blue Mountains and the renowned Hunter Valley vineyards. Although both these spots are worthy of an overnight stay, they're also close enough to visit on day trips from the city.

Numbers in the text correspond to numbers in the margin and on the Sydney Harbour, Sydney, Greater Sydney maps.

When to Visit Sydney

The best times to visit Sydney are in late spring and early fall. The spring months of October and November are pleasantly warm, although the ocean is slightly cool for swimming. The midsummer months of December through February are typically hot and humid, with February being quite rainy. In the early-autumn months of March and April, weather is typically stable and comfortable, outdoor city life is still in full swing, and the ocean is at its warmest. Even the coolest winter months of July and August typically stay mild and sunny, with average daily maximum temperatures in the low 60s.

Sydney Harbour

Captain Arthur Phillip, commander of the first European fleet to sail here and the first governor of the colony, called Sydney Harbour "in extent and security, very superior to any other that I have ever seen—containing a considerable number of coves, formed by narrow necks of land, mostly rocks, covered with timber." Two centuries later, few would dispute that the harbor is one of nature's extraordinary creations.

Officially titled Port Jackson, the harbor is in its depths a river valley carved by the Parramatta and Lane Cove rivers and the many creeks that flow in from the north. Several pockets of land are now protected within **Sydney Harbour National Park,** 958 acres of separate foreshores and islands, most of them on the north side of the harbor. To see the best areas, put on your walking shoes and head out on the many well-marked trails. The Hermitage Foreshore Walk skirts through bushland around Vaucluse's Nielsen Park, with sensational views and a fine beach backed by shady parkland. On the north side of the harbor, Bradleys Head and Chowder Head Walk is a 5-km (3-mi) stroll that starts from Taronga Zoo Wharf. The most inspiring trail is the 9½-km (6-mi) Manly Scenic Walkway, which joins the Spit Bridge with Manly by meandering along sandstone headlands, small beaches, and pockets of rain forest, and past Aboriginal sites and the historic Grotto Point Lighthouse. From Cadman's Cottage you can take day tours of Fort Denison and Goat Island, which have significant colonial buildings. The other three islands in the park—Rodd, Clark, and Shark—are recreational reserves that can be visited with permission from Australia's National Parks and Wildlife Service.

Fodor's Choice
★

a good cruise

The following tour is based on the route followed by the State Transit Authority ferries on their daily afternoon harbour cruise. The Coffee Cruise run by Captain Cook Cruises follows a similar course. The tour takes in the eastern half of the harbor, from the city to the Heads and Middle Harbour. This is Sydney at its most spectacular, but the harbor west of the city has its own areas of historic and natural distinction, as well as Homebush Bay, which was the main site for the Olympic Summer Games in 2000. Note that ferries don't actually stop at these locations—this is purely a sightseeing adventure, though you can visit many of these sights by car or public transportation. ⇨ For further details about these trips, *see* Boat Tours *in* Sydney A to Z.

As the vessel leaves the ferry wharves at Circular Quay ►—the transportation hub that runs between the Sydney Harbour Bridge and the Opera House—it crosses **Sydney Cove ❶**, where the ships of the First Fleet

1

Glorious Beaches

The boom of the surf could well be Sydney's summer theme song: 40 beaches, including world-famous Bondi, lie within the Sydney metropolitan area. Spoiled by a choice of ocean or sheltered harbor beaches—and with an average water temperature of 20°C (68°F)—many Sydneysiders naturally head for the shore on the weekends.

Exquisite Cuisine

In the culinary new world order Sydney is one of the glamorous global food centers, ranking right up there with London and New York. The Opera House has the Guillaume at Bennelong, and the Rocks has Quay. Then there are the food burbs of Bondi, Surry Hills, and Darlinghurst, where the smells of good espresso, sizzling grills, and aromatic stir-fry hover in the air. Of course, Sydney food always tastes better when enjoyed outdoors at a sidewalk table, in a sun-drenched courtyard—or best of all, in full view of that glorious harbor.

A Harbor Sail

Sydney Harbour offers many boating opportunities; whether aboard a cruise-boat tour or on an active sailing or kayaking trip. Being on the water is an essential element of the Sydney experience. *See* the Sydney Harbour section for tours of the harbor by boat.

National Parks & Wildlife

The numerous parks and reserves of Greater Sydney make it easy to experience the sights and sounds of wild Australia or the country's Aboriginal heritage. The lands protected by Sydney Harbour National Park provide a habitat for many unique native species of plants and animals. Ku-ring-gai Chase National Park has engravings and paintings by the area's original inhabitants, the Guringai Aboriginal people. Royal National Park encompasses large tracts of coastline and bushland where you can experience Australia's remarkable flora and fauna.

Sports

Whether it's watching or playing, Sydneysiders are devoted to sports, and the city's benign climate makes even water sports a year-round possibility. However, cricket—the most popular summer spectator sport—takes place on land. Australia plays both one-day and international test matches at the Sydney Cricket Ground. The biggest winter game is rugby league, but rugby union and Australian Rules Football also attract passionate followings. There are fine swimming pools, beaches, and boating activities on and around the harbor.

---

dropped anchor in January 1788. After rounding Bennelong Point, the site of the Sydney Opera House, the boat turns east and crosses **Farm Cove ❷**, passing the Royal Botanic Gardens. The tall Gothic Revival chimneys just visible above the trees belong to Government House, formerly the official residence of the state governor.

Garden Island ❸, the country's largest naval dockyard, is easily identifiable across Woolloomooloo (say "*wool*-oo-muh-loo") Bay by its squadrons of sleek gray warships. Dominated by several tall apartment

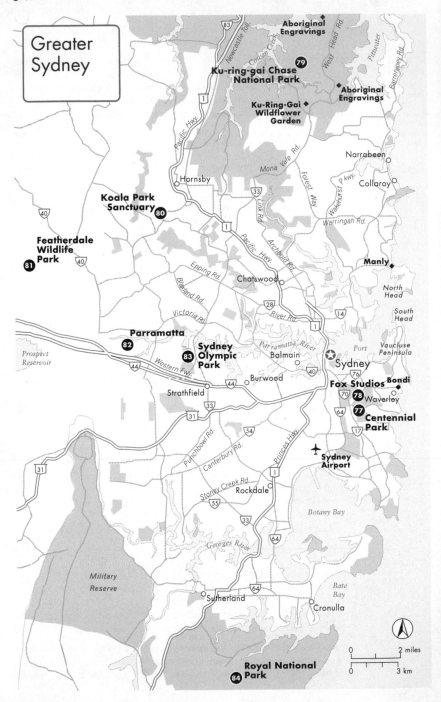

Greater
Sydney

Aboriginal
Engravings

83

Ku-ring-gai Chase
National Park   79

Aboriginal
Engravings

Ku-Ring-Gai
Wildflower
Garden

Narrabeen

Hornsby

Collaroy

Koala Park
Sanctuary   80

Chatswood

Featherdale
Wildlife
Park   81

Manly

North
Head

South
Head

Parramatta
82

Sydney
Olympic
Park   83

Balmain

Sydney

Vaucluse
Peninsula

Prospect
Reservoir

Port

Fox Studios   Bondi

78 Waverley
77 Centennial
Park

Burwood

Strathfield

Sydney
Airport

Rockdale

Botany Bay

Military
Reserve

Bate
Bay

Sutherland

Cronulla

0   2 miles
0   3 km

Royal National
84 Park

blocks, Darling Point, the next headland, marks the beginning of Sydney's desirable eastern suburbs. **Point Piper ❹**, across Double Bay, is famous as the ritziest address in the country. The large expanse of water to the east of Point Piper is **Rose Bay ❺**, bordered by another highly desirable, but somewhat more affordable, harborside suburb.

Beyond Rose Bay, **Vaucluse ❻** is yet another suburb that conveys social stature. The area is named after Vaucluse House, the sandstone mansion built by 19th-century explorer, publisher, and politician William Wentworth. The house is hidden from view, but you can see the Grecian columns of Strickland House, a former convalescent home. To the east is Shark Bay, part of Nielsen Park and one of the most popular harbor beaches. **Watsons Bay ❼**, a former fishing village, is the easternmost suburb on the harbor's south side. Beyond, the giant sandstone buttress of South Head rises high above the crashing Pacific breakers.

North Head is the boat's next landmark, followed by the beachside suburb of Manly and the **Quarantine Station ❽**. Once used to protect Sydney from disease, the station today documents a fascinating chapter in the nation's history. The vessel then enters **Middle Harbour ❾**, formed by creeks that spring from the forested peaks of Ku-ring-gai Chase National Park, and passes the beach at Clontarf to the right before sailing through the Spit Bridge. After exploring Middle Harbour, the boat passes the suburb of **Castlecrag ❿**, founded by Walter Burley Griffin, the American architect responsible for the design of Canberra.

Just before the vessel returns to the main body of the harbor, look right for the popular beach at Balmoral and **Middle Head ⓫**, part of Sydney Harbour National Park and the site of mid-19th-century cannons and fortifications. During that period, Sydney Harbour was a regular port of call for American whaling ships, whose crews were responsible for the name of nearby **Chowder Bay ⓬**. Sailing deeper into the harbor, the vessel passes **Taronga Zoo ⓭**, where you might spot some of the animals through the foliage.

The vessel now heads back toward the Harbour Bridge, passing the tiny island of **Fort Denison ⓮**, Sydney's most prominent fortification. On the point at **Kirribilli ⓯**, almost opposite the Opera House, you can catch glimpses of two colonial-style houses: the official Sydney residences of the governor-general and prime minister, John Howard, who understandably eschews Canberra for this gem of a spot. From the north side of the harbor, the vessel crosses back to Circular Quay, where the tour ends.

TIMING   This scenic cruise, aboard one of the State Transit Authority ferries, takes 2½ hours and operates year-round. Refreshments are available on the boat's lower deck. For the best views, begin the voyage on the right side of the vessel.

What to See

❿ **Castlecrag.** Walter Burley Griffin, an associate of Frank Lloyd Wright, founded this calm, prestigious Middle Harbour suburb after he designed the layout for Canberra. In 1924, after working on the national capital and in Melbourne, the American architect moved to Sydney and

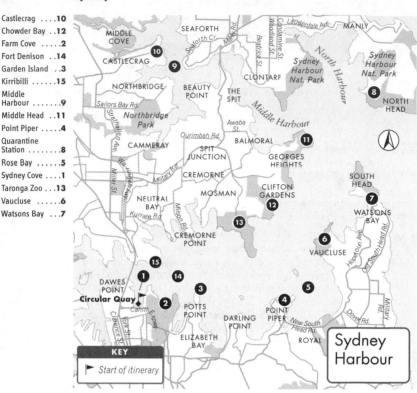

Sydney Harbour

KEY

► Start of itinerary

built a number of houses that are notable for their harmony with the surrounding bushland.

⑫ Chowder Bay. In the 19th century the American whalers who anchored here would collect oysters from the rocks and make shellfish soup—which gave the bay its name. Its location is identifiable by a cluster of wooden buildings at water's edge and twin oil-storage tanks.

② Farm Cove. The original convict-settlers established their first gardens on this bay's shores, now home to the **Royal Botanic Gardens.** The enterprise was not a success: the soil was too sandy for agriculture, and most of the crops fell victim to pests, marauding animals, and hungry convicts. The long seawall was constructed from the 1840s onward to enclose the previously swampy foreshore.

⑭ Fort Denison. For a brief time in the early days of the colony, convicts who committed petty offenses were kept on this harbor island, where they existed on a meager diet that gave the island its early name: Pinchgut. The island was progressively fortified from 1841, when it was also decided to strengthen the existing defenses at Dawes Point Battery, under the Harbour Bridge. Work was abandoned when cash ran out and not completed until 1857, when fears of Russian expansion in the Pacific spurred further fortification. Today the firing of the fort's cannon signals not an imminent invasion, but merely the hour—one o'clock. The National Parks and Wildlife Service runs 2½-hour tours to Fort Denison. Tours depart from Cadman's Cottage, 110 George Street, the Rocks. ⊠ *Sydney Harbour* ☎ *02/9247–5033* ⊕ *www.npws.nsw.gov.au/ parks/metro/harbour/shfortdenison.html* 🖼 *A$22* ☉ *Tours weekdays at 11:30 and 3, weekends at 11:30 and 2:30.*

❸ **Garden Island.** Although it's still known as an "island," this promontory was connected with the mainland in 1942. During the 1941–45 War of the Pacific, Australia's largest naval base and dockyard was a frontline port for Allied ships. Part of the naval base is now open to the public. This small park area has superb views of the Opera House and glimpses of the dockyard facilities, including the largest shipyard crane in the Southern Hemisphere. Access to the site is via ferry from Circular Quay.

⓯ **Kirribilli.** Residences of this attractive suburb opposite the city and Opera House have million-dollar views—and prices to match. Two of Sydney's most important mansions stand here. The more modest of the two is **Kirribilli House,** which is the official Sydney home of the prime minister and not open to the public. Next door and far more prominent is **Admiralty House** (☎ 02/9955–4095)—the Sydney residence of the governor-general, the Queen's representative in Australia. This impressive residence is occasionally open for inspection.

❾ **Middle Harbour.** Except for the yachts moored in the sandy coves, the upper reaches of Middle Harbour are almost exactly as they were when the first Europeans set eyes on Port Jackson, more than 200 years ago. Tucked away in idyllic bushland are tranquil suburbs just a short drive from the city.

⓫ **Middle Head.** Despite its benign appearance today, Sydney Harbour once bristled with armaments. In the mid-19th century, faced with expansionist European powers hungry for new colonies, the authorities erected artillery positions on the headlands to guard harbor approaches. At Middle Head you can still see the rectangular gun emplacements set into the cliff face, however the guns have never been fired at an enemy.

❹ **Point Piper.** The majestic Gatsbyesque houses in this harborside suburb are prized addresses for Sydney's rich and famous. This was once the Sydney neighborhood of Tom Cruise and Nicole Kidman, and the record for the suburb's—and Australia's—most expensive house is held by Altona, which fetched A$28.5 million when it sold in 2002.

❽ **Quarantine Station.** From the 1830s onward, ship passengers who arrived with contagious diseases were isolated on this outpost in the shadow of North Head until pronounced free of illness. You can access the station only as part of a guided tour; there's both a basic tour that departs from Manly Wharf, and a three-hour evening Ghost Tour (the station reputedly has its fair share of specters) which departs from the visitor center at the Quarantine Station. The Ghost Tour includes supper, and reservations are essential. Both tours are led by rangers from the National Parks and Wildlife Service, caretakers of the site. ⊠ *North Head, Manly* ☎ *02/ 9247–5033* ⊕*www.manlyquarantine.com* 🖼*Basic tour A$17, Ghost tour*

A\$27.50 ☻ *Basic tour Mon., Wed., Fri. and weekends at 1:10 PM; Ghost tour Wed., Fri., and weekends 7:30 PM, 8 PM in Dec. and Jan.*

❺ Rose Bay. This large bay was once a base for the Qantas flying boats that provided the only passenger air service between Australia and America and Europe. The last flying boat departed Rose Bay in the 1960s, but the "airstrip" is still used by floatplanes on scenic flights connecting Sydney with the Hawkesbury River and the Central Coast.

❶ Sydney Cove. Bennelong Point and the Sydney Opera House to the east and Circular Quay West and the Rocks to the west enclose this cove, which was named after Lord Sydney, the British home secretary at the time the colony was founded. The settlement itself was to be known as New Albion, but the name never caught on. Instead, the city took its name from this tiny bay.

★ ☾ ⑬ Taronga Zoo. In Sydney's zoo, in a natural bush area on the harbor's north shore, lives an extensive collection of Australian fauna, including everybody's favorite marsupial, the koala. The zoo has taken great care to create spacious enclosures that simulate natural habitats. The hillside setting is steep in parts, and a complete tour can be tiring, but you can use the map distributed free at the entrance gate to plan a leisurely route. Basic children's strollers are free. The easiest way to get here from the city is by ferry from Circular Quay. From Taronga Wharf a bus or the cable car will take you up the hill to the main entrance. The ZooPass, a combined ferry-zoo ticket (A\$33.50), is available at Circular Quay. ✉ *Bradleys Head Rd., Mosman* ☎ *02/9969–2777* ⊕ *www.zoo.nsw.gov. au* ☜ *A\$27* ☻ *Daily 9–5.*

❻ Vaucluse. The palatial homes in this glamorous harbor suburb provide a glimpse of Sydney's high society. The small beaches at Nielsen Park and Parsley Bay are safe for swimming, and both are packed with families in summer. The suburb takes its name from **Vaucluse House,** one of Sydney's most illustrious remaining historic mansions. The 15-room Gothic Revival house is furnished in period style, and its lush gardens, managed by the Historic Houses Trust, are open to the public. The tearooms, built in the style of an Edwardian conservatory, are a popular spot for lunch and afternoon tea on weekends. The house is one of the stops on the Bondi Explorer bus. ✉ *Wentworth Rd., Vaucluse* ☎ *02/9388–7922* ⊕ *www.hht.nsw.gov.au* ☜ *A\$7* ☻ *House Tues.–Sun. 10–4:30, grounds daily 10–5.*

❼ Watsons Bay. Established as a military base and fishing settlement in the colony's early years, Watsons Bay is a charming suburb that has held on to its village ambience, despite the exorbitant prices paid for tiny cottages here. In comparison to Watsons Bay's tranquil harborside, the side that faces the ocean is dramatic and tortured, with the raging sea dashing itself against the sheer, 200-foot sandstone cliffs of the Gap. When the sun shines, the 15-minute cliff-top stroll along South Head Walkway between the Gap and the **Macquarie Lighthouse** affords some of Sydney's most inspiring views. Convict-architect Francis Greenway (jailed for forgery) designed the original lighthouse here, Australia's first, in 1818. ✉ *Old South Head Rd., Vaucluse.*

The Rocks & Sydney Harbour Bridge

The Rocks is the birthplace not just of Sydney but of modern Australia. Here the 11 ships of the First Fleet, the first of England's 800-plus ships carrying convicts to the penal colony, dropped anchor in 1788, and this stubby peninsula enclosing the western side of Sydney Cove became known simply as the Rocks.

The first crude wooden huts erected by the convicts were followed by simple houses made from mud bricks cemented together by a mixture of sheep's wool, straw, and mud. The rain soon washed this rough mortar away, and no buildings in the Rocks survive from the earliest settlement. Most of the architecture dates from the Victorian era, by which time Sydney had become a thriving port. Warehouses lining the waterfront were backed by a row of tradesmen's shops, banks, and taverns, and above them, ascending Observatory Hill, rose a tangled mass of alleyways lined with the cottages of seamen and wharf laborers. By the late 1800s all who could afford to had moved out of the area, and it was widely regarded as a rough, tough, squalid part of town. As late as 1900, bubonic plague swept through the Rocks, prompting the government to offer a bounty for dead rats in an effort to exterminate their disease-carrying fleas.

It's only since the 1980s that the Rocks has become appreciated for its historic significance, and extensive restoration has transformed the area. Here you can see the evolution of a society almost from its inception to the present, and yet the Rocks is anything but a stuffy tutorial. History stands side by side with shops, cafés, and museums.

a good walk

Begin at Circular Quay ►, the lively waterfront area where Sydney's ferry, bus, and train systems converge. Follow the quay toward Harbour Bridge and, as you round the curve, turn left and walk about 20 yards into First Fleet Park. The map on the platform here describes the colony of 1808. The Tank Stream entered Sydney Cove at this very spot. This tiny watercourse, the colony's first source of fresh water, decided the location of the first European settlement on Australian soil.

Return to the waterfront and take the paved walkway toward Harbour Bridge. The massive art deco–style building to your left is the **Museum of Contemporary Art** ⑯, devoted to painting, sculpture, film, video, and performance art from the past 20 years.

Continue on the walkway around Circular Quay West; when you reach the Moreton Bay fig trees in the circular bed, look left. The bronze statue beneath the trees is the figure of **William Bligh** ⑰ of HMS *Bounty* fame. To the right is a two-story, cream-color stone house, **Cadman's Cottage** ⑱. Built in 1816, it's Sydney's oldest surviving house. The futuristic building ahead of you on the waterfront is the **Overseas Passenger Terminal** ⑲, the main mooring for passenger liners in Sydney.

Have a look inside Cadman's Cottage and then climb the stairs leading to George Street. Note the original gas street lamp at the top of these steps. Turn right, and immediately on the right stands the **Sydney Visi-**

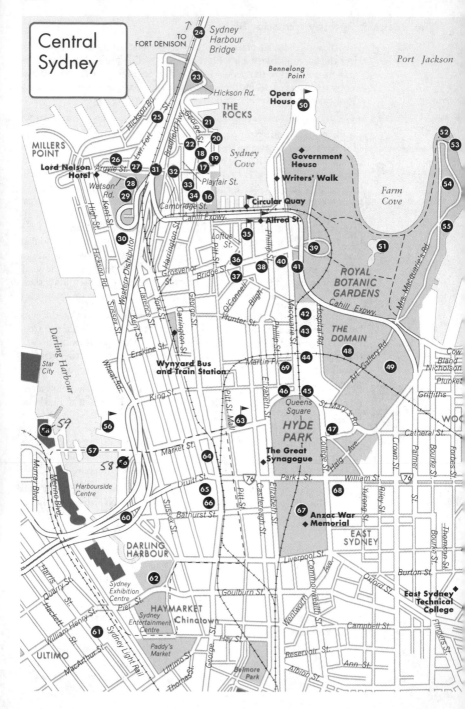

Central Sydney

TO FORT DENISON

Sydney Harbour Bridge

Port Jackson

Bennelong Point

Hickson Rd.

THE ROCKS

Opera House 50

MILLERS POINT

25

George St.

21

20

22 18 19

17

Sydney Cove

Government House

Writers' Walk

Lord Nelson Hotel 26 27

Argyle St.

31 32

Watson Rd.

28 29

33

34 16

Playfair St.

Farm Cove

Cambridge St.

Circular Quay

Cahill Expwy.

Alfred St.

51

ROYAL BOTANIC GARDENS

Hickson Rd.

Western Distributor

30

Harrington St.

Loftus St.

35

Phillip St.

39

Grosvenor St.

36

38

40 41

Bridge St.

37

O'Connell

Bligh

Cahill Expwy

Darling Harbour

Star City

Clarence St.

Kent St.

Erskine St.

Carrington St.

George St.

Hunter St.

42

43

THE DOMAIN

Macquarie St.

Hospital Rd.

Wynyard Bus and Train Station

Martin Pl.

44

69

48

Art Gallery Rd.

49

Mrs. Macquarie's Rd.

Port Jackson

52

53

54

55

Cow Bland Nicholson

Plunket

Griffiths

WOO

58 59

Wheat Rd.

56

King St.

Elizabeth St.

46

45

Queens Square

St Mary's Rd.

Cathedral St.

Crown St.

Palmer

Bourke St.

Forbes St.

57

58 60

Market St.

Pitt St. Mall

63

HYDE PARK

The Great Synagogue

47

College St.

Haig Ave.

William St.

76

EAST SYDNEY

Riley St.

Harbourside Centre

Merino Blvd.

64

Druitt St.

65

66

Bathurst St.

Castlereagh St.

Park St.

Elizabeth St.

68

67 **Anzac War Memorial**

Liverpool St.

Commonwealth Ave.

Yurong St.

Crown St.

College St.

76

Oxford St.

Burton St.

Thomson St.

Bourke St.

East Sydney Technical College

Harris St.

60

DARLING HARBOUR

Sussex St.

Goulburn St.

Wentworth Ave.

Campbell St.

Quarry St.

Sydney Exhibition Centre Pier

62

HAYMARKET Chinatown

Hay St.

George St.

Albion St.

Ann St.

ULTIMO

Sydney Light Rail

61

Sydney Entertainment Centre

Paddy's Market

Ultimo St.

Belmore Park

Reservoir St.

William Henry St.

Hackett St.

MacArthur St.

Thomas St.

tor Centre ⑳, which has a bookshop and an information counter with useful leaflets about the city.

After leaving the Information Centre, turn right past the redbrick facade of the Australian Steam Navigation Company. Continue down the hill and steps on the right to **Campbells Cove** ㉑ and its warehouses. The waterfront restaurants and cafés are a pleasant spot for a drink or meal, although you pay for the view. Walk back up the steps beside the warehouses and cross to Upper George Street, lined with restored 19th-century buildings. Just behind the Westpac Bank on the corner of George and Playfair streets is the **Westpac Banking Museum** ㉒, which exhibits early-Australian coinage.

Continue up George Street toward the Sydney Harbour Bridge until you are directly beneath the bridge's massive girders. The green iron cubicle standing on the landward side of George Street is a gentleman's toilet, modeled on the Parisian pissoir. Toilets such as this were fairly common in the early 1900s, but they have since been replaced by more discreet brick constructions—such as the modern restroom that stands behind this sole survivor.

Walk under the bridge to **Dawes Point Park** ㉓ for excellent views of the harbor, including the Opera House and the small island of Fort Denison. This park also provides an unusual perspective from underneath the **Sydney Harbour Bridge** ㉔—an unmistakable symbol of the city, and one of the world's widest long-span bridges.

Turn your back on the harbor and walk up **Lower Fort Street** ㉕, which runs to the right of the Harbour View Hotel. Continue to the corner of Windmill Street, where the wedge-shape Hero of Waterloo is one of the oldest pubs in the city.

Lower Fort Street ends at **Argyle Place** ㉖, built by Governor Macquarie and named after his home county in Scotland. The houses and other buildings here in the minisuburb of Millers Point are worth an inspection— particularly **Holy Trinity Church** ㉗ on the left-hand side and the Lord Nelson Hotel, which lies to one side of the village green.

Argyle Place is dominated by **Observatory Hill** ㉘, the site of the colony's first windmill and, later, a signal station. If you have the energy to climb the steps that lead to the hill, you can reach a park shaded by giant Moreton Bay fig trees; the reward is one of the finest views in Sydney. On top of the hill is the **Sydney Observatory** ㉙, now a museum of astronomy. You can also follow the path behind the Observatory to the National Trust Centre and the **S. H. Ervin Gallery** ㉚, which mounts changing exhibitions with Australian themes.

Leave Argyle Place and walk down Argyle Street into the dark tunnel of the **Argyle Cut** ㉛. On the lower side of the cut and to the left, the Argyle Stairs lead up through an archway. Several flights of steps and a 15-minute walk will take you onto Harbour Bridge and to the South East Pylon for a dizzying view of the Opera House and the city. To get to the Sydney Harbour Bridge walkway from the top of the stairs, cross the road, walk left for 20 yards, and then follow the signs to the walkway and pylon. You should allow at least one hour for this detour.

The walk resumes at the foot of the steps on Argyle Street. Continue down the street and turn left under the archway inscribed with the words **Argyle Stores ㉜**. The old warehouses around this courtyard have been converted to upscale fashion shops and galleries. Leave the Argyle Stores and cross onto Harrington Street.

The Gumnut Café is on the left-hand side of this street. Ten yards beyond the café is the **Suez Canal ㉝**, a narrow lane that runs down the incline toward George Street. Turn right at **Nurses Walk ㉞**, another of the area's historic and atmospheric backstreets, then left into Surgeons Court and left again onto George Street. On the left is the handsome sandstone facade of the former Rocks Police Station, now a crafts gallery. From this point, Circular Quay is only a short walk away.

TIMING The attractions of the Rocks are many, so to walk this route—even without lingering in museums or galleries or walking up to the Sydney Harbour Bridge—you should allow about three hours. The Museum of Contemporary Art, Sydney Observatory, and the S. H. Ervin Gallery each require an hour at the very least. The Rocks' numerous souvenir shops can absorb even more time.

The area is often very crowded on weekends, when the Rocks Market on George Street presents a serious distraction from sightseeing. At the end of the workweek, office workers in a TGIF mood flock to the local pubs, which become rowdy after about 10 PM.

What to See

㉛ **Argyle Cut.** Argyle Street links Argyle Place with George Street, and the thoroughfare is dominated by the Argyle Cut and its massive walls. In the days before the cut was made, the sandstone ridge here was a major barrier to traffic crossing between Circular Quay and Millers Point. In 1843 convict work gangs hacked at the sandstone with hand tools for 2½ years before the project was abandoned due to lack of progress. Work restarted in 1857, when drills, explosives, and paid labor completed the job. On the lower side of the Cut, an archway leads to the **Argyle Stairs**, which begin the climb from Argyle Street up to the Sydney Harbour Bridge walkway, and a spectacular view from the South East Pylon.

㉖ **Argyle Place.** With all the traditional requirements of an English green— a pub at one end, a church at the other, and grass in between—this charming enclave in the suburb of Millers Point is unusual for Sydney. Argyle Place is lined with 19th-century houses and cottages on its northern side and overlooked by Observatory Hill to the south.

need a break?

While in the west end of Argyle Place, consider the liquid temptations of the **Lord Nelson,** Sydney's oldest hotel, which has been licensed to serve alcohol since 1842. The sandstone pub has its own brewery on the premises. One of its specialties is Quayle Ale, named after the former U.S. vice president, who "sank a schooner" (drank a beer) here during his 1989 visit to Australia. ✉ *19 Kent St., Millers Point* ☎ *02/9251–4044* ⊕ *www.lordnelson.com.au.*

32 **Argyle Stores.** These solid sandstone warehouses date from the late 1820s and now house chic gift and souvenir shops, clothes boutiques, and cafés. ⊠ *Argyle St. opposite Harrington St., The Rocks.*

18 **Cadman's Cottage.** Sydney's oldest building, completed in 1816, has a history that outweighs its modest dimensions. John Cadman was a convict who was sentenced for life to New South Wales for stealing a horse. He later became superintendent of government boats, a position that entitled him to live in the upper story of this house. The water once practically lapped at Cadman's doorstep, and the original seawall still stands at the front of the house. The small extension on the side of the cottage was built to lock up the oars of Cadman's boats, since oars would have been a necessity for any convict attempting to escape by sea. The upper floor of Cadman's Cottage is now a National Parks and Wildlife Service bookshop and information center for Sydney Harbour National Park. ⊠ *110 George St., The Rocks* ☎ *02/9247–8861* ⊕ *www.cityofsydney. nsw.gov.au/hs_hb_cadmans_cottage.asp* ☉ *Tues.–Sun. 10–4:30.*

21 **Campbells Cove.** Robert Campbell was a Scottish merchant who is sometimes referred to as the "father of Australian commerce." Campbell broke the stranglehold that the British East India Company exercised over seal and whale products, which were New South Wales's only exports in those early days. The cove's atmospheric sandstone **Campbells Storehouse,** built from 1838 onward, now houses waterside restaurants. The pulleys that were used to hoist cargoes still hang on the upper level of the warehouses. The cove is also the mooring for Sydney's fully operational tall ships— including the HMAV *Bounty,* an authentic replica of the original 18th-century vessel—which conduct theme cruises around the harbor.

23 **Dawes Point Park.** The wonderful views of the harbor, Fort Denison, and, since the 1930s, the Harbour Bridge have made this park and its location noteworthy for centuries. Named for William Dawes, a First Fleet marine officer and astronomer who established the colony's first basic observatory nearby in 1788, this park was also once the site of a fortification known as Dawes Battery. The cannons on the hillside pointing toward the Opera House came from the ships of the First Fleet.

Harrington Street area. The small precinct around this street forms one of the Rocks' most interesting areas. Many old cottages, houses, and warehouses here have been converted into hotels. Between Harrington Street and George Street are some historical and creatively named alleyways to explore, including Nurses Walk and Suez Canal.

27 **Holy Trinity Church.** Every morning, redcoats would march to this 1840 Argyle Place church from Dawes Point Battery (now Dawes Point Park), and it became commonly known as the Garrison Church. As the regimental plaques and colors around the walls testify, the church still retains a close military association. The tattered ensign on the left wall was carried into battle by Australian troops during the Boer War, in which many Australians enlisted to help Great Britain in its war with South Africans of Dutch ancestry. ⊠ *Argyle Pl., Millers Point* ☎ *02/9247–1268* ☉ *Daily 9–5.*

㉕ **Lower Fort Street.** At one time the handsome Georgian houses along this street, originally a rough track leading from the Dawes Point Battery to Observatory Hill, were among the best addresses in Sydney. Elaborate wrought-iron lacework still graces many of the facades.

⑯ **Museum of Contemporary Art.** This ponderous art deco building houses one of Australia's most important collections of modern art, as well as two significant collections of Aboriginal art. There's no permanent collection, but the program of continually changing exhibits has included works by such luminaries as Andy Warhol, Roy Lichtenstein, Cindy Sherman, and Tracey Moffat. ⊠ *Circular Quay W, The Rocks* ☎ *02/9252–4033* ⊕ *www.mca.com.au* ⊠ *Free* ☉ *Daily 10–5.*

㉞ **Nurses Walk.** Cutting across the site of the colony's first hospital, Nurses Walk acquired its name at a time when "Sydney" and "sickness" were synonymous. Many of the 736 convicts who survived the voyage from Portsmouth, England, aboard the First Fleet's 11 ships arrived suffering from dysentery, smallpox, scurvy, and typhoid. A few days after he landed at Sydney Cove, Governor Phillip established a tent hospital to care for the worst cases. Subsequent convict boatloads had even higher rates of death and disease.

need a break?

The **Gumnut Café,** in the 1830 sandstone residence of blacksmith William Reynolds, serves delicious salads, pasta dishes, sandwiches, rolls, and cakes. The best tables are in the shady back garden, and reservations are necessary at lunch. ⊠ *28 Harrington St., The Rocks* ☎ *02/9247–9591.*

㉘ **Observatory Hill.** The city's highest point, at 145 feet, was known originally as Windmill Hill, since the colony's first windmill occupied this breezy spot. Its purpose was to grind grain for flour, but soon after it was built the canvas sails were stolen, the machinery was damaged in a storm, and the foundations cracked. The signal station at the top of the hill was built in 1848. This later became an astronomical observatory, and Windmill Hill changed its name to Observatory Hill.

⑲ **Overseas Passenger Terminal.** Busy **Circular Quay West** is dominated by this multilevel steel-and-glass port terminal, which is often used by visiting cruise ships. There are a couple of excellent waterfront restaurants at the terminal's northern end, and it's worth taking the escalator to the upper deck for a good view of the harbor and Opera House.

㉚ **S. H. Ervin Gallery.** This gallery, in the architecturally impressive National Trust Centre just behind Observatory Hill, concentrates on Australian art and architecture from a historical perspective. The changing exhibitions are of a consistently high standard and have shown the work of such well-known Australian artists as Lloyd Rees, Sidney Nolan, Hans Heysen, and Russell Drysdale. The gallery has a bookshop, and there's an outstanding National Trust gift shop next door. ⊠ *National Trust Centre, Observatory Hill, Watson Rd., Millers Point* ☎ *02/9258–0178* ⊕ *www.nsw.nationaltrust.org.au/ervin.html* ⊠ *A$6* ☉ *Tues.–Sun. 11–5, weekends noon–5.*

33 **Suez Canal.** So narrow that two people can't walk abreast, this alley acquired its name before drains were installed, when rainwater would pour down its funnel-like passageway and gush across George Street. Lanes such as this were once the haunt of the notorious late-19th-century Rocks gangs, when robbery was rife in the area. The "Pushes" (gangs) are remembered in a local wine bar known as the Rocks Push.

24 **Sydney Harbour Bridge.** Sydney's iron colossus, the Harbour Bridge was a monumental engineering feat when it was completed in 1932. The roadway is supported by the arch, not by the massive stone pylons, which were added for aesthetic rather than structural reasons. The 1,650-foot-long bridge is 160 feet wide and contains two sets of railway tracks, eight road lanes, a bikeway, and a footpath on both sides. Actor Paul Hogan worked for several years as a rigger on the bridge, long before he earned international fame as the star of *Crocodile Dundee*.

There are several ways to experience the bridge and its spectacular views. The first is to follow the walkway from its access point near the Argyle Stairs to the **South East Pylon** (☎ 02/9240–1100). This structure houses a display on the bridge's construction, and you can climb the 200 steps to the lookout and its unbeatable harbor panorama. The fee is A\$8.50 and the display is open daily 10–5. Another more expensive option is the **BridgeClimb tour** (☎ 02/8274–7777 ⊕ www.bridgeclimb.com.au), which takes you on a guided walking tour to the very top of the Harbour Bridge. The third option is to walk to the midpoint of the bridge to take in the views free of charge, but be sure to take the eastern footpath, which overlooks the Sydney Opera House. Access is via the stairs on Cumberland Street, close to the Shangri-La Hotel.

Fodor'sChoice
★

29 **Sydney Observatory.** Originally a signaling station for communicating with ships anchored in the harbor, this handsome building on top of Observatory Hill is now an astronomy museum. Within its sandstone walls, hands-on displays—including constellation charts, talking computers, and games—illustrate principles of astronomy. During evening observatory shows you can tour the building, watch videos, and, weather permitting, get a close-up view of the universe through a 16-inch mirror telescope. Reservations are required for the evening show, and times vary depending on the season. ⊠ *Watson Rd., Millers Point* ☎ *02/9217–0485* ⊕ *www.phm.gov.au/observe* ⊠ *Free, evening show A\$15* ⊙ *Daily 10–5.*

20 **Sydney Visitor Centre.** Once a mariners' mission, this building now offers insight into the history of the Rocks, with displays of artifacts and a short video. Staff members can answer questions and make travel bookings, and the informative Rocks Walking Tours depart from here. The building also contains the very popular Sailor's Thai restaurant and a less-expensive canteen. ⊠ *106 George St., The Rocks* ☎ *02/9255–1788* ⊕ *www.sydneyvisitorcentre.com* ⊙ *Mar.–Oct., daily 9–5; Nov.–Feb., daily 9–6.*

Upper George Street. The restored warehouses and Victorian terrace houses that line this part of George Street make this a charming section of the Rocks. The covered **Rocks Market** takes place here on weekends.

㉒ **Westpac Banking Museum.** This museum on a lane off George Street displays a collection of coins from the earliest days of the colony of New South Wales. ✉ *6–8 Playfair St., The Rocks* ☎ *02/9251–1419* 💲 *Free* ⊙ *Daily 10–4.*

⑰ **William Bligh statue.** Although history may have painted him as a tyrant, Captain William Bligh of HMS *Bounty* fame was perhaps more unlucky than cruel. In 1806, almost two decades after the infamous mutiny on the ship he commanded, Bligh became governor of New South Wales. Two years later he faced his second mutiny. Bligh had made himself unpopular with the soldiers of the New South Wales Corps, commonly known as the Rum Corps, who were the real power in the colony. When he threatened to end their lucrative monopoly on the liquor trade, he was imprisoned during the Rum Rebellion. He spent the next two years as a captive until his successor, Lachlan Macquarie, arrived. Ironically, the statue's gaze frequently rests on HMAV *Bounty,* a replica of Bligh's ship, as it sails around the harbor on charter cruises.

Macquarie Street & the Domain South

Some of Sydney's most notable Victorian-era public buildings, as well as one of its finest parks, can be found in this area. In contrast to the simple, utilitarian stone convict cottages of the Rocks, these buildings were constructed at a time when Sydney was experiencing a long period of prosperity, thanks to the gold rushes of the mid-19th century and an agricultural boom. The sandstone just below the surface of many coastal areas proved an ideal building material—easily honed into the ornamentation so fashionable during the Victorian era.

a good walk

This historical walk roughly follows the perimeter of the Royal Botanic Gardens and the Domain South. A shady park bench is never far.

Begin at Circular Quay. Turn your back on the harbor and cross Alfred Street, which runs parallel to the waterfront. The most notable historic building along Alfred Street is the **Customs House** ㉟ ▶. When it was built in the late 1880s, the sandstone structure was surrounded by warehouses storing the fleeces that were the colony's principal export.

Walk up Loftus Street, which runs to the right of the Customs House. In Customs House Lane at the rear you can still see a pulley that was used to lower the wool bales to the dockyard from the top floor of Hinchcliff's Wool Stores.

Follow Loftus Street to the small triangular park on your right, **Macquarie Place** ㊱, which has a number of historical monuments. The southern side of the park is bordered by busy Bridge Street, lined with a number of grandiose Victorian buildings. Across Bridge Street, the **Lands Department** ㊲ is one of the city's finest examples of Victorian public architecture. Walk up Bridge Street past the facade of the Department of Education. The **Museum of Sydney** ㊳ stands on the next block. Built on the site of the first Government House, the museum chronicles the history of the city between 1788 and 1850.

CloseUp

BUILDING SYDNEY

DESCENDED FROM SCOTTISH clan chieftains, Governor Lachlan Macquarie was an accomplished soldier and a man of vision. Macquarie, who was governor from 1810 to 1821, was the first governor to foresee a role for New South Wales as a free society rather than an open prison. He laid the foundations for that society by establishing a plan for the city, constructing significant public buildings, and advocating that reformed convicts be readmitted to society.

Macquarie's policies of equality may seem perfectly reasonable today, but in the early 19th century they marked him as a radical. When his vision of a free society threatened to blur distinctions between soldiers, settlers, and convicts, Macquarie was forced to resign. He was later buried on his Scottish estate, his gravestone inscribed with the words "the Father of Australia."

Macquarie's grand plans for the construction of Sydney might have come to nothing were it not for Francis Greenway. Trained as an architect in England, where he was convicted of forgery and sentenced to 14 years in New South Wales, Greenway received a ticket of prison leave from Macquarie in 1814 and set to work transforming Sydney. Over the next few years he designed lighthouses, hospitals, convict barracks, and many other essential government buildings, several of which remain to bear witness to his simple but elegant eye. Greenway was eventually even depicted on one side of the old A$10 notes, which went out of circulation early in the 1990s. Only in Australia, perhaps, would a convicted forger occupy pride of place on the currency.

Continue up Bridge Street to the corner of Macquarie Street. The figure on horseback about to gallop down Bridge Street is Edward VII, successor to Queen Victoria. The castellated building behind him is the **Sydney Conservatorium of Music** ㊴, originally built in 1819 as stables for Government House, which is screened by trees near the Opera House.

Your next stop is the lovely 1870s **History House** ㊵, headquarters of the Royal Australian Historical Society. It's just south of Bridge Street on Macquarie Street, Sydney's most elegant boulevard. Opposite History House are the fine wrought-iron **Garden Palace Gates** ㊶, flanking one of the entrances to the Royal Botanic Gardens. A little farther south along Macquarie Street is a ponderous brown building: the **State Library of New South Wales** ㊷. Cross the road toward this building, passing the Light Horse Monument and the Shakespeare Memorial. Australian cavalrymen fought with distinction in several Middle Eastern campaigns during World War I, and the statue is dedicated to their horses, which were not allowed to return due to Australian quarantine regulations.

Continue along Macquarie Street toward the gates of **State Parliament House** ㊸, in the north wing of the former Rum Hospital. In a stroke of political genius, Governor Macquarie persuaded two merchants to build a hospital for convicts in return for an extremely lucrative three-year monopoly on the importation of rum.

The next building on the left is the Victorian-style **Sydney Hospital** ⓐ, constructed to replace the central section of the Rum Hospital, which began to fall apart almost as soon as it was completed. Beyond the hospital is the **Hyde Park Barracks** ⓐ, commissioned by Macquarie and designed by Greenway to house prisoners. Opposite Hyde Park Barracks is the 1970s high-rise Law Court building. This area is the heart of Sydney's legal district.

Cross Queens Square to the other side of the road, where the figure of Queen Victoria presides over Macquarie Street. To Victoria's left is another Greenway building, **St. James Church** ⓐ, originally designed as a courthouse.

Return to the other side of Macquarie Street and walk along College Street to **St. Mary's Cathedral** ⓐ. This is Sydney's Roman Catholic cathedral, based on the design of Lincoln Cathedral in England. Both the pointed door arches and flying buttresses are signatures of the Gothic style.

At the rear of the cathedral, cross St. Mary's Road to Art Gallery Road. You are now in the parklands of the **Domain South** ⓐ. Continue past the statue of Robert Burns, the Scottish poet. The large trees on the left with enormous roots and drooping limbs are Moreton Bay figs. Despite their name, their fruit is inedible and poisonous—as Captain James Cook discovered when he fed some to his pigs. Directly ahead is the **Art Gallery of New South Wales** ⓐ, housed in a grand Victorian building with modern extensions. The gallery contains the state's largest art collection. From the Art Gallery you can return to Macquarie Street by crossing the Domain or wandering for 1 km (½ mi) through the Royal Botanic Gardens. If you have an Explorer bus pass, you can catch the bus back to the city center from the front of the gallery.

TIMING Half a day is sufficient to complete the outlined itinerary, even with stops to inspect the Museum of Sydney, Hyde Park Barracks, and the Art Gallery of New South Wales. Apart from the initial climb from Circular Quay to Macquarie Street, the terrain is flat and easy.

What to See

ⓐ **Art Gallery of New South Wales.** Apart from Canberra's National Gallery, this is the best place to explore the evolution of European-influenced Australian art, as well as the distinctly different concepts that underlie Aboriginal art. All the major Australian artists of the last two centuries are represented in this impressive collection. The entrance level, where large windows frame spectacular views of the harbor, exhibits 20th-century art. Below, in the gallery's major extensions, the Yiribana Gallery displays one of the nation's most comprehensive collections of Aboriginal and Torres Strait Islander art. ⊠ *Art Gallery Rd., The Domain* ☎ *02/ 9225–1700* ⊕ *www.artgallery.nsw.gov.au* ☞ *Free, special-exhibition fee varies* ☉ *Thurs.–Tues. 10–5, Wed. 10–9.*

ⓐ **Customs House.** The last surviving example of the elegant sandstone buildings that once ringed Circular Quay, this former customs house now holds the Centre for Contemporary Craft, a retail crafts gallery, and the Djamu Gallery, Australia's largest permanent exhibition of Aboriginal and Pacific Island artifacts. The rooftop Café Sydney, the standout in the clutch of restaurants and cafés in this late-19th-century structure, overlooks Sydney Cove. The building stands close to the site where the British flag was first raised on the shores of Sydney Cove in 1788. ✉ *Customs House Sq., Alfred St., Circular Quay* ☏ *02/9265–2007.*

48 Domain South. Laid out by Governor Macquarie in 1810 as his own personal "domain" and originally including what is now the Royal Botanic Gardens, this large park is a tranquil area at the city's eastern edge. Office workers flock here for lunchtime recreation, and the park holds free outdoor concerts during the Festival of Sydney in January.

41 Garden Palace Gates. These gates are all that remain of the Garden Palace, a massive glass pavilion that was erected for the Sydney International Exhibition of 1879 and destroyed by fire three years later. On the arch above the gates is a depiction of the Garden Palace's dome. Stone pillars on either side of the gates are engraved with Australian wildflowers. ✉ *Macquarie St. between Bridge and Bent Sts., Macquarie Street.*

40 History House. You're welcome to visit History House, the home of the Royal Australian Historical Society, and its collection of books and other materials. Note the balconies and the Corinthian columns, all made from iron, which was just becoming popular when this building was constructed in 1872. ✉ *133 Macquarie St., Macquarie Street* ☏ *02/9247–8001* ▥ *Library A$5* ◷ *Weekdays 9:30–4:30.*

45 Hyde Park Barracks. Before Governor Macquarie arrived, convicts were left to roam freely at night. Macquarie was determined to establish law and order, and in 1819 he commissioned convict-architect Francis Greenway to design this restrained, classically Georgian-style building. Today the Barracks houses compelling exhibitions that explore behind the scenes of the prison. For example, a surprising number of relics from this period were preserved by rats, who carried away scraps of clothing and other artifacts for their nests beneath the floorboards. A room on the top floor is strung with hammocks, exactly as it was when the building housed convicts. ✉ *Queens Sq., Macquarie St., Hyde Park* ☏ *02/9223–8922* ⊕ *www.hht.nsw.gov.au* ▥ *A$7* ◷ *Daily 9:30–5.*

need a break? On a sunny day, the courtyard tables of the **Hyde Park Barracks Café** provide one of the city's finest places to enjoy an outdoor lunch. The café serves light, moderately priced meals, salads, and open sandwiches, with a wine list including Australian vintages. ✉ *Queens Sq., Macquarie St., Hyde Park* ☏ *02/9361–6288.*

37 Lands Department. The figures occupying the niches at the corners of this 1890 sandstone building are early Australian explorers and politicians. James Barnet's building stands among other fine Victorian structures in the neighborhood. ✉ *Bridge St. near intersection of Macquarie Pl., Macquarie Street.*

36 Macquarie Place. This park, once a site of ceremonial and religious importance to Aboriginal people, contains a number of important monuments, including the obelisk formerly used as the point from which all distances from Sydney were measured. On a stone plinth at the bottom of the park is the anchor of HMS *Sirius,* flagship of the First Fleet, which struck a reef and sank off Norfolk Island in 1790. The bronze statue with his hands on his hips represents Thomas Mort, who in 1879 became the first to export refrigerated cargo from Australia. The implications of this shipment were enormous. Mutton, beef, and dairy products suddenly became valuable export commodities, and for most of the following century agriculture dominated the Australian economy.

Bridge Street runs alongside Macquarie Place. Formerly the site of the 1789 Government House and the colony's first bridge, this V-shape street was named for the bridge that once crossed the Tank Stream, which now flows underground. Today several grandiose Victorian structures line its sidewalks.

Macquarie Street. Sydney's most elegant boulevard was shaped by Governor Macquarie, who from 1810 until he was ousted in 1822 planned the transformation of the cart track leading to Sydney Cove into a stylish street of dwellings and government buildings. An occasional modern high-rise breaks up the streetscape, but many of the 19th-century architectural delights here escaped demolition.

38 Museum of Sydney. This museum, built on the site of the original Government House, documents Sydney's early period of European colonization. Aboriginal culture, convict society, and the gradual transformation of the settlement at Sydney Cove are woven into an evocative portrayal of life in the country's early days. One of the most intriguing exhibits, however, is outside: the striking Edge of the Trees sculpture, the first collaborative public artwork in Sydney between an Aboriginal and European artist.

Near the museum, at the intersection of Bridge and Phillip streets, is an imposing pair of sandstone buildings. The most impressive view of the mid-19th-century **Treasury Building,** now part of the Hotel Inter-Continental, is from Macquarie Street. The **Colonial Secretary's Office**—designed by James Barnet, who also designed the Lands Department—stands opposite the Treasury Building. Note the buildings' similarities, right down to the figures in the corner niches. ⊠ *Bridge and Phillip Sts., City Center* ☎ *02/9251–5988* ⊕ *www.hht.nsw.gov.au* ⊠ *A$7* ⊙ *Daily 9:30–5.*

46 St. James Church. Begun in 1822, the colonial Georgian–style St. James is Sydney's oldest surviving church, and another fine Francis Greenway design. Now lost among the skyscrapers, the church's tall spire once served as a landmark for ships entering the harbor. Enter through the door in the Doric portico. Plaques commemorating Australian explorers and administrators cover the interior walls. Inscriptions testify to the hardships of those early days. ⊠ *Queens Sq., Macquarie St., Hyde Park* ☎ *02/9232–3022* ⊙ *Daily 9–5.*

47 St. Mary's Cathedral. The first St. Mary's was built here in 1821, but fire destroyed the chapel, and work on the present cathedral began in 1868.

The spires weren't added until 2000. St. Mary's has some particularly fine stained-glass windows and a terrazzo floor in the crypt, where exhibitions are often held. The cathedral's large rose window was imported from England.

At the front of the cathedral stand statues of Cardinal Moran and Archbishop Kelly, two Irishmen who were prominent in Australia's Roman Catholic Church. Due to the high proportion of Irish men and women in the convict population, the Roman Catholic Church was often the voice of the oppressed in 19th-century Sydney, where anti-Catholic feeling ran high among the Protestant rulers. Australia's first cardinal, Patrick Moran, was a powerful exponent of Catholic education and a diplomat who did much to heal the rift between the two faiths. By contrast, Michael Kelly, his successor as head of the church in Sydney, was excessively pious and politically inept; Kelly and Moran remained at odds until Moran's death in 1911. ⊠ *College and Cathedral Sts., Hyde Park* ☎ *02/9220–0400* 🖭 *Tour free* ۞ *Weekdays 6:30–6:30, Sat. 8–7:30, Sun. 6:30 AM–7:30 PM; tour Sun. at noon.*

㊷ State Library of New South Wales. This large complex is based around the Mitchell and Dixson libraries, which make up the world's largest collection of Australiana. Enter the foyer through the classical portico to see one of the earliest maps of Australia, a copy in marble mosaic of a map made by Abel Tasman, the Dutch navigator, in the mid-17th century. Through the glass doors lies the vast Mitchell Library reading room, but you need a reader's ticket (establishing that you are pursuing legitimate research) to enter. You can, however, take a free escorted tour of the library's buildings. Inquire at the reception desk of the general reference library on Macquarie Street. ⊠ *Macquarie St., off Bent St., Macquarie Street* ☎ *02/9273–1414* ⊕ *www.sl.nsw.gov.au* ۞ *Weekdays 9–9, weekends 11–5; Mitchell Library closed Sun. General reference library tour Tues.–Thurs. at 2:30; Mitchell Library tour Tues. and Thurs. at 11.*

㊸ State Parliament House. The simple facade and shady verandas of this Greenway-designed 1816 building, formerly the Rum Hospital, typify Australian colonial architecture. From 1829, two rooms of the old hospital were used for meetings of the executive and legislative councils, which had been set up to advise the governor. These advisory bodies grew in power until New South Wales became self-governing in the 1840s, at which time Parliament occupied the entire building. The Legislative Council Chamber—the upper house of the parliament, identifiable by its red color scheme—is a prefabricated cast-iron structure that was originally intended to be a church on the goldfields of Victoria.

State Parliament generally sits between mid-February and late May, and again between mid-September and late November. You can visit the public gallery to watch the local version of the Westminster system of democracy in action. On weekdays, generally between 9:30 and 4, you can tour the building's public areas, which contain a number of portraits and paintings. You must reserve ahead. ⊠ *Macquarie St., across from Martin Pl., Macquarie Street* ☎ *02/9230–2111* ⊕ *www.parliament. nsw.gov.au* ۞ *Hrs vary when Parliament in session; call ahead.*

39 **Sydney Conservatorium of Music.** Providing artistic development for talented young musicians, this institution hosts free lunchtime and evening concerts (usually on Wednesday and Friday). The conservatory's turreted building was originally the stables for nearby Government House. The construction cost caused a storm among Governor Macquarie's superiors in London and eventually helped bring about the downfall of both Macquarie and the building's architect, Francis Greenway. ✉ *Conservatorium Rd. off Macquarie St., Macquarie Street* ☎ *02/9351–1222.*

44 **Sydney Hospital.** Completed in 1894 to replace the main Rum Hospital building, this institution offered an infinitely better medical option. By all accounts, admission to the Rum Hospital was only slightly preferable to death itself. Convict nurses stole patients' food, and abler patients stole from the weaker. The kitchen sometimes doubled as a mortuary, and the table was occasionally used for operations.

In front of the hospital is a bronze figure of a boar. This is *Il Porcellino,* a copy of a statue that stands in Florence, Italy. According to the inscription, if you make a donation in the coin box and rub the boar's nose, "you will be endowed with good luck." Sydney citizens seem to be a superstitious bunch because the boar's nose is very shiny indeed. ✉ *Macquarie St. and Martin Pl., Macquarie Street* ☎ *02/9382–7111.*

The Opera House, the RBG & the Domain North

Bordering Sydney Cove, Farm Cove, and Woolloomooloo Bay, this section of Sydney includes the iconic Sydney Opera House, as well as extensive and delightful harborside gardens and parks.

The colony's first farm was established here in 1788, and the botanical gardens were laid out in 1816. The most dramatic change to the area occurred in 1959, however, when ground was broken on the site for the Sydney Opera House at Bennelong Point. This promontory was originally a small island, then the site of 1819 Fort Macquarie, later a tram depot, and finally the Opera House, one of the world's most striking modern buildings. The area's evolution is an eloquent metaphor for Sydney's own transformation.

a good walk

From Circular Quay, walk around Sydney Cove along Circular Quay East. This walkway is also known as Writers' Walk. Brass plaques embedded in the sidewalk commemorate prominent Australian writers, playwrights, and poets. The apartment buildings, cafés, and restaurants along the street's landward side have some of Sydney's best views, yet they caused enormous controversy when they were built in the late 1990s—just as the Sydney Opera House had its own loud critics when it was first built. One look and it's easy to see why the building closest to the Opera House is known to all as the "Toaster."

Ahead, on the Bennelong Point promontory, is the unmistakable **Sydney Opera House** **50** ▶. Its distinctive white-tile "sails" and prominent position make this the most widely recognized landmark of urban Australia. The Opera House has fueled controversy and debate among Australians, but whatever its detractors may say, the structure leaves few people unmoved.

The **Royal Botanic Gardens** ㉛, on the landward side of the Opera House, combines with the rolling Domain park to form the city's eastern border. You can either walk around the Farm Cove pathway or head inland to explore the gardens, including a stop at **Government House**, before returning to the waterfront.

The pathway around the cove leads to a peninsula, **Mrs. Macquarie's Point** ㉜, in the northern part of the Domain. It's named for Elizabeth Macquarie, the governor's wife, who planned the road through the park. As you round the peninsula and turn toward the naval dockyard at Garden Island, notice the small bench carved into the rock with an inscription identifying it as **Mrs. Macquarie's Chair** ㉝.

Continue through the **Domain North** ㉞ on Mrs. Macquarie's Road to the **Andrew (Boy) Charlton Pool** ㉟, built over Woolloomooloo Bay. From the pool are views of the Garden Island naval base and the suburb of Potts Point, across the bay.

This road eventually takes you to the southern part of the Domain. The once-continuous Domain is divided into north and south sections by the Cahill Expressway, which leads up to the Sydney Harbour Bridge and down into the Sydney Harbour Tunnel.

At the end of the walk you can return to the city and Macquarie Street by reentering the botanical gardens through the Woolloomooloo Gate near the roadway over the Cahill Expressway.

TIMING   A walk around the Sydney Opera House, Royal Botanic Gardens, and the Domain North can easily be completed in a half day. The walk is highly recommended on a warm summer evening. Allow more time if you wish to explore the gardens more thoroughly. These are delightful at any time of year, though they're especially beautiful in spring.

What to See

㉟ **Andrew (Boy) Charlton Pool.** This heated outdoor, Olympic-size pool overlooking the navy ships tied up at Garden Island has become a local favorite. Complementing its stunning location is a radical design in glass and steel. The pool also has a chic terrace café above Woolloomooloo Bay. ⊠ *Mrs. Macquarie's Rd., Domain North, The Domain* ☎ *02/9358–6686* ⊕ *www.abcpool.org* ⊠ *A$5* ☉ *Daily 6 AM–7 PM.*

㉞ **Domain North.** The northern part of the Domain adjoins the Royal Botanic Gardens and extends from Mrs. Macquarie's Point to the Cahill Expressway. Surrounded by Farm Cove and Woolloomooloo Bay, this is a pleasant, harbor-fringed park.

Government House. Completed in 1843, this two-story, sandstone, Gothic Revival building in the Royal Botanic Gardens served as the residence of the Governor of New South Wales—who represents the British crown in local matters—until the Labor Party Government handed it back to the public in 1996. Prominent English architect Edward Blore designed the building without ever having set foot in Australia. The house's restored stenciled ceilings are its most impressive feature. Paintings hanging on the walls bear the signatures of some of Australia's best-known artists. You are free to wander on your own around Government House's gardens, which lie within the Royal Botanic Gardens, but you must join a guided tour to see the house's interior. ⊠ *Royal Botanic Gardens, The Domain* ☎ *02/9931–5200* 🏷 *Free* ⊗ *House Fri.–Sun. 10–3, gardens daily 10–4, tours Fri.–Sun. every ½ hr 10:30–3.*

⑤③ Mrs. Macquarie's Chair. During the early 1800s, Elizabeth Macquarie often sat on the point in the Domain at the east side of Farm Cove, at the rock where a seat has been hewn in her name.

⑤② Mrs. Macquarie's Point. The inspiring views from this point combine with the shady lawns to make this a popular place for picnics. The views are best at dusk, when the setting sun silhouettes the Opera House and Harbour Bridge.

★ **⑤① Royal Botanic Gardens.** More than 80 acres of sweeping green lawns, groves of indigenous and exotic trees, duck ponds, greenhouses, and some 45,124 types of plants—many of them flowering—grace these gardens. The elegant property, which attracts strollers and botany enthusiasts from all over the country, is a far cry today from what it once was: a failed attempt by convicts of the First Fleet to establish a farm. Though their early attempts at agriculture were disastrous, the efforts of these first settlers are acknowledged in the Pioneer Garden, a sunken garden built in their memory.

Among the many other feature gardens on the property are the Palm Grove—home to some of the oldest trees in Sydney, the Begonia and Rose Gardens, the Fernery, the Succulents Garden, and the Rare and Threatened Plants Garden. Plants throughout the gardens have various blooming cycles, so no matter when you visit, there are sure to be plenty of flowers. Other reasons to visit include the many striking sculptures scattered throughout the park; the bird- and wildlife (a hundred species of birds are estimated to make their homes here, along with a large colony of flying foxes, or fruit bats); spectacular views over the harbor and the Opera House; and two lovely restaurants, the Botanic Gardens Restaurant and Pavilion on the Park.

Tours leave from the visitor center, near the Art Gallery of New South Wales, several times daily. There are also maps available for a variety of themed, self-guided walks. ⊠ *Domain North, The Domain* ☎ *02/ 9231–8111* ⊕ *www.rbgsyd.gov.au* 🏷 *Free* ⊗ *Royal Botanic Gardens daily dawn–dusk; Sydney Fernery daily 10–4; tour daily at 10:30.*

▶ **⑤⓪ Sydney Opera House.** Sydney's most famous landmark had such a long
Fodor'sChoice and troubled construction phase that it's almost a miracle that the
★ building was ever completed. In 1954 the state premier appointed a committee to advise the government on the building of an opera house. The site chosen was Bennelong Point (named after an early Aboriginal inhabitant), which was, until that time, occupied by a tram depot. The premier's committee launched a competition to find a suitable plan, and a total of 233 submissions came in from architects the world over. One of them was a young Dane named Joern Utzon.

His plan was brilliant, but it had all the markings of a monumental disaster. The structure was so narrow that stages would have minuscule wings, and the soaring "sails" that formed the walls and roof could not be built by existing technology.

Nonetheless, Utzon's dazzling, dramatic concept caught the judges' imagination, and construction of the giant podium began in 1959. From the start, the contractors faced a cost blowout; the building that was projected to cost A$7 million and take 4 years to erect would eventually require A$102 million and 15 years. Construction was financed by an intriguing scheme. Realizing that citizens might be hostile to the use of public funds for the controversial project, the state government raised the money through the Opera House Lottery. For almost a decade, Australians lined up to buy tickets, and the Opera House was built without depriving the state's hospitals or schools of a single cent.

Initially it was thought that the concrete exterior of the building would have to be cast in place, which would have meant building an enormous birdcage of scaffolding at even greater expense. Then, as he was peeling an orange one day, Utzon had a flash of inspiration. Why not construct the shells from segments of a single sphere? The concrete ribs forming the skeleton of the building could be prefabricated in just a few molds, hoisted into position, and joined together. These ribs are clearly visible inside the Opera House, especially in the foyers and staircases of the Concert Hall.

In 1966 Utzon resigned as Opera House architect and left Australia, embittered by his dealings with unions and the government. He has never returned to see his masterpiece. A team of young Australian architects carried on, completing the exterior one year later. Until that time, however, nobody had given much thought to the *interior*. The shells created awkward interior spaces, and conventional performance areas were simply not feasible. It's a tribute to the architectural team's ingenuity that the exterior of the building is matched by the aesthetically pleasing and acoustically sound theaters inside.

In September 1973 the Australian Opera performed *War and Peace* in the Opera Theatre. A month later, Queen Elizabeth II officially opened the building in a ceremony capped by an astonishing fireworks display. Nowadays, the controversies that raged around the building seem moot. The Sydney Opera House, poised majestically on a harbor peninsula, has become a loved and potent national symbol, and a far more versatile venue than its name implies, hosting a diverse selection of performance arts and entertainment: dance, drama, films, opera, and jazz. It also has a restaurant, three cafés, and several bars that cater to its hordes of patrons. Guided one-hour tours depart at frequent intervals from the tour office, on the lower forecourt level, 9–5 daily. Tours can be limited or canceled due to performances or rehearsals. Call in advance. ⊠ *Bennelong Point, Circular Quay* ☎ *02/9250–7111* ⊕ *www. soh.nsw.gov.au* ✉ *Tour A$23.*

Darling Harbour

Until the mid-1980s this horseshoe-shape bay on the city center's western edge was a wasteland of disused docks and railway yards. Then, in an explosive burst of activity the whole area was redeveloped and opened in time for Australia's bicentennial in 1988. Now there's plenty to take in at the Darling Harbour complex: the National Maritime Museum, the large Harbourside shopping and dining center, the Sydney Aquarium, the Cockle Bay and Kings Street Wharf waterfront dining complexes, the LG IMAX Theatre, and the gleaming Exhibition Centre, whose masts and spars recall the square-riggers that once berthed here. At the harbor's center is a large park shaded by palm trees. Waterways and fountains lace the complex together.

The Powerhouse Museum is within easy walking distance of the harbor, and immediately to the south are Chinatown and the Sydney Entertainment Centre. The Star City entertainment complex, based around the Star City Casino, lies just to the west of Darling Harbour.

a good walk

Start at the Market Street end of Pitt Street Mall, Sydney's main pedestrian shopping precinct. Take the monorail—across Market Street and above ground level on the right-hand side of Pitt Street—from here to the next stop (Darling Park), passing the large Queen Victoria Building on your left. Get off at this stop and go down the steps and escalator. On your right is **Sydney Aquarium** ⑤⑥ ►.

From here, take the escalator back up to historic **Pyrmont Bridge** ⑤⑦. Cross below the monorail track to the other side of the walkway. The building immediately below is **Cockle Bay Wharf** ⑤⑧, a three-level waterfront dining-and-entertainment complex.

On the opposite side of the bridge stands the **Australian National Maritime Museum** ⑤⑨, the large white-roof building on your right, which charts Australia's vital links to the sea with lively interactive displays. After visiting the museum, grab a bite to eat at the adjacent Harbourside center, then walk through Darling Harbour, where a curved building with a checkerboard pattern sits beside the elevated freeway. This is the **LG IMAX Theatre** ⑥⓪, with an eight-story movie screen. Cross under the elevated freeway and walk past the carousel.

The intriguing **Powerhouse Museum** ⑥① , inside an old power station with extensive modern additions, makes a worthwhile detour from the amusements of Darling Harbour. Walk west to Merino Boulevard. Then continue south to William Henry Street and turn right. The museum is just south of the intersection of William Henry and Harris streets.

From the Powerhouse, walk back to William Henry Street and follow it east until it becomes Pier Street. Here the **Chinese Garden of Friendship** ⑥② is a small but serene park amid a sea of concrete and steel. Nearby, Chinatown itself is a bustling, energetic corner of the city that has been both home and headquarters to Sydney's Chinese citizens since the middle of the 19th century.

You can return to the city center by monorail—follow signs to the Haymarket station—or take a short walk around the colorful streets, shops, markets, and restaurants of Chinatown, south of the Chinese Garden.

TIMING It will take at least a half day to see the best of the area. If you want to skip the museums, a good time to visit is in the evening, when the tall city buildings reflect the setting sun and spill their molten images across the water. You might even pop over to Chinatown for dinner. Later, pubs, cafés, and nightclubs turn on lights and music for a party that lasts well past midnight. Darling Harbour is a family favorite on weekends, when entertainers perform on the water and in the forecourt area.

What to See

Ꙩ ➄ **Australian National Maritime Museum.** The six galleries of this soaring, futuristic building tell the story of Australia and the sea. In addition to figureheads, model ships, and brassy nautical hardware, there are antique racing yachts and the jet-powered *Spirit of Australia,* current holder of the world water speed record, set in 1978. The USA Gallery displays objects from such major U.S. collections as the Smithsonian Institution and was dedicated by President George Bush Sr. on New Year's Day 1992. An outdoor section showcases numerous vessels moored at the museum's wharves, including the HMAS *Vampire,* a World War II destroyer. ✉ *Wharf 7, Maritime Heritage Centre, 2 Murray St., Darling Harbour* ☎ *02/9298–3777* ⊕ *www.anmm.gov.au* ⌑ *Free* ⊗ *Daily 9:30–5.*

Chinatown. Bounded by the Entertainment Centre, George Street, and Goulburn Street, this neighborhood takes your senses on a galloping tour of the Orient. Within this compact grid are restaurants, traditional apothecary shops, Chinese grocers, clothing boutiques, and shops selling Asian-made electronic gear. The best way to get a sense of the area is to take a stroll along Dixon Street, now a pedestrian mall with a Chinese Lion Gate at either end.

Sydney's Chinese community was first established here in the 1800s, in the aftermath of the gold rush that originally drew many Chinese immigrants to Australia. By the 1920s the area around Dixon Street was a thriving Chinese enclave, although the fear and hostility that many white Australians felt toward the "Yellow Peril" gave it virtually the status of a ghetto. Chinatown was redeveloped in the 1970s, by which time Australians had overcome much of their racial paranoia and embraced the area's liveliness, multiculturalism, and food. These days, most of Sydney comes here regularly to dine, especially on weekends for dim sum lunches.

★ ➅ **Chinese Garden of Friendship.** Chinese prospectors came to the Australian goldfields as far back as the 1850s, and the nation's long and enduring links with China are symbolized by this tranquil walled enclave, the largest garden of its kind outside China. Designed by Chinese landscape architects, the garden includes bridges, lakes, waterfalls, sculpture, and Cantonese-style pavilions. The garden is a welcome refuge from sightseeing and Darling Harbour's crowds. ✉ *Darling Harbour* ☎ *02/9281–6863* ⌑ *A$6* ⊗ *Daily 9:30–5.*

58 **Cockle Bay Wharf.** Fueling Sydney's addiction to fine food, most of this sprawling waterfront complex is dedicated to gastronomy. Dining options include a tandoori takeout, a steak house, a Greek seafood spot, and an alfresco Italian-style café. This is also the site of Sydney's biggest nightclub, Home. If you have a boat you can dock at the marina—and avoid the hassle of parking a car in one of the city's most congested centers. ⊠ *201 Sussex St., Darling Harbour* ☎ *02/9264–4755* ⊕ *www. cocklebaywharf.com* ☉ *Weekends 10–4.*

60 **LG IMAX Theatre.** Both in size and impact, this eight-story-tall movie screen is overwhelming. One-hour presentations take you on astonishing, wide-angle voyages of discovery under the oceans, and to the summit of Mount Kilimanjaro. ⊠ *Southern Promenade, Darling Harbour* ☎ *02/ 9281–3300* ⊕ *www.imax.com.au* ⊠ *A$16* ☉ *Daily 10–10.*

61 **Powerhouse Museum.** Learning the principles of science is a painless process with this museum's stimulating, interactive displays, ideal for all ages. Exhibits in the former 1890s electricity station that once powered Sydney's trams include a whole floor of working steam engines, space modules, airplanes suspended from the ceiling, state-of-the-art computer gadgetry, and a 1930s art deco–style movie-theater auditorium. ⊠ *500 Harris St., Ultimo* ☎ *02/9217–0111* ⊕ *www.phm.gov.au* ⊠ *A$10* ☉ *Daily 9:30–5.*

57 **Pyrmont Bridge.** Dating from 1902, this is the world's oldest electrically operated swing-span bridge. The structure once carried motor traffic, but it's now a walkway that links the Darling Harbour complex with Cockle Bay and the city. The monorail runs above the bridge, but the center span still swings open to allow tall-masted ships into Cockle Bay, which sits at the bottom of the horseshoe-shape shore.

56 **Sydney Aquarium.** The larger and more modern of Sydney's public aquariums presents a fascinating view of the underwater world, with saltwater crocodiles, giant sea turtles, and delicate, multicolor reef fish and corals. Excellent displays highlight Great Barrier Reef marine life and Australia's largest river system, the Murray-Darling, and the marine mammal sanctuary and touch pool are favorites with children. Two show-stealing transparent tunnels give a fish's-eye view of the sea, while sharks and stingrays glide overhead. Although the adult admission price is high, family tickets are a good value, and prices are lower if you buy online. ⊠ *Aquarium pier, 1–5 Wheat Rd., Darling Harbour* ☎ *02/8251–7800* ⊕ *www. sydneyaquarium.com.au* ⊠ *A$26* ☉ *Daily 9 AM–10 PM.*

off the beaten path

SYDNEY FISH MARKET – Second in size only to Tokyo's giant Tsukiji fish market, Sydney's is a showcase for the riches of Australia's seas. Just a five-minute drive from the city, the market is a great place to sample sushi, oysters, octopus, spicy Thai and Chinese fish dishes, and fish-and-chips at the waterfront cafés overlooking the fishing fleet. It's open daily from 7 AM to about 5. ⊠ *Pyrmont Bridge Rd. and Bank St., Pyrmont West* ☎ *02/9004–1100* ⊕ *www. sydneyfishmarket.com.au.*

Sydney City Center

Shopping is the main reason to visit Sydney's city center, but there are several buildings and other places of interest among the office blocks, department stores, and shopping centers.

Begin at the Market Street end of Pitt Street Mall. With the mall at your back, turn left onto Market Street and walk a few steps to the entrance to **Sydney Tower** ⓺ ⏵. High-speed elevators will whisk you to the top of the city's tallest structure, and the spectacular view will give you an excellent idea of the lay of the land.

Return to Market Street and walk in the other direction to George Street. Turn left and continue to the Sydney Hilton Hotel, on the left-hand side. For a little refreshment, take the steps down below street level to the Marble Bar, an opulent basement watering hole with florid decor and architecture.

Back up on George Street, cross the street to enter the **Queen Victoria Building (QVB)** ⓺, a massive Victorian structure that occupies an entire city block. The shops are many and varied, and the meticulous restoration work is impressive. After browsing in the QVB, exit at the Druitt Street end and cross this street to the elaborate **Sydney Town Hall** ⓺, the domain of Sydney City Council and a popular performance space. Next door is the Anglican **St. Andrew's Cathedral** ⓺.

Cut across George Street and walk east along Bathurst Street to the southern section of **Hyde Park** ⓺. This is the city center's largest green space and the location of the Anzac War Memorial, which commemorates Australians who fought and died in the service of their country. Continue through the park to College Street, cross the street, and walk a few more feet to the **Australian Museum** ⓺, an excellent natural-history museum covering the Australia-Pacific region.

From the museum, cross College Street and then Park Street and follow the shady avenue through the northern half of Hyde Park to the Archibald Memorial Fountain, a focal point of this section of the park. Continue past the fountain and cross the road to Macquarie Street, walking north past the Hyde Park Barracks and Sydney Hospital. In front of the hospital, cross the road to the large pedestrian precinct of **Martin Place** ⓺ and walk the length of the plaza to George Street. This is Sydney's banking headquarters and the site of the cenotaph war memorial near the George Street end.

From here you can return to the Pitt Street Mall via Pitt Street, or walk north on George Street to Circular Quay.

TIMING The walk itself should take no longer than a couple of hours. Plan more time for an extended tour of the Australian Museum or for shopping in the Queen Victoria Building. Weekday lunchtimes (generally noon–2) in the city center are elbow-to-elbow affairs, with office workers trying to make the most of their brief break.

What to See

🐾 🟤68 **Australian Museum.** The strength of this natural-history museum, a well-respected academic institution, is its collection of plants, animals, geological specimens, and cultural artifacts from the Asia-Pacific region. Particularly notable are the collections of artifacts from Papua New Guinea and from Australia's Aboriginal peoples. The museum also has a comprehensive gems-and-minerals display, an excellent shop, and a lively café. ☒ *6 College St., near William St., Hyde Park* ☎ *02/9320–6000* ⊕ *www.austmus.gov.au* ☒ *A$10* ☉ *Daily 9:30–5.*

🟤67 **Hyde Park.** Declared public land by Governor Phillip in 1792 and used for the colony's earliest cricket matches and horse races, this area was turned into a park in 1810. The gardens are formal, with fountains, statuary, and tree-lined walks, and its tranquil lawns are popular with office workers at lunchtime. In the southern section of Hyde Park (near Liverpool Street) stands the 1934 art deco **Anzac Memorial** (☎ *02/ 9267–7668*), a tribute to the Australians who died in military service during World War I, when the acronym ANZAC (Australian and New Zealand Army Corps) was coined. The 120,000 gold stars inside the dome represent each man and woman of New South Wales who served. The lower level exhibits war-related photographs. It's open daily 9–5. ☒ *Elizabeth, College, and Park Sts., Hyde Park.*

> **need a break?**
>
> Stop in the **Marble Bar** for a drink, and to experience a masterpiece of Victorian extravagance. The 1890 bar was formerly in another building that was constructed on the profits of the horse-racing track, thus establishing the link between gambling and majestic public architecture that has its modern-day parallel in the Sydney Opera House. Threatened with demolition in the 1970s, the whole bar was moved—marble arches, color-glass ceiling, elaborately carved woodwork, paintings of voluptuous nudes, and all—to its present site. By night it serves as a backdrop for live music. ☒ *Sydney Hilton Hotel, basement level, 259 Pitt St., City Center* ☎ *02/9266–2000* ☉ *Closed Sun.*

🟤69 **Martin Place.** Sydney's largest pedestrian precinct, flanked by banks, offices, and shopping centers, is the hub of the central business district. There are some grand buildings here—including the beautifully refurbished Commonwealth Bank and the 1870s Venetian Renaissance–style General Post Office building with its 230-foot clock tower (now a Westin hotel). Toward the George Street end of the plaza the simple 1929 cenotaph war memorial commemorates Australians who died in World War I. Weekdays from about 12:30, the amphitheater near Castlereagh Street hosts free lunchtime concerts with sounds from all corners of the music world, from police bands to string quartets to rock-and-rollers. ☒ *Between Macquarie and George Sts., City Center.*

🟤64 **Queen Victoria Building (QVB).** Originally the city's produce market, this huge 1898 sandstone structure was handsomely restored with sweeping staircases, enormous stained-glass windows, and the 1-ton Royal Clock, which hangs from the glass roof. Shaped like Balmoral Castle, in Scotland, the clock chimes the hour from 9 AM to 9 PM with four tableaux: the second shows Queen Elizabeth I knighting Sir Frances Drake; the last ends with an executioner chopping off King Charles I's head. The complex includes more than 200 boutiques, with those on the upper floors generally more upscale and exclusive. The basement level has several inexpensive dining options. ✉ *George, York, Market, and Druitt Sts., City Center* ☎ *02/9264–9209* ☼ *Daily 8 AM–10 PM.*

66 **St. Andrew's Cathedral.** The foundation stone for Sydney's Gothic Revival Anglican cathedral—the country's oldest—was laid in 1819, although the original architect, Francis Greenway, fell from grace soon after work began. Edmund Blacket, Sydney's most illustrious church architect, was responsible for its final design and completion—a whopping 50 years later in 1869. Notable features of the sandstone construction include ornamental windows depicting Jesus's life and a great east window with images relating to St. Andrew. ✉ *Sydney Sq., George and Bathurst Sts., next to Town Hall, Hyde Park* ☎ *02/9265–1661* ☼ *Weekdays 10:30–3:30, Sun. for services only 8:30 AM, 10:30 AM, 6:30 PM; tours by arrangement.*

▶ **63** **Sydney Tower.** Short of taking a scenic flight, a visit to the top of this 1,000-foot golden-minaret-topped spike is the best way to see Sydney's spectacular layout. This is the city's tallest building, and the views from its indoor observation deck encompass the entire Sydney metropolitan area of more than 1,560 square km (600 square mi). You can often see as far as the Blue Mountains, more than 80 km (50 mi) away. Free guided tours, conducted hourly on the observation deck, cover the major sights and landmarks of the city below as well as details about the tower itself. ✉ *100 Market St., between Pitt and Castlereagh Sts., City Center* ☎ *02/9223–0933* ⊕ *www.sydneyskytour.com.au* ☞ *A$22* ☼ *Sun.–Fri. 9 AM–10:30 PM, Sat. 9 AM–11:30 PM.*

65 **Sydney Town Hall.** Sydney's most ornate Victorian building—an elaborate, multilayer sandstone structure—is often rather unkindly likened to a wedding cake. It does have some grand interior spaces, especially the vestibule and large Centennial Hall, and a massive 8,000-pipe Grand Organ, one of the world's most powerful, which is central to lunchtime concerts held here. Call for details of building tours. ✉ *George and Druitt Sts., City Center* ☎ *02/9265–9007, 02/9231–4629 for tour information* ☞ *Free* ☼ *Weekdays 8:30–6.*

The Eastern Suburbs

Sydney's eastern suburbs are truly the people's domain. They stretch from the mansions of the colonial aristocracy and the humble laborers' cottages of the same period to the modernized terrace houses of Paddington, one of Sydney's most charming suburbs and one of its most desirable. This tour also passes through Kings Cross and Darlinghurst, the country's best-known nightlife districts; visits a genteel colonial mansion in Elizabeth Bay; and takes you to the acclaimed Sydney Jewish Museum.

Begin at the bus stop on Alfred Street ➤, just behind Circular Quay, and catch Bus 311, which leaves from the stop on Bridge Street, between Pitt and Gresham streets. (This bus also reads either RAILWAY VIA KINGS CROSS or RAILWAY VIA ELIZABETH BAY.) Ask the driver to drop you off at Elizabeth Bay House and take a seat on the left side of the bus.

Wind your way through the city streets to Macquarie Street, past the State Library, the New South Wales Parliament, Hyde Park Barracks, and St. Mary's Cathedral. The bus then follows the curve of Woolloomooloo Bay, where it passes Harry's Café de Wheels, a unique Sydney institution, and beneath the bows of naval vessels at the Garden Island Dockyard, the main base for the Australian navy. Visiting ships from other Pacific Ocean navies can often be seen along this wharf.

Just before the Garden Island gates the bus turns right and climbs through the shaded streets of Potts Point and Elizabeth Bay to **Elizabeth Bay House** ⑳, an aristocratic Regency-style mansion and one of Australia's finest historic homes.

After a spin through Elizabeth Bay House, continue north to **Arthur McElhone Reserve** ㉑ for a pleasant rest with harbor glimpses. Take the stone steps leading down from the park to Billyard Avenue. Near the lower end of this street is a walled garden with cypress trees and banana palms reaching above the parapets. Through the black iron gates on the driveway you can catch a glimpse of Boomerang, a sprawling, Spanish-style villa built by the manufacturer of the harmonica of the same name. When it was last traded, in 2002, this was Sydney's second-most-expensive house, worth just a shade over A$20 million. Just beyond the house, turn left to **Beare Park** ㉒, overlooking the yachts in Elizabeth Bay.

Return to Billyard Avenue. Wait at the bus stop opposite Boomerang's first gate for Bus 311, but make sure that you catch one marked RAILWAY, *not* CIRCULAR QUAY. This bus threads its way through the streets of Kings Cross, Sydney's nightlife district, and Darlinghurst. During the day the Cross is only half awake, although the strip-club doormen are never too sleepy to lure passersby inside to watch nonstop video shows. Ask the driver to deposit you at the stop near the corner of Darlinghurst Road and Burton Street. From here the moving and thought-provoking **Sydney Jewish Museum** ㉓ is just across the road.

After leaving the museum, walk along the wall of the former Darlinghurst Jail, now an educational institution, to Oxford Street. Turn left, and on your right about 300 yards up Oxford Street is the long sandstone wall that is the perimeter of **Victoria Barracks** ㉔ and its Army Museum. These barracks were built in the middle of the 19th century to house the British regiments stationed in the colony.

Almost opposite the main entrance to the barracks is the start of **Shadforth Street** ㉕, which is lined with some of the oldest terrace houses in Paddington. From Shadforth Street turn right onto Glenmore Road, where the terrace houses become far more elaborate. Follow this road past the intersection with Brown Street to the colorful collection of shops known as Five Ways.

Walk up Broughton Street to the right of the Royal Hotel, which has a fine Victorian pub. Turn right at Union Street, left onto Underwood, and right at William Street. You are now among the boutique shops of Paddington, and you may want to spend some time browsing here before completing the walk. On the right is Just William, a shop for chocolate-lovers. If you're in the mood, don't miss Oxford Street's designer clothing and curio shops. The restored colonial mansion **Juniper Hall** ⓦ is also along Oxford.

You can take any bus back to the city from the other side of Oxford Street, but if the sun is shining, consider heading out to Bondi Beach, a mere 20-minute ride on Bus 380.

TIMING Allow the better part of a day to make your way through these neighborhoods, especially if you want to take a good look around Elizabeth Bay House and the Sydney Jewish Museum. If you wish to tour Victoria Barracks, take this trip on a Thursday and get there by 10 to hear the band (this will probably mean going there first and visiting the area's other sights in the afternoon). There is an additional diversion on Saturday, when the famous Paddington Bazaar brings zest and color to the upper end of Oxford Street.

The walk around Paddington is not particularly long, but some of the streets are steep. The walk can be shortened by continuing along Oxford Street from Victoria Barracks to Juniper Hall, rather than turning onto Shadforth Street.

What to See

ⓦ **Arthur McElhone Reserve.** One of the city's welcome havens, the reserve has tree ferns, a gushing stream, a stone bridge over a carp pond, and views up the harbor. ✉ *Onslow and Billyard Aves., Elizabeth Bay* ☞ *Free* ☉ *Daily dawn–dusk.*

ⓦ **Beare Park.** With its pleasant harbor views, this waterfront park is a favorite recreation spot among Elizabeth Bay locals. The adjoining wharf is often busy with sailors coming and going to their yachts, moored out in the bay. ✉ *Ithaca Rd., Elizabeth Bay* ☞ *Free* ☉ *Daily dawn–dusk.*

Elizabeth Bay. Much of this densely populated but still-charming harborside suburb was originally part of the extensive Elizabeth Bay House grounds. Wrought-iron balconies and French doors on some of the older apartment blocks give the area a Mediterranean flavor. During the 1920s and 1930s this was a fashionably bohemian quarter, and it remains a favorite among artists and writers.

ⓦ **Elizabeth Bay House.** Regarded in its heyday as the "finest house in the colony," this 1835–39 mansion retains little of its original furniture, although the rooms have been restored in Georgian style. The most striking feature is an oval-shape salon with a winding staircase, naturally lighted by glass panels in the domed roof. ✉ *7 Onslow Ave., Elizabeth Bay* ☎ *02/9356–3022* ⊕ *www.hht.net.au* ☞ *A$7* ☉ *Tues.–Sun. 10–4:30.*

off the
beaten
path

HARRY'S CAFÉ DE WHEELS – The attraction of this all-day dockyard food stall is not so much the delectable meat pies and coffee Harry dispenses as the clientele. Famous opera singers, actors, and international rock-and-roll stars have been spotted here rubbing shoulders with shift workers and taxi drivers. Drop in any time from 9 AM to the wee hours. ⊠ *1 Cowper Wharf Rd., Woolloomooloo* ☎ *02/9357–3074* ⊕ *www.harryscafedewheels.com.au.*

76 **Juniper Hall.** Built in 1824 by gin distiller Robert Cooper, this patrician Paddington residence was named for the juniper berries used to make the potent beverage. Cooper did everything on a grand scale, and that included raising and housing his family. He built Juniper Hall, with its simple and elegant lines typical of the Georgian period, for his third wife, Sarah, whom he married when he was 46 (she was just a teenager) and who bore 14 of his 24 children. Owing to lack of funds, the house is now closed to the public. It currently contains offices. ⊠ *248 Oxford St., Paddington.*

Paddington. Most of this suburb's elegant two-story houses were built during the 1880s, when the colony experienced a long period of economic growth following the gold rushes that began in the 1860s. The balconies are trimmed with decorative wrought iron, sometimes known as Paddington lace, which initially came from England and later from Australian foundries. Rebuilt and repainted, the now-stylish Paddington terrace houses give the area its characteristic, villagelike charm. Today an attractive, renovated terrace home will cost at least A$1 million.

75 **Shadforth Street.** Built at about the same time as Elizabeth Bay House, the tiny stone houses in this street were assembled to house the workers who built and serviced the **Victoria Barracks.**

need a
break?

The **Royal Hotel** has a fine Victorian pub with leather couches and stained-glass windows. It's a good place to stop for something cool to drink. On the floor above the pub is a balconied restaurant that's popular on sunny afternoons. ⊠ *237 Glenmore Rd., Paddington* ☎ *02/9331–2604.*

★ **73** **Sydney Jewish Museum.** Artifacts, interactive media, and audiovisual displays chronicle the history of Australian Jews and commemorate the 6 million killed in the Holocaust. Exhibits are brilliantly arranged on eight levels, which lead upward in chronological order, from the handful of Jews who arrived on the First Fleet in 1788 to the migration of 30,000 concentration-camp survivors to Australia—one of the largest populations of Holocaust survivors to be found anywhere. ⊠ *148 Darlinghurst Rd., Darlinghurst* ☎ *02/9360–7999* ⊕ *www. sydneyjewishmuseum.com.au* ⊠ *A$10* ☉ *Sun.–Thurs. 10–4, Fri. 10–2.*

74 **Victoria Barracks.** Built by soldiers and convicts from 1841 on to replace the colony's original Wynyard Barracks—and still occupied by the army—this vast building is an excellent example of Regency-style architecture. Behind the 740-foot-long sandstone facade is mostly a parade ground, where an army band performs most Thursdays at 10 AM during the free tours. In the former military prison on the parade grounds is the **Army Museum,** with exhibits covering Australia's military history from the early days of the Rum Corps to the Malayan conflict of the 1950s. Free tours of the barracks run most of the year. ✉ *Oxford St. and Oatley Rd., Paddington* ☎ *02/9339–3000* 🏷 *A$2* ☉ *Museum Thurs. 10–12:30, Sun. 10–3; tour at 10.*

Greater Sydney

The Sydney area has numerous attractions that are well away from the inner suburbs. These include historic townships, the Sydney 2000 Olympics site, national parks in which you can experience the Australian bush, and wildlife and theme parks that particularly appeal to children.

Other points of interest are the Bondi and Manly beaches; the historic city of Parramatta, founded in 1788 and located 26 km (16 mi) to the west; and the magnificent Hawkesbury River, which winds its way around the city's western and northern borders. The waterside suburb of Balmain, 5 km (3 mi) away, has an atmospheric Saturday flea market and backstreets full of character.

TIMING Each of the sights below could easily fill the better part of a day. If you're short on time, try a tour company that combines visits within a particular area—for example, a day trip west to the Olympic Games site, Australian Wildlife Park, and the Blue Mountains.

What to See

77 **Centennial Park.** More than 500 acres of palm-lined avenues, groves of Moreton Bay figs, paperbark tree–fringed lakes, and cycling and horse-riding tracks make this a popular park and Sydney's favorite workout circuit. In the early 1800s the marshy land at the lower end provided Sydney with its fresh water. The park was proclaimed in 1888, the centenary of Australia's foundation as a colony. The Centennial Park Café is often crowded on weekends, but a mobile canteen between the lakes in the middle of the park serves snacks and espresso. Bikes and blades can be rented from the nearby Clovelly Road outlets, on the eastern side of the park. ✉ *Oxford St. and Centennial Ave., Centennial Park* ⊕ *www. cp.nsw.gov.au* ☉ *Daily dawn–dusk.*

81 **Featherdale Wildlife Park.** If you don't have time to visit Tooronga Zoo, this is the place to see koalas, kangaroos, wombats, dingoes, and other extraordinary Australian fauna in native bush settings. ✉ *217 Kildare Rd., Doonside* ☎ *02/9622–1644* ⊕ *www.featherdale.com.au* 🏷 *A$18.50* ☉ *Daily 9–5.*

78 **Fox Studios.** Australia's largest movie production facility incorporates restaurants, cafés and bars, a retail center, weekend markets, and movie theaters. There are also bungee trampolines and minigolf. Children can play on a three-story jungle gym and jumping castle, and ride a merry-go-round in Lollipop's Playland (entry fee). ✉ *Driver Ave., Centennial Park, Moore Park* ☎ *02-9383–4333* ⊕ *www.foxstudios.com.au* 🏷 *Free, Lollipop's Playland A$5* ☉ *Daily 10 AM–11 PM.*

🐣 ⑧⓪ **Koala Park Sanctuary.** At this private park on Sydney's northern outskirts you can cuddle a koala or hand-feed a kangaroo. The sanctuary also has dingoes, wombats, emus, and wallaroos, and there are sheep-shearing and boomerang-throwing demonstrations. Feeding times are 10:20, 11:45, 2, and 3. ✉ *84 Castle Hill Rd., West Pennant Hills* ☎ *02/ 9484–3141* ⊕ *www.koalaparksanctuary.com.au* ✑ *A$18* ⊙ *Daily 9–5.*

⑦⑨ **Ku-ring-gai Chase National Park.** Nature hikes here lead past rock engravings and paintings by the Guringai Aboriginal tribe, the area's original inhabitants for whom the park is named. Created in the 1890s, the park mixes large stands of eucalyptus trees with moist, rain-forest-filled gullies where swamp wallabies, possums, goannas, and other creatures roam. The delightful trails are mostly easy to moderate, including the compelling 3-km (2-mi) Garigal Aboriginal Heritage Walk at West Head, which takes in ancient rock-art sites. From Mt. Ku-ring-gai train station you can walk the 3-km (2-mi) Ku-ring-gai Track to Appletree Bay, while the 30-minute, wheelchair-accessible Discovery Trail is an excellent introduction to the region's flora and fauna. Leaflets on all of the walks are available at the park's entry stations and from the Wildlife Shop at Bobbin Head.

The park is 24 km (15 mi) north of Sydney. Railway stations at Mt. Ku-ring-gai, Berowra, and Cowan, close to the park's western border, provide access to walking trails. On Sunday, for example, you can walk from Mt. Ku-ring-gai station to Appletree Bay and then to Bobbin Head, where a bus can take you to the Turramurra rail station. By car, take the Pacific Highway to Pymble. Then turn into Bobbin Head Road or continue on the highway to Mt. Colah and turn off into the park on Ku-ring-gai Chase Road. You can also follow the Pacific Highway to Pymble and then drive along the Mona Vale Road to Terry Hills and take the West Head turnoff.

Camping in the park is permitted only at **The Basin** on Pittwater (☎ 02/ 9974–1011). Sites must be booked in advance. The rate is A$10 per night. Supplies can be purchased in Palm Beach. For more information on the park, contact Ku-ring-gai Chase National Park Visitors Centre. ✑ *Box 834, Hornsby 2077* ☎ *02/9472–8949* ⊕ *www.nationalparks.nsw. gov.au.*

★ ⑧② **Parramatta.** This bustling satellite city 26 km (16 mi) west of Sydney is one of Australia's most historic precincts. Its origins as a European settlement are purely agrarian. The sandy, rocky soil around Sydney Cove was too poor to feed the fledgling colony, so Governor Phillip looked to the banks of the Parramatta River for the rich alluvial soil they needed. In 1789, just a year after the first convicts-cum-settlers arrived, Phillip established Rosehill, an area set aside for agriculture. The community developed as its agricultural successes grew, and several important buildings survive as outstanding examples of the period. The two-hour Harris Park Heritage Walk, which departs from the RiverCat Ferry Terminal, connects the key historic sites and buildings. The ferry departs at frequent intervals from Sydney's Circular Quay, and is a relaxing, scenic alternative to the drive from the city.

The site of the first private land grant in Australia, **Experiment Farm** was settled by James Ruse, a former convict who was given 1½ acres by Governor Phillip on condition that he become self-sufficient—a vital experiment if the colony was to survive. Luckily for Phillip, his gamble paid off. The bungalow, with its wide verandas, was built by colonial surgeon John Harris in the 1830s; it contains a fine collection of Australian colonial furniture, and the cellar now houses an exhibition on the life and work of James Ruse. The surrounding ornamental garden is most beautiful in early summer, when the floral perfumes are strongest. ☒ *9 Ruse St., Parramatta* ☏ *02/9365–5655* ▨ *A$5.50, joint ticket with Old Government House A$7* ☉ *Tues.–Fri. 10:30–3:30, Sun. 11–3:30.*

On the banks of the Parramatta River, **Old Government House** is Australia's oldest surviving public building, and a notable work from the Georgian period. Built by governors John Hunter and Lachlan Macquarie, the building has been faithfully restored in keeping with its origins, and contains the nation's most significant collection of early-Australian furniture. In the 260-acre parkland surrounding the house are Governor Brisbane's bathhouse and observatory and the Government House Dairy. ☒ *Parramatta Park, Parramatta* ☏ *02/9687–2662* ▨ *A$7* ☉ *Weekdays 10–4, weekends 10:30–4.*

The oldest European building in Australia, **Elizabeth Farm** was built by John and Elizabeth Macarthur in 1793. With its simple but elegant lines and long, shady verandas, the house became a template for Australian farmhouses that survives to the present day. It was here, too, that the merino sheep industry began, since the Macarthurs were the first to introduce the tough Spanish breed to Australia. Although John Macarthur has traditionally been credited as the father of Australia's wool industry, it was Elizabeth who largely ran the farm while her husband pursued his official and more lucrative unofficial duties as an officer in the colony's Rum Corps. Inside are personal objects of the Macarthur family, as well as a re-creation of their furnishings. ☒ *70 Alice St., Rosehill* ☏ *02/9635–9488* ⊕ *www.hht.net.au/museums/elizabeth_farm/ elizabeth_farm* ▨ *A$7* ☉ *Daily 10–5.*

★ ⑧④ **Royal National Park.** Established in 1879 on the coast south of Sydney, the Royal has the distinction of being the first national park in Australia and the second in the world, after Yellowstone National Park in the United States. Several walking tracks traverse the grounds, most of them requiring little or no hiking experience. The Lady Carrington Walk, a 10-km (6-mi) trek, is a self-guided tour that crosses 15 creeks and passes several historic sites. Other tracks take you along the coast past beautiful wildflower displays and through patches of rain forest. You can canoe the Port Hacking River upstream from the Audley Causeway; rentals are available at the Audley boat shed on the river. The Illawarra–Cronulla train line stops at Loftus, Engadine, Heathcote, Waterfall, and Otford stations, where most of the park's walking tracks begin. ✛ *Royal National Park Visitor Centre, 35 km (22 mi) south of Sydney via Princes Hwy. to Farnell Ave., south of Loftus, or McKell Ave. at Waterfall* ☍ *Box 44, Sutherland 1499* ☏ *02/9542–0648, 02/9542–0666 Na-*

tional Parks and Wildlife Service district office ✉ *A$11 per vehicle per day* ☉ *Daily 7:30 AM–8:30 PM.*

③ **Sydney Olympic Park.** The center of the 2000 Olympic and Paralympic Games lies 14 km (8½ mi) west of the city center. Sprawling across 1,900 acres on the shores of Homebush Bay, the site is a series of majestic stadiums, arenas, and accommodation complexes. Among the park's sports facilities are an aquatic center, archery range, athletic center, tennis center, and velodrome, and the centerpiece, an 85,000-seat, A$665 million Olympic Stadium. Since the conclusion of the 2000 Games it has been mostly used for concerts and sporting events. The Royal Sydney Easter Show, the country's largest agricultural show, with art displays and demonstrations by craftspersons, takes place here the two weeks before Easter. Some venues are open to the public only on guided tours.

The most scenic and relaxing way to get to Sydney Olympic Park is to take the RiverCat from Circular Quay to Homebush Bay. A bus is also available between the Olympic Park visitor center and Strathfield Station, reached by train from Town Hall or Central stations. ✉ *1 Herb Elliot Ave., Homebush Bay* ☎ *02/9714–7888* ⊕ *www. sydneyolympicpark.nsw.gov.au* ✉ *Tours A$18.50–A$27.50* ☉ *Daily during daylight hrs.*

BEACHES

Sydney is paradise for beach lovers. Within the metropolitan area there are more than 30 ocean beaches, all with golden sand and rolling surf, as well as several more around the harbor with calmer water for safe swimming. If your hotel is on the harbor's south side, the logical choice for a day at the beach is the southern ocean beaches between Bondi and Coogee. On the north side of the harbor, Manly is easily accessible by ferry, but beaches farther north involve a long trip by car or public transportation.

Lifeguards are on duty at most of Sydney's ocean beaches during summer months, and flags indicate whether a beach is being patrolled. "Swim between the flags" is an adage that is drummed into every Australian child, with very good reason: the undertow can be very dangerous. If you get into difficulty, don't fight the current. Breathe evenly, stay calm, and raise one arm above your head to signal the lifeguards.

Although there's no shortage of sharks inside and outside the harbor, these species are not typically aggressive toward humans. In addition, many Sydney beaches are protected by shark nets, and the risk of attack is very low. A more common hazard is jellyfish, known locally as bluebottles, which inflict a painful sting—with a remote risk of more serious complications (including allergic reactions). Staff at most beaches will supply a spray-on remedy to help relieve the pain, which generally lasts about 24 hours. Many beaches will post warning signs when bluebottles are present, but you can also determine the situation yourself by looking for the telltale bright-blue, bubblelike jellies washed up along the waterline.

Topless sunbathing is common at all Sydney beaches, but full nudity is permitted only at a couple of locations, including Lady Jane Beach, close to Watsons Bay on the south side of the harbor.

Details of how to reach the beaches by bus, train, or ferry are provided below, but some of the city's harbor and southern beaches are also on the Bondi Explorer bus route. These are Nielsen Park, Camp Cove, Lady Jane, Bondi, Bronte, Clovelly, and Coogee.

Numbers in the margin correspond to beaches on the Sydney Beaches map.

Inside the Harbor

★ **94** **Balmoral.** This 800-yard-long, rarely crowded beach—among the best of the inner-harbor beaches—is in one of Sydney's most exclusive northern suburbs. There's no surf, but it's a great place to learn to windsurf (sailboard rentals are available). The Esplanade, which runs along the back of the beach, has several snack bars and cafés, serving award-winning fish-and-chips. In summer you can catch performances of Shakespeare on the Beach. You could easily combine a trip to Balmoral with a visit to Taronga Zoo. To reach Balmoral, take the ferry from Circular Quay to Taronga Zoo and then board Bus 238. ⊠ *Raglan St., Balmoral.*

96 **Camp Cove.** Just inside South Head, this crescent-shape beach is where Sydney's fashionable people come to see and be seen. The gentle slope and calm water make it a safe playground for children. A shop at the northern end of the beach sells salad rolls and fresh fruit juices. The grassy hill at the southern end of the beach has a plaque to commemorate the spot where Captain Arthur Phillip, the commander of the First Fleet, first set foot inside Port Jackson. Parking is limited; arrive by car after 10 on weekends and there's a long walk to the beach. Take Bus 324 or 325 from Circular Quay. ⊠ *Cliff St., Watsons Bay.*

95 **Lady Jane.** Lady Jane—officially called Lady Bay—is the most accessible of the nude beaches around Sydney. It's also a popular part of Sydney's gay scene, although it attracts a mixed crowd. Only a couple of hundred yards long and backed by a stone wall, the beach has safe swimming with no surf. From Camp Cove, follow the path north and then descend the short, steep ladder leading down the cliff face to the beach.

97 **Nielsen Park.** By Sydney standards, this beach at the end of the Vaucluse Peninsula is small, but behind the sand is a large, shady park that's ideal for picnics. The headlands at either end of the beach are especially popular for their magnificent views across the harbor. The beach is protected by a semicircular net, so don't be deterred by the beach's correct name, Shark Bay. Surfable waves are rare here. The shop and café behind the beach sell drinks, snacks, and meals. Parking is often difficult on weekends. A 10-minute walk will take you to historic Vaucluse House and a very different harborside experience. Take Bus 325 from Circular Quay. ⊠ *Greycliffe Ave. off Vaucluse Rd., Vaucluse.*

South of the Harbor

98 **Bondi.** Wide, wonderful Bondi (pronounced *bon*-dye) is the most famous and most crowded of all Sydney beaches. It has something for just about everyone, and the droves who flock here on a sunny day give it a bustling,

Fodor's Choice
★

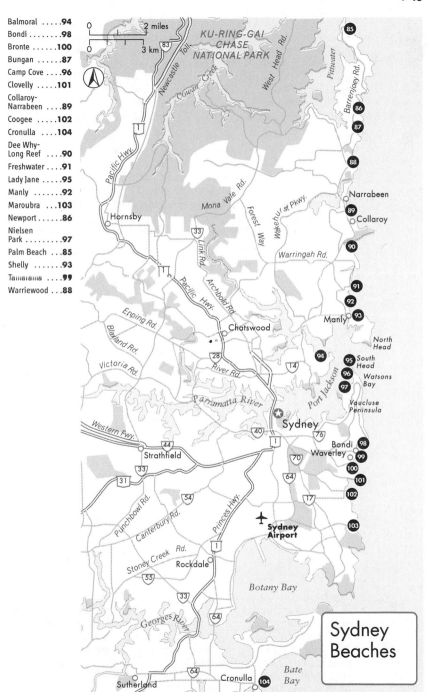

Sydney
Beaches

carnival atmosphere unmatched by any other Sydney beach. Facilities include toilets and showers. Cafés, ice-cream outlets, and restaurants line Campbell Parade, which runs behind the beach. Families tend to prefer the more sheltered northern end of the beach. Surfing is popular at the south end, where a path winds along the sea-sculpted cliffs to Tamarama and Bronte beaches. Take Bus 380 or 382 from Circular Quay via Elizabeth and Oxford streets, or take the train from the city to Bondi Junction and then board Bus 380 or 382. ⊠ *Campbell Parade, Bondi Beach.*

★ ⑩ **Bronte.** If you want an ocean beach that's close to the city, has both sand and grassy areas, and offers a terrific setting, this one is hard to beat. A wooded park of palm trees and Norfolk Island pines surrounds Bronte. The park includes a playground and sheltered picnic tables, and excellent cafés are in the immediate area. The breakers can be fierce, but swimming is safe in the sea pool at the southern end of the beach. Take Bus 378 from Central Station, or take the train from the city to Bondi Junction and then board Bus 378. ⊠ *Bronte Rd., Bronte.*

★ ⑩ **Clovelly.** Even on the roughest day it's safe to swim at the end of this long, keyhole-shape inlet, which makes it a popular family beach. There are toilet facilities but no snack bars or shops in the immediate area. This is also a popular snorkeling spot that usually teems with tropical fish. Take Bus 339 from Argyle Street, Millers Point (the Rocks), or Wynyard bus station; Bus 341 from Central Station; or a train from the city to Bondi Junction. Then board Bus 329. ⊠ *Clovelly Rd., Clovelly.*

☾ ⑩ **Coogee.** A reef protects this lively beach (pronounced *kuh*-jee), creating calmer swimming conditions than those found at its neighbors. A grassy headland overlooking the beach has an excellent children's playground. Cafés in the shopping precinct at the back of the beach sell ice cream, pizza, and the ingredients for picnics. Take Bus 373 from Circular Quay or Bus 372 from Central Station. ⊠ *Coogee Bay Rd., Coogee.*

⑩ **Cronulla.** Even on the hottest days you can escape the crowds by heading to Cronulla, the southernmost and largest beach in the metropolitan area. Good surf usually runs at this beach, and the sand is backed by a grassy park area. Cronulla is a long way from the city by train, however, and its attractions don't justify a long trip if you're not staying nearby. ⊠ *Kingsway, Cronulla.*

⑩ **Maroubra.** This expansive beach is very popular with surfers, although anyone looking for more than waves will probably be unimpressed by the rather scrappy surroundings and the lackluster shopping area. Take Bus 395 from Central Station or Bus 396 from Circular Quay. ⊠ *Marine Parade, Maroubra.*

★ ⑨ **Tamarama.** This small, fashionable beach—aka "Glam-a-rama"—is one of Sydney's prettiest, but the rocky headlands that squeeze close to the sand on either side make it less than ideal for swimming. The sea is often hazardous here, and surfing is prohibited. A café at the back of the beach sells open sandwiches, fresh fruit juices, and fruit whips. Take the train from the city to Bondi Junction. Then board Bus 391, or walk for 10 minutes along the cliffs from the south end of Bondi Beach. ⊠ *Tamarama Marine Dr., Tamarama.*

North of the Harbor

87 **Bungan.** If you *really* want to get away from it all, this is the beach for you. Very few Sydneysiders have discovered Bungan, and those who have would like to keep it to themselves. As well as being relatively empty, this wide, attractive beach is one of the cleanest, due to the prevailing ocean currents. Access to the beach involves a difficult hike down a wooden staircase, and there are no facilities. Take Bus 184 or 190 from the Wynyard bus station. ⊠ *Beach Rd. off Barrenjoey Rd., Mona Vale.*

89 **Collaroy–Narrabeen.** This is actually one beach that passes through two suburbs. Its main attractions are its size—it's almost 3 km (2 mi) long—and the fact that it's always possible to escape the crowds here. The shops are concentrated at the southern end of the beach. Take Bus 155 or 157 from Manly or Bus 182, 184, 189, or 190 from the Wynyard bus station. ⊠ *Pittwater Rd., Narrabeen.*

90 **Dee Why–Long Reef.** Separated from Dee Why by a narrow channel, Long Reef Beach is remoter and much quieter than its southern neighbor. However, Dee Why has better surfing conditions, a big sea pool, and several take-out shops. To get here take Bus 136 from Manly. ⊠ *The Strand, Dee Why.*

91 **Freshwater.** Sprawling headlands protect this small beach on either side, making it popular for families with kids. The surf club on the beach has dressing sheds with showers and toilets as well as a small shop that sells light refreshments. Take Bus 139 from Manly. ⊠ *The Esplanade, Harbord.*

92 **Manly.** The Bondi Beach of the north shore, Manly caters to everyone
Fodor'sChoice except those who want to get away from it all. On sunny days Syd-
★ neysiders, school groups, and travelers from around the world crowd the 1¼-mi-long sweep of white sand, and take to the waves to swim and ride boards. The beach is well equipped with changing and toilet facilities, and lockers. The promenade that runs along a good part of the beach, between the Norfolk Island pines, is great for people-watching and roller blading, and cafés, souvenir shops, and ice-cream parlors line the nearby shopping area, the Corso. Manly also has several nonbeach attractions. The ferry ride from the city makes a day at Manly feel more like a holiday than just an excursion to the beach. Take a ferry or Jet-Cat from Circular Quay. From the dock at Manly the beach is a 10-minute walk. ⊠ *Steyne St., Manly.*

86 **Newport.** With its backdrop of hills and Norfolk Island pines, this broad sweep of sand is one of the finest northern beaches. Although the relaxed town of Newport is known for its bodysurfing, it has one of the best selections of cafés and take-out shops of any Sydney beach, and there's a shopping center within easy walking distance. Take Bus 189 or 190 from the Wynyard bus station. ⊠ *Barrenjoey Rd., Newport.*

85 **Palm Beach.** The wide golden sands of Palm Beach run along one side of a peninsula separating the large inlet of Pittwater from the Pacific Ocean. Bathers can easily cross from the ocean side to Pittwater's calm waters and sailboats, and you can take a circular ferry trip around this waterway from the wharf on the Pittwater side. The view from the lighthouse at the northern end of the beach is well worth the walk. Nearby shops and cafés sell light snacks and meals. Take Bus 190 from Wynyard bus station. ⊠ *Ocean Rd., Palm Beach.*

93 Shelly. This delightful little beach is protected by a headland rising behind it to form a shady park, and it is well supplied with food options. The snack shop and restaurant on the beach sell everything from light refreshments to elaborate meals, and there are a couple of waterfront cafés at nearby Fairy Bower Bay. On weekends the beach is crowded and parking in the area is nearly impossible. It's best to walk along the seafront from Manly. Take a ferry or JetCat from Circular Quay to Manly. From there the beach is a 1-km (½-mi) walk. ⊠ *Marine Parade, Manly.*

88 Warriewood. Enticing and petite in its cove at the bottom of looming cliffs, Warriewood has excellent conditions for surfers and windsurfers. For swimmers and sunbathers, however, the beach does not justify the difficult journey down the steep cliffs. If you take public transportation, there's a long walk from the nearest bus stop to the beach. Basic toilet facilities are available on the beach, but there are no shops nearby. Take Bus 184, 189, or 190 from Wynyard bus station or Bus 155 from Manly. ⊠ *Narrabeen Park Parade, Warriewood.*

WHERE TO EAT

Sydney's dining scene is now as sunny and cosmopolitan as the city itself, and there are diverse and exotic culinary adventures to suit every appetite. Mod-Oz (modern Australian) cooking flourishes, fueled by local produce and guided by Mediterranean and Asian techniques. Look for such innovations as tuna tartare with flying-fish roe and wasabi; emu prosciutto; five-spice duck; shiitake mushroom pie; and sweet turmeric barramundi curry. A meal at Tetsuya's, Claude's, or Rockpool constitutes a crash course in this dazzling culinary language. A visit to the city's fish markets at Pyrmont, just five minutes from the city center, will also tell you much about Sydney's diet. Look for rudderfish, barramundi, blue-eye, kingfish, John Dory, ocean perch, and parrot fish, as well as Yamba prawns, Balmain and Moreton Bay bugs (shovel-nose lobsters), sweet Sydney rock oysters, mud crab, spanner crab, yabbies (small freshwater crayfish), and marrons (freshwater lobsters).

There are many expensive and indulgent restaurants in the city center, but the real dining scene is in the inner city and eastern suburbs. Neighborhoods like Surry Hills, Darlinghurst, Paddington, and beachside suburb Bondi are dining destinations unto themselves. Plus, you're more likely to find a restaurant that will serve on a Sunday night in one of these places than in the central business district—which can become a bit of a ghost town after offices close during the week, and on weekends (though the Rocks is always lively). If you find yourself hungry around Circular Quay on a weekend, you'll have to walk all the way to King Street Wharf in Darling Harbour or Chinatown to find a good meal, unless you're content with McDonald's or Hungry Jack's (the Australian name for the Burger King chain).

Surry Hills is a delight for diners with adventurous taste buds and limited budgets. Crown Street is lined with ethnic and gourmet restaurants where you can get a delicious meal for between A$20 and A$30. The restaurants in Darlinghurst are similarly diverse, though they tend to be a bit more trendy and expensive. Oxford Street in Paddington offers great upscale dining options as well as pub fare, and Bondi, which used to be a tourist trail of fast-food chains and cheap take-out joints, is now home to some of the most famous and beloved restaurants in the city.

Although most Sydney restaurants are licensed to serve alcohol, the few that aren't usually allow you to bring your own bottle (BYOB). Reservations are generally required, although some restaurants don't take bookings at all. Lunch hours are from around noon to 2:30; dinner is served between 7 and 10:30. The 10% Goods and Services Tax (GST) is already incorporated in the prices, but a 10% tip is customary for exemplary service. A corkage fee often applies in BYOB restaurants. Expect a 10% service surcharge on weekends and holidays. Smoking is prohibited inside all restaurants throughout New South Wales.

WHAT IT COSTS In Australian Dollars					
	$$$$	**$$$**	**$$**	**$**	**¢**
AT DINNER	over $65	$46–$65	$36–$45	$26–$35	under $25

Prices are for a main course at dinner.

The Rocks & Circular Quay

Italian

$–$$ ✕ **Aqua Luna.** The restaurant may look out onto the watery charms of Circular Quay, but the food harks back to the gently rolling hills of Tuscany. Little wonder, since Darren Simpson—the youngest cook ever to win Britain's Young Chef of the Year Award—was previously head chef of London's Italianate Sartoria restaurant. Flavors are rustic and authentic, and whenever possible dishes use organic ingredients. Favorites include wood-roasted lamb with pancetta, tagliolini with Spring Bay mussels, and baked oxtail orecchiette. ⊠ *Opera Quays, No. 2, Shop 18, Macquarie St., East Circular Quay* ☎ *02/9251–0311* ⊟ *AE, DC, MC, V* ⊗ *Closed Sun. No lunch Mon. or Sat.*

Japanese

$$$$ ✕ **Yoshii.** The eponymous restaurant of Sydney's finest sushi chef, Ryuichi Yoshii, has a calm, Zen-like decor that feels just like Japan. Lunchtime bento boxes start at A$38, but serious sushi fans book the special sushi menus (from A$70 at lunch). For the full Yoshii experience, order the set dinner menu (A$100–A$120), which, if you're lucky, may include roasted duck. You can also try the seared tuna marinated with parsley oil, sherry vinegar, and Dijon mustard for a perfect blend of East and West. ⊠ *115 Harrington St., The Rocks* ☎ *02/9247–2566* ⌀ *Reservations essential* ⊟ *AE, DC, MC, V* ⊗ *Closed Sun. No lunch Mon. and Sat.*

$–$$ ✕ **Galileo.** The gracious, salon-style look of the Observatory Hotel's dining room has become a hot spot, thanks to the innovative, Franco-

Japanese fusion cuisine of chef Harunobu Inukai. Start with the unique pizza tart of saffron potato and beetroot with truffle salsa; or splurge for the lamb shoulder, which is slow-cooked for 18 hours. The assiette of beef is a meal fit for the English nobility who inspired the restaurant's decor of Fortuny silk and polished cedar. ⊠ *89–113 Kent St., City Center* ☎ *02/9256–2215* ▭ *AE, DC, MC, V* ⊘ *No lunch.*

Modern Australian

$$$–$$$$
Fodor'sChoice
★
✕ **Rockpool.** A meal at Rockpool is a crash course in what modern Australian cooking is all about, conducted in a glamorous, long dining room with a catwalklike ramp. Chefs Neil Perry and Khan Danis weave Thai, Chinese, Mediterranean, and Middle Eastern influences into their repertoire with effortless flair and originality. Prepare to be amazed by the lobster tagine with spice stuffed dates, eggplant salad, and couscous, or try to snag one of the limited portions of slow-roasted aged beef with herb-and-curry spice butter, spinach puree, potato and cabbage gratin. If there's room (and there's always room), try the famous date tart. ⊠ *107 George St., The Rocks* ☎ *02/9252–1888* ⚖ *Reservations essential* ▭ *AE, DC, MC, V* ⊘ *Closed Sun. and Mon. No lunch.*

$$–$$$
Fodor'sChoice
★
✕ **Aria.** With windows overlooking the Opera House and the Harbour Bridge, Aria could easily rest on the laurels of its location. But instead, chef Matthew Moran creates a menu of extraordinary dishes that may easily prove to be your best meal in the antipodes. Make a reservation before you even get on the plane, and let your mouth begin to water for the double-cooked Bangalow sweet pork belly and the aged beef fillet in bourguignonne sauce. The wine list is superb, as is the service. Even the warm rolls with butter are memorable. ⊠ *1 Macquarie St., East Circular Quay* ☎ *02/9252–2555* ▭ *AE, DC, MC, V* ⊘ *No lunch weekends.*

★ **$$–$$$**
✕ **Quay.** In his take on Modern Australian cuisine, chef Peter Gilmore masterfully crafts such dishes as crisp-skinned Murray cod with brown butter; baby squid filled with potato puree, flowering chive, and spring onions; and seven-hour, slow-braised White Rocks veal with lentils. Desserts are sublime—the five-textured Valrhona chocolate cake may make you weak at the knees—and the wine list fits the flavors of the cuisine perfectly. Glass walls afford wonderful views of the bridge and Opera House, right at your fork's tip. ⊠ *Upper Level, Overseas Passenger Terminal, West Circular Quay, The Rocks* ☎ *02/9251–5600* ⚖ *Reservations essential* ▭ *AE, DC, MC, V* ⊘ *No lunch Sat.–Mon.*

$$
✕ **Guillaume at Bennelong.** Chef Guillaume Brahimi rattles the pans at possibly the most superbly situated dining room in town. Tucked into the side of the Opera House, the restaurant affords views of Sydney Harbour Bridge and the city lights. Brahimi's creations soar: try the fresh ink papardelle with seared Queensland scallops, roasted Moreton Bay bug, and blue swimmer crab meat in a tomato-and-coriander broth, or the Kangaroo Island chicken on Chinese cabbage with ravioli of duck foie gras and a veal jus. ⊠ *Bennelong Point, Circular Quay* ☎ *02/9241–1999* ⚖ *Reservations essential* ▭ *AE, DC, MC, V* ⊘ *Closed Sun. No lunch Sat.–Wed.*

$–$$
✕ **harbourkitchen & bar.** Dramatic harbor and Opera House views are democratically shared by this one-size-fits-all restaurant and its attendant bar. The food rivals the views of the Opera House and is best described as Modern Rustic, with a produce-driven menu revolving around

the rotisserie and wood-fired grill. The long list of dishes includes everything from duck and beetroot tart with mint and pine nuts to poached veal fillet with endive, sage, and crispy shallot. ✉ *Park Hyatt Sydney, 7 Hickson Rd., Circular Quay* ☎ *02/9256–1660* ✍ *Reservations essential* ▤ *AE, DC, MC, V.*

$ ✗ **Wharf Restaurant.** At one time only the Wharf's proximity to the Sydney Theatre Company (they share Pier 4) attracted diners, but with the restaurant now in the hands of one of Sydney's legendary chefs, the emphasis is firmly on the food. Fish dominates the menu, befitting the restaurant's name and locale, and there is a theme of Japanese-Western fusion in the flavoring: kingfish is wrapped in prosciutto with daikon and shiitake broth; salt-and-pepper squid is served with cucumber, mint, and red-pepper relish. You can see Sydney Harbour Bridge from some tables, but it's North Sydney and the ferries that provide the real floor show. Meal times and sizes are flexible to accommodate theatergoers. ✉ *End of Pier 4, Hickson Rd., Walsh Bay* ☎ *02/9250–1761* ✍ *Reservations essential* ▤ *AE, DC, MC, V* ◷ *Closed Sun.*

Thai

★ ¢–$$ ✗ **Sailor's Thai.** Sydney's most exciting and authentic Thai food comes from this glamorously restored restaurant in the Old Sailors Home. Downstairs, business types rub shoulders with sightseers and hard-core shoppers, devouring delicious red curries and salads fragrant with lime juice and fish sauce. Upstairs is the Sailors Thai Canteen (no reservations accepted), a casual noodle bar where long, communal zinc tables groan with *som dtam* (shredded papaya salad) and pad thai (rice noodles stir-fried with shrimp, egg, peanuts, and chili). ✉ *106 George St., The Rocks* ☎ *02/9251–2466* ✍ *Reservations essential* ▤ *AE, DC, MC, V* ◷ *Closed Sun.*

City Center Area

Chinese

¢–$$ ✗ **Golden Century.** For two hours—or as long as it takes for you to consume delicately steamed prawns, luscious mud crab with ginger and shallots, and *pipis* (triangular clams) with black bean sauce—you might as well be in Hong Kong. This place is heaven for seafood lovers, with wall-to-wall fish tanks filled with crab, lobster, abalone, and schools of barramundi, parrot fish, and coral trout. You won't have to ask if the food is fresh; most of it is swimming around you as you eat. The atmosphere is no-frills, and the noise level can be deafening, but the food is worth it. Supper is served late evenings from 10 until 4 AM. ✉ *393–399 Sussex St., Haymarket* ☎ *02/9212–3901* ▤ *AE, DC, MC, V.*

★ ¢ ✗ **BBQ King.** You can find better basic Chinese food elsewhere in town, but for duck and pork, barbecue-loving Sydneysiders know that this is the place to come. The ducks hanging in the window are the only decor at this small Chinatown staple, where the poultry is so fresh you can almost hear it clucking. Barbecued pork is the other featured dish, and the suckling pig is especially delicious. It's open until late at night, when the average customers are large groups of mates sprawled at the Formica tables feeding their drunken munchies, or Chinatown chefs kicking back after a day in the kitchen. The service is brusque, but it's all part

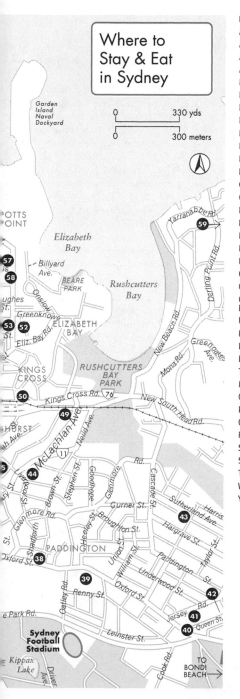

Where to
Stay & Eat
in Sydney

| 0 | 330 yds |
| 0 | 300 meters |

AUSTRALIAN CUISINE: WHAT, WHERE & WHY

AUSTRALIA SIMPLY DIDN'T HAVE TIME to sit back and wait for a homegrown cuisine to evolve in the traditional way. By the time the country was settled by the British 200 years ago, the industrial revolution had already made it virtually impossible for any single region to be isolated enough to gradually develop its own food resources and traditions without outside influence or interference.

So we borrowed an Anglo-Saxon way of eating that had little to do with where, what, or who we happened to be. We learned, of necessity, to include what was in our natural larder. The incredibly vast landmass of Australia means that somewhere in the country is a microclimate that is suitable for producing whatever we feel like eating, from the tropical fruit and sugarcane fields of northern Queensland to the grazing pastures and citrus groves of the temperate Riverina and Riverland areas, to the cool-climate dairy products of Victoria and Tasmania. It also didn't take us too long to realize that a country surrounded by water is a country surrounded by oysters, clams, crabs, lobsters, prawns, and fish.

The next great influence came from the southern Europeans who came to this country as refugees after World War II. Many were Spaniards, Greeks, and Italians, people who had lived with coastal breezes in their veins and whose lives and foods had been warmed by the Mediterranean sun.

But the emergence of a truly identifiable Australian way of eating came when we finally realized in the late 1970s that it was actually Asia's doorstep we were on, and not England's. These Asian and Mediterranean influences, together with a continual drive for superior produce and a spirit of experimentation, are the major factors that continue to define Australian cuisine. It's a cuisine that has many faces. Key dishes can immortalize indigenous produce, such as rare-roasted kangaroo with baby beets, or steamed barramundi with soy and ginger. At the same time, they can totally transform more universal ingredients, such as char-grilled Atlantic salmon with preserved lemon and couscous, or a miraculous checkerboard ice cream flavored with aniseed and pineapple.

But Australian cuisine is no slammed-together grab bag of fusion techniques or ingredients. It's brash, easygoing, big-flavored, fresh, and thoroughly natural. It's Japanese-born Tetsuya Wakuda's impossibly silky ocean trout confit with trout roe and konbu seaweed at Tetsuya's in Sydney. Or Malaysian native Cheong Liew's bravely conceived braised chicken with sea scallops, veal sweetbreads, roasted fennel, and black moss at the Grange restaurant in Adelaide. Or Sydneysider Neil Perry's adventure trek of mud crab, sweet pork, and green papaw salad at Rockpool in Sydney.

This is the sort of cooking that has made Australia a modern culinary force, and stamped Sydney as one of the three current food capitals of the world, along with New York and London. Let the academics ponder if it is a true cuisine or just a lifestyle. The rest of us will do the only sensible thing: head off to a great Australian restaurant and make up our own minds.

— Terry Durack

of the greasy charm. ✉ *18–20 Goulburn St., Haymarket* ☎ *02/ 9267–2586* ▭ *No credit cards.*

Malaysian

★ ¢–$ ✕ **The Malaya.** The cocktails are lethal, the view is captivating, and the food is extraordinary at this modern Asian restaurant on King Street Wharf. Signature dishes include beef Rendang (Indonesian-style beef curry), and marinated, sticky-sweet and crunchy Szechuan eggplant that's so good it may just be the food of the gods. Try one of the four set menus (for a minimum of three people) for a true feast on the extensive menu's flavor combinations. ✉ *39 Lime St., King Street Wharf, Darling Harbour* ☎ *02/9279–1170* ▭ *AE, DC, MC, V.*

Modern Australian

$$$$ ✕ **Forty One.** The view east over the harbor is glorious, the private dining rooms are plush, and Dietmar Sawyere's Asian-influenced classical food is top-notch. The set-price dinner menu (A$125) might include steamed Western Australian yabbie tails with asparagus and bread sauce, and espresso parfait with dark chocolate and Grand Marnier sauce for dessert. The vegetarian menu, with the likes of Ossau Iraty sheep's milk cheese with a salad of apples, dates, celeriac, and walnuts, is sublime. The restaurant's decadent Krug Room is a snug haven for those who still believe a glass of champagne and a little foie gras can cure most of the world's ills. ✉ *Level 42, Chifley Tower, 2 Chifley Sq., City Center* ☎ *02/9221–2500* ♠ *Reservations essential* ▭ *AE, DC, MC, V* ☽ *Closed Sun. No lunch Mon. and Sat.*

$$$$ ✕ **Tetsuya's.** It's worth getting on the waiting list—there's always a waiting list—to sample the unique blend of Western and Japanese-French flavors crafted by Sydney's most applauded chef, Tetsuya Wakuda. The serene, expansive dining room's unobtrusive Japanese aesthetic leaves the food as the true highlight. Confit of ocean trout served with unpasteurized ocean-trout roe and double-cooked, deboned spatchcock with braised daikon and bread sauce are typical items from a pricey set menu (A$175) that never fails to dazzle. Views of a Japanese garden complete with bonsai and a waterfall make this place seem miles from the city center. ✉ *529 Kent St., City Center* ☎ *02/9267–2900* ♠ *Reservations essential* ▭ *AE, DC, MC, V* ☽ *Closed Sun. and Mon. No lunch Tues.–Fri.*

Fodor'sChoice
★

$$–$$$ ✕ **Est.** This elegant, pillared dining room is the perfect setting for showing off chef Peter Doyle's modern, light touch with Mod-Oz cuisine. Anything Doyle cooks with scallops is divine; the crisp-skin John Dory fillet is also a sure bet, as is the lamb with sautéed spinach and eggplant caviar. The warm caramelized peach tart with peach-pistachio-nougat ice cream will test any dieter's resolve. ✉ *Level 1, Establishment Hotel, 252 George St., City Center* ☎ *02/9240–3010* ♠ *Reservations essential* ▭ *AE, DC, MC, V* ☽ *Closed Sun. No lunch Sat.*

$$ ✕ **Altitude.** The lure of this decadent restaurant, perched high above Sydney Harbour on the 36th floor of the luxurious Shangri-La Hotel, is the view, but the surprisingly unpretentious food is equally impressive. With a focus on Australia's best fish, meat, and poultry, chef George Jardine's flavorful dishes include a delicious steamed salmon cannelloni.

Gather a dozen friends with whom to dine in the opulent, egg-shape, glass private dining room, or reserve the communal table for a chef's-table-and-wine dinner. ⊠ *Level 6, Shangri-La Hotel, 176 Cumberland St., The Rocks* ☎ *02/9250–6123* ⌂ *Reservations essential* ⊟ *AE, DC, MC, V* ☉ *Closed Sun. No lunch Sat. or Mon.–Thurs.*

Steak

$–$$$ ✕ **Prime.** Steak houses in Sydney were once old-fashioned, macho affairs where men in dark suits scoffed down copious quantities of cheap red wine and charred red meat. Now, inspired by the likes of Smith & Wollensky and Maloney & Porcelli in New York, this subterranean diner elevates the image of the Aussie steak. The result is an elegant restaurant in what was once the staff canteen for postal workers under the General Post Office. As well as serving some of the best steaks in town, Prime also has knockout seafood tortellini and poached barramundi with clams. The oysters are also superb. ⊠ *1 Martin Pl., City Center* ☎ *02/ 9229–7777* ⌂ *Reservations essential* ⊟ *AE, DC, MC, V* ☉ *Closed Sun. No lunch Sat.*

Darlinghurst, Kings Cross & Woolloomooloo

Cafés

¢ ✕ **bills.** The Liverpool Street bills is a sunny corner café so addictive it
Fodor'sChoice should come with a health warning. It's a favorite hangout of everyone
★ from local nurses to semi-disguised rock stars, and you never know who you might be sitting next to at the big, communal, newspaper-strewn table. If you're not interested in the creaminess of what must be Sydney's best scrambled eggs, try the ricotta hotcakes with honeycomb butter. Lunch choices include the spring-onion pancakes with gravlax and the most famous steak sandwich in town, and dinner selections are similarly gourmet twists on comfort food staples like chicken fricassee. The newer branch in Surry Hills, bills 2, has less of a cult following for brunch—but be prepared to wait for a seat at either location. ⊠ *433 Liverpool St., Darlinghurst* ☎ *02/9360–9631* ⌂ *Reservations not accepted* ⊟ *AE, MC, V* ⌙ *BYOB* ☉ *No dinner Sun.* ⊠ *352 Crown St., Surry Hills* ☎ *02/9360–4762* ⌂ *Reservations not accepted* ⊟ *AE, MC, V* ⌙ *BYOB* ☉ *No dinner Sun.*

Italian

¢–$$ ✕ **Otto.** Few restaurants have the pulling power of Otto, a place where radio shock jocks sit side by side with fashion-magazine editors and foodies, all on the stylish Finger Wharf. Yes, it's a scene. But fortunately it's a scene with good Italian food and waiters who have just enough attitude to make them a challenge worth conquering. The homemade pastas are very good, the slow-roasted duck with green lentils a benchmark, and the selection of Italian wines expensive but rarely matched this far from Milan. Next door is a sister restaurant, Nove Cucina, offering pizzas and dishes from Otto's menu at lower prices. ⊠ *Wharf at Woolloomooloo, 8 Cowper Wharf Rd., Woolloomooloo* ☎ *02/9368–7488* ⌂ *Reservations essential* ⊟ *AE, DC, MC, V* ☉ *Closed Mon.*

Modern Australian

$$ ✕ **Salt.** Are you wearing black? Is your hand in martini position? Do you look like someone groovy and influential? Then you're ready to dine at Salt, the hippest, happiest Mod-Oz bistro in town. Chef Luke Mangan has worked with three-star chefs in London, and his skills shine in such dishes as snapper fillet baked in pastry with Indian spices, or the spiced Jerusalem artichoke-and-blue cheese tart. A five-, six-, or seven-course degustation menu is also available. ✉ *229 Darlinghurst Rd., Darlinghurst* ☎ *02/9332–2566* ⌖ *Reservations essential* ▤ *AE, DC, MC, V* ⊘ *Closed Sun. and Mon. No lunch Tues.–Thurs. or Sat.*

Pizza

¢–$ ✕ **Hugo's Bar Pizza.** Hugo's lounge is one of the hippest bars in Sydney, so when it launched a pizza restaurant it had a built-in mob of patrons willing to wait in line for a seat at its tiny tables with leather settees. Unless you're friends with the owners, you too should be prepared to wait, and wait, and wait to get into this hot spot on bar- and club-lined Bayswater Road. Nurse an expensive cocktail or overpriced beer while you wait to sink your teeth into the gourmet thin-crust pizzas which are absolutely worth every second that you've stood in line. Pizzas are fresh, flavorful, crispy, and creative; try the pork-belly or puttanesca pies, served on slabs of wood. The restaurant is so dimly lighted no one will be able to tell if you've got sauce on your face. ✉ *19 Bayswater Rd., Kings Cross* ☎ *02/9332–1227* ⌖ *Reservations not accepted* ▤ *AE, DC, MC, V* ⊘ *Closed Sun. and Mon. No lunch Tues.–Thurs. or Sat.*

Seafood

★ **¢–$** ✕ **Fishface.** Get here early, score one of the tiny, cramped tables, and you'll be able to dig into some of the most scrumptious seafood in Australia. The best sashimi-grade fish in the country—which is as good as it comes—is served up here to discerning locals. The pea and yabby (freshwater crayfish) soup is superb, the tuna always served rare and moist, and the fish-and-chips redefine the nation's favorite take-away order. Reservations aren't accepted after 7 PM. ✉ *132 Darlinghurst Rd., Darlinghurst* ☎ *02/9332–4803, 02/9332–4809 for takeout* ▤ *MC, V* ⛾ *BYOB, corkage fee A$3* ⊘ *Closed Sun. No lunch.*

Paddington & Woollahra

French

$$$$ ✕ **Claude's.** This tiny, unprepossessing restaurant proves that good
Fodor'sChoice things really do come in small packages. This was the first restaurant
★ to serve Australia's cultivated black truffles, and that interest in broadening the palates of its diners continues under the leadership of Singaporean chef-owner Chui Lee Luk. With an emphasis on East-West fusion, dishes like grilled breast of Muscovy duck in caramel, crisp battered marron (freshwater lobster), and an ethereal goat's-milk soufflé with peaches are masterly delights. ✉ *10 Oxford St., Woollahra* ☎ *02/9331–2325* ⌖ *Reservations essential* ▤ *AE, MC, V* ⛾ *BYOB, corkage fee A$10* ⊘ *Closed Sun. and Mon. No lunch.*

$–$$ ✕ **Bistro Moncur.** Archetypically loud and proud, this bistro spills over with happy-go-lucky patrons—mostly locals from around the leafy, moneyed suburb of Woollahra—who don't mind waiting a half hour for a table. The best dishes are inspired takes on Parisian fare, like the grilled Sirloin Café de Paris and the Bistro Moncur pure pork sausages with potato puree and Lyonnaise onions. There is a focus on fresh, high-quality ingredients—even the coffee at the end of the meal comes from a fancy espresso machine. ⊠ *Woollahra Hotel, 116 Queen St., Woollahra* ☎ *02/9363–2519* ⚑ *Reservations not accepted* ⊟ *AE, DC, MC, V* ⊙ *No lunch Mon.*

$ ✕ **Bistro LuLu.** Cozy and intimate, this woody bistro brings a touch of the Paris boulevards to Sydney's fashion catwalk. The food is essentially unfussy and unpretentious, but the essentials are all here in such dishes as seared chicken livers with beetroot, Parmesan, and sherry vinegar; grilled sardines with spiced cucumbers and feta; and the standout sirloin with Café de Paris butter and frites. On the lighter side, there's a selection of organic salads, which might include a platter of asparagus, avocado, boiled egg, and anchovy croutons dressed with lemon. A two- or three-course prix fixe menu is available at lunch and at dinner between 6 and 7 PM. ⊠ *257 Oxford St., Paddington* ☎ *02/9380–6888* ⚑ *Reservations essential* ⊟ *AE, DC, MC, V* ⊙ *No lunch Sun.–Wed.*

¢ ✕ **Four in Hand.** At this cute, popular little pub in Paddington, chef Mark Best turns out diner-friendly dishes with a strong French accent. His *boudin blanc* (sausage with minced white-meat filling) is a lesson in subtlety, while the accompanying apple-infused Puy lentils add a sweet, earthy hint. Don't leave without dessert—the dark-chocolate tart is a fitting finish. Note that reservations are only accepted for the 6:30 PM seating; otherwise, you run the risk of not getting a table later. ⊠ *105 Sutherland St., Paddington* ☎ *02/9362–1999* ⊟ *AE, DC, MC, V* ⊙ *No lunch Mon.–Sat.*

Italian

★ $$–$$$ ✕ **Buon Ricordo.** Walking into this happy, bubbly place is like turning up at a private party in the backstreets of Naples. Host, chef, and surrogate uncle Armando Percuoco invests classic Neapolitan and Tuscan techniques with inventive personal touches to produce such dishes as warmed figs with Gorgonzola and prosciutto, truffled egg pasta, and scampi with saffron sauce and black-ink risotto. The fettuccine *al tartufovo,* with eggs, cream, and reggiano cheese, is legendary. Everything comes with Italian-style touches that you can see, feel, smell, and taste. Leaving the restaurant feels like leaving home. ⊠ *108 Boundary St., Paddington* ☎ *02/9360–6729* ⚑ *Reservations essential* ⊟ *AE, DC, MC, V* ⊙ *Closed Sun. and Mon. No lunch Tues.–Thurs.*

Pizza

★ ¢ ✕ **Arthur's Pizza.** It's always crowded and hot in this tiny, narrow spot on Oxford Street. Easily Sydney's favorite—just look at the lines each day— Arthur's is the place for authentic, meaty, spicy thin-crust pies ranging in size from small to large. The TNT, with salami, onion, pepper, and bacon, is the most popular among meat lovers; the Zora, with olives, feta, red onions, and tomatoes is beloved by vegetarians and carnivores alike. Pick up some wine at one of the liquor stores nearby while you're waiting—there's a A$1.50 corkage fee. Or, call ahead and order your pizza to go. Delivery is also an option, though pizza with crust this thin and ingredients this fresh deserves to be eaten right out of the oven. ⊠ *260 Oxford St., Paddington* ☎ *02/9331–1779* ⊟ *AE, DC, MC, V* ⊗ *No lunch weekdays.*

Potts Point

Italian

¢–$ ✕**Fratelli Paradiso.** Fratelli (meaning brothers) is run by the Paradiso siblings, whose Italian heritage shows in everything from the *bomba* (like a donut) served in their adjoining bakery to the friendly service. Arrive early to find local devotees sipping their morning constitutional caffeine along with rice pudding, or at dinner for mouthwatering penne with a veal ragu. The zucchini-flower-and-fontina risotto is the stuff local legends are built on. ⊠ *12–16 Challis Ave., Potts Point* ☎ *02/9357–1744* ⌂ *Reservations not accepted* ⊟ *AE, DC, MC, V* ⊗ *No dinner weekends.*

Modern Australian

¢–$ ✕**Lotus.** With its fabulous back bar and pencil-thin diners, the food probably doesn't have to be as good as it is at this ultracool inner-city restaurant. Located on leafy Challis Avenue, just past where the riffraff of Kings Cross gives way to the urban chic of Potts Point, Lotus is a study in cool. Start with a salad of barbecued peppered squid with pancetta, watercress, and avocado and then try the char-grilled rump of Wagyu beef, served with incredible onion rings, for an entrée. Punctuate each course with an inventive, and potent, cocktail, and turn your evening meal into a big night out. ⊠ *22 Challis Ave., Potts Point* ☎ *02/9326–0488* ⌂ *Reservations not accepted* ⊟ *AE, DC, MC, V* ⊗ *Closed Sun. and Mon. No lunch.*

Surry Hills

Chinese

★ ¢–$$ ✕**Billy Kwong.** Locals rub shoulders while eating no-fuss Chinese food at chef Kylie Kwong's trendy drop-in restaurant. Kwong prepares the kind of food her family cooks, with Grandma providing not just the inspiration but also the recipes. Even the dumplings are made by specialty chefs from Shanghai. Although the table you're occupying is probably being eyed by the next set of adoring fans, staff members never rush you. But you could always play nice and ask for the bill through your last mouthful of scallops with XO sauce or steamed wontons. ⊠ *3/355 Crown St., Surry Hills* ☎ *02/9332–3300* ⌂ *Reservations not accepted* ⊟ *AE, MC, V* Ⓨ *BYOB, corkage fee A$5* ⊗ *Closed Mon. No lunch.*

French

$$ ✕**Marque.** Mark Best's promise as an award-winning, up-and-coming Sydney chef has been fulfilled at this sleek and elegant Darlinghurst restaurant. Few chefs approach French flavors with such passion and dedication (and stints alongside three-star demigods Alain Passard in Paris and Raymond Blanc in England haven't done any harm either). Best's roast South Australian Jewfish with potato Anglaise and shallot confit is a triumph, and the 500-day, grain-fed beef with *pied de mouton* (sheep's feet), lettuce, and bone marrow is worth writing home about. ⊠ *355 Crown St., Surry Hills* ☎ *02/9332–2225* ⌂ *Reservations essential* ⊟ *AE, DC, MC, V* ⊗ *Closed Sun. No lunch.*

Middle Eastern

¢ ✕ **Café Mint.** Breakfast and lunch are the focus at this tiny, modern Middle Eastern café, where Australian brunch staple Turkish toast accompanies some very inspired, and delicious, dishes. The breakfast couscous with honey yogurt, fruit compote, and pistachios is the perfect invention: a sweet, yet filling, carb-based breakfast that will keep you satisfied all day long. Lunch and dinner entrées are equally creative and flavorful, like the pomegranate lamb salad with tomato, cucumber, onion, roast eggplant, and pine nuts. As to be expected, the strong black coffee is a caffeine addict's dream. ✉ *259 Crown St., Surry Hills* ☎ *02/9319–0848* ▤ *No credit cards* ⊘ *Closed Sun. No lunch Wed.–Fri.*

Modern Australian

$ ✕ **Bécasse.** Foodies have been falling over each other to eat at this modest dining room. Bécasse so deftly combines inventive, flavorful cuisine with excellent service that oohs and aahs always seem to accompany the clink of silverware against dinner plates here. A salad of beetroot, leek, and lamb's tongue (*mache*) is giddily good and light, while a side dish of fried potatoes served with bone marrow is enough to stop your heart. Roasted barramundi with pipis and mussels should calm the nerves and please the cardiologist. ✉ *48 Albion St., Surry Hills* ☎ *02/9280–3202* ⌂ *Reservations essential* ▤ *AE, MC, V* ⊘ *Closed Mon. and Tues. No lunch.*

Thai

★ ¢–$$ ✕ **Longrain.** Start with a cocktail in the cool, minimalist bar, where Sydney's high life gathers around low-slung tables. Then make for the dining room, where the hip crowd jostles for a position at one of three giant wooden communal tables—it might be trendy, but the food is terrific. Chef Martin Boetz aimed to make this restaurant a leader among Sydney's Thai spots, and managed to score a double whammy: a smoldering bar scene and an outstanding eatery. His duck, venison, tuna, beef shin, and pork hock each marry style with substance. Reservations are not accepted for dinner. ✉ *85 Commonwealth St., Surry Hills* ☎ *02/9280–2888* ▤ *AE, DC, MC, V* ⊘ *Closed Sun. No lunch weekends.*

Bondi Beach & Eastern Suburbs

Chinese

$–$$ ✕ **Mu Shu.** This restaurant does marvelous things with duck—in particular, the fabulous pancakes, served Beijing-style. Zucchini flowers come fat with crabmeat and mint, while lamb is barbecued to melting tenderness. For the quintessential experience, score a seat on the daybed and imbibe a Green Fairy cocktail, made with France's legendary absinthe. ✉ *108 Campbell Parade, Bondi Beach* ☎ *02/9130–5400* ⌂ *Reservations essential* ▤ *AE, DC, MC, V* ⊘ *No lunch Mon.–Wed.*

Italian

$–$$ ✕ **Icebergs Dining Room and Bar.** The fashionable and famous just adore perching like seagulls here, over the Bondi Icebergs' swimming pool and Australia's most famous beach. The bar is a scene unto itself, with a tasty menu of bar snacks like polenta chips and oysters, and killer cocktails

FodorsChoice
★

like the Icebergs T—a proprietary mix of vodka, Nocello, crushed mint, and chilled black tea. Once you move into the restaurant and situate yourself on a low-back suede seat, check your reflection in the frosted glass and prepare to indulge in sophisticated Italian creations like Livornese-style fish stew and char-grilled quail with grape salad and verjus. The food is delectable, but above all else, Icebergs is a place to dine and be seen. ⊠ *1 Notts Ave., Bondi Beach* ☎ *02/9365–9000* ⌕ *Reservations essential* ▤ *AE, DC, MC, V* ⊙ *Closed Mon.*

Middle Eastern

$ ✕ **Moorish.** Local boy/girl, chef/owner team makes good, again, this time at the beach. Luke Mangan and Lucy Allon (of Salt and Bistro LuLu fame) score high marks with this modern Middle Eastern eatery with views of Bondi Beach. Here you can feast on grilled barramundi fillet with eggplant, pepper, mint, and red chili, and spiced veal loin with couscous, carrot, peas, and saffron. The dining room is appropriately dressed in pale aquamarine colors, and casually decked-out waiters chat like old friends. However, they're more tan and better looking than most people's best mates—and they serve the food more deftly as well. ⊠ *118–120 Ramsgate Ave., North Bondi* ☎ *02/ 9300–9511* ▭ *AE, DC, MC, V.*

Modern Australian

$–$$ ✕ **Sean's Panaroma.** It may look like a cross between a half-finished bomb shelter and a neglected shore house, but this beachside restaurant is home to Sean Moran, one of Sydney's brightest and most innovative chefs. Weekend lunches are easygoing affairs; things get a little more serious at night as Moran cooks up memorable dishes including Barossa Valley chicken with sweet-potato puree and peas, Illabo lamb shoulder with cannellini beans and sugar snap peas; and raspberry, blackberry, and blueberry trifle. ⊠ *270 Campbell Parade, Bondi Beach* ☎ *02/9365–4924* ⌕ *Reservations essential* ▤ *MC, V* 🍴 *BYOB* ⊙ *No lunch weekdays. No dinner Sun.–Tues.*

$ ✕ **Hugo's.** Snappy leisure wear and "cool dude" dispositions are the order of the day at Hugo's—and that's just the waitstaff. Like Bondi itself, this restaurant works effortlessly on many levels without ever taking itself too seriously. Weekend breakfasts are legendary. At night things get serious with the justly famous panfried prawn and avocado stack, roasted duck breast on bok choy, and spanner crab linguine. This is Nicole Kidman's favorite restaurant in Sydney—when she's in town there are reports of her dining here almost daily. It's easy to understand why she loves the joint, even though its location, behind a very popular stop on the bus route down to the beach, makes it a bit hectic. ⊠ *70 Campbell Parade, Bondi Beach* ☎ *02/9300–0900* ⌕ *Reservations essential* ▤ *AE, DC, MC, V* ⊙ *No lunch weekdays.*

Seafood

$$–$$$ ✕ **Pier.** With its wraparound harbor views and shipshape good looks, this wharf restaurant is a highly appropriate place to enjoy Australia's finest seafood. Chef Greg Doyle knows his fish, and manages to reach beyond the predictable char-grills and fish-and-chips without being

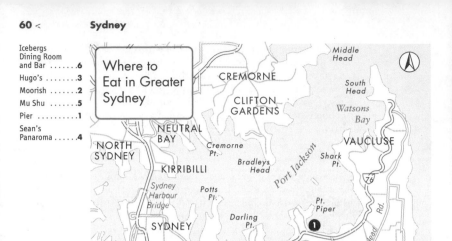

Where to Eat in Greater Sydney

gimmicky. The freshness of the produce itself sings in such choices as pot-roasted lobster with Kaffir lime leaf, Thai basil, and chili, and seared John Dory with scallop ravioli. ✉ *594 New South Head Rd., Rose Bay* ☎ *02/9327–6561* ▭ *AE, DC, MC, V.*

WHERE TO STAY

From grand hotels with white-glove service to tucked-away bed-and-breakfasts, there's lodging to fit all styles and budgets in Sydney. The best addresses in town are undoubtedly at the Rocks, where the tranquil setting and harbor views are right near major cultural attractions, restaurants, shops, and galleries. The area around Kings Cross is the city's second major hotel district, as well as a budget and backpacker lodging center. Keep in mind, however, that this is also the city's major nightlife district, and the scene can get pretty raucous after sunset.

If you arrive in Sydney without a hotel reservation, the best place to start looking is the Tourism New South Wales information counter at the international airport, which acts as a clearinghouse for unsold hotel rooms. It can often obtain a significant saving on published room rates.

WHAT IT COSTS In Australian Dollars				
$$$$	**$$$**	**$$**	**$**	**¢**
FOR 2 PEOPLE over $450	$301–$450	$201–$300	$151–$200	under $150

Prices are for two people in a standard double room in high season, including tax and service, based on the European Plan (with no meals) unless otherwise noted.

The Rocks & Circular Quay

★ $$$$ ▨ **Hotel Inter-Continental Sydney.** This sleek, sophisticated hotel rises from the sandstone facade of the historic Treasury Building. It's also near the harbor and within easy walking distance of Circular Quay, the Opera House, and the central business district. North-facing rooms overlook the Harbour Bridge, while those on the eastern side of the hotel overlook the Royal Botanic Gardens. Rooms have window seats for taking in the views, as well as remote-controlled blinds to tune out the bright Sydney sunshine; the decor features brown-and-white suede—including funky checkered, padded headboards on the beds. Four executive floors have meeting rooms, separate check-in/check-out, complimentary breakfast and cocktails, and access to the wonderful views of the rooftop lounge. The Mediterranean-inspired Mint restaurant and bar downstairs are major hot spots. ⊠ *117 Macquarie St., Circular Quay, 2000* ☎ *02/9253–9000* ⊟ *02/9240–1240* ⊕ *www.intercontinental.com* ⇆ *475 rooms, 28 suites ♺ 3 restaurants, room service, in-room safes, minibars, cable TV, in-room data ports, pool, gym, health club, bar, dry cleaning, laundry service, concierge, Internet room, business services, convention center, meeting rooms, parking (fee), no-smoking rooms* ⊟ *AE, DC, MC, V.*

$$$$ ▨ **Park Hyatt Sydney.** Moored in the shadow of Harbour Bridge, the Park
Fodor'sChoice Hyatt is the first choice for visiting celebrities (a minor irony, consider-
★ ing that the thousands who cross the bridge each day get a bird's-eye view of the guests lazing about the hotel's rooftop pool). Rooms here are decorated with reproductions of classical statuary, contemporary bronzes, and Australian artwork. Nearly all the spacious, elegant rooms have balconies and views of the Opera House. This is also the only hotel in Australia with full-time personal butler service in all rooms. Excellent Australian cuisine awaits at the harbourkitchen & bar restaurant. ⊠ *7 Hickson Rd., Circular Quay, 2000* ☎ *02/9241–1234* ⊟ *02/9256–1555* ⊕ *www.sydney.park.hyatt.com* ⇆ *120 rooms, 38 suites ♺ Restaurant, room service, in-room safes, minibars, cable TV, in-room data ports, pool, gym, hair salon, sauna, spa, 2 bars, dry cleaning, laundry service, concierge, Internet room, business services, convention center, meeting rooms, parking (fee), no-smoking rooms* ⊟ *AE, DC, MC, V.*

★ $$$–$$$$ ▨ **Four Seasons Hotel Sydney.** Although it's the oldest of Sydney's elite hotels, continual upgrades and refinement have kept this landmark a favorite. Silk furnishings, mahogany timbers, marble bathrooms, and warm hues create opulence in the large rooms (those above the 20th floor have better views). Thoughtful touches for business travelers are everywhere, including enormous room safes that can easily accommodate your laptop, and mobile phones for rent. Executive Club rooms on Level 32 come with extras like meeting rooms and complimentary breakfasts. The spa offers treatments, like the frangipani wrap, that marry exotic ingredients with Australian Aboriginal healing formulas. ⊠ *199 George St., Circular Quay, 2000* ☎ *02/9238–0000* 🖷 *02/9251–2851* ⊕ *www. fourseasons.com/sydney* ⤳ *417 rooms, 114 suites* ♨ *Restaurant, room service, in-room safes, minibars, cable TV, in-room data ports, pool, gym, spa, bar, dry cleaning, laundry service, concierge, Internet room, business services, convention center, meeting rooms, parking (fee), no-smoking rooms* ▤ *AE, DC, MC, V.*

★ **$$$–$$$$** 🏨 **Shangri-La Hotel Sydney.** Towering above Walsh Bay Cove from its prime position alongside the Sydney Harbour Bridge, the city's largest hotel is *the* place for a room with a view. North-facing rooms overlooking the water are the best; views on the other sides—Darling Harbour, the city, or the eastern suburbs—are less impressive. Rooms are large and modestly opulent, and decorated in pleasing autumnal colors. The Horizon Club floor offers impeccable service, with a private bar and lounge, breakfast, and a purser to look after your needs. Altitude restaurant and the adjacent Blu Horizon bar on the 36th floor provide terrific views of Sydney Harbour, especially in the evening. Look for deals on one-night stays over weekends. ⊠ *176 Cumberland St., The Rocks, 2000* ☎ *02/ 9250–6000* 🖷 *02/9250–6250* ⊕ *www.shangri-la.com/eng/hotel/index. asp* ⤳ *531 rooms, 32 suites* ♨ *3 restaurants, room service, in-room safes, minibars, cable TV, in-room data ports, pool, gym, hair salon, sauna, 2 bars, dry cleaning, laundry service, concierge, Internet room, business services, convention center, meeting rooms, parking (fee), no-smoking rooms* ▤ *AE, DC, MC, V.*

$$$ 🏨 **Harbour Rocks Hotel.** Formerly a wool-storage facility, this four-story hotel provides good value for its location, although its historic character is confined to the exterior of the 150-year-old building. Tidy rooms are modestly furnished in the style of British hotels from the 1980s, with a color scheme in red and cream, and overstuffed armchairs and settees. Top-floor rooms on the east side afford glimpses of Circular Quay and the Opera House. Note that the elevator is for luggage, not guests. ⊠ *34–52 Harrington St., The Rocks, 2000* ☎ *02/9251–8944* 🖷 *02/9251–8900* ⊕ *www. harbourrocks.com.au* ⤳ *55 rooms* ♨ *Restaurant, in-room safes, minibars, bar, laundry service, no-smoking rooms* ▤ *AE, DC, MC, V.*

$$$ 🏨 **Observatory Hotel.** More English country manor than inner-city hotel,
Fodor'sChoice this gorgeous property feels like a decadent, luxurious sanctuary. The
★ spacious rooms, with their Venetian- and Asian-inspired decor, have mahogany furnishings, antique reproductions, and plush fabrics. The spectacular indoor pool is surrounded by marble and potted palms, with a fresco of a starry night on the ceiling. You can have a drink and check your e-mail in the Globe Bar, which also is a Wi-Fi zone. The hotel's single weakness is its lack of views, but that's like saying the Mona Lisa's single weakness is her crooked smile. ⊠ *89–113 Kent St., The Rocks, 2000* ☎ *02/9256–2222* 🖷 *02/9256–2233* ⊕ *www.observatoryhotel. com.au* ⤳ *78 rooms, 22 suites* ♨ *Restaurant, room service, in-room safes, minibars, cable TV, in-room VCRs, in-room data ports, indoor pool, health club, sauna, steam room, bar, dry cleaning, laundry service, concierge, Internet room, business services, convention center, meeting rooms, parking (fee), no-smoking rooms* ▤ *AE, DC, MC, V.*

$$$ 🏨 **Quay West Suites Sydney.** Bordering the Rocks and the central business and shopping district, this statuesque tower combines the space and comforts of an apartment with the amenities of a five-star hotel. Luxurious one- and two-bedroom units, all on the eighth floor or higher, each have a lounge, dining room, full kitchen, and laundry. All apartments have either harbor or city views, and some of the more expensive Harbour View Suites have balconies. Round-the-clock room service, a glamorous health club, and a trendy restaurant and bar add even more panache. ⊠ *98 Gloucester St., The Rocks, 2000* ☎ *02/9240–6000* 🖷 *02/9240–6060* ⊕ *www.mirvac.com.au/hotelv3/* 🛏 *121 suites* ⚐ *Restaurant, room service, in-room safes, kitchens, minibars, microwaves, in-room VCRs, in-room data ports, indoor pool, health club, sauna, bar, dry cleaning, laundry service, concierge, Internet room, business services, convention center, meeting rooms, parking (fee), no-smoking rooms* ⊟ *AE, DC, MC, V.*

$$–$$$ 🏨 **Rendezvous Stafford Hotel Sydney.** Situated in the heart of the historic Rocks precinct, these self-contained studios and apartments offer easy access to the attractions around Circular Quay. The decor is neutral, and not particularly trendy—but this is a comfortable spot to wind down in after a long day of sightseeing. For something with a bit more charm, try one of the two historic terrace houses, spacious, two-story cottages that have been restored and refurbished. Good choices for families and extended vacationers, each has an upstairs bedroom and a downstairs kitchen and lounge. Fourth- through sixth-floor studio rooms in the main building have views across Circular Quay to the Opera House. ⊠ *75 Harrington St., The Rocks, 2000* ☎ *02/9251–6711* 🖷 *02/9251–3458* ⊕ *www.rendezvoushotels.com/html/sydney* 🛏 *59 apartments, 2 terrace houses* ⚐ *In-room safes, kitchenettes, cable TV, in-room VCRs, in-room data ports, pool, gym, sauna, outdoor hot tub, dry cleaning, laundry service, business services, parking (fee)* ⊟ *AE, DC, MC, V.*

¢–$$ 🏨 **The Russell.** For charm, character, and central location, it's hard to beat this ornate Victorian hotel. No two rooms are the same, but all have fresh flowers, down pillows, and Gilchrist & Soames toiletries. The spacious double rooms at the front have views of Circular Quay. There are also somewhat quieter, standard-size double rooms overlooking Nurses Walk or opening onto an internal courtyard. Ceiling fans and windows allow for a breeze in all rooms, and the rooftop garden is a delight, especially in the evening. Note that the Russell, a Heritage-listed building with four floors, does not have elevators; winding corridors and the steep, narrow staircase to the reception desk can be challenging for those with impaired mobility. ⊠ *143A George St., The Rocks, 2000* ☎ *02/9241–3543* 🖷 *02/9252–1652* ⊕ *www.therussell.com.au* 🛏 *26 rooms, 16 with bath; 1 suite; 1 apartment* ⚐ *Restaurant, fans, some cable TV; no a/c* ⊟ *AE, DC, MC, V* ⊙ *CP.*

City Center

★ $$$–$$$$ 🏨 **Westin Sydney.** The Westin hotel chain is world renowned for its heavenly beds—in Sydney it offers heavenly service, too. The staff here are cool, efficient, capable, and stylish as at a boutique hotel, but without the hipper-than-thou attitude. Located on gorgeous Georgian Martin

Place in the center of Sydney's central business district, the hotel's 31-story, modern atrium building incorporates the ornate, Victorian-era shell of Sydney's former General Post Office. Heritage Rooms, in the original GPO, have soaring ceilings, tall windows, and opulent decor. High-design Tower Rooms have stainless steel, aquamarine glass, and floor-to-ceiling windows for panoramic city views. ⊠ *1 Martin Pl., City Center, 2000* ☎ *02/8223–1111* 📠 *02/8223–1222* ⊕ *www.westin. com.au* 🛏 *370 rooms, 51 suites* ⚭ *2 restaurants, room service, in-room safes, minibars, cable TV, in-room data ports, indoor pool, gym, health club, hair salon, massage, sauna, bar, dry cleaning, laundry service, concierge, Internet room, business services, convention center, meeting rooms, parking (fee), no-smoking rooms* ▤ *AE, DC, MC, V.*

$$$ 🏨 **Grace Hotel.** Retaining traces of its original art deco style, this modernized structure has spacious, uncluttered rooms—although views have long been compromised by the surrounding buildings. During World War II the hotel was used as the Sydney headquarters for General Douglas MacArthur's Pacific campaign. Although room furnishings are sleek and comfy, the hotel overall still has a feel of purposeful, efficient functionality to it, as though everyone there is on a mission rather than a vacation. Owned by a Malaysian investment company, the hotel is especially popular with group travelers, especially from Asia. ⊠ *77 York St., City Center, 2000* ☎ *02/9272–6888* 📠 *02/9229–8189* ⊕ *www.gracehotel. com.au* 🛏 *382 rooms, 6 suites* ⚭ *3 restaurants, room service, in-room safes, cable TV, in-room data ports, indoor pool, gym, hot tub, sauna, steam room, 3 bars, dry cleaning, laundry service, Internet room, business services, convention center, meeting rooms, no-smoking floor, parking (fee)* ▤ *AE, DC, MC, V.*

$$$ 🏨 **Medina Grand Harbourside.** Water views, a Darling Harbour setting, and moderate rates make Medina a great choice for families who want apartment-style lodgings within walking distance of Sydney's major attractions. Large, bright studios and one-bedroom units approximate the look of a more stylish hotel, with bold-color velour couches and chairs. Most bathrooms lack bathtubs, but all apartments have kitchenettes with full cooking facilities. Book online for discounts. ⊠ *55 Shelley St., King St. Wharf, Darling Harbour, 2000* ☎ *02/9249–7000* 📠 *02/9249–6900* ⊕ *www.medinaapartments.com.au* 🛏 *114 apartments* ⚭ *Restaurant, room service, in-room safes, kitchenettes, in-room data ports, pool, gym, hot tub, sauna, steam room, dry cleaning, laundry service, business services, convention center, meeting rooms, parking (fee), no-smoking rooms* ▤ *AE, DC, MC, V.*

$$ 🏨 **Blacket Hotel.** A study in minimalist chic, this small hotel in a former bank building off busy George Street has been on Sydney's hot list since its debut in 2000. From the moment you step into the fashionably dim, charcoal-and-off-white reception area, the setting delivers the requisite degree of cool—although service can be patchy and indifferent. The one- and two-bedroom apartments and loft suites each have a kitchenette, whirlpool tub, and washing machine. The location provides easy access to the city and Darling Harbour. ⊠ *70 King St., City Center, 2000* ☎ *02/9279–3030* 📠 *02/9279–3020* ⊕ *www.theblacket.com* 🛏 *26 rooms, 5 suites, 9 apartments* ⚭ *Restaurant, some kitchenettes, minibars, in-room data ports, business services, parking (fee)* ▤ *AE, DC, MC, V.*

★ ¢ 🖼 **Y on the Park.** Comfortable, affordable lodgings in a prime city location means that rooms here are often booked months in advance. Dorms with shared bathrooms sleep four, while the family, deluxe, and corporate rooms come with a king bed, French-press coffeemaker, and toiletries. Studios have a kitchenette, in-room safe, and Internet connection. ✉ *5–11 Wentworth Ave., near corner of Hyde Park and Oxford St., East Sydney, 2010* ☎ *02/9264–2451* 🖷 *02/9285–6288* ⊕ *www.ywca-sydney.com.au/hotel.asp?HotelID=1* ⇨ *13 dorm rooms with shared baths, 38 studios, 106 rooms* ⌂ *Café, some in-room safes, some refrigerators, some in-room data ports, no-smoking rooms; no phones in some rooms, no TV in some rooms* ▭ *AE, DC, MC, V.*

Paddington & Woollahra

¢–$$ 🖼 **The Hughenden.** Modern behemoths not your style? Try this cozy, converted Victorian mansion. Rooms can be on the small side, and some have only showers, but all are individually decorated in modern country style with floral-print fabrics. After enjoying the full, made-to-order breakfast, you can relax on the porch or stroll among the well-manicured lawns of this Anglophile's dream estate. The prestigious eastern-suburbs address is close to Oxford Street, Centennial Park, and Paddington, while the city and the eastern beaches are just 10–15 minutes away by public transportation. ✉ *14 Queen St., Woollahra, 2025* ☎ *02/9363–4863* 🖷 *02/9362–0398* ⊕ *www.hughendenhotel.com.au* ⇨ *36 rooms* ⌂ *Restaurant, in-room data ports, bar, library, free parking, some pets allowed (fee); no smoking* ▭ *AE, DC, MC, V* ⍟ *BP.*

★ ¢ 🖼 **Sullivans Hotel.** Set on a quiet stretch in the picturesque shopping precinct of Paddington, this small, friendly, family-owned and -operated hotel has simple accommodations at an outstanding price. Garden rooms overlook an Italianate central courtyard and pool; the corner rooms, Numbers 116, 216, and 316, are the largest and quietest. Rooms that overlook bustling Oxford Street are more likely to be affected by traffic noise, though those on the third floor have harbor views. The location is close to shops, cafés, restaurants, movie theaters, and nightlife, and just a 15-minute walk from the city center. ✉ *21 Oxford St., Darlinghurst, Paddington, 2021* ☎ *02/9361–0211* 🖷 *02/9360–3735* ⊕ *www.sullivans.com.au* ⇨ *65 rooms* ⌂ *Café, refrigerators, in-room data ports, pool, bicycles, free parking* ▭ *AE, DC, MC, V.*

East of the City

★ $$$–$$$$ 🖼 **W Sydney.** Recrafted from the historic Finger Wharf, this member of the stylish international chain does little to disguise the fact that it was once a warehouse. Giant trusses and brontosaurus-like machinery that once formed the working core of the wharf have been left exposed, creating a funky, neo-Gothic interior. There's a background of pumping techno music, and minimalist furnishings in the public spaces are punctuated with splashes of red and chrome. Guest rooms, which have a light, bright, cappuccino color scheme, are arranged like the cabins on a luxury liner, rising in tiers on the outside of the central cavity. *Wharf at*

Woolloomooloo, ✉ *Cowper Wharf Rd., Woolloomooloo, 2011* ☎ *02/ 9331–9000* 📠 *02/9331–9031* ⊕ *www.whotels.com* 🛏 *104 rooms, 36 suites* ♿ *5 restaurants, in-room safes, minibars, in-room VCRs, in-room data ports, pool, gym, bar, dry cleaning, laundry service, concierge, Internet room, business services, convention center, meeting rooms, parking (fee), no-smoking rooms* 🚬 *AE, DC, MC, V.*

★ **$$** 🏨 **Medusa.** If you're tired of the standard traveler's rooms, this reno-vated Victorian terrace house may be just the tonic. Having undergone a massive conversion into 21st-century cool, it sports a decorating scheme of brash colors—blues, yellows, and creams splashed against reds—and furnishings (platform beds, chaise lounges, and so on) that might have come direct from a Milan design gallery. Every room is slightly different, and each has a kitchenette. Behind the glamour is a comfortable, well-run hotel with friendly, attentive staff. This is one of the few city hotels that welcomes guests' dogs. ✉ *267 Darlinghurst Rd., Dar-linghurst, 2010* ☎ *02/9331–1000* 📠 *02/9380–6901* ⊕ *www.medusa. com.au* 🛏 *18 rooms* ♿ *In-room safes, kitchenettes, minibars, cable TV, in-room data ports, bar, parking (fee), some pets allowed* 🚬 *AE, DC, MC, V.*

★ **$$** 🏨 **Regents Court.** Small, elegant, and known for its contemporary style, this boutique hotel is one of Sydney's best-kept secrets. The mood is in-timate yet relaxed, and the location in a cul-de-sac in Potts Point is quiet. Each room has its own well-equipped kitchenette, and many have an extra pull-down bed in addition to the queen-size bed. Bauhaus chairs and dark, moody lighting accent the cool, minimalist decor. You can get a breakfast basket (A$12–A$15) delivered to your room, but experienced patrons head upstairs to eat in splendor amid the glorious rooftop gar-dens. ✉ *18 Springfield Ave., Potts Point, Kings Cross, 2011* ☎ *02/ 9358–1533* 📠 *02/9358–1833* ⊕ *www.regentscourt.com.au* 🛏 *30 rooms* ♿ *Kitchenettes, in-room VCRs, dry cleaning, laundry service, con-cierge, Internet room, parking (fee)* 🚬 *AE, DC, MC, V.*

¢–**$$** 🏨 **De Vere Hotel.** "Simply Comfortable and Affordable" is the byline of this 1920s-style hotel at the leafy end of Potts Point, and it's hard to disagree on either count. No attempts are made to disguise the age of this property—or its furnishings—but the prices and friendly, helpful staff make it a good value. Rooms are spacious, though the linens are a bit worn and the TV a bit Jurassic; some have balconies. Studio apart-ments have basic kitchenettes. ✉ *44–49 Macleay St., Potts Point, Kings Cross, 2011* ☎ *02/9358–1211* 📠 *02/9358–4685* ⊕ *www.devere.com. au* 🛏 *100 rooms* ♿ *Restaurant, some kitchenettes, dry cleaning, laun-dry service, parking (fee)* 🚬 *AE, DC, MC, V.*

¢–**$$** 🏨 **Victoria Court Sydney.** A small, smart hotel on a Potts Point street lined with budget accommodations, the Victoria Court is appealing for more than just its reasonable rates. Hand-painted tiles and etched-glass doors recall the hotel's Victorian ancestry, yet the rooms come with the mod-ern blessings of en suite bathrooms and comfortable beds. Most rooms have marble fireplaces, some have four-poster beds, and some have bal-conies overlooking Victoria Street. ✉ *122 Victoria St., Potts Point, Kings Cross, 2011* ☎ *02/9357–3200* 📠 *02/9357–7606* ⊕ *www. victoriacourt.com.au* 🛏 *25 rooms* 🚬 *AE, DC, MC, V* 🍽 *CP.*

$ **The Chelsea.** The motto of this beautiful guesthouse is "Come home to the Chelsea"—and it won't be long before you're wishing it were *your* home. Occupying adjoining Victorian houses on a quiet, leafy street between Darlinghurst and Rushcutters Bay, this B&B is luxurious and warmly inviting. Rooms are either deluxe, done in a French provincial style with fireplaces and frosted glass bathrooms, or smaller and more contemporary, with shared facilities. Room 13 has a private courtyard with a fancy fountain; Room 7 is the largest of the contemporary units, with iron-trellised windows. You can use the modern, well-equipped kitchen to do your own cooking—although a Continental breakfast is included. ✉ *49 Womerah Ave., Darlinghurst, 2010* ☎ *02/9380–5594* 📠 *02/9332–2491* 🌐 *www.chelsea.citysearch.com.au* *13 rooms* *Dining room, fans, Internet room; no smoking* 💳 *AE, DC, MC, V* 🍴 *CP.*

Fodor'sChoice ★

¢–$ **Kirketon.** The small hotel is elevated to an art form in this stylish, intricately designed building. Striking glass doors at the entryway take you into a minimalist foyer, which then leads to coffee-and-cream-color guest rooms that are a study in simplicity. Furnishings blend 1950s classics with European imports, although the relentless pursuit of style sometimes intrudes into the comfort zone (for example, rooms lack couches or comfortable chairs). If you don't mind suffering slightly for fashion's sake, though, there's no better address. Tech junkies will appreciate the wireless Internet access; foodies will be excited about the restaurant, Sydney's famous Salt, and the adjacent bar, Fix. ✉ *229 Darlinghurst Rd., Darlinghurst, 2010* ☎ *02/9332–2011* 📠 *02/9332–2499* 🌐 *www.kirketon.com.au* *40 rooms* *Restaurant, in-room safes, kitchenettes, minibars, cable TV, in-room data ports, WiFi, bar, concierge, business services, meeting rooms, parking (fee), no-smoking rooms* 💳 *AE, DC, MC, V.*

¢ **Hotel 59 & Cafe.** In its character as well as its dimensions, this friendly B&B on a quiet part of a bar- and club-lined street is reminiscent of a *pensione* in a European capital city. Simple, tastefully outfitted rooms come with high-quality beds and linens, as well as wooden blinds over the windows. Access to rooms is via a small staircase and there is no elevator (the hotel has four floors). Despite its proximity to the heart of Kings Cross, the hotel has a relaxed, serene atmosphere. There's a two-night minimum stay; book online for cheaper rates. ✉ *59 Bayswater Rd., Kings Cross, 2011* ☎ *02/9360–5900* 📠 *02/9360–1828* 🌐 *www.hotel59.com.au* *9 rooms* *Café* 💳 *MC, V* 🍴 *BP.*

Bondi Beach and Manly

$$$ **Swiss Grand Resort & Spa.** With the beach just across the road, a rooftop pool and the Balinese-style Samsara day spa, a stay at the Swiss Grand makes it easy to forget that you're just 15 minutes away from the action of Sydney. The look of the hotel is a bit of pastiche: the fleur-de-lis patterned linens of the rooms match the lobby's Versailles-like ceiling, but clash with its jewel-tone suede club chairs. Sixty-five rooms are beachfront, the rest face the sometimes noisy side streets of this crowded beachside suburb. ✉ *Campbell Parade and Beach Rd., Bondi*

Beach, 2026 ☎ *02/9365–5666* 🖷 *02/9365–5330* ⊕ *www.swissgrand.com.au* ➽ *203 suites* ♨ *3 restaurants, health club, 2 pools, sauna, spa, 2 bars, Internet room, business services, babysitting, free parking* ▤ *AE, DC, MC, V.*

$$–$$$ 🏨 **Radisson Kestrel Hotel on Manly Beach.** Located on a secluded corner of the main beachside drag at Manly, the Radisson feels more like a boutique hotel than a chain. Rooms are subdued and comfortable, with couches in sitting areas, large fluffy beds, and immaculate bathrooms. All rooms have tiled patios, some have kitchenettes and Jacuzzis. Rooms 402, 403, and 405 are the most spacious and have the best views. Sorrel's on the Beach restaurant serves three meals daily to locals and hotel guests. ⊠ *8-13 S. Steyne , Manly, 2037* ☎ *02/9552–1141* 🖷 *02/9692–9462* ⊕ *www.radisson.com/manlyau* ➽ *83 rooms* ♨ *Restaurant, room service, 2 pools, sauna, bar, laundry facilities, Internet room, parking (fee)* ▤ *AE, DC, MC, V* ⦿| *CP.*

NIGHTLIFE & THE ARTS

The Arts

Nothing illustrates the dynamism of Sydney's arts scene better than its live theater. Some of the hottest names in Hollywood received their first taste of stardom in Sydney: Nicole Kidman got her first onstage kiss here; Guy Pearce rocked out in *Grease*; Mel Gibson, Cate Blanchett, and director Baz Luhrmann are products of Sydney's National Institute of Dramatic Arts; and Russell Crowe notched up a total of 416 Sydney performances in the *Rocky Horror Picture Show*—including the role of Dr. Frank N. Furter. At the root of these successes is a powerful, pithy theatrical tradition that has produced many talented Australian writers, directors, and performers. And though Sydney's contemporary theater pays tribute to the giants of world drama, it's also driven by distinctly Australian themes: multiculturalism, relating to the troubled relations between Aboriginal and white Australia, and the search for national identity, characterized by the famous Australian irreverence.

Dance, music, and the visual arts are celebrated with equal enthusiasm. At their best, Sydney's artists and performers bring a new slant to the arts, one that reflects the unique qualities of their homeland and the city itself. Standouts on the Sydney arts scene include the Sydney Dance Company, the Museum of Contemporary Arts, the Sydney Opera House, and Belvoir Street Theatre. The most comprehensive listing of upcoming events is in the Metro section of the *Sydney Morning Herald*, published on Friday. On other days, browse through the entertainment section of the paper. **Ticketek Phone Box Office** (☎ 13–2849 ⊕ premier.ticketek.com.au/) is the major ticket reservations agency, covering most shows and performances.

Ballet, Opera & Classical Music

Fodor'sChoice ★ **Sydney Opera House** (⊠ Bennelong Point, Circular Quay ☎ 02/9250–7777 ⊕ www.soh.nsw.gov.au) showcases all the performing arts in its five theaters, one of which is devoted to opera. The Australian Ballet, the Sydney Dance Company, and the Australian Opera Company also call the Opera House home. The complex includes two stages for theater and the 2,700-seat Concert Hall, where the Sydney Symphony Orchestra and the Australian Chamber Orchestra perform. The box office is open Monday–Saturday 9–8:30.

Dance

Bangarra Dance Theatre (⊠ Wharf 4, 5 Hickson Rd., The Rocks ☎ 02/9251–5333 ⊕ www.bangarra.com.au), an Aboriginal dance company, stages productions based on contemporary Aboriginal social themes, often to critical acclaim.

★ **Sydney Dance Company** (⊠ Pier 4, Hickson Rd., The Rocks ☎ 02/9221–4811 ⊕ www.sydneydance.com.au) is an innovative contemporary dance troupe with an international reputation from its many years under acclaimed director Graeme Murphy. The company generally performs at the Opera House when it's in town.

Theater

Belvoir Street Theatre (⊠ 25 Belvoir St., Surry Hills ☎ 02/9699–3444 ⊕ www.belvoir.com.au) has two stages that host innovative and challenging political and social drama. The smaller downstairs space is the home of "B Sharp," Company B's upstart company of brave, new Australian works. The theater is a 10-minute walk from Central Station.

Capitol Theatre (⊠ 13 Campbell St., Chinatown, Haymarket ☎ 02/9266–4800), a century-old city landmark, was redone with such modern refinements as fiber-optic ceiling lights that twinkle in time to the music. The 2,000-seat theater specializes in Broadway blockbusters.

Lyric Theatre (⊠ 20–80 Pyrmont St., Pyrmont, Darling Harbour ☎ 02/9777–9000 ⊕ www.starcity.com.au), at the Star City Casino complex, is Sydney's most spectacular dedicated performing-arts venue. Despite its size, there's no better place to watch the big-budget musicals that are its staple fare. Every seat in the lavishly spacious, 2,000-seat theater is a good one.

Stables Theatre (⊠ 10 Nimrod St., Kings Cross ☎ 02/9361–3817) has long been known as a proving ground for up-and-coming talents and plays. The avant-garde works of this small theater sometimes graduate to the big stage.

State Theatre (⊠ 49 Market St., City Center ☎ 02/9373–6655) is the grande dame of Sydney theaters, a mid-city venue that demands a dressed-up night to pay homage to a golden era. Built in 1929 and restored to its full-blown opulence in 1980, the theater has a Gothic foyer with a vaulted ceiling, mosaic floors, marble columns and statues, and brass and bronze doors. A highlight of the magnificent theater is the 20,000-piece chandelier that is supposedly the world's second largest.

Wharf Theatre (⊠ Pier 4, Hickson Rd., The Rocks ☎ 02/9250–1777), on a redeveloped wharf in the shadow of Harbour Bridge, hosts the Sydney Theatre Company, one of Australia's most original and highly regarded performing groups. Contemporary British and American plays and the latest offerings from leading Australian playwrights such as David Williamson and Nick Enright are the main attractions.

Nightlife

"Satan made Sydney," wrote Mark Twain, quoting a citizen of the city, and to some there can be no doubt that Satan was the principal architect behind Kings Cross. Strictly speaking, Kings Cross refers to the intersection of Victoria Street and Darlinghurst Road, although the name "The Cross" applies to a much wider area. Essentially, it is a ½-km (¼-mi) stretch of trendy bars and clubs, seedy sports bars and betting venues, burlesque shows, cafés, video shows, and massage parlors. The area is buzzing with backpackers checking in and out of hostels and checking their e-mail for most of the day, while farther down Bayswater Road and Victoria Street, inner-city hipsters lounge at classy cafés on tree-lined streets. The real action starts at 10 PM, and runs hot for most of the night.

Sydneysiders in search of late-night action are more likely to head for Oxford Street, between Hyde Park and Taylor Square, where the choice ranges from pubs to the hottest dance clubs in town. Oxford Street is also the nighttime focus for Sydney's large gay scene. Another nightlife district runs along Cockle Bay Wharf in Darling Harbour; the bars, restaurants, and nightclubs here are especially popular during the summer months. Nightlife in the Rocks is focused on the pubs along George Street, which attract a boisterous crowd. Several Spanish restaurants along the west side of Liverpool Street, just before Darling Harbour, serve delicious food and stay open late for salsa dancing.

The *Sydney Morning Herald*'s daily entertainment section is the most informative guide to the city's pubs and clubs. For club-scene coverage—who's been seen where and what they were wearing—pick up a free copy of *Beat,* available at just about any Oxford Street café or via the Internet (⊕ www.beat.com.au). The CitySearch Web site (⊕ sydney.citysearch.com.au) is another weekly source of entertainment information.

For all bars and clubs listed here, entry is free unless a cover charge is noted.

Bars & Dance Clubs

★ A former School of the Arts building, **Arthouse** (⊠ 275 Pitt St., City Center ☎ 02/9284–1200) has been renovated into a modern, belle epoque–style hot spot, with four bars and a restaurant spread over three cavernous floors. Art is the focus here, whether it's visual, aural, or comestible, and there is a full-time curator dedicated to programming events and installing exhibitions. Open Monday–Saturday until late.

★ The **Beach Road Hotel** (⊠ 71 Beach Rd., Bondi Beach ☎ 02/9130–7247), a Bondi institution, is famous for its Sunday Sessions, when locals come to drink and dance all day in one of several pub rooms. You can snack on a sausage grilled right out front or dine on Italian food on the back patio and settle in for a long night of partying like a Sydneysider. Open daily until late.

★ With its primo waterside location at the northern end of King Street Wharf, and famous mussels from its open kitchen, **Bungalow 8** (⊠ 8 the Promenade, King Street Wharf ☎ 02/9299–4660) invites a night of posing and partying. This is the place to be seen bobbing your head to the spinning of several ultracool resident DJs. Tuesday is especially packed for the all-you-can-eat mussel extravaganza. Open daily from noon until late.

The **Globe Nightclub** (⌧ 60 Park St., City Center ☎ 02/9264–4844) mutates from a business-district bar by day to a dance club after dark. The fake-velvet and chrome decor is a bit faded, but the club still draws elbow-to-elbow crowds to its state-of-the-art sound system. It's open Thursday–Saturday 10 PM–4 AM and Sunday 8 PM–4 AM. The cover charge hovers around A$12.

Fodor'sChoice ★ **Hemmesphere** (⌧ Level 4, 252 George St., City Center ☎ 02/9240–3040) is where Sydney's hippest pay homage to cocktail culture from low, leather divans. The mood is elegant, sleek, and cultish, and the guest list is usually sprinkled with whichever glitterati happen to be in town. Club members, who pay A$1,500 a year, get priority. Open Tuesday–Saturday until late.

Fodor'sChoice ★ **Home** (⌧ Cockle Bay Wharf, 101 Wheat Rd., Darling Harbour ☎ 02/9266–0600), Sydney's largest nightclub, is a three-story colossus that holds up to 2,000 party animals. The main dance floor has an awesome sound system, and the top-level terrace bar is the place to go when the action becomes too frantic. Outdoor balconies provide the essential oxygen boost. Arrive early or prepare for a long wait. Open Thursday–Sunday 10 PM–4 AM, with a cover charge of up to A$20.

Hugo's Lounge (⌧ Level 1, 33 Bayswater Rd., Kings Cross ☎ 02/9357–4411) is the place that transformed Kings Cross from a seedy crossroads of sex shops and smut to a sceney destination for Sydney's beautiful people. Red lamps are a nod to the neighborhood's skin trade, but the deep couches, opulent ottomans, and decadent cocktail menu are purely upmarket. Closed Monday, the lounge is open every other night until late.

Jimmy Liks (⌧ 188 Victoria St., Potts Point ☎ 02/8354–1400), a small, sexy Asian street-food restaurant, serves up drink concoctions with exotic flavors—like lemongrass martinis and "twisted and tasty" iced teas accented with basil—which you can sip under a honeycomb-like lantern that flatters with its golden light. It's open from 6 PM every night until late.

Fodor'sChoice ★ **Le Panic** (⌧ 20 Bayswater Rd., Kings Cross ☎ 02/9368–0763) is the perfect combination of bar and dance club. With its sleek, gentlemen's-club ambience and private back room, it's a great space for hanging out with a group. The dance floor is small and suitably crowded, though not people-keep-bumping-into-me-and-messing-up-my-dance-moves crowded, thanks to a rotating list of visiting DJs spinning in various styles. It's a major pickup scene for beautiful people who don't get their groove on until late—the action usually doesn't start until 11 PM. Closed Tuesday and Wednesday; there's sometimes a cover charge.

Fodor'sChoice ★ **Mars Lounge** (⌧ 16 Wentworth Ave., Surry Hills ☎ 02/9267–6440) takes its music as seriously as it takes its list of lethal, Martian-theme cocktails, like the "Marslide," with malt chocolate, Baileys, butterscotch, and cream. DJs spin everything from funk to fusion, and each night has a different theme, like the Thursday-night Squeeze party of sexy sounds, or Sunday night's soulful, funkified Red Velvet party. Closed Monday and Tuesday; no cover.

For a northern Sydney landmark, **The Oaks** (⊠ 118 Military Rd., Neutral Bay ☎ 02/9953–5515) encapsulates the very best of the modern pub. The immensely popular watering hole is big and boisterous, with a beer garden, a restaurant, and several bars offering varying levels of sophistication. It opens at 10 AM daily, and is packed on Friday and Saturday nights.

Fodor'sChoice
★ Perched beneath the concourse of the Opera House and at eye level with Sydney Harbour, **Opera Bar** (⊠ Lower Concourse, Sydney Opera House, Circular Quay ☎ 02/9247–1666) has the best location in all of Sydney. Cozy up for a drink in the enclosed bar area or grab a waterside umbrella table and take in the glimmering skyline. Live music plays under the stars nightly. The bar is open daily from 11:30 AM until late, and also has a full menu, though the attraction here is the scenery, not the cuisine.

★ A cross between a swinging '60s London nightspot and the back lot of a James Bond film, the small, groovy **Peppermint Lounge** (⊠ 281 Victoria St., Potts Point ☎ 02/9356–6634) is heavy on a mod mood, and, naturally, martinis. Tuck into an octagon-shape red-lighted booth surrounded by frosted glass and try one of the more than 70 libations on offer. Open Wednesday, Thursday, Friday, and Saturday nights until midnight.

The mood of the inner-city **Soho Bar** (⊠ 171 Victoria St., Kings Cross ☎ 02/9358–6511), a major celeb hangout for hometown favorites and visiting international stars, is relaxed and funky. The adjoining pool room is rated one of the city's finest. The bar is open daily 10 AM–3 AM, later on Friday and Saturday. Adjacent nightclub Yu pumps house music on weekends until sunrise.

★ **Tank** (⊠ 3 Bridge La., City Center ☎ 02/9240–3094) is the grooviest and best looking of all Sydney's nightclubs, with a polar-cool clientele and a slick dress code rigidly enforced at the door. The cover charge is A$20 on Saturday night, and you'll continue to shell out as much for drinks all evening. The interior is plush and relaxed, despite its space-capsule setting, and the techno music thumps. Hours are 10 PM–5 AM Friday and Saturday.

Comedy Club

Sydney's Original Comedy Store (⊠ Shop 102, Bldg. 207, Fox Studios, Bent St., Moore Park, Centennial Park ☎ 02/9357–1419 ⊕ www.comedystore.com.au), the city's oldest comedy club, is found in this plush 300-seat theater in a huge movie production facility. The difficult-to-find theater is at the rear of the complex, close to the parking lot. Shows are Tuesday–Saturday at 8, and admission runs A$15–A$29.50.

Gambling

Star City Casino (⊠ 20–80 Pyrmont St., Pyrmont, Darling Harbour ☎ 02/9777–9000 ⊕ www.starcity.com.au) is a glitzy 24-hour Las

Vegas–style casino with 200 gaming tables and 1,500 slot machines. Gambling options include roulette, craps, blackjack, baccarat, and the classic Australian game of Two-up.

Gay & Lesbian Bars & Clubs

Most of the city's gay and lesbian venues are along Oxford Street, in Darlinghurst. The free *Sydney Star Observer,* available along Oxford Street, has a roundup of Sydney's gay and lesbian goings-on, or check the magazine's Web site (⊕ www.ssonet.com.au). A monthly free magazine, *Lesbians on the Loose,* lists events for women, and the free *SX* (⊕ sxnews.com.au) also lists bars and events.

★ **ARQ** (⊠ 16 Flinders St., Darlinghurst ☎ 02/9380–8700), Sydney's biggest, best looking, and funkiest gay nightclub, attracts a clean-cut crowd who like to whip off their shirts and dance. There's a bar, multiple dance floors, and plenty of chrome and sparkly lighting. It's open from 9 PM until whenever Friday through Sunday, with a cover charge of A$5–A$20.

Beauchamp Hotel (⊠ 267 Oxford St., Darlinghurst ☎ 02/9331–2575) is a gay and lesbian pub mostly remarkable for what it lacks. There's no floor show, cruisy lighting, dance floor, or cocktail bar—just a comfortable, unpretentious, traditional Australian pub that appeals mostly to older gays. It's open daily 10 AM–1 AM, and is especially sociable on weekend afternoons.

Midnight Shift (⊠ 85 Oxford St., Darlinghurst ☎ 02/9360–4463) is Sydney's hard-core party zone, a living legend on the gay scene for its longevity and its take-no-prisoners approach. If anything, the upstairs nightclub is a little quieter than the ground-floor bars, where most of the leather-loving men go to shoot pool. Opening hours are daily from about midday to 6 AM.

Though the look, music, and decor of the **Newtown Hotel** (⊠ 174 King St., Newtown ☎ 02/9557–1329) do not approach the gloss and sophistication of Paddington's glamorous gay scene, you can't beat the laid-back attitudes and the bawdy, in-your-face drag shows. Open daily until late.

Jazz Clubs

Avery's Bar (⊠ 389 Pitt St., City Center ☎ 02/8268–1888), located in the Avillon hotel, is one of the few venues in Australia where soul music gets its due. Funk is also a focus here, and each night offers a different focus, like Hot Jazz Friday. Open daily until late.

★ **The Basement** (⊠ 29 Reiby Pl., Circular Quay ☎ 02/9251–2797) is a Sydney legend, the city's premier venue for top jazz and blues musicians. Dinner is also available. Expect a cover charge of A$15–A$20.

Soup Plus (⊠ 1 Margaret St., City Center ☎ 02/9299–7728), a small, subterranean jazz venue, hosts mainly contemporary jazz performers in a space that feels like a cross between a high school cafeteria and a rec room. Shows start at 8 PM Monday–Thursday, and there is a A$10 to A$12 cover charge. Shows are at 8:30 PM on Friday and Saturday nights, with an A$35 cover charge, which includes a two-course meal from the meat-and-potatoes-heavy menu.

Pubs with Music

Ettamogah Bar & Restaurant (⊠ 225 Harbourside, Darling Harbour ☎ 02/9281–3922), based on a famous Australian cartoon series depicting an Outback saloon, has three bars and an open-air restaurant. The pub varies from family-friendly by day to nightclub by evening. Hours are weekdays 11 AM–midnight, Saturday 11 AM–3 AM, and Sunday 11 AM–11 PM, with a cover charge of A$5–A$10 Thursday to Saturday.

Mercantile Hotel (⊠ 25 George St., The Rocks ☎ 02/9247–3570), in the shadow of Harbour Bridge, is Irish and very proud of it. Fiddles, drums, and pipes rise above the clamor in the bar, and lilting accents rejoice in song seven nights a week. Hours are Sunday–Wednesday 10 AM–midnight and Thursday–Saturday 10 AM–1 AM. There's no cover charge.

Rose, Shamrock and Thistle (⊠ 193 Evans St., Rozelle ☎ 02/9810–2244), popularly known as the Three Weeds, is a friendly, boisterous pub 5 km (3 mi) from the city center. It's one of the best places to hear live music, generally from Thursday through Saturday for a moderate cover charge of A$5–A$10. Otherwise, come for free Monday–Wednesday noon–midnight, Sunday noon–10.

SPORTS & THE OUTDOORS

Given its climate and its taste for the great outdoors, it's no surprise that Sydney is addicted to sports. In the cooler months rugby dominates the sporting scene, although these days the Sydney Swans, the city's flag bearer in the national Australian Rules Football competition, attract far bigger crowds. In summer, cricket is the major spectator sport, and nothing arouses more passion than international test cricket games—especially when Australia plays against England, the traditional enemy. Sydney is well equipped with athletic facilities, from golf courses to tennis courts, and water sports come naturally on one of the world's greatest harbors. **Ticketek Phone Box Office** (☎ 13–2849 ⊕ premier.ticketek.com.au) is the place to buy tickets for major sports events.

Australian Rules Football

A fast, demanding game in which the ball can be kicked or punched between teams of 22 players, Australian Rules Football has won a major audience in Sydney, even though the city has only one professional team compared to the dozen that play in Melbourne—the home of the sport. **Aussie Stadium** (⊠ Moore Park Rd., Centennial Park, Paddington ☎ 02/9360–6601 ⊕ www.scgt.nsw.gov.au) hosts games from April to September.

Bicycling

Sydney's favorite cycling track is Centennial Park's Grand Parade, a 3¾-km (2¼-mi) cycle circuit around the perimeter of this grand, gracious eastern suburbs park.

Centennial Park Cycles (⊠ 50 Clovelly Rd., Randwick, Centennial Park ☎ 02/9398–5027 ⊠ Grand Dr., 200 yds past restaurant inside Centennial Park, Centennial Park) rents bicycles for around A$15 per hour, A$40 per day.

Clarence Street Cyclery (✉ 104 Clarence St., City Center ☎ 02/9299–4962 ⊕ www.cyclery.com.au) is a major store for all cycling needs.

Boating & Sailing

EastSail (✉ D'Albora Marine, New Beach Rd., Rushcutters Bay, Darling Point ☎ 02/9327–1166 ⊕ www.eastsail.com.au) rents bareboat sailing and motored yachts from about A$465 per half day for a 31-foot sloop. Skippers' rates are around A$50 per hour.

Northside Sailing School (✉ Spit Rd., the Spit, Mosman ☎ 02/9969–3972 ⊕ www.northsidesailing.com.au) at Middle Harbour teaches dinghy sailing to individuals and children's groups. You can learn the ropes on a three-hour, one-on-one private lesson from A$130.

Sydney Harbour Kayaks (✉ 3/25 Spit Rd., Mosman ☎ 02/9960–4389) hires out one- and two-person kayaks. The location beside Spit Bridge offers calm water for novices, as well as several beaches and idyllic coves. Prices per hour start from A$20 for a one-person kayak to A$30 for a double.

Cricket

Cricket is Sydney's summer sport, and it's often played at the beach as well as in parks throughout the nation. For Australians, the pinnacle of excitement is the Ashes, when the national cricket team takes the field against the English. It happens every other summer and the two nations take turns hosting the event. The next Ashes series is in Australia December 2006–January 2007. Cricket season runs from October through March. International test series games are played at the **Sydney Cricket Ground** (✉ Moore Park Rd., Centennial Park, Paddington ☎ 02/9360–6601 ⊕ www.scgt.nsw.gov.au).

Golf

More than 80 golf courses, 35 of which are public, lie within a 40-km (25-mi) radius of the Sydney Harbour Bridge. Golf clubs and carts are usually available for rent.

Bondi Golf Club (✉ 5 Military Rd., North Bondi ☎ 02/9130–1981) is a 9-hole public course on the cliffs overlooking famous Bondi Beach. Although the par-28 course is hardly a challenge for serious golfers, the views are inspiring. The course is open to the public after noon on most days. The greens fee is A$18.50.

New South Wales Golf Course (✉ Henry Head, La Perouse ☎ 02/9661–4455 ⊕ www.nswgolfclub.com.au) is a rigorous, par-72, 18-hole championship course on the cliffs at La Perouse, overlooking Botany Bay. The course is generally open to nonmembers Monday, Thursday afternoons, and Friday mornings, but you must make advance arrangements with the pro shop. The greens fee is A$250.

Riverside Oaks Golf Club (✉ O'Brien's Rd., Cattai ☎ 02/4560–3299 ⊕ www.riversideoaks.com.au), on the bush-clad banks of the Hawkesbury River, is a spectacular 18-hole, par-72 course about a 90-minute drive northwest of Sydney. The greens fee is A$80 weekdays, A$92 weekends.

Hiking

Fine walking trails can be found in the national parks in and around Sydney, especially in **Royal National Park** (Royal National Park, *above*), **Ku-ring-gai Chase National Park** (Ku-ring-gai Chase National Park, above), and **Sydney Harbour National Park,** all of which are close to the city.

Rugby

Rugby League, known locally as footie, is Sydney's winter addiction. This is a fast, gutsy, physical game that bears some similarities to North American football, although the action is more constant and the ball cannot be passed forward. The season falls between April and September. **Aussie Stadium** (✉ Moore Park Rd., Centennial Park, Paddington ☎ 02/9360–6601 ⊕ www.scgt.nsw.gov.au) is the main venue.

Running

The path that connects the **Opera House to Mrs. Macquarie's Chair,** along the edge of the harbor through the Royal Botanic Gardens, is one of the finest in the city. At lunchtime on weekdays this track is crowded with corporate joggers.

Bondi Beach to Tamarama is a popular and fashion-conscious running path that winds along the cliffs south from Bondi. It's marked by distance indicators and includes a number of exercise stations.

Manly beachfront is good for running. If you have the legs for it, you can run down to Shelly Beach, or pop over the hill to Freshwater Beach and follow it all the way to check out the surf at Curl Curl beach.

Scuba Diving

Aquatic Explorers (✉ 40 the Kingsway, Cronulla Beach ☎ 02/9523–1518 ⊕ www.aquaticexplorers.com.au), in a southern seaside suburb, runs weekend boat dives (for a minimum of four people; midweek dives are also available by arrangement) to sites suitable for varying experience levels. Highlights include swim-through caves, 19th-century shipwrecks, and a gray nurse shark dive. PADI certification courses are also available. The cost for a two-dive boat trip starts at A$75.

Dive Centre Manly (✉ 10 Belgrave St., Manly ☎ 02/9977–4355 ⊕ www.divesydney.com), at the popular north Sydney beach, runs all-inclusive shore dives each day, which let you see weedy sea dragons and nudibranches, among other sea creatures. PADI certification courses are also available. The cost for two shore dives starts at A$95.

Pro Dive (✉ 27 Alfreda St., Coogee ☎ 02/9665–6333 ⊕ www.prodive.com.au) is a PADI operator conducting courses and shore- or boat-diving excursions around the harbor and city beaches. Some of the best dive spots—with coral, rock walls, and lots of colorful fish, including "Bazza" the grouper—are close to the eastern suburb beaches of Clovelly and Coogee, where Pro Dive is based. A four-hour boat dive with an instructor or dive master costs around A$169, including rental equipment.

Surfing

All Sydney surfers have their favorite breaks, but you can usually count on good waves on at least one of the city's ocean beaches. In summer, surfing reports are a regular feature of radio news broadcasts.

Let's go Surfing (✉ 128 Ramsgate Ave., North Bondi ☎ 02/9365–1800 ⊕ www.letsgosurfing.com.au) is a complete surfing resource for anyone who wants to hang five with confidence. Lessons are available for all ages, and you can rent or buy boards and wet suits. The basic three-class package of two-hour Surf Easy lessons costs A$155.

Manly Surf School (✉ North Steyne Surf Club, Manly Beach, Manly ☎ 02/9977–6977 ⊕ www.manlysurfschool.com) conducts courses for adults and children, and provides all equipment, including wet suits. Adults can join a two-hour group lesson (four per day) for A$50. Private instruction costs A$80 per hour.

Rip Curl (✉ 82 Campbell Parade, Bondi Beach ☎ 02/9130–2660) has a huge variety of boards and surfing supplies. It's conveniently close to Bondi Beach.

Surfcam (⊕ www.surfcam.com.au) has surf reports and weather details.

Swimming

Sydney has many heated Olympic-size swimming pools, some of which go beyond the basic requirements of a workout. Many Aussies, however, prefer to do their "laps" in the sea off Bondi and Manly.

Andrew (Boy) Charlton Pool (✉ Mrs. Macquarie's Rd., Domain North, The Domain ☎ 02/9358–6686) isn't just any heated, outdoor, and Olympic-size pool. Its stunning location overlooking the ships at Garden Island, its radical glass-and-steel design, and its chic terrace café above Woolloomooloo Bay make it an attraction unto itself. Admission is A$5 and it's open October–April, daily 6 AM–7 PM.

Cook and Phillip Park Aquatic and Fitness Centre (✉ College St., City Center ☎ 02/9326–0444) includes wave, hydrotherapy, children's, and Olympic-size pools in a stunning, high-tech complex on the eastern edge of the city center. There's also a complete fitness center and classes. Admission is A$5.80 and it's open weekdays 6 AM–10 PM, weekends 7 AM–8 PM.

Tennis

Cooper Park Tennis Centre (✉ Off Suttie Rd., Cooper Park, Double Bay ☎ 02/9389–9259) is a complex of eight synthetic-grass courts in a park surrounded by an expansive area of native bushland, about 5 km (3 mi) east of the city center. Weekday court fees are A$22 per hour from 7 to 5 and A$27 per hour from 6 to 10. On Saturday they are A$26 until 5 and A$27 afterward; Sunday A$26 until 1 and A$18 afterwards.

Parklands Sports Centre (✉ Lang Rd. and Anzac Parade, Moore Park, Centennial Park ☎ 02/9662–7033 ⊕ www.cp.nsw.gov.au/aboutus/sports.htm) has 11 courts in a shady park approximately 2½ km (1½ mi) from the city center. The weekday cost is A$16.50 per hour 9–5 and A$22 per hour 5–10:30; it's A$22 per hour 8–6 on weekends.

Windsurfing

Balmoral Windsurfing, Kite Surfing, Sailing, and Kayak School (✉ The Esplanade, Balmoral Beach ☎ 02/9960–5344 ⊕ www.sailboard.net.au) runs classes from its base at this north-side harbor beach. Kite-surfing, sailing, and kayaking lessons are also available. Kite-surfing lessons start from A$99, windsurfing from A$175, sailing from A$195.

Rose Bay Aquatic Hire (✉ 1 Vickery Ave., Rose Bay ☎ 02/9371–7036) rents motorboats, kayaks, catamarans, and Lasers. The cost is from A$35 per hour for a Laser and A$40 per hour for a catamaran; some sailing experience is required to rent these boats. Kayaks are also available for rent from A$20 per hour for a single; motorboat rentals cost A$30 per hour for the first two hours, then A$15 per hour.

SHOPPING

Sydney's shops vary from those with international cachet (Tiffany's, Louis Vuitton) to Aboriginal art galleries, opal shops, craft bazaars, and weekend flea markets. If you're interested in buying genuine Australian products, look carefully at the labels. Stuffed koalas and didgeridoos made anywhere but in Australia are a standing joke.

Business hours are usually about 9 or 10 to 6 on weekdays; on Thursday stores stay open until 9. Shops are open Saturday 9–5 and Sunday 11–5. Prices include the Goods and Services Tax (GST).

Department Stores

David Jones (✉ Women's store, Elizabeth and Market Sts., City Center ✉ Men's store, Castlereagh and Market Sts., City Center ☎ 02/9266–5544 ⊕ www.davidjones.com.au)—or "Dee Jays," as it's known locally—is the city's largest department store, with a reputation for excellent service and high-quality goods. Clothing by many of Australia's finest designers is on display here, and the store also markets its own fashion label at reasonable prices. The basement level of the men's store is a fabulous food hall with international treats.

Gowings (✉ Market and George Sts., City Center ☎ 02/9287–6394 ⊕ www.gowings.com.au) is Australia's answer to L. L. Bean: an old-fashioned store jam-packed with practical everyday items from hats to umbrellas to undergarments, mostly at no-frills prices. It's open Monday–Wednesday and Friday 8–6, Thursday 8–8, Saturday 9–5, and Sunday 11–4.

Grace Bros (✉ George and Market Sts., City Center ☎ 02/9238–9111 ⊕ www.gracebros.com.au), opposite the Queen Victoria Building, is the place to shop for clothing and accessories by Australian and international designers.

Flea Markets

Balmain Market (✉ St. Andrew's Church, Darling St., Balmain), in a leafy churchyard less than 5 km (3 mi) from the city, has a rustic quality that makes it a refreshing change from city-center shopping. Craft work, plants, handmade furniture, bread, tarot readings, massages, and toys are among the offerings at the 140-odd stalls. Inside the church hall you can buy international snacks, from Indian samosas to Indonesian satays to Australian meat pies. The market runs 8:30–4 on Saturday.

FodorsChoice **Paddington Bazaar** (✉ St. John's Church, Oxford St., Paddington), more ★ popularly known as Paddington Market, is a busy churchyard bazaar with more than 100 stalls crammed with clothing, plants, crafts, jewelry, and souvenirs. Distinctly new age and highly fashion conscious, the market is an outlet for a handful of avant-garde clothing designers. It also acts as a magnet for buskers and some of the area's flamboyant and entertaining characters. It's open Saturday 10–4.

The Rocks Market (⊠ Upper George St. near Argyle St., The Rocks), a sprawling covered bazaar, transforms the upper end of George Street into a multicultural collage of music, food, arts, crafts, and entertainment. It's open weekends 10–5.

Shopping Centers & Arcades

Harbourside (⊠ Darling Harbour), the glamorous, glassy pavilion on the water's edge, houses more than 200 clothing, jewelry, and souvenir shops. However, its appeal is not so much due to the stores as to its striking architecture and spectacular location. The shopping center, open daily 10–midnight, also has many cafés, restaurants, and bars that overlook the harbor.

Oxford Street, Paddington's main artery, is dressed to thrill. Lined with boutiques, home-furnishing stores, and Mediterranean-inspired cafés, it's a perfect venue for watching the never-ending fashion parade.

Pitt Street Mall (⊠ Between King and Market Sts., City Center), at the heart of Sydney's shopping area, includes the Mid-City Centre, Centrepoint Arcade, Imperial Arcade, Skygarden, Grace Bros, and the charming and historic Strand Arcade—six multilevel shopping plazas crammed with more than 450 shops, from mainstream clothing stores to designer boutiques.

Queen Victoria Building (⊠ George, York, Market, and Druitt Sts., City Center ☎ 02/9264–9209) is a splendid Victorian building with more than 200 boutiques, cafés, and antiques shops. The QVB is open 24 hours, so you can still window-shop after the stores have closed.

Specialty Stores

Aboriginal Art

Aboriginal art includes historically functional items, such as boomerangs, wooden bowls, and spears, as well as paintings and ceremonial implements that testify to a rich culture of legends and dreams. Although much of this artwork remains strongly traditional in essence, the tools and colors used in Western art have fired the imaginations of many Aboriginal artists. Works on canvas are now more common than works on bark, for example. Although the two most prolific sources of Aboriginal art are Arnhem Land and the Central Desert Region (close to Darwin and Alice Springs, respectively), much of the best work finds its way into the galleries of Sydney.

Aboriginal and Tribal Art Centre (⊠ Level 1, 117 George St., The Rocks ☎ 02/9247–9625) sells everything from large sculptures and bark paintings to fabric to such small collectibles as carved emu eggs. The store is open daily 10–5:30.

Coo-ee Aboriginal Art (⊠ 31 Lamrock Ave., Bondi Beach ☎ 02/9300–9233), open by appointment, exhibits and sells high-end Aboriginal paintings, sculptures, and limited-edition prints.

Hogarth Galleries (✉ 7 Walker La., Paddington ☎ 02/9360–6839 ⊕ www.aboriginalartcentres.com) showcases quality contemporary Aboriginal artworks from around the country. It's open Tuesday–Saturday 10–5.

Books

Ariel Booksellers (✉ 42 Oxford St., Paddington ☎ 02/9332 4581 ⊕ www. arielbooks.com.au ✉ 103 George St., The Rocks ☎ 02/9241–5622) is a large, bright browser's delight and the place to go for literature, pop culture, and anything avant-garde. It also has a fine selection of art books. Both stores are open daily 9 AM–midnight.

Dymocks (✉ 424 George St., City Center ☎ 02/9235–0155 ⊕ www. dymocks.com.au), a big, bustling bookstore packed to its gallery-level coffee shop, is the place to go for all literary needs. It's open Monday–Wednesday and Friday 9–6:30, Thursday 9–9, Saturday 9–6, and Sunday 10–5.

The **Travel Bookshop** (✉ Shop 3, 175 Liverpool St., Hyde Park ☎ 02/ 9261–8200) carries Sydney's most extensive selection of maps, guides, armchair-travel books, and histories.

Bush Apparel & Outdoor Gear

Mountain Designs (✉ 499 Kent St., City Center ☎ 02/9267–3822 ⊕ www. mountaindesigns.com.au), in the middle of Sydney's "Rugged Row" of outdoor specialists, sells camping and climbing hardware and dispenses the advice necessary to keep you alive and well in the wilderness.

Paddy Pallin (✉ 507 Kent St., City Center ☎ 02/9264–2685 ⊕ www. paddypallin.com.au) is the first stop for serious bush adventurers heading for the Amazon, Annapurna, or wild Australia. Maps, books, and mounds of gear are tailored especially for the Australian outdoors.

★ **R. M. Williams** (✉ 389 George St., City Center ☎ 02/9262–2228 ⊕ www. rmwilliams.com.au) is the place to go for the complete bush look, with accessories such as Akubra hats, Drizabone riding coats, plaited kangaroo-skin belts, and moleskin trousers.

Clothing

Artwear by Lara S (✉ 77½ George St., City Center ☎ 02/9247–3668) is Australian knitwear at its best, with the promise of years of warmth and style in every garment. Comfort as well as fashion are the keywords for these soft and luscious pure wool designs, which vary from eye-catching to understated, some in ultrafine wool for itch-free wearing.

Belinda (✉ 8 Transvaal Ave., Double Bay ☎ 02/9328–6288 ⊕ www. belinda.com.au) is where Sydney's female fashionistas go when there's a dress-up occasion looming. From her namesake store that scores high marks for innovation and imagination, former model Belinda Seper sells nothing but the very latest designs off the catwalks.

Collette Dinnigan (✉ 33 William St., Paddington ☎ 02/9360–6691 ⊕ www.collettedinnigan.com.au), one of the hottest names on Australia's fashion scene, has dressed Nicole Kidman, Cate Blanchett, and Sandra Bullock. Her Paddington boutique is packed with sensual, floating, negligee-inspired fashions crafted from silks, chiffons, and lace in soft pastel colors accented with hand-beading and embroidery.

Country Road (✉ 142–144 Pitt St., City Center ☎ 02/9394–1818 ⊕ www. countryroad.com.au) stands somewhere between Ralph Lauren and Timberland, with an all-Australian assembly of classic, countrified his 'n' hers, plus an ever-expanding variety of soft furnishings in cotton and linen for the rustic retreat.

Dorian Scott (✉ 61 Macquarie St., Circular Quay ☎ 02/9241–4114) specializes in bright, high-fashion Australian knitwear for men, women, and children, and carries sweaters and scarves in natural colors.

Marcs (✉ Shop 288, Mid-City Centre, Pitt Street Mall, City Center ☎ 02/9221–5575 ⊕ www.marcs.com.au) comes from somewhere close to Diesel-land in the fashion spectrum, with a variety of clothing, footwear, and accessories for the fashion-conscious. Serious shoppers should look for the Marcs Made in Italy sub-label for that extra touch of style and craftsmanship.

Orson & Blake (✉ 83–85 Queen St., Woollahra ☎ 02/9326–1155) is a virtual gallery dedicated to great modern design, with eclectic housewares, fashions, handbags, and accessories. There's even a coffee shop where you can mull over your purchases.

Scanlan & Theodore (✉ 443 Oxford St., Paddington ☎ 02/9361–6722) is the Sydney store for one of Melbourne's most distinguished fashion houses. Designs take their cues from Europe, with superbly tailored women's knitwear, suits, and stylishly glamorous evening wear.

Crafts

Object Store (✉ 88 George St., The Rocks ☎ 02/9247–7984 ⊕ www. object.com.au) sells beautiful glass, wood, and ceramic creations.

Music

Birdland Records (✉ 231 Pitt St., City Center ☎ 02/9267–6881) has an especially strong selection of jazz, blues, African, and Latin American music, and authoritative assistance. It's open Monday–Wednesday and Friday 10–5:30, Thursday 10–7:30, and Saturday 9–4:30.

Folkways (✉ 282 Oxford St., Paddington ☎ 02/9361–3980) sells Australian bush, folk, and Aboriginal recordings. The store is open Monday–Wednesday 10–6, Thursday 9–8, Friday 9–6, Saturday 10–6, Sunday 11–6.

Opals & Jewelry

Australia has a virtual monopoly on the world's supply of opals. The least expensive of these fiery gemstones are triplets, which consist of a thin shaving of opal mounted on a plastic base and covered by a plastic, glass, or quartz crown. Doublets are a slice of mounted opal without the capping. The most expensive stones are solid opals, which cost anywhere from a few hundred dollars to a few thousand. You can pick up opals at souvenir shops all over the city, but if you want a valuable stone you should visit a specialist. Sydney is also a good hunting ground for other jewelry, from the quirky to the gloriously expensive.

Dinosaur Designs (✉ Shop 77, Strand Arcade, George St., City Center ☎ 02/9223–2953 ⊕ www.dinosaurdesigns.com.au) sells luminous bowls, plates, and vases, as well as fanciful jewelry crafted from resin and Perspex® in eye-popping color combinations.

Flame Opals (⊠ 119 George St., The Rocks ☎ 02/9247–3446 ⊕ www. flameopals.com.au) sells nothing but solid opals—black, white, and Queensland boulder varieties, which have a distinctive depth and luster—set in either sterling silver or 18-karat gold. The sales staff is very helpful. The shop is open weekdays 9–6:45, Saturday 10–5, and Sunday 11:30–5.

★ **Makers Mark** (⊠ 72A Castlereagh St., City Center ☎ 02/9231–6800 ⊕ www.makersmark.com.au) has a gorgeous collection of handmade designer jewelry and objects by some of Australia's finest artisans.

The National Opal Collection (⊠ 176 Pitt St. Mall, City Center ☎ 02/ 9233–8844 ⊕ www.gemtec.com.au) is the only Sydney opal retailer with total ownership of its entire production process—mines, workshops, and showroom—making prices very competitive. In the Pitt Street showroom you can see artisans at work cutting and polishing the stones. Hours are weekdays 9–6 and weekends 10–4.

★ **Paspaley Pearls** (⊠ 142 King St., City Center ☎ 02/9232–7633 ⊕ www. paspaleypearls.com) derives its exquisite jewelry from pearl farms near the remote Western Australia town of Broome. Prices start high and head for the stratosphere, but if you're serious about a high-quality pearl, this gallery requires a visit.

Percy Marks Fine Gems (⊠ 60 Elizabeth St., City Center ☎ 02/9233–1355 ⊕ www.percymarks.com.au/welcome) has an outstanding collection of high-quality Australian gemstones, including dazzling black opals, pink diamonds, and pearls from Broome.

Rox Gems and Jewellery (⊠ Shop 31, Strand Arcade, George St., City Center ☎ 02/9232–7828 ⊕ www.rox.com.au) sells serious one-off designs, at the cutting edge of lapidary chic, that can be spotted on some exceedingly well-dressed wrists.

Souvenirs

ABC Shops (⊠ Level 1, Shop 48, Albert Walk, Queen Victoria Bldg., 455 George St., City Center ☎ 02/9286–3726 ⊕ www.shop.abc.net.au), the retail arm of Australia's national broadcaster, sells an offbeat collection of things Australian in words, music, and print. It's an unfailing source of inspiration for gifts and souvenirs. Hours are Monday–Wednesday and Friday 9–6, Thursday 9–9, Saturday 9–5, and Sunday 10–5.

Australian Geographic (⊠ Shop C14, Centrepoint, Market and Pitt Sts., City Center ☎ 02/9231–5055) is a virtual museum crammed with games, puzzles, experiments, and environmental science that promises endless fascination for the inquisitive mind.

T-Shirts & Beachwear

Beach Culture (⊠ 105 George St., The Rocks ☎ 02/9252–4551) is firmly rooted in the sand-and-surf ethos, and the place for one-stop shopping for Australia's great surf brands like Billabong and Mambo. As well as board shorts, towels, and T-shirts, there's a totally groovy collection of jewelry, footwear, and essential accessories for the après-surf scene.

Done Art and Design (⊠ 123 George St., The Rocks ☎ 02/9251–6099 ⊕ www.done.com.au) sells the striking artworks of prominent artist Ken Done, who catches the sunny side of Sydney with vivid colors and bold brushstrokes. His shop also carries practical products with his distinctive designs, including bed linens, sunglasses, beach towels, beach and resort wear, and T-shirts.

Mambo (✉ 80 Campbell Parade, Bondi Beach ☎ 02/9365-2255 ⊕ www. mambo.com.au) has designs inspired by bold beach colors and culture. The shirts, T-shirts, board shorts, and accessories are loud and funky—not for those who prefer their apparel understated.

SYDNEY A TO Z

AIR TRAVEL

International and domestic airlines serve Sydney's Kingsford–Smith International Airport from North America, Europe, and Southeast Asia. Qantas flights with numbers QF1 to QF399 depart from the Kingsford–Smith airport's international terminal. Flights QF400 and higher depart from the domestic terminal.

Air Canada, Air New Zealand, Air Paradise, Alitalia, Australian Airlines, British Airways, Cathay Pacific, Garuda, Japan Airlines, Lauda Air, Malaysia Airlines, Qantas, Singapore Airlines, Thai Airways, and United Airlines all have flights to Sydney.

Jetstar, Qantas, and Virgin Blue connect Sydney to other Australian cities.
🛪 **Airlines Air Canada** ☎ 1300/655767. **Air New Zealand** ☎ 13-2476. **Air Paradise** ☎ 13-6666. **Alitalia** ☎ 02/9244-2400. **Australian Airlines** ☎ 1300/799798. **British Airways** ☎ 1300/767177. **Cathay Pacific** ☎ 13-1747. **Garuda** ☎ 1300/365330. **Japan Airlines** ☎ 02/9272-1111. **Jetstar** ☎ 13-1538. **Lauda Air** ☎ 02/9251-6155. **Malaysia Airlines** ☎ 13-2627. **Qantas** ☎ 13-1313. **Singapore Airlines** ☎ 13-1011. **Thai Airways** ☎ 1300/651960. **United Airlines** ☎ 13-1777. **Virgin Blue** ☎ 13-6789.

AIRPORT

Sydney's main airport is Kingsford–Smith International, 8 km (5 mi) south of the city. Luggage carts are available in the baggage area of the international terminal. You can convert your money to Australian currency at the Travelex offices in both the arrival and departure areas. These are open daily from about 5 AM to 10 PM or later, depending on flight times.

Tourism New South Wales has two information counters in the arrival level of the international terminal. One provides free maps and brochures and handles general inquiries. The other deals with hotel reservations. Both counters are open daily from approximately 6 AM to 11 PM.

Kingsford–Smith's domestic and international terminals are 3 km (2 mi) apart. To get from one terminal to the other, you can take a taxi for about A$12 or use the Airport Shuttle Bus for A$4.
🛪 **Kingsford–Smith International Airport** ☎ 02/9667-9111 ⊕ www.sydneyairport.com.au.

TRANSFERS AirportLink rail service reaches the city in 13 minutes. Trains depart every 5–10 minutes during peak hours and at least every 15 minutes at other times. A one-way fare is A$11; a group ticket (three people) costs A$27. The link meshes with the suburban rail network at Central Station and

Circular Quay Station. On the downside, access to the platform is difficult for travelers with anything more than light luggage, trains do not have adequate stowage facilities, and for two traveling together a taxi is more convenient and costs only slightly more.

Taxis are available outside the terminal buildings. It's about A$33 to city hotels, and A$31 to Kings Cross.

A chauffeured limousine to the city hotels costs about A$80. Waiting time is charged at the rate of A$72 per hour. Astra Chauffeured Limousines has reliable services.

AirportLink ☎ 13-1500 ⊕ www.airportlink.com.au. **Astra Chauffeured Limousines** ☎ 1800/819797. **Transport Info Line (City Rail)** ☎ 13-1500.

BOAT & FERRY TRAVEL

Cunard, Holland America Line, Crystal Cruises, and P&O cruise ships call frequently at Sydney as part of their South Pacific itineraries. Passenger ships generally berth at the Overseas Passenger Terminal at Circular Quay. The terminal sits in the shadow of Harbour Bridge, close to many of the city's major attractions as well as to the bus, ferry, and train networks. Otherwise, passenger ships berth at the Darling Harbour Passenger Terminal, a short walk from the city center.

There is no finer introduction to the city than a trip aboard one of the commuter ferries that ply Sydney Harbour. The hub of the ferry system is Circular Quay, and ferries dock at the almost 30 wharves—which span the length and breadth of the harbor—between about 6 AM and 11:30 PM. One of the most popular sightseeing trips is the Manly ferry, a 30-minute journey from Circular Quay that provides glimpses of harborside mansions and the sandstone cliffs and bushland along the north shore. On the return journey, consider taking the JetCat, which skims the waves in an exhilarating 15-minute trip back to the city. But be warned: passengers are not allowed on deck, and the views are obscured.

The one-way Manly ferry fare is A$6, and the JetCat costs A$7.90. Fares for shorter inner-harbor journeys start at A$4.80. You can also buy economical ferry-and-entrance-fee passes, available from the Circular Quay ticket office, to such attractions as Taronga Zoo and Sydney Aquarium.

The sleek RiverCat ferries travel west from Circular Quay as far as Parramatta. These ferries are used overwhelmingly by commuters, although they also provide a useful and practical connection to Homebush Bay, site of Sydney Olympic Park. A one-way fare to Olympic Park is A$6.

A fun, fast, but somewhat expensive way to get around is by water taxi. (Circular Quay to Watsons Bay, for example, costs A$65 for two people.) These operate to and from practically anywhere on Sydney Harbour that has wharf or steps access.

The *Spirit of Tasmania III* passenger and vehicle ferry runs between Sydney and Devonport, in northern Tasmania. The vessel departs from Sydney's Darling Harbour thrice weekly mid-December to mid-January (Sunday, Tuesday, and Thursday), arriving in Devonport the following day; twice weekly September to mid-December and mid-January to

April; and weekly June to August. One-way fares run from A$160 for a hostel-style berth in off-peak season to A$340 per person for a double porthole cabin in peak season. Standard-size cars are transported for A$55. On-board facilities include restaurants, a movie theater, and a play area.

🚢 Cruise Ships Crystal Cruises ☎ 02/8247-7100. **Cunard** ☎ 13-2469. **Holland America Line** ☎ 02/8296-7072. **Overseas Passenger Terminal** ☎ 02/9299-5868. **P&O** ☎ 13-2469.

🚢 Ferries *Spirit of Tasmania III* ✉ Station pier, Port Melbourne ☎ 13-2010 or 1800/634906 ⊕ www.spiritoftasmania.com.au ✉ Berth 1, the Esplanade, Devonport ☎ 13-2010 or 1800/634906 ✉ Berth 7, 47–51 Hickson Rd., Darling Harbour ☎ 13-2010 or 1800/634906. **Transport Info Line (ferries)** ☎ 13-1500 ⊕ www.sydneyferries.info.

🚢 Water Taxis Harbour Taxi Boats ☎ 02/9555-1155. **Taxis Afloat** ☎ 02/9955-3222.

BUS TRAVEL TO & FROM SYDNEY

Greyhound Australia and Murrays bus services are available to all major cities from Sydney. Firefly Express caters mainly to backpackers. You can purchase tickets for long-distance buses from travel agents, by telephone with a credit card, or at bus terminals. Approximate travel times by bus are: Sydney to Canberra, 4 hours; Sydney to Melbourne, 11 hours; Sydney to Brisbane, 11 hours; Sydney to Adelaide, 13 hours. The main terminal is the Central Station (Eddy Avenue) terminus just south of the city center. Lockers are available in the terminal.

🚌 Firefly Express ☎ 1300/730740 ⊕ www.fireflyexpress.com.au. **Greyhound Australia** ☎ 13-1499 ⊕ www.greyhound.com.au. **Murrays** ☎ 13-2251 ⊕ www.murrays.com.au.

BUS TRAVEL WITHIN SYDNEY

Bus travel in Sydney is rather slow because of the city's congested streets and undulating terrain. Fares are calculated by the number of city sections traveled. The minimum two-section bus fare (A$1.60) applies to trips throughout the inner-city area. You would pay the minimum fare, for example, for a ride from Circular Quay to Kings Cross, or from Park Street to Oxford Street in Paddington. Tickets may be purchased from the driver, who will compute the fare based on your destination. Discounted fares are available in several forms, including Travelten passes (valid for 10 journeys), which start at A$12.70 and are available from bus stations and most newsagents.

🚌 Transport Info Line ☎ 13-1500 ⊕ www.sydneybuses.info.

CAR RENTAL

If you rent from a major international company, expect to pay about A$85 per day for a medium-size automatic and about A$75 for a standard compact. However, if you go with a local operator, such as Bayswater, you might pay as little as A$25 per day if you're prepared to shift gears on a slightly older vehicle with higher mileage (usually one or two years old). Some of these discount operators restrict travel to within a 50-km (30-mi) radius of the city center, and one-way rentals are not possible. A surcharge applies if you pick up your car from the airport.

🚗 Avis ☎ 13-6333. **Bayswater** ☎ 02/9360-3622. **Budget** ☎ 13-2727. **Hertz** ☎ 13-3039. **Thrifty** ☎ 13-6139.

CAR TRAVEL

With the assistance of a good road map or street directory, you shouldn't have too many problems driving in and out of Sydney, thanks to a decent freeway system. Keep in mind that Australia is almost as large as the United States minus Alaska. In computing your travel times for trips between Sydney and the following cities, allow for an average speed of about 85 kph (53 mph). The main roads to and from other state capitals are: the 982-km (609-mi) Pacific Highway (Highway 1) north to Brisbane; the 335-km (208-mi) Hume Highway (Highway 31) southwest to Canberra, and 874 km (542 mi) to Melbourne; also the 1,038-km (644-mi) Princes Highway (Highway 1) to the New South Wales south coast and Melbourne. Adelaide is 1,425 km (884 mi) away via the Hume and Sturt (Highway 20) highways, and Perth is a long and rather tedious 4,132-km (2,562-mi) drive via Adelaide.

Driving a car around Sydney is not recommended. Close to the city the harbor inlets plus the hilly terrain equal few straight streets. Parking space is limited, and both parking lots and parking meters are expensive. If you do decide to drive, ask your car-rental agency for a street directory or purchase one from a newsstand.

For details on emergency assistance, gasoline, road conditions, and rules of the road, *see* Car Travel *in* Smart Travel Tips A to Z.

CONSULATES

ⓘ **British Consulate General** ✉ Level 16, Gateway Bldg., 1 Macquarie Pl., Circular Quay ☎ 02/9247-7521. **Canadian Consulate General** ✉ Level 5, 111 Harrington St., The Rocks ☎ 02/9364-3000. **New Zealand Consulate General** ✉ Level 10, 55 Hunter St., City Center ☎ 02/9223-0222. **United States of America Consulate General** ✉ Level 59, 19-29 Martin Pl., City Center ☎ 02/9373-9200.

DISCOUNTS & DEALS

For the price of admission to two or three top attractions, the SmartVisit Card (available from the Sydney Visitor Centre in the Rocks, through the Web site, and from several other locations listed on the Web site) gets you into 40 Sydney sights and attractions—including the Opera House, Sydney Aquarium, and Koala Park Sanctuary. Several different cards are available, including single-day and weekly cards. Cards may also include public transportation. Prices start at A$65 for a single-day adult card without transportation.

SydneyPass (⇨ Transportation Around Sydney) allows unlimited travel on public transportation for between three and seven days. Passes start at A$100.

ⓘ **SmartVisit Card** ☎ 02/9960-3511 ⊕ www.seesydneycard.com. **SydneyPass** ☎ 13-1500 ⊕ www.sydneypass.info.

EMERGENCIES

Dial **000** for an ambulance, the fire department, or the police. Dental Emergency Information Service provides names and numbers for nearby dentists. It's available only after 7 PM daily. Royal North Shore Hospital is 7 km (4½ mi) northwest of the city center. St. Vincent's Public Hospital is 2½ km (1½ mi) east of the city center.

Your best bet for a late-night pharmacy is in the major ⬛
the Kings Cross and Oxford Street (Darlinghurst) areas. S⬛
overnight pharmacies work on a rotating basis, call the Pharm⬛
for 24-hour advice and referrals to the nearest open outlet.

🔂 **Dentist Dental Emergency** ☎ 02/9211-2224.

🔂 **Hospitals Royal North Shore Hospital** ✉ Pacific Hwy., St. Leonards ☎ 02/9926-⬛
St. Vincent's Public Hospital ✉ Victoria and Burton Sts., Darlinghurst ☎ 02/8382-111⬛

🔂 **Pharmacies Pharmacy Guild** ☎ 02/9966-8377.

🔂 **Police Bondi Beach** ✉ 77 Gould St., Bondi Beach ☎ 02/9365-9699. **City Central**
✉ 192 Day St., Darlinghurst ☎ 02/9265-6499. **Kings Cross** ✉ 1-15 Elizabeth Bay Rd.,
Kings Cross ☎ 02/8356-0099. **Manly** ✉ 3 Belgrave St., Manly ☎ 02/9977-9499. **The
Rocks** ✉ 132 George St., The Rocks ☎ 02/8220-6399.

MAIL, SHIPPING & THE INTERNET

If you need business services, such as faxing, using a computer, photo-
copying, typing, or translation services during your trip, plan to stay in
a hotel with a business center, since their services are normally available only to guests.

DHL and Federal Express both ship internationally overnight.

🔂 **Internet Cafés Global Gossip** ✉ 415 Pitt St., City Center ☎ 02/9281-6890 📠 111
Darlinghurst Rd., Kings Cross ☎ 02/9326-9777. **Hotel Sweeney's Internet Cafe** ✉ Level
2, 236 Clarence St., City Center ☎ 02/9261-5666. **Phone Net Café** ✉ 73-75 Hall St.,
Bondi Beach ☎ 02/9365-0681. **Surfnet Internet Cafe** ✉ 54 Spring St., Bondi Junction ☎ 02/9386-4066.

🔂 **Post Offices General Post Office** ✉ 1 Martin Pl., City Center ☎ 13-1318. **Glebe Post
Office** ✉ 181A Glebe Point Rd., Glebe ☎ 13-1318. **Kings Cross Post Office** ✉ Shop
501-502, Kingsgate Hotel, Victoria and William Sts., Kings Cross ☎ 13-1318.

🔂 **Overnight Shipping Services DHL** ☎ 13-1406 ⊕ www.dhl.com.au. **Federal Express**
☎ 13-2610 ⊕ www.fedex.com.au.

MONEY MATTERS

Any bank will exchange traveler's checks and most foreign currencies.
ATMs are ubiquitous in airports, shopping malls, and tourist areas. Cirrus and Plus cards are accepted at most ATMs, but check with your bank
to make sure that you can access your funds overseas and that you have
a four-digit PIN. Banks can be found in all areas where you are likely
to shop, including the city center, Kings Cross, Paddington, Double Bay,
and Darling Harbour.

🔂 **ANZ** ✉ 365 George St. City Center ☎ 13-1314. **Commonwealth Bank** ✉ 254 George
St. City Center ☎ 02/9241-6855. **Westpac Bank** ✉ 60 Martin Pl. City Center ☎ 13-2032.

MONORAIL & TRAM TRAVEL

Sydney Monorail is one of the fastest, most relaxing forms of public transportation in the city, but its use is limited to travel between the city center, Darling Harbour, and Chinatown. The fare is A$4 per one-way trip.
The A$8 Day Pass is a better value if you intend to use the monorail to
explore. You can purchase tickets at machines in the monorail stations.
The monorail operates every three to five minutes, generally from 7 AM
to 10 PM, and until midnight on Friday and Saturday. Stations are identified by a large white M against a black background.

… Light Rail, identifiable by signs with a large black M against … kground, is a limited system that provides a fast, efficient … n Central Station, Darling Harbour, the Star City casino and … nt complex, Sydney fish markets, and the inner-western … Glebe and Lilyfield. The modern, air-conditioned tram cars …)- to 30-minute intervals, 24 hours a day. One-way tickets … o A$3.90, and the Day Pass is a comparatively good value … You can purchase tickets at machines in Light Rail stations.

Metro Monorail and Light Rail ☎ 02/9285–5600 ⊕ www.metromonorail.com.au.

SIGHTSEEING TOURS

Dozens of tour operators lead guided trips through Sydney and the surrounding areas. Options include shopping strolls, tours of the Sydney fish markets, and rappelling the waterfalls of the Blue Mountains. The Sydney Visitors Information Centre and other booking and information centers can provide you with many more suggestions and recommendations. Most suburban shopping plazas have a travel agency—in addition to the many general and specialist travel agents in the city center.

BOAT TOURS **Fodor's Choice ★** The Sydney Harbour Explorer cruise, run by Captain Cook Cruises, allows you to disembark at the Opera House, Watsons Bay, Taronga Zoo, or Darling Harbour and catch any following Captain Cook explorer vessel throughout the day. Four Explorer cruises (A$27) depart daily from Circular Quay at 9:45 AM, 11:30 AM and then every two hours. The best introductory trip to Sydney Harbor is Captain Cook's 2½-hour Coffee Cruise, which follows the southern shore to Watsons Bay, crosses to the north shore to explore Middle Harbour, and returns to Circular Quay. Coffee cruises (A$44) depart daily at 10 and 2:15. Dinner, sunset, and showtime cruises are also available, and all cruises depart from Wharf 6, Circular Quay.

The State Transit Authority runs several Harboursights cruises aboard harbor ferries, at lower costs than those of privately operated cruises. Light refreshments are available on board. All cruises depart from Wharf 4 at the Circular Quay terminal. The Morning Harbour Cruise (A$18), a 1-hour journey, takes in the major sights of the harbor to the east of the city. The boat departs daily at 10:30. The Afternoon Harbour Cruise (A$24) is a leisurely 2½-hour tour that takes in the scenic eastern suburbs and affluent Middle Harbour. Tours leave weekdays at 1 and weekends at 12:30. The 1½-hour Evening Harbour Lights Cruise (A$22) takes you into Darling Harbour for a nighttime view of the city from the west, then passes the Garden Island naval base to view the Opera House and Kings Cross. Tours depart Monday through Saturday at 8 PM.

Captain Cook Cruises ☎ 02/9206–1122 ⊕ www.captaincook.com.au/sydney. **State Transit Authority** ☎ 13–1500 ⊕ www.sydneypass.info/harboursights.

BUS TOURS The only guided bus tour of the inner city is the Sydney Explorer bus, which makes a 35-km (22-mi) circuit of all the major attractions, including the Rocks, Kings Cross, Darling Harbour, Chinatown, and across Harbour Bridge to Milsons Point. Ticket holders can board or leave the bus at any of the 26 stops along the route and catch any following Explorer bus. The bright red buses follow one another every 18 minutes, and the service operates from 8:40 AM daily. The last bus to make the circuit departs from Circular Quay at 5:20 PM. If you choose to stay on board for the entire circuit, the trip takes around 100 minutes.

The Bondi Explorer bus runs a guided bus tour of the eastern suburbs. The blue bus begins its 30-km (19-mi) journey at Circular Quay and travels through Kings Cross, Double Bay, Vaucluse, and Watsons Bay to the Gap, then returns to the city via Bondi, Bronte, and Coogee beaches; Centennial Park; and Oxford Street. You can leave the bus at any of its 19 stops and catch a following bus, or remain on board for a round-trip of about 90 minutes. Buses follow one another at 30-minute intervals beginning at 8:45 AM. The last bus departs from Circular Quay at 4:15 PM.

Tickets for either Explorer bus, valid for one day, cost A$36 and can be purchased on board or from the New South Wales Travel Centre.

Several bus companies run day trips in and around the Sydney region, reaching as far as the Blue Mountains, the Hunter Valley wine region, Canberra, wildlife parks, and the 2000 Olympics site at Homebush Bay. ATT and Murrays both have a 24-hour information and reservation service.

🛈 AAT Kings ☎ 1300/556100. **Murrays Australia** ☎ 13-2251. **New South Wales Travel Centre** ✉ 11-31 York St., City Center ☎ 13-2077. **State Transit Authority, Explorer Bus routes** ☎ 13-1500 🌐 www.sydneybuses.info.

PARK & BUSH TOURS
Mount 'n Beach Safaris is a four-wheel-drive operator that arranges soft adventures to areas of outstanding beauty around Sydney. The company's Blue Mountains 4WD Wildlife Discovery gives you the chance to see koalas and kangaroos, enjoy morning tea in the bush, take in the scenic highlights of the Blue Mountains, lunch at a historic pub, and return to Sydney in time for a performance at the Opera House. Their Best of Hunter Wines & Dolphins tour of the Hunter Valley wine-growing district and the aquatic playground of Port Stephens is a two-day option.

🛈 Mount 'n Beach Safaris ☎ 02/9267-5899 🌐 www.mountnbeachsafaris.com.au.

SPECIAL INTEREST TOURS
BridgeClimb is a unique tour that affords the ultimate view of the harbor and city center. Wearing a special suit and harnessed to a static line, you can ascend the steel arch of the Sydney Harbour Bridge in the company of a guide. The hugely popular tour lasts for 3½ hours and costs from A$160 per person. Tours depart from 5 Cumberland Street, the Rocks. Twilight climbs (A$225) and night climbs are also available.

Easyrider Motorbike Tours conducts exciting chauffeur-driven (you ride as a passenger) Harley-Davidson tours to the city's beaches, the Blue Mountains, Royal National Park, Hawkesbury River, and the Hunter Valley wineries. A two-hour tour costs A$190 per person, and a full-day excursion starts at about A$400.

🛈 BridgeClimb ☎ 02/8274-7777 🌐 www.bridgeclimb.com.au. **Easyrider Motorbike Tours** ☎ 1300/882065 🌐 www.easyrider.com.au.

The Rocks Walking Tours will introduce you to Sydney's European set-tlement site, with an emphasis on the neighborhood buildings and per-sonalities of the convict period. The 1½-hour tour costs A$19 and involves little climbing. Tours leave weekdays at 10:30, 12:30, and 2:30 (in January 10:30 and 2:30 only), and weekends at 11:30 and 2.

Sydney Guided Tours with Maureen Fry are an excellent introduction to Sydney. Standard tours (two hours) cost A$18 and cover the colo-nial buildings along Macquarie Street, a ramble through the historic wa-terside suburbs of Glebe and Balmain, or Circular Quay and the Rocks. Theme tours include art galleries, food and markets, heritage hotels, and a tour of the Opera Centre, where operas are rehearsed before they move to the Sydney Opera House.

🚩 **The Rocks Walking Tours** ✉ 23 Playfair St., The Rocks ☎ 02/9247-6678 ⊕ www. rockswalkingtours.com.au. **Sydney Guided Tours** ☎ 02/9660-7157 🖷 02/9660-0805 ⊕ www.ozemail.com.au/mpfry.

TAXIS & LIMOUSINES

Taxis are a relatively economical way to cover short to medium distances in Sydney. A 3-km (2-mi) trip from Circular Quay to the eastern sub-urbs costs around A$16. Drivers are entitled to charge more than the metered fare if the passenger's baggage exceeds 55 pounds, if the taxi has been booked by telephone, or if the passenger crosses Harbour Bridge, where a toll is levied. Fares are 10% higher between 10 PM and 5 AM, when the numeral "2" will be displayed in the tariff indicator on the meter. At all other times, make sure the numeral "1" is displayed. Taxis are licensed to carry four passengers. Most drivers will accept pay-ment by American Express, Diners Club, MasterCard, and Visa, although a 10% surcharge is applied. Taxis can be hailed on the street, hired from a taxi stand, or booked by phone. Taxi stands can be found outside most bus and railway stations, as well as outside the larger hotels. Complaints should be directed to Taxi Cab Complaints.

Chauffeur-driven limousines are available for trips around Sydney. At your request, the driver will give commentary on the major sights. Limousines can be rented for approximately A$80 per hour.

🚩 **Limousine Company Astra Chauffeured Limousines** ☎ 1800/819797.
🚩 **Taxi Companies ABC Taxis** ☎ 13-2522. **Taxi Cab Complaints** ☎ 1800/648478.
Taxis Combined Services ☎ 02/8332-8888.

TELEPHONES

The telephone code for Sydney and New South Wales is 02. If you're calling a New South Wales number that is a nonlocal call, dial 02 be-fore the eight-digit local number. You can make interstate and interna-tional calls from any telephone. To make an interstate call, use the following codes: Australian Capital Territory (ACT), 02; Northern Ter-ritory (NT), 08; Queensland (QLD), 07; South Australia (SA), 08; Tas-mania (TAS), 03; Victoria (VIC), 03; and Western Australia (WA), 08. Public telephones are found throughout the city. The cost of a local call is 40¢. Some public phones will accept coins; more will accept phone cards, which are available in units of A$5, A$10, A$20, and A$50 from post offices and businesses that display the yellow PHONECARD sign.

TRAIN TRAVEL

The main terminal for long-distance and intercity trains is Central Station, about 2 km (1 mi) south of the city center. Two daily services (morning and evening) operate between Sydney and Melbourne; the trip takes about 11 hours. Two *Explorer* trains make the 4-hour trip to Canberra daily. The overnight *Brisbane XPT* makes the 15-hour Sydney–Brisbane journey every day. Call the state rail authority, Countrylink, between 6:30 AM and 10 PM daily for information about fares and timetables, or check the Countrylink Web site. The *Indian-Pacific* (operated by Great Southern Railways) leaves Sydney on Wednesday and Saturday afternoons for Adelaide (26 hours) and Perth (64 hours).

Tickets for long-distance train travel can be purchased from Countrylink Travel Centres at Central Station, Circular Quay, Wynyard Station, and Town Hall Station.

For journeys in excess of 7 km (4½ mi), Sydney's trains are considerably faster than buses. However, the City Rail network has been designed primarily for rapid transit between outlying suburbs and the city. Apart from the City Circle line, which includes the Circular Quay and Town Hall stations and the spur line to Kings Cross and Bondi Junction, the system does not serve areas of particular interest to tourists. If you plan on using the trains, remember the following axioms: all trains pass through Central Station; Town Hall is the "shoppers" station; the bus, ferry, and train systems converge at Circular Quay. Trains generally operate from 4:30 AM to midnight.

As an example of fare prices, a one-way ticket from Town Hall Station to Bondi Junction costs A$2.80. Several discounted fares are also available, including off-peak tickets that apply on weekends and after 9 AM on weekdays.

🚆 **Central Station** ⊠ Eddy Ave., City South. **City Rail** ☎ 13-1500 ⊕ www.cityrail.nsw. gov.au. **Countrylink Travel Centres** ⊠ Eddy Ave., Central Station, City South ⊠ Shop W6/W7, Alfred St., Circular Quay ⊠ Shop W15, Wynyard Concourse, Wynyard Station, City Center ⊠ Lower level, Queen Victoria Bldg., George and Park Sts., Town Hall Station, City Center ☎ 13-2232 ⊕ www.countrylink.nsw.gov.au. **Great Southern Railways** ☎ 13-2147 ⊕ www.gsr.com.au/indian

TRANSPORTATION AROUND SYDNEY

Despite its vast size, Sydney packs its primary attractions into a fairly small area. For the most part, public transportation is an efficient, economical way to see the city. Getting to and from such areas as the Rocks, Darling Harbour, and the Opera House is simple on Sydney's buses, ferries, and trains, except during rush hours. Once you're there, these areas are best explored on foot.

A TravelPass allows unlimited travel aboard buses, ferries, and trains, but not trams, within designated areas of the city for a week or more. The most useful is probably the weeklong Red TravelPass (A$32), which covers the city and eastern suburbs and inner-harbor ferries. (Ferries to Manly and Sydney Olympic Park cost extra.) TravelPasses are available from railway and bus stations and from most newsagents on bus routes.

If you're planning on spending three days or fewer in Sydney and taking the AirportLink rail service, the guided Sydney Explorer and Bondi Explorer buses, and any of the three sightseeing cruises operated by the State Transit Authority, SydneyPass (A$100 for three days; five- and seven-day passes available) will save you money. In addition to unlimited travel on all these services, the pass also allows unlimited travel on any public bus or harbor ferry and on most suburban train services. Purchase passes from the Tourism New South Wales counter on the ground floor of the international airport terminal or from the driver of any Explorer bus.

For route, timetable, and ticket price information on Sydney's buses, ferries, and trains call the State Transit Infoline, daily 6 AM–10 PM.
🚹 **State Transit Infoline** ☎ 13-1500 ⊕ www.sydneybuses.nsw.gov.au.

TRAVEL AGENCIES
The following travel agencies can help you arrange tours and excursions.
🚹 **American Express Travel Shop** ✉ 105 Pitt St., City Center ☎ 02/9236-4222. **Flight Centre** ✉ Shop 509, Kingsgate Centre, Darlinghurst Rd., Kings Cross ✉ 2/255 Elizabeth St., Hyde Park ☎ 02/9360-3800. **STA Travel** ✉ 855 George St., City Center ☎ 02/9212-1255. **Student Flights** ✉ 55-73 Oxford St., Darlinghurst ☎ 1800/069063. **YHA Travel Centre** ✉ 422 Kent St., City Center ☎ 02/9261-1111.

VISITOR INFORMATION
There are tourist information booths throughout the city, including Circular Quay, Martin Place, Darling Harbour, and the Pitt Street Mall.

Countrylink, the state rail authority, is a good source of Sydney and New South Wales travel information.

The Sydney Visitor Centre is the major source of information, brochures, and maps for Sydney and New South Wales.

The CitySearch Web site is a great resource for the latest on Sydney's arts, food, and nightlife scene. The Discover Sydney Web site also has accommodation and food guides, maps and what's on.
🚹 **CitySearch** ⊕ www.sydney.citysearch.com.au. **Countrylink** ✉ Shop W15, Wynyard Concourse, Wynyard Station, City Center ☎ 13-2829 ⊕ www.countrylink.info. **Discover Sydney** ⊕ www.discoversydney.com.au. **Sydney Visitor Centre** ✉ 106 George St., The Rocks ✉ 33 Wheat Rd., Darling Harbour ☎ 02/9255-1788 ⊕ www. sydneyvisitorcentre.com.

New South Wales

WORD OF MOUTH

"[If you like] to cuddle in front of the fire, drink mulled wine, eat fantastic stodgy food like baked puddings and . . . pot roasts, be able to hike to your heart's content without getting hot and uncomfortable and to get out there in nature's wilds and enjoy yourself . . . there is nowhere better than the Blue Mountains within a 5-hour drive from Sydney."

—lizF

Updated by
Melanie Ball

FOR MANY TRAVELERS, SYDNEY *IS* NEW SOUTH WALES, and they look to the other, less-populated states for Australia's famous wilderness experiences. There may be no substitute for Queensland's Great Barrier Reef or the Northern Territory's Kakadu National Park, but New South Wales has many of Australia's natural wonders within its borders. High on the list are the World Heritage areas of Lord Howe Island and the subtropical rain forests of the North Coast, as well as desert Outback, the highest mountain peaks in the country, moist river valleys, warm seas, golden beaches, and some of Australia's finest vineyards.

New South Wales was named by Captain James Cook during his voyage of discovery in 1770: the area's low, rounded hills reminded him of southern Wales. It was the first state to be settled by the British, whose plan to establish a penal colony at Botany Bay in 1788 was scrapped in favor of a site a short distance to the north—Sydney Cove. Successive waves of convicts helped swell the state's population, but the discovery in 1850 of gold at Bathurst on the western edge of the Great Dividing Range sparked a population explosion. The state's economic might was further strengthened by the discovery of huge coal seams in the Hunter Valley, and by the rich nickel, silver, and lead deposits at Broken Hill. Timber and wool industries also thrived.

Today, with approximately 6.7 million people, New South Wales is Australia's most populous state. Although this is crowded by Australian standards, it's worth remembering that New South Wales is larger than every U.S. state except Alaska. In the state's east, a coastal plain reaching north to Queensland varies in width from less than a mile to almost 160 km (100 mi). This plain is bordered to the west by a chain of low mountains known as the Great Dividing Range, which tops off at about 7,300 feet in the Snowy Mountains in the state's far south. On this range's western slopes is a belt of pasture and farmland. Beyond that are the western plains and Outback, an arid, sparsely populated region that takes up two-thirds of the state.

Eighty kilometers (50 mi) west of Sydney in the Great Dividing Range are the Blue Mountains, a rippling sea of hills covered by tall eucalyptus trees and dissected by deep river valleys—the perfect terrain for hiking and adventure activities. The mountains are also famous for their charming guesthouses and lush, cool-climate gardens. About 100 km (62 mi) south of Sydney, the Southern Highlands are a cool upland region that is geographically similar to the Blue Mountains. The difference here is a more genteel atmosphere, and the added attraction of the nearby temperate South Coast beaches. The Hunter Valley region, about 240 km (150 mi) northwest of Sydney, draws visitors for its wineries, food, historic towns, and tranquil countryside.

The North Coast stretches almost 600 km (373 mi) up to the Queensland border, and its seaside delights contrast with the rest of the state's rural splendor. With its sandy beaches, surf, and warm climate, the area is a perfect holiday playground. Finally, a tiny, remote speck in the Pacific Ocean, Lord Howe Island is the state's tropical island oasis, ringed with fringing coral, stacked with towering, forested volcanic peaks, and teeming with seabirds and marine life.

It's wise to decide in advance whether you'd like to cover a lot of ground quickly or choose one or two places to linger a while. If you have four days or fewer, stick close to Sydney. The most compelling choice would be the Blue Mountains, followed by the Hunter Valley or Southern Highlands. In a very busy week you could visit the Blue and Snowy mountains, plus either the Hunter Valley or Southern Highlands. Two weeks would allow a Blue Mountains–North Coast–Lord Howe circuit, or brief stops in most of the six regions.

2

If you have 4 days Start with a visit to the **Blue Mountains.** You could arrange a round-trip itinerary from Sydney in a fairly hectic day or, preferably, spend a night in **Katoomba, Blackheath,** or **Leura** and make it a two-day excursion. Return to Sydney, and then head north to the **Hunter Valley.** A two-day/one-night driving visit here would allow you enough time to see the main sights and spend time touring the wineries before traveling back to Sydney on the last day. An alternative would be a quick visit to the Blue Mountains, then a tour of the **Southern Highlands.** Lord Howe Island is a unique experience; its beaches, scenery, animal life, and quirky character set it apart from the rest of the state. Four days would be just sufficient for a visit.

If you have 7 days Head to the Blue Mountains and Hunter Valley as described above, then continue to the North Coast. In three days of driving you wouldn't get much farther than **Coffs Harbour ⓯** (with overnights there and in **Port Macquarie ⓬**), and this would be rushing it, but it's possible to fly back to Sydney from Coffs. If the North Coast holds special appeal, head straight there from Sydney and give yourself a chance to take in more of it. You could also spend three days in the Southern Highlands, then continue south to the Snowy Mountains for some alpine air, trout fishing, and bushwalking in Australia's highest alpine region.

If you have 14 days Divide and conquer: choose three areas and give yourself four days in each, taking into account travel time between them to round out the fortnight. The following combinations would allow for optimal encounters with the varied best of the state: wine, water, and wide-open spaces with the **Hunter Valley–North Coast–Snowy Mountains;** rocks, rain forests, and reefs with the **Blue Mountains–North Coast–Lord Howe Island;** or a watery triad of the **South Coast–North Coast–Lord Howe.**

Exploring New South Wales

New South Wales covers a large area that can broadly be divided into six popular regions. The Blue Mountains lie to the west of Sydney, while the Southern Highlands and South Coast stretch to the southwest, and the Hunter Valley dips north of the capital. The North Coast is exactly where its name suggests, while Lord Howe Island is 700 km (435 mi) northeast of Sydney, a distant offshore environment of its own. At the state's south edge are the Snowy Mountains, part of the Great Dividing Range, which parallels the New South Wales coastline from the northern state of Queensland to the southern state of Victoria.

There are good highways and paved rural roads connecting these major points, and driving is convenient and easy once you're outside Sydney. Although you can experience the Hunter Valley, the Southern Highlands, and the Blue Mountains on an organized day trip from Sydney, you'll get far more out of the experience if you stay at least one night. Bicycling is also an option along the scenic back roads and valleys of these three areas, and mountain-biking enthusiasts will find much to challenge them in the Blue Mountains. A bus network makes exploring an option for budget travelers. Trains run from Sydney north to Brisbane and south to Melbourne, providing access to the North Coast and the Snowy Mountains regions. You can fly to Lord Howe Island in about two hours from Sydney.

About the Restaurants

Dining varies dramatically throughout New South Wales, from superb city-standard restaurants to average country-town fare. As popular weekend retreats for well-heeled Sydneysiders, the Blue Mountains and Southern Highlands have a number of fine restaurants and cozy tea rooms that are perfect for light lunches or afternoon teas. In the Hunter Valley, several excellent restaurants show off the region's fine wines. And although the Snowy Mountains area isn't gastronomically distinguished, the succulent trout makes a standout meal.

In spite of the North Coast's excellent seafood and exotic fruits, fine dining is rare away from such major resort centers as Coffs Harbour and Port Macquarie. The small northern town of Byron Bay stands out, however, for its sophisticated cafés and restaurants. Despite its minuscule size and isolation, Lord Howe Island attracts a polished and well-heeled clientele who demand a high standard of dining. At restaurants throughout New South Wales, reservations are always a good idea.

WHAT IT COSTS In Australian dollars				
	$$$$	**$$$**	**$$**	**$**	**¢**
AT DINNER	over $50	$36–$50	$21–$35	$10–$20	under $10

Prices are per person for a main course at dinner.

About the Hotels

Accommodations include everything from run-of-the-mill motels to wilderness lodges, and from historic, cliff-perched properties in the Blue Mountains to large, glossy seaside resorts. Rates are often much lower on weekdays, particularly in the Blue Mountains, Hunter Valley, and Southern Highlands. In the Snowy Mountains prices are highest during the winter ski season, and some hotels close during the off-season (October through May). Although chains aren't typical, an upscale group of small Peppers resorts is scattered across the state and tends to have particularly lovely settings.

2

Flora & Fauna
Although you can get a close-up view of Australia's extraordinary plants and animals in the parks close to Sydney, nothing compares with seeing them in the wild. Exotic birds are prolific in the Blue Mountains and North Coast regions, while Lord Howe Island is a bird-watcher's paradise. Spring is the season for wildflowers. Kangaroos and emus are frequently seen in more isolated rural areas, especially in the evening.

The Great Australian Bite
Fine restaurants have taken root in the Hunter Valley wine region, as well as in the North Coast towns of Coffs Harbour and Byron Bay. Seafood can be excellent, although in many coastal towns the best you can hope for is fish-and-chips on the beach. Yuletide is celebrated from June to August in many hotels and guesthouse in the Blue Mountains, when feasts of stuffed turkey, Christmas cake, and fruit puddings are reminiscent of an English Christmas.

The Great Outdoors
The mountains and national parks of New South Wales are great spots for scenic walks and hikes, horseback riding, mountain biking, rappelling, canyoning, and rock climbing. Deep in the south of the state, the Snowy Mountains—Australia's winter playground—afford excellent cross-country skiing in particular. The North and South coasts are the place to go for surfing, snorkeling, scuba diving, and boating. The Blue Mountains, Lord Howe Island, and the rain forests of the Great Dividing Range are all included on UNESCO's World Heritage list.

Wineries
The Hunter Valley, the state's largest grape-growing region, has more than 120 wineries and an international reputation for producing excellent chardonnay, shiraz, and a dry semillon. Many well-known vineyards are based near the village of Pokolbin, where there are also antiques shops and art galleries.

WHAT IT COSTS In Australian dollars				
$$$$	**$$$**	**$$**	**$**	**¢**
FOR 2 PEOPLE over $300	$201–$300	$151–$200	$100–$150	under $100

Prices are for two people in a standard double room in high season, including tax and service, based on the European Plan (with no meals) unless otherwise noted.

When to Visit New South Wales
For many visitors the Australian summer (approximately December–February), which complements the northern winter, has great pull. The Blue Mountains and Southern Highlands provide relief from Sydney's sometimes stifling humidity, and it's the ideal season for bushwalking in the cool Snowy Mountains. The best times to visit the Hunter Valley are during the February–March grape harvest season and the September Hunter Food and Wine Festival.

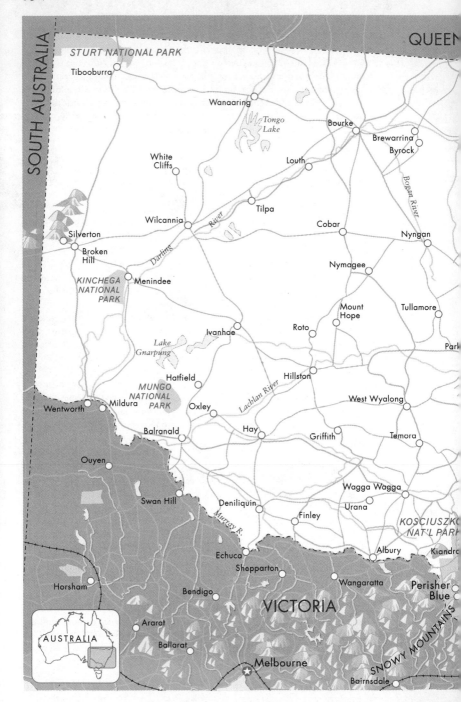

SOUTH AUSTRALIA

STURT NATIONAL PARK

Tibooburra

QUEEN

Wanaaring

Tongo
Lake

Bourke

Brewarrina

Byrock

White
Cliffs

Louth

Bogan River

Wilcannia

Tilpa

River

Cobar

Nyngan

Silverton

Darling

Nymagee

Broken
Hill

KINCHEGA
NATIONAL
PARK

Menindee

Mount
Hope

Tullamore

Lake
Gnarpung

Ivanhoe

Roto

Park

Hatfield

Hillston

MUNGO
NATIONAL
PARK

West Wyalong

Wentworth

Mildura

Oxley

Lachlan River

Balranald

Hay

Griffith

Temora

Ouyen

Wagga Wagga

Swan Hill

Deniliquin

Urana

Finley

KOSCIUSZK
NAT'L PARK

Murray R.

Echuca

Albury

Kiandro

Horsham

Shepparton

Wangaratta

Perisher
Blue

AUSTRALIA

Bendigo

VICTORIA

SNOWY MOUNTAINS

Ararat

Ballarat

Melbourne

Bairnsdale

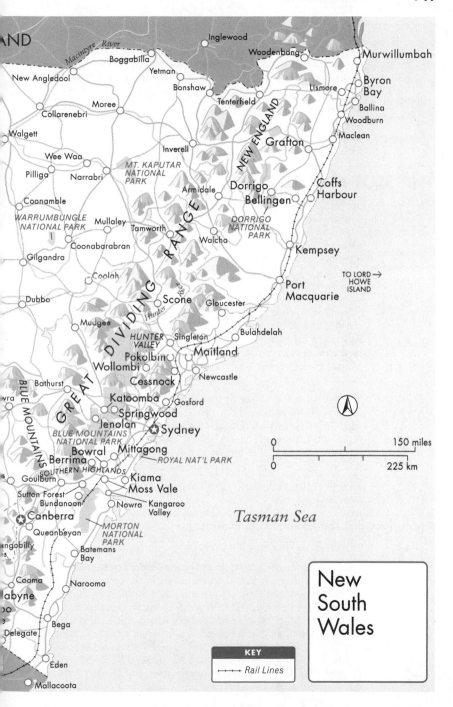

AND

Macintyre River

Inglewood

Woodenbong

Murwillumbah

Boggabilla

Yetman

New Angledool

Bonshaw

Lismore

Byron
Bay

Tenterfield

Ballina

Moree

Woodburn

Collarenebri

NEW ENGLAND

Maclean

Walgett

Inverell

Grafton

Wee Waa

MT. KAPUTAR
NATIONAL
PARK

Pilliga

Narrabri

Coffs
Harbour

Armidale

Dorrigo

Coonamble

Bellingen

WARRUMBUNGLE
NATIONAL PARK

Mullaley

Tamworth

DORRIGO
NATIONAL
PARK

Coonabarabran

Walcha

Gilgandra

Kempsey

RANGE

Coolah

TO LORD →
HOWE
ISLAND

Dubbo

Scone

Gloucester

Port
Macquarie

Mudgee

Hunter

DIVIDING

HUNTER
VALLEY

Singleton

Bulahdelah

Pokolbin

Maitland

Wollombi

Bathurst

Cessnock

Newcastle

GREAT

Katoomba

Gosford

BLUE

Springwood

MOUNTAINS

Jenolan

Sydney

wra

BLUE MOUNTAINS
NATIONAL PARK

Mittagong

150 miles

Bowral

ROYAL NAT'L PARK

Berrima

0

SOUTHERN HIGHLANDS

Kiama

225 km

Goulburn

Moss Vale

Sutton Forest

Kangaroo
Valley

Bundanoon

Nowra

Canberra

Tasman Sea

Queanbeyan

MORTON
NATIONAL
PARK

ngobilly

Batemans
Bay

Cooma

Narooma

abyne

New
South
Wales

Bega

Delegate

Eden

Mallacoota

KEY

┼──┼── *Rail Lines*

The North Coast resort region is often booked solid between Christmas and the first half of January, but autumn (March–May) and spring (September–November) are also good times to visit. Lord Howe Island is driest and hottest in February, while August is the windiest month. Many of the island's hotels and restaurants close between June and August.

There are some wonderful options if you are in New South Wales in winter (officially June, July, and August). The Snowy Mountains ski season runs from early June to early October. And the "Yulefest" season from June through August is a popular time to visit the Blue Mountains, with blazing log fires and Christmas-style celebration packages.

THE BLUE MOUNTAINS

Sydneysiders have been doubly blessed by nature. Not only do they have a magnificent coastline right at their front door, but a 90-minute drive west puts them in the midst of one of the most spectacular wilderness areas in Australia—World Heritage Blue Mountains National Park. Standing 3,500-plus feet high, these "mountains" were once the bed of an ancient sea. Gradually the sedimentary rock was uplifted until it formed a high plateau, which was etched by eons of wind and water into the wonderland of cliffs, caves, and canyons that exists today. Now the richly forested hills, crisp mountain air, cool-climate gardens, vast sandstone chasms, and little towns of timber and stone are supreme examples of Australia's diversity. The mountains' distinctive blue coloring is caused by the evaporation of oil from the dense eucalyptus forests. This disperses light in the blue colors of the spectrum, a phenomenon known as Rayleigh Scattering.

When a railway line from Sydney was completed at the end of the 19th century, the mountains suddenly became fashionable, and guesthouses and hotels flourished. Combined with the dramatic natural beauty of the region, the history and charm of local villages make the Blue Mountains one of the highlights of any tour of Australia. If your schedule allows just one trip out of Sydney, make the Blue Mountains your top priority.

Numbers in the margin correspond to points of interest on the Blue Mountains map.

Springwood & the Lower Blue Mountains

79 km (49 mi) northwest of Sydney.

★ ❶ The National Trust–listed **Norman Lindsay Gallery and Museum**, dedicated to the Australian artist and writer, is one of the cultural highlights of the Blue Mountains. Lindsay is best known for his paintings, etchings, and drawings (featured in the movie *Sirens,* starring other famous Australians Elle MacPherson and Portia di Rossi), but he also built model boats, sculpted, and wrote poetry and children's books, among which *The Magic Pudding* has become an Australian classic. Lindsay lived in this house during the latter part of his life until he died in 1969. The delightful landscaped gardens contain several of Lindsay's sculptures, and you can also take a short but scenic bush walk beyond the garden.

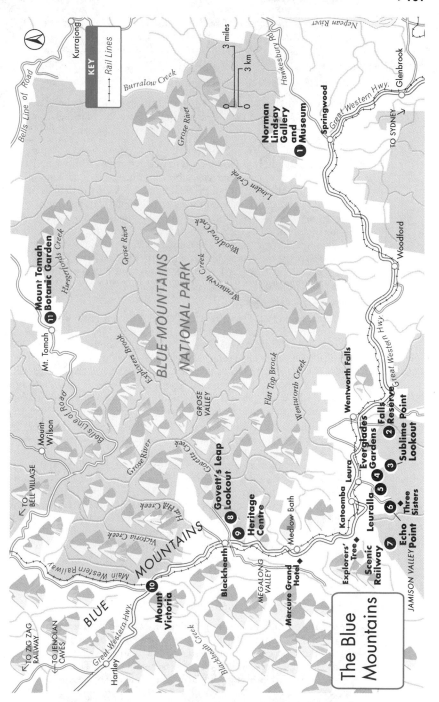

The Blue Mountains

KEY

- Rail Lines

Kurrajong

Bells Line of Road

Burralow Creek

Grose River

Norman Lindsay Gallery and Museum ①

Springwood

Great Western Hwy.

Glenbrook

Nepean River

Hawkesbury Rd.

TO SYDNEY

Linden Creek

Woodford Creek

Woodford

BLUE MOUNTAINS

NATIONAL PARK

Mount Tomah Botanic Garden ⑪

Mt. Tomah

Hartleys Creek

Grose River

Explorers Brook

Mount Wilson

Bells Line of Road

Grose River

GROSE VALLEY

Govetts Creek

Wentworth Creek

Flat Top Brook

Wentworth Creek

Wentworth Falls

Everglades Gardens ④

Sublime Point Lookout ②

Falls Reserve ③

Leura

Great Western Hwy.

Govett's Leap Lookout ⑧

Heritage Centre ⑨

Hat Hill Creek

Victoria Creek

Medlow Bath

Blackheath

Katoomba

Leuralla ⑤

⑥ Three Sisters

Echo Point ⑦

JAMISON VALLEY

Explorers' Tree

Scenic Railway

Mercure Grand Hotel

MEGALONG VALLEY

Mount Victoria ⑩

Blackheath Creek

BLUE MOUNTAINS

Main Western Railway

Great Western Hwy.

Hartley

TO ZIG ZAG RAILWAY

TO JENOLAN CAVES

TO BELL VILLAGE

0 3 miles

0 3 km

✉ *14 Norman Lindsay Crescent, Faulconbridge* ☎ *02/4751–1067*
🌐 *www.hermes.net.au/nlg* 🎫 *A$9* 🕐 *Daily 10–4.*

Wentworth Falls

26 km (16 mi) west of Springwood.

This attractive township has numerous crafts and antiques shops, a lake, and a popular golf course. Wentworth Falls straddles the highway, but most points of interest and views of the Jamison Valley and Blue Mountains National Park are south of the road.

★ ❷ From a lookout in **Falls Reserve,** south of the town of Wentworth Falls, you can take in magnificent views both out across the Jamison Valley to the Kings Tableland and of the 935-foot-high **Wentworth Falls** themselves. To find the best view of the falls, follow the trail that crosses the stream and zigzags down the sheer cliff face, signposted NATIONAL PASS. If you continue, the National Pass cuts back across the base of the falls and along a narrow ledge to the delightful Valley of the Waters, where it ascends to the top of the cliffs, emerging at the Conservation Hut. The complete circuit takes at least three hours and is a moderate walk. ✉ *End of Falls Rd.*

Where to Stay &Eat

¢–$ ✕ **Conservation Hut.** From its prime spot in Blue Mountains National Park, on a cliff overlooking the Jamison Valley, this spacious, mud-brick bistro serves simple, savory fare such as hearty soups, a beef pie, and perch fillets with baked fennel and sorrel sauce, as well as lovely dessert cakes. An open balcony is a delight on warm days, and a fire blazes in the cooler months. A hiking trail from the bistro leads down into the Valley of the Waters, one of the splendors of the mountains. It's a wonderful pre- or post-meal walk. ✉ *Fletcher St.* ☎ *02/4757–3827* 🍴 *AE, MC, V* 🍷 *BYO* 🕐 *No dinner.*

$ $$$ 🏠 **Bygone Beautys Cottages.** These nine country cottages, which are scattered around Wentworth Falls (a few are in other nearby villages), provide self-contained accommodations for couples, families, and small groups. Some of these are set among leafy gardens; all have wood-burning fireplaces. Fresh flowers, fruit, chocolates, and all the ingredients for a country-size breakfast are included in each unit. There's a two-night minimum stay. ✉ *Main office: Grose and Megalong Sts., Leura 2780* ☎ *02/ 4784–3117* 🖨 *02/4784–3078* 🌐 *www.bygonebeautys.com.au* 🛏 *9 cottages* 🛎 *Some BBQs, kitchens, microwaves, refrigerators, in-room VCRs, tennis court, hiking, laundry facilities; no a/c* 🍴 *AE, MC, V.*

Leura

5 km (3 mi) west of Wentworth Falls.

Leura, the prettiest of the mountain towns, is lined with excellent cafés, restaurants, and gift shops. From the south end of the main street (the Mall), the road continues past superb local gardens as it winds down to the massive cliffs overlooking the Jamison Valley. The dazzling 19-km (12-mi) journey along Cliff Drive skirts the rim of the valley—often only yards from the cliff edge—providing truly spectacular Blue Mountains views.

★ ❸ **Sublime Point Lookout,** just outside Leura, lives up to its name with a great view of the Jamison Valley and the generally spectacular Blue Mountains scenery. It's a quiet vantage point that provides a different perspective from that of the famous **Three Sisters** lookout at nearby Katoomba. ⊠ *Sublime Point Rd.*

❹ **Everglades Gardens,** a National Trust–listed, cool-climate arboretum and nature reserve established in the 1930s, is one of the best public gardens in the Blue Mountains region. Paths cut through settings of native bushland and exotic flora, a rhododendron garden, an alpine plant area, and formal European-style terraces. The views of the Jamison Valley are magnificent. ⊠ *37 Everglades Ave.* ☎ *02/4784–1938* ⊕ *www.evergladesgardens. info* ☞ *A$6* ⊙ *Oct.–Mar., daily 10–5, Apr.–Sept. daily 10–4.*

❺ **Leuralla,** a 1911 mansion, still belongs to the family of Dr. H. V. ("Doc") Evatt (1894–1965), the first president of the General Assembly of the United Nations and later the leader of the Australian Labor Party. A 19th-century Australian art collection and a small museum dedicated to Dr. Evatt are inside the home. Also on the grounds, the **New South Wales Toy and Railway Museum** has an extensive collection of railway memorabilia, including a toy display with tin-plate automobiles, ships, and planes, and antique dolls and bears. ⊠ *36 Olympian Parade* ☎ *02/ 4784–1169* ☞ *A$10* ⊙ *Daily 10–5.*

Where to Stay & Eat

$$ ✕ **Silks Brasserie.** Thanks to its Sydney-standard food, wine, and service,
Fodor's Choice Silks rates as one of the finest Blue Mountains restaurants. The menu
★ here changes seasonally, but might include pan-roasted Atlantic salmon with a honey–mustard-seed dressing on potato cake, or oven-baked lamb loin with mixed-herb mousseline and tomato compote. Rich desserts, such as warm Middle Eastern orange-and-almond pudding with cardamom and crème fraîche provide the perfect finish. In colder months a log fire warms the century-old shop's simple but elegant interior, where yellow ocher walls reach from a black-and-white checkerboard floor to high ceilings. ⊠ *128 the Mall* ☎ *02/4784–2534* ☞ *Reservations essential* ☰ *AE, DC, MC, V.*

$–$$ ✕ **Cafe Bon Ton.** If you're looking for a simple caffeine fix or a great night out, head to this bright, elegant café. Its famous coffee is an all-day draw, but most diners linger for breakfast, a slice of cake, or crowd-pleasers like pasta and pizza. In winter a log fire burns in the grate, and on warm summer days the shady front garden is ideal for lunch. Book ahead on weekends. ⊠ *192 the Mall* ☎ *02/4782–4377* ☰ *AE, MC, V* ⊙ *No dinner Sun.–Thurs. in winter, Mon.–Wed. in summer.*

$$$–$$$$ ▥ **Peppers Fairmont Resort.** Perched spectacularly on the edge of cliffs overlooking the Jamison Valley, this is the colossus of accommodations in the region. Although it can't hope to match the cozy warmth that's the hallmark of the more traditional mountain guesthouses, it's a good choice if you want a hotel with all the trimmings, like tennis courts, spa services, and a game room for the kids. The best rooms are on the valley side, and there's easy access to Leura Golf Course, the area's finest. There is a two-night minimum stay on weekends. ✉ *1 Sublime Point Rd., 2780* ☏ *02/4784–4144* ☒ *02/4784–1685* ⊕ *www.peppers.com. au* ⇌ *193 rooms, 17 suites ⚴ 2 restaurants, coffee shop, room service, IDD phones, some in-room hot tubs, some kitchenettes, some microwaves, some refrigerators, cable TV, in-room data ports, 3 tennis courts, 2 pools, health club, massage, sauna, spa, steam room, bicycles, basketball, billiards, Ping-Pong, squash, bar, video game room, shop, babysitting, dry cleaning, laundry service, Internet room, business services, meeting rooms, car rental, travel services, no-smoking rooms* ▭ *AE, DC, MC, V.*

Katoomba

2 km (1 mi) west of Leura.

The largest town in the Blue Mountains, Katoomba developed in the early 1840s as a coal-mining settlement, turning its attention to tourism later in the 19th century. The town center has shops and cafés, but most travelers find little reason to delay as they pass through en route to the scenic marvels at the lower end of town.

❻ Echo Point, which overlooks the densely forested Jamison Valley and three soaring sandstone pillars, has the best views around Katoomba. The formations—the **Three Sisters**—take their name from an Aboriginal legend that relates how three siblings were turned to stone by their witch-doctor father to save them from the clutches of a mythical monster. The area was once a seabed that rose over a long period and subsequently eroded, leaving behind tall formations of sedimentary rock. From Echo Point you can clearly see the horizontal sandstone bedding in the landscape. At night the Sisters are illuminated by floodlights. ✛ *Follow Katoomba St. south out of Katoomba to Echo Point Rd., or take Cliff Dr. from Leura.*

FodorsChoice
★

🖑 ❼ Far below Echo Point, the **Scenic Railway** was built into the cliff face during the 1880s to haul coal and shale from the mines in the valley. After the supply of shale was exhausted, the railway was abandoned until the 1930s, when the Katoomba Colliery began using the open carts to give tourists the ride of their lives on the steep incline. Today the carriages are far more comfortable, but the ride down to the foot of the cliffs is no less exciting. From the bottom of the railway a 1½-km (1-mi) boardwalk loops through ancient rain forest littered with mining relics to the base of the world's steepest cable car, the **Flyway.** This enclosed gondola car glides between the treed valley floor and the rim of the cliff 1,700 feet above. Your return ticket allows you to ride the railway down and the cable car up. Just a few steps from the top stations of both the railway and Flyway is the **Scenic Skyway,** a cable car that carries passengers for a short ride across the gorge, with a 1,000-foot drop below. If you're going to pick one, the railway is more spectacular. All three rides are part of **Scenic World.** ✉ *Cliff Dr. and Violet St.* ☏ *02/4782–2699* ⊕ *www.scenicworld.com.au.* ▦ *Round-trip Railway, Flyway, or Skyway A$14 each* ⊙ *Daily 9–5.*

The screen at the **Edge Maxvision Cinema** is the height of a six-story building. Specially filmed for this giant format, *The Edge,* shown six times daily starting at 10:20 (the last show is at 5:30) is an exciting 40-minute movie on the region's valleys, gorges, cliffs, waterfalls, and dramatic scenery. The complex includes a café and gift shop, and regular feature films screen three times a day, usually at 3 PM, 6 PM, and 8 or 9 PM. ⊠ *225–237 Great Western Hwy.* ☎ *02/4782–8928* ⌨ *A$14.50.*

Where to Stay & Eat

$–$$ ✕ **Paragon Restaurant.** With its chandeliers, gleaming cappuccino machine, and bas-relief figures above the booths, this wood-paneled 1916 restaurant recalls the Blue Mountains in their heyday. The menu has all-day fare, including waffles for breakfast, and homemade soups, burgers, and famous Paragon meat pies for lunch. There are also 52 varieties of homemade chocolates to take home with you. ⊠ *65 Katoomba St.* ☎ *02/4782–2928* ⊟ *MC, V* ⊙ *No dinner.*

$$$$ ✕⊡ **Echoes.** With a modern architectural style unique among the area's cozy guesthouses, this boutique hotel combines breathtaking Jamison Valley views with traditional Blue Mountains comforts. Simply furnished rooms have pin-striped drapes and upholstery; the top-floor Wentworth corner suite has particularly fine views of sandstone cliffs and deep, forested valleys. The excellent restaurant serves up Tuscan and Provençal cuisine, and the Three Sisters lookout and a network of walking trails are close by. ⊠ *3 Lilianfels Ave., 2780* ☎ *02/4782–1966* 🖶 *02/4782–3707* ⊕ *www.echoeshotel.com.au* ⇗ *13 suites* ⟋ *Restaurant, IDD phones, some fans, some in-room hot tubs, refrigerators, cable TV with movies, in-room data ports, hot tub, sauna, bar, Internet room, travel services; no a/c in some rooms, no smoking* ⊟ *AE, DC, MC, V* ❙⊙❙ *BP.*

★ **$$$$** ✕⊡ **Lilianfels Blue Mountains Resort & Spa.** Teetering close to the brink of Echo Point, this glamorous boutique hotel adds a keen sense of style to the traditional Blue Mountains guesthouse experience. Despite its old-fashioned feel, the hotel also has all the luxury you'd expect of a member of the prestigious Orient Express hotel group. Rooms are spacious and luxuriously furnished, with lush fabrics, silk curtains, and elegant marble bathrooms with deep baths. The upscale Darley's restaurant, in the Heritage-listed original 1889 homestead, serves a cutting-edge menu; a highlight is the rare roasted duck breast with red Persian lentils and figs. The first-class spa is the ultimate place to relax after exploring the Jamison Valley. There is a two-night minimum stay on weekends. ⊠ *Lilianfels Ave. and Panorama Drive., 2780* ☎ *02/4780–1200* 🖶 *02/ 4780–1300* ⊕ *www.lilianfels.com.au* ⟋ *Reservations essential* ⇗ *81 rooms, 4 suites* ⟋ *2 restaurants, room service, IDD phones, in-room safes, some in-room hot tubs, minibars, refrigerators, cable TV, in-room VCRs, in-room data ports, tennis court, 2 pools (1 indoors), gym, hot tub, sauna, spa, steam room, mountain bikes, billiards, bar, dry cleaning, laundry service, concierge, Internet room, meeting rooms, travel services, no-smoking rooms* ⊟ *AE, DC, MC, V.*

$–$$$ ✕⊡ **The Carrington.** It's unlikely you'll find a veranda, piazza, and ballroom elsewhere in the Blue Mountains. Established in 1880, this was the first of the region's truly grand lodgings, and today its Federation-style furnished public areas are graceful reminders of the hotel's glorious past. Guest rooms are less ornate, however; the views are of Katoomba township rather than the mountain valleys, and some have shared bathrooms. The enormous, chandelier-lighted dining room serves modern Australian and traditional dishes; you might try the pork fillet medallion with a sage-and-Parmesan crust, saffron gnocchi, and apple and calvados sauce. For dessert there's pavlova—Australia's famous meringue pie. ⊠ *15–47 Katoomba St., 2780* ☎ *02/4782–1111* 🖷 *02/4782–7033* ⊕ *www.thecarrington.com.au* 🛏 *59 rooms, 49 with private baths, 6 suites, 1 apartment* ⌂ *2 restaurants, IDD phones, some in-room hot tubs, some kitchenettes, refrigerators, massage, billiards, 2 bars, nightclub, dry cleaning, laundry service, meeting room, no-smoking rooms; no a/c* ⊟ *AE, DC, MC, V* ⏀⏀ *BP.*

$$$–$$$$ 🏨 **Mountain Heritage.** This home overlooking the Jamison Valley is steeped in history: it served as a "coffee palace" during the temperance movement, a rest-and-relaxation establishment for the British navy during World War II, and a religious retreat in the 1970s. Spacious rooms here are filled with welcoming country-house furnishings. If you're looking to splurge, try the round Tower Suite, or one of the two Valley View suites—each has its own veranda, kitchen, living room with fireplace, and hot tub. ⊠ *Apex and Lovel Sts., 2780* ☎ *02/4782–2155* 🖷 *02/4782–5323* ⊕ *www.mountainheritage.com.au* 🛏 *37 rooms, 4 suites* ⌂ *Restaurant, IDD phones, some in-room hot tubs, some kitchens, some kitchenettes, refrigerators, in-room VCRs, pool, gym, billiards, hiking, Ping-Pong, volleyball, bar, recreation room, laundry facilities, dry cleaning, Internet room, meeting rooms, travel services; no smoking* ⊟ *AE, DC, MC, V.*

★ **$$$** 🏨 **Melba House.** The Blaxland, Wentworth, and Lawson suites in this 19th century house are named after the explorers who toiled across the Blue Mountains in 1813 and opened up the Western Plains to settlers— and they offer a welcome retreat to visitors today. Two of the suites have king-size beds, hot tubs, and marble-framed wood fireplaces; all have decorative plaster ceilings and windows looking out at a garden full of birds. Afternoon tea is served when you arrive, and a sumptuous breakfast is brought to your room on a tray. ⊠ *98 Waratah St., 2780* ☎ *02/4782–4141* 🖷 *02/4782–7957* ⊕ *www.melbahouse.com* 🛏 *3 suites* ⌂ *Room service, some in-room hot tubs, refrigerators, in-room DVD, hiking, Internet room, no smoking rooms* ⊟ *AE, DC, MC, V* ⏀⏀ *BP.*

Blackheath

12 km (7½ mi) north of Katoomba.

Magnificent easterly views over the Grose Valley—which has outstanding hiking trails—and delightful gardens and antiques shops head the list of reasons to visit Blackheath, at the 3,495-foot summit of the Blue Mountains. The town was named by Governor Lachlan Macquarie, who visited in 1815 after a rough road had been constructed through here to the town of Bathurst, beyond the mountains.

8 Blackheath's most famous view is from the **Govett's Leap Lookout,** with its striking panorama of the Grose Valley and Bridal Veil Falls. Govett was a surveyor who mapped this region extensively in the 1830s. He calculated that the perpendicular drop near the falls is 528 feet. ⊠ *End of Govett's Leap Rd.*

❾ The **Heritage Centre,** operated by the National Parks and Wildlife Service, provides useful information on Aboriginal and European historic sites, as well as helpful suggestions for camping, guided walks, and hiking in Blue Mountains National Park. The center, which is a two-minute stroll from Govett's Leap Lookout, also has videos, interactive educational displays, exhibitions, and a nature-oriented gift shop. ⊠ *End of Govett's Leap Rd.* ☎ *02/4787–8877* ⊕ *www.npws.nsw.gov.au* ⊠ *Free* ۞ *Daily 9–4:30.*

☾ The **Megalong Australian Heritage Centre,** in a deep mountain valley off the Great Western Highway, is the place to saddle up and explore a country property. Both adults and children can go horseback riding around the farm's 2,000 acres, and bigger adults might get to ride a Clydesdale. If you'd like to go farther afield, you can join an overnight muster ride from A$165. There's a baby-animal nursery and children can get close to chickens, ducks, and pigs. The center puts on a cattle-and-horse show, and sheep shearing, for large groups. There is also cottage and guesthouse accommodation, and camping. ⊠ *Megalong Rd., Megalong Valley, 15 km (9 mi) south of Blackheath* ☎ *02/4787 8688* ⊠ *A$8* ۞ *Daily 9 5.*

Where to Stay & Eat

$$ ✗ **Vulcan's.** Don't let the concrete floor and rough redbrick walls fool
Fodor's Choice you: this tiny indoor-outdoor Blackheath café has revolutionized dining
★ in rural New South Wales. Operated by Phillip Searle (formerly one of the leading lights of Sydney's dining scene) and Barry Ross, Vulcan's specializes in slow-roasted dishes, often with Asian or Middle Eastern spices. The restaurant's checkerboard ice cream—with star anise, pineapple, licorice, and vanilla flavors—is a favorite that looks as good as it tastes. Smoking is not permitted. ⊠ *33 Govetts Leap Rd.* ☎ *02/4787–6899* ▤ *AE, DC, MC, V* ⛯ *BYOB* ۞ *Closed Mon.–Thurs. and Feb.*

★ $$ ▥ **Jemby Rinjah Eco Lodge.** Designed for urbanites seeking a wilderness experience, these rustic, self-contained wooden cabins are set deep in the bush. All have natural-wood furnishings and picture windows opening onto a small deck, and all sleep up to six. Eco-lodges have four bedrooms and are ideal for small groups or families, while the two-person tree houses elevate you to the same level as the kookaburras. There are also two-bedroom cabins with kitchens. Activities include free guided walks of the Grose Valley, feeding wild parrots, and spotlighting possums at night. ⊠ *336 Evans Lookout Rd., 2785* ☎ *02/4787–7622* ⚕ *02/4787–6230* ⊕ *www.jembyrinjahlodge.com.au* ⇔ *12 rooms without bath, 11 cabins, 3 tree houses* ☪ *Restaurant, BBQs, some fans, 1 in-room hot tub, some kitchenettes, refrigerators, hiking, Internet room, laundry facilities, meeting rooms, travel services; no a/c, no room phones, no smoking* ▤ *AE, DC, MC, V.*

Mount Victoria

❿ *7 km (4½ mi) northwest of Blackheath.*

The settlement of Mount Victoria has a Rip Van Winkle air about it—drowsy and only just awake in an unfamiliar world. A walk around the village reveals many atmospheric houses and stores with the patina of time spelled out in their fading paint. Mount Victoria is at the far side of the mountains at the western limit of this region, and the village serves as a good jumping-off point for a couple of out-of-the-way attractions.

Stalactites, stalagmites, columns, and lacelike rock on multiple levels fill **Jenolan Caves,** a labyrinth of vast limestone chasms sculpted by underground rivers. There are as many as 300 caves in the Jenolan area.

Three caves near the surface can be explored on your own, but a guide is required to reach the most intriguing formations. Standard tours lead through the most popular caves, while more rigorous Adventure tours last up to seven hours. The one- to two-hour walks depart every 15 minutes on weekends and every half hour on weekdays; note that even the easiest trails include 300 stairs. To get here, follow the Great Western Highway north out of Mount Victoria, then after Hartley turn southwest toward Hampton. There are also caves in Abercrombie and Wombeyan, to the west and south of Jenolan. ✉ *59 km (37 mi) from Mount Victoria, Jenolan* ☎ *02/6359–3311* ⊕ *www.jenolancaves.org. au* 🎫 *Standard tours A$15–A$22* ☉ *Daily 9:30–5:30.*

☺　The huff-and-puff vintage steam engine making the thrilling, cliff-hug-
Fodor's Choice　ging 16-km (10-mi) round-trip on the **Zig Zag Railway** looks spectacu-
★　lar from the road above. Built in 1869, this was the main line across the Blue Mountains until 1910. The track is laid on the cliffs in a giant "Z," and the train climbs the steep incline by chugging back and forth along switchback sections of the track—hence its name. The steam engine operates on weekends, public holidays, and Wednesday, and weekdays during the school holidays. A vintage self-propelled diesel-powered railcar is used at other times. ✉ *Bells Line of Rd., 19 km (12 mi) northwest of Mount Victoria, Clarence* ☎ *02/6353–1795* ⊕ *www. zigzagrailway.com.au* 🎫 *A$20* ☉ *Departures from Clarence Station daily at 11, 1, and 3.*

Where to Eat

$　✕ **Bay Tree Tea Shop.** A chilly afternoon, when a fire is burning in the grate and scones are piping hot from the kitchen, is the best time to dine at this cozy café. The menu includes hearty soups, salads, pasta dishes, and quiches. Everything is made on the premises—bread, cakes, and even the jam that comes with afternoon tea. At night the café reopens as the Bay Tree Thai restaurant. ✉ *26 Station St.* ☎ *02/4787–1275, 02/4787–1220 Bay Tree Thai* ▭ *V* ☉ *Closed Mon. and Tues. No dinner Wed.*

Mount Tomah

25 km (16 mi) southeast of Mount Wilson.

The area around the village of Mount Tomah, on the unusually named Bells Line of Road, holds strong appeal for garden lovers.

⓫　The cool-climate branch of Sydney's Royal Botanic Gardens, the **Mount Tomah Botanic Garden** is a spectacular setting for many native and imported plant species. At 3,280 feet above sea level, the moist, cool environment is perfect for rhododendrons, conifers, maples, and European deciduous trees. The gardens also have a shop, a visitor center, picnic areas, and a restaurant that serves modern Australian cuisine. Guided walks are available by arrangement. The family rate (A$8.80) is a good bargain. ⊠ *Bells Line of Rd.* ☎ *02/4567–2154* ⊕ *www.rbgsyd.nsw.gov. au* ✉ *A$4.40* ⊙ *Oct.–Mar., daily 10–5; Apr.–Sept., daily 10–4.*

Blue Mountains A to Z

BUS TRAVEL

Public buses operate between the Blue Mountains settlements. However, to see the best that the Blue Mountains have to offer, take a guided tour or rent a car and drive from Sydney.

CAR RENTAL

Since the most scenic Blue Mountains routes and attractions are outside the towns, it's best to rent a car. If you're not driving from Sydney, you can reserve a vehicle from RediCAR in Leura.

🚗 **RediCAR** ⊠ 80 Megalong St., Leura 2780 ☎ 02/4784-3443.

CAR TRAVEL

The 110-km (68-mi) journey to Katoomba takes between 90 minutes and two hours. Leave Sydney via Parramatta Road and the M4 Motorway, which leads to Lapstone at the base of the Blue Mountains. From there, continue on the Great Western Highway and follow the signs to Katoomba.

EMERGENCIES

In an emergency, dial **000** to reach an ambulance, the police, or the fire department.

🏥 Hospital **Blue Mountains District Anzac Memorial Hospital** ⊠ Great Western Hwy., 1 km [½ mi] east of town center, Katoomba ☎ 02/4784-6500.

TOURS

Since the Blue Mountains are one of Sydney's most popular escapes, you can take a day trip from there with a bus touring company or make your own way to the mountains and then link up with a guided tour. The region is also great for outdoor adventure and horseback-riding trips.

ADVENTURE-SPORTS TOURS Blue Mountains Adventure Company runs rappelling, rock-climbing, canyoning, bushwalking, and mountain-biking trips. Most outings (from about A$149) last one day, and include equipment, lunch, and transportation from Katoomba.

High 'n Wild conducts rappelling, canyoning, rock-climbing, and mountain-biking tours. One-day rappelling trips cost A$135; combination rappelling and canyoning tours cost A$160.

🚗 **Blue Mountains Adventure Company** ⊠ 84A Bathurst Rd., Katoomba 2780 ☎ 02/4782-1271 ⊕ www.bmac.com.au. **High'n Wild** ⊠ 3-5 Katoomba St., Katoomba 2780 ☎ 02/4782-6224 ⊕ www.high-n-wild.com.au.

BUS TOURS Fantastic Aussie Tours arranges trips ranging from bus tours to four-wheel-drive expeditions. They also operate the double-decker Blue Mountains Explorer Bus (A$25), which connects with trains from Sydney at the Katoomba Railway Station. Running hourly from 9:30 to 4:30 every day, it makes 30 stops at major attractions around Katoomba and Leura, and you're free to hop off and on as you please. If you're overnighting in the mountains, you can use the pass for the duration of your stay.

🚹 Fantastic Aussie Tours ✉ 283 Main St., Katoomba ☎ 02/4782-1866 ⊕ www. fantastic-aussie-tours.com.au.

FOUR-WHEEL-DRIVE TOURS
Tread Lightly Eco Tours operates small-group personalized tours of the Blue Mountains National Park and guided day and night walks. Luxury four-wheel-drive vehicles take you to lookouts, caves, and waterfalls. A full-day Wilderness Experience for two costs from A$160 to A$260, depending on destination and food (gourmet picnic or restaurant).

🚹 Tread Lightly Eco Tours ✉ 100 Great Western Hwy., Medlow Bath 2780 ☎☎ 02/ 4788-1229 or 0414/976752 ⊕ www.treadlightly.com.au.

HORSEBACK RIDING TOURS
At the foot of the Blue Mountains, 10 km (6 mi) south of Blackheath, Werriberri Trail Rides conducts reasonably priced half-hour (A$25) to full-day (A$180) horseback rides through the beautiful Megalong Valley. These guided rides are appropriate for both adults and children, and hard hats and chaps are supplied.

🚹 Werriberri Trail Rides ✉ Megalong Rd., Megalong Valley ☎ 02/4787-9171.

WALKING TOURS
Auswalk operates five- and seven-day guided and self-guided walking holidays in Blue Mountains National Park. You carry a day pack on spectacular day walks while your luggage is transferred from guesthouse to guesthouse. The seven-day self-guided walk (A$1,325) requires a minimum of two people and can be booked for any day of the year except July. Seven-day guided walking holidays (from A$1,595) depart Sunday on demand.

🚹 Auswalk ⏚ Box 516, Jindabyne 2627 ☎ 02/6457-2220 ⊕ www.auswalk.com.au.

TRAIN TRAVEL

Train services from Sydney stop at most stations along the line to Mount Victoria. The Blue Mountains are served by Sydney's Cityrail commuter trains, with frequent services to and from the city between 5 AM and 11 PM. On weekdays it's A$11.40 one-way between Sydney's Central Station and Katoomba, the main station in the Blue Mountains. If you travel on weekends, or begin travel after 9 on weekdays, it's A$14 round-trip.

🚹 Cityrail ☎ 13-1500 ⊕ www.cityrail.info.

VISITOR INFORMATION

Blue Mountains Visitor Information Centre offices are at Echo Point in Katoomba and at the foot of the mountains on the Great Western Highway at Glenbrook. The Echo Point office is open daily 9–5, and the Glenbrook office is open weekdays 9–5 and weekends 8:30–4:30. Sydney Visitor Centre, open daily 9:30–5:30, has information on Blue Mountains hotels, tours, and sights.

🚹 Blue Mountains Visitor Information Centre ✉ Echo Point Rd., Echo Point ☎ 1300/ 653408 ⊕ www.bluemountainstourism.org.au ✉ Great Western Hwy., Glenbrook ☎ 1300/653408. **Sydney Visitor Centre** ✉ 106 George St., The Rocks, Sydney 2000 ☎ 02/ 9255-1788 ⏚ 02/9241-5010 ⊕ www.sydneyvisitorcentre.com.

THE SOUTHERN HIGHLANDS & COAST

This fertile region just over 100 km (62 mi) southwest of Sydney was first settled during the 1820s by farmers in search of grazing lands. During the 19th century wealthy Sydney folk built grand country houses here as a refuge from the city's summer heat and humidity. Although the region is often compared with England, the steep sandstone gorges and impenetrable forests of Morton National Park bring an element of drama to this tranquil rural landscape. As a bonus, the South Coast—with its excellent beaches—is just a short drive away.

Mittagong

103 km (64 mi) southwest of Sydney.

Although it's known as the gateway to the Southern Highlands, the commercial center of Mittagong holds few attractions. Farther afield, at Berrima, Bowral, and Moss Vale, are antiques shops specializing in the quirky to the highly coveted. The Tourism Southern Highlands Information Centre on Main Street has maps and local brochures.

off the beaten path

WOMBEYAN CAVES – From Mittagong you can detour through rugged mountain scenery to these spectacular and delicate limestone formations. Five caves are open to the public, although the Fig Tree Cave is the only one that you can explore on your own. Guided tours to the others take place at regular intervals throughout the day. You can also wander along the bushwalking trails and look for wildlife. The caves are just 66 km (41 mi) from Mittagong, but the journey along the narrow, winding, and partly unpaved road takes about 1½ hours each way. There is unit, caravan, and cottage accommodation at the caves. ⊠ *Wombeyan Caves Rd. via Mittagong* ☎ *02/ 4843–5976* ⊕ *www.jenolancaves.org.au* ✉ *Self-guided cave tour A$12, guided cave tour A$16, 2-cave pass (1 guided, 1 self-guided) A$21, 3-cave pass (2 guided) A$28, 5-cave pass (available only to overnight guests) A$40* ☉ *Daily 8:30–5.*

Berrima

14½ km (9 mi) southwest of Mittagong.

Founded in 1829, Berrima is an outstanding example of an early Georgian colonial town, preserved in almost original condition. The settlement is a museum of convict-built sandstone and brick buildings, including the National Trust–listed Harpers Mansion and the Holy Trinity Church. The 1839 Berrima Gaol is still in use, and the 1834 Surveyor General Inn is one of Australia's oldest continuously licensed hotels. A self-guided walking tour pamphlet is available at the courthouse, and knowledgeable local guides are available.

The 1838 **Berrima Courthouse,** with its grand classical facade, is the town's architectural highlight. The impressive sandstone complex, now a museum, contains the original courtroom and holding cells. Inside is a reenactment—with wax mannequins and an audio track—of an infamous murder trial, as well as audiovisual and conventional displays of such items as iron shackles and cat-o'-nine-tails that were once used on recalcitrant convicts. ⊠ *Wilshire St.* ☏ *02/4877–1505* 🖃 *Museum A$6* ⊙ *Daily 10–4.*

Where to Eat

$–$$ ✕ **White Horse Inn.** Reputed to have a resident ghost, this meticulously restored, atmospheric 1832 inn is a fine example of colonial Australian architecture. It's also an ideal spot for lunch, and while there's nothing revolutionary on the menu of sandwiches, pastas, and steaks, the plain and simple fare is reliably good. The courtyard is a pleasant spot for tea. ⊠ *The Market Place near Old Hume Hwy.* ☏ *02/4877–1204* 🖃 *AE, DC, MC, V.*

Bowral

9½ km (6 mi) east of Berrima.

Since the 1880s the town of Bowral has been synonymous with opulent country dwellings. Fine old houses, antiques stores, and crafts shops line the tree-shaded streets. The parks and private gardens here are the focus of the colorful spring **Tulip Time Festival,** held over six weeks every September and October. For panoramas of Bowral, Mittagong, and the surrounding countryside, head up to 2,830-foot-high **Mt. Gibraltar,** which has four short walking trails at the summit.

Bowral's attraction for cricket fans is the **Bradman Museum.** Legendary cricketer Sir Donald (The Don) Bradman, although not a native Australian, spent his childhood in Bowral and captained the Australian team between 1928 and 1948. The museum, next to the town's idyllic cricket oval, has a shop and tea rooms. ⊠ *Glebe Park, Church and St. Jude Sts.* ☏ *02/4862–1247* ⊕ *www.bradman.org.au* 🖃 *A$8.50* ⊙ *Daily 10–5.*

Where to Stay & Eat

$$ ✕ **Grand Bar and Brasserie.** An extensive blackboard menu aims to please just about everyone at this lively brasserie. Specialties are seafood and meat dishes, such as the winter lamb shanks slow-roasted in red wine. The menu strays ambitiously between the Mediterranean and the Orient, and most of the time it succeeds. Wine is available by the glass. ⊠ *Grand Arcade, 295 Bong Bong St.* ☏ *02/4861–4783* 🖃 *AE, DC, MC, V.*

$ ✕ **Janeks.** One of the few Bowral eateries with outdoor seating, Janeks serves up hearty breakfasts of waffles and fresh baked goods, and lunches of sandwiches, soups, pastas, and salads. There are more substantial dishes, too, including chicken, mushroom and sage risotto, and Indian dal with naan bread. ⊠ *Corbett Plaza, 14 Wingecarribee St.* ☏ *02/4861–4414* 🖃 *AE, MC, V* ⊙ *No dinner.*

$$$$ ✕🖃 **Milton Park.** One of Sydney's elite families built this grand hotel with expansive English-style gardens as their country retreat 13 km (8 mi) east of Bowral. Adorned in a patrician country style, the building has spacious, modern rooms with slightly dated decor and furnishings;

some have fireplaces. The best reason to stay is the surrounding forested 300-acre estate, where you can stroll—or jog—among bluebells, wisteria, roses, and huge trees. There is a two-night minimum stay on weekends. The Hordern Room, the hotel's dining room, is suitably grand and distinguished, and the modern Australian cuisine makes especially fine use of local ingredients like duck and venison. ✉ *Horderns Rd., 2576* ☎ *02/4861–1522* 📠 *02/4861–7962* ⊕ *www.milton-park.com.au* 🛏 *34 rooms, 6 suites, 1 carriage house* ⚱ *2 restaurants, room service, some in-room hot tubs, minibars, refrigerators, cable TV, tennis court, pool, hot tub, billiards, boccie, croquet, bar, library, laundry service, Internet room, meeting rooms; no a/c, no smoking* ▭ *AE, DC, MC, V* 🍽 *BP.*

$$ 🏨 **Links House.** Directly opposite Bowral Golf Course, this friendly guesthouse has such modern amenities as comfortable beds, private showers, and Internet access. However, most rooms are small, and they're decorated in traditional country style. Number 20, a delightful cottage-style room in the hotel's gardens, is well worth the A$15 premium; the Cottage is the only room with a bathtub. In-house Eschalot restaurant serves modern Australian fare, and a full cooked breakfast is included in your room rate. ✉ *17 Links Rd., 2576* ☎ *02/4861–1977* 📠 *02/4862–1706* ⊕ *www.linkshouse.com.au* 🛏 *12 rooms, 4 suites, 1 cottage* ⚱ *Restaurant, IDD phones, refrigerators, tennis court, Internet room, travel services; no a/c, no smoking* ▭ *AE, DC, MC, V* 🍽 *BP.*

Moss Vale

10 km (6 mi) southeast of Berrima.

Founded as a market center for the surrounding farming districts, which now concentrate on horses, sheep, and dairy and stud cattle, the town of Moss Vale has several antiques galleries and crafts shops, although it lacks Bowral's charm. Leighton Gardens in the center of town are particularly attractive in spring and autumn.

The lagoon and swamplands of the **Cecil Hoskins Nature Reserve,** on the banks of the Wingecarribee River north of Moss Vale, have been a wildlife sanctuary since the 1930s. This important wetland area shelters more than 80 species of local and migratory waterfowl, including pelicans and black swans. You may even be fortunate enough to see a reclusive platypus here. The reserve has bird-watching blinds, a picnic area, and several easy walking tracks with excellent views of the river and wetlands. ⊹ *Highland Way (the Moss Vale–Bowral road, 2 km [1 mi]) north of Moss Vale* ☎ *02/4887–7270* 🎟 *Free* ☉ *Daily dawn–dusk.*

Golf

With its well-groomed greens and on-course accommodation, the 18-hole, par-72 **Moss Vale Golf Club** (✉ Arthur and Mark Sts. ☎ 02/4868–1503 or 02/4868–1811) is regarded as one of the best and most challenging courses in this golf-mad region. Nonmembers are welcome every day except Saturday, but phone first. Greens fees are A$17.50 for 9 holes and A$29.50 for 18 holes, and A$35 for 18 holes on weekends.

Sutton Forest & Bundanoon

6–13 km (4–8 mi) south of Moss Vale.

The drive from Moss Vale through the tranquil villages that lie to the south is particularly rewarding—a meandering journey that winds past dairy farms and horse stud farms. Although relatively unimportant today, **Sutton Forest** was the focus of the area's early settlement. In later years this small township became the country seat of the governors of New South Wales, who periodically based themselves at the grand country house Hillview. The village, 6 km (4 mi) from Moss Vale, also contains a few shops and the pleasant Sutton Forest Inn. At the nearby hamlet of **Exeter,** the 1895 St. Aidans Church has a vaulted timber ceiling and beautiful stained-glass windows.

South of Sutton Forest, **Bundanoon** (Aboriginal for "place of deep gullies") was once an extremely busy weekend getaway for Sydneysiders. Its popularity was due to its location—on the main rail line to Melbourne, at a bracing elevation of 2,230 feet and perched above the northern edge of spectacular Morton National Park. The tranquil village is still delightful and provides the best access to the park's western section. There are a few antiques and crafts shops, and Bundanoon is also the focus of the annual **Brigadoon Festival,** held in April, a lively event with pipe bands, Highland games, and all things Scottish.

Where to Stay & Eat

$$$–$$$$ ✕▦ **Peppers Manor House.** On 185 acres of gardens and pastureland adjoining Mt. Broughton Golf & Country Club, this elegant country resort is based around a grand 1920s family home. The baronial great hall has a high vaulted ceiling and leaded windows, and there are five traditionally decorated guest rooms on the floor above. The hotel also has a separate garden wing, which is furnished and decorated in plush country style. Set among groves of elm trees, the Elms Cottages have two bedrooms and two bathrooms apiece, with a connecting lounge room and broad verandas. The in-house Katers restaurant brings together flavors from around the world for its seasonal menu; offerings might include Szechuan-spiced duck or bleu-cheese gnocchi. ⊠ *Kater Rd., Sutton Forest 2577* ☎ *02/4868–2355* ⊟ *02/4868–3257* ⊕ *www.peppers.com. au* ⇆ *32 rooms, 9 suites* ⌂ *Restaurant, room service, IDD phones, refrigerators, in-room VCRs, golf privileges, tennis court, pool, mountain bikes, croquet, volleyball, 2 bars, babysitting, laundry service, concierge, Internet room, business services, meeting rooms, car rental, travel services; no smoking* ⊟ *AE, DC, MC, V* ⍻ *BP.*

Sports & the Outdoors

GOLF The exclusive, Scottish-style **Mt. Broughton Golf & Country Club** (⊠ Kater Rd., Sutton Forest ☎ 02/4869–1597 ⊕ www.mtbroughton.com.au) has an 18-hole, par-72 championship course that is considered by pros to be one of Australia's top 100. Facilities are of a very high standard. Nonmembers are welcome but should call in advance. Greens fees are A\$77 weekdays (including cart), A\$94 weekends (including cart).

HORSEBACK
RIDING

The superbly equipped **Highlands Equestrian Centre** (✉ Sutton Farm, Illawarra Hwy., Sutton Forest ☎ 02/4868–2584) runs cross-country rides and classes for everyone from beginners to advanced riders who are capable of dressage and show jumping. Pony rides cost A$20, and escorted trail rides start at A$50. Reservations are essential.

Morton National Park & Fitzroy Falls

19 km (12 mi) southwest of Moss Vale.

Sprawling across more than 400,000 acres, rugged **Morton National Park** ranks as one of the state's largest natural areas. This scenic region encompasses sheer sandstone cliffs and escarpments, scenic lookouts, waterfalls, and densely forested valleys. At **Fitzroy Falls,** the park's eastern highlight, water tumbles 270 feet from the craggy sandstone escarpment. A boardwalk leads to lookouts with spectacular views of the falls and the heavily forested Yarrunga Valley. Birdlife is prolific: look for kookaburras, parrots, and even the elusive lyrebird.

The **Fitzroy Falls Visitor Centre** (✉ Nowra Rd. ☎ 02/4887–7270), operated by the National Parks and Wildlife Service, has a shop, information displays, and a café. It's open daily 9–5:30.

Kangaroo Valley

18 km (11 mi) southeast of Fitzroy Falls.

After descending the slopes of Barrengarry Mountain, from which there are wonderful views of the plains and coast below, Moss Vale Road reaches Kangaroo Valley, a lush dairy farming region first settled during the early 1800s. Many old buildings remain, and the entire charming, verdant region is National Trust–classified. The Kangaroo Valley township has several cafés and crafts shops, and you can rent a canoe, golf, swim in the river, or hike. The grand, medieval-style Hampden Bridge, which was erected over the Kangaroo River in 1897, marks the entrance to the village.

The **Pioneer Museum Park,** next to Hampden Bridge, has a unique perspective on the valley's history. As well as a collection of rusting agricultural machinery, the site includes a re-creation of a late-19th-century homestead, and several forest and woodland bushwalks. ✉ *Moss Vale Rd. at Hampden Bridge* ☎ *02/4465–1306* 🖃 *A$4* ☉ *Fri.–Mon. 10–4 Nov.–Mar., 11–3 Apr.–Oct.*

Where to Stay

★ $$$ 🏠 **Woodbyne.** This refined and stylish white-painted villa radiates a sense of sanctuary and calm. Eleven spacious guest rooms, decorated in neutral tones, are sparingly furnished with design-conscious pieces, art, and fabrics. Each room has a view of the garden, which harks back to another era that delighted in precise composition. Despite its gracious airs, however, the hotel cannot disguise its proximity to the traffic that rushes along the Princes Highway. There's a two-night minimum at weekends. ✉ *4 O'Keefe's La., just off Princes Hwy. south of Berry, Jaspers Brush 2535* ☎ *02/4448–6200* 🖨 *02/4448–6211* ⊕ *www.woodbyne.com*

↵11 rooms & Dining room, fans, minibars, refrigerators, in-room DVD/
VCR, pool, boccie, Internet room, meeting rooms, travel services; no
a/c, no room phones, no kids, no smoking ⊟ AE, MC, V ⫶◯⫶ BP.

en route

After leaving Kangaroo Valley via Moss Vale Road, turn left after
about 3½ km (2 mi) onto the narrow, precipitous Kangaroo Valley
Road, which leads to the delightful town of **Berry**. Styling itself as the
"Town of Trees," this roadside settlement has carefully preserved its
19th-century heritage and architecture. The town's 1886 bank now
serves as the local history museum, and the main street is lined with
crafts and gift shops housed in attractive old buildings.

From Berry you can either travel to Kiama along the Princes
Highway or you can take a more scenic coastal route via the sands
and wild surf of spectacular **Seven Mile Beach** and the quiet seaside
villages of **Gerroa** and **Gerringong.** It is 26 km (16 mi) to Kiama
along the latter route.

Kiama

47 km (29 mi) northeast of Kangaroo Valley.

First "discovered" by the intrepid explorer George Bass, who sailed here
from Sydney in his small whaleboat in 1797, this attractive coastal township of 23,000 began life as a fishing port. There are several significant
19th-century buildings, such as the National Trust–listed weatherboard
cottages on Collins Street, the Presbyterian church, and Manning Street's
surprisingly grand post office. The Kiama Visitors Centre has a "Heritage
Walks" brochure that describes points of interest around the town center.

The town's beaches—including Kendalls, Easts, Surf, and Bombo—are
excellent for swimming and surfing. Other popular activities around Kiama
are fishing and scuba diving. Several boat operators based in the harbor offer game, sports, and deep-sea fishing trips, and others cater to
divers. At Blowhole Point are the blowhole itself, through which the sea
erupts, and the impressive 1887 Kiama Lighthouse.

Where to Eat

$–$$ ✕**Chachis.** Inside this converted 1880s weatherboard cottage is a friendly,
reasonably priced Italian-style restaurant. Meat, seafood, and vegetarian main courses are available, including a traditional *bistecca* (steak)
topped with garlic prawns, and the four pastas come with a choice of
eight sauces. The dessert menu is extensive and tempting; if you're lucky
it might include a red-wine-and-ricotta tiramisu. Dining is either indoors
or on the veranda. ✉ *The Terraces, 32 Collins St.* ☎ *02/4233–1144*
⊟ *AE, DC, MC, V* ⊘ *Closed Tues. No lunch Mon. and Wed.–Fri.*

en route

Exploring the lower half of the South Coast from Kiama to Eden is one
of this region's greatest pleasures. About 39 km (24 mi) past Ulladulla,
take the side road 8 km (5 mi) to **Pebbly Beach** to find hundreds of
kangaroos. About 110 km (68 mi) farther along the Princes Highway is
Central Tilba, a pleasant step back in time where you can visit arts-
and-crafts shops or sample locally produced wines and cheeses.

Eden

271 km (168 mi) southwest of Kiama.

On Twofold Bay, Eden is the third-deepest natural harbor in the world. It's also home to one of the state's largest fishing fleets and some of the best whale-watching on the East Coast. Visit the **Eden Killer Whale Museum** in the center of town to see Old Tom, the skeleton of the last of the killer whale pod that made Eden a famous whaling town more than 100 years ago. ⊠ *94 Imlay St.* ☎ *02/6496–2094* ☜ *A$6* ☉ *Mon.–Sat. 9:15–3:45, Sun. 11:15–3:45.*

Where to Stay & Eat

$$ ✕ **Wheelhouse Restaurant.** The best locally caught seafood is served with spectacular views of the wharf, Twofold Bay, and Mt. Imlay at this casual restaurant. Look for oysters in season and kingfish with salsa verde. ⊠ *Eden Wharf* ☎ *02/6496–3392* 🍴 *AE, D, MC, V* ☉ *Closed Mon. in winter (call ahead on other days).*

$–$$ 🏠 **Crown and Anchor.** This bed-and-breakfast is in Eden's oldest surviving building, dating from the 1840s—a splendid example of elegant Regency architecture. Carefully restored and filled with antiques by owners Judy and Mauro Maurilli, the B&B is aimed at those looking for a cozy, romantic getaway—with spectacular sea views (you can see humpback whales from the veranda in season). Some rooms have fireplaces, but everyone has access to the twin fireplaces in the lounge, where complimentary champagne and port can be enjoyed. ⊠ *239 Imlay St., 2551* ☎ *02/6496–1017* 🖷 *02/6496–3878* ⊕ *www.crownandanchoreden. com.au* ➪ *5 rooms* ⚬ *No a/c, no room phones, no room TVs, no kids, no smoking* 🍴 *AE, MC, V* ⍾ *BP.*

Whale-Watching

Cat Balou Cruises (⊠ Main Wharf ☎ 02/6496–2027) runs daily whale-watching trips October and November 7:30–noon. The A$70 fare includes refreshments, and if you don't see any whales you get a return free trip, or half of your fare back.

Southern Highlands & South Coast A to Z

BUS TRAVEL

Greyhound Australia has twice-daily service between Sydney and Mittagong. The journey takes 2½ hours, and the round-trip fare is about A$32. The same company also runs twice-daily buses from Canberra (two hours) at about A$28 round-trip. Local buses run between the main Highlands towns, but these will not take you to the out-of-the-way attractions.

🔋 **Greyhound Australia** ☎ 13-1499 ⊕ www.greyhound.com.au.

CAR RENTAL

Renting a car is the best way to see most of the area. You can reserve a car through Avis and Thrifty.

🔋 **Avis** ⊠ Shell Service Station, 571 Argyle St., Moss Vale ☎ 02/4868-1044. **Thrifty** ⊠ Mobil Service Station, 51 Hume Hwy., Mittagong ☎ 02/4872-1283.

CAR TRAVEL

From central Sydney, head for the airport and follow the signs to the M5 Motorway toll road (A$3.30). Connect with the Hume Highway and take the Mittagong exit. Mittagong is 103 km (64 mi) southwest of Sydney, and the drive should take 1½–2 hours.

Distances between towns and attractions are short, and roads are generally in good condition and scenic—all the more reason to drive them yourself.

EMERGENCIES

In an emergency, dial **000** to reach an ambulance, the police, or the fire department.

MAIL, INTERNET & SHIPPING

Most post offices are in the middle of town, on the main street. In Mittagong you can surf the Internet and check e-mail at Mittagong Mania. 🗐 **Internet Cafés Mittagong Mania** ⊠ Shop 7, Albion St., Mittagong ☎ 02/4871-7777.

TRAIN TRAVEL

Sydney's Cityrail commuter line trains have frequent daily service to Mittagong, Bowral, Moss Vale, and Bundanoon. Trains from Sydney also stop daily at Kiama. Round-trip fares to the Southern Highlands (Bowral) cost A$26 during peak hours and A$15.80 for an off-peak ticket. Round-trip fares to Kiama cost A$25.60 for a peak ticket and A$15.60 for an off-peak ticket. 🗐 **Cityrail** ☎ 13-1500.

VISITOR INFORMATION

Kiama Visitors Centre is open daily 9–5. Sydney Visitor Centre, open daily 9:30–5:30, has information on Southern Highlands and South Coast hotels, tours, and sights. Tourism Southern Highlands Information Centre is open 9–5 weekdays, 8:30–4:30 weekends. 🗐 **Kiama Visitors Centre** ⊠ Blowhole Point, Kiama 2533 ☎ 02/4232-3322 or 1300/ 654262. **Sydney Visitor Centre** ⊠106 George St., The Rocks, Sydney 2000 ☎02/9255-1788 🖶 02/9241-5010 ⊕ www.sydneyvisitorcentre.com. **Tourism Southern Highlands Information Centre** ⊠ 62-70 Main St., Mittagong 2575 ☎ 02/4871-2888 or 1300/657559 ⊕ www.southern-highlands.com.au.

THE HUNTER VALLEY

To almost everyone in Sydney, the Hunter Valley conjures up visions not of coal mines or cows—the area's earliest industries—but of wine. Hunter is the largest grape-growing area in the state, with more than 120 wineries and a reputation for producing excellent wines. Many of them have found a market overseas, and visiting wine lovers might recognize the Hunter Valley labels of Rosemount, Rothbury Estate, or Lindemans.

The Hunter Valley covers an area of almost 25,103 square km (9,692 square mi), stretching from the town of Gosford north of Sydney to 177 km (110 mi) farther north along the coast, and almost 300 km (186 mi) inland. The meandering waterway that gives this valley its name is also one of the most extensive river systems in the state. From its source on the rugged slopes of the Mt. Royal Range, the Hunter River flows through rich grazing country and past the horse stud farms around Scone in the upper part of the valley, home of some of Australia's wealthiest farming families. In the Lower Hunter region, the river crosses the vast coal deposits of the Greta seam.

Cessnock

185 km (115 mi) north of Sydney.

The large town of Cessnock is better known as the entrance to the Lower Hunter Valley than for any particular attraction in the town itself. Between 1890 and 1960 this was an important coal-mining area, but when coal production began to decline during the 1950s, the mines gradually gave way to vines.

At **Hunter Valley Zoo**, 4½ km (3 mi) north of Cessnock, animals from all over the world mingle with such Australian fauna as koalas, wallabies, kangaroos, wombats, snakes, and lizards in a 24-acre bushland park. There are more than 90 species of animals and birds here, including monkeys, deer, and antelope. Barbecue and picnic facilities are available. ⊠ 2 *Lomas La., Nulkaba 2325* ☎ *02/4990–7714* ⊠ *A$10* ☉ *Daily 9:30–4:30.*

Wollombi

31 km (19 mi) northwest of Cessnock.

Nothing seems to have changed in the atmospheric town of Wollombi since the days when the Cobb & Co. stagecoaches rumbled through town. Founded in 1820, Wollombi was the overnight stop for the coaches on the second day of the journey from Sydney along the convict-built Great Northern Road—at that time the only route north. The town is full of delightful old sandstone buildings and antiques shops, and there's also a museum in the old courthouse with 19th-century clothing and bushranger memorabilia. The local hotel, the Wollombi Tavern, serves its own exotic brew, which goes by the name of Dr. Jurd's Jungle Juice. The pub also scores high marks for its friendliness and local color.

Where to Stay

★ $$ 🏠 **Avoca House.** Overlooking the Wollombi Brook just outside town, this charming century-old house, with its vine-covered verandas and central courtyard, is a country classic with a layout that guarantees privacy. The owners, Russell and Kay Davies, pay great attention to detail to ensure that their guests have a comfortable and memorable stay. The largest of the three tasteful rooms is a self-contained suite with a queen bed, sitting room, and kitchenette. Rates include a hearty country-style breakfast, and dinner is available by arrangement. ⊠ *2699 Wollombi Rd., 2325* ☎ *02/4998–3233* 🖷 *02/4998–3319* 🛏 *2 rooms, 1 suite* ⚲ *BBQs, 1 kitchenette, billiards, hiking, laundry facilities, laundry service, some pets allowed; no room phones, no room TVs* ▤ *MC, V* ⦿*BP.*

Pokolbin

10 km (6 mi) northwest of Cessnock.

The Lower Hunter wine-growing region is centered around the village of Pokolbin, where there are antiques shops, good cafés, and dozens of wineries.

Any tour of the area's vineyards should begin at Pokolbin's **Hunter Valley Wine Country Visitors Information Centre,** which has free maps of the vineyards, brochures, and a handy visitor's guide. ✉ *455 Wine Country Dr.* ☎ *02/4990–0900* ⊕ *www.winecountry.com.au* ☉ *Mon.–Thurs. 9–5, Fri. and Sat. 9 6, Sun. 9 1.*

Drop into **Binnorie Dairy** (at Tuscany Wine Estate) to try and buy—-few can resist—Simon Gough's handcrafted soft cow and goat cheeses. You'd be hard-pressed to find a tastier marinated feta outside Greece—or even in it. ✉ *Hermitage Rd. and Mistletoe La.* ☎ *02/4998–6660* ☉ *Tues.–Sat. 10–5, Sun. 10–4.*

In a delightful rural corner of the Mount View region, **Briar Ridge Vineyard** is one of the Hunter Valley's outstanding small wineries. It produces a limited selection of sought-after reds, whites, and sparkling wines. The semillon, chardonnay, shiraz, and intense cabernet sauvignon are highly recommended. The vineyard is on the southern periphery of the Lower Hunter vineyards, about a five-minute drive from Pokolbin. ✉ *593 Mt. View Rd., Mount View* ☎ *02/4990–3670* ⊕ *www.briarridge. com.au* ☉ *Daily 10–5.*

On the lower slopes of Mt. Bright, one of the loveliest parts of the Lower Hunter region, is **Drayton's Family Wines.** Wine making is a Drayton family tradition dating from the mid-19th century, when Joseph Drayton first cleared these slopes and planted vines. Today the chardonnay, semillon, and shiraz made here are some of the most consistent award-winners around. ✉ *555 Oakey Creek Rd.* ☎ *02/4998–7513* ⊕ *www. draytonswines.com.au* ☉ *Weekdays 8–5, weekends 10–5.*

★ The **Lindemans Hunter River Winery** has been one of the largest and most prestigious winemakers in the country since the early 1900s. In addition to its Hunter Valley vineyards, the company also owns property in South Australia and Victoria, and numerous outstanding wines from these vineyards can be sampled in the tasting room. Try the red burgundy, semillon, or chardonnay. The winery has its own museum, displaying vintage wine-making equipment, as well as two picnic areas, one near the parking lot and the other next to the willow trees around the dam. ✉ *McDonalds Rd. just south of DeBeyers Rd.* ☎ *02/4998–7684* ⊕ *www.lindemans.com.au* ☉ *Daily 10–5.*

★ At **McWilliams Mount Pleasant Estate,** part of Australia's biggest family-owned wine company, chief winemaker Phil Ryan, the third since the winery was founded in 1921, continues the tradition of producing classic Hunter wines. Flagship Maurice O'Shea Shiraz and Chardonnay, and celebrated Elizabeth Semillon, are among the wines that can be sampled in the huge cellar door. You can also sit down on the terrace to a tasting plate in Elizabeth's Café; this matches three vintages of Elizabeth Semillon and one of premium Lovedale Semillon with four different foods. Guided winery tours run daily at 11 AM. ⊠ *Marrowbone Rd.* ☎ *02/4998–7505* ⊕ *www.mcwilliams.com.au* ✍ *Tours A$3.30* ⊗ *Daily 10–4:30.*

A leading light in the new wave of Hunter winemakers, **Margan Family Winegrowers** produces some of the valley's best small-volume wines. Try their full-bodied verdelho, rosé-style Saignee Shiraz, and House of Certain Views Cabernet Sauvignon. A riper-than-most semillon is the flagship, and the 2004 Decanter World Wine Awards rated Margan's botrytis semillon the world's best sweet wine under A$10—it's delicious. You can enjoy a glass of your pick with Mediterranean-inspired alfresco fare in the adjoining Beltree@Margan café. ⊠ *266 Hermitage Rd.* ☎☎ *02/ 6574–7004, 02/6574–7216 café* ⊕ *www.margan.com.au* ⊗ *Daily 10–5.*

The **Rothbury Estate,** set high on a hill in the heart of Pokolbin, is one of the Lower Hunter Valley's premier wineries, established in 1968 by Australian wine-making legend Len Evans. Rothbury grows grapes in many areas of New South Wales, but grapes grown in the Hunter Valley go into the Brokenback Range wine, its most prestigious. The fine semillon and earthy shiraz wines that make this vineyard famous are available in a delightful tasting room sample. A daily guided tour takes you from grapes to glass. The on-site Toby's Coffee House has good food and a terrific wine list. ⊠ *Broke Rd. near McDonalds Rd.* ☎ *02/ 4998–7555* ⊕ *www.rothburyestate.com.au* ✍ *Tour A$4* ⊗ *Sun.–Thurs. 9:30–4:30, weekends 9:30–5. Guided tour daily at 10:30.*

Founded in 1858, **Tyrrell's Wines** is the Hunter Valley's oldest family-owned vineyard. This venerable establishment crafts a wide selection of wines and was the first to produce chardonnay commercially in Australia. Its famous Vat 47 Chardonnay is still a winner. Enjoy the experience of sampling fine wines in the elegant tasting room, or take a picnic lunch to a site overlooking the valley. ⊠ *Broke Rd., 2½ km (1½ mi) west of McDonalds Rd.* ☎ *02/4993–7000* ⊕ *www.tyrrells.com.au* ⊗ *Weekdays 8:30–5, Sat. 8:30–4:30; free guided tour Mon.–Sat. at 1:30.*

The low stone-and-timber buildings of the **Hunter Valley Gardens** are the heart of the Pokolbin wine-growing district. This large complex includes a hotel and convention center, gift shops, restaurants, a pub, the underground **Hunter Cellars,** and 12 gardens covering 50 acres. At the far end of the complex is a large, shady picnic area with barbecues and a playground. ⊠ *Broke and McDonalds Rds.* ☎ *02/4998–7600* ⊕ *www. hvg.com.au* ⊗ *Daily 9:30–5.*

Adjoining the gardens is the cellar door complex of **McGuigan Wines.** Here you can taste wines and the **Hunter Valley Cheese Company**'s superb cheeses—look out for the washed-rind Hunter Valley Gold and the marinated soft, cows'-milk cheese—before you buy. You can also see the cheeses being made by hand. There is a cheese talk daily at 11, and winery tours are given on weekdays at noon, weekends at 11 and noon. ⊠ *Broke and McDonalds Rds.* ☎ *02/4998–7402* ⊕ *www.mcguiganwines. com.au* ⊗ *Daily 9:30–5.*

Where to Stay & Eat

$$$ ✕ **Robert's at Pepper Tree.** Incorporating an 1870s pioneer's cottage and
Fodor'sChoice encircled by grapevines, this stunning restaurant matches its surround-
★ ings with creative fare by chef Robert Molines. The modern Australian
menu draws inspiration from the recipes of regional France and Italy,
applied to local game, seafood, beef, and lamb. In the airy, country-style
dining room—with antique furniture, bare timber floors, and a big
stone fireplace—you might try char-grilled quail as a first course, and
then follow it with basil-and-pine-nut-crusted John Dory fillet with
trellis tomatoes and roast tomato sauce. The cozy fireside lounge is per-
fect for enjoying after-dinner liqueurs. ⊠ *Halls Rd.* ☎ *02/4998–7330*
🖃 *AE, DC, MC, V.*

$$ ✕ **Il Cacciatore Restaurant.** Serving up a vast selection of northern Italian specialties, the outdoor terrace at Il Cacciatore is the perfect place
for a leisurely weekend lunch. Don't be put off by the barnlike exterior;
once inside the restaurant your senses will be overwhelmed by the wonderful aromas wafting from the kitchen. Italian favorites crowd this menu:
try the char-grilled lamb fillets with oven-roasted tomato polenta and
rosemary pesto, or the citrus slow-roasted duck with caramelized figs.
Make sure you leave plenty of room for the long list of *dolci* (desserts)
too. An extensive list of local and imported wines complements the menu.
⊠ *McDonald and Gillard Rds.* ☎ *02/4998–7639* 🖃 *AE, MC, V* ☼ *No
lunch weekdays.*

$–$$ ✕ **Leaves & Fishes.** A rustic boathouse-style café with a deck that pro-
jects over a fish-stocked dam, this is the place to dip into a bucket of
prawns, down freshly shucked oysters, and graze antipasto plates any
time of day. Fish comes straight from farm to plate and wines from
local vineyards. Desserts from the specials board might include Sicil-
ian apple cake with fresh vanilla cream. Reservations are recommended, especially on weekends. ⊠ *737 Lovedale Rd., Lovedale 2320*
☎ *02/4930–7400* 🖃 *MC, V* ☼ *Closed Tues. No dinner Sun., Mon.,
Wed., and Thurs.*

$$$$ ✕🖪 **Casuarina Restaurant & Country Inn.** Lapped by a sea of grapevines,
this luxurious country resort has a powerful sense of fantasy about it.
Each of the palatial guest suites is furnished according to particular themes,
such as the French Bordello suite, with its pedestalled four-poster canopy
bed; Romeo's Retreat, with mirrors everywhere and a hot tub in the lounge
room; Susie Wong's suite, with its original opium couch for a bed; and
the movie-inspired Moulin Rouge suite. The on-site Casuarina Restaurant specializes in flambéed dishes theatrically prepared at your table.
There's a minimum two-night booking on weekends. ⊠ *Hermitage Rd.
between Broke and Deasys Rds., 2320* ☎ *02/4998–7888* 🖷 *02/
4998–7692* ⊕ *www.casuarinainn.com.au* ⇆ *9 suites, 3 cottages*
⚐ *Restaurant, IDD phones, some in-room hot tubs, some kitchenettes,
minibars, cable TV, some in-room DVDs, in-room data ports, tennis court,
saltwater pool, sauna, billiards, boccie, Internet room, meeting rooms,
travel services; no smoking* 🖃 *AE, DC, MC, V.*

$$$–$$$$ 🖪 **Cedars Mount View.** This property in the hills above the valley might
tempt you to forget about wine tasting for a few days; the peaceful sounds
of birds and wind in the eucalyptus leaves are that soothing. Each of

the three wooden cottages here is different: The Ridge—a honeymoon cottage—has an open plan with a king-size bed and leather sofas; there's a two-person daybed beneath a picture window in The Gums; and The Creek has a mezzanine main bedroom. All are comfortably luxurious, with fine bed linens, Jacuzzi tubs, stereos, and magazines to read beside the wood-burning fireplaces. There are full kitchens and you can cook your breakfast on the deck barbecue while watching the wildlife. Cellar doors are 15 minutes away. ⊠ *Mitchells Rd., Mount View 2325* ☎ *0414/533070 or 02/4959–3072* 🖷 *02/4950–4876* ⊕ *www.cedars. com.au* ⇋ *3 cottages* ♿ *BBQs, fans, in-room hot tubs, kitchens, microwaves, refrigerators, in-room DVD, hiking, travel services, no-smoking rooms* ▤ *AE, MC, V* ⑩ *BP.*

$$$–$$$$ ✕⌨ **Peppers Guest House.** Settled into a grove of wild peppercorn trees and surrounded by flagstone verandas, this cluster of long, low buildings imitates the architecture of a classic Australian country homestead. Guest rooms are stylishly furnished in subtle stripes and weaves in coffee-and-cream hues. In-house Chez Pok restaurant serves fine country-style fare with French, Asian, and Italian influences. You might try a boudin of quail and bacon, served with crushed green peas and an apple-and-walnut salad. The hotel has a devoted following and is booked well in advance for weekends. ⊠ *Ekerts Rd. just off Broke Rd., 2320* ☎ *02/4993–4993* 🖷 *02/4998–7739* ⊕ *www.peppers.com.au* ⇋ *47 rooms, 1 4-bedroom homestead* ♿ *Restaurant, room service, IDD phones, minibars, refrigerators, tennis court, pool, sauna, spa, bicycles, boccie, bar, babysitting, laundry service, concierge, Internet room, business services, meeting rooms, car rental, travel services, no-smoking rooms* ▤ *AE, DC, MC, V* ⑩ *BP.*

$$$$ ⌨ **Peppers Convent.** This former convent, the most luxurious property
Fodor's Choice in the Hunter Valley, was transported 605 km (375 mi) from its original home in western New South Wales. Despite the timber building's
★ imposing exterior, the 34-guest maximum makes for a relaxed atmosphere. White cane furniture, floral curtains, and fresh flowers decorate the spacious, light-filled rooms, each with French doors that open onto a wide veranda; the beds have crisp white duvets and romantic mosquito nets. The house is surrounded by Pepper Tree Winery's vines and is adjacent to Robert's at Pepper Tree, where you can get delicious meals. Rates include a full country breakfast plus predinner drinks and canapés. ⊠ *Halls Rd., 2320* ☎ *02/4998–7764* 🖷 *02/4998–7323* ⊕ *www.peppers. com.au* ⇋ *17 rooms* ♿ *IDD phones, minibars, refrigerators, in-room data ports, tennis court, pool, hot tub, bicycles, boccie, meeting rooms; no smoking* ▤ *AE, DC, MC, V* ⑩ *BP.*

$$–$$$ ⌨ **Carriages Country House.** Set on 36 acres at the end of a quiet country lane is this rustic-looking but winsome guesthouse. Each of its very private suites has antique country pine furniture and a large sitting area with cushy sofas, and many have open fireplaces. The two more expensive suites in the Gatehouse also have whirlpool tubs and share a lounge with full kitchen facilities. Breakfast—a basket of goodies delivered to your door or served in the Gatehouse Suites—is included. ⊠ *Halls Rd., 2321* ☎ *02/4998–7591* 🖷 *02/4998–7839* ⊕ *www. thecarriages.com.au* ⇋ *10 suites* ♿ *BBQs, IDD phones, some in-*

room hot tubs, 1 kitchen, some in-room DVDs, some in-room data ports, tennis court, saltwater pool, laundry service, Internet room, travel services; no kids ☱ AE, MC, V ⏃◎⏃ CP.

★ $–$$$ ⊞ **Vineyard Hill Country Motel.** Smart and modern, these one- and two-bedroom suites are far better than the "motel" tag suggests—and they're also an exceptional value. Each pastel-color suite has its own high-ceilinged lounge area, a private deck, and a kitchenette. The best views are from Rooms 4 through 8. Full, cooked breakfasts are available. There's a minimum stay of two nights on weekends. ⊠ *Lovedale Rd. just past Lodge Rd., Lovedale 2320* ☏ *02/4990–4166* 🖷 *02/ 4991–4431* ⊕ *www.vineyardhill.com.au* ⇝ *8 suites* ⚐ *BBQs, IDD phones, kitchens, microwaves, refrigerators, in-room VCRs, saltwater pool, outdoor hot tub, laundry service, Internet room, travel services; no smoking* ☱ *AE, MC, V.*

$–$$ ⊞ **Glen Ayr Cottages.** Tucked away in the Pokolbin bushland, yet close to the heart of the wine region, these trim, colonial-style wooden cottages are ideal for families. Built on a ridge, each has two to four bedrooms, with views of vineyards on one side and eucalyptus forest on the other. Furnishings are comfortable but simple: no televisions are allowed to compete with the songs of birds. ⊠ *776 DeBeyers Rd., 2320* ☏ *02/4998–7784* 🖷 *02/4998–7476* ⊕ *www.glenayrcottages.com.au* ⇝ *6 cottages* ⚐ *BBQs, fans, kitchens, microwaves, refrigerators; no a/c in some rooms, no room phones, no room TVs* ☱ *MC, V.*

Scone

137 km (85 mi) northwest of Pokolbin.

The delightful Upper Hunter Valley farming town of Scone contains several historic mid-19th-century buildings and a local museum, and there are particularly fine accommodations in the area. Sometimes called the horse capital of Australia, the town is also known for its high-quality horse and cattle stud farms and its enthusiasm for polo playing.

Where to Stay

$$$$ ⊞ **Belltrees Country House.** On a working cattle and horse ranch that dates from the 1830s, this outstanding rural retreat offers a taste of aristocratic Australian country life. Activities include horseback riding, polo, archery, clay pigeon shooting, and four-wheel-drive spins into the surrounding mountains. Bed-and-breakfast–style accommodations are in the modern wing, and there are three self-contained cottages. The Mountain Retreat, an all-inclusive two-bedroom house, is perched atop a 5,000-foot mountain, and reached by four-wheel drive. It's a two-hour drive to Belltrees from the Lower Hunter wineries. ⊠ *Gundy Rd., 2337* ☏ *02/6546–1123* 🖷 *02/6546–1193* ⊕ *www. belltrees.com* ⇝ *4 rooms, 4 cottages* ⚐ *Dining room, BBQs, fans, some in-room hot tubs, some kitchens, some in-room VCRs, tennis court, saltwater pool, laundry facilities, laundry service, Internet room, meeting rooms; no a/c, no room phones, no TV in some rooms, no smoking* ☱ *AE, MC, V* ⏃◎⏃ *BP.*

Maitland

121 km (75 mi) southeast of Scone.

Maitland was one of Australia's earliest European settlements, and you can best explore the town's history by strolling along High Street, which has a number of colonial buildings and is classified by the National Trust as an urban conservation area. Leading off this thoroughfare is Church Street, with several handsome two-story Georgian homes, a couple of which are open to the public.

The **Maitland Regional Art Gallery,** contains both permanent collections and changing exhibits of contemporary Australian art, historic photographs, East African sculptures, and Aboriginal paintings. ⊠ *230 High St.* ☎ *02/4934–9859* ✉ *Free* ☉ *Tues.–Sun. 10–5.*

The National Trust's **Grossman House** adjoins Maitland's art gallery. The restored 1870 home is furnished as a Victorian merchant's town house with an interesting collection of colonial antique furniture, costumes, and textiles. ⊠ *Church St. near Clive St.* ☎ *02/4933–6452* ✉ *A$5* ☉ *Thurs.–Sun. 10–3; also by appointment.*

Where to Stay & Eat

★ $$ ✕🏨 **Old George and Dragon.** With its sumptuous colors, green baize walls, oil paintings, Asian curios, and plush furnishings, this 19th-century coaching inn, where Cobb & Co. passengers would break their long journeys, takes you back to the full-blown opulence of the Victorian era. Guest rooms are filled with art and antiques, and there's a common lounge, kitchen facilities to share, and a leafy garden courtyard. The food is every bit as lavish as the surroundings, changing with the seasons and based on the classics of French cooking. You might try venison leg with blueberry sauce and roast parsnip, or roast local duck with oranges and red cabbage. The extensive wine list highlights Australia's finest vintages. It's not recommended for young children to stay here. ⊠ *48 Melbourne St., East Maitland 2323* ☎ *02/4933–7272* 🖨 *02/4934–1481* ⊕ *www.oldgeorgeanddragon.com.au* ➣ *5 rooms* ⚘ *In-room VCRs, laundry service, Internet room; no room phones, no kids under 12, no smoking* ▤ *AE, MC, V* ⊙⊩ *BP.*

Hunter Valley A to Z

BUS TRAVEL

Rover Coaches' Wine Country Xpress departs at 8:30 AM for the 2½-hour journey to Cessnock from Sydney's Central Coach Terminal on Eddy Avenue (near Central Station). The fare is A$35 one-way.

To avoid driving after sampling too many wines, hop aboard one of the Cessnock-based Wine Rover buses. Minibuses travel between area hotels, restaurants, and 18 wineries. A day pass (valid 10–5) with unlimited stops is A$35 weekdays, A$40 on weekends.

Locally based Shadows Hunter Wine Country Tours operates a local transfer service between wineries, restaurants, and your accommodation.
🚍 **Rover Coaches** ☎ 0427/001100 or 1800/801012. **Shadows Hunter Wine Country Tours** ☎ 02/4990–7002.

CAR RENTAL

▣ **Avis** ✉ Newcastle Airport, Lot 2, Williamtown Rd., Williamtown ☎ 02/4965-1451.
Budget ✉ Newcastle Airport, Lot 2, Williamtown Rd., Williamtown ☎ 02/4965-1671.
Hertz ✉ 1A Aberdare Rd., Cessnock ☎ 02/4991-2500.

CAR TRAVEL

A car is a necessity for exploring the area. Other than taking a guided tour on arrival, this is the most convenient way to visit the wineries and off-the-beaten-path attractions, such as Wollombi.

To reach the area, leave Sydney by the Harbour Bridge or Harbour Tunnel and follow the signs for Newcastle. Just before Hornsby this road joins the Sydney–Newcastle Freeway. Take the exit from the freeway signposted HUNTER VALLEY VINEYARDS VIA CESSNOCK. From Cessnock, the route to the vineyards is clearly marked. Allow 2½ hours for the 185-km (115-mi) journey from Sydney.

EMERGENCIES

In an emergency, dial **000** to reach an ambulance, the police, or the fire department.

MAIL & INTERNET

Post offices can be found in all major towns throughout the region. Most post offices are in the middle of town, on the main street. In Cessnock you can check e-mail and surf the Internet at L337gamerz cybercafé.
▣ **L337gamerz** ✉ Shop 7/34 Vincent St., Cessnock 2325 ☎ 02/4991-2300.

MONEY MATTERS

Cessnock has several banks, all of which will change foreign currency and travelers checks. There's an ATM in Pokolbin.

TOURS

Several Sydney-based bus companies tour the Hunter Valley. Alternative ways to explore the region are by horse-drawn carriage, Pontiac, bicycle, motorbike, or even in a hot-air balloon. Full details are available from the Hunter Valley Wine Country Visitors Information Centre.

AAT Kings operates a one-day bus tour of the Hunter Valley and Wollombi from Sydney daily. Buses collect passengers from city hotels, then make a final pickup from the Sydney Casino, departing at 8:30. The tour returns to the casino at 7. Tours cost A$135 and include lunch and wine tasting.

There's nothing quite like cruising the Hunter Valley in a 1960 Pontiac. Pickofthecrop Wine Expeditions offers customized tours from a few hours to several days. A day tour including restaurant lunch or gourmet picnic for two people costs A$350. Pickups from Newcastle can be arranged.

Drifting above the valley while the vines are still wet with dew is an unforgettable way to see the Hunter Valley. Balloon Aloft runs hour-long flights for A$280.

Hunter Valley Wine and Dine Carriages, based in Pokolbin, conducts half-day (from A$49) and full-day (from A$69) horse-drawn carriage tours of the wineries.

⑦ AAT Kings ☎ 02/9518-6095. **Balloon Aloft** ☎ 02/4938-1955 or 1800/028568. **Hunter Valley Wine and Dine Carriages** ☎ 0410/515358. **Pickofthecrop Wine Expeditions** ☎ 02/4990-1567 and 0416/187295

VISITOR INFORMATION

Scone Visitor Information Centre is open daily 9–5. Sydney Visitor Centre, open daily 9:30–5:30, has information on Hunter Valley accommodations, tours, and sights. Hunter Valley Wine Country Visitors Information Centre is open Monday–Thursday 9–5, Friday and Saturday 9–6, Sunday 9–4.

⑦ Hunter Valley Wine Country Visitors Information Centre ✉ 455 Wine Country Dr., Pokolbin 2325 ☎ 02/4990-0900 ⊕ www.winecountry.com.au. **Scone Visitor Information Centre** ✉ Kelly and Susan Sts., Scone 2337 ☎ 02/6545-1526. **Sydney Visitor Centre** ✉ 106 George St., The Rocks, Sydney 2000 ☎ 02/9255-1788 🖶 02/9241-5010 ⊕ www. sydneyvisitorcentre.com.

THE NORTH COAST

The North Coast is one of the most glorious and seductive stretches of terrain in Australia. An almost continuous line of beaches defines the coast, with the Great Dividing Range rising to the west. These natural borders frame a succession of rolling green pasturelands, mossy rain forests, towns dotted by red-roof houses, and waterfalls that tumble in glistening arcs from the escarpment.

A journey along the coast leads through several rich agricultural districts, beginning with grazing country in the south and moving into plantations of bananas, sugarcane, mangoes, avocados, and macadamia nuts. Dorrigo National Park, outside Bellingen, and Muttonbird Island, in Coffs Harbour, are two parks good for getting your feet on some native soil and for seeing unusual birdlife.

The tie that binds the North Coast is the Pacific Highway, but despite its name, this highway rarely affords glimpses of the Pacific Ocean. You can drive the entire length of the North Coast in a single day, but allow at least three—or, better still, a week—to properly sample some of its attractions.

Numbers in the margin correspond to points of interest on the North Coast map.

Port Macquarie

⑫ *417 km (260 mi) northeast of Sydney.*

Port Macquarie was founded as a convict settlement in 1821. Set at the mouth of the Hastings River, the town was chosen for its isolation to serve as an open jail for prisoners convicted of second offenses in New South Wales. By the 1830s the pace of settlement was so brisk that the town was no longer isolated, and its usefulness as a jail had ended. Today's

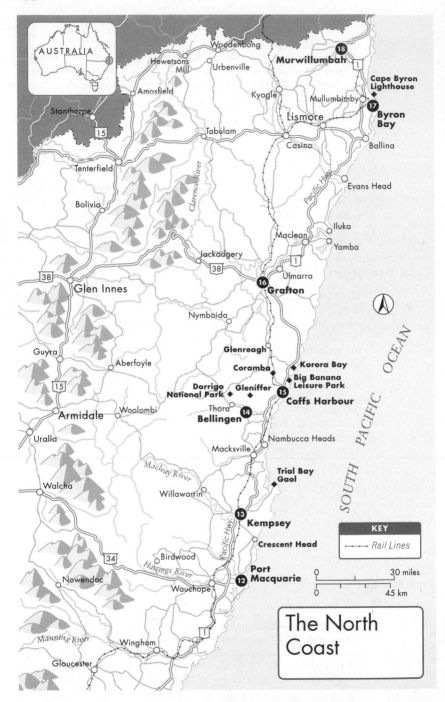

The North Coast

Port Macquarie has few reminders of its convict past and is flourishing as a vacation and retirement area. With its pristine rivers and lakes, and 13 regional beaches, including beautiful Town Beach and Shelley Beach, which both have sheltered swimming, it's a great place to get into water sports, catch a fish for dinner, and watch migrating humpback whales in season, usually May to July and September to November.

Operated by the Koala Preservation Society of New South Wales, the town's **Koala Hospital** is both a worthy cause and a popular attraction. The Port Macquarie region supports many of these extremely appealing but endangered marsupials, and the hospital cares for 150 to 250 sick and injured koalas each year. You can walk around the grounds to view the recuperating animals. Try to visit during feeding times—8 in the morning or 3 in the afternoon. There is a daily guided tour at 3. ⊠ *Macquarie Nature Reserve, Lord St.* ☎ *02/6584–1522* ⊕ *www. koalahospital.org* ⊡ *Donation requested* ⊙ *Daily 8–4:30.*

Fodor'sChoice
★ The **Sea Acres Rainforest Centre** comprises 178 acres of coastal rain forest on the southern side of Port Macquarie. There are more than 170 plant species here, including 300-year-old cabbage tree palms, as well as native mammals, reptiles, and prolific birdlife. An elevated boardwalk allows you to stroll through the lush environment without disturbing the vegetation. The center has informative guided tours, as well as a gift shop and a pleasant rain-forest café. ⊠ *Pacific Dr. near Shelley Beach Rd.* ☎ *02/6582–3355* ⊡ *A$6* ⊙ *Daily 9–4:30.*

Housed in a 19th century two-story shop near the Hastings River is the eclectic **Port Macquarie Historical Museum,** which displays period costumes, memorabilia from both world wars, farm implements, antique clocks and watches, and relics from the town's convict days. ⊠ *22 Clarence St.* ☎ *02/6583–1108* ⊡ *A$5* ⊙ *Mon.–Sat. 9:30–4:30.*

The 1828 **St. Thomas Church,** the country's third-oldest, was built by convicts using local cedar and stone blocks cemented together with powdered seashells. ⊠ *Hay and William Sts.* ☎ *02/6584–1033* ⊙ *Weekdays 9:30–noon and 2–4.*

Where to Stay & Eat

★ **$$** ✕ **Ça Marche.** This terrific Mod-Oz lunch spot is part of the Cassegrain Winery, 20 minutes from downtown Port Macquarie. Entrées such as honey-crusted beef fillet, or tempura of Tasmanian salmon with sesame noodles, sweet chili tamarind dressing, and toffeed lime complement the fine wines. The dining room has views of the vineyards and formal gardens, and the cellar door is open 9–5 for daily tastings. ⊠ *764 Fernbank Creek Rd.* ☎ *02/6582–8320* ▤ *MC, V* ⊙ *No dinner Sat.–Thurs.*

$$ ✕ **Portabellos.** The deceptively casual dining room here belies the sophisticated mix of Mod-Oz and French cuisines coming from the kitchen. Breakfast can be a simple affair of good coffee and homemade pastries, but lunch and dinner take things up a notch with saffron-poached chicken on sweet potato mash, and a salad of fennel, roasted corn, and seared scallops. ⊠ *124 Horton St.* ☎ *02/6584–1171*

⚕ *Reservations essential* ▤ *AE, DC, MC, V* ⛲ *BYOB* ⊘ *Closed Sun. and Mon.*

$$$$ ⌗ **Rydges Port Macquarie.** This imposing international-style hotel on the waterfront is an awkward fit in laid-back Port Macquarie. Decorated in soothing chocolate-and-cream tones, all the spacious rooms have balconies; the best views are over the beach. You're within easy walking distance of Port Macquarie's many attractions, and big discounts are often available outside school holidays. The hotel's Compass restaurant serves Mod-Oz food; you might start with Sydney rock oysters topped with garlic cream sauce and Brie, and move on to grilled seafood dusted with Moroccan spices on saffron risotto. ⊠ *1 Hay St., 2444* ☎ *02/ 6589–2888* ♨ *02/6589–2899* ⊕ *www.rydges.com* ⇘ *98 rooms, 18 apartments, 6 studios* ♿ *Restaurant, café, room service, IDD phones, in-room safes, some kitchens, minibars, some microwaves, refrigerators, cable TV with movies, in-room data ports, pool, gym, outdoor hot tub, bar, babysitting, dry cleaning, laundry service, concierge, meeting rooms, no-smoking floors* ▤ *AE, DC, MC, V.*

$–$$$ ⌗ **HW Boutique Motel.** Although the building dates from the late 1950s (when its sawtooth shape was considered very stylish) the amenities here are up-to-the-minute modern: the rooms have designer furnishings, flat-screen televisions, high-quality bed linens, marble bathrooms, and private balconies with views looking north along the New South Wales coast. Molton Brown bath products are supplied and, in some rooms, so are hot tubs in which to enjoy them. Town Beach is opposite, and it's just a five-minute walk into town. ⊠ *1 Stewart St., 2444* ☎ *02/6583–1200* ♨ *02/6584–1439* ⊕ *www.hwport.com.au* ⇘ *44 rooms, 4 apartments* ♿ *Room service, IDD phones, fans, some in-room hot tubs, kitchenettes, minibars, refrigerators, cable TV, in-room data ports, pool, laundry facilities, Internet room, airport shuttle, business services, no-smoking rooms* ▤ *AE, DC, MC, V.*

$ ⌗ **Azura Beach House B&B.** Standing opposite Shelley Beach, this small bed-and-breakfast is an easy walk from Sea Acres and coastal tracks. Inside, reproduction arts-and-crafts pieces and bright splashes of beach colors enhance minimalist-style furnishings. The more expensive rooms have their own bathrooms. There's also a shared lounge area with a refrigerator and microwave, and a library of some 200 videos. ⊠ *109 Pacific Dr., 2444* ☎♨ *02/6582–2700* ⊕ *www.azura.com.au* ⇘ *4 rooms, 2 with bath* ♿ *BBQs, fans, in-room VCRs, pool, outdoor hot tub, Internet room, no smoking rooms; no kids under 5* ▤ *MC, V* ⓧ *BP.*

Kempsey

⑬ *48 km (30 mi) north of Port Macquarie.*

Several historic buildings, the Macleay River Historical Society Museum and Settlers Cottage, an Aboriginal theme park, and arts-and-crafts shops are among the attractions of this Pacific Highway town, inland on the Macleay River. Kempsey is the business center for a large farming and timber region, as well as the place where Australia's famous Akubra hats are made.

> **off the beaten path**

TRIAL BAY GAOL – Occupying a dramatic position on the cliffs above the sea, this jail dates from the 1870s and 1880s. Its purpose was to teach useful skills to the prisoners who constructed it, but the project proved too expensive and was abandoned in 1903. During World War I the building served as an internment camp for some 500 Germans. To get here, follow Plummer's Road northeast from Kempsey to the village of South West Rocks and Trial Bay Gaol. ✛ *37 km (23 mi) from Kempsey* ☎ *02/6566–6168* ✉ *A$5* ☾ *Daily 9–4:30.*

Bellingen

⑭ *100 km (62 mi) north of Kempsey.*

In a river valley a few miles off the Pacific Highway, Bellingen is one of the prettiest towns along the coast. Many of Bellingen's buildings have been classified by the National Trust, and the museum, cafés, galleries, and crafts outlets are favorite hangouts for artists, craft workers, and writers.

From Bellingen, a meandering and spectacular road circles inland to meet the Pacific Highway close to Coffs Harbour. This scenic route first winds along the river, then climbs more than 1,000 feet up the heavily wooded escarpment to the **Dorrigo Plateau.** At the top of the plateau is

★ **Dorrigo National Park** (☎ 02/6657–2309), a small but outstanding subtropical rain forest that is included on the World Heritage list. Signposts along the main road indicate walking trails. The Satinbird Stroll is a short rain-forest walk, and the 6-km (4-mi) Cedar Falls Walk leads to the most spectacular of the park's many waterfalls. The excellent **Dorrigo Rainforest Centre,** open daily 8:30–5, has information, educational displays, and a shop, and from here you can walk out high over the forest canopy along the Skywalk boardwalk. The national park is approximately 31 km (19 mi) from Bellingen.

> **off the beaten path**

GLENIFFER – If you have an hour to spare, cross the river at Bellingen and take an 18-km (11-mi) excursion on the Bellingen–Gleniffer Road to the village of Gleniffer. This tranquil, rambling journey leads through farmlands and wooded valleys and across Never Never Creek to—believe it or not—the Promised Land, a peaceful, pastoral region with spots for picnics and swimming. Author Peter Carey once lived in this vicinity, and the river and its surroundings provided the backdrop for his novel *Oscar and Lucinda.*

Where to Stay

$$ ▦ **Koompartoo Retreat.** These self-contained, open-plan, elevated cottages on a hillside overlooking Bellingen are superb examples of local craftsmanship, particularly in their use of timbers from surrounding forests. Each has a complete kitchen, a family room, and a shower (no tub). Breakfast is available by arrangement. ✉ *Rawson and Dudley Sts., 2454* ⊕ *www.koompartoo.com.au* ☎ *02/6655–2326* ⬦ *4 cottages* ⚅ *BBQs, kitchens, in-room VCRs, outdoor hot tub, laundry facilities; no room phones, no smoking* ▭ *MC, V.*

en route
Beyond Dorrigo township, a gravel road completes the loop to the towns of Coramba and Moleton, the latter of which is the location for **George's Gold Mine** (⊠ Bushmans Range Rd. ☎ 02/ 6654–5355). Perched on a ridge high above the Orara Valley, this 250-acre cattle property still uses the slab huts and mustering yards built in the region's pioneering days. Owner George Robb is one of the legendary old-timers of the area, and his tour of his gold mine is a vivid account of the personalities and events from the days when "gold fever" gripped these hills. In addition to the mine and its historic equipment, the property has its own rain forest, mountain springs, stand of rare red cedars, and a barbecue-picnic area. Admission, which includes a tour, is A\$12.50. It's open Wednesday–Sunday 10–5, and daily during Christmas and Easter school holidays, with the last tour at 3.

Coffs Harbour

⑮ *35 km (22 mi) northeast of Bellingen via the Pacific Hwy., 103 km (64 mi) from Bellingen via the inland scenic route along the Dorrigo Plateau.*

The area surrounding Coffs Harbour is the state's "banana belt," where long, neat rows of banana palms cover the hillsides. Set at the foot of steep green hills, the town has great beaches and a mild climate. This idyllic combination has made it one of the most popular vacation spots along the coast. Coffs is also a convenient halfway point in the 1,000-km (620-mi) journey between Sydney and Brisbane.

The town has a lively and attractive harbor in the shelter of **Muttonbird Island,** and a stroll out to this nature reserve is delightful in the evening. To get here follow the signs to the Coffs Harbour Jetty, then park near the marina. A wide path leads out along the breakwater and up the slope of the island. The trail is steep, but the views from the top are worth the effort. The island is named after the muttonbirds (also known as shearwaters) that nest here between September and April. Between June and September Muttonbird Island is also a good spot from which to view migrating humpback whales.

Near the port in Coffs Harbour, the giant **Pet Porpoise Pool** aquarium includes sharks, colorful reef fish, turtles, seals, and dolphins. A 90-minute interactive sea-circus show takes place at 10:30 and 2:15 daily. Children may help feed the dolphins and seals. ⊠ *Orlando St. beside Coff's Creek* ☎ *02/6652–2164* 🔁 *A\$22* ◷ *Daily 9:30–4:30.*

Just north of the city, impossible to miss, is the Big Banana—the symbol of Coffs Harbour. This monumental piece of kitsch is part of the **Big Banana Leisure Park** complex, which takes a fascinating look at the past, present, and future of horticulture. A ride on the park's 2-km (1-mi) elevated railway includes a guided walk through a hydroponic growing area, packing shed, and plantation filled with an incredible selection of tropical fruits. At the end of the tour you can wander down the hill to the Nut House and the Banana Barn to purchase the park's own jams, pickles, and fresh tropical fruit. Other attractions include a toboggan run and an ice-skating rink. ☒ *351 Pacific Hwy.* ☎ *02/6652–4355* ⊕ *www.bigbanana.com* ⊠ *A$12* ⊙ *Daily 9–4:30; tours hourly from 10, last tour departs at 3.*

off the
beaten
path

GOLDEN DOG – This fine example of an atmospheric bush pub sits in the tiny village of Glenreagh, about 35 km (22 mi) northwest of Coffs Harbour. Full of character and old local memorabilia, the watering hole is also famous for its eccentricities: you might see a horse or even a motorbike in the bar. The bistro is open daily for lunch, as well as dinner Thursday to Sunday, and there is a pleasant beer garden. ☒ *Coramba Rd., Glenreagh* ☎ *02/6649–2162.*

Where to Stay & Eat

$–$$ ✕ **Shearwater Restaurant.** This open-air waterfront restaurant with views of Coffs Creek (which is spotlighted at night—look out for stingrays) leaves no culinary stone unturned in its search for novel flavors. The dinner menu might include Szechuan duck on roasted vegetables with bok choy and ginger relish, or barbecued lamb fillet on baked spinach, roast eggplant, and tomato. The room is relaxed, and the service friendly and attentive. ☒ *321 Harbour Dr.* ☎ *02/6651–6053* ▤ *AE, MC, V.*

$$–$$$ ▥ **Pelican Beach Resort Australis.** Children have plenty to keep them busy at this terraced beachfront complex. Rooms are bland and furnishings are plastic, but facilities like the giant free-form pool are ideal for making the most of the subtropical location. There's also a playground and miniature golf course. ☒ *740 Pacific Hwy., Korora 2450* ☎ *02/6653–7000 or 1800/028882* 🖷 *02/6653–7066* ⊕ *www.constellationhotels.com/hotels* ⇗ *101 rooms, 11 suites* ◬ *Restaurant, minibars, in-room VCRs, in-room data ports, miniature golf, 3 tennis courts, saltwater pool, gym, hot tub, massage, sauna, beach, volleyball, bar, babysitting, playground, dry cleaning, laundry service, Internet room, meeting rooms, no-smoking rooms* ▤ *AE, DC, MC, V.*

★ $$ ▥ **BreakFree Aanuka Beach Resort.** Teak furniture and antiques collected from Indonesia and the South Pacific fill the one-bedroom suites at this resort, which sits amid palms, frangipani, and hibiscus. Each suite has a kitchen, lounge, laundry, and glass-ceiling bathroom with a two-person whirlpool tub. There are also hotel-room studios and two-bedroom suites with standard furnishings. Outside, the landscaping is highly imaginative; the pool is immersed in a miniature rain forest with a waterfall and hot tub. The resort borders a secluded white-sand beach and the blue waters of the Pacific. ☒ *11 Firman Dr., 2450* ☎ *02/6652–7555* 🖷 *02/6652–7053* ⊕ *www.aanuka.com.au* ⇗ *29 studio rooms, 85 suites* ◬ *2 restaurants, room service, BBQs, IDD phones, some in-room hot tubs, some kitchens, some microwaves, refrigerators, cable TV with movies, 3 tennis courts, 3 pools, gym, hot tub, beach volleyball, 2 bars, laundry facilities, Internet room, meeting rooms, travel services; no smoking* ▤ *AE, DC, MC, V.*

Sports & the Outdoors

SCUBA DIVING The warm seas around Coffs Harbour make this particular part of the coast, with its moray eels, manta rays, turtles, and gray nurse sharks, a scuba diver's favorite. Best are the Solitary Islands, 7 km–21 km (4½ mi–13 mi) offshore. **Dive Quest** (☎ 02/6654–1930) also rents gear, schedules scuba and snorkeling trips, and hosts certification classes.

WHITE-WATER RAFTING   The highly regarded **Wildwater Adventures** (✉ 754 Pacific Hwy., Boambee ☎ 02/6653–3500) conducts one-, two-, and four-day rafting trips down the Nymboida River. Trips begin from Bonville, 14 km (9 mi) south of Coffs Harbour on the Pacific Highway, but pickups from the Coffs Harbour and Bellingen region can be arranged. One-day trips start at A$153, including meals.

Grafton

16   *84 km (52 mi) north of Coffs Harbour.*

This sizable city is at the center of the Clarence Valley, a rich agricultural district of sugarcane farms. The highway bypasses Grafton, but it's worth detouring to see some of the notable Victorian buildings on Fitzroy, Victoria, and Prince streets. The **Grafton Regional Gallery** museum displays traditional and contemporary Australian arts and crafts. ✉ *158 Fitzroy St.* ☎ *02/6642–3177* ⊘ *Tues.–Sun. 10–4.*

Grafton is famous for its jacaranda trees, which erupt in a mass of purple flowers in spring. During the last week of October, when the trees are at their finest, Grafton holds its **Jacaranda Festival.** The celebration includes arts-and-crafts shows, novelty races, children's rides, and a parade.

en route   Between Grafton and the far North Coast, the Pacific Highway enters sugarcane country, where tiny sugarcane trains and thick, drifting smoke from burning cane fields are ever-present. The highway passes the fishing and resort town of **Ballina,** where beaches are the prime feature.

Byron Bay

17   *176 km (109 mi) north of Grafton, exit right from the highway at Bangalow or Ewingsdale.*

Byron Bay is the easternmost point on the Australian mainland and perhaps earns Australia its nickname, the "Lucky Country." Fabulous beaches, storms that spin rainbows across the mountains behind the town, and a sunny, relaxed style cast a spell over practically everyone who visits. For many years Byron Bay lured surfers with abundant sunshine, perfect waves on Wategos Beach, and tolerant locals who allowed them to sleep on the sand. These days a more upscale crowd frequents Byron Bay, but the beachfront has been spared from high-rise resorts.

Byron Bay is also one of the must-sees on the backpacker circuit, and the town has a youthful energy that fuels late-night partying. There are many art galleries and crafts shops, a great food scene, and numerous adventure tours. The town is at its liveliest on the first Sunday of each month, when Butler Street becomes a bustling market.

Cape Byron Lighthouse, the most powerful beacon on the Australian coastline, dominates the southern end of the beach at Byron Bay. You can tour the lighthouse (no children under 5) on Tuesday and Thursday year round, and weekends during NSW summer and term school holidays. The headland above the parking lot near the lighthouse is a launching point for hang gliders, who soar for hours on the warm thermals. This is also a favorite place for whale-watching between June and September, when migrating humpback whales often come close inshore. Dolphins swim in these waters year-round and you can often see pods of them from the cape. Walk out on the rocks below the lighthouse and you're the most easterly person on the Australian mainland. ⊠ *Lighthouse Rd.* ☎ *02/6685–8565* 🖃 *Free; lighthouse tours A$8* ☉ *Lighthouse grounds daily 8–5:30; lighthouse tours Tues. and Sun. 11, 12:30 and 2, Sat. and Sun. 10, 11, 12:30, 2 and 3:30 during school holidays.*

Cape Byron Walking Track circumnavigates a 150-acre reserve and passes through grasslands and rain forest. The headland is the highlight of the route. From several vantage points along the track you may spot dolphins in the waters below. The best places in town to step onto the track are Captain Cook Lookout (off Lighthouse Road), and the lighthouse parking area.

Beaches

Several superb beaches lie in the vicinity of Byron Bay. In front of the town, Main Beach provides safe swimming, and Clarks Beach, closer to the cape, has better surf. The most famous surfing beach, however, is Wategos, the only entirely north-facing beach in the state. To the south of the lighthouse, Tallow Beach extends for 6 km (4 mi) to a rocky stretch of coastline around Broken Head, which has a number of small sandy coves. Beyond Broken Head is lonely Seven Mile Beach. Topless sunbathing is popular on many Byron Bay beaches.

Where to Stay & Eat

★ $$ ✕ **Fig Tree Country Restaurant.** In this century-old farmhouse with distant views of Byron Bay and the ocean, creative Mod-Oz cuisine blending Asian and Mediterranean flavors is served. Produce fresh from the owners' farm is featured on the regularly changing menu; there are always salads served with homemade bread, and lots of seafood dishes; you might try sesame yellowfin tuna with miso salad, or chicken-liver parfait with apple jelly. You can also tuck into a four-course "taste of Byron" menu. For dessert there's delicious homemade ice cream. Ask for a table on the veranda, amid the extravagant foliage. The restaurant is 5 km (3 mi) inland from Byron Bay. ⊠ *4 Sunrise La., Ewingsdale* ☎ *02/6684–7273* 🖃 *MC, V* 🍴 *BYOB* ☉ *Closed Mon. and Tues. No lunch Wed. No dinner Sun.*

$ ✕ **Beach Café.** A Byron Bay legend, this outdoor café is a perfect place to sit in the morning sun and watch the waves. It opens at 7:30 daily, and breakfasts run the gamut from wholesome—muesli with yogurt—to total calorific decadence—monstrous omelets with bacon, mushrooms, and more. For lunch you might try grilled fish with roast vegetables. The fresh juices and tropical fruits alone are worth the 15-minute stroll along the beach from town. ⊠ *Clarks Beach off parking lot at end of Lawson St.* ☎ *02/6685–7598* 🖃 *MC, V* ☉ *No dinner.*

$$$$
Fodor'sChoice
★
✕⊞ **Rae's on Watego's.** If a high-design boutique hotel is your cup of tea, you'd be hard-pressed to do better than this luxurious Mediterranean-style villa surrounded by a tropical garden. Each suite is individually decorated with an exotic collection of antiques, Indonesian art, Moroccan tables, and fine furnishings. The secluded rooms have gorgeous four-poster beds, tile floors, huge windows, in-room fireplaces, and private terraces; the service is top-notch, and the alfresco in-house restaurant serves creative Australian-Thai dishes. There's a minimum two-night stay on weekends. ⊠ *Watego's Beach, 8 Marina Parade, 2481* ☎ *02/ 6685–5366* 🖷 *02/6685–5695* 🌐 *www.raes.com.au* 🛏 *7 suites* ⌂ *Restaurant, room service, BBQs, IDD phones, refrigerators, some cable TV, in-room VCRs, pool, massage, steam room, Internet room, business services; no a/c some rooms, no kids under 13* 🖃 *AE, DC, MC, V.*

$$
⊞ **Julian's Apartments.** These studio apartments opposite Clarks Beach sleep up to three and are neat, spacious, and well equipped. All have a kitchen, a laundry, and either a balcony or a courtyard with rooms opening onto a generous private patio. Furnishings are simple, done in refreshing blond timbers, blue fabrics, and white walls. The beach is so close that the sound of the waves can rock you to sleep. ⊠ *124 Lighthouse Rd., 2481* ☎ *02/6680–9697* 🖷 *02/6680–9695* 🌐 *www. juliansbyronbay.com* 🛏 *11 apartments* ⌂ *Kitchens, microwaves, in-room DVD, laundry facilities, no smoking rooms* 🖃 *AE, DC, MC, V.*

Nightlife

For a small town, Byron rocks by night. Fire dancing—where bare-chested men dance with flaming torches—is a local specialty. Bars and clubs are generally open until about 2 AM on weekends and midnight on weekdays.

Head to the **Arts Factory** (⊠ Skinners Shoot Rd. ☎ 02/6685–7709) (also known as the Piggery) to catch a movie, grab a bite, or see a band. The **Beach Hotel** (⊠ Bay and Jonson Sts. ☎ 02/6685–6402) often hosts live bands. A bar, restaurant, and nightclub, **Cocomangas** (⊠ 32 Jonson St. ☎ 02/6685–8493) is a favorite of backpackers. Bands perform most evenings in the **Great Northern Hotel** (⊠ Jonson and Byron Sts. ☎ 02/ 6685–6454). Live music rocks the **Railway Friendly Bar** (⊠ Jonson St. Railway Station ☎ 02/6685–7662) most nights.

Sports & the Outdoors

KAYAKING
Dolphin Kayaking (☎ 02/6685–8044) has half-day trips twice daily (weather permitting) that take paddlers out to meet the local dolphins and surf the waves.

KITE BOARDING
The **Byron Bay Kiteboarding** (☎ 02/6687–2570 or 1300/888938) is an International Kiteboarding Organization–accredited school with beginner lessons and clinics. Two-day, two-student courses take place on a choice of local waterways.

SCUBA DIVING
The best local diving is at Julian Rocks Marine Reserve, some 3 km (2 mi) offshore, where the confluence of warm and cold currents supports a profusion of marine life. **Byron Bay Dive Centre** (⊠ 9 Marvel St. ☎ 02/ 6685–8333 or 1800/243483) has snorkeling and scuba-diving trips for all levels of experience, plus gear rental and instruction. **Sundive** (⊠ 8

Middleton St. ☎ 02/6685–7755) is a PADI dive center with courses for all levels of divers, as well as boat dives and snorkel trips.

Shopping

Byron Bay is one of the state's arts-and-crafts centers, with many innovative and high-quality articles for sale, such as leather goods, offbeat designer clothing, essential oils, natural cosmetics, and ironware. The community market, held on the first Sunday of every month, fills the streets with more than 300 stalls selling art, craft, and local produce.

Cape Gallery (✉ 2 Lawson St. ☎ 02/6685–7659) sells glasswork, sculptures, ceramics, and paintings by local craft workers. Hours are weekdays 9–5 and weekends 10–4. **Colin Heaney Hot Glass Studio** (✉ 6 Acacia St., Industrial Estate ☎ 02/6685–7044) sells exquisite handblown glass goblets, wineglasses, paperweights, and sculpture. The shop is open weekdays 9–5 and weekends 10–4. An additional attraction is watching the glassblowers at work on weekdays. **In Depth Creations** (✉ 2 Tasman Way, Byron Bay Arts & Industrial Estate ☎ 02/6628–8333) sells custom-made surfboards decorated with hand-painted silk art. It's open sporadic hours, so call ahead before visiting.

Murwillumbah

⑱ *53 km (33 mi) northwest of Byron Bay.*

Towering, conical **Mt. Warning,** the 3,800-foot central magma chamber of a now extinct volcano, dominates pleasant, rambling Murwillumbah, which rests amid sugarcane plantations on the banks of the Tweed River. Apart from the seaside resort of Tweed Heads, Murwillumbah is the last town of any size before the Queensland border.

★ A well-marked **walking track** winds up Mount Warning, which is a World Heritage national park, from the Breakfast Creek parking area at its base. The 4½-km (2½-mi) track climbs steadily through fern forest and buttressed trees where you can often see native brush turkeys and pademelons (small wallaby-like marsupials). The last 650 feet of the ascent is a strenuous scramble up a steep rock face using chain-link handrails. The local Aboriginal name for the mountain is Wollumbin, which means "cloud catcher," and the metal walkways on the summit are sometimes shrouded in clouds. On a clear day, however, there are fabulous 360-degree views of the massive caldera, one of the largest in the world: national parks crown the southern, western, and northern rims, and the Tweed River flows seaward through the eroded eastern wall.

For information about the walk and Mount Warning National Park visit the **Murwillumbah Visitors Centre** (✉ Pacific Hwy and Alma St. ☎ 02/6672–1340) in town. From here it is a 16½-km (10-mi) drive to the start of the walking track. Fill your water bottles in Murwillumbah; there is no drinking water in the park or on the mountain. Allow at least four hours up and back, and don't start the walk after 2 PM in winter.

Where to Stay

$$$–$$$$ **Crystal Creek Rainforest Retreat.** High in the forested hinterland behind Murwillumbah, handsome timber bungalows dot a former banana

plantation. Each spacious unit is modestly luxurious, with a king-size bed, a kitchen, and a big deck that lifts you into the rain forest. All have sunken whirlpool baths, where you can relax with only glass between you and the trees. The backdrop is Border Ranges National Park, a steep chunk of mossy rain forest furnished with huge trees and gushing creeks. You can breakfast on your veranda and listen to whipbirds calling from the depths of the forest. Dinners are also available, and served in your bungalow. ✉ *Box 69, 2484* ☎ *02/6679–1591* 🖷 *02/6679–1596* 🌐 *www.crystalcreekrainforestretreat.com.au* 🛏 *7 bungalows* ♿ *BBQs, fans, in-room hot tubs, kitchens, microwaves, refrigerators, in-room DVD/ VCR, massage, mountain bikes, hiking; no room phones, no kids, no smoking* 🖃 *AE, DC, MC, V.*

North Coast A to Z

AIR TRAVEL

From Sydney, REX (Regional Express) Airlines services Ballina (close to Byron Bay). Qantas Airways flies into Port Macquarie and Coffs Harbour.

🛈 **Qantas Airways** ☎13–1313 🌐 www.qantas.com.au. **REX Airlines** ☎13–1713 🌐 www. regionalexpress.com.au.

BUS TRAVEL

Greyhound Australia and Premier Motor Service frequently run between Sydney and Brisbane, with stops at all major North Coast towns. Sydney to Coffs Harbour is a nine-hour ride. Sydney to Byron Bay takes 12.

🛈 **Greyhound Australia** ☎ 13–1499 🌐 www.greyhound.com.au. **Premier Motor Service** ☎ 13–3410 🌐 www.premierms.com.au.

CAR RENTAL

A car is essential for touring the North Coast's off-highway attractions and traveling at your own pace. Avis, Budget, and Hertz offices are in Coffs Harbour, while Avis has another office in Ballina and Hertz has more in Port Macquarie and Byron Bay.

🛈 **Avis** ☎ 02/6686–7650 Ballina, 02/6651–3600 Coffs Harbour. **Budget** ☎ 02/6651–4994 Coffs Harbour. **Hertz** ☎ 02/6680–7925 Byron Bay, 02/6651–1899 Coffs Harbour, 02/ 6583–6599 Port Macquarie.

CAR TRAVEL

From Sydney, head north via the Harbour Bridge or Harbour Tunnel and follow the signs to Hornsby and Newcastle. Join the Sydney–Newcastle Freeway, then continue up the Pacific Highway (Highway 1), the main route along the 522-km (325-mi) Port Macquarie–to–Queensland coast. Port Macquarie is 417 km (260 mi) northeast of Sydney.

EMERGENCIES

In an emergency, dial **000** to reach an ambulance, the police, or the fire department.

MAIL, INTERNET & SHIPPING
Post offices are in the middle of most towns, on the main street. You can hook up to the Internet at the public library in Coffs Harbour, at Port Pacific in Port Macquarie, and at Precise PCs in Murwillumbah.
ℹ️ **Internet Access Coffs Harbour Public Library** ✉ Coff and Duke Sts., Coffs Harbour ☎ 02/6648-4900. **Port Pacific** ✉ Clarence St., Port Macquarie ☎ 02/6583-8099. **Precise PCs** ✉ 13 Commercial Rd., Shop 33, Murwillumbah ☎ 02/6672-8300.

TOURS
Mountain Trails Four-Wheel-Drive Tours conducts half- and full-day tours of the rain forests and waterfalls of the Great Dividing Range to the west of Coffs Harbour in style—a 7-seat Toyota Safari or a 14-seat, Australian-designed four-wheel-drive vehicle. The half-day tour costs A$65 and the full-day tour is A$95, including lunch and snacks.
ℹ️ **Mountain Trails** ☎ 02/6658-3333.

TRAIN TRAVEL
Trains stop at Kempsey, Coffs Harbour, Grafton, Byron Bay, and Murwillumbah, but much of the Sydney–Brisbane railway line runs inland and the service is not particularly useful for seeing the North Coast. Call Countrylink, the New South Wales rail operator, for fare and service details.
ℹ️ **Countrylink** ☎ 13-2232.

VISITOR INFORMATION
Byron Visitor Centre and Coffs Coast Visitors Information Centre are open daily 9–5. Tweed and Coolangatta Tourist Information Centre (in Murwillumbah) is open Monday–Saturday 9–4:30 and Sunday 9:30–4. Greater Port Macquarie Visitor Information Centre is open weekdays 8:30–5 and weekends 9–4. Sydney Visitor Centre, open daily 9:30–5:30, has information on North Coast accommodations, tours, and sights.
ℹ️ **Byron Visitor Centre** ✉ Jonson St., Byron Bay ☎ 02/6685-8050 🌐 www.visitbyronbay. com. **Coffs Coast Visitors Information Centre** ✉ Rose Ave. and Marcia St., Coffs Harbour ☎ 02/6652-1522 or 1300/369070 🌐 www.coffscoast.com.au. **Greater Port Macquarie Visitor Information Centre** ✉ Clarence and Hays Sts., Port Macquarie ☎ 02/6581-8000 or 1300/303155 🌐 www.portmacquarieinfo.com.au. **Sydney Visitor Centre** ✉ 106 George St., The Rocks, Sydney 2000 ☎ 02/9255-1788 🖨 02/9241-5010 🌐 www.sydneyvisitorcentre.com. **Tweed and Coolangatta Tourist Information Centre** ✉ Pacific Hwy. and Alma St., Murwillumbah ☎ 02/6672-1340.

LORD HOWE ISLAND

A tiny crescent of land 782 km (485 mi) northeast of Sydney, Lord Howe Island is the most remote and arguably the most beautiful part of New South Wales. With the sheer peaks of Mt. Gower (2,870 feet) and Mt. Lidgbird (2,548 feet) richly clad in palms, ferns, and grasses; golden sandy beaches; and the clear turquoise waters of the lagoon, this is a remarkably lovely place. Apart from the barren spire of Ball's Pyramid, a stark volcanic outcrop 16 km (10 mi) across the water to the southeast, the Lord Howe Island Group stands alone in the South Pacific. The island has been placed on UNESCO's World Heritage list as a "natural area of universal value and outstanding beauty."

Not only is the island beautiful, but its history is fascinating. The first recorded sighting was not until 1788, by a passing ship en route to the penal settlement on Norfolk Island, which lies to the east. And evidence, or lack of it, suggests that Lord Howe was uninhabited by humans until three Europeans and their Maori wives and children settled it in the 1830s. English and American whaling boats then began calling in for supplies, and by the 1870s the small population included a curious mixture of people from America (including whalers and a former slaves), England, Ireland, Australia, South Africa, and the Gilbert Islands. Many of the descendants of these early settlers still live on Lord Howe. In the 1870s, when the importance of whale oil declined, islanders set up an export industry of the seeds of the endemic Kentia (*Howea forsteriana*), the world's most popular indoor palm. It's still a substantial business, but rather than seeds, seedlings are now sold.

Lord Howe is a remarkably safe and relaxed place, where cyclists and walkers far outnumber the few cars. There are plenty of trails, both flat and rather precipitous, and fine beaches. Among the many bird species is the rare, endangered, flightless Lord Howe wood hen (*Tricholimnas sylvestris*). In the sea below the island's fringing reef is the world's southernmost coral reef, with more than 50 species of hard corals and more than 500 fish species. For its size, the island has enough to keep you alternately occupied and unoccupied for at least five days. Even the dining scene is of an unexpectedly high quality.

Fewer than 300 people live here, and visitor numbers are limited to 400 at any given time, though at present hotel beds can only accommodate 393 tourists. The allocation of those remaining seven tourists is the subject of local controversy.

Exploring Lord Howe Island

The first view of Lord Howe Island rising sheer out of the South Pacific is spectacular. The sense of wonder only grows as you set out to explore the island, which, at a total area of 3,220 acres (about 1 mi by 7 mi), is manageable. You don't have to allow much time to see the town. Most of the community is scattered along the low-lying saddle between the hills that dominate the island's extremities. There are a few shops, a hospital, a school, and three churches. Everything else is either a home or lodge.

As one of the very few impediments to winds sweeping across the South Pacific, the mountains of Lord Howe Island create their own weather. Visually, this can be amazing as you stand in sunshine on the coast watching cap clouds gather around the high peaks. The average annual rainfall of about 62 inches mostly comes down in winter. Note that, except during the period of Australia's summer daylight savings time (when Lord Howe and Sydney are on the same time), island time is curiously a half hour ahead of Sydney. Additionally, many of the lodges, restaurants, and tour operators close in winter—generally from June through August—and accommodation prices in the open establishments are reduced considerably during that period. A flight-and-accommodation package is the most economic way to visit Lord Howe.

What to See

Lord Howe Museum makes a good first stop in town. Inside, there's an interesting display of historical memorabilia and a less-impressive collection of marine life and stuffed land animals. ⊠ *Lagoon and Middle Beach Rds.* ☎ *02/6563–2111* ⊠ *Donation requested* ☉ *Sun.–Fri. 9–4, Sat 9–12:30.*

The ultimate challenge on Lord Howe is the climb up the southernmost peak of **Mt. Gower,** which rises straight out of the ocean to an astonishing 2,870 feet above sea level. The hike is rated medium to hard, and national park regulations require that you use a guide. Fifth-generation islander **Jack Shick** (☎ 02/6563–2218) is a highly recommended guide who makes the climb twice weekly, usually Monday and Thursday (call him to check). The cost is A$40 and reservations are essential. Meet at Little Island Gate at 7:30 AM sharp; bring lunch and drinks, and wear a jacket and sturdy walking shoes. After a scramble along the shore, the ascent into the forest begins. There's time for a break at the Erskine River crossing by the cascades. Then it's a solid march to the summit. The views, the lush vegetation, and the sense of achievement all make the hike worthwhile.

A very enjoyable way of filling a sunny day is to take a picnic down to **Ned's Beach,** on the eastern side of the island, where green lawns slope down to a sandy beach and clear blue waters. This is a fantastic place for swimming and snorkeling. Fish swim close to the shore, and the coral is just a few yards out. From Ned's Beach at dusk during shearwater (muttonbird) season, you can watch thousands of these birds returning to their burrows in the sand.

Several walks take you around the island. Easy strolls are to forested Stevens Reserve; surf-pounded Blinky Beach; great Clear Place and Middle Beach; and a snorkeling spot beneath Mt. Gower, by Little Island. The climbs up Mt. Eliza and Mt. Malabar at the island's northern end are more strenuous, although much less so than Mt. Gower. They afford tremendous views of the island, including its hulking, mountainous southern end and the waters and islets all around.

Where to Stay & Eat

$ ✕ **Blue Peter's Cafe.** Many patrons here drop in for cake and coffee or tea. Others come for the beer, wine, and afternoon cocktails. The bright, modern, indoor-outdoor café also serves generous salads and antipasto plates, fish-and-chips, burgers, cuttlefish linguine, and Tex-Mex fare. ⊠ *Lagoon Rd.* ☎ *02/6563–2019* ⊟ *AE, DC, MC, V* ☉ *Closed Mon. No lunch Fri.*

$$$ ✕ **Beachcomber Lodge.** The Beachcomber serves a traditional roast-meat dinner on Saturday, and a popular "island fish fry" buffet dinner on Sunday and Wednesday. The locally caught fish is cooked in beer batter and accompanied by chips and salads. Desserts, a cheese platter, and coffee follow the main courses. ⊠ *Anderson Rd.* ☎ *02/6563–2032* ⊕ *www. beachcomberlhi.com.au* ⊟ *AE, DC, MC, V.*

$$$$ ✕⊡ **Arajilla.** This intimate retreat is tucked away at the north end of the island amid banyan trees and Kentia palms. Spacious suites and two-bedroom apartments have well-equipped kitchens, separate lounge areas, and private decks. Snorkeling equipment and fishing tackle is provided; you can also rent mountain bikes. The excellent on-site restaurant serves fine Australian wine and modern cuisine with Asian and European influences for both guests and nonguests. You might try grilled local fish with a Mediterranean vegetable stack, or veal and herb sausages with potato mash and caramelized onion. Leave room, though, for desserts like chilled berry soup with raspberry mascarpone gelato. ⊠ *Old Settlement Beach, Lagoon Rd., 2898* ☎ *02/6563–2002* ⊞ *02/6563–2022* ⊕ *www. arajilla.com.au* ⟳ *10 suites, 2 apartments* ⟍ *Restaurant, BBQs, fans, kitchenettes, microwaves, refrigerators, in-room DVD/VCR, snorkeling, fishing, mountain bikes, bar, Internet room; no a/c* ▭ *AE, MC, V* ⦿ *BP.*

$$$$ ✕⊡ **Capella Lodge.** Lord Howe's most luxurious accommodation is a bit out of the way at the southern limit of settlement, but the reward is a truly dramatic panorama. The lodge's veranda overlooks beaches, the ocean, and the lofty peaks of Mt. Lidgbird and Mt. Gower. The nine high-ceiling guest suites are decked out in contemporary furnishings in soft sand and sea hues, and have shuttered doors that let light in while maintaining privacy. The equally stylish, glass-wall Capella Restaurant showcases local seafood. Nonguests are welcome to dine, but should call ahead for reservations. Your accommodation rate includes breakfast, a three-course dinner, and sunset drinks with canapes. ⊠ *Lagoon Rd., 2898* ☎ *02/6563–2008, 02/9544–2273 restaurant reservations, 02/ 9544–2387 Sydney booking office* ⊞ *02/6563–2180* ⊕ *www.lordhowe. com* ⟳ *9 suites* ⟍ *Restaurant, fans, 1 in-room hot tub, in-room DVD, pool, outdoor hot tub, massage, snorkeling, boating, mountain bikes, hiking, bar, laundry service, Internet room, airport shuttle, no-smoking rooms; no a/c* ▭ *AE, DC, MC, V* ⦿ *MAP.*

$$$$ ✕⊡ **Pinetrees.** Descendants of the island's first settlers run the largest resort on the island, one of the few that stays open year-round. The original 1884 homestead forms part of this central resort, but most accommodations are in undistinguished motel-style units, which have verandas leading into pleasant gardens. Five Garden Cottages and two luxury suites are a cut above the other rooms. At the in-house restaurant, a limited, changing menu might include seared local kingfish with jasmine rice, bok choy and red curry sauce, or satay-marinated Lord Howe trevally. Rates include all meals, and credit cards are accepted for advance reservations only. ⊠ *Lagoon Rd., halfway between airport and Middle Beach Rd., 2898* ☎ *02/9262–6585, 02/6563–2177 for restaurant* ⊞ *02/9262–6638* ⊕ *www.pinetrees.com.au* ⟳ *31 rooms, 2 suites, 5 cottages* ⟍ *Restaurant, some kitchenettes, refrigerators, tennis court, beach, snorkeling, bicycles, billiards, bar, library, laundry facilities, meeting rooms; no a/c, no room phones, no room TVs, no smoking* ▭ *AE, DC, MC, V* ⦿ *FAP.*

$$$–$$$$ ⊡ **Somerset.** Although it hails from the few-frills school of accommodation, this lodge has roomy units with balconies and a terrific location close to town and within walking distance from excellent beaches. Subtropical trees and flowers enliven the grounds, which contain barbecue areas. You can rent bikes and helmets. ⊠ *Neds Beach and Anderson Rds., 2898* ☏ *02/6563–2061* 🖷 *02/6563–2110* ⊕ *www.lordhoweisle.com.au* ↝ *25 suites* ⌂ *BBQs, fans, kitchenettes, microwaves, refrigerators, bicycles, laundry facilities, airport shuttle; no a/c, no room phones* ⊗ *Closed mid-May–mid Sept.* ☰ *MC, V.*

Sports & the Outdoors

Fishing

Fishing is a major activity on Lord Howe. Several well-equipped boats regularly go out for kingfish, yellowfin tuna, marlin, and wahoo. A half-day trip with **Obliviienne Sportsfishing Charters** (☏ 02/6563–2185) includes tackle and bait, for around A$85. It's best to arrange an excursion as soon as you arrive on the island.

Golf

Nonmembers are welcome at the spectacularly located—between the ocean on one side and two mountains on the other—9-hole, par-36 **Lord Howe Island Golf Club** (☏🖷 02/6563–2179), and you can rent clubs. The greens fee is A$20 for 9 or 18 holes.

Scuba Diving

Lord Howe Island's reefs provide a unique opportunity for diving in coral far from the equator. And, unlike many of the Queensland islands, superb diving and snorkeling is literally just offshore, rather than a long boat trip away. Even though the water is warm enough for coral, most divers wear a 5-millimeter wet suit. Dive courses are not available in June and July. If you're heading to Lord Howe specifically for diving, contact **Pro Dive Travel** (☏ 02/9281–5066 or 1800/820820 🖷 02/9281–0660 ⊕ www.prodive.com.au) in Sydney, which has packages that include accommodations, airfares, and diving.

Snorkeling

The best snorkeling spots are on the reef that fringes the lagoon, at Neds Beach and North Bay, and around the Sylph Hole off Old Settlement Beach—a spot that turtles frequent. You can likely rent snorkeling gear from your lodge. A good way to get to the reef, and view the coral en route, is on a glass-bottom boat trip. **Lord Howe Island Environmental Tours** (☏ 02/9563–2155, 02/6563–2045, 02/6563–2326 after hrs) runs two-hour glass-bottom boat cruises that include snorkeling gear in the A$25 charge.

Lord Howe Island A to Z

AIR TRAVEL

Unless you have your own boat, the only practical way of getting to Lord Howe Island is by Qantas from Brisbane or Sydney. In both cases, the flying time is about two hours. Your hosts on Lord Howe Island will pick you up from the airport. Note that the baggage allowance is only 14 kilograms (31 pounds) per person. Special discounts on airfares to the island are often available if you're coming from overseas and you purchase tickets outside Australia.

🔋 Qantas ☏ 13–1313 ⊕ www.qantas.com.au.

BIKE TRAVEL

Despite the island's hills and high peaks, much of the terrain is fairly flat, and bicycles, usually available at your lodge, are the ideal form of transportation. Helmets, which are supplied with the bikes, must be worn by law. If your hotel doesn't have free bikes, **Wilson's Hire Service** (✉ Lagoon Rd. ☎ 02/6563–2045) rents them for about A$12 a day.

CAR RENTAL

There are just six rental cars on the island, and only 24 km (15 mi) of roads, with a maximum speed of 24 kph (15 mph). Your lodge can arrange a car (if available) for about A$50 per day.

EMERGENCIES

In an emergency, dial **000** to reach an ambulance, the police, or the fire department.

ℹ **Emergency Contacts Doctor** Dr. Frank Reed ☎ 02/6563–2000. **Hospital** ✉ Lagoon Rd. and Bowker Ave. ☎ 02/6563–2000.

MAIL & SHIPPING

The Lord Howe Island Post Office is on Neds Beach Road at the heart of the small township. There are no Internet cafés on the island.

MONEY MATTERS

Although most major credit cards are accepted, there are no ATMs on the island. Be sure to carry adequate cash or traveler's checks in addition to credit cards.

TELEPHONES

International and long-distance national calls can be made from public phones, which you can find in tourist areas around the island. There are also four phones at the post office.

TOURS

Islander Cruises conducts several tours around the island, including ferries and cruises to North Bay for snorkeling, a two-hour sunset cocktail cruise on the lagoon, and a morning and evening cappuccino cruise around the lagoon. Prices run from A$30 to A$45 and private charters are also available.

Ron's Ramble is a scenic and highly informative three-hour stroll (A$15) around a small section of the island, with knowledgeable guide Ron Matthews explaining much about Lord Howe's geology, history, and plant and animal life. The rambles take place on Monday, Wednesday, and Friday afternoons starting at 2 in front of the hospital.

Whitfield's Island Tours runs a half-day air-conditioned bus tour (A$27) that provides a good overview of the island's history and present-day life. The tours include morning or afternoon tea at the Whitfield home.

ℹ **Islander Cruises** ☎ 02/6563–2021. **Ron's Ramble** ☎ 02/6563–2010. **Whitfield's Island Tours** ☎ 02/6563–2115.

VISITOR INFORMATION

Contact the Lord Howe Island Board for advance information on the island. The Lord Howe Visitor Centre is open daily 9:30–3 for information, fishing charters, and tour bookings. The Sydney Visitor Centre, open daily 9:30–5:30, also has information on Lord Howe Island.

Lord Howe Island Board ⊠ Middle Beach Rd. ☎ 02/6563–2066 🖷 02/6563–2127. **Lord Howe Visitor Centre** ⊠ Middle Beach and Lagoon Rds. ☎ 02/6563–2114 or 1800/ 240937 ⊕ www.lordhoweisland.info. **Sydney Visitor Centre** ⊠ 106 George St., The Rocks, Sydney ☎ 02/9255–1788 🖷 02/9241–5010 ⊕ www.sydneyvisitorcentre.com.

THE SNOWY MOUNTAINS

Down by Kosciuszko, where the pine-clad ridges raise
Their torn and rugged battlements on high,
Where the air is clear as crystal, and the white stars fairly blaze,
At midnight in the cold and frosty sky . . .

Fodor'sChoice Banjo Paterson's 1890 poem, "The Man from Snowy River," tells of
★ life in the Snowy Mountains—a hard life, to be sure, but one with its own beauty and rewards. It's still possible to experience the world that Paterson described by visiting any of the 100-odd old settlers' huts scattered throughout the Snowys. Hike the mountains and valleys with camera in hand, and breathe deeply the crystal-clear air.

Reaching north from the border with Victoria, this section of the Great Dividing Range is an alpine wonderland. The entire region is part of Kosciuszko (pronounced "koh-*shoosh*-ko", although Australians tend to say "kozee*o*sko") National Park, the largest alpine area in Australia, which occupies a 6,764-square-km (2,612-square-mi) chunk of New South Wales. The national park also contains Australia's highest point, 7,314-foot Mt. Kosciuszko. Mountain peaks and streams, high meadows, forests, caves, glacial lakes, and wildflowers provide for a wealth of outdoor activities.

This wilderness area lends itself to cross-country skiing in winter and, in other seasons, walking and adventure activities. The many self-guided walking trails are excellent, especially the popular Mt. Kosciuszko summit walk. Adventure tour operators arrange hiking, climbing, mountain biking, white-water rafting, and horseback riding tours and excursions.

A number of lakes—Jindabyne, Eucumbene, Tooma, and Tumut Pond reservoirs—and the Murray River provide excellent trout fishing. Khancoban's lake is another favorite for anglers. Tackle can be rented in a few towns, and a local operator conducts excursions and instruction. The trout fishing season extends from the beginning of October to early June.

Although the downhill skiing isn't what Americans and Europeans are used to, the gentle slopes and relatively light snowfalls are perfect for cross-country skiing. Trails from Cabramurra, Kiandra, Perisher Valley, Charlotte Pass, and Thredbo are very good; don't hesitate to ask locals about their favorites. The ski season officially runs from the June holiday weekend (second weekend of the month) to the October holiday weekend (first weekend).

Après-ski action in the Snowys is focused on the hotels in Thredbo, the large Perisher Blue resort, and the subalpine town of Jindabyne. Most hotel bars host live music in the evenings during the ski season, ranging from solo piano to jazz to rock bands. Thredbo tends toward the cosmopolitan end of the scale, and Jindabyne makes up with energy what it lacks in sophistication. Note, however, that many of the hotels close from October through May (room rates are considerably cheaper these months in hotels that stay open), and nightlife is much quieter outside the ski season.

Numbers in the margin correspond to points of interest on the Snowy Mountains map.

Jindabyne

19 *474 km (296 mi) southwest of Sydney, 170 km (106 mi) southwest of Canberra.*

This mountain resort area was built in the 1960s on the shores of Lake Jindabyne, which was created when the dam built by the Snowy Mountains Hydroelectric Scheme flooded the original town. (One of the world's modern engineering wonders, the Snowy Scheme—as most Australians call it—comprises kilometers of pipes, tunnels, and three power stations, and generates almost 4 million kilowatts of electricity distributed to Victoria, South Australia, New South Wales, and the Australian Capital Territory.) In winter, Jindabyne becomes a major base for budget skiers, with plenty of chalets and apartments at lower prices than on-snow lodges. In summer, outdoor activities center on the lake, and you can rent hiking, boating, and fishing equipment. The **Snowy Region Visitor Centre** (✉ Kosciuszko Rd. ☎ 02/6450–5600), open daily 8:30–5, has information on hikes, flora and fauna, and all that Kosciuszko National Park has to offer.

Where to Stay & Eat

★ **$$** ✕ **Crackenback Cottage.** This stone-and-timber bistro, on the road between Thredbo and Jindabyne, glows with rustic warmth. Expect generous servings of traditional favorites—soup, salad, roasts, pie, and mountain trout—as well as wood-fired pizzas with innovative toppings such as local smoked trout or goat cheese. The restaurant also serves scones and afternoon tea, but it's famous for its *gluhwein* (mulled wine) and Australia's largest selection of schnapps. Call ahead as the summer schedule varies. The Cottage is on Crackenback Farm, which also has guesthouse accommodation. ✉ *Alpine Way, 18 km (11 mi) west of Jindabyne, Thredbo Valley* ☎ 02/6456–2198 ⊕ *www.crackenback.com* ⊟ *AE, DC, MC, V* ⊗ *Closed Mon.–Wed. Oct.–early June. No dinner Thurs. Oct.–early June.*

$–$$ ✕ **Brumby Bar and Bistro.** Only the lighting is subdued at this hopping bistro, where the food is as popular as the varied live music. The menu includes grilled steaks, chicken, panfried trout and other seafood, lasagna, and schnitzels. You can help yourself to the salad-and-vegetable bar. ✉ *Alpine Gables Motel, Kalkite St. and Kosciuszko Rd.* ☎ 02/6456–2526 ⊟ *MC, V* ⊗ *No lunch.*

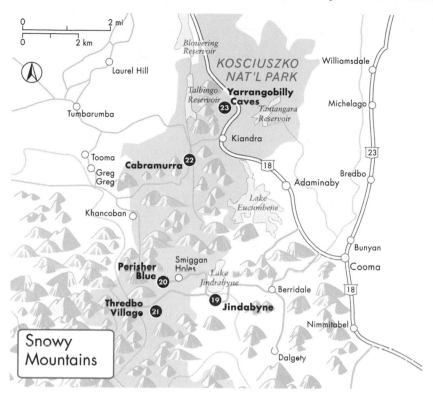

0 —— 2 mi
0 —— 2 km

Laurel Hill

Blowering
Reservoir

KOSCIUSZKO
NAT'L PARK

Williamsdale

Talbingo
Reservoir

**Yarrangobilly
Caves**
23

Tantangara
Reservoir

Michelago

Tumbarumba

Kiandra

23

Tooma
Greg
Greg

Cabramurra **22**

18

Bredbo

Adaminaby

Khancoban

Lake
Eucumbene

Bunyan

Cooma

**Perisher
Blue** **20**

Smiggan
Holes

Lake
Jindabyne

Berridale

18

**Thredbo
Village** **21**

19 **Jindabyne**

Nimmitabel

Snowy
Mountains

Dalgety

$$$$ 🏨 **Alpine Gables Motel.** These split-level suites each have a kitchenette, a lounge, and a separate bedroom in an upstairs loft. The modern decor makes extensive use of wood and glass, and some rooms have bunks for kids. Suites can accommodate up to six people. The on-site Brumby Bar and Bistro is one of the town's most popular watering holes. ⊠ *Kalkite St. and Kosciuszko Rd., 2627* ☎ *02/6456–2555 or 1800/ 645625* 🖷 *02/6456–2815* ⊕ *www.alpinegables.com.au* 📠 *42 suites* ♨ *Restaurant, fans, kitchenettes, room TVs with movies, sauna, hot tub, cross-country skiing, downhill skiing, ski shop, ski storage, bar, recreation room, laundry facilities, business services; no a/c, no smoking* 🚍 *AE, DC, MC, V.*

$$$$ 🏨 **Station Resort.** The largest resort in the Snowy Mountains accommodates more than 1,500 guests on its 50 rural acres. The lodgings here are utilitarian, the furnishings bland, but the relatively inexpensive prices make a ski vacation possible for families and students. Guest rooms, which are clustered around a central dining and activities complex, sleep from two to seven people. A daily shuttle service connects the hotel with the Skitube Terminal. Rates include breakfast and ski-lift tickets. Other packages are also available. There is a two-night minimum booking. The resort is 6 km (4 mi) north of Jindabyne. ⊠ *Dalgety Rd. and*

Barry Way, 2627 ☎ *02/6456–2895* 🖷 *02/6456–2544* ⊕ *www. stationresort.com.au* ⇖ *250 rooms* ⚬ *Restaurant, pizzeria, BBQs, refrigerators, downhill skiing, ski shop, 2 bars, nightclub, shops, meeting rooms, no-smoking rooms; no a/c, no room phones* ▤ *MC, V.*

★ **$$$** 🖃 **Eagles Range.** The big cedar lodge on this 300-acre sheep ranch rates as one of the region's outstanding finds. The five-bedroom lodge sleeps up to 16, but there's ample space for quiet reflection. The lodge is modern but rustic in character, with exposed wood rafters, country-style furniture, an open fireplace, and 180-degree views of the surrounding ranges, which you can also enjoy from the outdoor Jacuzzi. A full cooked breakfast is included, and dinners can be provided, if ordered (from a faxed menu) at time of booking. The property is about 12 km (7½ mi) from Jindabyne. ⬠ *Box 298, Dalgety Rd., 2627* 🖷🖷 *02/ 6456–2728* ⇖ *5-bedroom lodge* ⚬ *BBQs, in-room DVD/VCR, outdoor hot tub, hiking, laundry facilities, no smoking rooms; no a/c, no room phones* ▤ *MC, V* ⓘⓞⓘ *BP.*

> off the beaten path
>
> ★

REYNELLA – In undulating country near the highest point in Australia, this 2,000-acre, all-inclusive sheep and cattle station lets you saddle up and head off into "The Man from Snowy River" country. Basic but comfortable lodge-style accommodations—no phones, no air-conditioning, no televisions—share bathrooms, and you can eat roast lamb and Snowy Mountains trout in the dining room. It's a good winter base for downhill and cross-country skiing. The resort is renowned for its multiday horseback trips into Kosciuszko National Park. It's 72 km (45 mi) northeast of Jindabyne on the spectacular Snowy Mountains Highway. ⬠ *Kingston Rd., 2630* ☎ *02/6454–2386 or 1800/029909* 🖷 *02/6454–2530* ⊕ *www. reynellarides.com.au.*

Sports & the Outdoors

Alpine Angler (⬠ Snowy Mountains Hwy. ☎ 02/6452–5538 ⊕ www. alpineangler.com.au) runs trout fly-fishing excursions for anglers throughout the Snowy Mountains region. Lessons, equipment, transportation, and even accommodations are available.

BP Ski Hire (⬠ BP Service Station, Kosciuszko Rd. ☎ 02/6456–1959) rents snowboards and downhill and cross-country skis and equipment.

Paddy Pallin (⬠ Kosciuszko Rd., Thredbo turnoff ☎ 02/6456–2922) specializes in clothing and equipment for outdoor adventurers. In addition to retail sales, the shop rents out everything needed for a week in the wilderness, from Gore-Tex jackets to mountain bikes and all kinds of ski gear. The shop also conducts guided expeditions of all kinds.

> en route

From Jindabyne, divergent roads lead to two major destinations for walking, skiing, and generally exploring magnificent Kosciuszko National Park. **Kosciuszko Road** heads north to Sawpit Creek, from which point you need snow chains between June 1 and October 10. (You can rent chains from gas stations in Jindabyne). This road continues to the vast Perisher Blue ski region (including the resorts of

Smiggin Holes, Perisher Valley, Mt. Blue Cow, and Guthega), as well as the less-commercial skiing area around Charlotte Pass, which is at the very end of the road but accessible by over-snow transportation in winter. There are several excellent walks from Charlotte Pass, including a particularly scenic 10-km (6-mi) round-trip walk to Blue Lake, part of a 21-km (13-mi) loop that connects a number of peaks and a couple of other glacial lakes, and a more strenuous 18-km (11-mi) round-trip walk to the summit of Mt. Kosciuszko. From Jindabyne, the **Alpine Way** runs southwest to Thredbo Village and past the Skitube Terminal at Bullocks Flat, approximately 21 km (13 mi) from Jindabyne. The 8-km (5-mi) **Skitube** (☎ 02/6456–2010) has an underground/over-ground shuttle train that transports skiers to the terminals at Perisher (10 minutes) and Mt. Blue Cow (19 minutes). The service operates 24 hours daily in winter (June to early October), and is closed in summer.

Perisher Blue

㉟ *30 km (19 mi) west of Jindabyne.*

The four adjoining skiing areas of Smiggin Holes, Perisher Valley, Mt. Blue Cow, and Guthega have merged to become the megaresort of **Perisher Blue** (☎ 1300/655822 for general information, daily from early June to early October, other months weekdays only ⊕ www.perisherblue.com. au). This is the largest snowfield in Australia, with 50 lifts and T-bars that serve all standards of slopes, as well as more than 100 km (62 mi) of cross-country trails. Because it is a snowfield area—at 5,575 feet above sea level—Perisher Blue virtually closes down between October and May. Some lodges and cafés do stay open, especially around the Christmas holidays.

Mt. Blue Cow in particular has terrain to suit most skill levels, and in fine weather it has the best ski conditions at the resort. There are fast, challenging runs off the Ridge chair and in the traverse through the trees to Guthega. Smiggins is also for beginners. Guthega is a starting point for backcountry skiing, although chairlift access is less developed than in other parts of Perisher Blue.

Where to Stay & Eat

$$$$ ✗🏨 **Perisher Valley Hotel.** This ski-in, ski-out hotel is part of Perisher Centre, the retail and entertainment hub of the Perisher Valley ski fields. Luxurious suites with king-size beds accommodate up to six people, and the common areas include a cocktail bar with blazing fireplace, a billiard room, and a spa with sauna and massage available. Your room rate includes over-snow transportation to the hotel, as well as breakfast and dinner at the in-house Snow Gums Restaurant, which has stunning views of the ski slopes. The hotel is open only during the ski season. ✉ *Kosciuszko Rd., Perisher Valley 2624* ☎ *02/6459–4455* 🖷 *02/6457–5177* 🛏 *31 suites* ♨ *2 restaurants, IDD phones, minibars, refrigerators, cable TV, sauna, spa, cross-country skiing, downhill skiing, ski shop, ski storage, 2 bars, shops, dry cleaning, laundry service; no smoking* 🚫 *AE, DC, MC, V* ☺ *Closed Oct.–May* ⊙ *MAP.*

$$$$ ⌂ **Perisher Manor.** Accommodations at this hotel on the slopes vary from pocket-size basic rooms with tea and coffee facilities and shower-only bathrooms to stylish, deluxe rooms with views and tubs. All rooms are centrally heated and comfortable, and the hotel has 24-hour reception, a lobby lounge with an open fireplace, drying rooms, and ski lockers. It's open only in ski season, and there is a two-night minimum booking. Rates include a buffet breakfast and a three-course dinner. ⌧ *Kosciuszko Rd., Perisher Valley 2624* ☎ *02/6457–5291* 🖷 *02/ 6457–5064* ⊕ *www.perishermanor.com.au* 🖙 *49 rooms* ⌂ *Restaurant, café, some IDD phones, some minibars, some refrigerators, some room TVs with movies, cross-country skiing, downhill skiing, ski shop, ski storage, 2 bars; no a/c, no phones in some rooms, no TV in some rooms* ⊟ *AE, DC, MC, V* ⑂ *MAP* ⊙ *Closed Oct.–May.*

Nightlife

Perisher Manor stages rock bands throughout the ski season. If you want to mingle with the smart end of the after-ski set, drop in at the cocktail bar of the **Perisher Valley Hotel. Bazil's Bar** (☎ 02/6459–4430) in Perisher Centre, at the heart of the resort, is known for its Tuesday party nights and live entertainment. **Jax Nightclub** (☎ 02/6459–4437) (also in Perisher Centre) has live entertainment most nights in winter. You can have a drink and hear live music some evenings at the **Man From Snowy River Hotel** (☎ 02/6457–5234).

Skiing

Lift tickets for use at any of the ski areas at **Perisher Blue** (☎ 02/ 6459–4495) are A$87 per day, A$376 for five days. From the Bullocks Flat Skitube Terminal, combined Skitube and lift tickets are A$105 per day. From here skiers can schuss down the mountain to a choice of four high-speed quad chairlifts and a double chair. Blue Cow has a good choice of beginner- and intermediate-level runs, but no accommodations are available. Perisher, Smiggins, Guthega, and Bullocks Flat all have ski-hire facilities for children as well as adults. Skis, boots, and poles cost around A$50 per day, with discounted rates for multiday rentals.

Thredbo Village

㉑ *32 km (20 mi) southwest of Jindabyne.*

In a valley at the foot of the Crackenback Ridge, this resort has a European feel that is unique on the Australian snowfields. In addition to some of the best skiing in the country, this all-seasons resort has bushwalking, fly-fishing, canoeing, white-water rafting, tennis courts, mountain-bike trails, a 9-hole golf course, and a 2,300-foot alpine slide. The altitude at Thredbo Village is 5,000 feet above sea level.

The pollution-free, high-country environment is home to the **Australian Institute of Sport's Thredbo Leisure Centre** (⌧ Friday Dr. and Chimneys Way ☎ 02/6459–4138), which was primarily designed for elite athletes but is now open to the public. Facilities include an Olympic-size, heated, indoor swimming pool; a running track; an indoor, traverse climbing wall; squash, basketball, badminton, volleyball, and net ball courts; and a well-equipped gymnasium. It's open daily 7–7 in summer, 10 AM–8 PM in winter.

The **Crackenback Chairlift** provides easy access to Mt. Kosciuszko, Australia's tallest peak, with great views of the Aussie alps. From the upper chairlift terminal at 6,447 feet, the journey to the 7,314-foot summit is a relatively easy 12-km (7½-mi) round-trip hike in beautiful alpine country. You can also take a mile walk to an overlook. Be prepared for unpredictable and sometimes severe weather.

off the beaten path

②

CABRAMURRA – Beyond Thredbo, the Alpine Way heads south, west, and then north as it skirts the flanks of Mt. Kosciuszko. A 195-km (122-mi) drive through heavily forested terrain with occasionally spectacular views brings you to Cabramurra—which, at 4,890 feet, is the highest town in Australia. The scenic Goldseekers Track is a pleasant 3-km (2-mi) return walk that starts at Three Mile Dam, approximately 8 km (5 mi) beyond Cabramurra on the Kiandra road (known as the KNP5).

KIANDRA – Another 17 km (10 mi) east of Cabramurra, this small village was the site of a frantic early-1860s gold rush. At the height of the boom, 15 hotels and 30 stores serviced a large mining encampment. The town still has a few reminders of its mining history, including water sluices and an old graveyard. The self-guided heritage walks provide illumination as well as exercise.

㉓ YARRANGOBILLY CAVES – Twenty-one kilometers (13 mi) north of Kiandra up the Snowy Mountains Highway is this network of limestone grottoes. South Glory Cave has a self-guided tour, while two other caves—Jersey Cave is most visitors' favorite—must be toured with a guide. You can also bathe in 27°C (80°F) thermal pools, an enjoyable complement to the 12°C (53°F) chill inside the passages. The caves are within Kosciuszko National Park and the area contains pristine wilderness, including the spectacular Yarrangobilly Gorge. The caves are open daily from 9 to 5 (subject to winter road conditions); self-guided tours cost A$10.50, guided tours are A$13. ☎ 02/6454–9597.

Where to Stay & Eat

$$$$ ✕🏠 **Bernti's Mountain Inn.** The boutique-style accommodations here come with friendly service and superb food, all within walking distance of the chairlifts. Most rooms have delightful mountain views and king-size beds, and the lounge welcomes you with a fire, bar, and pool table. Outside, whirlpools, saunas, and plunge pools overlook the mountains. The popular terrace café serves snacks and drinks during the day, and innovative dishes alongside a comprehensive wine list at night. The inn is open year-round, and rates are considerably cheaper out of ski season. There's a two-night minimum if you stay in winter. ⊠ *Mowamba Pl. and Robuck La., 2625* ☎ *02/6457–6332* 🖨 *02/6457–6348* ⊕ *www. berntis.com.au* ⇌ *27 rooms ⚄ Restaurant, refrigerators, pool, hot tub, sauna, billiards, ski storage, bar, laundry service, meeting room; no smoking* ⊟ *AE, DC, MC, V* ⦿ *MAP.*

$$$$ ⬚ **Novotel Lake Crackenback Resort.** Perched on the banks of a lake that mirrors the backdrop peaks of the Crackenback Range, these luxury, all-season apartments make great family accommodations. One-bedroom-plus lofts sleep four, and there are also two- and three-bedroom units. Each has a modern kitchen, a laundry with drying racks, under-floor heating, a fireplace, under-cover parking, and lockable ski racks outside the rooms. There is a two-night minimum booking. ⊠ *Alpine Way, 21 km (13 mi) southwest of Jindabyne, 2627* ☎ *02/6456–2960 or 1800/020524* 🖷 *02/6456–1008* ⊕ *www.novotellakecrackenback.com.au* 🖙 *46 apartments* ⚐ *Restaurant, room service, BBQs, IDD phones, kitchens, cable TV with movies, 9-hole golf course, 3 tennis courts, indoor pool, gym, health club, massage, sauna, steam room, mountain bikes, archery, badminton, hiking, volleyball, cross-country skiing, downhill skiing, ski shop, ski storage, bar, babysitting, laundry facilities, Internet room, meeting rooms, no-smoking rooms; no a/c* ▭ *AE, DC, MC, V.*

$$$$ ⬚ **Thredbo Alpine Hotel.** Warm autumn colors and contemporary wood-and-glass furnishings fill the rooms at this spacious and comfortable hotel within easy reach of the ski lifts at Thredbo. You can also arrange to rent private apartments in the village through the hotel. From January to September the hotel also runs a popular nightclub, and the three on-site bars make it a favorite after-ski hangout. ⊠ *Friday Dr. near Thyne Reid Dr., 2625* ☎ *02/6459–4200 or 1800/026333* 🖷 *02/6459–4201* 🖙 *65 rooms* ⚐ *2 restaurants, café, some in-room hot tubs, in-room VCRs, tennis court, pool, outdoor hot tub, massage, sauna, cross-country skiing, downhill skiing, ski shop, ski storage, 3 bars, nightclub, Internet room, meeting rooms; no a/c* ▭ *MC, V* ⍾⊙⍾ *CP.*

Skiing

Among downhill resorts of the area, **Thredbo** (☎ 02/6459–4100 or 1800/020589 ⊕ www.thredbo.com.au) has the most challenging runs—with the only Australian giant-slalom course approved for World Cup events—and the most extensive snowmaking in the country. Lift tickets are A$87 per day, A$275 for five days.

Thredbo Sports (⊠ Ski-lift terminal ☎ 02/6459–4100) rents downhill and cross-country skis and snowboards.

Snowy Mountains A to Z

AIR TRAVEL

REX (Regional Express) Airlines operates daily flights between Sydney and Cooma. From Cooma's airport, it is a half-hour drive to Jindabyne.

🚩 **REX Airlines** ☎ 13–1713 ⊕ www.regionalexpress.com.au.

BUS TRAVEL

During ski season, Greyhound Australia makes twice-daily runs between Sydney and the Snowy Mountains via Canberra. The bus stops at Thredbo only. It's a seven-hour ride to Thredbo from Sydney, three hours from Canberra.

In winter, shuttle buses connect the regional towns with the ski fields. At other times of the year, the only practical way to explore the area is by rental car or on a guided tour.

🔃 **Greyhound Australia** ☎ 13-1499 ⊕ www.greyhound.com.au.

CAR RENTAL

You can rent cars in Cooma from Thrifty Car Rental.

🔃 **Thrifty Car Rental** ✉ 60 Sharpe St., Cooma ☎ 02/6452-5300.

CAR TRAVEL

From Sydney, head for the airport and follow the signs to the M5 Motorway toll road (A$3.30). The M5 connects with the Hume Highway, southwest of Sydney. Follow the highway to just south of Goulburn and then turn onto the Federal Highway to Canberra. The Monaro Highway runs south from Canberra to Cooma, where you turn onto the Barry Highway to Jindabyne. The 474-km (296-mi) journey takes at least five hours.

To visit anything beyond the main ski resort areas, a car is a necessity. Be aware, however, that driving these often steep and winding mountain roads in winter can be hazardous, and you must carry snow chains from June through October.

EMERGENCIES

In an emergency, dial **000** to reach an ambulance, the police, or the fire department.

🔃 **Cooma Hospital** ✉ Bent St., Cooma 2630 ☎ 02/6455-3222.

MAIL & SHIPPING

Post offices can usually be found in the middle of town, on the main street. It's best to mail outgoing letters and packages from post offices, as it's unusual for hotels to handle these transactions. Most hotels can, however, help organize delivery of skiing equipment before you arrive.

MONEY MATTERS

Most banks will cash traveler's checks and exchange money, as will tourist hotels and the visitor center in Jindabyne. The most common banks in the region include National and Commonwealth. You can find ATMs at the larger banks and in popular shopping areas and ski resorts. Credit cards are widely accepted.

SKITUBE TRAVEL

The Skitube shuttle train—running from Bullocks Flat on the Alpine Way, between Jindabyne and Thredbo, to the Perisher Blue area—operates year-round and is a useful means of reaching either of these resorts. You can access the parking lot at Bullocks Flat without the need to carry chains for your vehicle. The Skitube costs A$35 for a round-trip ticket.

🔃 **Skitube** ☎ 02/6456-2010.

TOURS

In addition to joining up with one of the tour operators listed here, you can also, if you are an experienced walker, undertake one of the area's many fine walks without a guide. Talk to staff at the Snowy Region Visitor Centre for suggestions and trail maps.

Jindabyne's Paddy Pallin arranges bushwalking, mountain biking, white-water rafting and canoeing, and horseback riding. Outstanding cross-country ski programs are also available, from introductory weekends to snow-camping trips.

Murrays Australia operates both skiing-accommodation packages and a transportation service (during the ski season only) to the Snowy Mountains from Canberra. These depart from Canberra's Jolimont Tourist Centre at Alinga Street and Northbourne Avenue.
🚗 **Murrays Australia** ☎ 13–2251. **Paddy Pallin** ✉ Kosciuszko Rd., Thredbo turnoff, Jindabyne 2627 ☎ 02/6456–2922 or 1800/623459.

VISITOR INFORMATION
Snowy Region Visitor Centre is open daily 8:30–5. Sydney Visitor Centre is open daily 9:30–5:30.
🚗 **Snowy Region Visitor Centre** ✉ Kosciuszko Rd., Jindabyne ☎ 02/6450–5600 ⊕ www.snowymountains.com.au. **Sydney Visitor Centre** ✉ 106 George St., The Rocks, Sydney 2000 ☎ 02/9255–1788 🖷 02/9241–5010 ⊕ www.sydneyvisitorcentre.com.

BROKEN HILL

1,160 km (720 mi) west of Sydney, 295 km (183 mi) north of Mildura, 508 km (316 mi) northeast of Adelaide.

Nicknamed the "Silver City," Broken Hill began as an isolated mining town, founded in the desert Outback in 1883. Boundary rider Charles Rasp discovered silver ore here at a broken hill jutting out into the arid plain, in land that originally belonged to the Wiljali Aborigines. Miners arrived not long after. They dug into the hill using both open-cut and tunneling methods, exploiting a lode that was 720 feet wide and over 7 km (4½ mi) long. They took the high-grade ore and left the rest behind, using the rock pile to fill in some of the open cut. This hill of waste now dominates the town's skyline.

Now a town of some 20,000 residents, Broken Hill is no longer the boomtown that it once was. However, sights still reflect the area's mining heritage and culture, and it's a chance to experience the unique flavor of Australia's Outback. Sitting amid the flat, baked landscape, the town has become an unlikely center for the arts, and many painters and sculptors now have studios there. The **Pro Hart Gallery** (✉ 108 Wyman St.) focuses on the work of well-known contemporary Australian artist Pro Hart, famous for his depictions of the Outback. The **Mutawintji National Park** (⊹ 120 km [74 mi] northeast of Broken Hill ☎ 08/8080–3200 ⊕ www.npws.nsw.gov.au) has one of the most important collections of Aboriginal rock art in New South Wales. The park has been managed by the Mutawintji Aboriginal Land Council since 1998. Because of the site's cultural and environmental value, viewings are by ranger-led tours only (Wednesday and Saturday, April–October).

Access to Broken Hill is difficult. It's isolated, expensive to reach by air, and not on the route between any major destinations. However, Broken Hill does lie on the Indian-Pacific rail line, and it's a potential stopover if you want to break the journey between Sydney and either Adelaide or Perth.

If you make it this far, head to Silverton, 24 km (15 mi) northwest of the city. A booming mining town briefly in the late 1880s, this virtual ghost town, where donkeys stroll the main street, has a fascinating 19th-century jail packed with memorabilia, several quirky art galleries in heritage buildings, and a traditional Outback pub. The town and surrounding country have been the setting for more than 100 music film clips, television shows, commercials, and movies, including *Mad Max 2* and *Razorback*.

Where to Stay & Eat

$$ ✕ **Broken Earth.** This café-restaurant with the best view in town is set on top of Mullock Hill. Over a coffee with cake, or dining on modern Australian grub—such as smoked emu pastrami tartlets with caramelized onion, or roasted lamb rack with Kakadu plum glaze—you can take in a vista of the Line of Load Miners Memorial and Visitors Centre. ⊠ *Federation Way* ☎ *08/8087–1345* ▤ *AE, DC, MC, V.*

$$ ▥ **Imperial Fine Accommodation.** This handsome, two-story hotel is two blocks from Broken Hill's town center. Large rooms are stylishly furnished, with duvet-draped, queen-size beds and art deco nightstands. A nifty games room includes a full-size billiards table, and you can meet fellow travelers around the large pool or over a complimentary port in the guest lounge. Cook-your-own breakfast provisions are provided in the shared kitchenette, and an attractive garden surrounds the property. It's not recommended for children to stay here. ⊠ *88 Oxide St., 2880* ☎ *08/8087–7444* ▤ *08/8087–7234* ⊕ *www.imperialfineaccommodation.com* ▱ *5 rooms* ♨ *IDD phones, in-room DVD, in-room data ports, saltwater pool, billiards, lounge, recreation room, dry cleaning, laundry service, free parking; no kids, no smoking* ▤ *AE, DC, MC, V* ❤❘ *BP.*

¢–$ ▥ **Old Willyama Motor Inn.** The desert to the town's northwest is a popular setting for movies, TV shows, and commercials, and actors often stay here when they're filming in the region. It's not fancy, but it's friendly and comfortable, with rooms decorated in a simple, casual style and more facilities than in many motels. ⊠ *30 Iodide St., 2880* ☎ *08/8088–3355* ▤ *08/8088–3956* ✑ *oldwilly@pcpro.net.au* ▱ *29 rooms* ♨ *Restaurant, room service, BBQs, IDD phones, minibars, refrigerators, cable TV, in-room data ports, pool, hot tub, laundry service, business services, free parking* ▤ *AE, DC, MC, V.*

¢ ▥ **Mulberry Vale Cabins.** Built around a central courtyard, these modern, self-contained cabins sleep up to four. The wilderness location is about 5 km (3 mi) southwest of Broken Hill. ⊠ *Menindee Rd., 2880* ☎ *08/8088–1597* ✑ *mulberry@ruralnet.net.au* ▱ *10 cabins* ♨ *BBQs, kitchens, pool, hiking, laundry facilities, some pets allowed, no smoking rooms; no phones in some rooms* ▤ *MC, V.*

¢ ▥ **Mario's Palace Hotel.** Fans of the 1994 camp Australian classic, *The Adventures of Priscilla, Queen of the Desert,* shouldn't leave Broken Hill without visiting this grand, old-style hotel. In its famous foyer is a colorful collection of mind-blowing murals—one of which (a copy of Botticelli's *Birth of Venus*) was painted by longtime owner, Mario Celotto.

The largest room, the Priscilla, was used in a scene for the film. Consider staying for the character rather than the comfort; only some rooms have private baths. ✉ *227 Argent St., 2880* ☎ *08/8088–1699* 📠 *08/8087–6240* ✉ *mariospalace@bigpond.com.au* 🛏 *20 rooms, 10 with private baths* ☖ *Refrigerators, no-smoking rooms; no phones in some rooms* ▭ *AE, MC, V.*

Broken Hill A to Z

AIR TRAVEL

To reach this remote Outback town, you can fly from Sydney and Adelaide with REX (Regional Express) Airlines.
🛈 **REX Airlines** ☎ 13-1713 ⊕ www.regionalexpress.com.au.

CAR TRAVEL

From Sydney, follow the Great Western Highway across the Blue Mountains, heading for Dubbo, from where the Mitchell Highway eventually joins with the Barrier Highway to Broken Hill. Travel time is at least 12 hours.

EMERGENCIES

In an emergency, dial **000** to reach an ambulance, the police, or the fire department.
🛈 **Broken Hill Base Hospital** ✉ Thomas St. ☎ 08/8080-1333.

MAIL & SHIPPING

🛈 **Australia Post** ✉ 260 Argent St. ☎ 02/8082-2533

MONEY MATTERS

Several banks can be found along Argent Street, in the city center. All will cash traveler's checks and exchange money. Credit cards are widely accepted.

VISITOR INFORMATION

🛈 **Broken Hill Visitor Information Centre** ✉ Bromide and Blende Sts. ☎ 08/8088-9700 ⊕ www.visitbrokenhill.com.au.

Canberra &
the A.C.T.

3

WORD OF MOUTH

"Check out the lavish Deep Space Communication Complex . . . giant radio dishes dot the valley, including those that are still tracking Voyager. And pay a visit to the Mt. Stromlo Observatory, where you can get a tour of the 74-inch research telescope. The National Science [and Technology] Centre, called Questacon, is one of the best I've seen."

—ALF

Updated by
Roger Allnutt

AS THE NATION'S CAPITAL, Canberra is often maligned by outsiders, who associate the city with poor decisions made by greedy politicians. The reality is vastly different, however. Canberra is Australian through and through, and those who live here will tell you that to know Canberra is to love it.

The need for a national capital arose in 1901, when the Australian states—which had previously operated separate and often conflicting administrations—united in a federation. An area of about 2,330 square km (900 square mi) of undulating sheep-grazing country in southeastern New South Wales was set aside and designated the Australian Capital Territory (A. C.T.). The inland site was chosen partly for reasons of national security and partly to end the bickering between Sydney and Melbourne, both of which claimed to be the country's legitimate capital. The name Canberry—an Aboriginal word meaning "meeting place" that had been previously applied to this area—was changed to Canberra for the new city. Like everything else about it, the name was controversial, and debate has raged ever since over which syllable should be stressed. These days, you'll hear *Can*-bra more often than Can-*ber*-ra.

From the very beginning this was to be a totally planned city. Walter Burley Griffin, a Chicago architect and associate of Frank Lloyd Wright, won an international design competition. Griffin arrived in Canberra in 1913 to supervise construction, but progress was slowed by two world wars and the Great Depression. By 1947 Canberra, with only 15,000 inhabitants, was little more than a country town.

Development increased during the 1950s, and the current population of more than 320,000 makes Canberra by far the largest inland city in Australia. The wide, tree-lined avenues and spacious parklands of present-day Canberra have largely fulfilled Griffin's original plan. The major public buildings are arranged on low knolls on either side of Lake Burley Griffin, the focus of the city. Satellite communities—using the same radial design of crescents and cul-de-sacs employed in Canberra—house the city's growing population.

Canberra gives an overall impression of spaciousness, serenity, and almost unnatural order. There are no advertising billboards, no strident colors, and very few buildings more than a dozen stories high. Framing the city are the separate areas of wooded hills and dry grasslands comprising Canberra Nature Park, which fills in much of the terrain just outside the suburban areas. It's paradoxically unlike anywhere else in Australia—the product of a brave attempt to create an urban utopia—and its success or failure has fueled many a pub debate.

EXPLORING CANBERRA

Canberra's most important public buildings stand within the Parliamentary Triangle. Lake Burley Griffin wraps around its northeast edge, while Commonwealth and Kings avenues radiate from Capital Hill, the city's political and geographical epicenter, to form the west and south boundaries. The triangle can be explored comfortably on foot, but a vehicle is re-

3

Most of Canberra's galleries, museums, and public buildings can be seen in a couple of days—but the capital's parks and gardens, as well as Namadgi National Park, the Deep Space complex, and Tidbinbilla Nature Reserve, to the south, can easily delay you for another day or so. Several lesser-known attractions, such as Lanyon Homestead, also warrant a visit.

If you have 2 days Two busy days will cover most of the main city attractions. You could start Day 1 with the spectacular view from the **Telstra Tower** ⑲, and then visit the **National Capital Exhibition** ⑧ for a good look into Canberra's planning and history. Your next stop should be the Parliamentary Triangle, where you might spend the remainder of the day visiting the **National Gallery of Australia** ⑫, **Questacon** ⑩, **Old Parliament House** ⑬, and **Parliament House** ⑭. Fill in the city-center gaps on the second day with the **National Museum of Australia** ⑳, **Australian National Botanic Gardens** ⑱, **Australian War Memorial** ❶, and the **National Film and Sound Archive** ㉑.

If you have 4 days After seeing all of the above, spend Days 3 and 4 visiting the **Australian Institute of Sport, St. John the Baptist Church and the Schoolhouse Museum** ❷, and the **Royal Australian Mint** ⑯. Then take a drive around the pleasant suburb of Yarralumla and the **Yarralumla Diplomatic Missions** ⑮ en route to the **National Zoo and Aquarium** ⑰. You should also be able to fit in a visit to **Lanyon Homestead** and **Tidbinbilla Nature Reserve,** to the city's south.

If you have 6 days With six days your itinerary could easily cover the above suggestions, plus a gentle bicycle ride around **Lake Burley Griffin,** a day hike in **Namadgi National Park,** and perhaps a visit to the **Canberra Deep Space Communications Complex** at Tidbinbilla. You could also take a trip a few miles north of the city to the **Gold Creek Village** complex and indulge in some souvenir hunting. Also in this area are **Cockington Green,** the **National Dinosaur Museum,** the **Australian Reptile Centre,** and the **Bird Walk.** Hikers, horseback riders, and skiers could head over to **Kosciuszko National Park,** in southern New South Wales.

quired for the rest of this tour. The monuments and other attractions within the Parliamentary Triangle and around Lake Burley Griffin are not identified by street numbers but all are clearly signposted.

Numbers in the text correspond to numbers in the margin and on the Canberra map.

When to Visit
February to April, when autumn leaves paint the city parks with amber hues, is a particularly good time to visit. This season also coincides with the February Canberra National Multicultural Festival. The event, which also incorporates the international Hot Air Balloon Fiesta, is just one of the celebrations leading up to Canberra Day festivities in March. The spring flower celebration, Floriade, lasts from mid-September to mid-

October. In early January, car enthusiasts gather for the popular Summernats, Australia's Ultimate Car Show.

CENTRAL CANBERRA

This self-drive tour takes in virtually all of central Canberra's major attractions, but in some places it's more convenient to park your car and walk between sites. Around town, you can use the local ACTION buses, which stop at most of the other sights, or join the hop-on, hop-off Canberra Tours bus. A car or a tour is necessary to reach the Telstra Tower.

a good tour

From the city center, head first to the **Australian War Memorial ❶** ▶, at the top of Anzac Parade, one of the nation's most popular attractions. From here, drive southwest on Anzac Parade to the **St. John the Baptist Church and the Schoolhouse Museum ❷**. Turn left on Constitution Avenue, which turns into Russell Drive, and continue to the **Australian-American Memorial ❸**. Notice that a section of the Canberra Nature Park lies just behind the marker.

Turn right and circle back on Parkes Way, then turn left on Wendouree Drive until you reach **Blundells' Cottage ❹**, which provides a glimpse into Australian farming life of a century ago. At the end of the road you can look across the water to the **National Carillon ❺**, which sits on Aspen Island in the middle of Lake Burley Griffin. From here, return to Parkes Way and drive northwest, then turn left on Commonwealth Avenue to reach Commonwealth Park. Stop at **Lake Burley Griffin ❻** for excellent views of the water, then look slightly southwest to spot the spectacular **Captain Cook Memorial Jet ❼** fountain. While you're here, take an hour to explore the **National Capital Exhibition ❽**, which provides an intriguing look into the city's history through exhibits, models, and audiovisual programs.

Cross the Commonwealth Avenue Bridge to the lake's southern shore and enter the Parliamentary Triangle. You can park and wander on foot through the grounds, heading southeast along Lake Burley Griffin from the **National Library of Australia ❾** to the interactive **Questacon—The National Science and Technology Centre ❿** and the **High Court of Australia ⓫**. Across the street from the High Court, at the southeast tip of the triangle, is the **National Gallery of Australia ⓬**, the country's premier art gallery. Walk two blocks southwest, to the center of the triangle, to see the gracious old **Old Parliament House ⓭** and National Portrait Gallery. Continue two blocks straight southwest to Capital Hill, where the sprawling **Parliament House ⓮** makes a striking contrast to its humble predecessor.

From here, head back to your vehicle and drive west to circle the **Yarralumla Diplomatic Missions ⓯**. Continue west on Adelaide Avenue and follow the signs to reach the **Royal Australian Mint ⓰**, 5 km (3 mi) from the city center. Turn north along the outer belt and, if you like, follow the signs to the **National Zoo and Aquarium ⓱** at the far western tip of Lake Burley Griffin.

To finish the tour, get back on Parkes Way and drive 5 km (3 mi) east toward the city. On the way, you can turn off Parkes Way and head north 1 km (½ mi) toward Black Mountain and the superb **Australian National**

3

City Dining

Despite the city's modest size, Canberra's dining scene has been spurred to culinary heights by the youth, affluence, and sophisticated tastes of its inhabitants. Many excellent restaurants are in suburban shopping areas, where you can look for cuisines to vary from classic and modern Australian to European, Middle Eastern, and all shades of Asian seasonings and spices. To accompany your dining experience, try a glass or two of the excellent local wines.

Hotels & Homesteads

Until the past decade or so, Canberra's hotels for the most part offered only modern utilitarian facilities. Today's hotels, however, provide luxurious rooms with modern fittings, plus top-class bars and restaurants. Serviced apartment-style hotels with kitchen facilities provide a more relaxed style of accommodations. Country homesteads tucked away in the surrounding mountain ranges give you the chance to experience life on working sheep and cattle farms—often in magnificently rugged surroundings—without sacrificing creature comforts.

Galleries, Museums & Public Buildings

With more than 30 national institutions, Canberra has an impressive selection of museums, art galleries, and public buildings to visit. The vast, modern Parliament House is the most famous of these, but the National Museum of Australia, National Gallery of Australia, Questacon—The National Science and Technology Centre, the Australian Institute of Sport, and the Australian War Memorial provide no less fascinating glimpses into the nation's history, character, and aspirations.

Parks, Reserves & the Great Outdoors

Canberra's surrounding mountain ranges and river valleys, combined with the crisp spring and autumn weather, allow for several invigorating outdoor pursuits. Within the A.C.T. itself lie a national park, a nature reserve, and vast areas of bushland and parkland that are great for walks. Lake Burley Griffin and its environs provide a scenic backdrop for walking and cycling. Kosciuszko National Park and the New South Wales snowfields are also within easy reach of the capital, far closer than they are to Sydney.

Botanic Gardens ⑱. Drive 2 km (1 mi) higher to find the 600-foot-high **Telstra Tower** ⑲ and spectacular views of the city, lake, and surrounding countryside. Return to Parkes Way and drive 3 km (2 mi) to the Acton Peninsula, where you can top off the day with a visit to the fascinating **National Museum of Australia** ⑳ and a relaxing stroll or boat ride along Lake Burley Griffin. Or, you could head east to check out the **National Film and Sound Archive** ㉑.

TIMING   You could squeeze this entire tour into one very busy day, but it would not do justice to Parliament House, the zoo, or any of the major museums or galleries. To accommodate these, split the tour into two parts. Wind up the first day with a visit to the Parliamentary Triangle and re-

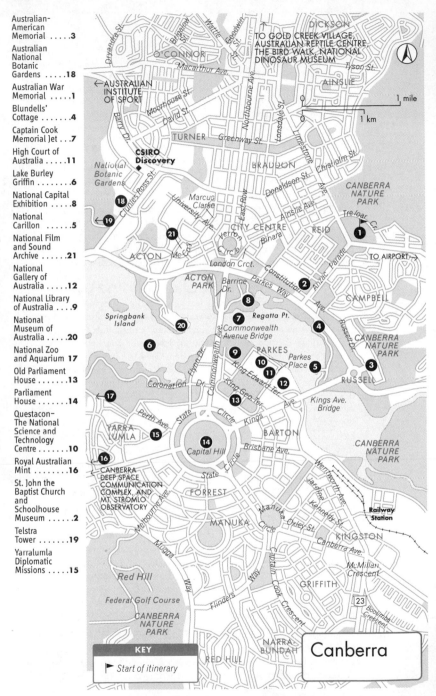

Canberra

KEY

► Start of itinerary

sume your sightseeing on the following day via the Yarralumla Diplomatic Missions.

The major galleries and museums—particularly the Australian War Memorial, the National Museum of Australia, the National Gallery, and Questacon—draw large crowds on weekends, so explore these on a weekday if you can.

What to See

③ Australian-American Memorial. This slender memorial with an eagle at its summit was unveiled in 1954 to commemorate the role of American forces in the defense of Australia during World War II. The monument stands near the northern side of Kings Avenue Bridge, surrounded by the government departments in charge of Australia's armed services. ⊠ *Russell Dr., Russell.*

⑱ Australian National Botanic Gardens. Australian plants and trees have evolved in isolation from the rest of the world, and these delightful gardens on the lower slopes of Black Mountain display the continent's best collection of this unique flora. The rain forest, rock gardens, Tasmanian alpine garden, and eucalyptus lawn—with more than 600 species of eucalyptus—number among the 125-acre site's highlights. Two self-guided nature trails start from the rain-forest gully, and free guided tours depart from the visitor center at 11 on weekdays, 11 and 2 on weekends. Parking is A\$1.20 per hour or A\$4.80 per day. ⊠ *Clunies Ross St., Black Mountain* ☎ *02/6250–9540* ⊕ *www.anbg.gov.au* ☞ *Free* ☉ *Gardens Jan. and Feb., daily 9–8; Mar.–Dec., daily 9–5. Visitor center daily 9:30–4:30.*

▶ ❶ Australian War Memorial. Both as a memorial to Australians who served their country in wartime and as a military museum, this is a shrine of great national importance and the most popular attraction in the capital. The museum, built roughly in the shape of a Byzantine church, explores Australian military involvement from the Sudan campaign of the late 19th-century through the 1970s and the Vietnam War. Displays include a Lancaster bomber, a Spitfire, tanks, landing barges, the giant German Amiens gun, and sections of two of the Japanese midget submarines that infiltrated Sydney Harbour during World War II. Each April 25 the memorial is the focus of Canberra's powerful Anzac Day ceremony, which honors fallen members of Australia's armed forces. Free guided tours take place daily at 10, 10:30, 11, 1:30, and 2.

Fodor'sChoice ★

You can best appreciate the impressive facade of the War Memorial from the broad avenue of **Anzac Parade.** Anzac is an acronym for the Australian and New Zealand Army Corps, formed during World War I. The avenue is flanked by several memorials commemorating the army, navy, air force, and nursing corps, as well as some of the campaigns in which Australian troops have fought, including the Vietnam War. The red gravel used on Anzac Parade symbolizes the blood of Australians spilled in war. ⊠ *Anzac Parade and Limestone Ave., Campbell* ☎ *02/6243–4211* ⊕ *www.awm.gov.au* ☞ *Free* ☉ *Daily 10–5.*

❹ Blundells' Cottage. The 1858 cottage, once home to three families of farmworkers, is a testimony to the pioneer spirit of the early European settlers in the Canberra region. Furnished to represent the lifestyle of a farming community in the late 1800s, the home now provides a hands-on experience for visitors and school groups. ☒ *Wendouree Dr., Kings Park, Parkes* ☎ *02/6273–2667 or 02/6257–1068* ⊕ *www.nationalcapital. gov.au* ☒ *A$4* ⊙ *Daily 11–4.*

❼ Captain Cook Memorial Jet. This water fountain in Lake Burley Griffin commemorates James Cook's discovery of Australia's east coast in 1770. On windless days the jet spurts a 6-ton plume of water 490 feet into the sky—making this one of the world's highest fountains.

Discovery. Set within the Commonwealth Scientific & Industrial Research Organisation (CSIRO), Australia's largest scientific organization, Discovery contains working labs where you can explore the latest technology in many pursuits. Try a cutting-edge computer that lets you view medical breakthroughs, ask questions about gene technology, and explore global warming at the finger touch of the screen. ☒ *Clunies Ross St., Black Mountain* ☎ *02/6246–4646* ⊕ *www.discovery.csiro.au* ☒ *A$6* ⊙ *Weekdays 9–5.*

⓫ High Court of Australia. As its name implies, this gleaming concrete-and-glass structure is the ultimate court of law in the nation's judicial system. The court of seven justices convenes only to determine constitutional matters or major principles of law. Inside the main entrance, the public hall contains a number of murals depicting constitutional and geographic themes. Each of the three courtrooms over which the justices preside has a public gallery, and you can observe the proceedings when the court is in session. ☒ *Parkes Pl. off King Edward Terr., Parkes* ☎ *02/ 6270–6811 or 02/6270–6850* ☒ *Free* ⊙ *Daily 9:45–4:30.*

❻ Lake Burley Griffin. Stretching through the very heart of the city, Lake Burley Griffin is one of Canberra's most captivating features. The parks that surround the lake are ideal for walking and cycling, and you can hire bikes and boats from Acton Park on the northern shore.

❽ National Capital Exhibition. Photographs, plans, audiovisual displays, and a laser model inside this lakeside pavilion illustrate the past, present, and future development of the national capital. Exhibits cover the time of the early settlers, Walter Burley Griffin's winning design for Canberra, and city plans for the coming decades. From the pavilion's terrace there are sweeping views of the Parliamentary Triangle across the lake: the National Library on the right and the National Gallery on the left form the base of the Parliamentary Triangle, which rises toward its apex at Parliament House on Capital Hill. The restaurant and kiosk on the terrace serve full meals and light snacks. ☒ *Regatta Point, Barrine Dr., Commonwealth Park* ☎ *02/6257–1068* ☒ *Free* ⊙ *Daily 9–5.*

❺ National Carillon. The elegant, 53-bell tower, a gift from the British government to mark Canberra's 50th anniversary in 1963, rises up from Aspen Island in Lake Burley Griffin. Free 45-minute recitals, which include everything from hymns to contemporary music, are played Monday, Wednesday, Friday, and Sunday at 12:30. Although you can only visit the inside of the tower by taking a tour, lots of people are happy sitting outside and just listening while the bells play. ☒ *Aspen Island off Wendouree Dr., Parkes* ☏ *02/6257–1068* ☞ *Tours A$8* ☉ *Tours Tues. and Thurs. 12:30 and 1:30, Sat. 11:30 and 12:30.*

㉑ **National Film and Sound Archive.** Australia's movie industry was booming during the early 20th century, but it ultimately couldn't compete with the sophistication and volume of imported films. Concern that film stock and sound recordings of national importance would be lost prompted the construction of this edifice to preserve Australia's movie and musical heritage. The archive contains an impressive display of Australian moviemaking skills, including a short film that was shot on Melbourne Cup Day in 1896—the oldest film in the collection. Special exhibitions focus on aspects of the industry ranging from rock music to historic newsreels. ☒ *McCoy Circuit, Acton* ☏ *02/6248–2000* ⊕ *www.screensound. gov.au* ☞ *Free* ☉ *Weekdays 9–5, weekends 10–5.*

⑫ **National Gallery of Australia.** The most comprehensive collection of Australian art in the country is on exhibit in the nation's premier art gallery, including superlative works of Aboriginal art and paintings by such famous native sons as Arthur Streeton, Sir Sidney Nolan, Tom Roberts, and Arthur Boyd. The gallery also contains a sprinkling of works by European and American masters, including Rodin, Picasso, Pollock, and Warhol. Free guided tours commence from the foyer at 11 and 2 each day. Although admission is free, there's usually a fee for special-interest exhibitions, which often display artwork from around the world. ☒ *Parkes Pl., Parkes* ☏ *02/6240–6502* ⊕ *www.nga.gov.au* ☞ *Free, fee for special exhibitions* ☉ *Daily 10–5.*

need a break? There are a couple of good spots to catch your breath amid the Parliamentary Triangle's mix of history, culture, and science. **Bookplate** (☒ Parkes Pl., Parkes ☏ 02/6262–1154), in the foyer of the National Library, extends out onto a patio overlooking the lake. Sandwiches, salads, cakes, and tea and coffee are served weekdays 8:30–6 and weekends 11–3. **Scribbles Café** (☒ Parkes Pl., Parkes ☏ 02/6240–6666), on the lower floor of the National Gallery, overlooks pleasant gardens and Lake Burley Griffin. A mix of salads and hot, hearty main dishes like spaghetti and *satay* (meat skewers) is served daily 10–4.

⑨ **National Library of Australia.** The library, constructed loosely on the design of the Parthenon in Athens, houses more than 5 million books and 500,000 aerial photographs, maps, drawings, and recordings of oral history. Changing exhibitions of old Australian photos, manuscripts, and art are displayed in the ground-floor gallery. One-hour behind-the-scenes tours take place Tuesday at 12:30. ☒ *Parkes Pl., Parkes* ☏ *02/6262–1111* ⊕ *www.nla.gov.au* ☞ *Free* ☉ *Mon.–Thurs. 9–9, Fri.–Sun. 9–5.*

⑳ **National Museum of Australia.** This comprehensive museum is spectacularly set on Acton Peninsula, thrust out over the calm waters of Lake **Fodor'sChoice** ★ Burley Griffin. The museum highlights the stories of Australia and Australians by exploring the key people, events, and issues that shaped and influenced the nation. The numerous exhibitions focus on rare and unique objects that illustrate the continent's complex origins. Memorabilia include the carcass of the extinct Tasmanian tiger, the old Bentley beloved by former Prime Minister Robert Menzies, and the black baby garments worn by dingo victim Azaria Chamberlain (whose story was made famous in the Meryl Streep film *A Cry in the Dark*). ⊠ *Lennox Crossing, Acton Peninsula* ☎ *02/6208–5000 or 1800/026132* ⊕ *www. nma.gov.au* ☞ *Free, fee for special exhibitions* ⊘ *Daily 9–5.*

⟳ ⑰ **National Zoo and Aquarium.** Display tanks alive with coral, sharks, rays, and exotic sea creatures let you take a fish-eye view of the underwater world. The adjoining 15-acre wildlife sanctuary is a bushland park that provides a habitat for the more remarkable species of Australia's fauna: emus, koalas, penguins, dingoes, kangaroos, and Tasmanian devils. Other exotic animals include cougars, pumas, snow leopards, tigers, and cheetahs. ⊠ *Lady Denman Dr., Scrivener Dam, Yarralumla* ☎ *02/ 6287–8400* ⊕ *www.zooquarium.com.au* ☞ *A$18.50* ⊘ *Daily 9–5.*

⑬ **Old Parliament House.** Built in 1927, this long white building was meant to serve only as a temporary seat of government, but it was more than 60 years before its much larger successor was finally completed on the hill behind it. Now that the politicians have moved out, the renovated building is open for public inspection. Guided tours, departing from Kings Hall on the half hour, take you through the legislative chambers, party rooms, and suites that once belonged to the prime minister and the president of the Senate. Old Parliament House also contains the expanding **National Portrait Gallery,** which displays likenesses of important Australians past and present. While you're in the area, take a stroll through the delightful **Rose Gardens** on both sides of the Old Parliament House building. Across the road from the entrance visit the controversial **Aboriginal Tent Embassy,** established in 1972 to proclaim the Aboriginals as Australia's "first people" and to promote recognition of their fight for land rights. ⊠ *King George Terrace, Parkes* ☎ *02/6270–8222* ⊕ *www. oph.gov.au* ☞ *A$2* ⊘ *Daily 9–5.*

⑭ **Parliament House.** Much of this vast futuristic structure is submerged,
Fodor's Choice covered by a domed glass roof that follows the contours of Capital Hill.
★ You approach the building across a vast courtyard with a central mosaic entitled *Meeting Place,* designed by Aboriginal artist Nelson Tjakamarra. Native timber has been used almost exclusively throughout the building, and the work of some of Australia's finest contemporary artists hangs on the walls.

Parliament generally sits Monday–Thursday mid-February–late June and mid-August–mid-December. Both chambers have public galleries, but the debates in the House of Representatives, where the prime minister sits, are livelier and more newsworthy than those in the Senate. The best time to observe the House of Representatives is during **Question Time** (☎ *02/6277–4889* sergeant-at-arms' office), starting at 2, when the government and the opposition are most likely to be at each other's throats. To secure a ticket for Question Time, contact the sergeant-at-arms' office. Book a week in advance, if possible. Guided tours take place every half hour from 9 to 4. ⊠ *Capital Hill* ☎ *02/6277–5399* ⊕ *www.aph. gov.au* ☞ *Free* ⊘ *Daily 9–5, later when Parliament is sitting.*

🔟 **Questacon—The National Science and Technology Centre.** This interactive science facility is the city's most entertaining museum. About 200 hands-on exhibits use high-tech computer gadgetry and anything from pendulums to feathers to illustrate principles of mathematics, physics, and human perception. Staff members explain the scientific principles behind the exhibits, and science shows take place regularly. ✉ *Enid Lyons St. off King Edward Terr., Parkes* ☎ *02/6270–2800* ⊕ *www.questacon. edu.au* 🎟 *A$14* ⊙ *Daily 9–5.*

🔟 **Royal Australian Mint.** The observation gallery has a series of windows where you can watch Australian coins being minted. Blanks are brought from the basement storage level up to the furnaces, where they are softened and finally sent to the presses to be stamped. The foyer has a display of rare coins, and silver and gold commemorative coins are for sale. There's no coin production on weekends or from noon to 12:40 on weekdays. ✉ *Denison St., Deakin* ☎ *02/6202–6800 or 1300/652020* ⊕ *www. ramint.gov.au* 🎟 *Free* ⊙ *Weekdays 9–4, weekends 10–4.*

② **St. John the Baptist Church and the Schoolhouse Museum.** These are the oldest surviving buildings in the Canberra district. When they were constructed in the 1840s, the land was part of a 4,000-acre property that belonged to Robert Campbell, a well-known Sydney merchant. The homestead, Duntroon, remained in the Campbell family until it was purchased by the government as a site for the Royal Military College. The schoolhouse is now a small museum with relics from the early history of the area. ✉ *Constitution Ave. near Anzac Parade, Reid* ☎ *02/6249–6839* 🎟 *Donation requested for museum, church free* ⊙ *Museum Wed. 10–noon, weekends 2–4; church daily 9–5.*

🔟 **Telstra Tower.** The city's tallest landmark, this 600-foot structure on the top of Black Mountain is one of the best places to begin any tour of the national capital. Three observation platforms afford breathtaking views of the entire city as well as the mountain ranges to the south. The tower houses an exhibition on the history of telecommunications in Australia and a revolving restaurant with a spectacular nighttime panorama. The structure provides a communications link between Canberra and the rest of the country and serves as a broadcasting station for radio and television networks. ✉ *Black Mountain Dr., Acton* ☎ *02/6219–6111 or 1800/806718* 🎟 *A$3.30* ⊙ *Daily 9 AM–10 PM.*

🔟 **Yarralumla Diplomatic Missions.** The expensive, leafy suburb of Yarralumla, west and north of Parliament House, contains many of the city's 70 or so diplomatic missions. Some of these were established when Canberra was little more than a small country town, and it was only with great reluctance that many ambassadors and their staffs were persuaded to transfer from the temporary capital in Melbourne. Today it's an attractive area where each building reflects the home country's architectural characteristics.

Around Canberra & the A.C.T.

Canberra's suburbs and the rural regions of the A.C.T. provide several lesser attractions. These include two national parks, a historic homestead, many wineries, a nature reserve with native animals, the Australian Institute of Sport, and Canberra's important contribution to the space race. A car is required to reach these sights.

TIMING   Don't try to cram all of these sights into one outing; instead, choose a few places to visit over the course of a day or two. The Australian Institute of Sport and Gold Creek Village are a 15-minute drive from the city center. To drive to the Canberra Deep Space Communication Complex, Tidbinbilla Nature Reserve, or Namadgi National Park (all of which are in proximity to one another at the southern end of the Australian Capital Territory), you should allow about an hour. Lanyon Homestead is on the way to Namadgi National Park.

What to See

Australian Institute of Sport (AIS). Established to improve the performance of Australia's elite athletes, this 150-acre site north of the city comprises athletic fields, a swimming center, an indoor sports stadium, and a sports-medicine center. Daily 1½-hour tours, some guided by AIS athletes, explore the facilities, where you may be able to watch some of the institute's Olympic-caliber squads in training for archery, gymnastics, swimming, soccer, and other sports. The latter half of the tour takes you through the **Sports Visitors Centre,** where displays, hands-on exhibits, and a video wall show the achievements of Australian sporting stars. Afterward, you can use the tennis courts and other facilities for a fee. ⊠ *Leverrier Crescent, Bruce* ☎ *02/6214–1010* ⊕ *www.aisport.com.au* ☒ *Guided tour A$13, tennis courts A$1 per hr* ⊙ *Weekdays 8:30–4:45, weekends 9:45–4:15. Tours daily at 10, 11:30, 1, and 2:30.*

⟳ **Australian Reptile Centre.** Australia has a remarkable diversity of snakes, lizards, and other reptilian creatures, and you can meet them face-to-face at this compact park. Those headed for the desert and bushland might want to spend some time becoming familiar with the collection of deadly snakes and other sorts. You can even meet (and be cuddled by) a python. ⊠ *O'Hanlon Pl., Gold Creek Village, Nicholls* ☎ *02/ 6253–8533* ⊕ *www.contact.com.au/reptile* ☒ *A$8* ⊙ *Daily 10–5.*

⟳ **Bird Walk.** More than 50 species of birds are housed in this enormous, walk-through aviary. Keepers have heaps of helpful details about each one, and they'll even let you help them with feedings. Note that the grounds close on rainy days. ⊠ *O'Hanlon Pl., Gold Creek Village, Nicholls* ☎ *02/ 6230–2044* ☒ *A$8* ⊙ *Daily 10–5.*

Canberra Deep Space Communication Complex. Managed and operated by the Commonwealth Scientific and Industrial Research Organization (CSIRO), this complex 40 km (25 mi) southwest of Canberra is one of just three tracking stations in the world linked to the Deep Space control center, the long-distance arms of the U.S. National Aeronautics and Space Administration (NASA). The function of the four giant antennae at the site is to relay commands and data between NASA and space vehicles or orbiting satellites. The first pictures of men walking on the moon were transmitted to this tracking station. The visitor information center houses models, audiovisual displays, and memorabilia from space missions. ⊠ *Discovery Dr. off Paddy's River Rd., Tidbinbilla* ☎ *02/*

6201–7838 ⊕ *www.cdscc.nasa.gov* ✉ *Free* ⊙ *Apr.–Oct., daily 9–5; Nov.–Mar., daily 9–6.*

Cockington Green. Set in lovely gardens, a delightful collection of miniature thatch-roof houses, castles, and canals creates a small-scale slice of England. The international section, which was constructed with the support of many of Canberra's embassies, highlights such world-renowned sights as the Bojnice Castle in Slovakia and Machu Picchu in Peru. ✉ *11 Gold Creek Rd., Nicholls* ☎ *02/6230–2273* ☎☎ *1800/ 627273* ⊕ *www.cockingtongreen.com.au* ✉ *A$13.50* ⊙ *Daily 9:30–4:30.*

Lanyon Homestead. When it was built in 1859 on the plain beside the Murrumbidgee River, this classic homestead from pioneering days was the centerpiece of a self-contained community. Many of the outbuildings and workshops have been magnificently restored and preserved. The adjacent **Nolan Gallery** (☎ 02/6235–5688) displays a selection of the well-known Ned Kelly paintings by the famous Australian painter Sir Sidney Nolan. ✉ *Tharwa Dr., Tharwa, 30 km (19 mi) south of Canberra off Monaro Hwy.* ☎ *02/6235–5677* ✉ *Homestead A$7, combined with gallery A$8* ⊙ *Tues.–Sun. 10–4.*

Mount Stromlo Observatory. Although terrible bushfires in January 2003 devastated the observatory, the facility is gradually being rebuilt. As of this writing you can attend stargazing evenings on Saturday nights; there are several rebuilt and brand-new telescopes. You can also stop by the visitor information center to learn about the ongoing astronomical research and the continuing restoration of the observatory. ✉ *Cotter Rd., Weston Creek* ☎ *02/6125–0232* ✉ *Donation requested for Sat.-night stargazing* ⊙ *Visitor center Wed.–Sun. 10–5; Sat.-night stargazing by booking only.*

Namadgi National Park. Covering almost half the total area of the Australian Capital Territory's southwest, this national park has a well maintained network of walking trails through mountain ranges, trout streams, and some of the most accessible subalpine forests in the country. Some parts of the park were severely burned in the January 2003 bushfires, but the recovery powers of the native bush have been truly remarkable. Check with park rangers to find out if any areas are off-limits. The park's boundaries are within 35 km (22 mi) of Canberra, and its former pastures, now empty of sheep and cattle, are grazed by hundreds of eastern gray kangaroos in the early mornings and late afternoons. The remote parts of the park have superb terrain, but you must be an experienced navigator of wild country to explore them. Snow covers the higher altitudes June–September. ✛ *Visitor center: Naas–Boboyan Rd., 3 km (2 mi) south of Tharwa* ☎ *02/6207–2900* ✉ *Free* ⊙ *Park daily 24 hrs; visitor center weekdays 9–4, weekends 9–4:30.*

☾ **National Dinosaur Museum.** Dinosaur-lovers will be dazzled by the display of full-size dinosaur skeletons here, many of which were found in Australia. An impressive collection of 700-million-year-old fossils is also on display, including the hardened remnants of plants, bugs, sea creatures, birds, and mammals. ✉ *Gold Creek Rd. and Barton Hwy.,*

Nicholls ☎ *02/6230–2655* ⊕ *www.nationaldinosaurmuseum.com.au*
▨ *A$9.50* ⊙ *Daily 10–5.*

Tidbinbilla Nature Reserve. Terrible bushfires in January 2003 burned down
more than 500 Canberra homes and devastated massive sections of the
surrounding countryside—including much of the Tidbinbilla Nature Reserve. Walking trails, wetlands, and animal exhibits are still returning,
so check out the latest details, including opening hours and admission
fees, with the park office before you visit. The park is 40 km (25 mi)
southwest of Canberra. ⊠ *Paddy's River Rd., Tidbinbilla* ☎ *02/*
6205–1233 ⊕ *www.environment.act.gov.au.*

WHERE TO EAT

Canberra has more restaurants per person than any other city in Australia, and their variety reflects the city's cosmopolitan nature. In addition to eclectic Australian and fusion restaurants are authentic French,
Italian, Turkish, Vietnamese, and Chinese dining options, among many
others. Overall, Canberra dining spots hold their own against the restaurants of Sydney and Melbourne, although the feeling is generally more
casual.

The main restaurant precincts are around the city center and in the trendy
suburbs of Manuka and Kingston. However, many fine eateries are
tucked away in such suburban centers as Griffith, Ainslie, Belconnen,
and Woden. In Dickson, Canberra's Chinatown, a line of inexpensive,
casual eateries along Woolley Street includes many little spots serving
Vietnamese, Malaysian, Chinese, Turkish, and Italian cuisine.

WHAT IT COSTS In Australian Dollars				
$$$$	**$$$**	**$$**	**$**	**¢**
AT DINNER over $50	$36–$50	$21–$35	$10–$20	under $10

Prices are for a main course at dinner.

Central Canberra & Northern Suburbs

ITALIAN
$$
✕ **Mezzalira on London.** Sleek and glossy, this city-center Italian restau-
rant is the fashionable gathering place for Canberra's smart set. The menu
varies from robust pasta dishes and pizzas to char-grilled salmon with
arugula and balsamic vinegar, grilled Italian sausages with truffle-oil
mashed potato, and grilled vegetables in a red-wine sauce. Pizzas from
the wood-fired oven make for good casual dining at a modest price. The
espresso enjoys a reputation as Canberra's finest. ⊠ *Melbourne Bldg.,*
W. Row and London Circuit, Canberra City ☎ *02/6230–0025* ▤ *AE,*
DC, MC, V ⊙ *Closed Sun.*

$
✕ **Tosolini's.** A long-standing favorite with Canberra's café society, this
Italian-accented brasserie offers a choice of indoor or sidewalk tables.
Coffee not your cup of tea? Sit back and sip a fresh fruit juice or shake.
A few heartier dishes like pasta, risotto, focaccia, and pizza are also avail-
able—but plan around the noon–2 lunch crush. You can bring your own
bottle of wine to dinner if you like. A more upscale branch is in Manuka.

✉ *E. Row and London Circuit, Canberra City* ☎ *02/6247–4317* ▭ *AE, DC, MC, V* Ⓨ *BYOB* ⊘ *No dinner Sun.–Tues.*

MODERN
AUSTRALIAN
$$–$$$

✕ **Boat House by the Lake.** There's something restful about looking out over the water of Lake Burley Griffin as you dine on the superb food of this modern, airy restaurant. High ceilings give the restaurant a spacious open feel, and tall windows provide lovely views of the lake. Unusual and innovative choices include rare-roasted kangaroo fillet served with lemon-balm salad and a spicy garlic sauce. Several excellent Australian wines are on hand to complement your meal. Leave room for scrumptious desserts like Black Forest brûlée with kirsch cream. ✉ *Menindie Dr., Grevillea Park, Barton* ☎ *02/6273–5500* ▭ *AE, DC, MC, V* ⊘ *Closed Sun. No lunch Sat.*

$$
Fodor$Choice
★

✕ **Anise.** This calm, relaxing haven sits amid Canberra's West Row dining strip. Have a drink at the quiet bar before being seated at one of the well-spaced, damask-covered tables. Filling selections include the roast veal rump with baby artichokes, peas, pancetta, and roasted garlic. The banana-and-frangipani tart, served with rum ice cream, is a superb way to finish a meal. ✉ *20 W. Row, Canberra City* ☎ *02/6257–0700* ▭ *DC, MC, V* ⊘ *Closed Sun. and Mon. No lunch Sat.*

$$

✕ **Courgette.** Creative food served in spacious, stylish surroundings is the specialty of this popular Canberra restaurant on the city's outer edge. The seasonal menu has such dreamy dishes as prawn-crusted salmon served with a mushroom velouté and poached oysters; but leave room for the decadent chocolate-and-almond fondant with bitter caramel ice cream. The wine cellar here is impressive, and you can sample vintages of Australian and overseas wines by the bottle or glass. ✉ *54 Marcus Clarke St., Canberra City* ☎ *02/6247–4042* ▭ *AE, DC, MC, V* ⊘ *Closed Sun. No lunch Sat.*

$$

✕ **Dijon.** A cozy space, white tablecloths, and touches of elegance provide the setting for an intimate dinner. The Mod-Oz menu is sprinkled with Asian flavorings, but includes classics like lamb saddle served with Lyonnaise potatoes, spinach, shallots, and mint. Rich desserts include raspberry ragout, and chocolate espresso mousse on vanilla shortbread. The extensive wine list includes local and overseas vintages, some available by the glass. You can also dine outside in warm weather. ✉ *24 W. Row, Canberra City* ☎ *02/6230–6009* ▭ *AE, DC, MC, V* ⊘ *No lunch weekends.*

PAN-ASIAN
$$
Fodor$Choice
★

✕ **Chairman and Yip.** The menu garners universal praise for its innovative mix of Asian and Western flavors against a backdrop of artifacts from Maoist China. Menu standouts include the duck pancakes, and the steamed barramundi with kumquats, ginger, and shallots. Finish with a delicious dessert, such as cinnamon-and-star-anise crème brûlée. The service and wine list are outstanding, and you can bring your own bottle of wine, if you like. ✉ *108 Bunda St., Canberra City* ☎ *02/6248–7109* ⏦ *Reservations essential* ▭ *AE, DC, MC, V* Ⓨ *BYOB* ⊘ *No lunch weekends.*

THAI
★ **$**

✕ **Zen Yai.** From the deliciously light, tangy stir-fried noodles with king prawns in tamarind sauce to the roast duck in red curry with lychees, the menu of this modern Thai restaurant is an inventive blend of tradi-

WINE TOURING AROUND CANBERRA

I N THE LATE 1990S the Canberra region saw huge growth in the number of regional wineries, where high-quality, cool-climate chardonnays, Rieslings, cabernets, shirazes, merlots, and pinots are produced. Though there have been vineyards in the area for more than a hundred years, the recent worldwide recognition of the area's vintages has contributed to the explosion of this mini–Wine Country: there are now about 140 vineyards set in the peaceful rural countryside around Canberra, producing more than 30 labels. Most are a maximum of 30 minutes from the city, and, despite the sophisticated product, the wineries are small and friendly— the wine-maker might even greet you at the door.

The area's wineries are concentrated in the villages of Hall and Murrumbateman, and Lake George and Bungendore. Many are open to visits on weekends only; you can explore the area on your own or with a guided tour. Depending on the number of wineries you wish to visit (and be careful if you intend to sample a few vintages as well as drive) then it's possible to cover the wineries in the Hall/Murrumbateman area along the Barton Highway in half a day. The wineries along the Federal Highway around Lake George and Bungendore would take at least another half day.

These wineries are small operations, and visiting the "cellar door" usually involves sampling the wines in the tasting room. There is no charge for tastings, although the vintners hope you'll be impressed enough with the wine to make some purchases. The Canberra District Wineries Guide is a good planning resource; you can pick one up from the Canberra and Region Visitor Centre, or from the **Kamberra Wine Centre** (✉ Flemington Rd. and Northbourne Ave., Lyneham ☎ 02/6262-2333 ⊕ www.brlhardy.com.au) at the northern entrance to Canberra overlooking the Canberra Racecourse. The wine center's excellent Meeting Place restaurant is a good place for a break between tours and tastings. If you don't want to combine driving with wine tasting, consider a wine tour. **Brindabella Wine Tours** (☎ 02/6231-6997 ⊕ www.actwine.com.au) provides escorted half- and full-day tours of the entire Canberra wine district. Half-day trips cost A$99; full days cost A$129 and include a restaurant meal (two courses) and the opportunity to meet the vintners. Groups are welcome. **Days of Delight Winery Tours** (☎ 02/6260-7773 ⊕ www.smallwineries.com.au) specializes in personally tailored itineraries. Tours range from half to full days and price is dependent on the size of the group.

Wineries Along the Barton Highway

From Canberra, take the Barton Highway in the direction of Yass. After 20 km (12 mi), you'll reach a trio of wineries around the village Hall: **Brindabella Hills Winery** (☎ 02/6230-2583, open weekends 10–5); **Pankhurst Wines** (☎ 02/6230-2592, open weekends 10–5); and **Surveyors Hill Winery** (☎ 02/6230-2046, open weekends 10–5). A few minutes farther along Barton Highway, a right turn onto Nanima Road will bring you to the **Wily Trout Winery** (☎ 02/6230-2487, open daily 10–5). This winery shares its premises with *Poachers Pantry*, which sells picnic-style smoked meats, poultry, and vegetables, and the *Smokehouse Cafe* (open Friday–Sunday 10–5), where you can have a decadent countryside dining experience.

About 15 minutes farther along the Barton Highway near Murrumbateman is another cluster of wineries. They're all well marked with signs: **Clonakilla Winery** (☎ 02/6227–5877, open daily 11–5); **Helm Wines** (☎ 02/6227–5953, open Thursday–Monday 10–5); **Jeir Creek Wines** (☎ 02/6227–5999, open Thursday–Monday 10–5); **Murrumbateman Winery** (☎ 02/6227–5584, open Thursday–Sunday 10–5); and **Doonkuna Winery** (☎ 02/6227–5811, open weekdays 8–4, weekends 11–4). If you need to refuel, you can stop by the **Barrique Cafe** (☎ 02/6227–5600, open Thursday–Saturday 10–late, Sunday 10–5); it serves a good selection of soups, open sandwiches, pizza, and other hearty fare.

Wineries Along the Federal Highway
From Canberra, take the Federal Highway for about 30 km (19 mi) north toward Sydney until you reach the Lake George area. Here you'll find **Lark Hill Winery** (☎ 02/6238–1393, open Wednesday–Monday 10–5); **Gidgee Estate Wines** (☎ 02/6236–9506, open weekends noon–4); **Lambert Vineyards** (☎ 02/6238–3866, open 10–5, Fri.–Sun.); and **Lerida Estate Wines** (☎ 02/4848–0231, open daily 10–5). At **Madew Wines** (☎ 02/4848–0026, open Wednesday–Sunday 10–5), you can stop by *grapefoodwine* restaurant, for modern Australian, seasonally inspired cuisine and great views over Lake George. It's open for lunch Thursday–Saturday, and for dinner on Friday and Saturday.

On the banks of the Molonglo River, close to the airport, is one other winery that's well worth visiting: **Pialligo Estate Wines and Cafe** (✉ 18 Kallaroo Rd., Pialligo ☎ 02/6247–6060), which is surrounded by beautiful rose gardens. Thursday through Sunday, 10–5, you can enjoy a wine tasting, lunch, or an antipasto platter here as the sun sets behind Parliament House.

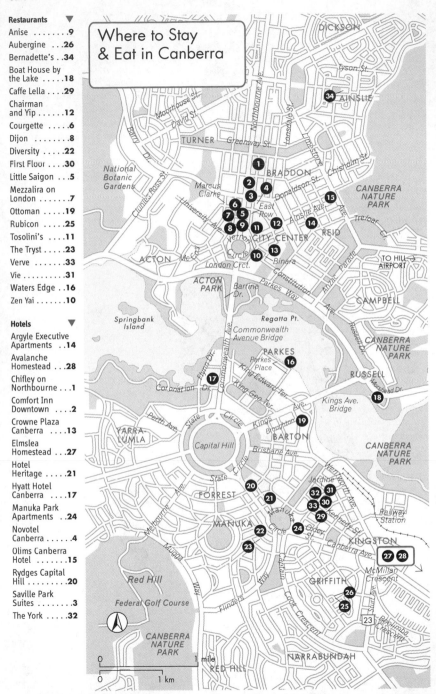

Where to Stay & Eat in Canberra

tional and contemporary flavors. The spacious, casual dining room makes a relaxing space to share new tastes, and the dedicated waitstaff is on hand to help you choose dishes that suit your spice tolerance. ⊠ *111–117 London Circuit, Canberra City* ☎ *02/6262–7594* ▭ *DC, MC, V* ⊘ *Closed Sun.*

TURKISH
$$
✕ **Ottoman.** Occupying an expansive space in the Parliamentary Triangle, this unique restaurant offers plush comfort amid Turkish decor. Though it's tempting to feast on the wonderful dips and appetizers, focus on the excellent entrées. Try the tender slices of veal, cooked in mild spices and served with a piquant lemon sauce on eggplant and baby spinach. ⊠ *Broughton and Blackall Sts., Barton* ☎ *02/6273–6111* ▭ *AE, DC, MC, V* ⊘ *Closed Sun. and Mon. No lunch Sat.*

VEGETARIAN
★ $
✕ **Bernadette's.** Gourmet vegetarian fare is the specialty of this indoor-outdoor café. Dig into Moroccan brochettes, or skewered slices of eggplant, zucchini, squash, and artichoke, both served with a savory combination of pine-nut couscous and *harissa* (a mix of chilies, garlic, cumin, and coriander) yogurt. Vegetarian pizzas are topped with creative combinations like slow-roasted pumpkin, caramelized onion, and goat cheese. Vegan and gluten-free choices are available. ⊠ *Wakefield Gardens at Ainslie Shops, Ainslie* ☎ *02/6248–5018* ▭ *MC, V* ⊘ *Closed Sun. and Mon.*

VIETNAMESE
$
✕ **Little Saigon.** Relaxed, indoor-outdoor dining areas are joined at this popular Vietnamese eatery. All the traditional favorites are here—including noodle dishes and salads—cooked with fresh ingredients and authentic spices. Groups often book banquets here, while locals grab quick, tasty take-away lunch boxes for A$5. ⊠ *Novotel Bldg., Alinga St., Canberra City* ☎ *02/6230–5003* ▭ *DC, MC, V.*

Southern Suburbs

ECLECTIC
$$
✕ **Rubicon.** Everything about this cozy restaurant speaks of attention to detail. For instance, savor the melded flavors of organic, pan-roasted lamb rump, served with crisp parsnip and grilled pear, along with brandied kumquats and mint jus. Later you can linger over such delicious desserts as ginger- and lime-infused crème brûlée. For a lighter meal, sample the cheese board and a few choice picks from the extensive collection of wines. ⊠ *6A Barker St., Griffith* ☎ *02/6295–9919* ▭ *DC, MC, V* ⊘ *Closed Sun. and Mon.*

$$
✕ **Waters Edge.** Tables are set with linen tablecloths and sparkling glasses, and huge glass windows look out over the sparkling waters of Lake Burley Griffin at this swanky spot adjacent to the lake. The menu cleverly blends French and Mod-Oz influences with dishes such as roast venison loin with roasted beetroot, garlic potato puree, and beetroot sauce; or a luscious dessert of bitter-chocolate fondant with star anise and white-chocolate ice cream. For a special night out try the degustation menu. An impressive wine list has many by-the-glass vintages. ⊠ *Commonwealth Pl. off Parkes Pl., Parkes* ☎ *02/6273–5066* ▭ *AE, DC, MC, V* ⊘ *Closed Mon. No lunch Sat.*

★ $–$$
✕ **The Tryst.** Set before the lush greenery of the Lawns at Manuka, this popular restaurant offers two very different settings. Inside, a serene din-

ing room and lovely garden views envelop you in sophistication, while outside tables place you right in the midst of the Bougainville Street shopping crowds. Cuisines are on hand to suit all moods and tastes, including spicy Moroccan panfried lamb, prepared with a hint of balsamic oil and served with couscous. Afterward, a stroll through the surrounding shops will work off at least a few calories from the rich desserts like panna cotta with blueberry jus and brandy snaps. ⊠ *The Lawns, Bougainville St., Manuka* ☎ *02/6239–4422* ▭ *AE, DC, MC, V* ☾ *No dinner Sun.*

$–$$ ✕ **Verve.** Tables spill out onto the sidewalk of this hip, casual café, or you can view the passing parade through the open front windows. Pasta, curries, and meat dishes form the bulk of the menu. Try the spaghetti *pescatore* (with seafood) with al dente pasta, served with garlic, parsley, basil, and olive oil. Weekends are busy with locals during breakfast and brunch, when the special menu lists a selection of old favorites: eggs, pancakes, waffles, and meats. ⊠ *Franklin St. and Flinders Way, Manuka* ☎ *02/6239–4666* ▭ *MC, V.*

¢–$ ✕ **Caffe Lella.** Friends often gather for coffee and snacks at this popular little local meet-and-eat spot. Munchies include bruschettas, frittatas, and pastas—or just go for a chunky slice from one of the mouthwatering .cakes. If it's too cozy inside, grab one of the tables on the nearby Green Square lawn. ⊠ *68 Green Sq., Kingston* ☎ *02/6239–6383* ▭ *MC, V* ☾ *No dinner Sat.–Tues.*

MODERN AUSTRALIAN

$$

Fodor'sChoice

★

✕ **Aubergine.** The large, plate-glass windows of this cozy restaurant look out onto relaxing parkland. A seasonal menu combines fresh produce, subtle spices, and pungent sauces into such delicacies as pan-seared salmon with crusted prawn mousse, served with tomato and avocado salsa. Calorie-rich desserts include date pudding drizzled with Bailey's ice cream and caramel fudge sauce. The wine list includes some rare vintages from Australian vineyards. ⊠ *18 Barker St., Griffith* ☎ *02/6260–8666* ▭ *AE, DC, MC, V* ☾ *No lunch weekends.*

$$ ✕ **Diversity.** This smart, casual restaurant has an innovative menu that gives basic Australian flavors an international twist. Spices are seamlessly blended in such dishes as Moroccan lamb with honey chili sauce, served with cinnamon-and-garlic rice and lemon salsa. Huge, wood-fired-oven pizzas are perfect for sharing. You can nosh in the warm dining room or sit at a sidewalk table amid the Franklin Street throng. ⊠ *36 Franklin St., Manuka* ☎ *02/6260–7398* ▭ *AE, DC, MC, V* ☾ *Closed Mon.*

$$ ✕ **Vie.** Huge glass windows look out onto a sun-drenched patio at this relaxing restaurant with Asian-spiced inspirations. Lunch includes delicacies like marinated rosemary chicken breast on roasted capsicum and tomatoes, while evenings bring Balinese coconut fish curry with tropical fruit chutney and jasmine rice. The excellent wine list includes many local and international varieties, some available by the glass. Warm weather draws diners out to the patio tables. ⊠ *15 Tench St., Kingston* ☎ *02/6234–8080* ▭ *AE, DC, MC, V* ☾ *No dinner Sun.*

$–$$ ✕ **First Floor.** A spacious dining room and modern decor add verve to this restaurant overlooking peaceful Kingston's Green Square. Here, above the gardens, Asian flavorings shake up the Mod-Oz menu in such dishes as garlic-and-chili squid sautéed in olive oil with parsley and onions, or fried fish fillet with watercress and red pepper salsa. Milder seasonings are used for the baked chicken breast, marinated in Indian spices and served with dal. There's an extensive list of wines by the glass. ⊠ *Green Sq., Jardine St., Kingston* ☎ *02/6260–6311* ▭ *AE, DC, MC, V* ✆ *Closed Sun. No lunch Sat.*

WHERE TO STAY

Canberra and its surrounding neighborhoods have comfortable, modern accommodations with basic room facilities and on-site activities. Most rooms have color TVs, coffee- and tea-making equipment, and refrigerators, and you can usually request hair dryers, irons, and other implements for personal grooming. Larger hotels have laundry and dry-cleaning services; those that don't usually have laundry facilities. Most hotels also have no-smoking rooms or floors, which you should be sure to reserve ahead of time.

WHAT IT COSTS In Australian Dollars					
	$$$$	**$$$**	**$$**	**$**	**¢**
FOR 2 PEOPLE	over $300	$201–$300	$151–$200	$100–$150	under $100

Prices are for two people in a standard double room in high season, including tax and service, based on the European Plan (with no meals) unless otherwise noted.

Central Canberra & Northern Suburbs

$$ ▤ **Crowne Plaza Canberra.** This atrium-style hotel, in a prime location between the city center and the National Convention Centre, has modern facilities and a moderate level of luxury. Decorated in cream and honey tones, guest rooms are large, comfortable, and well equipped. Public areas have a cool, contemporary style, with plenty of chrome and glass, giant potted plants, and fresh flowers. ⊠ *1 Binara St., Canberra City, 2601* ☎ *02/6247–8999* ▨ *02/6257–4903* ⊕ *www.crowneplazacanberra.com.au* ➔ *287 rooms, 6 suites* ♨ *2 restaurants, refrigerators, pool, gym, sauna, 2 bars, dry cleaning, laundry service, concierge, business services, free parking* ▭ *AE, DC, MC, V.*

$$
Fodor'sChoice
★
▤ **Saville Park Suites.** Most of the accommodations at this hotel a block away from the city center are self-contained one- and two-bedroom suites with spacious lounge and dining areas, full kitchens, and private balconies. Standard rooms are available for a lower price. Head down to the Zipp Restaurant and Wine Bar for delicious Mod-Oz fare—or enjoy it in the luxury of your room. ⊠ *84 Northbourne Ave., Canberra City, 2612* ☎ *02/6243–2500 or 1800/630588* ▨ *02/6243–2599* ⊕ *www.savillesuites.com.au* ➔ *52 rooms, 123 suites* ♨ *Restaurant, refrigerators, in-room data ports, indoor pool, gym, sauna, bar, meeting rooms, free parking* ▭ *AE, DC, MC, V.*

★ **$–$$** ▤ **Argyle Executive Apartments.** Small groups enjoy the good value of these smart, comfy, fully self-contained two- and three-bedroom apartments barely a five-minute walk from the city center. Each unit has a large living and dining area, a separate kitchen with a microwave and dishwasher, a secure garage, and free laundry facilities. Set amid gardens, units have either a balcony or a private courtyard. Rates are available with and without maid service. ⊠ *Currong and Boolee Sts., Reid, 2612* ☎ *02/ 6275–0800* 🖷 *02/6275–0888* ⊕ *www.argyleapartments.com.au* ⬎ *30 apartments* ⚄ *Kitchens, refrigerators, microwaves, laundry facilities, free parking* ☰ *AE, DC, MC, V.*

$–$$ 🏨 **Chifley on Northbourne.** The rooms and facilities here rival those of some of the city center's more expensive hotels. Dark timber furnishings, a piano, and an open fire create a cozy, clublike reception area, while the olive-and-cinnamon color scheme and gum-leaf motif in the rooms provide a very Australian feel. The hotel is close to the city center and overlooks one of the city's major arteries, so light sleepers should request a poolside room at the back of the hotel. ⊠ *102 Northbourne Ave., Braddon, 2601* ☎ *02/6249–1411* 🖷 *02/6249–6878* ⊕ *www.chifleyhotels.com* ⬎ *68 rooms, 10 suites* ⚄ *Restaurant, refrigerators, in-room data ports, pool, gym, bar, dry cleaning, laundry service, business services, free parking* ☰ *AE, DC, MC,.*

$–$$ 🏨 **Novotel Canberra.** Clean, crisp rooms; a heated indoor pool; and a central location (the hotel's part of the Jolimont Tourist Centre complex) make this an appealing choice. Rooms have desks with telephones and data ports. A large cluster of good restaurants is within easy walking distance. ⊠ *65 Northbourne Ave., Canberra City 2000* ☎ *02/ 6245–5000 or 02/6245–5100* ⊕ *www.accorhotels.com.au* ⬎ *149 rooms, 38 suites* ⚄ *Room service, minibars, refrigerators, in-room data ports, indoor pool, gym, sauna, free parking* ☰ *AE, DC, MC, V.*

$ 🏨 **Comfort Inn Downtown.** Travelers on a budget appreciate this excellent-value motel. Facilities are modern, and it's close to the city center. Tourist, business, and executive rooms are available, some of which have kitchenettes, and the place is kept absolutely spotless. ⊠ *82 Northbourne Ave., Braddon, 2601* ☎ *02/6249–1388 or 1800/026150* 🖷 *02/6247–2523* ⊕ *www.comfortinn.com.au* ⬎ *61 rooms, 4 suites* ⚄ *Restaurant, some kitchenettes, gym, laundry facilities, free parking* ☰ *AE, DC, MC, V.*

$ 🏨 **Olims Hotel Canberra.** Inside its original National Heritage–listed building and a modern addition built around a landscaped courtyard, this former pub—one of the city's first—has double rooms, split-level suites with kitchens, and two- and three-bedroom suites. Guest rooms and public spaces are contemporary in style, with laminated, pinelike wood finishes, fabrics and carpets tinged with red ocher, and beige walls. Rates are reduced Friday–Sunday. The hotel is about 1 km (½ mi) east of the city center, close to the Australian War Memorial. ⊠ *Ainslie and Limestone Aves., Braddon, 2601* ☎ *02/6248–5511* 🖷 *02/6247–0864 or 1300/656565* ⊕ *www.olimshotel.com* ⬎ *77 rooms, 49 suites* ⚄ *2 restaurants, kitchenettes, refrigerators, bar, dry cleaning, laundry service, free parking* ☰ *AE, DC, MC, V.*

Southern Suburbs

$$$–$$$$ 🏨 **Hyatt Hotel Canberra.** This elegant hotel, the finest in the city, occupies
Fodor'sChoice a 1924 National Heritage building that has been restored to its original
★ art deco style. Warm peach and earth tones decorate the large, luxurious rooms and spacious suites. Enormous marble bathrooms will appeal to anyone who enjoys a good soak in the tub. The hotel has extensive gardens and is within easy walking distance of the Parliamentary Triangle. Afternoon tea, held daily between 2:30 and 5 in the gracious Tea Lounge,

is one of Canberra's most popular traditions. ✉ *Commonwealth Ave., Yarralumla, 2600* ☎*13–1234 or 02/6270–1234* 🖷*02/6281–5998* ⊕*www. canberra.hyatt.com* ☞*231 rooms, 18 suites* ⌂ *3 restaurants, room service, in-room safes, minibars, refrigerators, in-room data ports, tennis court, saltwater pool, gym, sauna, 2 bars, dry cleaning, laundry service, concierge, business services, free parking* ☰ *AE, DC, MC, V.*

$$–$$$ 🏨 **Rydges Capital Hill.** With its atrium ceiling composed of immense fab-
Fodor'sChoice ric sails, this is one of Canberra's most luxurious hotels and a magnet
★ for a largely business-focused clientele. Spacious, airy, and comfortable rooms are filled with contemporary furnishings; sumptuous decor highlights the 38 Spa Suites and two Premier Suites. Close to Parliament House, the hotel and its bar have an ever-present flow of political gossip from parliamentary staff and members of the press, who drop in regularly. ✉ *Canberra Ave. and National Circle, Forrest, 2603* ☎ *02/6295–3144 or 1800/020011* 🖷 *02/6295–3325* ⊕ *www.rydges.com.au* ☞ *146 rooms, 40 suites* ⌂ *Restaurant, room service, refrigerators, pool, health club, sauna, bar, dry cleaning, laundry service, concierge, business services, free parking* ☰ *AE, DC, MC, V.*

★ **$–$$$** 🏨 **The York.** This family-owned boutique hotel in the heart of the trendy Kingston café area provides a blend of comfort and convenience. Choose from roomy one- and two-bedroom suites or attractive studios that include a fully equipped kitchen and separate dining and living areas. All have balconies, some overlooking a quiet garden courtyard. The chic Artespresso restaurant is also an art gallery displaying quality contemporary exhibitions. ✉ *Giles and Tench Sts., Kingston, 2603* ☎ *02/6295–2333* 🖷 *02/6295–9559* ⊕ *www. yorkcanberra.com.au* ☞ *9 studios, 16 suites* ⌂ *Restaurant, kitchens, laundry service, free parking* ☰ *AE, DC, MC, V.*

$–$$ 🏨 **Manuka Park Apartments.** The comfortable one- and two-bedroom apartments and interconnecting suites in this low-rise building all have cooking facilities, a living room, and a laundry area. Fully carpeted, open-plan rooms have a clean, contemporary feel. In a leafy suburb, the units are within easy walking distance of the restaurants, boutiques, and antiques stores of the Manuka shopping district. Landscaped gardens surround the apartments, all of which have a private balcony or courtyard. ✉ *Manuka Circle and Oxley St., Manuka, 2603* ☎ *02/6239–0000 or 1800/688227* 🖷 *02/6295–7750* ⊕ *www.manukapark.com.au* ☞ *40 apartments* ⌂ *Kitchens, refrigerators, saltwater pool, free parking* ☰ *AE, DC, MC, V.*

¢–$ 🏨 **Hotel Heritage.** Though it's in a quiet residential area, this two-story hotel built around a large courtyard and pool is a good budget option; it's only minutes from many of Canberra's attractions. Plain-Jane rooms are done in neutrals and might have patios or balconies; they cater to couples and family groups with varying rooms sizes and configurations. Public transportation stops near the hotel. The adjacent Capital Golf Course is open to visitors. ✉ *203 Goyder St., Narrabundah, 2604* ☎ *02/6295–2944 or 1800/026346* 🖷 *02/6239–6310* ⊕ *www. hotelheritage.com.au* ☞ *208 rooms* ⌂ *Restaurant, room service, refrigerators, pool, sauna, bar, babysitting, laundry facilities, free parking* ☰ *AE, DC, MC, V.*

Outside Canberra

$$$$ ⬚ **Avalanche Homestead.** Perched on a hillside in the Tinderry Mountains, this large, modern homestead offers a taste of the "real" Australia. Rooms are spacious and comfortable, and the inviting guest lounge is often warmed by an open fire. Dinners are splendid banquets served in a vast baronial hall. Daily activities include horseback riding, cattle mustering, sheep shearing, trout fishing, and bushwalking. The property is 45 km (28 mi) south of Canberra and adjoins an 80,000-acre nature reserve that abounds with kangaroos, wallabies, wombats, and colorful birds. Rates include all meals and activities. ⬚ *Box 544, Burra Creek, Queanbeyan 2620* ☎ *02/6236–3245* 🖷 *02/6236–3302* ⊕ *www. avalanchehomestead.com.au* ↪ *6 rooms* ⚓ *Pool, fishing, hiking, horseback riding, laundry service, free parking* ⊟ *AE, DC, MC, V* ⦿I *AI.*

$ ⬚ **Elmslea Homestead.** Surrounded by ancient elm trees and filled with a lifetime of history, this classic 1910 Federation-style homestead combines charm, grace, and character. The original dining room, kitchen, maid's room, laundry, and dairy, decorated in their original themes, have been transformed into guest quarters. Breakfast is included, and dinner can be provided by prior arrangement. Winery tours and balloon flights can be arranged, and there are several fine crafts shops in nearby Bungendore, a small, rustic village 25 minutes down the road from Canberra. ⊠ *80 Tarago Rd., Bungendore 2621* ☎ *02/6238–1651* ⊕ *www. elmslea.com.au* ↪ *5 rooms* ⚓ *Dining room, laundry service, free parking* ⊟ *DC, MC, V* ⦿I *CP.*

NIGHTLIFE & THE ARTS

Canberra after dark has a reputation for being dull. Actually, the city isn't quite as boring as the rest of Australia thinks, nor as lively as the citizens of Canberra would like to believe. Most venues are clustered in the city center and the fashionable southern suburbs of Manuka and Kingston. Except on weekends, few places showcase live music.

The Thursday edition of the *Canberra Times* has a "What's On" section (in the Times Out supplement) listing performances around the city. The Saturday edition's Arts pages also list weekend happenings.

The Arts

The **Canberra Theatre Centre** (⊠ Civic Sq., Canberra City) is the city's main live performance space. The center has two different theaters, which host productions by the Australian Ballet Company, touring theater companies, and overseas artists. The theater's ticketing agency, **Canberra Ticketing** (⊠ Civic Sq., Canberra City ☎ 02/6275–2700 or 1800/802025), is in a building adjacent to the theaters.

Smaller stage and musical companies perform at neighborhood venues like the **Erindale Theatre** (⊠ McBryde Crescent, Wanniassa ☎ 02/6207–2703). The Australian National University's School of Music has classical recitals and modern-style concerts on-campus at **Llewellyn Hall** (⊠ Childers St., Acton ☎ 02/6125–4993).

The **Street Theatre** (✉ Childers St. and University Ave., Canberra City ☎ 02/6247–1223), near the Australian National University campus, showcases the best in local talent with excellent productions ranging from musicals like *Les Miserables* and *Chicago* to avant-garde plays.

Art Galleries

Apart from the major galleries already listed above in the Exploring section, Canberra has a wealth of smaller private art galleries showcasing and selling the works of Australian artists. You can find paintings, sculpture, woodworks, glassware, and jewelry at these spots. Entry to most galleries is free, and most are open daily during regular business hours (9 or 10 AM to 5 PM).

Beaver Galleries (✉ 81 Denison St., Deakin ☎ 02/6282–5294) has four exhibition galleries and a sculpture garden, where works by contemporary Australian artists are showcased. There is also a licensed café.

Bungendore Wood Works Gallery (✉ Kings Hwy., Bungendore ☎ 02/6238–1682) exhibits the work of Australian wood artists, whose sculpture and contemporary furniture are made from the finest native timbers.

Chapman Gallery (✉ 31 Captain Cook Crescent, Manuka ☎ 02/6295–25503) has rotating exhibits by leading Australian artists, with a special emphasis on Aboriginal art.

Made from Australia Galleries (✉ 36 Grey St., Deakin ☎ 02/6273–7744) has five separate gallery spaces, where Australian-made wool garments, fashion accessories, and leather and glass works are displayed. There's also a selection of Australian gourmet foods.

Solander Gallery (✉ 10 Schlich St., Yarralumla ☎ 02/6285–2218) displays a range of paintings and sculpture by leading Australian artists.

Nightlife

Nightspots in the city center offer everything from laser light shows and noisy bands to dance and comedy clubs. Many waive cover charges except for special events.

Academy and Candy Bar. Canberra's hottest nightspot draws the hip crowd to its stylish, glitzy premises. The main club room, which hosts DJs, live bands, and mixed acts, attracts a young dance crowd. Upstairs, the Candy Bar serves innovative cocktails in a chic lounge-bar setting. ✉ *Centre Cinema Bldg., Bunda St., Canberra City* ☎ 02/6257–3355 ⚏ *A$5–A$20* ☉ *Academy Thurs.–Sat. 10 PM–late; Candy Bar Wed.–Mon. 5 PM–late.*

Bobby McGee's. The party crowds flock to this flamboyant American-style restaurant and entertainment lounge in the Rydges Lakeside Hotel. Service is slick and professional, and the staff is gregarious and spontaneous. ✉ *Rydges Lakeside Hotel, 1 London Circuit, Canberra City* ☎ 02/6257–7999 ⚏ *Free, except for special events* ☉ *Weekdays 5 PM–3 AM, Sat. 7 PM–4 AM.*

Casino Canberra. The European-style facility forgoes slot machines in favor of the more sociable games of roulette, blackjack, poker, minibaccarat, pai gow, and keno. There are 40 gaming tables here, and the complex includes a restaurant and two bars. ⊠ *21 Binara St., Canberra City* ☎ *02/6257-7074* ✆ *Free* ⊙ *Daily noon–6 AM.*

FMs. This modern club attracts a twentysomething crowd for hip DJ-spun music on weekends. ⊠ *40–42 Franklin St., Manuka* ☎ *02/6295-1845* ✆ *No cover* ⊙ *Tues.–Sat. 9 PM–3 AM.*

Holy Grail. With locations in the city center and south in Kingston, Holy Grail not only serves fabulous salads, pastas, and grills, but it also hosts great rhythm-and-blues bands. Grab a comfortable table and meet friends over a glass of wine. ⊠ *Bunda St. near Akuna St., Canberra City* ☎ *02/6257-9717* ✆ *Green Sq., Kingston* ☎ *02/6295-6071* ✆ *A$5 cover* ⊙ *Bar daily 10 PM–late, music Thurs.–Sat. at 10 PM.*

ICBM and Insomnia. Professionals and students in their twenties and thirties dance to Top 40 hits at this loud, modern bar. Wednesday is Comedy Night, and a DJ spins tunes on Saturday. ⊠ *50 Northbourne Ave., Canberra City* ☎ *02/6248-0102* ✆ *Comedy Night show A$5, Sat. DJ dance A$5* ⊙ *Wed.–Sat. 9 PM–2 AM.*

In Blue. Downstairs you can step up to the cocktail and vodka bar while sampling tapas and cigars. Then head upstairs to the nightclub, where DJs mix everything from dance to rhythm and blues. ⊠ *Mort and Alinga Sts., Canberra City* ☎ *02/6248-7405* ✆ *No cover* ⊙ *Daily 4 PM–3 AM.*

Minque. This relaxing bar is a great place to sit back and groove to the nightly music, which might be rock or rhythm and blues. ⊠ *17 Franklin St., Manuka* ☎ *02/6295-8866* ✆ *No cover* ⊙ *Tues.–Sun. 3–midnight.*

Tilley's Devine Café Gallery. This 1940s-style club was once for women only, but today anyone can sit at the wooden booths and listen to live bands, poetry readings, or comedy acts. Performances are held several times weekly. ⊠ *Wattle and Brigalow Sts., Lyneham* ☎ *02/6249-1543* ✆ *Café free, show fees vary* ⊙ *8 PM–late.*

SPORTS & THE OUTDOORS

Bicycling

Canberra has almost 160 km (100 mi) of cycle paths, and the city's relatively flat terrain and dry, mild climate make it a perfect place to explore on two wheels. One of the most popular cycle paths is the 40-km (25-mi) circuit around Lake Burley Griffin.

Mr. Spokes Bike Hire rents several different kinds of bikes as well as tandems and baby seats. Bikes cost A$12 for the first hour, including helmet rental, A$30 for a half day, and A$40 for a full day. ⊠ *Acton Ferry Terminal, Barrine Dr., Acton Park* ☎ *02/6257-1188* ⊙ *Closed Mon. and Tues. except during school holidays.*

If you're looking for a bit more action, **Row'n'Ride** rents mountain bikes and canoes, and will deliver them to where you're staying. Half-day bike rentals are A$30, full days are A$42; kayaks are A$30 for a half day.

The company also runs a range of adventure trips in areas around Canberra. ☎ *02/6228–1264* ⊕ *www.realfun.com.au.*

Boating

Southern Cross Cruises has daily one-hour sailings (A$14) around Lake Burley Griffin on the MV *Southern Cross* at 10 and 3. ⊠ *Lotus Bay, Mariner Pl. off Alexandrina Dr., Acton Park* ☎ *02/6273–1784.*

Ferry Cruises on Lake Burley Griffin employs two vessels that regularly crisscross the lake ($A11). The *Cygnet,* a small electric ferry, also runs between the Lake Burley docks (A$12). The SS *Maid Marion* has lake tours (A$11). ⊠ *Acton Ferry Terminal, Barrine Dr., Acton Park* ☎ *0418/ 828357.*

You can rent aqua bikes, surf skis, paddleboats, and canoes daily (except May–July) for use on Lake Burley Griffin from **Burley Griffin Boat Hire.** Rates start at A$12 for a half hour. ⊠ *Acton Ferry Terminal, Barrine Dr., Acton Park* ☎ *02/6249–6861.*

Golf

On the lower slopes of Red Hill, the 18-hole, par-73 **Federal Golf Course** is regarded as the most challenging of the city's greens. Nonmembers are welcome on most weekdays provided they make advance bookings. ⊠ *Red Hill Lookout Rd., Red Hill* ☎ *02/6281–1888* ⌣ *Greens fees A$55.*

Among the top four courses in Canberra, the 18-hole, par-72 **Gold Creek Country Club** is a public course—with the added bonus of three practice holes and a driving range. ⊠ *Harcourt Hill, Curran Dr., Nicholls* ☎ *02/ 6123–0600* ⌣ *Greens fees A$33 weekdays, A$44 weekends; cart hire A$30.*

Another highly rated course is the 18-hole, par-72 course at **Yowani Country Club,** 3 km (2 mi) north of the city. The club also has three first-class bowling greens, as well as convenient motel units for visitors. Built on flat terrain, the course is deceptively easy, with heavily wooded fairways, water storage lakes, and tricky bunkers all coming into play. ⊠ *Northbourne Ave., Lyneham* ☎ *02/6241–2303* ⌣ *Greens fees A$40 daily.*

Hiking & Walking

Namadgi National Park and Tidbinbilla Nature Reserve have excellent, well-marked bushwalking tracks. However, since many parts of the park and reserve were badly damaged in the bushfires of January 2003, you should stick to the trails to avoid harming the still-recovering vegetation. Maps of walking trails are available at the park visitor centers.

The urban area of Canberra has excellent walking paths around the three major lakes: Lake Burley Griffin, Lake Tuggeranong in the Tuggeranong Valley, and Lake Ginninderra in Belconnen. Many parts of the Canberra Nature Park have well-marked trails, such as Black Mountain, Mt. Ainslie, and Red Hill. Ask at the **Canberra Visitor Information Centre** (⊠ 330 Northbourne Ave., Dickson ☎ 02/6205–0044) for details.

Horseback Riding

The **National Equestrian Centre** (⊠ 919 Cotter Rd., Kerrabee, Weston Creek ☎ 02/6288–5555 ⊕ www.neqc.com.au), 10 minutes from Canberra, provides a country horseback riding experience. It's A$45 per person for one-hour rides (minimum two people), A$90 for ½-day rides (minimum four people), and full-day and overnight excursions are available.

Hot-Air Ballooning

Balloon Aloft (☎ 02/6285–1540) provides spectacular sunrise views over Canberra from around A$180. **Dawn Drifters** (☎ 02/6285–4450) offers sunrise panoramas over Lake Burley Griffin, Parliament House, and other local sights from around A$195.

Running

A favorite running track is the 3-km (2-mi) circuit formed by Lake Burley Griffin and its two bridges, Kings Avenue Bridge and Commonwealth Avenue Bridge.

Tennis

The **National Sports Club** offers play on synthetic grass courts. ⊠ *Riggall Pl. off Mouat St., Lyneham* ☎ *02/6247–0929* ⊡ *A$16–A$20 per hr during daylight, A$20 per hr under lights* ☉ *Daily 9 AM–10 PM.*

At the **Australian Institute of Sport** you can play on one of the establishment's six outdoor courts. ⊠ *Leverrier Crescent, Bruce* ☎ *02/6214–1281* ⊡ *A$12 per hr* ☉ *Weekdays 8 AM–9 PM, weekends 8–7.*

SHOPPING

Canberra is not known for its shopping, but there are a number of high-quality arts-and-crafts outlets where you are likely to come across some unusual gifts and souvenirs. The city's markets are excellent, and the galleries and museums sell interesting and often innovative items designed and made in Australia. In addition to the following suggestions, there are several malls and shopping centers in Canberra City (the main one is the Canberra Centre mall) and the major suburbs of Woden, Belconnen, and Tuggeranong.

Cuppacumbalong Craft Centre. A former pioneering homestead near the Murrumbidgee River, this is now a crafts gallery for potters, weavers, painters, and woodworkers, many of whom have their studios in the outbuildings. The quality of the work is universally high, and you can often meet and talk with the artisans. The center is about 34 km (21 mi) south of Canberra, off the Monaro Highway. ⊠ *Naas Rd., Tharwa* ☎ *02/6237–5116* ☉ *Wed.–Sun. 11–5.*

Gold Creek Village. The charming streets of this shopping complex on the city's northern outskirts are lined with all sorts of fun little places to explore. Peek into art galleries and pottery shops, browse through clothing boutiques and gift stores, and nosh at several eateries. ⊠ *O'Hanlon Pl., Nicholls* ☎ *02/6230–2273* ⊡ *Free* ☉ *Daily 10–5.*

Old Bus Depot Markets. South of Lake Burley Griffin, a lively Sunday market is in the former Kingston bus depot. Handmade crafts are the staples here, and buskers and exotic inexpensive food add to the shopping experience. ⊠ *Wentworth Ave., Kingston Foreshore, Kingston* ☎ *02/6292–8391* ☉ *Jan.–Nov., Sun. 10–4; Dec., weekends 10–4.*

CANBERRA A TO Z

AIR TRAVEL

Several domestic airlines connect Canberra with the rest of Australia, including Qantas and its subsidiaries Eastern, Southern, Airlink; and Virgin Blue. There are regular (about hourly) flights to Sydney and Melbourne, as well as frequent services to Brisbane. Some direct connections to Adelaide, the Gold Coast, and Perth are available, but most flights to these destinations are still via either Sydney or Melbourne.

Canberra International Airport is the only airport in the area, and is used by large commercial aircraft, small private planes, and the Air Force alike. Flights are about one-half hour to Sydney, an hour to Melbourne, and two hours to Brisbane. Early flights may be fogged in, so plan for delays. The airport is 7 km (4½ mi) east of the city center. Taxis are available from the line at the front of the terminal. The fare between the airport and the city is about A$16.

🛪 **Airlines Qantas Airways** ☎ 13-1313. **Virgin Blue** ☎ 13-6789.

🛪 **Airport Canberra International Airport** ☎ 02/6275-2236.

BUS TRAVEL

The main terminal for intercity buses is the Jolimont Tourist Centre. Canberra is served by two major bus lines, Greyhound Australia and Murrays Australia, both of which have at least three daily services to and from Sydney. Fares to Sydney start from A$25 one-way.

🛪 **Jolimont Tourist Centre** ✉ 61 Northbourne Ave., Canberra City ☎ No phone. **Greyhound Australia** ☎ 02/6249-6006, 13-1499, or 13-2030. **Murrays Australia** ☎ 13-2251.

BUS TRAVEL WITHIN CANBERRA Canberra's public transportation system is the ACTION bus network, which covers all of the city. Buses operate weekdays 6:30 AM–11:30 PM, Saturday 7 AM–11:30 PM, and Sunday 8–7. There's a flat fare of A$2.40 per ride. If you plan to travel extensively on buses, purchase a one-day ticket for A$6, which allows same-day unlimited travel on the entire bus network. If you're traveling only between 9:30 and 4:30, you're best bet is an off-peak daily ticket, which costs A$3.50. Tickets, maps, and timetables are available from the Canberra and Region Visitor Centre and the Bus Information Centre.

🛪 **Bus Information Centre** ✉ E. Row near London Circuit, Canberra City ☎ 13-1710 ⊕ www.action.act.gov.au.

CAR RENTAL

National car-rental operators with agencies in Canberra include Avis, Budget, Europcar, Hertz, and Thrifty. Rumbles Rent A Car is a local operator that offers discount car rentals. The major companies have pickup points at the airport.

🛪 **Avis** ✉ 17 Lonsdale St., Braddon ☎ 02/6249-6088 or 13-6333. **Budget** ✉ Shell Service Station, Mort and Girrahween Sts., Braddon ☎ 02/6257-2200 or 13-2727. **Europcar** ✉ 74 Northbourne Ave., Braddon ☎ 02/6284-5170 or 13-1390. **Hertz** ✉ 32 Mort St., Braddon ☎ 02/6257-4877 or 13-3039. **Rumbles Rent A Car** ✉ 11 Paragon Mall, Gladstone St., Fyshwick ☎ 02/6280-7444. **Thrifty** ✉ 29 Lonsdale St., Braddon ☎ 02/6247-7422 or 1300/367227.

CAR TRAVEL

From Sydney, take the Hume Highway to just south of Goulburn and then turn south onto the Federal Highway to Canberra. Allow 3–3½ hours for the 300-km (186-mi) journey. From Melbourne, follow the Hume Highway to Yass and turn right beyond the town onto the Barton Highway. The 655-km (406-mi) trip takes around 8 hours.

Although locals maintain otherwise, Canberra can be difficult to negotiate by car, given its radial roads, erratic signage, and often large distances between suburbs. Still, because sights are scattered about and not easily connected on foot or by public transport, a car is a good way to see the city itself, as well as the sights in the Australian Capital Territory. You can purchase maps with clearly marked scenic drives at the Canberra and Region Visitor Centre for A$2.20. Canberra's ACTION buses can get you around town comfortably and without stress.

EMBASSIES

The British High Commission is open weekdays 8:45–5 for visa and passport problems. The counter at the Consular Office is open weekdays 9–3; you can phone between 9 and 5. The Canadian High Commission is open weekdays 8:30–12:30 and 1:30–4:30, the New Zealand High Commission is open weekdays 8:45–5, and the U.S. Embassy is open weekdays 8:30–12:30.

🔳 Canada **Canadian High Commission** ✉ Commonwealth Ave. near Coronation Dr., Yarralumla ☎ 02/6270–4000.

🔳 New Zealand **New Zealand High Commission** ✉ Commonwealth Ave. near Coronation Dr., Yarralumla ☎ 02/6270–4211.

🔳 United Kingdom **British High Commission** ✉ Commonwealth Ave. near Coronation Dr., Yarralumla ☎ 02/6270–6666. **Consular Office** ✉ 39 Brindabella Circuit, Brindabella Business Park, Canberra Airport ☎ 1902/941555.

🔳 United States **U.S.Embassy** ✉ Moonah Pl. off State Circle, Yarralumla ☎ 02/6214–5600.

EMERGENCIES

In an emergency, dial **000** to reach an ambulance, the police, or the fire department. Canberra Hospital has a 24-hour emergency department.

If medical or dental treatment is required, seek advice from your hotel reception desk. There are doctors and dentists on duty throughout the city, but their office hours vary.

Pharmacies are in shopping areas throughout the city, and your hotel desk or concierge can help you find the closest one. Major chains include Capital Chemists and Amcal Chemists. Two convenient pharmacies with extended hours are Canberra Day and Night Chemist, open daily 9 AM–11 PM, and Manuka Amcal Pharmacy, open daily 9–9.

🔳 Hospitals **Calvary Hospital** ✉ Belconnen Way and Haydon Dr., Bruce ☎ 02/6201–6111. **Canberra Hospital** ✉ Yamba Dr., Garran ☎ 02/6244–2222.

🔳 Pharmacies **Canberra Day and Night Chemist (Capital Chemist)** ✉ O'Connor Shopping Centre, Sargood St., O'Connor ☎ 02/6248–7050. **Manuka Amcal Pharmacy** ✉ Shop 8, Manuka Arcade, Franklin St., Manuka ☎ 02/6295–0059.

MAIL, THE INTERNET & SHIPPING

The main post office is open weekdays 8:30–5:30. To send mail poste restante, address it with the recipient's name c/o GPO Canberra, A.C.T. Mail is held for one month. Post offices are in suburban shopping centers throughout the city, or look in the phone book under Australia Post.

Most larger hotels have rooms with data ports or Internet service. You can have free Internet access at any public library in Canberra. Internet cafés abound throughout town, including in the Canberra Centre shopping mall at City Walk, in Canberra City. Rates are about A$2 for 15 minutes.

🚩 **Main Post Office** ✉ 53–73 Alinga St., Canberra City ☏ 13-1318.

MONEY MATTERS

The major banks in Canberra are the National Australia Bank, Commonwealth Bank, ANZ, Westpac, and St. George. All have branches in all the main shopping precincts of Civic, Belconnen, Woden, Dickson, Coolemon Court, and Tuggeranong. ATMs are in shopping malls, petrol and transport stations, hotels, and clubs. Most ATMs take credit cards as well as bank cards. There are money-changing facilities at Canberra Airport, and American Express and Thomas Cook (*see* Travel Agencies) have offices in the city.

TAXIS

You can phone for a taxi, hire one from a stand, or flag one down in the street. Taxis in Canberra have meters, and fees are set based on the mileage. There's an extra fee for reservations by phone. You can bargain for an hourly rate for a day tour of the area. Tipping isn't customary, but drivers appreciate it when you give them the change.

🚩 **Canberra Cabs** ☏ 13-2227.

TOURS

A convenient (and fun!) way to see the major sights of Canberra is atop the double-decker Canberra Tour bus, operated by City Sightseeing, which makes a regular circuit around the major attractions. Tickets are A$25 and valid 24 hours, so you can hop on and off all day.

Idol Moments can tailor private chauffeur-driven tours to meet your interests, including customized tours of heritage houses, parks and gardens, or city highlights. Prices run A$38 to A$68.

Murrays Australia conducts half- and full-day tours that stop at the major tourist attractions. The full-day tour includes lunch at Parliament House. Rates are A$34.10 for a half-day tour and A$75.90 for a full-day tour.

Go Bush Tours runs relaxed half- and full-day tours of Canberra and the surrounding countryside, including morning tea and/or a picnic-style lunch outdoors, from A$45.

🚩 **City Sightseeing** ☏ 0500/505012 for cost of local call. **Go Bush Tours** ☏ 02/6231-3023. **Idol Moments** ☏ 02/6295-3822. **Murrays Australia** ☏ 13-2251.

TRAINS

The Canberra Railway Station is on Wentworth Avenue, Kingston, about 6 km (4 mi) southeast of the city center. Xplorer trains, operated by Countrylink, make the 4-hour trip between Canberra and Sydney twice daily. A daily bus-rail service by Countrylink makes the 10-hour run between Canberra and Melbourne, but first requires a bus to Cootamundra.

Countrylink has reservation and information offices at the Canberra Railway Station and at the Jolimont Tourist Centre.

⑦ Canberra Railway Station ☎ 02/6295-1198. **Countrylink** ☎ 13-2232 ⊕ www.countrylink.nsw.gov.au. **Jolimont Tourist Centre** ⊠ 61 Northbourne Ave., Canberra City ☎ 02/6257-1576.

TRAVEL AGENCIES

Reliable travel agencies include American Express Travel and Thomas Cook. The American Express Westpac Bank office exchanges money only. Many local, licensed travel agents are found throughout the city and in suburban shopping areas. Two reliable chains are Flight Centre and Harvey World Travel.

⑦ American Express ⊠ Shop 5, GIO Bldg., City Walk, Canberra City ☎ 02/6247-2333 ⊠ In Westpac Bank, City Walk at Petrie Plaza, Canberra City ☎ 1300/139060. **Flight Centre** ⊠ 111 Alinga St., Canberra City ☎ 02/6247-8199. **Harvey World Travel** ⊠ Shop DG18/19, Canberra Centre, Bunda St., Canberra City ☎ 02/6257-2222. **Thomas Cook** ⊠ Shop DG18/19, Canberra Centre, Bunda St., Canberra City ☎ 02/6257-2222.

VISITOR INFORMATION

The Canberra and Region Visitor Centre, open weekdays 9–5:30 and weekends 9–4, is a convenient stop for those entering Canberra by road from Sydney or the north. The staff makes accommodation bookings for Canberra and the Snowy Mountains.

Information booths are found at the airport, Canberra Centre shopping mall, and the Jolimont Tourist Centre. They're open during business hours on weekdays. Most hotels also have displays of brochures highlighting the city's attractions.

⑦ Canberra and Region Visitor Centre ⊠ 330 Northbourne Ave., Dickson ☎ 02/6205-0044 ⊕ www.visitcanberra.com.au. **Jolimont Tourist Centre** ⊠ 61 Northbourne Ave., Canberra City ☎ No phone.

Melbourne

WORD OF MOUTH

"St. Kilda is fun, particularly on a sunny day. There are lots of opportunities to people watch. If you walk a bit further along the Esplanade, you will end up at Acland, which has the most fantastic cake shops. Take the tram down St. Kilda Road, which will take you past some of the city gardens and the Shrine of Remembrance."

—marg

Updated by
Liza Power

MELBOURNE (SAY *MEL*-BURN) IS THE CULTIVATED SISTER of brassy Sydney. To the extent that culture is synonymous with sophistication—except when it comes to watching Australian Rules Football or the Melbourne Cup—some call this city the cultural capital of the continent. Melbourne is also known for its rich migrant influences, particularly those expressed through food: the espresso cafés on Lygon Street, Melbourne's "little Italy," Brunswick's Middle Eastern/Indian/Turkish enclave, Richmond's "little Vietnam," or the Chinatown district of the city center.

Named after then-British Prime Minister Lord Melbourne, the city of 3.5 million was founded in 1835 when Englishman John Batman and a group of businessmen bought 600,000 acres of land from the local Aborigines for a few trinkets. After gold was discovered in Victoria in the 1850s, Melbourne soon became the fastest-growing city in the British empire, and a number of its finer buildings were constructed during this period.

If, like its dowager namesake, Victoria is a little stuffy and old-fashioned, then the state capital of Melbourne is positively old world. For all the talk of Australia's egalitarian achievements, Melbourne society displays an almost European obsession with class. The city is the site of some of the nation's most prestigious schools and universities, and nowhere is it more important to have attended the right one. In a country whose convict ancestors are the frequent butt of jokes, Melburnians pride themselves on the fact that, unlike Sydney, their city was founded by free men and women who came to Victoria of their own accord.

Whatever appearances they maintain, Melburnians do love their sports, as evidenced by their successful bid to host the 2006 Commonwealth Games. The city is sports mad—especially when it comes to the glorious, freewheeling Melbourne Cup horse race that brings the entire nation to a grinding halt. The city also comes alive during the Australian Tennis Open, one of the four tennis Grand Slam events, which is held every January at Melbourne Park.

For years Melbourne's city center was seen as an inferior tourist attraction compared with Sydney's sparkling harbor. But a large-scale building development along the Yarra River in the early '90s transformed what was once an eyesore into a vibrant entertainment district known as Southgate. Starting from the charming Alexandria Bridge behind Flinders Street Station, pedestrians can tour through Southgate's myriad bars, shops, and restaurants on the south side of the Yarra River. An assortment of unusual water displays farther along mark the entrance to the Southbank's brash Crown Casino, where gasoline-fueled towers shoot bursts of flames on the hour after dark. Many changes have also taken place in the heart of the city, where Federation Square, a large civic landmark built in 2002, now houses a second branch of the National Gallery of Victoria, the Centre for the Moving Image, the Australian Racing Museum, the Melbourne Visitor Center, and an assortment of shops and restaurants.

If you have
1 day

If you're low on time, set your priorities: for those seeking boutique shopping, take a two-block tour down Little Collins Street, from Elizabeth Street to Russell Street in the city center. For a hipster's day of urban exploring, journey north to **Brunswick Street ㉒** in Fitzroy for wandering, shopping, and eating. Or, if you prefer natural sights, go marvel at the city's **Royal Botanic Gardens ㉖** or for a stroll along the bay on Kerford Road south of the city and continue along the boulevard to neighboring **St. Kilda.**

If you have
3 days

Do a little more exploring on the first day with a walk along the Southgate promenade to see the Crown Casino. Then jump aboard a Yarra River cruise boat, or take the kids to see the sharks at the **Melbourne Aquarium** opposite Southgate. On your second day, stroll through the **Royal Botanic Gardens** and see the **Shrine of Remembrance.** Then take a cable car on St. Kilda Road to the hip **Acland Street area ㉚**, in the suburb of **St. Kilda,** for dinner. On Day 3, take a tour of Chapel Street's shops, restaurants, and bars; it's Melbourne's hippest district.

If you have
5 days

Take in the farther-flung sights just outside the city. Head to Belgrave aboard the Puffing Billy steam railway through the fern gullies and forests of the Dandenongs, for example. On the way back, stop at a teahouse in Belgrave or Olinda to hand-feed the beautifully colored local birdlife. Or take an evening excursion to Phillip Island for the endearing sunset penguin parade at Summerland Beach. For these and other nearby activities and destinations, see the *Victoria* chapter.

4

EXPLORING MELBOURNE

Consistently rated among the "world's most livable cities" in quality-of-life surveys, Melbourne is built on a coastal plain at the top of the giant horseshoe of Port Phillip Bay. The city center is an orderly grid of streets where the state parliament, banks, multinational corporations, and splendid Victorian buildings that sprang up in the wake of the gold rush now stand. This is Melbourne's heart, which you can explore at a leisurely pace in a couple of days.

The symbol of Melbourne's civility, as in turn-of-the-20th-century Budapest or in Boston, is the streetcar. Solid, dependable, going about their business with a minimum of fuss, trams are an essential part of the city. For a definitive Melbourne experience, climb aboard a City Circle tram and learn about the city's history and sights.

As escapes from the rigors of urban life, the parks and gardens in and around Melbourne are among the most impressive features of the capital of the Garden State. More than one-quarter of the inner city has been set aside as recreational space. The profusion of trees, plants, and flowers creates a rural tranquillity within the thriving city.

In Southbank, one of the "neighborhoods" (suburbs) outside the city center, the Southgate development has refocused Melbourne's vision on the Yarra River. Once a blighted stretch of factories and run-down warehouses, the southern bank of the river is now a vibrant, exciting part of the city, and the river itself is finally taking its rightful place in Melbourne's psyche. Just a hop away, Federation Square—and its host of galleries—has become a civic landmark for Melburnians. Stroll along the Esplanade in the suburb of St. Kilda, amble past the elegant houses of East Melbourne, enjoy the shops and cafés in Fitzroy or Carlton, rub shoulders with locals at the Victoria Market, nip into the Windsor for afternoon tea, or hire a canoe at Studley Park to paddle along one of the prettiest stretches of the Yarra—and you may discover Melbourne's soul as well as its heart.

When to Visit Melbourne

Melbourne is at its most beautiful in fall, March to May. Days are crisp, sunny, and clear, and the foliage in parks and gardens is glorious. Melbourne winters can be gloomy, but by September the weather clears up, the football finals are on, and spirits begin to soar. Book early if you want to spend time in Melbourne in late October or early November when the Spring Racing Carnival and the Melbourne International Festival are in full swing. The same advice goes for early March when the city hosts a Formula 1 car-racing grand prix and in mid-January during the Australian Tennis Open.

City Center

Melbourne's center is framed by the Yarra River to the south and a string of parks to the east. On the river's southern bank, the Southgate development, the arts district around the National Gallery of Victoria in Federation Square, and the King's Domain–Royal Botanic Gardens areas also merit attention.

a good walk

One of the finest vistas of the city is from Southbank Promenade, looking across the Yarra River and its busy water traffic to the city's sparkling towers (this is an especially beautiful view at night). Start with a stroll around the shops, bars, cafés, and buskers of **Southgate ❶** ➤ and a visit to the **Victorian Arts Centre ❷** before crossing the ornate Princes Bridge to the city proper. Take a look to the east from the bridge. The Melbourne Cricket Ground and the Melbourne Park tennis center dominate the scene. On the green banks of the Yarra, boathouses edge toward the water and rowers glide across the river's surface.

At the corner of Swanston and Flinders streets are four major landmarks: **Flinders Street Station ❸**, with its famous clocks, **Young and Jackson's Hotel ❹** and its infamous *Chloe* painting, **St. Paul's Cathedral ❺**, and **Federation Square ❻**, a boldly designed landmark housing museums, restaurants, and shops. This corner also marks the beginning of Swanston Street, a pedestrian roadway intended to bring people off the sidewalks and onto the street. Ironically, though, once there, you have to dodge trams, tour buses, and even service and emergency vehicles. So it's better to keep to the sidewalk after all. **City Square ❼** has been overshadowed by an adjacent development, but the witty statues along this stretch of street are worth examining in some detail. Fifty yards up the Collins Street

4

The Arts
Melbourne regards itself as the artistic and cultural capital of Australia. It's home to the Australian Ballet and opera, theater, and dance companies—from the traditional to the avant-garde. The Melbourne International Arts Festival, the city's cultural highlight, runs throughout October and includes diverse theater, dance, visual arts, opera, and music events.

The Great Outdoors
Melbourne is an excellent jumping-off point for outdoor adventures, including bushwalking, a surf-and-turf trip down the Great Ocean Road, or a foray to one of Victoria's outstanding national parks. For details on these activities and destinations, *see* Chapter 5.

Markets
Melbourne has nearly a dozen major markets, from Prahran to South Melbourne. Fine cheeses and palate-pleasing wines are made right on Melbourne's doorstep, while butchers, bakers, and wholesalers keep chefs stocked with the latest, the freshest, and the best.

Nightlife
Melbourne's nightlife centers around King Street and Flinders Lane, with dozens of retro-style bars and clubs. The chic hotels tend to have hip cocktail lounges with an A-list clientele. Crown Casino's two nightclubs and the numerous bars along Southgate add life to the city center.

Sports
Melburnians, like Aussies in general, do love a good match. The Melbourne Cup horse race in November brings the entire city to a standstill. The same is true of Australian Rules Football, one of a few varieties of "footy." Scenic Albert Park Lake in South Melbourne is home to the Australian Grand Prix. The Australian Open is held at Melbourne Park in January.

What a Feast!
Melbourne's dining scene is a vast smorgasbord of cuisines and experiences. Chinese restaurants on Little Bourke Street are the equal of anything in Hong Kong. The Richmond neighborhood's Victoria Street convincingly reincarnates Vietnam. And a stroll down Fitzroy Street in St. Kilda finds everything from sushi and Singapore *laksa* (spicy Malaysian noodle soup) to spaghetti and *som tum* (Thai green papaya salad).

---

hill on the City Square side is the Regent Theatre, a fabulous 1930s picture palace transformed into a live theater and the latest in a series of rebirths in Melbourne's classic theater life. Go west on the north side of Collins Street to the **Block Arcade** ❽, the finest example of the many arcades that Melbourne planners built to defy the strictness of the grid pattern. Turn right between the Hunt Leather and Weiss clothing shops, cross Little Collins Street, and bear right to enter the airy, graceful **Royal Arcade** ❾. Standing guard over the shops are Gog and Magog, the mythical giants that toll the hour on either side of Gaunt's Clock.

Bourke Street Mall, which includes the large Myer department store, is a cluttered, lively pedestrian zone—although trams run through here,

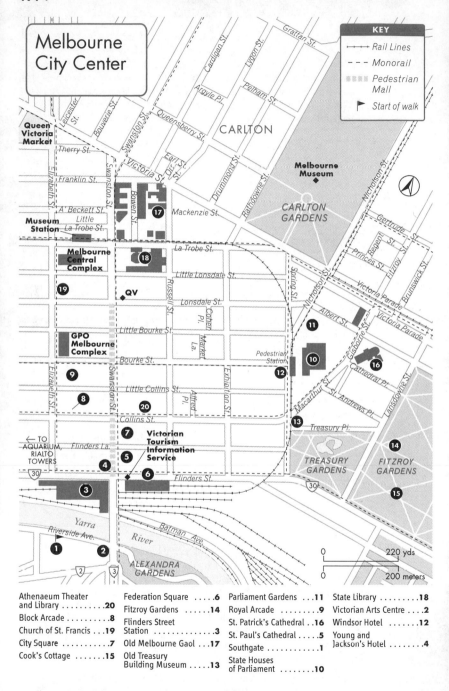

Melbourne City Center

too. From here, you can climb the Bourke Street hill to the east to reach the **State Houses of Parliament** ⑩ and adjacent **Parliament Gardens** ⑪ at the end. Or head across the street from the gardens to take a peek in the Princess Theatre, and then walk southeast for two blocks to the venerable **Windsor Hotel** ⑫, an ideal spot for high tea. Walk south to the **Old Treasury Building Museum** ⑬ and its Melbourne Exhibition, then cross the Treasury Gardens to the **Fitzroy Gardens** ⑭ and **Cook's Cottage** ⑮. Head along Lansdowne Street to see the towering **St. Patrick's Cathedral** ⑯.

You can call it quits now and visit the remaining historic sights on another day. If you've got the stamina, however, walk west along Albert Street, which feeds into Lonsdale Street, and then turn right at Russell Street. Two blocks north is the **Old Melbourne Gaol** ⑰, where you can briefly consort with assorted scoundrels. Backtrack down Russell Street, turning right into La Trobe Street. At the next corner is the **State Library** ⑱. Next, try a little shopping under the inverted glass cone of Lonsdale Street's Melbourne Central Complex. Walk to Elizabeth Street, where you can peek in the **Church of St. Francis** ⑲. Then turn and head south on Elizabeth for three blocks, past the general post office, and make a left on Collins Street. The **Athenaeum Theater and Library** ⑳ is on the left side of the second block, and the Paris End area is on the next block at Alfred Place.

TIMING From Southgate to St. Patrick's Cathedral—with time for the Victorian Arts Center, the Old Treasury Building Museum, the State Houses of Parliament, and refreshments—takes a good part of the day. It's possible to do a whirlwind walk, with a nod to all the sights in a couple of hours. However, plan a longer stroll if you can—perhaps also incorporating the Golden Mile heritage trail, which traces 150 years of Melbourne's history in a trek around the central business district.

What to See

⑳ **Athenaeum Theater and Library.** The first talking picture show in Australia was screened at this 1886 theater. Today the building also houses a library, and is used mainly for live theatrical performances. ⊠ *188 Collins St., City Center* ☎ *03/9650–3504* ☉ *Weekdays 8:30–5, Sat. 9–3.*

❽ **Block Arcade.** Melbourne's most elegant 19th-century shopping arcade dates from the 1880s, when "Marvelous Melbourne" was flushed with the prosperity of the gold rushes. A century later, renovations scraped back the grime to reveal a magnificent mosaic floor. ⊠ *282 Collins St., City Center* ☎ *03/9654–5244.*

Carlton Gardens. Forty acres of tree-lined paths, artificial lakes, and flower beds in this English-style 19th-century park form a backdrop for the outstanding Museum of Victoria, as well as other buildings that were erected in 1880. ⊠ *Victoria Parade and Nicholson, Carlton, and Rathdowne Sts., City Center* ☎ *No phone.*

⑲ **Church of St. Francis.** This 1845 Roman Catholic church was constructed when the city was barely a decade old. The simple, frugal design starkly contrasts with the Gothic exuberance of St. Paul's, built 40 years later. The difference illustrates just what the gold rush did for Melbourne. ⊠ *Elizabeth and Lonsdale Sts., City Center* ☎ *No phone.*

❼ City Square. Here bronze statues emerge from the crowd: a series of tall, thin men striding across the mall, or a snarling dog reaching for some unfortunate's ankles. The square also has the statue of Robert Burke and William Wills, whose 1860–61 expedition was the first to cross Australia from south to north. You can admire the parade from a stylish café on the square. ⊠ *Swanston St. between Collins St. and Flinders La., City Center.*

need a break?

Journal (⊠ 253 Flinders La., City Center ☎ 03/9650–4399) has leather couches, bookcases filled with magazines and newspapers, and communal tables where you can enjoy tapas, salads, antipasto platters, and selections from an excellent wine list.

At the **Transport Hotel** (⊠ Federation Sq., City Center ☎ 03/9654–8808) the steel-and-glass dining room with views across the Yarra River is a sophisticated place to enjoy a glass of wine and organic munchies.

⓯ Cook's Cottage. Once the property of the Pacific navigator Captain James Cook, the modest home was transported stone by stone from Great Ayton in Yorkshire and rebuilt in the lush Fitzroy Gardens in 1934. It's believed that Cook lived in the cottage between voyages. The interior is simple and sparsely furnished, a suitable domestic realm for a man who spent much of his life in cramped quarters aboard small ships. ⊠ *Fitzroy Gardens near Lansdowne St. and Wellington Parade, East Melbourne* ☎ *No phone* ⊡ *A$3* ⊙ *Apr.–Oct., daily 9–5; Nov.–Mar., daily 9–5:30.*

★ ❻ Federation Square. Encompassing a whole city block, the bold, abstract-style landmark was designed to house the second branch of the National Gallery of Victoria, which exhibits only Australian art. The square also incorporates the Centre for the Moving Image; the BMW Edge amphitheater, a contemporary music and theater performance venue; the Victorian Wine Precinct, showcasing the best of local wine; the Melbourne Racing Museum; the Melbourne Visitor Centre; and restaurants, bars, and gift shops. ⊠ *Flinders St. between Swanston and Russell Sts., City Center* ☎ *03/9655–1900* ⊕ *www.fedsq.com* ⊡ *Free* ⊙ *Mon.–Thurs. 10–5, Fri. 10–9, weekends 10–6.*

⓮ Fitzroy Gardens. This 65-acre expanse of European trees, manicured lawns, garden beds, statuary, and sweeping walks is Melbourne's most popular central park. Among its highlights is the **Avenue of Elms,** a majestic stand of 130-year-old trees that is one of the few in the world that has not been devastated by Dutch elm disease. ⊠ *Lansdowne St. and Wellington Parade, East Melbourne* ⊡ *Free* ⊙ *Daily sunrise–sunset.*

❸ Flinders Street Station. Melburnians use the clocks on the front of this grand Edwardian hub of Melbourne's suburban rail network as a favorite meeting place. When it was proposed to replace them with television screens, an uproar ensued. Today there are both clocks and screens. ⊠ *Flinders St. and St. Kilda Rd., City Center.*

off the beaten path

KING'S DOMAIN GARDENS – This expansive stretch of parkland includes Queen Victoria Gardens, Alexandra Gardens, the Shrine of Remembrance, Pioneer Women's Garden, the Sidney Myer Music Bowl, and the Royal Botanic Gardens. The temple-style **Shrine of Remembrance** is designed so that a beam of sunlight passes over the Stone of Remembrance in the Inner Shrine at 11 AM on Remembrance Day—the 11th day of the 11th month, when in 1918 armistice for World War I was declared. ⊠ *Between St. Kilda and Domain Rds., Anderson St., and Yarra River, City Center.*

🐾 **MELBOURNE AQUARIUM –** Become part of the action as you stroll through tubes surrounded by water and the denizens of the deep at play. Or take a ride on an electronic simulator. The aquamarine building illuminates a previously dismal section of the Yarra bank, opposite Crown Casino. If you're feeling brave, check out the shark dives—they're held daily, include scuba equipment, and are led by an instructor. ⊠ *Flinders and King Sts., City Center* ☎ *03/9620–0999* ⊕ *www.melbourneaquarium.com.au* 🎟 *A$23, shark dives from A$124* ☉ *Feb.–Dec., daily 9:30–6; Jan., daily 9:30–9.*

⑰ **Old Melbourne Gaol.** A museum run by the Victorian branch of the National Trust is housed in the city's first jail. The building has three tiers of cells with catwalks around the upper levels. Its most famous inmate was the notorious bushranger Ned Kelly, who was hanged here in 1880. Evening candlelight tours (reservations essential) are a popular, if macabre, facet of Melbourne nightlife. ⊠ *Russell and Mackenzie Sts., City Center* ☎ *03/9663–7228* 🎟 *Self-guided day tours A$12.50, candlelight tours A$20* ☉ *Daily 9:30–5 tours Sept.–May, Wed. and Sun. 8:30; June–Aug., Wed. and Sun. 7:30.*

⑬ **Old Treasury Building Museum.** The neoclassical bluestone-and-sandstone building, designed by 19-year-old architect J. J. Clark, was built in 1862 to hold the gold that was pouring into Melbourne from mines in Ballarat and Bendigo. Subsequently, underground vaults were protected by iron bars and foot-thick walls. Not to be missed is the Built on Gold show staged in the vaults. ⊠ *Treasury Pl. and Spring St., City Center* ☎ *03/9651–2233* ⊕ *www.oldtreasurymuseum.org.au* 🎟 *A$8.50* ☉ *Weekdays 9–5, weekends 10–4.*

⑪ **Parliament Gardens.** Stop here for a breath of cool green air in the center of the city. The gardens have a modern fountain and an excellent view of the handsome yellow Princess Theatre across Spring Street. The gardens are also home to the lovely St. Peter's Church. ⊠ *Parliament, Spring, and Nicholson Sts., East Melbourne* ☉ *Daily dawn–dusk.*

off the beaten path

RIALTO TOWERS OBSERVATION DECK – If you want a 360-degree panorama of Melbourne, there's no better (or more popular) place than from the 55th floor of the city's tallest building. Admission includes a 20-minute film and use of high-powered binoculars. ⊠ *Level 55, 525 Collins St., at King St., City Center* ☎ *03/9629–8222* 🎟 *Observation deck A$11.80* ☉ *Sun.–Thurs. 10–10, Fri. and Sat. 10–11.*

⑨ Royal Arcade. Built in 1869, this is the city's oldest shopping arcade and, despite alterations, it retains an airy, graceful elegance. Walk about 30 feet into the arcade to see the statues of Gog and Magog, the mythical monsters that toll the hour on either side of **Gaunt's Clock.** ⊠ *355 Bourke St., City Center* ☏ *No phone.*

⑯ St. Patrick's Cathedral. Ireland supplied Australia with many of its early immigrants, especially during the Irish potato famine in the middle of the 19th century. A statue of the Irish patriot Daniel O'Connell stands in the courtyard. Construction of the Gothic Revival building began in 1858 and took 82 years to finish. ⊠ *Cathedral Pl., East Melbourne* ☏ *03/ 9662–2233* ☉ *Weekdays 6:30–5, weekends 7:15–7.*

⑤ St. Paul's Cathedral. This 1892 headquarters of Melbourne's Anglican faith is one of the most important works of William Butterfield, a leader of the Gothic Revival style in England. Outside is the statue of Matthew Flinders, the first seaman to circumnavigate the Australian coastline, between 1801 and 1803. ⊠ *Flinders and Swanston Sts., City Center* ☏ *03/9650–3791* ☉ *Weekdays 7–6, Sat. 8:30–5, Sun. 8–7:30.*

St. Peter's Church. Two years after this 1846 church was built, Melbourne was proclaimed a city from its steps. One of Melbourne's oldest buildings, it's at the top end of Parliament Gardens. ⊠ *Albert and Nicholson Sts., East Melbourne* ☏ *03/9662–2391* ☉ *Weekdays 7–6, weekends 7–5:30.*

★ ☞ **① Southgate.** On the river's edge next to the Victorian Arts Center, the development is a prime spot for lingering—designer shops, classy restaurants, bars, and casual eating places help locals and visitors while away the hours. The promenade links with the forecourt of Crown Casino. ⊠ *Maffra St. and City Rd., Southbank* ☏ *03/9699–4311* ⊕ *www. southgate-melbourne.com.au.*

⑩ State Houses of Parliament. Dating from 1856, this building was used as the National Parliament from the time of federation in 1900 until 1927, when the first Parliament House was completed in Canberra. Parliament usually sits Tuesday to Thursday from March through July and again August–November. ⊠ *Spring and Nicholson Sts., East Melbourne* ☏ *03/ 9651–8911* ☒ *Free* ☉ *Weekdays 9–4; guided tour at 10, 11, noon, 2, 3, and 3:45 when parliament is not in session.*

⑱ State Library. On a rise behind lawns and heroic statuary, this handsome 1853 building was constructed during the gold-rush boom. Today, more than 1.5 million volumes are housed here. Large reading areas make this a comfortable place for browsing, and three galleries display works from the library's Pictures Collection. ⊠ *328 Swanston St., City Center* ☏ *03/8664–7000* ⊕ *www.statelibrary.vic.gov.au* ☒ *Free* ☉ *Mon.–Thurs. 10–9, Fri.–Sun. 10–6.*

off the beaten path

QUEEN VICTORIA MARKET – This sprawling, spirited bazaar is the city's prime produce outlet, and most of Melbourne comes here to buy its strawberries, fresh flowers, and imported cheeses. On Sunday you can find deals on jeans, T-shirts, bric-a-brac, and secondhand goods. The Gaslight Night Market, open from December to mid-February nightly from 5:30 to 10, has wandering entertainment and simple food stalls. ⊠ *Elizabeth and Victoria Sts., City Center* ☎ *03/ 9320–5822* ⊕ *www.qmv.com.au* ⊙ *Tues.–Thurs. 6 AM–2 PM, Fri. 6 AM–6 PM, Sat. 6 AM–3 PM, Sun. 9–4.*

② **Victorian Arts Centre.** Melbourne's most important cultural landmark is the venue for performances by the Australian Ballet, Australian Opera, and Melbourne Symphony Orchestra. It also encompasses the Melbourne Concert Hall, Arts Complex, and the original National Gallery of Victoria. One-hour tours begin from the information desk at noon and 2:30, Monday through Saturday. On Sunday a 90-minute backstage tour (no children) begins at 12:15. At night, look for the center's spire, which creates a magical spectacle with brilliant fiber-optic cables. ⊠ *100 St. Kilda Rd., Southbank* ☎ *03/9281–8000* ⊕ *www.vicartscentre.com.au* 🎫 *Tour A$10, backstage tour A$13.50* ⊙ *Mon.–Sat. 9 AM–11 PM, Sun. 10–5.*

⑫ **Windsor Hotel.** Not just a grand hotel, the Windsor is home to one of Melbourne's proudest institutions—the ritual of afternoon tea (from A$33), served daily 3:30–5:30. Ask about theme buffet teas served on weekends, such as the Chocolate Indulgence, available June–October (A$49), with a vast selection of chocolates and chocolate cakes and desserts. Although the Grand Dining Room—a belle epoque extravaganza with a gilded ceiling and seven glass cupolas—is open only to private functions, try to steal a look anyway. ⊠ *103 Spring St., City Center* ☎ *03/9633–6000* ⊕ *www.thewindsor.com.au.*

④ **Young and Jackson's Hotel.** Pubs are not generally known for their artwork, but climb the steps to the bar here to see *Chloe*, a painting that has scandalized and titillated Melburnians for many decades. The larger-than-life nude, painted by George Lefebvre in Paris in 1875, has hung on the walls of Young and Jackson's Hotel for most of the last century. ⊠ *1 Swanston St., City Center* ☎ *03/9650–3884.*

Richmond

Home of Victoria Street—Melbourne's "little Vietnam"—and the lively shopping stretch of Bridge Road, Richmond is 2 km (1 mi) east of the city center. If you're looking for a new wardrobe, a Vietnamese soup kitchen, a Korean barbecue, a Laotian banquet, or a Thai hole-in-the-wall, this is the place to come.

Victoria Street. Fast becoming one of Melbourne's most popular "eat streets," this 2-km (1-mi) stretch has restaurants ranging from simple canteens (eat until you drop for A$10) to dressy, tablecloth-and-candlelight dining spots. The street also features Vietnamese grocers, kitchenware stores, several art galleries, and several chichi drinking spots. Once a year in late September the street comes to life with a Moon Lantern Festival, during which children wander the streets carrying handmade paper lanterns. ⊠ *Victoria St., Richmond.*

Bridge Road. Once a run-down area of Richmond, this street is now a bargain shopper's paradise. It's chockablock with clothing shops, cafés, and factory outlets selling leather goods, shoes, and gourmet foods. ⊠ *Bridge Rd., Richmond.*

East Melbourne

The harmonious streetscapes in this historic enclave of Victorian houses, which date from the boom following the gold rushes of the 1850s, are a great excuse for a stroll. Start at the southeast corner of Fitzroy Gardens and head north on Clarendon to George Street; a right turn will lead you past a procession of superb terrace houses and mature European trees. Two blocks ahead, turn left on Simpson, then again on wide, gracious Hotham Street. On either side of the grassy median that divides the roadway, the mix of terrace houses and freestanding mansions includes some of the suburb's finest architecture. Back at Clarendon, turn north. Bishopscourt, the bluestone residence of the Anglican Archbishop of Melbourne, occupies the next block. Wind right again down Gipps Street and make your way to Darling Square. For different scenery on the way back, take Simpson Street south and turn right on Wellington Parade.

㉑ Melbourne Cricket Ground (MCG). A tour of this complex is essential for an understanding of Melbourne's sporting obsession. Outstanding museums here include the Australian Gallery of Sport and Olympic Museum, and the MCG Museum and Library. The site is a pleasant 10-minute walk from the city center or a tram ride to Jolimont Station. ⊠ *Jolimont Terr., Jolimont* ☎ *03/9657–8867* ⊕ *www.mcg.org.au* 🖃 *A$10* ⊙ *Tours daily on the hr 10–3, except on event days.*

South Melbourne & Albert Park

Best known as the site of Melbourne's annual Formula 1 Grand Prix, Albert Park and the adjoining suburb of South Melbourne are also known for their leafy streets, groovy cafés, and sea breezes straight off Port Phillip Bay. Regal mansions skirted by magnificent gardens make St. Vincents Place, an exclusive enclave of multimillion-dollar homes, a pleasant place to take a stroll. The square has its own quirky lawn bowling club, and an ever-present collection of eccentric residents who turn out to watch the games.

National Gallery of Victoria. This massive, moat-encircled, bluestone-and-concrete edifice houses works from renowned international painters, including Picasso, Renoir, and van Gogh. A second branch of the National Gallery, in Federation Square in the city center, exhibits only Australian art. ⊠ *180 St. Kilda Rd., South Melbourne* ☎ *03/9208–0222* ⊕ *www. ngv.vic.gov.au* 🖃 *Free* ⊙ *Daily 10–5.*

Fringed with quaint shops, gourmet cafés, and stylish boutiques, the leafy stretch of **Victoria Avenue in Albert Park** is a great spot for a long brunch, lunch, or simply a pleasant afternoon stroll. Nearby Albert Park Lake, dotted with the sails of boats most weekends, is a favorite spot for cycling, picnics, fun runs, and occasional festivals. The park is home to pelicans, black swans, terns, and eastern curlews, as well as a collection of native and exotic trees. Traces of the area's indigenous history also draw visitors; an ancient river red gum tree marks the spot where an-

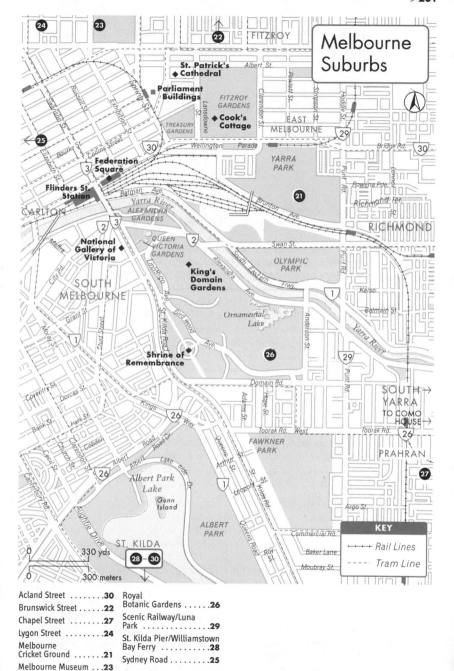

Melbourne Suburbs

FITZROY

St. Patrick's
◆ Cathedral

◆ Parliament
Buildings

FITZROY
GARDENS

EAST
MELBOURNE

◆ Cook's
Cottage

TREASURY
GARDENS

YARRA
PARK

Federation
Square

Flinders St.
Station

CARLTON

Yarra River

ALEXANDRA
GARDENS

RICHMOND

QUEEN
VICTORIA
GARDENS

National
Gallery of
Victoria

SOUTH
MELBOURNE

King's
Domain
Gardens

OLYMPIC
PARK

Ornamental
Lake

Shrine of
Remembrance

SOUTH
YARRA

TO COMO
HOUSE →

PRAHRAN

FAWKNER
PARK

Albert Park
Lake

Gunn
Island

ALBERT
PARK

ST. KILDA

0   330 yds

28 — 30

0   300 meters

KEY

⊢•••⊣ Rail Lines

- - - - Tram Line

cient corroborees (traditional dancing ceremonies) were once held. Said to be over 300 years old, it stands near Junction Oval on the corner of Fitzroy Street and Queens Road in St. Kilda.

St. Kilda

Once a seaside resort for genteel Melburnians, St. Kilda is now one of Melbourne's favorite playgrounds. In the 1970s and '80s it fell out of favor and took on a seedier edge as a red-light district. Today young professionals reside here, and the racy atmosphere has been largely replaced by a race to the next alfresco table. To reach the suburb from the Melbourne city center, take Tram 12, 16, 69, 79, or 96.

Begin a one-hour walk of the area at St. Kilda Pier, heading south along the foreshore, away from the city. Trendy cafés and eclectic restaurants emerge along the paved walkway, which is specially marked for either walking or wheeled traffic (the proliferation of rollerbladers, cyclists, and skateboarders gliding along the seaside). Set back from the water's edge, **Luna Park** is a five-minute stroll southeast of the pier. A Melbourne icon, the park's gates take the shape of an enormous mouth, swallowing visitors whole and delivering them into a world of ghost trains, pirate ships, and carousels. Built in 1912, the **Scenic Railway** is the park's most popular ride. Said to be the oldest continually operating roller coaster in the world (curious considering how many times it has been closed over the past few years for repairs), the railway is less roller coaster and more a relaxed loop-the-loop, offering stunning views of Port Phillip Bay between each dip and turn. Numerous music festivals, including Push Over (held each March) are held within the park's grounds each year. ⊠ *Lower Esplanade, St. Kilda* ☎ *03/9525–5033* ⊕ *www.lunapark. com.au* 🖭 *Free entry, A$7 per ride, A$33.95 for unlimited rides* ☉ *Sept. 20–Apr. 27, Fri. 7 PM–11 PM, Sat. 11 AM–11 PM, Sun. 11–6; Apr. 28–Sept. 19, weekends 11–6.*

③⓪ **Acland Street.** An alphabet soup of Chinese, French, Italian, and Lebanese eateries—along with a fantastic array of cake shops—lines the sidewalk of St. Kilda's ultrahip restaurant row. The street faces Luna Park. ⊠ *Acland St. between Barkly St. and Shakespeare Grove, St. Kilda.*

St. Kilda Festival. Five days of film, music, food, and general madness fill the streets of St. Kilda each February. The first four days, called Live n' Local, include a writers' festival, swimming races, uniquely Australian events (past efforts include rollerblade races and the Yooralla "Kiss for a Cause" Guinness Book of World Records attempt) and exhibitions. On the final day, known as Festival Day, some 50 bands perform across seven stages. ⊠ *St. Kilda* ☎ *03/9209–6306* ⊕ *www.stkildafestival.com.au.*

②⑧ **St. Kilda to Williamstown Bay Ferry.** A leisurely way to experience the area is to hop on this ferry service in the morning and head over to Williamstown for lunch at a seafood restaurant or café. Grab a cone (the town has famously good ice-cream shops) before heading back to St. Kilda Pier as the sun goes down. Views of Melbourne from the waters of Port Phillip Bay are breathtaking. Ferries depart from St. Kilda Pier each Saturday and Sunday and return from Gem Pier, Williamstown.

✉ *St. Kilda Pier, Lower Esplanade, St. Kilda; Williamstown* ☎ *03/ 9682–9555* ⌨ *A$17 one-way, A$28 round-trip* ◷ *Departures from St. Kilda Pier weekends at 11:30, 12:30, 1:30, 2:30, 3:30; departures from Gem Pier weekends at 11, noon, 1, 2, 3, 4.*

Fitzroy

Melbourne's bohemian quarter is 2 km (1 mi) northeast of the city center. If you're looking for an Afghan camel bag or a secondhand paperback, or yearn for a café where you can sit over a plate of tapas and watch Melbourne go by, Fitzroy is the place.

㉒ Brunswick Street. Along with Lygon Street in nearby Carlton, Brunswick Street is one of Melbourne's favorite places to dine. You might want to stop into a simple lunchtime café serving tasty focaccia for less than A$15, or opt for dinner at one of the stylish, highly regarded bar-restaurants. The street also has many galleries, bookstores, and arts-and-crafts shops. ✉ *Brunswick St. between Alexandra and Victoria Parades, Fitzroy.*

Melbourne Fringe Festival. From late September through the first week in October, this avant-garde festival brings more than 200 acts and exhibits—from fashion and art shows to live music, theater and comedy performances—to venues throughout the city. Nearly every gallery, bar, and open space in Melbourne gets in on the action. ✉ *25 Easey St., Collingwood* ☎ *03/8412–8788* ⊕ *www.melbournefringe.com.au* ◷ *Sept. and Oct.*

Hispanic-Latin American Festival. This colorful two-day street fiesta held in November celebrates the culture and heritage of Spanish-speaking nations. Street performers, music, and dance performances highlight the sights, smells, sounds, and tastes of these communities. ✉ *Johnston St., Fitzroy* ☎ *03/9205–5724* ⊕ *www.hispanicfiesta.com.au.*

Brunswick

Just 2 km (1 mi) north of the city center, Brunswick is Melbourne's multicultural heart. Here Middle Eastern spice shops sit next to avant-garde galleries, Egyptian supermarkets, Turkish tile shops, Japanese yakitori eateries, Lebanese bakeries, Indian haberdasheries, and secondhand bookstores.

㉕ Sydney Road. There's nowhere in Melbourne quite like Sydney Road. Cultures collide as Arabic mingles with French, Hindi does battle with Bengali, and the muezzin's call to prayer argues with Lebanese pop music. Scents intoxicate and colors beguile. Cafés serving everything from pastries to *tagines* (Moroccan stew) to Turkish delights huddle by the roadside, as do quirky record shops, antique auction houses, and Bollywood video stores. ✉ *Sydney Rd. between Brunswick Rd. and Bell St., Brunswick.*

Carlton

To see the best of Carlton's Victorian-era architecture, venture north of Princes Street, paying particular attention to Drummond Street, with its rows of gracious terrace houses, and Canning Street, which has a mix of workers' cottages and grander properties.

★ ② **Lygon Street.** Known as Melbourne's Little Italy, Lygon Street is a perfect example of the city's multiculturalism: where once you'd have seen only Italian restaurants, there are now Thai, Afghan, Malay, Caribbean, and Greek eateries. The city's famous café culture was also born here, with the arrival of Melbourne's first espresso machine at one of the street's Italian-owned cafés in the 1950s. The street has great color, particularly at night when the sidewalks are thronged with diners, strollers, and a procession of high-revving muscle cars rumbling along the strip. The Italian-inspired **Lygon Street Festival** in October gathers the neighborhood in music and merriment. ☒ *Lygon St. between Victoria and Alexandra Parades, Carlton.*

Ở ② **Melbourne Museum.** A spectacular, postmodern building surrounds displays of the varied cultures around Australia and the Pacific Islands. The Bunjilaka exhibit covers the traditions of the country's Aboriginal groups, while the Australia Gallery focuses on Victoria's heritage (and includes the preserved body of Australia's greatest racing horse, Phar Lap). There's lots for kids, too, with the wooded Forest Gallery, Children's Museum, Mind and Body Gallery, and Science and Life Gallery. ☒ *Carlton Gardens, Carlton* ☎ *13–1102* ⊕ *melbourne.museum.vic.gov. au* ⊠ *A$6* ☉ *Daily 10–5.*

South Yarra–Prahran

One of the coolest spots to be on any given night is in South Yarra and Prahran. If you're feeling alternative, head for Greville Street, which runs off Chapel near the former Prahran Town Hall and has more bars and eateries, groovy clothes, and music shops.

② **Chapel Street.** The heart of the trendy South Yarra–Prahran area, this
Fodor'sChoice long road is packed with pubs, bars, notable restaurants, and upscale
★ boutiques. The Toorak Road end of the avenue (nearest to the city) is the fashion-conscious, upscale section where Australian designers showcase their original designs. Walk south along Chapel Street to Greville Street, a small lane of hip bars, clothing boutiques, and record stores. Past Greville Street, the south end of Chapel Street is grungier, with pawnshops and kitschy collectibles stores. ☒ *Chapel St. between Toorak and Dandenong Rds., South Yarra–Prahran.*

★ Ở ② **Royal Botanic Gardens.** The present design and layout were the brainchild of W. R. Guilfoyle, curator and director of the gardens from 1873 to 1910. Within its 100 acres are 12,000 species of native and imported plants and trees, sweeping lawns, and ornamental lakes populated with ducks and swans that love to be fed. Guided walks leave from the visitor center, including the Aboriginal Heritage Walk, led by an Aboriginal cultural interpreter. Summer brings alfresco performances of classic plays, usually Shakespeare, children's classics like *Wind in the Willows,* and the popular Moonlight Cinema series. ☒ *Anderson St.,between Alexandra and Birdwood Aves., South Yarra* ☎ *03/9252–2300* ⊕ *www.*

rbg.vic.gov.au ✉ *Free* ☉ *Nov.–Mar., daily 7:30 AM–8:30 PM; Apr.–Oct., daily 7:30 AM–5:30 PM.*

Outside Melbourne

☪ **Melbourne Zoological Gardens.** Flourishing gardens and open-environment animal enclosures are hallmarks of this world-renowned zoo, which sits 4 km (2½ mi) north of the city center. A lion park, reptile house, and butterfly pavilion where more than 1,000 butterflies flutter through the rain-forest setting, are also on-site, as is a simulated African rain forest where the only group of gorillas in the country resides. The spectacular Trail of the Elephants, home of Asiatic elephants Mek Kapah and Bong Su, has a village, gardens, and a swimming pool. Twilight jazz bands serenade visitors on summer evenings. ✉ *Elliott Ave., Parkville* ☎ *03/9285–9300* ⊕ *www.zoo.org.au* ✉ *A$20* ☉ *Daily 9–5; Zoo Twilight evenings to 9 or 9:30.*

Rippon Lea. Begun in the late 1860s, Rippon Lea is a sprawling polychrome brick mansion built in the Romanesque style. By the time of its completion in 1903, the original 15-room house had swollen into a 33-room mansion. Notable architectural features include a grotto, a tower that overlooks a lake, a fernery, and humpback bridges. In summer, plays are performed on the grounds. To get here, take the Sandringham subway line 15 minutes south of the city center. ✉ *192 Hotham St., Elsternwick* ☎ *03/9523–6095* ⊕ *www.nattrust.com.au* ✉ *A$11* ☉ *Daily 10–5.*

☪ **Scienceworks Museum.** This hands-on museum of science-related activities entertains while it educates. At the popular Sportsworks you can test your speed against an Olympic sprinter and perform other athletic feats. The **Melbourne Planetarium** here uses a super computer and projection system to simulate 3-D travel through space and time on a 49-foot domed ceiling. ✉ *2 Booker St., Spotswood* ☎ *03/9392–4800* ⊕ *www.scienceworks.museum.vic.gov.au* ✉ *A$6* ☉ *Daily 10–4:30.*

WHERE TO EAT

Melbourne teems with top-quality restaurants, particularly in St. Kilda, South Yarra, and the Docklands. No serious foodies venture to the tourist trap of Lygon Street, but you can trawl the city's back-alley coffee shops for first-class java and pastries. Reservations are generally advised, and although most places are licensed to sell alcohol, the few that aren't usually allow you to bring your own. Lunch is served noon–2:30, and dinner is usually 7–10:30. A 10% tip is customary for exemplary service, and there may be a corkage fee in BYO restaurants.

WHAT IT COSTS In Australian Dollars				
$$$$	**$$$**	**$$**	**$**	**¢**
AT DINNER over $50	$36–$50	$21–$35	$10–$20	under $10

Prices are for a main course at dinner.

City Center

CAFÉS
$–$$

✕ **Brunetti.** This Romanesque bakery is still just as heavenly as when it opened nearly 30 years ago; it's still filled with perfect biscotti and mouthwatering cakes. More substantial pastas and risottos have recently been added to the menu, and you can finish off your lunch with a tremendous espresso and *cornetto con crema* (custard-filled croissant). ⊠ *198–204 Faraday St., Carlton* ☎ *03/9347–2801* 🗖 *AE, DC, MC, V.*

¢–$
✕ **Babka.** Although Fitzroy Street is the neighborhood's bustling hub, those in the know are often found loitering at this modest café. Try the excellent pastries, fresh-baked breads, or more substantial offerings like the omelet spiced with *dukkah* (an Egyptian-style spice and sesame blend). ⊠ *358 Brunswick St., Fitzroy* ☎ *03/9416–0091* ⚎ *Reservations not accepted* 🗖 *No credit cards* ⊘ *Closed Mon. No dinner.*

CHINESE
★ $$–$$$

✕ **Flower Drum.** Superb Cantonese cuisine is the hallmark of one of Australia's truly great Chinese restaurants. The restrained elegance of the decor, deftness of the service, and intelligence of the wine list puts most other restaurants to shame. Simply ask your waiter for the day's special and prepare yourself for a feast: perhaps crisp-skin Cantonese roast duck served with plum gravy, succulent dumplings of prawn and flying-fish roe, a perfectly steamed Murray cod, or huge Pacific oysters with black bean sauce. ⊠ *17 Market La., City Center* ☎ *03/9662–3655* ⚎ *Reservations essential* 🗖 *AE, DC, MC, V* ⊘ *No lunch Sun.*

ECLECTIC
★ $$

✕ **Taxi.** Housed in an innovatively designed steel-and-glass dining room above Federation Square, Taxi boasts both extraordinary food and spectacular views over Melbourne. East meets West on a menu that combines Japanese flavors—tuna tataki chased by udon noodles in a mushroom hot pot—with such traditional European fare as pork cutlets with red cabbage and date sauce. Kingfish with shredded ginger, roasted duck, and an impressive wine list complete the mix. ⊠ *Level 1, Transport Hotel, Federation Sq., Flinders St. and St. Kilda Rd., City Center* ☎ *03/9654–8808* ⚎ *Reservations essential* 🗖 *AE, DC, MC, V* ⊘ *Closed Sun.*

ITALIAN
$$–$$$

✕ **Grossi Florentino.** Since 1900, dining at Florentino has meant experiencing the height of Melbourne hospitality. After taking a seat in the famous mural room, with its wooden panels, Florentine murals, and hushed conversations, you can sample dishes like braised rabbit with muscatel and *farro* (a speltlike Italian grain), or tender veal shank with basil broth and black cabbage. Downstairs, the Grill Room has more businesslike fare, while the cellar bar is perfect for a glass of wine and pasta of the day. ⊠ *80 Bourke St., City Center* ☎ *03/9662–1811* ⚎ *Reservations essential* 🗖 *AE, DC, MC, V* ⊘ *Closed Sun. No lunch Sat.*

$$
✕ **Becco.** Every city center needs a place like this, with a drop-in bar, lively dining room, and groovy upstairs nightclub. At lunchtime, no-time-to-dawdle business types tuck into whitebait fritters, tagliolini with fresh tuna, and ricotta cake. Things get a little moodier at night, when a Campari and soda at the bar is an almost compulsory precursor to dinner. ⊠ *11–25 Crossley St., City Center* ☎ *03/9663–3000* ⚎ *Reservations essential* 🗖 *AE, DC, MC, V* ⊘ *Closed Sun.*

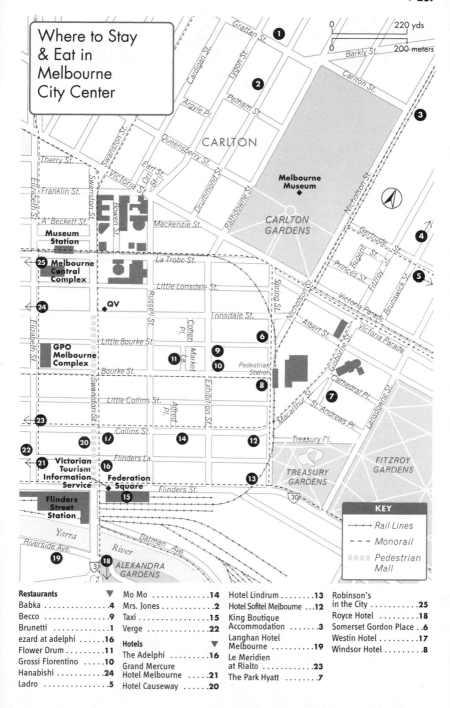

Where to Stay & Eat in Melbourne City Center

★ **$–$$** ✕ **Ladro.** Rita Macalli's stellar Italian bistro emphasizes flavor over starchy linen or stuffy attitude. Here eggplant is molded into gentle round *polpettes* (meatball-like mounds), lamb rump is scented with garlic and parsley and slow-roasted to impossible tenderness, and the service is as upbeat as the wine list. Delicious wood-fired pizzas are yet another reason to visit this suburban gem (thankfully, it's within walking distance from the city). ✉ *224 Gertrude St., Fitzroy* ☎ *03/9415–7575* ⌨ *Reservations essential* ▭ *MC, V* ⊗ *Closed Mon. and Tues. No lunch.*

JAPANESE ✕ **Hanabishi.** Touted as the city's best Japanese restaurant, Hanabishi
★ ¢ sits in slightly seedy King Street, an area known for its bars, club venues, and occasionally unsavory clientele. Featuring wooden floors, blue walls, and traditional ceramic serving trays, Hanabishi is the playground of Osakan chef Akio Soga, whose menu includes such gems as *hagi kimo* (salty steamed fish liver served with miso). The long list of hot and chilled sake, as well as the expansive wine list, ranges from reasonably to very pricey. ✉ *187 King St., City Center* ☎ *03/9670–1167* ⌨ *Reservations essential* ▭ *AE, DC, MC, V* ⊗ *Closed weekends.*

MIDDLE EASTERN ✕ **Mo Mo.** This exotic, pillow-laden basement restaurant offers a pun-
$$ gent mix of spicy Middle Eastern entrées; try *bastourma* (cured beef) salad with wild arugula and goat cheese, or *tagine* (Moroccan stew). ✉ *115 Collins St., basement, enter from George Parade, City Center* ☎ *03/9650–0660* ▭ *AE, DC, MC, V* ⊗ *Closed Sun. No lunch Sat.*

MODERN ✕ **ezard at adelphi.** Chef Teage Ezard's adventurous take on fusion pushes
AUSTRALIAN the boundaries between Eastern and Western flavors. Some combinations
$$ may appear unusual, even reckless—crème brûlée flavored with roasted Jerusalem artichoke and truffle oil, for example—but everything works, deliciously. ✉ *187 Flinders La., City Center* ☎ *03/9639–6811* ⌨ *Reservations essential* ▭ *AE, DC, MC, V* ⊗ *Closed Sun. No lunch Sat.*

$$ ✕ **Mrs. Jones.** Thank goodness there's a choice of only two starters and
Fodor'sChoice two main courses (both with a set price of A$35) at this restaurant; if
★ there were more, you might never be able to decide on a meal. Everything served up here is fabulous, whether it's chilled beetroot soup with crème fraîche or the pot-au-feu (boiled beef slow-cooked in broth with vegetables). There's also a lovely wine list—or, if you prefer, you can bring your own bottle. ✉ *312 Drummond St., Carlton* ☎ *03/9347–3312* ⌨ *Reservations essential* ▭ *AE, DC, MC, V.*

$$ ✕ **Verge.** A favorite of the local arty set, and also of office workers dropping in for after-work drinks and dinner, this eatery serves up modern bistro food with flair. Try the roast chicken with parsnips or angel hair pasta with prawns and chili. ✉ *1 Flinders La., City Center* ☎ *03/9639–9500* ▭ *AE, DC, MC, V.*

Melbourne Suburbs

CAFÉS ✕ **Richmond Hill Café and Larder.** Chef and food writer Stephanie Alexan-
$$ der is the force behind this bright and buzzy café–cum–produce store. The bistro fare brims with wonderful flavors, from the chicken, almond, and mushroom pie to a "hamburger as it should be." After you've eaten, pick up some marvelous cheese and country-style bread

FITZROY

Where to Stay
& Eat in the
Melbourne Suburbs

Albert St.

FITZROY
GARDENS

EAST
MELBOURNE

TREASURY
GARDENS

Wellington   Parade

Bridge Rd.

YARRA
PARK

Melbourne
Cricket
◆ Ground

Batman   Ave.

Yarra River

ALEXANDRA
GARDENS

Bruton   Ave.

RICHMOND

QUEEN
VICTORIA
GARDENS

Swan St.

SOUTH
MELBOURNE

KING'S
DOMAIN
GARDENS

OLYMPIC
PARK

Kelso

Ornamental
Lake

Batman St.

Yarra River

Domain Rd.

SOUTH
YARRA

Toorak Rd.   West

Toorak Rd.

PRAHRAN

FAWKNER
PARK

Argo St.

Gunn
Island

Albert Park
Lake

ALBERT
PARK

Commercial Rd.

Baker Lane

ST. KILDA

Moubray St.

0 .... 330 yds

0 .... 300 meters

KEY

⊢—⊢—⊢ *Rail Lines*

- - - - *Tram Line*

Restaurants ▼		Hotels ▼	
The Botanical **11**	Jacques Reymond **10**	Fountain Terrace **17**	Park Hyatt **2**
Café a Taglio **16**	Meccabah **21**	Hotel Como **8**	Richmond Hill Hotel ...**5**
Café di Stasio **15**	Melbourne Wine Room Restaurant **14**	Hotel Tolarno **20**	The Tilba **12**
Caffe e Cucina **9**	Pearl **6**	The Lyall **7**	
Circa the Prince **19**	Richmond Hill Café and Larder **4**	Magnolia Court Boutique Hotel **3**	
Dog's Bar **18**		Miami Motor Inn **1**	
Donovan's **13**			

from the adjoining cheese room and grocery. Cheese-making classes are offered here several times a year; call to learn more. ⊠ *48–50 Bridge Rd., Richmond* ☎ *03/9421–2808* ⊟ *AE, DC, MC, V* ☯ *No dinner Sun. and Mon.*

FRENCH ✕ **Circa the Prince.** Egyptian tea lights, white leather lounges, and walls
$$$ draped with organza and silk contribute to this restaurant's Arabian Nights feel. Here, chef Michael Lambie serves such French-inspired dishes as rabbit stew with white beans, alongside an exhaustive and tempting wine list. ⊠ *2 Acland St., St. Kilda* ☎ *03/9536–1122* ⚖ *Reservations essential* ⊟ *AE, DC, MC, V.*

ITALIAN ✕ **Café di Stasio.** This upscale bistro treads a very fine line between man-
$$-$$$ nered elegance and decadence. A sleek marble bar and modishly rav-
Fodor'sChoice aged walls contribute to the sense that you've stepped into a scene from
★ *La Dolce Vita.* Happily, the restaurant is as serious about its food as its sense of style. Crisply roasted duck is now a local legend, char-grilled baby squid is a sheer delight, and the pasta is always al dente. If the amazingly delicate lobster omelet is on the menu, do yourself a favor and order it. ⊠ *31 Fitzroy St., St. Kilda* ☎ *03/9525–3999* ⚖ *Reservations essential* ⊟ *AE, DC, MC, V.*

$-$$ ✕ **Café a Taglio.** Rarely has Roman-style pizza been this delicious, or this groovy. Although there's a blackboard menu of pastas and other Italian dishes, regulars prefer to cruise the counter, choosing from the giant squares of pizza on display. Toppings include bright-orange pumpkin rosemary and potato; tangy anchovy and olives; and wonderfully bitter radicchio. ⊠ *157 Fitzroy St., St. Kilda* ☎ *03/9534–1344* ⚖ *Reservations not accepted* ⊟ *AE, MC, V.*

$-$$ ✕ **Caffe e Cucina.** It's easy to imagine you're in Italy when dining at this always-packed café. Fashionable, look-at-me types flock here for coffee and pastry downstairs, or for more leisurely meals upstairs in the warm, woody dining room. Melt-in-your-mouth gnocchi, calamari San Andrea (lightly floured and deep fried), and prosciutto with figs are among the choices here; for dessert, the tiramisu is even better looking than the crowd. Reservations are essential upstairs, but not accepted downstairs. ⊠ *581 Chapel St., South Yarra* ☎ *03/9827–4139* ⊟ *AE, DC, MC, V.*

★ $-$$ ✕ **Melbourne Wine Room Restaurant.** Although the Wine Room itself buzzes day and night with young, black-clad types, the adjoining restaurant is far less frenetic. Elegantly whitewashed, with a moody glow that turns dinner for two into a romantic tête-à-tête, it possesses a gloriously down-at-the-heels sense of glamour. The Italianate fare, at once confident and determinedly single-minded, runs from powerful risottos to forceful pastas and grills that make you sit up and take notice. ⊠ *125 Fitzroy St., St. Kilda* ☎ *03/9525–5599* ⚖ *Reservations essential* ⊟ *AE, DC, MC, V* ☯ *No lunch Mon.–Thurs.*

MEDITERRANEAN ✕ **Dog's Bar.** With its blazing fires, artfully smoky walls, and striking
$-$$ wrought-iron chandeliers, this restaurant has a lived-in, neighborly look. The regulars at the bar look as if they grew there, while the young, artistic-looking groups who mooch around the front courtyard seem so

satisfied you can practically hear them purr. Wine is taken very seriously here, and you can find some particularly fine local pinot noir and sauvignon blanc at prices that won't break the bank. Put together a selection of antipasti from the tempting counter display, or opt for one of the daily pasta specials. ⊠ *54 Acland St., St. Kilda* ☎ *03/9525–3599* ⌣ *Reservations not accepted* ⊟ *AE, DC, MC, V.*

MIDDLE EASTERN
$

✕ **Meccabah.** Chef Cath Claringbold serves up delicious chicken and green-olive tagine, lemony grills, and sumac-dusted salads at this harbor-front eatery. It's the sort of good, honest food that mum would've served . . . if she were from Lebanon. In the evening you can enjoy splendid sunset views of the city skyline and the bay. ⊠ *55A New Quay Promenade, Docklands* ☎ *03/9642–1300* ⌣ *Reservations not accepted* ⊟ *AE, DC, MC, V.*

MODERN
AUSTRALIAN
$$$$

✕ **Jacques Reymond.** French and Asian flavors blend delightfully at this glamorous, century-old Victorian mansion-turned-eatery. The wine list is the stuff an oenophile dreams of, and the Burgundian-born chef uses the finest Australian produce to create such classics as roasted veal loin with ginger-and-soy butter, and fillet of barramundi hot pot with fresh rice noodles as part of set menus (A\$65–A\$115). Australian wines accompany each course, including dessert. Also available is the highly acclaimed six-course vegetarian option. ⊠ *78 Williams Rd., Prahran* ☎ *03/9525–2178* ⌣ *Reservations essential* ⊟ *AE, DC, MC, V* ☺ *Closed Sun. and Mon. No lunch Sat.*

$$–$$$

✕ **Donovan's.** Grab a window table at this bay-side hot spot and enjoy wide-open views of St. Kilda beach and its passing parade of rollerbladers, skateboarders, dog walkers, and ice-cream lickers. Chef Robert Castellani serves wonderful pasta and risotto, a thoroughly delicious fish soup, and a memorable baked Alaska in a homespun-style setting. Owners Kevin and Gail Donovan are such natural hosts you may feel like bunking down on the plush pillows near the cozy fireplace. ⊠ *40 Jacka Blvd., St. Kilda* ☎ *03/9534–8221* ⌣ *Reservations essential* ⊟ *AE, DC, MC, V.*

★ $$

✕ **The Botanical.** From one side it looks like a bottle shop—and it is. From the other it looks like a modern bistro, serving chateaubriand in an opened-out hotel space—and that it is, too. Here, Chef Paul Wilson redefines the art of eating out with a casual Aussie ambience and bucketloads of flavor. Retro touches mix effortlessly with 21st-century choices like flounder with a gaggle of wild mushrooms strewn across the top. ⊠ *169 Domain Rd., South Yarra* ☎ *03/9820–7888* ⌣ *Reservations essential* ⊟ *AE, DC, MC, V.*

$–$$

✕ **Pearl.** Geoff Lindsay's restaurant, with its white and shimmery interior, is a favorite hangout for Melbourne's beautiful people. But it's also home to some truly innovative dishes, such as watermelon and feta salad with satiny tomato jelly, and a sour yellow curry of Queensland scallops. ⊠ *631–633 Church St., Richmond* ☎ *03/9421–4599* ⊟ *AE, DC, MC, V* ☺ *No lunch Sat.*

WHERE TO STAY

WHAT IT COSTS In Australian Dollars					
	$$$$	$$$	$$	$	¢
FOR 2 PEOPLE	over $300	$201–$300	$151–$200	$100–$150	under $100

Prices are for two people in a standard double room in high season, including tax and service, based on the European Plan (with no meals) unless otherwise noted.

City Center

$$$$ ⊡ **Hotel Sofitel Melbourne.** Designed by world-famous architect I. M. Pei, this half of the twin-towered, 50-story Collins Place complex combines glamour and excellent facilities with a prime location. Rooms, which begin on the 35th floor, are built around a mirrored central atrium and have exceptional views. The 35th-floor Atrium bar is a good place to enjoy the scenery. The hotel's rooms and views are among the best in town, although service standards are patchy. ⊠ *25 Collins St., City Center, 3000* ☎ *03/9653–0000* 🖷 *03/9650–4261* ⊕ *www.sofitelmelbourne.com.au* ☞ *311 rooms, 52 suites ☖ 2 restaurants, in-room safes, cable TV with movies, in-room data ports, health club, spa, 3 bars, dry cleaning, laundry service, business services, no-smoking floors* ⊟ *AE, DC, MC, V.*

★ **$$$$**   ⊡ **Langhan Hotel Melbourne and Chuan Spa.** In the bustling Southgate river district, the Langhan (formerly Sheraton Hotel Southbank) has a terrific vantage point—the Melba Brasserie—from which to view passing pedestrian and Yarra River traffic. Autumn tones decorate the rooms, as do marble bathrooms, and a cascading fountain bubbles in the hotel's elegant foyer. This hotel is popular with a business travelers. ⊠ *1 Southgate Ave., Southbank, 3006* ☎ *03/8696–8888* 🖷 *03/9690–5998* ⊕ *www.langhamhotels.com* ☞ *387 rooms, 11 suites ☖ Restaurant, in-room safes, cable TV with movies, in-room data ports, pool, health club, massage, bar, dry cleaning, laundry service, business services, no-smoking floors* ⊟ *AE, DC, MC, V.*

★ **$$$$**   ⊡ **Windsor Hotel.** This century-old aristocrat of Melbourne hotels combines Victorian-era character with modern comforts. Plush rooms have Laura Ashley–style wall coverings and rosewood furnishings, although the marble bathrooms are modest in size. Standard rooms are also small; if you need space, book one of the vast Victorian suites, or a two-room executive suite. The 111 Spring Street Restaurant serves Continental-style dishes in a formal setting. The hotel commands a position opposite the State Houses of Parliament close to theaters, parks, and fine shops. ⊠ *103 Spring St., City Center, 3000* ☎ *03/9633–6000* 🖷 *03/9633–6001* ⊕ *www.thewindsor.com.au* ☞ *180 rooms, 20 suites ☖ Restaurant, some in-room safes, cable TV with movies, in-room data ports, gym, 2 bars, dry cleaning, laundry service, business services, no-smoking floors* ⊟ *AE, DC, MC, V.*

$$$–$$$$ ⊡ **The Adelphi.** This chic, design-conscious boutique hotel is decorated with minimalist-style furnishings of brushed-steel, maple, and glass. The best rooms are those at the front (with room numbers ending in 01). The pièce de résistance is the top-floor, 80-foot lap pool, which has a glass bottom jutting out from the edge of the building: bathers literally swim into space. Top-floor bar views, framed by the Gothic spires of St. Paul's, are heavenly. The restaurant ezard at adelphi serves daring Mod-Oz fusion fare. ✉ *187 Flinders La., City Center, 3000* ☎ *03/9650–7555* 📠 *03/9650–7555* ⊕ *www.adelphi.com.au* 🛏 *26 rooms* ⚭ *Restaurant, cable TV with movies, in-room data ports, pool, gym, 2 bars, babysitting, dry cleaning, laundry service, no-smoking floors* ▤ *AE, DC, MC, V* ⊙ *CP.*

$$$–$$$$
Fodor'sChoice
★
🏨 **Park Hyatt.** Set right next to Fitzroy Gardens and opposite St. Patrick's Cathedral, this elegant hotel overlooks some of the city's most beautiful historic buildings. Warm colors, rich wood paneling, and art deco–style furnishings adorn the rooms—all of which have walk-in wardrobes; king-size beds; Italian marble bathrooms; and roomy, modern work spaces. Suites are even more luxurious, some with fireplaces, terraces, and hot tubs. The five-level radii restaurant and bar is artsy and chic; and contemporary artworks by international talents are on exhibit throughout the hotel (some are for sale). ✉ *1 Parliament Sq., City Center, 3000* ☎ *03/9224–1234* 📠 *03/9224–1200* ⊕ *www.melbourne.hyatt.com* 🛏 *216 rooms, 24 suites* ⚭ *Restaurant, café, room service, in-room safes, cable TV with movies and video games, in-room data ports, indoor pool, health club, hot tub, sauna, spa, steam room, bar, babysitting, dry cleaning, laundry service, concierge, Internet room, business services, meeting rooms, car rental, travel services, parking (fee)* ▤ *AE, DC, MC, V.*

$$$–$$$$
🏨 **Royce Hotel.** Built in a former Rolls-Royce showroom, this elegant, 1920s-style hotel has rooms that are filled with natural light. The bathrooms here are spacious; many even have jetted double tubs. Two-story mezzanine rooms have separate sitting rooms. The Amber Room Bar schedules live jazz on weekends, and the Dish restaurant is on site. ✉ *379 St. Kilda Rd., City Center, 3004* ☎ *03/9677–9900* 📠 *03/9677–9922* ⊕ *www.roycehotels.com.au* 🛏 *71 rooms* ⚭ *Restaurant, kitchenettes, refrigerators, in-room data ports, bar, dry cleaning, laundry service, no-smoking floors, free parking* ▤ *AE, DC, MC, V.*

$$$–$$$$
🏨 **The Westin.** Overlooking Regent Place, the Westin sits in the heart of the city, a stone's throw from Federation Square, Southgate, and the boutique-lined alleys of Flinders Lane and Little Collins Street. Sophisticated and contemporary, the hotel features a spectacular lobby, an impressive collection of avant-garde Australian artwork, stunning rooms with Juliet balconies overlooking the city, a martini bar, wellness center (with lap pool, gym, hot tub, and sauna), and the Allegro restaurant. ✉ *Regent Pl., 205 Collins St., City Center, 3000* ☎ *03/9635–2222* 📠 *03/9635–2333* ⊕ *www.westin.com.au* 🛏 *262 rooms* ⚭ *Restaurant, in-room safes, cable TV with movies, in-room data ports, indoor hot tub, bar, dry cleaning, laundry service, business services, no-smoking floors* ▤ *AE, DC, MC, V.*

$$–$$$$
🏨 **Grand Mercure Hotel Melbourne.** The smallest of the city's upscale hotels, the Grand Mercure has a central location and a mix of lovely one- and two-bedroom suites. Rooms are beautifully furnished and decorated in apricot, burgundy, and pale-green tones. All have kitchenettes with microwaves and refrigerators. Guests have use of a small private court-

yard, inspired by the Renaissance gardens of Italy. ⊠ *321 Flinders La., City Center, 3000* ☎ *03/9629–4088* 🖷 *03/9629–4066* ⊕ *www.mercure. com* ↪ *59 suites* ⚸ *Restaurant, kitchenettes, microwaves, refrigerators, in-room data ports, health club, bar, dry cleaning, laundry service, no-smoking floors, free parking* ▤ *AE, DC, MC, V.*

$$–$$$$ 🏨 **Le Meridien at Rialto.** Within walking distance of the Crown Casino and Southgate, this 19th-century, European-style hotel is popular with business travelers. The suites here are spacious and decorated in soothing beige and citrus tones; some have Juliet balconies, and all have extras like hair dryers, tea- and coffee-making supplies, and fluffy bathrobes. For the ultimate luxury, try booking the Courtyard Suite, with its dramatic turreted bedroom. ⊠ *495 Collins St., City Center, 3000* ☎ *03/ 9620–9111* 🖷 *03/9614–1219* ⊕ *www.melbourne.lemeridien.com* ↪ *244 suites* ⚸ *Restaurant, IDD phones, in-room safes, cable TV with movies, 2 bars, dry cleaning, laundry facilities, Internet room, business services* ▤ *AE, DC, MC, V.*

$$$ 🏨 **Hotel Causeway.** Set among fashion boutiques, restaurants, and a host of hip cafés in the alleyways off Little Collins Street is this small, stylish hotel. Rooms have cream-colored walls, deep-walnut furnishings, and dark-red upholstery. Three split-level duplexes, which sleep four, are perfect for families. ⊠ *275 Little Collins St., City Center, 3000* ☎ *03/ 9660–8888* 🖷 *03/9660–8877* ⊕ *www.causeway.com.au* ↪ *42 rooms, 3 duplexes* ⚸ *Room TVs with movies, in-room data ports, gym, steam room, laundry facilities, business services, no-smoking floors* ▤ *AE, DC, MC, V* ⑂ *CP.*

$$$ 🏨 **Hotel Lindrum.** Housed in the Heritage-listed Lindrum family billiards center, this is one of Melbourne's savviest boutique properties. Spacious rooms with bay windows, high ceilings, and timber floors create an elegance similar to that of the city's swankiest big hotels. A smart restaurant, cozy cigar bar, and lounge with an open fire are the perfect settings for sipping local wines. Flinders Lane, lined with chic bars and eateries, is a short stroll away. ⊠ *26 Flinders St., City Center, 3000* ☎ *03/ 9668–1111* 🖷 *03/9668–1199* ⊕ *www.hotellindrum.com.au* ↪ *59 rooms* ⚸ *Restaurant, in-room safes, refrigerators, cable TV with movies, in-room data ports, billiards, bar, dry cleaning, laundry service, meeting room, no-smoking floors, free parking* ▤ *AE, DC, MC, V.*

$$–$$$ 🏨 **Robinsons in the City.** Melbourne's tiniest, and possibly quaintest hotel, Robinsons occupies a converted 1850s bakery. The six beautifully furnished rooms here have private bathrooms and are decorated with artworks from around the world. Homemade breakfasts—including fruit, smoked trout, sausage, bacon, eggs and toast—are a real highlight. ⊠ *405 Spencer St., City Center, 3000* ☎ *03/9329–2552* ⊕ *www. robinsonsinthecity.com.au* ↪ *6 rooms* ⚸ *Lounge, library, laundry facilities, Internet room, free parking* ▤ *AE, DC, MC, V* ⑂ *BP.*

★ $–$$ 🏨 **Somerset Gordon Place.** This historic 1883 structure is one of the most interesting and comfortable apartment hotels in the city. It's just steps from the Parliament building and is surrounded by excellent restaurants and theaters. Modern, comfortable flats contain washing machines, dryers, and dishwashers. The studios and one- and two-bedroom apartments face a courtyard with a 60-foot pool and a century-old palm tree.

✉ *24 Little Bourke St., City Center, 3000* ☎ *03/9663–2888* 🖷 *03/ 9639–1537* ⊕ *www.the-ascott.com* 🖘 *64 apartments* ⚲ *Kitchens, cable TV, in-room data ports, pool, gym, sauna, spa, dry cleaning, laundry facilities, business services, no-smoking floors* ▤ *AE, DC, MC, V.*

Melbourne Suburbs

$$$$ 🏨 **The Lyall.** The spacious suites at this exclusive hotel come with all the luxuries: CD and DVD players, velour bathrobes and slippers, gourmet minibars, a pillow menu. The in-house spa offers a full range of massages, facials, and body treatments (try the lime-and-ginger salt glow); the champagne bar is the perfect place to relax after a day of sightseeing. Mini–art galleries adorn each floor of the hotel. ✉ *14 Murphy St., South Yarra, 3141* ☎ *03/9868–8222* 🖷 *03/9820–1724* ⊕ *www.thelyall. com* 🖘 *40 suites* ⚲ *Restaurant, cable TV with movies, in-room data ports, gym, spa, bar, dry cleaning, laundry facilities, business services, no-smoking floors, parking (fee)* ▤ *AE, DC, MC, V.*

★ **$$$–$$$$** 🏨 **Hotel Como.** With its opulence and funky modern furnishings, this luxury hotel is as popular with business travelers as it is with visiting artists and musicians. Gray marble and chrome are prominent throughout the pop art–meets–art deco interior. Suites have king-size beds and bathrobes; several even have Jacuzzis. Some of the third-floor suites have access to private Japanese gardens, while others have fully equipped kitchenettes. Outstanding service and a swank clientele make this one of the best picks in the suburbs. ✉ *630 Chapel St., South Yarra, 3141* ☎ *03/9825 2222* 🖷 *03/9824–1263* ⊕ *www.mirvachotels.com.au* 🖘 *107 suites* ⚲ *In-room safes, some kitchenettes, cable TV with movies and video games, in-room data ports, pool, health club, massage, sauna, bar, dry cleaning, laundry service, meeting rooms, no-smoking floors* ▤ *AE, DC, MC, V.*

$$–$$$ 🏨 **Fountain Terrace.** Set on a tree-lined street in one of Melbourne's picturesque bay-side suburbs, this 1880 property has seven guest suites, all of them immaculate and furnished with opulent antiques. Each suite is named after a prominent Australian figure; the Henry Lawson, for example (named for a famous Aussie poet) is decorated in blue-and-gold brocade, and has a hot tub. The Dame Nellie Melba suite is the most spacious, and has French doors opening onto a private balcony. ✉ *28 Mary St., St. Kilda West, 3182* ☎ *03/9593–8123* 🖷 *03/9593–8696* ⊕ *www. fountainterrace.com.au* 🖘 *7 suites* ⚲ *Some in-room hot tubs, Internet room, meeting rooms; no room phones* ▤ *AE, DC, MC, V* ⦿ *BP.*

★ **$$–$$$** 🏨 **The Tilba.** Built as a grand residence at the turn of the 20th century, the Tilba became a hotel in 1920, and staying here feels like a sojourn in a luxurious private house. During World War II it was occupied by Ladies for the Armed Services and later fell on hard times until it was renovated in the mid-1980s. Now it's a small hotel with genuine charm, filled with antiques and eclectic pieces of furniture. In one room, for example, a bedstead was once the gate on a Queensland cattle ranch. The hotel overlooks Fawkner Park and is a short stroll from the chichi Toorak Road shops and restaurants. ✉ *30 Toorak Rd. W., South Yarra, 3141* ☎ *03/ 9867–8844* 🖷 *03/9867–6567* ⊕ *www.thetilba.com.au* 🖘 *14 rooms* ⚲ *In-room data ports, dry cleaning, laundry service, meeting rooms, no-smoking rooms; no a/c in some rooms* ▤ *AE, DC, MC, V.*

$-$$$ ⊞ **Hotel Tolarno.** Set in the heart of St. Kilda's café, bar, and club precinct, Hotel Tolarno was once owned by artists who ran a gallery out of the space. Even today the place has an artistic bent; many of the rooms and common spaces are decorated with paintings by students of the Victorian College of the Arts (VCA) and Royal Melbourne Institute of Tafe (RMIT). The color schemes here are a bit garish (red, purple, and orange dominate), and the furnishings are basic, but this is a friendly, funky place to stay (or to have a bite in the excellent on-site bistro). ⊠ *42 Fitzroy St., St. Kilda, 3182* 🕾 *03/9537–0200* 🖷 *03/9534–7800* ⊕ *www.hoteltolarno. com.au* ➾ *35 rooms* ᗉ *Restaurant, some kitchenettes, room TVs with movies, dry cleaning, laundry facilities* 🖃 *AE, DC, MC, V.*

$-$$$ ⊞ **Magnolia Court Boutique Hotel.** Although its name might imply modernity, the rooms and furnishings are slightly Victorian (and spotless) at this small inn. Standard rooms are modest in size, but the suites have more space and comfort at just a moderately higher rate. A family suite with a kitchen and space for six is also available. The hotel is separated from the city center by Fitzroy Gardens and is about a 12-minute walk from Spring Street. ⊠ *101 Powlett St., East Melbourne, 3002* 🕾 *03/9419–4222* 🖷 *03/9416–0841* ⊕ *www.magnolia-court.com. au* ➾ *25 rooms, 6 suites* ᗉ *In-room safes, some kitchenettes, in-room data ports, dry cleaning, laundry service, meeting rooms* 🖃 *AE, DC, MC, V.*

★ **$-$$** ⊞ **King Boutique Accommodation.** Overlooking the Carlton gardens, this regal Italianate mansion contains three meticulously decorated bedrooms, each featuring chic modern furniture and gorgeous picture windows. The two first-floor rooms have marble bathrooms. The common lounge has TV and a library with books and magazines. A sumptuous breakfast is served every morning in the dining room; other meals are available on request. ⊠ *122 Nicholson St., Fitzroy, 3065* 🕾 *03/ 9417–1113* 🖷 *03/9417–1116* ⊕ *www.kingaccomm.com.au* ➾ *3 rooms* ᗉ *Parking, no-smoking rooms; no room phones, no room TVs* 🖃 *AE, DC, MC, V* ⧉ *BP.*

$-$$ ⊞ **Richmond Hill Hotel.** Just a short tram ride from the city center, this pretty boutique hotel occupies a regal mansion skirted by a garden. Lodgings here range from basic single rooms to apartment-style rooms; the shared guest lounge has newspapers, a garden terrace, bar, and Internet access. ⊠ *353 Church St., Richmond, 3000* 🕾 *03/9428–6501* 🖷 *03/ 9427–0128* ⊕ *www.richmondhillhotel.com.au* ➾ *60 rooms* ᗉ *Lounge, laundry facilities, Internet room* 🖃 *AE, DC, MC, V* ⧉ *CP.*

¢ ⊞ **Miami Motor Inn.** Like a Motel 6, only fancier, Miami Motor Inn is an excellent value for the budget- and style-conscious. The first two levels contain standard motel rooms with large closets and private, streamlined bathrooms. The top floor has well-kept "economy rooms" with shared bathroom facilities. There are three TV lounge rooms, and the helpful staff can provide breakfast on request. ⊠ *13 Hawke St., at Spencer St., West Melbourne, 3003* 🕾 *03/9321–2444 or 1800/132333* 🖷 *03/9328–1820* ⊕ *www.themiami.com.au* ➾ *81 rooms, 41 with bath* ᗉ *In-room data ports, laundry facilities; no a/c in some rooms, no TV in some rooms* 🖃 *MC, V.*

NIGHTLIFE & THE ARTS

The Arts

Melbourne Events, available from tourist outlets, is a comprehensive monthly guide to what's happening in town. For a complete listing of performing arts events, galleries, and film, consult the "EG" (Entertainment Guide) supplement in the Friday edition of the *Age* newspaper. The *Age's* daily "Metro" section has a comprehensive listing of city events such as gallery openings, theater performances, public talks, bands, workshops, and festivals in its "If You Do One Thing Today" pages. Tourism Victoria hosts a fantastic Web site (thatsmelbourne.com.au), detailing all of Melbourne's upcoming and current events. The free local music magazine *Beat* is available at cafés, stores, markets, and bars. *Brother Sister* is the local gay paper.

Dance

In the 2,000-seat State Theatre at the Arts Centre, the **Australian Ballet** (⊠ Victorian Arts Centre, 100 St. Kilda Rd., Southbank ☎ 03/9669–2700 Ballet, 13–6100 Ticketmaster7) stages five programs annually and presents visiting celebrity dancers from around the world.

Music

The **Melbourne Concert Hall** (⊠ Victorian Arts Centre, 100 St. Kilda Rd., Southbank ☎ 03/9281–8000) stages classy concerts. Big-name, crowd-drawing contemporary artists perform at **Melbourne Park** (⊠ Batman Ave., City Center ☎ 03/9286–1600).

The **Melbourne Symphony Orchestra** (⊠ Victorian Arts Centre, 100 St. Kilda Rd., Southbank ☎ 13–6100 Ticketmaster7) performs year-round in the 2,600-seat Melbourne Concert Hall.

Open-air concerts take place December through March at the **Sidney Myer Music Bowl** (⊠ King's Domain near Swan St. Bridge, South Melbourne ☎ 13–6100 Ticketmaster7).

Summer Fun in the Parks (⊕ www.thatsmelbourne.com.au), which is open Jauary–March on Friday, Saturday, and Sunday evenings, brings green spaces around the city alive with the sound of world music, jazz, blues, soul, and hip-hop. Venues include Birrarung Marr, Fitzroy Gardens, Royal Botanic Gardens, Treasury Gardens, Carlton Gardens, and Federation Square. Stalls sell food and drinks; most concerts are free.

Opera

The **Opera Australia** (⊠ Victorian Arts Centre, 100 St. Kilda Rd., Southbank ☎ 03/9686–7477) has regular seasons, often with performances by world-renowned stars. The length and time of seasons vary, but all performances take place in the Melbourne Concert Hall.

Theater

The **Half-Tix** (⊠ Melbourne Town Hall, Swanston and Collins Sts., City Center ☎ 03/9650–9420) ticket booth in the Bourke Street Mall sells tickets to theater attractions at half price on performance days. It's open Monday and Saturday 10–2, Tuesday–Thursday 11–6, and Friday 11–6:30. Sales are cash only.

The **Melbourne Theatre Company** (✉ 129 Ferrars St., Southbank ☎ 03/9684–4500 ⊕ www.mtc.com.au) is the city's first and most successful theater company. The two annual seasons host classical, international, and Australian performances at the **Russell Street Theatre** (✉ 129 Ferrars St., Southbank ☎ 1300/136166). The city's second-largest company, the **Playbox at the CUB Malthouse Company** (✉ 113 Sturt St., Southbank ☎ 03/9685–5111), stages about 10 new or contemporary productions a year. The CUB Malthouse theater is a flexible space designed for drama, dance, and circus companies.

Revues and plays are staged at the **Comedy Theatre** (✉ 240 Exhibition St., City Center ☎ 03/9299–9800). **Her Majesty's Theatre** (✉ 219 Exhibition St., City Center ☎ 03/9663–3211) hosts international musicals like *Cats* and *Chicago*. **La Mama** (✉ 205 Faraday St., Carlton ☎ 03/9347–6142) puts on innovative and contemporary productions in a bohemian theater. The **Princess Theatre** (✉ 163 Spring St., City Center ☎ 03/9299–9800), an ornate, 1886 wedding cake–style edifice refurbished for the late-1980s hit *Phantom of the Opera,* is the home of Broadway-style blockbusters. The **Regent Theatre** (✉ 191 Collins St., City Center ☎ 03/9299–9500) presents mainstream productions. **Theatreworks** (✉ 14 Acland St., St. Kilda ☎ 03/9534–3388) concentrates on contemporary Australian plays.

Nightlife

Bars & Cocktail Lounges

Crown Casino, Melbourne's first gambling center, has blackjack, roulette, and poker machines. There are also dozens of restaurants, retail shops, bars, and two nightclubs open until late. Look for the impressive water and lighting displays on the first floor. The casino is on the south bank of the Yarra. *✉ Riverside Ave., Southbank ☎ 03/9292–8888 ⊕ www.crowncasino.com.au ⊗ Daily 24 hrs.*

The Atrium (✉ 25 Collins St., City Center ☎ 03/9653–0000), a cocktail bar on the 35th floor of the Hotel Sofitel, has spectacular views. **Cookie** (✉ 252 Swanston St., City Center ☎ 03/9663–7660), in a huge warehouse-style space with a balcony, focuses on imported beer and great Thai food. Find classic charm in the heart of the Windsor Hotel at the **Cricketeer's Bar** (✉ 103 Spring St., City Center ☎ 03/9633–6000).

The **George Hotel Bar** (✉ Fitzroy and Grey Sts., St. Kilda ☎ 03/9525–5599) is in a superb 19th-century building. Reminiscent of Hollywood opulence, **Gin Palace** (✉ 190 Little Collins St., City Center ☎ 03/9654–0533) has more than enough types of martinis to satisfy any taste. Enter from Russell Street. The **Hairy Canary** (✉ 212 Little Collins St., City Center ☎ 03/9654–2471) is one of the grooviest places in the city, but it's standing room only unless you get here early. The artsy, laid-back patrons of **Loop Bar** (✉ 23 Meyers Pl., South Yarra ☎ 03/9654–0500) watch avant-garde documentaries as they drink. The Grand Hyatt's **M. O. O.** (✉ Drivers La. behind 318 Little Bourke St., City Center ☎ 03/9639–3020) is a sophisticated spot. Antique leather sofas and cigars characterize the classy milieu at the **Melbourne Supper Club** (⌧ 161 Spring St., City Center ☎ 03/9654–6300). Stop by the **Polly** (⌧ 401 Brunswick St., Fitzroy ☎ 03/9417–0880), which combines antique red-velvet lounges, art deco mirrors, one of Melbourne's best wine lists, and colorful and quirky clientele with a magnificent fish tank, for which it is famous. **Revolver Upstairs** (⌧ 229 Chapel St., Prahran ☎ 03/9521–4644) caters to the young. The **Xchange** (⌧ 119 Commercial Rd., South Yarra ☎ 03/9867–5144) is a popular gay bar in the busy gay district of Prahran.

Comedy Clubs

Comedy Club Melbourne (⌧ 380 Lygon St., Carlton ☎ 03/9650–1977) is a popular place to see top-class Australian and international acts. In addition to being a hallowed live music venue, the **Esplanade Hotel** (⌧ 11 Upper Esplanade, St. Kilda ☎ 03/9534–0211) is a testing ground for local comedians.

Dance Clubs

Most of the central city's dance clubs are along the King Street strip or nestled in Little Collins Street. Clubs usually open at 9 or 10 weekends and some weeknights, and stay open until the early morning hours. Expect to pay a small cover at most clubs—between A$10 and A$15.

The action ranges from fast to furious at the multilevel, high-tech **Metro** (⌧ 20–30 Bourke St., City Center ☎ 03/9663–4288), which has eight bars, a glass-enclosed café, and three dance floors. This nightclub is one of the hottest clubs in town for Melbourne's twentysomethings. **The Saint** (⌧ 54 Fitzroy St., St. Kilda ☎ 03/9593–8333) is a glamorous hangout for the young and upwardly mobile. The city's enduring nightspot, **Seven** (⌧ 52 Albert Rd., South Melbourne ☎ 03/9690–7877) is a spot for chic young hipsters with fancy tastes in both fashion and cocktails.

Jazz Clubs

Bennetts Lane (⌧ 25 Bennetts La., City Center ☎ 03/9663–2856) is one of the city center's jazz mainstays. Cutting-edge cabaret acts are featured at **45 Downstairs** (⌧ 45 Flinders La., City Center ☎ 03/9662–9966). The **Night Cat** (⌧ 141 Johnston St., Fitzroy ☎ 03/9417–0090) hosts jazzy evening shows most nights of the week.

Music Clubs

The **Corner Hotel** (⌧ 57 Swan St., Richmond ☎ 03/9427–7300) has alternative, reggae, rock, blues, and jazz acts with an emphasis on homegrown bands. At the **Crown Casino** (⌧ Level 3, Crown Entertainment Complex, Riverside Ave., Southbank ☎ 03/9292–8888 ⊕ www.crowncasino.com.au) the Showroom and the Mercury Lounge attract big international and Australian headliners. You can catch rock headline acts at the **Ding Dong Lounge** (⌧ Level 1, 18 Market La., City Center ☎ 03/9662–1020).

The **Hi-Fi Bar** (⌧ 125 Swanston St., City Center ☎ 03/9654–0992) is a popular venue for live local and less-known international rock bands. The **Palace Entertainment Complex** (⌧ Lower Esplanade, St. Kilda ☎ 03/9534–0655) features alternative and hard-rock headline acts, such as Nick Cave and Queens of the Stone Age. A diverse range of Australian and international acts, including rap, rock, reggae, and hip-hop, play at **Pony** (⊠ 68 Little Collins St., City Center ☎ 03/ 9662–1026). For rock and roll, punk, and grunge, head to the **Prince of Wales** (⊠ 29 Fitzroy St., St. Kilda ☎ 03/9536–1166), which also has a gay bar downstairs.

SPORTS & THE OUTDOORS

Australian Rules Football

Tickets for Australian Rules Football are available through **Ticketmaster7** (☎ 13–6100) or at the playing fields. The **Melbourne Cricket Ground** (⊠ Brunton Ave., Yarra Park ☎ 03/9657–8867) is the prime venue for AFL games.

The multimillion-dollar residential and commercial Docklands, along the docks and former factory sites at the city's western edge, surrounds the high-tech, indoor **Telstra Dome** (⊠ Bourke St. W, Docklands ☎ 03/ 8625–7700). It's home to a number of Australian Rules Football clubs. You can reach the district on foot from the Spencer Street train station.

Bicycling

Melbourne and its environs contain more than 100 km (62 mi) of bike paths, including scenic routes along the Yarra River and Port Phillip Bay. Bikes can be rented for about A$25 per day from trailers alongside the bike paths.

Bicycle Victoria (⊠ Level 10, 446 Collins St., City Center ☎ 03/8636–8888 ⊕ www.bv.com.au) can provide information about area bike paths. Its excellent Web site has trail maps and descriptions as well as directions.

Boating

Studley Park Boathouse (⊠ Boathouse Rd., Kew ☎ 03/9853–1828) rents canoes, kayaks, and rowboats for journeys on a peaceful stretch of the lower Yarra River, about 7 km (4½ mi) east of the city center. Rentals are A$24 per hour for a two-person kayak or rowboat and A$28 per hour for a four-person rowboat. The boathouse is open daily from 9 until sunset.

Car Racing

Australian Formula 1 Grand Prix (⊠ 220 Albert Rd., South Melbourne ☎ 03/9258–7100 ⊕ www.grandprix.com.au) is a popular fixture on Melbourne's calendar of annual events. It's held every March in the suburb of Albert Park, a small neighborhood 4 km (2½ mi) south of the city, which encompasses the area surrounding Albert Park Lake.

Cricket

All big international and interstate cricket matches in Victoria are played at the **Melbourne Cricket Ground** (⊠ Brunton Ave., Yarra Park ☎ 03/ 9657–8867 stadium, 13–6100 Ticketmaster7) from October to March. The stadium has lights for night games and can accommodate 100,000 people. Tickets are available at the gate or through Ticketmaster7.

AUSTRALIAN RULES FOOTBALL

DESPITE ITS NAME, *novice observers frequently ask the question: "What rules?" This fast, vigorous game, played between teams of 18, is one of four kinds of football Down Under. Aussies also play Rugby League, Rugby Union, and soccer, but Australian Rules, widely known as "footy," is the one to which Victoria, South Australia, the Top End, and Western Australia subscribe. It's the country's most popular spectator sport.*

Because it is gaining an international television audience, the intricacies of Aussie-rules football are no longer the complete mystery they once were to the uninitiated: the ball can be kicked or punched in any direction, but never thrown. Players make spectacular leaps vying to catch a kicked ball before it touches the ground, for which they earn a free kick. The game is said to be at its finest in Melbourne, and any defeat of a Melbourne team—particularly in a Grand

Final—is widely interpreted as a sign of moral lassitude in the state of Victoria.

New South Wales and Queensland devote themselves to two versions of rugby. Rugby League, the professional game, is a faster, more exciting version of Rugby Union, the choice of purists.

Golf

Melbourne has the largest number of championship golf courses in Australia. Four kilometers (2½ mi) south of the city, **Albert Park Golf Course** (⊠ Queens Rd., South Melbourne ☎ 03/9510–5588) is an 18-hole, par-72 course that traverses Albert Park Lake, near where the Formula 1 Grand Prix is held in March. The 18-hole, par-67 **Brighton Public Golf Course** (⊠ 232 Dendy St., Brighton ☎ 03/9592–1388) has excellent scenery but is quite busy on weekends and midweek mornings. Club rental is available. **Ivanhoe Public Golf Course** (⊠ Vasey St., East Ivanhoe ☎ 03/9499–7001), an 18-hole, par-68 course, is well suited to the average golfer and is open to the public every day except holidays. Five minutes from the beach, **Sandringham Golf Links** (⊠ Cheltenham Rd., Sandringham ☎ 03/9598–3590) is one of the better public courses. The area is known as the golf links because there are several excellent courses in the vicinity. Sandringham is an 18-hole, par-72 course.

Horse Racing

Melbourne is the only city in the world to declare a public holiday for a horse race—the Melbourne Cup—held on the first Tuesday in November since 1861. The Cup is also a fashion parade, and most of Melbourne society turns out in full regalia. The rest of the country comes to a standstill, with schools, shops, offices, and factories tuning in to the action.

The city has four top-class racetracks. **Caulfield Race Course** (⊠ Station St., Caulfield ☎ 03/9257–7200), 10 km (6 mi) from the city, runs the Blue Diamond in February and the Caulfield Cup in October. **Flemington Race Course** (⊠ Epsom Rd., Flemington ☎ 03/9371–7171), 3 km (2 mi) outside the city, is Australia's premier racecourse and home of the Melbourne Cup. **Moonee Valley Race Course** (⊠ McPherson St., Moonee Ponds ☎ 03/9373–2222) is 6 km (4 mi) from town and holds the Cox Plate race in October. **Sandown Race Course** (⊠ Racecourse Dr., Springvale ☎ 03/9518–1300), 25 km (16 mi) from the city, hosts the Sandown Cup in November.

Soccer

Pickup or local-league soccer games are played in all seasons but summer in **Olympic Park** (⊠ Ovals 1 and 2, Swan St., Richmond ☎ 03/9286–1600).

Tennis

The **Australian Open** (☎ 03/9286–1175 ⊕ www.ausopen.com.au), held in January at the **Melbourne Park National Tennis Centre** (⊠ Batman Ave., City Center ☎ 03/9286–1244), is one of the world's four Grand Slam events. You can buy tickets at the event.

Brought your racket? **Melbourne Park Tennis Centre** (⊠ Batman Ave., City Center ☎ 03/9286–1244) has 22 outdoor and 4 hard indoor Rebound Ace courts. Play is canceled during the Australian Open in January. **East Melbourne Tennis Centre** (⊠ Powlett Reserve, Albert St., East Melbourne ☎ 03/9417–6511) has 5 synthetic-grass outdoor courts. **Fawkner Park Tennis Center** (⊠ Fawkner Park, Toorak Rd. W, South Yarra ☎ 03/9820–0611) has 6 synthetic-grass outdoor courts.

SHOPPING

Melbourne has firmly established itself as the nation's fashion capital. Australian designer labels are available on High Street in Armadale, on Toorak Road and Chapel Street in South Yarra, and on Bridge Road in Richmond. High-quality vintage clothing abounds on Greville Street in Prahran. Most shops are open Monday–Thursday 9–5:30, Friday until 9, and Saturday until 5. Major city stores are open Sunday until 5.

Department Stores

Bourke Street Mall. Once the busiest east–west thoroughfare in the city, Bourke is now a pedestrian zone (but watch out for those trams!). Two of the city's biggest department stores are here, **Myer** (⊠ 314 Bourke St., City Center ☎ 03/9661–1111) and **David Jones** (⊠ 310 Bourke St., City Center ☎ 03/9643–2222). An essential part of growing up in Melbourne is being taken to Myer at Christmas to see the window displays. ⊠ *Bourke St. between Elizabeth St. and Swanston Walk, City Center.*

Markets

Camberwell Market (✉ Bourke Rd., Camberwell ☎ 03/9813–2977), open Sunday only, is a popular haunt for memorabilia seekers. Stalls also display antiques, knickknacks, and food.

Chapel Street Bazaar (✉ 217–223 Chapel St., Prahran ☎ 03/9529–1727) has wooden stalls selling everything from stylish secondhand clothes to memorabilia and knickknacks. Open daily 10–6.

Prahran Market (✉ 177 Commercial Rd., Prahran ☎ 03/8290–8220) sells nothing but food—a fantastic, mouthwatering array imported from all over the world. Committed foodies seek out everything from star fruit and lemongrass to emu eggs and homemade relishes. Open Tuesday and Wednesday dawn to 5 PM, Thursday and Friday dawn to 6 PM, Saturday dawn to 5 PM and Sunday 10–3.

St. Kilda Esplanade Art and Craft Market (✉ Upper Esplanade, St. Kilda ☎ 03/9209–6777) has more than 200 stalls selling paintings, crafts, and homemade gifts. It's open Sunday from 10 to 5.

South Melbourne Market (✉ Cecil and Coventry Sts., South Melbourne ☎ 03/9209–6295) has a huge selection of fresh produce and foodstuffs. It's open Wednesday, Friday, and weekends from 8–4.

Shopping Centers, Malls & Arcades

Australia on Collins (✉ 260 Collins St., City Center ☎ 03/9650–4355) offers fashion, housewares, beauty, and an abundance of food. Labels include Gazman, Made in Japan, Country Road, and Siricco Leather.

Block Arcade (✉ 282 Collins St., City Center ☎ 03/9654–5244), an elegant 19th-century shopping plaza, contains the venerable Hopetoun Tea Rooms, the French Jewel Box, Orrefors Kosta Boda, Dasel Dolls and Bears, and Australian By Design.

Bridge Road, in the suburb of Richmond at the end of Flinders Street, east of the city, is a popular shopping strip for women's retail fashion that caters to all budgets.

★ **Brunswick Street,** east of the city in Fitzroy, has hip and grungy restaurants, coffee shops, gift stores, and clothing outlets selling the latest look.

Chapel Street, in South Yarra between Toorak and Dandenong roads, is where you can find some of the ritziest boutiques in Melbourne, as well as cafés, art galleries, bars, and restaurants.

Crown Entertainment Complex (✉ Riverside Ave., Southbank ☎ 03/9292–8888), the mall adjacent to the casino, sells Versace, Donna Karan, Gucci, Armani, and Prada, among others.

Dotted with chic boutiques, many of them selling merchandise by up-and-coming Australian designers, **Flinders Lane** will make fashionistas happy. Between Swanston and Elizabeth streets, look for shops like Christine and Alice Euphemia, which stock eclectic, sometimes whimsical, clothing designs by young designers.

Most Melburnians express a love-hate relationship for **GPO Melbourne** (✉ Between Elizabeth, Little Bourke, and Bourke Sts. and Postal La., City Center ☎ 03/9663–0066), but whether you like or loathe this landmark–post office–turned–shopping mall, you'll find it hard not to browse through its big-name designer-label shops. Built in 1859, the neo-Renaissance-style building is now Heritage-listed.

High Street, between the suburbs of Prahran and Armadale, to the east of Chapel Street, has the best collection of antiques shops in Australia. The **Jam Factory** (⊠ 500 Chapel St., South Yarra ☎ 03/9829–2641) is a group of historic bluestone buildings that house cinemas, fashion, food, and gift shops, as well as a branch of the giant Borders book-and-music store.

★ **Little Collins Street,** a precinct of stores frequented by shoppers with perhaps more money than sense, Little Collins is still worth a visit. In between frock shops, you'll find musty stores selling classic film posters, antique and estate jewelry, and Australian opals. At the eastern end of Collins Street, beyond the cream-and-red, Romanesque facade of St. Michael's Uniting Church, is **Paris End,** a name coined by Melburnians to identify the elegance of its fashionable shops as well as its general hauteur. The venerable **Le Louvre** salon (No. 74) is favored by Melbourne's high society.

Melbourne Central (⊠ 300 Lonsdale St., City Center ☎ 03/9922–1100) is a dizzying complex huge enough to enclose a 100-year-old shot tower (used to make bullets) in its atrium.

QV (⊠ Swanston and Lonsdale Sts., City Center ☎ 03/9658–0100) encompasses a site that was formerly occupied by the Victoria Women's Hospital. The shops here lie along six open-air lanes, and range from posh clothing boutiques like Christensen Copenhagen to chocolate shops and sushi restaurants. There are events most weekends—fashion parades, live music concerts, cooking classes, skateboard demonstrations—in the lanes.

Royal Arcade (⊠ 355 Bourke St., City Center ☎ No phone), built in 1846, is Melbourne's oldest shopping plaza. It remains a lovely place to browse, and it's home to the splendid Gaunt's Clock, which tolls away the hours.

★ **Southgate** (⊠ 4 Southbank Promenade, Southbank ☎ 03/9699–4311) has a spectacular riverside location. The shops and eateries here are a short walk both from the city center across Princes Bridge and from the Victorian Arts Center. There's outdoor seating next to the Southbank promenade.

Specialty Stores

Books

Borders (⊠ Jam Factory, Chapel St., South Yarra ☎ 03/9824–2299) is a gigantic book-and-music emporium.

Brunswick Street Bookstore (⊠ 305 Brunswick St., Fitzroy ☎ 03/9416–1030) sells modern Australian literature and art- and design-oriented books.

Hill of Content (⊠ 86 Bourke St., City Center ☎ 03/9662–9472), with a knowledgeable staff and an excellent selection of titles, is a Melbourne favorite.

Readings (⊠ 309 Lygon St., Carlton ☎ 03/9347–6633), with an exceptional range of books, magazines and CDs, is a Melbourne institution.

Clothing

Andrea Gold (✉ 110 Bridge Rd., Richmond ☎ 03/9428–1226) stocks a wide selection of women's wear, including dresses, suits, jewelry, and handbags.

Anthea Crawford (✉ 205 Bridge Rd., Richmond ☎ 03/9428–1670) attracts women who want high-quality dress wear, hats, and accessories.

Aquila Shoes (✉ 147 Bourke St., City Center ☎ 03/9650–4483) sells imported and locally made quality footwear for men and women.

Collette Dinnigan (✉ 553 Chapel St., South Yarra ☎ 03/9822–9433) is the upscale retail outlet for the famous Australian fashion designer Collette Dinnigan.

Cose Plus (✉ 3/286 Toorak Rd., South Yarra ☎ 03/9826–5788) is a popular women's shop.

Jean Pascal (✉ 144A Cotham Rd., Kew ☎ 03/9817–3671) is a local favorite of women shoppers.

Kookai (✉ 110 Greville St., Prahran ☎ 03/9529–8599) is a well-known international label. This chain of stores across Melbourne stocks women's fashions and accessories.

Sam Bear (✉ 225 Russell St., City Center ☎ 03/9663–2191), a Melbourne institution, sells everything from Aussie outerwear to Swiss Army knives.

Gifts

Aboriginal Art (✉ 73–77 Bourke St., City Center ☎ 03/9650–3277) sells arts and crafts created by Aborigines.

Aboriginal Handcrafts (✉ Mezzanine, 130 Little Collins St., City Center ☎ 03/9650–4717) stocks handcrafts created by Aborigines, including paintings, drawings, cooking implements, and more.

Alison Kelly (✉ 543A High St., Prahran ☎ 03/9533–8444) sells arts and crafts created by Aborigines from regional collectives.

Arts of Asia (✉ 1136 High St., Armadale ☎ 03/9576–0917), in a popular shopping strip, sells paintings, drawings, prints, and antiques from Southeast Asia.

Gallery Gabrielle Pizzi (✉ 141 Flinders La., City Center ☎ 03/9654–2944) represents the work of Aboriginal artists from the communities of Balgo Hills, Papunya, Utopia, Maningrida, Haasts Bluff, and the Tiwi Islands.

Kimberley Art (✉ 76 Flinders La., City Center ☎ 03/9654–5890) sells Aboriginal arts and crafts from Arnhem Land, the Kimberley, and the Western Desert.

Jewelry

Altmann and Cherny (✉ 120 Exhibition St., City Center ☎ 03/9650–9685) sells opals at tax-free prices to overseas tourists.

Dressed up to look like Victorian-era bedroom, complete with a dressing table draped in jewelry, plush armchairs, and old-fashioned wall hangings, **bqueen** (✉ 119 Hardware La., City Center ☎ 03/9602–4455) specializes in handmade wares by local designers.

Craft Victoria (✉ 31 Flinders La., City Center ☎ 03/9650–7775) has the best selection of international and local pottery and jewelry.

Exhibiting work from more than 80 Australian and New Zealand designers, **eg.etal** (✉ 185 Collins St., City Center ☎ 03/9663–4334) offers spectacular handmade one-off jewelry pieces.

A haunt of the incredibly affluent, **Kozminsky** (⌧ 421 Bourke St., City Center ☎03/9670–1277) has been a Melbourne institution since its opening in 1851. It's crowded with antiques, estate jewelry, and gilt-edged objects from days gone by.

Makers Mark Gallery (⌧ 88 Collins St., City Center ☎ 03/9650–3444) showcases the work of some of the country's finest jewelers and designers.

Music

Many of the too-cool staffers at **Au Go Go Records** (⌧ 1st fl., 2 Somerset Pl. [off Little Bourke St.], City Center ☎ 03/9670–0677) are well-known DJs or music-industry types; they're versed in all things independent, alternative, and underground.

CD Discounts (⌧ Shop 4, AMP Sq., 121 William St., City Center ☎ 03/9629–1662) sells CDs, records, DVDs, and tapes.

Discurio (⌧ 113 Hardware St., City Center ☎03/9600–1488) carries a cross section of pop, rock, and contemporary music by international artists.

Gaslight (⌧ 85 Bourke St., City Center ☎ 03/9650–9009) carries a range of pop, rock, and contemporary music by Australian and international artists, along with DVDs, T-shirts, and event tickets.

Greville Records (⌧ 152 Greville St., Prahran ☎03/9510–3012) is a Melbourne music institution. It carries rare releases in rock, alternative, and vinyl.

Gloomy, small and always crowded, **Record Collector's Corner** (⌧ 240 Swanston St., City Center ☎ 03/9663–3442) stocks an impressive range of CDs, vinyl, and (believe it or not) cassettes, from a wide cross section of genres. Secondhand CDs and hard-to-find import CD singles are the specialties of the house.

MELBOURNE A TO Z

AIR TRAVEL

Melbourne is most easily reached by plane, as it—like many places in Australia—is hours by car from even the nearest town. International airlines flying into Melbourne include Air New Zealand, British Airways, United, Singapore Airlines, Emirates, Japan Airlines, Alitalia, Thai Airways, and Malaysia Airlines.

Domestic carriers serving Melbourne are Qantas, Virgin Blue, O'Connor Airlines, and Regional Express. Qantas and Virgin Blue fly daily to Sydney, Adelaide, Perth, Brisbane, Hobart, and the Gold Coast, while smaller carriers like O'Connor Airlines and Regional Express fly to outer towns like Wagga Wagga, Mount Gambier, and Mildura.

🛪 Airlines **Air New Zealand** ☎ 13–2476. **Alitalia** ☎ 03/9920–3799. **British Airways** ☎ 03/9656–8133. **Emirates** ☎1300/303777. **Japan Airlines** ☎ 03/8662–8333. **Malaysia Airlines** ☎ 03/9279–9999. **O'Connor Airlines** ☎ 08/8723–0666. **Qantas Airways** ☎ 13–1313. **Regional Express** ☎ 13–1713. **Singapore Airlines** ☎ 13–1011. **Thai Airways** ☎ 1300/651960. **United** ☎ 13–1777. **Virgin Blue** ☎ 13–6789.

AIRPORTS

Melbourne Airport is 22 km (14 mi) northwest of the central business district and can be reached easily from the city on the Tullamarine Freeway. The international terminal is in the center of the airport complex. Domestic terminals are on either side.

Melbourne Airport ☎ 03/9297-1600 ⊕ www.melbourne-airport.com.au.

TRANSFERS Skybus, a public transportation bus service, runs between the airport and city center, making a loop through Melbourne before terminating at Spencer Street Station. The A$13 shuttle departs every 15 minutes from 7 AM to 7 PM, then every half hour until 12:30 AM, and hourly until 4:30 AM. The journey takes 20 minutes from the city center.

For three or more people traveling together, a taxi is a better value for airport connections. You can catch a taxi in front of the building. The cost into town is A$35. Limousines to the city cost about A$160. Astra is one of the larger companies.

Astra Chauffeured Limousines Of Australia ☎ 1800/819797. **Skybus** ☎ 03/9335-3066 ⊕ www.skybus.com.au.

BUS TRAVEL TO & FROM MELBOURNE

McCaffertys and Greyhound link the city with all Australian capital cities and with major towns and cities throughout Victoria. Terminals are on the corner of Swanston and Franklin streets. From Melbourne, it's about 10 hours to Adelaide, about 12 hours to Sydney, about 50 hours to Perth (consider flying), and about 8 hours to Canberra.

Greyhound ☎ 13-2030 ⊕ www.greyhound.com.au. **McCaffertys** ☎ 13-1499 ⊕ www.mccaffertys.com.au.

BUS & TRAM TRAVEL WITHIN MELBOURNE

The city's public transportation system is operated by Metropolitan Transit, which divides Melbourne into three zones. Zone 1 is the urban core, where most tourists spend their time. The basic ticket is the one-zone ticket, which can be purchased on board the bus or prepurchased from newsagents for A$3.10. It's valid for travel within a specific zone on any tram, bus, or train for two hours after purchase. For travelers, the most useful ticket is probably the Zone 1 day ticket, which costs A$5.90 and is available on board any tram. A free route map is available from the Victoria Tourism Information Service.

Trams run until midnight and can be hailed wherever you see a green-and-gold tram-stop sign. A free City Circle tram run by Metropolitan Transit operates every 10 minutes daily 10–6 on the fringe of the Central Business District, with stops in Flinders, Spencer, La Trobe, Victoria, and Spring streets. Look for the burgundy-and-cream trams.

Metropolitan Transit ☎ 13-1638 ⊕ www.victrip.com.au. **Victoria Tourism Information Service** ☎ 13-2842 ⊕ www.visitvictoria.com.

CAR RENTAL

Avis, Budget, and Hertz have branches at Melbourne Airport as well as downtown. If you rent from a major company, expect to pay about A$60 per day for a compact standard model. If you don't mind an older model and can return the car to the pick-up point, consider a smaller local rental agency, such as Rent-a-Bomb.

Airport Rent A Car ☎ 1800/331220. **Avis** ☎ 13-6333. **Budget** ☎ 13-2727. **Hertz** ☎ 13-3039. **Rent-a-Bomb** ☎ 13-1553.

CAR TRAVEL

The major route into Melbourne is Hume Highway, which runs north-east to Canberra, 646 km (400 mi) distant, and Sydney, which is 868 km (538 mi) away. Princes Highway follows the coast to Sydney in one direction and to Adelaide, 728 km (451 mi) northwest of Melbourne, in the other. The Western Highway runs northwest 111 km (69 mi) to Ballarat, and the Calder Highway travels north to Bendigo, a journey of 149 km (92 mi). From Melbourne it takes 10 to 12 hours to reach Sydney, about 9 hours to Adelaide, and about 1½ hours to Bendigo and Ballarat. The Royal Automobile Club of Victoria (RACV) is the major source of information on all aspects of road travel in Victoria.

Melbourne's regimented layout makes it easy to negotiate by car, but two unusual rules apply because of the tram traffic on the city's major roads. Trams should be passed on the *left,* and when a tram stops to allow passengers to disembark, the cars behind it also must stop unless there is a railed safety zone for tram passengers.

At some intersections within the city, drivers wishing to turn *right* must stay in the *left* lane as they enter the intersection, then wait for the traffic signals to change before proceeding with the turn. The rule is intended to prevent traffic from impeding tram service. For complete directions, look for the black-and-white traffic signs suspended overhead as you enter each intersection where this rule applies. All other right-hand turns are made from the center. It's far easier to understand this rule by seeing it in action rather than reading about it.

🚗 **Royal Automobile Club of Victoria (RACV)** ☎ 13-1955 ⊕ www.racv.com.au.

CONSULATES

Most embassies are in Canberra, but many countries also have consulates or honorary consuls in Melbourne. Others are usually listed in the telephone directory under the specific country.

🚗 **American Consulate-General** ✉ 553 St. Kilda Rd., St. Kilda ☎ 03/9526-5900. **British Consulate-General** ✉ 90 Collins St., City Center ☎ 03/9652-1600. **New Zealand Consulate-General** ✉ Level 3, 350 Collins St., City Center ☎ 03/9642-1279.

EMERGENCIES

In an emergency, dial **000** to reach an ambulance, the police, or the fire department. The Collins Place Pharmacy is open 9–6.

🚗 **Doctors & Dentists Medical Center** ✉ 115-125 Victoria Rd., Northacote ☎ 03/9482-2866. **Royal Dental Hospital** ✉ Elizabeth St. and Flemington Rd., Parkville ☎ 03/9341-0222. **Swanston Street Medical Centre** ✉ 393 Swanston St., City Center ☎ 03/9654-2722.

🚗 **Hospitals Alfred Hospital** ✉ Commercial Rd. and Hoddle St., Prahran ☎ 03/9276-2000. **Royal Women's Hospital** ✉ 132 Grattan St., Carlton ☎ 03/9344-2000. **St. Vincent's Hospital** ✉ Nicholson St. and Victoria Parade, Fitzroy ☎ 03/9288-2211.

🚗 **Pharmacy Collins Place Pharmacy** ✉ 45 Collins St., City Center ☎ 03/9650-9034.

MAIL, THE INTERNET & SHIPPING

The general post office is open from 8:15 to 5:30 weekdays and 10 to 3 Saturday. The post office's Express Post can send mail overnight within Australia; TNT handles 24-hour overseas packages.

Melbourne's larger hotels have business services and can recommend local resources for any additional tasks. Internet cafés are found throughout the city.

🖪 Internet Cafés Internet Café St. Kilda ⊠ 9 Grey St., St. Kilda ☎ 03/9534-2666. **ProGamer Internet and Games Café** ⊠ 208-210 La Trobe St., City Center ☎ 03/9639-7171.

🖪 Mail Services General Post Office ⊠ Elizabeth and Little Bourke Sts., City Center ☎ 03/9203-3076. **TNT** ⊠ Shed K 77 Millers Rd, City Center ☎ 13 1150.

MONEY MATTERS

Money changers are not as common in Melbourne as in other major international cities—try along Collins, Elizabeth, or Swanston streets. ATMs are plentiful throughout Victoria and accept CIRRUS, Maestro, PLUS, and credit cards. Other places to get and change money include large hotels, American Express, and Thomas Cook. If heading into regional Victoria, it's wise to cash up beforehand rather than relying on regional banking outlets, which may or may not cater to international travelers.

🖪 Banks ANZ ⊠ 6/530 Collins St., City Center ☎ 13-1314. **Commonwealth** ⊠ 463 Elizabeth St., City Center ☎ 13-2221 ⊠ 385 Bourke St., City Center ☎ 03/9675-8919 ⊠ Flinders and Elizabeth Sts., City Center ☎ 13-2221. **National Australia** ⊠ 164 Bourke St., City Center ⊠ 500 Bourke St., City Center ⊠ 271 Collins St., City Center ⊠ 460 Collins St., City Center ☎ 13-2265. **Westpac** ⊠ 447 Bourke St., City Center ⊠ 360 Collins St., City Center ⊠ Collins and Swanston Sts., City Center ⊠ 555 Collins St., City Center ☎ 13-1032.

🖪 Exchange Services American Express ⊠ 233 Collins St., City Center ☎ 1300/139060. **Custom House Currency Exchange** ⊠ Level 10, 224 Queen St., City Center ☎ 03/8622-8800. **Thomas Cook** ⊠ 257 Collins St., City Center ☎ 03/9650-2095.

SIGHTSEEING TOURS

BOAT TOURS One of the best ways to see Melbourne is to board the Parks Victoria ferry which takes in Federation Square and Docklands, with stops at Southgate, the aquarium, the casino, and Victoria Harbour. Daily pass tickets, which allow passengers to jump on and off en route, run daily and cost A$9. An even better option is the "What's in the Sky Tonight?" cruise which, run by Scienceworks and Melbourne Planetarium, includes a glass of champagne, planetarium show, stargazing through telescopes, and a return ferry trip to the city center. Cost A$25. The modern, glass-enclosed boats of the Melbourne River Cruises fleet take 1-, 2-, and 2½-hour Yarra River cruises daily (A$19, A$25, and A$30 respectively), traversing either west through the commercial heart of the city or east through the parks and gardens, or a combination of the two. Daily tours run every half hour from 10 to 4.

Yarra Yarra Water Taxis use a 1950s mahogany speedboat. The size of the boat makes it possible to follow the Yarra as far as Dight's Falls, passing some of Melbourne's larger houses in the wealthiest suburbs on the way. It costs A$100 per hour and can carry up to six passengers. If you want to plan a barbecue, the boat stops at a small island where you can cook your own.

Gray Line also has boat tours.

🖪 **Melbourne River Cruises** ✉ Vault 18, Banana Alley and Queensbridge St., City Center ☎ 03/9614-1215. **Parks Victoria** ✉ 535 Bourke St., City Center ☎ 13-1963. **Scienceworks and Melbourne Planetarium** ✉ 2 Booker St., Spotswood ☎ 03/9392-4819. **Melbourne Water Taxis** ✉ South Wharf Rd., South Melbourne ☎ 03/9686-0914.

BUS TOURS Gray Line has guided tours of Melbourne and its surroundings by bus and boat. The Melbourne Experience tour visits the city center's main attractions and some of the surrounding parks. The three-hour, A\$55 tour departs daily at 8:45 from the company's headquarters.

AAT Kings, Australian Pacific Tours, and Melbourne Sightseeing all have similar general-interest trips and prices.

🖪 **AAT Kings** ✉ 33 Palmerston Crescent, South Melbourne ☎ 1300/556100. **Australian Pacific Tours** ✉ 475 Hampton St., Hampton ☎ 1300/655965. **Gray Line** ✉ 180 Swanston St., City Center ☎ 1300/858687 ⊕ www.grayline.com.au. **Melbourne Experience** ✉ Melbourne Town Hall, Swanston St., City Center ☎ 03/9650-7000. **Melbourne Sightseeing** ✉ 184 Swanston Walk, City Center ☎ 03/9663-3377 ⊕ www. ozhorizons.com.au.

FOOD TOURS Foodies Dream Tours (A\$25) and cooking classes (2½ hours, A\$70–75) are available at the Victorian Arts Centre. The center is open Tuesday and Thursday 6–2, Friday 6–6, Saturday 6–3, and Sunday 9–4.

Chocoholic Tours offers several different Saturday touring options for chocolate lovers: the Chocoholic Brunch Walk (10–noon), the Chocoholic Indulgence Tour (12:15–2:15), and the Chocolate and Other Desserts Walk (2:15–4:30). Each offers a different combination of chocolate-fueled tastings and activities, and each costs A\$28.

Vietnam on a Plate runs a guided walking tour of the Asian precincts. Visiting traditional Chinese herbalists, food stalls, spice and herb specialists, and the "Little Saigon" shopping district, the tour includes lunch, numerous food tastings—from the weird (chilli pork blood and pickled pig's lung) to the wonderful (fresh ginger and lemongrass tea). It costs A\$49 and runs each Saturday from 9:30 to 12:30.

🖪 **Chocoholic Tours** ✉ 14 Rae St., Hawthorn ☎ 03/9815-1228 ⊕ www.chocoholictours. com.au. **Foodies Dream Tours** ✉ Queen and Victoria Sts., City Center ☎ 03/9320-5822 ⊕ www.qvm.com.au. **Vietnam on a Plate** ✉ Footscray Market, Footscray ☎ 03/ 9689-1186.

SHOPPING TOURS Serious shoppers might want to take advantage of a Shopping Spree tour, which includes lunch and escorted shopping at some at Melbourne's best manufacturers and importers. Tours depart Monday through Saturday at 8:30. The cost is A\$65 per person. More discerning shoppers or those with special interests in artwork, antiques, furniture, fabrics, home wares, or quirky gifts, should try Savvy Shop Tours. A personalized, four-hour tour in a chauffeur-driven car is A\$100 per person; morning or afternoon tea is included.

🖪 **Savvy Shop Tours** ✉ 4 Alamar Ave., Glen Huntly ☎ 03/9569-2529 ⊕ www. savvyshoptours.com.au. **Shopping Spree Tours** ✉ 2/ 77 Asling St., Gardenvale ☎ 03/ 9596-6600.

SPORTS TOURS Melbourne's excellent bicycle-path network and flat terrain makes cycling pleasurable. For around A$12 per hour you can rent a bike from Hire a Bicycle on the Yarra River near Princes Bridge in the city. For more information about cycling around Melbourne—with or without help—contact Bicycle Victoria.

Journey Events Travel specializes in sporting tours of Melbourne. Headed by ex-AFL football star Paul Salmon, the company organizes packages for major sporting events including Australian Rules Football games, tennis, golf, cricket, and the Formula 1 Grand Prix. Tours include accommodations and admission.

The Docklands Sailing School runs two-hour sailing tours of Melbourne's Victoria Harbour, Docklands precinct, or the Historic Maritime quarters of Hobson's Bay and Williamstown.

AFL is more a religion than a sport in Melbourne, so taking a Melbourne Sports Tour behind the scenes of Melbourne's top "footy" venues such as the Melbourne Cricket Ground and the Telstra Dome is the best way to get a real feel for the city. Other sights on the tour include Melbourne and Olympic parks, Melbourne Park National Tennis Centre (where the Australian Tennis Open is held each January, Albert Park Grand Prix racetrack, and Flemington Race Course (graced by the Melbourne Cup Carnival each November). If you want to experience the AFL ritual, which comprises a football match (with a host to explain the rules) and a meat pie (an Australian tradition), this is the way to do it.

Melburnians take their golf very seriously, and many of the area's pristine greens are members-only. To albatross on the drives many locals can't access, take a Gimme Golf tour, which takes in some of the city's most exclusive courses. Trips to regional courses on the Mornington and Bellarine peninsulas are also available.

🏡 **Bicycle Victoria** ✉ Level 10, 446 Collins St., City Center ☎ 03/8636–8888 🖷 03/8636–8800. **Docklands Sailing School** ✉ Victoria Harbour, Docklands ☎ 04/2575–2745. **Gimme Golf** ✉ Suite 254, 45 Glenferrie Rd., Malvern ☎ 03/9809–1022. **Hire A Bicycle** ✉ Under Batman Ave. at Yarra River, South Yarra ☎ 04/1733–9203. **Journey Events Travel** ✉ Level 7, 420 St. Kilda Rd. City Center ☎ 03/9639–6022 🖷 03/9639–7055. **Melbourne Sports Tours** ✉ Box 287, Mitcham ☎ 03/8802–4547.

TOWN HALL TOUR You can learn about the history and architectural significance of Melbourne's beautiful Town Hall with these tours. Among the sights you'll see are the Council Chambers and the 30-foot-high Town Hall Organ, which was built in 1929 and has 6,024 pipes. Tours are available weekdays at 11 AM and 1 PM; although they're free, reservations are essential.

🏡 **Melbourne Town Hall** ✉ Swanston and Little Collins Sts., City Center ☎ 03/9658–9658.

WALKING TOURS The Melbourne Greeters service, a Melbourne Information Centre program, provides free personalized tours by pairing you with a local volunteer who shares your interests. Melbourne's Golden Mile Heritage Trail runs guided walking tours of the city's architectural and historic sites. Tours, which cost A$20 and take 2½ to 3½ hours, depart daily at 1 from Federation Square and finish at the Melbourne Museum.

🚩 **Golden Mile Heritage Trail** ☎ 03/9650-3663 or 1300/130152 ⊕ www.visitvictoria. com. **Melbourne Greeters** ✉ Federation Sq., Flinders and Swanston Sts., City Center ☎ 03/9658-9524 🖷 03/9654-1054.

TAXIS

Melbourne's taxis are gradually adopting a yellow color scheme, and drivers are required to wear uniforms. Taxis are metered, and can be hailed on the street and at taxi stands or ordered by phone. Major taxi companies include Yellow Cabs, North Suburban, and Silver Top.

🚩 **North Suburban** ☎ 13 1119. **Silver Top** ☎ 13 1008. **Yellow Cabs** ☎ 13-2227.

TELEPHONES

The code for Victoria (and Tasmania) is 03. If you're in Melbourne, you don't need to dial the 03 before numbers in regional Victoria, but you must use the 03 for Tasmanian numbers. Public telephones are everywhere. Most accept both coins and phone cards, which can be purchased from newsagents, post offices, and corner food stores (milk bars).

TRAIN TRAVEL

Connex runs trains throughout metropolitan Melbourne from 4:30 AM until around 1 AM. The zone structure is similar to that of the city's buses and trams, and tickets can be prepurchased at the station or from newsagents. One-zone, two-hour tickets are A$3; all-day tickets are A$5.80. The main terminal for metropolitan trains is Flinders Street Station, at the corner of Flinders and Swanston streets.

Spencer Street Railway Station is at Spencer and Little Collins streets. From here the countrywide V-Line has eight-hour trips to Sydney. Public transportation is available, but if you have cumbersome luggage, you'd do better to head for the taxi stand outside the station.

🚩 **Connex** ☎ 13-1638 ⊕ www.connexmelbourne.com.au. **V-Line** ☎ 13-6196.

VISITOR INFORMATION

The Melbourne Information Centre at Federation Square provides touring details in six languages. Large-screen videos and touch screens add to the experience, and permanent displays follow the city's history. Daily newspapers are available, and there's access to the Melbourne Web site (www.visitmelbourne.com). The center is open daily 9–6. The Best of Victoria Booking Service here can help if you're looking for accommodations. It also has cheap Internet access.

City Ambassadors provided by the City of Melbourne rove the central retail area providing directions and information for anyone who needs their assistance (Monday–Saturday 10–5).

🚩 **Best of Victoria Booking Service** ☎ 03/9642-1055 or 1300/780045. **City of Melbourne Ambassadors Program** ☎ 03/9658-9658. **Melbourne Information Centre** ✉ Federation Sq., Flinders and Swanston Sts., City Center ☎ 03/9658-9658 ⊕ www. melbourne.vic.gov.au.

Victoria

WORD OF MOUTH

"In Melbourne, we hired a car and drove on the Great Ocean Road to Port Campbell to see the Twelve Apostles. LOOOONG DRIVE . . . but STUNNING DRIVE!!! One moment you are clinging to a cliff, the next you are driving through lush forests. Wow!!!"

—highness67

Updated by
Liza Power

SEPARATED FROM NEW SOUTH WALES BY THE MIGHTY MURRAY RIVER and fronted by a rugged and beautiful coastline, Victoria's terrain is as varied as any in the country. A collection of sweeping landscapes has been quilted together to make up this compact state. Along the West Coast, rugged, cliff-lined seascapes alternate with thick forests and charming resort towns; inland are historic goldfield communities, river towns along the Murray, and esteemed vineyards. The region also has some of Australia's most striking national parks, including the weathered offshore rock formations of Port Campbell; the waterfalls, flora, and fauna of Gariwerd; and the high-country solitude of Alpine National Park.

Many of Victoria's best sights are within a day's drive of Melbourne. Without venturing too far from the city limits, you can indulge in all sorts of nonurban pastimes—like following the spectacular western coastline to the stunning Twelve Apostles; toasting the sunrise over the Yarra Valley vineyards from the basket of a hot-air balloon; or taking in a Murray River sunset from the deck of a meandering paddle steamer.

Though it's younger than its neighbor, New South Wales, Victoria possesses a sense of history and continuity often missing in other Australian states, where humanity's grasp on the land appears temporary and precarious. Even the smallest rural communities in Victoria have some kind of museum.

Victoria's first permanent settlement was erected at Portland, on the state's treacherous West Coast, in 1834. When indigenous Aborigines resisted the European invasion, they were killed by the thousands; those who didn't fall victim to guns were eventually killed by smallpox, measles, and dysentery. Victoria was granted independence from New South Wales in 1851, the same year that goldfields were discovered across the state. When settlers from around the world came to join in the gold rush, towns such as Ballarat and Bendigo sprang up—pockets of extravagant 1880s architecture right in the middle of the bush, which still have the feel of living museums. Today Victoria's main industries include brown coal (the Latrobe Valley reefs comprise one of the world's largest deposits), timber, manufacturing, and agriculture.

Exploring Victoria

The best way to explore Victoria is by car. The state's road system is excellent, with clearly marked highways linking the Great Ocean Road to Wilson's Promontory, the Yarra Valley, the Murray River region, and the Mornington Peninsula. Although distances can be great, the changing scenery is entertainment in itself. From Melbourne, the capital, you can travel to Geelong in the Bellarine Peninsula, as well as the northwest settlements of Ballarat and Bendigo. If you're exploring the Murray River region, head for the towns of Echuca, Wodonga, Swan Hill, and Mildura. Buses and trains, which cost less but take more time, also run between most regional centers.

About the Restaurants

Chefs in Victoria take pride in their trendsetting preparations of fresh local produce. International flavors are found in both casual and up-

Victoria's relatively compact size makes the state's principal attractions appealingly easy to reach. Another region, another taste of this richly endowed state, is never too far away. Head off to the Melbourne suburbs for antiquing and nightlife, drive along the Great Ocean Road, explore Phillip Island, take a wine-tasting tour, hike through the forested mountains, or settle back into the Hepburn Springs spas. The longer you stay, the more you'll find to keep you in this fascinating state of myriad outdoor settings.

5

If you have
3 days

On the first morning that you leave Melbourne, head for the town of Belgrave. Here you can ride the **Puffing Billy** through the fern gullies and forests of the **Dandenongs.** In the afternoon, travel to **Phillip Island** for the endearing sunset penguin parade at Summerland Beach. Stay the night, and on the third morning meander along the coastal roads of the **Mornington Peninsula** through such stately towns as Sorrento and Portsea. Stop at a beach, or pick a Melbourne neighborhood or two to explore in the afternoon.

If you have
5 days

Make your way west from Melbourne along the Great Ocean Road. This is one of the world's finest scenic drives, offering stops at the irresistible beaches of the **West Coast Region.** Overnight in **Lorne,** beneath the Otway Ranges, then drive west to **Port Campbell National Park** on Day 3. Here you can view the Twelve Apostles rock formation, take a walk to the beach, and continue to **Warrnambool** for the night. On Day 4, take a morning tour of Flagstaff Hill Maritime Village, then drive northeast to the goldfields center of **Ballarat.** That evening you can explore the town's 19th-century streetscapes, then catch the sound-and-light show at Sovereign Hill Historical Park. Spend the night here, and in the morning, head to the wineries and spas around Daylesford before returning to Melbourne.

If you have
10 days

Spend your first day and night in **Melbourne,** and on Day 2 explore **Phillip Island** or head right to **Queenscliff;** you can spend the night in either place. On Day 3, take a drive along the West Coast via Anglesea, overnighting in **Lorne.** Spend Day 4 discovering the delights of **Port Campbell National Park** and **Warrnambool,** then drive to **Port Fairy** for the night. Start Day 5 early with a drive via **Gariwerd National Park.** Overnight in **Ballarat,** then on Day 6 take your time wandering through the spa towns of **Daylesford** and **Hepburn Springs** toward **Bendigo,** where you'll stay the night. On Day 7 tour the Golden Dragon Museum, examining the history of the Chinese on the goldfields. In the afternoon, drive to **Echuca,** a Murray River town, stopping in a couple of wineries on your way to **Beechworth.** Stay here two nights, taking Days 8 and 9 to discover **Alpine National Park.** On the last day, revisit your favorite regional highlights as you make your way back to the capital.

scale spots—and since prices are much lower here than in Sydney, you can have your fill without breaking the bank. On Sunday be sure to join in the Victorian tradition of an all-day "brekky."

WHAT IT COSTS In Australian dollars				
	$$$$	**$$$**	**$$**	**$**	**¢**
AT DINNER	over $50	$36–$50	$21–$35	$10–$20	under $10

Prices are for a main course at dinner.

About the Hotels

Accommodations in Victoria include grand country hotels, simple roadside motels, secluded bushland or seaside cabins, and backpacker hostels. Although you won't find large, modern resorts in this state, most of the grand old mansions and simple homes offering rooms have hot water, air-conditioning, and free parking. Rates are usually reduced after school and national holidays. Melbourne Visitor Centre (www.visitvictoria.com) has a list of the state's accommodations to help you plan.

WHAT IT COSTS In Australian dollars				
	$$$$	**$$$**	**$$**	**$**	**¢**
FOR 2 PEOPLE	over $300	$201–$300	$151–$200	$100–$150	under $100

Prices are for two people in a standard double room in high season, including tax and service, based on the European Plan (with no meals) unless otherwise noted.

Timing

Victoria is at its most beautiful in fall, March through May, when days are crisp, sunny, and clear, and the foliage in parks and gardens is glorious. Winter, with its wild seas and leaden skies, stretches May through August in this region, providing a suitable backdrop for the dramatic coastal scenery. It's dry and sunny in the northeast, however, thanks to the cloud-blocking bulk of the Great Dividing Range. Northeast summers, November through February, are extremely hot, so it's best to travel here and through Gold Country in spring and fall.

Victoria's mostly mild weather means that you can participate in outdoor activities from skiing to hiking almost any time you visit. The best white-water rafting, rock climbing, hang-gliding, and bushwalking options are in the high country around Bright and Mt. Buffalo. Wilson's Promontory, Warburton, and the Upper Yarra region around Marysville also have beautiful trails.

AROUND MELBOURNE

The Dandenongs/Yarra Valley

Melburnians come to the Dandenong Ranges for a breath of fresh air, especially in autumn when the deciduous trees turn golden, and in spring when the gardens explode into color with tulip, daffodil, azalea, and rhodo-

5

The Amazing Outdoors
Victoria has outstanding national parks. Bushwalking, canoeing, fishing, hiking, rafting, and riding are all choices here—it's a great state for getting out. Even on a day trip from Melbourne you can see some of Australia's best outdoor sights: the seascapes of Port Campbell, the rock spires and waterfalls in Gariwerd National Park, and the fairy penguin and sea lion colonies on Phillip Island.

Tasteful Dining
You'll eat well in this state of natural beauty and bounty, especially in Victoria's wine country. Regional specialties include kangaroo steaks, Gippsland cheeses, smoked meats, apples, organic blueberries from the Mornington Peninsula, and sun-dried citrus fruits and pistachios from Mildura. If you love seafood, head for Queenscliff and to towns along the Great Ocean Road, where lobster and prawns are particularly succulent. Also, don't miss the restaurants and wineries of the Yarra Valley and the Mornington Peninsula, which usually have a bountiful selection of labels to match their exquisite cuisine.

Old-Fashioned Lodging
Gracious B&Bs, host farms, and old-fashioned guesthouses are Victoria's welcome alternatives to hotel and motel accommodations. Bed-and-breakfasts are particularly good options, as they're run by locals who can advise you about regional history, activities, and attractions. Motels are best for those passing through towns quickly; travelers who want to linger should book a gracious historic hotel, where such sophisticated charms as silver tea service are combined with the luxuries of a modern resort. Queenscliff, Ballarat, and Mildura in particular have numerous charming B&Bs, but you'll need to book early in December and January.

Spas
New age–style treatments have taken Melbourne by storm, and even most small towns around the state have one or two natural or alternative therapy resorts. But it's the twin Gold Country towns of Daylesford and Hepburn Springs that have become the spa capital of Victoria. The naturally occurring mineral springs here are used as a foundation for all kinds of healing treatments, including mineral baths, mud wraps, massages, and facials.

Wineries
Victoria now has hundreds of wineries, particularly in the Yarra Valley and Pyrenees Ranges, and on the Mornington Peninsula. Travel agencies in Melbourne and the larger towns throughout the state have package tours that cover many wineries and regions. You can plan your own wine-tasting circuit as well with help from the regional tourist offices, which have maps of the wineries and details about tour times and labels.

---

dendron blooms. At Mt. Dandenong, the highest point (2,077 feet), a scenic lookout affords spectacular views over Melbourne and the bay beyond. Dandenong Ranges National Park, which encompasses five smaller parks, including Sherbrooke Forest and Ferntree Gully National Park, has dozens of walking trails, while the quaint townships of Olinda and

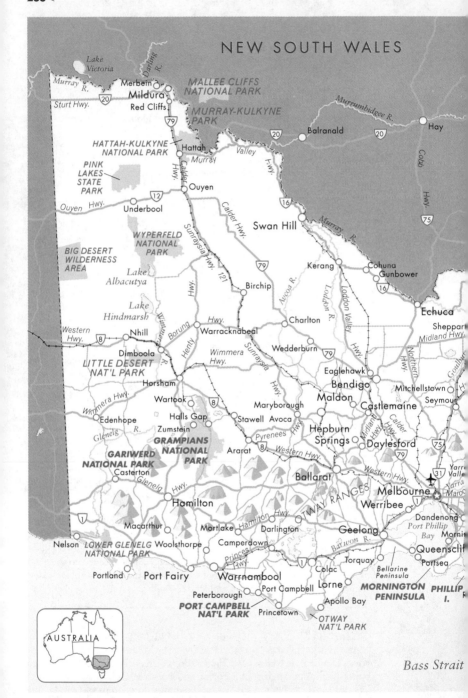

NEW SOUTH WALES

Lake Victoria

Murray R.

Sturt Hwy.

Darling R.

Merbein
Mildura
Red Cliffs

MALLEE CLIFFS NATIONAL PARK

MURRAY-KULKYNE PARK

Murrumbidgee R.

Hay

Balranald

HATTAH-KULKYNE NATIONAL PARK

Hattah

Murray Valley Hwy.

Calder Hwy.

PINK LAKES STATE PARK

Ouyen

Swan Hill

Murray R.

Cobb Hwy.

75

Ouyen Hwy.

Underbool

12

Calder Hwy.

16

WYPERFELD NATIONAL PARK

Sunraysia Hwy.

79

Kerang

Cohuna
Gunbower

Echuca

BIG DESERT WILDERNESS AREA

Lake Albacutya

121

Birchip

Avoca R.

Loddon R.

Loddon Valley

16

Sheppart

Lake Hindmarsh

Hwy.

Charlton

Midland Hwy.

Western Hwy.

8

Nhill

Borung Hwy.

Warracknabeal

Wedderburn

79

Eaglehawk

Hwy.

Northern Hwy.

Goulbur

Dimboola

Henty Hwy.

Wimmera Hwy.

Sunraysia Hwy.

Bendigo
Maldon

Mitchellstown

LITTLE DESERT NAT'L PARK

Horsham

Wimmera R.

Castlemaine

Seymour

Wimmera Hwy.

Wartook

8

Maryborough

Midland Hwy.

Calder Hwy.

75

Edenhope

Glenelg R.

Halls Gap

Zumstein

Stawell Avoca

Pyrenees

Hepburn Springs

Daylesford

79

Yarr Valle

GRAMPIANS NATIONAL PARK

8

Ararat

Western Hwy.

31

GARIWERD NATIONAL PARK

Casterton

Glenelg Hwy.

Ballarat

Western Hwy.

Melbourne

Yarra Maro

Hamilton

OTWAY RANGES

Werribee

1

Macarthur

Mortlake

Hamilton Hwy.

Darlington

Geelong

Dandenong

Port Phillip Bay

Mornin

Nelson

LOWER GLENELG NATIONAL PARK

Woolsthorpe

Camperdown

Barwon R.

Colac

1

Torquay

Bellarine Peninsula

Queenscli

Portsea

Portland

Princes Hwy.

Port Fairy

Warrnambool

Lorne

MORNINGTON PENINSULA

PHILLIP I.

Peterborough

Port Campbell

PORT CAMPBELL NAT'L PARK

Princetown

Apollo Bay

OTWAY NAT'L PARK

AUSTRALIA

Bass Strait

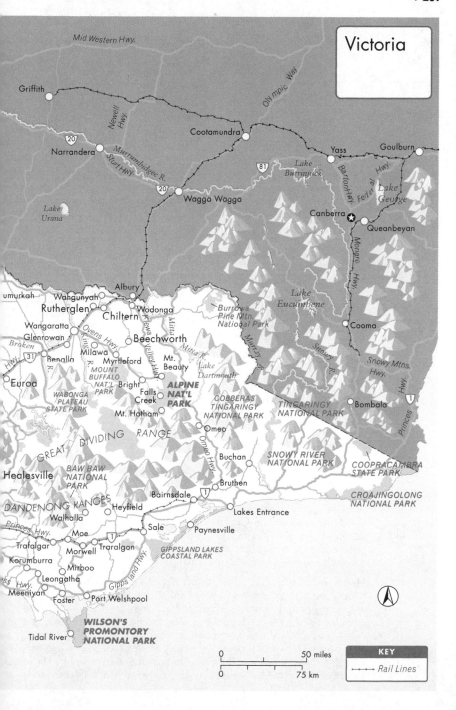

Victoria

Mid Western Hwy.

Olympic Way

Griffith

Newell Hwy.

Cootamundra

Yass

Goulburn

[20]

Narrandera

Sturt Hwy.

Murrumbidgee R.

[81]

Lake Burrinjuck

Barton Hwy.

Federal Hwy.

Lake George

[20]

Wagga Wagga

Canberra ★

Monaro Hwy.

Queanbeyan

Lake Urana

Lake Eucumbene

umurkah

Wahgunyah

Albury

Rutherglen

Chiltern

Wodonga

Burrowa Pine Mtn. National Park

Cooma

Wangaratta

Ovens Hwy.

Kiewa Valley Hwy.

Mitta

Glenrowan

King R.

Beechworth

Murray R.

Snowy R.

Broken

[31]

Benalla

Milawa

Myrtleford

Mt. Beauty

Lake Dartmouth

Snowy Mtns. Hwy.

Hwy.

Euroa

R.

MOUNT BUFFALO NAT'L PARK

Bright

ALPINE NAT'L PARK

COBBERAS TINGARINGY NATIONAL PARK

TINGARINGY NATIONAL PARK

Bombala

Princes Hwy.

WABONGA PLATEAU STATE PARK

Falls Creek

Mt. Hotham

[1]

GREAT DIVIDING RANGE

Omeo

Omeo Hwy.

Buchan

SNOWY RIVER NATIONAL PARK

COOPRACAMBRA STATE PARK

Healesville

BAW BAW NATIONAL PARK

Bruthen

CROAJINGOLONG NATIONAL PARK

DANDENONG RANGES

Heyfield

Bairnsdale

[1]

Lakes Entrance

Princes Hwy.

Walhalla

Moe

Sale

Paynesville

Trafalgar

Morwell

[1]

Traralgon

Gippsland Hwy.

GIPPSLAND LAKES COASTAL PARK

Korumburra

Mirboo

Leongatha

Gippsland Hwy.

ss

Hwy.

Meeniyan

Foster

Port Welshpool

Tidal River

WILSON'S PROMONTORY NATIONAL PARK

0   50 miles
0   75 km

KEY

╟──┼──┼─→ Rail Lines

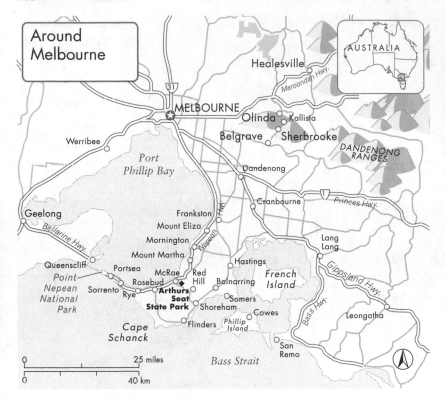

Around
Melbourne

AUSTRALIA

Healesville

Maroondah Hwy.

MELBOURNE Olinda Kallista

Werribee

Belgrave Sherbrooke

DANDENONG RANGES

Port
Phillip Bay

Dandenong

Cranbourne Princes Hwy.

Geelong

Bellarine Hwy.

Frankston

Mount Eliza

Mornington

Mount Martha

Lang
Lang

Gippsland Hwy.

Queenscliff

Portsea

McRae Red
Hill

Hastings

French
Island

Point
Nepean
National
Park

Sorrento Rye

Rosebud

Balnarring

**Arthurs
Seat
State Park**

Somers

Shoreham

Cowes

Leongatha

Bass Hwy.

Flinders Phillip
Island

Cape
Schanck

San
Remo

0   25 miles

0   40 km

Bass Strait

Sassafras Kallista have clusters of antiques, Devonshire tea, and bric-a-brac shops. Nearby, the vine-carpeted Yarra Valley—home of many top-class wines—is a favorite at all times of the year, although local reds always taste better by a crackling open fire in autumn or winter.

Healesville
60 km (37 mi) northeast of Melbourne.

The township of Healesville began its days in the 1860s as a coach stop along the road to the Gippsland and Yarra Valley goldfields. Two decades later, when the region's gold mining declined, Healesville became a logging center that grew by leaps and bounds, especially after it was linked by rail with Melbourne in 1889.

Healesville's main street, lined with antiques dealers, two old art deco hotels, and a huddle of shops, makes for a pleasant wander after lunch at a nearby winery. From here you can travel to Marysville, where pathways lead past the Steavensons Falls and through forests of beech and mountain ash trees. Another option is to take the spectacular **Acheron Way** drive, which winds over the summit of the Black Spur range, meandering through forests of towering mountain ash trees and tree ferns before circling back to Warburton. Along the way you'll hear the song of bellbirds and smell the pungent aroma of eucalyptus. If you feel like getting out of the car to stretch your legs, find the 4-km (2½-mi) Acheron Way Walk, just past Alexandra.

The most popular way to sample the wines and see the vineyards of the Yarra Valley is on a winery tour. Most tours depart from Melbourne and include four to five wineries and lunch; alternatively, you could concoct your own leisurely wine tour of the region. One of the best times to visit the Yarra Valley is in February, when the Grape Grazing Festival features wine tastings, music, and fine cuisine. On Grape Grazing Day 21, wineries present two meals designed by top regional chefs—and matched by two superb wines—to an accompaniment of live music.

★ Take one of the daily tours at **De Bortoli** (✉ Pinnacle La., Dixon's Creek ☎ 03/5965–2271) to follow the wine-making process through vineyards and barrel sheds. Chardonnays and rieslings are specialties, and tastings are offered. The restaurant, which has stunning views of the surrounding vines, landscaped gardens, and mountains, serves delectable dishes like Yarra Valley goat cheese panna cotta with pink grapefruit; kid goat slow-roasted with sage, oregano, and pumpkin; and double-roasted duck with braised chicory and a Campari–blood orange sauce.

Domaine Chandon (✉ Maroondah Hwy. between Coldstream and Healesville, Green Point ☎ 03/9739–1110) schedules tours that take visitors through the step-by-step production of sparkling wine, including visits to the vines, the bottling area, and the riddling room. Tastings are in the beautiful Green Point Room, where huge glass windows overlook the vines. Platters of regional cheeses and fruits are available to accompany your vintage choices.

Taking a walk through the tranquil bush exhibits at the **Healesville Sanctuary,** you can come face-to-face with wedge-tailed eagles, grumpy wombats, nimble sugar gliders, and shy platypus. ✉ *Badger Creek Rd.* ☎ *03/5957–2800* ✇ *A$19* ✇ *Daily 9–5.*

Several pungent reds and whites—including notable pinot noir, shiraz, cabernet merlot, and chardonnay—are ready for sampling at **Kellybrook Winery** (✉ Fulford Rd., Wonga Park ☎ 03/9722–1304), where visitors can attend tastings and then wander through the vineyards. The restaurant serves such delicacies as home-cured gravlax of Yarra Valley trout fillets; seafood salad poached in herb-and-wine broth; and porterhouse steak served with wild mushroom ragout and Kellybrook Shiraz jus.

Rochford Wines (formerly known as Eyton on Yarra) (✉ Maroondah Hwy. and Hill Rd., Coldstream ☎ 03/5962–2119) inhabits a striking-looking property; an architect-designed building crafted almost entirely of glass looks over the vineyards and rolling green paddocks here. There's a wine-tasting bar and a restaurant, and live music is played in the vineyard from December through March. Tastings are 10 to 5 daily except Christmas.

Skirted by acres of sprawling vineyards, **St. Huberts** (✉ St. Huberts Rd., Coldstream ☎ 03/9739–1118) produces a wide selection of highly regarded wines, including cabernet sauvignon, pinot noir, chardonnay, merlot, and roussanne. There's a picnic area and barbecue facilities, as well as free jazz performances on summer Sundays.

> **off the beaten path**

GEORGE TINDALE MEMORIAL GARDEN – This 6-acre garden has azaleas, camellias, and hydrangeas that spill down the hillsides, depending on the season. It's located just 8 km (5 mi) north of Belgrave in the little forest settlement of Sherbrooke, where whipbird calls echo calls through the trees. ⊠ *Sherbrooke Rd.* ☎ *13–1963* 🎟 *A$5.40* ☉ *Daily 10–5.*

PUFFING BILLY – This gleaming, narrow-gauge steam engine, located 40 km (25 mi) from Healesville in the town of Belgrave, was originally built in the early 1900s to assist 20th-century pioneers through the Dandenong mountains. Today the train still runs, and it's a great way to see the foothill landscapes. Daily trips between Belgrave and Emerald Lake pass through picture-book forests and trestle bridges. The standard 13-km (8-mi) trip takes an hour each way, and there are also lunch and evening trips. ⊠ *Old Monbulk Rd. (follow the signs), Belgrave* ☎ *03/9754–6800* ⊕ *www.puffingbilly.com.au* 🎟 *A$26 one-way, A$40 round-trip* ☉ *Call for hrs.*

WILLIAM RICKETTS SANCTUARY – Fern gardens, Aboriginal sculptures, moss-covered rocks, waterfalls, and mountain ash fill this 4-acre property on Mt. Dandenong. William Rickets, who established the sanctuary in the 1930s, meant it to stand as an embodiment of his philosophy: that people must act as custodians of the natural environment, as the Aborigines did. In 1960 the Victoria Government purchased the sanctuary and opened it to visitors. ⊠ *Mt. Dandenong Tourist Rd., Mt. Dandenong* ☎ *13–1963* 🎟 *A$6* ☉ *Daily 10–5.*

WHERE TO STAY & EAT
★ **$$$$**

✕🏨 **Chateau Yering.** Stockmen William, Donald, and James Ryrie built this homestead in the 1860s, and it was later one of the Yarra Valley's first vineyards. It's now a luxury hotel with opulent suites, as well as the upscale Eleanore's Restaurant. This is a favorite base for sunrise balloon flights over the Yarra Valley, followed by a champagne breakfast at the on-site Sweetwater Café. Balloon packages are A$1,015 for two. ⊠ *Melba Hwy., Yering 3770* ☎ *03/9237–3333 or 1800/237333* ⊕ *www. chateau-yering.com.au* ➥ *20 suites* ♨ *Restaurant, café, room service, tennis court, pool, hair salon, croquet* ☰ *AE, DC, MC, V* ¶◎¶ *MAP.*

¢–$
Fodor$Choice
★

✕🏨 **Healesville Hotel.** Housed in a restored 1910 building, this famous local lodge has bright, modern upstairs rooms with high ceilings, tall windows, and genteel touches such as handmade soaps. Downstairs, you can dine beneath pressed-metal ceilings on trout served with oil-drizzled yabbies (small, lobsterlike crustaceans), watercress, and capers, or lemon-roasted spatchcock served with eggplant. The adjoining Healesville Harvest Café serves and sells local wines, cheeses, and produce, and the cozy lounge has open fires in winter. The restaurant's wine list has won several Australian awards. ⊠ *256 Maroondah Hwy.* ☎ *03/5962–4002* ⊕ *www.healesvillehotel.com* ➥ *7 rooms* ♨ *Café, dining room, bar, lounge* ☰ *AE, DC, MC, V* ¶◎¶ *BP.*

★ **$$–$$$** ⊞ **Kangaroo Ridge.** These two cozy, mud-brick cabins are perched on a hillside with balconies overlooking the Yarra Valley. Inside you'll find polished jarrah wood floors, Persian rugs, and well-designed kitchens. Breakfast is included, and you can buy barbecue dinner hampers for A$25 per person. This a private and convenient base for exploring the nearby vineyards and orchards. ⊠ *38 Turners La. 3777* ☎ *03/5962–1122* ⊕ *www.kangarooridge.com.au* ⌫ *2 cabins* ⚲ *Kitchens* ☱ *AE, DC, MC, V* ❏◉❏ *BP.*

Olinda

48 km (30 mi) east of Melbourne, 10 km (6 mi) north of Belgrave, 8 km (5 mi) north of Sherbrooke.

The **National Rhododendron Gardens** are a sight to behold in October, when acres of white, mauve, and pink blooms make for spectacular countryside vistas. A small train provides transportation throughout the garden. For a perfect afternoon, combine your visit with tea and scones in one of the many little cafés dotting this part of the Dandenongs. ⊠ *Georgian Rd. off Olinda-Monbulk Rd.* ☎ *13–1963* ⊠ *A$6* ⊙ *Daily 10–5.*

WHERE TO EAT

$$ ✕ **Kenloch.** Built 90 years ago, and surrounded by 15 acres of terraced gardens, fern gullies, daffodils, and rhododendrons, this stately restaurant offers appropriately traditional English meals. The menu includes barbecued rack of lamb and beef rib eye, as well as finger sandwiches, small appetizers, and Devonshire teas. ⊠ *Mt. Dandenong Tourist Rd.* ☎ *03/9751–1008* ☱ *AE, DC, MC, V* ⊙ *No dinner Sun.–Thurs.*

$$ ✕ **Sacrebleu.** Succulent bistro fare is the specialty at this moderately priced restaurant, which is colorfully named for a mild, 14th-century Gallic expletive. The beef in red wine and tangy prawn salad are popular choices. The wine list mixes French and Australian labels. ⊠ *Shop 5, 1526 Mt. Dandenong Tourist Rd.* ☎ *03/9751–2520* ☱ *AE, DC, MC, V.*

$$ ✕ **Woods Sherbrooke.** Formerly a post office, this light-filled space is where chef Jason Dousset now whips up delicate, tantalizing fare. Menu choices include scallops grilled in the half shell with a citrus beurre blanc, and lobster-tail risotto served with sesame-ginger dressing. Meat lovers can order the Yarra Valley platter, with a five-spice venison burger, buffalo sausage, rabbit liver pâté, and venison prosciutto. ⊠ *21 Sherbrooke Rd.* ☎ *03/9755–2131* ☱ *MC, V* ⊙ *Closed Mon.–Wed. No dinner Sun.*

$ ✕ **Wild Oak Café.** At one of the oak tree–shaded outdoor tables here you can nibble on such delicate dishes as crab and pawpaw salad, accompanied by a glass of crisp chardonnay. Local musicians perform Friday night and Sunday afternoon. ⊠ *232 Ridge Rd.* ☎ *03/9751–2033* ☱ *AE, DC, MC, V* ⊙ *Closed Sun.–Wed.*

Mornington Peninsula

The Mornington Peninsula circles the southeastern half of Port Phillip Bay. Along the coast a string of seaside villages stretches from the larger towns of Frankston and Mornington to the summer holiday towns of Mount Martha, Rosebud, Rye, Sorrento, and Portsea. On the Western Port Bay side, the smaller settlements of Flinders, Somers, and Hastings have prettier, and quieter, beaches without the crowds.

Set aside at least a day for a drive down the peninsula, planning time for lunch and wine tasting. An afternoon cliff-top walk along the bluffs, or even a game of golf at Cape Schanck, is the perfect way to finish a day in this region. In summer pack a swimsuit and sunscreen for impromptu ocean dips as you make your way around the peninsula's string of attractive beaches.

Red Hill
121 km (75 mi) southeast of Melbourne.

Together with Main Ridge and Merricks, Red Hill is one of the state's premium producers of cool-climate wines, particularly pinot noir and shiraz. For an afternoon of fine wine, excellent seafood, and spectacular coastal views, plan a route that winds between vineyards. Red Hill has a busy produce and crafts market on the first Saturday morning of each month.

Dromana Estate (⌧ Harrisons Rd., Dromana ☏ 03/5987–3800) is one of the area's most beautiful wineries, run by Gary Crittenden, who produces three different varieties of wine under several labels. The Dromana Estate range is particularly notable, and includes chardonnay, pinot noir, cabernet, merlot, sauvignon blanc, and Schinus Molle chardonnay. Surrounded by rolling hills, the Vineyard Cafe overlooks a serene lake. Tastings are scheduled daily.

Red Hill Estate (⌧ Shoreham Rd., Red Hill South ☏ 03/5989–2838) is famous for its highly regarded Max's Restaurant, perched on a hillside with sweeping views over the 30-acre vineyards to Western Port Bay and Phillip Island. Dishes include coconut-and-coriander king prawns served on mango salsa, and Tuscan duck and red-wine sauce served with angelhair pasta. For dessert, don't miss the rich chocolate tart, served with Red Hill strawberries and double cream.

Established in 1977, **Stonier Winery** (⌧ Frankston–Flinders Rd., Merricks ☏ 03/5989–8300) is one of the peninsula's oldest vineyards. Notable wines here include chardonnay, pinot noir, and cabernet. Although there's no restaurant, cheeses and hors d'oeuvres accompany the daily tastings.

★ **T'Gallant Winemakers** (⌧ Corner of Mornington, Flinders, and Shand Rds., Main Ridge ☏ 03/5989–8660) produces such wines as the Imogen pinot gris, pinot noir, chardonnay, and muscat à petits grains. La Baracca Trattoria is always buzzing—the food is exceptional, with dishes made from local ingredients (some from the house herb garden). Try the tiny baked parcels of pecorino cheese wrapped in T'Gallant grapevine; piadina with prosciutto, taleggio, and arugula; or the spinach ricotta cannelloni drenched in zesty tomato sauce and shaved Parmesan.

WHERE TO EAT $$$ ✗ **Bittern Cottage.** Influenced by their adventures in northern Italy and southern France, chef-owners Jenny and Noel Burrows show off their provincial-style cooking skills using regional Australian produce. The set menu includes a trio of pâtés, plus wine-simmered duck breast. Blueberry *bavarois* (whipped cream and gelatin) makes a fine finish. ⌧ *2385*

Frankston–Flinders Rd., Bittern ☎ *03/5983–9506* ▭ *AE, DC, MC, V* ⊙ *Closed Mon.–Thurs.*

$$–$$$ ✕ **Poff's.** On a hillside with views across the vineyard and valley below, this modern restaurant is consistently rated one of the area's best. The menu is brief, and dishes are described with an austerity that downplays their caliber. Chef Sasha Esipoff's approach is to work with the best local ingredients in season, and the results—like mussels in a spicy broth, and other Asian-inspired creations—are delicious. The crème caramel is not to be missed. ⊹ *Red Hill Rd., 7 km (4½ mi) from McCrae* ☎ *03/ 5989–2566* ▭ *AE, DC, MC, V* ⊙ *Closed Mon.–Wed.*

$$–$$$ ✕ **Salix at Willow Creek.** While views through the restaurant's glass walls are spectacular year-round, Willow Creeks gardens break into a flurry of roses come autumn. The menu, which changes seasonally, always showcases local produce; if you're lucky, choices might include duck, venison, or fresh mushroom tart. Clever wine matches and a wonderfully friendly staff add to the experience. ✉ *166 Balnarring Rd., Merricks North* ☎ *03/5989–7640* ▭ *AE, DC, MC, V* ⊙ *No dinner weekdays; no lunch weekends.*

$–$$ ✕ **Monalto Vineyard & Olive Grove.** Overlooking an established vineyard **Fodor'sChoice** with vistas of rolling green hills, chef James Redfern prepares French-★ inspired food with the finest local ingredients: duck and chicken terrine with jack mushrooms; aged Red Hill goat cheese soufflé; roasted duck breast; and panfried blue-eye (a local fish) served with a sweet-pepper stew and herb emulsion. The wine list borrows from the best of Mornington's vintages. There are few better places in the state to while (or wine) away an afternoon. ✉ *33 Shoreham Rd., Red Hill South* ☎ *03/ 5989–8412* ▭ *AE, DC, MC, V.*

Arthurs Seat

76 km (47 mi) south of Melbourne, 10 km (6 mi) north of Red Hill.

Sweeping views of the surrounding countryside, Port Phillip Bay, Port Phillip Heads, and, on a clear day, the city skyline, the You Yangs and Mount Macedon are the attractions at **Arthurs Seat State Park.** Walking tracks meander through stands of eucalypts and a marked scenic drive snakes its way up the mountainside. Seawinds, a public garden established by a local gardener, Mr. Chapman, in the 1940s, also forms part of the park. Situated on the Mornington Peninsula, a short drive from Red Hill and Merricks, the park and its chairlift, which runs from the base of the mountain to the summit, are a draw both for local families and tourists. The mountain itself, also called Arthurs Seat, is the highest point on the Mornington Peninsula, and was named after Arthurs Seat in Edinburgh. Matthew Flinders was the first European to reach its summit after his ship entered the heads while making his circumnavigation of Australia in 1802. The chairlift, erected in 1960, has just reopened after an extensive makeover. Note that the road from Mornington is open at all times, so you can enjoy the spectacular mountaintop view even when the park is closed. ✉ *Arthurs Seat Rd. and Mornington Peninsula Hwy. Arthurs Seat* ☎ *03/5987–2565* ⛟ *Free; chairlift A$11 round-trip, A$8 one-way* ⊙ *Dec. and Jan., daily 10–6; Feb.–Nov., daily 11–5.*

en route | At the end of the Nepean Highway, in Portsea, turn left into Back Beach Road and make a right to **London Bridge,** a fantastic natural span carved by the ocean. Although the arch of the bridge connecting to the mainland actually collapsed in 1990, a beautiful island rock formation still remains, also in the shape of an arch. The sole of the Mornington Peninsula "boot" runs in a straight line for 28 km (17 mi), forming a long, narrow coastal park that ends at Cape Schanck. Here you can visit the **Cape Schanck Lighthouse and Museum** (⊠ Borneo Rd., Cape Schanck ☎ No phone). The sea can be violent along this coastline: in 1967 Australian prime minister Harold Holt drowned at Cheviot Beach just west of London Bridge. Swimming is advisable only where the beach is patrolled by lifeguards. Cape Schanck is also one of Victoria's largest golfing centers. The Moona Links course hosts the annual Australian Open Championships.

Sorrento

93 km (58 mi) southwest of Melbourne, 25 km (16 mi) west of Arthurs Seat.

An evocative Italian name befits one of the region's prettiest bay-side beach towns and most exclusive resorts. Sorrento is also the peninsula's oldest settlement, and thus is dotted with numerous historic buildings and National Trust sites (among them, the Collins Settlement Historical Site, which marks the first settlement site at Sullivan Bay; and the Nepean Historical Society Museum, with its displays of Aboriginal artifacts and settlers' tools). In summer the town transforms from a sleepy seaside village into a hectic holiday gathering place. Sorrento back beach, with its rock pools and cliff-side trails, and Point King, with its piers and boathouses, are the two most popular hangouts.

In the cooler months Sorrento's attractions include art galleries and numerous antiques, arts, and crafts shops. The main street is lined with little cafés and fish-and-chips shops tucked in between. After grabbing lunch, catch a ferry to Queenscliff and join the Great Ocean Road for its spectacular journey to Lorne, on the other side of the bay.

Bayplay Adventure Lodge offers a range of activities including sea- and surf-kayaking, scuba instruction, horse riding, surfing lessons, sailing, boat and fishing trips, and sky- and scuba diving. Half-day tours start from $75, full-day trips from $95. ⊠ *46 Canterbury Jetty Rd., Blairgowrie* ☎ *03/5988–0188.*

Moonraker Charters gives you the chance to swim with a pod of gentle wild dolphins that inhabits Port Phillip Bay. Your jaunt includes a boat ride out into the bay, where wet suits, snorkels, and flippers are supplied. ⊠*Sorrento car ferry terminal* ☎ *03/5984–4211* ⊞ *Sightseeing A$40, dolphin swim A$80, tour from Melbourne A$112* ☉ *Pier 24 hrs; boat departures: Dec.–Feb., daily at 8, noon, and 4; Mar.–Nov., daily at 9 and 1.*

Phillip Island

★ *125 km (78 mi) south of Melbourne.*

A nightly waddling parade of miniature fairy penguins from the sea to their burrows in nearby dunes is this island's main draw, attracting throngs of onlookers on summer weekends and holidays. But Phillip Island also has an unusually beautiful coast, wildlife parks where indigenous species including koalas and kangaroos make their homes, and enough good dining and lodging choices that you may be tempted to stay longer than a day. The island also marks the beginning of Victoria's Gippsland region, a spread of spectacular forests, beaches, and alpine national parks.

The seaside town of **Cowes** is an unpretentious place with beachwear stores, pizzerias, and a few decent eateries, most within walking distance of lodgings. Restaurant and hotel bookings are essential in the busy summer months.

The **Phillip Island Grand Prix Circuit** continues the island's long involvement with motor sport, dating back to 1928 when the Australian Grand Prix (motor racing) was run on local unpaved roads. The circuit was completely redeveloped in the 1980s, and in 1989 hosted the first Australian Motorcycle Grand Prix, which has made its home there. The circuit hosts regular club-car and motorcycle races as well as big-ticket events, and the museum and restaurant are surprisingly good. Guided tours of the track depart daily at 11 and 4. ⊠ *Back Beach Rd, Phillip Island.* ☎ *03/5952–9400* ✆ *Entry A$12, with guided tour A$20, plus $5 for museum entry* ۞ *Daily 9–5.*

The place to go for the nightly fairy penguin parade is **Summerland Beach.** It's memorable to see fluffy young penguin chicks standing outside their burrows, waiting for their parents to return from the sea with their dinner. Watching the parade is hardly a back-to-nature experience, however; the penguins emerge from the surf onto a floodlighted beach, while a commentator in a tower describes their progress over a public address system. Spectators, who watch from concrete bleachers, may number several thousand on a busy night. Camera flashbulbs are forbidden. The spectacle begins at around 8 PM each night—but if you don't mind getting up at the crack of dawn, you can have breakfast with the penguins too. ⊠ *Summerland Beach, eastern peninsula (follow signs)* ☎ *03/5956–8300, 03/5956–8691, or 1300/366422* ⊕ *www.penguins. org.au* ✆ *A$16* ۞ *Daily sunrise–sunset.*

Out past the penguin parade, at the end of the Summerland Peninsula, you can see two particularly captivating rock formations. At low tide you can walk across a basalt causeway to the **Nobbies** and take in the splendid views along the island's wild northern coast. Thousands of shearwaters (muttonbirds) nest here from September to April, when they return north to the Bering Strait in the Arctic. Farther out, **Seal Rocks** host Australia's largest colony of fur seals; more than 5,000 creatures bask on the rocky platforms and caper about here in midsummer.

Fine dining options are few and far between on the island. In summer, when crowds descend on the island in droves, visitors are best advised to pick up a bundle of fish-and-chips and head to the beach to eat them (throwing the last chips to the seagulls is an Australian tradition). The three eateries below are reliably good—but if your accommodation offers cooking facilities, pick up some fresh fish and prepare it yourself.

$–$$ ✗ **Harry's On The Esplanade.** Spilling onto an upstairs terrace above Cowes' picturesque jetty, Harry's is something of a Phillip Island institution. Its menu, which changes daily, draws heavily on local produce like Coffin Bay oysters and Phillip Island–raised beef and lamb. Menu favorites include German-style sausages served with mashed potato and sauerkraut, and duck with peppercorn sauce. The wine list has an Australian emphasis and features several vintages from the Gippsland region. ⊠ *115 Thompson Ave., Cowes* ☎ *03/5952–6226* ▤ *AE, DC, MC, V.*

$–$$ ✗ **The Inferno.** Generous portions of oysters, peppered blue swimmer crabs, braised lamb shanks, and squid-ink pasta accompany this restaurant's spectacular views over Western Port Bay. Reservations are essential in the busy summer months. ⊠ *The Continental, the Esplanade, Cowes* ☎ *03/5952–2316* ▤ *AE, DC, V.*

$–$$ ✗ **Jetty Restaurant.** The intimate yet modern dining room here has views overlooking Western Port Bay. An expansive menu begins with oysters and includes a range of pasta, salad, steak, and seafood dishes. You can opt for an old favorite such as rack of lamb or try a whole grilled barramundi, pepper squid, or Malaysian chicken curry. ⊠ *Thomas Ave and the Esplanade, Cowes* ☎ *03/5952–2060* ▤ *AE, DC, V.*

$$–$$$ ▣ **Abaleigh on Lovers Walk.** A fine beach right on the doorstep is just one of the pluses at this chic bed-and-breakfast. The property comprises one two-story apartment (which sleeps up to six people) and two luxury studios; all feature open fires, hot tubs, sun-drenched courtyards, and water views. Breakfast baskets, beach chairs and umbrellas, fishing lines, and even sunscreen are included in the tariff. Lovers Walk— a romantic waterfront pathway—leads right into the center of Cowes from the front door. ⊠ *2 and 6 Roy Ct., Cowes 3922* ☎ *03/5952–5649* ⇋ *1 apartment, 2 studios* ⚭ *Kitchens, outdoor hot tub, beach, fishing, laundry facilities, free parking; no room phones, no kids* ▤ *MC, V* ⦿*CP.*

$–$$ ▣ **Kaloha Resort.** A few minutes' walk from the beach and the center of Cowes, this quiet, leafy resort has one- and two-bedroom suites and a five-room apartment. Twelve of the suites have hot tubs. The restaurant, with an imaginative, Asian-inspired menu, is surprisingly good, and the prices are refreshingly moderate. Advance bookings are essential. ⊠ *Steele and Chapel Sts., Cowes 3922* ☎ *03/5952–2179* 🖷 *03/5952–2723* ⇋ *34 suites, 1 apartment* ⚭ *Restaurant, picnic area, some in-room hot tubs, some microwaves, in-room VCRs, pool, beach, bar, playground, laundry service, free parking; no phones in some rooms* ▤ *AE, MC, V.*

Around Melbourne A to Z

CAR RENTAL

Renting a car in Melbourne and driving south is the most practical way of seeing the Mornington Peninsula, although there are daily V-Line bus services from Melbourne to much of regional Victoria. To reach Phillip Island, you can drive from Melbourne along the B420, or catch a ferry from Stony Point on the Mornington Peninsula.

EMERGENCIES

In an emergency, dial **000** to reach an ambulance, the police, or the fire department.

The Phillip Island Medical Group has offices in Cowes and San Remo; both are open weekdays 9–5:30 PM and Saturday 9–11:30 AM. There's also a pharmacy right next to the offices in Cowes.

⑦ **Phillip Island Medical Group** ✉ 14 Warley St., Cowes ☎ 03/5952-2072 ✉ 123 Marine Parade, San Remo ☎ 03/5678-5402.

TOURS

Day trips from Melbourne are run by local tour operators, including Australian Pacific Tours, Gray Line, and AAT Kings. Tours of the Dandenongs cost A$66 (half day) to A$109 (full day), while those to the Phillip Island Penguin Parade cost A$86 (penguins only) to A$109 (with a full-day island tour).

⑦ **AAT Kings** ✉ 180 Swanston St., City Center, Melbourne ☎ 1300/556100. **Australian Pacific Tours** ✉ 180 Swanston St., City Center, Melbourne ☎ 03/9663-1611. **Gray Line** ✉ 180 Swanston St., City Center, Melbourne ☎ 03/9663-4455.

VISITOR INFORMATION

The Victoria Information Centre is open weekdays 9 to 6, weekends 9 to 5. The Phillip Island Information Centre and all other offices listed are open daily 9 to 5.

⑦ **Melbourne Visitor Centre** ✉ Federation Square, Flinders St. and St. Kilda Rd., Melbourne ☎ 03/9658-9658 🖶 03/9650-6168. **Mornington Peninsula Visitor Centre** ✉ 3598 Point Nepean Rd., Dromana ☎ 03/5987-3078. **Phillip Island Information Centre** ✉ Tourist Rd., Newhaven ☎ 03/5956-7447 or 1300/366422 🖶 03/5956-7905 ✉ Watt St., Wonthaggi 3995 ☎ 03/5671-2444. **Yarra Valley Visitor Information Centre** ✉ Old Courthouse, Harker St., Healesville ☎ 03/5962-2600 🖶 03/5962-2040.

WEST COAST REGION

Victoria's Great Ocean Road, which heads west from Melbourne along rugged, windswept beaches, is arguably the country's most spectacular coastal drive. The road, built during the Great Depression atop majestic cliffs, occasionally dips down to sea level. Here in championship surfing country some of the world's finest waves pound mile after mile of uninhabited, golden, sandy beaches. As you explore the coastline, be sure to check out Bell's Beach, site of the annual Easter Surfing Classic, one of the premier events of the surfing world. But you'll want to think twice before bringing your own board here; the fierce undertow all along this coast can be deadly.

Although this region is actually on the southeast coast of the Australian mainland, it lies to the west of Melbourne, and so Melburnians refer to it as the "West Coast." From the city, you should allow two or more days for a West Coast sojourn.

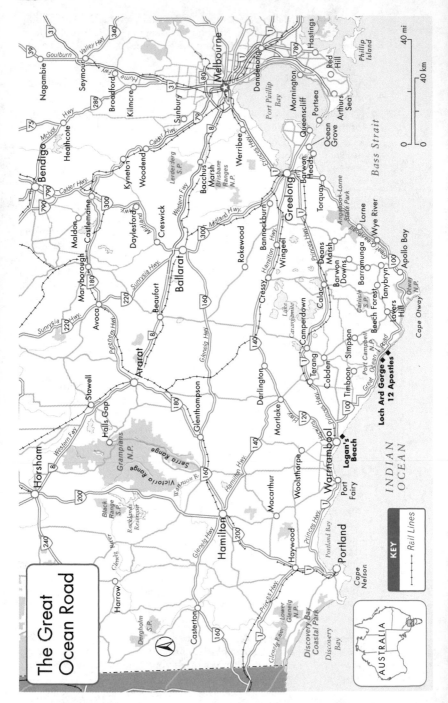

The Great Ocean Road

KEY

⊢⊢⊢⊢ Rail Lines

AUSTRALIA

Werribee

32 km (20 mi) southwest of Melbourne, 157 km (97 mi) west of Phillip Island.

Once a country town, now a generally undistinguished outer suburb of Melbourne, Werribee is notable for the glorious Werribee Park Mansion and its attendant safari-style zoo.

Victoria's Open Range Zoo, part of the original Werribee Park property, is a 200-acre safari-style zoo of the highest caliber. Safari buses travel through a landscape that replicates southern Africa, passing among giraffes, lions, rhinos, zebras, and hippos. A walk-through section houses cheetahs, apes, meerkats, and other African animals in natural conditions. Overnight slumber safaris (A$180), held September through April, let you watch wildlife at feeding time, partake in a "Rhythm of Africa" musical performance and drum lesson, and get close up and personal with a rhino or giraffe. Australian animals also live in the park. ☒ *K Rd.* ☎ *03/9731–9600* ⊕ *www.zoo.org.au* ☒ *A$19* ☉ *Daily 9–5, tours 10–3:40.*

The 60-room Italianate **Werribee Park Mansion,** dating from 1877, is furnished with period antiques. More than 25 acres of formal gardens surround the mansion. This was one of the grandest homes in the colony, built by wealthy pastoralists Thomas and Andrew Chirnside. Part of the mansion is now the luxurious Mansion hotel, winery, and day spa. You can take a self-guided tour of the property; or come on weekends for wine tasting, musical performances, and other special events. ☒ *K Rd.* ☎ *03/9741–2444* ☒ *Entry A$11.50, guided tour A$14.40* ☉ *Daily 10–5.*

en route

Set on the western shores of Corio Bay, the city of **Geelong**—Victoria's second largest—has a waterfront route that's worth driving along, even if you don't plan to stop. About 40 km (25 mi) west of Werribee on the Princes Highway, turn left into Bell Parade and follow the palm-lined esplanade as it meanders past gracious homes, gardens, and a harbor dotted with yachts. It's a good place to stretch your legs by the water and have lunch as you head down toward the Great Ocean Road.

Queenscliff

103 km (64 mi) southwest of Melbourne, 71 km (44 mi) south of Werribee.

The lovely coastal village of Queenscliff, and nearby sibling Point Lonsdale, make for a worthy—and well-signposted—detour on the drive between Werribee and Lorne. In the late 19th century Queenscliff was a favorite weekend destination for well-to-do Melburnians, who traveled on paddle steamers or by train to stay at the area's grand hotels. Some, like the Vue Grand and the Queenscliff Hotel, draw tourists to this day.

Good restaurants and quiet charm are also traits of Queenscliff. The best beach is at Lonsdale Bay, where a long stretch of golden sand and gentle surf makes a great place to wade, walk, or swim in summer. The playground of families during the day and dog walkers come dusk, Queenscliff is a restful alternative to the resort towns of Sorrento and Portsea on the other side of the bay. Point Lonsdale, once a sleepy little village known primarily for its lighthouse, is now a busy summer resort. The annual Queenscliff Music Festival, on the last weekend in November, draws hundreds of visitors to town.

Where to Stay & Eat

$$$$ ✕⛩ **Vue Grand Hotel.** Built by George Admans in 1881, the Vue Grand blends old-world elegance with modern trimmings (you'll realize this as you laze in the heated indoor swimming pool while listening to classical music). Billiard tables, a gymnasium, and a conservatory also beckon, although the hotel's prime focus is its grand dining room. Filled with flowers and with live piano music every Saturday night, it is one of the finest places on the peninsula to wine and dine. Guest rooms feature high ceilings, antique furniture, and period fittings. Snapshots depicting the hotel's history adorn walls in the foyer and bar-lounge. ⊠ *46 Hesse St., 3225* 🕾 *03/5258–1544* 🛏 *32 rooms, including 5 deluxe suites* ♦ *Pool, gym, indoor hot tub, free parking; no kids* ☴ *AE, DC, MC, V* ⦿| *BP.*

$$–$$$$ ✕⛩ **Queenscliff Hotel.** Gloriously restored to its original, 19th-century
Fodor'sChoice state, and resplendent with fresh flower arrangements, the Queenscliff
★ has soaring, pressed-metal ceilings, stained-glass windows, antique furnishings, and opulent sitting rooms graced with open fires and enormous armchairs. If you're after period charm, rather than spacious modernity, this is the place for you. Dining is offered in the small formal room, a leafy conservatory, or an outdoor courtyard; main courses might include braised rabbit leg with parsnip. There's a separate menu available for vegetarians. ⊠ *16 Gellibrand St., 3225* 🕾 *03/5258–1066* 🛏 *21 rooms, 2 with bath* ♦ *Restaurant, library, laundry facilities, free parking; no a/c, no room phones, no room TVs* ☴ *AE, DC, MC, V* ⦿| *BP.*

$$–$$$$ ✕⛩ **Athelstane House.** This charming, welcoming old home has been a guesthouse since 1860. Nine rooms include four standards, three balcony rooms, one deluxe balcony room (with a corner whirlpool tub), and one apartment. The restaurant is famed for dishes like butter lettuce–and–scallop salad, and paella with local mussels, scallops, chorizo, and fresh fish. Wines from the local Bellarine vineyards accompany lunch and dinner meals; at breakfast you can sit outside in one of the large courtyards. ⊠ *4 Hobson St., 3225* 🕾 *03/5258–1024* 🛏 *9 rooms* ♦ *Restaurant, room service, some in-room hot tubs, in-room VCRs, free parking; no kids* ☴ *AE, DC, MC, V* ⦿| *BP.*

⸠ **en route** ⸡ From Queenscliff, follow signs toward the Great Ocean Road for 45 km (28 mi) to **Torquay,** Australia's premier surfing and windsurfing resort, and Bell's Beach, famous for its Easter surfing contests and its October international windsurfing competitions. Great Ocean Road, a positively magnificent coastal drive, officially begins at Eastern View, 10 km (6 mi) east of Lorne. The seaside towns of Anglesea, Aireys Inlet, and Fairhaven also make good warm-weather swimming stops.

Lorne

140 km (87 mi) southwest of Melbourne, 95 km (59 mi) southwest of Queenscliff, 50 km (31 mi) southwest of Torquay.

A little town at the edge of the Otway Mountain Range, Lorne is the site of both a wild celebration every New Year's Eve and the popular Pier-to-Pub Swim held shortly thereafter. Some people make their reservations a year in advance for these events. It's also the home of the Great Otway Classic, a footrace held annually on the second weekend in June.

Where to Stay & Eat

★ **$$-$$$** ✕ **Marks.** Fresh seafood—from fried calamari to grilled flathead—is the draw at this sea-view Lorne institution. Sea bream on mashed potatoes with a parsley butter sauce, Moroccan fish cakes, or ocean trout with preserved lemon couscous are other options, while berry crumble will tempt those with a sweet tooth. ⊠ *124 Mountjoy Parade* ☎ *03/5289–2787* ▤ *AE, DC, MC, V.*

★ **$-$$** ✕ **Reifs.** Relaxed and laid back, this hangout and eatery is best known for its squid, made with chili pepper, lime, and mirin (a Japanese liqueur). Golden-skinned chicken with polenta wedges is another standout, while simple dishes such as nachos and fish-and-chips are served up with care. ⊠ *84 Mountjoy Parade* ☎ *03/5289–2366* ▤ *AE, DC, MC, V.*

¢-$$$$ ⌂ **Erskine on the Beach.** Some of the lodgings on this 12-acre property are in an 1868 guesthouse, surrounded by gracious gardens and perfectly manicured croquet lawns. Rooms are cozy, with open fireplaces and comfortable, if simple, furnishings. Grass tennis courts and a beach are nearby. The adjoining Erskine Resort is more upscale and is priced accordingly—although guesthouse patrons can use the facilities at no charge. Rates include breakfast and use of facilities. ⊠ *Mountjoy Parade, 3232* ☎ *03/5289–1209* ⊕ *www.erskinehouse.com.au* ⇖ *55 rooms (guesthouse), 120 suites (resort)* ♿ *Restaurant, putting green, 8 tennis courts, beach, croquet, laundry service, free parking; no room phones, no TV in some rooms* ▤ *AE, DC, MC, V* ☉ *BP.*

$-$$$ ⌂ **Stanmorr Bed and Breakfast.** Built in the 1920s, this gracious homestead sits a stone's throw from the water, just beyond Lorne's main huddle of shops. Rooms are spacious and private, with picture windows and private balconies offering water views and opportunities to meet colorful locals—including king parrots, rosellas, and kookaburras. Hot tubs, open fireplaces, and home-cooked breakfasts (included in the room rate) add to the appeal. ⊠ *64 Otway St., 3232* ☎ *03/5289–1530* ⊕ *www.stanmorr.com* ⇖ *3 rooms, 2 suites, 1 studio* ♿ *Dining room, lounge* ▤ *AE, DC, MC, V* ☉ *BP.*

> **en route** About an hour's drive and 70 km (43 mi) from Lorne (follow the Great Ocean Road until it joins Skenes Creek Road, then take Forrest Apollo Bay Road to Beech Forest Road, then Colac Lavers Hill Road until you reach the signed turnoff to Phillips Track) you'll find the entrance to the **Otway Fly,** a fabulous new attraction at Otway National Park (☎ 13–1963 or 1800/300477 ⊕ www.otwayfly.com). The Fly is a 1,969-foot-long elevated treetop walk, where you can

meander on a steel walkway structure (one section is springboard-cantilevered, and gently bounces as you pass over Young's Creek) above the rain-forest canopy. You'll see the tops of giant myrtle beech, blackwood, and mountain ash trees, as well as spectacular views of the surrounding region. It's open daily 9–5; tickets are A$15.

Port Campbell National Park

Fodor's Choice *225 km (140 mi) southwest of Melbourne, 56 km (35 mi) west of*
★ *Lorne.*

Stretching some 30 km (19 mi) along the southern Victoria coastline, Port Campbell National Park is the site of some of the most famously beautiful geological formations in Australia. Along this coast the ferocious Southern Ocean has gnawed at the limestone cliffs for centuries, creating a sort of badlands-by-the-sea, where strangely shaped columns of towering rock stand offshore amid the surf. The most famous of these formations is the Twelve Apostles, as much a symbol for Victoria as the Sydney Opera House is for New South Wales. Loch Ard Gorge, named after the iron-hulled clipper that wrecked on the shores of nearby Mutton Bird Island in 1878, is another spectacular place to walk. Four of the *Loch Ard*'s victims are buried in a nearby cemetery, while a sign by the gorge tells the story of the ship and its crew.

The best time to visit the park is January–April, when you can also witness the boisterous bird life on nearby Mutton Bird Island. Toward nightfall, hundreds of hawks and kites circle the island in search of baby muttonbirds emerging from their protective burrows. The hawks and kites beat a hasty retreat at the sight of thousands of adult shearwaters approaching with food for their chicks as the last light fades from the sky. ⊠ *Park Office: Tregea St., Port Campbell* ☎ *03/1319–63.*

The **Port Campbell Visitors Centre** (⊠ 26 Morris St., Port Campbell ☎ 03/5598–6089) is open daily 9 to 5. A self-guided, 1½-hour Discovery Walk begins near Port Campbell Beach, where it's safe to swim. The pounding surf and undertow are treacherous at other nearby beaches.

Where to Stay & Eat

$–$$ ✕ **Waves.** You won't see any waves from this relaxed, main-street eatery, but you will find enormous breakfasts and fireside seafood dinners, a spacious sundeck, and friendly waitstaff. The menu here has a little of everything and includes pickled whiting, chicken wontons, zucchini flowers stuffed with pancetta and goat cheese, and char-grilled rudderfish. ⊠ *29 Lord St. Port Campbell* ☎ *03/5598–6111* ⊟ *AE, DC, MC, V.*

$$–$$$ ⬚ **Southern Ocean Villas.** Ideally situated on the edge of Port Campbell National Park, within short walking distance of the town center and beach, these 20 architect-designed luxury villas are stylishly furnished, and fitted with polished wood floors, picture windows, and high ceilings. Each unit has two bedrooms and an upstairs loft. One villa accommodates six. ⊠ *2 McCue St., Port Campbell 3269* ☎ *03/5598–4200* ⊕ *www.southernoceanvillas.com* ⬚ *20 villas* ⚲ *Kitchens, cable TV with movies, laundry facilities* ⊟ *AE, DC, MC, V.*

$ ⊞ **Daysy Hill Country Cottages.** These six sandstone-and-cedar cottages, set alongside manicured gardens, have views over the Newfield Valley. Inside, the spacious rooms have comfortable couches, wooden furnishings, open fireplaces, TVs, and CD players. ⊠ *7353 Timboon/Port Campbell Rd., Port Campbell 3269* ☎ *03/5598–6226* ⊕ *www. greatoceanroad.nu/daysyhill* ⇨ *6 cottages* ⚒ *Kitchenettes, BBQs, laundry facilities* ⊟ *AE, DC, MC, V.*

Warrnambool

262 km (162 mi) southwest of Melbourne, 122 km (76 mi) west of Lorne, 66 km (41 mi) west of Port Campbell.

A friendly settlement of hardy souls who earn their living on both land and sea, Warrnambool makes the most of its location between the beaches and the big country farms inland. It's also the closest big town to Port Campbell National Park, and thus attracts tourists who come for the area's myriad swimming, surfing, and fishing opportunities. The February Wunta Fiesta is the town's main event, which includes whaleboat races, a seafood and wine festival, a carnival, and children's activities.

☾ A highlight in Warrnambool is **Flagstaff Hill Maritime Village,** a re-created 19th-century village built around a fort constructed in 1887 during one of the Russian scares that intermittently terrified the colony. In the village you can visit an 1853 lighthouse, wander through the old fort, or board the *Reginald M,* a trading ship from the South Australian Gulf. ⊠ *Merri and Banyan Sts.* ☎ *03/5564–7841* ⊡ *A$14* ⊙ *Daily 9–5.*

★ The sheltered bay at **Logan's Beach,** 3 km (2 mi) east of Warrnambool, has a beautiful setting and smooth sands for strolling. In winter southern right whales arrive to give birth to their calves, and sometimes swim close to shore. The whales take up residence here from June to September and are easily observed from a cliff-side viewing platform.

Tower Hill State Game Reserve, on an extinct volcano now green with vegetation, is a half-hour drive northwest of Warrnambool. The reserve is an attempt to return part of the land to a native state by introducing local flora and fauna. Spend some time at the park's natural history center and then walk around the trails. It's 14 km (8½ mi) from Warrnambool. ⊠ *Princes Hwy., Koroit* ☎ *03/5565–9202* ⊡ *Free* ⊙ *Reserve daily 8–5, natural history center daily 9:30–4:30.*

☾ The staff at the **Warrnambool Visitor Information Centre** can advise you of the southern right whales' presence and direct you to the best observation points. While here you can collect a Kid's Country Treasure Hunt Guide kit. Children who answer the questions on the "treasure map," which is designed to introduce them to Warrnambool and its surroundings, get a free badge, book, or decal. ⊠ *600 Raglan Parade* ☎ *03/5564–7837* ⊙ *Daily 9–5.*

Where to Stay & Eat

$$ ✕ **Pippies by the Bay.** Named after shellfish that live in the shallows off Warrnambool, this sophisticated eatery is the best place in town to eat

seafood. The local crayfish are not to be missed—nor are the fried Tasmanian oysters served with citrus aioli, or the braised pork belly served with white-bean confit. Vegetarians are catered to with a special three-course degustation menu. ☒ *Flagstaff Hill, Merri St.* ☎ *03/5561–2188* ▤ *AE, DC, MC, V.*

¢–$ ✗ **Puds Pantry & Deli.** This relaxed little spot serves casual fare like homemade quiche and fresh-baked pies. The famous homemade breads include a fruit-and-treacle loaf, and Chelsea buns packed with sugar-coated currants and cinnamon. In winter, daily hot pastas, soups, and curries take the chill off those icy gusts from the nearby Southern Ocean. ☒ *60 Kepler St.* ☎ *03/5562–5119* ▤ *No credit cards.*

★ $–$$ ✗▦ **Quamby Homestead.** Australian antiques fill this magnificent 1888 homestead, an ideal base from which to explore the Warrnambool area. Modern rooms in former staff quarters are set apart from the homestead and surrounded by an English-style garden, where native birdcalls compete with the shrieks of resident peacocks. The dining room, in the homestead, serves fine country meals, which are available to nonresident guests on weekends. Rates include breakfast and dinner. It's 26 km (16 mi) north of Warrnambool. ☒ *Caramut Rd., Woolsthorpe 3276* ☎ *03/5569–2395* 🖶 *03/5569–2244* ⇙ *7 rooms* ⚬ *Dining room, free parking; no a/c, no room phones, no room TVs, no kids* ▤ *AE, DC, MC, V* ⋈ *MAP.*

$–$$ ▦ **Girt by Sea.** Built in 1856 and beautifully restored, this delightful sandstone homestead sits a short stroll from the beach, lake, and restaurants. The sunny veranda, spacious lounge, and sumptuous home-cooked breakfasts (including ricotta hotcakes and scrambled eggs with smoked salmon) make this a home away from home. ☒ *52 Banyan St., 3280* ☎ *03/5562–3746* ⊕ *www.girtbyseabandb.com.au* ⇙ *3 rooms* ⚬ *Lounge, free parking, no-smoking rooms; no room TVs* ▤ *AE, DC, MC, V.*

$–$$ ▦ **Merton Manor.** Hosts Pamela and Ivan Beeche have lovingly refurbished this magnificent, 1880 Italianate villa. Classic antiques and paintings cram every room, including the formal lounge, the drawing room, and the music chamber complete with grand piano and Duke of Edinburgh billiard table. All rooms have king-size beds. Home-cooked meals, served in the tapestry-clad dining room, are a highlight. ☒ *62 Ardlie St., 3280* ☎ *03/5561–1220* ⇙ *6 rooms* ⚬ *Lounge; no room phones, no room TVs* ▤ *AE, DC, MC, V* ⋈ *BP.*

Port Fairy

291 km (180 mi) southwest of Melbourne, 29 km (18 mi) west of Warrnambool.

Port Fairy wins the vote of many as the state's prettiest village. The second-oldest town in Victoria, it was originally known as Belfast, and there are indeed echoes of Ireland in the landscape and architecture. Founded during the whaling heyday in the 19th century, Port Fairy was once a whaling station with one of the largest ports in Victoria. The town still thrives as the base for a fishing fleet, and as host to the Port Fairy Folk Festival, one of Australia's most famous musical events, every March. More than 50 of the cottages and sturdy bluestone buildings that line the banks of the River Moyne have been classified as landmarks by the National Trust, and few towns repay a leisurely stroll so richly.

The **Historical Society Museum** contains relics from whaling days and from the many ships that have foundered along this coast. ⊠ *Old Courthouse, Gipps St.* ☎ *No phone* ✍ *A$2* ⊙ *Wed. and weekends 2–5.*

Mott's Cottage is a restored limestone-and-timber cottage built by Sam Mott, a member of the 1830s whaling crew from the cutter *Fairy* who founded the town. ⊠ *5 Sackville St.* ☎ *03/5568–2682* ✍ *A$2* ⊙ *Wed. and weekends 1–4, or by appointment.*

The **Shipwreck Walk** is a 2-km (1-mi) trail that traces its way between the wrecks of the bark *Socrates,* which was battered by huge seas in 1843; the bark *Lydia,* wrecked off the coast in 1847; the schooner *Thistle,* wrecked in 1837; and the brigantine *Essington,* which sank while moored at Port Fairy in 1852. Other attractions en route include the town port, the wrecks of the *Sarah Louisa* and *Eliza,* and the historic lifeboat station. The walk begins at the local Surf Club (travel north on Gipps Street, cross the Moyne River, and turn into Hughes Avenue), and is well marked.

off the beaten path

HAMILTON – One of western Victoria's principal inland cities, Hamilton lies 82 km (51 mi) north of Port Fairy, surrounded by rich grazing country. The town has a lovely botanical garden and a trout-filled lake made from damming the Grange Burn. If you'd like to stay awhile, there's no better place than the **Arrandoovong Homestead Bed and Breakfast** (☎ 03/5578–6221), an antiques-filled, 1850s, bluestone homestead set on a 500-acre working sheep farm.

Where to Stay & Eat

$–$$$ ✕⌂ **Merrijig Inn.** Overlooking the riverbanks from lofty King George Square, this beautifully restored 1841 Georgian-style building is one of Australia's most authentic examples of a street-corner inn. Inside are a mix of cozy attic bedrooms and suites, with snug sitting rooms warmed by open fires. The licensed dining room and bar draw crowds on winter evenings, while spring weather brings colors to the wide lawns and charming cottage garden. ⊠ *Campbell and Gipps Sts., 3284* ☎ *03/5568–2324* 🖷 *03/9999–4332* ⊕ *www.merrijiginn.com* ⤿ *4 rooms, 4 suites* ⌂ *Dining room, bar; no a/c, no room phones* ☰ *AE, MC, V* ⧓ *BP.*

¢–$$$ ✕⌂ **Dublin House Inn.** This solid stone building dates from 1855 and is furnished in period style. Functional rooms incorporate 19th-century accents, although the modern two-bedroom cottage also has a dishwasher and laundry facilities. The 32-seat dining room, open for dinner daily in summer, is where Chef Glenn Perkins whips up dishes based on everything from seafood to free-range chicken, duckling, and local beef. ⊠ *57 Bank St., 3284* ☎ *03/5568–2022* 🖷 *03/5568–2158* 🖂 *dublin@standard.net.au* ⤿ *3 rooms, 1 cottage* ⌂ *Restaurant, some kitchenettes, laundry facilities, laundry service, free parking; no room phones, no kids* ☰ *AE, MC, V* ⧓ *BP.*

$$$ ⊞ **Oscars Waterfront Boutique Hotel.** Overlooking the waterfront and a marina of yachts, Oscar's takes French provincial style and gives it an Australian edge. Each room is individually decorated—some in stripes, others in florals—and various communal lounges have open fireplaces, armchairs, books and games, and regional artwork. Gourmet breakfasts, for which Oscars is renowned, include berry hotcakes and tomato bruschetta with basil butter. If the weather allows, breakfast is served on the veranda overlooking the river. ⊠ *41B Gipps St., 3284* ☎ *03/5568–3022* ⊕ *www.oscarswaterfront.com* ⇂ *6 rooms, 1 suite* ⚭ *Refrigerators, lounge* ⊟ *AE, DC, MC, V* ⅋ *BP.*

$–$$ ⊞ **Goble's Mill House.** An imaginative refurbishment of an 1865 flour mill on the banks of the Moyne River transformed its levels into six guest rooms with en suite bathrooms and a spacious sitting area, all furnished with antiques. The upper-story loft bedroom is especially appealing, with a balcony overlooking the ever-active river. The open fire makes the sitting room cozy, and a separate guest pantry is stocked with juices and freshly baked shortbreads. You can also enjoy fishing off the Mill House's private jetty. ⊠ *75 Gipps St., 3284* ☎ *03/5568–1118* 🖷 *03/5568–1178* ⇂ *6 rooms* ⚭ *Dock, fishing, free parking; no a/c, no room phones, no room TVs* ⊟ *MC, V* ⅋ *BP.*

West Coast Region A to Z

CAR TRAVEL

Driving is the most convenient way to see the region, and the only way to really enjoy the Great Ocean Road. Distances are considerable, and the going may be slow on the most scenic routes, especially during the summer holiday period.

Start out by taking the Princes Highway west from Melbourne to Geelong. From there, follow signs to Queenscliff and Torquay, where you'll connect with the Great Ocean Road. For an alternative inland route to Warrnambool (much quicker, but vastly less interesting), take the Princes Highway.

EMERGENCIES

In an emergency, dial **000** to reach an ambulance, the police, or the fire department.

🚩 **Geelong Private Hospital** ⊠ Ryrie and Bellerine Sts., Geelong ☎ 03/5226–1600. **Medical Centre Pharmacy** ⊠ 262 Shannon Ave., Geelong West ☎ 03/5229–7727. **Shannon Avenue Medical Centre** ⊠ 260 Shannon Ave., Geelong West ☎ 03/5229–0000.

TOURS

AAT Kings has a day tour of the Great Ocean Road from Melbourne for A$160. Passengers can stay overnight from a selection of accommodations before returning to Melbourne on a bus the next day.

The Wayward Bus is a minibus that takes 3½ days to meander from Melbourne to Adelaide via the Great Ocean Road, Mt. Gambier, and the Coorong, with overnight stops at Port Fairy, Apollo Bay, and Beachport. Passengers can leave the bus at either overnight stop and catch the following bus. Tours depart Melbourne on Tuesday, Thursday, and Saturday October–April. It's A$295 per person (with hostel accommodation) or A$460 (twin-share room with en suite), including three nights' accommodation and picnic lunches.

🚩 AAT Kings ✉ 180 Swanson St., City Center, Melbourne ☎ 03/9663-3377 or 1300/ 556100. **Wayward Bus** ✉ 180 Swanson St., City Center, Melbourne ☎ 1800/882823.

TRAIN TRAVEL

The West Coast Railway operates daily services between Melbourne and Warrnambool. Although the trains provide restful means of getting to the South West region, they run inland and don't provide the extraordinary views you can see by car.

🚩 West Coast Railway ☎ 03/5226-6500.

VISITOR INFORMATION

The Geelong Great Ocean Road Visitor Information Centre and the Port Fairy Tourist Information Centre are open daily 9–5. The Warrnambool Visitor Information Centre is open weekdays 9–5 and weekends 10–4. Contact the Department of Natural Resources and Environment for more information on area parks.

🚩 Geelong Great Ocean Road Visitor Information Centre ✉ Stead Park, Princes Hwy., Geelong ☎ 03/5275-5797. **Port Fairy Tourist Information Centre** ✉ Bank St., Port Fairy ☎ 03/5568-2682. **Warrnambool Visitor Information Centre** ✉ 600 Raglan Parade, Warrnambool ☎ 03/5564-7837.

THE GOLD COUNTRY & GARIWERD NATIONAL PARK

Victoria was changed forever in the early 1850s by the discovery of gold in the center of the state. Fantastic news of gold deposits caused immigrants from every corner of the world to pour into Victoria to seek their fortunes as "diggers"—a name that has become synonymous with Australians ever since. Few miners became wealthy from their searches, however. The real money was made by those supplying goods and services to the thousands who had succumbed to gold fever.

Gold towns like Ballarat, Castlemaine, Maldon, and Bendigo sprang up like mushrooms to accommodate these fortune seekers, and prospered until the gold rush receded. Afterward, they became ghost towns or turned to agriculture to survive. Today Victoria's gold is again being mined in limited quantities, while these historic old towns remain interesting relics of Australia's past.

About 160 km (100 mi) west of the Gold Country and close to the western border of Victoria are the Aboriginal lands known as *Gariwerd* (formerly called the Grampians). This 412,000-acre region combines stunning mountain scenery, abundant native wildlife, and invigorating outdoor activities. The sharp sandstone peaks here were long ago forced up from an ancient seabed, and sculpted by eons of wind and rain. Today the park has more than 160 km (100 mi) of walking trails, as well as some 900 wildflower species, 200 species of birds, and 35 species of native mammals. The best time to visit is October–December, when wild-flowers carpet the landscape, the weather is mild, and summer crowds have yet to arrive.

Gold Country

Although Victoria was not the first Australian state to experience a gold rush, when gold was discovered here in 1851 it became a veritable El Dorado. During the boom years of the 19th century, 90% of the gold mined in Australia came from the state. The biggest finds were at Ballarat and then Bendigo, and the Ballarat diggings proved to be among the richest alluvial goldfields in the world.

As well as providing a glimpse back to the gold-rush days, this region of Victoria is now considered a center for modern-day rejuvenation. Between Ballarat and other historic gold towns to the north are the twin hot spots of Daylesford and Hepburn Springs—which together constitute the spa capital of Australia.

Ballarat

106 km (66 mi) northwest of Melbourne, 146 km (91 mi) east of Halls Gap.

In the local Aboriginal language, the name Ballarat means "resting place." In pre-gold-rush days, nearby Lake Wendouree provided the area with a plentiful supply of food. Once the boom hit, however, the town became much less restful; in 1854 Ballarat was the scene of the battle of the Eureka Stockade, a skirmish that took place between miners and authorities over gold license fees that miners were forced to pay. More than 20 men died in the battle, the only time that Australians have taken up arms in open rebellion against their government.

All sorts of native animals, including saltwater crocodiles, snakes, lizards, wombats, echidnas, and kangaroos, can be found at **Ballarat Wildlife and Reptile Park.** Daily tours of the park are led at 11, with a koala show at 2, crocodile-feeding at 3, and a wombat show at 2:30. The park also has a café, and barbecue and picnic areas. ✉ *Fussel and York Sts., East Ballarat* ☎ *03/5333–5933* 💰 *A$17.50* ☉ *Daily 9–5:30.*

On the shores of Lake Wendouree, Ballarat's **Botanic Gardens** are identifiable by the brilliant blooms and classical statuary. At the rear of the gardens, the Begonia House is the focus of events during the town's Begonia Festival, held annually in February or March. ✉ *Wendouree Parade* ☎ *No phone* 💰 *Free* ☉ *Daily sunrise–sunset.*

The prosperity of the gold rush left Ballarat well endowed with handsome buildings, and the short stretch of **Lydiard Street** around Sturt Street has a number of notable examples. One of the most visited is the **Ballarat Fine Arts Gallery,** which has a large collection of contemporary Australian art. It also has some impressive historical exhibits, like the tattered remains of the Southern Cross flag that was flown defiantly by the rebels at the Eureka Stockade. ✉ *40 Lydiard St.* ☎ *03/5331–5622* 💰 *A$5* ☉ *Daily 10:30–5.*

Sovereign Hill Historical Park, built on the site of the Sovereign Hill Quartz Mining Company's mines, provides an authentic look at life, work, and play in this area during the gold rush. The main street features a hotel, blacksmith's shop, bakery, post office, and Chinese joss house—all perfectly preserved relics of their time. You can dress up in period costumes, take a mine shaft tour, pan for gold, or head to the "lolly shop" for penny candy. You can also see "Blood on the Southern Cross," a 90-minute sound-and-light spectacular that focuses on the Eureka uprising. The story is told with passion and dramatic technical effects, although the sheer wealth of historical detail clouds the story line. The climax of the show is the battle of the Eureka Stockade.

Included in Sovereign Hill Historical Park admission is the **Gold Museum,** across Bradshaw Street. It displays an extensive collection of nuggets from the Ballarat diggings as well as some examples of finished gold in the form of jewelry. There's an excellent souvenir shop on-site. ⊠ *Bradshaw St.* ☎ *03/5331–1944* ⊞ *A$29; gold museum only, A$7.20; Blood on the Southern Cross show A$35; Sovereign Hill and Blood on the Southern Cross A$60* ⊗ *Daily 9:30–5:20; sometimes closed for maintenance Aug. and Dec; no sound-and-light show Sun.*

Yuulong Lavender Estate. Resting on a property of rolling hills, the lovely estate features a retail nursery, a craft and tea-room complex, and a large garden fronting contoured fields of lavender. Music and farming festivals are scheduled throughout the year, and many culinary, craft, and skin-care products made from lavender are produced here. ⊠ *Yendon Rd., Mt. Egerton* ☎ *03/5368–9453* ⊞ *A$4.40* ⊗ *Wed.–Sun. 10–4:30.*

WHERE TO STAY & EAT

★ **$$–$$$**

✕ **Cincotta's.** Asian-, Middle Eastern-, and European-inspired dishes are paired here with wonderful wines. This restaurant, casual and relaxed by day, with tablecloths and candelight in the evening, is the perfect place for a leisurely brunch, afternoon tea, or a romantic dinner. The calamari in Parmesan batter, walnut-stuffed spatchcock, and Thai beef salad are best matched with local wines. ⊠ *102 Sturt St.* ☎ *03/5331–1402* ⊟ *AE, DC, MC, V.*

$$ ✕ **L'espresso.** Meals at this casual restaurant, which used to be a record shop back in the 1970s, taste like they're from Grandma's kitchen. It's open from breakfast through 6 PM, with specials like salmon fillet with lemon aioli or bruschetta with mascarpone and figs. ⊠ *417 Sturt St.* ☎ *03/5331–1789* ⊟ *No credit cards.*

$–$$ ✕ **Europa Cafe.** Italian, Middle Eastern, and Asian dishes are served with flair at this hip yet relaxed dining spot. The all-day breakfast is legendary, and lunches include such savory treats as smoked salmon bruschetta. For dinner, go for the delicious Moroccan chicken or slow-cooked lamb shanks. The restaurant closes at 6:30 Monday through Wednesday, open late Thursday through Sunday. ⊠ *411 Sturt St.* ☎ *03/5331–2486* ⊟ *AE, DC, MC, V.*

★ **$–$$$** ✕🛏 **The Ansonia.** Built in the 1870s as professional offices—and rescued by new owners, who refurbished it completely—the Ansonia is now an excellent boutique hotel and dining spot. Open from 7 AM, the restaurant serves sumptuous breakfast and lunch, in addition to an eclectic dinner (where linguine with baby beets shares the menu with salads and steaks). There are four different styles of accommodation, from two-room apartments to studios, all of which are beautifully furnished and appointed with soaring ceilings, antiques, regional artwork, and spectacular flower arrangements. ✉ *32 Lydiard St. S, 3350* ☎ *03/5332–4678* 📠 *03/5332–4698* ⤴ *20 rooms* ⚐ *Restaurant, dry cleaning, laundry service, meeting rooms, free parking; no kids* ▭ *AE, DC, MC, V.*

$–$$$ 🏨 **Ballarat Heritage Homestays.** This group manages a number of historic properties in Ballarat, including Ravenswood, Wilton House, Glen Eira, Kingsley Place, Quamby on Errard, and Tait's Cottage. These range from self-contained cottages to traditional B&B properties. Tucked behind a garden brimming with peach trees, pussy willows, fuchsias, and climbing roses, Ravenswood is a three-bedroom timber cottage ideal for families or small groups. The house, a bit less than 1½ km (1 mi) from the center of Ballarat, has contemporary decor and a full kitchen. Breakfast supplies are provided. ⌂ *185 Victoria St., 3354* ☎ *1800/813369* ⊕ *www.heritagehomestay.com* ⤴ *6 properties* ▭ *AE, DC, MC, V* ⚑| *CP.*

Daylesford & Hepburn Springs

109 km (68 mi) northwest of Melbourne, 45 km (28 mi) northeast of Ballarat.

Nestled in the slopes of the Great Dividing Range, Daylesford and its nearby twin, Hepburn Springs, are a spa lover's paradise. The water table here is naturally aerated with carbon dioxide and rich in soluble mineral salts, making it ideal for indulging in mineral baths and other rejuvenating treatments. The natural springs were first noted during the gold rush, and a spa was established at Hepburn Springs by Swiss-Italian immigrants in 1875, when spa resorts were fashionable in Europe. Today both towns are dotted with day spas, as well as private practitioners of massage and holistic remedies. The best time to visit the area is autumn, when the deciduous trees turn bronze and you can finish up a relaxing day next to an open fire with a glass of local red.

Perched on a hillside overlooking Daylesford, the **Convent Gallery** is a former nunnery that has been restored to its lovely Victorian state. It displays contemporary Australian pottery, glassware, jewelry, sculpture, and prints, all for sale. At the front of the gallery is Bad Habits, a sunny café that serves light lunches and snacks. ✉ *Daly St., Daylesford* ☎ *03/5348–3211* 🎟 *A$4.50* ⊘ *Daily 10–5.*

Fodor'sChoice Mineral baths and treatments are available at the bright, modern **Hep-** ★ **burn Spa Resort,** where the facilities include communal spa pools, private aerospa baths, float tanks, and saunas. This is the only spa in town that has direct access to the natural underground springs, whose water is rich in minerals including calcium, silica, magnesium, bicarbonate, and iron. Massages, facials, and other body treatments are available too. Services generally run between A$35 and A$95, although rates are slightly higher on weekends. The resort is set in a leafy valley, and skirted by herb gardens. The staff here is delightful. ✉ *Main Rd., Mineral Springs Reserve* ☎ *03/5348–2034* ⊕ *www.hepburnspa.com.au* 🎟 *Full access A$25; pool and spa only, A$10* ⊘ *Mon.–Thurs. 10–7, Fri. 10–8, weekends 9–8:30.*

Above the Hepburn Springs Spa Resort, a path winds through a series of mineral springs at the **Mineral Springs Reserve.** Each spring has a slightly different chemical composition—and a significantly different taste. You can bring empty bottles, if you like; they can be filled with the mineral water of your choice, for free.

WHERE TO
STAY & EAT
$-$$$
Fodor's Choice
★

✕🏠 **Lake House Restaurant.** Consistently rated one of central Victoria's best restaurants, this rambling lakeside pavilion brings glamour to spa country. The seasonal menu, which utilizes fresh Australian produce, lists such delicacies as hot gravlax of Atlantic salmon, as well as a selection of imaginative Asian-accented and vegetarian dishes. Guest rooms in the lodge are breezy and contemporary; those at the front have better views, but slightly less privacy, than those at the back, which are screened by rose-entwined trellises. ⊠ *King St., Daylesford 3460* ☎ *03/5348–3329* 🖷 *03/5448–3995* ⊕ *www.lakehouse.com.au* ➟ *33 rooms* ⟁ *Restaurant, dining room, tennis court, pool, sauna, bicycles, bar, laundry service, meeting rooms, free parking; no a/c in some rooms, no kids* ⊟ *AE, DC, MC, V* �𝄙 *BP.*

$$$
🏠 **Holcombe Homestead.** At this beautifully restored 1891 farmhouse you can fish for trout, wander the landscaped property, or spot kangaroos and kookaburras in between trips to the spa. The house is full of period Victorian furnishings, and the view from the top of the hillside is idyllic at sunset. Owners John and Annette Marshall live in a neighboring house and will prepare box lunches and dinner on request. ⊠ *Holcombe Rd., Glenlyon 3461, 15 km (9 mi) north-east of Daylesford* ☎ *03/5348–7514* 🖷 *03/5348–7742* ⊕ *www.holcombe.com.au* ➟ *6 rooms, 3 with bath* ⟁ *Dining room, tennis court, fishing, mountain bikes, laundry service, meeting rooms, free parking; no a/c in some rooms, no kids* ⊟ *AE, DC, MC, V* �𝄙 *BP.*

$-$$
🏠 **Dudley House.** Behind a neat hedge and picket gate, this fine example of timber Federation architecture sits on Hepburn Springs' main street. Rooms have been restored and furnished with antiques. A full English breakfast and afternoon tea with scones is included. The town's spas are within walking distance. Spa packages and dinner are available by arrangement. ⊠ *101 Main St., Hepburn Springs 3460* ☎ *03/5348–3033* ⊕ *www.netconnect.com.au/~dudley* ➟ *4 rooms* ⟁ *Dining room, free parking; no a/c, no room TVs, no kids under 16, no smoking* ⊟ *AE, MC, V* �𝄙 *BP.*

en route

As you head northeast from Daylesford toward Bendigo, you'll pass through the small but interesting goldfield town of **Castlemaine** (38 km [24 mi] north of Daylesford). Here you can see an impressive collection of jewelry, antique handcrafted furniture, and art at the historic Buda House (☎ 03/5472–1032), where a family of Hungarian artists lived for over a century. A 16-km (10-mi) drive northwest from Castlemaine will bring you to **Maldon,** another small, beautifully preserved gold mining town, where tea shops and antiques sellers line the main street. You can take a candlelight tour of the nearby Carman's Tunnel (☎ 03/5475–2667), a gold mine that's been preserved intact since it closed in 1884.

Bendigo

150 km (93 mi) northwest of Melbourne, 36 km (22 mi) northeast of Maldon, 92 km (57 mi) south of Echuca.

Gold was discovered in the Bendigo district in 1851, and the boom lasted well into the 1880s. The city's magnificent public buildings bear witness to the richness of its mines. Today Bendigo is a bustling, enterprising small city, with distinguished buildings lining both sides of Pall Mall in the city center. These include the **Shamrock Hotel, General Post Office,** and **Law Courts,** all majestic examples of late-Victorian architecture.

The refurbished **Bendigo Art Gallery** houses a notable collection of contemporary Australian paintings, including the work of Jeffrey Smart, Lloyd Rees, and Clifton Pugh. (Pugh once owned a remote Outback pub infamous for its walls daubed with his own pornographic cartoons.) The gallery also has some significant 19th-century French realist and impressionist works, bequeathed by a local surgeon. ⊠ *42 View St.* ☎ *03/ 5443–4991* ⊠ *Free* ⊗ *Daily 10–5.*

Central Deborah Gold Mine, with a 1,665-foot mine shaft, yielded almost a ton of gold before it closed in 1954. To experience life underground, take a guided tour of the mine. An elevator descends 200 feet below ground level. ⊠ *76 Violet St.* ☎ *03/5443–8322* ⊠ *A$16.90, A$26.50 including entry to Vintage Talking Tram A$26.50* ⊗ *Daily 9:30–5; last tour at 4:05.*

The superb **Golden Dragon Museum** evokes the Chinese community's role in Bendigo life, past and present. Its centerpieces are the century-old Loong imperial ceremonial dragon and the Sun Loong dragon, which, at more than 106 yards in length, is said to be the world's longest. When carried in procession, it requires 52 carriers and 52 relievers; the head alone weighs 64 pounds. Also on display are other ceremonial objects, costumes, and historic artifacts. ⊠ *5–9 Bridge St.* ☎ *03/5441–5044* ⊠ *A$7* ⊗ *Daily 9–5.*

Joss House was built in gold-rush days by Chinese miners on the outskirts of the city. At the height of the boom in the 1850s and 1860s, about a quarter of the miners were Chinese. These men were usually dispatched from villages on the Chinese mainland, and they were expected to work hard and return as quickly as possible to their villages with their fortunes intact. The Chinese were scrupulously law-abiding and hardworking—qualities that did not always endear them to other miners—and anti-Chinese riots were common. ⊠ *Finn St., Emu Point* ☎ *03/5442–1685* ⊠ *A$3.30* ⊗ *Daily 10–5.*

A good introduction to Bendigo is a tour aboard the **Vintage Talking Tram,** which includes a taped commentary on the town's history. The tram departs on its 8-km (5-mi) circuit every hour between 10 and 4:20 from the Central Deborah Gold Mine. ⊠ *76 Violet St.* ☎ *03/5443–8322* ⊠ *A$12.90* ⊗ *Daily 10–4:20.*

WHERE TO STAY & EAT
$$–$$$

✕ **Bazzani.** This restaurant fuses a mainly Italian menu with Asian influences under the capable stewardship of a second generation of Bazzanis. Try the ravioli with a tomato, chili, and coriander broth, or the wild mushroom risotto. A good selection of local and Pyrenees wines is very well priced, and coffee and snacks are also served. ⊠ *2-4 Howard Pl.* ☎ *03/5441-3777* ⊟ *AE, DC, MC, V.*

\$\$-\$\$\$ ✕ **Whirrakee.** This stylish, family-run restaurant and wine bar in one of Bendigo's many grand old buildings serves Mediterranean- and Asian-inspired dishes. The char-grilled baby octopus and the arugula salad with pesto and balsamic vinegar are standouts. The wine list showcases local wineries. ⊠ *17 View Point* ☎ *03/5441-5557* ⊟ *AE, DC, MC, V.*

\$\$-\$\$\$ ▦ **Warrenmang Vineyard Resort.** A wide valley full of flourishing grapevines surrounds this 250-acre estate, where the chalet-style cottages and luxury suites all have outdoor balconies and superb panoramas of the Australian countryside. You can ride bikes and horses, take bushwalks in the adjoining state forest, or simply watch kangaroos play on the lawn at dusk. The pleasant restaurant utilizes local fish, game, berries, and cheese, as well as wines from 12 regional vineyards. ⊠ *Mountain Creek Rd., Moonabel 3478* ☎ *03/5467-2233* ⊟ *03/5467-2309* ⌨ *11 suites, 3 cottages* ⚅ *Kitchens, hot tub, bicycles, hiking, horseback riding, laundry facilities* ⊟ *DC, MC, V* ⎮◯⎮ *BP.*

\$\$ ▦ **Langley Hall.** Housed in a circa-1903 Edwardian mansion, Langley Hall was originally built as a residence for the Anglican Archbishop of Bendigo. After incarnations as a restaurant and an antiques center, it was restored and refurbished as a B&B accommodation in the 1980s. Features include a billiard room, parlor, and drawing room, all dripping with antiques and period detail—testament to Bendigo's 1850s heyday. ⊠ *484 Napier St., 3550* ☎ *03/5443-3693* ⌨ *6 rooms* ⚅ *Billiards, shared sitting rooms, a/c, open fire place* ⊟ *MC, V* ⎮◯⎮ *CP.*

\$-\$\$ ▦ **Comfort Inn Shamrock.** The lodgings at this landmark Victorian hotel in the city center range from simple, traditional guest rooms with shared facilities to large suites. If you're looking for reasonably priced luxury, ask for the Amy Castles Suite. Rooms are spacious and well maintained, but furnishings are dowdy and strictly functional. The hotel's location and character are the real draws. ⊠ *Pall Mall and Williamson St., 3550* ☎ *03/5443-0333* ⊟ *03/5442-4494* ⌨ *26 rooms, 2 with bath; 4 suites* ⚅ *Restaurant, 3 bars, laundry facilities, meeting rooms, free parking; no a/c in some rooms, no room phones, no room TVs, no kids* ⊟ *AE, DC, MC, V.*

Gariwerd National Park

Fodor'sChoice *260 km (162 mi) west of Melbourne, 100 km (62 mi) north of Hamilton.*
★

Comprising four mountain ranges—Mt. Difficult, Mt. William, Serra, and Victoria—Gariwerd National Park, formerly known as the Grampians, spills over 412,000 acres. Its rugged peaks, towering trees, web of waterfalls and creeks, and plethora of wildlife make it a haven for bushwalkers, rock climbers, and nature lovers. In spring the region wears a carpet of spectacular wildflowers, while a number of significant Aboriginal rock art sites make it an ideal place to learn about Victoria's indigenous history. Dawn balloon flights over the park offer visitors the chance to see the park's hidden charms without working up a sweat.

Owned and operated by Aboriginal people, the **Brambuk Cultural Centre** provides a unique living history of Aboriginal culture in this part of Victoria. Displays of artwork, weapons, clothes, and tools here give a glimpse into the life of indigenous Koorie people (local to this area). In the Dreaming Theatre, dancing, music, and educational programs are presented daily. ⊠ *Dunkeld Rd., Halls Gap* ☎ *03/5356–4452* ⊠ *Free, Dreaming Theatre performances A$4.50 for* ☉ *Daily 9–5, show hourly 10–4.*

Where to Stay & Eat

The national park base is Halls Gap, which has motels, guesthouses, host farms, and RV parks. Eleven campgrounds are in the national park. The fee is A$8.60 per site for up to six people; permits are available from the Halls Gap and Grampians National Park Visitor Centre on Grampians Road, Halls Gap.

$$ ✕ **Kookaburra.** This place is the best dining option you'll find in the park area. Venison is popular here; you can try it prepared as steak, sausage, or pie. You can also choose duckling, milk-fed veal, or pork fillet smoked over cherrywood embers, and finish with a traditional bread-and-butter pudding. ⊠ *125 Grampian Rd., Halls Gap* ☎ *03/5356–4222* ⊟ *AE, DC, MC, V.*

$$$$
Fodor'sChoice
★
Boroka Downs. Set among 300 acres of bush, scrub, and grassland, Boroka's five architect-designed studios are nothing short of spectacular. Designed to meld with the environment, each studio features soaring ceilings, roof-to-floor windows—which frame the rugged, bush-clad ridges of the Grampians—handcrafted furniture, and enormous spa baths. You can wake to the sound of kookaburras laughing, while at sunset you'll find groups of grazing kangaroos, emus, and wallabies in the paddocks that skirt your studio. Each room also has its own fireplace, CD player, and kitchen. Bedside views of Gariwerd are exceptional. ⊠ *Birdswing Rd., Halls Gap 3381* ☎ *03/5356–6243* ⬛ *03/5356–6343* ⊕ *www.borokadowns.com.au* ⟿ *5 rooms* ⚲ *Kitchens, microwaves, in-room VCRs, free parking; no kids* ⊟ *AE, MC, V.*

$$ **Glenisla Homestead.** This 1870 heritage-classified B&B, built from local Grampians sandstone, nestles beside the Henty Highway in a valley between the Victoria and Black ranges. It's part of a 2,000-acre working sheep station that produces superfine merino wool, and guests are welcome to participate in farm activities. The homestead has two large colonial suites with their own lounge areas and bathrooms. There's also a large dining room and open courtyard. ⊠ *Off Hamilton-Horsham Rd. (follow the signs), Cavendish 3314* ☎ *03/5380–1532* ⬛ *03/5380–1566* ⊕ *www.grampians.net.au/glenisla* ⟿ *2 suites* ⚲ *Dining room, fishing, horseback riding, laundry service, free parking; no a/c, no room phones, no room TVs, no kids* ⊟ *AE, MC, V* ⦿ *BP.*

The Gold Country & Gariwerd National Park A to Z

CAR TRAVEL

For leisurely exploration of the Gold Country, a car is essential. Although public transportation adequately serves the main centers, access to smaller towns is less assured, and even in the bigger towns attractions tend to be widely dispersed.

To reach Bendigo, take the Calder Highway northwest from Melbourne; for Ballarat, take the Western Highway. The mineral springs region and Maldon lie neatly between the two main cities.

Halls Gap (the base town for Gariwerd National Park) is reached via Ballarat and Ararat on the Western Highway (Highway 8). The town is 260 km (162 mi) northwest of Melbourne, 97 km (60 mi) northeast of Hamilton, 146 km (91 mi) west of Ballarat.

EMERGENCIES
In an emergency, dial **000** to reach an ambulance, the police, or the fire department.
East Grampians Health Service ⊠ Girdlestone St., Ararat ☎ 03/5352-9300. **Stawell Medical Centre** ⊠ 26 Wimmera St., Stawell ☎ 03/5358-1410.

TELEPHONES
In the town of Halls Gap there are several public phones. There is limited cell reception in this area.

TOURS
Tour operators covering the Gold Country include Gray Line, Australian Pacific Tours, and AAT Kings; all three depart from 180 Swanston Street in Melbourne. Gray Line also operates a one-day tour of Gariwerd (A$112) that departs from Melbourne on Monday, Thursday, and Saturday.
AAT Kings ☎ 03/9663-3377 or 1300 556 100. **Australian Pacific Tours** ☎ 03/9663-1611. **Gray Line** ☎ 03/9663-4455.

TRAIN TRAVEL
Rail service to Ballarat or Bendigo is available from Melbourne. For timetables and rates, contact CountryLink or the Royal Automobile Club of Victoria (RACV).
CountryLink ☎ 13-2232. **Royal Automobile Club of Victoria (RACV)** ☎ 13-1955.

VISITOR INFORMATION
The visitor center in Ballarat is open weekdays 9–5 and weekends 10–4, the center in Bendigo is open daily 9–5, and the one in Daylesford is open daily 10–4. Visitor centers in Halls Gap and Stawell and the Grampians are open 9–5 daily.
Ballarat Tourist Information Centre ⊠ 39 Sturt St., Ballarat ☎ 03/5332-2694. **Bendigo Tourist Information Centre** ⊠ Old Post Office, Pall Mall, Bendigo ☎ 03/5444-4445. **Daylesford Regional Visitor Information Centre** ⊠ 49 Vincent St., Daylesford ☎ 03/5348-1339 🖷 03/5321-6193 ⊕ www.visitdaylesford.com. **Halls Gap Visitor Information Centre** ⊠ Grampians Rd., Halls Gap ☎ 03/5356-4616. **Stawell and Grampians Visitor Information Centre** ⊠ 50-52 Western Hwy., Stawell ☎ 03/5358-2314.

MURRAY RIVER REGION

From its birthplace on the slopes of the Great Dividing Range in southern New South Wales, the Mighty Murray winds 2,574 km (1,596 mi) on a southwesterly course before it empties into Lake Alexandrina, south of Adelaide. On the driest inhabited continent on earth, such a river, the country's largest, assumes great importance. Irrigation schemes that tap the river water have transformed its thirsty surroundings into a garden of grapevines and citrus fruits.

Once prone to flooding and droughts, the river has been laddered with dams that control the floodwaters and form reservoirs for irrigation. The lakes created in the process have become sanctuaries for native birds. In the pre-railroad age of canals, the Murray was an artery for inland cargoes of wool and wheat, and old wharves in such ports as Echuca bear witness to the bustling and colorful riverboat era.

Victoria, Tasmania, New South Wales, and Western Australia were planted with grapevines in the 1830s, fixing roots for an industry that has earned international praise. One of the earliest sponsors of Victorian viticulture was Charles LaTrobe, the first Victorian governor. LaTrobe had lived at Neuchâtel in Switzerland and married the daughter of the Swiss Counsellor of State. As a result of his contacts, Swiss winemakers emigrated to Australia and developed some of the earliest Victorian vineyards in the Yarra Valley, east of Melbourne.

Digging for gold was a thirst-producing business, and the gold rushes stimulated the birth of an industry. By 1890 well over half the total Australian production of wine came from Victoria. But then, in the mid-1800s, a strain of tiny plant lice, phylloxera, arrived from Europe and wreaked havoc in Victoria (it had similarly devastated the vineyards of France). In the absence of wine, Australians turned to beer, and not until the 1960s did the wineries here start to regain their footing. Today Victoria exports more than A$100 million worth of wine annually. High-quality muscat, Tokay, and port is still made in many parts of the Murray River region. The Rutherglen area, in particular, produces the finest fortified wine in the country, and anyone who enjoys the after-dinner "stickies" (dessert wines) is in for a treat when touring here.

Beechworth

131 km (82 mi) northeast of Euroa, 271 km (168 mi) northeast of Melbourne, 96 km (60 mi) northwest of Alpine National Park.

One of the prettiest towns in Victoria, Beechworth flourished during the gold rush. When gold ran out, the town was left with all the trappings of prosperity—fine Victorian banks, imposing public buildings, breweries, parks, and hotels wrapped in wrought iron—but with scarcely two nuggets to rub together. However, poverty preserved the town from such modern amenities as aluminum window frames, and many historic treasures that might have been destroyed in the name of progress have been restored and brought back to life.

A stroll along **Ford Street** is the best way to absorb the character of the town. Among the distinguished buildings are **Tanswell's Commercial Hotel** and the government buildings. Note the jail, antiques shops, and sequoia trees in **Town Hall Gardens.** Much of Beechworth's architecture is made from the honey-color granite quarried outside of town.

NED KELLY

THE ENGLISH HAD ROBIN HOOD, *the Americans Jesse James. People love a notorious hero, and Australian Ned Kelly was a natural: a tall, tough, idealistic youth who came to symbolize the struggle against an uncaring ruling class. Ned's attitudes were shaped by the forces of the time: corrupt local politics and unscrupulous squatters who tried to force small landholders—like members of the Kelly clan—off their land.*

Like many other lads from Irish working-class families, Ned got to know the police at a young age. At 15 he was charged with the assault of a pig-and-fowl dealer named Ah Fook and with aiding another bushranger, but was found not guilty on both charges. A year later, as a result of a friend's prank, he was convicted of assault and indecent behavior and sentenced to six months' hard labor. Within weeks of his release he was back in Melbourne's notorious Pentridge Prison serving three years for allegedly receiving a stolen horse. After this, Ned was determined to stay out of prison, but events were to dictate otherwise. It was matriarch Ellen Kelly's arrest—on what some claim were trumped-up charges—that was the turning point in the story. Warrants were issued for sons Ned and Dan, and a subsequent shoot-out left three policemen dead.

The heat was soon on the Kelly boys and their friends Joe Byrne and Steve Hart, whose occasional raids netted them thousands of pounds and worked the police into a frenzy. The gang's reputation was reinforced by their spectacular crimes, which were executed with humanity and humor. In 1878 they held scores of settlers hostage on a farm near Euroa en route to robbing the local bank, but they kept the folks entertained with demonstrations of horsemanship. The following year they took control of the town of Jerilderie for three days, dressing

in police uniforms and captivating the women. According to one account, Joe Byrne took the gang's horses to the local blacksmith and charged the work to the NSW Police Department.

The final showdown was ignited by the murder of a police informer and former friend, Aaron Sherritt. The gang fled to Glenrowan, where Ned ordered a portion of the train line derailed and telegraph wires cut to delay the police. Among other aims, the plan was to take the survivors prisoner and use them as pawns to secure the release of Mrs. Kelly. Meanwhile, the gang holed up in a local pub, where they played cards and danced. The police were warned of the plan by a captive who had managed to escape, and the scene was set for a bloody confrontation.

Although the gang had their trademark heavy body suits made from the mouldboards (board in a plough that turns the earth) of ploughshares (the main cutting blade of a plough), all were shot and killed except Ned, who took a bullet in his unprotected legs and was eventually captured. In hastily arranged proceedings in Melbourne, Ned appeared before Judge Redmond Barry, the same man who had sentenced his mother to three years' imprisonment. Barry ordered Ned Kelly to be hanged, a sentence carried out on November 11, 1880—despite a petition of 60,000 signatures attempting to have him spared. As the judge asked the Lord to have mercy on Ned's soul, the bushranger defiantly replied that he would meet him soon in a fairer court in the sky.

Twelve days after Ned Kelly's death, Judge Redmond Barry died.

— *Josie Gibson*

Burke Museum takes its name from Robert Burke, who, with William Wills, became one of the first white explorers to cross Australia from south to north in 1861. Burke was superintendent of police in Beechworth, 1856–59. Paradoxically, but not surprisingly, the small area and few mementos dedicated to Burke are overshadowed by the Ned Kelly exhibits, which include letters, photographs, and memorabilia that give genuine insight into the man and his misdeeds. The museum also displays a reconstructed streetscape of Beechworth in the 1880s. ☒ *Loch St.* ☎ *03/5728–1420* ☒ *A$5* ⊘ *Daily 10:30–3:30.*

The **Carriage Museum** occupies a corrugated-iron building that was a stable in the 19th century. On display is a collection of 20 horse-drawn vehicles from the 19th and early 20th century. Many vehicles were associated with Beechworth's past, having been used in the town and neighboring areas. Displays vary from simple farm carts and buggies to Cobb & Co. stagecoaches, some of which were modeled on U.S. designs. ☒ *Railway Ave.* ☒ *A$1.50* ⊘ *Daily 10:30–12:30 and 1:30–4:30.*

★ **Mt. Buffalo National Park.** You can visit this beautiful, much-loved corner of the Victorian Alps and see many of the same natural wonders you'd find at the better-known (but more distant) Alpine National Park. Anderson Peak and the Horn both top 5,000 feet, and the park is full of interesting granite formations, waterfalls, animal and plant life, and more miles of walking tracks than you're likely to cover. The gorge walk is particularly scenic. Lake Catani has swimming and a camping area. Primary access to the park is from Myrtleford and Porepunkah. Both towns have hotels and motels. ☒ *50 km (31 mi) south of Beechworth; from Bright, take the Mount Buffalo Tourist Rd. from Porepunkah to the summit* ☎ *13–1963 Parks Victoria* ☒ *Free* ⊘ *Daily sunrise–sunset.*

off the beaten path

EUROA – One of the main attractions of this small town, located 120 km (75 mi) from Beechworth, is the **Maygars Hill** boutique winery (☎ *03/5798–5417*). Guided walks through the vineyards (there are 2 acres of cabernet sauvignon and 4 acres of shiraz vines), are available, as are wine tastings by appointment. Another popular activity here is hot-air balloon flights; **Balloon Flights Victoria** (☎ *03/5798–5417*) runs year-round one-hour trips, which cost A$250 per person, and include a champagne breakfast upon touchdown.

Where to Stay & Eat

★ $$$$ ▦ **Howqua Dale Gourmet Retreat.** Owners Marieke Brugman and Sarah Stegley fully pamper their guests in this rural Victorian gem. Marieke's cooking is wonderful, and Sarah has an encyclopedic knowledge of wine, especially Victorian vintages. Accommodations are luxurious, with splendid views of willow-lined river valleys and manicured gardens, and each room is decorated and furnished in a particular theme—Asian, Victorian, modern, even Balinese. Horseback riding, boating on nearby Lake Eildon, or fishing can be arranged. Prices include all meals, accommodation, and wine. Brugman also conducts cooking classes on-site. ☒ *Howqua River Rd., Howqua 3722, 140 km (87 mi) southwest of Beechworth* ☎ *03/*

5777–3503 🖨 *03/5777–3896* 🛏 *6 rooms* ⚫ *Restaurant, tennis court, pool, boating, fishing, horseback riding, bar, meeting rooms, free parking; no a/c, no room phones, no room TVs* 🖃 *AE, DC, MC, V* 🍴 *FAP.*

$$ ✕🏠 **Bank Restaurant and Mews.** This restaurant's refined, dignified setting befits its status as a former Bank of Australasia. Built in the 1850s, the heritage-listed building features cathedral ceilings, antique furnishings, and the bank's original gold vault (which now holds a treasure of wines). The food, based on local produce and high-country beef, duck, and quail, is delicious and presented with style. Four luxurious garden suites, built overlooking manicured gardens and private courtyards, occupy what was originally the carriage house and stables. Rates include breakfast. ✉ *86 Ford St., 3747* 🕾 *03/5728–2223* 🖨 *03/5728–2883* 🛏 *4 suites* ⚫ *Restaurant, dining room, minibars, laundry facilities, free parking; no kids, no smoking* 🖃 *AE, DC, MC, V* 🍴 *BP.*

★ $–$$ ✕🏠 **Kinross.** Chintz fabrics and dark-wood antiques fill the rooms of this former manse, just a two-minute walk from the center of Beechworth. Each room here has its own fireplace, as well as an electric blanket and eiderdown bed pillows. Room 2, at the front of the house, is the largest. Rates include breakfast. Hosts Christine and Bill Pearse's Saturday-night dinners—created with regional produce and matched with local wines—are a highlight. ✉ *34 Loch St., 3747* 🕾 *03/5728–2351* 🖨 *03/5728–5333* 🛏 *5 rooms* ⚫ *Dining room, fans, laundry facilities, free parking; no a/c, no room phones, no kids* 🖃 *AE, MC, V* 🍴 *BP.*

$$–$$$ 🏠 **Country Charm Swiss Cottages.** Beautifully landscaped gardens overlooking the Beechworth Gorge surround these charming cottages. Each unit is self-contained, with such elegant touches as open fires, double jetted tubs, CD players, and fully equipped kitchens. You can request a TV and VCR if you like. This was the site of the original Beechworth vineyard, established in the 1800s, although a 130-year-old drystone wall is all that remains. While walking the grounds, note the views across the Woolshed Valley to Mt. Pilot. ✉ *22 Malakoff Rd., 3747* 🕾 *03/ 5728–2435* 🛏 *5 cottages* ⚫ *Kitchens, microwaves, refrigerators, in-room VCRs; no TV in some rooms* 🖃 *MC, V.*

en route   Originally known as Black Dog Creek, **Chiltern** is another gold-rush town that fell into a coma when gold ran out. The main street of this tiny village, located 31 km (19 mi) north of Beechworth on the way to Rutherglen, is an almost perfectly preserved example of a 19th-century rural Australian streetscape (a fact not unnoticed by contemporary filmmakers). Notable buildings include the **Athenaeum Library and Museum,** the **Pharmacy,** the **Federal Standard Office,** and the **Star Hotel,** which has in its courtyard the largest grapevine in the country, with a girth of almost 6 feet at its base.

Rutherglen

274 km (170 mi) northeast of Melbourne, 18 km (11 mi) northwest of Chiltern.

The surrounding red loam soil signifies the beginning of the Rutherglen wine district, the source of Australia's finest fortified wines. If the term conjures up visions of cloying ports, you're in for a surprise. In his authoritative *Australian Wine Compendium,* James Halliday says, "Like Narcissus drowning in his own reflection, one can lose oneself in the aroma of a great old muscat."

The main event in the region is the Rutherglen Wine Festival, held Labor Day weekend in March. The festival is a celebration of food, wine, and music—in particular jazz, folk, and country. Events are held in town and at all surrounding wineries. For more information on the wine festival, contact the **Rutherglen Tourist Information Centre** (⊠ Walkabout Cellars, 84 Main St. ☎ 02/6032–9166).

All Saints Vineyards & Cellars has been in business since 1864. Owned and operated by Peter Brown (one of the famous Brown Brothers of Milewain, one of the first families to produce wine in the region), the property features a National Trust–classified castle, which was built in 1878 and modeled on the castle of Mey in Scotland. Products include the Museum Muscat and Museum Tokay, both made from 50-year-old grapes. The Terrace restaurant is on-site. ⊠ *All Saints Rd., Wahgunyah, 9 km (5½ mi) southeast of Rutherglen* ☎ *02/6033–1922* ☎ *Free* ⊘ *Daily 9–5.*

Another long-established winery, **Buller's Calliope Vineyard,** has many vintage stocks of muscat and fine sherry distributed through its cellar outlet. Also on the winery's grounds is **Buller Bird Park,** an aviary of rare parrots and native Australian birds. ⊠ *3 Chain Rd. and Murray Valley Hwy.* ☎ *02/6032–9660* ☎ *Free* ⊘ *Mon.–Sat. 9–5, Sun. 10–5.*

Campbell's Rutherglen Winery is a family business that dates back more than 130 years. Famed for their award-winning Bobbie Burns Shiraz and Merchant Prince Muscat, the property spills over a picturesque 160 acres. You can wander freely through the winery on a self-guided tour. Campbell Family Vintage Reserve is available only at the cellar door. ⊠ *Murray Valley Hwy.* ☎ *02/6032–9458* ☎ *Free* ⊘ *Mon.–Sat. 9–5:30, Sun. 10–5:30.*

Chambers Rosewood Winery was established in the 1850s and is one of the heavyweight producers of fortified wines. Bill Chambers's muscats are legendary, with blending stocks that go back more than a century. Don't miss the chance to sample the vast tasting selection. ⊠ *Off Corowa Rd.* ☎ *02/6032–8641* ☎ *Free* ⊘ *Mon.–Sat. 9–5, Sun. 11–5.*

Along with exceptional fortified wine, **Pfeiffer Wines** has fine varietal wine, including chardonnay. It also has one of the few Australian plantings of gamay, the classic French grape used to make Beaujolais. At this small rustic winery you can order a picnic basket stuffed with crusty bread, pâté, cheese, fresh fruit, wine, and smoked salmon, but be sure to reserve in advance. Winemaker Chris Pfeiffer sets up tables on the old wooden bridge that spans Sunday Creek, where you can take your picnic provisions. Phone ahead to book a table. ⊠ *Distillery Rd., Wahgunyah, 9 km (5½ mi) southeast of Rutherglen* ☎ *02/6033–2805* ☎ *Free* ⊘ *Mon.–Sat. 9–5, Sun. 11–4.*

Where to Stay & Eat

$–$$ ✕ **Beaumont's Cafe.** Pasta tossed with local yabbies and veal rib eye with rich jus are highlights on the menu of this shop-front dining room. On warm nights the rear courtyard with its scented herb garden is the best place to enjoy a glass of Rutherglen red. Boutique regional labels dot the wine list. ✉ *84 Main St.* ☎ *02/6032–7428* ▤ *AE, DC, MC, V.*

$–$$ ✕ **The Terrace.** Part of the All Saints estate, this restaurant is a welcome spot for relaxing after a day of wine tastings. The brick floor and wide wooden tables add rustic charm to the dining room, which sits conveniently next to the cellar door. The menu lists light fare such as Mediterranean eggplant or more exotic choices like emu osso buco and smoked Lake Hume trout. Desserts are excellent, especially when combined with a formidable northeast fortified wine. ✉ *All Saints Rd., Wahgunyah* ☎ *02/6033–1922* ▤ *AE, DC, MC, V* ⊙ *No dinner.*

$$–$$$ ▥ **Tuileries.** Incorporating a vineyard, olive grove, lodgings, and a renowned restaurant, Tuileries offers boutique accommodation with a resort feel. Suites are spacious, modern, colorfully painted, and well appointed, with views over the estate's vines and orchard. ✉ *13-35 Drummond St., 3685* ☎ *02/6032–9033* ➥ *4 rooms, 5 suites* ♻ *Room service, minibars, microwaves, pool, tennis courts, free parking; no smoking* ▤ *AE, DC, MC, V* ⦿❘ *BP.*

Echuca

206 km (128 mi) north of Melbourne, 194 km (120 mi) west of Rutherglen, 92 km (57 mi) north of Bendigo.

Echuca's name derives from a local Aboriginal word meaning "meeting of the waters," a reference to the town's location at the confluence of the Murray, Campaspe, and Goulburn rivers. When the railway from Melbourne reached Echuca in 1864, the town became the junction at which wool and wheat cargo were transferred to railroad cars from barges on the Darling River in western New South Wales. In the second half of the 19th century, Echuca was Australia's largest inland port. River trade languished when the railway network extended into the interior, but reminders of Echuca's colorful heyday remain in the restored paddle steamers, barges, historic hotels, and the Red Gum Works, the town's sawmill, now a working museum.

Echuca's importance was recognized in the 1960s, when the National Trust declared the port a historic area. Nowadays it's a busy town of almost 10,000, the closest of the river towns to Melbourne. High Street, the main street of shops and cafés, leads to the river. Paddle-steamer trips along the Murray are especially relaxing if you've been following a hectic touring schedule.

A tour of the **Historic River Precinct** begins at the Port of Echuca office, where you can purchase a ticket (with or without an added river cruise) that gives admission to the Star and Bridge hotels and the Historic Wharf area. The **Bridge Hotel** was built by Henry Hopwood, ex-convict father of Echuca, who had the foresight to establish a punt, and then to build a bridge at this commercially strategic point on the river. The hotel is sparsely furnished, however, and it takes great imagination to re-create what must have been a roistering, rollicking pub frequented by river men, railway workers, and drovers. Built in the 1860s, the **Star Hotel** has an underground bar and escape tunnel, which was used by after-hours drinkers in the 19th century to evade the police. It also contains displays and memorabilia from the era. In the **Historic Wharf,** the heavy-duty side of the river-trade business is on view, including a warehouse, old railroad tracks, and riverboats. Unlike those of the Mississippi or the Danube, the small, squat, utilitarian workhorses of the Murray are no beauties. Among the vessels docked at the wharf, all original, is the PS *Adelaide,* Australia's oldest operating paddle steamer. The Adelaide cannot be boarded, but it occasionally is stoked up, with the requisite puff-puffs, chug-chugs, and toot-toots. ⊠ *Murray Esplanade* ☎ *03/5482–4248* ⊑ *A$17, A$23 with river cruise* ⊙ *Daily 9–5.*

Port of Echuca Woodturners is an old sawmill where timber from the giant river red gums that flourish along the Murray was once brought. Stop and watch the wood turners, blacksmith, and local businesses ply their trade today. Their work is for sale in the adjacent gallery. ⊠ *Murray Esplanade* ☎ *03/5480–6407* ⊑ *Free* ⊙ *Daily 9–5.*

Riverboats, including the PS *Pevensey* and the PS *Canberra,* make short, one-hour excursions along the Murray River several times daily. River traffic is limited to a few speedboats, small fishing skiffs, and an occasional kayak. The banks are thickly forested with river red gums, which require as much as half a ton of water per day. ⊠ *PS Pevensey tickets, Port of Echuca, Murray Esplanade* ☎ *03/5482–4248* ⊑ *A$18.50* ⊙ *Departs 5 times daily: 10:15, 11:30, 1:15, 2:30, 3:45* ⊠ *PS Canberra tickets, Bond Store, Murray Esplanade* ☎ *03/5482–2711* ⊑ *A$12.50* ⊙ *Departs daily at 10, 11:30, 12:45, 2, and 3:15.*

Sharp's Movie House and Penny Arcade is a nostalgic journey back to the days of the penny arcades. Have your fortune told; test your strength, dexterity, and lovability; or watch a peep show that was once banned in Australia. There are 60 machines here, the largest collection of operating penny arcade machines in the country. The movie house shows edited highlights of Australian movies that date back to 1896. ⊠ *Bond Store, Murray Esplanade* ☎ *03/5482–2361* ⊑ *A$13* ⊙ *Daily 9–5.*

Life-size wax effigies of U.S. presidents may be the last thing you would expect (or want) to find in Echuca, but the **World in Wax Museum** has Washington, Lincoln, and Kennedy—along with Fidel Castro, T. E. Lawrence (of Arabia), Queen Elizabeth II, Prince Charles, Lady Diana, and Australian celebrities and native sons. ⊠ *630 High St.* ☎ *03/ 5482–3630* ⊑ *A$9* ⊙ *Daily 9–5.*

Where to Stay & Eat

$$ ✕ **Oscar W's Wharfside.** Named after the last paddle steamer ever made
Fodor's Choice in this once-busy port, this is one of Echuca's finest restaurants. With
★ a beautiful, tree-fringed view of the Murray River, it's a comfortable, relaxed establishment with dishes as diverse as grilled flat bread with tomato tapenade and an intriguing fillet of ostrich with red onion jam. ⊠ *Murray Esplanade* ☎ *03/5482–5133* ▭ *AE, DC, MC, V.*

$$–$$$ 🏠 **PS *Emmylou*.** Departing Echuca around sunset, this paddle steamer shuffles downriver during a three-course dinner, a night in a cabin, and breakfast the following morning. The boat can accommodate 18 guests in eight bunk rooms and one double-bed cabin, all with shared showers and toilets. Sunrise over the river, as the boat churns past mist-cloaked gum trees and laughing kookaburras, is a truly memorable experience. ✉ *57 Murray Esplanade* ☎ *03/5480–2237* 🖷 *03/5480–2927* 🌐 *www. emmylou.com.au* 🛏 *9 rooms without bath* ⚐ *Dining room, bar; no a/c, no room phones, no room TVs, no kids, no smoking* 🝶 *MC, V* ⦿l *MAP.*

$$–$$$ 🏠 **River Gallery Inn.** In a 19th-century building around the corner from the historic port precinct, this hotel has large comfortable rooms at moderate prices. Each is decorated and furnished in a different theme: frilly French provincial, opulent Victorian, mock-rustic early Australian. Four rooms overlook the street but are still quiet. Five rooms have whirlpool tubs. Rates include breakfast. ✉ *578 High St., 3564* ☎ *03/5480–6902* 🛏 *6 rooms, 2 suites* ⚐ *Dining room, minibars, meeting rooms, free parking; no room phones, no kids* 🝶 *AE, MC, V* ⦿l *BP.*

$$ 🏠 **Murray House.** As soon as you step inside this inn you know that you're entering a much-loved home. Guest rooms are tastefully and individually decorated, and there's also a self-contained, two-bedroom cottage. The sitting room and the lovely cottage garden are ideal places to while away the hours. The breakfast menu changes daily. ✉ *55 Francis St., 3564* ☎ *03/5482–4944* 🖷 *03/5480–6432* 🛏 *5 rooms, 1 cottage* ⚐ *Meeting rooms; no room phones, no TV in some rooms, no kids* 🝶 *MC, V* ⦿l *BP.*

Sports & the Outdoors

BOATING **Echuca Boat and Canoe Hire** (✉ Victoria Park Boat Ramp ☎ 03/ 5480–6208) rents one-person kayaks, canoes, and motorboats, as well as fishing rods and bait. Combination camping/canoeing trips are also available. A canoe costs A$18 per hour, A$60 per day; a kayak is A$15 per hour, A$30 per day.

---

en route Named for the waterbirds that flourished here in the 1800s (and a few of the species are still around today), the prosperous town of **Swan Hill** makes a pleasant stop on the way to Mildura (it's 97 km [60 mi] northwest of Echuca). The biggest attraction here is the Swan Hill Pioneer Settlement (☎ 03/5036–2410), where life in a 19th-century Victorian river port is re-created. You can take a cruise aboard the century-old paddleboat *PYAP,* which departs twice a day, and see a snazzy sound-and-light show that brings the town's history to life.

Mildura

557 km (345 mi) northwest of Melbourne, 251 km (156 mi) northwest of Swan Hill.

Claiming more hours of sunshine per year than Queensland's Gold Coast, Mildura is known for dried fruit, wine, citrus, and avocados, as well as its hydroponic vegetable-growing industry. The town was developed in 1885 by two Canadians, George and William Chaffey, who were persuaded to emigrate by Victorian premier Alfred Deakin. The Chaffey brothers were world pioneers in irrigation, and the well-hydrated vineyards of the Riverland region are enormously productive. However, though they provide Australians with much of their inexpensive cask wines, a premium table wine rarely bears a Riverland label.

A popular option for kids, the **Aquacoaster** is a big complex of pools that includes an enormous waterslide. ⊠ *18 Orange Ave.* ☎ *03/5023–6955* 🖃 *A$11* ☉ *Dec.–Feb., weekdays 10–8.*

On the banks of the Murray, the **Golden River Fauna Gardens** has an extensive collection of native and exotic birds in walk-through aviaries. You can hand-feed kangaroos and wallabies; train rides along the river are included in the price. You can also sample a selection of locally produced boutique wines at the café. ⊠ *Flora Ave.* ☎ *03/5023–5540* 🖃 *A$12* ☉ *Daily 9–5.*

At the **Old Mildura Homestead,** which was the first home of settler William Chaffey, the life of Mildura's early European settlers is recreated through photos, furniture, clothes, and books. The property, which also features a woolshed and stables, is a favorite spot for locals to take picnic baskets to enjoy in the gardens. ⊠ *3 Hunter St.* ☎ *03/5023–3742* 🖃 *A$2* ☉ *Tues., Fri., and Sat. 10–4.*

Fodor'sChoice
★ **Trentham Estate Winery** is worth visiting as much for seeing the delightful vistas from a bend of the Murray River as for tasting its award-winning wines. Notable dishes at the on-site restaurant include yabbies, Murray perch, and kangaroo, which team admirably with the prize-winning wines available for tasting. In fine weather you can eat on the veranda or under towering gums overlooking the river. The restaurant serves lunch Tuesday–Sunday and dinner on Saturday. To find Trentham, head across the Murray and follow the Sturt Highway through Buronga until you see the Trentham Estate sign on the right. ⊠ *Sturt Hwy., Trentham Cliffs 2738, 15 km (9 mi) south of Mildura* ☎ *03/5024–8888* 🖃 *Free* ☉ *Daily 9–5.*

It's worth a peek into the **Workingman's Club** just to see the bar: at 300 feet, it's one of the world's longest, and seemingly the whole town turns out to drink at its 27 taps. ⊠ *Deakin Ave.* ☎ *03/5023–0531* 🖃 *Free* ☉ *Daily 11–10.*

Where to Stay & Eat

★ **$$–$$$** ✕ **Stefano's.** This restaurant became nationally known with the Australian television series *A Gondola on the Murray,* which showcased the skills and personality of chef-owner Stefano de Pieri. His northern Italian cuisine is tasty and prepared primarily from the Riverland's bountiful local produce. The extensive menu includes seasonal specialties like yabbies on a kipfler potato and caper salad, chicken-and-prosciutto tortellini, fresh vegetarian fettuccine, and a sumptuous European selection of desserts and cakes. ⊠ *Mildura Grand Hotel, 7th St., enter from Langtree Ave.* ☎ *03/5023–0511* ▭ *AE, DC, MC, V* ☉ *No dinner Sun.*

$$$$ ⌂ **Mildura Grand Hotel.** Perched beside the Murray River, the newly refurbished Grand Hotel offers visitors a taste of country Australia. There are luxury spa suites available here, as well as smaller, less-expensive rooms. There's also an in-house movie theater, tranquil rose gardens to wander through, and a wine center. Three eateries—Stefano's Restaurant, Dining Room One, and the Spanish Grill and Pizza Cafe—give you a range of dining choices. ⊠ *7th St., 3500* ☎ *03/5023–0511* 🖤 *95 rooms, 8 suites* ⚬ *Restaurants, room service, in-room VCRs, pool, hot tub, bar, dry cleaning, laundry facilities, meeting rooms, free parking* ⊟ *AE, DC, MC, V.*

$–$$$ ⌂ **Olive House.** Part of the original Chaffey brothers' property, this elegant Federation cottage has been fully restored and transformed into a self-contained accommodation. Two beautiful bedrooms, each with original pressed-metal walls and ceilings and period furniture, open onto a spacious lounge featuring a coal fire, stereo, and TV with DVD player. The fully appointed kitchen comes with breakfast provisions, a selection of homemade jams, teas, and percolator coffee. ⊠ *170 9th St., 3500* ☎ *03/5023–2826* 🖤 *2 rooms* ⚬ *Free parking* ⊟ *AE, DC, MC, V* ⦿ *CP.*

Murray River Region A to Z

CAR TRAVEL

The wide-open spaces of the northeast wineries and Murray River districts make driving the most sensible and feasible means of exploration. There's enough scenic interest along the way to make the long drives bearable, especially if you trace the river route. The direct run from Melbourne to Mildura is quite daunting (557 km [345 mi]). However, those towns accessed by the Calder Highway are easily reached from the capital city.

Beechworth and Rutherglen are on opposite sides of the Hume Freeway, the main Sydney–Melbourne artery. Allow four hours for the journey from Melbourne, twice that from Sydney. Echuca is a three-hour drive from Melbourne, reached most directly by the Northern Highway (Highway 75).

EMERGENCIES

In an emergency, dial **000** to reach an ambulance, the police, or the fire department.

🗐 Amcal Pharmacy ⊠ 192 Hare St., Echuca ☎ 03/5482-6666. **Echuca and District Hospital** ⊠ Francis St., Echuca ☎ 03/5482-2800.

TOURS

The Gray Line operates one-day bus tours of Echuca, departing from Melbourne on Friday and Sunday at 8:45 AM. The cost is A$110.

🗐 Gray Line ⊠ 180 Swanson St., City Center, Melbourne ☎ 03/9663-4455.

TRAIN TRAVEL

V-Line trains run to most of the major towns in the region, including Echuca, Rutherglen, Swan Hill, and Mildura—but not Beechworth.

This reasonable access is most useful if you do not have a car or want to avoid the long-distance drives. As with most country Victorian areas, direct train access from Melbourne to the main centers is reasonable, but getting between towns isn't as easy. The train to Swan Hill or Mildura may be an appealing option for those utterly discouraged by the long drive.

🚹 **V-Line** ☎ 1800/800120.

VISITOR INFORMATION

The information centers in Beechworth, Rutherglen, and Swan Hill are open daily 9–5:30; the center in Echuca is open daily 9–5; and the Mildura center is open weekdays 9–4 and weekends 10–4, but they close for lunch weekdays 12:30–1.

🚹 **Beechworth Tourist Information Centre** ⊠ Ford and Camp Sts., Beechworth ☎ 03/5728-1374. **Echuca Tourist Information Centre** ⊠ Leslie St. and Murray Esplanade, Echuca ☎ 03/5480-7555. **Mildura Tourist Information Centre** ⊠ Langtree Mall, Mildura ☎ 03/5023-3619. **Rutherglen Tourist Information Centre** ⊠ Walkabout Cellars, 84 Main St., Rutherglen ☎ 02/6032-9166. **Swan Hill Regional Information Office** ⊠ 306 Campbell St., Swan Hill ☎ 03/5032-3033.

ALPINE & WILSON'S PROMONTORY NATIONAL PARKS

More than 300 km (186 mi) separates these two national parklands, and their landscapes are very different: while Alpine National Park contains the highest peaks in the Victorian Alps and is a popular ski destination in winter, Wilson's Promontory occupies a peninsula at Australia's southernmost tip and is a great place for swimming, bird-watching, and other summertime activities. What both share in common, though, are spectacular landscapes and top-notch bushwalking year-round. Both parks are also a relatively easy easterly drive from Melbourne.

Alpine National Park

323 km (200 mi) northeast of Melbourne.

The name Alpine National Park actually applies to three loosely connected areas in eastern Victoria that follow the peaks of the Great Dividing Range. One of these areas, formerly called Bogong National Park, contains some of the highest mountains on the continent. As such, it is a wintertime mecca for skiers, who flock to the ski resorts at Falls Creek, Mt. Buller, Mt. Buffalo, and Mt. Hotham.

The land around here is rich in history. *Bogong* is an Aboriginal word for "big moth," and it was to Mt. Bogong that Aborigines came each year after the winter thaw in search of bogong moths, considered a delicacy. Aborigines were eventually displaced by cattlemen who brought their cattle here to graze. Since the creation of the park in the mid-1980s, grazing has become more limited.

Stately snow gums grace the hills, complemented by alpine wildflowers in bloom October–March. There are half- and full-day trails for bushwalkers, many of them in the Falls Creek area south of Mt. Beauty. In winter the area is completely covered in snow, and bushwalkers replace their hiking boots with cross-country skis.

For information on walks and parks in the area, contact the **Department of Natural Resources and Environment** (✉ 240 Victoria Parade, East Melbourne, Melbourne ☎ 03/9412–4011 ⊕ www.parkweb.vic. gov.au).

Where to Stay & Eat

Old cattlemen's huts are scattered throughout the park and may be used by hikers free of charge. These, however, are often occupied, and shelter is never guaranteed. Bush camping is permitted throughout the park, and there's a basic campground at Raspberry Hill.

Hotels, motels, commercial camping, and RV parks are in the major towns around the park, including Bright, Buckland, Mt. Beauty, Harrietville, Anglers Rest, Glen Valley, and Tawonga, as well as in the ski resorts of Falls Creek, Mt. Buller, and Mt. Hotham year-round.

$–$$ ✕ **Sasha's of Bright.** Crisp-skinned duck is the highlight of Czech-born chef Sasha Cinatl's menu. Hungarian goulash, smoked pork, and spatchcock in a rich port sauce are also dishes to look out for. For dessert, blueberry cheesecake, sticky date pudding, and lemon meringue pie join a range of daily specials. The well-priced wine list focuses on northeast Victorian vintages. ✉ 2D Anderson St., Bright ☎ 03/5750–1711 ▤ AE, DC, MC, V.

★ **$–$$** ✕ **Simone's Restaurant.** Bright's most popular restaurant is in a quaint terrace house near the main street. The fig salad with walnuts and pomegranate seeds is a must-try, as is the game ragout with wild mushrooms and chestnuts, served over ribbon pasta. Beautifully presented desserts include strawberry-and-ice-cream parfait sprinkled with dried rose petals. In summer you can dine on the balcony by candlelight, overlooking a profusely blooming cottage garden. ✉ 98 Gavan St., Bright ☎ 03/5755–2266 ▤ AE, DC, MC, V.

$$$–$$$$ ✕▣ **Villa Gusto.** This Tuscan-inspired villa occupies an elegant estate over-
Fodor'sChoice looking Mt. Buffalo. Cast-iron fountains, imported marble accents,
★ 17th-century antiques, and exquisite tapestries add Italianate authenticity to the suites and the restaurant here. Four-course set meals include entrées like Tuscan-style chicken and pumpkin agnolotti, and trout on fennel and kipfler potato ragout. Smooth desserts, like the Umbrian nectarine crostata topped with vanilla cream and chocolate sauce, perfect the experience. ✉ 630 Buckland Valley Rd., Buckland 3741 ☎ 03/ 5756–2000 ⊕ www.villagusto.com.au ⇨ 12 suites ᇰ Restaurant, outdoor hot tub, lounge, library, theater ▤ AE, DC, MC, V ⦿ BP.

Sports & the Outdoors

The Australian ski season is brief and unpredictable, but if you're keen to try one of the mountains in the Alpine area, it's best to check conditions and prices online first: ⊕ www.fallscreek.com.au, ⊕ www. mtbuller.com.au, ⊕ www.mtbuffalochalet.com.au, and ⊕ www. mthotham.com.au

Wilson's Promontory National Park

★ *231 km (144 mi) southeast of Melbourne.*

This granite peninsula, the continent's southernmost, once connected Tasmania with mainland Australia. Though this was eons ago, the area still maintains botanical and geological odds and ends common both to the mainland and the wayward island. More than 180 species of birds have been sighted here, and Corner Inlet, along Five Mile Beach, is a seabird sanctuary. Near the visitor center at Tidal River you may spot tame marsupials, including kangaroos, wombats, and koalas.

There are more than 20 well-marked trails here, some meandering past pristine beaches and secluded coves excellent for swimming, others more strenuous. One tough but popular trail is the 9½-km (6-mi) **Sealer's Cove Walk,** which traverses the slopes of Mt. Wilson Range before descending through Sealer's Swamp to the tranquil Sealer's Cove (where, as the name suggests, you can often see seals offshore). The **Lilly Pilly Gully Nature Walk,** a 5-km (3-mi) trip among tree ferns and giant mountain ash, gives a good introduction to the park's plant and animal life with the aid of informative signs posted along the way. And from the top of Mt. Oberon on a good day, you can see across the Bass Strait all the way to Tasmania.

Although Wilson's Promontory is perhaps the best-known sight in the Gippsland region, there are also notable seaside towns and inland parks worth visiting. **Tarra Bulga National Park,** about an hour's drive from Wilson's Promontory, has numerous walking tracks that wind through fern gullies and towering forests where rainbow parrots flit through the branches. Drive along the spectacular winding **Grand Ridge Road** through the Strzelecki Ranges, and stop in the historic towns of **Port Albert** and **Yarram.** Farther east of the Prom, Gippsland's **Lakes District** is a boater's haven, particularly around the towns of Metung and Painsville. Nearby, **Lakes Entrance** is a popular summer holiday resort where boats and water sports are easy to arrange.

Where to Stay & Eat

A few quality lodging establishments have sprung up in this once-rugged area. Dining is a bit more problematic: there's not much to be said about food in this particular corner unless you catch it and cook it yourself. The **Foster Motel** (⊠ 3800 S. Gippsland Hwy, Foster ☎ 03/5682—2022) has a dining room. The **Exchange Hotel** (⊠ 43 Main St., Foster ☎ 03/5682—2377) serves good pub dinners.

$$$
Fodor'sChoice
★ ⊞ **Bear Gully Coastal.** Overlooking Waratah Bay, Wilson's Promontory and the islands of the Glennie and Anser Groups, Bear Gully comprises four self-contained cottages. Each has a fully appointed kitchen, living room, bathroom/laundry, log heater, CD player, and electric barbecue. Large canopied decks open out from the living rooms—ideal for watching sunrise and sunset over Wilson's Promontory. Nearby, the waterfront unfolds in a series of sandy coves and rock pools that are perfect for swimming or snorkeling. ⊠ *33 Maitland Ct., Walkerville 3956*

☎ *03/5663–2364* ⊕ *www.beargullycottages.com.au* ⮑ *4 cottages* ⊟ *AE, DC, MC, V* ⎮◎⎮ *BP.*

$–$$ 🏠 **Larkrise House.** Set on 40 acres of rolling farmland with glorious sea
Fodor'sChoice views, this property has rooms with paintings, antique furnishings, and
★ lovely picture windows. Breakfasts, including freshly squeezed juice
and home-baked breads, are served outside in the gardens; dinners, served
by request and prepared from local ingredients, cost $40. Dishes might
include South Gippsland flathead with ginger and dill sauce, served with
grilled mixed vegetables, roasted young potatoes, and poached quince
slices. ✉ *395 Fish Creek Rd., Foster 3960* ☎ *03/5682–2953* ⊕ *www.
larkrise.com.au* ⮑ *2 rooms* ♨ *Lounge, library; no room phones, no room
TVs* ⊟ *AE, DC, MC, V* ⎮◎⎮ *BP.*

⚠ **Tidal River Campground.** With 480 campsites, this well-known
campground is among Australia's largest, and it can get crowded in
the January and February peak season. Trailer sites have access to electricity and water. Single-room huts each contain two double bunk beds,
a hot plate, a small refrigerator, heaters, and cold water. Heated cabins, which accommodate two to six people, have a one-week minimum
booking in peak season. Reservations, available up to 12 months
ahead, must be received by June for campsites, huts, and cabins.
✉ *Park Office, Wilson's Promontory National Park, South Gippsland*
☎ *03/5680–9555* ⮑ *480 campsites* ♨ *Flush toilets, pit toilets, full
hookups, drinking water, laundry facilities, showers, fire pits, grills,
picnic tables, electricity, public telephone, general store, ranger station* ▭ *A$20 ; A$18 ; A$49 ; A$840.*

Alpine & Wilson's Promontory National Parks A to Z

BUS TRAVEL

Bus services to Alpine National Park operate from Albury on the New
South Wales border in the north. In ski season, Pyles Coaches depart
from Mt. Beauty for Falls Creek and Mt. Hotham, and depart from Melbourne for Falls Creek.

🚏 **Pyles Coaches** ☎ 03/5754–4024.

CAR TRAVEL

Alpine National Park is 323 km (200 mi) northeast of Melbourne, and
you can reach it two ways. If you want to go to the park taking a short
detour through the historic town of Beechworth, take the Hume Freeway north out of Melbourne and turn southeast onto the Ovens Highway at Wangaratta. Beechworth is about a 30-km (19-mi) detour off
the Hume. You can also follow the Princes Highway east from Melbourne
through Sale and Bairnsdale. Pick up the Omeo Highway north from
here to Omeo, and then head west to Cobungra and Mt. Hotham. The
turnoff for Falls Creek is another 39 km (24 mi) north of Omeo.

To get to Wilson's Promontory National Park, 231 km (144 mi) south
of Melbourne, take the Princes Highway to Dandenong, and then the
South Gippsland Highway south to Meeniyan or Foster. Tidal River is
another 70 km (43 mi). There's no public transportation to the park.

VISITOR INFORMATION

The ranger station for the Alpine National Park is on Mt. Beauty, and there are information centers in Bright, Omeo, and Falls Creek. The station at Mt. Beauty has ranger-led programs.

Wilson's Promontory National Park headquarters sells guidebooks. Prom Country Information Centre handles all accommodation inquiries. Both are open daily 9–5.

🚩 **Alpine National Park** ✉ Kiewa Valley Hwy., Tawonga South ☎ 03/5754–4693. **Bright Visitor Center** ✉ 119 Gavan St., Bright ☎ 03/5755–2275. **Falls Creek Visitor Center** ✉ 1 Bogong High Plains Rd., Falls Creek ☎ 1800/033079. **Omeo Visitor Center** ✉ 199 Day Ave., Omeo ☎ 03/51591552. **Prom Country Information Centre** ✉ South Gippsland Hwy., Korumburra 3950 ☎ 1800/630704 ⊕ www.promcountry.com.au. **Wilson's Promontory National Park** ✉ Tidal River ☎ 03/5680–9555.

Tasmania

WORD OF MOUTH

"I am a bit biased toward Tassie wines. Although they are a bit more expensive than Mainland wines, I think they are worth it, and they go so nicely with Tasmania's fine foods. I still have fond memories of sitting with my wife on a headland overlooking the aqua blue waters of Binalong Bay (on the east coast of Tasmania), eating a fresh crayfish and sipping a Bream Creek Riesling."

—tropo

Updated by
Roger Allnutt

SEPARATED FROM THE MAINLAND by the rough Bass Strait, the island of Tasmania holds a bounty of natural diversity and old-fashioned hospitality. It's a hiker's dream, rich with rarely-tracked wilderness along its southwest and west coasts. Elegant English settlements with vast gardens fringe the east and north edges. Remnants of the island's volatile days as a penal colony await exploration in abundant museums and historic sites that preserve the lore of this fascinating piece of Australia.

About the size of West Virginia, and with a population of less than a half million, Tasmania is an unspoiled reminder of a simpler, slower lifestyle. It has been called the England of the south, as it, too, is richly cloaked in mists and rain, glows with russet and gold shades in fall, and has the chance of an evening chill year-round. Where the English tradition of a Christmas roast may strike you as strange in a steamy Sydney summer, such rites appear natural amid Tasmania's lush quilt of lowland farms and villages. Many towns retain an English look, with their profusion of Georgian cottages and commercial buildings, the preservation of which attests to Tasmanians' attachment to their past.

Aborigines, who crossed a temporary land bridge from Australia, first settled the island some 45,000 years ago. Europeans discovered it in 1642, when Dutch explorer Abel Tasman arrived at its southwest coast. First called Van Diemen's Land, after the Governor of the Dutch East Indies, Tasmania's violent history since the arrival of Europeans has episodes that many residents may wish to forget. The entire population of full-blooded Aborigines was wiped out or exiled to the Bass Strait islands by English troops and settlers. The establishment in 1830 of a penal settlement at Port Arthur for the colony's worst offenders ushered in a new age of cruelty.

Today, walking through the lovely grounds in Port Arthur or the unhurried streets of Hobart, it's difficult to picture Tasmania as a land of turmoil and tragedy. But in many ways Tasmania is still untamed. Twenty-eight percent of the land is preserved in national parks, where impenetrable rain forests and deep river gorges cut through the massive mountain valleys. The coastlines are scalloped with endless desolate beaches—some pristine white, fronting serene turquoise bays, and some rugged and rocky, facing churning, wind-whipped seas. The island's extreme southern position also results in a wild climate that's often hammered by Antarctic winds, so be prepared for sudden, severe weather changes. A snowstorm in summer isn't unusual.

Exploring Tasmania

Tasmania is compact—the drive from southern Hobart to northern Launceston takes little more than two hours. The easiest way to see the state is by car, as you can plan a somewhat circular route around the island. Begin in Hobart or Launceston, where car rentals are available from the airport city agencies, or in Devonport if you arrive on the ferry from Melbourne. Although distances seem small, allow plenty of time for stops along the way. Bring a sturdy pair of shoes for impromptu mountain and seaside walks; you'll most often have huge patches of forest

6

If you have 3 days

Spend your first morning in **Hobart,** where you can stroll around the docks, Salamanca Place, and Battery Point, and take a cruise on the Derwent River. After lunch, drive to **Richmond** and explore its 19th-century streetscape, then stay in a local B&B. On the second day head for **Port Arthur** and spend the morning exploring the town's historic park, the site of the island's former penal colony. Take the afternoon to drive through the dramatic scenery of the Tasman Peninsula, noting the tessellated pavement and Tasman Arch blowhole near Eaglehawk neck. Return to Hobart for the night, then on the third morning take a leisurely drive round the scenic **Huon Valley.** On return to Hobart, finish your tour with a trip to the summit of Mt. Wellington.

If you have 5 days

Explore **Hobart** on foot the first morning, then head for the Cadbury chocolate factory in Claremont, wandering through historic **Richmond** on the way back. Spend the night in Hobart, then on the second day drive through the scenic **Huon Valley.** Return to Hobart for the night, and on the third day drive to **Port Arthur,** taking in the beauty of the Tasman Peninsula on the way. Spend the night in Port Arthur, then drive early on the fourth day to **Freycinet National Park.** Climb the steep path to the outlook over Wineglass Bay, then descend to the sands for a picnic and swim. Stay the night in the park, then on Day 5 meander back to Hobart via **Ross** and **Oatlands.** Return to the capital, topping off the day with city views from Mt. Wellington.

If you have 10 days

Take a walking tour of **Hobart** on the first morning, then take an afternoon drive to **Richmond** before returning for the night. On the second day, drive to the Tasman Peninsula, enjoying the scenic backroads before heading to **Port Arthur** for the night. On the third day, head back southwest through Hobart toward the bucolic orchards of the **Huon Valley** and the Tahune Forest Airwalk. Stay the night, then depart early on the fourth morning for **Strahan,** stopping at Lake St. Clair. Spend the night, take an all-day cruise on the Gordon River, and stay another night. On Day 6 make the long drive north via Zeehan and Marrawah to **Stanley,** a lovely village set beneath the rocky majesty of the Nut. Have lunch here, then head back east to **Devonport** and stay the night. On Day 7, turn inland via Sheffield or Wilmot to reach **Cradle Mountain National Park.** Stay two nights, using Day 8 to fully explore the region's natural beauty. On the ninth day, leave early for **Launceston,** spend the night, then head back to Hobart through **Ross** and **Oatlands.**

and long expanses of white beaches all to yourself. In some cases the street addresses for attractions may not include building numbers (in other words, only the name of the street will be given). Don't worry— this just means either that the street is short and the attractions are clearly visible, or that signposts will clearly lead you there.

About the Restaurants
Although there are elegant dining options in the larger towns—especially Hobart—most eateries here serve filling meals in a casual setting. Local

seafood, steaks, hearty meat pies, produce, and wines are usually menu highlights; ask your waiter, or even the restaurant owner, for recommendations.

WHAT IT COSTS In Australian Dollars				
$$$$	**$$$**	**$$**	**$**	**¢**
AT DINNER	over $50	$36–$50	$21–$35	$10–$20	under $10

Prices are for a main course at dinner.

About the Hotels

In Tasmania, hotels of all levels usually include tea- and coffee-making facilities, room refrigerators, TVs, heating, electric blankets, irons, and hair dryers on request, and laundry facilities. Most hotels also have air-conditioning, but bed-and-breakfast lodgings often do not. Apart from a few hotels right in the main city center, most Hobart accommodations have free parking. In many smaller places, especially the colonial-style cottages, no smoking is allowed inside. For a comprehensive list of B&B establishments around Tasmania, look at ⊕ www.tasmanianbedandbreakfast.com.

WHAT IT COSTS In Australian Dollars				
$$$$	**$$$**	**$$**	**$**	**¢**
FOR 2 PEOPLE	over $300	$201–$300	$151–$200	$100–$150	under $100

Prices are for two people in a standard double room in high season, including tax and service, based on the European Plan (with no meals) unless otherwise noted.

Timing

Tasmanian winters can draw freezing blasts from the Antarctic, so this is not the season to explore the highlands or wilderness areas. It's better in the colder months to enjoy the cozy interiors of colonial cottages and the open fireplaces of welcoming pubs. Summer can be surprisingly hot—bushfires are common—but temperatures are generally lower than on the Australian mainland. Early autumn is beautiful, with deciduous trees in full color. Spring, with its splashes of pastel wildflowers, is the season for rainbows.

Tasmania is a relaxing island with few crowds, except during the mid-December to mid-February school holiday period and at the end of the annual Sydney-to-Hobart yacht race just after Christmas. Most attractions and sights, including the national parks, are open year-round.

HOBART

Straddling the Derwent River at the foot of Mt. Wellington's forested slopes, Hobart was founded as a penal settlement in 1803. It's the second-oldest city in the country after Sydney, and it certainly rivals its mainland counterpart as Australia's most beautiful state capital. Close-set colonial brick-and-sandstone shops and homes line the narrow, quiet streets, creating a genteel setting for this historic city of 185,000. Life

Tassie Tastes

Tasmania's clean air, unpolluted waters, and temperate climate provide a pristine environment in which fresh seafood, beef, dairy goods, fruits and vegetables, and wine are produced year-round. In particular, the island's culinary fame is based on its superb, bountiful seafood. Tasmanian dairy products are worth the indulgence, notably King Island's cheese and thick double cream. With more than 100 vineyards, Tasmania is also establishing itself as a force in Australian wine making, and the quality reds and whites from small producers are gaining accolades locally and overseas. And no one should miss a tour of the famous Cadbury-Schweppes chocolate and cocoa factory near Hobart, where you can sample from the richly flavored treats that have long been an Australian favorite.

Colonial Homes & Cottages

Tasmania nurtures the architectural gems that have survived its colonial past. With only a small population to support, the state has rarely found it necessary to demolish the old to make way for the new. Many cottages built during the first days of the colony are now B&Bs, guesthouses, and self-catering apartments. They are in the best-preserved towns and villages, as well as in the major cities of Hobart and Launceston. Georgian mansions, country pubs, colonial cottages, charming boutique hotels, and welcoming motels are all part of the quality accommodation network ready to invite you in for some real "Tassie" hospitality.

Outdoor Adventures

Tasmania is an explorer's playground, with some of Australia's best and most challenging walking terrain. Large sections of mountains and coasts are incorporated into regulated natural areas like Mt. Field, Southwest, and Franklin-Gordon Wild Rivers National Park in the southwest. The state's western wilderness is still virtually untouched, and it's the domain of serious trekkers. You can find less-strenuous and relatively pristine walking around Cradle Mountain, in the center of Tasmania, and on the Freycinet Peninsula on the east coast. The island has myriad opportunities for cycling, diving, bushwalking (hiking), rafting, sailing, sea kayaking, and game and trout fishing.

---

revolves around the broad Derwent River port, one of the deepest harbors in the world. Here, warehouses that once stored Hobart's major exports of fruit, wool, and corn, and products from the city's former whaling fleet still stand alongside the wharf today.

Hobart sparkles between Christmas and New Year's—summer Down Under—during the annual Sydney-to-Hobart yacht race. The event dominates conversations among Hobart's citizens, who descend on Constitution Dock to welcome the yachts and join in the boisterous festivities of the crews. The new year also coincides with the Tastes of Tasmania Festival, when the dockside area comes alive with the best of Tasmanian food and wine on offer in numerous cafés, bars, and waterfront

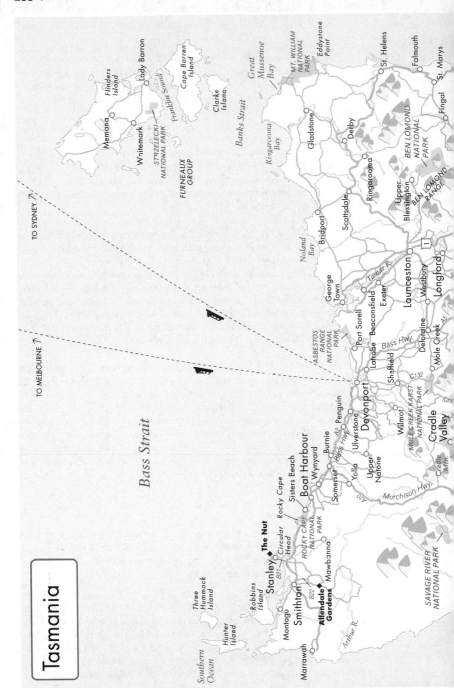

Tasmania

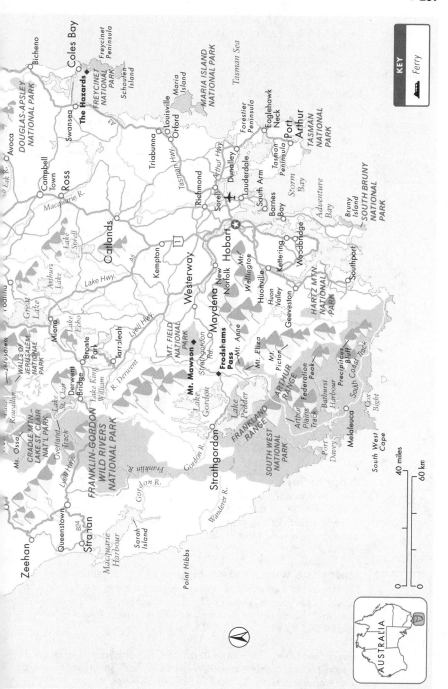

Ferry

stalls. Otherwise, Hobart is a placid city whose nightlife is largely confined to excellent restaurants, jazz clubs, and the action at the Wrest Point Casino in Sandy Bay.

Exploring Hobart

Numbers in the text correspond to numbers in the margin and on the Downtown Hobart map.

a good tour

Begin your tour of Hobart at the **Brooke Street Pier** ❶ ⌐, near Franklin Wharf and the old Macquarie Street warehouses. Walk northwest to Davey Street, then northeast one block to visit the **Maritime Museum of Tasmania** ❷ and the adjacent **Tasmanian Museum and Art Gallery** ❸. Across from the museums is **Constitution Dock** ❹, from which you can follow the line of the wharves to **Parliament House** ❺. A block southeast is **Salamanca Place** ❻, Hobart's most vibrant shopping district, where the colorful Salamanca morning market opens on Saturday. From here, climb Montpelier Road onto Hampden Road, which leads to the **Narryna Heritage Museum** ❼ and antiques shops, charming cottages, and other historic buildings. Head back toward Castray Esplanade, but this time turn left into Runnymede Street and walk by the delightful homes of **Arthur's Circus** ❽.

From here you'll need a car to drive north to one or all of the following sights: the **Penitentiary Chapel and Criminal Courts** ❾, the **Royal Tasmanian Botanical Gardens** ❿, or the **Cadbury-Schweppes Chocolate Factory** ⓫. At the end of the day, tour the **Cascade Brewery** ⓬ in South Hobart, then stop at the **Shot Tower** ⓭ for spectacular views over the city and Derwent River.

TIMING Allow at least 2 hours for the docks, the museums, and the Salamanca Place market. A wander through the Arthur's Circus neighborhood might take a half hour, while the Cascade Brewery makes a good stop for lunch before the 2-hour tour. Add an hour each to explore the Penitentiary Chapel, the Botanical Gardens, and the Shot Tower, all of which are pleasant places to wander in the late afternoon. Tours of the Cadbury factory take 1½ hours.

What to See

❽ **Arthur's Circus.** Hobart's best-preserved street is an enchanting collection of tiny houses and cottages in a circle around a village green on Runnymede Street, in the heart of historic Battery Point. Most of these houses, which were built in the 1840s and 1850s, have been nicely restored.

off the beaten path

BONORONG WILDLIFE PARK – Situated 25 km (16 mi) north of Hobart on the highway to Launceston, the park has a wide selection of Australian species, including koalas, wombats, quolls (indigenous cats), and the notorious Tasmanian devil. ✉ *Briggs Rd., Brighton* ☏ *03/6268–1184* 🎫 *A$11* ⏱ *Daily 9–5.*

⌐ ❶ **Brooke Street Pier.** The busy waterfront at Brooke Street Pier is the departure point for harbor cruises. Nearby **Elizabeth Street Pier** has trendy restaurants and bars. ✉ *Franklin Wharf, Hobart City.*

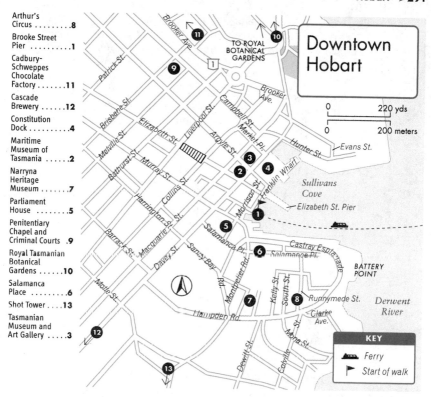

🐾 ⑪ **Cadbury-Schweppes Chocolate Factory.** Very few children (or adults!) can resist a trip to the best chocolate and cocoa factory in Australia. Visits are by 1½-hour guided tour only; book through the visitor information center. Of course, the best part of the tour is getting to sample some of the scrumptious products. ✉ *Cadbury Estate, Cadbury Rd., Claremont, 12 km (7½ mi) north of Hobart* ☎ *03/6249–0333 or 1800/627367* ⊕ *www.cadbury.com.au* 💰 *A$12.50* ☉ *Tours weekdays at 9, 9:30, 10:30, and 1.*

⑫ **Cascade Brewery.** This is Australia's oldest brewery, producing fine beers since 1824. You can see its inner workings only on the two-hour tours, which require lots of walking and climbing, but you're rewarded with a free drink at the end. Note that appropriate attire—no shorts, no sandals—is required, and tour reservations are essential. ✉ *140 Cascade Rd., South Hobart* ☎ *03/6221–8300* 💰 *A$14* ☉ *Tours weekdays at 9:30 and 1.*

❹ **Constitution Dock.** Yachts competing in the annual Sydney-to-Hobart race moor at this colorful marina dock from the end of December through the first week of January. Buildings fronting the dock are century-old reminders of Hobart's trading history. ✉ *Argyle and Davey Sts., Hobart City* ☎ *No phone* 💰 *Free* ☉ *Daily 24 hrs.*

② **Maritime Museum of Tasmania.** The old state library building houses one of the best maritime collections in Australia, including figureheads, whaling implements, models, and photographs dating from as far back as 1804. ⊠ *Argyle and Davey Sts., Hobart City* ☎ *03/6234–1427* 🖅 *A$6* ☉ *Daily 10–4:30.*

⑦ **Narryna Heritage Museum.** Exhibits in this gracious old town house depict the life of Tasmania's upper-class pioneers. Of particular interest are the collections of colonial furniture, clothes, paintings, and photos. ⊠ *103 Hampden Rd., Battery Point* ☎ *03/6234–2791* 🖅 *A$5* ☉ *Aug.–June, weekdays 10:30–5, weekends 2–5.*

⑤ **Parliament House.** Built by convicts in 1840 as a customs house, this building did not acquire its present function until 1856. Although it's closed to the general public, tours run on weekdays. Contact the Clerk of the House if you'd also like to watch a session of parliament from the viewing gallery. The grounds are maintained by the Royal Botanic Gardens. ⊠ *Morrison St. between Murray St. and Salamanca Pl., Hobart City* ☎ *03/6233–2374* 🖅 *Free* ☉ *Guided tours weekdays 10–2.*

⑨ **Penitentiary Chapel and Criminal Courts.** Built and used during the early convict days, these buildings vividly portray Tasmania's penal, judicial, and religious heritage in their courtrooms, old cells, and underground tunnels. If you want to get spooked, come for the nighttime ghost tour (reservations recommended). ⊠ *Brisbane and Campbell Sts., Hobart City* ☎ *03/6231–0911* 🖅 *A$7.70, ghost tour A$8.80* ☉ *Tour weekdays 10–3, ghost tour daily 7:45 PM.*

need a break? Drop into **Sugo** (⊠ Shop 9, Salamanca Pl., Hobart City ☎ 03/6224–5690) if you get hungry while strolling the shops of Salamanca Place. This funky café serves great breakfasts, as well as tasty pizzas, pastas, and coffee. You're welcome to bring your own bottle of wine. It's open Tuesday–Friday 8–5, and weekends 9–5,

⑩ **Royal Tasmanian Botanical Gardens.** The largest area of open land in Hobart, these well-tended gardens are rarely crowded and provide a welcome relief from the city. Plants from all over the world are here—more than 6,000 exotic and native species in all. (The collection of Tasmania's unique native flora is especially impressive.) One section has been specially designed for wheelchairs. The Japanese Garden is dominated by a miniature Mt. Fuji. ⊠ *Lower Domain Rd., Queen's Domain* ☎ *03/6234–6299* 🖅 *Free* ☉ *Daily 8–4:45, education center noon–4.*

⑥ **Salamanca Place.** Old whaling ships used to dock at Salamanca Place. *Fodor's*Choice Today many of the warehouses that were once used by whalers along ★ this street have been converted into crafts shops, art galleries, and restaurants. At the boisterous Saturday market, dealers of Tasmanian arts and crafts, antiques, old records, and books—and a fair bit of appalling junk—display their wares between 8 and 3. Keep an eye open for items made from beautiful Tasmanian timber, particularly Huon pine.

⑬ **Shot Tower.** Built in the 1860s, this 160-foot structure adjacent to the road in the town of Taroona is now the only remaining circular sandstone tower in the world. Lead bullets were once manufactured here for use in the firearms of the day. Climb the internal, 259-step staircase to breathtaking views of the Derwent estuary, then reward yourself at the ground-level café with delicious scones, homemade jam, and fresh cream. ⊠ *Channel Hwy., Taroona* ☎ *03/6227–8885* 🖃 *A$4.50* ☉ *Daily 9–5.*

❸ **Tasmanian Museum and Art Gallery.** This building overlooking Constitution Dock houses many exhibits on Tasmania's history. It's the best place in Hobart to learn about the island's Aborigines (the last native Aboriginal inhabitants here died in the late 1800s), and unique wildlife. ⊠ *40 Macquarie St., Hobart City* ☎ *03/6211–4177* 🖃 *Free* ☉ *Daily 10–5.*

Where to Eat

Constitution Dock is the perfect place for yacht-watching, as well as for gobbling fresh fish-and-chips from one of the punts (floating fish-and-chips shops) moored on the water. Ask for the daily specials, such as local blue grenadier or trevally, which cost A$6–A$8. The city's main restaurant areas include the docks and around Salamanca Place.

$$–$$$ ✕ **Lickerish.** Casual and affordable, this hip restaurant-cum-bistro with a clever name is very popular and you may have to wait for a table. However the food is well worth the wait. Try the heavenly creamy semolina gnocchi with beetroot sorbet. Be sure to leave room for dessert, too—like the fabulous honey panna cotta crowned with a thin layer of strawberry jam. ⊠ *373 Elizabeth St., North Hobart* ☎ *03/6231–9186* 🖃 *AE, DC, MC, V* ☉ *Closed Mon. No lunch.*

$$–$$$ ✕ **Steam Packet.** Part of the Henry Jones Art Hotel, this restaurant lets
FodorʼsChoice you dine in either a glassed-in atrium courtyard or alfresco on Hunter
★ Street's Old Wharf. Local seafood, beef, lamb, game, and seasonal produce are featured in dishes like sashimi-style ocean trout with wasabi mayonnaise, or spice-roasted loin of fallow deer with butternut squash and beetroot jus. The wine list boasts selections from only the finest Tasmanian, mainland Australia, and overseas wineries. ⊠ *25 Hunter St. Hobart City* ☎ *03/6231–6391* 🖃 *AE, DC, MC, V.*

★ **$$** ✕ **Elbow Room.** Chef-proprietor Charlie Shoobridge earns his reputation for innovative cuisine at this stylish basement restaurant. White linen, crystal glassware, fresh flowers, and attentive service lend an elegant feel to the dining room. The roast saddle of lamb served with preserved lemon and vegetable couscous is a showstopper, as are the tournedos topped with red wine and shallot butter. There are excellent wines, including vintage Australian reds and French champagne and sauternes, to complement every choice on the menu. ⊠ *9–11 Murray St., entrance off Despard St., Hobart City* ☎ *03/6224–4254* 🖃 *AE, DC, MC, V* ☉ *Closed Sun. No lunch Mon. or Sat.*

$$ ✕ **Lebrina.** Elegant surroundings in an 1849 brick colonial home inspire classic Tasmanian cooking. The best of the island's fresh produce is well utilized in such dishes as the twice-cooked Gruyère soufflé appetizer, or the seared loin of venison with fresh horseradish, served with red cabbage salad. Leave room for the superb Tasmanian cheese plate. The wine list includes many fine Tasmanian vintages. ⊠ *155 New Town Rd., New*

Town ☎ *03/6228–7775* ☱ *AE, DC, MC, V* ☉ *Closed Sun. and Mon. No lunch.*

$$ ✕ **Meehan's.** Superb views of Hobart's bustling waterfront surround the dining room at the Hotel Grand Chancellor's signature restaurant. Seasonal menu choices here include aged King Island porterhouse steak with artichoke mash, grilled onion, and red wine au jus; or barbecued, boned quail marinated in lemon, garlic, herbs, and wine and served with couscous and Mediterranean vegetables. The wine list is excellent. ☒ *1 Davey St., Hobart City* ☎ *03/6235–4535 or 1800/222229* ☖ *Reservations essential* ⛺ *Jacket and tie* ☱ *AE, DC, MC, V* ☉ *No lunch Sun. or Mon.*

$$ ✕ **The Point.** This revolving restaurant atop one of Hobart's tallest buildings offers breathtaking views, and the food is equally rewarding. The savory smoked Tasmanian salmon appetizer is a wonderful starter; for a main course, try the prawns flambéed at your table, or the venison served with stewed figs and a poached pear Shiraz glaze. Tables are widely spaced around a mirrored central column, so everyone gets to enjoy the view. ☒ *Wrest Point Hotel, 410 Sandy Bay Rd., Sandy Bay* ☎ *03/6225–0112* ☖ *Reservations essential* ⛺ *Jacket required* ☱ *AE, DC, MC, V.*

$–$$ ✕ **Ball and Chain Grill.** Set in an old sandstone warehouse, this eatery is the place to go if you like your meat, game, and seafood cooked over a real charcoal fire. The huge, succulent hunks of meat here will leave even the biggest eater satisfied; there's also a self-serve salad bar. ☒ *87 Salamanca Pl., Battery Point* ☎ *03/6223–2655* ☱ *AE, DC, MC, V* ☉ *No lunch weekends.*

$–$$ ✕ **Blue Skies.** You can practically see the fish jumping out of the river from the waterfront tables here—especially those on the outdoor deck. The menu focuses on top-quality Tasmanian seafood, like oven-baked blue-eye trevally with steamed asparagus, served on a creamy potato mash and roasted pepper coulis. If it's too hard to choose, try the Pirates Bay combo, which includes calamari, scallops, and prawns in a creamy white wine, garlic, and basil sauce, served with potato gnocchi. ☒ *Murray St. Pier, ground fl., Hobart City* ☎ *03/6224–3747* ☱ *AE, DC, MC, V.*

$–$$ ✕ **Cornelian Bay Boat House.** This former boathouse and bathing pavilion on the edge of the Derwent River has views over the water and the Tasman Bridge. You can admire the scenery while enjoying crisp-skinned Tasmanian salmon, served with oven-dried tomato puree—or, if you're a vegetarian, eggplant au gratin, with baby onions, fresh pasta, and goat cheese. ☒ *Queens Walk, Cornelian Bay* ☎ *03/6228–9289* ☱ *AE, MC, V* ☉ *No dinner Sun.*

$–$$ ✕ **Kelleys.** Some of Hobart's best seafood is served up in this 200-year-old sailmaker's cottage, where an open fireplace glows on chilly nights. **Fodor'sChoice** ★ Feast on lightly spiced sea trout fillets, panfried and served with shaved Parmesan; blue-eye trevally topped with basil pesto, and wrapped in parchment with fresh spring vegetables; or the fabulous seafood platter—a smorgasbord of shellfish, prawns, fish and squid, served with an array of dipping sauces. ☒ *5 Knopwood St., Battery Point* ☎ *03/6224–7225* ☖ *Reservations essential* ☱ *AE, MC, V* ☉ *No lunch weekends.*

★ **$–$$** ✕ **Mures Fish House Complex.** On the top floor of this complex on the wharf, Mures Upper Deck Restaurant has superb indoor and alfresco views of the harbor. Try the flathead—a house version of the local fish, trevally, panfried with smoked trout pâté and Brie. Downstairs, Mures Lower Deck is a less-expensive, cash-only alternative: you order, take a number, pick up your food, and eat it at tables outside. Also in the complex, Orizuru has Hobart's best and freshest sushi and sashimi. ⊠ *Victoria Dock, Hobart City* ☎ *03/6231–1999 Upper Deck, 03/6231–2121 Lower Deck, 03/6231–1790 Orizuru* ▤ *AE, DC, MC, V.*

$ ✕ **Hope and Anchor Tavern.** Antiques, old prints, weapons, and other relics of bygone days are tastefully integrated into this cozy, historic 1807 pub, which is part of the oldest continually licensed hotel in Australia. The hearty menu choices here cater to trenchermen (local lingo for people with hearty appetites); you can try the 17½-ounce porterhouse or Scotch Fillet steaks, and finish up with a huge helping of chocolate mud cake. ⊠ *65 Macquarie St., Hobart City* ☎ *03/6236–9982* ▤ *DC, MC, V* ☺ *No lunch.*

$ ✕ **Maldini.** Reminiscent of an Italian café in a charming country village, this popular spot lets you watch the parade of Salamanca Place shoppers as you dine on appetizers like antipasto or char-grilled sardines. Heartier fare includes pastas, osso buco, and free-range-chicken breast with potato gnocchi and creamy Gorgonzola. Although Australian wines dominate the list, there are a few Italian labels to match the setting. ⊠ *47 Salamanca Pl., Hobart City* ☎ *03/6223–4460* ▤ *AE, DC, MC, V.*

¢ ✕ **Jackman and McRoss.** A perfect place to refuel when you're exploring Battery Point and Salamanca Place, this lively café serves up fantastic breads, pies, cakes, and pastries accompanied by a selection of coffees. The hearty, slow-cooked beef pie is a Tasmanian classic. For a sandwich with an unusual twist, try the pastrami and spiced pear with mustard on sunflower rye bread. ⊠ *57–59 Hampden Rd., Battery Point* ☎ *03/ 6223–3186* ▤ *No credit cards* ☺ *No dinner.*

Where to Stay

Area accommodations include hotels, guesthouses, B&Bs, and self-catering cottages. Although there are several new hotels in Hobart, as well as many chain accommodations, the greatest attractions are the lodgings in old, historic houses and cottages, most of which have been beautifully restored.

$$$–$$$$ ✕▣ **Henry Jones Art Hotel.** Right on the Hobart waterfront, this row of
Fodor'sChoice historic warehouses and former jam factory have been transformed into
★ a sensational, art-theme hotel, where the work of Tasmania's finest visual and performing artists is displayed. The spacious guest suites, also artistically decorated, reflects the influences of a rich colonial trading history with India and China: all suites have natural wood furnishings and king-size beds with exotic silk covers. Bathrooms are supermodern, with stainless-steel and translucent-glass fittings. Some suites have harbor views; others overlook the stunning glassed-in courtyard atrium. ⊠ *25 Hunter St., Hobart City 7000* ☎ *03/6231–6391 or 1300/665581* 🖷 *03/6231–6393* ⊕ *www.thehenryjones.com* 🛏 *50 suites* ⚹ *Restaurant, room service, bar, concierge, laundry service, parking, no-smoking rooms* ▤ *AE, DC, MC, V.*

★ **$$–$$$$** 🏨 **Hotel Grand Chancellor.** Across the street from the old wharves and steps from some of the best restaurants in Hobart, this imposing glass-and-stone building seems a bit out of place amid Hobart's colonialism. What it lacks in period charm, however, it more than makes up for in luxury. All rooms have large wooden desks and thick, white guest bathrobes. Some rooms overlook the harbor. ⊠ *1 Davey St., Hobart City, 7001* ☎ *03/6235–4535 or 1800/222229* 🖷 *03/6223–8175* ⊕ *www.hotelchancellor.com.au* 🛏 *212 rooms, 12 suites* ⟋ *2 restaurants, pool, health club, hair salon, massage, sauna, bar, laundry service, airport shuttle, car rental, free parking* ▤ *AE, DC, MC, V.*

$$$ 🏨 **Moorilla Vineyard Chalets.** These stylish cottages, built in 1958, occupy a lush private peninsula along the Derwent River. Four spacious, light-filled, self-contained chalets—two with two bedrooms and two with one bedroom—have views of the Derwent River and the estate's small but impressive vineyard, known for its merlot, chardonnay, and pinot noir. Day guests can enjoy a complimentary wine tasting. Moorilla is 13 km (8 mi) north of Hobart. ⊠ *655 Main Rd., Berridale 7011* ☎ *03/6277–9900* 🖷 *03/6249–4093* ⊕ *www.moorilla.com.au* 🛏 *4 chalets* ⟋ *Restaurant, kitchens, in-room data ports, in-room hot tubs, wineshop, free parking* ▤ *AE, DC, MC, V.*

$$$ 🏨 **Zero Davey.** Located close to Hobart's waterfront, this hotel's apartments and studios are exquisitely furnished in contemporary designer style. You can dine in-house, choose from the many local restaurants within walking distance, or buy supplies at the hotel's gourmet convenience store and use your apartment's kitchenette. ⊠ *15 Hunter St., Hobart City, 7000* ☎ *03/6270–1444, 03/6270–1400, or 1300/733422* ⊕ *www.escapesresorts.com.au* 🛏 *31 apartments* ⟋ *Restaurant, minibars, some kitchenettes, cable TV, gym, Internet room, parking (free)* ▤ *AE, DC, MC, V.*

$$–$$$ 🏨 **Hadley's Hotel.** In 1912 this venerable city-center hotel played host to South Pole discoverer Roald Amundsen upon his return from the icy wasteland. Legend has it that at first he was turned away because in his bearded, bedraggled state he looked like a penniless bum. Today the rooms reflect early Tasmanian style with plush carpets and soaring ceilings. The Ritz Atrium Restaurant serves contemporary Australian cuisine with an emphasis on seafood. ⊠ *34 Murray St., Hobart City, 7000* ☎ *03/6223–4355 or 1800/131689* 🖷 *03/6224–0303* 🛏 *63 rooms* ⟋ *Restaurant, room service, bar, laundry facilities, free parking* ▤ *AE, DC, MC, V.*

$$–$$$ 🏨 **Salamanca Inn.** These elegant, self-contained apartments blend in well with the surrounding historic district. Queen-size sofa beds, modern kitchens, and free laundry facilities make the accommodations perfect for families. Ask for a room on the sunny western side, but don't expect great views from a three-story building. ⊠ *10 Gladstone St., Battery Point, 7000* ☎ *03/6223–3300 or 1800/030944* 🖷 *03/6223–7167* ⊕ *www.salamancainn.com.au* 🛏 *68 rooms* ⟋ *Restaurant, kitchens, pool, hot tub, laundry facilities, free parking* ▤ *AE, DC, MC, V.*

$–$$$ 🏨 **Corus Hotel.** On the edge of the central business district, this bright, breezy hotel is ideally situated for both work and pleasure. Large rooms have plenty of light, while suites include king-size beds, whirlpool tubs, and luxury fittings. The modern bistro, Embers Bar and Grill, serves meals with a Tasmanian flavor. ⊠ *156 Bathurst St., Hobart City, 7000* ☎ *03/6232–6255 or 1800/030003* 🖷 *03/6234–7884* 🛏 *126 rooms, 14 suites* ⚴ *Restaurant, bar, laundry facilities, free parking* ☰ *AE, DC, MC, V.*

★ **$–$$$** ⌑ **Old Woolstore.** Formerly an early-20th-century wool store, this intriguing complex now houses a combination of lodgings. Hotel-style rooms are bright and airy, while all the studio, one- and two-bedroom, and executive spa apartments have kitchens and laundry facilities. Equipment and old photos of the original wool store are displayed throughout the buildings, the Baa Bar, and Stockmans Restaurant. The central setting near the waterfront makes this an ideal base for exploring the city on foot. ⊠ *1 Macquarie St., Hobart City, 7000* ☎ *03/6235–5355 or 1800/814676* 🖷 *03/6234–9954* ⊕ *www.oldwoolstore.com.au* 🛏 *59 rooms, 183 apartments* ⚴ *Restaurant, some kitchens, minibars, bar, some laundry facilities, meeting rooms, free parking* ☰ *AE, DC, MC, V.*

$–$$$ ⌑ **Wrest Point Hotel Casino.** This 17-floor hotel earned its fame in 1973 when it opened the first legalized gambling casino in Australia. The more expensive rooms and suites in the tower and the Water's Edge section have grand views over Mt. Wellington and the Derwent River; some have whirlpool baths. The motor inn overlooks relaxing gardens and has access to the main hotel and casino facilities. ⊠ *410 Sandy Bay Rd., Sandy Bay, 7005* ☎ *03/6225–0112* 🖷 *03/6225–2424* ⊕ *www.wrestpoint. com.au* 🛏 *Tower: 159 rooms, 16 suites; Water's Edge: 42 rooms; motor inn: 33 rooms* ⚴ *2 restaurants, room service, tennis court, pool, health club, hair salon, casino, car rental, travel services, free parking* ☰ *AE, DC, MC, V.*

$$ ⌑ **Colville Cottage.** From the moment you pass through the white picket fence into the garden surrounding this property, you can't help but feel relaxed. The interior of the large Victorian house (rather incongruously called a cottage) exudes warmth and welcome, and has hardwood floors, fireplaces, and antique furniture. Fresh flowers and bay windows trimmed with iron lace add to the sense of coziness. Children are welcome here. ⊠ *32 Mona St., Battery Point, 7000* ☎ *03/6223–6968* 🖷 *03/6224–0500* ⊕ *www.salamanca.com.au/colvillecottage* 🛏 *6 rooms* ⚴ *Dining room, lounge, free parking; no smoking* ☰ *MC, V* ⦿ *BP.*

★ **$$** ⌑ **Corinda's Cottages.** This charming residence was built in the 1880s for Alfred Crisp, a wealthy timber merchant who later became Lord Mayor of Hobart. Three historic outbuildings—including a gardener's residence, servants' quarters, and coach house—have been lovingly converted into delightful self-contained cottages filled with period antiques. The B&B is close to the woodland, yet it's only a few minutes from the city center. ⊠ *17 Glebe St., Glebe, 7000* ☎ *03/6234–1590* 🖷 *03/6234–2744* ⊕ *www.corindascottages.com.au* 🛏 *3 cottages* ⚴ *Kitchens, laundry service, free parking* ☰ *AE, MC, V* ⦿ *BP.*

★ **$$** ⌑ **Somerset on the Pier.** Located on one of Hobart's historic piers, this all-suite complex is just a five-minute walk from the city, Salamanca Place, and many popular restaurants and nightspots. Spacious, modern-furnished units have loft-style bedrooms, stereos, DVD players, and full kitchens with dishes and cutlery; many have balconies with harbor views. The adjacent conference facility makes this a favorite of business travelers. ⊠ *Elizabeth St. Pier, Hobart City, 7000* ☎ *03/6220–6600 or 1800/620462* 🖷 *03/6224–1277* ⊕ *www.the-ascott.com* ⊐ *56 suites* ⌂ *Restaurant, room service, kitchens, microwaves, refrigerators, room TVs with movies, gym, sauna, bar, laundry facilities, free parking* ⊟ *AE, DC, MC, V.*

$–$$ 🏠 **Barton Cottage.** Built in 1837, this refurbished lodge still maintains its colonial grace while offering modern conveniences like in-room TVs and air-conditioning. Seven rooms with such names as Footman, Pantry-maid, and Chambermaid are simply decorated with antiques, and all have private baths. An old coach house has been restored into a private hideaway. Hearty breakfasts are served in the period chancery room. ⊠ *72 Hampden Rd., Battery Point, 7000* ☎ *03/6224–1606* 🖷 *03/6224–1724* ⊕ *www.bartoncottage.com.au* ⊐ *7 rooms, 1 cottage* ⌂ *Dining room, some kitchens, free parking* ⊟ *AE, DC, MC, V* ⏐◯⏐ *BP.*

$–$$ 🏠 **Islington Private Hotel.** Colonial-style rooms in this converted 1845 mansion are graced with antiques, and matching curtains and bedspreads. Although minutes from the city center, the hotel seems comfortably isolated, with a lush garden, outdoor pool, and stunning view of Mt. Wellington. Ask for a room with garden access. Your room rate includes a complimentary Continental breakfast served in the sunny conservatory. ⊠ *321 Davey St., South Hobart, 7000* ☎ *03/6223–3900* 🖷 *03/6224–3167* ⊐ *8 suites* ⌂ *Pool, laundry service, free parking* ⊟ *AE, DC, MC, V* ⏐◯⏐ *CP.*

$–$$ 🏠 **Lodge on Elizabeth.** This opulent grand manor, convict-built in 1829, and home over the years to many Hobart notables, is within walking distance of the city center, but far enough removed to feel like a sanctuary. The courtyard garden is a fine place to relax, as is the fireside common room, where you can sip a glass of wine before retreating upstairs to your room with private hot tub. ⊠ *249 Elizabeth St., Hobart City 7000* ☎ *03/6231–3830* ⊕ *www.thelodge.com.au* ⊐ *13 rooms* ⌂ *Dining room, in-room hot tubs, refrigerators, laundry facilities, free parking* ⊟ *MC, V* ⏐◯⏐ *CP.*

$ 🏠 **Bluff Lodge.** Built in 1889 as a "gentleman's residence," this lodge on the eastern shore of the Derwent River has been lovingly restored with antique Tasmanian furnishings. The rooms all have either queen- or king-size beds, and the guest lounge is the perfect place to enjoy a glass of port before the open fire. The full breakfast will set you up for a day's sightseeing. ⊠ *40 King St., Bellerive, 7018* ☎ *03/6244–5502* ⊕ *www.blufflodge.com.au* ⊐ *3 rooms* ⌂ *BBQs, lounge, library, parking (free); no room phones* ⊟ *AE, DC, MC, V.*

Nightlife & the Arts

Although Hobart has the only true nightlife scene in Tasmania, it's extremely tame compared to what's in Melbourne and Sydney. There are few dance clubs, and most bars have live music only on Friday and Saturday. Consult the Friday or Saturday editions of the *Mercury* newspaper before heading out. *This Week in Tasmania*, available at most hotels, is a comprehensive guide to current stage performances and contemporary music concerts.

Casino

The **Wrest Point Casino** (✉ 410 Sandy Bay Rd., Sandy Bay ☎ 03/6225–0112) in the Wrest Point Hotel has blackjack, American roulette, minibaccarat, keno, minidice, craps, federal wheel, federal poker and stud poker, and Two-up. It's open Monday–Thursday 1 PM–3 AM, Friday and Saturday 1 PM–4 AM, and Sunday noon–3 AM.

Bars & Dance Clubs

Bakers (✉ Barrack and Macquarie Sts., Hobart City ☎ 03/6223–5206) pub often hosts live music. **Bar Celona** (✉ 24 Salamanca Sq., Hobart City ☎ 03/6224–7557), a wine bar, has a good selection of local vintages by the glass or bottle.

The **Grand Chancellor** (✉ 1 Davey St., Hobart City ☎ 03/6235–4535) has a relaxing piano bar popular with the professional crowd and visitors alike. **Isobar** (✉ 11 Franklin Wharf, Hobart City ☎ 03/6231–6600) is a colorful and cool place to listen to live bands while relaxing over a drink. The contemporary crowd heads for the raucous, art deco **Republic Bar and Cafe** (✉ 299 Elizabeth St., North Hobart ☎ 03/6234–6954). **Round Midnight** (✉ 39 Salamanca Pl., Battery Point ☎ 03/6223–2491) has a mix of youthful live bands and DJs.

Syrup (✉ 39 Salamanca Pl., Battery Point ☎ 03/6224–8249), in the same building as Round Midnight, also mixes spun music with stage bands to draw in crowds under 30. **T42** (✉ Elizabeth St. Pier, Hobart City ☎ 03/6224–7742), a cleverly named waterfront spot, is popular for both dining and drinking; though the food is good, the main draw is the lively bar.

Music

Federation Concert Hall (✉ 1 Davey St., Hobart City ☎ 03/6235–4535) is the permanent home of the world-acclaimed Tasmanian Symphony Orchestra. Adjacent to the Hotel Grand Chancellor, the 1,100-seat auditorium also often welcomes touring musicians and speakers.

Theater

Playhouse Theatre (✉ 106 Bathurst St., Hobart City ☎ 03/6234–1536) stages a mix of traditional, locally cast plays and cutting-edge works. **Theatre Royal** (✉ 29 Campbell St., Hobart City ☎ 03/6233–2299), an 1834 architectural gem with portraits of composers painted on its magnificent dome, stages classic and contemporary plays by Australian and international playwrights.

Sports & the Outdoors

Walking is excellent around Mt. Wellington, which has a number of well-marked trails. The best hiking is a bit farther away, in Southwest National Park or in Mt. Field National Park.

Bicycling

Although most of Hobart and its surrounding areas are too hilly to make for easy cycling, some old railway lines along the western bank of the Derwent River (which are quite flat) have been transformed into bicycle paths. These offer a relaxing way to explore parts of the city. Bikes can be rented from **Derwent Bike Hire** (✉ Regatta Grounds, Queens Domain ☎ 03/6234–2910), from A$7 per hour to A$90 for a week. **Island Cycle Tours** (☎ 1300/880334) also rents bikes.

Boating

Blackaby's Sea Kayak Tours (✉ 1 Jessica Ct., Howrah ☎ 03/6267–1509 ⊕ www.blackabyseakayaks.com.au) runs sea kayaking tours around Hobart's waterfront, as well as at Port Arthur and on the Gordon River on the west coast.

Bushwalking

The Tasmanian Travel and Information Centre has details on local hiking trails; many are within easy reach of Hobart. Although shops around town stock outdoor equipment, you should bring your own gear if you're planning any serious bushwalking. Sneakers are adequate for walking around Mt. Wellington and along beaches. A car is necessary to access several of the trails around Mt. Wellington.

Fishing

Tasmania's well-stocked lakes and streams are among the world's best for trout fishing. The season runs from August through May, and licensed trips can be arranged through the Tasmanian Travel and Information Centre.

Several professional fishing guides are based on the island. For information on these guides, as well as related tours, accommodations, and sea charters, check out **www.troutguidestasmania.com.au** and **www.scboot. com.au.**

Golf

There are about 80 golf courses around Tasmania and visitors are welcome to play on many of them. Prices and accessibility vary, though (for example, some courses may require that you be introduced by a member), so it's always best to check first by phoning ahead.

There are several excellent golf courses within the Hobart area. The 9-hole **Bothwell Golf Course** (☎ 03/6259–5628), about 75 km (47 mi) north of Hobart in the village of Bothwell, is the oldest in Australia—and is part of a working farm. The 18-hole course at **Claremont Golf Club** (☎ 03/ 6249–1000) occupies a spit of land that juts into the Derwent River. The 18-hole course at **Kingston Beach** (☎ 03/6229–4298) is also an official bird sanctuary. The 18-hole course at **North West Bay** (☎ 03/6267–2166), located 15 minutes south of Hobart, has challenging, hilly terrain. The par-72 championship course at the **Royal Hobart Golf Club** (☎ 03/ 6248–6161) is often said to be one of the best in Australia. The 3rd hole at the **Tasmania Golf Club** (☎ 03/6248–5098), which sits atop a cliff overlooking Barilla Bay, has been compared to the 18th at Pebble Beach.

Skiing & Snowboarding

Tasmania's main snowfield is at **Ben Lomond,** 32 km (20 mi) east of Launceston. There's also a snowfield at **Mt. Mawson,** in the Mt. Field National Park, 81 km (50 mi) northwest of Hobart. Both of these ski areas, however, are only 4,000 feet above sea level, and the ski season is short (lasting from about mid-July to mid-September). Some years there is virtually no snow. It's best to contact the Tasmanian Travel and Information Centre for information on conditions, accommodations, and equipment rental.

Spectator Sports

Cricket, soccer, and Australian Rules Football matches all take place in Hobart. Buy tickets (A$10–A$40) at the gates.

Cricket matches run November to March at the **Bellerive Oval** (⊠ Derwent and Church Sts., Bellerive ☎ 03/6244–7099) on the scenic eastern shore. Football matches are Saturday afternoons April to August at **North Hobart Sports Ground** (⊠ Argyle and Ryde Sts., North Hobart ☎03/6234–3203).

Shopping

Tasmanian artisans and craftspeople work with diverse materials to fashion unusual pottery, metalwork, and wool garments. Items made from regional timber, including myrtle, sassafras, and Huon pine, are very popular. The wonderful scenery around the island is an inspiration for numerous artists.

Along the Hobart waterfront at Salamanca Place are a large number of shops that sell art and crafts. On Saturday the area turns into a giant market, where still more local artists join produce growers, bric-a-brac sellers, and itinerant musicians to sell their wares.

Aspect Design (⊠79 Salamanca Pl., Battery Point ☎03/6223–2642) stocks blown glass, wooden products, pottery, and jewelry. **Handmark Gallery** (⊠ 77 Salamanca Pl., Battery Point ☎ 03/6223–7895) sells Hobart's best wooden jewelry boxes as well as art deco jewelry, pottery, painting, and sculpture. **Tasmania Shop** (⊠ 120A Liverpool St., Hobart City ☎ 03/6231–5200) specializes in products made in Tasmania, including wood, pottery, food, and wine. The **Wilderness Society Shop** (⊠ 33 Salamanca Pl., Battery Point ☎ 03/6234–9370) sells prints, cards, books, and T-shirts, all made in Australia.

Hobart A to Z

AIR TRAVEL

Hobart International Airport is 22 km (14 mi) east of Hobart, one hour by air from Melbourne or two hours from Sydney. Although most interstate flights connect through Melbourne, both Qantas and Virgin Blue also run direct flights to Sydney and Brisbane. On the island, TasAir can get you to the northwest, to bucolic King Island, and to Flinders Island (charter flights only). Tickets can be booked through the airlines, or through Tasmanian Travel and Information Centres.

🛫 Airport **Hobart International Airport** ⊠ Holyman Ave., Cambridge ☎03/6216–1600.
🛫 Airlines **Qantas** ☎ 13–1313 ⊕ www.qantas.com.au. **TasAir** ☎ 03/6248–5088 ⊕ www.tasair.com.au. **Virgin Blue** ☎ 13–6789 ⊕ www.virginblue.com.au.

AIRPORT
TRANSFERS It's 20 minutes between the airport and Hobart along the Eastern Outlet Road. Tasmanian Redline Coaches has airport shuttle service for A$10 per person between the airport and its downtown depot. Metered taxis

are available at the stand in front of the terminal. The fare to down-town Hobart is approximately A\$30.

🏛 **Tasmanian Redline Coaches** ⊠ 199 Collins St., Hobart City ☎ 03/6231-3233 or 1300/ 360000 ⊕ www.tasredline.com.au.

BUS TRAVEL TO & FROM HOBART

Tasmanian Redline Coaches run daily to towns and cities across the state. Buses also meet the ferries arriving in northern Devonport from Melbourne and Sydney.

TassieLink also has daily services around the state, including daily buses to Geeveston via Huonville for easy access to Southwest National Park. The TassieLink Explorer Pass is a one-week ticket (to be used within 10 days) for unlimited travel around Tasmania (A\$172). A two-week pass (to be used in 20 days) costs A\$237, and other passes are also available.

The "Metro," operated by Metropolitan Tasmania, runs a bus system from downtown Hobart to the surrounding suburbs daily from 6 AM to midnight. Special "Day Rover" tickets for A\$4 permit unlimited use of buses for a day from 9 AM onward.

🏛 **Metro** ⊠ GPO Bldg., 9 Elizabeth St., Hobart City ☎ 13-2201. **Tasmanian Redline Coaches** ⊠ 199 Collins St., Hobart City ☎ 03/6231-3233 or 1300/360000 ⊕ www. tasredline.com.au. **TassieLink** ⊠ Hobart Transit Ctr., 199 Collins St., Hobart City ☎ 1300/ 300520 ⊕ www.tassielink.com.au.

CAR RENTALS

Cars, campers, caravans, and minibuses are available for rent. The largest rental-car companies are Autorent Hertz, Avis, Budget, Curnow's, and Thrifty, all of which have airport locations. Lower-price rental companies include Lo-Cost Auto Rent. Companies with motor-home and camper-van rental include Cruisin' Tasmania, Tasmanian Campervan Hire, and Trailmaster Campervan.

🏛 **Autorent Hertz** ☎ 03/6237-1111 or 13-3039. **Avis** ☎ 03/6234-4222 or 13-6333. **Budget** ☎ 03/6234-5222 or 13-2727. **Cruisin' Tasmania** ☎ 1800/772758. **Curnow's** ☎ 03/ 6236-9611. **Lo-Cost Auto Rent** ☎ 03/6231-0550. **Rent-a-Bug** ☎ 03/6231-0300. **Tasmanian Campervan Hire** ☎ 1800/807119. **Thrifty** ☎ 03/6234-1341. **Trailmaster Campervan** ☎ 1800/651202.

CAR TRAVEL

If you're arriving in Devonport on the *Spirit of Tasmania* ferry from Melbourne or Sydney, Hobart is about four hours south by car. Most places in Tasmania are within easy driving distance, rarely more than three or four hours in a stretch, although some of the narrow, winding secondary roads are unsuitable for camper vans and motor homes. If you drive in Hobart, be wary of the one-way street system.

DISCOUNTS & DEALS

If you're planning to explore all of the island, the See Tasmania Smartvisit Card provides unbeatable convenience and value. Three-, 7-, and 10-day cards give you free (or greatly reduced) admission at more than 60 of Tasmania's most popular attractions. A 3-day card costs A\$149; a 7-day card costs A\$189; and a 10-day card costs A\$269.

🏛 **See Tasmania Smartvisit Card** ☎ 1300/661771 ⊕ www.seetasmaniacard.com.

EMERGENCIES

In an emergency, dial **000** to reach an ambulance, the police, or the fire department.

Corby's Pharmacy and Macquarie Pharmacy, both in the city center, are open 8 AM to 10 PM daily.

🔢 **Hospitals Calvary Hospital** ✉ 49 Augusta Rd., Lenah Valley 📞 03/6278-5333. **Royal Hobart Hospital** ✉ 48 Liverpool St., Hobart City 📞 03/6222-8308. **St. Helen's Private Hospital** ✉ 186 Macquarie St., Hobart City 📞 03/6221-6444.

🔢 **Pharmacies Corby's Pharmacy** ✉ 170 Macquarie St., Hobart City 📞 03/6223-3044. **Macquarie Pharmacy** ✉ 180 Macquarie St., Hobart City 📞 03/6223-2339.

MAIL, SHIPPING & THE INTERNET

Hobart's main post office is at the corner of Elizabeth and Macquarie streets. Post restante services are available.

Internet services are available in public libraries, Internet cafés, business centers, and larger hotels. Mouse on Mars has broadband facilities at locations around Tasmania from their base cyber lounge at 27 Salamanca Place. Prepaid cards (A$5 for 30 minutes, A$10 for 70 minutes) allow users to log on and off at will.

🔢 **Post Office Hobart GPO** ✉ Elizabeth and Macquarie Sts., Hobart City 📞 13-1818.

🔢 **Internet Café Mouse on Mars** ✉ 27 Salamanca Pl., Hobart City 📞 03/6224-0513 🌐 www.mouseonmars.com.au.

MONEY MATTERS

You can cash traveler's checks and change money at ANZ Bank, Commonwealth Bank, National Bank, and Westpac in downtown Hobart.

🔢 **ANZ Bank** ✉ 22 Elizabeth St., Hobart City 📞 03/6221-2601. **Commonwealth Bank** ✉ 81 Elizabeth St., Hobart City 📞 03/6238-0673 or 13-2221. **National Bank** ✉ 76 Liverpool St., Hobart City 📞 13-2265. **Westpac** ✉ 28 Elizabeth St., Hobart City 📞 13-2032.

TAXIS

You can hail metered taxis on the street or find them at designated stands and major hotels. Cabs for hire have lighted signs on their roofs. Contact City Cabs or Taxi Combined.

🔢 **City Cabs** 📞 13-1008. **Taxi Combined** 📞 13-2227.

TELEPHONES

Tasmania's area code is 03, the same as Victoria. Mobile phones are widely used in the main towns, but reception is patchy in remote areas.

TOURS

AIRPLANE TOURS Par Avion Tours and TasAir have some of the most exciting ways to see Hobart and its surroundings. One flight by Par Avion goes to Melaleuca Inlet on the remote southwest coast and includes lunch, tea, and a boat trip and bushwalking around Bathurst Harbour ($A275). Shorter, less-expensive flights by both Par Avion Tours and TasAir cover just as much territory but don't include meals or time for exploring. Other flights from Hobart include the Tasman Peninsula, the Derwent River estuary, the Freycinet Peninsula, and Maria Island.

🔢 **Par Avion Tours** 📞 03/6248-5390 🌐 www.paravion.com.au. **TasAir** 📞 03/6248-5088 🌐 www.tasair.com.au.

BIKE TOURS Island Cycle Tours has many trips around Tasmania, including three-, four-, six-, and seven-day coastal tours. Prices include equipment, accommodations, meals, guides, van service, and entry to nearby attractions and activities. The exhilarating descent from the top of Mt. Wellington into Hobart (A$55) is a must.

🚲 **Island Cycle Tours** ✉ Box 2014, Lower Sandy Bay 7005 ☎ 1300/880334 ⊕ www. islandcycletours.com.

BOAT TOURS The Hobart Cruises catamaran zips through the majestic waterways of the Derwent River and the D'Entrecasteaux Channel to Peppermint Bay at Woodbridge. Wildlife is abundant, from sea eagles and falcons soaring above the weathered cliffs to pods of dolphins swimming alongside the boat. Underwater cameras explore kelp forests and salmon in the floating fish farms. Dine on local produce at Peppermint Bay. Prices start around A$75.

Captain Fell's Historic Ferries makes daily trips around Derwent Harbour on the MV *Emmalisa*. An excellent commentary on Hobart and its environs is included on the 1-hour trip, which costs A$8.

The 1912 MV *Cartela* makes one-hour harbor cruises, as well as three-hour trips to Cadbury's and a local winery. Trips depart in the morning, at lunch, and in the afternoon, and fares start at A$15. The *Lady Nelson* sailing ship takes 90-minute cruises around the harbor on Saturday and Sunday for A$6.

🚢 **Captain Fell's Historic Ferries** ✉ Franklin Wharf Pier, Hobart Waterfront ☎ 03/6223-5893. **Hobart Cruises** ✉ Brooke St. Pier, Hobart Waterfront ☎ 1300/137919. *Lady Nelson* ✉ Elizabeth Wharf, Hobart Waterfront ☎ 03/6234-3348. **MV** *Cartela* ✉ Franklin Wharf Ferry Pier, Hobart Waterfront ☎ 03/6223-1914.

BUS TOURS Hobart City Explorer operates a hop-on, hop-off tram bus between the main sights. Tickets are A$30. Tigerline Coaches and Gray Line run half- and full-day tours to Salamanca Place, Mt. Wellington, the Huon Valley, Bruny Island, Bonorong Wildlife Center, Port Arthur, and Richmond.

🚌 **Gray Line** ✉ Brooke St. Pier, Hobart Waterfront ☎ 03/6234-3336. **Hobart City Explorer** Tasmanian Travel and Information Centre ✉ 20 Davey St., at Elizabeth St., Hobart City ☎ 03/6230-8233. **Tigerline Coaches** ✉ Roche O'May Terminal, Pier One, Hobart Waterfront ☎ 1300/653633.

WALKING TOURS Walks led by the National Trust provide an excellent overview of Battery Point, including visits to mansions and 19th-century houses. Tours, which depart Saturday at 9:30 from the wishing well (near the Franklin Square post office), include morning tea. The National Trust also conducts daily tours (hourly 10–2) of the courthouse, Campbell Street chapel, and the old penitentiary (there's also a spooky night tour).

Hobart Historic Tours offers guided walks through old Hobart, around the waterfront and maritime precinct, and a historic pub tour.

🚶 **Hobart Historic Tours** ✉ 27 Carr St., North Hobart ☎ 03/6278-3338. **National Trust** ✉ 6 Brisbane St., Hobart City ☎ 03/6223-5200.

The Tasmanian Travel and Information Centre hours are weekdays 9–5 and Saturday 9–noon, often longer in summer.

🛈 Tasmanian Travel and Information Centre ✉ 20 Davey St., at Elizabeth St., Hobart City, 7000 ☎ 03/6230–8233 ⊕ www.tourism.tas.gov.au or wwwvisittasmania.com.au.

SIDE TRIPS FROM HOBART

Hobart is a perfect base for short trips to some of Tasmania's most historic and scenic places. Although you can visit them in a day, it's best to stay the a night or two and experience their delights at a leisurely pace.

The Huon Valley

★ *40 km (25 mi) south of Hobart.*

En route to the vast wilderness of South West National Park is the tranquil Huon Valley. Sheltered coasts and sandy beaches are pocketed with thick forests and small farms. Vast orchards cover the undulating land; in fact, William Bligh planted the first apple tree here, founding one of the region's major industries. Lush pastures shelter trim rows of fruit trees. Farmed salmon and trout caught fresh from churning blue rivers are other delicious regional delicacies.

The valley is also famous for the Huon pine, much of which has been logged over the decades. The trees that remain are strictly protected, so other local timbers are used by the region's craftspeople.

The **Forest and Heritage Centre** has fascinating displays on the history of forestry in the area, as well as some beautiful tables, vases, and cabinetry that have been crafted from the timber. ✉ *Church St., Geeveston* ☎ *03/6297–1836* 💲 *A$5* ⊙ *Daily 9–5.*

En route to Huonville, the **Huon Valley Apple Museum** is in a former apple packing shed. Some 500 varieties of apples are grown in the valley, and the museum displays farming artifacts, picking and processing equipment, and early-settler memorabilia from the area's vast orchards. ✉ *Main Rd., Grove* ☎ *03/6266–4345* 💲 *A$5* ⊙ *Sept.–May, daily 9–5; June–Aug., daily 10–4.*

Beyond Geeveston, the cantilevered, 1,880-foot-long **Tahune Forest Airwalk** rises to 150 feet above the forest floor, providing a stunning panorama of the Huon and Picton rivers and the Hartz Mountains. The best views are from the platform at the end of the walkway. ✉ *Arve Rd.* ☎ *03/6297–0068* 💲 *A$9* ⊙ *Daily 9–5.*

Spectacular cave formations and thermal pools amid a fern glade await at the **Hastings Caves and Thermal Springs.** The caves are about 110 km (70 mi) from Hobart, past Huonville and Dover. You can take a tour of the chambers, or just relax at the well-equipped picnic areas. The route to the site is well marked from the town of Dover on. ☎ *03/6298–3209* 💲 *A$16* ⊙ *Daily 9–5.*

Where to Stay & Eat

$-$$ ✕ **Home Hill Restaurant.** Large plate-glass windows here open to the Home Hill winery's endless hillside vineyards. The seasonal menu includes such delicacies as oven-baked salmon smothered in black olives, tomatoes, and homemade noodles—perfect for pairing with the Home Hill chardonnay. The crisp Sylvaner (a light, Alsace-style white wine) goes beautifully with the quail salad. After dinner, you can head down to the cellar to sample more of the winery's excellent cool-climate labels. ⊠ *38 Nairn St., Ranelagh* ☎ *03/6264–1069* ⊕ *www.homehillwines. com.au* ⊟ *DC, MC, V* ⊗ *No dinner Sun.–Thurs.*

$-$$ 🖬 **Matilda's of Ranelagh.** The official greeters at this delightful, 1850
Fodor'sChoice Heritage-listed B&B are five golden retrievers. Elegant Victorian and Ed-
★ wardian furnishings provide the ultimate in refinement and comfort—and two of the rooms even have spa baths. Outside, it's a pleasure to stroll through the 5-acre English-style gardens, which are filled with trees, shrubs, and thousands of flowers that bloom seasonally. A hearty breakfast is served each morning in the pretty blue-and-white dining room. ⊠ *44 Louisa St., Ranelagh 7109* ☎ *03/6264–3493* 🖷 *03/6264–3491* ⊕ *www. matildasofranelagh.com.au* ⌗ *5 rooms* ⌂ *Dining room, laundry facilities, some in-room hot tubs, free parking; no kids, no smoking* ⊟ *MC, V* ⟊ *BP.*

$ 🖬 **Heron's Rise Vineyard.** Mornings in either of the vineyard's two self-contained cottages are bucolic and gorgeous; you'll wake to glorious water views out over the flower gardens, where you might see rabbits nibbling. Both cottages have queen-size beds and wood-burning fireplaces. Dinner is available in your cottage by prior arrangement. ⊠ *Saddle Rd., Kettering 7155* ☎ *03/6267–4339* 🖷 *03/6267–4245* ⊕ *www.heronrose. com.au* ⌗ *2 cottages* ⌂ *Kitchens, laundry facilities, free parking; no smoking* ⊟ *DC, MC, V* ⟊ *CP.*

Bruny Island

★ From the village of Kettering 25 km (16 mi) south of Hobart, a ferry crosses the narrow D'Entrecasteaux Channel to reach Bruny Island, a little-publicized, gemlike satellite of Tasmania. Names here reflect the influence of the French explorers who sailed through this region in the 1770s and 1780s. At Bruny's southern tip are a convict-built lighthouse and magnificent coastal scenery.

To fully appreciate the dramatic panorama, take the three-hour, 50-km (31-mi) ecologically focused cruise run by **Bruny Island Charters.** You'll sail past towering cliffs and hidden caves, and likely see dolphins, seals, and penguins gliding all around the boat. Eagles, albatrosses, and shorebirds also dart and dive overhead, and can often be seen nesting amid the craggy outcrops. Cruise reservations are required in winter. ⊠ *915 Adventure Bay Rd, Adventure Bay, Bruny Island* ☎ *03/6293–1465* ⌸ *A$85* ⊗ *Cruises daily year-round.*

Richmond

★ *24 km (15 mi) northeast of Hobart.*

Twenty minutes' drive from Hobart and a century behind the big city, this colonial village in the Coal River valley is a major tourist magnet.

On weekends parking is tight, and crowds stroll and browse through the crafts shops, antiques stores, and cafés along the main street. Richmond is also home to a number of vineyards, all of which produce excellent cool-climate wines.

Richmond Bridge, Australia's oldest bridge, a scenic counterpoint to the village's church-spired skyline, is a convict-built stone structure dating from 1823. You can stroll over the bridge any time. It's at the eastern end of the main street.

The well-preserved **Richmond Jail,** built in 1825, has eerie displays of chain manacles, domestic utensils, and instruments of torture. ⊠ *37 Bathurst St.* ☎ *03/6260–2127* *A$5.50* ⊙ *Daily 10–5.*

Where to Stay & Eat

$–$$ ✕ **Coal Valley Vineyard.** This winery restaurant, accessible via the road from Cambridge, is set amid scenic vineyards with views over a golf course to the waters of Barilla Bay. It's open daily for lunch from 10 to 4. Try the roasted free-range-chicken breast filled with King Island double Brie and baby spinach, and served with Coal Valley chardonnay sauce. ⊠ *257 Richmond Rd., Cambridge* ☎ *03/6248–5367* *AE, DC, MC, V* ⊙ *No dinner.*

$–$$ ✕ **Meadowbank.** Wine tasting and an art gallery complement this restaurant with its views over the vineyards of Meadowbank Estate and the waters of Barilla Bay. Local oysters make a fine starter; main courses include duck breast with savoy cabbage and rabbit braised in cider. Save room for the warm, caramel-soaked sponge pudding served with vanilla crème anglaise and Tasmanian blackberries. ⊠ *699 Richmond Rd., Cambridge* ☎ *03/6248–4484* *DC, MC, V* ⊙ *No dinner.*

$–$$ 🏠 **Daisy Bank Cottages.** These two superbly converted cottages are nestled within a sandstone barn on a farm overlooking Richmond. Each dwelling has loft bedrooms, a modern kitchen, and private bathroom facilities. Antique furnishings fill the rooms, and full breakfast fixings are provided. ⊠ *Middle Tea Tree Rd., 7025* ☎ *03/6260–2390* *03/6260–2635* ⊕ *www.cottagesofthecolony.com.au/daisybankcottages. html* ➭ *2 cottages* ⚬ *Kitchens, laundry facilities, free parking; no smoking* *MC, V* 🍽 *BP.*

★ $–$$ 🏠 **Millhouse on the Bridge.** Originally built in 1853, this stately restored mill overlooking the Richmond Bridge is now a cozy B&B. Comfortable guest rooms have homespun touches, such as handmade preserves, and you can gather with the hosts in front of a roaring fire in the large, beamed sitting room after meals. The quiet garden, blossoming orchard, and river trails make for peaceful morning and afternoon strolls. ⊠ *2 Wellington St., 7000* ☎ *03/6260–2428* *03/6260–2148* ⊕ *www. millhouse.com.au* ➭ *4 rooms, 1 self-contained cottage* ⚬ *Dining room, laundry service, free parking* *MC, V* 🍽 *BP.*

Mt. Field National Park

70 km (43 mi) northwest of Hobart.

This popular park contains easily navigable trails, picnic areas, and well-maintained campsites that are ideal for family outings. Especially notable is the 1-km (½-mi) **Russell Falls Nature Walk,** which winds up a hill to the gorgeous Horseshoe Falls, then to the fascinating Tall Trees Walk, then another 20 minutes to Lady Barron Falls. Animals, including wallabies and possums, are often out and about around dusk.

South West National Park

Maydena is 98 km (61 mi) northwest of Hobart, Geeveston is 60 km (37 mi) southwest of Hobart.

The South West National Park encompasses the entire southwestern portion of the state, creating an extraordinary World Heritage wilderness area. This is one of the few virgin land tracts in Australia, whose mountain ranges and lakes were virtually unknown to all but the most avid bushwalkers until the 1970s. Although the park holds the greatest appeal for the hardy and adventurous, within its boundaries are some pleasant but quite underpublicized easy-access locales.

Roads in the park are few, and those that exist skirt only the edges of the wilderness area. The two main ways to access the park are through the town of Maydena, north of Hobart, and the town of Geeveston in the Huon Valley.

Maydena is located a few miles west of the entrance to Mt. Field National Park. From there the Gordon River Road takes you through to Strathgordon, close to where Lake Pedder was dammed in 1972 for hydroelectricity production. The scenery is magnificent, with lakes surrounded by mountains in pristine wilderness. Take care if you are tempted to walk away from the road, however; the terrain is rugged and weather conditions can change rapidly, even in summer.

Beyond Geeveston and the Tahune Forest Airwalk, the Arve River Road takes you to a number of parking areas from where you can walk on trails on the edge of the Hartz Mountain part of the South West National Park.

For more information on exploring the park, contact the **main park office** (⊠ Park Rd., Maydena ☎ 03/6288–1283), or the **Southern District Office** (⊠ Main Rd., Huonville ☎ 03/6264–8460).

PORT ARTHUR

102 km (63 mi) southeast of Hobart.

When Governor George Arthur, Lieutenant-Governor of Van Diemen's Land (now Tasmania) was looking for a site to dump his worst convict offenders in 1830, the Tasman Peninsula was a natural choice. Joined to the rest of Tasmania only by the narrow Eaglehawk Neck, the spit was easy to isolate and guard. And so evolved Port Arthur, where between 1830 and 1877 more than 12,000 convicts served sentences in Britain's equivalent of Devil's Island. Dogs patrolled the narrow causeway, and guards spread rumors that sharks infested the waters. Reminders of those dark days remain in some of the area names—Dauntless Point, Stinking Point, Isle of the Dead.

Apart from the main penal colony, a number of outstations were also established at other strategic locations around the Tasman Peninsula. The "Convict Trail," which you can follow by car, takes in seven such sites, including the remains of a coal mine. This once-foreboding peninsula has become Tasmania's major tourist attraction, filled with beautiful scenery and historic sites that recapture Australia's difficult beginnings.

Exploring Port Arthur

Fodor's Choice **Port Arthur Historic Site.** This property, formerly the grounds of the Port
★ Arthur Penal Settlement, is now a lovely—and quite large—historical park. Be prepared to do some walking between widely scattered sites. Begin at the excellent visitor center, which introduces you to the experience by "sentencing, transporting, and assigning" you before you ever set foot in the colony. Most of the original buildings were damaged by bushfires in 1895 and 1897, shortly after the settlement was abandoned, but you can still see the beautiful church, round guardhouse, commandant's residence, model prison, hospital, and government cottages.

The old **lunatic asylum** is now an excellent museum with a scale model of the Port Arthur settlement, a video history, and a collection of tools, leg irons, and chains. Along with a walking tour of the grounds and entrance to the museum, admission includes a harbor cruise, of which there are eight scheduled daily in summer. There's a separate twice-daily cruise to and tour of the **Isle of the Dead,** which sits in the middle of the bay. It's estimated that 1,769 convicts and 180 others are buried here, mostly in communal pits. Ghost tours (reservations are essential) leave the visitor center at dusk and last about 90 minutes. ⊠ *Arthur Hwy.* ☎ *03/6251–2310 or 1800/659101* 🖃 *2-day entry ticket A$24; Isle of the Dead tour A$8.80; ghost tour A$14.30* ⊙ *Daily 8:30–dusk.*

Tasmanian Devil Park. This is probably the best place in the state to see Tasmanian devils (burrowing carnivorous marsupials about the size of a dog), as well as quolls, boobooks (small, spotted brown owls), masked owls, eagles, and other native fauna. The park is also a wildlife refuge for injured Australian animals. Watch the live "Kings of the Wind" show, which stars birds of prey and other species in free flight. ⊠ *Arthur Hwy., Taranna, 11 km (7 mi) north of Port Arthur* ☎ *03/6250–3230* 🖃 *A$19* ⊙ *Daily 9–5.*

Where to Stay & Eat

$–$$ ✕ **Felons.** This restaurant at the Port Arthur Historic Site serves fresh Tasmanian seafood and game. The ever-succulent local fish of the day is served New Orleans style (with a spicy Cajun coating), oven-baked with lemon butter, or deep-fried tempura-style in a light batter. If it's teatime, pop in for one of the exceedingly rich desserts. ⊠ *Port Arthur Historic Site, Port Arthur* ☎ *03/6251–2314 or 1800/659101* 🖃 *AE, DC, MC, V.*

$–$$ 🏠 **Cascades Colonial Accommodation.** Part of a onetime convict outstation that dates to 1841, the original buildings here have been transformed into luxury accommodations. Each has kitchen facilities with breakfast

CloseUp

TASMANIA'S CONVICT PAST

THEY CAME IN CHAINS to this hostile island where the seasons were all the wrong way around and the sights and smells unfamiliar. They were the men and women whom Great Britain wanted to forget, the desperately poor refuse of an overcrowded penal system that considered seven years of transportation an appropriate penalty for stealing a loaf of bread that might have meant the difference between survival and starvation. They were mostly young, usually uneducated, and often—from 1830 onward—they were Irish. Sending "troublemakers" halfway around the world was one good way of ridding the land of voices calling for its freedom.

When Lieutenant John Bowen inaugurated the first permanent incursion into Van Diemen's Land in September 1803, he brought with him as servants 21 male convicts and 3 female prisoners. In just under 50 years, when the last convict ship arrived, that total had soared to 57,909 male prisoners, and 13,392 women prisoners. Tasmania, Governor George Arthur observed, had become an island prison.

Port Arthur, established in 1830, was—contrary to today's legend—never the most ghastly hellhole of the convict gulag. That dubious honor was shared by Sarah Island on Tasmania's west coast and Norfolk Island in the South Pacific. There was a classification system to keep hardened felons apart from those who had strayed a bit. The latter worked at Maria Island or as domestic servants on Midlands estates. Repeat offenders and the violent miscreants, though, ended up on the Tasman Peninsula.

First established as a logging site for Hobart, the Port Arthur penal settlement opened with 68 prisoners and soon became Australia's main convict center. Its natural advantages—two narrow necks and steep cliffs pounded by surging surf—could hardly be overlooked. With the closure of the Maria Island colony in 1832 and Macquarie Harbour a year later, numbers at Port Arthur increased to 675 prisoners in 1833. More buildings went up, and a semaphore system advising of escapes linked Port Arthur with Hobart via numerous hilltop stations. The penal colony became a self-sufficient industrial center where prisoners sawed timber, built ships, laid bricks, cut stone, and made tiles, shoes, iron castings, and clothing.

Convict banishment to Van Diemen's Land ceased in 1853. Most of the Port Arthur inmates were given tickets of leave or were sent to the countryside as agricultural laborers. Insane convicts (and there were many who had gone quite mad here) were incarcerated in the old wooden barracks until a special asylum was finished in 1868.

The settlement closed in 1877 after some 12,000 sentences had been served. For a while the authorities tried to expunge all memories of the peninsula's shame. They even changed the name for a time to Carnarvon. This halfhearted cover-up failed. Today, memories of Tasmania's convict past burn brighter than ever as society once again wrestles with the same dilemmas of good and evil, crime and punishment.

— Steve Robertson

provisions included. A small museum related to the property is also on-site and there are some lovely bushwalks on the property. ✉ *531 Main Rd., Koonya 7187, 20 km (12 mi) north of Port Arthur* 🕾 *03/6250–3873* 🖶 *03/6250–3013* 🛏 *4 cottages* ⚒ *Kitchens, laundry facilities, free parking* 🖃 *No credit cards* 🍴 *CP.*

$ 🖭 **Comfort Inn Port Arthur.** On a ridge behind an old church, this motel overlooks the entire historic penal settlement site. There's a range of lodging options here, from interconnecting "Guards' Rooms," which are great for families, to more standard hotel rooms. As well as providing excellent food, the Commandant's Table Restaurant and Bistro has arguably the best view over the historic site. ✉ *29 Safety Cove Rd., 7182* 🕾 *03/6250–2101 or 1800/030747* 🖶 *03/6250–2417* ⊕ *www.comfortinn.com* 🛏 *35 rooms* ⚒ *Restaurant, bar, laundry facilities, free parking* 🖃 *AE, DC, MC, V.*

$ 🖭 **Port Arthur Villas.** A 10-minute walk from the penal colony, these modern apartments have verandas, old-fashioned brickwork, and pleasant cottage gardens typical of Port Arthur dwellings. Studio and two-bedroom units have fully equipped kitchens. Barbecue facilities are also on-site. ✉ *52 Safety Cove Rd., 7182* 🕾 *03/6250–2239 or 1800/815775* 🖶 *03/6250–2589* 🛏 *9 apartments* ⚒ *Kitchens, BBQs, playground, laundry facilities, free parking* 🖃 *AE, DC, MC, V.*

Port Arthur A to Z

CAR TRAVEL
Port Arthur is an easy 90-minute drive from Hobart via the Arthur Highway. Sights along the route include the Tessellated Pavement, a checkered-pattern geological formation; the Blowhole, spectacular in wild weather; and Tasman Arch, a naturally formed archway at Eaglehawk Neck. At the peninsula's far northwest corner is the fascinating Coal Mines Historic Site where convicts mined Australia's first coal in dreadful conditions.

A private vehicle is essential if you want to explore parts of the Tasman Peninsula beyond the historic settlement.

EMERGENCIES
In an emergency, dial **000** to reach an ambulance, the fire department, or the police.

TOURS
You can visit Port Arthur on a tour run by the Port Arthur Historic Site, take a sea kayak through the surrounding waters, or fly above the cliffs by plane.

AIRPLANE TOURS Tasmanian Seaplanes has three scenic flights over Port Arthur and the massive sea cliffs of the Tasman Peninsula and its national park. Costs start at A$80 for a 20-minute flight.
🚩 **Tasmanian Seaplanes** 🕾 03/6227–8808.

BUS TOURS The Tasmanian Travel and Information Centre organizes day trips from Hobart to Port Arthur by bus. The Port Arthur Historic Site conducts daily tours around Port Arthur. The popular torchlight ghost tour has guides who recount stories of apparitions and supposed hauntings at the site. Tigerline Coaches and Gray Line conduct full-day tours to the penal settlement at Port Arthur.

⚡Gray Line ⊠ Brooke St. Pier, Hobart City, Hobart ☎ 03/6234–3336. **Port Arthur Historic Site** ⊠ Arthur Hwy. ☎ 1800/659101. **Tasmanian Travel and Information Centre** ⊠ 20 Davey St., at Elizabeth St., Hobart City, Hobart ☎ 03/6230–8233. **Tigerline Coaches** ⊠ 199 Collins St., Hobart City, Hobart ☎ 1300/653633.

FREYCINET NATIONAL PARK & EAST-COAST RESORTS

The east coast of Tasmania has a mild climate, beautiful swimming and surfing beaches, and excellent fishing spots. The stretches of white sand here are often so deserted you can pretend you're Robinson Crusoe. The towns in this region are quiet but historically interesting; in Louisville, for example, you can catch a ferry to the Maria Island National Park, which was a whaling station and penal settlement in the mid-19th century. Farther north, the town of Swansea has numerous stone colonial buildings that have been restored as hotels and restaurants, as well as the unusual Spiky Bridge (so named because of its vertically placed sandstone "spikes") and the convict-built Three Arch Bridge, both of which date from 1845.

One of the jewels of the eastern coast is Freycinet National Park, renowned among adventure seekers and those who appreciate stunning scenery. The spectacular granite peaks of the Hazards, and the idyllic protected beach at Wineglass Bay have been dazzling visitors to this peninsula since it became a park in 1916.

East-Coast Resorts

From Hobart the east-coast Tasman Highway travels cross-country to Orford, then passes through beautiful coastal scenery with spectacular white-sand beaches, usually completely deserted, before reaching Swansea. Bicheno, just north of Freycinet National Park, and St. Helens, which is farther north, are both fishing and holiday towns with quiet, sheltered harbors.

Where to Stay

$$ 🏨 **Wybalenna Lodge.** English-style gardens welcome you to this impressive, high-ceilinged lodge above Georges Bay in the town of St. Helens. The elegant rooms, all recently renovated and furnished with country antiques, have water views. There's a lovely veranda where you can have breakfast alfresco (weather permitting) and a formal dining room, where a full set menu of local seafood is cooked to perfection (with 24 hours' notice). ⊠ *56 Tasman Hwy., St. Helens 7216* ☎ *03/6376–1611* 🖨 *03/6376–2612* ⊕ *www.wybalennalodge.com* ➪ *4 rooms* ◊ *Dining room, laundry facilities, free parking; no kids under 14* ▤ *MC, V.*

$$ 🏨 **Meredith House.** Exquisite red-cedar furnishings and antiques decorate this 1853 refurbished residence in the center of Swansea. Comfortable rooms overlook the tranquil waters of Great Oyster Bay. You can request morning and evening meals in the dining room or choose from the many cafés and restaurants in town. ⊠ *15 Noyes St., Swansea 7190* ☎ *03/6257–8119* 🖷 *03/6257–8123* ⊕ *babs.com.au/meredith* ⚲ *11 rooms* ⚭ *Dining room, free parking* ⊟ *AE, MC, V* ⦿ *BP.*

$–$$ ⊞ **Diamond Island Resort.** Located 2½ km (1½ mi) north of Bicheno's town center, this property overlooks the Tasman Sea and has direct beach access. Twelve duplex units, each of which has two bedrooms, are set among the 7 acres of landscaped gardens; there are also three smaller, one-bedroom units. All have private bathrooms. Between September and February, the resort hosts group tours to see wild fairy penguins, who come ashore each night after a day of fishing; be sure to reserve a spot when you book your room. ⊠ *69 Tasman Hwy., Bicheno 7215* ☎ *03/6375–1161 or 1800/030299* 🖷 *03/6375–1349* ⚲ *15 rooms* ⚭ *Restaurant, BBQs, pool, tennis courts, recreation room, laundry, parking* ⊟ *DC, MC, V.*

$–$$ ⊞ **Wagners Cottages.** These four charming stone cottages, two of which date from the 1850s, sit amid rambling gardens. Each is decorated with country antique-style furniture, and has its own fireplace and spa tub. There are also two guest rooms in the main house, each with a private bathroom. A full breakfast is served in the sunny atrium overlooking the rose garden. ⊠ *Tasman Hwy. near Francis St., 2 mi south of town, Swansea 7190* ☎ *03/6257–8494* 🖷 *03/6257–8267* ⊕ *www.wagnerscottages.com. au* ⚲ *4 cottages, 2 rooms* ⚭ *Some in-room hot tubs, some kitchens, laundry facilities, free parking* ⊟ *AE, DC, MC, V* ⦿ *BP.*

$ ⊞ **Kabuki by the Sea.** You can look out over Schouten Island and the Hazards from the terraces of this cliff-top inn for some of the most stunning coastal views in the state—then watch the moon rise over Great Oyster Bay while dining at the on-site Japanese restaurant. Cottages have all the comforts of a true Japanese *ryokan* (a traditional style of Japanese inn), including private sitting and dining rooms, and kitchen facilities. ⊠ *Tasman Hwy., 7190, 8 km (5 mi) south of Swansea* ☎ *03/ 6257–8588* ⊕ *www.view.com.au/kabuki* ⚲ *5 cottages* ⚭ *Restaurant, kitchens, laundry service, free parking* ⊟ *AE, MC, V.*

¢–$ ⊞ **Eastcoaster Resort.** This seaside complex in the town of Louisville is a great jumping-off point for exploring Maria Island National Park; the resort's catamaran, the *Eastcoaster Express,* makes three or four trips a day to the island. There are motel-type rooms here with kitchenettes, and also detached cabins (four of which have spa baths). The on-site Marlin restaurant specializes in local seafood and Tasmanian wines. ⊠ *Louisville Point Rd., Louisville 7190* ☎ *03/6257–1172* ⚲ *48 rooms, 8 cabins* ⚭ *Restaurant, some kitchenettes, BBQs, 2 pools, some in-room hot tubs, tennis court, playground* ⊟ *DC, MC, V.*

Freycinet National Park

Fodor's Choice ★ *238 km (149 mi) north of Port Arthur, 214 km (133 mi) southwest of Launceston, 206 km (128 mi) northeast of Hobart.*

The road onto the Freycinet Peninsula ends just past the township of Coles Bay; from that point the Freycinet National Park begins and covers 24,700 acres.

It took the early European explorers of Van Diemen's Land four voyages and 161 years to realize that this peninsula, a thickly forested wedge of granite jutting east into the Southern Ocean, was not an island. In 1642 Abel Tasman saw it through fierce squalls and, thinking it separate from the mainland, named it Van Der Lyn's Island, after a member of the Dutch East India Company's council of governors. It was not until 1803, when Nicolas Baudin's hydrographer, Pierre Faure, took a longboat and crew into what is now Great Oyster Bay, that Van Der Lyn's Island was proven to be attached. It was named the Freycinet Peninsula after the expedition's chief cartographer. It became a national park in 1916.

Highlights of the dramatic scenery here include the mountain-size granite rock formations known as the **Hazards.** On the ocean side of the peninsula, there are also sheer cliffs that drop into the deep-blue ocean; views from the lighthouse at Cape Tourville (reached by a narrow dirt road) are unforgettable. A series of tiny coves called the Honeymoon Bays provide a quieter perspective on the Great Oyster Bay side. **Wineglass Bay,** a perfect crescent of dazzling white sand, is best viewed from the lookout platform, about a 30-minute walk from the parking lot; if you're feeling energetic, though, the view from the top of Mt. Amos, one of the Hazards, is worth the effort. A round-trip walk from the parking lot to Wineglass Bay takes about 2½ hours. The park's many trails are well signposted.

Daily entry to the park costs A$20 per car or A$10 for pedestrians and bus passengers.

Where to Stay & Eat

$$–$$$$
Fodor'sChoice
★
✕ Freycinet Lodge. These 60 plush cabins are scattered among the densely wooded forest above Great Oyster Bay. They range from relatively simple one-bedroom units to "Premier Wineglass cabins," which have double spa tubs, CD players, and fluffy bathrobes. All have private balconies—essential for drinking in the views—and are outfitted with Tasmanian wood furnishings. The on-site Bay Restaurant ($$) has breathtaking sunset views, as well as an extensive wine list; the more casual Richardson's is the place for light lunches and coffee, while Hazards Bar and Lounge is a relaxing place to swap stories or curl up with a book by the open fire. ✉ *Freycinet National Park, Coles Bay 7215* ☎ *03/6257–0101* 🖷 *03/6257–0278* ⊕ *www.freycinetlodge.com.au* ➥ *60 cabins* ⌂ *Some in-room hot tubs, 3 restaurants, tennis court, boating, hiking, recreation room, laundry facilities, free parking; no room phones, no room TVs* ☰ *AE, DC, MC, V.*

$–$$$
✕ **Edge of the Bay.** The views from these modern, minimalist-style beachfront suites and cottages stretch across Great Oyster Bay to the Hazards. All have private decks and kitchenettes. The Edge restaurant ($$) uses Tasmanian produce and has local wines. Activities like tennis, as well as bicycles and rowboats for exploring, are all free. There's a minimum stay of two nights. ✉ *2308 Main Rd., Coles Bay 7215* ☎ *03/6257–0102* 🖷 *03/6257–0102* ⊕ *www.edgeofthebay.com.au* ➥ *8 suites, 15 cottages* ⌂ *Restaurant, kitchenettes, beach, tennis, boating, hiking, bar, laundry facilities, free parking* ☰ *AE, MC, V.*

Freycinet National Park & East-Coast Resorts A to Z

BUS TRAVEL
Tasmanian Redline Coaches and TassieLink regional coaches run between Hobart and Bicheno, where you can connect with a local bus to Coles Bay. A shuttle bus runs from Coles Bay to the parking lot within the national park.

7 Tasmanian Redline Coaches ☎ 1300/360000. **TassieLink** ☎ 1300/300520.

CAR TRAVEL
The Tasman Highway is a paved road, and though it's narrow in places it's easy to drive. Picnic and rest spots are frequent and there are some wonderful coastal views along the way, especially across to the Freycinet Peninsula from around Swansea. Gas stations can be found in all the towns.

TOURS
Freycinet Adventures has sports tours, including sea kayaking, rappelling, and rock climbing, that range from a half day to five days in length. Costs range from A$85 to A$1,190 per person.

Other ways to experience the wonders of the Freycinet Peninsula include cruises on the MV *Kahala* with Freycinet Sea Charters, which cost between A$55 and A$88. Scenic flights with Freycinet Air start at A$82 per person. At Bicheno the nightly tour to see the penguins emerge from the water and clamber up to their nesting area is popular; it costs around A$16 per person.

7 Bicheno Penguin Tour ☎ 03/6375-1333 **Freycinet Adventures** ☎ 03/6257-0500 🖥 03/6257-0447. **Freycinet Air** ☎ 03/6375-1694. **Freycinet Sea Charters** ☎ 03/6257-0355.

VISITOR INFORMATION
Contact Freycinet National Park directly for information about hiking, camping, and wildlife. The office is open daily from 9 to 5.

7 Freycinet National Park ✉ Park Office ☎ 03/6256-7000.

THE MIDLANDS

The first real road through the Midlands appeared more than 175 years ago, blazed by brave explorers who linked Hobart with Launceston. Back then, the journey between the two cities could take as long as eight days, but today you can speed between them on the 200-km (124-mi) Highway 1 (Midlands Highway; locals sometimes call it Heritage Highway) in less than 2½ hours. To do so, however, would mean bypassing many of Tasmania's appealing historic sites and English-style villages. The Great Western Tiers mountains on the Midlands' horizon form a backdrop to verdant, undulating pastures that are strongly reminiscent of England. Off the beaten trail you can discover trout-filled streams and lakes, snow-skiing slopes, grand Georgian mansions, and small towns redolent with colonial character.

Oatlands

85 km (53 mi) north of Hobart.

Situated alongside Lake Dulverton, the Georgian town of Oatlands was built in the 1820s as a garrison for the local farming community. The settlement was also a center for housing the convicts building the Hobart-to-Launceston highway. It was named in June 1821 by Governor Macquarie for what he predicted would be the best use for the surrounding fertile plains. Today many of the original buildings, built from the glorious golden sandstone of the region, still remain. These include the Council Chambers and Town Hall, which were built in 1880, and the town's courthouse, which dates from 1829. The town also has a number of fine old churches, and a wind-powered mill—Callington Mill—which gives a glimpse into early Tasmanian industry.

Where to Stay

$ ☷ **Oatlands Lodge.** This tranquil 1830 guesthouse has a lovely cottage garden and sandstone interior walls complemented by charming country furnishings and quilts. A complete English-style breakfast is included with your room rate; dinners and picnic lunches are also available. ⊠ *92 High St., 7120* ☎ *03/6254–1444* ➳ *3 rooms* ♿ *Dining room, laundry facilities, free parking* ⊟ *AE, MC, V* ❍| *BP.*

$ ☷ **Waverley Cottage Collection.** These four convict-built but cleverly restored cottages, two in the Oatlands township and two just outside town, make great places to stay. Amelia Cottage was once a changing station for horses riding the dusty road between Hobart and Launceston. It contains many of its original features, including shutters, a fuel stove, a baker's oven, and a flagstone kitchen floor. Another unit, Forget-me-not Cottage, is built in the old stables. ⊠ *104 High St., 7120* ☎ *03/6254–1264* 🖷 *03/6254–1527* ➳ *4 cottages* ♿ *Kitchens, free parking* ⊟ *AE, MC, V.*

Ross

55 km (34 mi) northeast of Oatlands, 140 km (87 mi) north of Hobart.

This quaint village of 500-odd residents has some wonderful historic buildings dating from the mid-19th century. Some of the best examples of colonial architecture include the Macquarie Store, the Old Ross General Store, and the old Scotch Thistle Inn, built around 1840.

The 1836 **Ross Bridge** (⊠ Bridge St.) is architect John Lee Archer's best-loved work. Graceful arches are highlighted by local sandstone and the decorative carvings of a convicted highwayman, Daniel Herbert, who was given freedom for his efforts. Herbert's work can also be seen on headstones throughout the graveyard where he's buried.

The buildings at the intersection of **Church Street,** the main road, and Bridge Street are often said to summarize life neatly. They include the **Man-O-Ross Hotel** (temptation), the **Town Hall** (recreation), the **Catholic Church** (salvation), and the **Old Gaol** (damnation).

The **Tasmanian Wool Centre** details the region's famous industry, which produces Australia's top-rated superfine wool and some of the best fibers in the world. After feeling the difference between wools and their divergent thicknesses, you'll leave with hands soft from lanolin. ⊠ *Church St.* ☎ *03/6381–5466* ✍ *Donation suggested* ☉ *Daily 9–4:30.*

Where to Stay

$ 🏠 **Colonial Cottages of Ross.** These four self-contained cottages, built between 1830 and 1880, provide charming and historic accommodation. Apple Dumpling Cottage (circa 1880) and Hudson Cottage (circa 1850) each sleep four adults. Church Mouse Cottage (circa 1840) is just for two. Captain Samuel's Cottage (circa 1830) accommodates six or more people. ⊠ *12 Church St., 7209* ☎ *03/6381–5354* ✍ *03/6381–5408* ⊕ *www.interbed.com.au/colonialcottages.htm* ➪ *4 cottages* ⚒ *Kitchens, laundry service, free parking* ⊟ *AE, MC, V.*

$ 🏠 **Ross Bakery Inn.** Right next to St. John's Church of England, this 1832 sandstone colonial building takes its name from the bakery that has occupied part of the property for the past 100 years. The main house now has four cozy guest bedrooms (all with private bathrooms) and a common lounge with a blazing fireplace where tea, coffee, and bakery treats are served. Breakfast includes bread that comes straight from the woodfire oven. ⊠ *Church St., 7209* ☎ *03/6381–5246* ✍ *03/6381–5360* ⊕ *www.rossbakery.com.au* ➪ *4 rooms* ⚒ *Dining room, free parking* ⊟ *AE, MC, V* ⬤❘ *BP.*

$ 🏠 **Somercotes.** Snuggled into a bucolic pasture and riverside property just outside town, this 1823 National Trust property of 2,000 acres has a blacksmith shop and gorgeous gardens on-site. You can stay in original colonial cottages once occupied by families who emigrated from England. Don't worry—the bathrooms and other amenities are up-to-date. Historic tours of the property are available. ⊠ *Mona Vale Rd., 7209* ☎ *03/6381–5231* ✍ *03/6381–5356* ⊕ *www.beautifulaccommodation. com/somercotes.html* ➪ *4 cottages* ⚒ *Kitchens, fishing, free parking* ⊟ *AE, MC, V.*

Longford

72 km (45 mi) northwest of Ross, 212 km (131 mi) north of Hobart, 25 km (16 mi) south of Launceston.

It's worth taking a short detour from the Midlands (Heritage) Highway to visit this town, a National Trust historic site. Settled in 1813, Longford was one of northern Tasmania's first towns. The original major landowners in the Longford district were the Archer family who settled from England, and their family name is still prominent in the district.

Of particular early historic interest is **Christ Church** (⊠ Archer and Wellington Sts.), built in 1839. William Archer designed the west window of the church, which is regarded as one of the country's finest. Currently, the building is only open on Sunday.

There are a number of other **historic villages** in the vicinity of Longford that are worth a visit. Hadspen, Carrick, Hagley, Perth, and Evandale are all within a short 25-km (16-mi) radius of Longford and all have their own unique charm. Near Evandale on the road toward Nile, **Clarendon House** is one of the great Georgian houses of Australia, restored by the National Trust. You can explore the main house, which is furnished with fine period antique furniture, as well as the stables, woolshed, and coach houses. ⊠ *234 Clarendon Station Rd., Evandale* ☏ *03/6398–6220* ⊡ *A$7.70* ☉ *Daily 10–5.*

Where to Stay

$$ ⊡ **Woolmers.** If you like the idea of being transported back in time to Australia's early farming days, this is the place for you. Built by a branch of the Archer family in 1816, Woolmer's has retained the collections, family possessions, and working farm just as they were close to two centuries ago. The original fireplace has just one duplicate outside Tasmania—at the White House. You can tour the estate (A$12) or spend the night in a superbly restored worker's cottage on the property. Allow yourself time to stroll through the National Rose Garden and have a picnic—packed to order—by the river. ⊠ *Woolmers La., 7301* ☏ *03/6391–2230* ⊟ *03/6391–2270* ⊕ *www.vision.net.au/~woolmers* ⇆ *7 cottages* ⚿ *Picnic area, kitchens, free parking* ⊟ *AE, DC, MC, V.*

$–$$ ⊡ **Brickendon.** More than just a historic farm property, this 1824 site **Fodor'sChoice** near Longford, which has been in the Archer family for seven genera- **★** tions, is also a true colonial village, with 20 National Trust–classified buildings on-site. After you've toured the lovingly restored chapel and barns, try your luck at trout fishing in the Macquarie River while the kids frolic with the animals. Afterward, you can relax in one of the rustic but romantic cottages, all of which have open fires, deep baths, antique furnishings, and private gardens. ⊠ *Woolmers La., 7301* ☏ *03/6391–1383 or 03/6391–1251* ⊟ *03/6391–2073* ⊕ *www.brickendon.com.au* ⇆ *5 cottages* ⚿ *Kitchens, playground, laundry service, free parking* ⊟ *AE, DC, MC, V.*

Midlands A to Z

CAR TRAVEL

Highway 1 (Midland Highway) bypasses the heart of Oatlands, Ross, and Longford, which is one reason they've kept their old-fashioned characters. These towns can be seen as part of a day trip from the capital or as stops along the drive between Hobart and Launceston.

TOURS

Fielding's Historic Tours has a daytime Convict Tour (A$7), available by appointment, and an evening Ghost Tour at 9 (A$8), which inspects Oatlands' jails and other historic buildings by lamplight.

Specialty Tours of Ross is operated by the informative and genial Tim Johnson, a local history buff who also runs Colonial Cottages of Ross. His Ross Historic Tour has a minimum rate of A$25 for up to five people. Reservations are essential.

🛈 **Fielding's Historic Tours** ☏ 03/6254-1135. **Specialty Tours of Ross** ☏ 03/6381-5354.

LAUNCESTON

200 km (124 mi) north of Hobart.

Nestled in a fertile agricultural basin where the South and North Esk rivers join to form the Tamar, the city of Launceston (pronounced *Lon-sess-tun*) is the commercial center of Tasmania's northern region. Its abundance of unusual markets and shops is concentrated downtown (unlike Hobart, which has most of its stores in the historic center, set apart from the commercial district).

Launceston is far from bustling, and has a notable number of pleasant parks, late-19th-century homes, historic mansions, and private gardens. However, refurbished restaurants, shops, and art galleries along the banks of the Tamar and North Esk rivers have turned rundown railway yards into a glitzy new social scene. Another appeal of this city is the sumptuous countryside surrounding it: rolling farmland and the rich loam of English-looking landscapes are set off by the South Esk River meandering through towering gorges.

Exploring Launceston

The **Queen Victoria Museum and Art Gallery,** opened in 1891, combines items of Tasmanian historical interest with natural history. The museum has a large collection of stuffed birds and animals (including the now-extinct thylacine, or Tasmanian, tiger), as well as a joss house (a Chinese shrine) and a display of coins. ⊠ *Wellington and Paterson Sts.* ☎ *03/ 6323-3777* ☜ *Free* ☉ *Mon.–Sat. 10–5, Sun. 2–5.*

Almost in the heart of the city, the South Esk River flows through **Cataract Gorge** on its way toward the Tamar River. A 1½-km (1-mi) path leads along the face of the precipices to the **Cliff Gardens Reserve,** where there are picnic tables, a pool, and a restaurant. Take the chairlift in the first basin for a thrilling aerial view of the gorge—at just over 900 feet, it's the longest single chairlift span in the world. Self-guided nature trails wind through the park. ⊠ *Paterson St. at Kings Bridge* ☎ *03/ 6331-5915* ☜ *Gorge free, chairlift A$7* ☉ *Daily 9–4:40.*

★ Along both sides of the Tamar River north from Launceston the soil is perfect for grape cultivation. A brochure on the **Wine Route of the Tamar Valley and Pipers Brook Regions,** available from Tasmanian Travel and Information Centre, can help you to plan a visit to St. Matthias, Ninth Island, Delamere, Rosevears, and Pipers Brook wineries. Many establishments serve food during the day so you can combine your tasting with a relaxing meal.

Waverly Woollen Mills. Opened in 1874, these mills on the North Esk River are still powered by a waterwheel. The store sells wool yarn and products made on-site from fine Tasmanian wool, such as sweaters, rugs, and blankets. ⊠ *Tasman Hwy. and Waverly Rd.* ☎ *03/6339–1106* ☜ *A$4* ☉ *Weekdays 9–5.*

Penny Royal World. This historic, amusement-park-type complex has been built around the riverfront Penny Royal Gunpowder Mills, which are some of the last operational gunpowder mills in the world. Rides on sailboats, barges, and trams are included in the ticket price, as are exhibits in the historic foundry, the museum, and the mills where cannons are periodically fired. Hit the Powderkeg Café for provisions if you're feeling peckish. ⊠ *145 Paterson St.* ☏ *03/6331–6699* ≣ *A$15* ⊙ *Daily 9–4:30 (except for 2 wks in July).*

J. Boag & Son Brewery. Since 1881, J. Boag & Son has been brewing quality Tasmanian beer in this imposing brick building. Tours of the brewery, which are available on weekdays, show you the entire process, from brew house to packaging, and end with a beer tasting. Advance bookings are essential. ⊠ *9 William St.* ☏ *03/6332–6300* ≣ *Tour A$16* ⊙ *Weekdays 8:45–4:30.*

Franklin House. Built in 1838, this fine Georgian house was a private boarding school before being purchased in 1960 by the National Trust. The building is notable for its beautiful cedar architecture, and its collection of period English furniture, clocks, and fine china. Morning and afternoon teas are served in the tea room. ⊠ *413 Hobart Rd., Franklin Village* ☏ *03/6344–6233* ≣ *A$7.70* ⊙ *Aug.–June, daily 9–4.*

Where to Eat

$$–$$$
Fodor'sChoice
★
✕ **Fee and Me.** One of Tasmania's top dining venues, this popular restaurant has won more culinary accolades than you could poke a mixing spoon at. ("Fee" refers to the talented chef, Fiona Hoskin.) You might begin your meal here with Tasmanian Pacific oysters or chicken dumplings in a fragrant broth, then choose from entrées like roasted quail with honeyed chili sauce, and roasted loin of Tasmanian venison. Wine from Australia's top vineyards is also served here. ⊠ *190 Charles St.* ☏ *03/6331–3195* ⌂ *Reservations essential* ⚐ *Jacket required* ≣ *AE, MC, V* ⊙ *Closed Sun.*

★ **$$**
✕ **Stillwater.** Part of Ritchie's Mill (a beautifully restored 1830s flour mill beside the Tamar River) and directly across from the Penny Royal World, this restaurant serves casual fare during the day. The dinner menu, however, includes some wonderfully creative seafood dishes, such as shaved baby Tasmanian abalone with ginger-and-miso panna cotta, and lime-grilled trevally with wilted Asian greens, saffron sabayon, and wasabi crisps. There's also a great selection of Tasmanian wines. ⊠ *Paterson St.* ☏ *03/6331–4153* ≣ *AE, MC, V.*

★ **$$**
✕ **Synergy.** This popular, stylish restaurant serves modern Australian seasonally based cuisine and provides impeccable service. Tingle your taste buds with the unusual wallaby fillet, served with preserved lemon and roast pepper couscous, or, alternatively, the Japanese tea-smoked trout. Tasmanian wines are featured on the excellent wine list. ⊠ *135 George St.* ☏ *03/6331–0110* ≣ *AE, DC, MC, V* ⊙ *Closed Sun. No lunch.*

$–$$
✕ **Fluid.** The boardwalk tables here overlooking the North Esk River are the perfect place to linger; you can choose from light snack fare, or more savory entrées like duck breast on buckwheat noodles, double-roasted with a soured black currant jus. Meals are easily paired with

choices from the long list of local wines. ⊠ *Launceston Seaport Blvd.* ☎ *03/6334–3220* ⊟ *AE, MC, V.*

$–$$ ✕ **Hallams.** The menu at this restaurant overlooking the Tamar River highlights local fresh seafood. You can try such dishes as scallops baked in a white wine, dill, and Freycinet cheddar Mornay, or seafood curry of the day with jasmine rice (it might be prawns, scallops, mussels, clams, or fish). There's always a friendly, exuberant crowd to make you feel part of the waterfront scene. ⊠ *13 Park St.* ☎ *03/6334–0554* ⊟ *AE, MC, V.*

$–$$ ✕ **Jailhouse Grill.** If you have to go to jail, this is the place to do it; you can have a delectable steak as soon as you get there. Surrounded by chains and bars, you can feast on prime beef (or fish and chicken), vegetable dishes, and a salad bar. The wine list—all Tasmanian—is comprehensive. ⊠ *32 Wellington St.* ☎ *03/6331–0466* ⊟ *AE, DC, MC, V* ⊗ *No lunch Sat.–Thurs.*

¢–$ ✕ **Fresh on Charles.** Step into this casual, busy place to choose from a variety of fresh juices, thick open sandwiches, hearty hot dishes, and tasty desserts. ⊠ *178 Charles St.* ☎ *03/6331–4299* ⊟ *No credit cards* ⊗ *Closed Sun.*

Where to Stay

$$–$$$ ▦ **Alice's Cottages.** Constructed from the remains of three 1840s buildings, this delightful B&B is full of whimsical touches. Antique furniture drawers might contain old-fashioned eyeglasses or books; an old turtle shell and a deer's head hang on the wall; and a Victrola and a four-poster canopy bed lend colonial charm. ⊠ *129 Balfour St., 7250* ☎ *03/6334–2231* ⊠ *03/6334–2696* ➷ *9 rooms* ⟁ *Some in-room hot tubs, minibars, laundry facilities, free parking* ⊟ *AE, MC, V* ⊙¶ *BP.*

$$–$$$ ▦ **Country Club Resort and Villas.** At this luxury property on the outskirts of Launceston you can choose between resort rooms and villas, some of which have fully equipped kitchens. The Terrace Restaurant serves specialties such as smoked duck breast and local scallops. The curved driveway to the club is lined with flowers and manicured gardens, and the championship golf course is one of the best in Australia. ⊠ *Country Club Ave., Prospect Vale 7250* ☎ *03/6335–5777 or 1800/030211* ⊠ *03/6343–1880* ⊕ *www.countryclubcasino.com.au* ➷ *88 rooms, 16 suites* ⟁ *Restaurant, dining room, room service, some kitchens, 18-hole golf course, tennis court, pool, hot tub, sauna, horseback riding, squash, casino, Internet room, free parking* ⊟ *AE, DC, MC, V.*

$$–$$$ ▦ **Hatherley House.** This magnificent 1830s mansion, set among lavish
Fodor'sChoice English gardens, has been transformed into a hip, intimate hotel. The guest
★ suites here, which are all individually decorated according to theme (you can choose, for example, from the Ballroom Suite, with its high ceilings and French doors; or the Oriental Suite, furnished with Asian antiques and art). All suites have ultramodern bathrooms with spa tubs, king-size beds, and flat-screen TVs with DVD players. Afternoon tea and cappuccino are served daily in the library and salon, which looks over the gardens. ⊠ *43 High St., 7250* ☎ *03/6334–7727* ⊠ *03/6334–7728* ⊕ *www. hatherleyhouse.com.au* ➷ *9 suites* ⟁ *Minibars, in-room hot tubs, laundry facilities, Internet room, free parking* ⊟ *AE, DC, MC, V.*

$$–$$$ 🏨 **Launceston International Hotel.** This modern, six-story building in the city center has big rooms that blend classic furnishings with modern conveniences. Its convention center and function rooms make it a favorite with business travelers, but pleasure seekers will appreciate that it's just a short walk from the shops and restaurants of downtown. After a day of meetings or sightseeing, you can dine at the Avenue Restaurant, or join the crowds at Jackson's Tavern and the Lobby Bar. ⊠ *29 Cameron St., 7250* ☎ *03/6334–3434 or 1800/642244* 🖨 *03/6331–7347* 🖈 *162 rooms, 7 suites* ♿ *3 restaurants, room service, 2 bars, babysitting, laundry service, convention center, meeting rooms, travel services, free parking* ☰ *AE, DC, MC, V.*

★ **$$–$$$** 🏨 **Waratah on York.** Built in 1862, this grand Italianate mansion has been superbly restored. Spacious modern rooms are tastefully decorated to reflect the era in which the building was constructed; six rooms have spa baths. Many rooms have panoramic views over the Tamar, and the property is just a quick walk away from the city center. Continental breakfast is served in the elegant dining room. ⊠ *12 York St., 7250* ☎ *03/6331–2081* 🖨 *03/6331–9200* ⊕ *www.waratahonyork.com.au* 🖈 *9 rooms* ♿ *Dining room, some in-room hot tubs, laundry service, free parking; no smoking* ☰ *AE, MC, V* ❙❙❙ *BP.*

$$–$$$ 🏨 **York Mansions.** Luxurious 19th-century elegance is the lure of these self-contained, serviced apartments. Room names like the Gamekeeper, the Countess, and the Duke of York hint at their opulence; indeed, each room has its own theme and style—and a fireplace. The garden at the rear, where you can sip drinks beneath a 130-year-old oak tree, enriches this sumptuous 1840 National Trust property. ⊠ *9 York St., 7250* ☎ *03/6334–2933* 🖨 *03/6334–2870* ⊕ *www.yorkmansions.com.au* 🖈 *5 apartments* ♿ *Some in-room hot tubs, kitchens, laundry facilities, laundry service, free parking* ☰ *AE, DC, MC, V.*

$–$$$ 🏨 **Prince Albert Inn.** First opened in 1855, this splendid colonial hotel has been lovingly restored to provide award-winning fine boutique accommodation. It is conveniently situated in the historic heart of Launceston, a short walk from the river wharves. Once you cross the threshold of the building's Italianate facade, you'll feel you've entered a Victorian time warp, where wall-to-wall portraits of British royalty hang in the plush dining room. Renovations in seven of the guest rooms have not broken the spell; lace curtains, velvet drapery, and fluffy comforters maintain the posh setting while maximizing comfort. ⊠ *22 Tamar St., 7250* ☎ *03/6331–7633* 🖨 *03/6334–1579* ⊕ *www.princealbertinn.com.au* 🖈 *17 rooms* ♿ *Some in-room hot tubs, lounge, travel services, free parking; no smoking* ☰ *AE, DC, MC, V.*

$$ 🏨 **Freshwater Point.** About 15 minutes' drive from Launceston center, this circa-1820 homestead sits on the western bank of the Tamar River, surrounded by acres of gardens. Two luxurious rooms are available in the main house; there are also three separate restored cottages, which come with kitchenettes and provisions for breakfast. Dinner is available by prior arrangement only on weeknights. ⊠ *56 Nobelius Dr., Legana, 7277* ☎ *03/6330–2200* 🖨 *03/6330–2030* 🖈 *2 rooms, 3 cottages* ♿ *BBQs, some kitchenettes, pool, laundry facilities, parking* ☰ *MC, V.*

$ 🏨 **Old Bakery Inn.** You can choose from three areas at this colonial complex: a converted stable, the former baker's cottage, or the old bakery. A loft above the stables is also available. All rooms reflect colonial style, with antique furniture and lace curtains. One room in the old bakery was actually the oven. Its walls are 2 feet thick (and bound to keep you toasty at night.) ⊠ *York and Margaret Sts., 7250* ☎ *03/6331–7900 or 1800/641264* 🖷 *03/6331–7756* 🗩 *23 rooms* ⚕ *Restaurant, free parking* ▤ *AE, MC, V.*

Nightlife & the Arts

The local *Examiner* is the best source of information on local nightlife and entertainment. The **Country Club Casino** (⊠ Country Club Ave., Prospect Vale ☎ 03/6335–5777) has blackjack, American roulette, minibaccarat, keno, minidice, federal and stud poker, federal wheel, and Two-up. There's also late-night dancing. It's open daily until early morning.

Live bands and jazz are a feature of the entertainment at the **Royal on George** (⊠ 90 George St. ☎ 03/6331–2526), a refurbished 1852 pub. The **Lounge Bar** (⊠ 63 St. John St. ☎ 03/6334–6622), in a 1907 former bank, has bands upstairs and a vodka bar in the old vault.

The curtain at the **Princess Theatre** (⊠ 57 Brisbane St. ☎ 03/6323–3666) rises for local and imported stage productions. The **Silverdome** (⊠ 55 Oakden Rd. ☎ 03/6344–9988) holds regular music concerts—everything from classical to heavy metal.

Shopping

Launceston is a convenient place for a little shopping, with most stores central on George Street and in nearby Yorktown Mall. The **Design Centre of Tasmania** (⊠ Brisbane and Tamar Sts. ☎ 03/6331–5506) carries wonderful items made from Tasmanian wood, including custom-designed furniture. Other choice products are the high-quality woolen wear, pottery, and glass. One of the best arts-and-crafts stores in town is the **Old Umbrella Shop** (⊠ 60 George St. ☎ 03/6331–9248), which sells umbrellas and gifts such as tea towels and toiletries. The **Sheep's Back** (⊠ 53 George St. ☎ 03/6331–2539) sells woolen products such as sweaters, blankets, and rugs.

Launceston A to Z

AIR TRAVEL

Launceston airport is located at Western Junction, 16 km (10 mi) south of central Launceston. It's served by Southern Australia Airlines, Island Airlines, Virgin Blue, Jetstar, and Qantas.

🛈 Airport **Launceston Airport** ☎ 03/6391-8699.

🛈 Airlines **Australia Airlines** ☎ 13-1313. **Island Airlines** ☎ 1800/645875. **Jetstar** ☎ 13-1538, **Qantas** ☎ 13-1313. **Virgin Blue** ☎ 13-6789.

BUS TRAVEL

TassieLink and Tasmanian Redline Coaches serve Launceston from Devonport, Burnie, and Hobart.

🛈 **Tasmanian Redline Coaches** ✉ 16-18 Charles St. ☎ 03/6336-1444 or 1300/360000 ⊕ www.tasredline.com.au. **TassieLink** ✉ Gateway Tasmania, St. John and Bathurst Sts. ☎ 1300/30052 ⊕ www.tassielink.com.au.

CAR RENTAL

Cars, campers, caravans, and minibuses are available for rent from the airport and several locations in Launceston. The main companies for car rental are Autorent Hertz, Avis, Budget, and Thrifty.

🛈 **Autorent Hertz** ✉ 58 Paterson St. ☎ 03/6335-1111. **Avis** ✉ 29 Cameron St. ☎ 03/6334-7722. **Budget** ✉ Launceston Airport ☎ 03/6391-8566. **Thrifty** ✉ 151 St. John St. ☎ 03/6333-0911.

EMERGENCIES

In an emergency, dial **000** to reach an ambulance, the police, or the fire department.

🛈 Hospitals **Launceston General Hospital** ✉ Charles St. ☎ 03/6348-7111. **St. Luke's Hospital** ✉ 24 Lyttleton St. ☎ 03/6335-3333. **St. Vincent's Hospital** ✉ 5 Frederick St. ☎ 03/6331-4999.

🛈 Pharmacy **Healthwise Pharmacy** ✉ 84 Brisbane St. ☎ 03/6331-7777.

MONEY MATTERS

You can cash traveler's checks and change money at ANZ Bank, Commonwealth Bank, National Bank, and Westpac.

🛈 **ANZ Bank** ✉ 69 Brisbane St. ☎ 13-1314. **Commonwealth Bank** ✉ 97 Brisbane St. ☎ 03/6337-4444. **National Bank** ✉ 130 Brisbane St. ☎ 13-2265. **Westpac** ✉ 75 Brisbane St. ☎ 13-2032.

TAXIS

Central Cabs and Taxi Combined can be hailed on the street or booked by phone.

🛈 **Central Cabs** ☎ 13-1008. **Taxi Combined** ☎ 13-2227.

TOURS

You can book a city sights tour of Launceston by replica tram through the Coach Tram Tour Company or at the Tasmanian Travel and Information Centre. Tours run November through April twice daily and cost A$28. Launceston Historic Walks conducts a leisurely stroll through the historic heart of the city. Walks leave from the Tasmanian Travel and Information Centre weekdays at 9:45 AM and cost A$15.

Tasmanian Wilderness Travel leads day and multiday tours to Cradle Mountain and the Tamar Valley. Tigerline Coaches, Tiger Wilderness Tours, and Treasure Island Coaches all run tours from Launceston, including to city highlights, Tamar River and wineries, and Cradle Mountain. Prices vary depending on the tour selected.

Tamar River Cruises conducts relaxing trips on the Tamar, past many wineries and into Cataract Gorge. An afternoon tour costs A$38.

🛈 **Coach Tram Tour Company** ☎ 03/6336-3133. **Launceston Historic Walks** ☎ 03/6331-3679. **Tamar River Cruises** ☎ 03/6334-9900. **Tasmanian Wilderness Travel**

☎ 03/6334-4442. **Tigerline Coaches** ☎ 1300/653633. **Tiger Wilderness Tours** ☎ 03/6394-3212 ⊕ www.tigerwilderness.com.au. **Treasure Island Coaches** ☎ 03/6343-2056 ⊕ www.treasureislandcoaches.com.au.

VISITOR INFORMATION

The Tasmanian Travel and Information Centre is open weekdays 9–5 and Saturday 9–noon.

🚩 Tasmanian Travel and Information Centre ⊠ St. John and Paterson Sts. ☎ 03/6336-3122.

THE NORTHWEST & CRADLE MOUNTAIN–LAKE ST. CLAIR NATIONAL PARK

The Northwest

Tasmania's northwestern region is one of the most exciting and least-known areas of the state. Most of the local inhabitants are farmers, fisherfolk, or lumberjacks. They're a hardy bunch and some of the friendliest folk in Tasmania. The rugged coastline here has long been the solitary haunt of abalone hunters, and from the area's lush grazing land comes some of Australia's best beef and cheese. Tasmanian farmers are the only legal growers of opium poppies (for medicinal use) in the Southern Hemisphere, and fields in the northwest are blanketed with their striking white and purple flowers.

Inland from the coast the mountain ranges rear up in dramatic fashion and these regions, especially in the Cradle Mountain National Park, are a major draw for hikers and sightseers. The western side of the northwest tip of Tasmania bears the full force of the Roaring Forties winds coming across the Indian Ocean, and this part of Tasmania contains some of the island's most dramatic scenery. Mining was a major industry a century ago and although some mines still operate, the townships have a rather forlorn look.

It should be noted that the northern part of the Cradle Mountain–Lake St. Clair National Park (that is, Cradle Mountain itself) is accessed by roads inland from Devonport and the nearby town of Sheffield. The southerly Lake St. Clair end of the park, though, is reached by the Lyell Highway between Hobart and Queenstown at Derwent Bridge.

Devonport & Environs

89 km (55 mi) northwest of Launceston, 289 km (179 mi) northwest of Hobart.

In the middle of the north coast, Devonport is the Tasmanian port where the ferries from Melbourne and Sydney dock. Visitors often dash off to other parts of Tasmania without realizing that the town and its surroundings have many interesting attractions.

The **Maritime Museum** contains a fascinating collection of local and maritime history artifacts, including examples of rope work, ironwork, and whaling equipment. It's the collection of boat models, though—ranging from Aboriginal canoes to modern passenger ferries—that will really interest nautical buffs. ✉ *6 Gloucester Ave.* ☎ *03/6424–7100* 🖃 *A$3* ⊙ *Tues.–Sun. 10–4.*

At the **Tiagarra Aboriginal Cultural and Art Centre,** remnants of Tasmania's Aboriginal past are housed in a series of reproduced Aboriginal huts. Among the exhibits are many beautiful Aboriginal rock engravings, which were discovered on the nearby Mersey Bluff headland in 1929 and subsequently collected here for protection. ✉ *Mersey Bluff* ☎ *03/ 6424–8250* 🖃 *A$3.80* ⊙ *Daily 9–5.*

The **Don River Railway** re-creates an early-20th-century passenger railway with working steam and diesel engines. The hour-long journey along the banks of the Don River, which leads through native vegetation and has lovely water views, is well worth the price. The train departs from the restored railway station, where there's a large collection of vintage engines, carriages, and wagons. ✉ *4th Main Rd.* ☎ *03/6424–6335* 🖃 *A$10* ⊙ *Daily 10–5.*

South from Devonport along the Bass Highway toward Launceston, the **House of Anvers** specializes in making exquisite chocolates—and you can watch the confectionery staff as they mold and dip different truffles, pralines, and fudges. The on-site "museum of chocolate" describes the history of this favorite sweet, and the café serves wonderful coffee, chocolate desserts, and cocoa drinks in many flavors. ✉ *9025 Bass Hwy., Latrobe* ☎ *03/6426–2958* ⊙ *Daily 7–5.*

The **Ashgrove Farm Cheese Factory** makes delicious English-style cheeses like cheddar, Lancashire, and Cheshire. Stop in to sample some of the varieties, and also to browse through other locally produced goods, like jams, olive oils, and honey. ✉ *6173 Bass Hwy., Elizabeth Town* ☎ *03/ 6368–1105* 🖃 *Free* ⊙ *Daily 9–5.*

In the small village of **Sheffield**, 32 km (20 mi) south of Devonport, more than 30 murals painted on the exterior walls of local buildings depict scenes of local history. Similar to murals found at Chemainus, British Columbia, they were painted in the late 1980s and depict industries (farming, cement manufacture) that had been carried out over the previous century but were then in decline.

WHERE TO STAY & EAT
$$

✗ **Essence.** Two separate dining rooms grace this intimate restaurant, where three cozy fireplaces add warmth in cooler months. Local produce figures in such succulent choices as Flinders Island lamb rump, served with local pink-eye potatoes and tomato-braised vegetables. Desserts include the rich chocolate praline marquis with raspberry coulis and toffee wafer. There's also a bar and lounge area, and an excellent selection of Tasmanian and Australian wines by the glass. ✉ *28 Forbes St., Devonport* ☎ *03/6424–6431* ▤ *AE, DC, MC, V* ⊙ *Closed Sun. and Mon. No lunch Sat.*

$ ✗ **Pedro's.** Tasty seaside bounty is caught fresh and cooked up daily in this kitchen on the edge of the Leven River. You can relax above the flowing water while sampling local crayfish, calamari, Tasmanian scallops, flounder, or trevally. The take-away fish-and-chips window lets you make a picnic of your feast in a nearby park. ✉ *Wharf Rd., Ulverstone* ☎ *03/6425–6663 restaurant, 03/6425–5181 take-away counter* ☰ *MC, V.*

$–$$ 🏨 **Killynaught Spa Cottages.** Five cozy, decorative one- and two-bedroom cottages comprise this property 15 km (9 mi) west of the town of Wynyard. Each has a spa bath, fireplace, a fully equipped kitchen, laundry facilities, and an antique queen-size brass or iron bed. The adjacent renovated 1890s main homestead also has a two-bedroom apartment and a one-bedroom suite. ✉ *17266 Bass Hwy., Boat Harbour 7321* ☎ *03/6445–1041* 🖷 *03/6445–1556* ⊕ *www.killynaught.com.au* 🛏 *1 apartment, 5 cottages* ⚴ *Café, kitchens, some in-room hot tubs, laundry facilities, free parking; no smoking* ☰ *DC, MC, V.*

$ 🏨 **Birchmore.** This elegant B&B is housed in a beautifully restored old mansion in the heart of Devonport. Rooms are luxuriously appointed, and have writing desks and faxes (on request) for business travelers. ✉ *10 Oldaker St., Devonport 7310* ☎ *03/6423–1336* 🖷 *03/6423–1338* ⊕ *www.view.com.au/birchmore* 🛏 *6 rooms* ⚴ *Some in-room faxes, laundry service, meeting rooms, free parking* ☰ *DC, MC, V.*

$ 🏨 **Rannoch House.** Set amid rambling gardens and orchards, this spacious, early-1900s Federation-style home is a convenient place to stay if you've just come off the *Spirit of Tasmania* ferry. Each of the guest rooms has a view of the gardens, and a full country-style breakfast is served each morning in the elegant dining room. ✉ *5 Cedar Ct., East Devonport 7310* ☎ *03/6427–9818* 🖷 *03/6427–9181* 🛏 *5 rooms* ⚴ *Dining room, free parking* ☰ *MC, V* ⦿ *BP.*

$ 🏨 **Westella House.** This charming 1885 period homestead has stunning sea views. Wood-burning fireplaces in each room, handcrafted banisters and mantles, and antique furnishings draw you into the cozy setting. A hearty, home-cooked breakfast starts the day. ✉ *68 Westella Dr., Ulverstone 7315* ☎ *03/6425–6222* 🖷 *03/6425–6276* ⊕ *www.westella.com* 🛏 *3 rooms* ⚴ *Dining room, laundry facilities, free parking* ☰ *MC, V* ⦿ *BP.*

Stanley
140 km (87 mi) northwest of Devonport, 430 km (267 mi) northwest of Hobart.

Stanley is one of the prettiest villages in Tasmania and a must for anyone traveling in the northwest. A gathering of historic cottages at the foot of the Nut, Tasmania's version of Uluṟu (Ayers Rock), it's filled with friendly tea rooms, interesting shops, and old country inns.

The **Highfield Historic Site** should be your first stop. Here, you can explore the town's history at the fully restored house and grounds where Van Diemen's Land Company once stood. ✉ *Just outside Stanley* ☎ *03/6458–1100* 🎟 *A$6* ◷ *Sept.–May, daily 9–5; June–Aug., daily 10–4.*

★ The **Nut**, a sheer volcanic plug some 12.5 million years old, rears up right behind the village. It's almost totally surrounded by the sea. You can ride a chairlift to the top of the 500-foot-high headland, where the views are breathtaking; or, you can make the 20-minute trek on a footpath leading to the summit, where walking trails lead in all directions. ☎ *03/6458–1286 Nut chairlifts* 🎟 *1-way chairlift A$6, round-trip A$9* ◷ *Chairlift runs 9–5 daily.*

✕ **Julie and Patrick's.** Some say this restaurant serves the best fish-and-chips in Tasmania. Formal diners stay upstairs, while snackers head to the casual downstairs café, and those on the run grab meals from the take-out counter. Whatever's fresh, from crayfish and king crabs to local salmon and flathead, you'll find it swimming live in the huge water tanks—the choice is yours. ⊠ *2 Alexander Terr.* ☎ *03/6458–1103* ▭ *MC, V.*

★ $–$$ ✕ **Stanley's on the Bay.** Set on the waterfront in the fully restored old Bond Store, this restaurant specializes in fine steaks and seafood. Try the eye fillet of beef—Australian terminology for the top-quality beef cut—topped with prawns, scallops, and fish fillets, served in a creamy white-wine sauce. ⊠ *15 Wharf Rd.* ☎ *03/6458–1404* ▭ *DC, MC, V* ☾ *Closed July and Aug.*

★ $–$$ ▦ **Beachside Retreat West Inlet.** These modern-lined, environmentally friendly cabins are set on waterfront sand dunes overlooking the sea. The 180-plus-acre farmland property is also adjacent to protected wetlands, which are perfect for bird-watching (keep an eye out for white-breasted sea eagles) and other wildlife-spotting. Many of the furnishings in the cabins are made by the owners and other local artisans from hand-turned Tasmanian wood. You can relax on your private deck after a morning on the beach and shuck your own oysters for lunch. ⊠ *253 Stanley Hwy., 7331* ☎ *03/6458–1350* ▤ *03/6458–1350* ⊕ *www.beachsideretreat. com* ⌖ *3 cabins* ⚿ *Kitchens, laundry facilities, travel services, free parking* ▭ *DC, MC, V* ⦿ *CP.*

$ ▦ **Touchwood Cottage.** Built in 1840 right near the Nut, this is one of Stanley's oldest homes, and it's furnished with plenty of period pieces. The cottage is known for its doorways of different sizes and its oddly shaped living room. Rooms are cozy, with open fires that add romance. Afternoon tea is served on arrival. The popular Touchwood crafts shop, where guests receive a discount, is part of the cottage complex. ⊠ *31 Church St., 7331* ☎ *03/6458–1348* ⌖ *3 rooms without bath* ⚿ *Dining room, free parking* ▭ *MC, V* ⦿ *BP.*

Smithton
140 km (87 mi) northwest of Devonport, 510 km (316 mi) northwest of Hobart.

Travelers come here to get away, to venture outdoors in remote places, and to explore the rugged northwest coast. Two rain forest–clad nature reserves in the area are Julius River and Milkshakes Hills. There are lots of opportunities to spot wildlife in this region, particularly Tasmanian devils. About 65 km (40 mi) west of Smithton the road reaches the wild west coast at Marrawah and continues on to Arthur River and down the west coast.

Around each corner of the private **Allendale Gardens** is a surprise: a cluster of native Tasmanian ferns or a thicket of shrubs and flowers. Self-guided forest walks of 10 to 25 minutes take you past trees more than 500 years old. The gardens shelter many birds; you may see pheasants, peacocks, guinea fowl, and pigeons wandering freely. ⊠ *Allendale La., Edith Creek, 14 km (9 mi) from Smithton* ☎ *03/6456–4216* ▧ *A$7.50* ☾ *Oct.–Apr., daily 10–4.*

WHERE TO
STAY & EAT
$$

✕ ⊡ **Tall Timbers.** This lodge is one of the finest establishments in the northwest. Rooms, in a building away from the main house, are simply yet elegantly decorated. A bistro and a cozy bar are found in the main lodge, which was built with Tasmanian wood. The more formal Grey's Fine Dining restaurant, also in the main house, serves such specialties as rock crayfish, chicken breast, rabbit hot pot, Atlantic salmon, and crêpes suzette for dessert. ⊠ *Scotchtown Rd., Box 304, 7330* ☎ *03/6452–2755* 🖶 *03/ 6452–2742* ⌑ *59 rooms* ♺ *2 restaurants, tennis court, bar, playground, laundry service, convention center, free parking* ⊟ *AE, DC, MC, V.*

Cradle Mountain–Lake St. Clair National Park

★ *173 km (107 mi) northwest of Hobart to Lake St. Clair at the southern end of the park, 85 km (53 mi) southwest of Devonport, 181 km (113 mi) from Launceston, 155 km (97 mi) from Strahan to Cradle Mountain at the northern end of the park.*

Cradle Mountain–Lake St. Clair National Park contains some of the most spectacular alpine scenery and mountain trails in Australia. Popular with hikers of all abilities, the park has several high peaks, including Mt. Ossa, the highest in Tasmania (more than 5,300 feet). The Cradle Mountain section of the park lies in the north. The southern section of the park, centered on Lake St. Clair, is popular for boat trips and hiking. Many walking trails lead from the settlement at the southern end of the lake, which is surrounded by low hills and dense forest.

One of the most famous trails in Australia, the **Overland Track** traverses 85 km (53 mi) between the park's north and south boundaries. The walk usually takes four or five days, depending on the weather, and on clear days the mountain scenery seems to stretch forever. Tasmania's Parks and Wildlife Service has provided several basic sleeping huts that are available on a first-come, first-served basis. Because space in the huts is limited, hikers are advised to bring their own tents. If you prefer to do the walk in comfort, you can use well-equipped, heated private structures managed by Cradle Mountain Huts (☎ 03/6391–9339, ⊕ www.cradlehuts.com.au).

Several of Cradle Mountain's most alluring natural attractions can be enjoyed on short (20-minute to three-hour) walks. The best include the Enchanted Walk, Wombat Pool, Lake Lilla, Dove Lake Loop, and Marion's Lookout. These walks take you along the edge of Lake Dove, up ridges with panoramic views to the mountains or to secluded small pools of water surrounded by dense forest. In late April you can make your way up the Truganini Track to see the native fagus bushes turn the hillsides a dazzling yellow and orange. It's the closest thing Australia has to Vermont in autumn.

Where to Stay

$$$–$$$$ ⊡ **Cradle Mountain Lodge.** This wilderness lodge with its collection of cabins is the most comfortable place to stay at Cradle Mountain. The high-ceilinged guest rooms, two per cabin, are cheerfully decorated and homey. A couple of walking trails begin at the lodge door. Breakfast is included in your room rate, and there's a minimum two-night stay. ⚓ 60

km (37 mi) from Sheffield ⊡ Box 153, Sheffield 7306 ☎ 03/6492–1303
🖷 03/6492–1309 ⊕ www.cradlemountainlodge.com.au ⟲ 96 rooms
⚲ Dining room, business services, travel services ▤ MC, V ⦿ BP.

★ $$$ ▥ **Lemonthyme Lodge.** Perhaps the largest log cabin in the Southern
Hemisphere, this huge lodge lies about 12 km (7½ mi) east of the park,
near the tiny village of Moina. With its huge stone fireplace and soar-
ing ceiling, this hotel has a grander look than Cradle Mountain Lodge
but is not as close to the park. Guided walks let you view the towering
trees and native wildlife. ⊡ Locked Bag 158, Devonport 7310 ☎ 03/
6492–1112 🖷 03/6492–1113 ⊕ www.lemonthyme.com.au ⟲ 31 rooms
⚲ Dining room, some kitchenettes, hiking, laundry service, free park-
ing ▤ AE, MC, V.

¢ ⛰ **Cradle Mt. Tourist Park,** near the forest at the northern edge of the park,
has campgrounds, RV sites, four-bed bunkhouses with cooking facilities,
and self-contained cabins with kitchens. Fees for tent and RV sites and
bunkhouse rooms are per person, per night, and advance booking is es-
sential for all accommodations. The tour desk can help you plan trips around
the area. ⚲ Grills, flush toilets, partial hookups, guest laundry, showers,
picnic tables ⊠ 3832 Cradle Mountain Rd., Cradle Mountain 7306
☎ 03/6492–1395 🖷 03/6492–1438 ⟲ 38 unpowered sites, 10 powered
sites, 75 bunkhouse beds, 36 cabins ⊠ A$8–A$10 campsites, A$10–A$12
RV sites, A$18–A$30 bunkhouse, A$75–A$95 cabins ▤ MC, V.

The Northwest & Cradle Mountain–Lake St. Clair National Park A to Z

AIR TRAVEL

QantasLink connects Devonport with the Australian mainland, while
TasAir connects Devonport to King Island. The airport is on the east-
ern side of the Mersey River in East Devonport, about 10 km (6 mi)
from the city center.

🛈 Airport **Devonport Airport** ☎ 03/6424–7088.
🛈 Airlines **QantasLink** ☎ 13–1313. **TasAir** ☎ 03/6427–9777 or 1800/062900 ⊕ www.
tasair.com.au.

BOAT & FERRY TRAVEL

Spirit of Tasmania I and *II* ferries operate in reverse directions between
Melbourne and Devonport across Bass Strait, making the 10-hour, overnight
crossing daily. In peak periods, extra daylight sailings are added to meet
the demand. Each ferry carries a maximum of 1,400 passengers and up
to 600 vehicles. *Spirit of Tasmania III* links Sydney with Devonport on a
20-hour journey that departs thrice weekly in each direction. A standard-
size car is free except during the December and January summer school
holiday period; *however, most rental car companies do not allow their ve-
hicles on the ferries.* Accommodations are in airlines-type seats or cabins,
and facilities include children's playrooms, a games arcade, gift shops, and
several restaurants and bars. Advance bookings are essential.

🛈 *Spirit of Tasmania* ⊠ Station Pier, Port Melbourne ☎ 13–2010 or 1800/634906 ⊕ www.
spiritoftasmania.com.au ⊠ Berth 1, Esplanade, Devonport ☎ 13–2010 or 1800/634906
⊠ Berth 7, 47–51 Hickson Rd., Darling Harbour, Sydney ☎ 13–2010 or 1800/634906.

BUS TRAVEL

Tasmanian Redline Coaches has offices in Devonport, Burnie, and Smithton. TassieLink operates daily buses from Hobart and Strahan to Derwent Bridge, near Cradle Mountain–Lake St. Clair National Park's southern entrance, and also from Launceston, Devonport, and Strahan to Cradle Mountain at the northern entrance to the park.

🚌 **Tasmanian Redline Coaches** ✉ 9 Edward St., Devonport ☎ 03/6421–6490 or 1300/360000 ✉ 117 Wilson St., Burnie ☎ 03/6434–4488 ✉ 19 Smith St., Smithton ☎ 03/6452–1262. **TassieLink** ☎ 1300/300520.

CAR RENTAL

Cars, campers, and minibuses are available for rent in Devonport.

🚌 **Autorent Hertz** ✉ 26 Oldaker St., Devonport ☎ 03/6424–1013. **Avis** ✉ Devonport Airport, Devonport ☎ 03/6427–9797. **Budget** ✉ Airport Rd., Devonport ☎ 03/6427–0650 or 13–2727. **Thrifty** ✉ 10 Esplanade, Devonport ☎ 03/6427–9119.

CAR TRAVEL

Many of the northwest roads are twisty and even unpaved in the more remote areas. A few may require four-wheel-drive vehicles. However, two-wheel drive is sufficient for most touring. Be prepared for sudden weather changes. This is one of the colder parts of Tasmania, and snow in the summertime is not uncommon in the highest areas.

Lake St. Clair is 173 km (107 mi) northwest of Hobart and can be reached via the Lyell Highway, or from Launceston via Deloraine or Poatina. Cradle Mountain is 85 km (53 mi) south of Devonport and can be reached by car via Claude Road from Sheffield or via Wilmot. Both lead 30 km (19 mi) along Route C132 to Cradle Valley. The last 10 km (6 mi) are unpaved, but the road is in very good condition.

EMERGENCIES

In an emergency, dial **000** to reach an ambulance, the police, or the fire department.

🚌 **Hospitals Mersey Community Hospital** ✉ Bass Hwy., Latrobe ☎ 03/6426–5111. **North West Regional Hospital** ✉ Brickport Rd., Burnie ☎ 03/6430–6666.

TOURS

Seair Adventure Charters conducts scenic flights that depart from Cradle Valley Airstrip and take you over sights in the area. Doors on the planes are removable for photography. A 50-minute flight, including a landing near Cradle Mountain, costs A$185. Flights are also available from Wynyard Airport.

Arthur River Cruises runs boat trips on the serene Arthur River 14 km (9 mi) south of Marrawah. Glide through pristine rain forest unchanged for centuries. Half-day excursions start at A$60.

An evening of spotting Tasmanian devils in their natural habitat is the highlight of Joe King's Kings Run Tours. The cost is A$75.

🚌 **Arthur River Cruises** ✉ Arthur River ☎ 03/6457–1158 ⊕ www.arthurrivercruises. com. **Kings Run Tours** ✉ Marrawah ☎ 03/6457–1191. **Seair Adventure Charters** ✉ Cradle Valley Airstrip, Cradle Valley ☎ 03/6492–1132 ✉ Wynyard Airport, Wynyard ☎ 03/6442–1220.

VISITOR INFORMATION
Tasmanian Travel and Information Centre has offices in Devonport and Burnie. Hours are usually weekdays 9–5 and Saturday 9–noon, and often longer in summer.

i **Cradle Mountain Visitor Center** ⊠ Park Rd. ☎ 03/6492–1133. **Lake St. Clair Visitor Center** ⊠ Park Rd. ☎ 03/6289–1172. **Tasmanian National Parks** ⊠ 134 Macquarie St., Hobart City, Hobart ☎ 03/6233–6191 ⊕ www.parks.tas.gov.au. **Tasmanian Travel and Information Centre** ⊠ 92 Formby Rd., Devonport ☎ 03/6424–4466 ⊠ 48 Civic Sq., off Little Alexander St., Burnie ☎ 03/6434–6111.

THE WEST COAST

The wildest and least-explored countryside in Australia lies on Tasmania's west coast. Due to the region's remoteness from the major centers of Hobart and Launceston, as well as its rugged terrain, the intrepid pioneers who developed this part of the island endured incredible hardships and extremely difficult living conditions. Though the area is now internationally recognized as one of the world's richest mineral provinces, with vast deposits of tin, gold, silver, copper, lead, and zinc, even today the viability of towns depends on the fluctuations in the price of the metals. The region still seems like part of the frontier.

Much of the land lies in protected zones or conservation areas, and there are lingering tensions among conservationists, loggers, and local, state, and federal government agencies. Strahan is the major center for tourism, and the departure point for cruises along the pristine Gordon River and Macquarie Harbour. The area's rich mining history is kept alive in smaller towns such as Queenstown and Zeehan.

The wildness and remoteness of the region, however, is what makes the area a major tourist draw. Pristine, untouched ocean beaches are readily accessible from Strahan; and cruises on Macquarie Harbour and to the lower reaches of the Gordon River reveal spectacular scenery, including majestic Huon pine trees growing right down to the water's edge.

In the heyday of mining in Queenstown at the beginning of the 20th century, ore was taken by train to be loaded at ports on Macquarie Harbour in Strahan. A former rack-and-pinion train line carrying ore is now the restored **West Coast Wilderness Railway** (⊠ Esplanade, Strahan ☎ 1800/628288 ⊕ www.westcoastwildernessrailway.com.au ⊠ Driffield St., Queenstown), which makes the 35-km (22-mi) journey between Queenstown and Strahan. The line passes through one of the world's last pristine wilderness areas, as well as through historic settlements and abandoned camps, across 40 bridges and wild rivers, and up and down steep gradients. Tickets are A$90 one-way, A$102 round-trip (one way by train, return by bus). Lunch is included.

The **West Coast Pioneers' Memorial Museum,** housed in the old Zeehan School of Mines and Metallurgy (established in 1894), displays a remarkable selection of minerals, historical items, and personal records of the region. Some exhibits are in a re-created underground mine. ⊠ *Main St., Zeehan 7469* ☎ *03/6471–6225* 🖂 *A$6* ⊙ *Daily 8:30–5.*

Strahan

265 km (164 mi) southeast of Smithton, 305 km (189 mi) northwest of Hobart.

This lovely, lazy fishing port, once a major stop for mining companies, has one of the deepest harbors in the world. The brown color that sometimes appears on the shoreline isn't pollution, but naturally occurring tannin from the surrounding vegetation. The town, which has a population of less than 750, sits on the edge of Macquarie Harbour and mixes a still-active fishing industry with tourism. The foreshore walking track gives an excellent view of the Strahan area. Don't overlook the short easy trail from the foreshore through the rain forest to Hogarth Falls.

Fodor's Choice **Franklin-Gordon Wild Rivers National Park** is the main reason to visit Stra-
★ han. This is the best-known section of the Tasmanian Wilderness World Heritage Area, with its rugged mountain peaks, areas of untouched rain forest, and deep gorges carved by the wild river valleys that wind through the wilderness. In the late 1970s and early '80s this area was the focus of one of Australia's most bitter conservation battles, when a hydroelectric power scheme was proposed that called for damming the Franklin River and flooding the river valley. Conservationists eventually defeated the proposal, but tensions remained high in the community for years.

About 50 km (31 mi) of the Lyell Highway, which stretches from Hobart to Queenstown, winds through the heart of the park to the west of Derwent Bridge. Making this drive is a great way to appreciate the area's natural beauty; there are several well-signposted walks along the way that let you do some easy exploring. Among these are the **Franklin River Nature Trail,** a 1-km (½-mi) wheelchair-accessible route through the rain forest; and the **Nelson Falls Nature Trail,** which takes you to the waterfall of the same name. The more challenging **Donaghys Hill Wilderness Lookout Walk** is one you should bring your camera for; it brings you to a beautiful panoramic lookout dominated by the peak called Frenchman's Cap.

The park is also accessible by boat from the town of Strahan; cruises from there take you across Macquarie Harbour and into the early reaches of the Gordon River, where you can stop for a short walk in the rain forest. Some cruises include a stop at **Sarah Island,** once one of the harshest penal settlements in Tasmania, and venture out through the narrow entrance to Macquarie Harbour for a glimpse of the tempestuous ocean beyond. Half- and full-day cruises run daily; some include a smorgasbord lunch and other refreshments.

Other worthwhile destinations around Strahan include the towering Henty Dunes north of town, the lush forest along the walk to Teepookana Falls, and—for the adventurous—a true rain-forest trek along the Bird River Track to some eerie overgrown ruins on the shores of Macquarie Harbour.

The **Strahan Visitor Centre** is also a museum that concentrates on local subjects and isn't afraid to tackle such controversial issues as past conservation battles over the area's rivers, and the fate of Tasmania's Aborigines. Don't miss performances of the play *The Ship That Never Was,* based on a true story of convict escape and a loophole in British justice. ⊠ *Esplanade at Harold St.* ☎ *03/6471–7622* 🎫 *A$12* ⊙ *Daily 10–6.*

Where to Stay & Eat

$ ✕ **Hamers Hotel.** This basic, bar-style restaurant specializes in seafood and steak, and the food is better than most pub counter meals for about the same price. Dessert includes a choice of fresh cakes. ⊠ *Esplanade at Harold St.* ☎ *03/6471–7191* 🖃 *MC, V.*

$$–$$$ 🏨 **Franklin Manor.** Located on a hillside overlooking the harbor, this century-old mansion is surrounded by landscaped gardens that skirt the edge of the forest wilderness. Charmingly decorated rooms, some with fireplaces and hot tubs, are in the main house, while the separate, self-contained, open-plan Stables cottages each sleep five. The restaurant serves lobster, oysters, pot-roasted quail, and sea trout. ⊠ *Esplanade at Vivian St., 7468* ☎ *03/6471–7311* ⊕ *www.strahanaccommodation.com* ➪ *14 rooms, 4 cottages* ⚐ *Restaurant, room service, some kitchens, some in-room hot tubs, bar, lounge, laundry facilities, free parking; no smoking* 🖃 *AE, DC, MC, V* ⦾ *BP.*

★ $$–$$$ 🏨 **Ormiston House.** Utterly luxurious, this mansion has been faithfully restored to ultimate elegance. Four-poster beds, spacious rooms, and cozy fireplaces make this the best romantic hideaway on the west coast. You can still keep in touch with the modern world, though, as the hotel provides fax and e-mail services. ⊠ *Esplanade at Bay St., 7468* ☎ *03/6471–7077 or 1800/625745* 🖷 *03/6471–7007* ⊕ *www.ormistonhouse. com.au* ➪ *4 rooms* ⚐ *Restaurant, bar, free parking* 🖃 *AE, DC, MC, V.*

$–$$$ 🏨 **Strahan Village.** A row of waterfront and hilltop cottages, all in different styles, and hotel rooms make up this extensive property. Family-style units have kitchens, and some have hot tubs. Dining options include the spectacular, cliff-top Macquarie Restaurant and the more casual Hamers Hotel and waterside Fish Cafe. ⊠ *Esplanade at Esk St., 7468* ☎ *03/6471–4200* 🖷 *03/6471–4389* ➪ *64 rooms, 39 cottages* ⚐ *2 restaurants, café, some kitchens, some in-room hot tubs, laundry facilities, travel services* 🖃 *AE, DC, MC, V.*

$$ 🏨 **Risby Cove.** Art is a main theme at this elegant waterfront property— a gallery of contemporary paintings, sculpture, and weaving graces the main building. The room furnishings are bright and modern, made of native woods. Whirlpool tubs add to the comfort. The restaurant, with a menu that lists Tasmanian wines and such seafood delicacies as ocean trout risotto, overlooks the marina. Sea kayaks and dinghies are available for hire. ⊠ *Esplanade at Trafford St., 7468* ☎ *03/6471–7572* 🖷 *03/6471–7582* ⊕ *www.risby.com.au* ➪ *4 rooms* ⚐ *Restaurant, boating, marina, mountain bikes, free parking* 🖃 *AE, MC, V.*

The West Coast A to Z

BUS TRAVEL

TassieLink serves the West Coast from Hobart to Strahan via Lake St. Clair and Queenstown five times a week and from Launceston via Devonport, Cradle Mountain, and Queenstown three times a week.
🗷 **TassieLink** ☎ 1300/300520.

CAR TRAVEL

A vehicle is absolutely essential on the west coast. The road from Hobart travels through the Derwent Valley and past lovely historic towns such as Hamilton before rising to the plateau of central Tasmania, famous for its lake and stream fishing. Craggy mountain peaks and dense forests are scenic highlights along the road to Queenstown; the denuded hillsides resemble a moonscape.

The north highway snakes down from Burnie (a link road joins Cradle Mountain with the highway) to the mining towns of Rosebery and Zeehan. From here, a newer link road to Strahan passes the Henty Dunes and Ocean Beach, (often battered by the storms of the Roaring Forties). The adventurous can head north from Zeehan, cross the Picman River (by barge) and then track through pristine forest and plains to rejoin the coast at the Arthur River.

EMERGENCIES

In an emergency, dial **000** to reach an ambulance, the police, or the fire department.
🗷 **Hospital West Coast District Hospital** ✉ 53 McNamara St., Queenstown ☎ 03/6471–3300.

TOURS

Wilderness Air flies seaplanes from Strahan Wharf over Frenchman's Cap, the Franklin and Gordon rivers, Lake Pedder, and Hells Gates, with a landing at Sir John Falls. It's a great way to see the area's peaks, lakes, coast, and rivers. Seair Adventures Charters has similar tours by helicopter and small plane.

Gordon River Cruises has half- and full-day tours on Macquarie Harbour and the Gordon River; the full-day tour includes a smorgasbord lunch. An informative commentary accompanies the trip to historic Sarah Island, and you can disembark at Heritage Landing and take a half-hour walk through the vegetation to a 2,000-year-old Huon pine tree. Reservations are essential.

World Heritage Cruises has half- and full-day cruises, which sail daily from Strahan Wharf. Meals and drinks are available on board. The leisurely journey pauses at Sarah Island, Heritage Landing, and the Saphia Ocean Trout Farm on Macquarie Harbour. From November through April they also operate the luxury three-day and two-night Wilderness Escape Cruise on the MV *Discovery*; limited to 24 passengers, this is the ultimate way to experience the Gordon River.

West Coast Yacht Charters has daily Macquarie Harbour twilight cruises aboard the 60-foot ketch *Stormbreaker*; a crayfish dinner is included. A two-day and two-night sailing excursion, a morning fishing trip, and overnight cruises on the Gordon River are also available.

Offices of all tour operators are on Strahan Wharf. Prices of tours vary depending on length and inclusions (some have options for meals as part of the package); but costs for cruises generally start at around A$60, and flights at around A$150.

🚩 Air Tours **Seair Adventure Charters** ☎ 03/6471-7718. **Wilderness Air** ☎ 03/6471-7280.

🚩 Boat Tours **Gordon River Cruises** ☎ 03/6471-4300 ⊕ www.strahanvillage.com.au. **West Coast Yacht Charters** ☎ 03/6471-7422. **World Heritage Cruises** ☎ 03/6471-7174 🖷 03/6471-7431 ⊕ www.worldheritagecruises.com.au.

VISITOR INFORMATION
🚩 **Strahan Visitor Centre** ✉ Esplanade, Strahan ☎ (03/6471-7622. **Tasmanian National Parks** ✉ 134 Macquarie St., Hobart City, Hobart ☎ 03/6233-6191 ⊕ www.parks.tas.gov.au.

Queensland

WORD OF MOUTH

"One of the most fabulous things about [the Carnarvon] area is that at night the sky is so close, clear and bright and it is really worth taking a map of the heavens if you go."

—lizF

Updated by
Caroline
Gladstone

A FUSION OF FLORIDA, LAS VEGAS, AND THE CARIBBEAN, Queensland attracts crowd lovers and escapists alike. Name your outdoor pleasure and it's here, whether you want to soak in the Coral Sea, stroll from cabana to casino with your favorite cocktail, or cruise rivers and rain forests with crocs and other intriguing creatures of the tropics.

At 1,727,999 square km (667,180 square mi) and more than four times the size of California, Queensland has enormous geographic variety. Its eastern seaboard stretches 5,200 km (3,224 mi)—about the distance from Rome to Cairo—from the subtropical Gold Coast to the wild and steamy rain forests of the far north. Up until the 1980s the northern tip and the Cape York Peninsula had not yet been fully explored, and even today crocodiles still claim a human victim once in a while. Away from the coastal sugar and banana plantations, west of the Great Dividing Range Queensland looks as arid and dust-blown as any other part of Australia's interior. Few paved roads cross this semidesert, and, as in the Red Centre, communication with remote farms is mostly by radio and air. Not surprisingly, most of the state's 3.6 million inhabitants reside on the coast.

Local license plates deem Queensland the "Sunshine State," a sort of Australian Florida—a laid-back stretch of beaches and sun where many Australians head for their vacations. The state has actively promoted tourism, and such areas as the Gold Coast in the south and Cairns in the north have exploded into mini-Miamis, complete with high-rise buildings, casinos, and beachfront amusements. The major attraction for Australians and foreign tourists alike is the Great Barrier Reef, the 1,900-km (1,178-mi) ecological masterpiece that supports thousands of animal species. For more information on the reef, an integral part of any trip to the state, *see* Chapter 8.

Queensland was thrust into the spotlight when Brisbane hosted the Commonwealth Games in 1982, the World Expo '88, and the 2001 Goodwill Games. Such big-name competitions have exposed Brisbane to the wider world and helped bring the city, along with other provincial capitals, to full-fledged social and cultural maturity. Consequently, Queensland is a vibrant place to visit, and Sunshine Staters are far more likely to be city kids who work in modern offices than stereotypical "bushies" who work the land. And, as with so many other lands blessed with hot weather and plenty of sunshine, the pace of life here is relaxed.

Exploring Queensland

Queensland is the huge northeast section of the Australian continent that stretches from the northern point of the Cape York Peninsula south through Brisbane and Lamington National Park. The Great Barrier Reef parallels most of the state's edge, all the way south to Hervey Bay. A coastal road makes for easy travel between the major cities and little towns that are jumping-off points to Fraser Island, the Whitsundays, and Magnetic Island, but vast distances make flying the best option between mainland cities and the offshore resorts.

If you have
3 days

Fly into **Cairns** and take a boat out to one of the reef islands for a day, then head up to **Cape Tribulation** for the next two days to take in the sights and sounds of the rain forest. If you'd rather have a Miami Beach–style trip, fly into **Brisbane** and head straight for the glitzy **Gold Coast,** overnighting in **Surfers Paradise.** You could end the spree with a final night and day in **Lamington National Park** for its subtropical wilderness and birdlife.

If you have
5 days

Spend three days on shore and two days on the reef. Stay the first night in **Brisbane,** then head up the **Sunshine Coast** for a hike up one of the **Glass House Mountains** on the way to **Noosa Heads.** Apart from beach and surf time, take in the Sunshine Coast's monument to kitsch, **Big Pineapple,** and indulge in one of their famous ice-cream sundaes. Then make your way back to Brisbane for a flight to **Cairns** and either a boat to the reef or a drive to the rain forest north of Cairns for cruising the rivers, listening to the jungle, relaxing on the beach, and looking into the maw of a crocodile.

If you have
7 or more days

Unless you're keen on seeing everything, limit yourself to a couple of areas, such as **Brisbane,** its surrounding **Sunshine and Gold Coasts,** and the rain forests north from Cairns, and take three to four days in each—Queensland's warm climate is conducive to slowing down. Extended stays will also allow you to take a four-wheel-drive trip all the way to the top of **Cape York Peninsula** from **Cairns,** go for overnight bushwalks in national parks, spend a few days on a dive boat exploring islands and reefs north of Cairns, trek inland to the ancient **Undara lava tubes,** take the **Matilda Highway** through the Outback, or just lie back and soak in the heat.

The southern end of the state bordering New South Wales is known as the Gold Coast, where sprawling beach towns mimic Miami Beach and Waikiki. North of Brisbane is the quieter Sunshine Coast, where you can kick back on nearly deserted beaches or take four-wheel-drive expeditions into beautiful rain forests. North of Cairns, the Cape York Peninsula is all tropical terrain, where you can hike and camp in the jungle. In the western hinterlands, mountains stretch into the central deserts that border the country's Northern Territory and South Australia.

About the Restaurants

The concept of specialized rural cuisines is virtually unknown in Queensland. Steak and seafood predominate once you leave city limits behind. Brisbane, however, has its share of Mediterranean- and Asian-influenced menus. The coastal towns are full of casual, open-air restaurants that take advantage of the tropical climate. For upscale dining, head to Brisbane, where most restaurants have views of the river, while casual eateries are in Fortitude Valley and trendy New Farm.

WHAT IT COSTS In Australian Dollars				
$$$$	**$$$**	**$$**	**$**	**¢**
AT DINNER over $50	$36–$50	$21–$35	$10–$20	under $10

Prices are for a main course at dinner.

About the Hotels

Accommodations in this state run the gamut from rain-forest lodges, Outback pubs, colonial "Queenslander" bed-and-breakfasts—beautiful, large timber houses built above the ground on stilts, with big wraparound verandas—and backpacker hostels to deluxe beachside resorts and big-city hotels. The luxury resorts are clustered around the major tourist areas of Cairns, the islands, and the Gold Coast. In the smaller coastal towns, accommodation is mostly in motels, apartments, and bed-and-breakfasts.

WHAT IT COSTS In Australian Dollars				
$$$$	**$$$**	**$$**	**$**	**¢**
FOR 2 PEOPLE over $300	$201–$300	$151–$200	$100–$150	under $100

Prices are for two people in a standard double room in high season, including tax and service, based on the European Plan (with no meals) unless otherwise noted.

When to Visit Queensland

North of Cairns, the best time for visiting is between May and September, when the daily maximum temperature averages around 27°C (80°F) and the water is comfortably warm. From about December through March, expect monsoon conditions. Elsewhere in the state, the tropical coast is besieged from October through April by deadly box jellyfish and the tiny transparent Irukandji jellyfish, which make ocean swimming impossible. Because of school holidays, sea- and reef-side Queensland tends to fill up around Christmas. When making travel plans, remember that there's no daylight savings time in the state.

BRISBANE

Founded in 1823 on the banks of the wide, meandering Brisbane River, the former penal colony of Brisbane was for many years thought of as just a big country town. Many beautiful timber Queenslander homes, built in the 1800s, still dot the riverbanks and suburbs, and the numerous parks erupt in a riot of colorful jacaranda, flame tree, and bougainvillea blossoms in spring. However, the Queensland capital today is one of Australia's up-and-coming cities, where glittering high-rises mark its polished business center and a string of sandy beaches beckon to endless outdoor attractions. In summer, temperatures here are broilingly hot, a reminder that this city is part of a subtropical region.

The inner suburbs, just a 5- to 10-minute drive or a 15- to 20-minute walk from the city center, have a mix of intriguing eateries and quiet accommodations. Fortitude Valley combines Chinatown with a cos-

Reef Visits

The Great Barrier Reef, which teems with extraordinary sea life, is one of the certified wonders of the world. Boats leave from Cairns and Townsville every day (though Cairns is a better base) on diving, snorkeling, and deep-water fishing excursions; for those that would rather not get wet, there are glass-bottom boat trips, as well.

National Parks

Queensland has one of the most extensive and organized park systems in Australia, from the varied ecosystems of Lamington National Park on the New South Wales border to the gorges and Aboriginal rock paintings of Carnarvon National Park northwest of Brisbane, and the rain forests of Daintree north of Cairns. National Park entry is free, and many have ranger stations, walking tracks, and well-equipped campgrounds. Parks are also the ideal places to spot local wildlife, including fresh- and saltwater crocodiles (although the latter are only safe to look at from a distance).

7

Wild Queensland

If you have the time, an explorer's curiosity, or just wish to see one of the world's last wild jungles, take a trip north from Cairns. The remaining pockets of ancient untouched wilderness that warrant the area's listing as a World Heritage Site provide one of the most archetypal Australian adventures you can have.

---

mopolitan influx of clubs, cafés, and boutiques. Spring Hill has several high-quality hotels, and Paddington, New Farm, and the West End in South Brisbane are full of restaurants and bars. Brisbane is also a convenient base for trips to the Sunshine and Gold coasts, the mountainous hinterlands, and the Moreton Bay islands.

Exploring Brisbane

City Center

Brisbane's inner-city landmarks—a combination of Victorian, Edwardian, and slick high-tech architecture—are best explored on foot. Most of them lie within the triangle formed by Ann Street and the bends of the Brisbane River. Hint: the streets running toward the river are named after female (British) royalty, and those streets running parallel to the river are named after male royalty.

Numbers in the text correspond to numbers in the margin and on the Brisbane map.

a good walk

Start at **St. John's Anglican Cathedral ❶ ▶**, near the corner of Wharf and Ann streets. Walk southeast along Wharf Street, across Queen Street, south on Eagle Street, and southwest on Elizabeth Street to **Old St. Stephen's Church ❷**, which stands in the shadow of St. Stephen's Catholic Cathedral. Both buildings are in Gothic Revival style. One block northwest of the church, on Queen Street, is the **National Bank Building ❸**;

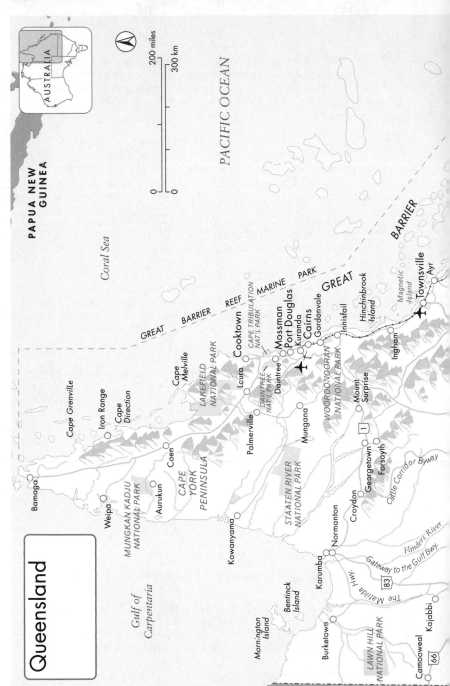

Queensland

PAPUA NEW GUINEA

PACIFIC OCEAN

Coral Sea

Gulf of Carpentaria

CAPE YORK PENINSULA

200 miles

300 km

Bamaga

Weipa

Cape Grenville

Iron Range

Cape Direction

Coen

Aurukun

MUNGKAN KADJU NATIONAL PARK

Kowanyama

Cape Melville

LAKEFIELD NATIONAL PARK

Palmerville

Lcura

Cooktown

CAPE TRIBULATION NAT'L PARK

DAINTREE NAT'L PARK

Daintree

Mossman

Port Douglas

Kuranda

Cairns

Gordonvale

Innisfail

GREAT

BARRIER REEF MARINE PARK

GREAT BARRIER

BARRIER

Magnetic Island

Townsville

Ayr

Hinchinbrook Island

Ingham

Mungana

WOOROONOORAN NATIONAL PARK

Mount Surprise

STAATEN RIVER NATIONAL PARK

Georgetown

Forsayth

Croydon

Cattle Corridor Byway

Normanton

Karumba

Gateway to the Gulf Bwy.

Flinders River

The Matilda Hwy.

Beninck Island

Mornington Island

Burketown

LAWN HILL NATIONAL PARK

Camooweal

Kajabbi

AUSTRALIA

1

83

66

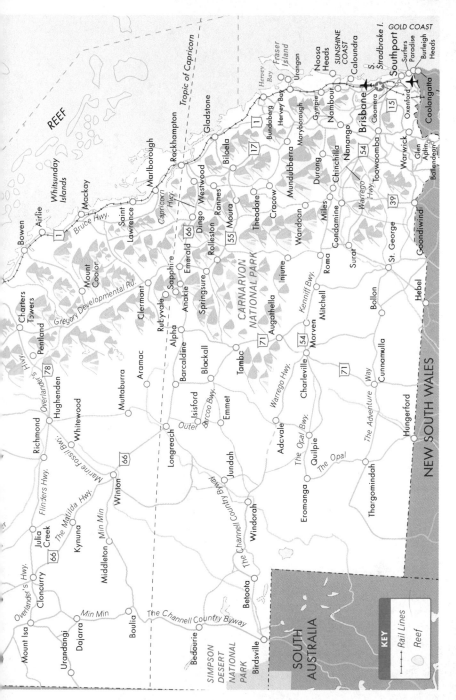

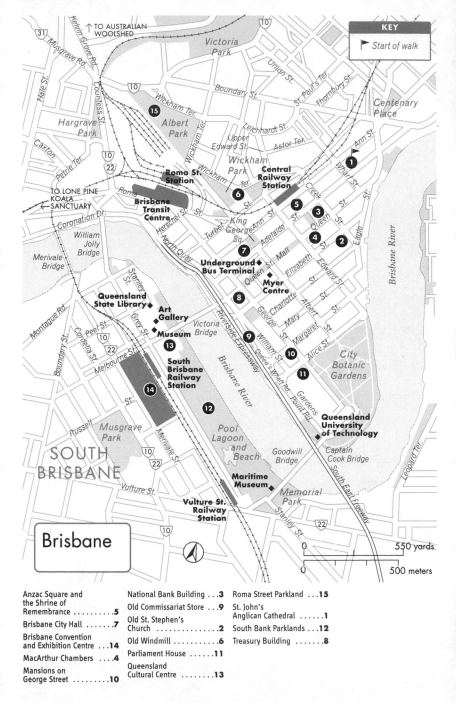

KEY

▶ Start of walk

TO AUSTRALIAN
WOOLSHED

31

Kelvin Grove Rd.

Musgrave Rd.

Hale St.

Caxton St.

*Hargrave
Park*

Petrie Ter.

TO LONE PINE
KOALA
SANCTUARY

Coronation Dr.

*William
Jolly
Bridge*

*Merivale
Bridge*

Montague Rd.

Cordelia St.

Boundary St.

Peel St.

Stanley St.

Grey St.

Melbourne St.

Russell St.

*Musgrave
Park*

SOUTH
BRISBANE

Vulture St.

Countess St.

Roma St.

Herschel St.

North Quay

Victoria
Park

Boundary St.

Wickham Ter.

Albert
Park

Wickham Ter.

Upper
Edward St.

Wickham
Park

Leichhardt St.

Astor Ter.

**Roma St.
Station**

**Brisbane
Transit
Centre**

Turbot St.

Roma St.

King
George
Sq.

Ann St.

Adelaide St.

Queen St. Mall

Elizabeth St.

**Queensland
State Library**

**Art
Gallery**

Museum

Victoria
Bridge

Riverside Expressway

Queen St.

**Myer
Centre**

**Underground
Bus Terminal**

George St.

Charlotte St.

Mary St.

**South
Brisbane
Railway
Station**

Merivale St.

Brisbane River

William St.

Queen's Wharf Rd.

Margaret St.

Alice St.

*Pool
Lagoon
and
Beach*

Goodwill
Bridge

Gardens Point Rd.

*City
Botanic
Gardens*

**Queensland
University
of Technology**

Captain
Cook Bridge

**Maritime
Museum**

*Memorial
Park*

Stanley St.

South East Freeway

Leopard Ter.

**Vulture St.
Railway
Station**

22

Union St.

St. Paul's Ter.

Thornbury St.

*Centenary
Place*

Wharf St.

Ann St.

Creek St.

**Central
Railway
Station**

Old Windmill 6

Wickham Ter.

Eagle St.

Queen St.

Edward St.

Albert St.

Brisbane River

Brisbane

550 yards

500 meters

① St. John's Anglican Cathedral
⑤ Anzac Square and the Shrine of Remembrance
③ National Bank Building
② Old St. Stephen's Church
④ MacArthur Chambers
⑤ Anzac Square
⑥ Old Windmill
⑦ Brisbane City Hall
⑧ Treasury Building
⑨ Old Commissariat Store
⑩ Mansions on George Street
⑪ Parliament House
⑫ South Bank Parklands
⑬ Queensland Cultural Centre
⑭ Brisbane Convention and Exhibition Centre
⑮ Roma Street Parkland

note the doors and interior of this classical palazzo. Continue southwest along Queen Street for one block to **MacArthur Chambers** ❹, General Douglas MacArthur's main Pacific office during World War II, which now houses **Dymocks,** one of Australia's largest chain bookstores, and **MacArthur Central Mall.**

At the corner of Elizabeth and Edward streets, head northwest along Edward Street and turn right onto Adelaide Street. On the left look for **Anzac Square and the Shrine of Remembrance** ❺, built in memory of Australian casualties in World War I. Return to Edward Street and head northwest to Wickham Terrace. Turn left and follow the street as it curves to the **Old Windmill** ❻, one of the city's two remaining convict-built structures. Back on Edward Street, walk two blocks southeast and turn right onto Adelaide Street. Abutting King George Square is the classical **Brisbane City Hall** ❼, where a bell tower provides great views of the city.

From here, walk to Queen Street Mall, between George and Edward streets, where there's often free midday entertainment. Head southwest to the **Treasury Building** ❽ (aka the Conrad Treasury Casino), then walk southeast on William Street to the **Old Commissariat Store** ❾, the city's other surviving convict-built structure. Farther along William Street, turn left onto Margaret Street and then right onto George Street to reach the brick and sandstone **Mansions on George Street** ❿.

Cross Alice Street and on your right will be the splendid French Renaissance **Parliament House** ⓫. Now step into the City Botanic Gardens, which stretch over to the river. To the south is the pedestrian- and cycle-only Goodwill Bridge, which crosses the Brisbane River to connect with the **South Bank Parklands** ⓬. Adjacent is the **Queensland Cultural Centre** ⓭, while the imposing **Brisbane Convention and Exhibition Centre** ⓮ lies at the Parklands' northwest corner. Follow Melbourne Street northeast to the Victoria Bridge, then head northwest along George Street to end your tour at the **Roma Street Parkland** ⓯.

TIMING This walk takes about two hours, including the hike up to the Old Windmill. To explore the sights or play in the parklands, allow several more hours. The free **Loop bus** (☎ 13–1230 ⊕ www.qld.gov.au), which runs weekdays on 10-minute intervals from 7 AM to 5:50 PM, connects the Queensland University of Technology (near Parliament House) to the Queen Street Mall, City Hall, Central Station, and Riverside.

What to See

❺ **Anzac Square and the Shrine of Remembrance.** Walking paths stretch across green lawns toward the Doric Greek Revival shrine, constructed of Queensland sandstone. An eternal flame burns here for Australian soldiers who died in World War I. Equally spine-tingling is the **Shrine of Remembrance,** where a subsurface crypt stores soil samples collected from battlefields on which Australian soldiers perished. On April 25, Anzac Day, a moving dawn service is held here in remembrance of Australia's fallen soldiers. ⊠ *Adelaide St. between Edward and Creek Sts., City Center* ⌸ *Free* ☉ *Shrine weekdays 11–3.*

❼ **Brisbane City Hall.** Built in 1930, this substantial Italianate structure was once referred to as the "million-pound town hall" because of the massive funds poured into its construction. Today it's a major symbol of Brisbane's civic pride, where visitors and locals "ooh" and "aah" at the grand pipe organ and circular concert hall. You can take a tour of City Hall on weekdays (A$4.75), but it's essential to book first. This is also the home of the free **Museum of Brisbane.** The museum portrays the social history of the city; its changing exhibitions have included entries in the Lord Mayor's photographic awards (an annual photographic competition that has a different, distinctly Brisbane theme each year) and "Brisbane Buddhas" (a display of 2,549 Buddhas owned by local residents). Other attractions include a ground-floor art gallery, a tower housing one of Australia's largest civic clocks, and an observation platform with superb city views. ⊠ *King George Sq. and Adelaide St., City Center* ☎ *07/3403–8888* ⊠ *City Hall entry, museum, and clock tower free; City Hall tours A$4.75* ⊗ *Clock Tower weekdays 10–3, Sat. 10–2:30; City Hall weekdays 8–5, weekends 10–5; museum daily 10–5.*

⓮ **Brisbane Convention and Exhibition Centre.** This 4½-acre building is equipped with four exhibition halls, a 4,000-seat Great Hall, and a Grand Ballroom, and apart from conferences it is the venue for large rock concerts. Sixties' legends the Moody Blues and Jethro Tull played here in 2005. ⊠ *Glenelg and Merivale Sts., South Brisbane* ☎ *1800/036308* ⊕ *www.brisconex.com.au.*

❹ **MacArthur Chambers.** As commander-in-chief of the Allied Forces fighting in the Pacific, General Douglas MacArthur came to Australia from the Philippines, leaving the Japanese in control there with his famous vow, "I shall return." This present-day bookstore, mall, and apartment block was MacArthur's World War II headquarters. A museum displaying countless photographs of the period and newspaper stories, together with military memorabilia, opened in late 2004 on the eighth floor where MacArthur's office was located. ⊠ *Queen St., entrance at 201 Edward St., City Center* ☎ *07/3211–7052* ⊠ *Gold coin donation (A$1 or A$2)* ⊗ *Tues., Thurs., and Sun. 10–3.*

need a break?　Duck around the corner from MacArthur Chambers, taking a right on Elizabeth Street, and stop in at the locally owned American Bookstore. Work your way to the back, where **Caffé Libri** serves coffee, cakes (try the Dutch Apple), and extravagantly filled sandwiches. The bookstore carries literary fiction, academic, and foreign-language titles, and has been run by the same family (who are not Americans!) for 50 years. ⊠ *197 Elizabeth St. City Center* ☎ *07/3229–4677* ⊟ *AE, DC, MC, V* ⊗ *Closed Sun.*

❿ **Mansions on George Street.** Constructed in 1890 as six fashionable town houses, these splendid Victorian terrace homes are well worth a visit. Elegant, wrought-iron lace trim garnishes the buildings' exterior; inside are the National Trust gift shop, a restaurant, bookshops, and professional offices—all open during regular business hours. ⊠ *40 George St., City Center.*

❸ **National Bank Building.** Brisbane's National Bank went up in 1885 and is one of the country's finest Italian Renaissance–style structures. Aside from the majestic entrance hall with its ornate ceilings and eye-catching dome, the most interesting features are the front doors, which were crafted from a single cedar trunk. The bank is open during regular business hours. ⊠ *308 Queen St., City Center.*

⑨ Old Commissariat Store. Convict-built in 1829, and erected over the location of the city's original timber wharf, this was the first stone building in Brisbane. It has served variously as a customs house, storehouse, and immigrants' shelter and is currently the headquarters of the Royal Historical Society of Queensland. A model of early-19th-century Brisbane is on display. The Royal Historical Society library and museum are open to visitors, and hold a collection of historical documents, manuscripts, and artifacts dating back to Brisbane's early colonial days. ⊠ *115 William St., City Center* ☎ *07/3221–4198* ⊡ *A$4* ⊙ *Tues.–Sat. 10–4.*

❷ Old St. Stephen's Church. The tiny 1850 church that adjoins St. Stephen's Catholic Cathedral is Brisbane's oldest house of worship, and a particularly fine example of Gothic Revival architecture. The church is believed to have been designed by Augustus Pugin, a noted English architect who designed much of London's Houses of Parliament. The church is not open to the public. ⊠ *Elizabeth St. near Creek St., City Center.*

⑥ Old Windmill. This 1828 construction is the oldest remaining convict building in Brisbane. Because it never worked very well, it was dubbed the "Tower of Torture" by the convicts who were forced to power a treadmill to crush grain for the colony's bread whenever the wind died down. When fire erupted across the city in 1864, scorching almost everything in its path, the windmill survived with only minimal damage. Stripped of its blades, the tower now looks much like a lighthouse. It's closed to the public. ⊠ *Wickham Park, Wickham Terr., City Center.*

⑪ Parliament House. Opened in 1868, this splendid, stone-clad, French Renaissance building with a Mount Isa copper roof earned its colonial designer a meager 200-guinea (A$440) salary. A legislative annex was added in the late 1970s. The interior is fitted with polished timber, brass, and frosted and engraved glass. On weekdays, building tours take place. The adjacent **City Botanic Gardens** have native and exotic plants and themed areas, including the Bamboo Grove and Weeping Fig Avenue, along with fountains, sculptures and ornamental ponds. ⊠ *George and Alice Sts., City Center* ☎ *07/3406–7562* ⊡ *Free* ⊙ *Weekdays 9–5; tours Tues., Wed., Thurs. 10:30 and 2:30; Fri. on request; last tour at 4:15. Gardens open 24 hrs.*

⑬ Queensland Cultural Centre. The Queensland Art Gallery, Queensland Museum, State Library, Performing Arts Complex, and a host of restaurants, cafés, and shops are all here. On weekdays at noon there are free tours of the Performing Arts Complex. Backstage peeks at the 2,000-seat concert hall and Cremorne Theatre are often included. ⊠ *Melbourne and Grey Sts., South Brisbane* ☎ *07/3840–7303 art gallery, 07/3846–1918 museum, 07/3840–7810 library, 13–6246 Performing Arts Complex* ⊡ *Free* ⊙ *Gallery daily 10–5, museum daily 9:30–5, library Mon.–Thurs. 10–8 and Fri.–Sun. 10–5.*

⑮ Roma Street Parkland. The world's largest subtropical garden within a city is a gentle mix of forest paths and structured plantings surrounding a lake. Look for unique Queensland artwork on display along the walkways. Highlights include the Lilly Pilly Garden, which displays native evergreen rain-forest plants. Pack a picnic, lunch at the café, or hop aboard the park's train for a 15-minute ride with commentary (A$5). ⊠ *1 Parkland Blvd., City Center* ☎ *07/3006–4545* ⊕ *www.romastreetparkland.com; www.trains4u.com.au* ⊠ *Free* ⊙ *Daily 24 hrs.*

➤ ❶ St. John's Anglican Cathedral. Built in 1901 with porphyry rock, this is a fine example of Gothic Revival architecture. Free guided tours are available Monday through Saturday and most Sundays. Inside the cathedral grounds is the **Deanery** (the residence of the ecclesiastical dean) which predates the construction of the cathedral by almost 50 years. ⊠ *373 Ann St., City Center* ☎ *07/3835–2248* ⊙ *Tours Mon.–Sat. at 10 and 2, most Sun. at 2.*

⑫ South Bank Parklands. One of the most appealing urban parks in Australia, and the site of Brisbane's World Expo '88, this 40-acre complex includes gardens, shops, a maritime museum, foot- and cycling paths, a sprawling beach lagoon (complete with lifeguards), a Nepalese-style carved-wood pagoda, and excellent views of the city. The Friday-night Lantern Markets and weekend Crafts Village are main events. The park lies alongside the river just south of the Queensland Cultural Centre, stretching along Grey Street to the Goodwill Bridge. ⊠ *Grey St. south of Melbourne St., South Brisbane* ☎ *07/3867–2000, 07/3867–2020 for entertainment information* ⊠ *Parklands free, maritime museum A$6* ⊙ *Parklands daily 5 AM–midnight, museum daily 9:30–4:30, Lantern Markets Fri. 5–10 PM, Crafts Village Sat. 11–5 and Sun. 9–5.*

❽ Treasury Building. This massive Edwardian baroque edifice overlooking the river stands on the site of the officers' quarters and military barracks from the original penal settlement. Bronze figurative statuary surrounds the structure. Constructed between 1885 and 1889, the former treasury reopened as the **Conrad Treasury Casino.** In addition to floors of game rooms, the casino also houses five restaurants and seven bars. ⊠ *William and Elizabeth Sts., City Center* ☎ *07/3306–8888* ⊠ *Free* ⊙ *Daily 24 hrs.*

Around Brisbane

Ⓒ **Australian Woolshed.** Eight rams from the major sheep breeds found in Australia perform in this park's one-hour stage show, giving an insight into the dramatically different appearances—and personalities—of sheep. Next to perform are the sheepdogs who show how adept they are at rounding up their wooly charges. Waterslides, miniature golf, an animal nursery, and a crafts shop are also on-site, and you can get your photo taken with a koala (A$14.50) at the koala sanctuary. The woolshed is 14 km (8½ mi) west of Brisbane city and the nearest train station is at Ferny Grove. Trains arrive regularly from Roma Street and Central stations; the trip from either of these takes about 25 minutes. From Ferny Grove it's about a 10-minute walk to the theme park. ⊠ *148 Samford Rd., Ferny Hills* ☎ *07/3872–1100* ⊕ *www.auswoolshed. com.au* ⊠ *Ram and dog shows and animal farm A$18; shows, farm,* *and unlimited waterslide rides A$23* ☉ *Daily 8:30–4.30, shows daily at 9:30, 11, 1, and 2:30.*

ⓒ **Lone Pine Koala Sanctuary.** Queensland's most famous fauna park,
Fodor'sChoice founded in 1927, claims to be the oldest animal sanctuary in the world.
★ The real attraction for most people are the koalas (130 in all), although emus, wombats, and kangaroos also reside here. You can pet and feed some of the animals, have a snake wrapped around you, and even cuddle with a koala for free. However, a photo with a koala costs A$15. The MV *Mirimar* (☎ 07/3221–0300), a historic 1930s ferry, travels daily to Lone Pine sanctuary from Brisbane's North Quay at the Victoria Bridge departing at 10, returning at 2:50 (A$25 round-trip). Bus 430 from the Myer Centre and Bus 445 from outside City Hall also stop at the sanctuary. ⊠ *Jesmond Rd., Fig Tree Pocket* ☎ *07/3378–1366* ⊕ *www. koala.net* ⓈⒶ *A$18* ☉ *Daily 8:30–5.*

Where to Eat

Contemporary

$$$ ✕ **Siggi's at The Port Office.** Socialites rub shoulders with visiting celebrities at this comfortable restaurant in the Stamford Plaza hotel. The service is impeccable, and the dining and bar areas make full use of the architecture of the 19th-century Port of Brisbane Office. Monthly set menus supplement ever-changing Continental dishes, which might include cappuccino of lobster bisque with chestnuts and porcini dust, or glazed truffle honey double-roasted duckling over Lyonnaise-scented potatoes. Desserts are just as worthy. ⊠ *Edward and Margaret Sts., City Center* ☎ *07/3221–1999* ⚑ *Reservations essential* ⊟ *AE, DC, MC, V* ☉ *Closed Sun. and Mon. No lunch.*

Eclectic

$$–$$$ ✕ **Oxley's on the River.** By day the dining room at Brisbane's only floating restaurant is sunny and has a bird's-eye view of boat traffic. By night, light from the city and the moon dimple the water and lend an intimate, romantic feel. This purpose-built restaurant with floor-to-ceiling windows on three sides is permanently moored to the wharf at the inner-city suburb of Milton. Queensland barramundi and Thai-style curry of swordfish are on the à la carte menu, while the three-course set menu— at A$41.95 per head (with four choices of appetizers and main courses, and three desserts) is very popular. Oxley's is a five-minute taxi ride from the city center. ⊠ *330 Coronation Dr., Milton* ☎ *07/3368–1866* ⊟ *AE, DC, MC, V.*

Italian

$$–$$$ ✕ **Il Centro.** No expense has been spared in fitting this handsome eatery with gleaming wood floors, terra-cotta tiles, and enormous windows that take advantage of the river view. Wondrous aromas spill out of the open kitchen, where the staff whips up potato gnocchi with Torres Strait lobster tail, sand-crab lasagna, and duck with tarragon jus, mustard fruits, and caramelized sweet-potato frittata. Throw your diet out the window and try *semifreddo* (chilled dessert) with varying fruits and sauces, or the warm chocolate tart with gelato and caramel sauce. The predomi-

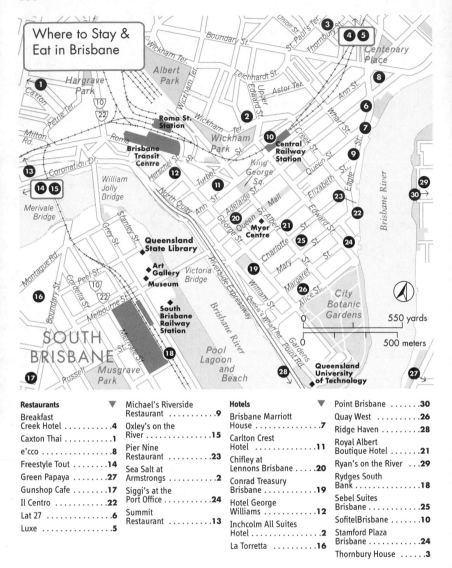

Where to Stay &
Eat in Brisbane

nantly Australian wine list is excellent, and there's a vegetarian menu. ⊠ *Eagle Street Pier, 1 Eagle St., City Center* ☎ *07/3221–6090* ⊕ *www. ilcentro.com.au* ☰ *AE, DC, MC, V* ⊘ *No lunch Sat.*

Mediterranean

$$ ✕ **Lat 27.** It takes its name from Brisbane's position on the globe—Latitude 27—and in a very short time has placed itself firmly on the city's map. This spacious, almost all-white restaurant in the heart of town has great views of the Story Bridge and Brisbane River. Chef Brad Jolly worked in some well-known restaurants in the United Kingdom (and even with TV's Naked Chef, Jamie Oliver) before opening his own place with his wife Angelica. His signature dish is the 24-hour-marinated *daube de boeuf* (a classic beef stew) served with creamy mash, bacon, button mushrooms, and shallots. A decadent way to end a meal is to crack open the chocolate *marbre* with vanilla ice-cream and watch the chocolate melt out of this self-saucing pudding. ⊠ *471 Adelaide St., Petrie Bight, City Center* ☎ *07/3838–2727* ⊕ *www.lat27.com.au* ☰ *AE, DC, MC, V* ⊘ *No lunch weekends, no dinner Sun.*

Modern Australian

$$ ✕ **e'cco.** Consistently rated as the best restaurant in town, this petite

Fodor'sChoice eatery serves innovative food to a loyal following. The white-columned

★ entry leads into a maroon-and-black dining room, where an open kitchen and bar await. The menu lists a wide selection of seasonally changing, Mediterranean- and Asian-inspired dishes, which use local produce and are beautifully presented. Superb choices include field mushrooms on olive toast with arugula, truffle oil, and lemon; salmon poached in tomato, chili, and lemongrass broth; crab ravioli; and mussels. For dessert, the buttermilk panna cotta with passion-fruit syrup is wonderful. Pay attention to the waiter's suggestions for accompanying wines. ⊠ *100 Boundary St., City Center* ☎ *07/3831–8344* ⊕ *www.eccobistro.com* ⌲ *Reservations essential* ☰ *AE, DC, MC, V* ⊘ *Closed Sun. and Mon. No lunch Sat.*

$$ ✕ **Luxe.** This casual restaurant-cum-bar serves delicious tapas-style starters and meals with a Euro-Mediterranean edge. Sample smoked sardines with kipfler potatoes, French beans, and a grain mustard dressing; or oxtail ravioli with wild mushrooms, baby spinach, and *duxelles* (chopped mushrooms, shallots, and onions sautéed in butter). Char-grilled asparagus and artichokes with Parmesan crackling and tomato jelly is one of the many vegetarian options. The wine and cocktail lists are impressive. In nice weather, try for a table outside on the sidewalk. ⊠ *39 James St., Fortitude Valley* ☎ *07/3854–0671* ☰ *AE, DC, MC, V.*

$$ ✕ **Summit Restaurant.** Perched beside the lookout on the slope of Mt. Cootha, this restaurant affords unbeatable views of the city, especially at night. Since the view is a bigger attraction than the food, diners tend to be from out of town. The original building dates from 1925 and has been patronized by such lights and dignitaries as Katharine Hepburn and Britain's Princess Alexandra. Treat yourself to grilled kangaroo loin on rosemary skewers, and follow it with iced mango-and-coconut parfait with mango coulis and crisp macaroons. Taxi fare to the Summit from the city center is about A$17. ⊠ *Sir Samuel Griffith Dr., Toowong* ☎ *07/ 3369–9922* ☰ *AE, DC, MC, V.*

$–$$ ✕ **Gallery Dining Room.** The old, ornate General Post Office of Fortitude Valley has had a complete internal face-lift and reopened for business in March 2005. The whole complex is known as the GPO Hotel and this elegant, palm-filled restaurant with high, arched windows is on the top floor. The menu has something to suit all tastes: try the panfried, crispy Atlantic salmon or the Eye fillet filled with Pont l'Evêque (cheese) wrapped in Parma ham, and finish with mango and Malibu (a rum liqueur) parfait. The restaurant has an adjoining bar which serves small tasting plates (as aperitifs) of several of the dishes available in the dining room. The new-look GPO Hotel, which also includes the Beluga Lounge champagne-and-caviar bar, is now attracting a mature, creative clientele. ✉ *740 Ann St., Fortitude Valley* ☎ *07/3252–1322* ⊕ *www.gpohotel. com.au* ⊟ *AE, DC, MC, V.*

$–$$ ✕ **Gunshop Cafe.** Named for its previous business, this West End café is the place to go for breakfast on weekends (the potato-and-feta hash cakes are locally famous). The unfinished brick walls display an ever-changing selection of local art where guns used to hang. Tin buckets of lilies fill the arches separating the open kitchen from the wooden tables; you can also dine outside on the deck or in the fern-filled garden. Australian foodies also flock here for lunch and dinner, or coffee and a slice of fig, pistachio, and ginger tart. ✉ *53 Mollison St., West End* ☎ *07/3844–2241* ⊟ *AE, DC, MC, V* ⊗ *Closed Mon. and Tues.*

$–$$ ✕ **Sea Salt at Armstrongs.** Well-known local chef Russell Armstrong works seafood magic at this popular, intimate, 30-seat restaurant tucked away in the back of the boutique Inchcolm All-Suites Hotel. Choices include blue mussels braised with vermouth and served with garlic toast, or confit of tuna niçoise, quail eggs, and green beans. Old favorites include Steak Dianne West, named in honor of the chef's partner. ✉ *73 Wickham Terr., City Center* ☎ *07/3832–4566* ⊟ *AE, DC, MC, V* ⊗ *Closed Sun. No lunch Sat.*

★ **¢–$** ✕ **Freestyle Tout.** Tucked away in an inner-city suburb, this art-gallery café is famous for the 24 beautiful desserts that grace its menu. Savvy owner Martin Duncan focuses on healthy main dishes, so you can indulge in wonderful sweets (like artfully designed sundaes, served in a vase) without guilt. Live music is often scheduled, and the flamboyant flowers and modern Australian artwork are for sale. An extensive assortment of teas, coffees, and wines is available. ✉ *21 Nash St., Rosalie* ☎ *07/3876–2288* ⊕ *www.freestyle-online.com* ⊟ *AE, DC, MC, V* ⊗ *No dinner.*

Seafood

$$–$$$$ ✕ **Michael's Riverside Restaurant.** Of Michael Platsis's two very different restaurants in the Riverside Centre, this silver-service establishment is the jewel. You can enjoy sweeping views of the Brisbane River and the Story Bridge here, as well as a menu that changes daily and focuses on Queensland seafood. A popular dish is the crispy-skin barramundi on roasted fennel. Michael's has what just might be the best wine cellar in town. ✉ *123 Eagle St., City Center* ☎ *07/3226–2100* ⊕ *www. michaelsrestaurant.com.au* ✍ *Reservations essential* ⊟ *AE, DC, MC, V* ⊗ *No lunch weekends.*

★ **$$–$$$** ✕ **Pier Nine Restaurant.** The city's most stylish seafood restaurant prepares everything from fish-and-chips to lobsters and has fantastic views of the Brisbane River and the Story Bridge. Only the best catches from the Northern Territory to Tasmania appear here, and fresh oysters are delivered daily and shucked to order. Try the three-crab lasagna (made with sand, spanner, and mud crabs), or the barbecued Moreton Bay bugs (lobsterlike crustaceans) if they're available. ⊠ *Eagle Street Pier, 1 Eagle St., City Center* ☎ *07/3229–2194* ▭ *AE, DC, MC, V.*

Steak

$$ ✕ **Breakfast Creek Hotel.** A Brisbane institution, this enormous hotel is perched right on the wharf at Breakfast Creek. It's undergone a major interior makeover, but its trademark steaks are still as superb as ever. Just choose your cut, how you'd like it cooked, and a sauce to go with it. Vegetarians also have options. Look around as you dig in; many Australian sports notables dine here. ⊠ *2 Kingsford Smith Dr., Albion* ☎ *07/3262–5988* ▭ *AE, DC, MC, V.*

Thai

¢–$ ✕ **Caxton Thai.** This traditional Thai restaurant, where you dine between red and yellow walls surrounded by Thai art and sculptures, is popular with both locals and tourists. The most requested dish is the pork chop with basil—a bit of Aussie fusion, perhaps? In this otherwise traditional Thai restaurant, you can find a warm Thai salad, a mixture of chicken, prawn, glass noodles, and vegetables. There's a generous vegetarian menu. ⊠ *47B Caxton St., Paddington* ☎ *07/3367–0300* ⊕ *www. caxtonthai.com.au* ▭ *AE, DC, MC, V* ☽ *No lunch.*

Vietnamese

$–$$$ ✕ **Green Papaya.** The small selection of simple dishes here is beautifully prepared in traditional North Vietnamese style; among the most popular choices are chili-dusted chicken with lemongrass, and prawns in coconut juice. Lunches are available by reservation on Friday. ⊠ *898 Stanley St., East Brisbane* ☎ *07/3217–3599* ⊕ *www.greenpapaya.com. au* ▭ *AE, DC, MC, V* ☽ *Closed Sun. and Mon. No lunch Sat.–Thurs.*

Where to Stay

$$$$ ▦ **Brisbane Marriott Hotel.** This narrow, 28-story, riverfront hotel is easy to recognize by its distinctive bronze dome. The top floor houses the fantastic Dome Retreat Day Spa, which offers just about every treatment imaginable, from body scrubs and wraps to foot baths and a lap pool. It also serves healthy cuisine to spa clients. The rooms are decorated in elegant cream tones and tasteful wood furnishings, and have marble bathrooms. Fitness facilities include a Grecian-style indoor-outdoor swimming pool with a sundeck overlooking the river. The hotel is a short walk from the City Cat high-speed ferry wharf, and several restaurants and bars in the Riverside Centre. ⊠ *515 Queen St., City Center, 4000* ☎ *07/3303–8000 or 1800/899899* ▦ *07/3303–8088* ⊕ *www. marriott.com/bnedt* ⇆ *263 rooms, 4 suites* ☖ *Restaurant, room service, cable TV, in-room data ports, 2 pools, gym, outdoor hot tub, massage,* sauna, spa, bar, laundry service, concierge, Internet room, business services, meeting rooms, parking (fee) 🖿 AE, DC, MC, V.

★ **$$$$** 🖼 **Conrad Treasury Brisbane.** Like the Conrad Treasury Casino one block to the north, this National Heritage–listed hotel represents a beautiful sandstone example of Edwardian baroque architecture. Rooms have antique furniture and large, luxurious bathrooms. The hotel has five very different restaurants to suit all budgets and tastes. ✉ *130 William St., City Center, 4000* ☎ *07/3306–8888* 🖷 *07/3306–8880* ⊕ *www.conrad. com.au* ➾ *114 rooms, 16 suites* ⚖ *5 restaurants, room service, in-room safes, minibars, refrigerators, gym, sauna, 7 bars, casino, laundry service, business services, free parking* 🖿 *AE, DC, MC, V.*

$$$$ 🖼 **Rydges South Bank.** Sandwiched between the Brisbane Convention and Exhibition Centre and South Bank Parklands, this hotel is an excellent choice for both business and leisure travelers. It's within walking distance of the Queensland Museum, Art Gallery, Performing Arts Centre, and Conservatorium of Music. Rooms have modern furnishings and computer workstations. Although there's no pool, the beach at South Bank Parklands is within easy walking distance. ✉ *9 Glenelg St., South Brisbane, 4101* ☎ *07/3364–0800* 🖷 *07/3364–0801* ⊕ *www.rydges. com* ➾ *240 rooms, 65 suites* ⚖ *Restaurant, café, room service, microwaves, refrigerators, in-room data ports, gym, sauna, spa, 2 bars, laundry service, business services, parking (fee)* 🖿 *AE, DC, MC, V.*

$$$–$$$$ 🖼 **SofitelBrisbane.** Despite its position above the city's main rail station, this hotel is a quiet and pleasant place to stay. After over 20 years as a Sheraton, it was taken over by the French Accor group in early 2005 and rebranded Sofitel. A six-month refurbishment program has produced a new-look lobby with rich wood panelling. All the spacious rooms and suites have been upgraded to include marble bathrooms and what are advertised as "the world's most comfortable beds." Floors 26 through 29 are the pricier executive floors, where the rate includes breakfast, hors d'oeuvres, and cocktails in a club lounge. The bar on the 30th floor—which has sweeping views across the city—has been turned into an ultrahip lounge with sleek decor, and is expected to attract a corresponding clientele. ✉ *249 Turbot St., City Center, 4000* ☎ *07/3835–3535* 🖷 *07/ 3835–4960* ⊕ *www.accorhotels.com.au* ➾ *385 rooms, 25 suites* ⚖ *3 restaurants, room service, in-room fax, in-room safes, minibars, cable TV, pool, gym, hair salon, hot tub, massage, sauna, 2 bars, lounge, nightclub, laundry service, business services, Internet room, meeting room, free parking, no-smoking rooms* 🖿 *AE, DC, MC, V.*

★ **$$$–$$$$** 🖼 **Stamford Plaza Brisbane.** This refined riverfront hotel next to the City Botanic Gardens is a quiet retreat from the bustling city. The soaring lobby, full of artwork, flower arrangements, and an expanse of natural woods, is warm and inviting and looks out onto a leafy courtyard. Guest rooms, decorated in neoclassical style in muted yellow and beige, enjoy clear views over the river. Three dining spots include the hotel's signature restaurant, Siggi's, and the lively Kabuki, considered the best teppanyaki restaurant in the city. Probably the most famous of the many celebrities and performers who have stayed here is Queen Elizabeth II, who visited in 2002. ✉ *Edward and Margaret Sts., City Center, 4000* ☎ *07/3221–1999 or 1800/773700* 🖷 *07/3221–6895 or 1800/773900* ⊕ *www.stamford.com.*

au 🛏 *252 rooms, 10 suites* 🍴 *4 restaurants, room service, pool, gym, sauna, spa, 2 bars, shops, babysitting, laundry service, business services, no-smoking floors* 🖃 *AE, DC, MC, V.*

$$$ 🏨 **Quay West.** This modern hotel opposite the City Botanic Gardens has sophisticated pressed-metal ceilings, sandstone columns, hammered-iron decorations, and white-louvered windows. The suites are fitted with plantation teak furniture and include fully equipped kitchens and laundry facilities. The pool on the first floor is surrounded by a tropically landscaped area, where intricately carved early-19th-century teak columns from South Africa support a poolside pergola. ✉ *132 Alice St., City Center, 4000* 🕾 *07/3853–6000 or 1800/672726* 🖷 *07/3853–6060* 🌐 *www.mirvachotels.com.au* 🛏 *74 suites* 🍴 *Restaurant, room service, in-room fax, kitchens, minibars, room TVs with movies, in-room data ports, pool, gym, sauna, spa, bar, laundry facilities, free parking* 🖃 *AE, DC, MC, V.*

$$–$$$ 🏨 **Chifley at Lennons Brisbane.** A feature of Brisbane's skyline for many years, this hotel has a winning location in front of the Queen Street Mall at the river end. Most of the spacious rooms have city views; those on Floors 15 to 20 afford river panoramas. There are eight rooms with spa baths; if you don't score one, you can relax in the hotel's rooftop pool. ✉ *66–76 Queen St., City Center, 4000* 🕾 *07/3222–3222* 🖷 *07/ 3221–9389* 🌐 *www.chifleyhotels.com* 🛏 *130 rooms, 24 suites* 🍴 *Restaurant, room service, refrigerators, pool, sauna, spa, 2 bars, babysitting, laundry facilities, laundry service, business services, meeting room, travel services, parking (fee)* 🖃 *AE, DC, MC, V.*

$$–$$$ 🏨 **Point Brisbane.** Across the Brisbane River from the central business district, this modern hotel has great views of the city skyline, the Story Bridge, or the trendy precinct of New Farm from each balcony. Accommodations include studios and one- and two-bedroom apartments with fully equipped kitchens and private laundry facilities. The hotel provides a courtesy shuttle bus to the city, and the Inner City Ferry (dock-side ferry stop) is 100 yards from the front door. ✉ *21 Lambert St., Kangaroo Point, 4169* 🕾 *07/3240–0888 or 1800/088388* 🖷 *07/ 3392–1155* 🌐 *www.thepointbrisbane.com.au* 🛏 *43 rooms, 3 suites, 60 apartments* 🍴 *Restaurant, room service, room TVs with movies, in-room data ports, tennis court, pool, gym, bar, babysitting, dry cleaning, laundry facilities, laundry service, business services, meeting room, travel services, free parking, no-smoking rooms* 🖃 *AE, DC, MC, V.*

$$–$$$ 🏨 **Sebel Suites Brisbane.** Minimalist furnishings create an elegant, un-cluttered look in the rooms here, which are decorated in a color scheme of navy, cream, and red. Suites have kitchens and laundry facilities. Palettes Brasserie and Bar is a popular dining venue for the after-work crowd. The hotel is just two blocks from the Queen Street Mall. ✉ *Albert and Charlotte Sts., City Center, 4000* 🕾 *07/3224–3500 or 1800/888298* 🖷 *07/ 3211–0277* 🌐 *www.mirvachotels.com.au* 🛏 *46 rooms, 110 suites* 🍴 *Restaurant, room service, some kitchenettes, room TVs with movies, in-room data ports, pool, wading pool, sauna, bar, laundry facilities, meeting rooms, parking (fee), no-smoking floors* 🖃 *AE, DC, MC, V.*

$$ 🏨 **Royal Albert Boutique Hotel.** This Heritage-listed building is right in the heart of Brisbane and offers more than you might expect from a standard hotel. Each larger-than-average room has a self-contained kitchen and laundry. The reproduction antique furniture and cream-and-plum plush carpets add elegant finishing touches. This is a small hotel where staff members are very friendly and take pride in greeting guests by name. There is a licensed brasserie on the ground floor. ⊠ *Elizabeth and Albert Sts., City Center, 4000* ☎ *07/3291–8888 or 1800/655054* 🖷 *07/3229–7705* ⊕ *www.atlantisproperties.com.au* 🖘 *28 rooms, 25 suites, 3 apartments* ⚬ *Restaurant, kitchenettes, cable TV, laundry facilities, parking (fee), no-smoking rooms* 🖃 *AE, DC, MC, V.*

$–$$ 🏨 **Carlton Crest Hotel.** The largest hotel in Brisbane is ideally situated opposite City Hall and close to the center of town. A central lobby, elegantly furnished with French-style sofas and carpets, is flanked by the deluxe rooms and Jacuzzi suites of the Carlton Tower on one side and the standard rooms of the Crest Tower on the other. The heated rooftop pool provides cooling relief in summer. Picasso's restaurant, on the ground level, serves Mediterranean cuisine. ⊠ *Ann and Roma Sts., City Center, 4000* ☎ *07/3229–9111 or 1800/777123* 🖷 *07/3229–9618* ⊕ *www.carltoncrest-brisbane.com.au* 🖘 *432 rooms, 7 suites* ⚬ *2 restaurants, room service, in-room VCRs, in-room data ports, pool, gym, sauna, 3 bars, laundry service, concierge, business services, meeting rooms, parking (fee), no-smoking floors* 🖃 *AE, DC, MC, V.*

$–$$ 🏨 **Ryan's on the River.** If you're standing at Eagle Street Pier or the City Botanic Gardens, you can't miss this aqua-color hotel perched on Kangaroo Point directly across the river. You cross the Story Bridge to get to this small, friendly hotel; you can also take a short ferry ride from either Eagle Street Pier or the Edward Street wharf to Thornton Street wharf. It's popular with businesspeople and tourists alike due to its position virtually on the city's doorstep. Every room has a river view from its balcony and each has a double bed and a pull-down single bed. A Continental breakfast is available for A$12. ⊠ *269 Main and Scott Sts., Kangaroo Point, 4169* ☎ *07/3391–1011* 🖷 *07/3391–1824* ⊕ *www.ryans. com.au* 🖘 *23 rooms* ⚬ *Dining room, refrigerators, in-room data ports, saltwater pool, lobby lounge, wineshop, babysitting, laundry facilities, travel services, free parking* 🖃 *MC, V.*

$ 🏨 **Inchcolm All Suites Hotel.** Converted from Heritage medical chambers, this boutique hotel now provides doses of personalized service amid intimate oak surroundings. Spacious rooms are fitted with timber louvers, hand-carved fretwork, and cream fabrics. Some one- and two-bedroom suites have spa baths. A lounge chair by the rooftop Lilliputian pool is an ideal place to enjoy the Brisbane skyline. Sea Salt at Armstrongs restaurant serves creatively prepared seafood. ⊠ *73 Wickham Terr., City Center, 4000* ☎ *07/3226–8888* 🖷 *07/3226–8899* ⊕ *www.inchcolmhotel. com.au* 🖘 *35 suites* ⚬ *Restaurant, kitchenettes, pool, bar, free parking* 🖃 *AE, DC, MC, V.*

$ 🏨 **Ridge Haven.** This late-19th-century bed-and-breakfast is for those who would rather stay outside the hubbub of central Brisbane. With high ceilings, ornate cornices, and reproduction antiques, the rooms exude both comfort and old-fashioned romance. Breakfast is served in the dining room or on a patio with a view of the suburbs. Proprietors Peter and Morna Cook allow guests to use the kitchen or barbecue for lunch or dinner. Complimentary homemade aromatherapy toiletries are a classy touch. ⊠ *374 Annerley Rd., Annerley, 4103, 4 km (2½ mi) south of Brisbane, via the southeastern freeway* ☎ *07/3391–7702* 🖷 *07/3392–1786* ⊕ *www.uqconnect.net/ridgehaven* 🖙 *3 rooms* ⟁ *Dining room, BBQ; no a/c in some rooms, no phones in some rooms, no room TVs, no smoking* ⊟ *MC, V* ⊺◉⊺ *BP.*

$ ⊞ **Thornbury House.** Buttermilk-color walls, polished floors, thick carpets, and wood furnishings decorate this three-level 19th-century merchant's house. Two bedrooms have attached en suite bathrooms, while the other three rooms each have a private bathroom located separately off a hallway. The attic suite has two bedrooms, a bathroom, and a separate lounge and dining room. Continental breakfast is served in the palm-filled courtyard; there's a formal sitting room, where you can sip a complimentary glass of port in the evening. ⊠ *1 Thornbury St., Spring Hill, 4000* ☎ *07/3839–5334* 🖷 *07/3839–5336* ⊕ *www.babs.com.au/thornbury* 🖙 *5 rooms, 1 suite* ⟁ *Dining room, some kitchens, laundry facilities; no kids under 4, no smoking* ⊟ *AE, MC, V* ⊺◉⊺ *BP.*

¢–$ ⊞ **Hotel George Williams.** This modern hotel is right in the heart of the city, 150 yards from the Brisbane Transit Center. Rooms are decorated in sandstone and green or blue color schemes; some have outdoor terraces, and family rooms have a queen-sized bed and double bunks. Cerellos Bar and Café, which serves Asian and Mediterranean cuisine, has budget steaks on Tuesday nights, and tapas and jazz on Friday. If your room doesn't have a data port, you can log on at the on-site Internet café. ⊠ *317–325 George St., City Center, 4000* ☎ *07/3308–0700 or 1800/064858* 🖷 *07/3308–9733* ⊕ *www.hgw.com.au* 🖙 *81 rooms* ⟁ *Café, refrigerators, some in-room data ports, bar, dry cleaning, Internet room, business center, travel services* ⊟ *AE, DC, MC, V* ⊺◉⊺ *BP.*

¢ ⊞ **La Torretta.** A 10-minute walk from the South Bank Parklands takes you to this sprawling, early 1900s West End Queenslander. There are two simple, comfortable rooms, and a large guest lounge looks out onto a tropical Brisbane garden. The price includes a breakfast of strong Italian coffee with homemade bread and jam, juice, cereal, and yogurt. The owners, Charles and Dorothy Colman, speak Italian, French, and German. Guests can use the kitchen to make their own lunch and dinner. The lounge has a TV and Internet connection. ⊠ *8 Brereton St., West End, 4101* ☎ *07/3846–0846* 🖷 *07/3342–7863* ⊕ *www.users.bigpond.com/colmanwilliams* 🖙 *2 rooms* ⟁ *Dining room, library, Internet room, free parking; no a/c, no room phones, no room TVs* ⊟ *MC, V* ⊺◉⊺ *CP.*

Nightlife & the Arts

The Arts

The Saturday edition of the *Courier–Mail* newspaper lists concerts, ballet, opera, theater, jazz, and other events. Thursday's paper includes a free *What's On* magazine, which is Brisbane's most comprehensive entertainment guide.

The **Brisbane Powerhouse** (⊠ 119 Lamington St., New Farm ☎ 07/3358–8600 ⊕ www.brisbanepowerhouse.com), built in a former power plant, hosts avant-garde live performances in flexible 200- and 400-seat theaters. Cafés, restaurants, bikeways, boardwalks, and picnic areas complement the funky art space.

At the **Queensland Art Gallery** (✉ Melbourne and Grey Sts., South Brisbane ☎ 07/3840–7303) you can see old favorites—such as the paintings *Evicted* by Blandford Fletcher (1887) and *Under the Jacaranda* by R. Godfrey Rivers (1903)—as well as a large selection of contemporary Australian Aboriginal and Asian-Pacific artworks. The gallery contains 11,000 Australian and international paintings, sculptures, and other artworks. Its new building, the Queensland Gallery of Modern Art, will open in late 2006, at Kurilpa Point, some 200 yards from the current site.

The **Queensland Performing Arts Complex** (✉ Melbourne and Grey Sts., South Brisbane ☎ 07/3840–7444 or 13–6246 ⊕ www.qpac.com.au), the city's cultural heart, hosts both international and Australian entertainers. In 2005, artists included songstress Norah Jones, folk-rocker Jackson Browne, the Soweto Gospel Choir, and Australia's hit folk group from the 1960s, the Seekers.

Nightlife

Adrenalin Sports Bar (✉ 127 Charlotte St., City Center ☎ 07/3229–1515) is a large American-style haunt with pool tables, 40 television screens broadcasting sporting events, and a large open bar surrounded by tables and chairs. It's open Sunday–Thursday 11:30 AM–midnight, and until 2:20 AM on Friday and Saturday.

Conrad Treasury Casino (✉ Queen and George Sts., City Center ☎ 07/3306–8888)—with a "neat and tidy" dress code geared toward securing an upscale clientele—is a 24-hour, European-style casino. It has three levels of gaming, with 104 tables and more than 1,000 machines, plus four restaurants and five bars.

Cru Bar (✉ James Street Market, 22 James St., Fortitude Valley ☎ 07/3252–2400) is one of Brisbane's newest places to see and be seen. The decor is sleek and sophisticated, with leather ottomans, a long onyx bar, and a circa-1800 French chandelier. The staff here describes the clientele as "people who love good wine, and those who just like to spend money on it." There's a huge adjacent wine cellar, a restaurant open for lunch and dinner, and low-key jazz and mood music to listen to as you sip long into the night.

Empire Hotel (✉ 339 Brunswick St., Fortitude Valley ☎ 07/3852–1216 ⊕ www.empirehotel.com.au) packs in four bars under one roof. You can make yourself at home in the Family Bar, or relax with a cocktail and cool jazz at the ultrahip Press Club, fitted with leather sofas and arty lamps. Dance-music fans flock to the Empire Bar, while those who prefer alternative and rock music mingle upstairs in the Moonbar. It's open Monday–Saturday until 5 AM.

The Monastery (✉ 621 Ann St., City Center ☎ 07/3257–7081) is anything but an ascetic retreat for quiet contemplation. It is, however, the place to dance to house music that rips through the airwaves at 200 beats per minute. The cool blue interior echoes the techno atmosphere, and the dance floor is rarely less than full. It has two bars and is open until late from Thursday to Saturday.

No. 12 Lounge Bar (⊠ 12 McLachlan St., Fortitude Valley ☎ 07/3852–5200) serves cocktails in a hip setting with old comfy lounges and sofas, funky drop lights, and contemporary art displays. It's sophisticated yet relaxed, with a casual dress code, affordable drink prices, and live music some nights.

Sports & the Outdoors

Biking

An extensive network of bicycle paths crisscrosses Brisbane. A highlight is to follow the Bicentennial Bikeway southeast along the Brisbane River, across the Goodwill Bridge, and then along to South Bank Parklands or the Kangaroo Point cliffs.

Brisbane's "Bicycle Guide," detailing more than 400 km (250 mi) of cycling paths, is available from the **Brisbane City Council** (⊠ 69 Ann St., City Center ☎ 07/3403–8888 ⊕ www.brisbane.qld.gov.au). **Brisbane Bicycle Sales and Hire** (⊠ 87 Albert St., City Center ☎ 07/3229–2433 ⊕ www.brizbike.com) rents out bikes from the heart of the city. **Valet Cycle Hire and Tours** (☎ 0408–003198 ⊕ www.valetcyclehire.com) conducts guided bike trips and will deliver a rental bike right to your hotel.

Cricket

Queensland Cricketers' Club (⊠ 411 Vulture St., East Brisbane ☎ 07/3896–4533) provides playing schedules and ticket information for the nation's favorite sport, which is played during the Australian summer.

Golf

St. Lucia Golf Links (⊠ Indooroopilly Rd. and Carawa St., St. Lucia ☎ 07/3870–2556) is an 18-hole, par-71 course open to visitors. You can dine at one of two stylish options: the Clubhouse or the 19th Café, overlooking the 18th green.

Tennis

Contact **Tennis Queensland** (⊠ 83 Castlemaine St., Milton ☎ 07/3368–2433) for information about playing at Brisbane's municipal or private courts and for details on upcoming tournaments.

Shopping

Department Stores

The renowned **David Jones** (⊠ 194 Queen St., City Center ☎ 07/3243–9000), downtown in the Queen Street Mall, is open Monday–Thursday 9:30–5:30, Friday until 9 PM, Saturday 9–5, and Sunday 9:30–5. **Myer** (⊠ 91 Queen St., City Center ☎ 07/3232–0121), also in Queen Street Mall, is open Monday–Thursday 9–5:30, Friday 9–9, Saturday 9–5, and Sunday 10–5.

Discount Stores

Stones Corner (⊠ Logan and Old Cleveland Rds., Stones Corner), a business and residential area about 10 km (6 mi) south of the city center, is a popular shopping area where discount outlets sell seconds, end-of-season styles, and housewares.

Malls & Arcades

The historic and aesthetically pleasing **Brisbane Arcade** (⊠ City Center) joins Queen Street Mall and Adelaide Street and has elegant designer boutiques and jewelry shops. **Broadway on the Mall,** which runs between the Queen Street Mall and Adelaide Street, connects via a walkway to David Jones department store, and has a very good—and enormous—food center on the lower ground floor. The stores of **Brunswick Street Mall** (⊠ Brunswick St., Fortitude Valley 🕾 No phone) and other parts of the "Valley," including Ann Street, are in one of downtown's hippest fashion districts. **Chopstix** (⊠ 249 Brunswick St., Fortitude Valley 🕾 No phone) is a collection of 20 Asian shops and restaurants in the heart of Chinatown. **MacArthur Central** (⊠ Edward and Queen Sts., City Center 🕾 07/3221–5977) also houses boutiques and specialty shops, a bookstore, and a food court.

Myer Centre (⊠ Queen, Elizabeth, and Albert Sts., City Center 🕾 No phone) houses the national department store of the same name, as well as boutiques, specialty shops, delis, restaurants, and cinemas. The **Pavilion** (⊠ Queen and Albert Sts., City Center) has two levels of exclusive shops. **Queen Street Mall** (⊠ City Center 🕾 No phone) is considered the best downtown shopping area, with numerous buskers and a generally festive crowd. **Rowes Arcade** (⊠ 235 Edward St., City Center 🕾 No phone) is a rebuilt 1920s ballroom and banquet hall with boutique clothing stores. **Savoir Faire** (⊠ 20 Park Rd., Milton 🕾 No phone) is an upscale shopping and dining complex 10 minutes from the business district. **Tattersalls Arcade** (⊠ Queen and Edward Sts., City Center 🕾 No phone) caters to discerning shoppers with a taste for upscale designer labels. **Wintergarden Complex** (⊠ Queen Street Mall, City Center 🕾 No phone) houses boutiques and specialty shops, as well as a food court.

Markets

The **Brisbane Powerhouse** (⊠ 119 Lamington St., New Farm 🕾 07/3358–8600 ⊕ www.brisbanepowerhouse.com) hosts a farmers' market 6 AM to noon on the second Saturday of the month. The **Riverside Markets** (⊠ Riverside Centre, 123 Eagle St., City Center), an upscale arts-and-crafts bazaar, are open Sunday 8–4. **South Bank Parklands** (⊠ Grey St. between Melbourne St. and the Goodwill Bridge, City Center) hosts a Friday-night Lantern Market that is open 5–10, and a Crafts Village that sells good-quality homemade clothing and arts and crafts Saturday 11–5 and Sunday 9–5.

Specialty Stores

ABORIGINAL CRAFTS **Aboriginal Art Culture Craft Centre** (⊠ Grey St., South Bank Parklands, Southbank 🕾 07/3844–0255) sells genuine Aboriginal hunting paraphernalia and boomerangs, woomeras, didgeridoos, bark paintings, pottery, and carvings. Books, T-shirts, and other Australian-made gifts and souvenirs are also for sale.

ANTIQUES **Brisbane Antique Market** (⊠ 791 Sandgate Rd., Clayfield 🕾 07/3262–1444), near the airport, collects more than 40 dealers of antiques, collectibles, and jewelry under one roof.

Cordelia Street Antique and Art Centre (⊠ Cordelia and Glenelg Sts., South Brisbane ☎ 07/3844–8514), housed inside an old church, purveys an interesting selection of antiques, books, and jewelry.

Paddington Antique Centre (⊠ 167 Latrobe Terr., Paddington ☎ 07/3369–8088) is a converted theater filled with antiques and bric-a-brac. More than 50 dealers operate within the center.

AUSTRALIAN PRODUCTS **Australia The Gift** (⊠ 150 Queen St. Mall, City Center ☎ 07/3210–6198 ⊕ www.australiathegift.com.au) sells quality Australian-made handicrafts, plus postcards, books, and novelty items.

Greg Grant Country Clothing (⊠ Myer Centre, Queen St., City Center ☎ 07/3221–4233) specializes in the legendary Driza-Bone oilskin coats, Akubra and leather hats, whips, R. M. Williams boots, and moleskins.

My Country Clothing Collection (⊠ Level 1, Broadway on the Mall, Queen Street Mall, City Center ☎ 07/3221–2858) sells country-style clothing for the whole family, plus stock whips, moleskins, and steer-hide belts, all made in Australia.

OPALS **Quilpie Opals** (⊠ Lennons Plaza Bldg., 68 Queen St. Mall, City Center ☎ 07/3221–7369) carries a large selection of Queensland boulder opals as well as high-grade opals, available as individual stones or already set.

Side Trip to Southern Downs

If the cityscapes of Brisbane have given you a thirst for pastoral rolling hills—and fabulous wine—the two-hour drive west on the Cunningham Highway to the Southern Downs is a must. This area, which ranges from Cunninghams Gap in the east to Goondiwindi in the west, to Allora in the north and Wallangarra in the south, is one of Queensland's premier wine-producing areas.

Spring brings the scent of peach and apple blossoms to the air here; in autumn the 40-odd vineyards are ripe for harvest. Winter invites wine-tasting tours. One tour company, the **Grape Escape** (☎ 07/4681–4761 or 1800/361150 ⊕ www.grapeescape.com.au), runs both full-day and overnight winery excursions, as well as very popular progressive dinner tours (A$85 includes five courses, each at a different winery) every Saturday night June through August.

In the tiny, blink-and-you'll-miss-it town of Glen Aplin, 235 km (146 mi) southwest of Brisbane, is **Felsberg Winery.** Known for both its red and white wines (including award-winning Rhine Riesling and merlot) and honey mead, this winery has a tasting room inside a German-inspired château, with hilltop views over the Severn River Valley and the Granite Belt area. ⊠ *116 Townsends Rd., Glen Aplin* ☎ *07/4683–4332* ☜ *Free* ☉ *Daily 9:30–4:30.*

Just south of Glen Aplin is the town of Ballandean, home to the award-winning **Ballandean Estate Wines.** This property includes the oldest family-owned and -operated vineyard and winery in Queensland; the first grapes were grown on the site in 1931. The tasting room is the original brick shed built in 1950, and the Barrel Room Cafe behind it—complete with huge, wine-filled, 125-year-old wooden barrels lining one wall—serves light lunches and coffee. ⊠ *354 Sundown Rd., Ballandean* ☎ *07/4684–1226* ⊕ *www.ballandean-estate.com.au* ☲ *Free* ⊙ *Daily 8:30–5; free tours at 11, 1, 3, and by request.*

Girraween National Park, one of the most popular parks in southeast Queensland, sits at the end of the New England Tableland, a stepped plateau area with elevations ranging from 1,968 feet to 4,921 feet. The 17 km (11 mi) of walking tracks here wind past granite outcrops, boulders and precariously balanced rocks, eucalyptus forests, and wildflowers in spring. If you want to camp, you'll need a permit from the park's ranger. ⊠ *Ballandean 4382, 11 km (7 mi) north of Wallangarra or 26 km (16 mi) south of Stanthorpe on the New England Hwy.* ☎ *07/4684–5157.*

Where to Stay & Eat

$$
Fodor'sChoice
★

✕▥ **Vineyard Cottages and Café.** Built around a turn-of-the-20th-century church that is now the Vineyard Café, this property has four cottages and a row of two-story joined houses (known as terrace houses) set amid 2 acres of beautiful gardens, hedgerows, and arbors. The lodgings, built in the 1990s but in a style that complements the rustic church, are furnished with comfortable sofas, colonial antique furniture, and vases brimming with roses from the gardens. One-bedroom cottages—which have in-room hot tubs built for two—and the terraces can sleep four people; the two-story, two-bedroom cottage accommodates up to seven. Chef Janine Cumming, who co-owns the property with her husband Peter, varies her menus seasonally to take advantage of fresh produce from local farms, including Granite Belt beef fillet and New England rainbow trout. ⊹ *Two blocks from Ballandean village on New England Hwy., near Bents Rd.* ☎ *07/4684–1270* 🖶 *07/4684–1324* ⊕ *www.vineyard-cottages.com.au* ⊅ *4 cottages, 3 terraces* � & *Restaurant, room service, bar, some in-room hot tubs; no room phones, no a/c in some rooms* ▤ *AE, MC, V.*

Brisbane A to Z

AIR TRAVEL

Flight time from Brisbane to Bundaberg is 45 minutes; to Cairns, 2 hours; to Coolangatta, 30 minutes; to Emerald, 1 hour 40 minutes; to Gladstone, 1 hour 15 minutes; to Hamilton Island, 1 hour 45 minutes; to Hervey Bay, 55 minutes; to Mackay, 1 hour 35 minutes; to Maroochydore, 25 minutes; to Maryborough, 45 minutes; to Rockhampton, 1 hour 10 minutes; to Townsville, 1 hour 50 minutes, and to Sydney 1 hour 30 minutes.

AIRLINES   Brisbane is Queensland's major travel crossing point. Many international airlines have head offices in the city center as well as information booths at the airport. Qantas and Virgin Blue Airlines fly to all Australian capital cities and most cities within Queensland. Jetstar links Brisbane with Cairns, Hamilton Island, Mackay, Proserpine, and Rockhampton, as well as Newcastle, in New South Wales, and Avalon, in Victoria. Norfolk Jet Express flies from Brisbane to Norfolk Island in the South Pacific twice weekly.

Many international carriers fly to and from Brisbane. Air Nauru, Air Vanuatu, and Solomon Airlines link Brisbane with islands in the South Pacific. Air New Zealand, Air Pacific, Cathay Pacific, EVA Airways, Garuda Indonesia, Malaysian Airlines, Royal Brunei Airlines, Singapore Airlines, and Thai Airways fly between Brisbane and points throughout Asia, with connections to Europe and the U.S. West Coast.

✈ Air Nauru ✉ Level 4, 97 Creek St., City Center, Brisbane ☎ 07/3229-6455. **Air New Zealand** ✉ Level 7, 360 Queen St., Brisbane ☎ 13-2476. **Air Pacific** ✉ Level 5, 217 George St., Brisbane ☎ 1800/230150. **Air Vanuatu** ✉ Level 5, 293 Queen St., City Center, Brisbane ☎ 1300/780737. **Cathay Pacific Airways** ✉ Level 1, Brisbane International Airport, Airport Dr., Eagle Farm, Brisbane ☎ 13-1747 ⊕ www.cathaypacific.com.au. **EVA Airways** ✉ 127 Creek St., City Center, Brisbane ☎ 07/3229-8000. **Garuda Indonesia** ✉ 288 Edward St., City Center, Brisbane ☎ 1300/365330. **Jetstar** ☎ 13-1538. **Malaysian Airlines** ✉ Level 17, 80 Albert St., City Center, Brisbane ☎ 13-2627. **Norfolk Jet Express** ✉ Level 4, 97 Creek St., City Center, Brisbane ☎ 1800/81647. **Qantas** ✉ 247 Adelaide St., City Center, Brisbane ☎ 07/3238-2700 or 13-1313 ⊕ www.qantas.com. **Royal Brunei Airlines** ✉ 60 Edward St., City Center, Brisbane ☎ 07/3017-5000. **Singapore Airlines** ✉ Level 19, 344 Queen St., City Center, Brisbane ☎ 13-1011 ⊕ www.singaporeair.com.au. **Solomon Airlines** ✉ Level 5, 217 George St., City Center, Brisbane ☎ 07/3407-7266. **Thai Airways** ✉ Level 4, 145 Eagle St., City Center, Brisbane ☎ 07/3215-4700. **Virgin Blue** ✉ Level 7, Centenary Sq., 100 Wickham St., Fortitude Valley, Brisbane ☎ 13-6789 ⊕ www.virginblue.com.

AIRPORT &TRANSFERS Brisbane International Airport is 9 km (5½ mi) from the city center. Coachtrans provides a daily bus service, called SkyTrans Shuttle, to and from city hotels every 30 minutes 5 AM–8:30 PM. The fare is A$11 per person one way, A$18 round trip.

Airtrain has train services to Central Station and other stations throughout Brisbane and the Gold Coast. The fare is A$10 per person one way to Central Station, A$20 round-trip. Trains depart up to four times an hour and it takes 20 minutes to reach the City Center.

Taxis to downtown Brisbane cost approximately A$32.

✈ Airtrain ☎ 07/3216-3308 or 13-1230 ⊕ www.airtrain.com.au. **Brisbane International Airport** ✉ Airport Dr., Eagle Farm ☎ 07/3406-3190. **Coachtrans** ☎ 07/3238-4700 ⊕ www.coachtrans.com.au.

BOAT & FERRY TRAVEL

Speedy CityCat ferries, operated by the Brisbane City Council, call at 13 points along the Brisbane River, from Bretts Wharf to the University of Queensland. They run daily 6 AM–10:30 PM about every half hour. The CityCat ferries are terrific for taking a leisurely look at Brisbane river life. From the city skyline to the homes of the well-heeled, there's always something of interest to see.

✈ CityCat ferries ☎ 13-1230.

BUS TRAVEL

Greyhound Australia travels to all parts of Australia from Brisbane. Bus stops are well signposted, and vehicles run on schedule. It's 1,716 km (1,064 mi) and 25 hours between Brisbane and Cairns.

Crisps Coaches operates regular daily service to the Southern Downs area from Brisbane.

Trans Info's help line and Web site can help you find which bus lines run to your destination.

🚌 **Crisps Coaches** ☎ 07/3236-5266. **Greyhound Australia** ✉ Brisbane Transit Centre, Roma St., City Center ☎ 07/3236-3035 or 13-1499 ⊕ www.greyhound.com.au. **Trans Info** ☎ 13-1230 ⊕ www.transinfo.qld.gov.au.

CAR RENTAL

All major car-rental agencies have offices in Brisbane, including Avis, Thrifty, and Budget. Four-wheel-drive vehicles, motor homes, and campervans (which sleep two to six people) are available from Britz Campervan Rentals, Maui Rentals, and Kea Campers. If you're heading north along the coast or northwest into the bush, you can rent in Brisbane and drop off in Cairns or other towns. One-way rental fees usually apply.

🚗 **Avis** ✉ 275 Wickham St., Fortitude Valley ☎ 07/3252-7111. **Britz Campervan Rentals** ✉ 647 Kingsford Smith Dr., Eagle Farm ☎ 03/8379-8890 or 1800/331-454 ⊕ www.britz.com. **Budget** ✉ 105 Mary St., City Center ☎ 13-2727. **Hertz** ✉ 55 Charlotte St., City Center ☎ 13-3039. **Kea Campers** ✉ 348 Nudgee Rd., Hendra ☎ 1800/252555 ⊕ www.keacampers.com. **Maui Rentals** ✉ 647 Kingsford Smith Dr., Eagle Farm ☎ 1300/363800 ⊕ www.maui-rentals.com. **Thrifty** ✉ 49 Barry Parade, Fortitude Valley ☎ 1300/367227.

CAR TRAVEL

Brisbane is 1,002 km (621 mi) from Sydney, a 12-hour drive along the Pacific Highway (Highway 1). Another route follows Highway 1 to Newcastle, then heads inland on Highway 15 (the New England Highway). Either drive can be made in a day, although two days are recommended for ample time to sightsee.

EMERGENCIES

In an emergency, dial **000** for an ambulance, the police, or the fire department.

Travellers Medical Service is a 24-hour medical center with a travel health clinic, a women's health clinic, and 24-hour hotel visits. The staff can also recommend dentists and pharmacies to suit your needs. Two pharmacies with extended hours are Delahunty's and Queen Street Mall.

🏥 **Doctors & Hospitals Royal Brisbane Hospital** ✉ Herston Rd., Herston ☎ 07/3636-8111. **Travellers Medical Service** ✉ Level 1, 245 Albert St., City Center ☎ 07/3211-3611.

🏥 **Pharmacies Delahunty's City Day & Night Pharmacy** ✉ 245 Albert St., City Center ☎ 07/3221-8155. **Queen Street Mall Day & Night Pharmacy** ✉ 141 Queen St., City Center ☎ 07/3221-4586.

MAIL, SHIPPING & THE INTERNET

You can send faxes, make photocopies, retrieve e-mail, and find other business services at most major hotels, including the Conrad Treasury Brisbane, Stamford Plaza Brisbane, and Sofitel.

You can also send faxes and make photocopies at the General Post Office, which is open weekdays 7 AM–6 PM. Australia Post provides overnight mail services. Federal Express has international door-to-door mail services and is open weekdays 9–5:30. Internet cafés include Dialup Cyber Lounge, open Monday–Saturday 10–7 and Sunday 10–6; the International Youth Service Centre (everyone welcome); and the Purrer Cyber Space Café.

🔢 Internet Cafés **Dialup Cyber Lounge** ✉ 126 Adelaide St., City Center ☎ 07/3211-9095. **International Youth Service Centre (IYSC)** ✉ 2/69 Adelaide St., City Center ☎ 07/3229-9985. **Purrer Cyber Space Café** ✉ 751 Stanley St., Woolloongabba ☎ 07/3392-1377.

🔢 Mail Services **Australia Post** ✉ 261 Queen St., City Center ☎ 13-1317. **Federal Express** ✉ 11-15 Gould Rd., Herston ☎ 13-2610.

MONEY MATTERS

You can cash traveler's checks and change money at most banks and financial institutions around town. ATMs, usually next to banks, are reliable and will accept most cards that are enabled for international access. ANZ Bank is one of the biggest banks in Australia. Commonwealth Bank of Australia is easily recognizable due to its distinctive black-and-yellow logo. National Australia Bank has several branches in the heart of Brisbane.

🔢 Banks **ANZ Bank** ✉ 324 Queen St., City Center ☎ 07/3228-3228. **Commonwealth Bank of Australia** ✉ 240 Queen St., City Center ☎ 13-2221. **National Australia Bank** ✉ 225 Queen St., City Center ☎ 13-2265.

TAXIS

Taxis are metered and relatively inexpensive. They are available at designated taxi stands outside hotels, downtown, and at the railway station, although it is usually best to phone for one.

Black and White Cabs, as its name suggests, has a fleet of black-and-white taxis. Yellow Cabs has the largest taxi fleet in Brisbane.

🔢 **Black and White Cabs** ✉ 11 Dryandra Rd., Eagle Farm ☎ 13-1008 ⊕ www.blackandwhitecabs.com.au. **Yellow Cabs** ✉ 116 Logan Rd., Woolloongabba ☎ 13-1924.

TELEPHONES

The Queensland code is 07 when dialing within Australia. Drop the 0 when calling from outside Australia.

Public telephones are plentiful in Brisbane's city center. They accept coins, credit cards, and phone cards, which are available at stores and newsstands in increments of A$5 to A$50. Mobile phone service is reliable in the major centers but can be nonexistent in some rural areas.

I Country Direct provides international access to operators in other countries via a credit card or collect call. A telephone interpreter service operates 24 hours.

🔢 **I Country Direct** ☎ 1800/801800. **Interpreter Service** ☎ 13-1450.

TOURS

Australian Day Tours conducts half- and full-day tours of Brisbane, as well as trips to the Gold Coast, Noosa Heads, and the Sunshine Coast.

City Nights tours depart daily from the Brisbane City Hall, City Sights Bus Stop 2 (Adelaide Street), at 6:30 PM for a trip up scenic Mt.

Coot-tha. After enjoying the city's lights you are taken on a CityCat ferry ride down the Brisbane River before joining the bus for a ride back to town through the historic Valley precinct. The A$18 tour finishes at 9.

City Sights, run by the Brisbane City Council, operates open tram-style buses that make half-hourly circuits of city landmarks and other points of interest. They leave from Post Office Square every 30 minutes, starting at 9 AM, with a break from 12:20 to 1:40. You can buy tickets on the bus, and you can get on or off at any of the 19 stops. The A$18 ticket is also valid for use on the CityCat ferries and commuter buses.

Kookaburra River Queens is a paddle wheeler that runs lunch and dinner cruises on the Brisbane River. The lunch cruise includes scenic and historic commentary; live entertainment and dancing are highlights of the dinner cruise. Tours run A$38–A$65 per person.

"Historic Walks" is an informative brochure put out by the National Trust, available from the Queensland Government Travel Centre and hotels.

🛈 Australian Day Tours ✉ Level 3, Brisbane Transit Centre, Roma St., City Center ☎ 07/3236–4155 or 1300/363436. **City Nights** ✉ Brisbane City Council, 69 Ann St., City Center ☎ 13–1230. **City Sights** ✉ Brisbane City Council, 69 Ann St., City Center ☎ 13–1230. **Kookaburra River Queens** ✉ Eagle Street Pier, 1 Eagle St., City Center ☎ 07/3221–1300. **National Trust** ✉ Edward and Adelaide Sts., City Center ☎ 13–1801.

TRAIN TRAVEL

CountryLink trains make the 15-hour journey between Sydney and Brisbane. Service from Brisbane to the Gold Coast runs 5:30 AM until midnight. The *Sunlander* and the luxurious *Queenslander* trains make four runs weekly between Brisbane and Cairns. Other long-distance passenger trains from Brisbane are the *Spirit of the Tropics* (twice weekly), to Townsville; the *Spirit of Capricorn* (once weekly), to Rockhampton; the *Westlander,* to Charleville (twice weekly); and the *Spirit of the Outback,* to Longreach (twice weekly). The *Inlander* connects Townsville and Mount Isa (twice weekly). Trains depart from the Roma Street Station. For details contact Queensland Rail's Traveltrain or the City Booking Office.

🛈 City Booking Office ☎ 13–2232. **Queensland Rail's Traveltrain** ✉ 305 Edward St., City Center ☎ 07/3235–2222 or 13–2232 ⊕ www.traveltrain.qr.com.au.

VISITOR INFORMATION

The Brisbane Marketing Visitor Information Centre is open Monday–Thursday 9–5:30, Friday 9–8, Saturday 9–5, and Sunday 9:30–4:30. Queensland Holiday Xperts is open 8:30–5 weekdays only. The Southern Downs Tourist Association is open 8:30–5 daily (but closed Christmas Day and Good Friday).

🛈 Brisbane Marketing Visitor Information Centre ✉ Elizabeth St., Box 12260, 4001 ✉ Queen Street Mall, City Center ☎ 07/3006–6200 ⊕ www.brisbanemarketing.com.au. **Queensland Holiday Xperts** ✉ 30 Makerston St., City Center ☎ 07/3535–4557 or 13–8833 ⊕ www.qhx.com.au. **Southern Downs Tourist Association** ✉ 49 Albion St., Warwick ☎ 07/4661–3401 ⊕ www.qldsoutherndowns.org.au.

THE GOLD COAST

Three hundred days of sunshine a year and an average temperature of 24°C (75°F) ensure the popularity of the Gold Coast, the most developed tourist destination in Australia, with plenty of amusement complexes and resorts. Christmas, Easter, and December through the last week of January are peak seasons. An hour south of Brisbane, the Gold Coast stretches some 70 km (43 mi) from Labrador in the north to Coolangatta–Tweed Heads in the south, and has now sprawled as far inland as Nerang. It has 35 patrolled beaches and 446 km (277 mi) of canals and tidal rivers, nine times the length of the canals of Venice.

Coomera & Oxenford

48–51 km (30–32 mi) south of Brisbane.

The biggest draw of these two northern Gold Coast suburbs are the family-oriented theme parks—Dreamworld, Warner Bros. Movie World, and Wet 'n' Wild. The large complexes have many attractions and each takes about a day for a leisurely visit.

Fodor'sChoice ★ At Coomera's **Dreamworld** you can ride on the fastest, tallest ride in the world, the Tower of Terror, and the tallest high-speed gravity roller coaster in the Southern Hemisphere, the Cyclone. You can also watch Bengal tigers play and swim with their handlers on Tiger Island, cuddle a koala in Koala Country, cool off in a water park, or cruise the park on a paddle wheeler through the man-made waterways. The Big Brother house, used for the Australian version of the hit reality TV show, is situated in the park and you can go inside when the show isn't filming. The park is 40 minutes outside Brisbane and 20 minutes from Surfers Paradise along the Pacific Highway. ⊠ *Dreamworld Pkwy.* ☎ *07/5588–1111 or 1800/073300* ⊕ *www.dreamworld.com.au* ☐ *A$60* ⊙ *Daily 10 5.*

Warner Bros. Movie World, one of the few movie theme parks outside the United States, lets you wander through set re-creations of the *Harry Potter Movie Magic Experience,* laugh at the antics of the *Police Academy* stunt show, or rocket through the *Lethal Weapon* roller coaster. Young children enjoy Looney Tunes Village, while shoppers take heart at the numerous shops selling Warner Bros. souvenirs. The park is in Oxenford, about 10 minutes' drive from Dreamworld along the Pacific Highway. A three-park pass, which gives you entry to Movie World, Wet'n'Wild, and Sea World, as well as a return visit to one of the parks, costs A$158. ⊠ *Pacific Hwy.* ☎ *07/5573–3999 or 07/5573–8485* ⊕ *www.movieworld.com.au* ☐ *A$60* ⊙ *Daily 10–5:30.*

When you're looking for Oxenford's **Wet 'n' Wild Water Park,** keep your eyes peeled for Matilda, the giant kangaroo mascot of the 1982 Brisbane Commonwealth Games. The park has magnificent waterslides, as well as a wave pool with a 3-foot-high surf. There's also Calypso Beach, a tropical island fringed with white-sand beaches, surrounded by a slow-moving river where you can laze about in brightly colored tubes.

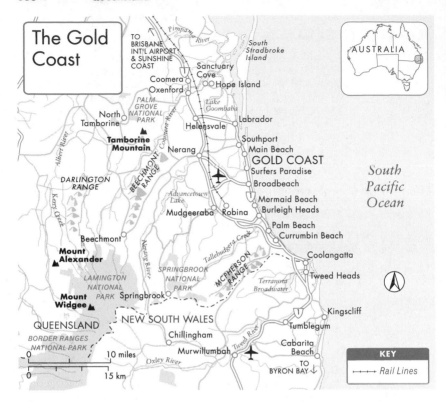

The Gold Coast

TO BRISBANE INT'L AIRPORT & SUNSHINE COAST

Pimpama River

South Stradbroke Island

AUSTRALIA

Coomera
Oxenford

Sanctuary Cove

Hope Island

Lake Coombaba

PALM GROVE NATIONAL PARK

North Tamborine

Helensvale

Labrador

Tamborine Mountain

Nerang

Southport
Main Beach

GOLD COAST

Surfers Paradise

DARLINGTON RANGE

Advancetown Lake

Broadbeach

Mermaid Beach
Burleigh Heads

Mudgeeraba
Robina

Palm Beach
Currumbin Beach

Beechmont

Nerang River

Tallebudgera Creek

Coolangatta

Mount Alexander

SPRINGBROOK NATIONAL PARK

MCPHERSON RANGE

Terranora Broadwater

Tweed Heads

LAMINGTON NATIONAL PARK

Springbrook

Kingscliff

Mount Widgee

QUEENSLAND

NEW SOUTH WALES

Chillingham

Tumblegum

BORDER RANGES NATIONAL PARK

Murwillumbah

Oxley River

Tweed River

Cabarita Beach

TO BYRON BAY ↓

South Pacific Ocean

10 miles

15 km

KEY

⊢—⊢ Rail Lines

For a little more excitement, plunge down a thrilling waterslide ride on a tandem tube at Terror Canyon. The park is ½ km (¼ mi) down the Pacific Highway from Warner Bros. Movie World. ⊠ *Pacific Hwy.* ☎ *07/5573–6233* ⊕ *www.wetnwild.com.au* ⊡ *A$38* ⊙ *Daily 10–4:30.*

Where to Stay

$$$$ ⊞ **Ruffles Lodge.** The lodge is 5 km (3 mi) from Dreamworld, but its tranquil location makes it seem worlds away. Set high on a hill, surrounded by forests and manicured gardens, three private villas and an executive lodge suite with a separate living room have views to the Gold Coast beaches and high-rises as well as the surrounding bushland. The suite has a wood-burning fireplace for winter, plasma TV, hot tub, and high-speed Internet. Owners John and Jan Nicholls create a comfortable environment, with a choice of dinner-party-style or private meals in the main lodge. Predinner drinks, hors d'oeuvres, and a three-course set dinner cost A$50 per person. ⊠ *423 Ruffles Rd., Willow Vale 4209* ☎ *07/5546–7411* 🖷 *07/5546–7358* ⊕ *www.ruffleslodge.com. au* ➫ *3 villas, 1 suite* ⚒ *Dining room, cable TV, in-room VCRs, in-room data ports, putting green, pool; no kids, no smoking* ⊟ *AE, DC, MC, V* ⦿*| BP.*

Hope Island

6 km (4 mi) east of Oxenford.

This isn't your average island with swaying palm trees and white-sand beaches. Like several Gold Coast islands, it is actually a mile or two inland, and is circled by the Coomera River and a series of canals. The island's main attraction is Sanctuary Cove Resort, the first gated tourism and residential precinct in Australia. Frank Sinatra, Peter Allen, and Whitney Houston sang at the complex's lavish opening in 1988, an event that placed it squarely on the map. The resort has a marina full of luxury launches and yachts, two golf courses, a swanky hotel, beautiful condos, and upscale restaurants, nightclubs, and shops. Beyond the gates of Sanctuary Cove there are also a handful of other hotels and a shopping center.

Hope Island is accessed by car via bridges from both the west side (the towns of Oxenford and Coomera) and the eastern, coastal side (from Paradise Point, Hollywell, and Runaway Bay). Route 4, also known as the Oxenford–Southport Road, begins in Oxenford at Pacific Highway's Exit 57 and travels through Hope Island on its way to the coast.

Where to Stay

★ $$$–$$$$ ▦ **Hyatt Regency Sanctuary Cove.** Landscaped tropical gardens surround this opulent low-rise hotel, which resembles a monumental Australian colonial mansion. It's one of the best hotels on the Gold Coast, and each luxuriously appointed room has either a king-sized sleigh bed or two double sleigh beds and a large, private balcony. The main building, known as the Great House, leads past a cascading waterfall to the courtyard and swimming pool–hot tub area. The sandy beach lagoon next to the hotel's main harbor is fed with filtered saltwater, and a walkway from the hotel leads directly into the main resort village. ⊠ *Manor Circle, Sanctuary Cove, 4212* ☎ *07/5530–1234* 🖷 *07/5577–8234* ⊕ *www. sanctuarycove.hyatt.com* ⊅ *223 rooms, 24 suites* ⌂ *3 restaurants, room service, refrigerators, room TVs with movies, in-room data ports, driving range, 2 18-hole golf courses, 10 tennis courts, 2 pools, health club, hair salon, hot tub, sauna, beach, boating, marina, fishing, bowling, 2 bars, babysitting, children's programs (ages 4–12), laundry service, meeting rooms, travel services, free parking, no-smoking rooms, no-smoking floors* ▤ *AE, DC, MC, V.*

South Stradbroke Island

1 km (½ mi) east of the Gold Coast.

White-sand beaches, diverse flora and fauna, and a peaceful interior draw visitors to South Stradbroke Island, which is just 22 km (12 mi) long and 2 km (1 mi) wide. The island and its northern neighbor (North Stradbroke Island) were once connected, but in 1896 a fierce storm separated them at a narrow neck called Jumpinpin. Unlike its northern namesake, South "Straddie" is less populated and does not have a public ferry service. It's a good spot for fishing and boating.

You can get to the island by taking one of the boat services operated by the three island resorts. Couran Cove Island Resort (☎ 1800/268726) operates three return trips a day leaving Hope Harbour terminal at 10:30, 2, and 6, and returning at noon, 3, and 7.

Where to Stay

$$$$ 🏨 **Couran Cove Island Resort.** Just 15 minutes by boat from the glitz of the Gold Coast, this ecotourism resort is a haven of peace and harmony. The vision of Olympic athlete Ron Clarke, a long-distance runner, the property has an amazing selection of sports opportunities: biking, swimming, tennis, rock climbing, baseball, basketball, and more. The marine resort area includes hotel rooms, suites, and two- and four-bedroom lodges (all with kitchenettes and cooking facilities), while the nature resort area has fan-cooled bush cabins with full kitchens. Some accommodations are built over the water so you can fish right off the balcony. There's a strong pro-environment focus throughout the resort, with recycling, solar power, and organic products used to help protect the island's wildlife. ☝ *South Stradbroke Island, Box 224, Runaway Bay, Gold Coast, 4216* ☎ *07/5597–9000 or 1800/632211* 📠 *07/5597–9090* ⊕ *www.courancove.com* ⇘ *100 rooms, 92 suites, 91 cabins, 29 lodges, 10 villas* ⚐ *Restaurant, 3 cafés, some fans, in-room safes, kitchenettes, putting green, 3 tennis courts, 2 pools, health club, spa, beach, snorkeling, windsurfing, boating, jet skiing, parasailing, waterskiing, fishing, bicycles, basketball, bar, shops, children's programs (ages 3–12), Internet room, business services, convention center, travel services; no a/c in some rooms, no smoking* ⊟ *AE, DC, MC, V.*

Southport & Main Beach

16 km (10 mi) southeast of Oxenford.

South of Southport, look for the turnoff to the **Spit**, a natural peninsula that stretches 4 km (2½ mi) north, almost to the tip of South Stradbroke Island. Sea World Drive runs the full length of the Spit, from Mariner's Cove (a popular covered area with affordable restaurants and fast-food outlets) to a nature reserve. This narrow peninsula is bordered by the Pacific Ocean to the east and the calm waters of the Broadwater (a long lagoon) to the west. Two of the Gold Coast's best hotels face each other across Sea World Drive and are connected to Marina Mirage, the most elegant shopping precinct on the Gold Coast. Farther up the road is Sea World itself.

♻ **Seaworld,** Australia's largest marine theme park, has six daily shows that highlight the resident whales, dolphins, and sea lions. Rides include a monorail, a corkscrew roller coaster, and waterslides. Shark Bay is a dual enclosure with dangerous tiger sharks in one lagoon and harmless reef sharks in another: patrons can snorkel or scuba dive in the latter and then peer at the man-eaters through a clear wall that separates the two lagoons. All rides except helicopter and parasailing flights and swimming with the sharks are included in the ticket price. ✉ *Seaworld Dr. (at end of this long street), The Spit, Main Beach* ☎ *07/5588–2222* ⊕ *www.seaworld.com.au* 🎫 *A$60* ⊘ *Daily 10–5.*

Where to Stay & Eat

$–$$$ ✕ **Omeros Bros. Seafood Restaurant.** The Omeros brothers, who arrived from Greece in 1953, have operated seafood restaurants in eastern Australia for more than 30 years. This one on the waterfront at the lovely Marina Mirage center provides an entire menu of seafood—from bouillabaisse, barbecued prawns, mussels, and barramundi to classic surf-and-turf (steak and lobster tail) with live lobster and mud crabs. The three-course lunch and dinner prix-fixe menus are well priced at A$29.90. ⊠ *Marina Mirage, Seaworld Dr.* ☎ *07/5591–7222* ☐ *AE, DC, MC, V.*

$–$$$ ✕ **Saks.** Perched on the edge of the Broadwater and just a short boardwalk away from Palazzo Versace is this hip restaurant and bar, with both indoor and outdoor areas. Relax on faux-suede lounge seats and ottomans while nibbling tapas, or nab a waterside table with crisp white linens. Savor one of the Italian-inspired seafood dishes or opt for the Peking duck risotto with Asian greens. The live music on Friday nights and Sunday afternoons attracts a crowd. ⊠ *Marina Mirage, 74 Seaworld Dr., Main Beach* ☎ *07/5591–2755* ☐ *AE, DC, MC, V.*

$$$$ 🏨 **Palazzo Versace.** Sink into one of the Versace-monogrammed silk sofas, armchairs, or circular banquettes in the sensational lobby and watch the beautiful people walk by. The Italian fashion house lent its flair to this stunning hotel, the first Versace hotel in the world. Marble columns topped with ornate capitals, a marble-and-mosaic tiled floor, and a gigantic chandelier in the middle of a white-and-gold ceiling all add up to over-the-top opulence. Rooms in low-rise wings surround a lagoon pool edged with palm trees and a sandy beach. Some have balconies with views over the Broadwater; others look out at the pool. The signature restaurant, Vanitas, serves contemporary Australian cuisine. ⊠ *Seaworld Dr. next door to Marina Mirage, 4217* ☎ *07/5509–8000* ☐ *07/5509–8889* ⊕ *www.palazzoversace.com* ➲ *205 rooms, 72 condos* ♤ *4 restaurants, room service, in-room safes, in-room hot tubs, in-room data ports, pool, health club, spa, beach, dock, marina, bar, shops, babysitting, laundry service, concierge, business services, convention center, meeting rooms, car rental, travel services, no-smoking rooms* ☐ *AE, DC, MC, V* ⦿I *BP.*

FodorśChoice
★

$$$$ 🏨 **Sheraton Mirage.** A cascading waterfall, floor-to-ceiling glass walls, and cream marble floors create a Zen atmosphere in the light-filled lobby of this low-rise resort. Tasteful rooms have either terraces or balconies that overlook 35 acres of gardens, the surf, or the lagoon on which glide the resort's signature white swans. A secluded gate leads from the sprawling grounds to a long, often-deserted strip of beach. The health club is a branch of the renowned Golden Door Spa, which has holistic treatments. An aerial bridge links the hotel with the elegant Marina Mirage shopping center. ⊠ *Seaworld Dr., The Spit, Main Beach, 4217* ☎ *07/5591–1488* ☐ *07/5591–2299* ⊕ *www.starwood.com/sheraton* ➲ *284 rooms, 10 suites, 39 villas* ♤ *3 restaurants, room service, in-room safes, some kitchenettes, in-room data ports, 4 tennis courts, pool, health club, hot tub, spa, beach, bar, babysitting, laundry service, concierge, business services, convention center, meeting room, car rental, travel services, free parking, no-smoking rooms* ☐ *AE, DC, MC, V.*

FodorśChoice
★

Shopping

Marina Mirage (✉ Seaworld Dr., The Spit, Main Beach ☎ 07/5577–0088 ⊕ www.marinamirage.com.au) is perhaps the most beautiful place on the Gold Coast for retail and food therapy. Among the 80 stores are designer boutiques including Nautica, Aigner, Louis Vuitton, and Hermès, along with upscale Australian brand stores, many fine restaurants, a medical center, and marina facilities.

en route

Although the Spit strip is also called Main Beach by its upscale inhabitants, the real **Main Beach** is a little gem of a beach community, off the radar of many tourists. It's a popular swimming spot with good surf (and without the crowds of nearby Surfers Paradise), and Tedder Avenue has a strip of elegant coffee shops, cafés, bars, and clubs. From the Spit drive south along Sea World Drive and turn left into Main Beach Parade, rather than turning right to rejoin the Gold Coast Highway.

Surfers Paradise

5 km (3 mi) south of Southport, 72 km (45 mi) south of Brisbane.

Before the Gold Coast existed as a tourism entity, there was Surfers Paradise, a long, 3-km (2-mi) stretch of beach and great surf. Though Surfers has been overrun with a glut of high-rises all jammed into a few square miles, it's still a vibrant beachside town that draws a mix of Japanese travelers, planeloads of Aussie teenagers invading the area during "schoolies" week in November, surfies who live nearby or drive up the coast from the south, or families enjoying all the school-holiday fun. Bare-chested swimmers walk past designer stores on their way to the beach, towels slung casually over their shoulders; locals on roller skates glide down the beachfront promenade; and bronzed lifeguards (called lifesavers in Australia) park their patrol vans right on the sand.

The heart of Surfers is bordered by Elkhorn and Cavill avenues, the beachfront Esplanade, and Surfers Paradise Boulevard. Here you'll find an array of souvenir shops, restaurants and bars, fun parlors such as the Wax Museum and the Infinity futuristic maze, and hair-raising attractions like rocket bungee. You'll also find upscale stores like Prada and Gucci steps away from outlet stores advertising "nothing over A$20." By day, office workers and visitors lunch along Cavill Avenue; at night the young and the boisterous (and the tourists) fill the bars and parlors.

Locals and more discerning visitors prefer the refinement of Broadbeach, to the south, or the upmarket residential area set around the canals of the Nerang River, west of the hub of Surfers Paradise. You'll find a smattering of classy apartment hotels and a handful of fun bars and restaurants in these areas.

If the attractions and crowds haven't satisfied your need for visual stimulation in Surfers Paradise, the displays at **Ripley's Believe It or Not! Museum** may give you that extra thrill. Here you'll find models of the world's tallest man and the world's largest man, and a pair of African fertility statues that bring good luck to women who rub them—according to Ripley's, they have been responsible for 50 confirmed pregnancies. ✉ *Raptis Plaza, Cavill Ave.* ☎ *07/5592–0040* ⊕ *www.ripleys. com.au* 🖼 *A$13.50* ⊙ *Daily 9 AM–11 PM.*

Surfers Paradise hosts the annual **Indy Car Race** (☎ 07/5588–6800 Gold Coast Indy Office ⊕ www.indy.com.au) for four days in late October. It's the biggest event on the local calendar, with streets blocked off to create a challenging course for the world's top speed demons. The track follows a loop around the streets of Surfers Paradise, Main Beach, and MacIntosh Island. The event brings revelers from around the globe.

On Wednesday and Friday nights the beachfront promenade spills over with crafts and gifts at the **Surfers Paradise Friday Night Beachfront Lantern Market,** held throughout the year. The market's theme is "make it, bake it, grow it," and finds include exotic home wares, ceramics, jewelry, cosmetics, children's toys and games, leather goods, and oils and potions. ✉*Esplanade beachfront promenade between Hanlan St. and Elkhorn Ave.* ☎ *07/5584–3700 or 04/1159–7979* 🖼 *Free* ⊙ *Wed. and Fri. 5:30–10.*

Where to Stay & Eat

$$ ✗ **Grumpy's Wharf Surfers Paradise.** Towering coconut palms shade this quiet restaurant on the banks of the Nerang River, but it's still just a short walk to all the action of Surfers Paradise. Eat on the terrace before fine river views, or take an exquisitely prepared meal in the elegant Sante Fe dining room. The Adobe Bar is a popular watering hole, while the candlelit Courtyard is frequented by couples on romantic dinner dates. Seafood platters, fish cooked to order, mud crabs, and lobsters are the main fare. ✉ *Tiki Village, Cavill Ave.* ☎ *07/5532–2900* ▭ *AE, DC, MC, V.*

$$ ✗ **Sayas Restaurant Café Bar.** A magnificent Inca-style bungalow lends an exotic feel to this eatery on the grounds of the Outrigger Sun City Resort. The signature dish is the barramundi, cooked in Chermoula spices (a Moroccan marinade of herbs, oil, garlic, and lemon juice) and served with crisp Asian greens and sweet tomato-and-lime salsa—the classic Australian fish with Mediterranean and Asian flavors. ✉ *Ocean Ave. and Gold Coast Hwy.* ☎ *07/5584–6060* ▭ *AE, DC, MC, V* ⊙ *No lunch.*

$$$$ 🏨 **Moroccan Beach Resort.** Opposite a lifeguard-patrolled section of the beach, these white Mediterranean-style apartments contrast strikingly with the blue of the sky and water. The pick of the development's three towers is the Esplanade, which faces the beach. The one- and two-bedroom apartments are spacious and luxurious. All are well equipped with kitchen and laundry facilities; many have air-conditioning. There's a minimum stay requirement of seven days in high season. ✉ *14 View Ave., 4217* ☎ *07/5526–9400* 🖨 *07/5555–9990* ⊕ *www.moroccan.com.au* 🛏 *150 apartments* ⚒ *Kitchens, cable TV, in-room data ports, 3 pools, wading pool, 3 hot tubs, babysitting, free parking; no a/c in some rooms* ▭ *AE, DC, MC, V.*

$$$ 🏨 **Surfers Paradise Marriott Resort.** The lobby's giant columns and grand
Fodor's Choice circular staircase, cooled by a colorful Indian *punkah* (a decorative, rope-
★ operated fan), typify this hotel's opulent style. The large guest rooms, decorated in gentle hues of beige, light plum, and moss green, have walk-in closets, marble bathrooms, balconies, and ocean and river views. The

coral- and fish-filled lagoon swimming pool has a sandy beach and a cave grotto with a waterfall and is deep enough for scuba lessons or snorkeling. There's also a meandering freshwater pool. You can rent windsurfing equipment, water skis, and catamarans to take on the river. ⊠ *158 Ferny Ave., 4217* ☎ *07/5592–9800* 🖷 *07/5592–9888* ⊕ *www.marriott. com* ⇀ *300 rooms, 30 suites* ৬ *3 restaurants, room service, in-room fax, in-room safes, in-room VCRs, in-room data ports, 2 tennis courts, pool, gym, health club, hair salon, sauna, spa, steam room, dive shop, dock, windsurfing, boating, marina, waterskiing, 2 bars, shops, babysitting, children's programs (ages 4–14), playground, dry cleaning, laundry facilities, laundry service, concierge, business services, meeting room, travel services, free parking, no-smoking floor* ⊟ *AE, DC, MC, V.*

$$–$$$ ⊡ **Royal Pines Resort.** Nestled beside the Nerang River, this resort combines a beautiful natural setting with state-of-the-art sports facilities. Within the 500 acres of manicured gardens and small lakes are a native wildlife sanctuary, two championship golf courses, a PGA-accredited golf school, tennis courts, and a marina. All accommodations have views, some of the Gold Coast high-rises, some of the forested hinterland, and some over the golf course and gardens. Suites, which are either split-level or two-story, have marble jetted tubs. The resort hosts major golf events, including the Australian Ladies Masters in late February or early March. The rooftop restaurant affords sensational views to the coast. ⊠ *7 km (4½ mi) west of Surfers Paradise, Ross St., Ashmore 4214* ☎ *07/5597–1111 or 1800/074999* 🖷 *07/5597–2277* ⊕ *www. royalpinesresort.au-hotels.com* ⇀ *285 rooms, 45 suites* ৬ *4 restaurants, driving range, 2 18-hole golf courses, putting green, 7 tennis courts, pro shop, 3 pools, health club, hair salon, 2 bars, children's programs (ages 5–14), business services, convention center, meeting room, travel services, free parking, no-smoking floors* ⊟ *AE, DC, MC, V.*

$$ ⊡ **Chateau Beachside Resort.** If you hanker after a view of Surfers Paradise beach and want to stay within walking distance of all the action, this comfortable, budget-style hotel across the road from the famous beach is for you. Each room, studio, or one- or two-bedroom apartment is done in bright blues and whites, accented by a tropical bedspread and cane tables and chairs. All have views of the surf. The A$9.90 all-you-can-eat buffet breakfast is legendary. ⊠ *The Esplanade and Elkhorn Ave., 4217* ☎ *07/5538–1022* 🖷 *07/5538–5460* ⊕ *www.strand.com.au* ⇀ *20 rooms, 50 studios, 20 apartments* ৬ *Café, IDD phones, fans, some kitchens, some microwaves, in-room DVD, in-room data ports, tennis court, pool, hot tub, sauna, steam room, bicycles, bar, playground, laundry facilities, Internet room, travel services, free parking; no a/c in some rooms* ⊟ *MC, V.*

$–$$ ⊡ **Gold Coast International Hotel.** In the heart of Surfers Paradise, this hotel is a block from the beach, with views of the Pacific Ocean or the Gold Coast hinterland from every luxurious room. Wander down from your relaxed, beachy quarters, decorated in pastel colors and cane furniture, to the stylish lobby bar or the Yamagen Japanese Restaurant, where the entertaining chefs perform culinary magic at teppanyaki tables. ⊠ *Gold Coast Hwy. and Staghorn Ave., 4217* ☎ *07/5584–1200* 🖷 *07/ 5584–1280* ⊕ *www.gci.com.au* ⇀ *296 rooms, 24 suites* ৬ *2 restau-*

rants, café, room service, room TVs with movies and video games, in-room data ports, 2 tennis courts, pool, health club, hair salon, sauna, spa, steam room, 2 bars, shops, laundry service, concierge, meeting rooms, travel services, free parking ⊟ *AE, DC, MC, V.*

Nightlife

Surfers Paradise is the entertainment hub of the Gold Coast, full of bars, clubs, restaurants, and live entertainment venues. But it's unmistakably the domain of the young party animal out on the town. Miniskirted young girls and the guys looking to meet them seem to make up the bulk of the Surfers crowd on a typical Saturday night. Most nightclubs can be found on Orchid, Elkhorn, and Cavill avenues, though there are some scattered elsewhere in Surfers and in the more upscale enclave of Chevron Island. Most clubs are free during the week, but may have a cover charge of A$10–A$15 on Friday and Saturday nights. You'll also pay to play pool and other games.

The Drink (⊠ 4 Orchid Ave. ☎ 07/5570–6155) claims to be "the sexiest club on the coast." Popular with the rich and famous—especially during the Indy Car festival in October—the club mainly plays commercial dance music. It's open daily 9 PM–5 AM.

Howl at the Moon (⊠ Shop 7, Paradise Centre, Cavill Ave. ☎ 07/5527–5755) is a fun place to go, especially if you like a good sing-along and know the words of popular songs. Every night it's a case of dueling pianos as two (often very different) pianists with great voices belt out a medley of tunes (some requested by patrons) to an appreciative crowd of thirty- to fortysomethings. Even the bar staff join the fun, dressing up in silly costumes with 1970s Afro wigs and putting on a bit of a show. Grab a vanilla-chocolate martini and hit the always-jumping—even midweek—dance floor. There's also a restaurant with good meals at reasonable prices.

Melba's (⊠ 46 Cavill Ave. ☎ 07/5538–7411), one of Surfers Paradise's oldest clubs, has been in business for more than two decades. It attracts an upscale crowd and plays the latest dance and pop music. A Melba's Tickle (butterscotch schnapps, Bailey's, Advocaat liqueur, and milk) is just one of the cocktails on a long list. A café, open 7 AM–3 AM daily, is also on-site.

Another trendy spot is **mybar** (⊠ Lower level, Mark Complex, Orchid Ave. ☎ 07/5592–4111), which claims to have an "invitation-only" guest list. The sophisticated dress code ensures that it's the fabulous and beautiful who groove to the funky house music spun by cool DJs well into the early hours. It's open 9 PM to 5 AM, Wednesday to Sunday.

Shooters Saloon Bar (⊠ Mark Complex, Orchid Ave. ☎ 07/5592–1144), with an American saloon theme, has a nightclub, sports bar, and pool hall. It's a floor above mybar, but the crowd is ultrayoung and not likely to begin partying until 10 PM. Though Shooters hosts magazine swimsuit contests and other male fantasy events, it has surprisingly tasteful decor and is extremely large with a variety of different bars. It stays open until 5 AM.

Broadbeach

8 km (5 mi) south of Southport.

With clean beaches, great cafés, and trendy nightspots, Broadbeach is one of the most popular areas on the Gold Coast, especially with the locals. It's home to Pacific Fair, one of Australia's leading shopping centers, and is also a good base for visiting the wildlife parks south of town.

David Fleay's Wildlife Park, located in the town of Burleigh Heads and named for an Australian wildlife naturalist, takes you along a boardwalk trail through pristine wetlands and rain forests. Koalas, kangaroos, dingoes, platypuses, and crocodiles, grouped together in separate zones according to their natural habitat, are just some of the creatures you might see. ✚ *7 km (4½ mi) south of Broadbeach, Tallebudgera Creek Rd. near W. Burleigh Rd.,* ✉ *Burleigh Heads* ☎ *07/5576–2411* 🎟 *A$13* ☉ *Daily 9–5.*

★ ☾ A Gold Coast institution, the **Currumbin Wildlife Sanctuary** is a 70-acre National Trust Reserve that shelters Australian species like lorikeets, bilbies, kangaroos, and koalas. There are daily shows, animal talks, and Aboriginal dancers, as well as kangaroo feedings and koala cuddling. Come between 8 and 9 or 4 and 5 when the lorikeets are fed and you'll be surrounded by them. ✉ *28 Tomewin St., off Gold Coast Hwy., 14 km (8½ mi) south of Broadbeach, Currumbin* ☎ *07/5534–1266* ⊕ *www.currumbin-sanctuary.org.au* 🎟 *A$23* ☉ *Daily 8–5.*

Where to Stay & Eat

$–$$$ ✕ **Sopranos.** The wooden tables here spill out onto the terra-cotta-tile sidewalk of Surf Parade, Broadbeach's restaurant strip. With a well-stocked bar, a frequently changing menu that takes advantage of the local seafood, and a generous display of desserts, the restaurant is rarely empty. The dishes combine Mediterranean and pan-Asian flavors and include marinated barramundi in lemongrass, cilantro, garlic, chili, and lime, and barbecued octopus tossed with chili, garlic, and olive oil. ✉ *Shop 11, Surf Parade* ☎ *07/5526–2011* ▤ *AE, DC, MC, V.*

$$$ ✕🖼 **Hotel Conrad and Jupiters Casino.** This hotel-casino is always bustling. Rooms have cream-color walls, gold curtains, bright bedspreads, and wood furniture, and most have either a balcony or a sun terrace. Front-facing Conrad rooms lack balconies, but they have great views of the Gold Coast; other rooms have views across the hinterland. Restaurants include Andiamo, a local Italian star, as well as Charters Towers, where fresh mud crab and lobster are popular choices. ✉ *Gold Coast Hwy., 4218* ☎ *07/5592–1133 or 1800/074344* 📠 *07/5592–8219* ⊕ *www.conrad.com.au* 🛏 *573 rooms, 29 suites, 2 penthouses* ☁ *5 restaurants, coffee shop, in-room safes, cable TV, in-room data ports, 4 tennis courts, pool, gym, hair salon, sauna, squash, 8 bars, pub, casino, showroom, shops, babysitting, laundry service, concierge, business services, convention center, meeting room, car rental, travel services, free parking, no-smoking floors* ▤ *AE, DC, MC, V* ⬤ *BP.*

$$ 🖼 **Antigua Beach Resort.** Less than a minute's walk from the beach and around the corner from shopping centers and restaurants, this three-story, bright peach-and-blue hotel has balconies on all sides. Self-contained

apartments are decorated in bright tropical colors. The pool and terrace outside are ringed by landscaped gardens with barbecues. There's a minimum seven-night stay during the three-week period starting on Christmas Day. ⊠ *6 Queensland Ave., 4218* ☎ *07/5526–2288* 🖷 *07/5526–2266* ✎ *antigua@onthenet.com.au* ⌨ *23 apartments* ♿ *Kitchens, microwaves, refrigerators, pool, hot tub, sauna, laundry facilities, travel services, free parking* 🚫 *MC, V.*

Nightlife

Jupiters Casino (⊠ Gold Coast Hwy. ☎ 07/5592–1133) provides flamboyant round-the-clock entertainment. Besides two levels of gaming tables with blackjack, baccarat, craps, sic bo, pai gow, and keno, there are more than 100 round-the-clock gaming machines. The 950-seat showroom hosts glitzy Las Vegas–style productions.

Shopping

Oasis Shopping Centre (⊠ Victoria Ave. near Burleigh Rd. ☎ 07/5592–3900) is the retail heart of beachside Broadbeach, with more than 100 shops and an attractive mall where open-air coffee shops stand umbrella-to-umbrella. A monorail runs from the center to Jupiters Casino.

Fodor'sChoice
★ **Pacific Fair** (⊠ Hooker Blvd. and Gold Coast Hwy., next to Jupiters Casino ☎ 07/5539–8766), a sprawling outdoor shopping center, is Queensland's largest. Its major retailers and 260 specialty stores should be enough to satisfy even die-hard shoppers. Myer (one of Australia's two leading department stores) is the largest store on-site; other Australian stores include Tony Barlow menswear and Maggie T, which specializes in designer clothes for larger women. There are also undercover malls, landscaped grounds with three small lakes, a children's park, movie theaters, and a village green.

Side Trip to the Gold Coast Hinterland

A visit to the Gold Coast wouldn't be complete without a short journey to the nearby **Gold Coast Hinterland**. Be forewarned, however, that this can induce culture shock: the natural grandeur of this area contrasts dramatically with the human-made excesses of the coastal strip. Three national parks have waterfalls and rock pools where you can cool off on a steamy day, mountain lookouts with expansive views to the coast, walking trails that traverse dense rain forest and some very ancient trees, a handful of wineries, and quaint country villages where high-rise is anything over one story. The parks form part of a geological region known as the Scenic Rim, a chain of mountains running parallel to the coast along southeast Queensland and northern New South Wales.

Because it's high above sea level—up to 3,000 feet—some areas of the hinterland are about 4°C–6°C (7°F–11°F) cooler than the coast. The three main areas—Tamborine Mountain, Lamington National Park, and Springbrook—can be reached from a number of exits off the Pacific Highway (the motorway connecting the Gold Coast to Brisbane) or via Beaudesert from Brisbane. Each takes about 30 to 40 minutes to reach from the Gold Coast.

Nine fragmented parks make up **Tamborine National Park,** on Tamborine Mountain. More than 20 million years ago, volcanic eruptions created rugged landscapes of exceptional beauty while fertile volcanic soils produced luxuriant vast patches of rain forest. Tamborine Mountain is both the collective term for several small villages stretching along an 8-km (5-mi) ridge of the mountain range and an actual geological phenomenon. Tamborine Mountain is the most developed region of the Gold Coast Hinterland, and it's worth spending a day or two to enjoy it. Apart from the natural environment, there are five wineries, many lodges and B&Bs, restaurants, and the famous Gallery Walk, a 1-km-long (½-mi-long) street full of art galleries.

To reach Tamborine, take Exit 57 off the Pacific Highway at Oxenford (north of Warner Bros. Movie World) to Oxenford–Tamborine Road. Or, take Exit 71 off the Pacific Highway and proceed along the Nerang–Beaudesert Road to Canungra. Follow the signs to Tamborine.

Queensland's first national park, **Witches Falls** (☎ 07/5545–1171), is a good spot for families, with picnic facilities and a 3-km (2-mi) walk which snakes down a steep slope through open rain forest and past lagoons en route to the falls. To the east of Witches Falls is **Joalah National Park** (☎ 07/5545–1171). There's a 1½ km (1 mi) round-trip walk to Curtis Falls that descends to a rock pool at the falls' base. There's also a longer, 4-km (2½-mi) Joalah Circuit walk that links up with the Curtis Falls Walk. Access is off Eagle Heights Road. **MacDonald National Park** (☎ 07/5545–1171) at Eagle Heights has a flat, easy 1½-km (1-mi) walk. This small park is adjacent to Tamborine Mountain's Botanic Gardens.

The peaks of **Springbrook National Park** (☎ 07/5533–5147), which rise to around 2,700 feet, dominate the skyline west of the Gold Coast. This park has three separate regions (Springbrook, Natural Bridge, and Mt. Cougal); because the roads are steep and winding in parts and the distances between each area are long, it takes about a day to explore. It's about 30 km (19 mi) from the tiny hamlet of Springbrook itself to Natural Bridge—a lovely waterfall that cascades through the roof of a cave into an icy pool, making a popular swimming spot. This cave is also home to Australia's largest glowworm colony, and at night hundreds of them light up the cavern to stunning effect. Several waterfalls, including Purling Brook Falls (the area's largest), can be reached via a 4-km (2½-mi) walking path that takes you under the cliff face. The path includes some stairs and uphill walking; if you want to skip the path, there's a lookout about 100 yards from the parking lot that has views of the falls. The park has some wonderful lookouts that provide wide vistas over the forest to the coast and south to New South Wales' mountain peaks: the aptly named Best of All Lookout is a must.

To get to Springbrook take Exit 80 off the Pacific Highway and travel through the village of Mudgeeraba along Springbrook Road. Or take Exit 71 off the Pacific Highway and drive along the Nerang–Beaudesert Road for about 10 to 15 minutes, until you reach the Nerang–Murwillumbah Road to Springbrook.

Lamington National Park (✉ Binna Burra Rd. ☎ 07/5533–3584) is a tropical-subtropical-temperate ecological border zone with a complex abundance of plant and animal life that's astounding. Its 50,600-acre expanse is made up of two sections: Binna Burra and Green Mountains. Lamington National Park is listed as part of the Central Eastern Rainforest Reserves World Heritage Area, which protects the park's extensive and varied rain-forest regions. In places you can see ancient Antarctic Beech trees that date back 2,000 years. It has 160 km (100 mi) of bushwalking tracks, waterfalls, mountain pools, and some 120 native bird species. To reach the park take Exit 71 (Nerang) off the Pacific Highway and drive along the Nerang–Beaudesert Road toward Canungra. For Green Mountain, proceed to Canungra and then follow the signs to Lamington. For Binna Burra, turn off (to the left) before you reach Canungra at the sign to Beechmont.

Where to Stay

Binna Burra has a campground at the entrance to Lamington National Park (call 07/5533–3584) that charges A$10 per person per night, and 17 on-site tents cost A$40 per night for two people, A$60 per night for four. Amenities include shower and toilet facilities, coin-operated gas barbecue stoves and hot plates, coin-operated laundry facilities, and a café. The views across the hinterland from this campground are spectacular. If camping, you must bring your own linens, as Binna Burra Mountain Lodge does not provide this service.

$$$$ 🏨 **Binna Burra Mountain Lodge.** Founded in 1933, this group of hilltop cabins has sweeping views across the hinterland to the Gold Coast. The cabins are cozy, secluded, and furnished with basics; some have shared bathrooms. Rates include meals and guided activities, such as bushwalks and rappelling; bed-and-breakfast–only rates are slightly less. There are also kids-only bushwalks, picnics, and rain-forest adventures. The Hill Top Dining Room has fantastic views over the Numinbah Valley in the distance. Four-night and five-night minimum stays are required during Easter and Christmas/New Year's, respectively. The Binna Burra bus (☎ 1800/074260) makes a daily round-trip from the property to the Surfers Paradise Transit Centre. ✉ *Binna Burra Rd., Beechmont 4211* ☎ *07/5533–3622 or 1800/074260* ⊕ *www.binnaburralodge.com.au* ⤷ *40 cabins ⚬ Restaurant, some in-room hot tubs, mountain bikes, hiking, bar, babysitting, children's programs (5–16), playground, laundry facilities, Internet room, free parking; no a/c, no room phones, no room TVs, no smoking* ⊟ *AE, DC, MC, V* ⚭ *AI.*

★ **$$$$** 🏨 **Pethers Rainforest Retreat.** In 12 acres of privately owned rain forest, this couples-only resort is comprised of 10 spacious tree houses with timber floors, verandas, and Chinese furnishings and antiques. Each house is an open room with a bed, lounge area, dining area, and balcony with floor-to-ceiling glass doors. There's also a fireplace and a hot tub. Undercover walkways link each tree house with the main lodge, a stunning building with 16-foot-high glass walls that provide views of the surrounding rain forest. Guests can while away the hours in the library, picnic on the banks of Sandy Creek, and explore the rain forest on walking trails, where they might be lucky enough to spot wallabies and koalas. Restaurants are nearby, but for those who want to dine in, there's a A$40 three-course dinner available for guests. ⊠ *28B Geissmann St., North Tamborine 4272* ☎ *07/5545–4577* 🖷 *07/5545–4463* ⊕ *www.pethers.com.au* ⇨ *10 tree houses* ⌂ *Dining room, picnic area, fans, minibars, in-room DVD, massage, free parking; no room phones, no a/c, no kids, no smoking* ⊟ *AE, MC, V* ⎁ *BP.*

★ $$–$$$$ 🏨 **O'Reilly's Rainforest Guesthouse.** Since 1926 the O'Reilly family has welcomed travelers into their forested world. Four types of accommodations include bedrooms with a shared bath in a 1930s-style house and one- and two-bedroom canopy suites with spa baths, where you can literally soak in the mountain views through floor-to-ceiling windows. The canopy-walk suspension bridge takes you high above the rain-forest floor, and rates include activities like guided forest walks, children's programs, four-wheel-drive trips, and flying fox (zip-line) rides. The three-meals-daily package is an extra A$84, while the dinner-and-breakfast package is A$69. ⊠ *Green Mountains via Canungra, 4275* ☎ *07/5544–0644 or 1800/688722* ⊕ *www.oreillys.com.au* ⇨ *70 rooms* ⌂ *Restaurant, café, dining room, refrigerators, pool, outdoor hot tub, massage, sauna, hiking, bar, library, recreation room, theater, shop, children's programs (ages 5–16), laundry facilities, free parking; no a/c in some rooms, no room phones, no room TVs* ⊟ *AE, DC, MC, V.*

¢ 🏨 **Canungra Hotel.** Perhaps the best thing about this sprawling, two-story Tudor-style house with a wraparound veranda is its location: it's 20 km (14 mi) from Lamington National Park near a village green in the friendly, rural town of Canungra. Though rooms are basic, the atmosphere here is lively—mostly due to the popularity of the hotel's bar, which is always filled with locals. If you relish your peace and quiet, it's probably best to choose another hotel, as this one can get a little rowdy on weekends. Nearby are the Canungra Valley Vineyards, a lovely rural setting for a picnic and wine tasting. ⊠ *18 Kidston St., Canungra 4275* ☎ *07/5543–5233* 🖷 *07/5543–5617* ⇨ *11 rooms* ⌂ *Restaurant, bar, casino; no a/c in some rooms, no room phones, no room TVs* ⊟ *AE, DC, MC, V.*

Gold Coast A to Z

AIR TRAVEL

Gold Coast Airport, also known as Coolangatta Airport, is the region's main air transit point. From the Gold Coast it's 30 minutes to Brisbane, 2 hours 10 minutes to Melbourne, and 1 hour 25 minutes to Sydney. Qantas, Virgin Blue, and Jetstar operate domestic flights. Australian Airlines flies to several Asian cities, and Freedom Air flies to New Zealand.

🛈 **Airport Gold Coast Airport** (Coolangatta Airport) ⊠ Gold Coast Hwy., Bilinga ☎ 07/5589-1100.

🛈 **Airlines Australian Airlines** ☎ 13-1313. **Freedom Air** ☎ 1800/122000. **Jetstar** ☎ 13-1538. **Qantas** ☎ 13-1313. **Virgin Blue** ☎ 13-6789.

BUS TRAVEL

Long-distance buses traveling between Sydney and Brisbane stop at Coolangatta and Surfers Paradise.

Allstate Scenic Tours leaves Brisbane for O'Reilly's Rainforest Guesthouse in the Gold Coast Hinterland (A$44 round-trip) Sunday–Friday at 9:30 AM from the Brisbane Transit Centre.

Greyhound Australia runs an express coach from the Gold Coast to Brisbane International Airport and Gold Coast Airport, as well as day trips that cover southeast Queensland with daily connections to Sydney and Melbourne.

From the Gold Coast, Mountain Coast Company buses pick passengers up from the major bus depots, most of the major hotels, and from Coolangatta Airport for O'Reilly's Rainforest Guesthouse in the Gold Coast Hinterland (A$39 round-trip).

Surfside Buslines run every 15 minutes around the clock between Gold Coast attractions, along the strip between Tweed Heads and Southport. 🚩 **Allstate Scenic Tours** ✉ Brisbane Transit Centre, Roma St., Brisbane ☎ 07/3003-0700. **Greyhound Australia** ✉ 6 Beach Rd., Surfers Paradise ☎ 13-2030 ⊕ www.greyhound.com.au. **Mountain Coast Company** ☎ 07/5524-4249. **Surfside Buslines** ✉ 1-10 Mercantile Ct., Southport ☎ 07/5571-6555.

CAR RENTAL
All major car-rental agencies have offices in Brisbane, Surfers Paradise, and at Gold Coast Airport. Companies operating on the Gold Coast include Avis, Budget, and Thrifty. Four-wheel-drive vehicles are available. 🚩 **Avis** ✉ Ferny and Cypress Aves., Surfers Paradise ☎ 07/5539-9388. **Budget** ✉ Gold Coast Airport, Gold Coast Hwy., Bilinga ☎ 07/5536-5377. **Thrifty** ✉ 3006 Gold Coast Hwy., Surfers Paradise ☎ 07/5570-9999 ✉ Gold Coast Airport, Gold Coast Hwy., Bilinga ☎ 07/5536-6955.

CAR TRAVEL
The Gold Coast begins 65 km (40 mi) south of Brisbane. The M1 highway (the Pacific Highway) south bypasses the Gold Coast towns, and you'll see well-marked signs to guide you to your destination. If you're leaving from Brisbane International Airport, take the toll road over the Gateway Bridge to avoid having to drive through Brisbane, then follow the signs to the Gold Coast. Driving distances and times from the Gold Coast are 859 km (533 mi) and 12 hours to Sydney via the Pacific Highway, 105 km (65 mi) and 1 hour to Brisbane, and 1,815 km (1,125 mi) and 22 hours to Cairns.

EMERGENCIES
In an emergency, dial **000** for an ambulance, the police, or the fire department. 🚩 **Hospital Gold Coast Hospital** ✉ 108 Nerang St., Southport ☎ 07/5571-8211. 🚩 **Pharmacies Broadbeach Pharmacy** ✉ 2717 Main Pl., Broadbeach ☎ 07/5539-8751. **Renaissance Chemmart Pharmacy** ✉ Elkhorn Ave., Surfers Paradise ☎ 07/5561-0850.

MAIL, SHIPPING & THE INTERNET
Internet Express Café is a good place to retrieve e-mail and surf the Web. The Gold Coast Mail Centre has Australia Post and overnight services; it's open weekdays 8:30–5. 🚩 **Internet Café Internet Express Café** ✉ Level 1, Australia Fair Shopping Centre, Marine Parade, Southport ☎ 07/5527-0335.

🖪 Mail Services **Gold Coast Mail Centre** ✉ 26 Crombie Ave., Bundall ☎ 13–1318. **Surfers Paradise Post Office** ✉ Paradise Centre, 5-10 Cavill Ave., Surfers Paradise ☎ 13–1318.

MONEY MATTERS

You can cash traveler's checks and change money at most banks and financial institutions on the Gold Coast. Commonwealth Bank of Australia and ANZ have ATM machines. There are money changers in all tourist areas.

🖪 **ANZ** ✉ 3171 Gold Coast Hwy. ☎ 13–1314. **Commonwealth Bank of Australia** ✉ Pacific Fair Shopping Center, Hooker Blvd. ☎ 07/5526–9071.

TOURS

Coachtrans provides theme-park transfers and has several day tours of the Gold Coast.

🖪 **Coachtrans** ✉ 64 Ourimbah Rd., Tweed Heads ☎ 07/5506–9700.

TRAIN TRAVEL

Regular Queensland Rail service from 5:30 AM until midnight connects Brisbane and the Helensvale, Nerang, and Robina stations on the Gold Coast.

🖪 **Queensland Rail** ✉ 305 Edward St., Brisbane ☎ 07/3235–1323 or 13–2232 ⊕ www.qr.com.au.

VISITOR INFORMATION

🖪 **Gold Coast Information Centres** ✉ Griffith and Warner Sts., Coolangatta ☎ 07/5536–7765 ✉ Cavill Mall Kiosk, Cavill Ave., Surfers Paradise ☎ 07/5538–4419. **Gold Coast Tourism Bureau** ✉ Level 2, 64 Ferny Ave., Surfers Paradise 4217 ☎ 07/5592–2699 ⊕ www.goldcoasttourism.com.au.

THE SUNSHINE COAST & AIRLIE BEACH

One hour from Brisbane by car to its southernmost point, the Sunshine Coast is a 60-km (37-mi) stretch of white-sand beaches, inlets, lakes, and mountains. It begins at the Glass House Mountains and extends to Rainbow Beach in the north. Kenilworth is its inland extent, 40 km (25 mi) from the ocean. For the most part, the Sunshine Coast has avoided the high-rise glitz of its southern cousin, the Gold Coast. Although there are plenty of stylish restaurants, endearing bed-and-breakfasts, and luxurious hotels, the Sunshine Coast is best loved for its abundant national parks, secluded coves, and charming mountain villages.

More than 970 km (600 mi) to the north, Airlie Beach shares many of the same characteristics as its more southerly coastal neighbors. Like Noosa, Maroochydore, and other beach towns along the Pacific, the town enjoys great weather throughout the year. And since it's very popular with the young adventurous set, who use it as a jumping-off point for trips to the Whitsunday Islands and the Great Barrier Reef, its main street is packed with cafés and bars, travel agencies, and hotels.

Numbers in the margin correspond to points of interest on the Sunshine Coast map.

Glass House Mountains Area

16 *65 km (40 mi) north of Brisbane.*

More than 20 million years old, the Glass House Mountains consist of nine dramatic, conical outcrops. These eroded remnants of volcanoes are a spectacular sight, seeming to appear from nowhere out of the ground. They lie along the old main road about a half hour outside Brisbane to the west of the Bruce Highway.

One of the best places to view the mountains is from the Glass House Mountains Lookout. It's accessed via the Glass House Mountains Tourist Route, which begins in the quaint Glass House Mountains Village off the Bruce Highway. From the lookout you can take a short 25-minute walk. Several other longer walks begin from other lookouts and summits (such as Mt. Beerburrum and Wild Horse Mountain Lookout) that are all about 6 km (4 mi) from Glass House Mountains Lookout. For further information, contact Queensland Parks and Wildlife Service (☎ 07/5494–0150) or Naturally Queensland Information Centre (☎ 07/3227–8185).

Australia Zoo, crocodile hunter Steve Irwin's home base, has all manner of Australian animals: pythons, taipans, adders, kangaroos, eagles, wallabies—and, naturally, crocodiles. ✉ *Glass House Mountains Tourist Rte., 5 km (3 mi) north of Glass House Mountains, Beerwah* ☎ *07/ 5494–1134* ⊕ *www.crocodilehunter.com* 💰 *A$29* ◷ *Daily 8:30–4.*

There's a large, red-roof parody of a classic Australian pub on the left side of the Bruce Highway a few kilometers north of Palmview (21 km [13 mi] north of Glass House Mountains). A vintage car perches precariously on the roof, and the whole building appears on the verge of **17** collapse. This is the **Ettamogah Pub** (☎ 07/5494–5444), whose name and design are based on the famous pub featured for decades in the work of Australian cartoonist Ken Maynard. It has an upstairs bistro, a beer garden, and bar. Next door, the **Ettamogah Bakery** sells excellent pies.

The **Aussie World** amusement area adjacent to Ettamogah Pub has a large shed with pool tables, as well as long wooden tables that form the pub's beer garden. There is also a fairground with 30 rides set in beautiful gardens; pony rides are the perennial favorite for children. The **Aboriginal Cultural Centre** displays Aboriginal art. ✉ *Bruce Hwy. at Frizzo Rd.* ☎ *07/5494–5444* 💰 *Free, rides extra* ◷ *Daily 9–5.*

18 The expansive **Forest Glen Sanctuary** is a drive-through park that covers 60 acres of forest and pastures. Several species of deer, such as rusa, fallow, chital, and red, come right up to your car, especially if you have purchased a 50¢ feed bag. Koala shows take place daily at 11 and 2. ✉ *Tanawha Tourist Dr. off Bruce Hwy., 10 km (6 mi) northwest of Palmview* ☎ *07/5445–1274* 💰 *A$10* ◷ *Daily 9–4.*

Montville

19 *16 km (10 mi) northwest of Forest Glen.*

This charming mountain village, settled in 1887, is known as the creative heart of the Sunshine Coast, as many artists have made their home

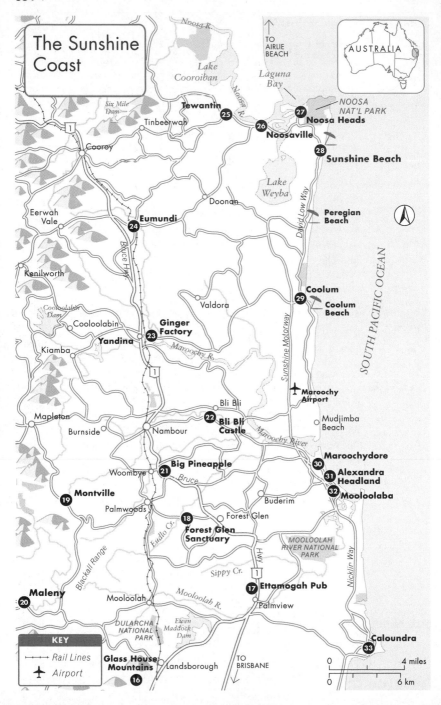

The Sunshine Coast

Noosa R.

Lake Cooroiban

Six Mile Dam

Tinbeerwah

Cooroy

Eerwah Vale

Kenilworth

Cooloolabin Dam

Cooloolabin

Yandina

Kiamba

Mapleton

Burnside

Montville 19

Palmwoods

Maleny 20

Mooloolah

DULARCHA NATIONAL PARK

Ewen Maddock Dam

Glass House Mountains 16

Landsborough

Tewantin 25

Eumundi 24

Bruce Hwy

Ginger Factory 23

Maroochy R.

Nambour

Big Pineapple 21

Woombye

Bruce

Eudlo Cr.

18 Forest Glen Sanctuary

Forest Glen

Buderim

Sippy Cr.

17 Ettamogah Pub

Palmview

Mooloolah R.

Blackall Range

TO BRISBANE

Noosa R.

TO AIRLIE BEACH

Laguna Bay

27 Noosa Heads

26 Noosaville

28 Sunshine Beach

NOOSA NAT'L PARK

Doonan

Lake Weyba

David Low Way

Peregian Beach

Coolum 29

Coolum Beach

Valdora

Sunshine Motorway

Maroochy Airport

Bli Bli

22 Bli Bli Castle

Mudjimba Beach

Maroochy River

Maroochydore

30 31 Alexandra Headland

32 Mooloolaba

MOOLOOLAH RIVER NATIONAL PARK

Hwy

Nicklin Way

Caloundra 33

AUSTRALIA

SOUTH PACIFIC OCEAN

KEY
- Rail Lines
- ✈ Airport

0   4 miles

0   6 km

here. There are panoramic views of the coast from the main street, which was built with a blend of Tudor, Irish, and English cottages of log or stone; Bavarian and Swiss houses; and old Queenslanders. Shops in town are filled with a browser's delight of curiosities and locally made crafts; art galleries have more serious pieces by local artists.

Kondalilla National Park (⊠ Kondalilla Falls Rd. off Montville–Mapleton Rd., near Flaxton ☎07/5494–3983 or 07/5459–6110), with its swimming hole, waterfall, picnic grounds, and walking trails, is a popular local attraction. Three different bushwalks begin near the large grassy picnic area: the Picnic Creek circuit, the Rock Pools walk, and the Kondalilla Falls circuit. They're all rated easy to moderate and range from 2 km (1 mi) to 5 km (3 mi) in length.

Where to Stay & Eat

$–$$ ✕ **Montville Views.** The large veranda, providing cool breezes on a steamy summer's day, overlooks the rain forest, banana plantations, and the coast at this restaurant tucked below Montville's main street. The modern Australian fare borrows freely from other cuisines; try the barramundi dusted in Cajun seasoning and served with a flambéed banana and salad. The signature dish is the creole salad, seasoned with cayenne pepper and known as "the firecracker." ⊠ *171–183 Main St.* ☎ *07/5442–9204* ⊟ *MC, V* ⊗ *No dinner Mon.–Wed.*

$–$$ ✕ **Poets Café.** Pictures of famous poets adorn the walls of this daytime restaurant, which gives you the feeling of being immersed in culture. French doors open out on to a balcony where you can dine surrounded by tall rain-forest trees. The menu focuses on open sandwiches, seafood platters, a full range of exotic curries, and pasta dishes. Save room for Utopia, the chocolate macadamia tart. ⊠ *167 Main St.* ☎ *07/5478–5479* ⊟ *AE, DC, MC, V* ⊗ *No lunch Fri.*

$–$$$$ ⊞ **Clouds of Montville.** This colonial-style motel set in 5 acres of rain forest along the Blackall Mountain Range overlooks the lush valleys leading to the Sunshine Coast. Generously sized rooms and self-contained cottages, all with exposed brick walls, floral-print furnishings, and verandas, are scattered amid the trees. All cottages have kitchen facilities; some also have hot tubs in the bathroom. A free-form saltwater pool is surrounded by rocks and tropical plants. Nearby restaurants provide complimentary pickup and drop-off services most evenings. ⊠ *166 Balmoral Rd., 4560* ☎ *07/5442–9174* ⊟ *07/5442–9475* ⊕ *www.cloudsofmontville.com.au* ☞ *10 rooms, 4 cottages* ⚿ *Kitchens, tennis court, saltwater pool, laundry facilities, free parking; no phones in some rooms* ⊟ *AE, DC, MC, V* ⦿ *BP.*

$$$ ⊞ **Falls Cottages.** Adjacent to the forest of Kondalilla Falls National Park and built in the style of traditional Queensland houses, these secluded cottages make for a lovely romantic getaway. Hardwood floors, floral upholstery, country furnishings, and wood-burning fireplaces fill the spacious cottages, which also have whirlpool tubs and cooking facilities. A breakfast basket each morning is included in the price. ⊠ *20 Kondalilla Falls Rd., 4560* ☎ *07/5445–7000* ⊕ *www.thefallscottages.com.au* ☞ *6 cottages* ⚿ *In-room hot tubs, kitchenettes, free parking; no room phones, no kids, no smoking* ⊟ *AE, DC, MC, V* ⦿ *CP.*

$$–$$$ ⊡ **Spotted Chook Ferme Auberge.** A French provincial touch infuses this newly built timber Queenslander home. Four rooms and a self-contained cottage are brightly painted and furnished with a combination of antique and modern furniture; some rooms have fireplaces. Each has sweeping views of the property's 100 acres of rain forest and the Obi Gorge in the distance. The garden and its gazebo provide a tranquil haven. A four-course dinner (at A$60 per person) is available on request and may include such delights as crayfish risotto. If you have children, call ahead to see if the Snowpea suite (which has an adjoining children's room) is available. There's a two-night minimum stay on weekends (either Friday/Saturday or Saturday/Sunday). ⊠ *176 Western Ave. 4560* ☎ *07/5442–9242* ⊕ *www.spottedchook.com* ⇆ *4 rooms, 1 cottage* ⬡ *Dining room, refrigerators, in-room DVD; no a/c in some rooms, no room phones, no smoking* ⊟ *AE, DC, MC, V* ⦿ *BP.*

Shopping

The **Montville Craft Collective** (⊠ Shop 4, 192 Main St. ☎ 07/5442–9355) has a good selection of local art, including paintings, handicrafts, and pottery.

Verde (⊠ 174 Main St. ☎ 07/5478–5855) stocks a wide selection of locally made skin-care products.

Maleny

㉒ *14 km (8½ mi) west of Montville.*

The hinterland village of Maleny is a lively mix of rural life, the arts, wineries, and cooperative community ventures. First settled around 1880, Maleny is now a working dairy town and popular tourist resort that has managed to hold on to its strong community spirit. One place not to be missed is **Maleny Cheese** (⊠ 1 Clifford St. ☎ 07/5494–2207), a boutique dairy-goods manufacturer where you can watch cheese and yogurt being made. A large number of arts-and-crafts festivals take place here, such as the Scarecrow Carnival in September and the Spring Festival of Color, held in late October. **Lake Baroon,** accessible from Maleny's main street, offers sailing, canoeing, fishing, and swimming, as well as walking trails along the shore to where the Obi Obi Creek flows into the lake.

Mary Cairncross Scenic Reserve (☎ 07/5499–9906), one of the most popular picnic spots in the area, is about 5 km (3 mi) southeast of Maleny (at the intersection of the Landsborough–Maleny and Mountainview roads). The 130 acres of rain forest shelter an array of wildlife that includes bandicoots, goannas, echidnas, wallabies, and even pythons. Whether you eat in the café or at picnic tables on the grass, you'll have a magnificent view of the Glass House Mountains.

Where to Stay & Eat

¢–$ ✕ **Colin James Fine Goods.** Savor homemade ice creams and gelati (flavors include crème caramel and lychee sorbet) at this popular gourmet food outlet and café. Owner Colin James Cunningham is a master cheese maker and sells more than 25 different cheeses. Light meals include sandwiches on homemade grain bread, smoked beef or chicken salads, and dip and cheese platters. The café serves wine by the glass and exceptional coffee. ⊠ *57 Maple St.* ☎ *07/5494–2860* ▤ *MC, V.*

¢–$ ✗ **Maple 3 Café.** A covered veranda and courtyard surround this local favorite. The menu changes daily, but there are always salads, focaccias, and many dessert options. Come in for brunch, grab a sandwich and a huge slice of cake, and head down to Lake Baroon for a picnic, or just sit out front and watch the eclectic mix of Maleny townsfolk go about their day. ⊠ *3 Maple St.* ☎ *07/5499–9177* ▤ *AE, DC, MC, V.*

$$ ▣ **Maleny Tropical Retreat.** At the end of a steep, winding driveway is a dense, misty rain-forest valley; in its midst is this Balinese-style bed-and-breakfast. Tropical gardens surround the small, two-story house furnished with Balinese touches—right down to the piped-in music. Each room has a balcony overlooking the rain forest and a glass-wall spa bath, both of which provide fabulous views of Lake Baroon. Hiking trails from the house lead to the creek. There's a two-night minimum stay on weekends. ⊠ *304 Maleny–Montville Rd., 4552* ☎ *07/5435–2113* 🖷 *07/ 5435–2114* ⊕ *www.malenytropicalretreat.com* ↗ *2 rooms* ⅄ *In-room hot tubs, in-room VCRs, hiking, free parking; no room phones, no kids, no smoking* ▤ *AE, DC, MC, V* ▯◉ *BP.*

Nambour

9 km (5½ mi) northwest of Forest Glen, 101 km (63 mi) north of Brisbane.

★ ☽ ㉑ Sunshine Plantation is home to the impossible-to-miss **Big Pineapple.** The 50-foot fiberglass monster towers over the highway, and you can climb inside to learn how pineapples are grown. The plantation is a tourist-oriented operation, incorporating a large souvenir shop, jewelry store, arts-and-crafts shop, flume rides, train rides, and an animal nursery. The culinary focus of the on-site restaurants is, of course, pineapple—it's used in imaginative ways in a number of dishes. It's also a good place to see how macadamia nuts and other tropical fruits are cultivated. ⊹ *Nambour Connection Rd., 6 km (4 mi) south of Nambour* ☎ *07/5442–1333* ⊕ *www.bigpineapple.com.au* ⊠ *Free, rides extra* ☉ *Daily 9–5.*

☽ ㉒ Children love **Bli Bli Castle,** a surprisingly realistic 1973 replica of a Norman castle. The castle is starting to show its age but still has everything necessary for a rousing game of make-believe, including dungeons and a torture chamber. The turnoff for Bli Bli is at the north end of Nambour, opposite a Toyota dealership. ⊠ *David Low Way, Bli Bli* ☎ *07/ 5448–5373* ⊠ *A$12* ☉ *Daily 9–5.*

Yandina

9 km (5½ mi) north of Nambour.

☽ ㉓ The **Ginger Factory** is one of the legendary establishments of Queensland tourism. It now goes far beyond its original factory-door sale of ginger, although you can still observe the factory at work by taking a tour for A$11. A restaurant and a large shop sell ginger in all forms—from crystallized ginger to ginger incorporated into jams, chocolates, and herbal products. There's also a miniature train ride (A$6). ⊠ *50*

Pioneer Rd. (Coolum Rd.), 1 km (½ mi) east of Bruce Hwy. ☎ *07/ 5446–7100* ⊕ *www.buderimginger.com* 🖅 *Free* ⊙ *Daily 9–5.*

Where to Stay & Eat

$$–$$$ 🏨 **Ninderry Manor.** On the ridge of Mt. Ninderry in the hinterland, this luxury bed-and-breakfast in an elegant modern manor house has three rooms that open out onto a garden. Bright, comfortable furnishings are enhanced by romantic touches, like beds gracefully draped with sheer white mosquito nets. Three cottages have hot tubs, kitchens, and separate bedrooms. Owners Aki and Miyukie Kitabatake have added some Asian touches, including "easy" Japanese cooking classes, calligraphy lessons, and a tea ceremony on request. At dusk, relax with cocktails and canapés while enjoying views of the rain-forest-covered rolling hills and valleys. ⊠ *12 Karnu Dr., Ninderry 4561, 7 km (4½ mi) northeast of Yandina* ☎ *07/5472–7255* 🖷 *07/5446–7089* ⊕ *ninderrymanor.com. au* ⇆ *3 rooms, 3 cottages* ⚿ *Dining room, some kitchens, saltwater pool, laundry facilities, business services, meeting rooms, free parking; no a/c in some rooms, no room phones, no room TVs in some rooms, no kids, no smoking* ☰ *AE, DC, MC, V* ⊙⃥ *BP.*

$$ ✕ **Spirit House.** Mention you are going to eat in Yandina, and locals and
FodorsChoice   even Brisbane foodies say "Spirit House" with an envious grin. Own-
★   ers Peter and Helen Brierty, who lived in Thailand for five years, have done a remarkable job re-creating contemporary Asian cuisine on Queensland soil. The menu changes seasonally, but a worthy signature dish is the whole crispy fish with tamarind, chili, and garlic sauce. Be sure to save room for desserts such as coconut lime syrup cake with tropical fruit. The lush garden setting has a lagoon and Buddhist shrines. A hydroponic farm and cooking school are on-site. ⊠ *4 Ninderry Rd.* ☎ *07/ 5446–8994* ⊕ *www.spirithouse.com.au* ⚞ *Reservations essential* ☰ *AE, DC, MC, V* ⊙ *No dinner Sun.–Tues.*

Eumundi

❷❹   *18 km (11 mi) north of Nambour, 21 km (13 mi) southwest of Noosa Heads.*

A walk through the streets of this late-1800s town will take you past the original (and still operational) bank, bakery, museum, and school of arts. Locally brewed beer is on tap at the Imperial Hotel, where memorabilia covers the walls and ceiling. The big attractions, though, are
FodorsChoice   the Wednesday and Saturday **Eumundi Markets** (☎ 07/5442–7106)—
★   the best street markets on the Sunshine Coast—when 300 stall holders gather along Memorial Drive to sell fresh produce, arts, crafts, and clothing from 6:30 to 2 on Saturday and 8–1 on Wednesday. Buses run to Eumundi from Noosa (via Cooroy and Trewantin) on market days, when the town swells to near-cosmopolitan proportions.

Where to Stay & Eat

$$ ✕🏨 **Taylor's Damn Fine Bed and Breakfast.** A short stroll from Eumundi's main street, this gracious old Queenslander overlooks 4 acres of lush paddock bordering the North Maroochy River. A blend of Australian and Asian furnishings fills the common areas and guest rooms, which each have a private veranda. You can also stay in a restored, circa-1946 railway carriage, which holds two additional rooms with private baths. The dining room serves Mod-Oz cuisine; the four-course dinners may include kangaroo fillets on beetroot risotto followed by bamboo skewers of lycee, mango, and pineapple, as well as a dessert wine. Ingredients are fresh from the Eumundi markets. ⊠ *1502 Eumundi–Noosa Rd., 4562* ☎ *07/5442–8685* 🖷 *07/5442–8168* ⊕ *www.taylorsbandb.com. au* 🛏 *5 rooms* ⌂ *Dining room, driving range, pool, free parking, some pets allowed; no a/c, no room phones, no TV in some rooms* 🖃 *AE, DC, MC, V* ⑪ *BP.*

Tewantin

㉕ *18 km (11 mi) northeast of Eumundi, 7 km (4½ mi) west of Noosa Heads.*

Originally a timber town, Tewantin is now a relaxed place to go fishing or boating on the Noosa River or enjoy a tranquil riverside dinner. You can rent canoes, catamarans, Windsurfers, paddle skis, and motorboats at **Everglades Tourist Park and Boat Hire** (☎ 07/5485–3164) at Boreen Point, north of Tewantin on the western side of Lake Cootharaba. They also run a water taxi to the Everglades, a wetlands area of swamps and forests teaming with birdlife where you can hire a canoe to explore.

Where to Eat

$–$$ ✗ **Amici's on the Water.** An open, informal restaurant with tables on the deck overlooking the marina, this Italian restaurant highlights veal steaks, wood-fired pizzas, and handmade pasta. The casual waitstaff and generous portions ensure its popularity with both locals and tourists. ⊠ *Noosa Harbour Marine Village* ☎ *07/5449–0515* 🖃 *MC, V.*

Noosaville

㉖ *4 km (2½ mi) east of Tewantin, 3 km (2 mi) west of Noosa Heads.*

A snug little town dotted with small hotels and apartment complexes, Noosaville is the access point for trips to the **Teewah Coloured Sands,** an area of multicolor sand dunes that were created by natural chemicals in the soil. Dating from the Ice Age, some of the 72 different hues of sand form cliffs rising to 600 feet and stretch inland from the beach to a distance of about 17 km (11 mi). A four-wheel-drive vehicle is essential for exploring both this area and interesting sites to the north, such as Great Sandy National Park, the wreck of the *Cherry Venture* near the beachside hamlet of Freshwater, and Rainbow Beach. Access is by ferry across the Noosa River at Tewantin.

Tour operators run day trips that take in these sights, and some include an overnight or longer visit to Fraser Island, north of Rainbow Beach. **Beyond Noosa** (☎ 97/5448–9177 or 1800/657666) runs cruises along the Noosa River and the Everglades, and a combined cruise and four-wheel-drive tour to the Colored Sands and Rainbow Beach area.

Where to Stay & Eat

$ ✗ **A Taste of Spice.** A short stroll from the river is this popular Asian eatery which once hosted the Sultan of Brunei, his entourage, and a host of government officials from Sri Lanka. It's a simple, colorful restaurant with indoor-outdoor dining areas. The wide range of curries includes tamarind curry prawns, wok-tossed and stir-fried dishes, and hawker-style noodle dishes. The pepper lamb simmered in spices and tomato puree melts in your mouth, while the perfect dish to finish with is coconut crepe with mango and banana. ⊠ *Thomas St. at No. 5 Island Resort* ☎ *07/5474–2833* ⊟ *DC, MC, V.*

¢–$ ✕ **Nourish Bar.** This riverside café specializes in fresh-fruit smoothies and juices, which you can enjoy out on the patio or take down to the bank of the Noosa River. A favorite is the "Noosaville Tropics" blend of pineapple, strawberries, banana, honey, and coconut cream. The café also serves fresh-fruit gelati, espresso, and such delicacies as panini, pumpkin-and-chickpea salad, and pancakes with caramelized apple. ⊠ *Shop 1, 253 Gympie Terr.* ☎ *07/5449–9449* ⊟ *AE, DC, MC, V.*

$$$ ⊞ **Montpellier Boutique Resort.** This modern apartment hotel is a mere stroll from the lovely Noosa River, where you can swim, fish, hire a boat, picnic by the shore, or dine at several riverside restaurants. Two-bedroom apartments, which can accommodate four, have a kitchen, two bathrooms, and laundry, plus a balcony accessed through sliding-glass doors. ⊠ *7–11 James St., 4566* ☎ *07/5455–5033* 🖷 *07/5455–8022* ⊕ *www.montpelliernoosa.com.au* ✑ *20 apartments* ⟁ *Kitchens, in-room VCRs, cable TV, in-room data ports, pool, hot tub, laundry facilities, free parking* ⊟ *AE, DC, MC, V.*

Noosa Heads

❷❼ *39 km (24 mi) northeast of Nambour, 17 km (11 mi) north of Coolum, 140 km (87 mi) north of Brisbane.*

Set along the calm waters of Laguna Bay at the northern tip of the Sunshine Coast, Noosa Heads is one of the most stylish resort areas in Australia. The town consisted of nothing more than a few shacks until the mid-1980s, but then surfers discovered the spectacular waves that curl around the sheltering headland of Noosa National Park. Today, Noosa Heads is a charming mix of surf, sand, and sophistication, with a serious reputation for its unique and evolving cuisine. Views along the trail from Laguna Lookout to the top of the headland take in miles of magnificent beaches, ocean, and dense vegetation.

Where to Stay & Eat

$$–$$$ ✕ **Sails.** "Super fresh and super simple" could be the motto at Sails, which serves modern Australian cuisine with an emphasis on seafood. Try the sushi platter, the char-grilled Moreton Bay bugs, or the seafood plate. The open dining pavilion backs straight onto Noosa's famous beach. ⊠ *Park Rd. and Hastings St.* ☎ *07/5447–4235* ⊕ *http://sailsnoosa. citysearch.com.au* ⊟ *AE, DC, MC, V.*

$–$$ ✕ **Aromas.** This coffee shop was at the forefront of Noosa's famous café culture, and it's still one of the best sipping spots in town. The loyal clientele comes for the film-noir setting and great people-watching. There's a modern Mediterranean slant to the menu, which also lists an impressive selection of cakes, biscuits, and coffees. ⊠ *32 Hastings St.* ☎ *07/5474–9788* ⊟ *AE, DC, MC, V.*

$–$$ ✕ **Cato's Restaurant and Bar.** This split-level restaurant attached to the Sheraton Noosa Resort has a bar downstairs next to bustling Hastings Street, and a relaxed dining section above. Seafood dominates the menu at both; among the favorites are Caesar salad with seared scallops and prosciutto, and spiced tuna steak with baby beets. A fantastic seafood buffet is available every evening for A$58, and you can help yourself to the all-you-can-drink "wine buffet" for A$19.50 per person. ✉ *16 Hastings St.* ☎ *07/5449–4787* ▭ *AE, DC, MC, V.*

$–$$ ✕ **Berardo's on the Beach.** Expatriate New Yorker Jim Berardo came to Noosa to retire, but he ended up with two restaurants. Berardo's on the Beach, the more casual one, has a prime location open to the Noosa shores, and attracts a constant stream of customers. Quirky fish sculptures line the walls, and handblown chartreuse carafes are on every table. The weekly menu lists fresh juices, cocktails, extravagant open sandwiches, and light meals such as steamed mussels with *gremolata* (Italian seasonings), oregano, tomato, and toasted sourdough. ✉ *49 Hastings St., on the beach* ☎ *07/5448–0888* ⊕ *www.berardos.com.au* ▭ *AE, DC, MC, V.*

$–$$ ✕ **Bistro C.** Spectacular views of the bay from the open dining area make a stunning backdrop for this restaurant's modern Australian cuisine. The menu highlights seafood, though landlubbers can partake of several vegetarian and meat dishes. Try the seafood antipasti plate, the justly famous egg-fried calamari, or grilled prawn skewers on a mango, snow pea, and cherry-tomato salad, served with ginger syrup and lime oil. ✉ *On the Beach Complex, Hastings St.* ☎ *07/5447–2855* ⊕ *www. bistroc.com.au* ▭ *AE, DC, MC, V.*

$–$$ ✕ **Ricky Ricardo's River Bar and Restaurant.** A glassed-in dining room overlooking the Noosa River makes this restaurant perfect for a relaxed lunch or a romantic dinner. The menu has a loose Mediterranean theme, with an emphasis on the best local, organic produce. Start off with a few tapas and a drink before moving on to a main course of a crispy-skin barramundi or reef fish with rock salt and lemon. ✉ *Noosa Wharf, Quamby Pl.* ☎ *07/5447–2455* ⊕ *www.rickyricardos.com* ▭ *AE, DC, MC, V.*

$$$$ ▥ **Netanya Noosa.** Most of the airy suites in this low-rise beachfront complex look straight over the main beach; a few are in a garden wing. All suites come with soft bathrobes, and most have large verandas. The Presidential suite has a private terrace with an outdoor Jacuzzi, as well as a magnificent dining room where a local chef serves special dinners on request. ✉ *75 Hastings St., 4567* ☎ *07/5447–4722 or 1800/072072* ▤ *07/ 5447–3914* ⊕ *www.netanyanoosa.com.au* ⊷ *48 suites* ⟁ *Room service, some in-room hot tubs, kitchenettes, pool, gym, outdoor hot tub, sauna, spa, laundry service, travel services, free parking* ▭ *AE, DC, MC, V.*

★ **$$$$** ▥ **Sheraton Noosa Resort.** You can't miss this stepped, six-story, horseshoe-shape complex as you drive into Noosa Heads from Noosaville. It faces fashionable Hastings Street on one side and the river on the other, and is playfully painted apricot pink with lavender-blue balconies and sea-green trim. The foyer area is equally colorful, though the adjoining River Lounge is stylish and subdued. It's hard to find fault with the spacious rooms: each has a kitchenette, balcony, and hot tub, and a terrace or balcony with river or pool views. ✉ *16 Hastings St., 4567* ☎ *07/ 5449–4888* ▤ *07/5449–2230* ⊕ *www.sheratonnoosa.com.au* ⊷ *140* rooms, 19 suites, 8 villas, 2 penthouses ♨ Restaurant, in-room hot tubs, kitchenettes, cable TV with movies and video games, pool, health club, sauna, spa, bar, babysitting, laundry service, concierge, Internet room, business services, meeting room, travel services, free parking, no-smoking floor ⊟ AE, DC, MC, V.

¢ ⌸ **Halse Lodge.** This Heritage-listed guesthouse with colonial-style furnishings sits in 2 acres of gardens on the edge of Noosa National Park. Pictures of Noosa from yesteryear decorate the large functional rooms. Double rooms, twin rooms, and bunk rooms that sleep either four or six people all have shared baths. Reservations are essential at this very popular place. ⊠ 2 Halse La., at Noosa Dr., near Lions Park, 4567 ☎ 07/5447-3377 or 1800/242567 ⍐ 07/5447-2929 ⊕ www.halselodge.com. au ↪ 26 rooms without bath ♨ Cafeteria, billiards, Ping-Pong, bar, travel services, free parking; no a/c, no room phones, no room TVs ⊟ MC, V.

Sunshine Beach

28 4 km (2½ mi) south of Noosa Heads.

Ten minutes away from the bustle and crowds of Hastings Street and Noosa Beach, south of the headland and Noosa National Park, is the serene suburb of Sunshine Beach. It's home to a number of good restaurants, a small shopping village, and, as the name suggests, 16 km (10 mi) of beachfront which stretches north to the national park.

Where to Stay & Eat

★ $$ ✕ **Sabai Sabai.** A terra-cotta-tiled courtyard lined with bougainvillea, banana palms, and bamboo leads to the dining room here. The mostly Vietnamese and Thai menu changes seasonally, but signature dishes include whole crispy fish with sweet-and-sour ginger-and-lime sauce or the roasted duck in steamed coconut pancakes with fragrant green curry. An extensive Australian and New Zealand wine list is on hand, as is a vegetarian menu. ⊠ 46 Duke St. ☎ 07/5473-5177 ⊟ AE, DC, MC, V.

$$-$$$ ⌸ **La Mer.** This two-story hotel has apartment-style suites with balconies facing the water. The large rooms have woven cane furniture, tile floors, and gorgeous sunrise views. The beach is across the road and down a short bush trail that leads to the Esplanade. You can walk to Sunshine Beach's shopping village and restaurants, and book most tours in the hotel lobby. There's a three-night minimum stay in high season, a five-night minimum from mid-December through January. ⊠ 5-7 Belmore Terr., 4567 ☎ 07/5447-2111 ⍐ 07/5449-2483 ⊕ www. lamersunshine.com.au ↪ 18 suites ♨ Fans, kitchens, in-room VCRs, pool, recreation room, babysitting, laundry facilities, travel services, free parking; no a/c ⊟ AE, DC, MC, V.

Coolum

29 17 km (11 mi) south of Noosa Heads, 25 km (16 mi) northeast of Nambour.

At the center of the Sunshine Coast, Coolum makes an ideal base for exploring the countryside. It has what is probably the finest beach along the Sunshine Coast, and a growing reputation for good food.

Where to Stay & Eat

$$ ✕ **Beachhouse Restaurant and Bar.** Across the street from Coolum Beach and beneath the Baywatch Resort, this laid-back restaurant reflects the nature of the town. Windows are thrown wide open to let sea breezes waft across the indoor and outdoor tables. The menu combines local seasonal produce with Asian and Mediterranean flavors: try seared scallops with smoked eggplant purée; cucumber and tzatziki salad; or soy-glazed duck with roasted sweet potatoes and baby bok choy. ⊠ *172 David Low Way* ☎ *07/5446–4688* ⊟ *AE, DC, MC, V.*

★ $$$$ ✕⌨ **Hyatt Regency Resort.** Spread out at the foot of Mount Coolum, this is one of the best health resorts in Australia. Accommodations, grouped in low-rise clusters throughout the large complex, include studio suites, two-bedroom villas, and luxurious three-bedroom residences. Villas and residences have kitchens and laundry facilities; residences also have rooftop terraces and hot tubs. The spa has pools, an aerobics room, a supervised gym, hot tubs, a hair and beauty salon, and dozens of beauty, pampering, and health treatments. Fish Tales restaurant specializes in seafood while McKenzie Grill serves a juicy steak. A shuttle will transport you around the 370-acre property. ⊠ *1 Warran Rd., 4573* ☎ *07/5446–1234* 🖷 *07/ 5446–2957* ⊕ *www.coolum.hyatt.com* ➱ *156 suites, 162 villas, 5 residences* ⚘ *4 restaurants, in-room safes, kitchenettes, some microwaves, cable TV with movies, 18-hole golf course, 7 tennis courts, pro shop, 8 pools, wading pool, fitness classes, gym, health club, hair salon, hot tub, spa, beach, 4 bars, wineshop, dance club, nightclub, shops, babysitting, children's programs (ages 6 wks–12 years), dry cleaning, laundry service, Internet room, business services, convention center, meeting rooms, travel services, free parking; no smoking* ⊟ *AE, DC, MC, V* ⃝ *CP.*

$$–$$$ ⌨ **Coolum Seaside.** These spacious sunny apartments have excellent views of the coast, and are just around the corner from the beach and the town's main restaurant drag. Each unit has a large balcony or terrace, and some have a private roof garden. Bright seaside prints line the off-white walls, and tropically colored furniture stands atop bleached terra-cotta tiles. Several apartments can accommodate 10 guests. ⊠ *23 Beach Rd., 4573* ☎ *07/ 5455–7200 or 1800/809062* 🖷 *07/5455–7288* ⊕ *www.coolumseaside. com* ➱ *30 apartments* ⚘ *Kitchens, in-room VCRs, cable TV, 2 pools, hot tub, spa, laundry facilities, free parking* ⊟ *MC, V.*

Maroochydore

30 *18 km (11 mi) south of Coolum, 21 km (13 mi) north of Caloundra, 18 km (11 mi) east of Nambour.*

Maroochydore, at the mouth of the Maroochy River, has been a popular beach resort for years, and has its fair share of high-rise towers. It's draw is excellent surfing and swimming beaches.

Where to Stay & Eat

$$ ✕ **ebb.** Faux-suede sofas, dining chairs, and ottomans in varying shades of cool blue set the mood at this riverside seafood restaurant. Floor-to-ceiling windows line one side of this long dining room, while the other side is an open kitchen. Start with one of four oyster dishes, including natural and ebb margarita shots, before moving onto an exquisite sim-

mering champagne lobster and sand-crab bisque, or chicken ballotine with duck farce, pomme purée, and duck jus. Finish with orange-and-praline semifreddo or peruse the chocolate menu. ⊠ *Duporth Riverside, Duporth Ave.* ☎ *07/5452–7771* ⊟ *AE, MC, V.*

\$–\$\$ ✕ **Maroochy Surf Club.** Relax with a drink and an inexpensive meal after a day in the sun at this beachside surf club (also known as Flags restaurant). Hearty surf-and-turf dishes like barbecued king prawns, grilled swordfish, and steaks dominate the menu, although there are vegetarian choices too. Although you can lounge in beachwear by day, smart-casual dress is the rule in the evenings, when live bands often play. A weekend courtesy bus provides transportation between the club and local hotels. ⊠ *34–36 Alexandra Parade* ☎ *07/5443–1298* ⊟ *MC, V.*

\$\$\$–\$\$\$\$ ✕▥ **Novotel Twin Waters Resort.** Nestled on 660 private acres 9 km (5½ mi) north of Maroochydore, this hotel was built around a 15-acre salt-water lagoon bordering the Maroochy River and Mudjimba Beach (a board-walk joins the resort and the beach). The family-style resort has one of Queensland's finest golf courses, where kangaroos and ducks make their home. There are resident golf, surfing, and tennis pros, and catamaran sailing, windsurfing, and canoeing on the lagoon is free for guests. The excellent restaurant, Lily's-on-the-Lagoon, perches over one section of the lake. ⊠ *Ocean Dr., 4558* ☎ *07/5448–8000* 🖷 *07/5448–8001* ⊕ *www.twinwatersresort.com.au* ⇆ *244 rooms, 120 suites* ⧉ *4 restaurants, room service, some microwaves, refrigerators, room TVs with movies, driving range, 18-hole golf course, 6 tennis courts, pool, hair salon, spa, beach, windsurfing, boating, bicycles, volleyball, 3 bars, babysitting, children's programs (ages 2–12), Internet room, business services, convention center, meeting room, travel services, free parking* ⊟ *AE, DC, MC, V.*

\$\$\$\$ ▥ **Sebel Maroochydore.** Each of the two-bedroom apartments in this stylish hotel has a curved wall and a separate media room with all the latest entertainment wizardry. Glass doors lead to spacious balconies with views over of the Maroochy River, Maroochydore Beach, or the hinterland. Airy rooms have cream walls, blond-wood furniture, and cream sofas in the living and bedrooms; stainless-steel appliances and stone benches in the kitchen; and two bathrooms, one with hot tub. The rooftop bar-becue area is the perfect place to unwind. A clutch of cafés and restaurants is a five-minute walk away, as is the beach itself. ⊠ *20 Aerodrome Rd., 4558* ☎ *07/5478–8000 or 1800/137106* 🖷 *07/5478–8100* ⊕ *www.mirvachotels.com.au* ⇆ *104 apartments, 6 penthouses* ⧉ *BBQs, IDD phones, in-room hot tubs, kitchens, microwaves, refrigerators, room TVs with movies, in-room DVD, pool, wading pool, outdoor hot tub, steam room, laundry facilities, concierge, Internet room, meeting rooms, airport shuttle, free parking, no-smoking rooms* ⊟ *AE, DC, MC, V.*

Alexandra Headland

❸❶ *4 km (2½ mi) south of Maroochydore, 1 km (½ mi) north of Mooloolaba.*

The development between Maroochydore, Alexandra Headland, and Mooloolaba is continuous, so you're often unaware of passing through different townships. Alexandra Headland is the smallest of the three and has a very good surf beach.

Where to Stay

$–$$ ⊞ **Alexandra Beach Resort.** This sprawling complex is opposite the patrolled beach of Alexandra Headland and is a popular place for families and couples. The centerpiece is a huge 150-m lagoon pool with two waterslides and rapids, and a hot tub and heated pool at one end. There are studio, one-, two-, and three-bedroom apartments as well as a penthouse. Rooms are simply furnished with cane furniture and have kitchen and laundry facilities. Lagoon rooms have steps from the balcony straight into the pool. ⊠ *Alexandra Parade and Pacific Terr., 4572* ☎ *07/5475–0600 or 1300/651046* 🖷 *07/5475–0611* ⊕ *www.alexbeach. com* ⟲ *214 apartments, 1 penthouse* ⚭ *In-room safes, kitchens, kitchenettes, cable TV, 3 pools, gym, 2 outdoor hot tubs, bar, shops, babysitting, playground, laundry facilities, laundry service, meeting room, free parking* ☰ *AE, DC, MC, V.*

Mooloolaba

32 *5 km (3 mi) south of Maroochydore.*

Mooloolaba stretches along lovely areas of beach and riverbank, which are an easy walk from town. The Esplanade has many casual cafés, upscale restaurants, and fashionable shops. You can also stroll to the town outskirts for lovely picnic spots and prime coastal views.

🖑 **Underwater World** has round-the-clock marine presentations including a stringray feeding, a guided shark tour, seal shows, and a croc feeding, all accompanied by informative talks. A clear underwater tunnel lets you get face-to-face with giant sharks, stingrays, and other creatures of the deep. The aquarium is part of Mooloolaba's Wharf Complex, which also has a marina, restaurants, and a tavern. ⊠ *Parkyn Parade, The Wharf* ☎ *07/5444–8488* 🖾 *A$24* 🕗 *Daily 9–5.*

Where to Stay & Eat

★ **$–$$** ✕ **Bella Venezia Italian Restaurant.** A large wall mural of Venice, simple wooden tables, and terra-cotta floor tiles decorate this popular restaurant at the back of an arcade, near the Esplanade. You can eat in or take out traditional and modern Italian cuisine, such as the *involtini di vitello,* thin slices of veal, rolled and stuffed with cacciatore sausage, olives, sun-dried tomatoes, bacon, and spinach. ⊠ *Pacific Bldg., 95 the Esplanade* ☎ *07/5444–5844* ☰ *MC, V* 🕗 *No lunch.*

¢–$ ✕ **Coffee Club.** Although it's part of a national restaurant chain, this open-air restaurant-bar-café has top-notch flavored coffees and desserts. Try the *affogatto,* a long (tall), black espresso with ice cream, paired with a slice of Coffee Club mud cake or a piece of mango-and-macadamia strudel. Open sandwiches, salads, and light meals can be ordered any time. The dinner menu highlights an eclectic mix of specials like spinach-ricotta ravioli and Cajun-seasoned chicken breast. ⊠ *The Esplanade at Syrenuse Plaza* ☎ *07/5478–3688* ☰ *DC, MC, V.*

$$$$ ⊞ **Sirocco Resort.** The stylish, futuristic curves of this apartment complex stand out on Mooloolaba's main drag, just across the road from the beach. Apartments have two, three, and five-bedroom plans, each with sleek modern furniture, a hot tub, a balcony, and magnificent beach views. Apartments have different themes; you might have tribal decor with bold colors and interesting artifacts. A minimum five-night stay is required during the high season from late December through January. Several smart restaurants are just outside the resort's front doors. ⊠ *59–75 the Esplanade, Box 798, 4557* ☎ *07/5444–1400 or 1800/ 303131* ⊕ *www.sirocco-resort.com* 🛏 *69 apartments* ♨ *In-room hot tubs, kitchens, cable TV, pool, wading pool, gym, spa, laundry facilities, car rental, travel services, free parking* ⊟ *MC, V.*

\$\$–\$\$\$ 🏨**Landmark Resort.** Floor-to-ceiling windows with balconies over the water are the memorable traits of this lovely resort. Rooms have wood and wicker furniture, tropical floral prints, marble breakfast bars, and whirlpool tubs. Several restaurants are underneath the complex, and the Mooloolaba Surf Club—a good place for snacks and a drink—is across the road. A minimum of seven nights must be booked during the high season from mid-December to late January, and two nights for the rest of the year. ⊠ *The Esplanade and Burnett St., 4557* ☎ *07/5444–5555 or 1800/888835* 🖷 *07/5444–5055* ⊕ *www.landmarkresorts.au.com* 🛏 *132 rooms* ♨ *BBQs, in-room hot tubs, kitchens, cable TV, pool, wading pool, gym, sauna, recreation room, laundry facilities, Internet room, meeting rooms, car rental, travel services, free parking* ⊟ *AE, DC, MC, V.*

Caloundra

➌ *29 km (18 mi) south of Maroochydore, 63 km (39 mi) south of Noosa Heads, 91 km (56 mi) north of Brisbane.*

This southern seaside town has nine beaches of its own, which include everything from placid wading beaches (King's Beach and Bulcock Beach are best for families) to bays with thundering surf. The town is much less glitzy than the more touristy Queensland resorts.

Where to Stay & Eat

\$–\$\$ ✕ **Alfie's on the Beach.** Owned by legendary (and now retired) Queensland Rugby League footballer Allan "Alfie" Langer, this restaurant has an ideal setting right on Bulcock Beach. It overlooks the sheltered inlet known as Pumicestone Passage. The decor and design are light and bright, and there's both indoor and outdoor dining. Try the Mexican oysters with avocado, salsa, and chili cream, then move on to the sand-crab ravioli or salt-and-pepper cuttlefish. There are also light meals such as burgers and salads. ⊠ *The Esplanade and Oranto St.* ☎ *07/5492–8155* ⊟ *AE, DC, MC, V.*

\$\$\$ 🏨 **Rolling Surf Resort.** The white sands of King's Beach front this resort, which is set among tropical gardens. Wooden blinds, cane furniture, and beach prints fill well-equipped, one- to three-bedroom apartments. All rooms have hot tubs; many also have large, curved balconies overlooking the beach. The pool, which can be accessed from the door of several of the ground-floor units, is long enough to do laps in. The resort has its own café and a restaurant with white-linen service. The Sun Air Bus Service delivers you to the front door from Brisbane Airport. ⊠ *Levuka Ave., King's Beach, 4551* ☎ *07/5491–9777* ⊕ *www. rollingsurfresort.com.au* 🛏 *74 apartments* ♨ *Restaurant, café, cable TV, pool, gym, sauna, laundry facilities, Internet room, travel services, free parking* ⊟ *MC, V.*

¢ ▦ **Caloundra City Backpackers.** This modern hostel prides itself on being the best value in town. There are twin rooms (without bathrooms), doubles, and one triple, plus two dorms that sleep eight. All rooms share two fully equipped kitchens. It's a five-minute walk to the beach, two minutes into town. ⊠ *84 Omrah Ave., 4551* ☎ *07/5499–7655* 🖷 *07/5499–7644* ⊕ *www.caloundracitybackpackers.com.au* ⟳ *18 rooms, 5 with bath; 2 dorms* ⚖ *Laundry facilities, free parking; no a/c, no room phones, no room TVs* ⊟ *MC, V.*

Airlie Beach

1,130 km (702 mi) north of Brisbane, 1,039 km (636 mi) north of Caloundra, 635 km (395 mi) south of Cairns.

Although it's not part of the Sunshine Coast, Airlie Beach has a similar feel to many of the Pacific beach towns far to the south. The waterfront Esplanade, with its boardwalk, landscaped gardens, and Saturday-morning crafts markets, is a lively gathering place. So is the main street, which is chockablock with hotels, restaurants, bars, and shops—many catering to the backpacker crowd.

The beachfront, man-made Airlie Beach Lagoon is a popular spot for locals and tourists, and provides a stinger-free swimming enclosure open all day, seven days a week. It is patrolled by lifeguards from 9 to 5 daily and has two adjoining children's pools.

Shute Harbour, 11 km (7 mi) southeast from Airlie Beach, is the main ferry terminal and gateway to the islands and the reef. The large sheltered inlet is sprinkled with boats and flanked by steep wooded banks. Shute Harbour is such a hive of marine activity that it's ranked as the second-busiest commuter port in Australia after Sydney's Circular Quay. Though some accommodation is available, the harbor is geared toward transferring visitors to the islands or used as the departure point for yachters or commercial launches to the reef. For a great view over the harbor and Whitsunday Passage, take a drive to the top of Coral Point.

Conway National Park, a 10-minute drive southeast from Airlie Beach, is a 54,000-acre expanse that hugs the coast from Shute Harbour south and has a diverse range of plant life including mangrove, open forest, canopy, and tropical lowland. You'll also see ferns and orchids, and, if you're very lucky, the endangered Proserpine rock wallaby. Two of Australia's mound-building birds—the Australian brush-turkey and the orange-footed scrub fowl—can also be found here. Four walking trails range in length from 1 km (½ mi) to 16 km (10 mi), and most start at the park's picnic area on Shute Harbour Road (4 km [2½ mi] from the information center). The Mount Rooper Walking Track meanders past a variety of plant life and up to the lookout for breathtaking views of the Whitsunday Islands. The Swamp Bay track follows the creek at the base of Mount Rooper and leads to a beach with coral-strewn sand. Take note: although a dip in the deep-blue sea is tempting, it's wise to play it safe and avoid swimming in any beaches north of Rockhampton during the "stinger" or box-jellyfish season (November to May), unless stinger nets are in use. ⊠ *Whitsunday Information Centre, Shute Harbor Rd. and Mandalay Rd.* ☎ *07/4926–7022.*

⟳ At the **Barefoot Bushman's Wildlife Park** you can view a comprehensive collection of Australian wildlife, including cassowaries and crocodiles, and walk among the roaming kangaroos and wallabies. Wildlife shows, such as croc feedings and snake handling, take place throughout the day. ⊠ *Shute Harbour Rd.* ☎ *07/4946–4848* ⌑ *A$20* ☉ *Daily 9–4:30.*

Where to Stay & Eat

$–$$ ✕ **Capers at the Beach Bar and Grill.** Tables spill out across bleached terra-cotta tiles at this busy, beachside restaurant in the Airlie Beach Hotel. The menu leans toward Asian and Mediterranean flavors, and favorite menu items include coconut-crusted fish braised in Thai curry, and char-grilled chicken with garlic, chili, and lemon zest. Save room for the warm, chocolate sticky date pudding, served with Kahlua-and-pistachio caramel sauce and gelati. There's live music on Friday nights. ⊠ *The Esplanade and Coconut Grove* ☎ *07/4964–1777* ⊟ *AE, DC, MC, V.*

¢–$ ✕ **Airlie Thai.** Overlooking the water from the second floor of a beach-front building, this authentic Thai restaurant is a very popular spot for dinner. The local favorite dish is the Thai fish cakes (lightly fried patties of minced fish and spices). The jungle curry spiced with *kachai* (a sweet, aromatic spice in the ginger family) lime leaves, red curry paste, and fresh chilies is another great dish. There are also plenty of vegetarian options such as the hot-and-sour coconut soup. The sweet sticky rice wrapped in banana leaf is the only dessert, but it's perfect. ⊠ *Beach Plaza, the Esplanade* ☎ *07/4946–4683* ⊟ *AE, DC, MC, V.*

¢–$ ✕ **Chatz Bar and Brasserie.** Choose from an array of burgers or fresh fish dishes at this affordable pub-style eatery. There's a large selection of local and imported bottled beers and eight basic cocktails (which can be bought by the glass or the jug) to round out your meal. Locals and tourists alike fill the indoor and outdoor areas until closing time at 11 PM each night. ⊠ *390 Shute Harbour Rd.* ☎ *07/4946–7223* ⊟ *MC, V.*

¢–$$ ▥ **Airlie Beach Hotel.** With the beach right at its doorstep and the main street directly behind it, this hotel is arguably the most convenient base from which to explore the region. Spacious rooms are decorated with photographs of the reef, ocean, and islands, and each opens onto a balcony overlooking the palm-lined beachfront. ⊠ *The Esplanade and Coconut Grove, 4802* ☎ *07/4964–1999 or 1800/466233* ⎙ *07/4964–1988* ⊕ *www.airliebeachhotel.com.au* ↩ *80 rooms* ⌂ *2 restaurants, minibars, cable TV, in-room data ports, saltwater pool, beach, laundry facilities, travel services, free parking* ⊟ *AE, DC, MC, V.*

$ ▥ **Whitsunday Moorings Bed and Breakfast.** Overlooking Abel Point Ma-
Fodor's Choice rina, this property has a patio view that's fantastic at dusk. The house
★ is surrounded by mango and frangipani trees, where an abundance of lorikeets frolic. Although host Peter Brooks is extraordinarily helpful with regard to activities in the area (and an excellent breakfast chef), the lure of his poolside hammock can overcome even the most energetic guest. Rooms are tiled in terra-cotta, with bamboo mat ceilings and cedar blinds. Breakfast is a five-course affair, combining white linen with tropical fruits and flowers, homemade jams, freshly squeezed juice, and a wide choice of dishes. ⊠ *37 Airlie Crescent, 4802* ☎ *07/4946–4692* ⊕ *www.whitsundaymooringsbb.com.au* ↩ *2 rooms* ⌂ *Kitchens, cable TV, pool, laundry facilities; no room phones* ⊟ *AE, DC, MC, V.*

¢ 🔲 **Beaches Backpackers.** With the liveliest bar and bistro in Airlie Beach on the premises, this hostel in the center of town attracts the party crowd. You can stay in an eight-bed dorm or opt for a more private double or twin room; each is air-conditioned, serviced daily, and has an en suite bathroom, TV, bar fridge, and balcony. There's a palm tree–shaded on-site pool and a year-round lagoon pool across the street. A free shuttle bus service runs from the bus terminal to the hostel. ✉ *356-362 Shute Harbour Rd., 4802* 🕾 *07/4946–6244 or 1800/636630* 🖷 *07/4946–7764* ⊕ *www.beachers.com.au* 🗪 *24 dorms, 6 double or twin rooms* ⚐ *Restaurant, refrigerators, pool, beach, bar, laundry facilities, Internet room, travel services, free parking* 🟰 *MC, V.*

Nightlife

Shute Harbour Road is where it all happens in Airlie Beach. Bars and nightspots offer the young backpacker crowd all kinds of undergraduate entertainment, from Jell-O wresting to wet-T-shirt and pole-dancing competitions (the latter are open to both women and men). Some clubs have live music on weekends.

The crowd's friendly at **Beaches** (✉ 362 Shute Harbour Rd. 🕾 072/ 4946–6244), part of the backpackers' hostel of the same name. Catch one of the nightly live bands or watch one of the sports games playing on TV.

Head to **Magnums** (✉ 366 Shute Harbour Rd. 🕾 1800/624634) to join the party. The club is split into two venues: M@ss has wilder activities, like toad racing, Jell-O wresting, foam parties (you're sprayed with foam guns while dancing), and pole dancing; The Boardwalk has live music and happy-hour drinks.

Sunshine Coast A to Z

AIR TRAVEL

Maroochy Airport (also known as Sunshine Coast Airport) is the main airport for the Sunshine Coast. Qantas, Virgin Blue, and Sunshine Express Airlines have domestic flights. By air from Maroochydore, it's 25 minutes to Brisbane, 2 hours 25 minutes to Melbourne, and 1 hour 35 minutes to Sydney.

The Whitsunday Coast Airport (also known as Proserpine Airport) in Proserpine, 25 km (16 mi) southeast from Airlie Beach, has daily flights by Sunshine Express Airlines from Brisbane and Cairns and Jetstar and Virgin Blues flights from Sydney.

🛈 **Airports Maroochydore Airport** (Sunshine Coast Airport) ✉ Friendship Dr. off David Low Way, Marcoola 🕾 07/5448-7662. **Proserpine Airport** (Whitsunday Coast Airport) ✉ Air Whitsunday Dr. off Shute Harbour Rd., Proserpine 🕾 07/4946-9180.

🛈 **Airlines Jetstar** 🕾 13-1538. **Qantas** 🕾 13-1313. **Sunshine Express Airlines** 🕾 07/ 5448-8700. **Virgin Blue** 🕾 13-6789.

BUS TRAVEL

SunCoast Pacific offers daily bus service from Brisbane Airport and the Roma Street Transit Centre in Brisbane. Distances are short: from Brisbane to Caloundra takes 1½ hours; from Caloundra to Mooloolaba takes

30 minutes; from Mooloolaba to Maroochydore takes 10 minutes; from Maroochydore to Noosa takes 30 minutes; and from Noosa to Tewantin takes 10 minutes. Sun Air Bus Service has daily links from Brisbane and Maroochy airports to Sunshine Coast towns. Henry's Transport Group runs services from Maroochy Airport to the northern Sunshine Coast as far as Tewantin.

Greyhound Australia and Oz Experience offer approximately 12 services daily into Airlie Beach from Sydney and Brisbane, and many towns between, as well as from Cairns.

🚌 **Greyhound Australia** ☎ 13-1499. **Henry's Transport Group** ☎ 07/5474-0199. **Oz Experience** ☎ 1300/300028. **Sun Air Bus Service** ☎ 07/5478-2811. **SunCoast Pacific** ☎ 07/3236-1901or 07/5449-9966.

CAR RENTAL

Several international companies have offices on the Sunshine Coast. Avis has offices in Maroochydore, Maroochy Airport, and Noosa Heads. Budget has one of the biggest rental-car fleets on the Sunshine Coast. Hertz has offices in Noosa Heads and at Maroochy Airport. Thrifty has an office at Maroochy Airport. Europcar has an office in Airlie Beach.

🚗 **Avis** ✉ Shop 6, Beach Rd. and Ocean St., Maroochydore ☎ 07/5443-5055 ✉ Maroochy Airport, Friendship Dr., Mudjimba ☎ 07/5443-5055 ✉ Shop 1, Hastings St. and Noosa Dr., Noosa Heads ☎ 07/5447-4933. **Budget** ✉ 146 Alexandra Parade, Alexandra Headland ☎ 07/5443-6555. **Europcar** ✉ 269 Shute Harbour Rd., Airlie Beach ☎ 07/4946-6359. **Hertz** ✉ 16 Noosa Dr., Noosa Heads ☎ 07/5447-2253 ✉ Maroochy Airport, Friendship Dr., Mudjimba ☎ 07/5448-9731. **Thrifty** ✉ Maroochy Airport, Friendship Dr., Mudjimba ☎ 07/5443-1733.

CAR TRAVEL

A car is a necessity on the Sunshine Coast. The traditional route to the coast from Brisbane is along the Bruce Highway (Highway 1) to the Glass House Mountains, with a turnoff at Cooroy. This makes for about a two-hour drive to Noosa, the heart of the area. However, the motorway may be marginally faster. Turn off the Bruce Highway at Tanawha (toward Mooloolaba) and follow the signs. The most scenic route is to turn off the Bruce Highway to Caloundra and follow the coast to Noosa Heads.

EMERGENCIES

In an emergency, dial **000** to reach an ambulance, the police, or the fire department.

🏥 **Hospitals Caloundra Hospital** ✉ West Terr., Caloundra ☎ 07/5491-1888. **Nambour General Hospital** ✉ Hospital Rd., Nambour ☎ 07/5470-6600. **Whitsunday Medical Centre** ✉ 400 Shute Harbour Rd., Airlie Beach ☎ 07/4946-6275.

🏥 **Pharmacies Caloundra Central Pharmacy** ✉ 45 Bulcock St., Caloundra ☎ 07/5491-1050. **Noosa Heads Day and Night Pharmacy** ✉ 32 Hastings St., Noosa Heads ☎ 07/5447-3298.

MAIL, SHIPPING & THE INTERNET

The Australia Post branches are open weekdays 8:30–5:30. Internet Arcadia in Noosa is open weekdays 9–7 and 9–5 on Saturday.

🌐 **Internet Café Internet Arcadia** ✉ Shop 3, Arcadia Walk, Noosa Junction ☎ 07/5474-8999.

⚡ Mail Services Australia Post ✉ 21 Ocean St., Maroochydore ☎ 13-1318 ✉ Shop 6A, 366-370 Shute Harbour Rd., Shute Harbour ☎ 07/4946-6515.

MONEY MATTERS

Commonwealth Bank of Australia will cash traveler's checks and change money. ATMs and money changers are plentiful and reliable along the Sunshine Coast.

⚡ Banks Commonwealth Bank of Australia ✉166 Horton Parade, Maroochydore ☎ 07/5443-8693 ✉ 380 Shute Harbour Rd., Airlie Beach ☎ 07/4746-7433 ✉ 25 Brisbane Rd., Mooloolaba ☎ 07/5444-3166 ✉ 24 Sunshine Beach Rd., Noosa Heads ☎ 07/5447-5555.

TOURS

Adventures Sunshine Coast offers one-day trips from Noosa Heads and Caloundra that take you walking, canoeing, rock climbing, and/or rappelling among rain forests and mountains.

Clip Clop Treks conducts horse-riding treks, ranging from half-day excursions to weeklong camping expeditions.

Southern Cross Motorcycle Tours provides one of the best ways to get a feel for the Sunshine Coast: by riding a Harley-Davidson motorcycle from the beach to the Blackall Range. The company has a team of experienced guides who know the area and will take you on a half- or full-day's excursion on the back of a bike.

Koala Adventures, part of a chain of backpacker hostels along the Queensland coast, runs three-night/two-day sailing trips around the Whitsunday Islands. Oz Sail runs leisurely sailing and snorkeling trips around the islands on any of its eight vessels.

⚡ Adventures Sunshine Coast ✉ 69 Alfriston Dr., Buderim ☎ 07/5444-8824. **Clip Clop Treks** ☎ 07/5449-1254. **Koala Adventures** ✉ Koala Backers Lodge, Shute Harbour Rd. ☎ 07/4946-6001 or 1800/466444. **Oz Sail** ✉ 344 Shute Harbour Rd., Airlie Beach ☎ 07/4948-1388. **Southern Cross Motorcycle Tours** ✉ Box 7175, Sippy Downs 4556 ☎ 1300/665386 ⊕ www.motorcycle-tours.com.au.

TRAIN TRAVEL

Trains leave regularly from Roma Street Transit Centre in Brisbane en route to Nambour, the business hub of the Sunshine Coast. They continue on to Yandina and Eumundi and other noncoastal towns. Once in Nambour, however, a car is a necessity, so it may make more sense to drive from Brisbane.

Queensland Rail operates approximately eight trains weekly into the Proserpine Railway Station, about 27 km (17 mi) from Airlie Beach.

⚡ Proserpine Railway Station ✉ Hinschen St., Proserpine ☎ 13-1617. **Roma Street Transit Centre** ✉ Roma St., Brisbane ☎ 13-2232.

VISITOR INFORMATION

⚡ Caloundra Tourist Information Centre ✉ 7 Caloundra Rd., Caloundra ☎ 07/5491-0202 or 1800/644969. **Maroochy Tourist Information Centre** ✉ Aerodrome Rd. and 6th Ave., Maroochydore ☎ 07/5479-1566 or 1800/882052. **Noosa Information Centre** ✉ Hastings St. and the roundabout, Noosa Heads ☎ 07/5447-4988 or 1800/

448833 ⊕ www.tourismnoosa.com.au. **Whitsunday Information Centre** ⊠ Airlie Beach 4802 ☎ 07/4945-3711 or 1800/801252 ⊕ www.whitsundayinformation.com.au.

FRASER ISLAND

Some 200 km (124 mi) north of Brisbane, Fraser Island, at 1,014 square km (630 square mi), is both the largest of Queensland's islands and the most unusual. Originally known as K'gari to the local Butchulla Aboriginal people, the island was later named after Eliza Fraser, who in 1836 was shipwrecked here and lived with local Aborigines for several weeks. It's the world's largest sand island—instead of coral reefs and coconut palms, it has wildflower-dotted meadows, freshwater lakes, a teeming bird population, dense stands of rain forest, towering sand dunes, and sculpted, multicolor sand cliffs along its east coast. That lineup has won the island a place on UNESCO's World Heritage list. The surf fishing is legendary, and humpback whales and their calves can be seen wintering in Hervey Bay between May and September. The island also has interesting Aboriginal sites dating back more than a millennium.

Hervey Bay is the name given to the expanse of water between Fraser Island and the Queensland coast. It's also the generic name given to a conglomeration of four nearby coastal towns—Urangan, Pialba, Scarness, and Torquay—that have grown into a single settlement. This township is the jumping-off point for most excursions. (Note that maps and road signs usually refer to individual town names, not Hervey Bay.)

Fraser's east coast marks the intersection of two serious Australian passions: an addiction to the beach and a love affair with the motor vehicle. Unrestricted access has made this coast a giant sandbox for four-wheel-drive vehicles during busy school-holiday periods. All vehicles entering the island by car ferry from the mainland towns of Hervey Bay, River Heads, or Rainbow Beach must have a one-month Vehicle Access Permit (A\$31.85 for mainland vehicles, A\$42.80 if bought on the island). There are a number of places in southeast Queensland where you can obtain these and camping permits for the island. (If you prefer your wilderness *sans* dune-buggying, head for the unspoiled interior of the island.) For the closest permit center, contact **Naturally Queensland** (⊠ 160 Ann St., Brisbane 4000 ☎ 07/3227-8185 ⊕ www. epa.qld.gov.au).

Exploring Fraser Island

Note that swimming in the ocean off the east coast is not recommended because of the rough conditions and sharks that hunt close to shore.

Highlights of a drive along the east coast, which is known as Seventy-Five Mile Beach for its sheer distance, include **Eli Creek,** a great freshwater swimming hole. North of this popular spot lies the rusting hulk of the *Maheno,* half buried in the sand, a roost for seagulls and a prime hunting ground for anglers when the tailor are running. Once a luxury passenger steamship that operated between Australia and New Zealand (and served as a hospital ship during World War I), it was wrecked during a cyclone in 1935 as it was being towed to Japan to be sold for scrap metal. North of the wreck are the **Pinnacles**—dramatic, deep-red cliff formations. About 20 km (14 mi) south of Eli Creek, and surrounded by massive sand-blow (or dune), is **Lake Wabby,** the deepest of the island's lakes.

Great Sandy National Park (☎ 07/4121–1800) covers the top third of the island. Beaches around Indian Head are known for their shell middens—shell heaps that were left behind after Aboriginal feasting. The head's name is another kind of relic: Captain James Cook saw Aborigines standing on the headland as he sailed past, and he therefore named the area after inhabitants he believed to be "Indians." Farther north, past Waddy Point, is one of Fraser Island's most magnificent variations on sand: wind and time have created enormous dunes, and nearby at Orchid Beach are a series of bubbling rock pools known as Champagne Pools.

The center of the island is a quiet, natural garden of paperbark swamps, giant satinay and brush box forests, wildflower heaths, and 40 freshwater lakes. The spectacularly clear **Lake McKenzie,** ringed by a beach of incandescent whiteness, is the perfect place for a refreshing swim.

The island's excellent network of walking trails converges at **Central Station,** a former logging camp at the center of the island. Services here are limited to a map board, parking lot, and campground. It's a promising place for spotting dingoes, however. Comparative isolation has meant that Fraser Island's dingoes are the most purebred in Australia. They're also wild animals, so remember: don't feed them, watch from a distance, and keep a close eye on children.

A boardwalk heads south from Central Station to **Wanggoolba Creek,** a favorite spot for photographers. The little stream snakes through a green palm forest, trickling over a bed of white sand between clumps of rare angiopteris fern. One trail from Central Station leads through rain forest—incredibly growing straight out of the sand—to **Pile Valley,** which has a stand of giant satinay trees.

Where to Stay & Eat

Because the entire island is a World Heritage national park, permits for camping (A\$4 per person per night) are required. You also need a one-month Vehicle Access Permit, which is A\$31.85 for mainland vehicles, A\$42.80 for vehicles bought on the island. Although you can pitch a tent anywhere you don't see a NO CAMPING sign, there are also designated camping areas with toilet blocks, picnic tables, and walking trails. At the island's only official campground, Frasers at Cathedral Beach, campsites cost A\$18 per night for one or two people (A\$4 permit not required). The Department of Environment and Heritage manages the island, and you can obtain permits from their offices and some travel agencies in southeast Queensland. For the name of the closest center, contact **Naturally Queensland** (✉ 160 Ann St., Brisbane 4000 ☎ 07/ 3227–8186 ⊕ www.epa.qld.gov.au).

$$$–$$$$ ✕▨ **Kingfisher Bay Resort and Village.** This stylish, high-tech marriage of
Fodor's Choice glass, stainless steel, dark timber, and corrugated iron nestles in the tree-
★ covered dunes of the island's west coast. The impressive lobby, with its
cathedral ceiling and high-gloss polished floorboards, leads out to
wraparound decks for outdoor dining areas and one of the resort's four
pools. Lodgings here include villas, elegantly furnished hotel rooms with
balconies, and wilderness lodges for groups. Rangers conduct informa-
tive four-wheel-drive tours and free nature walks, and children can join
junior ranger programs. Free fishing classes are available, as are boat rentals;
the chefs here will even cook your catch! The first-class menu at Seabelle's
incorporates kangaroo, emu, and crocodile, as well as local island fruits.
Maheno Restaurant has nightly buffet dinners from A$40 to A$55 per
person. ⌂ *Box 913, Brisbane 4001* ☎ *07/4120–3333 or 1800/072555*
🖨 *07/3221–3270* ⊕ *www.kingfisherbay.com* ➱ *152 rooms, 110 villas,
180 beds in lodges* ♢ *3 restaurants, 2 tennis courts, 4 pools, hair salon,
spa, boating, fishing, hiking, volleyball, 4 bars, shops, babysitting, chil-
dren's programs (ages 6–14), dry cleaning, laundry facilities, business ser-
vices, convention center, meeting rooms, car rental, travel services, free
parking, no-smoking rooms; no a/c in some rooms* ▤ *AE, DC, MC,.*

$ ✕▨ **Eurong Beach Resort.** Right on the beach and set in lush rain forest,
this east-coast resort has the best of Fraser Island at its doorstep. Lake
McKenzie and Central Station are only 20 minutes away, and the fa-
mous Seventy-Five Mile Beach, Eli Creek, and other coastal attractions
are an easy drive away. Lodgings here range from rooms with double
or twin beds to two-bedroom apartments and A-frame cottages with full
kitchens that can accommodate eight people. Some units overlook the
ocean; others the resort and pool area. You can choose from one of three
alternating theme buffet dinners (Australian, Mexican, or Mediter-
ranean—A$22 per person), or order from an à la carte menu of seafood
specialties. The resort has a store that sells just about everything from
food to fuel and fishing gear. ⌂ *Box 7332, Hervey Bay 4655* ☎ *07/
4127–9122* 🖨 *07/4127–9179* ⊕ *www.eurong.com* ➱ *24 rooms, 16
apartments, 2 cottages* ♢ *Restaurant, grocery, BBQs, some kitchens,
tennis, 2 pools, beach, boating, fishing, bar, meeting rooms, travel ser-
vices, car rental, free parking* ▤ *AE, MC, V.*

$ ▨ **Fraser Island Wilderness Retreat.** This cluster of wooden beachside cot-
tages—some one-bedroom, some family size—is nestled in the Happy
Valley hillsides, halfway down the island's eastern coast. Each cottage
has a kitchen, but there's also a bar, and a bistro that serves three meals
daily. This is the most central location on the island, just a 15-minute
drive from Eli Creek and 20 minutes from the *Maheno* shipwreck and
the Pinnacles. ⌂ *Box 5224, Torquay 4655* ☎ *07/4125–2342 or 1800/
446655* 🖨 *07/4125–5514* ➱ *9 cottages* ♢ *Restaurant, grocery, cable
TV, pool, bar, free parking; no a/c, no room phones* ▤ *AE, MC, V.*

Fraser Island A to Z

AIR TRAVEL

Sunshine Express, a subsidiary of Qantas, has several flights daily be-
tween Brisbane and Hervey Bay Airport on the mainland. The airport

runway was extended in August 2005, and the island now has direct services from Sydney, operated by both Jetstar and Virgin Blue.

🛪 **Airport Hervey Bay Airport** ⊠ Don Adams Dr., Hervey Bay ☎ 07/4124-9313 or 07/4125-3600.

🛪 **Airlines Jetstar** ☎ 13-1538. **Sunshine Express** ☎ 07/5448-8700. **Virgin Blue** ☎ 13-6789.

BOAT & FERRY TRAVEL

Several vehicle and passenger ferry services connect the mainland with Fraser Island. The Rainbow Venture & Eliza Fraser ferries run continuously 7 AM–5 PM between Inskip Point near Rainbow Beach on the mainland (between Brisbane and Hervey Bay via the Bruce Highway) and Hooks Point at the southern end of the island. The round-trip fare is A$60 per vehicle, including driver and passengers.

The Fraser Dawn ferry departs from Hervey Bay Boat Harbour (on the mainland) for the one-hour journey to Moon Point (on Fraser Island) three times a day. Round-trip fare is A$110 for a vehicle, driver, and three passengers. The Kingfisher Bay ferry connects River Heads (on the mainland) with Kingfisher Bay Resort in 45 minutes. Trips run three times daily, and round-trip fare is A$110 for a vehicle, driver, and three passengers.

🚢 **Fraser Dawn** ☎ 07/4125-4444. **Kingfisher Bay** ☎ 1800/072555. **Rainbow Venture & Eliza Fraser** ☎ 07/5486-3227.

BUS TRAVEL

Greyhound Australia and Sunshine Pacific operate from Brisbane to Hervey Bay and Maryborough, a township just south of Hervey Bay.

🚌 **Greyhound Australia** ⊠ Bay Central Coach Terminal, 1st Ave., Pialba ☎ 13-2030 ⊕ www.greyhound.com.au. **Sunshine Pacific Coaches** ⊠ 11 Renee St., Noosaville ☎ 07/5449-9966 ⊕ www.greyhound.com.au.

CAR RENTAL

You can rent four-wheel-drive vehicles at Kingfisher Bay Resort and Village, the Eurong Beach Resort, and Fraser Island Wilderness Retreat for around A$195 a day.

🚗 **Fraser Island Wilderness Retreat** ☎ 07/4127-9144. **Kingfisher Bay Resort and Village** ☎ 07/4120-3333.

CAR TRAVEL

The southernmost tip of Fraser Island is 200 km (124 mi) north of Brisbane. The best access is via vehicle ferry from Rainbow Beach, or from the Hervey Bay area, another 90 km (56 mi) away. For Rainbow Beach, take the Bruce Highway toward Gympie, then follow the signs to Rainbow Beach. For Hervey Bay, head north to Maryborough, then follow signs to Urangan.

Four-wheel-drive rentals may be cheaper on the mainland, but factoring in the ferry ticket makes it less expensive to get your rental on-island. Most commodities, including gas, are more expensive on the island than the mainland.

EMERGENCIES

In an emergency, dial **000** to reach an ambulance, the police, or the fire department.

Fraser Island does not have a resident doctor. Emergency medical assistance can be obtained at the ranger stations in Eurong, Central Station, Waddy Point, and Dundubara. Kingfisher Bay Resort has first-aid facilities and resident nursing staff.

🚩 **Central Station Ranger Station** ☎ 07/4127-9191. **Dundubara Ranger Station** ☎ 07/4126-9138. **Eurong Ranger Station** ☎ 07/4127-9128. **Waddy Point Ranger Station** ☎ 07/4127-9190.

TOURS

Air Fraser Island operates whale-watching flights of 45 minutes or more across Hervey Bay between July and October, and scenic flights and day trips to the island year-round. Prices start at A$50 per person. You can also get packages that include renting a four-wheel-drive vehicle for A$110 per person.

For day-trippers, the Kingfisher passenger ferry runs between Urangan and North White Cliffs, near Kingfisher Bay Resort. The A$35 fare includes morning tea, lunch, and a ranger-led walking tour.

Whale Connections has daily whale-watching tours July to November. These begin at Urangan Boat Harbour in Hervey Bay.

🚩 **Air Fraser Island** ☎ 07/4125-3600. **Kingfisher** ☎ 07/4125-5155. **Whale Connections** ☎ 07/4124-7247.

VISITOR INFORMATION

Fraser Coast Tour Booking Office and Whale Watch Centre, on the mainland, is a good source of information, maps, and brochures. The center will also help you with tour and accommodations bookings. Another good information source is the Hervey Bay Tourist and Visitors Centre.

🚩 **Fraser Coast Tour Booking Office and Whale Watch Centre** ✉ Buccaneer Ave., Urangan ☎ 07/4128-9800. **Hervey Bay Tourist and Visitors Centre** ✉ 353 the Esplanade, Hervey Bay ☎ 07/4124-4050.

TOWNSVILLE & MAGNETIC ISLAND

Townsville—and its adjacent twin city of Thuringowa—make up Australia's largest tropical city, with a combined population of 150,000. It's the commercial capital of the north, and a major center for education, scientific research, and defense. Spread along the banks of Ross Creek and around the pink granite outcrop of Castle Hill, Townsville is a pleasant city of palm-fringed malls, historic colonial buildings, and lots of parkland and gardens. It's also the stepping-off point for Magnetic Island, one of the state's largest islands and a haven for wildlife.

Townsville

The summit of **Castle Hill,** 1 km (½ mi) from the city center, provides great views of the city as well as the islands of the Great Barrier Reef.

While you're perched on top, think about the proud local resident who, along with several scout troops, spent years in the 1970s piling rubble onto the peak to try to add the 23 feet that would officially make it Castle Mountain. (Technically speaking, a rise has to exceed 1,000 feet to be called a mountain, and this one tops out at just 977 feet.) Most people walk to the top, along a steep walking track that doubles as one of Queensland's most scenic jogging routes.

Reef HQ, on the waterfront, only a few minutes' walk from the city center, has the largest natural-coral aquarium in the world—a living slice of the Great Barrier Reef. There are more than 100 species of hard coral, 30 soft corals, and hundreds of fish. Also here are an enclosed underwater walkway, touch pool, theater, café, and shop. ⊠ *2–68 Flinders St. E* ☎ *07/4750–0800* ⊒ *A$19.50* ◷ *Daily 9–5.*

The **Museum of Tropical Queensland,** next door to Reef HQ, displays relics of the HMS *Pandora,* which sank in 1791 while carrying 14 crew members of the *Bounty* to London to stand trial for mutiny. Also on display are Australian dinosaur fossils and cultural exhibits about the Torres Strait Islands and Aboriginal peoples. ⊠ *70–102 Flinders St. E (near Reef HQ at very end of road)* ☎ *07/4726–0600* ⊒ *A$9* ◷ *Daily 9–5.*

A stroll along **Flinders Street** will show you some of Townsville's turn-of-the-20th-century colonial architecture. **Magnetic House,** the **Bank** (now a lounge bar), and other buildings have been beautifully restored. The old **Queens Hotel** is built in Classical Revival style, as is the 1885 **Perc Tucker Regional Gallery,** which was originally a bank. The former post office, which is now the Brewery, had an impressive **masonry clock tower** (⊠ Flinders and Denham Sts.) when it was erected in 1889; though the tower was dismantled in 1942 so it wouldn't be a target for World War II air raids, it was put up again in 1964.

The Strand, a spectacular 2½-km (1½-mi) beachfront boulevard, is lined with restaurants, cafés, bars, picnic and barbecue areas, swimming enclosures, restaurants, water-sports facilities, and a water playground for children. The avenue runs along Cleveland Bay, with wonderful views to Magnetic Island.

At the **Townsville Common** nature preserve, spoonbills, jabiru storks, pied geese, herons, and ibis, plus occasional wallabies, goannas, and echidnas, make their homes without cages or enclosures. You might even spot a dingo. Most of the birds leave the swamplands from May through August, the dry months, but they're all back by October. The Common is open every day from 6:30 AM to 6:30 PM and entrance is free. To get there, take the Cape Pallarenda Road at the north of the city to the northern suburb of Pallarenda, 7 km (4½ mi) away.

Queen's Gardens is a popular spot for weddings, as well as a lovely place to spend a cool couple of hours away from the scorching coast. The park, which is about a tenth of an acre, is bordered with frangipani and towering Moreton Bay Fig trees, whose unique hanging roots and branches create a mysterious veiled entryway to the grounds. ⊠ *Gregory St. near Warburton St.* ☎ *No phone* ⊒ *Free* ◷ *Daily dawn–dusk.*

THE OUTBACK

QUEENSLAND'S OUTBACK REGION is a vast and exciting place to visit, filled with real Crocodile Dundee types and people used to relying on each other in isolated townships. If you choose to tour this vast, rugged region, there are three popular routes.

The Warrego Highway Route

If you travel northwest from Brisbane on the Warrego Highway you'll pass through the rich farming country known as the Downs and Western Downs for some 500 km (300 mi), passing through the towns of Toowoomba, Dalby, Chinchilla, and Roma. The scenery starts to change and become more arid and dusty as you approach Mitchell, which is said to be the gateway to the Outback.

Located 587 km (364 mi) northwest of Brisbane, Mitchell became something of an oasis town with the opening of the **Great Artesian Spa** (⊠ 4 Cambridge St., Mitchell ☎ 07/4623–1073) in 1998. The spa's two lagoon-shape pools are fed by mineralized waters from the Great Artesian Basin, a vast underground natural spring that covers an area of more than 1,711,000 square km (660,450 square mi), or about one-fifth of Australia. The pools, which are in a modern complex with landscaped grounds, are for soaking—not swimming—and an hour spent in the waters is said to revive the spirits and ease aches and pain. Admission is A$5; the spa is open daily 9–5.

The Capricorn Highway Route

Heading inland from Rockhampton along Route 66 means you can stop at the **gem fields** near the towns of Rubyvale, Sapphire, Anakie, and the Willows. These towns have a Wild West, frontier feel, and the 25,000-acre area around them comprises one of the world's richest source of sapphires. Commercial and tourist mines are scattered throughout the fields, so you can fossick for your own gems; if you make a find you can visit one of the 100-plus gem cutters in the area to have your jewel cut and and polished. At **Gemfest** (☎ 07/4985–4225 ⊕ www.gemfest.com.au), held in the second week of August, miners, merchants, and traders converge to swap, sell, and barter their wares.

Before continuing to Longreach, 400 km (320 mi) to the west, you might think about swinging southward and spending a night or two at **Carnarvon Gorge.** This amazing series of towering sandstone cliffs, which stretches for more than 30 km (19 mi), is the most-visited site in Carnarvon National Park. Walking trails here lead to the Gallery and Cathedral Cave, painted with ancient Aboriginal rock art. The park has a campsite and other accommodations; phone the **Park Ranger's Office** (☎ 07/4987–4505) for information. Carnarvon National Park is 230 km (144 mi) south of Emerald via the Gregory and Dawson highways.

At Longreach you'll find one of the highlights of the Queensland Outback, the **Stockman's Hall of Fame,** which brings to life the early days of European settlers in Australia. Exhibits on everything from Aboriginal history to droving (moving cattle from town to market over vast areas of land), mustering (rounding up cattle), and bush crafts pay tribute to the pioneers who sought to tame the Australian Outback. ⊠ Off Matilda Hwy., Longreach ☎ 07/4658–2166 ⊕ www.outbackheritage.com.au ⊠ A$20 ⊙ Daily 9–5.

If you continue northwest of Longreach for another 200 km (125 mi), you'll come to the town of Winton, home of the interactive **Waltzing Matilda Centre.** An art gallery, history museum, restaurant, and sound-and-light show are all here, as is the Qantilda Museum, a diverse collection of Outback pioneering memorabilia.

✉ Elderslie St., Winton ☎ 07/4657–1466 🎟 A$14 ⊙ Daily 9–5.

A bit farther north, just outside the little town of Kyuna, you can stop to dip your toes in **Combo Waterhole**, where A. B. "Banjo" Paterson wrote the lyrics for "Waltzing Matilda," Australia's unofficial national anthem.

The Overlander's Highway Route

Heading west from Townsville on the Flinders Highway (also known as the Overlander's Way) will give you the chance to stop at the once-prosperous gold-mining town of **Charters Towers**, arguably the most beautiful Queensland inland city, with more than 60 buildings of historical significance. Farther west is Hughenden, known as dinosaur country because of the many ancient fossils found in the region. (The area was once on the edge of a vast, prehistoric inland sea, where terrestrial dinosaurs and marine reptiles roamed.) "Hughie," a Muttaburrasaurus skeleton, is on display at the **Flinders Discovery Centre** (✉ 37 Gray St., Hughenden ☎ 07/4741–1021), along with other exhibits.

From Hughenden you can continue via Cloncurry to Mount Isa, a city of 22,000 people from 50 different nations, where the sprawling Mount Isa Mine comprises Australia's deepest underground mine and the world's largest producer of copper, silver, lead, and zinc. The largest rodeo in the Southern Hemisphere takes place here each July. Mount Isa is also a good jumping-off point for exploring the spring-fed rivers and gorges of **Lawn Hill National Park** (☎ 07/3737–5572), where you can canoe amid freshwater crocodiles and camp in the wilderness.

Mount Isa is also home to the **Outback@Isa Explorers Park,** an interpretative center in the heart of Mount Isa, which has fossil exhibits from the Riversleigh Fossil site, some 300 km (186 mi) away. Here, you can participate in the Mount Isa Underground Mine Experience, where you'll dress in a miner's outfit—hard hat, white suit, and headlamp—and tour a "mock-up" mine shaft 49½ feet below the surface. ✉ 19 Marion St., Mount Isa ☎ 1300/659660 🎟 Mine and all museums A$50, mine only A$40, Riversleigh Fossil and Mount Isa history museum only A$10 ⊙ Daily 8:30–5.

If you're a fan of the movie Crocodile Dundee, you might want to head south from Cloncurry via Route 66 to the tiny dusty town of McKinlay. This little hamlet's claim to fame is the low-framed, rustic **Walkabout Creek Hotel** (✉ Middleton St., McKinlay ☎ 07/4746–8424), which was featured in the movie. You can stay here for the night or just have a pint at the pub and pretend you're Paul Hogan.

When traveling any of these routes by car, be sure to take the necessary precautions. Use a four-wheel-drive vehicle—some roads are unpaved and become slippery after it rains—and always carry spare water, a first-aid kit, a map, and sufficient fuel to get to the next town (this often means carrying spare gas tanks). If you're traveling into remote areas, advise local police or another responsible person of your travel plans and report back to them when you return; and if you have an emergency while on the road, call **000** from the nearest phone to reach an ambulance or the police.

If you prefer to let someone else do the driving, you can travel through the Outback by bus, as well. **Greyhound Australia** (☎ 13–1499 ⊕ www.greyhound.com.au) services all of the towns on the Flinders Highway between Townsville and Mount Isa, with connections to the Northern Territory. It also travels between Brisbane, Charleville, Longreach, and Winton to Cloncurry and from Rockhampton to Longreach via the gemstone towns.

off the beaten path

BILLABONG SANCTUARY – This 22-acre nature park 17 km (11 mi) south of Townsville shelters crocodiles, koalas, wombats, dingoes, wallabies, and birds—including cassowaries, kookaburras, and beautiful red-tailed black cockatoos. Educational shows throughout the day give you the chance to learn more about these native animals and their habits. The sanctuary is a 20-minute drive south of Townsville and is well signposted. ⊠ *Bruce Hwy., Nome 4810* ☎ *07/ 4778–8344* 🖾 *A$23* ◷ *Daily 8–5.*

Where to Stay & Eat

$–$$ ✕ **Australian Hotel Café.** This restored 1888 building, with its beautiful bull-nose veranda and original iron lacework, is a classic example of Townsville colonial architecture. Rumor has it that, back when it was a hotel, actor Errol Flynn once stayed here and paid for his keep by selling autographs. Today the building contains a public bar, a wine bar (open on Friday and Saturday nights), and a courtyard restaurant serving everything from gourmet pizzas and curries to a "reef and beef" speciality of steak and seafood. ⊠ *11 Palmer St.* ☎ *07/4722–6910* ⊕ *www. theaussie.com* ▤ *AE, DC, MC, V.*

$–$$ ✕ **Yotz Watergrill + Bar.** Right on the seafront, this restaurant has great views across Cleveland Bay. The clientele and atmosphere are casual chic, and if you're looking to "see and be seen" or to impress a client, this is the perfect spot. Seafood is the specialty, and grazing menus let you design your own platters with treats like Moreton Bay bugs and salt-and-pepper squid, warm Asian duck salad, and seafood chowder. Main courses include the medley of oysters and the sizzling octopus platter. ⊠ *Gregory St. Headland, the Strand* ☎ *07/4724–5488* ⊕ *www.yotz. com.au* ⚑ *Reservations essential* ▤ *AE, DC, MC, V.*

$$–$$$ ✕🍴 **Jupiter's Townsville Hotel and Casino.** Dominating Townsville's waterfront area, this hotel complex is the city's entertainment center. Rooms, which have terrific views across the bay to Magnetic Island from all 11 floors, are large, bright, and colorful—and surprisingly quiet, given their proximity to North Queensland's first casino. The Quarterdeck restaurant is on the marina and is a great place for sunset drinks, while Aqua overlooks the tropical pool and serves a great seafood buffet (A$35) every night. ⊠ *Sir Leslie Thiess Dr., Box 1223, 4810* ☎ *07/ 4722–2333* 🖨 *07/4772–4741* ⊕ *www.jupiterstownsville.com.au* ⚑ *193 rooms, 16 suites* ♿ *3 restaurants, room service, room TVs with movies, 2 tennis courts, pool, gym, massage, sauna, spa, 5 bars, casino, babysitting, laundry service, business services, meeting room, travel services, free parking, no-smoking rooms* ▤ *AE, DC, MC, V.*

$–$$ 🍴 **Historic Yongala Lodge.** This late-19th-century lodge was originally the home of building magnate Matthew Rooney, whose family was shipwrecked off the Townsville coast on the SS *Yongala* in 1911. Rooms here are decorated with antiques, old photographs, and wrought-iron ceiling fittings. The dining room serves traditional Greek and Australian meals; you can also eat outside on the wide, colonial-style veranda. ⊠ *11 Fryer St., 4810* ☎ *07/4772–4633* 🖨 *07/4721–1074* ⊕ *www. historicyongala.com.au* ⚑ *18 rooms* ♿ *Restaurant, room service, refrigerators, in-room VCRs, saltwater pool, bar, laundry facilities, meeting rooms, free parking* ▤ *AE, DC, MC, V.*

$ ▦ **Seagull's Resort on the Seafront.** Three acres of palm tree–studded tropical gardens form the backdrop for this very pleasant, two-story brick complex. Cane furniture and tropical color schemes decorate the spacious hotel rooms; self-contained apartments and suites with kitchenettes are also available. Seagull's restaurant serves generous portions of local seafood. The resort is 2½ km (1½ mi) from the city center (with free shuttle service) and about a 10-minute walk from the beach. ⊠ *74 the Esplanade, 4810* ☎ *07/4721–3111* ⊕ *www.seagulls.com.au* ⇗ *55 rooms, 11 suites, 4 apartments* � *Restaurant, room service, some kitchenettes, some in-room hot tubs, room TVs with movies, tennis court, 2 pools, bar, playground, dry cleaning, laundry facilities, Internet room, business services, convention center, meeting room, travel services, free parking* ⊟ *AE, DC, MC, V.*

¢–$ ▦ **Rocks Guesthouse.** In its past incarnations this 1886 Victorian-style home has functioned as a hospital, upscale guesthouse, and housing for U.S. Army personnel during World War II. Today it's an elegant B&B with a vast dining room, billiard room, polished wood floors, and bric-a-brac everywhere, thanks to collectors and owners Joe Sproats and Jenny Ginger. Complimentary sherry is provided on the veranda evenings at 6 PM. You can walk to the city and surrounding attractions. ⊠ *20 Cleveland Terr., 4810* ☎ *07/4771–5700* 🖶 *07/4771–5711* ⊕ *www.therocksguesthouse.com* ⇗ *7 rooms, 4 with bath; 1 self-contained apartment* ⅃ *Dining room, outdoor hot tub, billiards, Internet room, croquet, bar, meeting room, free parking; no room phones, no TV in some rooms, no smoking* ⊟ *MC, V* ⧖ *CP.*

Nightlife & the Arts

THE ARTS **Civic Theatre** (⊠ 41 Boundary St. ☎ 07/4727–9797 ⊕ www.townsville. qld.gov.au/theatre) hosts some of the state's finest performances from opera, musicals, comedy, ballet, and popular singers. Sixties' legend Gene Pitney trod the boards in 2005, as did Canadian country singer Terri Clark.

Perc Tucker Gallery (⊠ Denham St. and Flinders Mall ☎ 07/4727–9671), housed in one of Townsville's finest heritage buildings, has a diverse program of local, national, and international exhibitions, with an emphasis on North Queensland art and musical performances. It's open weekdays 10–5, weekends 10–2.

Townsville Entertainment and Convention Centre (⊠ Entertainment Dr. ☎ 07/4771–4000 ⊕ www.tecc.net.au) can seat 4,000 and has hosted such international acts as Tom Jones and Tina Turner. The center is also the home of the Townsville Crocodiles National Basketball League team.

NIGHTLIFE For gamblers, the main attraction in Townsville is the **Jupiters Townsville Hotel and Casino** (⊠ Sir Leslie Thiess Dr. ☎ 07/4722–2333), which has a full choice of gaming opportunities including minibaccarat, sic bo, blackjack, roulette, keno, and slot machines, as well as the Australian game of Two-up. It's open from 10 AM to 3 AM daily.

Bank Lounge Bar (⊠ Flinders St. E ☎ 07/4721–1916) is another one of Townsville's first buildings—it dates from 1888—that's now seeing a lot of modern, and late-night, action. It's the place to go if you want to dance to the latest sounds played by the city's coolest DJs.

The Brewery (✉ 252 Flinders St. ☎ 07/4724–2999), once the original Townsville Post Office, now houses a bar that also serves light meals and a microbrewery. The owners have done a fine job of combining ultramodern wood-and-chrome finishing with the original design and furnishings from its days as a post office; the bar itself is the old stamp counter. It's open 7 AM–2 AM every day.

For a rollicking Irish-style night on the town, hit **Molly Malone's** (✉ Flinders St. E near intersection with Wickham St. ☎ 07/4771–3423). You can choose to listen to live bands or groove to the latest tunes spun by DJs at the adjoining Mantax nightclub on weekends.

Palmer Street, on the city's south bank, is regarded as the cosmopolitan precinct. It's become the place to be seen on Friday and Saturday nights; there's always a new bar or restaurant to sample here. Overlooking Ross Marina, the avenue is lined with alfresco restaurants and popular watering holes like Cactus Jack's Bar and Grill (famed for its frozen margaritas), Michel's Café and Bar, and the Rhino Bar, where the latest drink is the Vodkatini.

Sports & the Outdoors

BEACHES Townsville is blessed with a golden, 2-km (1-mi) strand of beach along the northern edge of the city. Four man-made headlands jut into the sea, and a long pier is just the spot for fishing. There is no surf, as the beach is sheltered by the reef and Magnetic Island. The Strand has a permanent swimming enclosure known as the Rockpool, which is fitted with temporary nets (to keep the box jellyfish out) during the summer months.

BOATING **Magnetic Island Sea Kayaks** (✉ 93 Horseshoe Bay Rd., Horseshoe Bay ☎ 07/4778–5424) organizes kayak trips to the quiet bays of Magnetic Island. Tours include a tropical breakfast on a secluded beach, and cost A$59 per person.

Mud Hut Mangrove Adventures (✉ 32 Surrey St. ☎ 07/4728–4499 ⊕ www. mudhutadventures.com) hires modern boats from Townsville, Magnetic Island, and Hinchinbrook Island, halfway between Townsville and Cairns. Safety equipment and shade canopies are included, and a boat license is required. Full-day rates start at A$120. For fishermen who yearn to get away from it all, there's also a six- to eight-person air-conditioned fishing hut, called the "Mud Hut," that can be hired for a minimum of three nights (A$300). It's at Cungulla, an area renowned for its fish and mud crabs, 30 minutes or 27 km (17 mi) south of Townsville.

SCUBA DIVING Surrounded by tropical islands and warm waters, Townsville is a topnotch diving center. Diving courses and excursions here are not as crowded as in the hot spots of Cairns or the Whitsunday Islands.

The wreck of the *Yongala,* a steamship that sank just south of Townsville in 1911, lies in 99 feet of water about 16 km (10 mi) offshore, 60 km (37 mi) from Townsville. Now the home of teeming marine life, it's one of Australia's best dive sites and can be approached as either a one- or two-day trip. All local dive operators conduct trips to the wreck.

Adrenalin Dive (✉ 121 Flinders St. ☎ 07/4724–0600 ⊕ www.adrenalindive.com.au) has day trips to a number of popular sites in the region, including the wreck of the *Yongala*.

Pro-Dive (✉ Reef HQ, Flinders St. E ☎ 07/4721–1760) arranges day and overnight trips. Sites include the *Yongala* and the outer Barrier Reef.

Tropical Diving (✉ 14 Palmer St. ☎ 07/4771–6150) operates day trips to the reef and the *Yongala*.

Shopping

Castletown Shoppingworld (✉ 35 Kings Rd., Pimlico ☎ 07/4772–1699) houses two supermarkets and more than 80 specialty shops, as well as a post office and a medical center. **Flinders Street Mall**, a bright and sunny street closed to vehicular traffic, is Townsville's main shopping area. On Sunday it holds the long-running Cotters Markets, where local foods, arts, and crafts are sold. There are also many suburban shopping centers.

Magnetic Island

The bulk of Magnetic Island's 52 square km (20 square mi) is national parkland, laced with miles of walking trails and rising to a height of 1,640 feet on Mount Cook. The terrain is punctuated with huge granite boulders and softened by tall hoop pines, eucalyptus forest, and small patches of rain forest. A haven for wildlife, the island shelters rock wallabies, koalas, and an abundance of birdlife. You can also escape to 23 beaches and dive nine offshore shipwrecks.

The 2,500-odd residents, who fondly call their island "Maggie," mostly live on the eastern shore at Picnic Bay, Arcadia, Nelly Bay, and Horseshoe Bay. Many locals are artists and craftspeople, and there are numerous studios and galleries around the island.

The island has 24 km (15 mi) of hiking trails, most of which are relatively easy. The most popular walk leads to World War II gun emplacements overlooking Horseshoe and Florence bays. At a leisurely pace it takes 45 minutes each way from the Horseshoe–Radical Bay Road. The best views are on the 5-km (3-mi) Nelly Bay to Arcadia walk, which is rewarding if you take the higher ground. Carry plenty of water, sunscreen, and insect repellent.

Swimming and snorkeling are other popular activities, particularly around Alma Bay's beach near Arcadia, and at Nelly Bay. Geoffrey Bay has a well-marked snorkel trail, and free, self-guiding trail cards identifying local corals and sea life are available at the information center adjacent to the Picnic Bay Jetty. Near the northeastern corner of the island, Radical Bay has a small, idyllic beach surrounded by tree-covered rock outcrops. Horseshoe Bay has the largest beach, with boat rentals and a campground.

☾ The **Koala and Wildlife Park** in Horseshoe Bay has exhibits of Australian animals, including koalas, kangaroos, and wombats. You can walk among the trees housing sleepy koalas, or feed the kangaroos, wallabies, wombats, and birds. Each day at 2 PM there's free "koala hold-ing" for those who want to cuddle these furry animals. The daily lori-keet feeding at 11:30 is always a noisy affair. ⊠ *Pacific Dr., Horseshoe Bay* ☎ *07/4778–5260* ⊠ *A$10* ☉ *Daily 9–5.*

One way to get an overview of Magnetic Island is to ride the **Magnetic Island Bus Service,** whose drivers provide commentary. Your A$10 ticket allows one day of unlimited travel to different points on the island, en-abling you to return to the places you like most. A three-hour guided tour, including morning or afternoon tea, is A$35. Reservations are es-sential, and tours depart daily at 9 and 1. ⊠ *44 Mandalay Ave., Nelly Bay* ☎ *07/4778–5130.*

Where to Stay & Eat

Magnetic Island began "life" as a holiday-home getaway for Townsville residents, and never attracted the kind of large-scale development that other tropical islands near the Barrier Reef have. As a result, accom-modations here are a mix of functional but not very attractive 1970s properties, small backpacker lodges, and a new wave of upmarket, but relatively small apartment complexes and resorts.

$–$$ ✕⊡ **Magnetic International Resort.** This comfortable resort nestles amid 11 acres of lush gardens 2 km (1 mi) from the beach. Rooms have a pas-tel-yellow color scheme, kitchenettes, tile floors, and cane furniture. At the terrace restaurant, MacArthur's, beef and seafood are the mainstays; try grilled coral trout on a bed of crisp snow peas, topped with tiger prawns and finished with a lemon-and-chive beurre blanc. Hiking trails into the national parkland are nearby, and the energetic can take advantage of flood lighted tennis courts in the cool evenings. Courtesy bus transfers from Picnic Bay to the resort are available. ⊠ *Mandalay Ave., Nelly Bay, 4819* ☎ *07/4778–5200* ⊠ *07/4778–5806* ⊕ *www.magneticresort.com* ⤵ *80 rooms, 16 suites* ⊘ *Restaurant, room service, fans, kitchenettes, refrigerators, 2 tennis courts, pool, wading pool, gym, volleyball, bar, babysitting, playground, dry cleaning, laundry service, convention cen-ter, meeting room, travel services, free parking* ⊟ *AE, DC, MC, V.*

$$$ ⊡ **Sails on Horseshoe.** As the name suggests, this low-rise, modern com-plex is located at Horseshoe Bay, the biggest of Magnetic Island's 23 beaches. It's also the farthest from the ferry terminal—but on Maggie, that's still not very far. The one- and two-bedroom apartments and two-bedroom town houses here are decorated in pastels or tropical designs, with cane furniture. The units are set around a palm-shaded pool with a hot tub and barbecue area. ⊠ *13–15 Pacific Dr., Horseshoe Bay, 4819* ☎ *07/ 4124–9943 or 1800/248824* ⊠ *07/4125–6833* ⊕ *www.sailsonhorseshoe. com.au* ⊘ *BBQs, IDD phones, kitchens, microwaves, cable TV, in-room VCRs, in-room data ports, pool, massage, outdoor hot tub, beach, laun-dry facilities, car rental, free parking* ⊟ *AE, DC, MC, V.*

¢ ⊡ **Maggie's Beach House.** Right on the beach at Horseshoe Bay, this bud-get lodging has dormitories with five or six beds each. There are also double rooms, deluxe doubles with bathrooms, twin rooms, and fam-ily rooms that each have a double bed and two singles. The dorms, and all but two rooms, have air-conditioning. The on-site Gecko's bar and restaurant is great place for breakfast, or for watching the sun set over the bay. This property is a member of the Nomads group and gives discounts to Nomads club members. ⊠ *Pacific Dr., Horseshoe Bay, 4918* ☎ *07/4778–5144 or 1800/001544* 🖷 *07/4778–5194* ⊕ *www. maggiesbeachhouse.com.au* ↪ *7 five-bed dorms; 8 six-bed dorms, 2 with bath; 19 rooms, 17 with bath* ᗒ *Restaurant, kitchen, pool, bar, laundry facilities, Internet room* ▭ *AE, DC, MC, V.*

Sports & the Outdoors

HORSEBACK RIDING

★

With **Bluey's Horseshoe Ranch Trail Rides** you can take a one-hour bush ride or a more extensive two-hour bush-and-beach ride with a chance to take the horses swimming. Half-day rides are also offered. ⊠ *38 Gifford St., Horseshoe Bay* ☎ *07/4778–5109.*

SNORKELING & SCUBA DIVING

The **Dive Shack** (⊠ Shop 2, Arkie's Backpacker Resort, 7 Marine Parade, Arcadia ☎ 07/4778005697) is the place to learn to scuba dive on Magnetic Island. Lessons take place on the beach only yards from the "Shack," and can also include trips to the Outer Great Barrier Reef. Snorkeling trips can also be arranged. **Pleasure Divers** (⊠ 10 Marine Parade, Arcadia ☎ 07/4778–5788) rents snorkeling and diving gear (including stinger-proof suits for protection against jellyfish) and runs trips to sites including the coral gardens and canyons off Alma Bay.

TOAD RACES

One of the more unusual evening activities on Magnetic Island is the weekly toad racing at **Arkie's Backpacker Resort** (⊠ 7 Marine Parade, Arcadia ☎ 07/4778–5177). Held every Wednesday night at 8 PM for 20 years, the event raises funds for local charities. The crowd is generally a mix of tourists and locals. Once the race has been won, the winning owner kisses his or her toad and collects the proceeds.

WATER SPORTS

Adrenalin Jet Ski Tours (⊠ 46 Gifford St. ☎ 07/4778–5533) provides half-day tours around Magnetic Island on two-seater sports boats. **Horseshoe Bay Watersports** (⊠ 97 Horseshoe Bay Rd. ☎ 07/4758–1336) has sailing, parasailing, waterskiing, and aqua bikes and canoes for hire. **Magnetic Island Sea Kayaks** (⊠ 93 Horseshoe Bay Rd. ☎ 07/4778–5424) provides tours to several of Magnetic Island's more secluded, quiet beaches. A tropical breakfast is included.

Townsville & Magnetic Island A to Z

AIR TRAVEL

Qantas flies frequently from Townsville Airport to Brisbane, Cairns, interstate cities, and overseas destinations. Virgin Blue also connects Townsville to Brisbane and Sydney. There are no air connections to Magnetic Island, only the ferry from Townsville.

Airport Transfers and Tours runs shuttle buses that meet each flight. The cost of the transfer to Townsville is A$7 one-way, A$11 round-trip. Townsville Taxis are available at the airport. The average cost of the journey to a city hotel is A$10.

🛪 **Airport** Townsville Airport ☎ 07/4774-6302.
🛪 **Airlines** Qantas ☎ 13-1313. Virgin Blue ☎ 13-6789.
🛪 **Taxis & Shuttles** Airport Transfers and Tours ☎ 07/4775-5544. Townsville Taxis ⊠ 11 Yeatman St., Hyde Park, Townsville ☎ 07/4772-1555 or 13-1008.

BIKE & MOPED TRAVEL

Townsville's flat terrain is well suited to cycling. You can rent a bike for A$10 a day at Coral Sea Skydiving Company, which also offers tandem sky dives.

Magnetic Island Holiday Photos rents bicycles for A$14 a day. Road Runner Scooter Hire rents scooters and trail bikes, and also conducts Harley-Davidson tours.

🚲 **Coral Sea Skydiving Company** ⊠ 14 Plume St., South Townsville ☎ 07/4772-4889. **Magnetic Island Holiday Photos** ⊠ The Esplanade, Picnic Bay ☎ 07/4778-5411. **Road Runner Scooter Hire** ⊠ The Esplanade, Picnic Bay ☎ 07/4778-5222.

BOAT & FERRY TRAVEL

The 40-minute Magnetic Island Passenger and Car Ferry runs three to six departures daily. Round-trip fares are A$127 for a car with up to three people, A$14 for passengers only.

Sunferries has 25-minute catamaran service daily from Townsville (leaving from 168–192 Flinders Street East and from the Breakwater Terminal on Sir Leslie Thiess Drive) to Nelly Bay on Magnetic Island. Bus and island transfers meet the ferry during daylight hours. There are up to 15 departures daily; a round-trip ticket costs A$23.

🚢 **Magnetic Island Passenger and Car Ferry** ☎ 07/4772-5422. **Sunferries** ☎ 07/4771-3855.

BUS TRAVEL

Greyhound Australia coaches travel regularly to Cairns, Brisbane, and other destinations throughout Australia from the Townsville Transit Center.

Magnetic Island Bus Service meets each boat at Picnic Bay in the south and travels across to Horseshoe Bay in the north of the island. An unlimited day pass costs A$11.

🚌 **Greyhound Australia** ⊠ Palmer and Plume Sts., South Townsville ☎ 13-1499 ⊕ www.greyhound.com.au. **Magnetic Island Bus Service** ☎ 07/4778-5130.

CAR RENTAL

Avis, Budget, and Thrifty all have rental cars available in Townsville.

The tiny Mini Moke, a soft-top convertible version of the Minor Mini car, provides an ideal means of exploring Magnetic Island. Magnetic Mokes rents Mini Mokes for A$65 for 24 hours.

🚗 **Avis** ⊠ 81-83 Flinders St. E, Townsville ☎ 07/4721-2688. **Budget** ⊠ 251 Ingham Rd., Townsville ☎ 07/4725-2344. **Magnetic Mokes** ⊠ 4 the Esplanade, Picnic Bay ☎ 07/4778-5377. **Thrifty Car Rental** ⊠ 289 Ingham Rd., Townsville ☎ 07/4725-4600.

CAR TRAVEL

Townsville is 1,400 km (868 mi) by road from Brisbane—a colossal, dull drive. The 370-km (230-mi) journey from Townsville to Cairns, with occasional Hinchinbrook Island views, is more appealing.

EMERGENCIES

In an emergency, dial **000** to reach an ambulance, the police, or the fire department.

🚑 Hospitals **Aitkenvale Medical Centre** ⊠ 295 Ross River Rd., Aitkenvale, Townsville ☎ 07/4775-7444. **Townsville Hospital** ⊠ 100 Angus Smith Dr., Douglas, Townsville ☎ 07/4796-1111.

MAIL, SHIPPING & THE INTERNET

The Australia Post office is open weekdays 8:30–5:30.

🚑 Internet Café **Internet Den** ⊠ 265 Flinders Mall, Townsville ☎ 07/4721-4500. 🚑 Mail Services **Australia Post** ⊠ Shaws Arcade, Sturt St., Townsville ☎ 07/4760-2020.

MONEY MATTERS

ANZ Bank can change money and cash traveler's checks. Commonwealth Bank of Australia accepts most overseas cards. Westpac is one of Australia's largest banks.

🚑 Banks **ANZ Bank** ⊠ 298 Ross River Rd., Aitkenvale, Townsville ☎ 13-1314. **Commonwealth Bank of Australia** ⊠ 370 Flinders Mall, Townsville ☎ 07/4721-1290. **Westpac** ⊠ 153 Charters Towers Rd., Hermit Park, Townsville ☎ 07/4775-9777.

TAXIS

You can flag Townsville Taxis on the street or find one at stands or hotels. Magnetic Island Taxi has a stand at the ferry terminal at Picnic Point.

🚑 **Magnetic Island Taxi** ☎ 07/4772-1555 or 13-1008. **Townsville Taxis** ⊠ 11 Yeatman St., Hyde Park, Townsville ☎ 07/4772-1555 or 13-1008.

TOURS

Coral Princess has several three- to seven-night cruises that leave from Townsville and Cairns. The comfortable, 54-passenger, minicruise ship stops for snorkeling, fishing, and exploring resort islands. The crew includes marine biologists who give lectures and accompany you on excursions. Divers can rent equipment on board. Lessons are also available.

Tropicana Guided Adventures runs island tours of normally inaccessible bays and beaches in a converted, extra-long jeep. Bush tucker adventures let you taste native foods, while other trips let you meet and feed island wildlife.

🚑 *Coral Princess* ⊠ Breakwater Marina, Townsville ☎ 07/4040-9999 ⊕ www.coralprincess.com.au. **Tropicana Guided Adventures** ☎ 07/4758-1800 ⊕ www.tropicanatours.com.au.

TRAIN TRAVEL

The *Sunlander* line travels along the coast between Brisbane and Townsville four times weekly, taking approximately 24 hours. Twice a week the train schedules *Queenslander* class, a sleeper service with first-class and economy-style compartments and seats. Trains are operated by Queensland Rail (QR). For more information, call the Railways Booking Office in Brisbane.

🚑 **Queensland Rail** ☎ 13-1617. **Railways Booking Office** ☎ 13-2232 ⊕ www.traveltrain.qr.com.au.

VISITOR INFORMATION

The Environmental Protection Agency has an office in Picnic Bay on Magnetic Island with information on walking trails. Magnetic Island Tourist Bureau is the island's primary oracle.

Townsville Enterprise has the widest selection of material and information on all local attractions and is open weekdays 8:30–5. Townsville Tourism Information Centre has a kiosk in Flinders Mall.

🚩 **Environmental Protection Agency** ✉ 22 Hurst St., Picnic Bay, Magnetic Island ☎ 07/4778-5378. **Magnetic Island Tourist Bureau** ✉ 10 Endeavour Rd., Arcadia 4819 ☎ 07/4778-5256. **Townsville Enterprise** ✉ Enterprise House, 6 the Strand, Townsville 4810 ☎ 07/4726-2728. **Townsville Tourism Information Centre** ✉ Flinders Mall between Stokes and Stanley Sts., Townsville 4810 ☎ 07/4721-3660.

CAIRNS

With its lush green mountains hugged by low-slung clouds, its sugarcane fields and laid-back pace, Cairns feels South Pacific, not Antipodean—which isn't surprising considering the capital of the region known as Tropical North Queensland is closer to Papua New Guinea than it is to most of Australia. Stepping off the plane at Cairns International Airport into the tropical heat and humidity, you might think you've mistakenly arrived in Taiwan or Guam.

Indeed, Cairns (pronounced *Caans*) feels worlds away from the bustle of Brisbane or the cobblestone streets of Melbourne. Cairns's central business district (CBD), which ambles along the Esplanade built around Cairns Harbour and Trinity Inlet, feels like a country town, not a capital city. It's devoid of the vestigial colonial influences that shape Australia's other big cities—most of the two- or three-story buildings in town are made of wood, not sandstone, and shopkeepers and businesspeople are more likely to sport loud, floral-print shirts than suits.

Tourism is the life blood of Cairns. The city makes a perfect base for exploring the wild top half of Queensland, and thousands of international travelers use it as a jumping-off point for activities like scuba diving and snorkeling trips to the Barrier Reef, boating and parasailing, and rain-forest treks.

It's a tough environment, with intense heat and fierce wildlife. Instead of the cuddly koalas and hop-happy kangaroos of the south, you'll find stealthy saltwater crocodiles, poisonous snakes, and jellyfish so deadly that they keep the stunning beaches unswimmable for most of the year. Yet despite the formidable setting, Cairns and Tropical North Queensland are far from intimidating. The people here are warm and friendly, the sights spectacular, and the beachside lounging world class—at the right time of year.

Fodor's Choice
★
A beautiful drive is along what locals call the **Great Green Way,** the main road connecting Townsville to Cairns. The road heads through sugarcane, papaya, and banana plantations, passing dense rain forest, white beaches, and bright blue water dotted with tropical islands. The 345-km (215-mi) drive along the single-lane Bruce Highway takes around

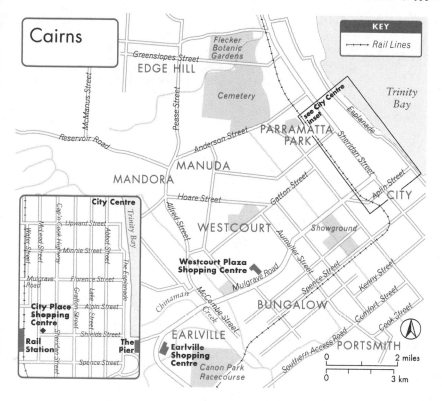

Cairns

KEY

⊢——⊣ Rail Lines

four hours—longer if you get caught behind a tractor or if the sugar-cane rail is running—plus stops to explore towns, parks, waterfalls, and rain-forest tracts along the way.

Babinda Boulders is a popular swimming hole, as well as a sacred Aboriginal site. It's located 7 km (4½ mi) inland from Babinda, which is accessible via the Bruce Highway. Stop in at the volunteer-run information center for more information and to check weather advisories; the swimming hole can sometimes get flooded during the wet season. If you'd rather hike than drive to the boulders, you can take the 19-km (12-mi) **Goldfield Track**, which starts in Goldsborough Valley, about 90 minutes southwest of Cairns. ⊠ *Babinda Information Centre, Munro St., Babinda 4861* ☎ *07/4067–1008, 07/4067–6304 park ranger weather conditions* ⊙ *Information center daily 9 AM–4:30 PM.*

Paronella Park Heritage Gardens. A sprawling Spanish-style castle and accompanying gardens grace this National Trust site, which is set in the lush Mena Creek Falls rain forest. It's an unusual place, in that it lets you explore both horticulture and Aboriginal culture. After taking a self-guided botanical walk or a bush-tucker walk with members of the area's indigenous Baddagun people, you can enjoy a traditional Devonshire tea on the deck of the castle. You should allow 3 hours to fully explore the grounds and buildings. It's about 1½ hours south of Cairns via the Bruce Highway. ⊠ *Japoonvale Rd., Box 88, Mena Creek 4871* ☎ *07/4065–3225* ⊕ *www.paronellapark.com.au* ⊠ A$22 ⊙ *Daily 9* AM*–9:30* PM.

Tully Gorge. Located in the wettest zone of the wet tropics, the mighty Tully River is a haven for white-water rafters. You can access the gorge via Tully township, which is about 100 km (62 mi) south of Cairns, then drive 40 minutes to the Kareeya Hydroelectric Station, where the parking lot and viewing platform are. Contact the Queensland Parks and Wildlife Service for more information. ☎ *07/4095–3768* ⊕ *www. wettropics.gov.au.*

Wooroonooran National Park, which extends from just south of Gordonvale and stretches to the Palmerston Highway between Innisfail and Milla Milla, is one of the most densely vegetated areas in Australia. Rain forest dominates Wooroonooran—from lowland tropical rain forest to the stunted growth on Mt. Bartle Frere, at 5,287 feet the highest point in Queensland, and Australia's largest remaining area of upland rain forest. Bush camping is allowed, with ranger permission, throughout the park, except at Josephine Falls. Permits cost A$3.50 per person per night. You'll need to bring all supplies with you, including food and water. To reach the park, look for signs about 50 km (31 mi) south of Cairns along the Bruce Highway—the trip should take 2½ hours. ⊠ *Off Bruce Hwy., Box 93, Miriwinni 4871* ☎ *07/4067–6304.*

Exploring Cairns

The **Esplanade,** which fronts Cairns Harbour between Minnie and Spence streets, is the focal point of life in Cairns. A man-made lagoon-style swimming pool—common throughout Queensland, where the temperatures are hot and the beaches often inhospitable—that's open well after the sun sets is always buzzing with activity. As well as being a free and convenient place to cool off from the sticky air, it's situated at a great spot for viewing the boats around the Marlin Marina. Many of the town's best shops, hotels, and restaurants are found on the Esplanade, and this is also where many of the backpackers who throng to Cairns like to gather, giving it a lively feel. If you're looking for inspiration about what to do with your time in this part of town, visit one of the many tour shops and information kiosks along here.

Trinity Bay is a shallow stretch of hundreds of yards of mangrove flats, uncovered at low tide, that attract birds like herons, cranes, sea eagles, and egrets. In the late 1980s some of the waterfront was filled in, and **Pier Market Place,** a shopping-hotel complex, was constructed.

Cairns can trace its beginnings to the point where the Esplanade turns into **Wharf Street.** In 1876 this small area was a port for the gold and tin mined inland. Chinese and Malaysian workers, as well as immigrants from other countries, settled in the area during that period to participate in the gold trade, and Cairns eventually grew into of the most multicultural cities in Australia. As the gold rush receded and the sugarcane industry around the surrounding Atherton Tableland grew, Cairns turned its attention to fishing. It is still a thriving port.

Charter fishing boats moor at **Marlin Marina.** Big-game fishing is a major industry, and fish weighing more than 1,000 pounds have been caught in the waters off the reef. The docks for the catamarans that conduct Great Barrier Reef tours are found here at Marlin Marina and at nearby Trinity Wharf.

The actual center of Cairns is **City Place,** a pedestrian mall at the corner of Lake and Shields streets. Some of the town's few authentic pubs, as well as the major shopping area, are around this square.

The **Cairns Museum,** located next to City Place, houses a collection of Aboriginal artifacts, including musical instruments and paintings, as well as photographs documenting the city's history. ✉ *Lake and Shields Sts., CBD* ☎ *07/4051–5582* ⊕ *www.cairnsmuseum.org.au* ✐ *A$5* ⊙ *Mon.–Sat. 9–4:30.*

★ The largest regional gallery in Queensland, the **Cairns Regional Gallery,** is housed in the former Public Office building at City Place. Designed and built in the early 1930s, the magnificent, two-story edifice has high ceilings and maple-paneled rooms with native wood floors. A diverse collection of artwork by local, national, international, and indigenous artists is on display, with a particular emphasis on photography from around Australia. One-hour guided tours are on Wednesday and Friday: be sure to book ahead. Workshops are often held in conjunction with exhibits. ✉ *City Place, Shields and Abbott Sts., CBD* ☎ *07/4046–4800* ⊕ *www.cairnsregionalgallery.com.au* ✐ *A$5* ⊙ *Mon.–Sat. 10–5, Sun. 1–5.*

At **Reef Teach,** Professor Paddy Colwell presents a unique, informative, and entertaining lecture series on the Great Barrier Reef six nights a week to a packed house. A marine biologist, Colwell uses slides and samples of coral to inform prospective divers and general sightseers about the reef's evolution and the unique inhabitants of this delicate marine ecosystem. He's considered such an authority on marine life that dive instructors around Cairns are often required to attend his lectures before they're hired. Be sure to sign up for a seat at the lecture by midday. ✉ *Bolands Centre, 14 Spence St., CBD* ☎ *07/4031–7794* ⊕ *www.reefteach.com.au* ✐ *A$13* ⊙ *Shows Mon.–Sat. 6:15–8:30.*

Around Cairns

The **Kuranda Scenic Railway** makes a 40-minute ascent through rain forest, via the Barron River Gorge, and through 15 hand-hewn tunnels before arriving in tiny, tropical Kuranda, the gateway to the Atherton Tablelands. This elevated area of rich volcanic soil that produces some of Australia's finest beef, dairy, and produce was also home to several strategic sites during World War II. Excerpts from that point in history, as well as a narration of the railway's construction, are broadcast on the historic railway car by a high-tech audiovisual presentation system. Several tours are available, from full-day rain-forest safaris to simple round-trip train and bus rides. Many visitors take the train out to Kuranda and return via the Skyrail Rainforest Cableway. ✉ *Cairns Railway Station, Bunda St. behind Cairns Central Shopping Centre, CBD* ☎ *07/4036–9249* ⊕ *www.ksr.com.au* ✐ *1-way ticket A$35, round-trip A$50* ⊙ *Train departs Cairns Sun.–Fri. 8:30 AM and 9:30 AM, Sat. 8:30 only.*

Fodor's Choice
★

From the remarkable **Skyrail Rainforest Cableway,** six-person cable cars carry you on a 7½-km (5-mi) journey across the top of the rain-forest canopy to the tiny highland village of Kuranda, where you can visit some local attractions or shop for Aboriginal art. At the second stop you can walk to the magnificent Barron Falls waterfall or into the rain forest. The base station for the cableway is 15 km (9 mi) north of Cairns. Many visitors take the Kuranda Scenic Railway out to Kuranda and the cableway on the return trip. ⊠ *Caravonica Lakes, Kamerunga Rd. and Cook Hwy., Smithfield* ☎ *07/4038–1555* ⊕ *www.skyrail.com.au* ☒ *1–way ticket A$35, round-trip A$50* ⊘ *Daily 8:15–5:15, last round trip boards at 3; last 1-way trip boards at 3:45.*

Tiny, tropical Kuranda offers several nature-oriented attractions, including the Australian Butterfly Sanctuary, Bird World, and Koala Gardens. You can visit these sites individually, or buy a Kuranda Wildlife Experience pass (A$33), which lets you visit them as part of a package with both the Scenic Railway and the Skyrail. More information on the Wildlife Experience Pass is available at ⊕ www.skyrail.com.au.

The **Australian Butterfly Sanctuary,** an aviary where thousands of tropical butterflies flitter within a rain-forest environment, is home to the the largest butterfly in Australia, the Cairns. ⊠ *Kuranda Heritage Market, Kuranda* ☎ *07/4093–7575* ⊕ *www.australianbutterflies.com* ☒ *A$12* ⊘ *Daily 10–4.*

You'll get your best chance to see the prehistoric, emu-like cassowary at **Bird World,** also home to 500 avian species. ⊠ *Kuranda Heritage Market, Kuranda* ☎ *07/4093–9957* ⊕ *www.birdworldkuranda.com* ☒ *A$12* ⊘ *Daily 9–4.*

All kinds of Australian wildlife make their homes at **Koala Gardens,** but the namesake marsupials are the starring attractions. The admission price is a bit high for such a small park—plus, you'll pay an additional fee to have your photo taken with a "teddy," as they're known locally. ⊠ *Kuranda Heritage Market, Kuranda* ☎ *07/4093–9957* ⊕ *www.koalagardens.com* ☒ *A$14* ⊘ *Daily 9–4.*

★ **Tjapukai Aboriginal Cultural Park,** a unique Aboriginal cultural center located at the base of the Skyrail Rainforest Cableway, provides many opportunities to learn about the history and lifestyle of the indigenous Djabugay people. Not only is this one of the most unique and informative cultural attractions in the country, it's also one of very few that actually returns its profits back to the Aboriginal community. Watch a dance performance, learn traditional songs, throw a spear, chuck a boomerang, or play a didgeridoo; you also can learn about bush foods and medicines. The staff and performers are friendly and knowledgeable—there's no better way to learn about a culture, especially one so often ignored in Australia, than to ask questions of its people. Aboriginal artworks, from modern works to traditional Dreamtime interpretations are on display and for sale. Ticket options include a lunch package or the Tjapukai by Night buffet dinner and performance. ⊠ *Kamerunga Rd., Smithfield, 15 km (9 mi) north of Cairns* ☎ *07/4042–9999* ⊕ *www.tjapukai.com.au* ☒ *A$29* ⊘ *Daily 9–5.*

off the beaten path

UNDARA VOLCANIC NATIONAL PARK – The lava tubes here are a fascinating geological oddity in the Outback, attracting an ever-increasing number of visitors. A volcanic outpouring 190,000 years ago created the hollow basalt tubelike tunnels, many of which you can wander through. The tunnels are 35 km (22 mi) long in total—some are 62 feet high and half a mile long, covering a total of 19,700 acres. Undara is the Aboriginal word for "long way." **Undara Experience** (⊠ Mt. Surprise ☎ 1800/990992 🖷 07/4097–1450 ⊕ www.undara.com.au) conducts two-hour (A$37), half-day (A$65), full-day (A$97), and wildlife at sunset tours (A$30).

Old railway cars have been converted into comfortable (if compact) motel rooms at the **Undara Lava Lodge** (⊠ Mt. Surprise ☎ 07/4097–1411 🖷 07/4097–1450 ⊕ www.undara.com.au). The lodge, 275 km (171 mi) from Cairns, is set amid savanna and woodlands. It supplies the complete Outback experience: bush breakfasts, campfires, and evening wildlife walks. Packages start at A$135 per night.

Where to Eat

$$–$$$ ✕ **Mangostin's.** Combining traditional Asian flavors with Australian ingredients, Mangostin's seafood offerings are among the most creative in town. The pan-seared scallops with nashi pear and champagne butter is melt-in-your-mouth decadent, and the classic salt-and-pepper Szechuan calamari is spicy and tart. The chic Lagoon tapas bar and oyster lounge is a great spot for light meals and people-watching. ⊠ *65 the Esplanade, CBD* ☎ *07/4031–9888* ⊕ *www.mangostins.com* 🖃 *AE, DC, MC, V.*

$$–$$$
Fodor$Choice
★ ✕ **Red Ochre Grill.** Local seafood and native ingredients have top billing at this elegant spot that specializes in bush dining. Try the Australian antipasto platter of emu pâté, crocodile wontons, and smoked ostrich for starters, followed by kangaroo sirloin with quandong-chili glaze. Some dishes have a Mediterranean flavor, like the chicken served with tahini and yogurt. The hot Turkish doughnuts with lemon-myrtle coconut ice cream make a fine finish; or you can linger and sip a glass of Australian wine while nestled into a violet velvet booth. ⊠ *43 Shields St., CBD* ☎ *07/4051–0100* ⊕ *www.redochregrill.com.au* 🖃 *AE, DC, MC, V* ☾ *No lunch Sun.*

★ $$ ✕ **Breezes Brasserie.** The floor-to-ceiling windows overlooking Trinity Inlet at this Hilton Cairns restaurant make you feel like you're dining right in the middle of the water. The decor is bright, with tropical greenery, white tablecloths, and candles. The Mod-Oz fare includes such delights as smoked Tasmanian salmon served with a bug mush (Australian lobster mixed with mashed potato), accompanied by red-wine jus. A spectacular seafood and Mediterranean buffet is available nightly, and a table d'hôte menu featuring North Queensland's specialties changes every two weeks. ⊠ *Hilton Cairns, Wharf St., CBD* ☎ *07/4052–6786* 🖃 *AE, DC, MC, V* ☾ *No lunch.*

$-$$$ ✕ **Bay Leaf Balinese Restaurant.** Dining alfresco under the glow of tiki
Fodor'sChoice torches, you can enjoy some of the most delicious, innovative cuisine you'll
★ find in North Queensland. The expansive menu combines traditional Balinese spices with native Australian ingredients—this may be the only place where you'll have the opportunity to try crocodile satay. The pork in sweet soya sauce sounds simple, but is one of the most memorable, mouthwatering dishes you'll find anywhere. The classic rijsttafel course for two—which includes rice and lots of different curry and pickle dishes—is the best way to sample the Bali–trained chefs' masterly cooking. ✉ *Lake and Gatton Sts., CBD* ☎ *07/4047–7955* ▭ *AE, DC, MC, V.*

$-$$ ✕ **Barnacle Bill's Seafood Inn.** Complete with netting and mounted, shellacked fish on the walls, Barnacle Bill's serves fresh, delicious seafood while also dabbling in Aussie specialties. Try the crocodile with mint seasoning and mango or the Taste of Australia plate, with grilled barramundi, kangaroo, and crocodile. Lunch is served only on Friday. ✉ *103 the Esplanade, near Aplin St., CBD* ☎ *07/4051–2241* ⊕ *www. barnaclebills.com.au* ▭ *AE, DC, MC, V* ☉ *No lunch Sat.–Thurs.*

$-$$ ✕ **Villa Romana.** This classic Italian chain doesn't feel like one—in fact, its Tuscan-style, terra-cotta decor seems unique among the Esplanade's Mod-Oz restaurants. Serving authentic cuisine like pizza and pasta with a focus on fresh seafood, Villa Romana also prepares specialty dishes like quail picante and bistecca. Open until 2 AM, the restaurant becomes more like an Italian wine bar and less like a restaurant as the night draws on. ✉ *Aplin St. and the Esplanade, CBD* ☎ *07/4051–9000* ▭ *AE, DC, MC, V.*

¢-$$ ✕ **Perrotta's at the Gallery.** This outdoor café with galvanized steel tables and chairs at the Cairns Regional Gallery also has a wine bar. Sumptuous breakfasts are served here from 8 AM, including French toast with star anise–scented pineapple and lime mascarpone. Lunch fare includes warm lamb salads and prawn club sandwiches with taramosalata (a spread made from spiced, puréed fish roe). Desserts like vanilla-bean panna cotta with poached cherries are memorable. ✉ *Gallery Deck, Cairns Regional Gallery, Abbott and Shields Sts., CBD* ☎ *07/ 4031–5899* ⊕ *www.cairnsregionalgallery.com* ▭ *AE, DC, MC, V.*

¢-$ ✕ **Night Markets Food Court.** The food court in the night owl–friendly Night Markets offers something for every palate, from spicy Malaysian *laksa* (coconut-milk soup) to meaty kebabs to Kentucky Fried Chicken. It's open daily with the markets, from 4:30 to 11 PM. ✉ *71–75 the Esplanade, CBD* ☎ *07/4051–7666* ▭ *No credit cards.*

Where to Stay

★ **$$$$** ▦ **Hotel Sofitel Reef Casino.** Part of an entertainment complex in the heart of Cairns, this all-suites hotel has gambling tables, several bars, and a nightclub. This is the place to stay if having a big room is a priority. Accommodations have tropical-style ceiling fans, louver doors, floor-to-ceiling windows, and garden balconies. Asian-inspired dishes are served at Pacific Flavours Brasserie, while Tamarind serves Thai-Australian cuisine. Flinders Bar & Grill is a suprisingly cheap and tasty dining option for such an upscale hotel. ✉ *35–41 Wharf St., CBD, 4870* ☎ *07/ 4030–8888 or 1800/808883* 🖷 *07/4030–8788* ⊕ *www.reefcasino.com.*

au ⏩ 128 suites ⚹ 3 restaurants, room service, in-room safes, room TVs with movies, in-room data ports, pool, gym, hot tub, massage, sauna, 3 bars, lounge, casino, nightclub, babysitting, laundry service, business services, meeting room, car rental, travel services, free parking ⊟ AE, DC, MC, V.

$$$$ **Shangri-La Marina Hotel.** With an ultra-minimalist lobby featuring
Fodor'sChoice golden-orb chandeliers and suede backless lounges, this resort is Cairns's
★ swankiest, hippest place to stay. Everything about the property indicates quiet elegance: outside, the swimming pools are shaded by palms; inside, rooms are decorated in muted colors, and have plasma TVs and flow-through views of the adjacent marina. Should you decide to tear yourself away, the savvy concierge and tour desk can arrange for your entertainment, such as a reef excursion from a terminal just a stone's throw from the hotel. ⊠ *Pierpoint Rd., CBD, 4870* ☎ *07/4031–1411* 🖷 *07/4031–3226* ⊕ *www.shangri-la.com* ⏩ *235 rooms, 21 suites* ⚹ *Restaurant, room service, in-room safes, room TVs with movies, in-room data ports, 2 pools, health club, outdoor hot tub, sauna, marina, babysitting, laundry service, concierge, Internet room, business services, meeting room, car rental, travel services, free parking, no-smoking rooms* ⊟ *AE, DC, MC, V.*

★ **$$$–$$$$** **Hilton Cairns.** Curving along the shoreline, this seven-story hotel affords wonderful sea views. The mood here is distinctly tropical: the lobby features an atrium filled with rain-forest palms and ferns; plants from a rooftop garden dangle along the outdoor walkways; and rooms on the lowest level open onto a palm forest. Rooms are tastefully, if not imaginatively, furnished, in soft neutral hues. All units have Playstations available for the kids; executive-floor rooms have balconies. The hotel is near the business district and a famous game-fishing club. ⊠ *Wharf St., CBD, 4870* ☎ *07/4050–2000* 🖷 *07/4050–2001* ⊕ *www.hilton. com* ⏩ *263 rooms, 5 suites* ⚹ *2 restaurants, room service, in-room safes, room TVs with movies, in-room data ports, pool, health club, hot tub, sauna, marina, 2 bars, babysitting, laundry service, concierge, Internet room, business services, meeting room, car rental, travel services, free parking, no-smoking rooms* ⊟ *AE, DC, MC, V.*

$$$–$$$$ **Pacific International Cairns.** A soaring three-story lobby makes an impressive entrance to this hotel facing the waterfront and the marina. Cane-and-rattan chairs, soft pastel colors, tropical plants, and Gauguin-style prints fill the guest rooms, all of which have private balconies. The South Pacific theme extends to the pool, which has a large fish painted on the bottom. Within the hotel are three restaurants and a coffee shop. ⊠ *The Esplanade and Spence St., CBD, 4870* ☎ *07/4051–7888 or 1800/ 079001* 🖷 *07/4051–0210* ⊕ *www.pacifichotelcairns.com* ⏩ *163 rooms, 13 suites* ⚹ *3 restaurants, coffee shop, minibars, room TVs with movies, in-room data ports, pool, spa, bar, babysitting, laundry service, meeting room, travel services* ⊟ *AE, DC, MC, V.*

$$$ **Holiday Inn Cairns.** This seven-story hotel affords views of Trinity Bay and the Coral Sea, but the daily feeding of the hotel's pool of barramundi is a much better show. A marble floor, luxurious rugs, and cane sofas decorate the glass-walled lobby, which overlooks a tropical garden atrium. Rooms are done in muted shades of blues and yellows, with wicker and wood furnishings. The hotel is within walking distance of shops, restaurants, and the business district. All room rates are quoted online, so check out the Web site before booking. ✉ *The Esplanade and Florence St., CBD, 4870* ☎ *07/4050–6070* 🖷 *07/4031–3770* ⊕ *www. holiday-inn.com* 🛏 *227 rooms, 5 suites* ⚬ *Restaurant, room service, in-room safes, room TVs with movies, in-room data ports, pool, wading pool, hot tub, bar, babysitting, laundry service, business services, meeting room* ⊟ *AE, DC, MC, V.*

$$–$$$ 🖼 **Cairns Colonial Club.** Though it's just a few minutes outside the city center, this resort's 11 acres of tropical gardens make you feel a world away from the hubbub of Cairns. The colonial-style compound is built around three lagoonlike swimming pools, including a toddler pool. A children's playground and babysitting services make it a great spot for families. Rooms have simple furnishings, ceiling fans, and vivid tropical patterns; apartments also have cooking facilities (there are microwaves in some, full kitchens in others). A free shuttle makes the run to the city center hourly, and courtesy airport transfers are provided. ✉ *18–26 Cannon St., Manunda, 4870* ☎ *07/4053–5111* 🖷 *07/ 4053–7072* ⊕ *www.cairnscolonialclub.com.au* 🛏 *264 rooms, 82 apartments* ⚬ *3 restaurants, some kitchens, some microwaves, refrigerators, room TVs with movies, tennis court, 2 pools, wading pool, gym, sauna, 2 spas, bicycles, 4 bars, shops, babysitting, playground, dry cleaning, laundry service, Internet room, business services, car rental, airport shuttle, free parking* ⊟ *AE, DC, MC, V.*

★ $$ 🖼 **Il Palazzo Boutique Hotel.** Cairns might be a long way from Europe, but you can easily imagine yourself at the Italian Rivera at this Continental boutique hotel. A 6½-foot Italian marble replica of Michelangelo's *David* greets you in the foyer, and other intriguing objets d'art appear throughout. Spacious suites have a soft-green color scheme, forged-iron and glass tables, and cane furniture; they also have fully equipped kitchens and laundry machines. Matsuri, a Japanese-style cafeteria, is on-site. ✉ *62 Abbott St., CBD, 4870* ☎ *07/4041–2155 or 1800/813222* 🖷 *07/4041–2166* ⊕ *www.ilpalazzo.com.au* 🛏 *38 suites* ⚬ *Cafeteria, room service, kitchens, pool, hair salon, dry cleaning, some laundry facilities, free parking* ⊟ *AE, DC, MC, V.*

$ 🖼 **Bay Village Tropical Retreat.** Resident managers Klaus and Lyn Ullrich have taken their expertise in hospitality, culled from years working at Sydney's poshest hotels and restaurants, to create this family-friendly, low-key, and comfortable hotel. Rooms are clean and serviceable—more a place to flop after a hard day of adventure around Queensland than a destination themselves. The adjacent Bay Leaf restaurant, though, should be on anyone's itinerary; its fresh and creative Balinese cuisine will leave a stronger impression than the rooms. The staff here is accommodating and helpful. The property offers both standard rooms and one-, two-, and three-bedroom apartments. ✉ *Corner of Lake and Gatton Sts., CBD, 4870* ☎ *07/4051–4622* 🖷 *07/4051–4057* ⊕ *www. bayvillage.com.au* 🛏 *92 rooms, 36 apartments* ⚬ *Restaurant, room TVs with movies, pool, bar, laundry service, travel services, some free parking* ⊟ *AE, DC, MC, V.*

¢–$ ⊞ **Club Crocodile Hides Hotel.** This 1880s building with breeze-buffeted verandas is a superb example of colonial Outback architecture. The adjoining motel has modern rooms, all with tropical decor and some with private baths. Rates include Continental breakfast and a light evening meal from PJ O'Brien's pub, which can get rowdy on weekends. The hotel is in the center of the Cairns Mall. ⊠ *Lake and Shields Sts., CBD, 4870* ☎ *07/4051–1266* 🖷 *07/4031–2276* ⇋ *102 rooms* ⚫ *In-room safes, refrigerators, pool, hot tub, 5 bars, laundry facilities, travel services* ☰ *AE, DC, MC, V* ⏐◯⏐ *CP.*

¢–$ ⊞ **Lilybank.** In the early 1900s this two-story Queenslander was the home of the mayor of Cairns, as well as the homestead of North Queensland's first tropical-fruit plantation. A wooden veranda surrounds the entire building, and each high-ceilinged room has a private porch. The saltwater pool, surrounded by a brick patio and trees, is particularly pleasant on hot afternoons. Hosts Pat and Mike Woolford are happy to book tours and share the affections of their pet poodles and cockatoo. ⊠ *75 Kamerunga Rd., Stratford 4870* ☎ *07/4055–1123* 🖷 *07/4058–1990* ⊕ *www.lilybank.com.au* ⇋ *5 rooms* ⚫ *Dining room, saltwater pool, library, laundry facilities, free parking* ☰ *AE, MC, V.*

¢ ⊞ **Gilligan's Backpackers Hotel & Resort.** If you're headed to Cairns for the action, not relaxation, this upscale budget property is the perfect place to rest your head. Offering both hostel-type dorm beds and private rooms with en suite facilities, Gilligan's offers a cheap and cheerful way to travel on a budget, without feeling like you've compromised on anything. It's earned a reputation as a no-brainer must-stay spot for younger travelers, but tourists who wheel their luggage rather than carry it on their backs are welcome, too—thought they might find the open-air beer garden a bit hectic. Rooms are clean and modern. ⊠ *57–89 Grafton St., CBD, 4870* ☎ *07/4041–6566* 🖷 *07/4041–6577* ⊕ *www. gilligansbackpackers.com.au* ⇋ *120 rooms* ⚫ *Restaurant, pool, kitchen, spa, bar, lounge, laundry facilities, Internet room, shop, travel services* ☰ *MC, V.*

Fodor'sChoice
★

Nightlife

The entire Esplanade comes alive at night, with most restaurants serving until late, and wine being a staple with the evening meal. Several rowdy pubs catering to backpackers and younger travelers line the center of City Place, while a few hotel venues manage to be upscale while remaining true to the easygoing spirit of Cairns. Unless noted, bars are open every night and there's no cover charge.

If you're looking for a fiesta, **Casa de Meze** (⊠ Aplin St. and the Esplanade, CBD ☎ 07/4051–5550), with its tapas bar and Latin dance club, is the place for you. It's open daily until 2 AM.

1936 (⊠ Hotel Sofitel Reef Casino, 35–41 Wharf St., CBD ☎ 07/4030–8888), is an art deco space inspired by Manhattan in the 1930s. It has nightly live bands and dancing and is open Thursday through Saturday from 8 PM until dawn. Hotel guests get in free; others pay A$5.

The **Pier Tavern** (✉ Pier Marketplace, Pierpoint Rd., CBD ☎ 07/ 4031–4677), overlooking the waterfront, is a lively, upscale watering hole where local folk and rock bands play on Sunday nights.

PJ O' Brien's (✉ 87 Lake St., CBD ☎ 07/4031–5333), a traditional Irish pub chain, is always buzzing with backpackers swapping travel tales over pints, and generally having a *craic* (Gaelic for "good time").

Verdi's (✉ Sheridan and Shields Sts., CBD ☎ 07/4052–101), a steak-and-seafood restaurant, comes alive as a local favorite for casual (but not shabby) drinks and dancing after 10 PM.

Sports & the Outdoors

Adventure Trips

Cairns is chockablock full of adventure tour companies and activities, and there's no shortage of tourist offices, booking agents, and tour desks around the Esplanade to help you choose what to do and who to do it with.

Raging Thunder (✉ 52–54 Fearnley St., CBD ☎ 07/4030–7990 ⊕ www. ragingthunder.com.au) conducts adventure packages that let you dive, snorkel, or sail around the Great Barrier Reef; white-water raft through the rain forest; visit the Tjapukai Aboriginal Cultural Park and the Kuranda Scenic Railway or Skyrail; and hot-air balloon over the Atherton Tablelands. Day trips and longer trips are available.

RNR Rafting (✉ 4 Shields St., CBD ☎ 07/4051–7777) runs overnight white-water expeditions on the Tully River for adults of all levels.

Beaches

Since Cairns has no city beaches, most people head right out to the reef to swim and snorkel. North of the airport, the neighborhood beach communities of **Machans Beach, Holloways Beach, Yorkey's Knob, Trinity Beach,** and **Clifton Beach** are prime for swimming from June through September. It's crucial to avoid the water at other times, however, when deadly box jellyfish (marine stingers) and invisible-to-the-eye Irukandji jellyfish float in the water along the coast. The jellyfish aren't usually found around the Great Barrier Reef or any nearby islands.

Diving

Be sure to ask at a tour desk or tourist office before you book a diving tour. Tours vary in size and some specifically cater to certain people; if you're an experienced diver, for example, you won't want to be stuck on a daylong introductory dive trip with aquaphobic tourists. If you're a relatively new diver, on the other hand, you'll need to make sure to visit a dive site that doesn't require advanced skills, and where plenty of qualified, certified staff will be on hand to assist you if necessary.

Deep Sea Divers Den (✉ 319 Draper St., CBD ☎ 1800/612223) has a roaming permit that allows them to go to any part of the reef. They organize day trips on one of their three boats that include three dives, equipment, and lunch.

American **Mike Ball Dive Expeditions** (✉ 143 Lake St., CBD ☎ 07/4031–5484 ⊕ www.mikeball.com) has dive trips along the Queensland coastline. Live-aboard dive boats depart Monday and Thursday—they are pricey, but all-inclusive. From mid-June to July you might just see the rare, and curious, minke whales.

Pro Dive (✉ 116 Spence St., CBD ☎ 07/4031–5255 ⊕ www.prodive-cairns.com.au) conducts two-night trips to the Great Barrier Reef as well as live-aboard and night dives for all levels.

★ **Quicksilver** (✉ Pier Marketplace, the Esplanade, CBD ☎ 07/4031–4299 ⊕ www.quicksilver-cruises.com) is the best one-stop shop for getting out to the reef, especially if you're a beginner. The staff is excellent. They run sightseeing, snorkeling, and diving tours on their sleek catamarans to the outer Barrier Reef. They also have two-day/two-night trips to Cod Hole and the Ribbon Reefs, three-day/four-night trips to Osprey Reef, and scenic helicopter flights.

Reef Magic Cruises (✉ 13 Shields St., CBD ☎ 07/4031–1588) runs day trips to 10 different pontoon locations on the Great Barrier Reef.

Fodor'sChoice **Tusa Dive** (✉ Shield St. and the Esplanade, CBD ☎ 07/4031–1448
★ ⊕ www.tusadive.com) is renowned as being the best day dive boat. The groups here are small (about 10 people each), and they visit a wide range of dive and snorkel sites—often two per trip. Their super-fast boats can get you out to the reef in 90 minutes.

Shopping

Malls

Cairns Central (✉ McLeod and Spence Sts., CBD ☎ 07/4041–4111), adjacent to the Cairns railway station, houses 180 specialty stores, a Myer department store, an international food court, and cinemas. **Orchid Plaza** (✉ 79–87 Abbott St., CBD ☎ 07/4051–7788) has clothing stores, cafés, record stores, a pearl emporium, an art gallery, and a post office. **Pier Marketplace** (✉ Pierpoint Rd., CBD ☎ 07/4051–7244) houses such international chains as Brian Rochford and Country Road, and the offices of yacht brokers and tour operators. Many of the cafés, bars, and restaurants open onto verandas on the waterside. **Trinity Wharf** (✉ Wharf St., CBD ☎ 07/4031–1519) has everything from designer clothes and souvenirs to resort wear, hairdressers, restaurants, and a bus terminal. You can request complimentary transportation from your hotel to this waterfront shopping spot.

Markets

If you're looking for cheap, disposable beachwear, Indian-style long cotton shirts, or T-shirts, the crowded, nightly **Cairns Night Markets** are the place to go. Bring lots of cash—merchants charge an additional fee for credit cards—and check out the souvenirs, arts, and crafts. (✉ The Esplanade and Aplin St., CBD).

The best street market in Cairns is **Rusty's Bazaar** (✉ Grafton and Sheridan Sts., CBD), with homegrown produce, antiques, and many more items on sale Friday afternoon, all day Saturday, and Sunday morning.

Specialty Stores

Australian Craftworks (✉ Shop 20, Village La., Lake St., CBD ☎ 07/4051–0725) sells one of the city's finest collections of local crafts, including didgeridoos, wind chimes, and the like. **Jungara Gallery** (✉ 99 the Esplanade, CBD ☎ 07/4051–5355) has Aboriginal and New Guinean arts and artifacts for sale. The well-respected **Original Dreamtime Gallery** (✉ Orchid Plaza, Lake St., CBD ☎ 07/4051–3222) carries top-quality artwork created by the Aborigines of the Northern Territory. The **Queensland Aborigine** (✉ Shop 4, Tropical Arcade, Shield St., CBD ☎ 07/4041–2800) has Aboriginal art and crafts for sale. There's also a small museum on-site, and weaving workshops are held here occasionally. **Reef Gallery** (✉ Pier Marketplace, CBD ☎ 07/4051–0992) sells paintings by local Anglo and Aboriginal artists.

Cairns A to Z

AIR TRAVEL

Cairns Airport is a main international gateway and a connection point for flights to south Queensland and the Northern Territory. Express Chauffeured Coaches provide bus service from the airport to town—an 8-km (5-mi) trip that takes about 10 minutes. Private taxis make the trip as well.

Airlines based at Cairns Airport include Air New Zealand, Cathay Pacific, Continental, Qantas, and Virgin Blue.

🛪 **Airport & Transfers Cairns Airport** ✉ Airport Rd. ☎ 07/4052–9703. **Express Chauffeured Coaches** ✉ 5 Opal St., Port Douglas ☎ 07/4098–5473.

🛪 **Airlines Air New Zealand** ☎ 13–2476. **Cathay Pacific** ☎ 1300/361060. **Continental** ☎ 1300/361400. **Qantas** ☎ 13–1313. **Virgin Blue** ☎ 13–6789.

BUS TRAVEL

Greyhound Australia operates daily express buses from major southern cities to Cairns. By bus, Cairns to Brisbane takes 25 hours, to Sydney it's 42 hours, and to Melbourne it's 50 hours.

🚌 **Greyhound Australia** ✉ Trinity Wharf Center, Wharf St., CBD ☎ 13–2030 ⊕ www.greyhound.com.au.

CAR RENTAL

Avis, Budget, Hertz, and Thrifty all have rental cars and four-wheel-drive vehicles available in Cairns.

🚗 **Avis** ✉ Lake and Aplin Sts., CBD ☎ 07/4035–9100. **Budget** ✉ 153 Lake St., CBD ☎ 07/4051–9222. **Hertz** ✉ 147 Lake St., CBD ☎ 07/4051–6399 or 13–3039. **Thrifty** ✉ Sheridan and Aplin Sts., CBD ☎ 1300/367227.

CAR TRAVEL

The 1,712-km (1,061-mi), 20-hour route from Brisbane to Cairns runs along the Bruce Highway (Highway 1), which later becomes the Captain Cook Highway. Throughout its length, the often monotonous road rarely touches the coast. Unless you're planning to spend time in Central Queensland, Airlie Beach, and the Whitsundays, or exploring the

Fraser Island, Hervey Bay, and South Burnett region, it's best to fly to Cairns and rent a car there.

EMERGENCIES

In an emergency, dial **000** to reach an ambulance, the police, or the fire department.

🖪 **Hospital Cairns Base Hospital** ✉ The Esplanade and Florence St., CBD ☎ 07/4050-6333. **Cairns City 24 Hour Medical Centre** ✉ Grafton and Florence Sts., CBD ☎ 07/4052-1110.

🖪 **Pharmacies Esplanade Day & Night Pharmacy** ✉ Shop 10, 85 the Esplanade, CBD ☎ 07/4041-4545.

MAIL, SHIPPING & THE INTERNET

The main post office in Cairns is on the corner of Grafton and Hartley streets, and is open weekdays 9 AM–4:30 PM. There's no phone.

Most backpacker accommodations have Internet services. The Inbox Café, which has a restaurant, live DJs, and CD burners, is open 7 AM to midnight Sunday to Thursday and until 2 AM Friday and Saturday.

🖪 **Internet Café Inbox Café** ✉ 119 Abbott St., CBD ☎ 07/4041-4677 🌐 www.inboxcafe. com.au.

MONEY MATTERS

Commonwealth Bank will cash traveler's checks and change money. National Bank of Australia is one of Australia's largest banks. Westpac has automatic teller machines that accept most overseas cards.

🖪 **Commonwealth Bank** ✉ 76 Lake St., CBD ☎ 07/4041-2760. **National Bank of Australia** ✉ 14 Shields St., CBD ☎ 07/4080-4111. **Westpac** ✉ 63 Lake St., CBD ☎ 13-2032.

TOURS

BOAT TOURS *Coral Princess* has three- to seven-night cruises from Cairns and Townsville on a comfortable, 54-passenger expedition-style ship. There are plenty of stops for snorkeling, guided coral-viewing, rain-forest hikes, fishing, and beach barbecues. The crew includes marine biologists who give lectures and accompany you on excursions. Divers can rent equipment on board; lessons are also available.

Great Adventures Outer Barrier Reef and Island Cruises, which caters primarily to Japanese tourist groups, runs a fast catamaran daily to Green Island and the outer Barrier Reef, where diving, snorkeling, and helicopter overflights are available. Some trips include a buffet lunch and coral viewing from an underwater observatory and a semisubmersible.

Ocean Spirit Cruises conducts a full-day tour aboard the *Ocean Spirit,* a catamaran, and the smaller *Ocean Spirit II.* A daily trip to Michaelmas or Upolo Cay includes four hours at the Great Barrier Reef, coral viewing from a semisubmersible or a glass-bottom boat at Upolo Cay, swimming and snorkeling, and a fresh seafood lunch. Introductory diving lessons are available.

🖪 *Coral Princess* ✉ 5/149 Spence St., CBD, Cairns 4870 ☎ 07/4040-9999 or 1800/079545 🌐 www.coralprincess.com.au. **Great Adventures Outer Barrier Reef and Island Cruises** ✉ 1 Spence St., Reef Fleet Terminal ☎ 07/4044-9944 or 1800/079080 🌐 www.

greatadventures.com.au. **Ocean Spirit Cruises** ✉140 Mulgrave Rd., CBD ☎1800/644227 ⊕ www.oceanspirit.com.au.

Blazing Saddles organizes half-day horse rides (A$89) through the rain forest and to lookouts over the northern beaches.

🛈 **Blazing Saddles** ✉ Captain Cook Hwy., Palm Cove ☎ 07/4059-0955 ⊕ www. blazingsaddles.com.au.

Daintree Wildlife Safari runs 1½-hour motorboat tours on the Daintree River.

Daintree Rainforest River Trains organizes full-day and half-day tours through mangrove swamps and thick rain forest to see native orchids, birds, and crocodiles.

Wilderness Challenge runs trips to the top of the Cape York Peninsula from June through November.

Reef and Rainforest Connections organizes excursions out of Cairns and Port Douglas. One day trip includes visits to the Kuranda Scenic Railway, Skyrail Rainforest Cableway, and Tjapukai Aboriginal Cultural Park. You can also journey to Cape Tribulation and Bloomfield Falls, the Daintree River and Mossman Gorge, and the Low Isles on the Great Barrier Reef. Down Under Tours makes day trips and four-wheel-drive excursions to Kuranda, Cape Tribulation, and the Daintree.

🛈 **Daintree Rainforest River Trains** ☎ 800/808309 ⊕ www.daintreerivertrain.com. **Daintree Wildlife Safari** ☎ 07/4098-6125. **Down Under Tours** ✉ 26 Redden St., Cairns ☎ 07/4035-5566 ⊕ www.downundertours.com. **Reef and Rainforest Connections** ✉ 40 Macrossan St., Port Douglas ☎ 07/4099-5777 ⊕ www.reefandrainforest. com.au. **Wilderness Challenge** ✉ 15 Panguna St., Trinity Beach, 4870 ☎ 07/4055-6504 🖷 07/4057-7226 ⊕ www.wilderness-challenge.com.au.

TRAIN TRAVEL

Trains arrive at the Cairns Railway Station on Bunda Street. The *Sunlander* and the luxury *Queenslander* each make the 32-hour journey between Brisbane and Cairns twice weekly. On Wednesday the *Savannahlander* winds its way from Cairns to Forsayth in the heart of the Gulf of Savannah.

The Great South Pacific Express provides first-class "Orient Express"–type luxury between Sydney, Brisbane, and Cairns. It's 22 hours by train from Sydney to Brisbane, and three days from Brisbane to Cairns. The train runs twice weekly each way and includes many extra sightseeing tours during the journey.

🛈 **Cairns Railway Station** ✉ Bunda St., CBD ☎ 07/4036-9250 ⊕ www.qr.com.au. **Great South Pacific Express** ☎ 1800/627655.

VISITOR INFORMATION

The main tourism office in Cairns, open daily from 8 AM–8 PM, offers regional literature and brochures, and recommends accommodations and tour options. You can also check out ⊕ www.wettropics.gov.au, a great Web site with an overview of the whole region.

🛈 **Tourism Tropical North Queensland** ✉ Fogarty Rd. and the Esplanade, CBD ☎ 07/ 4051-3588 ⊕ www.tropicalaustralia.com.au.

NORTH FROM CAIRNS

The Captain Cook Highway runs from Cairns to Mossman, a relatively civilized stretch known mostly for the resort town of Port Douglas. Past the Daintree River, wildlife parks and sunny coastal villages fade into one of the most sensationally wild corners of the continent. If you came to Australia in search of high-octane sun, pristine coral cays, steamy jungles filled with exotic bird noises and riotous vegetation, and a languid beachcomber lifestyle, then head straight for the coast between Daintree and Cooktown.

The southern half of this coastline lies within Cape Tribulation National Park, part of the Greater Daintree Wilderness Area, a region named to UNESCO's World Heritage list because of its unique ecology. If you want to get a peek at the natural splendor of the area, there's no need to go past Cape Tribulation. However, the Bloomfield Track does continue on to Cooktown, a destination that will tack two days onto your itinerary. This wild, rugged country breeds some notoriously maverick personalities and can add a whole other dimension to the far North Queensland experience.

Prime time for visiting the area is from May through September, when the daily maximum temperature averages around 27°C (80°F) and the water is comfortably warm. During the wet season, which lasts from about December through March, expect rain, humidity, and lots of bugs. Highly poisonous box and transparent Irukandji jellyfish make the coastline unsafe for swimming during this time, but the jellies hardly ever drift out as far as the reefs, so you'll be safe there.

Numbers in the margin correspond to points of interest on the North from Cairns map.

Palm Cove

35 *23 km (14 mi) north of Cairns.*

Fodor'sChoice
★

A mere 20-minute drive north of Cairns, Palm Cove is one of the jewels of Queensland and an idyllic, though expensive, base for exploring the far north. It's a quiet place that those in the know seek out for its magnificent trees, calm waters, and excellent restaurants. The loudest noises you're likely to hear in this place are the singing of birds and the lapping of the Pacific Ocean against the shore.

At the **Outback Opal Mine** you can glimpse huge specimens of this unique Australian gemstone and opalized seashells and fossils. Owners Joe and Sue Clyde, who were once opal miners at Coober Pedy, demonstrate how an opal is formed, cut, and polished. The mine is adjacent to the Tropical Zoo. ⊠ *Captain Cook Hwy.* ☎ *07/4055–3492* ⊕ *www. outbackopalmine.com.au* ⊠ *Free* ☺ *Daily 8–6.*

The 10-acre **Cairns Tropical Zoo** is home to many species of Australian wildlife, including kangaroos, crocodiles and other reptiles, pelicans, and cassowaries. Most distinguished among its residents is Sarge, a 17-foot, 1,540-pound crocodile that the park claims is more than 100 years old

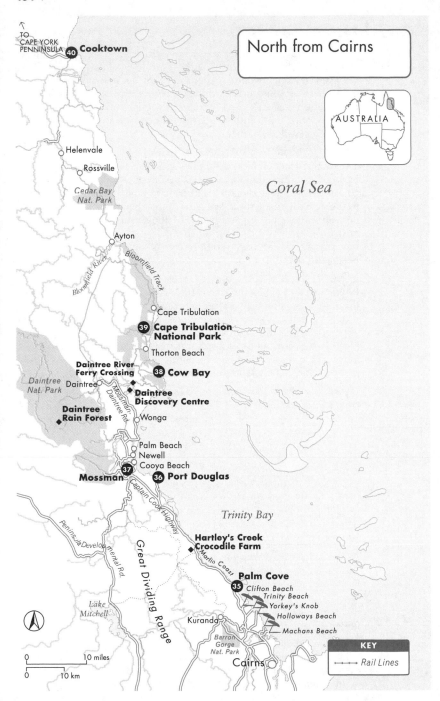

North from Cairns

AUSTRALIA

Coral Sea

TO CAPE YORK PENNINSULA

40 **Cooktown**

Helenvale

Rossville

Cedar Bay Nat. Park

Ayton

Bloomfield River

Bloomfield Track

Cape Tribulation

39 **Cape Tribulation National Park**

Thorton Beach

Daintree River Ferry Crossing

38 **Cow Bay**

Daintree Nat. Park

Daintree

Daintree Discovery Centre

Mossman/Daintree Rd.

Daintree Rain Forest

Wonga

Palm Beach

Newell

Cooya Beach

37

Mossman

36 **Port Douglas**

Captain Cook Highway

Trinity Bay

Peninsula Developmental Rd.

Great Dividing Range

Hartley's Creek Crocodile Farm

Marlin Coast

Palm Cove

35 *Clifton Beach*

Trinity Beach

Yorkey's Knob

Holloways Beach

Machans Beach

Lake Mitchell

Kuranda

Barron Gorge Nat. Park

Cairns

0   10 miles

0   10 km

KEY

⊢⊢⊢⊢ *Rail Lines*

and the largest female in captivity. The park also has a snake show and a giant North Queensland cane toad race. ⊠ *Captain Cook Hwy.* ☎ *07/ 4055–3669* ⊕ *www.cairnstropicalzoo.com.au* 💲*A$25* ⊙ *Daily 8:30–5.*

Where to Stay & Eat

$$ ✕ **Casmar.** The ocean's bounty is the focus at this innovative waterfront restaurant. You can try scallops served on the half shell with tropical fruit salsa, or grilled Moreton Bay bugs that are just the right combination of smoky and buttery. The service here can be staggeringly slow, but the food is a pleasure to linger over, and the creative cocktails make everything seem all right. ⊠ *Harpa St. and Williams Esplanade* ☎ *07/ 4059–0013* ▭ *AE, MC, V* ⊙ *No lunch.*

$–$$ ✕ **Nunu.** The sexy suede lounges here, combined with the unspoiled view of Palm Cove beach and the spicy, sweet vanilla–ginger mojitos, make lingering easy at this spot adjacent to the Outrigger Beach Club. The chefs, decamped from Melbourne, pride themselves on an ever-changing menu that serves Aussie seafood creations with a cutting-edge, flavorful twist, such as blue swimmer crab tortellini, and a "jungle curry" of quail and wok-fried squid with grilled chilies. ⊠ *123 Williams Esplanade* ☎ *07/4059–1880* ▭ *AE, MC, V.*

$$$$ 🏨 **Angsana Resort and Spa.** Fine landscaping, pools, barbecues, and plenty of sunny areas in which to relax enhance this colonial-style complex of vacation apartments, which opens directly onto a large, white sand beach. Each apartment has a large private veranda, a comfortable sitting and dining area, and one, two, or three bedrooms with king-sized beds. The furnishings are all modern and custom-designed; kitchens have granite-top counters, and there are laundry facilities in every apartment. ⊠ *1 Veivers Rd., 4879* ☎ *07/4055–3000 or 1800/672236* 🖷 *07/ 4055–3090* ⊕ *www.angsana.com* 🛏 *67 apartments* ⌂ *Restaurant, room service, in-room safes, kitchens, cable TV, 3 pools, spa, shop, dry cleaning, laundry facilities* ▭ *AE, DC, MC, V.*

★ $$$$ 🏨 **Sebel Reef House & Spa.** Set amid lovely gardens, this charming hotel seems more like a private club, with a waterfall that spills into one of three swimming pools. The lobby, along with its mural of the Queensland rain forest, is decorated with a superb collection of New Guinea Sepik River handicrafts. The main building dates from 1885, and the comfortable rooms have a turn-of-the-20th-century decor characterized by mosquito netting, whitewashed walls, and pastel furnishings. Some rooms have bars and refrigerators; all have DVDs. At the spa you can unwind with the Mala-Mayi, a 90 minute treatment that includes exfoliation, a mud bath, scalp massage, rain therapy, and deep-tissue massage. ⊠ *99 Williams Esplanade, 4879* ☎ *07/4055–3633* 🖷 *07/4059–3305* ⊕ *www.reefhouse.com.au* 🛏 *65 rooms, 4 suites* ⌂ *Restaurant, kitchenettes, some refrigerators, in-room DVD, 3 pools, spa, bar, library, laundry service, Internet room* ▭ *AE, DC, MC, V.*

★ $$$–$$$$ 🏨 **Outrigger Beach Club &Spa.** The open-air reception area of this gorgeous tropical resort flows seamlessly into the first of three pools, where a cascading wall of water immediately soothes the spirit. This is a great place to have a drink at the swim-up, thatched-roof bar. The sparkling white buildings here house large, modern, sophisticated rooms and suites, but with the beautifully landscaped grounds and dazzling Palm Cove beach just a few steps away, you won't want to stay inside for long. A few kinks that undermine the resort's elegance—like the requirement that you exchange chips for a towel to guard against theft—are easily forgotten once you walk along the sandy white beaches of the clear-blue man-made lagoon pool. ⊠ *123 Williams Esplanade, 4879* ☎ *07/4059–9200 or 1800/134444* 🖷 *07/4059–9222* ⊕ *www.outrigger.com* ➳ *220 rooms, 83 suites* ♿ *Restaurant, in-room safes, some kitchens, refrigerators, cable TV, in-room DVD, 3 pools, spa, bar, business services, library, laundry facilities* ▤ *AE, DC, MC, V.*

en route

★ North of Palm Cove, where the Captain Cook Highway swoops toward the sea, a sign announces the beginning of the **Marlin Coast,** and for the next 30 km (19 mi) the road plays hide-and-seek with a glorious stretch of shoreline, ducking inland through tunnels of coconut palm and curving back to the surf.

🐊 **Hartley's Creek Crocodile Farm,** 40 km (25 mi) north of Cairns, houses crocodiles farmed for meat and skin, plus koalas, kangaroos, snakes, lizards, and colorful cassowaries. The crocodile attack show, held daily at 3, manages to both induce and reduce fear by showing off terrifying crocodile tricks and then explaining how to avoid being a victim of them. ⊠ *Cook Hwy.* ☎ *07/4055–3576* ⊕ *www.crocodileadventures.com* 🎫 *A$25* ⊗ *Daily 8:30–5.*

Port Douglas

36 *61 km (38 mi) northwest of Cairns.*

Known simply as "Port" to locals, Port Douglas offers a similarly wide range of outdoor adventures as Cairns, but in a smaller, quainter tropical setting. As a small, holiday-making town, there's a palpable buzz of energy and excitement, despite the sleep-inducing tropical haze and humidity. Travelers from around the world flock here to be close to the north's wild rain forests and the Great Barrier Reef, and to take advantage of the varied lodgings and the restaurants and bars of Macrossan Street.

Like most of North Queensland, Port Douglas was settled on the promise of, and the search for, gold. When the gold rush receded in the 1880s, Port Douglas became a sugar town, and it remained the port for the sugar milled in nearby Mossman until the 1950s. The many old Queensland colonial buildings give it the authentic feel of a humble seaside settlement, despite its modern resorts and, some might say, overbuilt landscape of holiday accommodations. The rain forests and beaches—like Four Mile Beach—surrounding the town are World Heritage sites, so the bounteous natural beauty of the region will remain untouched, no matter how popular Port Douglas remains with travelers.

★ 🐊 You'll have many chances to dine with animals around Australia, but the breakfast with the birds experience at the **Rainforest Habitat Wildlife Sanctuary**—where birds surround you and even sit on your shoulders as you dine—is among the best. The park houses more than 180 species of native rain-forest wildlife, including cassowaries, parrots, wetland waders, kangaroos, and crocodiles. The sumptuous buffet breakfast is A$38, including admission and a guided tour. ⊠ *Port Douglas Rd. and Agincourt St.* ☎ *07/4099–3235* ⊕ *www.rainforesthabitat.com.au* ⊠ *A$25* ☼ *Daily 8–5:30, breakfast with the birds daily 8–11.*

Where to Stay & Eat

$$–$$$$
Fodor'sChoice
★
✕ **Catalina.** Huge bird-of-paradise plants flank the entrance of this sprawling restaurant, built to resemble a gracious old Queenslander. In the elegant dining room, tables are surrounded by tall wrought-iron candelabras and plants. The Pan-Asian cuisine here is every bit as dramatic as the setting; you can try coral trout steamed in banana leaf with pepper, cilantro, and coconut salsa, and seared Moreton Bay bugs with avocado, grapefruit, papaya, and French-Asian aioli. Be sure to leave room, though, for the flourless chocolate cake and homemade banana ice cream. ⊠ *22 Wharf St.* ☎ *07/4099–5287* ⚑ *Reservations essential* ⊟ *AE, DC, MC, V* ☼ *Closed Mon.*

$–$$$
✕ **Il Pescatore.** This modern, glass-walled restaurant in the Sheraton Mirage is one of the best spots for classy dining in Port Douglas. High-quality antiques, floor-length white tablecloths, and elegant silver settings complement the cuisine: dishes are prepared with fresh seafood and local produce. The food is artfully presented, usually with a garnish of exotic fruit. Try the Mossman prawns if they are available, and don't miss the soufflé of the day. ⊠ *Davidson St.* ☎ *07/4099–5888* ⊟ *AE, DC, MC, V* ☼ *No lunch.*

$–$$
✕ **Ironbar.** Built like a ramshackle, corrugated-iron shack, this restaurant has a menu scattered with Aussie colloquialisms. But don't be fooled into thinking the food is as slap-happy as the surroundings; here you can "dip your lid" to taste the prime rib-eye fillet served with a red-wine-and-garlic sauce, or kangaroo steak served with roasted vegetables, bush tomato dust, and a semidried-tomato pesto. If you time it right, you may catch the cane toad races held in the back-room bar. ⊠ *5 Macrossan St.* ☎ *07/4099–4776* ⊟ *AE, DC, MC, V.*

★ **$–$$**
✕ **Nautilus Restaurant.** Tables with high-backed cane chairs stand under a canopy of magnificent coconut palms at this family-owned, but not completely family friendly, restaurant (no children under age eight are allowed). The Mod-Oz cuisine is fresh and original, with plenty of seafood on the menu, and all dishes are beautifully presented. The restaurant's most famous dish is the cooked-to-order mud crabs. Superb desserts include the tropical soufflé of the day. ⊠ *17 Murphy St.* ☎ *07/4099–5330* ⚑ *Reservations essential* ⊟ *AE, DC, MC, V* ☼ *No lunch.*

$–$$
✕ **Salsa Bar and Grill.** This lively seaside restaurant is a Port Douglas institution; it's been visited by Australian prime ministers, and has also been a favorite local hangout for ages. The interior is bright and beachy, and a huge wooden deck becomes an intimate dining area once the sun goes down. Seafood, steaks, salads, and light snacks all grace the menu, and happy hour comes daily between 3 and 5. ⊠ *Wharf St.* ☎ *07/4099–5390* ⊟ *AE, DC, MC, V.*

$–$$
✕ **Sardi's Italian Seafood Restaurant and Bar.** Cool terra-cotta tiles and brown-and-cream stucco walls set the mood here for a wonderfully genuine Italian experience. The mouthwatering *bruschetta al pomodoro* combines fresh tomatoes, herbs, and olive oil on crispy toasted bread. The

lightly crumbed, grilled calamari comes with a parsley sauce and a green salad, and the tagliatelle is served with fresh red-claw yabbies. You can dine at formal tables, in relaxed lounge suites, or next to a small pool in a peaceful garden. A well-stocked bar lines two sides of the restaurant. ⊠ *123 Davidson St.* ☎ *07/4099–6585* ☰ *AE, DC, MC, V* ☺ *Closed Sun. Dec.–June. No lunch.*

$$$–$$$$ ☷ **Sheraton Mirage Port Douglas.** Elegant guest rooms at this deluxe resort have tropical-print bedspreads and cane furniture upholstered in blues and greens. Wood-shuttered windows overlook the hotel gardens, golf course, or 5 acres of swimmable saltwater lagoons. On-call valets will assist you with everything from replenishing ice buckets to arranging special candlelight dinners in your room. You're free to use the gym and tennis courts at the neighboring Mirage Country Club. ⊠ *Davidson St., 4871* ☎ *07/4099–5888* ☷ *07/4099–4424* ⊕ *www.sheraton-mirage.com* ⤳ *291 rooms, 3 suites, 100 villas* ⚭ *4 restaurants, coffee shop, room service, some in-room hot tubs, minibars, room TVs with movies, 18-hole golf course, 9 tennis courts, 3 pools, health club, hair salon, beach, 3 bars, shops, babysitting, dry cleaning, laundry service, concierge, business services, convention center, meeting room, helipad, travel services, no-smoking rooms* ☰ *AE, DC, MC, V.*

★ **$$–$$$** ☷ **Hibiscus Gardens Spa Resort.** Four Mile Beach is just a short walk from this Balinese-inspired resort and spa. Terra-cotta-tile floors contrast nicely with warm teak and cedar furnishings in each apartment. Most have private balconies affording spectacular views of Mossman Gorge and the mountains of the Daintree rain forest. You can try the spa's relaxing mud wraps and rain therapy treatments (if you haven't already gotten your fill of rain and mud) which incorporate native Australian ingredients and Aboriginal healing techniques. The friendly, knowledgeable staff is on a par with those at the region's more expensive resorts. ⊠ *22 Owen St., 4871* ☎ *07/4099–5315 or 1800/995995* ☷ *07/4099–4678* ⊕ *www.hibiscusportdouglas.com.au* ⤳ *66 apartments* ⚭ *BBQ, kitchens, cable TV, in-room data ports, pool, spa, hiking, laundry facilities* ☰ *AE, DC, MC, V.*

$$ ☷ **Rydges Reef Resort.** An extensive choice of accommodation styles—from standard hotel rooms to self-contained villas, all set against a backdrop of rain forest—is available here. Cane furniture and brightly colored bedspreads fill standard rooms, while villas have modern furnishings. Water enthusiasts can take advantage of the free snorkeling on weekdays; dive lessons are also provided through local dive shops. Excellent amenities for children include babysitting, miniature golf, a games room, toddler-friendly pools, and a free kid's club. ⊠ *87–109 Port Douglas Rd., 4871* ☎ *07/4099–5577 or 1800/445644* ☷ *07/4099–5559* ⊕ *www.rydges.com* ⤳ *207 rooms, 16 suites, 181 villas* ⚭ *2 restaurants, in-room safes, some kitchens, minibars, room TVs with movies, miniature golf, 2 tennis courts, 6 pools, gym, snorkeling, 2 bars, recreation room, babysitting, children's programs (ages 5–12)* ☰ *AE, DC, MC, V.*

Shopping

The **Marina Mirage** (⊠ Wharf St. ☎ 07/4099–5775) houses 40 fashion and specialty shops for souvenirs, jewelry, accessories, resort wear, and designer clothing.

Sports & the Outdoors
Poseidon Diving (✉ Marina Mirage, Shop 2, 34 Macrossan St. ☎ 07/ 4099–4772 ⊕ www.poseidon-cruises.com.au) conducts daily snorkeling and diving trips to the Great Barrier Reef. A marine naturalist will explain the biology and history of the reef before you dive down to see it yourself. Prices are A$140 to A$195 and include a buffet lunch.

Quicksilver (✉ Marina Mirage ☎ 07/4087–2100 ⊕ www.quicksilver-cruises.com) runs daily high-speed catamarans to the Agincourt Reef for sailing, snorkeling, and diving trips. The staff is patient, efficient and knowledgable—important considering many passengers are non-English-speaking tourists who may not feel exactly at home on the water. Prices start at A$185. Also available are scenic helicopter flights over the spectacular coastline, starting at A$98.

Mossman

③⑦ *14 km (8½ mi) northwest of Port Douglas, 75 km (47 mi) north of Cairns.*

Mossman, a sugar town 20 minutes drive from Port Douglas, has a population of less than 2,000. Its appeal lies not in the village itself but 5 km (3 mi) out of town where you find the beautiful waterfalls and river at **Mossman Gorge.** The ice-cold water flows here all year round, and there are several boulder-studded swimming holes where you can take a crocodile-free, cool dip. Be careful during the rainy season, though—swimming holes may overflow. There's a suspension bridge across the Mossman River, and a 2½-km (1½ mi) rain forest walking track. ⊹ *Take the signposted turnoff in Mossman and drive 6 km (4 mi)* ☎ *07/ 4098–2188 Queensland National Parks and Wildlife Service.*

FodorsChoice ★

Where to Stay
$$$$ ▦ **Silky Oaks Lodge and Restaurant.** On a hillside surrounded by national
FodorsChoice parkland, this hotel is reminiscent of the best African safari lodges. Air-
★ conditioned, tropically inspired tree-house villas on stilts overlook either the rain forest and the river below or a natural rock swimming pool. The lodge is the starting point for four-wheel-drive, cycling, and canoeing trips into otherwise inaccessible national park rain forest. You can recharge at the Healing Waters Spa, where the treatments use all-natural Australian products. Fabulous gourmet breakfast and dinners are included in the price. ✉ *Finlayvale Rd., Mossman Gorge, 4871* ☎ *07/ 4098–1666* 🖨 *07/4098–1983* ⊕ *www.silkyoakslodge.com.au/* 🔑 *50 rooms ⌂ Restaurant, in-room hot tubs, minibars, tennis court, pool, spa, bar, lounge, library, shops, laundry facilities, laundry service, travel services, free parking* ▭ *AE, DC, MC, V* ⦿ *MAP.*

⏵ en route ⏴ New species of fauna and flora are still being discovered in the **Daintree Rain Forest,** the world's oldest living tropical rain forest, where the tropical vegetation is as impressive as anything found in the Amazon Basin. You can collect information and maps for exploring from on-site park rangers, since the best areas for walking are off the main road. You can also arrange guided four-wheel-drive tours, which include walking within the rain forest, or a ride on a riverboat. The national park is 35 km (22 mi) northwest of Mossman off the Mossman–Daintree Road. **Daintree Discovery Centre,** a World Heritage–accredited organization, provides information on the rain forest and its ecosystem. You also can take an aerial walkway across part of the bush, and climb the 75-foot-high Canopy Tower. ⊠ *Cape Trip Rd., 10 km (6 mi) north from the Daintree River ferry station* ☎ *07/4091–9171* ⊕ *www.daintree-rec.om.au* ⊘ *Daily 8:30–5.*

The intrepid can follow the Mossman–Daintree Road as it winds through sugarcane plantations and towering green hills to the **Daintree River ferry crossing.** The Daintree is a relatively short river, yet it's fed by heavy monsoonal rains that make it wide, glossy, and brown—and a favorite inland haunt for saltwater crocodiles. On the other side of the river a sign announces the beginning of Cape Tribulation National Park. There's only one ferry, so although the crossing itself is only five minutes, the wait can be a half hour. The road beyond the ferry crossing is paved. ☎ *07/4098–7536* ⊠ *A$20 per car, A$1 per walk-on passenger* ⊘ *Ferry crossings every 20 mins daily 6 AM–midnight.*

Cow Bay

38 *17 km (11 mi) northeast of the Daintree River crossing, 47 km (29 mi) north of Mossman.*

The sweep of sand at Cow Bay is typical of the beaches north of the Daintree, with the advantage that the fig trees at the back of the beach provide welcome shade. Follow Buchanans Creek Road north from the Daintree River crossing, which after about 10 km (6 mi) turns toward the sea and Cow Bay.

Where to Stay

¢ 🏠 **Crocodylus Village.** Adventurous and budget-conscious travelers appreciate the Village, in the rain forest about 3 km (2 mi) from Cow Bay. Accommodations are in fixed-site tents, which, since they're raised off the ground and enclosed by a waterproof fabric and insect-proof mesh, resemble cabins more than tents. Some tents are set up as dormitories with bunk beds, others are private and have showers. Both styles are basic, but the entire complex is neat and well maintained, and it has an excellent activities program including sea kayaking, reef trips, and crocodile cruises. ⊕ *2 km (1 mi) from turnoff to Buchanan Creek Rd., in Baileys Creek section of Cape Tribulation National Park* ☎ *07/4098–9166* 🖶 *07/4098–9131* ⊕ *www.crocodyluscapetrib.com* ⟿ *5 dormitory tents, 10 private tents* ⚐ *Restaurant, pool, snorkeling, fishing, bicycles, hiking, bar, library, laundry facilities, travel services* ▭ *MC, V.*

Cape Tribulation

27 km (17 mi) north of Cow Bay, 34 km (21 mi) north of the Daintree River crossing, 139 km (86 mi) north of Cairns.

Set dramatically at the base of Mt. Sorrow, Cape Tribulation was named by Captain James Cook after a nearby reef snagged the HMS *Endeav-*

our, forcing him to seek refuge at the site of present-day Cooktown. Today the tiny settlement, which has just a shop and a couple of lodges, is the activities and accommodations base for the surrounding national park. All of the regional tours—including rain-forest walks, reef trips, horseback riding, and fishing—can be booked through Mason's Store (no phone), or PK's Jungle Village backpackers' lodge (☎ 07/4098–0040). Both places are the last stops for food, supplies, and fuel as you head north. Also, there are no banks north of the Daintree River; most outlets in the region accept credit cards, but Mossman is the last town with ATM facilities.

39   **Cape Tribulation National Park** is an ecological wonderland, a remnant
Fodor'sChoice   of the forests in which flowering plants first appeared on Earth—an evo-
★   lutionary leap that took advantage of insects for pollination and provided an energy-rich food supply for the early marsupials that were replacing the dinosaurs. Here experts can identify species of angiosperms, the most primitive flowering plant, many of which are found nowhere else on the planet. The park is approximately 22,000 acres, although the entire Wet Tropics region (which stretches from Townsville to Cooktown, and is 12,000 square km [4,633 square mi]) was declared a World Heritage site in 1998.

The park stretches along the coast and west into the jungle from Cow Bay to Aytor. The beach is usually empty, except for the tiny soldier crabs that move about by the hundreds and scatter when approached. If you hike among the mangroves you're likely to see an incredible assortment of small creatures that depend on the trees for survival. Most evident are mudskippers and mangrove crabs, but keen observers may spot green-backed herons crouched among mangrove roots.

The prime hiking season is May through September, and the best method is by walking along dry creek beds. Bring plenty of insect repellent.

Where to Eat

$$ ✕ **Cape Restaurant & Bar.** Set in an A-frame wooden building with 30-foot ceilings, this restaurant at Coconut Beach Rainforest Lodge has floor-to-ceiling windows and a (free) pool surrounded by rain forest. Wicker tables and chairs surround a giant palm growing up through a hole in the floor, a classic tropical environment in which to sample creative cuisine. The signature dish may well be the tropics platter for two: garlic lobster tails, emu, crocodile-and-kangaroo satay, asparagus wrapped in prosciutto, crab-stuffed mushrooms, and macadamia-nut-crumbed Camembert. ⊠ *Lot 10, Cape Tribulation Rd.* ☎ *07/4098–0033* ▭ *AE, DC, MC, V.*

$–$$ ✕ **Le Bistrot Floravilla.** A cute café with a small menu, this spot is a welcome change from the Mod-Oz or bush tucker you'll find elsewhere in these parts. Local ingredients flavor Continental dishes, with a focus on meat rather than seafood. The property also has an on-site art gallery. ⊠ *Baileys Creek Rd.* ☎ *07/4098–9016* ▭ *AE, DC, MC, V.*

¢–$ ✕ **Dragonfly Gallery Café.** Constructed by local craftspeople from native timber and stone, this gallery sits among rain-forest gardens and overlooks natural barramundi pools. The café is open all day for coffee, sweets, and lunch, as well as for dinner or drinks. A book and gift store and Internet service are also on-site. The gallery showcases local artwork in timber, stone, oils, watercolor, photography, and weaving. ⊠ *9 Camelot Close* ☎ *07/4098–0121* ▤ *AE, DC, MC, V.*

Where to Stay

Camping is permitted at **Noah's Beach** (☎ 07/4098–2188), about 8 km (5 mi) south of Cape Tribulation, for A$4 per person. Privately run campgrounds and small resorts can be found along the Daintree Road at Myall Creek and Cape Tribulation.

$$　**⊡ Coconut Beach Rainforest Lodge.** The most splendid accommodations
FodorśChoice　at Cape Tribulation sit in a jungle of fan palms, staghorn ferns, giant
★　melaleucas, and strangler figs about 2 km (1 mi) south of the cape itself. The resort makes much of its eco-awareness: whether you choose to stay at the Daintree or Rainforest Retreat lodges, both are fan-cooled rather than air-conditioned. Daintree Retreats have daybeds, CD players, and Internet access, while Rainforest Retreats forgo high-tech amenities and focus on the serenity of the natural setting. Both have modern wood furnishings. The beach is a two-minute walk away, and there's an elevated walkway set into the nearby rain-forest canopy. The resort offers a nightly "rain-forest orientation," as well as night walks, day hikes, four-wheel-drive tours, and trips out to the reef. ⊠ *Cape Tribulation Rd., 4873* ☎ *1300/134044* ☐ *07/4098–0033* ⊕ *www.coconutbeach.com.au* ⌁ *27 rooms, 39 villas* ⌂ *Restaurant, fans, 3 pools, beach, mountain bikes, hiking, bar, recreation room, babysitting, laundry service, Internet room, travel services; no a/c, no room TVs* ▤ *AE, DC, MC, V.*

$　**⊡ Ferntree Rainforest Lodge.** This property has the same owners as the Coconut Beach Rainforest Lodge, and a similar emphasis on eco-awareness and nature. The vaulted front windows and roofs of the large, split-level villas and bungalows here peek out from among palm trees and tropical shrubs. Garden rooms have lofts and verandas, poolside rooms allow you to roll straight from bed into the water. Dorm accommodations are also available. The Cassowary Café, which serves casual food and drinks all day, is actually two dining huts built into the rain forest. ᵈ *Box 334H, Edge Hill 4870* ☎ *1300/134044* ☐ *07/4098–0011* ✍ *travel@voyages.com.au* ⌁ *17 bungalows, 20 villas, 8 suites* ⌂ *Restaurant, 2 pools, laundry service, meeting room, travel services, free parking; no room TVs* ▤ *AE, DC, MC, V.*

¢–$$　**⊡ Cape Trib Beach House.** These cabins set on the border of the rain forest are simple and airy, with verandas that lead right down to the beach. The beachfront St. Crispin cabins, which have air-conditioning and private balconies, are the most luxurious; the Escape Cabins, with their multiple bed configurations, are best for families. Much of the hotel, including the bistro, is set outdoors—partially under a man-made canopy and partially under the rain forest's own ceiling of Fan Palms. ⌖ *38 km (23 mi) north of ferry crossing, at far end of Cape Tribulation Rd.* ☎ *07/4098–0030* ☐ *07/4098–0120* ⊕ *www.capetribbeach.com.au* ⌁ *130 cabins* ⌂ *Restaurant, BBQ, kitchens, pool, bar, shop, laundry facilities, Internet room, travel services; no a/c in some rooms, no room phones, no room TVs* ▤ *AE, DC, MC, V.*

¢–$ ▣ **PK's Jungle Village.** This backpacker's haven is where young international travelers settle in for multiday stays of rain-forest touring and partying. The on-site Jungle Bar is legendary in this part of the bush for its theme nights and karaoke, and the restaurant serves three cheap and cheerful meals daily. The cabins have varying sleeping configurations, with eight beds in the dorm accommodation; up to four people can stay in the triple cabin. Camping at the unpowered site is A$15 per person. ⊠ *Cape Tribulation Rd., 4873* ☎ *07/4098–0040* 🖷 *07/4098–0055* ⊕ *www.pksjunglevillage.com.au* ☞ *19 cabins, 8 with bath; 14 dorm rooms* ♻ *Restaurant, kitchens, pool, bar, shop, laundry facilities, Internet room; no room phones, no room TVs* ▭ *AE, DC, MC, V.*

Sports & the Outdoors

Several tour companies conduct day trips to the rain forest in four-wheel-drive buses and vans, and have river cruises for crocodile-spotting. The oldest and most established is **BTS Tours** (⊠ 49 Macrossan St., Port Douglas 4871 ☎ 07/4099–5665).

Cape Trib Horse Rides (☎ 1800/111124) has two daily rides including tea, with transportation from Cape Tribulation hotels at 8 and 1:30. Trips wind through rain forest, along Myall Beach, and in open paddocks, with opportunities to swim in the rain forest.

Daintree Rainforest River Trains (⊠ Daintree River Ferry Crossing ☎ 07/4090–7676 or 1800/808309 ⊕ www.daintreerivertrain.com) has what's billed as the world's only floating river train, the *Spirit of Daintree,* which cruises down the Daintree River. There are stops for strolls down the rain forest and mangrove boardwalk for tropical-fruit tasting at farms and at Daintree Village for lunch. You can book a number of different cruises, with the river train as the main mode of transportation. Keep an eye out for estuarine (saltwater) crocodiles. There's free pickup at your accommodation, from Cairns through to Port Douglas. The full-day tour (A$119) departs from Cairns at 7:30 AM and from Port Douglas at 9. The 2½-hour river cruise (A$38), which includes a guided boardwalk tour and tea, departs at 10:30 and 1:30. The 90-minute river cruise (A$26) also departs at 10:30 and 1:30. The 1-hour river cruise (A$20), departing at 9:15 and 4, is for groups only.

Cooktown

40 *96 km (60 mi) north of Cape Tribulation, 235 km (146 mi) north of Cairns.*

The last major settlement on the east coast of the continent, Cooktown is a frontier town on the edge of a difficult wilderness. Its wide main street consists mainly of two-story pubs with four-wheel drives parked out front. Despite the temporary air, Cooktown has a long and impressive history. It was here in 1770 that Captain James Cook beached HMS *Endeavour* to repair her hull. Any tour of Cooktown should begin at the waterfront, where a statue of Captain Cook gazes out to sea, overlooking the spot where he landed.

The town was established a hundred years after Cook's landfall when gold was discovered on the Palmer River. Cooktown mushroomed and quickly became the largest settlement in Queensland after Brisbane, but as in many other mining boomtowns, life was hard and often violent. Chinese miners flooded into the goldfields, and anti-Chinese sentiment flared into race riots, echoing events that had occurred at every other goldfield in the country. Further conflict arose between miners and local Aborigines, who resented what they saw as a territorial invasion and the rape of the region's natural resources; such place-names as Battle Camp and Hell's Gate testify to the pattern of ambush and revenge.

Cooktown is now just a sleepy shadow of those dangerous days—when 64 pubs once lined the 3-km-long (2-mi-long) main street—but a significant slice of history has been preserved at the **James Cook Historical Museum,** formerly a convent of the Sisters of Mercy. The museum houses relics of the gold-mining era, Chinese settlement, and both world wars, as well as Aboriginal artifacts, canoes, and a notable collection of seashells. The museum also contains mementos of Cook's voyage, including the anchor and one of the cannons that were jettisoned when the HMS *Endeavour* ran aground. ✉ *Helen and Furneaux Sts.* ☎ *07/ 4069–5386* 🖃 *A$7* ☉ *Daily 9:30–4.*

Where to Stay & Eat

$–$$ ✕🏨 **Sovereign Resort.** This attractive, colonial-style hotel in the heart of town is the best bet in Cooktown. With verandas across the front, terra-cotta tiles, and soft colors, the two-story timber-and-brick affair has the air of a plantation house. Appealing guest rooms are trimmed with rustic wooden doors and tiled floors, and overlook either tropical gardens or the Endeavour River. The Balcony restaurant is the most upscale dining spot around this part of the country, serving classic Aussie dishes with Asian flavors—try the salt-and-pepper prawn and crocodile. The Turkish donuts with lime syrup and honey ice cream are excellent for dessert. The Café bar serves light lunches. ✉ *Charlotte and Green Sts., 4871* ☎ *07/4069–5400* 🖷 *07/4069–5582* ⊕ *www.sovereign-resort. com.au* 🛏 *24 rooms, 5 suites* ⚭ *Restaurant, minibars, pool, bar, meeting room* 🖃 *AE, DC, MC, V* ☉ *Restaurant and café closed Sun.*

North from Cairns A to Z

BUS TRAVEL

Coral Coaches runs buses from Cairns to Port Douglas (1½ hours), Cape Tribulation (4 hours), and Cooktown (5½ hours). Coral Coaches also has a bus that makes the 1½-hour run between the Daintree Ferry crossing and Cape Tribulation twice daily in each direction.

🚺 **Coral Coaches** ☎ 07/4031-7577.

CAR RENTAL

This is tough driving territory. Most of the roads near the Top End are unpaved; major thruways around Daintree are regularly closed in the wet season due to flooding. You must have a four-wheel-drive vehicle anywhere north of the river, and you'd do well to have one south of it, too. Avis has four-wheel-drive Toyota Land Cruisers for rent from Cairns. The cost varies daily depending on availability of vehicles. Cooktown Car Hire rents four-wheel-drive jeeps from A$90 per day.

🚗 **Avis** ✉ Lake and Aplin Sts., Cairns ☎ 07/4035-9100 or 07/4035-5911. **Cooktown Car Hire** ✉ Annan Rd., Cooktown ☎ 07/4069-5007.

CAR TRAVEL

To head north by car from Cairns, take Florence Street from the Esplanade for four blocks and then turn right onto Sheridan Street, which is the beginning of northbound Highway 1. Highway 1 leads past the airport and forks 12 km (7½ mi) north of Cairns. Take the right fork for Cook Highway, which goes as far as Mossman. From Mossman, the turnoff for the Daintree River crossing is 29 km (18 mi) north on the Daintree–Mossman Road. The road north of the river winds its way to Cape Tribulation, burrowing through dense rain forest and onto open stretches high above the coast, with spectacular views of the mountains and coastline. Stock up on everything—food, cash, fuel, and water—before you cross the Daintree. Very limited services are available north of the river, and you'll pay dearly for them.

EMERGENCIES

Be advised that doctors, ambulances, firefighters, and police are scarce to nonexistent between the Daintree River and Cooktown.

In an emergency, dial **000** to reach an ambulance, the police, or the fire department.

🚑 **Cooktown Hospital** ✉ Hope St., Cooktown ☎ 07/4069-5433. **Mossman District Hospital** ✉ Hospital St., Mossman ☎ 07/4098-2444. **Mossman Police** ☎ 07/4098-1200. **Port Douglas Police** ☎ 07/4099-5220.

MAIL, SHIPPING & THE INTERNET

The main post office in Port Douglas is open weekdays 9–5, Saturday 9–noon. You can retrieve e-mail and check the Internet at a number of locations including backpackers' and youth hostels.

Port Douglas Cyberworld Internet Café is open Monday–Saturday 9–5. Uptown Internet Café is open daily 10–10.

💻 Internet Cafés **Port Douglas Cyberworld Internet Café** ✉ 38A Macrossan St., Port Douglas ☎ 07/4099-5661. **Uptown Internet Café** ✉ 48 Macrossan St., Port Douglas ☎ 07/4099-5568.

✉ Mail Service **Main post office** ✉ Owen and Macrossan Sts., Port Douglas ☎ 07/4099-5210.

MONEY MATTERS

ANZ Bank can change money and cash traveler's checks. National Australia Bank accepts most overseas cards. Westpac is one of Australia's largest banks.

🏦 **ANZ Bank** ✉ Macrossan St., Port Douglas ☎ 13-1314. **National Australia Bank** ✉ Port Douglas Shopping Center, Macrossan St., Port Douglas ☎ 07/4099-5688. **Westpac** ✉ Charlotte St., Cooktown ☎ 13-2032.

TOURS

ABORIGINAL
TOURS

Kuku-Yalanji Aborigines are the indigenous inhabitants of the land between Cooktown in the north, Chillagoe in the west, and Port Douglas in the south. Kuku-Yalanji Dreamtime Tours employs tribal guides who lead one-hour rain-forest walks to important Aboriginal sites. You'll also learn about traditional bush tucker and medicine, and try tea and damper (camp bread) under a bark *warun* (shelter). The office is open weekdays 8:30–5; walks leave at 10, 11:30, 1, and 2:30, and cost A$18.

Hazel Douglas, an Aboriginal woman, conducts one-day Native Guide Safari Tours. Departing from Port Douglas, you'll sample edible flora, learn Aboriginal lifestyles, and hear tribal legends. Pack swimwear, insect repellent, and good walking shoes. A maximum of 11 passengers is allowed on each tour. The price—A$130 (A$140 from Cairns)—includes pickup, a picnic lunch, and the Daintree River Ferry crossing.

⭐ **Kuku-Yalanji Dreamtime Tours** ⊠ Gorge Rd., 24 km (15 mi) northwest of Port Douglas ☎ 07/4098-1305. **Native Guide Safari Tours** ⊠ 58 Pringle St., Mossman 4873 ☎ 07/4098-2206 ☐ 07/4098-1008 ⊕ www.nativeguidesafaritours.com.au.

BOAT TOURS

Crocodile Express, a flat-bottom boat, cruises the Daintree River on crocodile-spotting excursions. The boat departs from the Daintree River crossing at 10:45 and midday for a 1-hour cruise. Trips also depart from the Daintree Village regularly from 10 to 4 for a 1½-hour cruise. The 1-hour cruise costs A$20, and the 1½-hour cruise costs A$26.

⭐ *Crocodile Express* ☎ 07/4098-6120 or 1800/658833.

NATURE TOURS

BTS Tours captures the best of northern Queensland with several day tours: you can glide over the Daintree rain-forest canopy in a six-person cable car, swim in the natural spas of the Mossman Gorge, or zip up to Cape Tribulation in a four-wheel-drive vehicle. Prices are A$75 to A$280.

Reef and Rainforest Connections organizes several day trips and excursions out of Cairns and Port Douglas. One day trip includes visits to the Kuranda Scenic Railway, Skyrail Rainforest Cableway, and Tjapukai Aboriginal Cultural Park. Excursions are also available to Cape Tribulation and Bloomfield Falls, the Daintree River and Mossman Gorge, and the Low Isles on the Great Barrier Reef.

⭐ **BTS Tours** ⊠ 49 Macrossan St., Port Douglas ☎ 07/4099-5665. **Reef and Rainforest Connections** ⊠ 40 Macrossan St., Port Douglas ☎ 07/4099-5777 ⊕ www.reefandrainforest.com.au.

FOUR-WHEEL-
DRIVE TOURS
★

Australian Wilderness Safari has a one-day Daintree and Cape Tribulation Safari aboard air-conditioned four-wheel-drive vehicles. All tours depart from Port Douglas or Mossman, are led by naturalists, and include a Daintree River Cruise, barbecue lunch at Myall Creek, and afternoon tea. Groups are limited to 12 people. This A$170 rain-forest tour is one of the longest established and one of the best.

Deluxe Safaris conducts three daylong safaris in luxury four-wheel-drive vehicles. You can visit Mossman Gorge and Cape Tribulation, rough it on the rugged track to the magnificent Bloomfield River Falls, or spot kangaroos and other wildlife in the Outback region of Cape York. Lunch and refreshments, included in the A$160–A$185 price, keep your strength up for these energetic journeys.

🚩 **Australian Wilderness Safari** ☎ 07/4098-1766. **Deluxe Safaris** ✉ Port Douglas ☎ 07/4099-6406 ⊕ deluxesafaris.com.au.

VISITOR INFORMATION
🚩 **Cape Tribulation Tourist Information Centre** ✉ Cape Tribulation Rd., Cape Tribulation ☎ 07/4098-0070. **Cooktown Travel Centre** ✉ Charlotte St., Cooktown ☎ 07/4069-5446.

The Great Barrier Reef

8

WORD OF MOUTH

"The reef is amazing to behold. The first thing you see when you put your head into the water while preparing for a dive is a hundred football-sized fish sheltering under the boat where it's cool. I saw (small) sharks, a ray, a turtle, a 4-foot-long Maori wrasse, coral of every color, squid, giant clams (just like in the bad horror flicks!): fish colorful enough for any aquarium, but far too big and running wild in their natural environment."

—MD

Updated by
Emily Burg

A MAZE OF 3,000 INDIVIDUAL REEFS and 900 islands stretching for 2,600 km (1,616 mi), the Great Barrier Reef is one of the world's most spectacular natural attractions, and one of which Australia is extremely proud. Known as Australia's "Blue Outback," the reef was established as a marine park in 1975, and is a collective haven for thousands of species of sea life, as well as turtles and birds. In 1981 the United Nations designated the Great Barrier Reef a World Heritage Site. In 2004, strict legislation was enacted prohibiting fishing along most of the reef—a further attempt to protect the underwater treasures of this vast, yet delicate ecosystem. Any visitor over the age of four must pay an A$4 reef tax to help support the preservation of the reef.

The reef system began to form approximately 6,000–7,000 years ago, according to scientists. It's comprised of 2,500 individual reefs and 1,000 islands, which lie to the east of the Coral Sea and extend south into the Pacific Ocean. Most of the reef is about 65 km (40 mi) off the Queensland coast, although some parts extend as far as 300 km (186 mi) offshore. Altogether it covers an area bigger than Great Britain, forming the largest living feature on Earth and the only one visible from space.

Most visitors explore this section of Australia from one of the 26 resorts necklaced along the islands in the southern half of the marine park. Although most are closer to the mainland than to the more spectacular outer reef, all offer chartered boats to outer-reef sites. Live-aboard dive boats ply the more remote sections of the northern reef and Coral Sea atolls, exploring large cartographic blank spots on maritime charts that simply read, in bold purple lettering, "Area unsurveyed."

Exploring the Great Barrier Reef

This chapter is arranged in three geographical sections covering islands off the mid-Queensland coast from south to north. The sections group together islands that share a common port or jumping-off point. Addresses for resorts often include the word "via" to indicate which port town to use to reach the island.

If you had the time, money, and patience, you could string together a long holiday that would take you to all the major island resorts. The map linking these coastal ports and offshore resorts would look like a lace-up boot 1,600 km (1,000 mi) long—but it would also take most of a month even if you only spent one night in each place. Just from Lady Elliot Island north to Lizard Island you'd only see half the reef, which continues north along the roadless wilderness of Cape York to the shores of Papua New Guinea.

While most travelers are aware of the reef's expanse, they still tend to say that they're visiting the reef, rather than naming a particular destination. But the specific island you choose to base your travels from is actually very important. Each island—and each accommodation option—has its own unique charms.

It's worth noting that if you'd like to visit the reef briefly, as just one stop on a packed Australia itinerary, it's easiest and most economical to simply day-trip from the mainland. Some of the reef-island resorts are accessible by boat, but many others can only be reached by plane, and both airfare and lodging rates can be prohibitively expensive. Day trips to the reef, however, depart several times each day from major coastal cities like Cairns, Port Douglas, Townsville, and Airlie Beach. These tours let you dive, snorkel, sail, or beach comb on the reef—some of the island resorts will even let you visit and use their facilities for the day—and then return you to the mainland at day's end to continue your traveling.

About the Restaurants

Most restaurants are part of each island's main resort, and so many of the resort rates include all meals. Some resorts have a range of restaurants, with formal dining rooms, outdoor barbecues, and seafood buffets; some have a premium dining option for which you pay extra.

WHAT IT COSTS In Australian Dollars				
$$$$	$$$	$$	$	¢
AT DINNER over $65	$46–$65	$36–$45	$25–$35	under $25

Prices are for a main course at dinner.

About the Hotels

You can't pick and choose hotels on the Great Barrier Reef islands—each island usually has just one main resort, offering a range of lodging types and prices. You should choose your destination based on your budget, and also on the kind of vacation you want—active, relaxed, or a mix of both. Resorts on Bedarra and Lizard islands offer white-glove service to a discerning international clientele, who take their leisure, and their privacy, very seriously. A vacation at Hayman Island is almost like a trip to sleepaway camp: activities from diving to go-cart racing are scheduled from early morning until late at night across the island. Daydream Island, with its focus on kids and family entertainment, can seem more like it belongs in Orlando, Florida, than the Australian tropics.

With some exceptions, sporting activities like sailing, snorkeling, and tennis are included in basic lodging rates. However, reef excursions, fishing charters, scuba diving, and what are termed "motorized sports"—Jet Skis and waterskiing—usually cost extra.

Dress in general is island casual. Some upscale restaurants, however—like those on Hayman Island—require men to wear sports jackets, and frown on flip-flop sandals. All but the most rustic resorts have air-conditioning, telephones, televisions, tea- and coffeemakers, and refrigerators.

WHAT IT COSTS In Australian Dollars				
$$$$	$$$	$$	$	¢
FOR 2 PEOPLE over $450	$301–$450	$201–$300	$150–$200	under $150

Prices are for two people in a standard double room in high season, including tax and service, based on the European Plan (with no meals) unless otherwise noted.

8

Most visits to the Great Barrier Reef combine time on an island with time in Queensland's mainland towns and parks. With a week or more, you could stay at two very different resorts, perhaps at a southern coral cay and a mountainous northern island, allowing a day to travel between them. For the good life, try Orpheus, Hayman, Bedarra, or Lizard islands. If you want to resort-hop, pick the closely arranged Whitsundays.

To fully experience the Great Barrier Reef, divers should jump on one of the many live-aboards that run from Port Douglas to Lizard Island and back, or those that explore the uncharted reefs of the far north and the Coral Sea. Live-aboard trips, which can be surprisingly affordable, run from 2 to 10 days. For land-based diving, consider such islands as Heron or Lizard, which have fringing reefs.

If you have 1 day Take a boat from Cairns or Port Douglas to a pontoon on the outer reef for a day on the water. A helicopter flight back will provide an astounding view of the reef and islands from above. Or, catch an early boat from Cairns to **Fitzroy Island,** or from Shute Harbour to **Daydream Island.** Spend a couple of hours snorkeling, take a walk around the island to get a look at its wilds, then find a quiet beach for an idyllic afternoon.

If you have 3 days Pick one island that has the water sports and on-land attractions you appreciate—flora and fauna, beaches and pools, or resort nightlife—and give yourself a taste of everything.

If you have 7 or more days Planning a full week on an island probably means that you're a serious diver, a serious lounger, or both. Divers should hop on one of the Lizard Island–Port Douglas live-aboards for several days, then recuperate on an island that has fringing coral, such as **Lady Elliot, Heron,** or **Lizard.** Beach lovers can skip the boat altogether and simply concentrate on exploring one or two islands with great beaches and hiking terrain.

When to Visit the Great Barrier Reef

The majority of Barrier Reef islands lie north of the tropic of Capricorn and have a distinctly monsoonal climate. In Australian summer (roughly December–February), expect tropical downpours that can mar underwater visibility for days. It's hot everywhere—and the farther north you go, the hotter it gets. The water temperature is mild to cool, but not really a factor: you'll likely be required to wear at least a half a wet suit when going in the water to help keep you buoyant, or a Lycra suit to protect you against unexpected stings from coral while you're exploring the water. The warm days, clear skies, and balmy nights of winter are ideal for traveling around and above Cairns. If you choose an island on the southern end of the chain, keep in mind that some winter days are too cool for swimming.

MACKAY–CAPRICORN ISLANDS

Despite its name, this group of islands is closer to the southern half of Queensland—between Bundaberg and Rockhampton—than they are to the Queensland city of Mackay. These islands comprise the section of the reef known as Capricorn Marine Park, which stretches for 140 km (87 mi) and through the Tropic of Capricorn (Heron Island is the closest point). This is a great area for nonmarine wildlife: turtles use several of the islands as breeding grounds, and seabirds nest here as well. Humpback whales also pass through while migrating to Antarctica each spring (between approximately July and October).

Lady Elliot Island

Fodor's Choice Lady Elliot Island is a 104-acre coral cay on the southern tip of the Great
★ Barrier Reef, positioned 85 km (50 mi) off the Queensland coast, within easy reach of Bundaberg. Wildlife here easily outnumbers the guests (a maximum of 105 can visit at once)—and that reality is underscored by the ammoniac odor of thousands of nesting seabirds. Avianphobes, be warned: if you don't like birds, and don't want to worry about dodging bird droppings as you explore the island, you might want to holiday elsewhere.

Divers will enjoy the easy access to the reef and the variety of diving sites around Lady Elliot. Fringed on all sides by the reef and graced with a white coral beach, this oval isle seems to have been made for diving—there's even a budding reef education center complete with saltwater fish exhibits. The land is often battered by waves, which can sometimes cancel dives and wash out underwater visibility. However, when the waters are calm you'll see turtles, morays, sharks, and millions of tropical fish. Many divers visit Lady Elliot specifically for the large population of manta rays that feed off the coral.

From October to April Lady Elliot becomes a busy breeding ground for crested and bridled terns, silver gulls, lesser frigate birds, and the rare red-tailed tropic bird. Between November and March green and loggerhead turtles emerge from the water to lay their eggs; hatching takes place after January. During the hatchling season staff biologists host guided turtle-watching night hikes. From about July through October pods of humpback whales are visible from the restaurant.

Lady Elliot is one of the few islands in the area where camping—albeit modified—is part of the resort, and a back-to-basics theme pervades the accommodations. There are no televisions, no air-conditioning, and only one guest phone is available. Social activities revolve around diving, reef walking, and the lively bar and restaurant.

Where to Stay & Eat

¢–$$ ✕🏨 **Lady Elliot Island Resort.** Here you're more like a marine biologist at an island field camp than a tourist at a luxury resort. Your linens are only changed every third day, and the absence of television and air-conditioning reinforce the resort's focus on simplicity and functional-

8

Deep Blue Views

Sometimes, just getting out to the reef is an adventure, especially if you travel by helicopter or seaplane. Once you get there, the undersea views vary greatly, but even in the shallower or murkier spots you'll still see creatures you'd never otherwise encounter outside an aquarium, or a fancy fish tank. In prime viewing spots along the outer reef, and especially around Orpheus Island, the variety of coral and fish is incredible, and well worth the price you'll have to pay to access it.

Island Time

Life in and around the water is why most people visit the Great Barrier Reef, but flora and fauna on the islands themselves can be fascinating. Some have rain forests, or hills and rocky areas, or postcard-perfect beaches. Island resorts can be havens of sports and sociability or hideaways of solitude and natural splendor. The vast surrounding reef is a true wilderness filled with diverse wildlife, and huge stretches—particularly north of the diving gateway, Cairns—have only a handful of visitors a year and are a boat ride away.

Reef Explorations

There are literally thousands of spectacular dive sites scattered up and down the coral spine of the Great Barrier Reef. Some of the most famous, like Briggs Reef off Cairns, might have several hundred divers a day threading through the reefs, admiring moray eels, stingrays, and the occasional white-tipped reef shark. More remote dive sites, like the famous Cod Hole off Lizard Island, will only see 30 divers a day. Still other dive sites, like those in the far north of the Coral Sea, are only accessible after a weeklong journey by live-aboard dive boat. In the truly wild reefs you could run into anything from a pod of dwarf minke whales to a graceful tiger shark.

---

ity rather than amenities and aesthetics. There are four types of rooms: beachfront island suites; reef units, which have multiple bed configurations and private facilities; shearwater rooms; and permanent, powered safari-style tents. All rooms are sparsely decorated; windows are framed with cerulean blue curtains, further emphasis on the resort's big attraction—the water. Dinner and breakfast are served buffet-style in the dining room. Meals emphasize seafood, grilled dishes, and salads. ⌂ *Box 5206, Torquay, QLD 4655* ☎ *07/5536-3644 or 1800/072200* ☒ *07/5536-3644* ⊕ *www.ladyelliot.com.au* ⮐ *24 rooms, 5 suites, 8 tents with shared bath* ⌂ *Restaurant, miniature golf, pool, dive shop, snorkeling, boating, fishing, hiking, babysitting, playground, laundry facilities, airstrip; no a/c, no room phones, no room TVs* ▭ *AE, DC, MC, V* ⍇ *MAP.*

Sports & the Outdoors

You can rent equipment at the resort dive shop and arrange scuba-diving courses through the dive school. It's A$27.50 for a refresher course, A$485 for an open-water course, and A$39 and up for a two-tank boat dive. Diving here is weather-dependent, so plan accordingly if you're

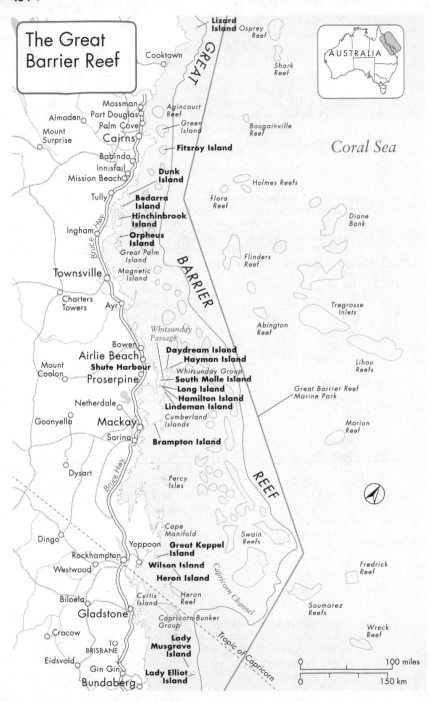

The Great Barrier Reef

AUSTRALIA

Coral Sea

Lizard Island
Osprey Reef
Cooktown
Shark Reef
GREAT
Mossman
Agincourt Reef
Almaden
Port Douglas
Palm Cove
Green Island
Bougainville Reef
Mount Surprise
Cairns
Fitzroy Island
Babinda
Innisfail
Mission Beach
Dunk Island
Holmes Reefs
Tully
Flora Reef
Bedarra Island
Diane Bank
Hinchinbrook Island
Ingham
Orpheus Island
Great Palm Island
BARRIER
Flinders Reef
Townsville
Magnetic Island
Charters Towers
Ayr
Tregrosse Inlets
Abington Reef
Whitsunday Passage
Bowen
Daydream Island
Airlie Beach
Hayman Island
Lihou Reefs
Mount Coolon
Shute Harbour
Whitsunday Group
Proserpine
South Molle Island
Long Island
Great Barrier Reef Marine Park
Hamilton Island
Netherdale
Lindeman Island
Cumberland Islands
Goonyella
Marion Reef
Mackay
Sarina
Brampton Island
REEF
Dysart
Percy Isles
Cape Manifold
Swain Reefs
Dingo
Yeppoon
Great Keppel Island
Rockhampton
Wilson Island
Fredrick Reef
Westwood
Heron Island
Curtis Island
Heron Reef
Biloela
Gladstone
Capricorn-Bunker Group
Saumarez Reefs
Capricorn Channel
Cracow
TO BRISBANE
Lady Musgrave Island
Tropic of Capricorn
Wreck Reef
Eidsvold
Gin Gin
Lady Elliot Island
Bundaberg

Bruce Hwy.

0   100 miles
0   150 km

pursuing an advanced course over multiple days. Five-day/four-night packages including three dives and shared accommodation start at A$500, while eight-day/seven-night packages with six dives and shared accommodation start at A$875. Snorkeling, reef walks, glass-bottom boat rides (A$11), and hiking are also possible. There's a onetime A$5 reef tax charge.

Arriving & Departing

BY PLANE Lady Elliot is the only coral cay with its own airstrip. Small aircraft make the flight from Hervey Bay and Bundaberg, though pickups can be arranged from as far south in Queensland as the Gold Coast. The 30-minute round-trip flight from Bundaberg or the 35-minute flight from Hervey Bay to Lady Elliot on **Seair Pacific** (☎ 07/5599–4509 ⊕ www.seairpacific.com.au) costs A$219 from the mainland and A$175 for island guests. Strict luggage limits allow 10 kilograms (22 pounds) per person (the sum of both hand and checked baggage). If you exceed this limit, you can repack at the ticket-counter scale or wave good-bye to the plane.

Day Trips

You can day-trip to Lady Elliot with **Seair Pacific**. The cost—including scenic flight, buffet lunch, glass-bottomed boat ride and snorkeling lesson—is A$599 per person from Brisbane or the Gold Coast. Tours require a minimum of 2 passengers to go out, and use planes that can carry an average of 10 passengers.

Lady Musgrave Island

★ Lady Musgrave Island sits at the southern end of the Great Barrier Reef Marine Park, about 40 km (25 mi) north of Lady Elliot. Five kilometers (3 mi) of coral reef and a massive yet calm 3,000-acre lagoon surround the island, a true coral cay of 35 acres—500 yards wide. When day-trippers, yachties, divers, and campers converge, traffic gets heavy, but the island has some of the best diving and snorkeling in Queensland. In quiet times, campers have a chance to view the myriad sea life surrounding this tiny speck of land in the Pacific.

In summer (November through March) the island is a bird and turtle rookery with white-capped noddies, wedge-tailed shearwaters, and green and loggerhead turtles. There's also an abundance of flora, including casuarina and pisonia trees.

Camping

The island is uninhabited and has only basic facilities (one toilet block and emergency radio equipment) for campers. Commercial tour operators from the interestingly named Town of 1770 on the mainland have all camping equipment and necessary provisions available for hire. More information can be learned when purchasing a required camping permit from the **Environmental Protection Agency** (☎ 07/3405–0970) for A$4 per person per night, or a maximum of A$16 per family (children under five free). No more than 40 campers may visit the island at any one time, and camping reservations must be made a year in advance (and even then, school breaks and holidays book fast).

CloseUp

DANGERS OF THE REEF

T'S TRUE: *there are creatures in the water here that can kill you, or at least inflict some serious pain. The most ubiquitous offenders near the tropical mainland are jellyfish; the sting of the tiny, transparent Irukandji, no bigger than a thumbnail, can cause severe pain, vomiting, and soaring blood pressure, which may be life threatening to people with already high blood pressure or diabetes. Even more dangerous, however, are the deadly Chrionex jellyfish— commonly known as sea wasps or box jellyfish. These transparent, cube-shape creatures are the most venomous sea creatures on Earth; their stings, which cause the lungs and heart to stop functioning, are fatal unless they are treated within three minutes. Jellyfish season unfortunately coincides with the tourist season and prime beach weather; many of the most popular beaches in North Queensland have stinger nets, which will keep box jellyfish out of the swimming areas.*

The good news is that on the outer reef and islands jellyfish aren't a problem. Here, though, another danger you need to be careful of is the coral. Millepora, or stinging coral, ranges in form from large upright sheets and blades to branching, antlerlike stalks with a yellow-brown color. If this coral inadvertently scrapes or tears your skin, you'll get painful, burning welts. Try to swim with your arms and legs close to your body, and of course notify someone if you think you have rubbed up against anything.

Sharks are present in the waters of the inner and outer reef, but unlike jellyfish aren't likely to come near you. The small sharks that live in the shallow waters off the shores of North Queensland and around the inner reef islands only eat fish. Tiger sharks and hammerheads, which hunt in deeper waters, tend to swim away from people, not toward them. You are unlikely to see a great white shark while on the reef; they tend to prefer the colder waters of the southern Pacific. But even if you do see one, remember that these mythically fearsome creatures aren't hard-wired to make a meal out of you. There are plenty of delicious and convenient nonhuman feeding options available on the reef, so they're only likely to pursue a human if provoked, or if the irresistible smell of blood is flowing in the water.

There are other, more exotic, but equally dangerous creatures lurking around the reef, such as stonefish and sea snakes. But your worst enemy in this part of Australia—whether you're in or out of the water—is the sun. The ozone layer in Australia is almost nonexistent, and one in three Australians develops some form of skin cancer in their lifetime. Many a snorkeler has had a day on the water ruined by a nasty sunburn on the back of his or her legs. Be sure to coat yourself in sunblock consistently the whole time you're visiting the reef.

Arriving & Departing

BY BOAT You can reach the island on the catamaran MV *Lady Musgrave*, or the trimaran MV *Spirit of Musgrave*, both run by **Lady Musgrave Cruises** (☎07/ 4159–4519 or 1800/072110 ⊕ www.lmcruises.com.au). Boats depart from Port Bundaberg, 20 minutes northeast of Bundaberg, Monday, Thursday, Saturday, and Saturday at 8 AM, returning at 5:45 PM. The trip takes 2½ hours in each direction and costs A$150 for day-trippers, A$280 for campers (to secure return passage). Scuba diving (including equipment) is an extra A$58 for one dive, A$80 for two dives, or A$70 for an introductory lesson. Boats depart from Port Bundaberg, but a coach will pick you up and drop you off at your accommodation in Bundaberg for A$10 round-trip.

Heron Island

Fodor'sChoice
★ Most resort islands lie well inside the shelter of the distant reef, but Heron Island, some 70 km (43 mi) northwest of the mainland port of Gladstone, is actually part of the reef. The waters off this 41-acre island are spectacular, teeming with fish and coral, and ideal for snorkeling and scuba diving. The water is clearest in June and July and cloudiest during the rainy season, January and February.

Heron is also a national park and bird sanctuary, which makes it a good place to learn about indigenous life on a coral island. Thousands of birds live here, including noddy terns, silver eyes, rails, and gray and white herons. From September through March the indigenous birdlife is joined by large numbers of migrating birds, some from as far away as the Arctic. From November through March, hundreds of migrating green and loggerhead turtles arrive to mate and lay their eggs on the sandy foreshores, and thousands of tiny hatchlings emerge from the nests from December through April. Between July and October (September is best), humpback whales pass here on their journey from the Antarctic.

You won't find many activities and entertainment on Heron, as the island's single accommodation accepts a cozy maximum of only 250 people—and there are no day-trippers. But these might be reasons why you decide to come here.

Only guests of the Heron Island Resort can visit uninhabited **Wilson Island,** a coral cay 10 km (6 mi) north, a 40-minute day trip from Heron Island. In January and February Wilson Island becomes the breeding ground for roseate terns and green and loggerhead turtles. The island also has its own exclusive resort, catering to a maximum of 12 guests (and no children under 16). Combination packages are available, allowing for two nights at Heron Island and three nights at Wilson Island, starting at A$1,995, including meals.

Where to Stay & Eat

$$–$$$$ ✕🖼 **Heron Island Resort.** Set among palm trees and connected by sand paths, the six types of accommodations here range from the deluxe, modern Beach House (with its private outdoor shower) to the compact, garden-level Turtle Rooms. The large modern suites, which include amenities like CD players and minibars, as well as lounge areas and private outdoor space, merit the extra expense. Among the included activities are a range of nature and reef walks, as well as snorkeling lessons and tennis. All snorkeling and diving excursions cost extra, as does the kids' program (A$55), open during Australian school holidays. Rates include breakfast and lunch buffets and four-course set dinners, including a weekly seafood smorgasbord. The island closes in February to protect nesting birds. ⌂ *Voyages, GPO 3859, Sydney, NSW 2001* ☎ *02/ 8296–8000* ⊕ *www.heronisland.com* ➳ *1 beach house, 76 suites, 32 rooms* ⌂ *Coffee shop, dining room, minibars, tennis court, 2 pools, spa, dive shop, snorkeling, fishing, paddle tennis, bar, recreation room, children's programs (ages 7–12), laundry service, Internet room, meeting rooms; no a/c in some rooms, no room TVs* ▤ *AE, DC, MC, V* ⚬l *FAP.*

Sports & the Outdoors

You can book snorkeling, scuba diving, and fishing excursions through the dive shop. Snorkeling boat trips are A$25; children under 8 aren't permitted and those under 14 must be accompanied. Open-water diving courses are available for A$400, and resort diving costs A$50 per dive. A full-day excursion dive and tour of the neighboring islands is A$1,500.

Nondivers who want to explore the reef's underwater world can take semisubmersible tours with a naturalist guide for A$30. Also available are free guided reef walks, interpretive nature walks, a turtle-watching tour, or a visit to the island's Marine Research Station.

Arriving & Departing

BY BOAT   All transfers are booked with your accommodations through the resort. The high-speed launch makes the 2-hour run to Heron Island from Gladstone, on the Queensland coast, for A$196 round-trip. This is a rough journey by any standards, so take some anti-nausea medicine ½ hour before the boat departs.

BY HELICOPTER   **Australian Helicopters** makes the 25-minute helicopter flight to Heron Island from Gladstone for A$495 round-trip. The baggage restriction is 15 kilograms (33 pounds) per person and one piece of 4-kilogram (9-pound) hand luggage. Lockup facilities for excess baggage are free.

Great Keppel Island

The Contiki Great Keppel Island Resort used to have a party reputation similar to that of Fort Lauderdale at spring break. Only people ages 18 to 35 were allowed in, and the focus was on raucous fun, adventure sports, and showing off tanned bodies on the beach and on the dance floor. Now under new management by the Accor Mercure hotel group, however, the resort is expanding its target audience to include young families, as well as singles. Although at this writing many of the resort's changes hadn't been finalized, plans are in place to add a kids' club to the list of amenities—so that young parents can still party at night knowing their kids are well taken care of.

Although Great Keppel is large, at 8 km (5 mi) by 11 km (7 mi), it lies 40 km (25 mi) from the Great Barrier Reef, which makes for a long trip from the mainland. There's lots to do, though, with walking trails, 17 stunning beaches, 40 sports activities, and excellent coral growth in many sheltered coves. An underwater observatory at nearby Middle Island allows you to watch marine life without getting wet. A confiscated Taiwanese fishing boat has been sunk alongside the observatory to provide shelter for tropical fish.

Where to Stay

¢ ▦ **Great Keppel Island Holiday Village.** Tucked in among the welcome shade of gum trees is this modest, quiet alternative for couples and older travelers looking to get back to basics without a party scene. Centered around a reception hall that doubles as a grocery store, the village includes a house, several simple cabins, double and single rooms, tents, and dorm accommodations. All have shared bathroom facilities. There are barbecues for cooking out, and you can hike or take a canoe or kayak tour of the island, or flop on one of the island's 17 beaches. The store carries basic supplies. ✉ *Community Mailbag, Great Keppel Island, QLD 4700* ☎ *07/4939–8655* 🖷 *07/4939–8755* ⊕ *www.gkiholidayvillage.com. au* ↘ *1 house, 2 cabins, 8 tents, 4 rooms, 2 dormitories—all without bath* ☕ *Café, pizzeria, snorkeling, boating, hiking; no a/c, no room phones, no TV in some rooms* ⊟ *AE, DC, MC, V.*

¢–$ ▦ **Mercure Great Keppel Island Resort.** The same sports, activities, dining, and nightlife options exist as when this resort was a Generation X party haven, but now the tone is more *Rugrats* than *Friends.* The villas and two-story accommodation buildings stand among gardens and extend up the island's hills. Bright tropical colors and terra-cotta tiles decorate many of the garden and beachfront rooms and villas. Villas have wonderful rooms but are some distance from the beach. Rates include breakfast and dinner at the buffet-style restaurant. Otherwise, you can dine on wood-fired pizzas or à la carte dishes on your own dime. ↘ *PMB 8001, North Rockhampton, QLD 4702* ☎ *07/4939–5044* 🖷 *07/ 4939–1775* ⊕ *www.accorhotels.com* ↘ *181 rooms* ☕ *2 restaurants, 9-hole golf course, 3 tennis courts, 5 pools, fitness classes, hair salon, 2 outdoor hot tubs, snorkeling, windsurfing, boating, jet skiing, parasailing, waterskiing, fishing, archery, badminton, basketball, paddle tennis, racquetball, squash, volleyball, 5 bars, nightclub, Internet room; no a/c in some rooms, no room phones, no room TVs* ⊟ *AE, DC, MC, V* ⊠ *MAP.*

Sports & the Outdoors

Great Keppel Island is a beachcombers' and water lovers' spot, with 17 beaches and great snorkeling and diving sites. The Great Keppel Island resort offers 40 activities, from tennis to jet skiing. Book all activities through the main resort.

Arriving & Departing

BY BOAT **Mercure Great Keppel Island Resort** transfers guests to the island from Rockhampton Airport or Yeppoon Marina. A coach and launch service from the airport costs A\$68 round-trip; the launch alone costs A\$31 round-trip. **Keppel Bay Marina** (☎ 07/4933–6244) operates daily island launch services, for A\$35 round-trip, from Rosslyn Bay aboard the catamaran *Freedom Flyer.* Departures are at 9, 11:30, and 3. Return trips are at 10, 2, and 4.

BY PLANE **Mercure Great Keppel Island Resort** (☎ 1300/305005) can arrange flights to the island from Rockhampton. Low-cost carrier **Jetstar** (☎ 13-1538 ⊕ www.jetstar.com) has daily flights from Sydney and Brisbane only. **Virgin Blue** (☎ 13-6789 ⊕ www.virginblue.com.au) flies to Rockhampton from all major Australian cities. You can also fly to Great Keppel from Brisbane with one of the resort's package tours.

THE WHITSUNDAY ISLANDS

The Whitsundays are a group of 74 islands situated within 161 km (100 mi) of each other, just 50 km (35 mi) from Shute Harbour, the mainland departure point. Discovered by Captain James Cook of the HMS *Endeavour* in 1770 (though not actually discovered on Whitsunday, due to a time-zone change oversight on his part), the Whitsundays are a favorite sailing destination, as well as an easy-access base point for exploring the reef. Some of the islands' beaches, particularly famous Whitehaven Beach, are picture-postcard gorgeous, though the islands themselves look more scrubby than tropical. The entire region is actually subtropical, making for very moderate air and water temperatures year-round. Almost all of the Whitsunday islands are national parks; although animals aren't very plentiful on them, birds are—more than 150 species make their homes here. Only seven islands have resorts on them; others are destinations for day trips, beach and bush walks, or simply serve as backdrop at scenic mooring spots.

Brampton Island

Seven coral-and-white sandy beaches encircle Brampton Island, and kangaroos, colorful rainbow lorikeets, and butterflies populate the hilly interior's rain forests. Located at the southern entrance to the Whitsunday Passage, this 195-acre island, which is 40 km (25 mi) offshore from Mackay, is one of the prettiest in the area. Most of the island is a designated national park, although the resort area is lively, with nightly dances and poolside drinking. The biggest attraction is the water—especially snorkeling over the reef between Brampton and adjoining Carlisle islands.

Where to Stay & Eat

$$–$$$ ✕🏨 **Brampton Island Resort.** As if in recognition that its greatest assets are outside, this resort has rooms that are clean, modern, and functional, but nothing to write home about. Why would you want to spend time in your room, though, when you could be exploring the reef or lounging by the beautiful ocean-view pool? The premium ocean-view rooms, which sit right on the beach, are the most lavish, with turndown service and waffle-weave bathrobes. The other categories of rooms look very similar to each other, with rattan furniture and fabrics in soft blues and corals. The Bluewater Restaurant serves a buffet breakfast, smorgasbord lunch, and a set four-course seafood dinner. All are included in the lodging rate. ⌂ *Voyages, GPO 3859, Sydney, NSW 2001* ☎ *1300/334034* 🖷 *02/9299–0203* ⊕ *www.brampton-island.com* ↩ *106 rooms* ⚓ *Restaurant, minibars, refrigerators, room TVs with movies, 6-hole golf course, 3 tennis courts, 2 pools, fitness classes, gym, spa, beach, snorkeling, jet skiing, waterskiing, archery, badminton, basketball, boccie, volleyball, bar, lounge, babysitting, laundry service* ▤ *AE, DC, MC, V* ⦿ *AI.*

Sports & the Outdoors

Brampton Island's resort has extensive facilities and activities included in the rate. For an extra charge, you can also take boom-netting cruises (where you get trailed behind a boat by a net), guided walks, Jet Ski island tours, fishing trips, flights to the Great Barrier Reef, island and sunset cruises, waterskiing, tube rides (where you ride in an inner tube pulled along behind the ski boat), and guided snorkeling safaris.

Arriving & Departing

BY BOAT The *Heron II* (☎ 13–2469), a modern, high-speed monohull, leaves Mackay Outer Harbour daily at 11:30. Fare is A$50 one-way and A$100 round-trip. Complimentary coach transfers from Mackay airport are available.

BY HELICOPTER **Australian Helicopters** depart from Mackay airport daily, for a 15- to 25-minute scenic flight to Brampton Island. The fare is A$198 round-trip. Contact the resort to make arrangements.

Lindeman Island

More than half of Lindeman Island—which at 2,000 acres, is one of the largest in the Whitsunday group—is national park, with 20 km (12 mi) of walking trails that wind through tropical growth and up hills for fantastic views. Bird-watching is excellent here, although the blue tiger butterflies that you can see in Butterfly Valley may be even more impressive than the birds. With its nature-viewing and sporting possibilities, the island draws lots of families. The island lies 40 km (25 mi) northeast of Mackay near the southern entrance to the Whitsunday Passage.

Where to Stay & Eat

$$$–$$$$ ✕🏠 **Club Med Lindeman Island.** This three-story, palm-tree-filled resort sits on 1,750 acres on the southern end of the island. Rooms are sparsely furnished, as is the habit at Club Med (this is the only one in Australia), and those that are poolside or have hot tubs cost more. All rooms overlook the sea and have a balcony or patio, and all border the beach and pool. Away from the main village are the golf clubhouse, sports center, dance club, and restaurant. Prices include meals, nonmotorized sports, and evening entertainment shows, and packages cover round-trip airfares within Australia on Jetstar, though prices differ slightly depending on point of embarkation. ⊠ *PMB Mackay Mail Centre, QLD 4741* ☎ *07/4946–9333 or 1800/646933* 🖷 *07/4946–9776* ⊕ *www.clubmed. com.au* ⌁ *218 rooms* ⍦ *2 restaurants, in-room safes, 9-hole golf course, 5 tennis courts, 2 pools, fitness classes, beach, snorkeling, windsurfing, boating, jet skiing, fishing, archery, badminton, basketball, hiking, volleyball, 3 bars, cabaret, dance club, theater, children's programs (ages 2–14), laundry facilities, Internet room, airstrip, travel services; no room phones, no room TVs* 🖃 *AE, DC, MC, V* ⍩ *AI.*

Sports & the Outdoors

Club Med's basic price includes most activities, including their trademark flying trapeze school, a 9-hole golf course, tennis, and swimming, although you have to pay for motorized water sports. You can also take refresher scuba-diving courses or enjoy offshore excursions to Whitehaven Beach for an additional fee. Dive excursions to the outer reef by air are 30 minutes each way. By boat it's two hours each way.

Arriving & Departing

BY BOAT   There are direct half-hour water-taxi transfers to Lindeman Island from **Hamilton Island Airport** (☎ 07/4946–9999).

BY PLANE   **Island Air Taxis** (☎ 07/4946–9933) fly to the Lindeman airstrip on demand. The one-way cost is A$105 from Proserpine, A$60 from Shute Harbour, A$60 from Hamilton Island, and A$135 from Mackay.

Long Island

This aptly named narrow island lies off the coast south of Shute Harbour. Although it's 9 km (5½ mi) long and no more than 1½ km (1 mi) wide—7,680 acres total—it has walking trails through large areas of thick, undisturbed rain forest, which is protected as national parkland. Some of the beaches here are pretty and picturesque, others are rocky and windblown. As it's so close to the mainland, box jellyfish are a problem here. The tides are mercurial, too, coming in and out drastically, which makes for murky waters, low visibility, and uneven coastlines. It's a better spot for walking and hiking, along 13 km (8 mi) of tracks, than for sunbathing.

Where to Stay & Eat

$$$$ ✕🖾 **South Long Island Nature Lodge.** With a maximum of 10 guests, this intimate lodge accessible only by helicopter is free of TVs and phones. You'll be so relaxed by the simple beauty of it, not to mention the sound of the ocean lapping against the beach, that you won't remember what day it is, let alone what you might be missing on HBO. Each of the private cabins has both a king-sized and a single bed, and a private veranda with a double hammock—perfect for watching romantic sunsets. Walls are adorned with photos from around the island. Unlike some other exclusive resorts, this one welcomes those traveling on their own: it doesn't impose a single surcharge for sole occupancy of a bungalow. There's a five-night minimum stay, but a 10% rate discount if you book online. The lodge owns and operates a sailing catamaran; excursions with lunch are included. The tariff includes meals, snorkeling equipment, sailing excursions, wet suits, helicopter transfers, and even seaplane excursions to the outer reef. ⌕ *Box 842, Airlie Beach, QLD 4802* ☎🖷 *07/4946–9777* ⊕ *www.southlongisland.com* ⇆ *10 cabins* ⚐ *Dining room, beach, snorkeling, boating, hiking, bar, shop, helipad; no a/c, no room phones, no room TVs, no kids under 15* ☰ *MC, V* ¶⃝¶ *AI.*

★ $$$–$$$$ ✕🖾 **Peppers Palm Bay Hideaway.** The Peppers luxury hotel chain has a great reputation in Australia—and this elegant property, with its attentive service and gorgeous setting, lives up to the hype. All 21 rooms, in A-frame bungalows of varying size, have private balconies with hammocks overlooking the beach. Cabins are equivalent to standard rooms, with beds and en suite facilities decorated in dark wood and neutral colors; *bures* (tropical-style bungalows with thatched roofs) have lounges; bungalows are full suites with two separate lounge areas. Packages include restaurant meals, or you can pay a room-only rate. The saltwater pool is a unique feature, and the lagoon pool is also delightful. ⊠ *Palm Bay Hideaway, PMB 28, via Mackay, QLD 4740* ☎ *07/ 4946–9233 or 1800/095025* 🖷 *07/4946–9309* ⊕ *www.peppers.com. au* ⇦ *15 bungalows, 6 cabins* ⚲ *Restaurant, fans, minibars, pool, out-door hot tub, library, shop, laundry service; no room phones, no room TVs* ⊟ *AE, DC, MC, V* ⫝̸ *CP.*

¢–$$ ✕🏠 **Long Island Resort.** Just a short walk over the hill from Palm Bay, this family-focused resort might as well be on an entirely different is-land. This is not the place to commune quietly with nature, because the resort focuses on outdoor activities, particularly on water sports such as jet skiing and windsurfing. While the no-cost kids' club for children ages 4–14 is meant to enable the adults to enjoy their leisure time un-interrupted, the club is adjourned from noon to 5 PM, which means there are lots of little ones running around. Air-conditioned beachfront and garden-view rooms have en suite bathrooms and private balconies; bud-get lodge rooms are fan-cooled and have shared facilities. The island and the resort are easily accessed via ferry, launch, and two airports, making it a great base for island-hopping. ⊠ *Box 798, Airlie Beach, QLD 4802* ☎ *07/4946–9400 or 1800/075125* 🖷 *07/4946–9555* ⊕ *www.clubcroc.com.au* ⇦ *160 rooms, 60 with shared bath* ⚲ *Restau-rant, café, tennis court, 2 pools, sauna, spa, snorkeling, windsurfing, boating, jet skiing, waterskiing, fishing, basketball, nightclub, babysit-ting, children's programs (ages 4–14), laundry facilities, Internet room; no a/c in some rooms* ⊟ *AE, DC, MC, V* ⫝̸ *MAP.*

Arriving & Departing

BY BOAT You can reach Long Island (but not South Long Island Nature Lodge) by **Fantasea Cruises** (☎ 07/4946–5111 ⊕ www.fantasea.com.au) from either Shute Harbour or Hamilton Island. Boats leave Shute Harbour for Long Island Resort and Palm Bay daily; the 30-minute journey costs A$44 round-trip. A water taxi meets each flight into Hamilton Island, and the 30- to 45-minute transfer to either resort costs A$77 round-trip.

Hamilton Island

Though it's the most heavily populated and developed island in the Whit-sunday group, more than 70% of Hamilton Island has been carefully preserved in its natural state, which translates into beautiful beaches (such as the long, curving palm-dotted Catseye Beach), native bush trails, and spectacular lookouts. Yet for all its natural beauty the 1,482-acre island is more of a place to have an action-packed, sociable holiday than to get away from it all.

Only 30 minutes by ferry from Shute Harbour, Hamilton (called "Hamo" by locals) buzzes with activity. Guests of the resort, and its four types of accommodations, make up most of the population, but there are pri-vate residences here as well as throngs of day-trippers who wander the island's studio-back-lot-style marina and village each day.

Hamilton is set up as a small city, with its own school, post office, su-permarket, video store, shops, restaurants, and bars that both guests and day-trippers are free to visit. But little on Hamilton is free. Because amenities are targeted to resort guests, prices for everything are steep, and access to most of the island's attractions, from the koala gallery zoo to the motorized water sports, cost even more. Even the ubiquitous golf carts that guests use to zip around the island in are A$35 per hour, or A$75 a day, to rent.

Perhaps because of the volume of visitors, the quality of the service and the restaurant meals on Hamo tends to be lower than on some of the more private, exclusive islands. Still, for a family-friendly, one-stop-shop reef experience in a beautiful setting, Hamo is a good bet.

Where to Eat

Hamilton Island Resort has more than a dozen dining options, including several casual cafés and restaurants.

$–$$$ ✕ **Beach House.** This is Hamilton Island's signature dress-up restaurant, set right on Catseye Beach in a beach house overlooking the cerulean waters. Extravagant seven-course lunches and à la carte dinners focus on choices like barramundi served with roast-pepper salsa, or char-grilled chicken breast with ratatouille and balsamic syrup. ⊠ *Main resort complex* ☎ *07/4946–8580* ▭ *AE, DC, MC, V* ☾ *Closed Mon.*

$–$$$ ✕ **Romanos Italiano Restaurant.** With polished wood floors and a balcony overlooking the marina, Romanos is the place to come for casual, fine dining. The kitchen produces traditional Italian favorites such as *amatriciana* (pasta with tomato, bacon, onion, and chili), but the real focus is on seafood and seafood-pasta combination dishes. ⊠ *Marina Village, Harbourside* ☎ *07/4946–9999* ▭ *AE, DC, MC, V* ☾ *Closed Tues. No lunch.*

¢–$ ✕ **Toucan Tango Café.** Vibrant summer colors, high ceilings, an Italian terrazzo floor, and potted palms fill this tropical-theme restaurant overlooking the waters of both Catseye Beach and the main resort. This is the island's relaxed all-day dining option, with a large menu of snacks and a seafood buffet on Friday and Saturday nights. The daily buffet breakfast by the beach is the best offering. ⊠ *Main resort complex* ☎ *07/4946–9999* ▭ *AE, DC, MC, V.*

Where to Stay

You can make reservations for all accommodations on Hamilton Island with the **Hamilton Island Resort** (⊠ Hamilton Island, Whitsunday Islands, QLD 4803 ☎ 1800/075110 ⊕ www.hamiltonisland.com.au).

★ $$$$ ▦ **Beach Club Resort.** If you never left the gorgeous infinity pool at the Beach Club, which overlooks a picture-perfect stretch of beach, took all your meals poolside and your cocktails in the Club Lounge and Bar, you would believe, as the staff want you to, that you're in the ultimate beach resort. The rooms, however, don't match the rest of the lavish property. Many of them are dark, and the modern wood furniture has a chain-hotel drabness. They do, however, have stereos and VCRs, and staying here also get you buggy chauffeur service around the island, daily newspapers, and free Internet access. The staff are efficient, but not especially friendly—especially if you ask them for too many favors. ⊠ *Hamilton Island, Whitsunday Islands, QLD 4803* ☎ *1800/075110* ⊕ *www. hamiltonisland.com.au* ⌔ *55 rooms* ☖ *Room service, refrigerators,* *in-room VCRs, pool, beach, laundry service, Internet; no kids* ▤ *AE, DC, MC, V.*

$$$–$$$$ 🏨 **Reef View Hotel.** This hotel only lives up to its name on the higher floors; the rooms here have spectacular vistas of the Coral Sea, while others overlook a landscaped, tropical garden. All have private balconies. Rooms are spacious and comfortable, although many give the impression of having been decorated more than 10 years ago. There are Caribbean-tropical print linens, tile floors, bright walls, and floral-print furnishings. Suites are also available. ⊠ *Hamilton Island, Whitsunday Islands, QLD 4803* ☎ *1800/075110* ⊕ *www.hamiltonisland.com.au* ⌁ *370 rooms, 12 suites* ⚘ *Restaurant, room service, minibars, refrigerators, pool, spa, laundry facilities, concierge, no-smoking floor* ▤ *AE, DC, MC, V.*

$$$ 🏨 **Whitsunday Holiday Apartments.** These twin 13-story towers, which overlook the Coral Sea toward Whitsunday Island, have the only self-contained apartments on Hamilton Island. The one- and two-bedroom accommodations have pastel walls, comfortable wooden and cane furniture, large balconies, fully equipped kitchens, and dining and sitting areas—everything you need to feel at home. ⊠ *Hamilton Island, Whitsunday Islands, QLD 4803* ☎ *1800/075110* ⊕ *www.hamiltonisland. com.au* ⌁ *176 apartments* ⚘ *Kitchens, refrigerators, in-room VCRs, 2 pools, outdoor hot tub, laundry facilities* ▤ *AE, DC, MC, V.*

$$–$$$ 🏨 **Palm Bungalows and Terrace.** The steep-roofed, freestanding bungalows at this accommodation complex resemble Polynesian huts. Each has a private furnished balcony, cool tile floors, a small bar, and a king-sized bed with bright floral bedspread. Budget-friendlier, contemporary hotel rooms are also available at the Terrace part of the property—a series of town-house-style buildings. ⊠ *Hamilton Island, Whitsunday Islands, QLD 4803* ☎ *1800/075110* ⊕ *www.hamiltonisland.com.au* ⌁ *50 bungalows, 60 rooms* ⚘ *Minibars, pool, outdoor hot tub* ▤ *AE, DC, MC, V.*

Nightlife

At **Boheme's Bar & Nightclub** (⊠ Main resort complex ☎ 07/4946–9990) you can dance to live or DJ-spun music and shoot a round of pool. The bar opens Wednesday to Sunday at 9 PM, while the nightclub is open 11 PM–3 AM.

Sports & the Outdoors

Hamilton Island Resort has the widest selection of activities in the Whitsundays. Activities include bushwalking, go-carts, a golf driving range, miniature golf, a health club, a target-shooting range, parasailing, game fishing, scuba diving, waterskiing, speedboats, Jet Skis, catamarans, sea kayaking, and windsurfing, as well as six swimming pools and floodlighted tennis courts. Reserve ahead through the **Tour Booking Desk** (☎ 07/4946–8305).

Hamilton Island is so family-friendly it allows kids to stay free, provided they use existing bedding in the rooms (no roll-away beds or cribs). Kids under age 14 also can eat free at six of the island's restaurants when accompanied by their parents. The **Clownfish Club** (☎ 07/4946–8941 ⊕ www.clownfishclub.com.au), for children ages 6 weeks to 14 years, has organized sand-castle making, snorkeling, water polo, beach sports, and more. Babysitting services are also available for A$15 per hour (minimum three hours).

FISHING The 40-foot deep-sea game-fishing boat, *Balek III* and the *Drag-n-Fly* catamaran make two-hour trips to the outer reef for marlin, sailfish, Spanish mackerel, and tuna. Charters can be arranged through Hamilton Island's **Tour Booking Desk** (☎ 07/4946–8305) year-round. Private charters cost A$1,600 for a full day on *Balek III,*; shared charters are A$225. All equipment is included.

SCUBA DIVING Hamilton runs a complimentary introductory scuba course including instruction, equipment, and a dive. If you're already qualified, equipment can be rented and trips arranged. A single dive with **H2O Sportz** (☎ 07/4946–8217), the island's dive shop, runs A$55; a two-tank dive costs A$70.

Shopping
Hamilton Island's Marina Village houses many shops selling resort wear, children's clothes, souvenirs, and gifts. An art gallery, art studio, florist, small supermarket, pharmacy, realty agent, medical center, video store, and beauty salon are also on the premises.

Arriving & Departing
BY BOAT **Blue Ferries** (☎ 1800/650851) makes the 35-minute journey from Shute Harbour eight times daily for A$62 round-trip.

BY PLANE **Qantas** (☎ 13–1313) and **Jetstar** (☎ 13–1538) fly directly to the island daily from Sydney, Brisbane, Cairns, and Townsville. Flights from other interstate capitals are available. Boat transfers to Whitsunday resort islands can be made from the wharf adjoining the airport.

Tour Operators
The resort's **Tour Booking Desk** (☎07/4946–8305) can organize scenic flights over the Whitsunday Islands and the reef by plane or helicopter, plus seaplane flights to the reef. Transfers to the other islands are available.

★ **Fantasea Cruises** (☎ 07/4946–5111 tour booking desk) runs reef trips daily from Hamilton and other islands, as well as from all mainland Whitsunday resorts. From Hamilton it's a 75-km (47-mi) trip to the company's own Reefworld pontoon on magnificent **Hardy Reef Lagoon,** where you can swim, snorkel, ride in a semisubmersible, or simply relax. Cost is A$166 with a buffet lunch. You can do a dive lesson and introductory dive for A$243. It's also possible to overnight on the Reefworld pontoon (A$360 per person in a shared, four-bunk dorm, or A$424 per double room).

Fodor's Choice
★
Fantasea also runs daily high-speed catamaran trips (starting at A$77) to **Whitehaven Beach,** a justifiably famous and spectacular stretch of pure white silica sand as fine (and a messy) as talcum powder. Slather yourself in sunblock when you lie out here—the sand acts as a reflector for the sun, so you can get a bad burn here—or swim in the crystal clear, temperate, jellyfish-free water. The beach, which is its own island, is 6½ km (4 mi) long.

Hamilton Island's **Sunsail Australia** (✉ Front St. ☎ 07/4946–9900 or 1800/ 803988 ⊕ www.sunsail.com.au) has 29 boats available for charter and group trips.

South Molle Island

South Molle, a 1,040-acre island close to Shute Harbour, was originally inhabited by Aborigines, who collected basalt here to use for their axes. Much later, it became the first of the Whitsundays to be used for grazing, hence its extensive grassy tracts. Now the island is a national park with a single, family-oriented resort settled on sheltered Bauer Bay in the north. Protected between two headlands, the bay often remains calm when wind rips through the rest of the Whitsundays.

Where to Stay & Eat

$$$–$$$$ ✕🏨 **South Molle Island Resort.** Known as an Aussie budget getaway, this resort offers great value as well as easy reef access. Nestled in a bay at the northern end of the island, the property includes a long jetty reaching out beyond the fringing reef. Every room has a balcony, a whirlpool tub, and sea or garden views. Meals and most activities are included in the rate, with the exception of motorized sports. This is one of the few islands on the reef that has a golf course, and the family-oriented setting means first-timers never feel intimidated trying to windsurf or waterski. ✉ *South Molle Island, via Shute Harbour, QLD 4741* ☎ *07/ 4946–9433 or 1800/075080* 🖷 *07/4946–9580* ⊕ *www.southmolleisland. com.au* ✑ *200 rooms* ⚇ *2 restaurants, in-room hot tubs, refrigerators, 9-hole golf course, 2 tennis courts, pool, wading pool, gym, outdoor hot tub, massage, beach, dive shop, snorkeling, windsurfing, jet skiing, waterskiing, archery, volleyball, babysitting, children's programs (ages 6–12), laundry service* ▭ *AE, DC, MC, V* ⦿ *AI.*

Arriving & Departing

BY BOAT **Fantasea Cruises** (☎ 07/4946–5111) ferries passengers from Shute Harbour (A$40 round-trip) and Hamilton Island (A$62 round-trip).

Daydream Island

The resort on this small, 42-acre island is especially welcoming to day-trippers. Just 20 minutes from Shute Harbour, it's a perfect place to relax or pursue outdoor activities such as hiking and snorkeling—all of which are relatively affordable. The resort has lush gardens that blend into a rain forest, which is, of course, surrounded by clear blue water and fringing coral reef.

Where to Stay & Eat

$$$–$$$$ ✕🏨 **Daydream Island Resort.** Decorated in colors so bright you might want sunglasses, this family-focused resort has a staff that's similarly cheerful. Spacious garden- or ocean-view condo-style apartments have modern cane and wooden furniture, terra-cotta-tile floors, and brightly colored beach-theme fabrics. Activities—all free except boating—vary from snorkeling the sunny reef to catching an open-air movie under the stars. Breakfast is the only meal included, but you can dine at the à la

CloseUp

THE REEF

THE GREAT BARRIER REEF IS A LIVING ANIMAL. *Early scientists, however, thought it was a plant, which is forgivable. Soft corals have a plantlike growth and a horny skeleton that runs along the inside of the stem. In contrast, the hard, calcareous skeletons of stony corals are the main building blocks of the reef. There are also two main classes of reefs: platform or patch reefs, which result from radial growth, and wall reefs, which result from elongated growth, often in areas of strong water currents. Fringing reefs occur where the growth is established on sub-tidal rock, either on the mainland or on continental islands.*

It's hard to imagine that the reef, which covers an area about half the size of Texas, is so fragile that even human sweat can cause damage. However, despite its size, the reef is a finely balanced ecosystem sustaining zillions of tiny polyps, which have been building on top of each other for thousands of years. So industrious are these critters that the reef is more than 1,640 feet thick in some places. These polyps are also fussy about their living conditions and only survive in clear, salty water around 18°C (64°F) and less than 98 feet deep.

Closely related to anemones and jellyfish, marine polyps are primitive, sacklike animals with a mouth surrounded by tentacles. Coral can consist of one polyp (solitary) or many hundreds (colonial), which form a colony when joined together. These polyps create a hard surface by producing lime; as they die, their coral "skeletons" remain, which form the reef's white substructure. The living polyps give the coral its colorful appearance.

The Great Barrier Reef begins south of the tropic of Capricorn around Gladstone and ends in the Torres Strait below Papua New Guinea, making it about 2,000 km (1,240 mi) long and 356,000 square km (137,452 square mi) in area. Declared a World Heritage Site in 1981, it is managed by the Great Barrier Reef Marine Park Authority, which was itself established in 1976. Consequently, detailed observations and measurements of coral reef environments only date back to around this time. Thus, annual density bands in coral skeletons, similar to rings formed in trees, are important potential storehouses of information about past marine environmental conditions.

The Great Barrier Reef attracts thousands of divers and snorkelers every year. Apart from the coral, divers can swim with 2,000 species of fish, dolphins, dugongs, sea urchins, and turtles. There are also about 400 species of coral and 4,000 species of mollusk, as well as a diversity of sponges, anemones, marine worms, and crustaceans.

Dive sites are unlimited, set around approximately 3,000 individual reefs, 300 coral cays, 890 fringing reefs, and 2,600 islands (including 618 continental islands that were once part of the mainland). Despite the vast amount of water surrounding the islands, though, freshwater is nonexistent here and thus is a precious commodity; self-sufficiency is particularly important for explorers and campers. Removing or damaging any part of the reef is a crime, so divers are asked to take home only photographs and memories of one of the world's great natural wonders.

— Jane Carstens

carte Mermaids Restaurant or choose the Tavern restaurant-bar for contemporary Australian and seafood plates. Child care is available at additional cost, so you can drop the kids off and head to the Daydream Rejuvenation Spa, the best in the Whitsundays. The island is owned by a vitamin magnate, whose interest in naturopathy is reflected in the spa's diverse services, including computerized iridology and instant blood typing. ⊠ *Daydream Island, PMB 22, via Mackay, QLD 4740* ☎ *07/ 4948–8488 or 1800/075040* 🖷 *07/4948–8479* ⊕ *www.daydream.net. au* 🛏 *296 rooms* ♨ *3 restaurants, coffee shop, miniature golf, 2 tennis courts, 3 pools, gym, sauna, spa, dive shop, snorkeling, windsurfing, jet skiing, waterskiing, badminton, 3 bars, cinema, recreation room, babysitting, children's programs (ages 6 wks–12 years), laundry service, travel services* ▭ *AE, DC, MC, V* ⦺ *CP.*

Sports & the Outdoors

Most sports are included in room rates. Parasailing, fishing, snorkeling, waterskiing, jet skiing, and miniature golf are provided for an additional charge. Day excursions to the surrounding islands and the Great Barrier Reef are also available. The resort also offers introductory dives for A$110 and one-tank dives for A$70. Nonguests can also book activities through the resort.

Arriving & Departing

BY BOAT **Fantasea Cruises** (☎ 07/4946–5111) runs regularly to Daydream from Shute Harbour (A$40 round-trip). The company also runs boats to Hamilton Island for A$62 round-trip.

BY PLANE Although most people come by boat from Hamilton Airport, an alternative is to fly to **Proserpine Airport** on the mainland, catch a bus to Shute Harbour, and take a boat to the island. Boat transportation can be booked through the island's reservations office. **Virgin Blue** (☎ 13–6789), **Qantas** (☎ 13–1313), and **Jetstar** (☎ 13–1538) operate flights to and from Proserpine Airport. Check with each carrier for weight restrictions.

Hayman Island

Fodor'sChoice Hayman Island, in the northern Whitsunday Passage, is a 900-acre
★ crescent with a series of hills along its spine. The closest of the Whitsundays to the Outer Barrier reef, Hayman's renowned resort is one of the oldest and most opulent in the region, and is consequently very popular with jet-setters who take their play and leisure seriously. The service here—understated yet completely attentive—truly merits the price you pay for it; staff members even traverse the resort via underground tunnels so they're not too much of a "presence." Reflecting pools, sandstone walkways, manicured tropical gardens, and sparkling waterfalls provide the feel of an exclusive club within the resort grounds, while beautiful walking trails crisscross the island around it. The main beach sits right in front of the hotel, but more secluded sands, as well as fringing coral, can be reached by boat.

Where to Eat

All restaurants are in the resort. Reservations are recommended and can be booked through the resort's concierge.

★ $$$　✕ **La Fontaine.** With Waterford chandeliers and Louis XVI furnishings, this elegant French restaurant is the resort's culinary showpiece. The cuisine rivals the finest restaurants on the mainland and highlights such innovative dishes as chicken breast and wing stuffed with lobster in cream sauce, and roast medallions of lamb with compote of shallots and red-pepper coulis. Live music usually accompanies dinner. A private dining room, where you can design your own menu in consultation with the chef, is available. ⬜ *Jacket required* ▭ *AE, DC, MC, V* ☺ *No lunch.*

$$–$$$　✕ **Oriental Restaurant.** This Asian establishment overlooks a teahouse and Japanese garden, complete with soothing rock pools and waterfalls. Black lacquer chairs, shoji screens, and superb Japanese artifacts fill the dining room. Menu choices include both exotic and classic pan-Asian creations like *hoi man poo* (Thai-style mussels in black-bean sauce) and shark-fin soup. ▭ *AE, DC, MC, V* ☺ *No lunch.*

$$　✕ **La Trattoria.** With its red-and-white–checkered tablecloths and casual furnishings, "Tratt's" is a classic provincial Italian restaurant that may make you feel you've been whisked to Portofino. Seated either inside or outdoors, you can choose from an extensive list of pastas and traditional Italian dishes. ▭ *AE, DC, MC, V* ☺ *No lunch.*

★ $–$$　✕ **Azure.** Right in front of the island's main beach, this casual restaurant affords gorgeous views. Dining is indoors or alfresco, with seating extending to the sand. There's a splendid buffet breakfast each morning, with tropical fruits and juices, and contemporary Australian cuisine throughout the day and night. The specialty is fresh local seafood. ▭ *AE, DC, MC, V.*

Where to Stay

$$$$　⬚ **Hayman Island Resort.** Well-heeled types come here to be seen, and to brag about having stayed here. Lavish decor, including Asian and Australian artifacts, European tapestries, Persian rugs, and exquisite objets d'art, enliven this property's lobby, restaurants, and rooms. Lagoon, Pool, Beach Garden, or Beachfront suites are all beautifully appointed and overlook the different areas of the resort they're named for. For complete luxury, nothing tops the penthouse suites, decorated in different themes like French Provincial or Italian Palazzo. Expect to pay handsomely for all this finery—even little things like bar drinks cost a small fortune. ✉ *Hayman Island, QLD 4801* ☎ *07/4940–1234 or 1800/ 075175* ⊟ *07/4940–1567* ⊕ *www.hayman.com.au* ⬗ *216 rooms, 18 suites, 11 penthouses* ᗑ *5 restaurants, room service, in-room safes, minibars, refrigerators, putting green, 6 tennis courts, 3 pools, health club, hair salon, sauna, spa, steam room, beach, dive shop, snorkeling, windsurfing, parasailing, waterskiing, fishing, badminton, billiards, volleyball, 2 bars, library, babysitting, children's programs (ages 5–15), laundry service, Internet room, business services, convention center, helipad* ▭ *AE, DC, MC, V.*

Sports & the Outdoors

All nonmotorized water sports on Hayman Island are included in the rates. The resort's water-sports center has a training tank for diving lessons, and a dive shop sells everything from snorkel gear to complete wet suits and sports clothing. The marina organizes parasailing, waterskiing, sailing, boating, fishing, coral-viewing, windsurfing, and snorkeling, as well as dive trips. Contact the resort's **Recreation Information Centre** (☎ 07/4940–1725) for reservations and information.

Arriving & Departing

BY PLANE Hayman doesn't have an airstrip of its own, but you can fly into Hamilton Island on Qantas or Jetstar and transfer onto one of Hayman's luxury motor yachts. Australian sparkling wine is served during the 60-minute trip to the island. Upon your arrival at the wharf, a shuttle whisks you to the resort about 1 km (½ mi) away. Make sure you are ticketed all the way to Hayman Island, including the motor-yacht leg, as purchasing the round-trip yacht journey from Hamilton Island to Hayman separately will cost upward of A$300. **Air Whitsunday** (☎ 07/4946–9111) provides seaplane connections from Hamilton to Hayman for A$675 one way.

Tour Operators

The Hayman Island Resort's **Recreation Information Centre** (☎ 07/4940–1725) provides information on all guided tours from or around the island.

A 90-minute coral-viewing trip aboard the *Reef Dancer* (A$66 per person) departs three or four times daily. The coral is viewed from a semisubmersible sub. A Whitehaven Beach Picnic Cruise (A$152) departs Tuesday and Friday at 9:45, the price includes lunch.

Reef Goddess, Hayman Island's own boat, makes Great Barrier Reef excursions Monday, Wednesday, Thursday, and Saturday from 9:15 to 3:30. The A$178 per-person charge includes snorkeling, some drinks, and a light lunch. There's a dive master on board, and the day-trip cost for divers is A$310, which includes weight belt, two tanks, and lunch. Additional equipment can be hired.

You can take **scenic flights** over or to the Great Barrier Reef by seaplane or helicopter; rates start at A$250 per person. At the reef, activities include snorkeling, coral viewing from a semisubmersible sub, and refreshments.

NORTH COAST ISLANDS

Orpheus Island

Volcanic in origin, this narrow island—11 km (7 mi) long and 1 km (½ mi) wide, 3,500 acres total—uncoils like a snake in the waters between Halifax Bay and the Barrier Reef. It's part of the Palm Island Group, which consists of 10 islands, 8 of which are Aboriginal reservations which you need permission to visit. Orpheus is a national park, occupied only by a marine research station and its fantastic resort. Although there are patches of rain forest in the island's deeper gullies and around the sheltered bays, Orpheus is a true Barrier Reef island, ringed by seven unspoiled sandy beaches and superb coral. Incredibly, 340 of the known 350 species of coral inhabit these waters, as well as some amazing giant clams. The marine life is so easily accessed and so extraordinary here, it's no wonder the island is the sole domain of the maximum 42 guests allowed at the resort. You may occasionally see unfamiliar boats offshore, which is their right according to a marine park treaty, but you'll know everyone on Orpheus at any given time, maybe even by name.

Where to Stay & Eat

$$$$
Fodor'sChoice
★

✕⊡ **Orpheus Island Resort.** Nestled among palm trees and lush tropical gardens, this intimate island sanctuary offers two types of beachfront accommodation: the Nautilus Suites and the Orpheus Retreats. Both choices are immaculate, comfortable, and decorated with tasteful sophistication, but suites are considerably larger, with private outdoor areas and lounge rooms. You won't want to spend too long in your room, though—not when the coral gardens thriving under clear blue waters and the white sand are beckoning you. With only 42 guests (and no clocks) on the island, activities can be scheduled at any time you like. You'll need to do a lot of swimming, diving, and hiking, though, to work off the extravagant gourmet meals served every night. Dining with the tides on the jetty and feeding the mullet fish by candlelight is a unique and unforgettable experience. ⊠ *Orpheus Island, PMB 15, Townsville Mail Centre, QLD 4810* ☎ *07/4777–7377* 📠 *07/4777–7533* ⊕ *www. orpheus.com.au* ⬩ *17 rooms, 4 suites* ⬩ *Restaurant, tennis court, 2 pools, gym, hot tub, spa, beach, snorkeling, boating, fishing, hiking, 2 bars, recreation room, Internet room; no room phones, no room TVs, no kids under 15* ⊟ *AE, DC, MC, V* ¶◎¶ *AI.*

Sports & the Outdoors

The resort is surrounded by walking trails, and there's spectacular snorkeling and diving right off the beaches. Dive courses cost A$250, two-tank dives are A$175. Most nonboating activities are included in the rate, and outer-reef fishing charters can be arranged. Trips are subject to weather conditions. A minimum of six passengers is required.

Arriving & Departing

BY PLANE   Orpheus Island lies 24 km (15 mi) offshore of Ingham, about 80 km (50 mi) northeast of Townsville, and 190 km (118 mi) south of Cairns. The 25-minute flight from Townsville to Orpheus aboard a Nautilus Aviation seaplane costs A$450 per person round-trip. Book flights when you make your reservation with Orpheus Island Resort. A maximum of 15 kilograms (33 pounds) of luggage is allowed on board, though special arrangements can be made to ship excess baggage by barge for longer stays.

Tour Operators

The coral around Orpheus is some of the best in the area, and cruises to the outer reef can be arranged through the resort. Whereas most of the islands are more than 50 km (31 mi) from the reef, Orpheus is just 15 km (9 mi) away.

Hinchinbrook Island

This 97,000-acre national park is the largest island on the Great Barrier Reef. It's a nature-lover's paradise, with dense tropical rain forests, mangroves, mountain peaks, sandy beaches. When Captain Cook discovered it in 1770, he didn't realize it was an island, and mistakenly named it Mount Hinchinbrook (likely imagining that 3,746-foot Mt. Bowen, Australia's third-highest mountain, was part of the mainland). Dolphins and sea turtles inhabit the waters, as well as fish you are allowed to catch (a rarity given the strict protection of the reef's marine life). The island is virtually untouched, save for a small resort on the northeast corner of the island and some well-placed toilets and campsites, compliments of the **Queensland National Parks and Wildlife Service** (☎ 07/4066–8601)—contact them for essential information and camping permits. These permits are essential for camping, and need to be reserved up to eight weeks in advance of your visit. **Hinchinbrook Visitor Information** (☎ 07/4776–5221) can also provide information.

Where to Stay & Eat

$$$ ✕▣ **Hinchinbrook Wilderness Lodge & Resort.** Limited to 50 guests, this small resort specializes in quiet enjoyment. Set amid the beautiful bush on the northeast corner of the island, clean, modern tree houses and self-contained cabins offer unspoiled sea views from private balconies. Experienced chefs cater to guests' specific requests, with a focus on modern Australian cuisine. Self-catering is an option for guests of the beach cabins; you can bring your own provisions or the resort will have them sent over from the mainland for you. Service is responsive, but understated. The resort is closed annually between February 2 and March 23. ⬧ *Box 3, Cardwell, QLD 4849* ☎ *07/4066–8270* ⬧ *07/4066–8271* ⊕ *www. hinchinbrooklodge.com.au* ⬧ *15 tree houses, 7 beach cabins* ⬧ *Restaurant, refrigerators, some kitchens, pool, snorkeling, boating, fishing, bar, lounge, library, laundry facilities* ▭ *AE, DC, MC, V* ⬧⬧ *MAP*.

Sports & the Outdoors

The focus here is on the island's environment, not the one underwater. Snorkeling and swimming are both good here, but nature walks through the varied and spectacular landscapes are the primary attraction.

Arriving & Departing

BY BOAT Hinchinbrook is a 50-minute ferry ride from the mainland town of Cardwell, which is 190 km (118 mi) south of Cairns and 161 km (100 mi) north of Townsville. Scheduled ferries depart from Cardwell at 9 AM and return at 4 PM. Round-trip fare is A$96. Nonscheduled departures can be arranged for A$120. Contact the lodge of the Queensland National Parks and Wildlife Service for more information.

Dunk Island

A member of the Family Islands, this 2,397-acre island is divided by a hilly spine that runs its entire length. The eastern side consists mostly of national park, with dense rain forest and secluded beaches accessible only by boat. Beautiful paths have been created through the rain forest, where you might be lucky enough to glimpse a Ulysses butterfly—a beautiful blue variety with a wingspan that can reach 6 inches. Dunk is located 4½ km (2 mi) from Mission Beach on the mainland, making it a popular spot for day-trippers.

Where to Stay & Eat

$$–$$$ ✕▦ **Dunk Island Resort.** Coconut palms, flowering hibiscus, and frangipani surround this informal, family-oriented resort on the island's west side. Cool tile floors, wicker furniture, and pastel color schemes make the Beachfront Units the best value, while latticed balconies assure the most privacy. The airy Garden Cabanas lack beach views but sit among tropical gardens. Wood beams, cane furniture, and potted plants fill the Beachcomber Restaurant, which serves pasta and seafood. BB's on the Beach serves snacks, burgers, and pizzas. While the resort touts itself as an activity-fueled holiday spot (a widely varied menu of activity options is available each day), relaxation is easily found beachside, poolside, or at the resort's Spa of Peace and Plenty. *⌂ Voyages, GPO 3859, Sydney, NSW 2001 ☎ 02/8296–8010 ⊕ www.dunk-island.com ⤴ 144 rooms, 24 suites, 32 cabanas ☼ 2 restaurants, 2 cafés, refrigerators, 18-hole golf course, 3 tennis courts, 2 pools, fitness classes, gym, hair salon, spa, beach, boating, jet skiing, parasailing, waterskiing, archery, badminton, basketball, boccie, croquet, horseback riding, squash, volleyball, 2 bars, babysitting, children's programs (ages 3–14), playground, laundry service, Internet room, airstrip ⊟ AE, DC, MC, V ⦿ MAP.*

Sports & the Outdoors

In addition to reef cruises and fishing charters, the resort has many choices of water sports. Rates include all sports except horseback riding, scuba diving, and activities requiring fuel. The resort also provides a bushwalking map of the island's well-maintained trails.

Arriving & Departing

BY BOAT **Dunk Ferry** (☎ 07/4068–7211) runs launches that depart from the mainland from Clump Point Jetty in Mission Beach daily for the 20-minute ride to Dunk Island. Departures are at 9:30 and 4:30, returning at 5 and 10 PM. The round-trip fare is A$34, resort transfers are A$50. Coach connections to Cairns are available.

The **Dunk Island Express water taxi** (☎ 07/4068–8310) is the best option for day-trippers. It departs Mission Beach for Dunk Island five times daily, for a very choppy 10-minute ride. It's necessary to disembark in shallow waters, so you should take care to keep your luggage from getting wet. The round-trip fare costs A$26 for a day trip, A$30 for resort guests.

BY PLANE Dunk Island has its own landing strip. **Macair Airlines** (☎ 13–1313 ⊕ www.macair.com.au) serves the island three times daily from Cairns for A$380 round-trip. You can check up to 16 kilograms (35 pounds) of luggage and bring an additional 4 kilograms (9 pounds) on board as hand luggage.

TOUR OPERATORS The **Dunk Ferry's *MV Kavanaugh*** (☎ 07/4068–7211), a large passenger catamaran, makes the 45-minute trip to the island daily, with a buffet lunch, for A$90.

Bedarra Island

This tiny, 247-acre island 5 km (3 mi) off the coast of Mission Beach has natural springs, a dense rain forest, and eight separate beaches. Bedarra Island is a tranquil getaway popular with affluent executives and entertainment notables who want complete escape. It's the only Great Barrier Reef resort with an open bar, and the liquor—especially champagne—flows freely. Bedarra accommodates only 30 people, and you stay in freestanding villas hidden amid thick vegetation but still steps from golden beaches.

Where to Stay & Eat

$$$$
Fodor'sChoice
★
✕🎬 **Bedarra Island Resort.** Elevated on stilts, these two-story, open-plan, tropical-style villas blend into the island's dense vegetation. Polished wood floors, ceiling fans, and exposed beams make for bright, airy accommodations that bear little resemblance to standard hotel rooms. Each villa has a balcony with a double hammock, a view of the ocean, a king-sized bed, and a complimentary minibar. Secluded bungalows with private reflecting pools for ocean-view soaking are a short walk from the main compound. All meals and drinks are included in the price—and although there's no room service there is a 24-hour, fully stocked open bar. The restaurant emphasizes seafood and tropical fruit, and despite the full à la carte menu, you are urged to request whatever dishes you like. No children under 16 are allowed, but this isn't a place for anyone who's not of legal drinking age. 🕊 *Voyages, GPO 3589, Sydney, NSW 2001* ☎ *02/8296–8010* ⊕ *www.bedarraisland.com* ↪ *12 villas, 4 bungalows* ⚴ *Restaurant, in-room safes, minibars, cable TV with movies, in-room DVD/VCR, in-room data ports, 6-hole golf course, tennis court, pool, spa, beach, dock, snorkeling, laundry service, Internet room; no kids under 16* ☰ *AE, DC, MC, V* ⦿*AI.*

Sports & the Outdoors

Snorkeling is possible around the island, although the water can get cloudy during the January and February rains. You can also windsurf, scuba dive, sail, fish, or boat. Other sporting activities, including transfers, can be organized on nearby Dunk Island, and fishing charters can also be arranged.

Arriving & Departing

BY BOAT
Bedarra Island lies a few minutes away by boat from Dunk Island. Round-trip fare is included in the accommodation price.

Tour Operators

To get to the Barrier Reef from Bedarra you have to return to Dunk Island, from which all reef excursions depart.

Fitzroy Island

This rugged, heavily forested national park has vegetation ranging from rain forest to heath, and an extensive fringing reef for snorkeling and diving. Only 6 km (4 mi) from Cairns (less than an hour's cruise), the 988-acre island is popular with day-trippers. The cabins and dormitory-style rooms also make it an affordable overnight option. From June to August manta rays and humpback whales swim around the island as part of their migratory route.

Where to Stay & Eat

¢–$$ ✕▢ **Fitzroy Island.** This affordable reef retreat is very popular with backpackers and young travelers, who are attracted to its easy mainland access and dormitory-style bunk rooms that sleep up to four people. There are also eight two-bedroom cabins here with showers, which are furnished in natural woods and bright prints, with ceiling fans and shaded verandas. The Raging Thunder Beach Bar and Restaurant, billed as the only nightclub on the reef, serves dinner before the dancing and drinking begin—Saturday night features a North Queensland seafood buffet. The Flare Grill provides barbecue lunches, and the kiosk sells take-away foods. ⌂ *Fitzroy Island Resort, Box 1109, Cairns, QLD 4870* ☎ *07/4051–9588* 🖷 *07/4052–1335* ⊕ *www.fitzroyisland.com.au* ⟐ *8 cabins, 32 bunk rooms* ⌂ *Restaurant, snack bar, pool, dive shop, snorkeling, boating, fishing, hiking, bar, laundry facilities, no a/c, no room phones, no TV in some rooms* ▤ *AE, DC, MC, V.*

Sports & the Outdoors

Even day-trippers can rent catamarans, paddle-skiing equipment, and fishing and snorkeling gear at the resort. Sea kayaking tours are A$88, introductory scuba dives are A$65, and guided certified dives cost A$50.

Arriving & Departing

BY BOAT The **Fitzroy Island Ferry** (☎07/4051–9588), which takes 45 minutes to reach the island, departs daily at 8:30, 10:30, and 4 from Marlin Marina in Cairns. Round-trip fare is A$38. Return trips are at 9:30, 3, and 5.

Lizard Island

★ The small, upscale resort on secluded Lizard Island is the farthest north of any Barrier Reef hideaway. At 2,500 acres, it's larger than and quite different from other islands in the region. Composed mostly of granite, Lizard has a remarkable diversity of vegetation and terrain, where grassy hills give way to rocky slabs interspersed with valleys of rain forest.

Ringed by stretches of white-sand beaches, the island is actually a national park with some of the best examples of fringing coral of any of the resort areas. Excellent walking trails lead to key lookouts with spectacular views of the coast. The highest point, Cook's Look (1,180 feet), is the historic spot from which, in August 1770, Captain Cook finally spied a passage through the reef that had held him captive for a thousand miles. Large monitor lizards, for which the island is named, often bask in this area.

★ Diving and snorkeling in the crystal-clear waters off Lizard Island are a dream. **Cod Hole,** 20 km (12 mi) from Lizard Island, ranks as one of the best dive sites in the world. Here massive potato cod swim right up to you like hungry puppies—an awesome experience, considering these fish weigh 300 pounds and are more than 6 feet long. In the latter part of the year, when black marlin are running, Lizard Island becomes the focal point for big-game anglers.

Where to Stay & Eat

$$$$ ✗▦ **Lizard Island Lodge.** One of Australia's premier resorts, this prop-
Fodor'sChoice   erty has beachside suites and sumptuous villas with sail-shaded decks
★   and views of the turquoise bay. The large, comfortable rooms, decorated
in pastels, have polished wood floors and blinds, soft furnishings with
Balarinji Aboriginal motifs, CD players, and private verandas. Meals,
which are included, emphasize seafood and tropical fruits; dishes include
fresh coral trout panfried and served with a passion-fruit sauce. An excellent wine list complements the menu. No children under are 10 allowed. ⌖ *Voyages, GPO 5329, Sydney, NSW 2001* ☎ *02/8296–8010*
⊕ *www.lizardisland.com.au* ⏎ *6 rooms, 18 suites, 15 villas, 1 pavilion* ⚹ *Restaurant, minibars, tennis court, pool, beach, snorkeling, windsurfing, boating, waterskiing, fishing, boccie, bar, laundry service,
Internet room; no kids under 10* ▤ *AE, DC, MC, V* ⊚ *AI.*

Sports & the Outdoors

The lodge has an outdoor pool, a tennis court, catamarans, outboard
dinghies, Windsurfers, paddle skis, and fishing supplies. There is superb
snorkeling around the island's fringing coral. Arrange a picnic hamper
with the kitchen staff ahead of time and you can take a rowboat or sail-
boat out for an afternoon on your own private beach. All these activities are included as part of your lodging rate.

DEEP-SEA GAME   Lizard Island is one of the big-game-fishing centers in Australia, with
FISHING   several world records set here in the last decade. Fishing is best between
August and December, and a marlin weighing more than 1,200 pounds
is no rarity here. **Lizard Island Charters** (☎ *07/4043–1976* ⊕ *www.
lizardislandcharters.com.au*) runs day trips on the outer reef; the cost,
including tackle, is A$1,550. Inner reef and night fishing are also avail-
able. One day's inner reef fishing with light tackle costs A$1,420.

SCUBA DIVING   The resort arranges supervised scuba-diving trips to the inner and outer
reef, as well as local dives and night dives. An introductory one-dive course,
including classroom and beach sessions, is A$175. One-tank boat dives
are A$70. If you have a queasy stomach, take seasickness tablets before
heading out for an afternoon on the reef, as crossings between dive sites
in the exposed ocean can make for a bumpy ride.

Arriving & Departing

BY PLANE   Lizard Island has its own small airstrip served by **Macair Airlines**
(☎ *13–1313* ⊕ *www.macair.com.au*). One-hour flights depart twice
daily from Cairns and cost from A$630 round-trip.

Tour Operators

The reefs around Lizard island have some of the best marine life and
coral anywhere. The 16-km (10-mi), full-day snorkeling and diving trip
to the outer reef, which takes you to the world-famous Cod Hole, is
A$180. Half-day inner reef trips are A$130. Glass-bottom boat and
snorkeling trips and the use of motorized dinghies are included in
guests' rates.

GREAT BARRIER REEF A TO Z

AIR TRAVEL

Regular boat and air services are available to most of the Great Barrier Reef resorts, but because all of the destinations are islands, they require extra travel time. Schedule the last leg of your trip for the early morning, when most charters and launches depart.

Airplane and helicopter pilots follow strict weight guidelines, usually no more than 15 kilograms (33 pounds) permitted per person (including hand baggage). To avoid repacking at the ticket counter where your gear is weighed, travel light. If you're a diver, you'll do well to just bring a mask and snorkel, then rent the rest of the gear from your resort's dive shop. For information about reaching the islands, *see* Arriving and Departing *under* individual island headings.

BOAT TRAVEL

Several operators provide uncrewed charters to explore the Great Barrier Reef. Cumberland Charter Yachts has a five-day minimum for all charters. Queensland Yacht Charters has been operating for more than 20 years. Whitsunday Rent a Yacht has a fleet of 58 vessels including yachts, catamarans, and motor cruisers.

Crewed charters can be booked through several operators. Whitsunday Private Yacht Charters has a minimum of five nights/six days for all charters. Sunsail Australia has a fleet of 29 boats.

Cumberland Charter Yachts ⊠ Abel Point Marina, Airlie Beach, QLD 4802 ☎ 07/4946-7500 or 1800/075101 ⊕ www.ccy.com.au. **Queensland Yacht Charters** ⊠ Abel Point Marina, Airlie Beach, QLD 4802 ☎ 07/4946-7400 ⊕ www.yachtcharters.com.au. **Sunsail Australia** ⌖ Box 65, Hamilton Island, QLD 4803 ☎ 07/4946-9900 or 1800/803988 ⊕ www.sunsail.com.au. **Whitsunday Private Yacht Charters** ⊠ Abel Point Marina, Airlie Beach, QLD 4802 ☎ 07/4946-6880 or 1800/075055 ⊕ www.whitsundayyacht.com.au. **Whitsunday Rent a Yacht** ⊠ Shute Harbour, Airlie Beach, QLD 4802 ☎ 07/4946-9232 or 1800/075111 ⊕ www.rentayacht.com.au.

CAMPING

Camping is popular on the myriad islands of the Whitsunday group. To pitch a tent on islands lying within national parks, you need prior permission from the Queensland Parks and Wildlife Service, open weekdays 8:30–5. The Whitsunday Information Centre of the Queensland Parks and Wildlife Service, 3 km (2 mi) from Airlie Beach toward Shute Harbour, is open weekdays 9–5:30 and weekends 9–4.

Queensland Parks and Wildlife Service ⊠ Naturally Queensland Information Centre, Dept. of Environment, 160 Ann St., Brisbane, QLD 4002 ☎ 07/3227-8186. **Whitsunday Information Centre** ⌖ Box 83, Airlie Beach, QLD 4802 ☎ 07/4945-3711 or 1800/801252 🖷 07/4945-3182 ⊕ www.epa.qld.gov.au.

EMERGENCIES

Emergencies are handled by the front desk of the resort on each island, which can summon aerial ambulances or doctors. Remote islands have what are known as flying doctor kits, which contain a range of medicines and medical equipment. Hamilton Island has its own doctor.

MAIL, SHIPPING & THE INTERNET

E-mail and Internet access is available everywhere, though connectivity may be limited.

Australia Post has an official outlet on Hamilton Island. The other islands offer postal services from the reception desk at each resort. You can also arrange special mail services, such as DHL and Federal Express, but overnight delivery isn't guaranteed.

🛈 **Mail Services** Australia Post ⊠ Hamilton Island ☎ 07/4946–8238.

MONEY MATTERS

Resorts on the following islands have money-changing facilities: Daydream, Fitzroy, Hamilton, Hayman, Lindeman, Lizard, Long, Orpheus, and South Molle. However, you should change money before arriving on the island, as rates are better elsewhere. Hamilton Island has a National Australia Bank branch with an ATM. Bedarra, Brampton, Dunk, and Heron islands have limited currency-exchange facilities and no ATMs.

🛈 **Bank** National Australia Bank ⊠ Hamilton Island ☎ 13–2265.

TELEPHONES

There's only one area code (07) for Queensland and the Great Barrier Reef islands. You don't need to use the code when dialing in-state. International direct-dial telephones are available throughout the islands. You can use calling cards at any resort, and most islands listed in this chapter have decent cell-phone reception.

TOURS

BOAT CHARTERS FROM AIRLIE BEACH The Whitsundays are a boat-lover's haven, and there's an entire cottage industry of boating charters that will take you out to the reef for longer than a day trip. Barefoot Cruises operates three- and six-night cruises around the Whitsunday Islands on a variety of vessels that vary in terms of level of comfort and price. The 115-foot *Reef Odyssey,* is the largest, taking 39 passengers, and the 72-foot luxury schooner *Windjammer* is the smallest, with capacity for only 9 passengers. Backpackers favor Koala Adventures, which runs three-day/two-night tours on racing yachts *Anaconda II* and *The Card.* The *Pride of Airlie* is more upscale, offering day sails around the Whitsundays and night stays on South Molle Island at the resort.

OzSails's skippered yacht charters provide a high level of service on a variety of vessels, including the racing trimaran *Avatar* and the meticulously restored *Enid* for three-day/two-night cruises. ProSail also offers crewed charters, and is the largest crewed sailing company in Australia. With no fixed itineraries, passengers can choose their reef destinations, as well as vessel type from among 20 yachts. Southern Cross Sailing Adventures, the longest-running crewed sailing operator in Airlie, runs two- to six-day sailing holidays on one of five famous sailing vessels (including the onetime World Cup racer *Ragamuffin II,* the Whitbread Around the World racing maxi *British Defender,* and the 103-year-old tall ship *Solway Lass*). Sunsail, the world's largest boating holiday company, has a fleet of 30 ships, and runs charters for a minimum of five nights.

🛈 Barefoot Cruises ☎ 07/4946-1777 ⊕ www.barefootcruises.com.au. **Koala Adventures** ☎ 07/4946-0001 ⊕ www.koalaadventures.com. **OzSail** ☎ 07/4948-1388 ⊕ www.ozsail.com.au. **ProSail** ☎ 07/4946-5433 ⊕ www.prosail.com.au. **Southern Cross Sailing Adventures** ☎ 07/4946-4999 ⊕ www.soxsail.com.au **Sunsail** ☎ 07/4948-9514 ⊕ www.sunsail.com.au.

BOAT CHARTERS FROM CAIRNS — Divers can hop on Explorer Venture's 72-foot, 18-passenger *Nimrod Explorer,* which runs 5-day trips between Port Douglas and Lizard Island (A$595 per diver). The fare includes a return flight. The *Nimrod Explorer* also ventures north into the Coral Sea on 10-day trips that skirt the North Queensland coastline.

Coral Princess runs cruises from three to seven nights that leave from either Cairns or Townsville on a comfortable 54-passenger minicruise ship. Divers can rent equipment on board. Lessons are also available. Great Adventures operates fast catamaran service daily from Cairns to Green and Fitzroy islands and to the Outer Barrier Reef. Some trips include barbecue luncheon and coral viewing from an underwater observatory and a semisubmersible.

Ocean Spirit Cruises conducts full-day tours aboard the *Ocean Spirit* and the smaller *Ocean Spirit II.* A daily trip to Michaelmas Cay (a seabird nesting island located 43 km [27 mi] from Cairns) or Upolu Cay (a sand island 29 km [18 mi] from Cairns) includes four hours at the Great Barrier Reef, coral viewing in a semisubmersible at Upolu Cay only, swimming and snorkeling, and a seafood lunch. Introductory diving lessons are available. Ocean Spirit Cruises also has a three-hour dinner cruise, with live entertainment and a seafood buffet.

Quicksilver Connections operates tours to the reef from Cairns, Palm Cove, and Port Douglas.

🛈 Coral Princess ☎ 07/4040-9999 or 1800/079545 ⊕ www.coralprincess.com.au. **Explorer Ventures** ☎ 07/4031-5566 ⊕ www.explorerventures.com. **Great Adventures** ☎ 1800/079080 ⊕ www.greatadventures.com.au. **Ocean Spirit Cruises** ☎ 07/4031-2920 ⊕ www.oceanspirit.com.au. **Quicksilver Connections** ☎ 07/4087-2100 ⊕ www.quicksilver-cruises.com.

VISITOR INFORMATION

🛈 Tourist Information Queensland Travel Centre ⊠ Roma and Makerston Sts., Brisbane, QLD 4000 ☎ 13-8833 ⊕ www.tq.com.au.

Adelaide & South Australia

WORD OF MOUTH

"Kangaroo Island is beautiful. Very pretty beaches, interesting rock formations, lots of animals (we saw tons of koalas, a couple of kangaroos, lots of wallabies, fairy penguins, pelicans, black swans, fur seals, and sea lions) and had a great time. I wished we could have stayed an extra day!"

—MaeT

Updated by
Liza Power

RENOWNED FOR ITS CELEBRATIONS of the arts, its multiple cultures, and its bountiful harvests from vines, land, and sea, South Australia is both diverse and divine. Here you can taste some of the country's finest wines, sample from its best restaurants, and admire some of the world's most valuable gems. Or, skip the state's sophisticated options and unwind on wildlife-rich Kangaroo Island, hike in the Flinders Ranges, or live underground like opal miners in the vast Outback.

Spread across a flat saucer of land between the Mt. Lofty ranges and the sea, the capital city of Adelaide is easy to explore. The wide streets of its 1½-square-km (½-square-mi) city center are organized in a simple grid that's filled with parklands. The plan was originally laid out in 1836 by William Light, the colony's first surveyor-general, making Adelaide the only early Australian capital not built by English convict labor. Today Light's plan is recognized as being far ahead of its time. This city of 1.1 million still moves at a leisurely pace, free of the typical urban menace of traffic jams and glass canyons.

Nearly 90% of South Australians live in the fertile south around Adelaide, because the region stands on the very doorstep of the harshest, driest land in the most arid of the earth's populated continents. Jagged hills and stony deserts fill the parched interior, which is virtually unchanged since the first settlers arrived. Desolate terrain and temperatures that top 48°C (118°F) have thwarted all but the most determined efforts to conquer the land. People who survive this region's challenges do so only through drastic measures, such as in the far northern opal-mining town of Coober Pedy, where residents live underground.

Still, the deserts hold great surprises, and many clues to the country's history before European settlement. The scorched, ruggedly beautiful Flinders Ranges north of Adelaide hold Aboriginal cave paintings and fossil remains from when the area was an ancient seabed. Lake Eyre, a great salt lake, filled with water in the year 2000 for only the fourth time in its recorded history. The Nullarbor ("treeless") Plain stretches west across state lines in its tirelessly flat, ruthlessly arid march into Western Australia.

Adelaide's urban character combines laid-back city living with respect for South Australia's tough environment. Poles supporting the city's electric wires are made from steel and cement, not wood: timber is precious. Toward the end of summer the city parks are crowded with brilliantly colored parrots escaping the parched desert. Bushfires are always a major threat, and the city is still haunted by the memory of the Ash Wednesday flames that devastated the Adelaide Hills in 1983.

Yet South Australia is, perhaps ironically, gifted with the good life. It produces most of the nation's wine, and the sea ensures a plentiful supply of lobster, famed King George whiting, and tuna. Cottages and guesthouses tucked away in the countryside around Adelaide are among the most charming and relaxing in Australia. Farther afield, unique experiences like watching seal pups cuddle with their mothers on Kangaroo Island would warm any heart. South Australia may not be grand in reputation, but its attractions are extraordinary, and after a visit you'll know you've indulged in one of Australia's best-kept secrets.

Many of the state's attractions are an easy drive or bus ride from Adelaide. However, for a taste of the real South Australia a trip to a national park or up to the Outback is definitely worth the extra travel time. Short flights between destinations make any journey possible within a day or overnight, but the more time you leave yourself to explore the virtues of this underrated state, the better.

9

If you have
3 days

Spend a leisurely day in **Adelaide** enjoying the museums and historical sights, as well as the bustling Central Market. Take a sunset stroll along the Torrens, then have dinner and drinks at one of the city's vibrant restaurants or wine bars. Spend the night, then take Day 2 to tour the **Adelaide Hills,** strolling the 19th-century streets of **Hahndorf** and taking in the panorama from atop **Mt. Lofty.** Stay the night in a charming bed-and-breakfast in one of the region's small towns, or come back down to North Adelaide and rest among the beautiful sandstone homes. Save Day 3 for wine tasting in the **Barossa Region.**

If you have
5 days

Expand your horizons beyond **Adelaide** and take a tram-car ride to the beach at Glenelg, where you can laze on the white sands and dine at tasty outposts. Spend the night here or at a B&B on the **Fleurieu Peninsula,** then take Day 3 to explore the vineyards and catch the ferry to **Kangaroo Island.** After a night here, use Day 4 to explore and appreciate the island's wildlife and untamed beauty. Return to Adelaide in the afternoon on Day 5 and drive up to the **Adelaide Hills** for sunset at **Mt. Lofty.**

If you have
7 days

Spend Day 1 in **Adelaide** nosing through museums and picnicking in a park or on the banks of the Torrens River. After a night in the city, head into the leafy **Adelaide Hills** to meet nocturnal Australian wildlife at Warrawong Earth Sanctuary. Stay the night in a local bed-and-breakfast, then on Day 3 travel to the **Barossa Region,** where German and English influences are strong and the dozens of wineries offer tempting free tastings. Spend the evening at a country house, then on Day 4 cross to **Kangaroo Island.** Stay two nights, giving you Day 5 to fully explore the island's remote corners and unwind. On Day 6, plunge into the Outback at extraordinary **Coober Pedy** (consider flying to maximize your time). There you can eat, shop, and stay the night underground as the locals do and "noodle" (rummage) for opal gemstones. If you're a hiker, consider heading for **Flinders Ranges National Park** on Day 7 to explore one of the country's finest Outback parks.

Exploring Adelaide & South Australia

South Australia comprises the dry hot north and the greener, more temperate south. The green belt includes Adelaide and its surrounding hills and orchards, the Barossa Region and Clare Valley vineyards, the beautiful Fleurieu Peninsula, and the Murray River's cliffs and lagoons. Offshore, residents of Kangaroo Island live at a delightfully old-fashioned pace, savoring their domestic nature haven. A trip to the almost extraterrestrial Coober Pedy provides a glimpse of Outback living, complete with larger-than-life cattle ringers and opal miners.

The best way to experience this diverse state is by road. In general, driving conditions are excellent, although minor lanes are unpaved. It's two hours from Adelaide to the wine regions, the southern coast, and most other major sights.

The most direct route to the Flinders Ranges is via the Princes Highway and Port Augusta, but a more interesting route takes you through the Clare Valley vineyards and Burra's copper-mining villages. Travelers with limited time can enjoy aerial views of expansive desert and the Outback on a flight from Adelaide to Coober Pedy, or one soaring over Wilpena Pound in the Flinders. The Kangaroo Island ferries have sweeping views of Australia's massive mainland. Two classic train journeys also wind through this state: the *Ghan,* which runs north via Alice Springs to Darwin, and the *Indian Pacific,* which crosses the Nullarbor Plain to reach Perth.

About the Restaurants

Adelaide has more restaurants per capita than anywhere else in Australia, so travelers are spoiled for choice when dining in town. Cafés are the favorite dining spots, and inexpensive, bustling casual eateries—with occasionally quirky service—abound in Adelaide and the regional towns. However, there are also many fine-dining establishments with prim-and-proper service, starched napkins, and polished wine glasses.

Most restaurants are closed Monday and Tuesday, and even Wednesday in more rural spots. Same-day reservations are recommended across the board as a courtesy to the restaurant. Some upscale institutions require booking well in advance, and tables are tight during major city festivals and holidays.

Restaurants in Adelaide and the surrounding regions favor Mod-Oz cuisine, with main dishes showcasing oysters, crayfish, and whiting prepared with Asian and Mediterranean flavors. Bush foods are also popular; look for *quandongs* (native plums), wattle seed, and kangaroo (delicious served as a rare steak). Metwursts and sausages, culinary and cultural links with the region's 19th-century German immigrants, are particular popular in the Adelaide Hills and the Barossa Valley.

WHAT IT COSTS In Australian Dollars				
	$$$$	**$$$**	**$$**	**$**	**¢**
AT DINNER	over $50	$36–$50	$21–$35	$10–$20	under $10

Prices are for a main course at dinner.

About the Hotels

South Australia abounds with delightful lodgings. Self-contained accommodations—rooms or cabins with full cooking facilities and, in most cases, the prized spa bath (Jacuzzi)—are the most common. Bed-and-breakfasts are tucked into contemporary studios, converted cottages and stables, restored homesteads, and grand mansions. Modern resorts

9

Arts & Music
Adelaide's Festival Centre is the focus of the city's cultural life. Its name hints at the highlight of South Australia's arts calendar—the biennial Adelaide Festival of Arts, a tremendously successful celebration that was the forerunner to other artistic festivities throughout Australia. Beginning a week before, but concluding the same day, is the Fringe Festival, presenting all that's new in the independent arts. Adelaide also hosts the internationally acclaimed youth festival Come Out in off-festival years, and the annual WOMADelaide celebration of world music. Country towns and regions have their own festivals, the most notable of which is the Barossa Under the Stars music concert each February.

Bush Tucker
South Australia, along with the Northern Territory, led the way in educating the Australian palate in the pleasures of bush tucker—the wild foods in the Australian countryside that have been used for millennia by the Aboriginal people. Kangaroo, crocodile, emu, and other regional fare were introduced to a skeptical public who now embrace it and seek ever-more inventive preparations of native ingredients. Many menus also have local seafood, especially tuna, King George whiting, and oysters from the waters of Spencer Gulf and the Great Australian Bight, the expanse of ocean off Australia's curved central southern coast.

Historic Homes
Adelaide's accommodations are bargains compared with those in any other Australian capital city. Even so, you might consider staying outside the city in one of the historic properties in North Adelaide or in the Adelaide Hills to have the best of both worlds: easy access to the pleasures of the city as well as to the vineyards, orchards, and rustic villages that are tucked away in this idyllic, rolling landscape. Wonderfully restored 19th-century homes and guesthouses are plentiful in Adelaide and throughout the state.

Outdoor Escapes
Kangaroo Island's Flinders Chase and the Outback's Flinders Ranges national parks are great places to take in South Australia's geographical diversity. Coastal expanses and seascapes stretch into lowland meadows and open forests toward rugged Outback mountain terrain. Australian creatures abound at Cleland Wildlife Park. Carry water in this dry state, and drink it often—the dry heat is deceptively dehydrating.

Wonderful Wines
South Australia is considered Australia's premier wine state and produces more than half the total Australian vintage. The premium wines of the Barossa Region, Clare Valley, McLaren Vale, Adelaide Hills, and Coonawarra are treasured by connoisseurs worldwide, and many South Australian producers and wines have been awarded international honors. Whether or not you make it to any cellar doors, be sure to schedule a trip to the National Wine Centre in Adelaide to get a good working knowledge of Australian wines. Then test your knowledge by ordering a glass with dinner.

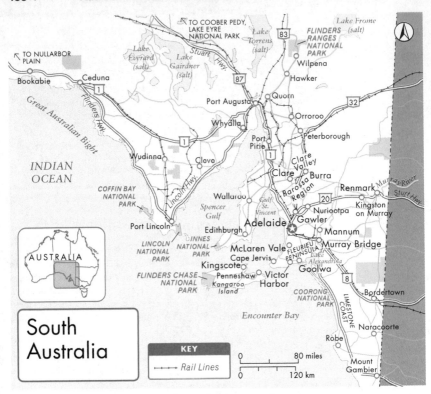

South Australia

KEY

0   80 miles

0   120 km

—— Rail Lines

sprawl along the coastal suburbs, the Barossa Valley, and other tourist centers, while intimate properties for 10 or fewer guests nestle in hidden corners of the land. Budget hotels have basic rooms with beds and coffee-making facilities, while upscale places pamper you with organic soaps and lotions, plush bathrobes, multiple pillows, premium bed linens, and space-age audiovisual equipment.

Most large hotels are in Adelaide, and although they offer the best prices on weekends, many offer discounts during much of the year, sometimes up to 50% off. So shop around for great deals. Outside the city, weekday nights are usually less expensive and two-night minimum bookings often apply. On Kangaroo Island, lodgings outside the major towns accent conservation; hence, there are few hot tubs or in-house restaurants, and water is often limited. Reservations for all accommodations are recommended year-round.

	WHAT IT COSTS In Australian Dollars				
	$$$$	**$$$**	**$$**	**$**	**¢**
FOR 2 PEOPLE	over $300	$201–$300	$151–$200	$101–$150	under $100

Prices are for two people in a standard double room in high season, including tax and service, based on the European Plan (with no meals) unless otherwise noted.

Timing

Adelaide has the least rainfall of all Australian capital cities, and the mid-day summer heat is oppressive. The Outback in particular is too hot for comfortable touring during this time, but Outback winters are pleasantly warm. South Australia's national parks are open year-round, and the best times to visit are in spring and autumn. In summer, extreme fire danger may close walking tracks, and in winter heavy rain can make some roads impassable. Boating on the Murray River and Lake Alexandrina are best from October to March, when the long evenings are bathed in soft light. The ocean is warmest from December to March.

Culture lovers can plan their South Australia visit around Adelaide's biggest events: the Adelaide Festival of Arts, the Adelaide Fringe Festival, and WOMADelaide, all in February and March. For sports fans, the Milang-Goolwa Freshwater Classic in late January is Australia's largest freshwater sailing regatta. Professional cycling teams from Australia, Europe, and the United States compete in the Jacob's Creek Tour Down Under in January, riding city sprints and country stages over six days. V8 Supercars roar around Adelaide's street circuit during the Clipsal 500 in March, and the Oakbank Easter Racing Carnival in the Adelaide Hills is one of the world's biggest horse-race meetings.

ADELAIDE

Australians' first reference to Adelaide is the city of churches, but Adelaide has outgrown its reputation as a sleepy country town dotted with cathedrals and spires. The Adelaide of this millennium is infinitely more complex, with a large, multiethnic population and thriving urban art and music scenes.

Big, bright, green, and clean, leafy Adelaide is a breeze to explore, with a grid pattern of streets surrounded by parks. The heart of the green belt is divided by the meandering River Torrens, which passes the Festival Centre at its prettiest stretch.

Exploring Adelaide

City Center

Numbers in the text correspond to numbers in the margin and on the Adelaide map.

Victoria Square ❶ ⌐ is Adelaide's geographical heart and an appropriate place to begin a walking tour. Head north along King William Street, with the General Post Office on your left. A short distance away is the **Town Hall ❷**, built to designs by Edmund Wright, mayor of Adelaide, in 1859.

Walk north on King William Street to North Terrace, home to Adelaide's cultural, historic, and government buildings. Dominating this busy corner is the formidable Greco-Roman facade of **Parliament House ❸**. To its left is Old Parliament House, the rooms of which are open to the public on Parliament House tours. The **South African War Memorial ❹**, a bronze statue of a mounted trooper commemorating the Boer War, stands op-

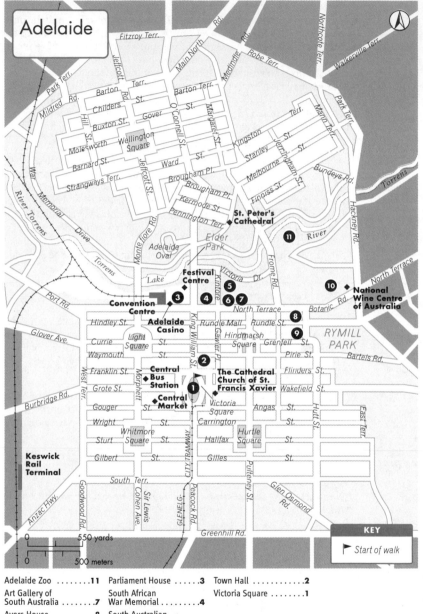

Adelaide

Fitzroy Terr.
Park Terr.
Mildred Rd.
Barton Terr.
Childers St.
Buxton St.
Molesworth
Wellington Square
Barnard St.
Strangways Terr.
Jeffcott Rd.
Main North Rd.
Medindie Rd.
Robe Terr.
Barton Terr.
O'Connell St.
Margaret St.
Kingston Terr.
Stanley St.
Melbourne St.
Jerningham St.
Finniss St.
Bundeys Rd.
Northcote Terr.
Mann Terr.
Park Terr.
Walkerville Terr.

Brougham Pl.
Brougham Pl.
Kermode St.
Pennington Terr.

St. Peter's Cathedral

River Torrens
Memorial Drive
Torrens
Port Rd.
Glover Ave.

Elder Park
Adelaide Oval
Lake

Festival Centre
Victoria Dr.
Frome Rd.
Kintore
⑪ River
⑩ ◆ **National Wine Centre of Australia**
North Terrace

Convention Centre
③
④
⑤
⑥ ⑦
⑧
Botanic Rd.
North Terrace

Adelaide Casino
Hindley St.
Rundle Mall
Rundle St.
RYMILL PARK
Currie St.
Light Square
Hindmarsh Square
Grenfell St.
⑨
Bartels Rd.
Waymouth St.
Pirie St.
Franklin St.
King William St.
Gawler Pl.
Flinders St.

Central Bus Station
②
The Cathedral Church of St. Francis Xavier
Morphett St.
Grote St.
Wakefield St.
Hutt St.
East Terr.

Central Market
①
Victoria Square
Angas St.
Gouger St.
Wright St.
Carrington
Whitmore Square
Hurtle Square
Sturt St.
Halifax St.
Gilbert St.
Gilles St.
Pulteney St.

Keswick Rail Terminal
CITY TRAMWAY
South Terr.
Goodwood Rd.
Cohen Ave.
Sir Lewis
GLENELG
Peacock Rd.
Glen Osmond Rd.
Anzac Hwy.
Burbridge Rd.
West Terr.
Greenhill Rd.

0 ——— 550 yards
0 ——— 500 meters

Adelaide Zoo **11**
Art Gallery of South Australia **7**
Ayers House **8**
Botanic Gardens **10**
Migration Museum **5**

Parliament House **3**
South African War Memorial **4**
South Australian Museum **6**
Tandanya Aboriginal Cultural Institute **9**

Town Hall **2**
Victoria Square **1**

posite. Walk up Kintore Avenue, past the white marble City of Adelaide Lending Library, to the **Migration Museum** ❺, one of Australia's most evocative museums.

Return to North Terrace and walk past the Royal Society of the Arts and the library. Turn left at the grassy courtyard to the **South Australian Museum** ❻, which holds a particularly rich collection of Aboriginal artifacts. Next along North Terrace is the **Art Gallery of South Australia** ❼, with its neoclassical exterior. Continue on North Terrace and cross to **Ayers House** ❽, once the scene for the highlights of Adelaide's social calendar and the home of seven-time state premier Sir Henry Ayers.

Two blocks south on East Terrace, the **Tandanya Aboriginal Cultural Institute** ❾ showcases the work of Australia's indigenous people. Head north again on East Terrace. If you need a rest, take a detour onto Rundle Street, to the left, which is lined with restaurants and bars. Continue straight across North Terrace and walk east along Botanic Road, the shady avenue that leads to the magnificent **Botanic Gardens** ❿. To the north, off Frome Road, is **Adelaide Zoo** ⓫. From here you can follow the riverside trail back to the Festival Centre.

TIMING   A walk past Adelaide's attractions will take a couple of hours. However, the South Australian Museum deserves at least 90 minutes, as does the Art Gallery. In summer, time your visits to indoor attractions such as museums and the art gallery so you are under cover at the hottest time of day.

WHAT TO SEE   **Adelaide Zoo.** The second-oldest in Australia, Adelaide's zoo still retains much of its original architecture. Enter through the 1883 cast-iron gates to see such animals as Sumatran tigers, Australian rain-forest birds, and chimpanzees, housed in modern, natural settings. The zoo is world renowned for its captive breeding and release programs, and rare species including the red panda and South Australia's own yellow-footed rock wallaby are among its successes. ⊠ *Frome Rd. near War Memorial Dr., City Center* ☎ *08/8267–3255* ⊕ *www.adelaidezoo.com.au* ⌨ *A$15* ⊙ *Daily 9:30–5.*

★ ❼   **Art Gallery of South Australia.** Many famous Australian painters, including Charles Conder, Margaret Preston, Clifford Possum Tjapaltjarri, Russell Drysdale, and Sidney Nolan, are represented in this collection. Extensive Renaissance and British artworks are on display, and a separate room houses Aboriginal pieces. A café and bookshop are also on-site. ⊠ *N. Terrace near Pulteney St., City Center* ☎ *08/8207–7000* ⊕ *www.artgallery.sa.gov.au* ⌨ *Free* ⊙ *Daily 10–5.*

❽   **Ayers House.** Between 1855 and 1897 this sprawling colonial structure was the home of Sir Henry Ayers, South Australia's premier and the man for whom Uluru was originally named Ayers Rock. Most rooms have been restored with period furnishings, and the state's best examples of 19th-century costumes are displayed in changing exhibitions. Admission includes a one-hour tour. ⊠ *288 N. Terrace, City Center* ☎ *08/8223–1234* ⊕ *www.nationaltrustsa.org.au* ⌨ *A$8* ⊙ *Tues.–Fri. 10–4, weekends 1–4.*

★ ⑩ **Botanic Gardens.** These magnificent formal gardens include an international rose garden, giant water lilies, an avenue of Moreton Bay fig trees, acres of green lawns, and duck ponds. The Bicentennial Conservatory—the largest single-span glass house in the Southern Hemisphere—provides an environment for lowland rain-forest species, many of them endangered, such as the Cassowary Palm and Torch Ginger; native Noisy Pitta birds fly free inside. Daily free guided tours leave from the trees at the restaurant at 10:30. ✉ *N. Terrace, City Center* ☎ *08/8222–9311* ⊕ *www.environment.sa.gov.au/botanicgardens* ▭ *Gardens free, conservatory A$3.50* ⊙ *Weekdays 8–sunset, weekends 9–sunset.*

Cathedral Church of St. Francis Xavier. This church faced a bitter battle over construction after the 1848 decision to build a Catholic cathedral. It's now a prominent, decorative church with a soaring nave, stone arches through to side aisles with dark wood ceilings, and beautiful stained-glass windows. The tower was only completed in 1996. ✉ *Wakefield St. and Victoria Sq., City Center* ☎ *08/8231–3551* ▭ *Free* ⊙ *Mass weekdays 8 AM, 12:10, and 5:45 PM; Sat. 8 and 11 AM; Sun. 7, 9, 11 AM, and 6 PM.*

> **need a break?**
>
> Many locals insist that you haven't been to Adelaide unless you've stopped at a curbside **pie cart,** found outside the General Post Office on Franklin Street during the day, on North Terrace near the railway station, and the SkyCity Casino after 6 PM. The floater—a meat pie in tomato sauce (ketchup) submerged in pea soup—is South Australia's original contribution to the culinary arts. More traditional pie options, like beef, or chicken with veggies, are also available.

❺ **Migration Museum.** Chronicled in this converted 19th-century Destitute Asylum (where Adelaide's destitute, homeless, sick, and aged lived, worked, and died from the 1850s to 1918), are the origins, hopes, and fates of some of the millions of immigrants who settled in Australia during the past two centuries. The museum is starkly realistic, and the bleak welcome that awaited many migrants is graphically illustrated in the reconstructed quarters of a migrant hostel. ✉ *82 Kintore Ave., City Center* ☎ *08/8207–7580* ⊕ *www.history.sa.gov.au* ▭ *Free* ⊙ *Weekdays 10–5, weekends 1–5.*

National Wine Centre of Australia. Bold architecture, using timber, steel, and glass to evoke the ribs of a huge wine barrel, and a soaring, open-plan concourse make this the perfect place to showcase Australian wines. Using displays, audiovisuals, and touch-screen technology, the Wine Discovery Journey takes you from neolithic pottery jars to a stainless steel tank; you can even make your own virtual wine on a computer. You can also taste some of the best vintages from more than 50 Australian wine-growing regions here, or take a wine-appreciation class. ✉ *Hackney and Botanic Rds., City Center* ☎ *08/8222–9222, 08/8222–9277 wine courses* ⊕ *www.wineaustralia.com.au, www.winesa.asn.au/winecourses/courses* ▭ *Free; tastings A$2 per wine, A$5 for 4 wines, A$19.50 for 4 premium wines* ⊙ *Daily 10–5.*

❸ **Parliament House.** Ten Corinthian columns are the most striking features of this classical parliament building. It was completed in two stages 50 years apart: the west wing in 1889 and the east wing in 1939. Alongside is **Old Parliament House,** which dates from 1843. There's a free guided tour of both houses weekdays at 10 and 2 during nonsitting weeks, and on Friday only when parliament is in session. ⊠ *N. Terrace between King William and Montefiore Sts., City Center* ☎ *08/8237–9467* 🖅 *Free* ⊗ *Tours only.*

St. Peter's Cathedral. The spires and towers of this cathedral, founded in 1869 and completed in 1904, dramatically contrast with the nearby city skyline. St. Peter's is the epitome of Anglican architecture in Australia and an important example of grand Gothic Revival. Free 45-minute guided tours are available Wednesday at 10:30 and Sunday at 3. ⊠ *1–19 King William St., North Adelaide* ☎ *08/8267–4551* 🖅 *Free* ⊗ *Services Mon., Tues., Thurs. and Fri. 7:30 AM; Wed. 7:30 AM, 10 AM and 5:15 PM; Sat. 7:30 AM and 5:30 PM; Sun. 8 AM, 10:30 AM, and 7 PM.*

④ South African War Memorial. This statue was unveiled in 1904 to commemorate the volunteers of the South Australian Bushmen's Corps who fought with the British in the Boer War. Through the gates behind the statue you can glimpse **Government House,** the official residence of the state governor, which was completed in 1878. The building is not open to visitors. ⊠ *King William St. and N. Terr., City Center* ☎ *No phone.*

❻ South Australian Museum. The Australian Aboriginal Cultures Gallery in this museum—the world's largest—houses 3,000 items, including ceremonial dress and paintings, in high-tech exhibits. Old black-and-white films show traditional dancing, and touch screens convey desert life. Aboriginal guides lead tours (Thursday and Friday) and share personal insights. You can use interactive multimedia computers to find out more, and watch animated films of Dreaming (Creation) stories, in the Indigenous Information Centre. Also in the museum is an exhibition commemorating renowned Antarctic explorer Sir Douglas Mawson, after whom Australia's main Antarctic research station is named; a Fossil Gallery housing the opalized partial skeleton of a 19-foot-long plesiosaur (marine dinosaur) found in Coober Pedy; and a café. ⊠ *N. Terrace near Gawler Pl., City Center* ☎ *08/8207–7500* ⊕ *www.samuseum. sa.gov.au* 🖅 *Museum and general tours free, Aboriginal tours A$10* ⊗ *Daily 10–5; tours weekdays at 11, weekends at 2 and 3; Aboriginal tours Thurs. and Fri. at 11:30.*

❾ Tandanya Aboriginal Cultural Institute. The first major Aboriginal cultural facility of its kind in Australia, Tandanya houses high-quality changing exhibitions of works by Aboriginal artists and a theater where you can watch didgeridoo and dance performances. ⊠ *253 Grenfell St., City Center* ☎ *08/8224–3200* ⊕ *www.tandanya.com.au* 🖅 *A$4* ⊗ *Daily 10–5.*

❷ Town Hall. An imposing building constructed in 1863 in Renaissance style, the Town Hall was modeled after buildings in Genoa and Florence. Free guided tours on Monday visit civic rooms, including the Colonel Light Room, where objects used to map and plan Adelaide are exhibited, and the grand main auditorium with its 4,500-pipe organ; bookings are required. ⊠ *128 King William St., City Center* ☎ *08/8203–7203* 🖅 *Free* ⊗ *Tours by appointment on Mon. at 10.*

► ❶ **Victoria Square.** The fountain in the square, which is floodlighted at night, celebrates the three rivers that supply Adelaide's water: the Torrens, Onkaparinga, and Murray are each represented by a stylized man or woman paired with an Australian native bird. Shady trees and park benches attract lunching office workers, while shoppers and tourists come and go from the Glenelg Tram, which terminates here. Surrounding the square are several beautiful stone colonial buildings. Note the three-story **Torrens Building** on the east side and the **Adelaide Treasury** on the northeast corner, one of the city's oldest buildings and now an upscale hotel. ⊠ *King William, Grote, and Wakefield Sts., City Center* ☏ *No phone.*

Greater Adelaide

☺ **National Railway Museum.** Steam-train buffs will delight in this collection of locomotive engines and rolling stock in the former Port Adelaide railway yard. The finest of its kind in Australia, the collection includes enormous "Mountain"-class engines and the "Tea and Sugar" train, once the lifeline for camps scattered across the deserts of South and Western Australia. Miniature trains run inside the grounds, and exhibits depict the social history of the regional railways. ⊠ *Lipson St. near St. Vincent's St., Port Adelaide* ☏ *08/8341–1690* ⊕ *www.natrailmuseum.org. au* 🎫 *A$10* ☺ *Daily 10–5.*

★ **Penfolds Magill Estate.** Founded in 1844 by immigrant English doctor Christopher Rawson Penfold, this working vineyard in Adelaide's eastern suburbs is the birthplace of Australia's most famous wine, Penfolds Grange. Introduced in 1951, Grange is the flagship of a huge stable of wines priced from everyday to special occasion (collectors pay thousands of dollars to complete sets of Grange). Reds and whites can be tasted at cellar door, and 45-minute winery tours (A$15) leave daily at 11, 1, and 3; bookings are essential. The Great Grange Tour is the ultimate Magill Estate experience; over three hours you visit the original Penfold family cottage, tour the winery, and enjoy a seated, tutored tasting of premium wines, including Grange. This tour is by arrangement for a minimum of five people, and costs A$150 per person. ⊠ *78 Penfolds Rd., Magill* ☏ *08/8301–5569* ⊕ *www.penfolds.com.au* 🎫 *Free; winery tour A$15, Great Grange Tour A$150* ☺ *Daily 10:30–4:30.*

☺ **South Australian Maritime Museum.** Inside a restored stone warehouse, this museum brings maritime history vividly to life with ships' figureheads, relics of shipwrecks, and intricate scale models. Lists of past passengers and vessel arrivals in South Australia can be accessed for a small fee. In addition to the warehouse displays, the museum also includes a lighthouse and a restored steam tug tied up at the nearby wharf; the lighthouse can be climbed (closed Saturday) for a great view, and the tug cruises Port Adelaide and the wharf area in summer, over the Easter weekend, and during end-of-term school holidays. ⊠ *126 Lipson St., Port Adelaide* ☏ *08/8207–6255* ⊕ *www.history.sa.gov.au/maritime/maritime. htm* 🎫 *A$8.50, family A$22 (lighthouse entry included); steam tug tours from A$5 per person* ☺ *Daily 10–5.*

Where to Eat

Adelaide teems with restaurants that deliver fresh, delicious, and inexpensive international cuisine. With an emphasis on locally grown products, even the most worldly menus have South Australian connections. South Australia's chefs are also at the forefront in developing innovative regional cuisine, and menus often change weekly or even daily.

Melbourne, Gouger, O'Connell, and Rundle streets, along with the Norwood Parade and Glenelg neighborhoods, are the main eating strips. In any of these areas it's fun to stroll around until a restaurant or café takes your fancy.

Argentine

$$ ✕ **Gaucho's.** Forget the spurs and big hat. What you need to enjoy this spacious Argentine restaurant is a cowboy-size appetite. The menu celebrates carnivorousness, combining dishes such as pan-roasted duck in Campari fruit glaze with classic charcoal-grilled meat dishes. A traditional *churrasco grande* steak is accompanied by your choice of rich salsas. Typical of Argentine steak houses worldwide, the restaurant is fun and festive, with large parties often dominating the room. ⊠ *91 Gouger St., City Center* ☏ *08/8213–2299* ▭ *AE, DC, MC, V.*

Cafés

$–$$ ✕ **Garage Bistro & Bar.** Gilded nudes adorn the raw brick walls, and mirrors reflect exposed beams and pipes in this funky reborn garage facing Light Square, a grassy square containing the grave of William Light, Adelaide's founder. The chefs here have fun with Asian, European, and Australian flavors, tossing together a menu that might include a risotto of chicken, porcini mushrooms, pine nuts, basil and lemon, or a roast-duck pancake accompanied by minted yogurt dipping sauce. Wash it down with a glass or bottle from the extensive wine list, perhaps the Barossa shiraz cabernet "just like Apocalypse Now but without the war" or the "very gluggable" house sparkling. You can play boccie in the courtyard bar by day; by night, the corporate crowd makes way for DJs and dancers. The Garage is a bar only on Friday and Saturday evening. ⊠ *163 Waymouth St., City Center* ☏ *08/8212–9577* ▭ *AE, DC, MC, V* ☉ *No lunch Sat. No dinner Tues., Wed., Fri.–Sun.*

$–$$ ✕ **Paul's on Gouger.** Get hooked on King George whiting at this Greek-influenced café, which is hailed as one of Adelaide's best—and best-priced—seafood restaurants. The deep-fried baby prawns with sweet chili sauce are another local favorite. For a great view of the bustle in the open kitchen, request a table upstairs on the ship's-deck-like mezzanine floor. ⊠ *79 Gouger St., City Center* ☏ *08/8231–9778* ▭ *AE, DC, MC, V* ☉ *No lunch Sun.*

$–$$ ✕ **Universal Wine Bar.** Adelaide's fashionable crowd loves this high-gloss, split-level bar-café with its giant mirrors and exposed wine racks. Join their ranks for a coffee or organic tea, or settle in for a tasty lunch or dinner inside or at a sidewalk table. If you're lucky, the seasonal menu might include shredded spicy beef salad with asparagus, fresh coriander and chili; or whole baby barramundi with leeks and brown butter.

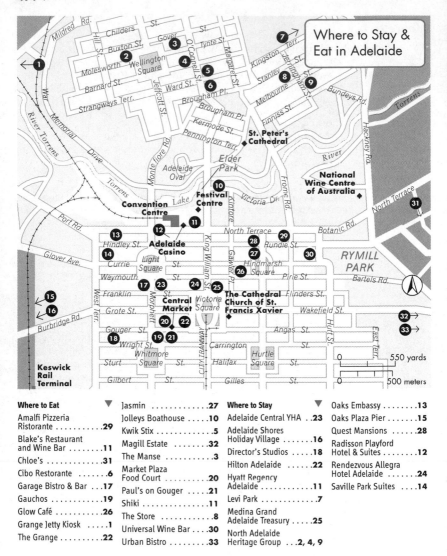

Where to Stay & Eat in Adelaide

St. Peter's Cathedral

National Wine Centre of Australia

Elder Park

Adelaide Oval

Convention Centre

Festival Centre

Adelaide Casino

RYMILL PARK

Central Market

The Cathedral Church of St. Francis Xavier

Keswick Rail Terminal

0   550 yards
0   500 meters

Where to Eat

Amalfi Pizzeria Ristorante **29**

Blake's Restaurant and Wine Bar **11**

Chloe's **31**

Cibo Restorante **6**

Garage Bistro & Bar . . . **17**

Gauchos **19**

Glow Café **26**

Grange Jetty Kiosk **1**

The Grange **22**

Jasmin **27**

Jolleys Boathouse **10**

Kwik Stix **5**

Magill Estate **32**

The Manse **3**

Market Plaza Food Court **20**

Paul's on Gouger **21**

Shiki **11**

The Store **8**

Universal Wine Bar **30**

Urban Bistro **33**

Where to Stay

Adelaide Central YHA . . **23**

Adelaide Shores Holiday Village **16**

Director's Studios **18**

Hilton Adelaide **22**

Hyatt Regency Adelaide **11**

Levi Park **7**

Medina Grand Adelaide Treasury **25**

North Adelaide Heritage Group . . . **2, 4, 9**

Oaks Embassy **13**

Oaks Plaza Pier **15**

Quest Mansions **28**

Radisson Playford Hotel & Suites **12**

Rendezvous Allegra Hotel Adelaide **24**

Saville Park Suites **14**

For A$2 a swallow you can down South Australian oysters soused with wasabi, flying-fish roe, and lime juice. Many of the wines on the huge list are sold by the glass. ✉ *285 Rundle St., City Center* ☎ *08/8232–5000* ▭ *AE, DC, MC, V* ⊘ *Closed Sun.*

$ ✕ **Glow Cafe.** Fed up with boring health food? Being good rocks at this organic café, with its Tracy Chapman sound track and modern artworks hung on brightly colored walls. Join office workers checking fat content of the menu choices as you design a take-out sandwich or a cooked breakfast—using free-range eggs, of course. For a more substantial lunch, vegans can tuck into baked vegetable and chickpea curry, while carnivores can opt for an omega 3–rich tuna steak. ✉ *98 Gawler Pl., City Center* ☎ *08/8231–2228* ▭ *MC, V* ⊘ *Closed weekends. No dinner.*

¢–$ ✕ **The Store.** North Adelaide yuppies fuel up on aromatic coffee, fresh-squeezed juices, and simple, wholesome food here before trawling the adjacent delicatessen and upscale supermarket. Try the bacon sandwich with smoked cheddar and tomato jam for brunch. More substantial meals and a hearty wine list are available after 11 AM. Service can be slow, so grab a sidewalk table, kick back, and watch the comings and goings of couples, families, and dogs (there's a water bowl for thirsty pooches). ✉ *157 Melbourne St., North Adelaide* ☎ *08/8361–6999* ▭ *AE, DC, MC, V.*

Eclectic

$$$ ✕ **Magill Estate.** Do you inhale deeply from your wine glass before drinking? Do you know your back palate from your front? Then you're ready to join the wine buffs and enthusiasts at this pavilion-style vineyard restaurant, where Australia's most famous wine, Penfolds Grange, was created. The restaurant looks across vines to the city skyline and coast, and sunset is a spectacle that makes eating here a memorable experience. The menu might include such European-flavored Oz delights as olive oil–poached marron (farmed freshwater crayfish) served with a ragout of mussels, broad beans, and chorizo sausage. The wine list is a museum of Penfolds's finest, including Grange by the glass. ✉ *78 Penfold Rd., Magill* ☎ *08/8301–5551* ⌕ *Reservations essential* ▭ *AE, DC, MC, V* ⊘ *Closed Sun. and Mon. No lunch.*

★ $$–$$$ ✕ **Blake's Restaurant and Wine Bar.** Rustic timber and small, cozy spaces lighted by floating candles create a wine-cellar intimacy in this sophisticated spot. The innovative seasonal menu might include tomato consommé with red-claw crayfish bavarois and Parmesan biscotti, or Moroccan-spiced lamb rack on saffron and pine-nut couscous; and there are four different dessert soufflés. The highly regarded wine list of more than 600 vintages includes some of the finest labels in the country; your selection is served by South Australia's sommelier of the year 2004, Louise Radman. ✉ *Hyatt Regency Adelaide, N. Terrace, City Center* ☎ *08/8238–2381* ⌕ *Reservations essential* ▭ *AE, DC, MC, V* ⊘ *Closed Sun. and Tues. No lunch.*

French

$$ ✕ **Chloe's.** Silver-service dining, an extraordinary wine list, and the omnipresent owner and maître d' of maître d's, Nick Papazahariakis, define this elegant yet unpretentious restaurant. Georgian chairs, crystal decanters, Lalique chandeliers, and gleaming silver make every meal an

occasion—and often at surprisingly modest prices. The menu marries Australia's best produce with French flavors in such dishes as compote of soft herbs, pear, and mustard on cured salmon, and roast local duck with a spiced quince glaze. ⊠ *36 College Rd., Kent Town* 🕾 *08/ 8362-2574* ⚖ *Reservations essential* ▤ *AE, DC, MC, V* ⊗ *Closed Sun.*

$$ ✕ **The Manse.** Bustles and tailcoats were de rigueur dinner attire when this Victorian mansion was built in the heart of North Adelaide, but the dress code for the modern French gem it houses is thankfully more relaxed. Continental cuisine, such as the terrine of feathered game, is prepared with flair, and special effort is made to add local ingredients to classic dishes (try the South Australian crayfish on a braised leek tart). Wood-burning fireplaces and an outdoor terrace make dining a pleasure any time of year. The wine list includes both cellar-aged and boutique vintage bottles. ⊠ *142 Tynte St., North Adelaide* 🕾 *08/8267–4636* ▤ *AE, DC, MC, V* ⊗ *Closed Tues. and Sun.*

Indian

$ ✕ **Jasmin.** Wooden filigree screens, bejeweled Buddhas, and beaten-metal horses amid gleaming dark-wood tables bring India to life in this restaurant downstairs from lively Hindmarsh Square. Mostly Punjabi-style food, such as prawn sambal and tandoori barramundi, and the ever-popular Goan fish curry, complemented by more than 100 wines from Australia's smaller vineyards, has attracted Adelaide regulars and touring international cricketers for 25 years. Bats signed by teams who have dined here line the short corridor to the bathrooms. While awaiting your order, gaze at the evocative scenic paintings by local Australian artist Tom Gleghorn hanging on the walls; at 81 he's still prolific. ⊠ *31 Hindmarsh Sq., City Center* 🕾 *08/8223–7837* ▤ *AE, DC, MC, V* ⊗ *Closed Sun. and Mon. No lunch Tues., Wed., and Sat.*

Italian

$$ ✕ **Cibo Restorante.** Step through the colonnaded front door of this Adelaide favorite and you face a dilemma: buy a take-out mixed gelati (the green apple and roasted almond are delicious), enjoy a cappuccino and traditional torte on the outdoor terrace, or take a red-leather seat at a white-clothed table for some of the city's best Italian food? You could start with a twice-baked broad-bean-and-pecorino-cheese soufflé, and follow it with thin egg noodles tossed with South Australian blue swimmer crabmeat, chili, cream, and tomato. Truffles imported from Italy flavor the menu in season, and pizza comes hot and crisp from the wood-fired oven in the corner. There are 13 grappas on the wine list. ⊠ *10 O'Connell St., North Adelaide* 🕾 *08/8267–2444* ▤ *AE, DC, MC, V* ⊗ *No lunch Sat.*

$ ✕ **Amalfi Pizzeria Ristorante.** If not for the Australian accents here, you'd swear you were in an Italian students' local eatery. The dark, brick dining room is furnished with long wooden tables, around which Adelaide intelligentsia sit reading newspapers and discussing city life. The simple pizza-and-pasta menu lists everything in two sizes—appetizer and entrée—so you can sample from lots of different plates. For the anti-carb crowd there are several veal dishes, plus the classic *bistecca* (a thick loin steak on the bone). ⊠ *29 Frome St., City Center* 🕾 *08/8223–1948* ▤ *AE, DC, MC, V* ⊗ *Closed Sun. No lunch Sat.*

Japanese

$$–$$$$ ✕ **Shiki.** Sculptures and elaborate floral arrangements set the scene at this Japanese restaurant, where six set menus are available in addition to à la carte dining. Unusual dishes include smoked and seared kangaroo fillet served with *ponzu* sauce (a tangy blend of soy sauce and balsamic vinegar); barramundi tempura; and sushi, sashimi, and teriyaki. At the teppanyaki and tempura tables, chefs put on a lively show as they cook. ✉ *Hyatt Regency Adelaide, N. Terrace, City Center* ☎ *08/8238–2382* ⊟ *AE, DC, MC, V* ☺ *Closed Sun. and Mon. No lunch.*

Modern Australian

$$$$ ✕ **The Grange.** World-renowned chef Cheong Liew's creative philoso-
Fodor'sChoice phy is to "pursue the flavor of things," and Liew—who pioneered East-
★ West fusion cuisine in Australia in the early 1970s—works nightly culinary magic. Eight-course tasting menus, which open with the famous "Four Dances of the Sea"—snook, raw calamari with black-ink noodles, octopus, and spiced prawn sushi—pair exquisite taste sensations with thrilling wines. (Matched wine packages are extra.) Be prepared to splurge, though; this is one of South Australia's most expensive, as well as inventive, restaurants. ✉ *233 Victoria Sq., City Center* ☎ *08/8217–2000* ⌕ *Reservations essential* ⊟ *AE, DC, MC, V* ☺ *Closed Jan., and Sun. and Mon. No lunch.*

$$–$$$ ✕ **Jolleys Boathouse.** Blue canvas directors' chairs and white-clothed wooden tables create a relaxed, nautical air here—which perfectly suits the location on the south bank of the River Torrens. Sliding glass doors open onto a full-width front balcony for alfresco dining. The imaginative modern Australian menu changes seasonally, but might include a salad of grilled Kangaroo Island marron, green mango, basil and shallots, or sweet pork belly with red dates. Executives make up most lunch crowds, and warm evenings attract couples. ✉ *King William St. and Victoria Dr., City Center* ☎ *08/8223–2891* ⊟ *AE, DC, MC, V* ☺ *No dinner Sun.*

★ **$$** ✕ **Urban Bistro.** The interior of this restaurant is an almost clinical interpretation of modern minimalism, with scalpel-blade-edge furnishings—yet the food is as imaginative as it gets. The quick-witted, friendly twentysomething staff serve up such pleasures as crisp-fried smoked ocean trout fillet with green mango and lime salad, and ginger-marinated spatchcock with spiced potato, mint yogurt, and coriander. This place also has one of the best breakfasts in town; don't miss the roast Swiss brown mushrooms with thyme, olive toast, and truffle Parmesan. ✉ *160 Fullarton Rd., Rose Park 5067* ☎ *08/8331–2400* ⌕ *Reservations recommended.* ⊟ *AE, DC, MC, V.*

★ **$–$$** ✕ **Grange Jetty Kiosk.** Local couples and families come from all over town to enjoy the beach view from this spot's glass-fronted restaurant and umbrella-shaded deck; and then there is the scrumptious Mod-Oz seafood. Standouts include crisp fried baby squid with an orange chili dipping sauce; or pan-seared scampi, bacon, apple, and snow-pea salad with mustard vinaigrette. This is also a perfect place to discover the joy of South Australian oysters. Breakfast is served on Sunday. ✉ *Esplanade and Jetty Rd., Grange* ☎ *08/8235–0822* ⌕ *Reservations essential* ⊟ *AE, DC, MC, V* ☺ *No lunch Tues., no dinner Sun.–Tues. June–Aug.*

Pan Asian

★ $ ✕ **Kwik Stix.** Terrific Asian food packs people in at the dark-wood tables and black-upholstered booths of this O'Connell Street eatery (one of a three-restaurant franchise). Food sizzles, woks clang, voices are loud, and service is borderline frantic when there's a crowd—which is often. You can walk past the open kitchen to order and pay at the high-gloss bar, then drink Australian or New Zealand wine while eating your way from Indonesia to Japan; don't miss the spicy barramundi with crispy basil leaves. Food arrives on huge white plates and a spoon and fork are standard; you'll need to ask for chopsticks. ⊠ *42 O'Connell St., North Adelaide* ☎ *08/8239–2023* ⊠ *Main North Rd. near Parafield Rd., Parafield* ☎ *08/8258–3522* ⊠ *8 Rupert Ave., Bedford Park* ☎ *08/8177–0035* 🖃 *AE, DC, MC, V.*

¢ ✕ **Market Plaza Food Court.** This bustling pan-Asian food hall is a beef-with-black-bean-sauce–free zone. Instead, stalls including Mum's Kimbap and Li's Mouth Magic produce such dishes as salty fish and chicken fried rice, special hot pot, and *pho gà* (Vietnamese chicken noodle soup with fresh mint and coriander). Shoppers and tourists crowd the Formica tables next door to the Central Market, yet you never have to wait more than a few minutes for a delicious, cheap meal. ⊠ *Moonta St. between Gouger and Grote Sts., City Center* ☎ *08/8212–8866* 🖃 *No credit cards* ☉ *No dinner Sat.–Thurs.*

Seafood

$$ ✕ **Sammy's on the Marina.** Enormous fishbowl windows frame a 270-degree view of beach and million-dollar yachts at this restaurant—one of Adelaide's best seafood eateries—in Glenelg's upscale Holdfast Marina development. Watch the setting sun silhouette playing dolphins or a storm rolling across Gulf St. Vincent as you tuck into Port Lincoln tuna sashimi or a bowl of steaming bouillabaisse. The menu here charts South Australia's ocean bounty and the hot seafood platter (for two people) would feed a school of sharks. ⊠ *Restaurant 1–12 Holdfast Promenade, Glenelg* ☎ *08/8376–8211* ⚓ *Reservations essential* 🖃 *AE, DC, MC, V.*

Where to Stay

At first glance, large international, business-style hotels seem to dominate Adelaide, but there's actually a wide choice of places to rest your head. Adelaide's accommodations are a mix of traditional mid-rise hotels, backpacker hostels, self-contained apartments, and charming bed-and-breakfasts, many in century-old sandstone buildings. City-center hotels are convenient to the sights, but for a better taste of local life head outside the central business district (CBD). If you have a car, you'll be within easy reach of a Glenelg beach house or an Adelaide Hills bed-and-breakfast.

Higher city rates mean a hotel is closer to downtown Adelaide and has more facilities. Weekend discounts are usually available for hotels and apartments. Accommodations should be prebooked for visits coinciding with major festivals and sporting events.

$$$$ ⌂ **Oaks Plaza Pier.** Sea air wafts through open balcony doors in this all-apartment complex on Adelaide's favorite beach, where floor-to-ceiling windows frame either Glenelg and parkland views or white sand and turquoise sea. The spacious suites are decorated in neutral colors, with splashes of black and bright red; all have fully equipped kitchens and every mod-con imaginable, including Sony Playstations. After a night spent exploring Glenelg's waterfront restaurants and bars, you can fall asleep in your huge, comfortable bed listening to waves washing ashore. ⌧ *16 Holdfast Promenade, Glenelg 5045* ☎ *08/8350–6688 or 1300/551111* 🖷 *08/8350–6699* ⊕ *www.theoaksgroup.com.au* ⇥ *121 1-bed apartments, 34 2-bedroom apartments, 1 3-bedroom apartment ⌂ Restaurant, 2 cafés, coffee shop, room service, IDD phones, in-room safes, some in-room hot tubs, kitchens, minibars, microwaves, refrigerators, cable TV with movies, in-room data ports, indoor pool, gym, sauna, spa, beach, 2 bars, babysitting, dry cleaning, laundry facilities, laundry service, concierge, business services, travel services, parking (fee); no smoking* ⊟ *AE, DC, MC, V.*

★ **$$$$** ⌂ **Radisson Playford Hotel and Suites.** Showy chandeliers illuminate a movie-set-like celebration of art nouveau in the lobby of this luxury hotel. Check your reflection in an enormous gilt mirror before relaxing in a club lounge or around the grand piano in the bar, where the tables have statue bases and marble tops. Room decorations in gilt, purple, sage green, and chocolate are a subtler nod to the art nouveau era. In the unusual loft suites, wrought-iron stairs climb to a king size bed on the mezzanine floor. The colonnaded indoor hotel pool feels like a Roman bathhouse. ⌧ *120 North Terr., City Center 5000* ☎ *08/8213–8888* 🖷 *08/8213–8833* ⊕ *www.radisson.com* ⇥ *110 rooms, 72 suites ⌂ Restaurant, room service, IDD phones, some in-room hot tubs, some in-room safes, some kitchenettes, minibars, some microwaves, refrigerators, cable TV, in-room data ports, indoor pool, gym, sauna, spa, bar, laundry facilities, laundry service, concierge, Internet room, convention center, car rental, travel services, parking (fee), no-smoking rooms* ⊟ *AE, DC, MC, V.*

$$$$ ⌂ **Rendezvous Allegra Hotel Adelaide.** Black-tile–and–timber columns frame the Hollywood-glamorous marble lobby of this ultrasleek, upscale boutique hotel. Beveled-glass elevators with marble floors, designed to resemble the interior of a diamond, whisk you to snazzy, contemporary quarters drawn in clean lines of glass, ivory marble, and red wood. A picture window separates bathroom and bedroom. The first-floor Glasshouse restaurant can deliver treats day and night; you can work them off in the cerulean-blue tile pool, which has underwater portholes for watching the hotel entrance. ⌧ *55 Waymouth St., City Center, 5000* ☎ *08/8115–8888* 🖷 *08/8115–8800* ⊕ *www.rendezvoushotels.com* ⇥ *200 rooms ⌂ Restaurant, IDD phones, minibars, room TVs with movies, in-room data ports, pool, gym, sauna, spa, babysitting, dry cleaning, laundry service, concierge, Internet room, business services, car rental, travel services, no smoking rooms* ⊟ *AE, DC, MC, V* ⍩ *CP.*

Fodor's Choice ★

$$$–$$$$ ⌂ **Hilton Adelaide.** Overlooking Victoria Square, this grand hotel is in the middle of Adelaide's shopping, theater, and business district. There are two styles of spacious room, as well as suites. Refurbished rooms are elegant in taupe, white, and golden wood, and have all-marble bathrooms with separate showers. Older-style rooms are furnished in black, cream, and ocher. Crisp white duvets set off large wooden headboards in all rooms. You can meander downstairs to sip a cocktail in the swanky lobby, where the wraparound rock pool holds a 119-pound raw amethyst; dine at the Grange restaurant; or have a pint in Charlie's bustling bar. ✉ *233 Victoria Sq., City Center, 5001* ☎ *08/8217–2000* 🖶 *08/8217–2001* ⊕ *www.hilton.com* 🛏 *380 rooms, 10 suites* ♿ *2 restaurants, café, room service, IDD phones, in-room safes, minibars, refrigerators, cable TV with movies, in-room data ports, tennis court, pool, gym, hair salon, sauna, spa, 2 bars, dry cleaning, laundry service, concierge, Internet room, business services, convention center, car rental, travel services, parking (fee); no smoking* 🚭 *AE, DC, MC, V* ⑩ *CP.*

$$$–$$$$ 🏨 **Hyatt Regency Adelaide.** Views, luxury, service, and location (right next to the Festival Centre) define this landmark atrium-style city hotel. Gilt-framed mirrors and modern artworks decorate the octagonal rooms in the four towers; the best views are from the riverside sections above the eighth floor. All rooms have portable keyboards and high-speed Internet access through the TV. Four Regency Club floors include separate concierge service and complimentary Continental breakfast. The first-rate Blake's, Shiki, and Riverside restaurants all provide room service. ✉ *N. Terrace near King William Rd., City Center, 5000* ☎ *08/8231–1234* 🖶 *08/8231–1120* ⊕ *www.adelaide.hyatt.com* 🛏 *346 rooms, 21 suites* ♿ *3 restaurants, room service, IDD phones, in-room safes, minibars, refrigerators, cable TV with movies, in-room data ports, pool, gym, sauna, spa, bar, nightclub, babysitting, dry cleaning, laundry service, concierge, Internet room, business services, convention center, car rental, travel services, parking (fee), no-smoking floors* 🚭 *AE, DC, MC, V* ⑩ *CP.*

$$$–$$$$ 🏨 **Oaks Embassy.** Service is top priority at this modern, ultraslick all-apartment hotel, where the concierge has been a member of the Australian chapter of the Clefs d'Or international fraternity of concierges (motto: "Service through friendship") since 1995. Frosted glass, polished steel, and muted earth tones splashed with blood plum prevail throughout the property, and every high-tech, luxury convenience is available. All units have balconies; the two- and three-bedroom apartments on the higher floors have spa baths. ✉ *96 N. Terr., City Center, 5000* ☎ *08/8124–9900 or 1300/551111* 🖶 *08/8124–9901* ⊕ *www.theoaksgroup.com.au* 🛏 *137 apartments* ♿ *Restaurant, room service, in-room safes, some in-room hot tubs, kitchens, minibars, microwaves, refrigerators, cable TV with movies, in-room data ports, indoor pool, gym, sauna, spa, steam room, wine bar, dry cleaning, laundry facilities, laundry service, car rental, travel services, parking (fee); no smoking* 🚭 *AE, DC, MC, V.*

$$–$$$$ 🏨 **North Adelaide Heritage Group.** Tucked into the city's leafy, oldest section, these 21 lodgings are stunningly unique. Antiques dealers Rodney and Regina Twiss have converted Heritage-listed mews houses, a meeting chapel, an Arts & Crafts manor house, and a fire station (complete with fire engine) into apartments and suites, and filled them with Australian antiques and contemporary furnishings. Each one- to four-bedroom unit has a bath or hot tub, sitting room, and kitchen with a milk-shake maker; all are charming. The Bishop's Garden apartment is the most luxurious and secluded spot in Adelaide, with a sophisticated kitchen and lounge opening into a private garden with a rock-adorned

Fodor'**s**Choice
★

fish pool. American, lactose-free, kosher—any breakfast can be arranged. ✉ *Office: 109 Glen Osmond Rd., Eastwood 5063* 🖷 *08/ 8272–1355* 🌐*www.adelaideheritage.com* ⇕*10 cottages, 3 suites, 7 apartments* ♻ *Room service, BBQs, some IDD phones, some fans, some in-room hot tubs, kitchens, some cable TV, some in-room DVD/VCR, in-room data ports, laundry facilities, laundry service, travel services, free parking; no smoking* 🖃 *AE, DC, MC, V.*

★ **$$$** 🏨 **Medina Grand Adelaide Treasury.** Contemporary Italian furnishings in white, slate gray, and ocher are juxtaposed with 19th-century Adelaide architecture in this stylish Victoria Square hotel. Cast-iron columns, archways, and barrel-vaulted ceilings—original features of the former Treasury building—add texture to clean lines in the studio rooms and serviced apartments. The lobby lounge incorporates an 1839 sandstone wall, one of the oldest remaining colonial structures in South Australia. Great food is as close as the adjoining Treasury Restaurant. ✉ *2 Flinders St., City Center, 5000* 🖷 *08/8112–0000 or 1300/300232* 🖷 *08/8112–0199* 🌐 *www.medinaapartments.com.au* ⇕ *20 studio rooms, 59 apartments* ♻ *Restaurant, in-room safes, some kitchens, some refrigerators, room TVs with movies, in-room data ports, indoor pool, gym, bar, babysitting, dry cleaning, laundry facilities, car rental, travel services, parking (fee); no smoking* 🖃 *AE, DC, MC, V.*

$$$ 🏨 **Saville Park Suites.** Step out your door at this three-story redbrick complex and you might think you're in the tropics; open-air walkways and huge palm trees suggest you're closer to the beach than the western-parkland end of Hindley Street. The compact apartments are decked out in pin-striped charcoal, chocolate, and beige. All have full kitchens and free pantry service; some have washing machines and dryers. The open-plan one-bed studios feel roomier than the two-bedroom standard apartments. The complex is on the CityFree bus route. ✉ *255 Hindley St., City Center 5000* 🖷 *08/8217–2500* 🖷 *08/8217–2519* 🌐 *www.savillesuites.com* ⇕ *47 studios, 94 2-bedroom apartments* ♻ *Restaurant, room service, IDD phones, kitchens, minibars, microwaves, refrigerators, room TVs with movies, some in-room data ports, babysitting, laundry service, laundry facilities, concierge, business services, car rental, travel services, parking (fee); no smoking* 🖃 *AE, DC, MC, V.*

$–$$ 🏨 **Director's Studios.** The friendly and efficient staff at this central Saville Hotel Group property have you in and out of the small reception area in minutes. Standard rooms are in a wing punched with skylights and decorated with hanging plants and vintage movie posters (the only connection to the property's name). The self-contained studios have kitchens. All rooms have irons and ironing boards. You can take your meals in the adjoining Director's Hotel restaurant or wander down Gouger Street into Chinatown and the Central Market. It's a pleasant walk to the city's sights, and there's free covered parking. ✉ *259 Gouger St., City Center, 5000* 🖷 *08/8213–2500* 🖷 *08/8216–2519* 🌐 *www. savillesuites.com* ⇕ *22 rooms, 36 studios* ♻ *Restaurant, room service, IDD phones, some kitchenettes, minibars, some microwaves, refrigerators, in-room data ports, babysitting, dry cleaning, laundry facilities, laundry service, Internet room, car rental, travel services, free parking, no smoking rooms* 🖃 *AE, DC, MC, V.*

$ ▦ **Quest Mansions.** Suites, self-catering studios, and one-bedroom serviced apartments are housed in this handsome, Heritage-listed building between North Terrace and Rundle Mall. All rooms are spacious and comfortable and have complete kitchens; also there's a free pantry-shopping service. There's also a rooftop terrace with a communal barbecue and sauna. The basement Mansions Tavern serves good counter grub, and you can charge meals back to your room at several local restaurants. ⊠ *21 Pulteney St., City Center, 5000* ☎ *08/8232–0033* ⊟ *08/ 8223–4559* ⊕ *www.questapartments.com.au* ⌁ *6 suites, 6 studios, 33 apartments* ⚇ *Room service, BBQ, kitchens, room TVs with movies, in-room data ports, sauna, pub, babysitting, laundry facilities, business services, parking (fee); no smoking* ⊟ *AE, DC, MC, V.*

¢–$ ▦ **Adelaide Shores Holiday Village.** The breeze is salty, the lawns are green, and white sand is only a few lazy steps from this summery resort on the city's coastal fringe. Beyond the dunes is a seldom-crowded beach, which fronts a mix of raised two-bedroom villas with private balconies, standard apartment units, and cabins with shared facilities. It's a 20-minute drive to the city, but the pool, many sports facilities, and barbecue are reasons enough to stay put. ⊠ *Military Rd., West Beach, 5045* ☎ *08/8353–2655* ⊟ *08/8353–3755* ⊕ *www.adelaideshores.com.au* ⌁ *30 villas, 32 apartments, 32 cabins* ⚇ *BBQ, grocery, tennis court, pool, wading pool, beach, basketball, billiards, Ping-Pong, volleyball, recreation room, playground, laundry facilities, Internet room, free parking, no-smoking rooms; no room phones* ⊟ *AE, DC, MC, V.*

¢ ▦ **Adelaide Central YHA.** Mostly young people buzz around this purpose-built, city-center hostel like bees at a hive. It's the only YHA in Adelaide, and it far exceeds the standards of its affiliation. There's a true community feel throughout the property, from the declaration of human rights on the front door to the free movie nights. Bright, airy doubles, family rooms, and dorms (six beds maximum) have metal-frame beds and individual luggage lockers. There's a large, well-equipped communal kitchen, TV rooms, recreation areas, and a smoking lounge. Nightclubs, restaurants, and city attractions are close by in Light Square. Doors lock at 11 PM, but if you pick up the external phone, the night staff will let you in whatever the hour. ⊠ *135 Waymouth St. City Center 5000* ☎ *08/8414–3010* ⊟ *08/8414–3015* ⊕ *www.yha.com.au* ⌁ *63 rooms* ⚇ *Grocery, mountain bikes, billiards, Ping-Pong, shop, laundry facilities, Internet room, travel services, parking (fee); no-smoking rooms; no room phones, no room TVs* ⊟ *AE, DC, MC, V.*

⚠ **Levi Park.** Green Port Lincoln parrots and black ducks are regulars at this caravan park overlooking the River Torrens, 5 km (3 mi) from the center of Adelaide. From here it's a scenic walk or cycle along a shared river path to the city, and a bus passes the front gate. Grassy tent sites have river frontage, with en suite cabins and campervans parked behind. A fully equipped camp kitchen and separate children's and disabled-access bathrooms are bonuses. You can play tennis in the adjoining sports field. In the middle of the park, beside a historic fig tree, is Adelaide's oldest surviving colonial home, Vale House, now a four-suite upscale Heritage accommodation. ⚇ *Flush toilets, partial hookups (electric and water), dump station, drinking water, guest laundry, showers, grills, pic-*

nic tables, electricity, public telephone, general store, play area ⚡ 15 *unpowered sites, 77 powered sites, 30 cabins* ✉ 69 *Lansdowne Terr., Walkerville, 5081* ☎ 08/8344–2209 *or* 1800/442209 🖷 08/8344–2209 ⊕ *www.levipark.com.au* 🖃 *unpowered site A$23, powered site A$29, cabins A$76–A$106, Vale House A$130/double* 🖃 *MC, V.*

Nightlife & the Arts

The Arts

The three-week Adelaide Festival of Arts, the oldest arts festival in the country, takes place in February and March of even-numbered years. It's a cultural smorgasbord of outdoor opera, classical music, jazz, art exhibitions, comedy, and cabaret presented by some of the world's top artists. Recent performers have included the Ballet Nacional de España and Welsh bass-baritone Bryn Terfel. Visit ⊕ www.adelaidefestival. com.au or contact the South Australian Visitor and Travel Centre for more information. The annual, three-day WOMADelaide Festival of world music, arts, and dance, which takes place in early March, makes noise and raises consciousness on stages in Botanic Park and other near-city venues; see ⊕ www.womadelaide.com.au for details.

For a listing of performances and exhibitions, look to the entertainment pages of the *Advertiser,* Adelaide's daily newspaper. The *Adelaide Review,* a free monthly arts paper, reviews exhibitions, galleries, and performances and lists forthcoming events. Tickets for most live performances can be purchased in person or by phone from **BASS Ticket Agency** (✉ Adelaide Festival Centre, King William St., City Center ☎ 13–1246).

The **Adelaide Festival Centre** (✉ King William St. near N. Terrace, City Center ☎ 13–1246) is the city's major venue for the performing arts. The State Opera, the South Australian Theatre Company, and the Adelaide Symphony Orchestra perform here regularly. Performances are in the Playhouse, Festival, and Space theaters, the outdoor amphitheater, and the Majestic Theatre at 58 Grote Street. The box office is open Monday–Saturday 9–6. The Backstage Bistro at the Centre serves modern Australian food.

Nightlife

BARS & CLUBS There's something going on every evening in Adelaide, although clubs are especially packed on the weekends. Cover charges vary according to the night and time of entry. Nightlife for the coming week is listed in *The Guide,* a pull-out section of Thursday's edition of *The Advertiser. Rip It Up* is a free Thursday music-and-club publication aimed at the younger market. *Onion,* published biweekly on Thursday, is Adelaide's top dance music magazine. *dB,* a twice-monthly free independent publication, covers music, arts, film, games, and dance.

Bars along Rundle Street and East Terrace are trendy, while Hindley and Waymouth streets are lined with traditional pubs. North Adelaide's O'-Connell Street buzzes every night, and the popular Sunday-evening beer-and-banter sessions really pack in the crowds.

Austral Hotel (✉ 205 Rundle St., City Center ☎ 08/8223–4660), the first bar in South Australia to put Coopers beer on tap, is a local favorite. You can sample a series of shots called the Seven Deadly Sins here, while listening to a DJ spin groovy tunes. It's open daily 11 AM–3 AM. Meals are available all day on weekends and at lunch and dinner hours during the week.

Botanic Bar (✉ 309 N. Terr., City Center ☎ 08/8227–0799), a cool city lounge, has cordovan banquettes encircling the U-shape, marble-top bar. Muddlers (crushed ice drinks) are the specialty, and they bring in mostly young professionals. It's open Wednesday–Sunday, 3 PM–3 AM.

Cargo Club (✉ 213 Hindley St., City Center ☎ 08/8231–2327) attracts a stylish clientele with funk, acid rock, jazz, and house music. It's open Wednesday, Friday, and Saturday 10 PM–5 AM; covers are between A$5–A$10.

★ **The Gov** (✉ 59 Port Rd., Hindmarsh, 5007 ☎ 08/8340–0744) was voted the country's best live-music venue at the Australian Live Music Awards in 2004. A two-story stone hotel (its full name is the Governor Hindmarsh), this is the favorite venue of a mixed crowd. Young homeowners and long-term regulars come for Irish music sessions, all-weekend metal fests, and everything in between. Cabaret, comedy, Latin music—if you can name it, you can probably hear it here. There's good pub grub, too. It's open weekdays 11 AM to late, Saturday noon to late, and Sunday 3 PM–8 PM.

Grace Emily (✉ 232 Waymouth St., City Center ☎ 08/8231–5500), a multilevel music lover's pub, has barmen spouting the mantra, "No pokies, no TAB, no food." (The first two declarations refer to gambling: pokies are the poker machines found in many traditional Aussie pubs, and TAB, Australia's version of OTB, lets you place bets on horse races and football games.) Instead, there's live music near-nightly, and a jukebox and pool table for when there's no band. The beer garden out back is one of the city's best, with secluded spots for those wanting a quiet tipple and big round tables for groups to drink en masse and alfresco. It's open daily 4 PM–late.

Heaven (✉ N. and W. Terr., City Center ☎ 08/8216–5200) is where the young party crowd dances to contemporary music. Live bands play some weeknights. Doors open Wednesday at 8:30 PM, Thursday at 10 PM, and Friday and Saturday at 9 PM, and don't close until around 6 AM. Cover charges are A$8 on Wednesday, from A$5 on Thursday (depending on the act), A$5 until midnight and A$8 after on Friday, and A$10 on Saturday.

The **Wellington Hotel** (✉ 36 Wellington Sq., North Adelaide ☎ 08/8267–1322), first licensed in 1851, is hops-lovers' heaven, with 30 Australian-brewed beers on tap. Line up six "pony" (sample) glasses, then enjoy a schooner (large glass) of your favorite. The adjoining Welly Tap & Grill also serves great food.

CASINO Head to **SkyCity** for big-time casino gaming, including the highly animated Australian Two-up, in which you bet against the house on the fall of two coins. Three bars and three restaurants are also within the complex. It's one of a handful of places in Adelaide that keep pumping until dawn. ⊠ *N. Terrace, City Center* ☎ *08/8212–2811* ⊙ *Sun.–Thurs. 10 AM–4 AM, Fri. and Sat. 10 AM–6 AM.*

Sports & the Outdoors

Participant Sports

BICYCLING Adelaide's parks, flat terrain, and wide, uncluttered streets make it a perfect city for two-wheel exploring. **Linear Park Mountain Bike Hire** (⊠ Elder Park, adjacent to Adelaide Festival Centre, City Center ☎ 0400/ 596065) rents 21-speed mountain bikes by the hour or for A$20 per day and A$80 per week, including a helmet, lock, and maps. They're open daily 9–5 in winter, 9–6 in summer, or by appointment.

GOLF One short (par-3) and two 18-hole courses are run by the **City of Adelaide Golf Links** (⊠ Entrance to par-3 course is off War Memorial Dr.; 18-hole courses are off Strangways Terr. and War Memorial Dr., North Adelaide ☎ 08/8267–2171). You can rent clubs and carts from the pro shop. Greens fees are from A$15.70 weekdays and A$18.45 weekends for the north course, A$18.50 weekdays and A$21.75 weekends for the south course. Playing hours are dawn to dusk daily.

TENNIS & Across the Torrens from the city, the **Next Generation** (⊠ War Memo-
SWIMMING rial Dr., North Adelaide ☎ 08/8110–7777) club has hard, grass, synthetic, and clay tennis courts (35 in total), squash courts, two pools, and a gym, hot tub, and sauna. Admission is A$55 per day, and it's open weekdays 5:30 AM–11 PM, weekends 7 AM–10 PM.

Spectator Sports

Venue*Tix (⊠ Shop 24, Da Costa Arcade, 68 Grenfell St., City Center ☎ 08/ 8225–8888) sells tickets for domestic and international one-day and test (five-day) cricket matches, other major sporting events, and concerts.

CRICKET The main venue for interstate and international competition is the Ade-
★ laide Oval. During cricket season October–March, the **Cricket Museum** (⊠ Adelaide Oval, War Memorial Dr. and King William St., North Adelaide ☎ 08/8300–3800) has 2½-hour tours (A$10) weekdays (except on match days).

FOOTBALL Australian Rules Football is the most popular winter sport in South Australia. Games are played on weekends at **AAMI Stadium** (⊠ Turner Dr., West Lakes ☎ 08/8268–2088). Teams play in the national AFL competition on Friday, Saturday, or Sunday. The season runs March to August. Finals are in September.

Shopping

Shops in Adelaide City Center are generally open Monday–Thursday 9–5:30, Friday 9–9, Saturday 9–5, and Sunday 11–5. In the suburbs shops are often open until 9 PM on Thursday night instead of Friday. As the center of the world's opal industry, Adelaide has many opal shops, which are around King William Street. Other good buys are South Australian regional wines, crafts, and Aboriginal artwork.

Malls

Adelaide's main shopping area is **Rundle Mall** (⊠ Rundle St. between King William and Pulteney Sts., City Center ☎ 08/8203–7611), a pedestrian plaza lined with boutiques, department stores, and arcades. Heritage-listed Adelaide Arcade is a Victorian-era jewel, with a decorative tiled floor, skylights, and dozens of shops behind huge timber-framed windows.

Markets

★ One of the largest produce markets in the Southern Hemisphere, **Central Market** (⊠ Gouger St., City Center ☎ 08/8203–7494) is chock-full of stellar local foods, including glistening-fresh fish, meat, crusty Vietnamese and Continental breads, German baked goods, cheeses of every shape and color, and old fashioned lollies (candy). You can also buy souvenir T-shirts, CDs, books, cut flowers, and a great cup of coffee. Hours are Tuesday 7–5:30, Thursday 9–5:30, Friday 7 AM–9 PM, and Saturday 7–3.

Specialty Stores

ANTIQUES **Megaw and Hogg Antiques** (⊠ 118 Grote St., City Center ☎ 08/ 8231–0101) sells antique furniture and decorative arts.

CHOCOLATE **Haigh's Chocolates** (⊠ 2 Rundle Mall and King William St., City Cen-
★ ter ☎ 08/8231–2844 ⊠ Haigh's Visitor Centre, 154 Greenhill Rd., Parkside ☎ 08/8372–7077), Australia's oldest chocolate manufacturer, has tempted people with corner shop displays since 1915. The family-owned South Australian company produces exquisite truffles, pralines, and creams—as well as the chocolate Easter bilby (an endangered Australian marsupial), Haigh's answer to the Easter bunny. Shop hours are Monday–Thursday 8:30–6, Friday 8:30 AM–9:30 PM, Saturday 9–5:30, and Sunday 11–5:30. Free chocolate-making tours at the visitor center run Monday–Saturday at 1 and 2, and bookings are essential.

HOMEWARES The **Jam Factory** (⊠ 19 Morphett St., City Center ☎ 08/8410–0727), a contemporary craft-and-design center, exhibits and sells unique Australian glassware, ceramics, wood, and metal designs. For quirky locally made jewelry, pottery, glass, and sculptures, visit **Urban Cow Studio** (⊠ 11 Frome St., City Center ☎ 08/8232–6126).

JEWELRY & GEMS **Adelaide Exchange** (⊠ 10 Stephens Pl., City Center ☎ 08/8212–2496), off Rundle Mall, sells high-quality antique jewelry. The **Australian Opal Collection** (⊠ 14 King William St., City Center ☎ 08/8211–9995), sells and manufactures superb handcrafted one-of-a-kind opal jewelry. **Opal Field Gems Mine and Museum** (⊠ 33 King William St., City Center ☎ 08/ 8212–5300) has an excellent selection of opals and other gems, an authentic opal-mining display, an Aboriginal art gallery, and video screenings of opal production. It's open daily (Mon.–Thurs. 9–6, Fri. 9–7:30, Sat. 9–5:30 and Sun. 10–5) and it's free.

Side Trips to the Adelaide Hills

With their secluded green slopes and flowery gardens, the Adelaide Hills are a pastoral shelter in this desert state. The patchwork quilt of vast orchards, neat vineyards, and avenues of tall conifers resembles the

Bavarian countryside, a likeness fashioned by the many German immigrants who settled here in the 19th century. During the steamy summer months the Adelaide Hills are consistently cooler than the city, although the charming towns and wineries are pleasant to visit any time of year. To reach the region from Adelaide, head toward the M1 Princes Highway or drive down Pulteney Street, which becomes Unley Road and then Belair Road. From here, signs are marked to Crafers and the freeway.

Mt. Lofty
16 km (10 mi) southeast of Adelaide.

There are splendid views of Adelaide from the lookout atop 2,300-foot Mt. Lofty. A 3½-km (2-mi) round-trip walk from the Waterfall Gully parking lot in Cleland Conservation Park (15 minutes' drive from Adelaide) takes you along Waterfall Creek before climbing steeply to the giant white obelisk on the summit; the track is closed on Total Fire Ban days. Much of the surrounding area was devastated during the Ash Wednesday bushfires of 1983. By car from Adelaide, take the Crafers exit off the South Eastern Freeway and follow Summit Road.

Mt. Lofty Botanic Gardens, with its rhododendrons, magnolias, ferns, and exotic trees, is glorious in fall and spring. Free guided walks leave the lower parking lot on Thursday at 10 in spring and autumn. ⊠ *Picadilly entrance off Lampert Rd.* ☎ *08/8370–8370* ⊕ *www.environment. sa.gov.au/botanicgardens* ☞ *Free* ⊙ *Weekdays 8:30–4, weekends 10–6.*

A short drive from Mt. Lofty Summit brings you to **Cleland Wildlife Park,** where animals roam free across three different but linked forest habitats. Walking trails crisscross the park and its surroundings, and you're guaranteed to see wombats, emus, and kangaroos in the fields and swampy billabongs. Guided day tours cover the park's highlights, while monthly two-hour night walks let you stroll among nocturnal species such as potoroos and brush-tailed bettongs. Private guided tours of park highlights can be arranged for A\$60 per hour. Reservations are essential for tours, and the park is closed when there's a fire ban (usually between December and February). ⊠ *Summit Rd.* ☎ *08/8339–2444, 08/ 8231–4144 Adelaide sightseeing tours* ⊕ *www.environment.sa.gov.au/ parks/cleland* ☞ *A\$13, night walks A\$21.50* ⊙ *Daily 9:30–5.*

WHERE TO
STAY & EAT
★ \$\$

✕ **Summit.** If you suffer from vertigo, think twice about dining here; this glass-front building atop Mt. Lofty is all about dining with altitude. The menu here is a frequently changing play of Australian, French, and Asian flavors; dishes might include hills venison with cider-glazed apples and horseradish cream, or cumin-, coriander-, and paprika-spiced chicken with hummus and eggplant chutney. Spectacular views of the hills, city, and coast across to Yorke Peninsula complement samplings from local markets, gardens, and bakeries. The wine list similarly promotes Adelaide Hills vintages. ⊠ *Mt. Lofty Lookout* ☎ *08/8339–2600* ⌂ *Reservations essential* ⊟ *AE, DC, MC, V* ⊙ *No dinner Mon. and Tues.*

\$\$\$–\$\$\$\$

▥ **Mercure Grand Mt. Lofty House.** From very English garden terraces below the summit of Mt. Lofty, this refined country house overlooks a distant patchwork of vineyards, farms, and bushland. This is country living at its finest; relax over dinner in the glass-fronted restaurant, read the daily paper on a settee in the lounge, then retreat to a large bedroom sumptuously decorated with silks and brocades in lush Victorian hues and florals. Heritage rooms have their own wood-burning fireplaces. ⊠ *74 Summit Rd., Crafers 5152* ☏ *08/8339–6777* ☐ *08/8339–5656* ⊕ *www. mtloftyhouse.com.au* ➯ *27 rooms, 2 suites* ♿ *Restaurant, some in-room hot tubs, minibars, cable TV with movies, in-room data ports, tennis court, pool, billiards, boccie, volleyball, 2 bars, 2 lounges, library, dry cleaning, laundry service, concierge, convention center, travel services* ▭ *AE, DC, MC, V.*

Mylor

10 km (6 mi) south of Mt. Lofty via the town of Crafers, the South Eastern Fwy., and Stirling; 25 km (16 mi) southeast of Adelaide.

The attractive little village of Mylor draws in crowds for its wildlife.

★ ☺   The 85-acre **Warrawong Earth Sanctuary,** a lovely combination of rain forest, gurgling streams, and black-water ponds, is the place to spot kangaroos, wallabies, bandicoots, and platypuses—particularly on one of the daily guided dawn (6:30 AM) or dusk walks. Because most of the animals are nocturnal, the evening walk is more rewarding. Facilities include a café-restaurant and bush cabin accommodations. Entrance is by tour only, and reservations for walks are essential. ⊠ *Stock Rd.* ☏ *08/ 8370–9197* ⊕ *www.warrawong.com* ➯ *Walks A$22, dinner A$19–A$25; 2-course dinner & walk packages A$49* ☉ *Daily 6:30 AM–late.*

Bridgewater

6 km (4 mi) north of Mylor, 22 km (14 mi) southeast of Adelaide.

Bridgewater came into existence in 1841 as a refreshment stop for bullock teams fording Cock's Creek. More English than German, with its flowing creek and flower-filled gardens, this leafy, tranquil village was officially planned in 1859 by the builder of the first Bridgewater flour mill.

The handsome, 145-year-old **stone flour mill** with its churning waterwheel stands at the entrance to the town. These days the mill houses the first-class Bridgewater Mill Restaurant and serves as the shop front for Petaluma Wines, one of Australia's finest labels; try the chardonnay and viognier. The prestigious Croser champagne is matured on the lower level of the building, and you can tour the cellars by appointment. ⊠ *Bridgewater and Mt. Barker Rds.* ☏ *08/8339–3422* ➯ *Free* ☉ *Daily 10–5.*

WHERE TO   ✕ **Bridgewater Mill Restaurant.** A stylish and celebrated restaurant in a
STAY & EAT   converted flour mill, this is one of the state's best dining spots. Using
$$$$ mostly local produce, chef Le Tu Thai creates a contemporary Australian
Fodor'sChoice   menu of imaginative food as unique as the setting; dishes might include
★   double-baked blue-cheese souffle with roasted eggplant, or saddle of venison and quail sausage with roasted beetroot and sour cherries. In summer, book ahead to get a table on the deck beside the waterwheel. If you're feeling flush, ask to see the special wine list. ⊠ *Bridgewater and Mt. Barker Rds.* ☏ *08/8339–3422* ▭ *AE, DC, MC, V* ☉ *Closed Tues. and Wed. No dinner.*

$-$$ ✕ **Aldgate Pump Bistro.** This friendly double-story country pub 2 km (1 mi) from Bridgewater, in the delightful village of Aldgate, has an extensive, eclectic selection of hearty fare such as Mediterranean-style sausage with tomato chili relish and double-cooked roast duckling dressed with tamarind glaze and stone-fruit chutney. Warmed by log fires in winter, the dining room overlooks a shaded beer garden. It's a good place for a leisurely glimpse into the local character. ✉ *1 Strathalbyn Rd., 2 km (1 mi) from Bridgewater, Aldgate* ☎ *08/8339–2015* ▭ *AE, DC, MC, V.*

★ **$$$$** ▥ **Thorngrove Manor Hotel.** This romantic Gothic castle is "Lifestyles of the Rich and Famous" writ large, with valet Kenneth Lehmann making your every wish his command. Seven opulent suites, set amid glorious gardens, have different configurations and decorative themes. A four-poster bed carved with crowned heraldic lions is the centerpiece of the satin-and-brocade-draped Queen's Chambers, while there are exposed beams, stained-glass windows, and a piano in the King's Chambers. All the suites have entrances that ensure total privacy. It's the place for the holiday of a lifetime. ✉ *2 Glenside La., Stirling 5152* ☎ *08/8339–6748* 🖷 *08/8370–9950* ⊕ *www.slh.com/thorngrove* ➦ *7 suites* ♨ *Dining room, room service, IDD phones, in-room safes, some in-room hot tubs, some microwaves, refrigerators, room TVs with movies, in-room data ports, boccie, croquet, dry cleaning, laundry service, airport shuttle, travel services, free parking; no smoking* ▭ *AE, DC, MC, V* ⦿ *CP.*

$$$ ▥ **The Orangerie.** Gardens filled with statuettes, gazebos, and fountains surround the two self-contained suites in this delightful 1890s sandstone residence. French provincial is the tone of the sunlit one-bedroom suite, which has an elegantly furnished garden sitting room opening onto a private vine-covered terrace. Large gilt mirrors, chandeliers, and antiques furnish the classic Parisian atelier-style two-bedroom suite (two-night minimum booking). There's an extensive library with a wood-burning fireplace for cozy reading, and you can stargaze from the hideaway rooftop terrace. ✉ *4 Orley Ave., Stirling 5152* ☎ *08/8339–5458* 🖷 *08/8339–5912* ⊕ *www.orangerie.com.au* ➦ *2 suites* ♨ *BBQs, kitchens, microwaves, refrigerators, some cable TV, in-room DVD, in-room VCRs, in-room data ports, tennis court, saltwater pool, boccie, library, laundry facilities, free parking, no-smoking rooms* ▭ *AE, MC, V* ⦿ *BP.*

Hahndorf

7 km (4½ mi) east of Bridgewater, 29 km (18 mi) southeast of Adelaide.

This Bavarian-style village might have sprung to life from a chocolate-box lid. Founded in 1839 by German settlers, Hahndorf consists of a single shaded main street lined with stone-and-timber shops and cottages. Most are now arts-and-crafts galleries, antiques stores, and souvenir outlets; however, German traditions survive in bakeries and a butcher's shop. The village is extremely crowded on Sunday.

The Cedars is the original home, studio, and gardens of Sir Hans Heysen, a famous Australian landscape artist who lived in this area at the turn of the 20th century. Beautifully preserved, the 1920s house is filled with original artifacts, antiques, and an impressive collection of the artist's work. The surrounding gardens, where his studio can be seen, inspired many of his paintings. Entrance to the studio and house is by guided tour, which take place at 11, 1, and 3 in summer (11 and 2 in winter). ✉ *Heysen Rd. off Ambleside Rd.* ☎ *08/8388–7277* ⊕ *www. visitadelaidehills.com.au/thecedars* 🎫 *A$10, garden only A$4* ⏱ *Tues.–Sun. 10–4:30.*

The **Hahndorf Academy** contains 10 works by Sir Hans Heysen, and holds exhibitions by local artists. Here, too, are seven artists' studios, some open to the public, and a German migration museum. ✉ *68 Main St.* ☎ *08/8388–7250* 🎫 *Free* ⏱ *Daily 10–4.*

Named after the famous landscape painter, the **Heysen Trail** is Australia's longest dedicated walking track. Beginning—or ending—at Cape Jervis, on the Fleurieu Peninsula, the trail wends north for about 1,200 km (750 mi) to Parachilna Gorge, in the Flinders Ranges. Suitable for day walkers and long-distance hikers, the trail passes through national and state parks, and tourist destinations such as the Barossa Valley and Hahndorf. Most sections are closed from December to April because of the high fire danger. For details on routes, equipment, and events, contact **Friends of the Heysen Trail** (✉ 10 Pitt St., City Center Adelaide 5000 ☎ 08/8212–6299 ⊕ www.heysentrail.asn.au).

WHERE TO STAY & EAT

$–$$

✕ **Cafe Bamburg.** Cow bells, antlers, and lederhosen festoon this tiny German settler's cottage. Delicious *wurst* (sausage), *kassler* (smoked pork cutlet), and other hearty fare fill the plates brought to dark-wood tables in the front room and on the narrow veranda abutting the main street. The choice of German beers is huge, the wine list short. ✉ *81 Main St.* ☎ *08/8388–1797* ☐ *No credit cards* ⏱ *Closed Mon.–Wed. No dinner.*

★ **$$–$$$**

🏨 **Adelaide Hills Country Cottages.** Amid 200 acres of orchards and cattle pastures near Hahndorf, these secluded luxury hideaways are idyllic refuges from the city. You can spend an afternoon rowing a boat on the lake beside Apple Tree, an 1860s English cottage, or enjoy the golden glow of Baltic pine in Gum Tree, a pioneer-style stone cottage overlooking a valley. There's room for two couples in Lavender Fields Cottage, a French country–style gem nestled in rolling lavender gardens. All cottages have log fireplaces, whirlpool tubs, and breakfast provisions. Weekend bookings have a two-night minimum. ✉ *Box 100, Oakbank 5243* ✛ *8 km (5 mi) northeast of Hahndorf* ☎ *08/8388–4193* 🖨 *08/ 8388–4733* ⊕ *www.ahcc.com.au* 🛏 *5 cottages* 🍴 *BBQs, kitchens, microwaves, refrigerators, in-room VCRs, lake, hiking, some laundry facilities, travel services, free parking; no room phones, no kids, no smoking* ☐ *AE, DC, MC, V* ⏱ *BP.*

off the beaten path

MANNUM – The "Mighty Murray" is Australia's longest river and one of the longest on the planet. From its source in the Snowy Mountains of New South Wales it travels some 2,415 km (1,500 mi) through 11 locks before entering the ocean southeast of Adelaide. Vital to South Australia's economy and life, the Murray provides water for the vast irrigation schemes that turned the desert into a fruit bowl—the Riverland is one of the country's largest growers of citrus fruits and produces most of the nation's bulk wine—and supplies Adelaide with its domestic water.

During the second half of the 19th century, before railways eased the difficulty of overland transportation, the river reverberated with the churning wheels and shrieking whistles of paddle steamers carrying wool and livestock from remote pastoral properties to bustling river ports. This most colorful period lives on in the town of Mannum, 85 km (53 mi) northeast from Hahndorf and 84 km (52 mi) east of Adelaide.

Murray River paddle steamers had their origins in Mannum when the first riverboat, the *Mary Ann,* was launched here in 1853. There are a number of reminders of the town's past at the **Mannum Dock Museum** (⊠ 6 Randell St., Mannum ☎ 08/8569–1303 ☉ Weekdays 9–5, weekends 10–4 ☞ A$5), including the 1897 paddle steamer *Marion.* You can take cruises and book overnight cabins on the fully restored boat; when not operating, it's open for exploring (entry included in museum ticket).

The *Murray Princess* (☎ 02/9206–1122 ⊕ www.captaincook.com.au/murray/index.htm), a replica Mississippi River paddle wheeler, also operates from Mannum. You can explore the river-region Outback on two-, three- and five-night cruises.

Adelaide A to Z

AIR TRAVEL
Adelaide Airport, 6 km (4 mi) west of the city center, is small and modern. The international and domestic terminals are very close.

Airlines serving Adelaide include United Airlines, British Airways, Singapore Airlines, Malaysia Airlines, and Cathay Pacific. Qantas also connects Adelaide with many international cities (usually via Melbourne or Sydney). Domestic airlines flying into Adelaide include Airlines of South Australia, Emu Airways, Jetstar, REX/Regional Express, and Virgin Blue.
🖪 **Airport Adelaide Airport** ⊠ 1 James Schofield Dr. ☎ 08/8308-9211.
🖪 **Airlines Airlines of South Australia** ☎ 1800/018234. **British Airways** ☎ 1300/767177. **Cathay Pacific Airways** ☎ 08/8234-4737 or 13-1747. **Emu Airways** ☎ 08/8234-3711. **Jetstar** ☎ 13-1538. **Malaysia Airlines** ☎ 13-2627. **Qantas Airways** ☎ 13-1313. **REX/ Regional Express** ☎ 13-1713. **Singapore Airlines** ☎ 08/8203-0800 or 13-1011. **United Airlines** ☎ 13-1777. **Virgin Blue** ☎ 13-6789.

AIRPORT TRANSFERS The Skylink Airport Shuttle costs A$7.50 and links the airport terminals with city hotels, Keswick Rail Terminal (interstate and country trains), and central bus stations. The bus leaves hourly from the terminals 6:15 AM–9:40 PM and from the city 6 AM–9:15 PM. Extra services operate 7 AM–1 PM Monday–Saturday. Taxis are available from the stands outside the air terminal buildings. The fare to the city is about A$15, and all credit cards are accepted.
🖪 **Skylink Airport Shuttle** ☎ 08/8332-0528.

BOAT TRAVEL
Pop-Eye Motor Launches connect Elder Park, in front of the Adelaide Festival Centre, with the rear gate of the Zoological Gardens. Trips run

weekends 11–5, with departures every 20 minutes, and weekdays 11–3, with hourly departures. Tickets are A$5 one-way, A$8 round-trip.

🚩 **Pop-Eye Motor Launches** ✉ Elder Park ☎ 08/8223–5863.

BUS TRAVEL

The Central Bus Station, open daily 6:30 AM–9 PM, is near the city center. From here, Premier Stateliner operates buses throughout South Australia, and V-Line, Firefly Express, and Greyhound Australia run interstate and some local services.

🚩 **Bus Station Central Bus Station** ✉ 111 Franklin St., City Center ☎ 08/8415–5533.

🚩 **Bus Lines Firefly Express** ☎ 1300/730740 ⊕ www.fireflyexpress.com.au. **Greyhound Australia** ☎ 08/8212–5066 ⊕ www.greyhound.com.au. **Premier Stateliner** ☎ 08/8415–5555 ⊕ www.premierstateliner.com.au. **V-Line** ☎ 08/8231–7620 ⊕ www.vlinepassenger.com.au.

BUS TRAVEL WITHIN ADELAIDE

Fares on the public transportation network are based on morning peak and off-peak travel 9–3. A single-trip peak ticket is A$3.40, off-peak A$2. Tickets are available from most railway stations, newsstands, post offices, and the Adelaide Metro Info Centre. If you plan to travel frequently you can economize with a multitrip ticket (A$22.20), which allows 10 rides throughout the three bus zones. Off-peak multitrip tickets are A$12.20. Another economical way to travel is with the day-trip ticket, which allows unlimited bus, train, and tram travel throughout Adelaide and most of its surroundings from first until last service. It costs A$6.40.

No-cost CityFree buses make about 30 stops in downtown Adelaide. The BeeLine Bus runs on 5- to 10-minute intervals around King William Street and North Terrace weekdays 7:40 AM–6 PM and every 10 minutes Friday only 6:10 PM–9.20 PM; every 15 minutes Saturday 8:30 AM–5:30 PM and Sunday 10 AM–5:30 PM. The City Loop Bus runs every 15 minutes in two central city directions, weekdays 8 AM–8:45 PM, and every 30 minutes Saturday 8:15 AM–5:45 PM and Sunday 10 AM–5:15 PM. The free Adelaide Connector, which links North Adelaide and the City, runs weekdays 9–5:30. Buses have ramp access for wheelchairs and baby carriages, and they stop at most major attractions.

Wandering Star is a late-night bus service that operates on Friday and Saturday. From 12:30 to 5 AM you can travel from the city to your door (or as near as possible) in 11 suburban zones for A$6.

The Adelaide metropolitan network also serves the Adelaide Hills, but you need to catch two or more buses to some of the more remote attractions, such as Mt. Lofty and Cleland Wildlife Park.

Free guides to Adelaide's public bus lines are available from the Adelaide Metro Info Centre, open weekdays 8–6, Saturday 9–5, and Sunday 11–4.

🚩 **Adelaide Metro Info Centre** ✉ Currie and King William Sts., City Center ☎ 08/8210–1000 ⊕ www.adelaidemetro.com.au.

CAR RENTAL

Most of the major car-rental agencies have offices both at the airport and in downtown Adelaide.

🚗 **Avis** ✉ 136 North Terr., City Center ☎ 08/8410-5727 or 13-6333. **Budget** ✉ 274 N. Terr., City Center ☎ 08/8223-1400 or 13-2727. **Thrifty** ✉ 296 Hindley St., City Center ☎ 08/8211-8788 or 1300/367227.

CAR TRAVEL

A car gives you the freedom to discover the country lanes and villages in the hills region outside the city, and Adelaide also has excellent road connections with other states. Highway 1 links the city with Melbourne, 728 km (451 mi) southeast, and with Perth, 2,724 km (1,689 mi) to the west, via the vast and bleak Nullarbor Plain. The Stuart Highway provides access to the Red Centre. Alice Springs is 1,542 km (956 mi) north of Adelaide. The Royal Automobile Association (RAA) offers emergency and roadside assistance to members, and allows you to join on the spot if you're in a jam.

🚗 **Royal Automobile Association** ✉ 101 Richmond Rd., Mile End ☎ 08/8202-4600 🌐 www.raa.com.au.

EMERGENCIES

In an emergency, dial **000** to reach an ambulance, the police, or the fire department.

🚗 **Royal Adelaide Hospital** ✉ N. Terrace and Frome Rd., City Center ☎ 08/8222-4000.

MAIL, SHIPPING & THE INTERNET

Full postal services are available at Australia Post outlets throughout the city. Adelaide's General Post Office is open weekdays 8:30–5:30; the City POSTshop is open weekdays 8:30–5:30 and Sat. 9–12:30.

Free Internet access is available at Adelaide's public libraries. However, you must book each half-hour session in advance, and in person. There are several Internet cafés in Hindley and Rundle streets, including Enigma Bar (free connection), and Kiss Café & Business Centre.

🚗 **Internet Cafés Enigma Bar** ✉ 173 Hindley St., City Center ☎ 08/8212-2313. **Kiss Café & Business Centre** ✉ 165 Hindley St., City Center ☎ 08/8211-6663.

🚗 **Mail Services City POSTshop** ✉ Shop 18, City Centre Arcade, Rundle Mall, City Center ☎ 13-1318. **General Post Office** ✉ 141 King William St., City Center ☎ 13-1318.

MONEY MATTERS

Most banks exchange traveler's checks and foreign currencies, as do large city hotels. Most ATMs accept Cirrus, Maestro, and Plus cards, but check with your bank to ensure that you can access your funds overseas, and that you have a four-digit PIN. Banks and ATMs are common in all areas where you are likely to shop, including the city center, North Adelaide, and Glenelg.

🚗 **Banks ANZ** ✉ 148 Rundle Mall, City Center ☎ 13-1314. **Commonwealth Bank** ✉ 96 King William St., City Center ☎ 08/8206-4467. **Westpac** ✉ 2-8 King William St., City Center ☎ 13-2032.

TAXIS

Taxis can be hailed on the street, booked by phone, or collected from a taxi stand, and most accept credit cards. Outside the CBD it's best to phone for a taxi. Expect a wait if you're heading into town on Friday and Saturday night.

🚖 **Suburban Taxi Service** ☎ 13-1008. **Yellow Cabs** ☎ 13-2227.

TOURS

Mary Anne Kennedy, the owner of A Taste of South Australia, is one of the most knowledgeable regional food and wine guides. Her private tours (A$300 and up) are a taste treat. Adelaide's Top Food and Wine Tours showcases Adelaide's food and wine lifestyle—as in the behind-the-scenes guided tour of the central market (A$32), which lets you meet stall holders, share their knowledge, and taste the wares. Tours are scheduled Tuesday and Thursday–Saturday at 9:30 AM.

The Adelaide Explorer (a bus tricked up to look like a tram) makes city highlights tours, which can be combined with a trip to Glenelg. Passengers may leave the vehicle at any of the attractions along the way and join a following tour. Trams depart every 90 minutes and cost A$25 for just the city, A$30 for the city and Glenelg.

Adelaide Sightseeing operates a morning city sights tour for A$45. The company also runs a daily afternoon bus tour of the Adelaide Hills and Hahndorf village for A$49. For A$47, Gray Line Adelaide provides morning city tours that take in all the highlights. They depart from 101 Franklin Street at 9:30 AM.

Tourabout Adelaide has private tours with tailored itineraries. Prices run from around A$30 for an Adelaide walking tour to A$400 for daylong excursions to the Barossa Valley. Sandy Pugsley, the owner and chief tour guide, can arrange almost anything.

Rundle Mall Information Centre hosts 45-minute free guided walks. The First Steps Tour points out the main attractions, facilities, and transportation in central Adelaide. Tours depart weekdays at 9:30 AM from outside the booth. Bookings are not required.

🚖 **Food & Wine Tours** **Adelaide's Top Food and Wine Tours** ☎ 0412/726099 ⊕ www.topfoodandwinetours.com.au. **A Taste of South Australia** ᗡ Box 250, Adelaide 5001 ☎ 0419/861588 ⊕ www.tastesa.com.au.

🚖 **Van Tours** **Adelaide Explorer** ✉ 101 Franklin St., City Center ☎ 08/8231-7172 ⊕ www.adelaideexplorer.com.au. **Adelaide Sightseeing** ✉ 101 Franklin St., City Center ☎ 08/8231-4144 ⊕ www.adelaidesightseeing.com.au. **Gray Line Adelaide** ✉ 101 Franklin St., City Center ☎ 1300/858687 ⊕ www.grayline.com. **Tourabout Adelaide** ᗡ Box 1033, Kent Town 5071 ☎ 08/8333-1111 ⊕ www.touraboutadelaide.com.au.

🚖 **Walking Tour** **Rundle Mall Information Centre** ✉ Rundle Mall and King William St., City Center ☎ 08/8203-7611.

TRAIN TRAVEL

Four suburban train lines serve north- and south-coast suburbs, the northeast ranges, and the Adelaide Hills. Trains depart from Adelaide station. The station for interstate and country trains is the Keswick Rail Terminal, west of the city center. The terminal has a small café, and taxis are available from the stand outside. The *Overland* connects Adelaide and Melbourne (11 hours) Thursday through Sunday. The *Ghan* makes the 20-hour journey to Alice Springs on Sunday and Friday, continuing north to Darwin on Monday. The *Indian Pacific* links Adelaide with Perth (37½ hours) and Sydney (25 hours) twice a week.

🏠 **Keswick Rail Terminal** ✉ Keswick, 2 km (1 mi) west of city center ☎ 13–2147 ⊕ www.gsr.com.au.

TRAM TRAVEL

The city's only surviving tram route runs between Victoria Square and beachside Glenelg. Ticketing is identical to that on city buses.

TRAVEL AGENTS

Budget travel agents Flight Centre and STA Travel have offices throughout Adelaide and its suburbs. International firms Harvey World Travel and Bunnick Travel/American Express are reliable travel agents where you can arrange tour packages and book flights.

🏠 **Bunnik Travel/American Express** ✉ 122 Pirie St., City Center ☎ 08/8359–2295. **Flight Centre** ✉ 136 N. Terr., City Center ☎ 08/8231–0044. **Harvey World Travel** ✉ 200 the Parade, Norwood ☎ 08/8332–9933. **STA Travel** ✉ 235 Rundle St., City Center ☎ 08/8223–2426.

VISITOR INFORMATION

The South Australian Visitor and Travel Centre, open weekdays 8:30–5 and weekends 9–2, has specialist publications and tourism brochures on South Australia and excellent hiking and cycling maps.

Sightseeing South Australia is a comprehensive monthly newspaper with feature articles on current events, destinations, and experiences throughout the whole state. It's free at most tourist outlets, hotels, and transportation centers.

The Discover Adelaide Card gives you up to 50% off admission at 14 top Adelaide attractions. Cards are available from local travel agencies and through Best Available Seating Service (BASS).

The Adelaide Hills Visitor Information Centre is open weekdays 9–5 and weekends 10–4.

🏠 **Adelaide Hills Visitor Information Centre** ✉ 41 Main St., Hahndorf ☎ 08/8388–1185 ⊕ www.visitadelaidehills.com.au. **BASS** 🗐 Box 1269, Adelaide 5001 ☎ 13–1246 ⊕ www.bass.net.au. **South Australian Visitor and Travel Centre** ✉ 18 King William St., City Center ☎ 1300/655276 ⊕ www.southaustralia.com.

THE BAROSSA REGION

Some of Australia's most famous vineyards are in the Barossa Region, an hour's drive northeast of Adelaide. More than 70 wineries across the two wide, shallow valleys that make up the region produce numerous wines, including aromatic Rhine Riesling, Seppelt's unique, century-old Para Port—which brings more than A$1,000 a bottle—and Penfolds Grange, Australia's most celebrated wine.

Cultural roots set the Barossa apart. The area was settled by Silesian immigrants who left the German-Polish border region in the 1840s to escape religious persecution. These farmers brought traditions that you can't miss in the solid bluestone architecture, the tall slender spires of the Lutheran churches, and the *kuchen,* a cake as popular as the Devonshire tea introduced by British settlers. Together, these elements give the Barossa a charm that no other Australian wine-growing area can match.

Most wineries in the Barossa operate sale rooms, called cellar doors, which usually have 6 to 12 varieties of wine available for tasting. Generally you begin with a light, fragrant white, such as Riesling, move on through a soft, fruity white like a semillon, and then repeat the process with reds such as merlot, grenache, and the full-bodied shiraz. Sweet and fortified wines should be left until last. You are not expected to sample the entire selection; to do so would overpower your taste buds. It's far better to give the tasting-room staff some idea of your personal preferences and let them suggest wine for you to sample.

Numbers in the margin correspond to points of interest on the Barossa Region map.

Lyndoch

⓭ *58 km (36 mi) northeast of Adelaide.*

This pleasant little town surrounded by vineyards was established in 1840 and is the oldest settlement site of the Barossa. It owes the spelling of its name to a draftsman's error—it was meant to be named after the British soldier Lord Lynedoch. **Lyndoch Lavender Farm,** a family-friendly tribute to the purple flower that adorns the hills, grows more than 60 varieties on 6 lush acres high above Lyndoch. Light café meals are available, and the farm shop sells essential oils, creams, and other lavender products. ⊠ *Hoffnungsthal and Tweedies Gully Rds.* ☎☎ *08/8524–4538* 🖃 *A$2* ⊙ *Sept.–Feb., daily 10–4:30; Mar.–Aug., weekends 10–4:30.*

⓬ **Burge Family Wine Makers.** You can drink in a leafy vineyard while tasting among the wine barrels in this understated cellar door. Winemaker Rick Burge's best include the powerful yet elegant Draycott Shiraz and Olive Hill shiraz-grenache-mourvedre blend. There is also A Nice Red—read the label! ⊠ *Barossa Valley Way near Hermann Thumm Dr.* ☎ *08/8524–4644* ⊕ *www.burgefamily.com.au* 🖃 *Free* ⊙ *Thurs.–Mon. 10–5.*

Where to Stay

$$$ 🏨 **Abbotsford Country House.** Tranquillity reigns at this property on 50
Fodor'sChoice acres of rolling beef farm with Barossa views. Silence and blissfully com-
★ fortable beds with super-high thread count linens make drifting off easy. Collected antiques decorate the eight rooms, one of which has a jetted tub, another a deep, claw-foot enamel bathtub, and the rest double showers. All have complementary port and chocolate. Relax in your room (TVs are available on request) or venture out to sit by the fireplace in the main house. The abundant, home-cooked breakfast, which uses farm-grown and local ingredients, will fuel you up for a day of exploring the valley. ⊠ *Yaldara Dr. and Fuss Rd., Lyndoch 5351* ☎ *08/*

AUSTRALIAN WINE

PREPARE TO BE *thoroughly taken aback, or at least a touch startled, at Australia's refreshing wine-and-food pairings. From the wineries of northeast Victoria, an area known for its full-bodied reds, come some truly remarkable fortified Tokays and muscats, all with a delicious, wild, untamed quality that is so rich and sticky you don't know whether to drink them or spread them. Among the more notable varieties are the All Saints Classic Release Tokay, Campbell's Liquid Gold Tokay, and Bailey's Old Muscat. Believe it or not, these are perfect with Australia's distinctive farmhouse cheeses, such as Milawa Gold (northeast Victoria), Yarra Valley Persian Feta, and Meredith Blue (from Victoria's Western District).*

Practically unknown beyond these shores is what was once affectionately but euphemistically known as sparkling burgundy, an effervescent red made mainly from shiraz grapes using the traditional méthode champenoise. A dense yet lively wine with fresh, fruity tones, it's suited to game and turkey and is now an integral part of a festive Australian Christmas dinner. Look for labels such as Seppelts Harpers Range, Yalumba, and Peter Lehmann's Black Queen.

Then there are the classic Rieslings of South Australia's Barossa Region and Clare Valley, first introduced by German and Silesian settlers. Today wines such as Heggies Riesling, Petaluma Riesling, and Wirra Wirra Hand Picked Riesling are as much at home with Middle Eastern merguez sausage and couscous as they are with knockwurst and sauerkraut.

Also very Australian in style are the big, oaky semillons of the Hunter Valley (try Tyrrell's Vat 1 Semillon and Lindeman's Hunter River Semillon) and the powerful steak-and-braised-meat–loving cabernets

from the rich, red "terra rossa" soil of the Coonawarra district in South Australia. These wines, including Petaluma Coonawarra, Lindeman's Pyrus, and Hollick Coonawarra, have a habit of knocking first-timers' socks off.

As a breed, the Australian shiraz style has delicious pepper-berry characteristics and food-friendly companionability. A clutch of worthy labels includes Penfolds's Bins 128 and 389, Elderton Shiraz from the Barossa Region, Brokenwood Graveyard Vineyard from the Hunter Valley, and Seppelts Great Western Shiraz from the Grampians in Victoria.

Shiraz is very much at home with modern Australian cooking, working beautifully with Moroccan-inspired lamb, Mediterranean roasted goat, pasta, and yes, even kangaroo with beetroot. Also worth a mention are the elegant, berry-laden pinot noirs of Tasmania and Victoria's Mornington Peninsula (perfect with Peking duck); the fresh, bright-tasting unwooded chardonnays of South Australia (fabulous with fish); and the fragrant sauvignon blancs of Margaret River (excellent with Sydney Rock oysters).

So there you have it. Australian wines have been stopping people in their tracks ever since the first grapes were grown in the first governor's garden back in 1788. If you are about to embark on your own personal discovery of Australian wine and food pairing, get ready to be amazed, astonished, and shocked—into having another glass.

— Terry Durack

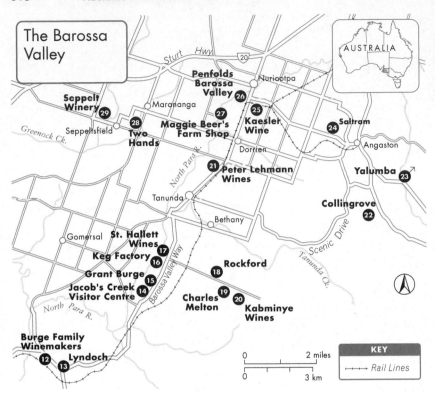

8254–4662 🖨 *08/8524–4186* ⊕ *www.abbotsfordhouse.com* ➥ *8 rooms* ♿ *Dining room, refrigerators, 1 in-room hot tub, boccie, laundry service, Internet room, free parking; no room phones, no room TVs, no kids, no smoking* 🚭 *AE, DC, MC, V* 🍴 *BP.*

$$$ 🏨 **Novotel Barossa Valley Resort.** Active vacationers need never leave this complex of studios and two-bedroom apartments nestled in a natural amphitheater overlooking Jacobs Creek and the North Para River. Suede room curtains draw back to reveal rustic vineyard and river views and a private balcony from which to enjoy the vista. All rooms have CD players, hair dryers, irons and ironing boards, and sleek kitchenettes with blond-wood countertops. Kids are well attended at the Club Dolfi daycare center, and Tanunda Golf Course is next door. ⊠ *Golf Links Rd. off Barossa Valley Way, Rowland Flat 5352, 8 km (5 mi) from Lyndoch* 🖼 *1300/657697* 🖨 *08/8524–0100* ⊕ *www.novotelbarossa.com* ➥ *116 studio rooms, 24 2-bedroom apartments* ♿ *Restaurant, café, room service, IDD phones, some in-room hot tubs, kitchenettes, minibars, microwaves, refrigerators, cable TV with movies, in-room data ports, golf privileges, tennis court, pool, health club, massage, sauna, spa, bicycles, archery, badminton, basketball, billiards, boccie, croquet, hiking, Ping-Pong, volleyball, 2 bars, dry cleaning, laundry service, Internet room,* *business services, convention center, travel services, free parking, no-smoking rooms, no-smoking floors* ☰ *AE, DC, MC, V.*

$$–$$$ ⊞ **Belle Cottages.** Rose-filled gardens surround these classic Australian accommodations. Wood-burning fireplaces in the lounges invite you to relax with a bottle of red after a day in the Barossa region, and comfy brass beds tempt you to sleep late. In Christabelle Cottage, an 1849 Heritage-listed former chapel, a spiral staircase winds up to a mezzanine bedroom. The other cottages have two or three bedrooms, country kitchens, and jetted tubs. ⌂ *Box 481, 5351* ☎ *08/8524–4825* 🖷 *08/8524–4046* ⊕ *www.bellescapes.com* ⇆ *4 cottages* ⚷ *Some BBQs, some in-room hot tubs, kitchens, microwaves, refrigerators, in-room VCRs, some laundry facilities, travel services, free parking, some pets allowed; no smoking* ☰ *AE, MC, V* ⦿⦿ *BP.*

Tanunda

13 km (8 mi) northeast of Lyndoch, 70 km (43 mi) northeast of Adelaide.

The cultural heart of the Barossa, Tanunda is its most German settlement. The four Lutheran churches in the town testify to its heritage, and dozens of shops selling German pastries, breads, and wursts (sausages)—not to mention wine—line the main street. Many of the valley's best wineries are close by.

⑲ **Charles Melton Wines.** Tasting is relaxing and casual at this brick-floor, timber-wall cellar door, which is warmed by a log fire in winter. After making sure the resident cats have vacated it first, settle into a director's chair at the long wooden table and let staff pour. Nine Popes, a huge, decadent red blend, is the flagship wine, and the rich, ruby red Rose of Virginia is arguably Australia's best rosé. ✉ *Krondorf Rd. near Nitschke Rd.* ☎ *08/8563–3606* ⊕ *www.charlesmeltonwines.com.au/* ⊠ *Free* ☉ *Daily 11–5.*

⑮ **Grant Burge** is one of the most successful of the Barossa's young, independent wine labels. Wines include impressive chardonnays, crisp Rieslings, and powerful reds such as Meshach shiraz. Don't miss the Holy Trinity—a highly acclaimed Rhône blend of grenache, shiraz, and mourvedre. ✉ *Barossa Valley Way near Koch Rd., 5 km (3 mi) south of Tanunda* ☎ *08/8563–3700* ⊕ *www.grantburgewines.com.au* ⊠ *Free* ☉ *Daily 10–5.*

⑭ An impressive block of glass, steel and recycled timber, **Jacob's Creek Visitor Centre** overlooks the creek whose name is familiar to wine drinkers around the world. Inside the building, plasma screens and pictorial displays tell the history of viticulture, wine making, the Barossa Valley, and the Jacob's Creek label. Cabernet sauvignon, merlot, red blends, chardonnay, and the new shiraz-rosé, served chilled, can be tasted at a 60-foot-long counter. There is a lunch-only restaurant with broad glass doors opening onto a grassy lawn edged with towering eucalyptus trees. ✉ *Barossa Valley Way near Jacob's Creek* ☎ *08/8521–3000* ⊕ *www.jacobscreek.com* ⊠ *Free* ☉ *Daily 10–5.*

★ ⑳ Built from local mud brick and corrugated iron, with a winglike roof, the light-filled cellar door at **Kabminye Wines** was a controversial addition to the valley—but there's no argument about the wines and the food. Each wine has its own unique and surprising taste, particularly the excellent Ilona rosé and the full-frontal HWG cabernet sauvignon. The café cooks up traditional Silesian fare such as free-range chicken with bacon and fresh herbs, and *Blitztorte,* a sinfully rich butter cake topped with meringue, cinnamon, and toasted almonds. Changing art exhibitions are displayed in the upstairs gallery. ✉ *Krondorf Rd. near Nitschke Rd.* ☎ *08/8563–0899* ⊕ *www.kabminye.com* ⌨ *Free* ⊙ *Daily 11–5.*

🐾 ⑯ **Keg Factory** uses traditional methods to repair oak casks for wineries. You can watch coopers (barrel makers) working the American and French oak staves inside the iron hoops. Small, handmade port kegs make wonderful souvenirs of the Barossa. ✉ *St. Halletts Rd.* ☎ *08/8563–3012* ⌨ *Free* ⊙ *Daily 8–5.*

㉑ **Peter Lehmann Wines** is owned by a larger-than-life Barossa character whose wine consistently wins international awards and medals. Stonework and a wood-burning fireplace make the tasting room one of the most pleasant in the valley. This is the only place to find Black Queen Sparkling Shiraz; also look for semillon, Riesling, and the premium Ambassador range. Wooden tables on a treed lawn encourage picnicking on Barossa lunch platters, served daily. ✉ *Para Rd. off Stelzer Rd.* ☎ *08/8563–2500* ⊕ *www.peterlehmannwines.com.au* ⌨ *Free* ⊙ *Weekdays 9:30–5, weekends 10:30–4:30.*

★ ⑱ **Rockford,** nestled in a cobbled stable yard, is a small winery with a tasting room in an old stone barn. The specialties are heavy, rich wines made from some of the region's oldest vines. Several notable labels have appeared under the Rockford name—be sure to try the cabernet sauvignon and the Basket Press Shiraz, outstanding examples of these most traditional of Australian varieties. ✉ *Krondorf Rd. near Nitschke Rd.* ☎ *08/8563–2720* ⊕ *www.rockfordwines.com.au* ⌨ *Free* ⊙ *Mon.–Sat. 11–5.*

★ ⑰ **St. Hallett Wines,** one of the region's best, welcomes you with the chatter of "Stewy" the parrot as you're ushered from rose-studded gardens into the tasting room. The signature Old Block Shiraz, a classic and fantastic Australian red, is harvested from century-old vines. Poacher's Blend Semillon and cabernet sauvignon are also good sampling choices. ✉ *St. Halletts Rd.* ☎ *08/8563–7000* ⊕ *www.sthallett.com.au* ⌨ *Free* ⊙ *Daily 10–5.*

Where to Stay & Eat

$–$$ ✕ **1918 Bistro & Grill.** This rustic restaurant in a restored villa makes exemplary use of the Barossa's distinctive regional produce. Local olive oil, almonds, and sausages enhance the dishes, which are served beside a two-sided fireplace in winter and alfresco in the garden in summer. The cellar collection lists wines that are about to become extinct and those which are new additions to the menu. ✉ *94 Murray St.* ☎ *08/ 8563–0405* ▭ *AE, DC, MC, V.*

¢–$ ✕ **Die Barossa Wurst Haus & Bakery.** For a hearty German lunch at a reasonable price, no place beats this small, friendly café and shop. The wurst is fresh from the butcher down the street, the sauerkraut is direct from Germany, and the potato salad is made on-site from a secret recipe. ⊠ *86A Murray St.* ☎ *08/8563–3598* ▭ *No credit cards* ☾ *No dinner.*

★ $$–$$$ 🏨 **Lawley Farm.** Amid 20 acres of grapes, in a courtyard shaded by gnarled peppercorn trees, these delightful stone cottage-style suites were assembled from the remains of barns dating from the Barossa's pioneering days. A wood-burning stove warms the Krondorf Suite, in the original 1852 cottage with low-beam doors, while in the Para Suite—former stables with ceiling beams from Adelaide shearing sheds—you can soak in a spa tub and then sleep late in a brass bed. Breakfast feasts of local German bacon and salmon, free-range farm eggs, and fresh-ground coffee are brought on a tray to your cottage each morning. The farm is within easy walking distance of six wineries. ⌂ *Box 103, Krondorf and Grocke Rds., 5352* ☎ *08/8563–2141* ⊕ *www.lawleyfarm.com.au* ⇨ *4 suites* ⚙ *Room service, refrigerators, in-room data ports, boccie, horseshoes, dry cleaning, laundry service, Internet room, free parking; no room phones, no smoking* ▭ *AE, DC, MC, V* ⍟ *BP.*

$–$$ 🏨 **Blickinstal Vineyard Retreat.** Its name means "view into the valley," which understates the breathtaking panoramas from this delightful B&B on 20 acres: it might better be known as "Blissinstal." Amid vineyards in foothills five minutes from the Barossa's heart, the retreat is a tranquil base for exploring. Gardens surround the self-contained lodge apartments and studios, and breakfast is served under the almond tree, weather permitting. You can also indulge in afternoon tea. ⌂ *Box 17, Rifle Range Rd., 5352* ☎ *08/8563–2716* ⊕ *www.users.bigpond.com/blickinstal* ⇨ *4 studios, 2 apartments* ⚙ *BBQ, kitchenettes, microwaves, refrigerators, in-room DVD, boccie, laundry facilities, Internet room, free parking; no room phones, no smoking* ▭ *AE, MC, V* ⍟ *BP.*

¢–$ 🏨 **Valley Hotel.** Peace, quiet, and light-filled space await you in the stone motel block tucked behind a parking lot, across which rises the beautiful spire of Tabor Lutheran Church. All rooms have hair dryers, settees, and tea- and coffee-making facilities; one has a hot tub. ⊠ *73 Murray St., 5352* ☎ *08/8563–2039* ⇨ *5 rooms* ⚙ *Restaurant, 1 in-room hot tub, refrigerators, pub, free parking; no room phones, no smoking* ▭ *AE, DC, MC, V.*

Angaston

16 km (10) northeast of Tanunda via Menglers Hill Rd. Scenic Drive, 86 km (53 mi) northeast of Adelaide.

Named after George Fife Angas, the Englishman who founded the town and sponsored many of the German and British immigrants who came here, Angaston is full of jacaranda and Moreton Bay fig trees. Along the main street are stately stone buildings and tiny shops. Schulz Butchers has been making and selling wurst (German sausage) for 67 years; 17 varieties hang above the counter.

㉒ **Collingrove** was until 1975 the ancestral home of the Angas family, the descendants of George Fife Angas, one of the founders of modern South

Australia. The family carved a pastoral empire from the colony and at the height of its fortunes controlled 14.5 million acres from this house. Today the property is administered by the National Trust, and you can inspect the Angas family portraits and memorabilia, including Dresden china, a hand-painted Louis XV cabinet, and Chippendale chairs. You can also stay overnight at Collingrove. ⊠ *Eden Valley Rd. near Collingrove Rd.* ☎ *08/8564–2061* ⊕ *www.collingrovehomestead.com.au* ⊠ *A$5* ⊙ *Weekdays 1–4:30, weekends 11–4:30.*

❷❹ Low-beamed ceilings and ivy-covered trellises give **Saltram** an urbanized sort of rustic charm. The robust wine list includes the Pepperjack Barossa Grenache Rosé, a delightful vintage available only in summer. Billed as "the red to drink when you're not in the mood for a red," it's a delicious accompaniment to the Italian-influenced menu at the adjacent—and excellent—Salters restaurant. ⊠ *Nuriootpa Rd., 1 km (½ mi) west of Angaston* ☎ *08/8561–0200* ⊕ *www.saltramwines.com.au* ⊠ *Free* ⊙ *Weekdays 9–5, weekends 10–5.*

❷❸ **Yalumba,** Australia's oldest family-owned winery, sits within a hugely impressive compound resembling an Italian monastery. The cellar door is decorated with mission-style furniture, antique wine-making materials, and mementos of the Hill Smith family, five generations of whom have been involved in wine making since English brewer Samuel Hill Smith first planted vines in the Barossa in 1849. The Octavius shirazes are superb, and the "Y Series" Viognier 2003 is thoroughly enjoyable. ⊠ *Eden Valley Rd. just south of Valley Rd.* ☎ *08/8561–3200* ⊕ *www.yalumba.com* ⊠ *Free* ⊙ *Daily 10–5.*

Where to Eat

★ $$ ✕ **Barr-Vinum.** Prepare for a long, lazy meal that leaves your table festooned with empty wine bottles; this restaurant encourages loitering. You can plant yourself at a sunny garden table, on the shady wooden veranda overlooking the rose beds, or around a white-papered table in the 19th-century home of Angaston's first magistrate and doctor. The menu suggests food-wine partnerships such as crisp ocean trout with a Valencia-orange-and-olive dressing and Barossa Riesling. The bruschetta trio is a simple delight of tomato, mushrooms, feta, and caramelized onion on wood-oven-baked bread. ⊠ *10 Washington St.* ☎ *08/8564–3688* ⊟ *AE, DC, MC, V* ⊙ *Closed Mon. No lunch Sat., no dinner Sun.*

★ $$ ✕ **Vintners Bar & Grill.** The Barossa region is at its best in this sophisticated spot, where wide windows look out on rows of vineyards, and artwork adorns the walls. The menu blends Australian, Mediterranean, and Asian flavors in such dishes as blue swimmer crab and seaweed salad, and roasted local squab with cumin and sweet-potato gâteau. Scarlet suede chairs and an upbeat jazz sound track make it easy to relax; top winemakers often come here to sample from the cellar's 280 wines. ⊠ *Nuriootpa Rd. near Stockwell Rd.* ☎ *08/8564–2488* ⊟ *AE, DC, MC, V* ⊙ *No dinner Sun.*

Nuriootpa

8 km (5 mi) northwest of Angaston, 74 km (46 mi) northeast of Adelaide.

Long before it was the Barossa's commercial center, Nuriootpa was used as a bartering place by local Aboriginal tribes, hence its name: Nuriootpa means "meeting place."

㉕ Kaesler Wine is a charming boutique winery, where shiraz and sparkling shiraz are made from century-old vines and sold at a cellar door that was once a farm stable. This remarkable little place also has a restaurant serving lunch and dinner, and cottage accommodations for A$160–A$180 per night. ✉ *Barossa Valley Way near Kaiser Stuhl Ave.* ☎ *08/8562–4488, restaurant and cottages 08/8562–2711* ⊕ *www.kaesler.com.au* ▦ *Free* ☉ *Mon.–Sat. 10–5, Sun. 11:30–4.*

Renowned cook, restaurateur, and food writer Maggie Beer is a Barossa personality and an icon of Australian cuisine. Burned-fig jam, quince paste, *verjus* (a golden liquid made from unfermented grape juice and used for flavoring), and her signature Pheasant Farm Pâté are some of ★ ㉗ the delights you can taste and buy at **Maggie Beer's Farm Shop.** Light lunches are served 12:30–3, while fresh-baked scones with cream and jam are delicious anytime. Wine and coffee are also available. The shop and café area overlook a tree-fringed pond full of fish and turtles. ✉ *End of Pheasant Farm Rd. off Samuel Rd.* ☎ *08/8562–4477* ⊕ *www.maggiebeer.com.au* ▦ *Free* ☉ *Daily 10:30–5.*

off the
beaten
path

BANROCK STATION WINE & WETLAND CENTRE – The salt-scrub-patched Murray River floodplain 150 km (94 mi) east of Nuriootpa is an unlikely setting for a winery, but it is worth making the journey to this spot at Kingston-on-Murray. Within the stilted, mud-brick building perched above the vineyard and river lagoons here you can select a wine to accompany a grazing platter or lunch on the outdoor deck—try the River Murray silver perch and leek in filo pastry with curried apple pepperleaf dressing, or *quandong* (a native fruit) pie with lemon-myrtle ice cream. Afterward, you can take the 4½-km (3-mi) Boardwalk Trail (advance bookings essential), which highlights Banrock's ongoing work to restore the surrounding wetlands. There are several bird blinds around the lagoon. The winery donates some of the proceeds from wine sales to environmental projects around Australia. ✉ *Holmes Rd. just off Sturt Hwy., Kingston-on-Murray* ☎ *08/8583–0299 information and Boardwalk Trail bookings* ⊕ *www.banrockstation.com.au* ▦ *Wine and Wetland Centre free,; Boardwalk Trail A$5* ☉ *Daily 10–5.*

㉖ PENFOLDS BAROSSA VALLEY – A very big brother to the 19th-century Magill Estate in Adelaide, this massive wine-making outfit in the center of Nuriootpa lets you taste shiraz, cabernet merlot, chardonnay, and Riesling blends—but not the celebrated Grange—at the cellar door. (✉ Barossa Valley Hwy. and Railway Terr. Nuriootpa ☎ *08/8568–9408* ⊕ *www.penfolds.com.au* ▦ *Free* ☉ *Weekdays 10–5, weekends 11–5)*

Marananga

6 km (4 mi) west of Nuriootpa, 68 km (42 mi) northeast of Adelaide.

The tiny hamlet of Marananga inhabits one of the prettiest corners of the Barossa. This area's original name was Gnadenfrei, which means "freed by the grace of God"—a reference to the religious persecution the German settlers suffered under the Prussian kings before they emigrated to Australia. Marananga, the Aboriginal name, was adopted in 1918, when a wave of anti-German sentiment spurred many name changes in the closing days of World War I.

Marananga marks the beginning of a 3-km (2-mi) avenue of date palms planted during the 1930s depression as a work-creation scheme devised by the Seppelts, a wine-making family. Look for the Doric temple on the hillside to the right—it's the Seppelt family mausoleum.

★ ㉙ Joseph Seppelt was a Silesian farmer who purchased land in the Barossa after arriving in Australia in 1849. Under the control of his son, Benno, the wine-making business flourished, and today **Seppelt Winery** and its splendid grounds are a tribute to the family's industry and enthusiasm. Fortified wine is a Seppelt specialty; this is the only winery in the world that has vintage ports for every year as far back as 1878. Most notable is the 100-year-old Para Vintage Tawny. The grenache, chardonnay, cabernet, and sparkling shiraz are also worth tasting. Tours of the distillery and its wine-making artifacts are run daily. ⊠ *Seppeltsfield Rd., 3 km (2 mi) west of Marananga, Seppeltsfield* 🕾 *08/8568–6217* ⊕ *www. seppelt.com* ✉ *Free, tour A$7* ☉ *Weekdays 10–5, weekends 11–5; tours weekdays at 11, 1, 2, and 3; weekends at 11:30, 1:30, and 2:30.*

★ ㉘ **Two Hands.** The inside of this 19th-century sandstone cottage is every bit as suprising as the wines produced here. A modern stainless-steel counter, polished wood, and glass surround you once you enter, and the attantive staff leads you through the tasting of several "out of the box" red and white varietals and blends. The main event is shiraz sourced from six premium Australian wine regions. Compare and contrast shiraz from Victoria and Padthaway (South Australia); and try the Barossa-grown Bad Impersonator. Groups of up to eight can arrange private tastings or dinners in the adjoining bake house, which has a glass floor over the original cellar. ⊠ *Neldner Rd. just off Seppeltsfield Rd.* 🕾 *08/ 8562–4566* ⊕ *www.twohandswines.com* ✉ *Free* ☉ *Weekdays 11–5, weekends 10–5.*

Where to Stay & Eat

$$ ✕ **Barossa Picnic Baskets.** Stuffed with meat, pâté, cheese, salad, and fruit, these baskets make for a perfect outdoor lunch. Vegetarian baskets are also available. Each comes with all crockery and cutlery and directions to the best picnic spots. Red wine only can be purchased separately at the cellar door, open 11–5 Tuesday to Sunday. Phone 24 hours ahead to order. ⊠ *Gnadenfrei Estate Winery, Seppeltsfield and Radford Rds.* 🕾 *08/8562–2522* ▭ *AE, MC, V.*

★ $$$$ ▦ **Lodge Country House.** Rambling and aristocratic, this bluestone homestead 3 km (2 mi) south of Marananga was built in 1903 for one of the

13 children of Joseph Seppelt, founder of the showpiece winery across the road. Barossa vintages fill the wine cellar, polished timber gleams in the formal dining room, and big, comfortable sofas inspire relaxing in the sitting room, perhaps with a book from the library. The four large guest rooms are furnished in period style; a bay window seat in each looks out at the gorgeous, leafy garden. Set menu dinners, available by reservation, make good use of local produce. There's a minimum two-night stay on weekends. ⊠ *Seppeltsfield Rd., 3 km (2 mi) west of Marananga, Seppeltsfield 5355* ☎ *08/8562–8277* 🖷 *08/8562–8344* ⊕ *www.thelodgecountryhouse.com.au* ➱ *4 rooms* ⚭ *Dining room, tennis court, pool, boccie, library, laundry service, free parking; no room phones, no room TVs, no kids under 16, no smoking* ⊟ *AE, MC, V* ⚭ *BP.*

$$$–$$$$ 🏨 **Peppers Hermitage.** Scarlet roses line the entry to this deluxe country house on a quiet back road with glorious valley views. Vines fringe the Mediterranean-style courtyard off which open 10 stylish rooms. Each is named after a different grape, which influences the colors of the elegant furnishings. Grape names continue in the five luxurious Estate Suites; however, the duvets and pillows and the marble bathrooms with double showers are charcoal, chocolate, and cappuccino. Courtyard rooms have large sitting areas with woodstoves adjoining open bedrooms; all accommodations have spa tubs and complimentary port. The restaurant, which serves interesting regional cuisine, spills onto a terrace. ⊠ *Seppeltsfield and Stonewell Rds., 5352* ☎ *08/8562–2722* 🖷 *08/8562–3133* ⊕ *www.peppers.com.au* ➱ *15 suites, 1 apartment* ⚭ *Restaurant, room service, IDD phones, in-room safes, some microwaves, refrigerators, room TVs with movies, in-room DVD, in-room data ports, pool, massages, sauna, badminton, boccie, lounge, laundry service, Internet room, free parking; no smoking* ⊟ *AE, DC, MC, V* ⚭ *BP.*

Barossa Region A to Z

CAR TRAVEL

The most direct route from Adelaide to the Barossa Region is via the town of Gawler. From Adelaide, drive north on King William Street. About 1 km (½ mi) past the Torrens River Bridge, take the right fork onto Main North Road. After 6 km (4 mi) this road forks to the right—follow signs to the Sturt Highway and the town of Gawler. At Gawler, leave the highway and follow the signs to Lyndoch on the southern border of the Barossa. The 50-km (31-mi) journey should take about an hour. A more attractive, if circuitous, route travels through the Adelaide Hills' Chain of Ponds and Williamstown to Lyndoch.

Because the Barossa wineries are relatively far apart, a car is by far the best way to get around. But keep in mind that there are stiff penalties for driving under the influence of alcohol. Police in patrol cars can pull you over for a random breath test anywhere in the state, and roadside mobile breath-testing stations—locally known as "Booze Buses"—are particularly visible during special events, such as the Barossa Vintage Festival, held March–April each year.

EMERGENCIES

In an emergency, dial **000** to reach an ambulance, the police, or the fire department.

TOURS

Gray Line Adelaide operates a full-day tour of the Barossa Region (A\$96) from Adelaide, including lunch at a winery. Enjoy Adelaide's full-day (A\$70) Barossa tour, which visits five vineyards and includes lunch. Groovy Grape Getaways offers full-day (A\$65) Barossa tours with a visit to the Adelaide Hills and a barbecue lunch. Mirror Image Touring Company operates "Classic Times Amongst the Vines." This personalized full-day (A\$199) Barossa tour, hosted by knowledgeable local guides, includes winery visits and a three-course lunch. Hotel pickups can be arranged, and one- and two-night packages are available.

🚹 **Enjoy Adelaide** ⊠ 74 Charles St., Norwood, Adelaide ☎ 08/8332-1401 ⊕ www.enjoyadelaide.com.au. **Gray Line Adelaide** ⊠ 101 Franklin St., City Center, Adelaide ☎ 1300/858687. **Groovy Grape Getaways** ⊠ 39 Raglan Ave., Edwardstown ☎ 08/8371-4000 or 1800/661177 ⊕ www.groovygrape.com.au. **Mirror Image Touring Company** ⊠ 168 Paynham Rd., Evandale 5069 ☎ 08/8362-1400 ⊕ www.mirror-image.com.au.

VISITOR INFORMATION

The Barossa Visitor Information Centre has printed information and displays on the area's attractions. The center is open weekdays 9–5, weekends 10–4. Internet access is free at the Tanunda Public Library 9–5 weekdays and 9–noon Saturday.

🚹 **Barossa Visitor Information Centre** ⊠ 66–68 Murray St., Tanunda ☎ 08/8563-0600 ⊕ www.barossa-region.org. **Tanunda Public Library** ⊠ 79–81 Murray St., Tanunda ☎ 08/8563-2729.

THE CLARE VALLEY

Smaller and less well known than the Barossa, the Clare Valley nonetheless holds its own among Australia's wine-producing regions. Its robust reds and delicate whites are among the country's finest, and the Clare is generally regarded as the best area in Australia for fragrant, flavorsome Rieslings. On the fringe of the vast inland deserts, the Clare is a narrow sliver of fertile soil about 30 km (19 mi) long and 5 km (3 mi) wide, with a microclimate that makes it ideal for premium wine making.

The first vines were planted here as early as 1842, but it took a century and a half for the Clare Valley to take its deserved place on the national stage. The mix of small family wineries and large-scale producers, 150-year-old settlements and grand country houses, snug valleys and dense native forests has rare charm. And beyond the northern edge of the valley, where the Outback begins, is the fascinating copper-mining town of Burra, which is a natural adjunct to any Clare Valley sojourn.

Sevenhill

126 km (78 mi) north of Adelaide.

Sevenhill is the geographic center of the Clare Valley, and the location of the region's first winery, established by Jesuit priests in 1851 to pro-

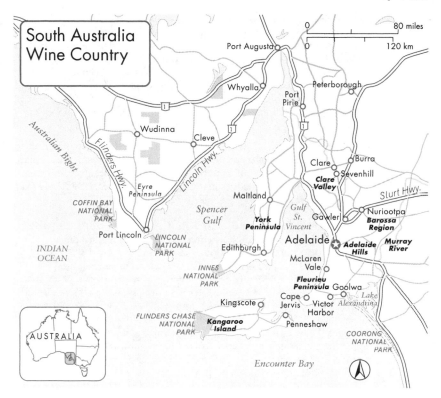

South Australia Wine Country

duce altar wine. The area had been settled three years earlier by Austrian Jesuits who named their seminary after the seven hills of Rome.

The Riesling Trail, a walking and cycling track that follows an old Clare Valley railway line, runs through Sevenhill. The 25 km (16 mi) trail passes wineries and villages in gently rolling country between Auburn and Clare, and three loop trails take you to vineyards off the main track. Bikes can be rented from some wineries and accommodations, and from **Clare Valley Cycle Hire** (☎ 08/8842–2782).

Kilikanoon Wines. A rising star of the Clare Valley and Australian wine making, Kilikanoon is already renowned for multilayered reds, such as the dense, richly colored Oracle Shiraz; Prodigal Grenache is another beauty. Taste your way from Riesling to the big ones before choosing a bottle to enjoy with an à la carte lunch in the 1880s stone-cottage restaurant. ✉ *Penna La., Penwortham, 2 km (1 mi) off Main North Rd.* ☎ *08/8843–4377* ⊕ *www.kilikanoon.com.au* ✉ *Free* ☉ *Fri. 11–4, weekends 10–5.*

Fodor'sChoice The area's first winery, **Sevenhill Cellars** was created by the Jesuits, and ★ they still run the show, with any profits going to education, mission work, and the needy within Australia. In the 1940s the winery branched out from sacramental wine into commercial production, and today 12 wine varieties, including Riesling, verdelho, grenache, and fortified wines, account for 75% of its business. You can wander on your own or book a guided tour with the charming director of wine making, Brother John May; he takes you to the cellars, the oldest vines, the cemetery, and St. Aloysius Church—and its crypt where Jesuits have been interred since 1865. You can also rent bicycles here to explore the rolling hills and vineyards. ⊠ *College Rd. just off Main North Rd.* ☎ *08/8843–4222* ⊕ *www.sevenhillcellars.com.au* ⊠ *Free, tours A$5* ⊙ *Daily 9–5, tours (bookings essential) Tues. and Thurs. at 2.*

Skillogalee Winery is known for its excellent Riesling, gewürztraminer, and shiraz, as well as its wonderful restaurant. Wine tasting takes place in a small room in the 1850s cottage (the restaurant occupies the others). Don't miss the sparkling Riesling. ⊠ *Hughes Park Rd.* ☎ *08/8843–4311* ⊕ *www.skillogalee.com* ⊠ *Free* ⊙ *Daily 10–5.*

off the beaten path

★ ☯

MARTINDALE HALL – Just outside the hamlet of Mintaro, 10 km (6 mi) southeast of Sevenhill, is where a wealthy bachelor named Edmund Bowman built this gracious manor house in 1879—as legend has it, to lure his fiancée from England to the colonies. He failed, and spent the next decade buying more properties, entertaining lavishly, and enjoying sports. In 1891 a near-bankrupt Bowman sold the grand house to the Mortlock family, who in 1965 willed it—and its contents—to the University of Adelaide. Filled with the Mortlocks' books, beds, furniture, crockery, glassware, and billiard table, Martindale Hall is a museum of late-19th- and early-20th-century rural life. The house was featured in director Peter Weir's first film, *Picnic at Hanging Rock*, and now doubles as an upscale B&B with butler and maid service. ⊠ *Mintaro Rd., 3 km (2 mi) south of Mintaro* ☎ *08/8843–9088* ⊕ *www.martindalehall.com.au* ⊠ *A$7* ⊙ *Weekdays 11–4, weekends noon–4.*

Where to Stay & Eat

★ $–$$ ✕ **Skillogalee Winery.** The dining area here spills from an 1850s cottage onto a beautiful veranda overlooking a flower-filled garden and rows of grapevines. The menu changes seasonally, but you can't go wrong with the "vine pruner's lunch," chef Diana Palmer's spin on the British ploughman's meal, a platter of rum-glazed ham, cheddar cheese, chutney, and crusty bread. Entrées might include duck-leg curry or Atlantic salmon; rich whiskey chocolate cake with raspberry coulis is the long-term favorite dessert. Gourmet picnic baskets can be ordered and group dinners are available by prior arrangement. Skillogalee also has self-contained cottage accommodation. ⊠ *Hughes Park Rd.* ☎ *08/8843–4311* 🚪 *AE, DC, MC, V.*

$$$$ 🏨 **Thorn Park Country House.** Saved from ruin by owners David Hay and
Fodor'sChoice Michael Speers, this is one of Australia's finest dining retreats. Gorgeous
★ antiques fill the mid-19th-century sandstone house, and wood-burning fireplaces warm the sitting room and small library on wintry days. Each room is named for a color: the largest and most inviting is the blue-and-white room, which is adorned with artworks of geishas; the white room, which has a second bedroom, is perfect for children. Bay windows look

out on hawthorns, elms, and heritage roses. The cooked breakfasts and dinners (reservations necessary) are scrumptious—sometimes sinfully so. David also runs cooking classes. ⊠ *1½ km (1 mi) off Main North Rd., 5453* ☎ *08/8843–4304* 🖨 *08/8843–4296* ⊕ *www.thornpark.com.au* ⇨ *6 rooms* ⚂ *Dining room, some in-room VCRs, library, laundry service, Internet room, free parking; no room phones, no TV in some rooms, no smoking* ⊟ *AE, MC, V* �🍴⎮ *BP.*

<table>
<tr><td>en route</td><td>The Clare Valley's southern gateway town (it's 16 km [10 mi] south of Sevenhill), Auburn is famous as the birthplace of Australian poet C. J. Dennis, and is now a great place to take a break on your way south. You can wander past the 19th-century stone post office and courthouse, then drop into the Rising Sun Hotel for a beer or to taste Clare Valley wines over a delicious meal. You can also stop by the small, highly regarded Grosset Wines (⊠ King St. off Main North Rd. ☎ 08/8849–2175 ⊕ www.grosset.com.au), established in 1981 in an old butter factory. Jeffrey Grosset's wines include Polish Hill and Watervale Rieslings, as well as Gaia, a blend of cabernet sauvignon, cabernet franc, and merlot grapes. The vineyard, at an 1,870-foot elevation, is the highest in the Clare Valley.</td></tr>
</table>

Clare

10 km (6 mi) north of Sevenhill, 136 km (84 mi) north of Adelaide.

The bustling town of Clare is the Clare Valley's commercial center. Unusual for ultra-English South Australia, many of its early settlers were Irish—hence the valley's name, after the Irish county Clare, and place-names such as Armagh and Donnybrook.

Ↄ The **Old Police Station Museum** has an interesting collection of memorabilia from Clare's early days, as well as Victorian furniture and clothing, horse-drawn vehicles, and agricultural machinery. The 1850 stone building was Clare's first courthouse and police station. ⊠ *Neagles Rock Rd., 1 km (½ mi) west of Main North Rd.* ☎ *08/8842–2376* ⎘ *A$2* ⊙ *Weekends 10–noon and 2–4.*

On Clare's fringe is **Leasingham Wines,** among the biggest producers in the valley. The winery began operation in 1893, which also makes it one of the oldest vineyards. The tasting room is in an old two-story stone still house. Leasingham's reputation of late has been forged by its red wines, particularly the peppery shiraz. ⊠ *7 Dominic St.* ☎ *08/8842–2785* ⊕ *www.leasingham-wines.com.au* ⎘ *Free* ⊙ *Weekdays 8:30–5, weekends 10–4.*

★ The small, no-frills tasting room means there is nothing to distract you from discovering why **Tim Adams Wines** has a big reputation. The standout in an impressive collection of reds and whites, which includes a botrytis (fungus)-tinged semillon and a celebrated Riesling, is the purply red Aberfeldy Shiraz, made from hundred-year-old vines. ⊠ *Warenda Rd. just off Main North Rd., 5 km (3 mi) south of Clare* ☎ *08/8842–2429 or 1800/356326* ⊕ *www.timadamswines.com.au* ⎘ *Free* ⊙ *Weekdays 10:30–5, weekends 11–5.*

Where to Stay

$$$$
Fodor'sChoice
★

▦ **North Bundaleer.** The spoils of wealthy pastoral life await you at this century-old sandstone homestead 61 km (38 mi) north of Clare. Beyond the jewel-box hall lined with hand-painted wallpaper is a ballroom where you can play the piano, and a peppermint-pink drawing room that's perfect for reading. After dining with hosts Marianne and Malcolm Booth at a Georgian table you can slip into the canopy bed in the Red Room Suite, the most luxurious of four bedrooms. Rural isolation is a great excuse for taking a dinner/bed-and-breakfast package here; this is a deliciously decadent stop on the drive to or from the Flinders Ranges. ⊠ *Spalding–Jamestown Rd., Jamestown 5491* ☎ *08/ 8665–4024* 🖷 *08/8665–4080* ⊕ *www.northbundaleer.com.au* ☜ *3 rooms, 1 suite* △ *Dining room, hiking, bar, library, piano, Internet, travel services; no a/c in some rooms, no room phones, no room TVs, no smoking* ⦿ *BP, MAP.*

★ $$

▦ **Clausens of Clare.** Built of glass, iron, and recycled timbers, and powered mostly by solar panels and wind, this contemporary Australian home sits on 80 flower- and bird-filled acres high above the Clare Valley. Fire-engine red is splashed against white bed linen and golden timber floors in the airy, spacious rooms opening onto the veranda. There is a rainwater shower in each en suite room. Co-host Diane Clausen's breakfasts, dinners, and gourmet picnic hampers are on a par with the incredible valley views from the dining room and deck. ⌑ *Box 133, 5453* ☎☎ *08/8842–2323* ⊕ *www.clausensofclare.com* ☜ *4 rooms* △ *Dining room, BBQ, IDD phones, refrigerators, in-room DVD, sauna, bicycles, boccie, laundry service, Internet room, business services, travel services, meeting room; no kids, no smoking* ▤ *AE, DC, MC, V* ⦿ *BP.*

$–$$

▦ **Chaff Mill Village.** The spacious, elevated-country-style apartments here have all the modern amenities, including kitchenettes and spa baths. Although it's conveniently located on a main road, the property overlooks a wooded backdrop of pepper trees along the Hutt River, so it feels like a country retreat. A pub and Chinese restaurant are next door, and other dining options are within walking distance. ⊠ *310 Main North Rd., 5453* ☎ *08/8842–1111* 🖷 *08/8842–1303* ⊕ *www.countryclubs.com. au* ☜ *6 apartments* △ *BBQs, in-room hot tubs, kitchenettes, cable TV, in-room data ports, laundry facilities, free parking; no smoking* ▤ *AE, DC, MC, V.*

$–$$

▦ **Quality Resort Clare Country Club.** Bordering the 11th fairway of the Clare Golf Course, this country club is a place for active travelers who want to enjoy sports facilities. Several types of rooms are available, from two-room family apartments with kitchenettes to deluxe balcony rooms. All have high-quality furnishings and whirlpool tubs. ⊠ *White Hutt Rd., 5453* ☎ *08/8842–1060* 🖷 *08/8842–1042* ⊕ *www.countryclubs.com. au/clare* ☜ *38 rooms, 15 2-room kitchenettes, 3 suites, 1 apartment* △ *Restaurant, room service, IDD phones, in-room hot tubs, some kitchenettes, minibars, some microwaves, some refrigerators, cable TV, in-room data ports, tennis court, pool, health club, sauna, hot tub, billiards, bar, babysitting, laundry facilities, laundry service, convention center, travel services, free parking; no smoking* ▤ *AE, DC, MC, V.*

$ 🏠 **Bungaree Station.** Your journey back to colonial Australia begins at check-in at this family-owned farm; the reception area is in the original station store. Outlying cottages and the Heritage-listed stables beside the stone homestead have been converted into family-friendly accommodations, some with shared facilities. The sandstone stallion box is now the honeymoon cottage! Rooms have fans only and can heat up in summer; wood-burning, slow- combustion stoves give winter warmth. Take time exploring the property; down the hill is an unusual sandstone woolshed. Bungaree is popular with groups and may be booked out for private functions. ⊠ *Main North Rd., 11 km (7 mi) north of Clare, 5453* ☎ *08/8842–2677* 🖷 *08/8842–3004* ⊕ *www.bungareestation.com.au* ⇗ *6 cottages, 4 rooms, 1 apartment* ⚴ *BBQs, fans, some kitchens, some microwaves, some refrigerators, pool, gym, free parking; no a/c, no TVs in some rooms, no smoking* 🖃 *AE, DC, MC, V.*

Burra

44 km (27 mi) northeast of Clare, 156 km (97 mi) north of Adelaide.

Although it's actually outside the Clare Valley, Burra is a mining-era town that is full of character—and characters—so it's well worth a detour from the wine region. In harsh, stony country where summer temperatures can soar, the town also offers a taste of the Outback close to vineyard greenery.

The discovery of copper in Burra in 1845 made it Australia's largest inland town, and its seventh-largest settlement overall. Miners from all parts of the world swelled the population to 5,000 in 1851, when only 18,000 people lived in Adelaide. The find also saved the struggling young colony of South Australia from potential bankruptcy. The ore ran out quickly, however—the biggest mine closed 32 years after it opened—and Burra settled into a comfortable existence as a service town.

Today the Heritage Trail leads you to sites related to Burra's rich mining past. The innovative Burra Heritage Passport, available at the **Burra Visitor Centre** (⊠2 Market Sq. ☎08/8892–2154 ⊕www.visitburra.com) makes touring the 11-km (7-mi) Heritage Trail simple and enjoyable. The Burra Heritage Passport (A$15 per person) includes a guidebook, map, and a key that gives access to eight locked historic sites, including the Monster Mine area. The Museum Pass (A$15) gets you into four museums, including Morphett's Engine House. The Heritage Passport and the Museum Pass can be combined for A$25. The visitor center is open daily 9–5.

The **Burra Mine Historic Site** contains the huge open-cut, so-called Monster Mine, weathered machinery, chimneys, and many other relics of the mining era. Also within the site is **Morphett's Engine House Museum,** which once housed the huge Cornish beam engine used to pump water from the mine; the three floors in the restored redbrick building have excellent displays about the history of engine houses and beam engines. Adjoining the mine site is the mine's Heritage-listed powder magazine (separate keyed entry). ⊠ *West and Linkson Sts.* ☎ *08/8892–2154* 🖾 *Mine and Museum entry with Heritage Passport key and Museum*

Pass from visitor center, or A$4.50 separate ticket for Museum ☉ Mine site daily during daylight hrs, Engine House Museum daily 11–2.

The **Bon Accord Mine,** unlike the phenomenally successful Monster Mine, was a failure. However, the canny Scottish owners made the best of a bad lot by selling the mine shaft, which hit the water table, to the town as a water supply. The mine complex is now an interesting museum, where you can see documents, old tools, photographs, and many more artifacts related to the history of the Bon Accord Mine and Burra. There's also a 9-foot by 6-foot model of the Burra Mine. ⊠ Linkson St. ☎ 08/8892–2154 ☜ Entry with Museum Pass from visitor center, or A$4.50 separate ticket ☉ Daily 1–4.

With no formal accommodation available, most of the Cornish miners who flocked to Burra after the discovery of copper dug dwellings into the banks of dry Burra Creek. Many of these **dugouts** were surprisingly comfortable, with whitewashed walls, doors, and even glass windows, and up to 2,000 people lived in 600 dugouts along "Creek Street" before a devastating flood in 1851. You can visit the two surviving, unfurnished dugouts on the Heritage Trail. ⊠ Blyth St. ☎ 08/8892–2154 ☜ Entry with Heritage Passport key from visitor center ☉ Daily during daylight hrs.

Redruth Gaol, a colonial prison that later served as a girls' reformatory, houses an informative display on its checkered history. The jail appeared in the Australian film Breaker Morant. ⊠ Tregony St. ☎ 08/8892–2154 ☜ Entry with Heritage Passport key from visitor center ☉ Daily during daylight hrs.

One of the series of villages that made up the "Burra," as the town was originally called, **Hampton** was built in 1857 for English miners (the Scottish lived in "Aberdeen" and the Welsh in "Llwchwr"). The ruined village has the best view of the town, but it was the last to get electricity and water. You can walk around and through the site. To get here, drive north on Tregony Street from Redruth Gaol and take the first right turn. At the T-junction, turn left into the Hampton parking lot. ☎ 08/8892–2154 ☜ Entry with Heritage Passport key from visitor center ☉ Daily during daylight hrs.

Malowen Lowarth is one of several dozen cottages at Paxton Square built between 1849 and 1852 as housing for miners who had moved from the creek dugouts. It's now owned by the National Trust and operates as a museum showcasing period furniture and fittings. ⊠ Paxton Sq. ☎ 08/8892–2154 ☜ Entry with Museum Pass from visitor center, or A$4.50 separate ticket ☉ Weekdays 9.30–11.30, weekends either 9:30–12:30 or 2–5 (check with visitor center).

The tiny **Market Square Museum** re-creates a typical general store and residence circa 1880–1920. ⊠ Market Sq. ☎ 08/8892–2154 ☜ Entry with Museum Pass from visitor center, or A$3.50 separate ticket ☉ Daily 1–3.

The **Unicorn Brewery Cellars** are cool and inviting in the desert heat of a Burra summer, even though there's no longer any beer in the house. The

1873 brewery operated for 30 years and was regarded as one of Australia's best producers. ⊠ *Bridge Terr.* ☎ *08/8892–2154* ☜ *Entry with Heritage Passport key from visitor center* ☉ *Daily during daylight hrs.*

Clare Valley A to Z

CAR TRAVEL

The Clare Valley is about a 90-minute drive from Adelaide via Main North Road. From the center of Adelaide, head north on King William Street through the heart of North Adelaide. King William becomes O'-Connell Street. After crossing Barton Terrace, look for Main North Road signs on the right. The road passes through the satellite town of Elizabeth, bypasses the center of Gawler, and then runs due north to Auburn, the first town of the Clare Valley when approaching from the capital. Main North Road continues down the middle of the valley to Clare. From Clare town, follow signs to Burra, on the Barrier Highway.

As with the Barossa, a car is essential for exploring the Clare Valley in any depth. Taste wine in moderation if you're driving; as well as keeping yourself and others safe, you'll avoid paying the extremely high penalties for driving while intoxicated.

EMERGENCIES

In an emergency, dial **000** to reach an ambulance, the police, or the fire department.

TOURS

The Grape Express Winery Tour visits six wineries each Saturday for A\$45 (bookings required), departing from the Clare Valley Visitor Information Centre at 9:30 AM. Clare Valley Tours combines wine tasting with history and culture on its daylong tour of the regions's major towns (A\$78), departing from Clare.

🛈 **Clare Valley Tours** ☎ 0418/832812 or 08/8843-8066 ⊕ www.cvtours.com.au. **Grape Express Winery Tour** ☎ 08/8842-2131 or 1800/242131 ⊕ www.clarevalley.com.au.

VISITOR INFORMATION

The Clare Valley Visitor Information Centre is open Monday–Saturday 9–5 and Sunday 10–4.

🛈 **Clare Valley Visitor Information Center** ⊠ Town Hall, 229 Main North Rd., Clare ☎ 08/8842-2131 ⊕ www.clarevalley.com.au.

FLEURIEU PENINSULA

The Fleurieu has traditionally been seen as Adelaide's backyard. Generations of Adelaide families have vacationed in the string of beachside resorts between Victor Harbor and Goolwa, near the mouth of the Murray River. McLaren Vale wineries attract connoisseurs, and the beaches and bays bring in surfers, swimmers, and sunseekers. The countryside, with its dramatic cliff scenery, is a joy to drive through.

Although the region is within easy reach of Adelaide, you should consider spending the night if you want to enjoy all it has to offer. You can also easily combine a visit here with one or more nights on Kangaroo Island. The ferry from Cape Jervis, at the end of the peninsula, takes less than an hour to reach Penneshaw on the island, and there are coach connections from Victor Harbor and Goolwa.

McLaren Vale

39 km (24 mi) south of Adelaide.

This region has a distinctly modern, upscale look, even though many of the 60 wineries in and around town are as old as their Barossa peers. The first vines were planted in 1838 at northern Reynella by Englishman John Reynell, who had collected them en route from the Cape of Good Hope. The McLaren Vale region has always been known for its big reds, shiraz, white varietals, and softer reds.

The stone cellar door at **Coriole Vineyards** sits among nasturtiums and hollyhocks, on a hill with St. Vincent Gulf views. From the surrounding vines, winemaker Mark Lloyd makes some of Australia's best Italian varietal wines, such as Sangiovese and Nebbiolo, and a fine chenin blanc that tastes of guava. Also look out for "The Old Barn" limited-release shiraz cabernet. Coriole grows olives, too, and you can taste olive oils as well as wine. Enjoy a platter of local produce—cheeses, roast turkey, and chutney—in the flagstone courtyard (weekend lunch only). ⊠ *Chaffeys Rd. near Kays Rd.* ☎ *08/8238–0000* ⊕ *www.coriole.com* ⌹ *Free* ⊗ *Weekdays 10–5, weekends 11–5.*

At **d'Arenberg Wines,** family-run since 1912, a fine restaurant complements excellent wine. Winemaker Chester d'Arenberg Osborn is known for his quality whites, including the luscious Noble Riesling dessert wine, as well as powerful reds and fortified wines with equally compelling names. Reservations are recommended for dining at d'Arry's Verandah restaurant, which overlooks the vineyards, the valley, and the sea. The seasonal menu uses local produce for pan-national dishes. Lunch is served daily. ⊠ *Osborn Rd.* ☎ *08/8323–8410* ⊕ *www.darenberg.com. au* ⌹ *Free* ⊗ *Daily 10–5.*

★ On a clear day you can indeed see forever from the cellar door at **Hugh Hamilton Wines.** Floor-to-ceiling windows in the geometric building offer 360-degree views down to the sea and up to the Mt. Lofty ranges. The crisp white Verdelho is as refreshing as the scenery. ⊠ *McMurtrie Rd. just east of McLaren Vale-to-Willunga cycling/walking track* ☎ *08/ 8323–8689* ⊕ *www.hamiltonwines.com.au* ⌹ *Free* ⊗ *Weekdays 10–5:30, weekends 11–5:30.*

The absence of wine at its cellar door is one of many unique factors that makes the **Olive Grove** special. Instead of sampling and spitting out wines, you'll be tasting and spitting out pits as you enjoy the varieties of olives and gourmet foods. The delicate macadamia-nut oil pairs well great with the homemade *dukkah* (crushed nuts eaten with bread and oil). ⊠ *Warners Rd. near Olivers Rd.* ☎ *08/8323–8792* ⊕ *www. olivegroves.com.au* ⌹ *Free* ⊗ *Daily 10–5.*

McLaren Vale's most historic winery is **Rosemount Estates,** which has vines dating from 1850. You can stroll around the buildings and the old, carved vats lining the large tasting room, but there are no organized tours. A superb selection of reds and whites, including fantastic sparkling wines, is for sale. ⊠ *Chaffeys and Neills Rds.* ☎ *08/8323–8250* ⊕ *www. rosemountestates.com* ⊠ *Free* ⊗ *Mon.–Sat. 10–5, Sun. 11–4.*

A lane of giant tree stumps leads to the cellars at **Wirra Wirra Vineyards,** which were built in 1894. The Mrs. Wigley Rosé is a favorite throughout McLaren Vale, and each of the three varieties of shiraz is delicious. Don't forget to try the good-value Church Block Dry Red. ⊠ *McMurtrie Rd. near Stroutt Rd.* ☎ *08/8323–8414* ⊕ *www.wirrawirra.com* ⊠ *Free* ⊗ *Mon.–Sat. 10–5, Sun. 11–5.*

Where to Stay & Eat

$$ ✕**Salopian Inn.** First licensed in 1851, this former inn and celebrated restaurant overlooks rolling vineyards in the heart of McLaren Vale. Fresh local produce is used to create seasonal treats prepared with a Mediterranean-Australasian flavor, such as crisp-skin duck served with spiced Fleurieu cherries. Instead of a wine list you get to pick from the well-stocked basement cellar. ⊠ *Willunga and McMurtrie Rds.* ☎ *08/8323–8769* ▭ *AE, DC, MC, V* ⊗ *Closed Wed. No dinner Sun.–Tues. and Thurs.*

★ **$$** ✕ **Star of Greece.** More for the linen-slacks-and-deck-shoes set than the board-shorts-and-sunscreen crowd, this extended weatherboard kiosk on the cliffs at Port Willunga, 10 km (6 mi) southwest of McLaren Vale, is beach-ball bright. Wooden chairs painted in mandarin, lime, and sky-blue stripes sit at paper-draped tables, and windows frame the aqua sea. (The buoy offshore marks where the three-masted *Star of Greece* foundered in 1888.) Looking through the menu nets mostly seafood. You could order coconut-dressed yellowfin tuna carpaccio or whole bream, but every white-plated dish the hip staff carry past may make you question your choice. Take a lead from the surfers below and go with the flow. ⊠ *The Esplanade, Port Willunga 5173* ☎ *08/8557–7420* ▭ *AE, DC, MC, V.*

★ **$** ✕**Market 190.** With its worn floorboards and pressed-metal ceilings, this café-shop feels like a country corner store. Bottled olive oil and local jams line the shelves, and cakes and cheeses fill the glass-front counter. Read a magazine over coffee and buy a bunch of flowers on the way out. The menu shows off Fleurieu Peninsula produce: for a taste of McLaren Vale, order a regional platter, or for something spicier tuck into Thai flathead fillets with lime, coriander, and coconut cream. To finish, try a lemon-curd tart or the Swiss ice cream. ⊠ *190 Main Rd.* ☎ *08/8323–8558* ▭ *AE, DC, MC, V* ⊗ *No dinner Sun.–Thurs.*

¢–$ ✕**Blessed Cheese.** It's hard to disappoint when cheese and chocolate are your specialties, particularly when they're adeptly paired with local wines. Cheese maker and co-owner Mark Potter uses his PhD in biochemistry to mix up flavorful combinations of small-vineyard wines and cheese, available in A\$10-per-head platters. He also runs daylong home cheese-making courses. The organic coffee is the best in the Vale, and the baked cherry cheesecake is its perfect match. ⊠ *150 Main Rd.* ☎ *08/8323–7958* ▭ *AE, DC, MC, V* ⊗ *No dinner.*

$$$ 🖭 **Wine and Roses B&B.** Its exterior may look like a regular residential house, but the inside of this luxury B&B is far from ordinary. Liqueur-filled chocolates and port await you in your suite, where you can set the mood for romance with music CDs or a DVD, and relax in the double jetted tub or wrapped in a plush bathrobe beside the wood-burning fire. Choose from the pillow menu for bedtime. The house is five minutes from the main McLaren Vale road. ⊠ *39 Caffrey St., 5171* 🕾 *08/ 8323–7654* 🖷 *08/8323–7653* ⊕ *www.wineandroses.com.au* ⇨ *3 suites* ⌂ *Dining room, in-room safes, in-room hot tubs, some kitchens, some microwaves, some refrigerators, some in-room DVDs, some in-room VCRs, massage, laundry service, Internet room, travel services, free parking; no kids, no smoking* ⊟ *MC, V* ⍾◎⍿ *BP.*

$$–$$$ 🖭 **Willunga House B&B.** Polished parquet floors, pressed-metal ceilings, and marble fireplaces are among the restored, original features in this inviting, Heritage-listed, Georgian stone residence. Once the town's post office and general store, the house now has five double guest rooms with antique brass-and-iron beds. In winter a log fire blazes in the large, communal sitting room, which opens onto the first-floor balcony. The hearty complimentary breakfast includes produce fresh from the organic garden. Willunga is 7 km (4½ mi) south of McLaren Vale. ⊠ *1 St. Peter's Terr., Willunga 5172* 🕾 *08/8556–2467* 🖷 *08/8556–2465* ⊕ *www. willungahouse.com.au* ⇨ *5 rooms* ⌂ *Dining room, pool, massage, laundry service, Internet room, free parking; no a/c in some rooms, no room phones, no kids, no smoking* ⊟ *MC, V* ⍾◎⍿ *BP.*

Goolwa

44 km (27 mi) southeast of McLaren Vale, 83 km (51 mi) south of Adelaide.

Beautifully situated near the mouth of the mighty Murray River, Goolwa grew fat on the 19th-century river paddle-steamer trade. South Australia's first railway line was built to Port Elliott, Goolwa's seaport, in 1854, and at one point the town had 88 pubs. Today, with its enviable position close to the sea and the combined attractions of Lake Alexandrina and Coorong National Park, tourism has replaced river trade as the main source of income.

☉ **Goolwa Wharf** is the launching place for daily tour cruises. The *Spirit of the Coorong,* a fully equipped motorboat, has a six-hour cruise (A$84) to Coorong National Park that includes three guided walks, lunch, and afternoon tea. ⊠ *Goolwa Wharf* 🕾 *08/8555–2203, 1800/442203 tour cruises* ⊕ *www.coorongcruises.com.au.*

★ Goolwa is also the home port of paddle-steamer **Oscar W.** Built in 1908, it's one of the few remaining as-is, wood-fired boiler ships. This boat holds the record for bringing the most bales of wool (2,500) down the Darling River, which flows into the Murray River. When not participating in commemorative cruises and paddleboat races (no public passengers), the boat is open for inspection. ⊠ *Goolwa Wharf* 🕾 *08/ 8555–1144 tourist office* 🖾 *Donations suggested.*

Signal Point is an excellent interpretive center that uses audiovisual techniques, artifacts, models, and interactive displays to demonstrate historical and environmental aspects of the Murray River. Exhibits include stories of the indigenous Ngarrindjeri people and the river trade. ⊠ *Goolwa Wharf* ☎ *08/8555–1144 tourist office* ≊ *A$5.50* ⊘ *Daily 9–5.*

Coorong National Park (⊠ 34 Princes Hwy., Meningie ☎ 08/8575–1200), a sliver of land stretching southeast of the Fleurieu Peninsula and completely separate from it, hugs the South Australian coast for more than 150 km (94 mi). Many Australians became aware of the Coorong's beauty from the 1970s film *Storm Boy,* which told the story of a boy's friendship with a pelican. These curious birds are one reason why the Coorong is a wetland area of world standing. You can visit any time as long as you drive on the designated tracks. Campers must first get a permit (A$6.50 per vehicle per night) from the park office.

Where to Stay

$ ⊞ **Hays Street Cottage.** Calico curtains, coconut-fiber mats, and sky-blue furniture bring the sea inside this airy house opposite Goolwa's wharf. Stripped timbers lend the kitchen a weathered charm; the old refrigerator could have washed up in a storm. A potbellied stove in the adjoining sitting room provides winter warmth. Off the sitting room are two simply furnished double bedrooms that share a bathroom. ⊠ *4 Hays St. 5214* ☎ *08/8555–5557* ✐ *liz.liv@bigpond.com* ⤳ *1 cottage* ⚭ *Fan, microwave, refrigerator, in-room DVD/VCR, free parking; no room phones* ⊟ *MC, V* ⊙ *BP.*

Victor Harbor

18 km (11 mi) west of Goolwa, 83 km (51 mi) south of Adelaide.

As famous for its natural beauty and wildlife as for its resorts, Victor Harbor is the seaside getaway town of South Australia. In 1802 English and French explorers Matthew Flinders and Nicolas Baudin met here at Encounter Bay, and by 1830 the harbor was a major whaling center. Pods of southern right whales came here to breed in winter, and they made for a profitable trade through the mid-1800s. By 1878 the whales were hunted nearly to extinction, but the return of these majestic creatures to Victor Harbor in recent decades has established the city as a premiere source of information on whales and whaling history.

★ ☾ The **South Australian Whale Centre** tells the often graphic story of the whaling industry along the South Australia coast, particularly in Encounter Bay. Excellent interpretive displays spread over three floors focus on dolphins, seals, penguins, and whales—all of which can be seen in these waters. In whale-watching season (May–October) the center has a 24-hour information hotline on sightings. There's a Discovery Trail and craft area for children. ⊠ *2 Railway Terr.* ☎ *08/8552–5644, 1900/931223 whale information* ⊕ *www.sawhalecentre.com* ≊ *A$6* ⊘ *Daily 11–4:30.*

Visit the **Bluff,** 7 km (4½ mi) west of Victor Harbor, to see where whalers once stood lookout for their prey. Today the granite outcrop, also known as Rosetta Head, serves the same purpose in very different circumstances. It's a steep, 1,400-foot climb to the top, on a formed trail, to enjoy the Bluff views. For cycling enthusiasts, there's also the **Encounter Bikeway,** a paved track that runs 30 km (19 mi) from the Bluff along a scenic coastal route to Laffin Point (east of Goolwa). Almost flat, the bikeway is suitable for riders of most ages and experience levels.

☺ **Granite Island** is linked to the mainland by a causeway, along which trundles a double-decker tram pulled by Clydesdale horses. A self-guided walk leads to the island's summit. Inside Granite Island Nature Park a penguin interpretive center runs guided tours to view the large, native colony of fairy penguins. There are also dolphin-watching cruises, whale-watching cruises (May–October), a shark oceanarium (a floating platform comprising several glass-walled saltwater tanks), a kiosk, and an excellent bistro with deck dining overlooking the harbor and ocean. Access to the oceanarium is by boats that depart every 30–60 minutes. Penguin center tours depart daily at dusk and take 1½ hours. The dolphin-watching cruise departs daily at 2 and lasts 1½ hours. The 2½-hour whale-watching cruises (minimum eight people) operate daily May–October. ⊠ *Granite Island* ☎ *08/8552–7555* 🚋 *Round-trip tram A$7, penguin tours A$12.50, oceanarium A$15, dolphin-watching cruises A$40, whale-watching cruises A$55* ⊙ *Interpretive center daily 12:30–3:30 and ¾ hr before tours; oceanarium summer daily 11–3, winter daily 1–3, subject to weather and water conditions.*

The steam-powered **Cockle Train** travels the original route of South Australia's first railway line on its journey to Goolwa. Extended from Port Elliot to Victor Harbor in 1864, the line traces the lovely Southern Ocean beaches on its 16-km (10-mi), half-hour route. The train runs by steam power daily over the Easter weekend and during summer school holidays and end-of-term breaks. A diesel locomotive pulls the heritage passenger cars Sunday and public holidays. ⊠ *Railway Terr., near Coral St.* ☎ *1300/655991* ⊕ *www.steamranger.org.au* 🚋 *Round-trip A$23.*

☺ Head to **Urimbirra Wildlife Park** if you feel like gawking at a menagerie of native animals and birds, more than 70 species in all. Among the collection at this open-range zoo are kangaroos, saltwater and freshwater crocodiles, Cape Barren geese, and pelicans. ⊠ *Adelaide Rd., 2 km (1 mi) north of Victor Harbor* ☎ *08/8554–6554* 🚋 *A$9* ⊙ *Daily 9–dusk.*

Where to Stay

$–$$$ 🏨 **Whalers Inn Resort.** The vibe is more tropical than maritime at Victor Harbor's upscale resort complex, with palm trees and spectacular surf as the backdrop for spacious, well-equipped rooms of varying configurations. Suites can be joined together to make family quarters, and apartments are totally self-contained; all are decorated in hazy seaside hues. Cook meals in your ultramodern kitchen or head down to the Waterside restaurant and bar for fresh seafood and shoreline views. ⊠ *121 Franklin Parade 5211* ☎ *08/8552–4400* 🖨 *08/8552–4240* ⊕ *www. whalersinnresort.com.au* 🛏 *47 rooms, 14 apartments, 14 studios, 14 suites, 4 pool studios, 1 cottage* ♿ *Restaurant, BBQs, some kitchens,* *some in-room VCRs, some in-room data ports, tennis court, pool, bicycles, bar, babysitting, laundry facilities, laundry service, convention center, free parking* ▭ *AE, MC, V.*

⚠ **Port Elliot Caravan & Tourist Park.** Six kilometers (4 mi) east of Victor Harbor, and a third of the way to Goolwa, this grassy park fronts beautiful tree-lined Horseshoe Bay, one of South Australia's best swimming beaches. Choose from foreshore campsites and self-contained cabins and villas (basic linens are provided). The park is within a regional reserve and close to cycling tracks and coastal walking paths. In whale-watching season (usually May to October) you can sometimes see southern right whales from the park. ⚖ *Flush toilets, partial hookups (electric and water), dump station, drinking water, guest laundry, showers, picnic tables, electricity, public telephone, general store, play area, swimming (ocean)* ⛺ *7 unpowered and 251 powered campsites, 9 villas, 3 cottages, 4 units, 4 cabins* ✉ *Off Goolwa Rd., near Hussey St., Port Elliot 5212* ☎ *08/8554–2134 or 1800/008480* 📠 *08/8554–3454* ⊕ *www. portelliotcaravanpark.com.au* ▦ *A$32–A$120* ▭ *AE, DC, MC, V.*

Fleurieu Peninsula A to Z

CAR TRAVEL

Renting a car in Adelaide and driving south is the best way to visit the Fleurieu Peninsula, especially if you wish to tour the wineries, which aren't served by public transportation.

The Fleurieu is an easy drive south from Adelaide. McLaren Vale itself is less than an hour away. Leave central Adelaide along South Terrace or West Terrace, linking with the Anzac Highway, which heads toward Glenelg. At the intersection with Main South Road, turn left. This road takes you almost to McLaren Vale. After a detour to visit the wineries, watch for signs for Victor Harbor Road. About 20 km (12 mi) south the highway splits. One road heads for Victor Harbor, the other for Goolwa. Those two places are connected by a major road that follows the coastline. Drivers heading to Cape Jervis and the Kangaroo Island ferries should stay on Main South Road.

EMERGENCIES

In an emergency, dial **000** to reach an ambulance, the police, or the fire department.

VISITOR INFORMATION

Inside the Victor Harbor Visitor Information Centre try the Fleurieu and Kangaroo Island Booking Centre for planning tours and accommodations. The large, open-plan McLaren Vale and Fleurieu Visitor Centre in the heart of the vineyards resembles a winery. In addition to tourist information, it has a café and wine bar and a wine interpretative counter. The center is open daily 9–5.

🚩 **Fleurieu and Kangaroo Island Booking Centre** ✉ The Causeway, Victor Harbor ☎ 08/8552–7000 or 1800/088552. **McLaren Vale and Fleurieu Visitor Centre** ✉ Main St., McLaren Vale ☎ 08/8323–9944. **Victor Harbor Visitor Information Centre** ✉ The Causeway, Victor Harbor ☎ 08/8552–5738.

KANGAROO ISLAND

Kangaroo Island, Australia's third largest (after Tasmania and Melville), is barely 16 km (10 mi) from the Australian mainland. Yet the island belongs to another age—a folksy, friendly, less-sophisticated time when you'd leave your car unlocked and knew everyone by name.

The island is most beautiful along the coastline, where the land is sculpted into a series of bays and inlets teeming with bird and marine life. The stark interior has its own Outback charm, however, with pockets of red earth between stretches of bush and farmland. Wildlife is probably the island's greatest attraction; in a single day you can stroll along a beach crowded with sea lions and watch kangaroos, koalas, pelicans, and fairy penguins in their native environments.

Many people treasure Kangaroo Island for what it lacks. Although it's within sight of the mainland, there are few resorts and virtually no nightlife. Its main luxuries are salty sea breezes, sparkling clear water, solitude, and food—local marron (freshwater crayfish), yabbies, seafood, corn-fed chicken, lamb, honey, and cheese. Eucalyptus oil–based products are also produced here (in the 1930s and 1940s there were 40 eucalyptus stills), and the island has 28 vineyards.

The towns and most of the accommodations are on the eastern third of the island. The most interesting sights are on the southern coast, so if you've only got one day—you could easily spend a week—it's best to tour the island in a clockwise direction, leaving the north-coast beaches for the afternoon. Before heading out, fill your gas tank and pack a picnic lunch. Shops are few and far between outside the towns, with general stores being the main outlets for food and gas.

The Island Parks Pass (A$42; A$110 families) is available from any National Parks and Wildlife site, or from the **National Parks and Wildlife SA Office** (⌷ 37 Dauncey St., Kingscote ☎ 08/8553–2381 ⊕ www. environment.sa.gov.au/parks/parks.html). The pass covers a selection of guided tours and park entry fees (except camping) and is valid for a year.

Kingscote

121 km (75 mi) southwest of Adelaide.

Kangaroo Island's largest town, Kingscote is a good base for exploring. Reeves Point, at the northern end of town, is where South Australia's colonial history began. Settlers landed here in 1836 and established the first official town in the new colony. Little remains of the original settlement except Hope Cottage, now a small museum; several graves; and a huge, twisted mulberry tree that grew from a cutting the settlers brought from England—locals still use the fruit to make jam. Today American River, about halfway between Kingscote and Penneshaw, the island's second-largest town, is another accommodation and restaurant hub.

★ ☾ Make sure you catch the **Pelican Feeding** "show" at 5 PM daily on the rock wall beside Kingscote Jetty. A guide in fishing waders gives an informative and entertaining talk as he feeds handfuls of seafood to a comic mob of noisy pelicans. This is great fun. ⊠ *Kingscote Jetty* ☎ *08/8553–3112 Kangaroo Island Marine Centre* ☉ *Daily 5 PM.*

Where to Stay & Eat

$–$$ ✕ **Restaurant Bella.** This modern Italian restaurant serves dishes prepared with the freshest local ingredients. Classic starters such as garlic prawns and gnocchi with basil and sun-dried tomato evoke the Mediterranean, while Asian flavors spice up some of the main courses. Be sure to try the duck salad on marinated Chinese cabbage with honey and lime dressing. You can also order gourmet pizza, cooked in the adjoining café. A simplified café menu is available at lunchtime under the sidewalk awning. ⊠ *54 Dauncey St.* ☎ *08/8553–0400* ▤ *AE, DC, MC, V.*

$–$$ ✕▦ **Kangaroo Island Lodge.** The island's oldest resort faces beautiful Eastern Cove at American River. Rooms overlook open water or the saltwater pool; the most attractive are the "water-view" rooms, which have mud-brick walls, warm terra-cotta tones, and king-sized beds. You can taste some of Kangaroo Island's bounty in the restaurant, one of the island's best. A great choice is grilled American River whiting on a bed of bean-and-preserved-lemon salad. It's 39 km (24 mi) southeast of Kingscote. ☐ *Box 232, American River 5221* ☎ *08/8553–7053 or 1800/355581* ☐ *08/8553–7030* ⊕ *www.kilodge.com.au* ☜ *38 rooms* ⚘ *Restaurant, room service, some in-room hot tubs, some kitchens, some microwaves, tennis court, pool, sauna, beach, bar, laundry facilities, Internet room, business services, meeting rooms, travel services, free parking; no smoking* ▤ *AE, DC, MC, V.*

$$$ ▦ **Acacia Apartments.** A huge video library in the reception area confirms that the self-contained one- and two-bedroom units at this Reeve's Point complex are family-friendly. All the units have tile floors, brick walls, and enough room for different generations to have their own space. Allergy sufferers can check into apartments cleaned with natural products rather than chemicals. Special units for travelers with disabilities and restricted mobility have easy access and bathroom doors that open both ways. Four-wheel-drive tours can be arranged. The state's first British colonial settlement, Reeve's Point, is ½ km (¼ mi) down the hill. Book two nights or more for reduced rates. ⊠ *3–5 Rawson St., Reeve's Point 5223* ☎ *08/8553–0088 or 1800/247007* ☐ *08/8553–0008* ⊕ *www.acacia-apartments.com.au* ☜ *8 apartments, 2 executive suites* ⚘ *BBQs, some in-room hot tubs, kitchens, microwaves, refrigerators, in-room VCRs, in-room data ports, indoor pool, hot tub, volleyball, playground, laundry facilities, travel services, free parking; no smoking* ▤ *AE, DC, MC, V* ⍾ *CP.*

$$$ ▦ **Wanderers Rest.** Marvelous local artworks dot the walls in this country inn's stylish units. The elevated veranda and à la carte restaurant, where breakfast is served, have splendid views across American River to the mainland. ☐ *Bayview Rd., Box 34, American River 5221* ☎ *08/8553–7140* ☐ *08/8553–7282* ⊕ *www.wanderersrest.com.au* ☜ *9 rooms* ⚘ *Restaurant, minibars, refrigerators, pool, bar, travel services, free parking; no room phones, no kids under 10, no smoking* ▤ *AE, DC, MC, V* ⍾ *BP.*

★ **$$–$$$** 🏨 **Correa Corner.** Named after an indigenous flowering plant, this gorgeous, owner-hosted B&B nestles in a rambling mix of native and formal gardens. Lace and old-fashioned lamps add romantic touches to the deluxe rooms (Rose, Lavender, and Willow), where private reading nooks look out at the garden and floral spreads decorate the king-sized beds. You can even book dinner by candlelight. Wallabies and emus in the garden make it feel like a magical hideaway. It's 2 km (1 mi) from Kingscote, and one minute from the beach. ✉ *The Parade and 2nd St., Box 232, Brownlow 5223* ☎ *08/8553–2498* 🖨 *08/8553–2355* ⊕ *www. correacorner.com.au* 🛏 *3 rooms* △ *Dining room, BBQs, massage, beach, fishing, bicycles, bar, library, laundry service, Internet room, airport shuttle, travel services, free parking; no room phones, no kids under 5, no smoking* ☱ *MC, V* ⃝❘ *BP.*

$–$$ 🏨 **Comfort Inn Wisteria Lodge.** This small hotel overlooking a black-swan–and boat-dotted stretch of Nepean Bay challenges preconceptions of this budget-friendly chain. With big rooms and a VCR available on request, a pool, tennis court, and well-regarded restaurant that serves a mix of Italian, French, and Australian dishes-with-a-view, it's like staying at a private resort. ✉ *7 Cygnet Rd., 5223* ☎ *08/8553–2707* 🖨 *08/ 8553–2200* ⊕ *www.wisterialodgeki.com* 🛏 *20 rooms* △ *Restaurant, some in-room hot tubs, minibars, refrigerators, tennis court, pool, hot tub, bar, laundry facilities, Internet room, car rental, travel services, free parking; no smoking* ☱ *MC, V* ⃝❘ *CP.*

$ 🏨 **Ozone Seafront Hotel.** The ornate Victorian-look facade on this two-story 1920s hotel hides surprisingly modern and spacious rooms that overlook either Nepean Bay or the pool. Each room has an iron and ironing board, and tea- and coffee-making facilities. The huge bistro menu stars local seafood, and the wine list runs to 100 wines, many of them local. There are daily wine tastings in the bar. The airport is a 15-minute drive away. ✉ *Chapman Terr. and Commercial St., 5223* ☎ *08/8553–2011 or 1800/083133* 🖨 *08/8553–2249* ⊕ *www. ozonehotel.com* 🛏 *37 rooms* △ *Restaurant, BBQs, refrigerators, room TVs with movies, pool, sauna, hot tub, 3 bars, laundry facilities, Internet room, car rental, travel services, free parking, no-smoking rooms* ☱ *AE, DC, MC, V.*

Penneshaw

62 km (39 mi) east of Kingscote.

This tiny ferry port has a large population of penguins, which are visible on nocturnal tours. Gorgeous shoreline, views of spectacularly blue water, and rolling green hills are a few lovely surprises here.

☙ **Penneshaw Penguin Centre** offers two ways to view the delightful fairy penguins indigenous to Kangaroo Island. From the indoor interpretive center, where you can read about bird activity—including mating, nesting, and feeding—a boardwalk leads to a viewing platform above rocks and sand riddled with burrows. Because the penguins spend most of the day fishing at sea or inside their burrows, the best viewing is after sunset. You can take a self-guided walk or an informative guided tour, which starts with a talk and video at the center. You might see penguins waddling ashore, chicks emerging from their burrows to feed, or scruffy adults moulting. ⊠ *Middle Terr. and Bay Terr.* ☏☏ *08/8553–1103 or 08/ 0553–1016* 🖃 *Interpretive center free, guided tours A$8.80, self-guided tours A$6.50* ⊙ *Tours at 7:30 and 8:30* PM *in winter, 8:30 and 9:30* PM *in summer.*

Sunset Winery. Sip smooth chardonnay while overlooking Eastern Cove at this calm, cool, and pristine addition to Kangaroo Island's thriving wine industry. A selection of local cheeses accompanies your drink, and island olive oil, candles, pottery, and artworks are also available. ⊠ *Hog Bay Rd.* ☏ *08/8553–1378* 🖃 *08/8553–1379* 🖃 *Free* ⊙ *Daily 11–5.*

off the
beaten
path

CAPE WILLOUGHBY – Australia's oldest lighthouse sits on Kangaroo Island's easternmost point, 27 km (17 mi) from Penneshaw, on a mostly unpaved, often rutted road. You can explore the property around the lighthouse, but only guided tour groups can enter the 1852 building itself. Tours (A$10.50) depart from the National Parks office in one of the three 1920s lighthouse keepers' cottages. The other two cottages have been converted into self-contained accommodations that let you experience Kangaroo Island at its most remote and wild—it's always windy here. Because rain is the only water supply, there are no washing machines in the cottages; there are no TVs either, and the phone is for emergencies only. However, there's a claw-foot bathtub, lots of room, and spectacular scenery all around.

Below the light station is the cellar door of **Dudley Wines** (☏ 08/ 8553–1333). This corrugated-iron–and–timber building with a wavelike roof overlooks Backstairs Passage, the quirkily named strait between Kangaroo Island and the mainland. Open daily 11–5, Dudley has a small menu—including a bucket of king prawns—to complement their wines, which you can taste for free and buy by the glass, bottle, and case.

Where to Stay & Eat

★ ¢–$$ ✕ **Fish.** Belly up to the counter in this tiny shop for a cheap and cheer-ful take-out feast of local seafood. Choose your fish—whiting, John Dory, garfish—from the blackboard menu and have it beer-battered, crumbed, or grilled. Or you might prefer a paper-wrapped parcel of scallops, prawns, lobster, and oysters (in season) shucked to order. The team be hind the shop also runs 2 Birds & A Squid, which prepares seafood packs and cooked meals for pickup or delivery to your accommodation any-where on the island; minimum orders apply and seven days' notice is required. ⊠ *43 N. Terr.* ☏ *08/8553–1177* ⊕ *www.2birds1squid.com* 🖃 *No credit cards* ⊙ *Closed June–Aug. No lunch.*

$ ✕ **Penneshaw Pizza Kitchen.** Piping-hot pizza in all sizes and flavors is a great way to fuel up for an evening of penguin-spotting. Take your meal to the adjacent park on the water, or dine in and enjoy the tra-ditional pizzeria setting. The lasagna is great, too. ⊠ *N. Terrace near Nat Thomas St.* ☏ *08/8553–1227* 🖃 *AE, MC, V* ⊙ *No lunch Mon. and Tues.*

$–$$$ ⊞ **Kangaroo Island Seafront.** This hotel has an ideal position near the ferry terminal and overlooking Penneshaw Bay. You can choose an ocean-view room or stay amid tropical gardens in freestanding, one-room Heritage chalets. There are also two- and three-bedroom, self-contained cottages with full kitchens. The sky-blue-and-sand-yellow restaurant, which spills out onto a seafront terrace, serves marron, oysters, whiting, and other fresh local produce. Admission to the local nightly penguin tour is included in your room rate. ✉ *49 N. Terr., 5222* ☎ *08/ 8553–1028* 🖷 *08/8553–1204* ⊕ *www.seafront.com.au* 🛏 *12 rooms, 6 chalets, 3 cottages* ⌂ *Restaurant, some kitchens, some kitchenettes, tennis court, pool, sauna, bar, laundry facilities, free parking* ▤ *AE, DC, MC, V.*

$$ ⊞ **Seaview Lodge.** Hosts Jude and Milton MacKay welcome you into their 1860s home at this elegant yet relaxing B&B. Roses fill the cottage garden, and the cane chairs on the wide veranda are perfectly positioned for watching the sun set over the sea. Three of the five rooms have original timber floors and wood-burning fireplaces; all are decorated with colonial-style furniture. From the lace-draped four-poster beds in the Rose and Jasmine rooms and the temptingly deep claw-foot bathtub in Tecoma, to the full-size shampoo in your large, powerful shower, you're pampered all the way. ✉ *Willoughby Rd., 5222* ☎ *08/8553–1132* 🖷 *08/8553–1183* ⊕ *www.seaviewlodge.com.au* 🛏 *5 rooms* ⌂ *Dining room, bar, free parking* ▤ *AE, DC, MC, V.*

★ **$** ⊞ **Beach House.** Apple-green, hot-pink, and crimson cushions on white cane couches make this tiny sky-blue weatherboard a colorful seaside treasure. Opening off the glass-fronted sitting room are two bedrooms, and there are more stainless steel utensils in the compact adjoining kitchen than even a holidaying chef could find a use for. Feel the polished floorboards underfoot as you read a book or listen to a CD; then stroll across the road and get white sand between your toes on Hog Bay Beach. ✉ *Frenchman's Terr. near Cheops St., 5222* ☎ *08/8339–3103 or 0428/339310* ✎ *pma48979@bigpond.net.au* 🛏 *2 bedrooms, 1 bungalow* ⌂ *BBQs, kitchen, microwave, refrigerator, in-room VCR, beach, laundry facilities, free parking; no room phones, no smoking* ▤ *No credit cards.*

Seal Bay Conservation Park

🕒 *60 km (37 mi) southwest of Kingscote via South Coast Rd.*

Fodor'sChoice
★ This top Kangaroo Island attraction gives you the chance to visit one of the state's largest Australian sea lion colonies. About 300 animals usually lounge on the beach, except on stormy days, when they shelter in the sand dunes. You can only visit the beach, and get surprisingly close to females, pups, and bulls, on a tour with an interpretive officer; otherwise, you can follow the self-guided boardwalk to a lookout over the sand. Two-hour sunset tours depart on varied days in December and January; a minimum of four people (or equivalent payment) is required, as is 24-hour advance booking. The park visitor center has fun and educational displays, and a touch table covered in sea lion skins and bones. There is also a shop. ✉ *End of Seal Bay Road, Seal Bay* ☎ *08/*

8559–4207 ✉ Group tour A$12.50 per person, sunset tour A$25, boardwalk A$9 ⊙ Tours Dec. and Jan., daily 9–7, every 15–45 mins; Feb.–Nov., daily 9–4:15, every 30–45 mins.

en route 7 km (4½ mi) west of Seal Bay Conservation Park, towering white-sand dunes cover several square miles at **Little Sahara**. It's hard to resist a short walk to climb the dunes and slide down their faces; it's a popular place for sandboarding. To get here from Seal Bay Road, turn left onto South Coast Road and continue until immediately before a narrow bridge lined with metal safety barriers. The rough track on the left, marked with a "Heritage Area" sign, leads to Little Sahara.

A further 7 km (4½ mi) along South Coast Road, another red-earth side road leads to Vivonne Bay, a Mediterranean-looking fisherman's cove with electrifyingly colorful waters and stark white sands. There's no better view of the bay than from **Island Beach-House** (☎ 08/8357–7555 ⊕ www.fergusonaustralia.com/ki_accom.html). A stilted house with a glass-fronted semicircular lounge room facing the sea, this self-contained house has everything you need for a holiday, including a bread-making machine. You can order fresh-cooked lobster steaks from the owners, who operate professional lobster boats.

Continue on to **Point Ellen** for superb views of the bay and Vivonne Bay Conservation Park.

Flinders Chase National Park

★ *102 km (64 mi) west of Kingscote.*

Some of the most beautiful coastal scenery in Australia is on the western end of Kangaroo Island in Flinders Chase National Park. Much of the island has been widely cultivated and grazed, but the park has protected a huge area of original vegetation since it was declared a national treasure in 1919.

The seas crashing onto Australia's southern coast are merciless, and their effects are visible in the oddly shaped rocks off Kangaroo Island's shores. A limestone promontory was carved from underneath at Cape du Couedic on the island's southwestern coast, producing what is now known as **Admiral's Arch**. From the boardwalk you can see the New Zealand fur seals which have colonized the rocks around the Arch. About 4 km (2½ mi) farther east are the aptly named **Remarkable Rocks**, huge fantastically shaped boulders balanced precariously on the promontory of Kirkpatrick Point. This is a great place to watch the sun set or rise.

Starting in the 1920s, more than 20 animal species becoming endangered on the mainland were introduced—and reintroduced—to the island; these included koalas and Cape Barren geese. Today the park is full of wallabies, kangaroos, koalas, possums, goannas, and countless birds. Many of the animals are very friendly, but you shouldn't feed them. Doing so can make the animals sick, and can cause aggression in kangaroos.

Flinders Chase has several 1½-km- to 9-km- (1 mi- to 5½-mi-) loop walking trails, which take one to three hours to complete. The trails meander along the rivers to the coast, passing mallee scrub and sugar gum forests, and explore the rugged shoreline. The 4-km (2½-mi) Snake Lagoon Hike follows Rocky River over and through a series of broad rocky terraces to the remote sandy beach where it meets the sea. The sign warning of freak waves is not just for show.

The park is on the island's western end, bounded by the Playford and West End highways. The state-of-the-art visitor center, open daily 9–5, is the largest National Parks and Wildlife office. Displays and touch screens explore the park's history and the different habitats and wildlife in Flinders Chase. The center provides park entry tickets and camping permits, and books stays at the Heritage cabins. A shop sells souvenirs and provisions and there is also a café.

Where to Stay & Eat

Accommodations within the national park (and in Cape Willoughby Conservation Park at the other end of the island) are controlled by the **Flinders Chase National Park Office** (☎ 08/8559–7235 ⊕ www.environment.sa.gov.au/parks/flinderschase). Rustic sofas, chairs, and tables furnish Heritage-listed huts, cottages, homesteads, and lighthouse lodgings at Cape Willoughby (at the far end of the island), Cape du Couedic (southwest), and Cape Borda (northwest). All accommodations have kitchens or cooking facilities; blankets and pillows are supplied and you can rent bed linens and towels. Camping is allowed only at designated sites at Rocky River and bush campgrounds permits are essential.

¢–$$$$ ✕▣ **Kangaroo Island Wilderness Resort.** This eco-friendly retreat is everything a wallaby-loving traveler could desire. Wallabies see the grounds as part of the surrounding bush and at dusk there can be a dozen of them on the grass. Low-line, log-construction courtyard rooms decorated in sky-blue and terra-cotta have furniture made from recycled Oregon pine. Private decks in the two corner suites open onto thick banksia scrub. Motel-style rooms and dorm-style bunk rooms that sleep up to four share the barnlike Lodge at the back of the property. Rain is the only water source and showers are heated by solar power. The restaurant serves local specialties, such as American River oysters (in season) and whiting. The gas pump here is the last one for 35 km (21 mi). ⊠ *1 S. Coast Rd., Flinders Chase 5223* ☎ *08/8559–7275* 🖷 *08/8559–7377* ⊕ *www.kiwr.com* 🛏*23 courtyard rooms, 2 suites, 20 lodge rooms, 4 dorm rooms* ♻ *Restaurant, café, 1 in-room hot tub, some minibars, some refrigerators, laundry service, Internet room, meeting rooms, free parking; no a/c in some rooms, no phones in some rooms* ▤ *AE, DC, MC, V.*

⚠ **Rocky River Campground.** Birds sing rousing morning choruses and wallabies and possums are everywhere—so keep everything shut and zipped—in this campground a few hundred yards behind the Flinders Chase visitor center. There are tent and campervan sites (but no electricity), a covered communal eating area, and a rainwater tank. The camp abuts a beautiful grassy swamp and you can follow walking trails from here to platypus-viewing platforms on Rocky River; look for koalas in the trees along the way. ♿ *Flush toilets, drinking water, showers, picnic tables, public telephone, general store, ranger station ❤ 21 campsites, group camping area ✉ just off Cape Couedic Rd., 5223 ☎ 08/ 8559–7235 ⊕ www.environment.sa.gov.au/parks/kangaroo_is.html ✑ A$19 per car (up to 5 people), A$5.50 per person with no vehicle ▤ DC, MC, V.*

Kangaroo Island A to Z

AIR TRAVEL

REX/Regional Express flies twice daily between Adelaide and Kingscote, the island's main airport. Ask about 14-day advance-purchase fares and holiday packages in conjunction with SeaLink. Flights to the island take about 30 minutes. Emu Airways also operates daily flights.

✈ Airlines **Emu Airways** ☎ 08/8234-3711 ⊕ www.emuair.com.au. **REX/Regional Express** ☎ 13-1713 ⊕ www.rex.com.au.

BOAT & FERRY TRAVEL

Vehicular ferries allow access for cars through Penneshaw and Kingscote. The most popular option, and the shortest sea trip, is the SeaLink ferry from Cape Jervis at the tip of the Fleurieu Peninsula, a 90-minute drive from Adelaide. Kangaroo Island Ferries sail to Kingscote from Wirrina, 1¼ hours' drive from Adelaide.

SeaLink operates the passenger ferry *Sea Lion 2000* and MV *Island Navigator,* a designated freight boat with limited passenger facilities. These ferries make respective 45-minute and one-hour crossings between Cape Jervis and Penneshaw. There are usually 2 or 3 daily sailings each way, but at peak times there are up to 10 crossings. Kangaroo Island Ferries schedules 2 crossings (two hours) each day, with more in peak seasons. Ferries are the favored means of transportation between the island and the mainland, and reservations are advisable during the holidays.

Adelaide Sightseeing operates coaches in conjunction with the SeaLink ferry services from Cape Jervis and Penneshaw, linking Adelaide, Victor Harbor, and Goolwa with Cape Jervis.

✈ **Adelaide Sightseeing** ✉ 101 Franklin St., City Center, Adelaide ☎ 08/8231-4144. **Kangaroo Island Ferries** ☎ 13-2233 ⊕ www.kiferries.com. **SeaLink** ☎ 13-1301 ⊕ www. sealink.com.au.

CAR TRAVEL

Kangaroo Island's main attractions are widely scattered; you can see them best on a guided tour or by car. The main roads form a sealed loop, which branches off to such major sites as Seal Bay, and Admirals Arch and Remarkable Rocks in Flinders Chase National Park. Stretches of unpaved road lead to lighthouses at Cape Borda and Cape Willoughby, South Australia's oldest. Roads to the island's northern beaches, bays, and camping areas are also unpaved. These become very rutted in summer, but they can be driven carefully in a conventional vehicle. Be alert for wildlife, especially at dawn, dusk, and after dark. Slow down and dip your lights so you don't blind the animals you see.

CAR RENTAL

🚹**Budget** ✉1 Commercial St., Kingscote 5223 ☎08/8553-3133. **Kangaroo Island Rental Cars** ✉ Telegraph Rd. and Franklin St., Kingscote ☎ 08/8553-2390.

EMERGENCIES

In an emergency, dial **000** to reach an ambulance, the police, or the fire department.

In Kingscote there is a health clinic and a hospital with an emergency department. General practitioners make twice-monthly visits to health centers in Penneshaw, American River, and Parndana.

🚹**American River Health Service** ✉Tangara Dr., American River 5221 ☎08/8553-7110. **Kangaroo Island Health Service & Hospital** ✉ The Esplanade, Kingscote 5223 ☎08/8553-4200. **Kangaroo Island Medical Clinic** ✉64 Murray St., Kingscote 5223 ☎08/8553-2037. **Parndana Health Centre** ✉Jones St., Parndana 5220 ☎08/8559-6116.**Penneshaw Community Health Centre** ✉ Howard Dr., Penneshaw 5222 ☎08/8553-1101.

MONEY MATTERS

The ANZ bank in Kingscote can exchange foreign currency; agencies in American River, Penneshaw, and Parndana handle limited banking transactions. There are ATMs in Kingscote, Penneshaw, American River, and Parndana.

🚹 **Bank ANZ** ✉ 62 Dauncey St., Kingscote ☎ 13-1314.

TOURS

Adventure Charters of Kangaroo Island has quality four-wheel-drive and bushwalking tours from A$295 per person per day. Tailor-made itineraries, including bird-watching and photography, and flight-accommodation packages can also be arranged. Kangaroo Island Odysseys operates luxury four-wheel-drive nature tours from one to three days priced from $285 per person. Kangaroo Island Wilderness Tours has four personalized four-wheel-drive wilderness tours with full accommodations ranging from one to four days and starting at A$310 per person.

SeaLink Kangaroo Island operates one-day (A$181) bus tours of the island, departing from Adelaide, in conjunction with the ferry service from Cape Jervis. They also can arrange fishing and self-drive tours and extended packages. Two-day/one-night tours are A$302 and up per person; two-day/one-night self-drive tours start at A$160 per person.

🚹 **Adventure Tours Adventure Charters of Kangaroo Island** 🗋 Box 169, Kingscote 5223 ☎ 08/8553-9119 🖶 08/8553-9122 🌐 www.adventurecharters.com.au. **Kangaroo Island Odysseys** 🗋 Box 494, Penneshaw 5222 ☎ 08/8553-0386 🖶 08/8553-0387 🌐 www.kiodysseys.com.au. **Kangaroo Island Wilderness Tours** 🗋 Box 84, Parndana 5220 ☎ 08/8559-5033 🖶 08/8559-5088 🌐 www.wildernesstours.com.au.

🚹 **Bus Tour SeaLink Kangaroo Island** ✉ 7 N. Terr., Penneshaw 5222 ☎ 08/8553-1122 or 13-1301 🌐 www.sealink.com.au.

VISITOR INFORMATION

The Gateway Visitor Information Centre in Penneshaw is a model for tourist-information offices. Ask for the *Fast Fact Finder* to get an overview of where to shop, bank, surf the Web, and fuel up your car on the island. Kingscote has its own smaller tourist office and gift shop. ⓕ **Gateway Visitor Information Centre** ⊠ Howard Dr., Penneshaw ☎ 08/8553-1185 🖷 08/8553-1255 ⊕ www.tourkangarooisland.com.au. **Kingscote Tourist Centre** ⊠ 78 Dauncey St., Kingscote ☎ 08/8553-2165.

THE OUTBACK

South Australia is the country's driest state, and its Outback is an expanse of desert vegetation. But this land of scrubby salt bush and hardy eucalyptus trees is brightened after rain by wildflowers—including the state's floral emblem, the blood-red Sturt's desert pea, with its black, olivelike heart. The terrain is marked by geological uplifts, abrupt transitions between plateaus broken at the edges of ancient, long-inactive fault lines. Few roads track through this desert wilderness—the main highway is the Stuart, which runs all the way to Alice Springs in the Northern Territory.

The people of the Outback are as hardy as their surroundings. They are also often eccentric, colorful characters who happily bend your ear over a drink in the local pub. Remote, isolated communities attract loners, adventurers, fortune-seekers, and people simply on the run. In this unyielding country, you must be tough to survive.

Coober Pedy

850 km (527 mi) northwest of Adelaide.

Known as much for the way most of its 3,500 inhabitants live—underground in dugouts gouged into the hills—as for its opal riches, Coober Pedy is arguably Australia's most singular place. The town is ringed by mullock heaps, pyramids of rock and sand left over after mining shafts are dug.

Opals are Coober Pedy's reason for existence. Australia has 95% of the world's opal deposits, and Coober Pedy has the bulk of that wealth; this is the world's richest opal field.

Opal was discovered here in 1915, and soldiers returning from World War I excavated the first dugout homes when the searing heat forced them underground. In midsummer temperatures can reach 48°C (118°F), but inside the dugouts the air remains a constant 22°C–24°C (72°F–75°F).

Coober Pedy is a brick–and–corrugated-iron settlement propped unceremoniously on a scarred desert landscape. It's a town built for efficiency, not beauty. However, its ugliness has a kind of bizarre appeal. There's a feeling that you're in the last lawless outpost in the modern world, helped in no small part by the local film lore—*Priscilla Queen of the Desert, Pitch Black, Kangaroo Jack*, and *Mad Max 3* were filmed here. Once you go off the main street you get an immediate sense of the apocalyptic.

Exploring Coober Pedy

Fossicking for opal gemstones—locally called noodling—requires no permit at the Jewelers Shop mining area at the edge of town. Take care in unmarked areas and always watch your step, as the area is littered with abandoned opal mines down which you might fall. (Working mines are off-limits to visitors.)

Although most of Coober Pedy's devotions are decidedly material in nature, the town does have its share of spiritual houses of worship. Keeping with the town's layout, they, too, are underground. **St. Peter and St. Paul's Catholic Church** is a National Heritage–listed building, and the **Catacomb Anglican Church** is notable for its altar fashioned from a windlass (a winch) and lectern made from a log of mulga wood. The **Serbian Orthodox Church** is striking, with its scalloped ceiling, rock-carved icons, and brilliant stained-glass windows. The **Revival Fellowship Underground Church,** adjacent to the Experience Motel, has lively gospel services.

Goanna Land (⊠ Lot 374 Post Office Hill Rd. ☎ 08/8672–5965), an arts-and-crafts shop at Underground Books, rents clubs for A$10 and arranges play at the 18-hole, par-72 Coober Pedy Golf Club (A$10 per round). Instead of greens, be prepared for oil and red sand.

★ The **Old Timers Mine** is a genuine opal mine turned into a museum. Two underground houses, furnished in 1920s and 1980s styles, are part of the complex, where mining equipment and memorabilia are exhibited in an extensive network of hand-dug tunnels and shafts. Tours are self-guided. ⊠ *Crowders Gully Rd. near Umoona Rd.* ☎☎ *08/8672–5555* ⊕ *www.oldtimersmine.com* ☜ *A$10* ⊙ *Daily 9–5.*

Umoona Opal Mine and Museum is an enormous underground complex with an original mine, a noteworthy video on the history of opal mining, an Aboriginal Interpretive Centre, and clean, underground bunk camping and cooking facilities. Guided tours of the mine are available. ⊠ *14 Hutchison St.* ☎ *08/8672–5288* ⊕ *www.umoonaopalmine.com.au* ☜ *Tour A$10* ⊙ *Daily 8–7; tours at 10, 2, and 4.*

Around Town

Breakaways, a striking series of buttes and jagged hills centered on the Moon Plain, is reminiscent of the American West. There are fossils and patches of petrified forest in this strange landscape, which has appealed to makers of apocalyptic films. *Mad Max 3—Beyond Thunderdome* was filmed around here, as was *Ground Zero.* The scenery is especially evocative early in the morning. The Breakaways area is 30 km (19 mi) northeast of Coober Pedy.

Fodor'sChoice
★ The Coober Pedy–Oodnadatta **Mail Run Tour** (⊠ Post Office Hill Rd. ☎ 08/ 8672–5226 or 1800/069911 ⊕ www.mailruntour.com), a 12-hour, 600-km (372-mi) tour through the Outback (A$145), is one of the most unusual experiences anywhere. Former miner–turned–entrepreneur Peter Rowe runs the twice-weekly tour, delivering mail and supplies to remote cattle stations and Outback towns like Anna Creek, the world's largest cattle ranch, and William Creek, population 12. You also get a good look at the Dog Fence, and at the dingoes it was built to keep away. Be

sure to stop by the **Transcontinental Hotel** in Oodnadatta—proprietors Bev and Alan are happy to share their resident orphan baby kangaroos for a cuddle and a photo. Tours depart at 8:45 AM from the Underground Book Shop on Post Office Hill Road.

Martin's Night Sky Presentation (☎ 08/8672–5223 ⊕ www. martinsmithsnightsky.com.au) is a one-hour introduction to the southern sky, including the famous Southern Cross constellation depicted on the Australian flag. Ideal for beginners and suitable for all ages, the show takes place at the Moon Plain Desert, about 6 km (4 mi) outside of Coober Pedy. Martin will pick you up at your hotel immediately after dark. Trips are A$25.

Where to Stay & Eat

$–$$ ✗ **Umberto's.** Perched atop the monolithic Desert Cave Hotel, this eatery named after the hotel's founding developer is Coober Pedy's most urbane restaurant. The Outback's softer hues and more colorful wildlife are seen in the prints of native birds that decorate the walls. There are many Italian dishes on the menu, as well as more exotic modern Australian fare. ✉ Hutchison St. ☎ 08/8672–5688 ⊟ AE, DC, MC, V ⊘ No lunch.

¢–$ ✗ **Ampol Restaurant.** Although it's right by the bus station, this is no ordinary station diner. Hearty Aussie favorites like pasties (pastry-wrapped vegetables and meat) and schnitzel, plus top wines and beer, are served in an airy, glass-fronted restaurant. Locals come for breakfast, and there's even a shaded beer garden in which to wash down the desert dust. ✉ Hutchison St. near Malliotis Blvd. ☎ 08/8672–5199 ⊟ MC, V.

¢–$ ✗ **Stuart Range Caravan Park Pizza Bar.** Locals swear that the pizzas at this popular Caravan Park are among Australia's best. The toppings combinations can be classic or creative, such as the Noon (with tomato, mushrooms, and onions) and the Mexicana (with hot peppers). ✉ Stuart Hwy. and Hutchison St. ☎ 08/8672–5179 ⊟ MC, V.

$$ ▦ **Desert Cave Hotel.** What may be the world's only underground hotel presents a contemporary, blocky face to the desert town. In the 19 spacious, subsurface rooms, luxurious furnishings in Outback hues complement and contrast the red striated rock walls that protect sleepers from sound and heat. Aboveground rooms are also available. The hotel has an excellent interpretive center and offers daily tours of the town and surrounding sights. ✉ Hutchison St. and Post Office Hill Rd., 5723 ☎ 08/8672–5688 or 1800/088521 ⊟ 08/8672–5198 ⊕ www. desertcave.com.au ⋫ 50 rooms ⚴ Restaurant, café, room service, IDD phones, in-room data ports, minibars, refrigerators, room TVs with movies, pool, gym, sauna, hot tub, bar, shops, laundry facilities, Internet room, convention center, travel services, free parking, no-smoking rooms; no a/c in some rooms ⊟ AE, DC, MC, V.

$ ▦ **Mud Hut Motel.** Mud brick is the building material used here, and desert hues in the guest rooms continue the earthy theme. Two-bedroom apartments have cooking facilities. One unit is available for travelers with disabilities. The à la carte restaurant has outside dining and serves international fare. ✉ Lot 102 St. Nicholas St., 5723 ☎ 08/8672–3003, 1800/646962 South Australia and Northern Territory only ⊟ 08/ 8672–3004 ⊕ www.mudhutmotel.com.au ⋫ 24 rooms, 4 apartments

⛢ *Restaurant, room service, IDD phones, some kitchenettes, some microwaves, refrigerators, in-room DVD, bar, shop, laundry facilities, Internet room, car rental, travel services, free parking, no-smoking rooms* ▤ *AE, DC, MC, V.*

¢–$ ▦ **Opal Inn.** This combined hotel and motel, owned by the same folks who run the Desert Cave, is the place to meet Coober Pedy characters and opal buyers. You can chat with them over a drink in the bistro (a favorite local gathering spot) or play a game of pool on one of two tables. The lodgings include some in-house, pub-style rooms with shared bathrooms; some courtyard budget rooms with private baths; standard motel rooms; and family suites. You can also pitch a tent or bring your camper. ⊠ *Hutchison and Wright Sts., 5723* ☎ *08/8672–5054 or 1800/088523* 🖷 *08/8672–5501* ⊕ *www.opalinn.com.au* ⌁ *55 powered campsites, 10 tent sites, 12 hotel rooms, 12 budget rooms, 75 motel rooms, 2 family suites* ⛢ *Restaurant, some IDD phones, refrigerators, some in-room data ports, 3 bars, shop, laundry facilities, Internet room, business services, meeting rooms, travel services, free parking, no-smoking rooms; no phones in some rooms, no TV in some rooms* ▤ *AE, DC, MC, V.*

¢ ▦ **Radeka's Downunder.** Part backpackers' accommodation, part underground motel, this desert compound is a hit among travelers because of its many facilities. Quiet family motel rooms that sleep up to eight, an on-site video library, communal kitchen, Internet kiosks, and a billiards table in a bar 30 feet below street level make it a good base for touring. Backpackers have a private lounge and access to outdoor areas. The daily tours to the Breakaways (A$40) are excellent. ⊠ *Oliver & Hutchison Sts., 5723* ☎ *08/8672–5223, 1800/633891 South Australia and Northern Territory only* 🖷 *08/8672–5821* ⊕ *www.radekadownunder. com.au* ⌁ *22 rooms, 12 with shared bath* ⛢ *Some kitchenettes, some refrigerators, billiards, bar, laundry facilities, Internet room, car rental, travel services, free parking, no-smoking rooms; no a/c in some rooms, no room phones, no TV in some rooms* ▤ *AE, MC, V.*

¢ ▦ **Underground Motel.** The Breakaways sometimes seem close enough to touch at this hilltop motel, where you can lounge on a veranda watching the sun set on the rock formations 30 km (19 mi) across the desert. Each room is uniquely shaped, comfortably furnished, and decorated with Aboriginal designs. Two secluded suites have kitchenette facilities, and main rooms share a communal kitchen. A complimentary light breakfast is provided. ⊠ *1185 Catacomb Rd., 5723* ☎ *08/ 8672–5324 or 1800/622979* 🖷 *08/8672–5911* ✉ *elsaunderground@sa86.net* ⌁ *6 rooms, 2 suites* ⛢ *BBQs, IDD phones, fans, some kitchenettes, some microwaves, some refrigerators, some in-room VCRs, playground, laundry facilities, car rental, travel services, free parking, some pets allowed; no a/c, no smoking* ▤ *AE, DC, MC, V* ❍ *CP.*

Shopping

More than 30 shops sell opals in Coober Pedy. The **Opal Cave** (⊠ Hutchison St. ☎ 08/8672–5028) has a huge opal display, arts and crafts, and adjoining B&B accommodations within one neat, self-contained unit. The **Opal Cutter** (⊠ 880 Post Office Hill Rd. 🖷🖷 08/8672–3086) has stones valued from A$7 to A$25,000. Displays of opal cutting can be requested. You can see the world's largest opal matrix at the **Opal Factory** (✉ Hutchison St. ☎ 08/8672–5300).

Underground Books (✉ Lot 374 Post Office Hill Rd. ☎ 08/8672–5558) has an excellent selection of reading material, arts, and crafts, but the best buy is a postcard by local photographer Peter Caust, who captures the essence of the desert landscape. This is also the booking office for the Coober Pedy–Oodnadatta Mail Run Tour.

Underground Potteries (✉ Off 17 Mile Rd. ☎ 08/8672–5226), adjacent to the golf course, is owned by Peter Rowe, who also created the Mail Run Tour. Watch potters in basement studios creating handmade products, then walk up and buy them in the main gallery.

Flinders Ranges National Park

690 km (430 mi) southeast of Coober Pedy, 460 km (285 mi) northeast of Adelaide.

Extending north from Spencer Gulf, the mountain chain of the Flinders Ranges includes one of the most impressive Outback parks in the country. These dry, craggy mountain peaks, once the bed of an ancient sea, have been cracked, folded, and sculpted by millions of years of rain and sun. Cypress pine and casuarina cover this furrowed landscape of deep valleys, which slope into creeks lined with river red gums. The area is utterly fascinating—both for geologists and for anyone else who revels in wild, raw scenery and exotic plant and animal life.

★ The scenic center of the Flinders Ranges is **Wilpena Pound,** an 80-square-km (31-square-mi) bowl ringed by hills that curve gently upward, only to fall away from the rims of sheer cliffs. The only entrance to the Pound is a narrow cleft through which Wilpena Creek sometimes runs. A mud-brick **Visitor Centre** (✉ Wilpena Rd. ☎ 08/8648–0048), part of the Wilpena Pound Resort, has information about hiking trails and campsites within the park.

The numerous steep trails make the Flinders Ranges ideal for bushwalking, even though the park has few amenities. Water in this region is scarce and should be carried at all times. The best time for walking is during the relatively cool months between April and October. This is also the wettest time of year, so you should be prepared for rain. Wildflowers, including the spectacular Sturt's desert pea, are abundant between September and late October.

The park's most spectacular walking trail leads to the summit of 3,840-foot **St. Mary's Peak,** the highest point on the Pound's rim and the second-tallest peak in South Australia. The more scenic of the two routes to the summit is the outside trail (15 km [9 mi] return); give yourself a full day to get up and back. The final ascent is difficult, but views from the top—including the distant white glitter of the salt flats on Lake Frome—make the climb worthwhile. ✉ *End of Wilpena Rd., 156 km (97 mi) off Princes Hwy., via town of Hawker* ☎ *08/8648–4244* ⊕ *www. flinders.outback.on.net.*

Where to Stay

★ $–$$ ⊞ **Wilpena Pound Resort.** This popular resort at the entrance to Wilpena Pound has chalets (10 with kitchenettes); well-equipped, spacious motel-style rooms; and backpacker units, as well as permanent tents and campsites with and without electrical hookups. Kangaroos frolic on the lawn by the kidney-shape pool to the sound track of birds singing and chirping. A licensed restaurant serves meals throughout the day, and you can stock up on goods at the small supermarket. The resort runs four-wheel-drive tours, guided walks, and scenic flights, and the visitor center is a major attraction. You couldn't ask for a more idyllic and civilized nature outpost. ⊠ *End of Wilpena Rd., Wilpena Pound 5434, 156 km (97 mi) off the Princes Hwy. via the town of Hawker* ☎ *08/8648–0004* 🖷 *08/8648–0028* 🌐 *www.wilpenapound.com.au* 🖙 *34 rooms, 26 chalets* ♿ *2 restaurants, grocery, BBQs, some kitchenettes, some microwaves, refrigerators, room TVs with movies, pool, hiking, bar, shops, laundry facilities, Internet room, travel services, free parking; no room phones, no smoking* ▭ *AE, DC, MC, V.*

The Outback A to Z

AIR TRAVEL

REX/Regional Express Airlines flies direct to Coober Pedy from Adelaide daily, except Saturday. Because it's the only public carrier flying to Coober Pedy, prices are sometimes steep. However, anyone holding a valid ISIC, YHA, or VIP card is eligible for unlimited air travel throughout Australia on the Backpackers pass for a flat rate of A$499 for one month, or A$949 for two months.

🖪 **Airport Coober Pedy Airport** ⊠ Stuart Hwy, 2 km (1 mi) north of town Coober Pedy ☎ 08/8672–5688 Desert Cave Hotel.

🖪 **Airline REX/Regional Express** ☎ 13–1713 🌐 www.rex.com.au.

BUS TRAVEL

Greyhound Australia buses leave Adelaide's Central Bus Terminal for Coober Pedy daily. Tickets for the 12-hour ride cost A$129 each way. Premier Stateliner's Friday-morning bus from the Central Bus Terminal to Port Augusta ($39.70 one-way) links with the Gulf Getaways bus to Wilpena Pound at Flinders Ranges National Park via Quorn ($40 one-way). The total journey takes 6½ hours.

🖪 **Greyhound Australia** ☎ 13–1499 🌐 www.greyhound.com.au. **Gulf Getaways** ☎ 0408–445133 or 1800/170170. **Premier Stateliner** ☎ 08/8415–5555 🌐 www. premierstateliner.com.au.

CAR TRAVEL

The main road to Coober Pedy is the Stuart Highway from Adelaide, 850 km (527 mi) to the south. Alice Springs is 700 km (434 mi) north of Coober Pedy. The drive from Adelaide to Coober Pedy takes about nine hours. From Alice Springs it's about seven hours.

A rental car enables you to see what lies beyond Hutchison Street, but an organized tour is a much better way to do so. Budget is the only rental-car outlet in Coober Pedy. Although some roads are unpaved—those to the Breakaways and the Dog Fence, for example—surfaces are generally suitable for conventional vehicles. Check on road conditions with the police if there has been substantial rain.

The most interesting route to Flinders Ranges National Park from Adelaide takes you north through the Clare Valley vineyards and Burra's copper-mining villages. For a more direct journey to Wilpena Pound, follow the Princes Highway north to Port Augusta, and then head east toward Quorn and Hawker. A four-wheel-drive vehicle is highly recommended for traveling on the many gravel roads around the national park.

🚗 **Budget** ☎ 08/8672-5333 or 1300/362848.

EMERGENCIES

In an emergency, dial **000** to reach an ambulance, the police, or the fire department. There are hospitals with accident and emergency departments in Coober Pedy and in Hawker, the nearest town to Wilpena Pound.

🚗 **Hospitals Coober Pedy Hospital** ✉ Hospital Rd., Coober Pedy ☎ 08/8672-5009. **Great Northern War Memorial Hospital** ✉ Craddock St., Hawker ☎ 08/8648-4007.

MONEY MATTERS

There are banks in Coober Pedy and Hawker with currency exchange facilities. The larger Outback towns and some accommodations, such as Wilpena Pound Resort, have ATMs.

🚗 **Banks ANZ** ✉ 11 Wilpena Rd., Hawker ☎ 13-1314. **Westpac** ✉ Lot 1 Hutchison St., Coober Pedy ☎ 13-2032.

VISITOR INFORMATION

The Coober Pedy Visitor Information Centre is open weekdays 8:30–5. More information about national parks can be obtained through the Department for Environment and Heritage, or from the Wilpena Pound Visitor Centre.

🚗 **Coober Pedy Visitor Information Centre** ✉ Coober Pedy District Council Bldg., Hutchison St., Coober Pedy ☎ 08/8672-5298 or 1800/637076 ⊕ www.opalcapitaloftheworld.com.au. **Department for Environment and Heritage** ✉ 77 Grenfell St., City Center, Adelaide ☎ 08/8204-1910 ⊕ www.environment.sa.gov.au/parks/outback.html. **Wilpena Pound Visitor Centre** ✉ Wilpena Rd., Wilpena Pound ☎ 08/8648-0048.

The Red Centre

WORD OF MOUTH

"Ayers Rock has a wonderful spiritual feel to it. The Aborigines are an integral part of the area's tourism, and this adds greatly to the experience. The spirit of the place does not get lost in commercialism, and I was glad to know that development is limited to preserve the sacredness of the area."

—nibblette

"You cannot tell from the one picture of Uluru (Ayer's Rock) how stunning and varied the features of the rock are. There are no images of these because they are sacred to the aboriginal people, who ask that photos not be taken."

—kerikeri

Updated by
Caroline
Gladstone

THE LUMINESCENT LIGHT OF THE RED CENTRE—named for the deep color of its desert soils—has a purity and vitality that photographs only begin to approach. For tens of thousands of years, this vast desert territory has been home to Australia's indigenous Aboriginal people. Uluru, also known as Ayers Rock, is a great symbol in Aboriginal traditions, as are many sacred sites among the Centre's mountain ranges, gorges, dry riverbeds, and spinifex plains. At the center of all this lies Alice Springs, Australia's only desert city.

The essence of this ancient land is epitomized in the paintings of the renowned Aboriginal landscape artist Albert Namatjira and his followers. Viewed away from the desert, their images of the MacDonnell Ranges may appear at first to be garish and unreal in their depiction of purple-and-red mountain ranges and stark-white ghost gum trees. Seeing the real thing makes it difficult to imagine executing the paintings in any other way.

Uluru (pronounced oo-loo-*roo*), that magnificent stone monolith rising from the plains, is but one focus in the Red Centre. The rounded forms of Kata Tjuta (*ka*-ta *tchoo*-ta), also known as the Olgas, are another. Watarrka National Park and Kings Canyon, Mt. Conner, and the cliffs, gorges, and mountain chains of the MacDonnell Ranges are other worlds to explore.

Exploring the Red Centre

The primary areas of interest are Alice Springs, which is flanked by the intriguing eastern and western MacDonnell Ranges; Kings Canyon; and Uluru–Kata Tjuta National Park, with neighboring Ayers Rock Resort. Unless you have more than three days, focus on only one of these areas.

To reach the Red Centre, you can fly from most large Australian cities into either Alice Springs or from Sydney direct to Ayers Rock Resort. You can also fly the 440 km (273 mi) between the two centers. By rail, you can take one of the world's classic train journeys from Adelaide to Alice Springs (16 hours) and Darwin (23 hours) on the *Ghan*, named after the Afghan camel-train drivers who once traveled the Adelaide–Alice Springs route.

Bus tours run between all Red Centre sites, as well as between Alice and Ayers Rock Resort. The best way to get around, though, is by car, and vehicles can be rented at Alice Springs and Ayers Rock Resort. The Central Australian Tourism Industry Association in Alice Springs books tours and rental cars, and provides motoring information.

About the Restaurants

Restaurants in Alice Springs and at Ayers Rock Resort surprise visitors with fabulous produce, innovative cuisine, and such unusual Australian dishes as crocodile, kangaroo, and camel. Meals are often served with local fruits, berries, and plants. Definitely try this "bush tucker," perhaps within the pioneer setting of a saloon or steak house.

Whatever your dining style, you'll find it in Alice Springs, where the streets are lined with everything from fast-food chains and pubs to stylish cafés and quality hotel restaurants. Ayers Rock Resort, on the other hand, groups together a campsite and six different hotels, most of which have their own restaurant. The resort also has barbecue areas where you can cook your own meals. If you can, be sure to book the prime Ayers Rock dining experience, the unforgettable Sounds of Silence dinner in the desert under the stars. At Kings Canyon you can take the similar, couples-only Sounds of Starlight dining tour.

WHAT IT COSTS In Australian Dollars				
	$$$$	**$$$**	**$$**	**$**	**¢**
AT DINNER	over $50	$36–$50	$21–$35	$10–$20	under $10

Prices are for a main course at dinner.

About the Hotels

Alice Springs has all kinds of accommodation choices: youth hostels and motels, a casino-hotel, and top-quality resorts. Caravan and camping parks are also popular, and have numerous facilities and even entertainment. The Ayers Rock Resort hotel complex—which is the only place to stay in the vicinity of Uluṟu–Kata Tjuṯa National Park—is actually a group of seven different accommodations with different price ranges, all of which are managed by Voyages Hotels and Resorts. Homesteads and cattle stations also abound, and you can stay on the ranch or camp on the property.

The high season runs from April to September, so book ahead during this time. The Central Australian Tourism Industry Association in Alice Springs has hotel details, and Voyages Hotels and Resorts handles Ayers Rock Resort bookings. Ask about low-season discounts.

WHAT IT COSTS In Australian Dollars				
	$$$$	**$$$**	**$$**	**$**	**¢**
FOR 2 PEOPLE	over $300	$201–$300	$151–$200	$100–$150	under $100

Prices are for two people in a standard double room in high season, including tax and service, based on the European Plan (with no meals) unless otherwise noted.

Timing

May through September are the best months to visit, as nights are crisp and cold, and days are pleasantly warm. Summer temperatures—which can rise above 43°C (110°F)—make hiking and exploring uncomfortable. The third Saturday of September brings the Henley-on-Todd Regatta in Alice Springs, a colorful race along the dry Todd River bed where the racers scamper along inside bottomless boats. Camel jockeys race around a sand track at the **Alice Springs Camel Cup Carnival** on the second Saturday in July. The Bangtail Muster cattle and float parade wanders along Alice's main street on May Day. National parks are open daily year-round, but a handful of attractions close during the hot summer months.

It doesn't take long for the desert's beauty to capture your heart. Still, allow yourself enough time in the Red Centre to really let it soak in. If you don't fly directly to Ayers Rock Resort, start in Alice Springs, which also has spectacular scenery. Poke in and around town for a couple of days, then head out to the nearby hills.

If you have 3 days

You can hardly ignore one of Australia's great icons: Uluru. Drive straight down from Alice Springs to **Ayers Rock Resort** for lunch, followed by a circuit of the rock and a look at the **Uluru–Kata Tjuta Cultural Centre** near its base. Spend the night, then make an early start to catch dawn at **Kata Tjuta** before exploring its extraordinary domes. End the day with sunset at the rock, then return to Alice Springs for the second night via the **Henbury Meteorite Craters.** If you fly in and out of Ayers Rock Resort and have more time, take the final day for a Mala or Uluru Experience walk and a flightseeing tour of the area.

10

If you opt to spend your days around **Alice Springs,** stay in town the first morning to walk around the city center and shops. In the afternoon, head out to the **Alice Springs Desert Park** or **Alice Springs Telegraph Station Historical Reserve.** Spend the night, then drive out into either the eastern or western MacDonnell Ranges to explore the gorges and gaps and dip into a water hole. Overnight at **Glen Helen Resort.** Make your way back to town through the western MacDonnells scenery on the third day.

If you have 5 days

Take in the best of Alice Springs and the MacDonnell Ranges before heading down to Uluru, with a detour to Rainbow Valley. To see more of the desert, start out in Uluru as in the above itinerary, but head west to **Watarrka National Park** for a day and two nights exploring **Kings Canyon** with one of the Aboriginal guided tours. Surprisingly little-visited, the canyon is one of central Australia's hidden wonders. Stop by **Mt. Conner,** which looks like Uluru except that it's flat on top.

If you have 7 days

Start with three days in and around **Alice Springs,** then two days and a night in **Watarrka National Park.** For the remaining two days, knock around **Uluru–Kata Tjuta National Park,** leaving yourself at least a few hours for absorbing the majesty of the desert. Fly out from the resort to your next destination.

ALICE SPRINGS

Once a ramshackle collection of dusty streets and buildings, Alice Springs—known colloquially as "the Alice"—is today an incongruously suburban tourist center with a population of 27,000 in the middle of the desert. The town's ancient sites, a focus for the Arrernte Aboriginal tribe's ceremonial activities, lie cheek by jowl with air-conditioned shops and hotels. The MacDonnell Ranges dominate Alice Springs, changing color according to the time of day from brick red to purple. Another striking feature of the town is the Todd River. Water rarely runs in the desert, and the Todd's deep sandy beds, fringed by majestic ghost gum trees, suggest a timelessness far different from the bustle of the nearby town.

Until the 1970s the Alice was a frontier town servicing the region's pastoral industry, and life was tough. During World War II it was one of the few (barely) inhabited stops on the 3,024-km (1,875-mi) supply lines between Adelaide and the front line at Darwin. First established at the Old Telegraph Station as the town of Stuart, it was moved and renamed Alice Springs—after the wife of the telegraph boss Charles Todd—in 1933.

Exploring Alice Springs

Numbers in the margin correspond to points of interest on the Alice Springs map.

a good walk

Anzac Hill ❶ ▶, the highest point in Alice Springs, is the ideal place to start a walking tour. After taking in the views south to the MacDonnell Ranges, walk down the path on the town side of the hill. From the base, head east along Wills Terrace to the Todd River. If you walk partway across the raised footbridge and look up and down the broad, usually dry, sandy riverbed, you might be hard-pressed to imagine it swirling with muddy water—but rare flash floods do close both the road below and the raised walkway. Backtrack to Leichhardt Terrace and stroll south among the wonderfully colored and textured ghost gums along the river.

At Parsons Street, turn right (west), then left at the shade awnings into Todd Mall, Alice Springs' main shopping precinct. Wander past the cafés and Aboriginal art galleries, and down the mall to the **Adelaide House Museum ❷**, the town's first hospital. Continue down Todd Street to the **Aboriginal Art & Culture Centre ❸**, where you can learn to play the didgeridoo. Keep walking south to Stuart Terrace. Three short blocks west is the **Royal Flying Doctor Service ❹**, an Australian icon that provides medical care to residents across some 2 million square km (772,000 square mi) of Outback. Opposite is the **Alice Springs Reptile Centre ❺**. Turn back along Stuart Terrace and turn up Hartley Street, noting the row of historic 1930s government buildings on your immediate left. In the next block, on the right, is **Panorama Guth ❻**, a unique circular indoor mural that depicts many of the natural features of the Red Centre. Continuing north brings you to the **Old Hartley Street School ❼**, and beyond it to the Parsons Street intersection. Behind the hedge on the southeast corner is the Old Residency (closed to the public), built in 1927 for John Cawood, the first government resident to be appointed to central Australia. Behind the opposite hedge is the **Old Courthouse ❽**, home to the National Pioneer Women's Hall of Fame. Detour about 40 yards west up Parsons Street to **Old Stuart Town Gaol ❾**, the oldest surviving building in Alice Springs.

TIMING Four hours will cover the sights on this walk. It's a comfortable stroll all day in winter (approximately May–September), but it's best done early morning in summer (November–February). Several sights close in summer.

10

Aboriginal Art & Legends

Virtually all the natural features in the Red Centre—and particularly around Uluṟu (Ayers Rock), Kata Tjuṯa (the Olgas), and Watarrka (Kings Canyon)—play a part in the Aboriginal creation legend, often referred to as the Dreamtime. The significance of these sacred sites is best discovered on a walking tour led by Aboriginal guides, who will also introduce you to such true Outback bush tucker as witchetty grubs. There are ancient Aboriginal rock paintings inside caves at Uluṟu's base and in N'Dhala Gorge, while rock carvings abound in Ewaninga Rock Carvings Conservation Reserve. Aboriginal crafts include beautiful dot paintings, wood carvings, baskets, and didgeridoos.

Amazing Geology

Uluṟu and Kata Tjuṯa are the Red Centre's most fascinating geological features, but there are many more natural wonders—evidence of past inland seas, of uplift and erosion, and of cataclysmic events. One particularly violent occurrence was the crash-landing of a meteor 140 million years ago, which created the spectacular 5-km-wide (3-mi-wide) Gosse Bluff. In the MacDonnell Ranges, gorges and plunging chasms cradle crystal-clear water holes, while oases of thousands of cabbage palms thrive in Palm Valley. Towering red walls and sheer quartzite cliffs make spectacular scenery for hikes like the breathtaking Kings Canyon rim walk. Other impressive land forms are Rainbow Valley, the Mt. Conner mesa near Ayers Rock Resort, and the 164-foot, red-and-yellow sandstone Chamber's Pillar south of Alice Springs.

Desert Camping

Sleeping in the desert under a full moon and the Milky Way is an experience that you will carry with you for the rest of your life. Few travelers realize that far more stars and other astronomical sights, like the fascinating Magellanic Clouds, are visible in the southern hemisphere than in the northern. Nights can be very cold in winter, but the native mulga wood makes for terrific fires, burning hot and long for cooking and for curling up beside in your sleeping bag—a tent is unnecessary. To avoid ants, make your campsite in a dry, sandy riverbed, preferably near a grove of tall ghost gums for shade in the daytime.

Outback Grub

"Bush tucker" and "Territory tucker" best describe the unique dishes found on Red Centre menus—be they concoctions made with kangaroo, emu, and crocodile, or desert fruits and flavorings. Picnics are a delight in the Outback, where national parks provide spectacular backdrops for outdoor meals in the shade of a gum tree or by a water hole. But perhaps the most unique dining experience in the Red Centre is riding a camel along a dry creek bed or across desert sands and then taking your meal by campfire light.

Photo Opportunities

Landscape photography in the Red Centre is challenging and rewarding. Amazing light and intense colors change through the day, and sunset at Uluṟu is but one of hundreds of panoramic sights that will inspire you to pick up your camera. Heat and dust can be a problem, so be sure to bring insulated, dust-proof bags for your cameras and film stock. Also bring a good UV filter to deflect the fierce light of midday.

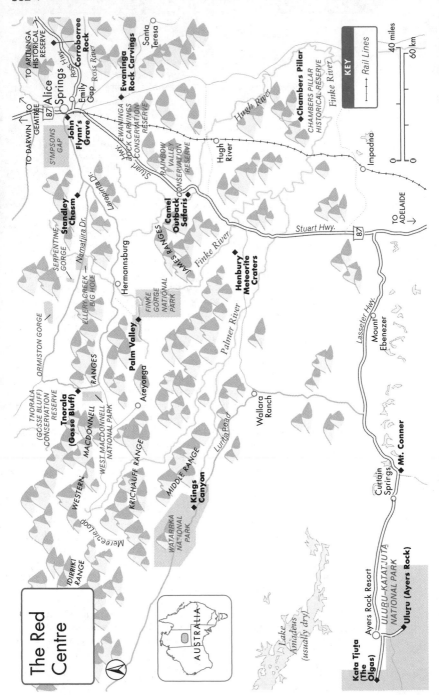

The Red Centre

What to See: City Center

❸ Aboriginal Art & Culture Centre. You can learn all about Arrernte Aboriginal culture and music in this gallery of western desert art and artifacts. Try playing the didgeridoo at the music school, or wandering through the Living History Museum. The Centre also runs half-day cultural tours of the Alice Springs region. ⊠ *125 Todd St.* ☎ *08/8952–3408* ⊕ *www.aboriginalaustralia.com* ▦ *Free* ⊙ *Daily 8–5.*

❷ Adelaide House Museum. This was the first hospital in Alice Springs, designed by the Reverend John Flynn and run by the Australian Inland Mission (which Flynn founded) from 1926 to 1939. An ingenious system of air tunnels and wet burlap bags once cooled the hospital rooms in hot weather. The building is now a museum devoted to the mission and pioneering days in Alice Springs. The stone hut at the rear was the site of the first field radio transmission in 1926, which made viable Flynn's concept of a flying doctor. The Royal Flying Doctor Service continues to maintain its "mantle of safety" all over Australia's remote settlements. ⊠ *Todd Mall* ☎ *08/8952–1856* ▦ *A$4* ⊙ *Mar.–Nov., weekdays 10–4, weekends 10–noon.*

❺ Alice Springs Reptile Centre. Thorny devils, frill-neck lizards, and some of the world's deadliest snakes inhabit this park in the heart of town, opposite the Royal Flying Doctor Service. Viewing is best from May to August when the reptiles are most active. You can even feed the snakes by hand and pick up the pythons. ⊠ *9 Stuart Terr.* ☎ *08/8952–8900* ⊕ *www.reptilecentre.com.au* ▦ *A$9* ⊙ *Daily 9:30–5.*

❶ Anzac Hill. North of downtown, Anzac Hill has an excellent view of Alice Springs and the surrounding area, including the MacDonnell Ranges. From atop the hill you can see that Todd Mall, the heart of Alice Springs, is just one block west of the Todd River, which at best flows only every few years. To reach the top, head up Lions Walk, which starts opposite the Catholic church on Wills Terrace downtown.

❽ Old Courthouse. This ex-government building's wide, simple rooflines are typical of pioneer-era architecture. The building houses the National Pioneer Women's Hall of Fame, dedicated to Australia's women. Founded in 1993 by Molly Clark, owner of Old Andado Station cattle station 200 km (124 mi) southeast of Alice Springs, the hall includes photographs and memorabilia of pioneering central Australian women. ⊠ *27 Hartley St.* ☎ *08/8952–9006* ⊕ *www.pioneerwomen.com.au* ▦ *A$2.20* ⊙ *Daily 10–5.*

❼ Old Hartley Street School. Alas, little remains here that recalls the blackboards and lift-top desks in use in 1930, when Mrs. Ida Standley was the school's first teacher, but it's worth a peek anyway. The school is also the headquarters of the Alice Springs National Trust branch, and brochures on local sights are available. ⊠ *Hartley St. between Parsons St. and Gregory Terr.* ☎ *08/8952–4516* ▦ *Free* ⊙ *Feb.–Nov., weekdays 10–2.*

❾ Old Stuart Town Gaol. The 1908 jail is the oldest surviving building in Alice Springs—and it looks it. With almost no air coming through the jail's tiny barred windows, imprisonment here on a long, hot summer

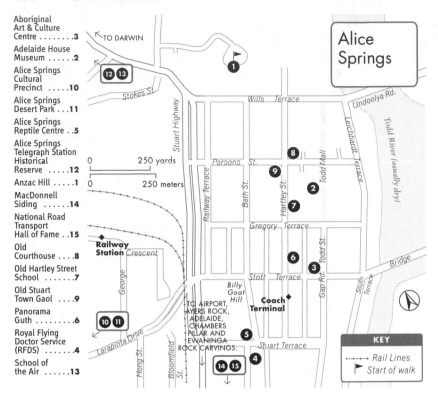

day must have been punishment indeed. ⊠ *Parsons St. next to the police station* 🖅 *A$3* ⊙ *Mar.–Nov., weekdays 10–12:30, Sat. 9:30–noon.*

❻ Panorama Guth. Dutch artist Henk Guth found canvases too restrictive for his vision of central Australia, so he painted his panoramic, unstintingly realistic landscape paintings in the round. Panorama Guth, inside an unusual crenellated building, has a circumference of 200 feet and stands 20 feet high. There's also a collection of Aboriginal artifacts downstairs. ⊠ *65 Hartley St.* 🕿 *08/8952–2013* 🖅 *A$5.50* ⊙ *Feb.–Nov., Mon.–Sat. 9–5, Sun. noon–5.*

❹ Royal Flying Doctor Service (RFDS). Directed from this RFDS radio base, doctors use aircraft to make house calls on settlements and homes hundreds of miles apart. Like the School of the Air, the RFDS is a vital part of Outback life. The visitor center has historical displays and an audiovisual show. Tours run every half hour throughout the year. ⊠ *8–10 Stuart Terr.* 🕿 *08/8952–1129* ⊕ *www.rfds.org.au* 🖅 *A$6.50* ⊙ *Mon.–Sat. 9–4, Sun. 1–4.*

Todd Mall. Cafés, galleries, banks, and tourist shops line this pedestrian area, the heart of Alice Springs. ⊠ *Todd St. between Wills and Gregory Terrs.*

Around Alice Springs

★ ❿ **Alice Springs Cultural Precinct.** The most distinctive building in this complex is the multiroof Museum of Central Australia. Anthropologist Theodor Strehlow (1908–78) grew up with and later spent many years studying the Arrernte (Aranda) Aborigines of central Australia. Exhibits include a skeleton of the 10½-foot-tall duck relative Dromornis stirtoni, the largest bird to walk on earth, which was found northeast of Alice. Also in the precinct are the Aviation Museum, the Araluen Galleries, and the Namatjira Gallery, with a collection of renowned Aboriginal landscapes. The precinct is 2 km (1 mi) southwest of town and is on the Alice Wanderer tourist bus itinerary. ⊠ *61 Larapinta Dr.* ☎ *08/8951–1120* ⊕ *www.nt.gov.au/dam* ▱ *A$9* ◷ *Daily 10–5.*

★ ☽ ⓫ **Alice Springs Desert Park.** This combined zoo, botanic gardens, and museum makes a fun and educational stop on the way to the western ranges. Focusing on the desert, which makes up 70% of the Australian landmass, the 75-acre site presents 320 types of plants and 120 animal species in several Australian ecosystems—including the largest nocturnal house in the Southern Hemisphere. The park is 6½ km (4 mi) west of Alice Springs and is on the Alice Wanderer bus itinerary. ⊠ *Larapinta Dr.* ☎ *08/8951–8788* ⊕ *www.alicespringsdesertpark.com.au* ▱ *A$19* ◷ *Daily 7:30–6.*

⓬ **Alice Springs Telegraph Station Historical Reserve.** The first white settlement in the area was at this reserve 3 km (2 mi) north of Alice Springs, beside the original freshwater spring named after the wife of Charles Todd. As the South Australian Superintendent of Telegraphs, Todd planned and supervised construction of 12 repeater stations—including this one—along the telegraph line to Darwin, completed in 1872. The restored telegraph-station buildings evoke the Red Centre as it was at the turn of the 20th century. Within the buildings, exhibits of station life and a display of early photographs chronicle its history. A scenic walking and cycling path runs along the Todd River between Alice Springs and the reserve. ⊠ *Stuart Hwy.* ☎ *08/8952–3993* ▱ *A$7* ◷ *Daily 8–5.*

⓮ **MacDonnell Siding.** Set on an old section of rail line, this station 10 km (6 mi) south of Alice Springs is the resting place of the restored *Old Ghan,* a train named for the Afghans who led camel trains on the route from Adelaide. The train began passenger service to Alice Springs on August 6, 1929, and over the next 51 years it provided a vital, if erratic, link with the south. In times of flood it could take up to three months to complete the journey. Today the *Ghan* uses modern trains to connect towns between Adelaide and Darwin.

The site comprises a museum chockfull of *Ghan* memorabilia, and original rolling stock. You can even climb aboard steam and diesel locomotives. The Alice Wanderer bus stops here. ⊠ *Stuart Hwy.* ☎ *08/8955–5047* ▱ *A$5.50* ◷ *Mar.–Oct., Mon., Wed., Fri., and Sun. 9–3:30.*

⓯ **National Road Transport Hall of Fame.** Wander among exhibits of the huge road trains, which replaced the camel trains that formerly hauled supplies and equipment through central Australia. Look for the first road train, which arrived from England in 1934. A 1942 former U.S. Army

Diamond T, the first commercially operated cattle train, is also on display. Adjoining MacDonnell Siding, but separately run, this museum is 10 km (6 mi) south of Alice Springs. ⊠ *Stuart Hwy.* ☎ *08/8952–7161* ⊕ *www.roadtransporthall.com* ⊠ *A$8* ⊘ *Daily 9–5.*

🔞 **School of the Air.** Operating in many remote areas of the country, and unique to Australia, the School of the Air teaches faraway students in an ingenious way: children take their classes by correspondence course, supplemented by lessons over the Royal Flying Doctor radio network. Observing the teacher-student relationship by way of radio is fascinating. The school is 3 km (2 mi) northwest of town, on the Alice Wanderer route. ⊠ *80 Head St.* ☎ *08/8951–6834* ⊕ *www.assoa.nt.edu.au* ⊠ *A$4* ⊘ *Mon.–Sat. 8:30–4:30, Sun. 1:30–4:30.*

Where to Eat

$–$$ ✕ **Barra on Todd.** Seafood—especially the famed Northern Territory barramundi—is the main draw at this funky restaurant and bar at the Alice Springs Resort. You can have your fish char-grilled (accompanied by lemon risotto and champagne-salmon caviar butter); cooked in foil with garlic butter and prawns; grilled to perfection; or deep-fried in a beer batter with lemon-pepper fries. Non-seafood choices include a very tasty five-spice duck. ⊠ *34 Stott Terr.* ☎ *08/8952–3523* ▤ *AE, DC, MC, V.*

$–$$ ✕ **Bojangles Saloon and Restaurant.** Cowhide seats, tables made from old *Ghan* railway benches, and a life-size replica of bushranger Ned Kelly give this lively restaurant true Outback flavor. Food is classic Northern Territory tucker: barramundi, kangaroo, camel, emu, thick slabs of ribs, and huge steaks. Jangles, an 8-foot python, lives with a rusty motorbike in a glass case left of the bar. ⊠ *80 Todd St.* ☎ *08/8952–2873* ▤ *AE, DC, MC, V.*

$–$$ ✕ **Casa Nostra.** Red-and-white gingham tablecloths, Chianti bottles and plastic grapes festoon this family-run Alice old-timer. Locals crowd in for traditional meat dishes, pizza, and pasta (try the specialty pasta, with chicken, mushrooms, and cream-and-black pepper sauce). Take a tip from the regulars and preorder your serving of vanilla slice for dessert, or you might miss out on this scrumptious cake of layered papery pastry and custard cream. ⊠ *Undoolya Rd. and Sturt Terr.* ☎ *08/8952–6749* ▤ *MC, V* ⊘ *No lunch; no dinner Sun.*

$–$$ ✕ **Hanuman Thai.** The grilled Hanuman oysters—seasoned with lemongrass and tangy lime juice—are the big draw at this comfortably plush, plum-walled spot; reportedly they've converted even avowed seafood-haters. The *Pla Sam Rod* (three-flavor—sweet, sour, spicy—fish) is also popular. Desserts include black rice brûlée and banana spring rolls with dates and malted ice cream. If you like the flavors here and you're traveling north, visit the sister property in Darwin. ⊠ *Crown Plaza Resort, 82 Barrett Dr.* ☎ *08/8953–7188* ⊴ *Reservations essential* ▤ *AE, DC, MC, V.*

FodorsChoice
★

$–$$ ✕ **Oriental Gourmet.** This plain but historic weatherboard government building—1939 is old for Alice Springs—is the place to come for the best Chinese food in the Red Centre. There are no surprises on the menu—

honey prawns, beef with black bean sauce, duck with lemon sauce—but all the dishes are fresh, simple, and well prepared. Step inside to dine or sit in the garden waiting area until your take-out order is ready. ⊠ *80 Hartley St.* ☎ *08/8953–0888* ▤ *AE, DC, MC, V* ⊘ *No lunch.*

★ **$–$$** ✕**Overlanders Steakhouse.** When locals take out-of-town guests to dinner, this is the restaurant they usually choose. Expect a full-throttle Outback experience, including a nightly Australian floor show, among weathered saddles, lamps, and equipment from local cattle stations. Hearty cooking presents Northern Territory specialties. Dip into an appetizer of vol-au-vent filled with crocodile, or try the popular "Drover's Blow-Out" five-course meal that includes a mixed grill of kangaroo, camel, and barramundi for A$50 per person. ⊠ *72 Hartley St.* ☎ *08/8952–2159* ▤ *AE, DC, MC, V* ⊘ *No lunch.*

★ **$–$$** ✕**Red Ochre Grill.** Check out Aboriginal art while eating your way around the Outback at this café-style restaurant in the Aurora Alice Springs Hotel. Look for emu pâté, bush-myrtle tomato salsa, and honey-and-wattleseed-marinated duck. The "Taste of the Territory" combines camel and kangaroo, served with saffron rice and lemon myrtle-flavor tzatziki. Sampling from the cosmopolitan wine list while sitting at an outdoor table under the grapevines might tempt you to linger for hours. ⊠ *11 Leichhardt Terr.* ☎ *08/8952–9614* ▤ *AE, DC, MC, V.*

¢–**$** ✕**Bar Doppio.** At this street-side alfresco café you can sip one of Alice's top-notch espressos as you watch Todd Mall shoppers stroll by. A casual crowd comes for filling, inexpensive offerings, which include vegetarian dishes, fish, and Turkish bread with several dips. ⊠ *Fan Arcade off Todd Mall* ☎ *08/8952–6525* ▭ *No credit cards* ⊘ *No dinner Sun.–Thurs.*

¢–**$** ✕**Todd Tavern.** The only traditional Australian pub in Alice Springs serves cheap, hearty meals all day. Theme-dinner nights, which cost from A$8.95, include fish and all-you-can-eat salad on Wednesday, schnitzel on Thursday, and a traditional roast and vegetables dinner on Sunday. Pick your wine from the on-site bottle shop. ⊠ *1 Todd Mall* ☎ *08/8952–1255* ▤ *AE, DC, MC, V.*

Where to Stay

Hotels & Motels

$$$ ▦**Alice Springs Resort.** At dusk, hungry pink-and-gray galah birds crowd the broad, foliage-fringed lawns at this hotel on the Todd River's east bank, just a short stroll from downtown. Many of the earth-tone rooms open directly onto lawns or gardens where dozens of native birds chatter. A popular place for human conversation is the in-pool bar, while a classy new restaurant and bar called Barra on Todd (so-called because it specializes in barramundi and other seafood dishes) has quickly become a popular place to dine or meet for a drink. ⊠ *34 Stott Terr., 0870* ☎ *08/8951–4545* ▤ *08/8953–0995* ⊕ *www.voyages.com.au* ⤴ *144 rooms* ♻ *Restaurant, room service, some in-room data ports, minibars, refrigerators, room TVs with movies, pool, bicycles, 2 bars, shop, dry cleaning, laundry facilities, laundry service, Internet, business services, meeting rooms, travel services, free parking; no smoking* ▤ *AE, DC, MC, V.*

★ **$$$** ⊞ **Crowne Plaza Resort Alice Springs.** Landscaped lawns with elegant eucalyptus and palm trees greet you at the entrance of Alice's best hotel, about a mile outside town. Inside, the rooms have bleached-wood furniture and balcony views of either the garden and pool or of the Alice Springs golf course and the low, barren mountains behind. The on-site Hanuman Thai restaurant is a local favorite. ⊠ *82 Barrett Dr., 0870* ☎ *08/8950–8000* 📠 *08/8952–3822* ⊕ *www.crowneplaza.com.au* ⊅ *228 rooms, 7 suites* ⚬ *2 restaurants, room service, in-room data ports, in-room safes, some in-room hot tubs, minibars, refrigerators, room TVs with movies, 2 tennis courts, pool, health club, sauna, 2 bars, laundry facilities, laundry service, Internet, meeting rooms, travel services, free parking, no-smoking rooms* ⊟ *AE, DC, MC, V.*

★ **$$–$$$** ⊞ **Orangewood B&B.** The owners of this cozy property, Ross and Lynne Peterkin, know the Red Centre like the back of their hands. (Ross used to work for the Royal Flying Doctor Service at Ayers Rock, and Lynne is a member of the Central Australian Tourism Industry Association.) Their former family home now features three double rooms (one with a hot tub) in the main house, and a one-bedroom self-contained cottage near the pool. Breakfast is served in a sunny room overlooking the garden, and there's a formal lounge with an open fireplace, TV and stereo, and adjoining reading room. The property is just a seven-minute walk—across the dry Todd River bed—from the heart of Alice. ⊠ *9 McMinn St., 0870* ☎ *08/8952–4114* 📠 *08/8952–4664* ⊕ *www.orangewood-bnb.au.com* ⊅ *3 rooms, 1 cottage* ⚬ *Dining room, pool, lounge; no room phones, no room TVs, no kids, no smoking* ⊟ *MC, V.*

$ ⊞ **Desert Palms Resort.** Dip your toes in the 24-hour island pool with a waterfall and you might just stay put, lounging and gazing up at the umbrella-like palm trees and red-and-pink bougainvillea. Accommodation, should you choose to get out of the water, is in self-contained, freestanding A-frame units, each with one bedroom and a private balcony. ⊠ *74 Barrett Dr., 0870* ☎ *08/8952–5977* 📠 *08/8953–4176* ⊕ *www.desertpalms.com.au* ⊅ *80 cabins* ⚬ *Grocery, kitchenettes, microwaves, refrigerators, tennis court, pool, wine shop, laundry facilities, laundry service, Internet, airport shuttle, travel services* ⊟ *AE, DC, MC, V.*

$ ⊞ **Heavitree Gap Outback Lodge.** Wild, black-footed rock wallabies are fed nightly in this resort at the base of the MacDonnell Ranges, a few hundred yards south of the break in the ranges known as Heavitree Gap. Lodge rooms and four-bed bunkhouses all have air-conditioning and kitchenettes. Nightly entertainment—thrice weekly December to February—includes a bush balladeer and a hands-on reptile show. A free shuttle runs from the resort to Alice Springs, which is five minutes away. ⊠ *Palm Circuit off Stuart Hwy., 0870* ☎ *08/8950–4444* 📠 *08/8952–9394* ⊕ *www.aurora-resorts.com.au* ⊅ *60 rooms, 16 bunkhouses* ⚬ *Restaurant, grocery, picnic area, kitchenettes, microwaves, refrigerators, room TVs with movies, pool, playground, laundry facilities, Internet, travel services, no-smoking rooms* ⊟ *AE, DC, MC, V.*

$ ⊞ **Mercure Inn Diplomat Hotel.** Don't have a car? This motel is ideally set 100 yards from the town center, just far enough to guarantee peaceful evenings. However, avoid ground-floor rooms if you want privacy, as the glass doors open onto the central pool and parking lot. The hotel has a tavern serving breakfast and casual bar meals. Guests can also dine at the nearby Keller's Restaurant (which serves up Swiss, Indian, and innovative Australian dishes) and the Overlander's Steakhouse and charge their meals back to the hotel. ⊠ *Gregory Terr. and Hartley St., 0870* 🕾 *08/ 8952–8977 or 1800/804885* 🖷 *08/8953–0225* ⊕ *www.accorhotels.com. au* ➔ *82 rooms* ⚹ *Restaurant, room service, some in-room hot tubs, some minibars, refrigerators, some room TVs with movies, pool, bar, dry cleaning, laundry facilities, laundry service, Internet, travel services, free parking, no-smoking rooms* 🚭 *AE, DC, MC, V.*

$ 🏨 **Novotel Outback Alice Springs.** Shadowed by the mountain range along the town's southern periphery, this modern resort has rooms with exposed-brick walls, desert-hue furnishings, and molded fiberglass bathrooms. A pool and barbecue area invite families to gather. Hop onto the courtesy shuttle for the 1½-km (1-mi) transfer to town. ⊠ *46 Stephens Rd., 0870* 🕾 *08/8952–6100 or 1800/810664* 🖷 *08/8952–1988* ⊕ *www.accorhotels.com.au* ➔ *138 rooms* ⚹ *Restaurant, room service, some kitchenettes, minibars, some microwaves, refrigerators, room TVs with movies, tennis court, pool, hot tub, bicycles, bar, dry cleaning, laundry facilities, laundry service, Internet, meeting room, travel services, free parking, no-smoking rooms* 🚭 *AE, DC, MC, V.*

★ **¢–$** 🏨 **Alice on Todd Apartments.** On the banks of the Todd River about a mile south of Todd Mall, these self-contained accommodations are priced at a steal and are perfect for families. Studios sleep two, one-bedrooms sleep four, and two-bedrooms sleep six. Light fills each desert-hue apartment through a patio or balcony. You can make friends at the barbecue area, then hop across the dry riverbed to try your luck at Lasseters Hotel Casino. ⊠ *South Terr. and Strehlow St., 0870* 🕾 *08/ 8953–8033* 🖷 *08/8952–9902* ⊕ *www.aliceontodd.com* ➔ *15 studios, 4 1-bedroom and 15 2-bedroom apartments* ⚹ *Picnic area, in-room data ports, some kitchens, some kitchenettes, microwaves, refrigerators, pool, recreation room, laundry facilities, Internet, free parking; no smoking* 🚭 *MC, V.*

¢ 🏨 **Pioneer YHA Hostel.** Past moviegoers would barely recognize Alice's old open-air cinema. Instead of looking up at a screen you can now lounge around a small, grassy pool area, but a wonderful old projector in the communal lounge-cum-kitchen is a reminder of the property's colorful history. With corrugated-iron cladding and a timber ramp, the two-story main accommodation block resembles a ship. Doors open into bright, spotless 4-, 6-, and 8-bed dorms, all with shared bath. Older 16-bed dorms are behind the main building. ⊠ *Leichhardt Terr. and Parsons St., 0870* 🕾 *08/8952–8855* 🖷 *08/8952–4144* ⊕ *www.yha.com.au* ➔ *22 rooms without bath* ⚹ *Pool, bicycles, billiards, recreation room, laundry facilities, Internet, car rental, travel services; no room phones, no room TVs, no kids under 7, no smoking* 🚭 *MC, V.*

★ ⛺ **MacDonnell Ranges Holiday Park.** Hidden behind the ranges 5 km (3 mi) south of town, this extensive, well-planned park has many trees, good children's facilities, Internet access, nightly entertainment—and a free pancake breakfast on Sunday. Most sites are powered, and 48 have private showers and toilets. Facilities for people with disabilities are also provided. A free shuttle bus runs from the airport. ⊠ *Palm Pl. off Palm*

Circuit, Box 9025, 0871 ☎ *08/8952–6111 or 1800/808373* 🖷 *08/8952–5236* ⊕ *www.macrange.com.au* ✉ *A\$57–A\$140* ⌁ *360 sites* ♿ *Flush toilets, full hookups, drinking water, showers, picnic tables, restaurant, electricity, public telephone, general store, service station, playground, 2 pools* ▤ *AE, MC, V.*

⚠ **Heavitree Gap Caravan Park.** Tucked between the Stuart Highway and the MacDonnell Ranges beside the Todd River, this small campground shares facilities with the adjoining Heavitree Gap Lodge. Located five minutes south of town, the park is popular with coach camping companies, which have a designated camping and cooking area. It can be crowded in winter. ✉ *Palm Circuit off Stuart Hwy., 0871* ☎ *08/8950–4444* 🖷 *08/8952–9394* ⊕ *www.aurora-resorts.com.au* ✉ *A\$18–A\$20* ⌁ *78 powered sites, 100 tent sites* ♿ *Flush toilets, partial hookups, drinking water, laundry facilities, showers, picnic tables, restaurant, snack bar, electricity, public telephone, general store, service station, playground, pool* ▤ *AE, DC, MC, V.*

Nightlife & the Arts

Lasseters Hotel Casino (✉ 93 Barrett Dr. ☎ 08/8950–7777 or 1800/808975) has blackjack, roulette, slot machines, keno, and the lively heads/tails Australian gambling game of Two-up. It's free to get into this late-night local haunt, which is open from midday until about 3 AM. The Irish pub has evening entertainment Wednesday through Sunday.

Sounds of Starlight (✉ 40 Todd Mall ☎ 08/8953–0826) is the place to enjoy Outback theater performances and didgeridoo music accompanied by a slide show of Red Centre images. Concerts (A\$25) are held at 8 PM Tuesday–Saturday April–November, and Tuesday, Friday, and Saturday other months. A pre-theater dinner and show package (with dinner at the Red Ochre Grill) costs A\$60.

Todd Tavern (✉ 1 Todd Mall ☎ 08/8952–1255), the only traditional Australian pub in town, is naturally a lively spot every night. Besides the bar, restaurant, and bottle shop, there are gambling facilities. You can bet on horse races across the country with TAB (the Australian equivalent of OTB). Keep some change aside for the slot machines.

Sports & the Outdoors

Camel Riding

🕭 You can take a camel to dinner or breakfast, or just ramble along the dry Todd River bed, astride a "ship of the desert" at **Frontier Camel Farm** (✉ Ross Hwy., 5 km [3 mi] southeast of Alice Springs ☎ 08/8953–0444). Short rides, river rambles, and breakfast rides begin daily at 6:30 AM, and 4 PM dinner rides include a three-course meal, wine, and beer. Dinner rides depart at 5 PM from October through April. Prices run from A\$10 for a short ride to A\$105 for a dinner date. Transfers from Alice Springs hotels are included with the breakfast and dinner tours.

Hot-Air Ballooning

At dawn on most mornings, hot-air balloons float in the sky around Alice Springs. **Outback Ballooning** (✉ 35 Kennett Ct. ☎ 1800/809790) makes hotel pickups about an hour before dawn and returns between 9 AM and 10 AM. The A$220 fee covers 30 minutes of flying time, insurance, and a champagne breakfast. A 60-minute flight costs A$340 including insurance.

Quad-Bike Riding

Hop aboard a motorbike with four huge wheels and explore the Red Centre's oldest working cattle station with **Outback Quad Adventures** (⊠ Undoolya Station, Undoolya Rd. ☎ 08/8953–0697). The company collects you from Alice Springs and takes you to the station, 17 km (10 mi) out of town on the edge of the MacDonnell Ranges. No special license is needed and all tours are escorted by guides with two-way radios. Two-hour rides (A$99), 3½-hour rides (A$189), and overnight tours—which include barbecue dinner with wine, sleeping bags, and breakfast (A$329)—operate year-round.

Shopping

Apart from the ubiquitous souvenir shops, the main focus of shopping in Alice Springs is Aboriginal art and artifacts. Central Australian Aboriginal art is characterized by intricate patterns of dots, commonly called sand paintings because they were originally drawn on sand as ceremonial devices. The **Aboriginal Desert Art Gallery** (⊠ 87 Todd Mall ☎ 08/8953 1005) is one of the best local galleries. For books on all things central Australian, from bush tucker and Aboriginal culture to settlement and birdlife, visit **Big Kangaroo Books** (⊠ 79 Todd Mall ☎ 08/8953–2137). **Gallery Gondwana** (⊠ 43 Todd Mall ☎ 08/8953–1577) sells wonderful contemporary and traditional Aboriginal art. Aboriginal and wildflower print fabrics for dressmaking and patchwork are available from **SewForU** (⊠ Reg Harris La. off Todd Mall ☎ 08/8953–5422). The **Todd Mall Markets** (⊠ Todd St. ☎ 08/8952–9299) are held every second Sunday morning from late February to December. Local arts, crafts, and food are displayed in stalls against a background of live entertainment.

Alice Springs A to Z

AIR TRAVEL

Alice Springs Airport, with its bright, cool passenger terminal, is 15 km (9 mi) southeast of town. Qantas has daily direct flights from Sydney, Melbourne, Adelaide, Perth, and Cairns. Virgin Blue has direct flights three times a week from Adelaide, and these connect with flights originating in Melbourne, Sydney, and Brisbane. It's three hours flying time from Sydney, Melbourne, and Brisbane, and two hours from Adelaide.

🛪 Airlines **Qantas** ☎ 13-1313 ⊕ www.qantas.com. **Virgin Blue** ☎ 13-6789 ⊕ www.virginblue.com.au.

🛪 Airport **Alice Springs Airport** ☎ 08/8951-1211 ⊕ www.aliceairport.com.au.

AIRPORT TRANSFERS Alice Springs Airport Shuttle Service meets every flight. The ride to all hotels and residential addresses in town costs A$11 each way. On request, the bus will also pick you up at your hotel and take you back to the airport. Alice Springs Taxis maintains a stand at the airport. The fare to most parts of town is about A$25.

Alice Springs Airport Shuttle Service ⊠ Shop 6, Capricornia Centre, Gregory Terr. ☎ 08/8953-0310 or 1800/621188. **Alice Springs Taxis** ☎ 08/8952-1877.

BUS TRAVEL

Greyhound-operated interstate buses arrive and depart from the Coles Complex. AAT Kings coaches, which run day and extended tours, have a separate terminal.

AAT Kings ⊠ 74 Todd St. ☎ 08/8952-1700 or 1800/334009 ⊕ www.aatkings.com. **Greyhound Australia** ⊠ Coles Complex, Gregory Terr. ☎ 08/8952-7888 ⊕ www. greyhound.com.au.

CAR RENTAL

Avis, Budget, Hertz, Thrifty, and the local Territory Rent-a-Car have offices in Alice Springs. All rent conventional and four-wheel-drive vehicles, which are essential for getting off the beaten track. Britz and Maui rent motor homes, which are another popular way to explore the Red Centre.

Avis ⊠ 52 Hartley St. ☎ 08/8953-5533 or 13-6333 ⊕ www.avis.com.au. **Britz** ⊠ Stuart Hwy. and Power St. ☎ 08/8952-8814 or 1800/331454 ⊕ www.britz.com. **Budget** ⊠ Shop 6, Capricorn Centre, Gregory Terr. ☎ 08/8952-8899 or 13-2727 or 13-2727 ⊕ www.budget.com.au. **Hertz** ⊠ 76 Hartley St. ☎ 08/8952-2644 or 1300/132105 ⊕ www.hertznt.com. **Maui** ⊠ Stuart Hwy. and Power St. ☎ 08/8952-8049 or 1300/363800 ⊕ www.maui-rentals.com **Thrifty-Territory Rent-a-Car** ⊠ 71 Hartley St. ☎ 08/8952-9999 or 1800/626515 ⊕ www.rentacar.com.au.

CAR TRAVEL

The Stuart Highway, commonly called the Track, is the only road into Alice Springs. The town center lies east of the highway. The 1,693-km (1,000-mi) drive from Adelaide takes about 24 hours. The drive from Darwin is about 160 km (100 mi) shorter than the drive from Adelaide.

If you plan on going into the desert, renting a car is a smart idea. The five-hour, 440-km (273-mi) trip from Alice Springs to Ayers Rock Resort is on a paved, scenic road that's in good condition. However, a four-wheel-drive vehicle is necessary for visiting some of the attractions off this route, as access roads can be hard and corrugated or soft and sandy; rain can make them impassable. Fatigue is also a danger on desert drives. Stop often to rest—and to admire the scenery.

The N.T. Road Report provides the latest information about conditions on the many unpaved roads in the area. In the event of a breakdown, contact the Automobile Association of N.T. contractor in Alice Springs. And whatever happens, don't leave your vehicle.

Automobile Association of N.T. contractor ⊠ 58 Sargent St. ☎ 08/8952-1087 ⊕ www. aant.com.au. **N.T. Road Report** ☎ 1800/246199 ⊕ www.roadreport.nt.gov.au.

EMERGENCIES

In an emergency, dial **000** to reach an ambulance, the police, or the fire department.

Doctors & Dentists Central Clinic ⊠ 76 Todd St. ☎ 08/8952-1088. **Community Dental Centre** ⊠ Flynn Dr. off Memorial Dr. ☎ 08/8951-6713.

⚕ Hospital Alice Springs Hospital ⊠ Gap Rd. between Traeger Ave. and Stuart Terr. ☎ 08/8951-7777.

⚕ Pharmacies Alice Springs Pharmacy ⊠ Shop 19, Yeperenye Centre, Hartley St. ☎ 08/8952-1554. **Amcal Chemist** ⊠ Alice Plaza, Todd Mall ☎ 08/8953-0089.

MAIL & THE INTERNET

Alice Springs Post Office provides all mailing services, including post restante. There are numerous Internet cafés in town, many connected to tour booking services. E-mail connection is free with any booking at the Outback Travel Shop.

⚕ Internet Café Outback Travel Shop ⊠ 2a Gregory Terr. ☎ 08/8955-5288.

⚕ Mail Services Alice Springs Post Office ⊠ 31-33 Hartley St. ☎ 13-1318. Money Matters

ANZ Bank, National Australia Bank, and Westpac have branches on or just off Todd Mall, with counter service and ATM facilities.

⚕ ANZ Bank ⊠ Todd Mall and Parsons St. ☎ 13-1314. **National Australia Bank** ⊠ 51-53 Todd Mall ☎ 13-2265. **Westpac** ⊠ 19 Todd Mall ☎ 13-2032.

TELEPHONES

The Alice Springs area code is 08, the same code for all of the Northern Territory, South Australia, and Western Australia. Cell-mobile phone coverage extends into Alice's immediate surroundings, but there's no reception in the far East or West MacDonnell Ranges or the desert. There's a bank of public phones at the central post office.

⚕ Alice Springs Post Office ⊠ 31-33 Hartley St. ☎ 13-1318.

TOURS

The *Alice Wanderer* bus completes a 70-minute circuit (with narration) of 16 tourist attractions in and around Alice Springs 9–5 daily. You can leave and rejoin the bus whenever you like over two days for a flat rate of A$38. Entry into attractions is extra. It is part of the Alice Wanderer & Centre Sightseeing, a company that also runs half-day tours of Alice. AAT Kings and Tailormade Tours operate three-hour trips and all companies include visits to the Royal Flying Doctor Service Base, School of the Air, Telegraph Station, and Anzac Hill scenic lookout.

⚕ AAT Kings ⊠ 74 Todd St. ☎ 08/8952-1700 or 1800/334009 ⊕ www.aatkings.com. **Alice Wanderer** ⊡ Box 2110, Alice Springs, NT 0871 ☎ 08/8952-2111 or 1800/669111 ⊕ www.alicewanderer.com.au. **Tailormade Tours** ⊡ Box 2230, Alice Springs, NT 0871 ☎ 08/8952-1731 or 1800/806641 ⊕ www.tailormadetours.com.au.

TRAIN TRAVEL

The *Ghan* train leaves Adelaide at 5:15 PM Sunday and Friday, arriving in Alice Springs at 11:55 AM Monday and Saturday. Return trains leave Alice Springs at 12:45 PM Thursday and 2 PM Saturday, arriving in Adelaide at 9 AM on Friday and 9:10 AM on Sunday. On Monday at 4:10 PM the *Ghan* continues to Darwin via Katherine, arriving at 4:30 PM Tuesday. Trains from Darwin depart Wednesday at 10 AM. Trains from Sydney and Melbourne to Adelaide also connect with the *Ghan*. You can transport your car by train for an extra charge. The Alice Springs railway station is 2½ km (1½ mi) west of Todd Mall.

⚕ Ghan Great Southern Railway ☎ 13-2147 bookings, 1300/132147 holiday packages ⊕ www.gsr.com.au.

VISITOR INFORMATION
The Central Australian Tourism Industry Association dispenses information, advice, and maps and will book tours and cars. For additional information on buildings of historical significance in and around Alice Springs, contact the National Trust, open February–November, weekdays 10:30–2:30.

🗊 **Central Australian Tourism Industry Association** ⊠ 60 Gregory Terr., 0870 🕾 08/8952–5800 or 1800/645199 ⊕ www.centralaustraliantourism.com. **National Trust** ⊠ Old Hartley Street School, Hartley St. 🕾 08/8952–4516.

SIDE TRIPS FROM ALICE SPRINGS

East MacDonnell Ranges

Spectacular scenery and Aboriginal rock art in the MacDonnell Ranges east of the Alice are well worth a day or more of exploration. Emily Gap (a sacred Aboriginal site), Jessie Gap, and Corroboree Rock, once a setting for important men-only Aboriginal ceremonies, are within the first 44 km (27 mi) east of Alice Springs. Beyond these are Trephina Gorge, John Hayes Rockhole, and N'Dhala Gorge Nature Park (with numerous hide-and-seek Aboriginal rock carvings).

Arltunga Historical Reserve, 110 km (69 mi) northeast of Alice, contains the ruins of a former 19th-century gold-rush site. If you fancy fossicking for your own semiprecious stones, you can take your pick—and shovel—at Gemtree in the Harts Ranges, 140 km (87 mi) northeast of Alice.

Where to Stay

🛆 **Gemtree.** You can fossick for gems by day and sleep under the stars at night at this bush-style caravan park. Powered sites are A$22, campsites are A$18 for two adults, and two-person cabins cost A$65 per night. It's A$60 to join a tag-along gem-fossicking tour, including equipment. Although it's rustic, and 140 km (87 mi) northeast of Alice Springs, the park has its own golf course. ⊹ *Plenty Hwy., approximately 70 km (43 mi) from Stuart Hwy. junction.* 🕾 *08/8956–9855* 🖷 *08/8956–9860* ⊕ *www.gemtree.com.au* 🖾 *A$18–A$65* 🖙 *50 powered sites, 50 campsites, 2 cabins* ⚬ *Flush toilets, partial hookups, drinking water, laundry facilities, showers, fire pits, grills, picnic tables, electricity, public telephone, general store, service station* ⊟ *MC, V.*

West MacDonnell Ranges

The MacDonnell Ranges west of Alice Springs are, like the eastern ranges, broken by a series of chasms and gorges, many of which can be visited in a single day. To reach the sights, most within the West MacDonnell National Park, drive out of town on Larapinta Drive, the western continuation of Stott Terrace.

John Flynn's Grave memorializes the Royal Flying Doctor Service founder. It's on a rise with the stark ranges behind, in a memorable setting 6 km (4 mi) west of Alice Springs. ⊠ *Larapinta Dr.* 🕾 *No phone* 🖾 *Free* ⊙ *Daily 24 hrs.*

THE HEARTLAND

FOR MOST AUSTRALIANS, the Red Centre is the mystical and legendary core of the continent, and Uluru is its beautiful focal point. Whether they have been there or not, locals believe its image symbolizes a steady pulse that radiates deep through the red earth, through the heartland, and all the way to the coasts.

Little more than a thumbprint within the vast Australian continent, the Red Centre is barren and isolated. Its hard, relentless topography and lack of the conveniences found in most areas of civilization make this one of the most difficult areas of the country in which to survive, much less explore. But the early pioneers—some foolish, some hardy—managed to set up bases that thrived. They created cattle stations, introduced electricity, and implemented telegraph services, enabling them to maintain a lifestyle that, if not luxurious, was at least reasonably comfortable.

The people who now sparsely populate the Red Centre are a breed of their own. Many were born and grew up here, but many others were "blow-ins," immigrants from far-flung countries and folk from other Australian states who took up the challenge to make a life in the desert and stayed on as they succeeded. Either way, folks out here have at least a few common characteristics. They're laconic and down-to-earth, canny and astute, and very likely to try to pull your leg when you least expect it.

No one could survive the isolation without a good sense of humor: where else in the world would you hold a bottomless-boat race in a dry riverbed? The Henley-on-Todd, as it is known, is a sight to behold, with dozens of would-be skippers bumbling along within the bottomless-boat frames.

As the small towns grew and businesses quietly prospered in the mid-1800s, a rail link between Alice Springs and Adelaide was planned. However, the undercurrent of challenge and humor that touches all life here ran through this project as well. Construction began in 1877, but things went wrong from the start. No one had seen rain for ages, and no one expected it; hence, the track was laid right across a floodplain. It wasn't long before locals realized their mistake, when intermittent, heavy floods regularly washed the tracks away. The railway is still in operation today and all works well, but its history is one of many local jokes here.

For some, the Red Centre is the real Australia, a special place where you will meet people whose generous and sincere hospitality may move you. The land and all its riches offer some of the most spectacular and unique sights on the planet, along with a sense of timelessness that will slow you down and fill your spirit. Take a moment to shade your eyes from the sun and pick up on the subtleties that nature has carefully protected and camouflaged here, and you will soon discover that the Red Centre is not the dead center.

— Bev Malzard

Simpsons Gap isn't dramatic, but it's the closest gorge to town. Stark-white ghost gums, red rocks, and the purple-haze mountains will give you a taste of the scenery to be seen farther into the ranges. The gap itself can be crowded in the morning and late afternoon, since these are the best times to see rock wallabies, but unlike Standley Chasm, it's only a short walk from the parking lot. ⊕ *Larapinta Dr., 17 km (10 mi) west of Alice Springs, then 5½ km (3½ mi) on side road* ☎ *No phone* ✉ *Free* ⊗ *Daily 8–8.*

★ **Standley Chasm** is one of the most impressive canyons in the MacDonnell Ranges. At midday, when the sun is directly overhead, the 10-yard-wide canyon glows red from the reflected light. The walk from the parking lot takes about 20 minutes and is rocky toward the end. There's a kiosk selling snacks and drinks at the park entrance. ✉ *Larapinta Dr., 40 km (25 mi) west of Alice Springs, then 9 km (5½ mi) on Standley Chasm Rd.* ☎ *08/8956–7440* ✉ *A$7* ⊗ *Daily 8:30–5.*

Namatjira Drive

A ride along Namatjira Drive takes you past striking, diverse desert landscape and into scenic, accessible national parks and gorges. Beyond Standley Chasm the mileage starts adding up, and you should be prepared for rough road conditions.

Ellery Creek Big Hole (✉ Namatjira Dr.), 88 km (55 mi) west of Alice Springs, is one of the coldest swimming holes in the Red Centre. It's also the deepest and most permanent water hole in the area; thus, you may glimpse wild creatures like wallabies or goannas (monitor lizards) quenching their thirst. Take the 3-km (2-mi) Dolomite Walk for a close-up look at this fascinating geological site.

Serpentine Gorge (✉ Namatjira Dr.), 99 km (61 mi) west of Alice Springs, is best seen by taking a refreshing swim through the narrow, winding gorge. Aboriginal myth has it that the pool is the home of a fierce serpent; hence the name.

Ormiston Gorge (✉ Namatjira Dr.), 128 km (79 mi) west of Alice Springs, is one of the few truly breathtaking sights in the western ranges. A short climb takes you to Gum Tree Lookout, from where you can see the spectacular 820-foot-high red gorge walls rising from the permanent pool below. Trails include the 7-km (4½-mi) Ormiston Pound Walk.

Glen Helen Gorge (✉ Namatjira Dr.), 140 km (87 mi) west of Alice Springs, slices through the MacDonnell Range, revealing dramatic rock layering and tilting. The gorge was cut by the rather sporadic coursing Finke River, often described as the oldest river in the world. Here the river forms a broad, cold, permanent water hole that's perfect for a refreshing swim.

Where to Stay

★ ¢–$ 🏠 **Glen Helen Resort.** With a huge natural swimming hole at its front door, this homestead resort in the West MacDonnell Ranges doesn't need a conventional pool—but it has both. You can camp, stay in one of the 10 four-person Stockman's Quarters with shared facilities, or splurge on a motel room. There's a restaurant, plus entertainment thrice weekly March through November. Take a helicopter ride for a fantastic view of the range, or simply enjoy a glass of wine as you watch the sun sink over the gorge. ✛ *Namatjira Dr., 135 km (84 mi) west of Alice Springs* ☎ *08/8956–7489* 🖷 *08/8956–7495* ⊕ *www.glenhelen.com.au* ➳ *25 rooms, 105 unpowered sites, 22 powered sites* ⚐ *Restaurant, grocery, picnic area, some refrigerators, hiking, bar, beer garden, laundry facilities, travel services; no room phones, no room TVs* ▤ *AE, MC, V.*

Hermannsburg & Beyond

One alternative after passing Standley Chasm is to continue on Larapinta Drive toward Hermannsburg to see a restored mission, and beyond that to a national park. Hermannsburg itself has tea rooms, a supermarket, and a service station. The buildings of the early **Lutheran Mission,** dating from the late 19th century, have been restored, and visitors are welcome. Aboriginal artist Albert Namatjira was born into the Arrernte community at the mission in 1902. There's a camping ground 500 yards from the mission that has 10 powered sites and full amenities from A\$11 a night. ✛ *Larapinta Dr., 132 km (82 mi) from Alice Springs* ☎ *No phone at mission, campsite 08/8956–7480* 🖾 *A\$5* ⊙ *Daily 9–4.*

Palm Valley in **Finke Gorge National Park** is a remnant of a time when Australia's climate was wetter and palm trees grew over large areas. The flora here includes *Livistonia mariae,* an ancient, endemic type of cabbage palm. The area is like a slice of the tropical north dropped into the middle of the Red Centre. To get here you'll need to travel about 20 km (14 mi) from Hermannsburg to Palm Valley; a four-wheel-drive, high-clearance vehicle is essential for driving on the unpaved road and entering Palm Valley.

A scenic option to backtracking to Alice Springs lies west of the Palm Valley turnoff, where Larapinta Drive veers northwest on a 109-km (68-mi) loop to Glen Helen Gorge in the West MacDonnell Ranges. After 41 km (25 mi) the road branches left into the Mereenie Loop (A\$2.20 permit is required), a spectacular route through remote Aboriginal land to Uluṟu via Kings Canyon and Watarrka National Park. As the road is often rutted or muddy (and closed to even four-wheel-drive vehicles after heavy rain), check conditions by calling the N.T. Road Report (☎ 1800/246199) before setting out.

The right (north) road at the Mereenie Loop junction brings you to Tnorala (Gosse Bluff) Conservation Reserve. Created when a meteor crashed into Earth about 140 million years ago, Gosse Bluff is a 5-km-wide (3-mi-wide) crater on an otherwise featureless plain. Entry is strictly four-wheel-drive only, and inside there's only a short trail and picnic tables. The best perspectives of the crater are from the roadside and Tylers Pass, some 30 km (19 mi) beyond the reserve, where you can stop for a picnic with a view. From here, the road continues north before turning east to Glen Helen Gorge, where the paved road starts again.

ULUṞU & KATA TJUṮA

It's easy to see why the Aborigines attach spiritual significance to Uluṟu (Ayers Rock). It's an awe-inspiring sight, rising above the plain and dramatically changing color throughout the day. The Anangu people are the traditional owners of the land around Uluru and Kata Tjuta. They believe they are direct descendants of the beings—which include a python, an emu, a blue-tongue lizard, and a poisonous snake—who formed the land and its physical features during the Tjukurpa (creation period). Tjukurpa also refers to the Anangu religion, law, and moral system, a knowledge of past and present handed down from memory through stories and other oral traditions.

Rising more than 1,100 feet from the surrounding plain, Uluru is one of the world's largest monoliths, and because it's a sacred site, visitors should not climb the rock. Kata Tjuta (the Olgas), 53 km (33 mi) west, is a series of 36 gigantic rock domes hiding a maze of fascinating gorges and crevasses. The names Ayers Rock and the Olgas are used out of familiarity alone; at the sites themselves, the Aboriginal Uluru and Kata Tjuta are the respective names of preference.

Uluru and Kata Tjuta have very different compositions. Monolithic Uluru is a type of sandstone called arkose, while the rock domes at Kata Tjuta are composed of conglomerate. It was once thought that they rested upon the sandy terrain like pebbles; however, both formations are the tips of tilted rock strata that extend thousands of yards into the earth. The rock strata tilted during a period of intense geological activity more than 300 million years ago—the arkose by nearly 90 degrees and the conglomerate only about 15 degrees. The surrounding rock fractured and quickly eroded about 40 million years ago, leaving the present structures standing as separate entities. But this is just one interpretation—ask your Aboriginal guide to relate the ancient stories of the rock.

Both of these intriguing sights lie within Uluru–Kata Tjuta National Park, which is protected as a World Heritage Site. As such, it's one of just a few parks in the world recognized in this way for both its landscape and cultural values. The whole experience is a bit like seeing the Grand Canyon turned inside out, and a visit here will be remembered for a lifetime.

On the Way to Uluru

The 440-km (273-mi) drive to Uluru from Alice Springs along the Stuart and Lasseter highways takes about five hours, but you can see some interesting sights along the way if you make a few detours.

Rainbow Valley Conservation Reserve. Amazing rock formations take on rainbow colors in early-morning and late-afternoon light in the sandstone cliffs of the James Range. The colors were caused by water dissolving the red iron in the sandstone, and further erosion created dramatic rock faces and squared towers. To reach the reserve, turn left off the Stuart Highway 76 km (47 mi) south of Alice. The next 22 km (13 mi) are on a dirt track, requiring a four-wheel-drive vehicle. ⊠ *Stuart Hwy.* ☎ *08/8999–5511* ⊠ *Free* ⊙ *Daily 8–8.*

Neil and Jayne Waters, owners of **Camels Australia,** offer everything from quick jaunts to five-day safaris. Day trips include a light lunch. Book all rides at least a day in advance. It's A$40 for a one-hour ride, and

A\$150 for a day trek with lunch; safaris, which include camping gear and meals, are A\$450 for three days and A\$750 for five days. ✥ *Stuarts Well, Stuart Hwy., 91 km (57 mi) south of Alice Springs* ☎ *08/8956–0925* 🖷 *08/8956–0909* ⊕ *www.camels-australia.com.au.*

The **Henbury Meteorite Craters,** 12 depressions between 6 feet and 600 feet across, are believed to have been formed by a meteorite shower about 5,000 years ago. One is 60 feet deep. To get here, you must travel off the highway on an unpaved road. ✥ *Ernest Giles Rd., 114 km (71 mi) south of Alice Springs and 13 km (8 mi) west of Stuart Hwy.*

An important navigational landmark for 19th-century explorers and pioneers—you can still see their signatures in its base—is the **Chamber's Pillar Historical Reserve,** a solitary sandstone column rising 170 feet above the red plains of the northwest Simpson Desert. Over millions of years, oxidation and minerals created the pillar's red-and-gold hues, which are most dramatic in the late-afternoon sunlight. To reach the reserve, drive 119 km (74 mi) south of Alice Springs on Old South Road (mostly unpaved), then turn west at Maryvale Station homestead. The next 41 km (25 mi) is suitable only for high-clearance, four-wheel-drive vehicles. ⊠ *Chamber's Pillar Track* ☎ *08/8951–8211* 💲 *Free.*

On the road to Chamber's Pillar, more than 3,000 ancient Aboriginal rock engravings (petroglyphs) are etched into sandstone outcrops at the **Ewaninga Rock Carvings Conservation Reserve.** Early-morning and late-afternoon light are best for photographing the lines, circles, and animal tracks. A 2-km (1-mi) half-mile trail leads to several art sites. The reserve is open all day, year-round. ✥ *Old South Rd., 39 km (24 mi) south of Alice Springs* ☎ *08/8951–8250* 💲 *Free.*

A drive through **Watarrka National Park** takes you past desert foliage and wildflowers to **King's Canyon.** The park is accessible by car on the Mereenie loop road from Glen Helen Gorge. To make this loop around the West MacDonnell Ranges, an Aboriginal Land Entry Permit is required. It's A\$2.20 from the **Central Australian Tourism Industry Association** (☎ *08/8952–5800* or *1800/645199*) in Alice Springs. ✥ *Luritja Rd., 167 km (104 mi) from the turnoff on Lasseter Hwy.*

Fodor'sChoice **Kings Canyon,** in **Watarrka National Park,** is one of the most spectacu-
★ lar sights in central Australia. The canyon's sheer cliff walls shelter a world of ferns and woodlands, permanent springs and rock pools. The main path is the 6-km (4-mi) Canyon Walk, which starts with a short but steep climb to the top of the escarpment. It then leads through a colony of beehive sandstone domes, known as the Lost City, to a refreshing water hole in the so-called Garden of Eden halfway through the four-hour walk. It's all visible during the half-hour scenic helicopter flight over the canyon and range from Kings Canyon Resort (A\$195 or A\$100 for 15 minutes). ✥ *Luritja Rd., 167 km (104 mi) from turnoff on Lasseter Hwy.*

South of Kings Canyon, on the Lasseter Highway heading toward Uluṟu, you can see **Mt. Conner** from the side of the road. Set on Curtain Springs Cattle Station, and often mistaken for Uluṟu from a distance, it's actually a huge mesa. Nearby on the highway is Curtain Springs Roadhouse, a good stopover for refreshments; you can also arrange guided tours of Mt. Conner, the 1,028,960-acre cattle station, and Lake Amadeus, as well as scenic flights. The roadhouse has cabins with private facilities, caravan sites, and free camping. ✛ *Lasseter Hwy., 41 km (25 mi) west of the Luritja Rd. junction.* ☎ *08/8956–2906.*

Where to Stay

$–$$$$ ⊞ **Kings Canyon Resort.** The only place to stay within Watarrka National **Fodor'sChoice** Park, this resort is 6 km (4 mi) from the canyon. Check into one of the ★ deluxe spa rooms so you can relax in the whirlpool bath after taking the four hour Canyon Walk. There's only a glass wall separating the whirlpool from views of the George Gill Range, but each room is totally private. Accommodations include two- and four-bed lodge rooms and a campground. Book the six-course Sounds of Firelight Dinner (A$130) to nosh in style around a desert campfire under the stars. ⌂ *PMB 136, Alice Springs, NT 0871* ☎ *08/8956–7442 or 1800/817622* 🖷 *08/ 8956–7410* ⊕ *www.voyages.com.au* ⊃ *164 rooms, 52 powered caravan sites, 200 tent sites* ⌂ *Restaurant, café, grocery, some in-room hot tubs, some minibars, refrigerators, some room TVs with movies, tennis court, 2 pools, hiking, 2 bars, shop, laundry facilities, Internet, free parking, no-smoking rooms* ▭ *AE, DC, MC, V.*

Uluru

Fodor'sChoice An inevitable sensation of excitement builds as you approach the great ★ monolith. If you drive toward it in a rental car, you may find yourself gasping at the first glimpse of it through the windshield; if you're on a tour bus, you'll likely want to grab the person sitting next to you and point out the window as it looms larger and larger. Rising like an enormous red mountain in the middle of an otherwise completely flat desert, Uluru really is a marvel to behold.

The **Uluru–Kata Tjuta Cultural Centre** (✉ Off Lasseter Hwy. ☎ 08/ 8956–3138) is the first thing you'll see after entering the park through a tollgate. The two buildings are built in a serpentine style, reflecting the Kuniya and Liru stories about two ancestral snakes who fought a long-ago battle on the southern side of Uluru. Inside, you can learn about Aboriginal history, and the return of the park to Aboriginal ownership in 1983. There's also an excellent park's ranger station where you can get maps and hiking guides, an art shop, and a pottery store with lovely collectibles.

As you work your way around Uluru, your perspective of the great rock changes significantly. You should allow four hours to walk the 10 km (6 mi) around the rock and explore the several deep crevices along the way; you can also drive around it on the paved road. Be aware that some places are Aboriginal sacred sites and cannot be entered. These are clearly signposted. Aboriginal art can be found in caves at the rock's base.

There's only one trail that leads to the top of the rock. Though many people visit Uluru with the explicit intention of climbing it, there are a few things you should bear in mind before attempting this. First, Aboriginal people consider climbing the rock to be sacrilege—so if you believe in preserving the sanctity of sacred native sites, you may have to be content with admiring it from below. Second, if you do decide to make the climb, be aware that it's a very strenuous hike, and not suitable for those who aren't physically fit. The trail is about 1½ km (1 mi) from the base; the round-trip walk takes about two hours. Sturdy hiking boots, a hat, sunscreen, and drinking water are absolute necessities (there are no food or water available at the summit). The climb is closed when temperatures rise above 36°C (97°F)—which means most afternoons in the summertime. Tour buses that bring groups to climb the rock often arrive at the site as early as 4:30 AM for this reason.

Another popular way to experience Uluṟu is far less taxing but no less intense: watching the natural light show on it from one of the two sunset-viewing areas. As the last rays of daylight strike, the rock positively glows, as if lighted from within. Just as quickly, the light is extinguished and the color changes to a somber mauve and finally to black.

Shopping

The **Cultural Centre** (☎ 08/8956–3138) not only has information about the Anangu people and their culture, but houses the **Ininti Store** (☎ 08/8956–2214), which carries souvenirs. The adjoining **Maṟuku Arts and Crafts Centre** (☎ 08/8956–2558) is owned by Aborigines and sells Aboriginal painting and handicrafts. There's also a display of traditional huts and shelters. The Cultural Centre is open daily 7–6; Ininti Store is open daily 7–5:15; Maṟuku is open daily 8–5:30 October–March and 8:30–5.30 April–September.

Kata Tjuṯa

FodorsChoice In many ways, Kata Tjuṯa is more satisfying to explore than Uluṟu. The
★ latter rock is one immense block, so you feel as if you're always on the outside looking in—but you can really come to grips with Kata Tjuṯa. As the Aboriginal name, Kata Tjuṯa (many heads), suggests, this is a jumble of huge rocks containing numerous hidden gorges and chasms. There are three main walks, the first from the parking lot into **Olga Gorge,** the deepest valley between the rocks. This is a 2-km (1-mi) walk, and the round-trip journey takes about one hour. More rewarding but also more difficult is a walk that continues through the major cleft between the Olgas, known as the Valley of the Winds. Experienced walkers can complete this 6-km (4-mi) walk in about four hours. The Valley of the Winds walk is closed when temperatures rise above 36°C (97°F). The **Kata Tjuṯa Viewing Area,** 26 km (16 mi) along the Kata Tjuṯa Road, offers a magnificent vista and is a relaxing place for a break. Interpretive panels give you an understanding of the natural life around you.

Ayers Rock Resort

This complex of lodgings, restaurants, and facilities, which along with the airport is officially known as the township of Yulara, is base camp for exploring Uluṟu and Kata Tjuṯa. The accommodations and services here are the only ones in the vicinity of the national park. Uluṟu is about a 20-minute drive from the resort area (there's a sunset-viewing area on the way); driving to Kata Tjuṯa will take another 30 minutes. The park entrance fee of A$25 is valid for three days.

The properties at the resort, which range from luxury hotels to a campground, are all run by Voyages Hotels and Resorts and share many of the same facilities. The resort "village" includes a bank, newsstand, supermarket, several souvenir shops, Aboriginal art gallery, hair salon, and child-care center.

Where to Eat

Indoor dining is limited to hotel restaurants and the less-expensive Geckos Cafe. If you eat away from your hotel, you can have the meals billed to your room. All hotel reservations can be made through Voyages Hotel and Resorts on-site, or the resort's central reservations service in Sydney. **Central reservations service** (☎ 02/9339–1030 or 1300/ 134044 ⊕ www.voyages.com.au).

★ The most memorable group dining experience in the region is the A$139 **Sounds of Silence,** an elegant (although heavily attended) outdoor dinner served away from civilization. Champagne and Northern Territory specialty dishes—including bush salads—are served on tables covered with crisp white linens, right in the desert. An astronomer takes you on a stargazing tour of the southern sky while you dine. In winter, hot mulled wine is served around a campfire. Dinners can be reserved through the resort's central service.

$$$–$$$$ ✕ **Rockpool Restaurant.** Take a culinary cruise through Asia without leaving poolside at this casual alfresco eatery at Sails in the Desert hotel. Start with chicken satay, then move on to Thai vegetable curry or spiced snapper oven-roasted in a banana leaf. Because it's outside, this restaurant closes seasonally during the hottest part of summer (January) and the worst of winter (July). ⊠ *Sails in the Desert hotel, Yulara Dr., Yulara* ☎ *08/ 8957–7417* ⌸ *Reservations essential* ▭ *AE, DC, MC, V* ⊘ *No lunch.*

$$$
Fodor'sChoice ✕ **Kuniya Restaurant.** Named after the python that battled the Liru snake ★ in Aboriginal creation stories, this restaurant is the best in town. The decor reflects local legends, with images of Kuniya and Liru burned into two magnificent wooden panels at the entrance. A "Kuniya Dreaming" mural covers the rear wall. Appetizers and main courses are named after the Australian states. Specialties include barramundi, duck, and crayfish. ⊠ *Sails in the Desert hotel, Yulara Dr., Yulara* ☎ *08/8957–7714* ⌸ *Reservations essential* ▭ *AE, DC, MC, V* ⊘ *No lunch.*

$–$$ ✕ **Geckos Cafe.** Yellow walls and deep-blue, exposed ceiling struts and pipes add interest to this barnlike eatery in the main shopping center. All-day dining options include inexpensive appetizers, yellowfin tuna kebabs, and several pastas and wood-fired pizzas—there's even a dessert pizza. You can also drop in for a quick coffee or slice of cake. ⊠ *Town Sq., Yulara Centre, Yulara* ☎ *08/8957–7722* ▭ *AE, DC, MC, V.*

★ **$–$$** ✕ **Outback Pioneer BBQ.** Discover why Australians love cooking and dining outdoors at this casual open-air eatery. Order steak, prawn skewers, or a kangaroo kebab from the server, then cook it to your liking on huge barbecues. Pile your plate with greens from the salad bar, and tuck in at

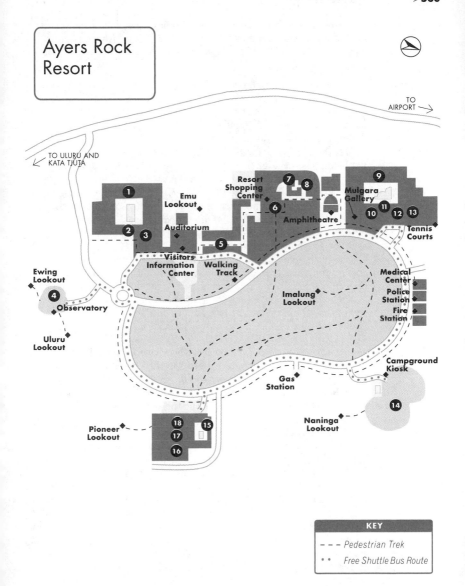

Ayers Rock Resort

TO AIRPORT →

← TO ULURU AND KATA TJUTA

KEY

– – – *Pedestrian Trek*

• • *Free Shuttle Bus Route*

long tables beneath corrugated iron canopies. This place buzzes with life even at the height of summer. ⊠ *Outback Pioneer Hotel & Lodge, Yulara Dr., Yulara* ☎ *08/8957–7606* ⊟ *AE, DC, MC, V* ⊘ *No lunch.*

Where to Stay

$$$$ 🏨 **Desert Gardens Hotel.** Clusters of rooms in this one- and two-story hotel are surrounded by extensive native gardens. Blond-wood furniture complements desert hues in the small, neat rooms, all of which are named after different Australian flora and have a balcony or courtyard. Although standard rooms have a shower only, deluxe rooms have whirlpool baths and twin hand basins. Whitegums restaurant prepares tempting breakfast and dinner buffets. For a lunch snack with an emphasis on fresh and healthful, pop into the Bunya Bar. ⊠ *Yulara Dr., Yulara 0872* ☎ *08/8957–7714* 🖶 *08/8957–7716* ⊕ *www.voyages.com.au* ⟱ *218 rooms* ⟱ *2 restaurants, room service, in-room data ports, some in-room safes, some in-room hot tubs, minibars, refrigerators, room TVs with movies, pool, 2 bars, babysitting, dry cleaning, laundry service, travel services, free parking; no smoking* ⊟ *AE, DC, MC, V.*

$$$$ 🏨 **Emu Walk Apartments.** Fancy a fully equipped kitchen (complete with champagne glasses), a separate living room, and daily maid service? These one- and two-bedroom apartments are just the thing. Each unit contains a sofa bed, so one-bedrooms can sleep four, and the balconied two-bedrooms can accommodate six or eight. There's no on-site restaurant, but you're welcome to dine in any of Ayers Rock Resort's eateries. ⊠ *Yulara Dr., Yulara 0872* ☎ *08/8957–7714* 🖶 *08/8957–7742* ⊕ *www.voyages.com.au* ⟱ *40 1-bedroom and 20 2-bedroom apartments* ⟱ *Kitchens, minibars, microwaves, refrigerators, room TVs with movies, babysitting, dry cleaning, laundry service, airport shuttle* ⊟ *AE, DC, MC, V.*

$$$$ 🏨 **Longitude 131°.** Popping out of the desert like a row of white cones, a
Fodor'sChoice gathering of 14 luxury "tents" make up this unique resort, which is about
★ 3 km [2 mi] away from the other hotels at Ayers Rock Resort, on its own in the desert. Each raised, fully enclosed, prefabricated unit has a balcony with floor-to-ceiling sliding-glass doors for a panoramic view of the rock from the king-size bed. Set 2 km (1 mi) from the boundary of Uluru–Kata Tjuta National Park, it's the closest accommodation to the main sites. There's a two-night minimum stay, but the price includes meals, drinks, and tours. You can park free at Sails in the Desert and hop a free transfer bus here. ⊠ *Yulara 0872* ☎ *08/8957–7131* ⊕ *www.voyages.com.au* ⟱ *14 tents* ⟱ *Restaurant, in-room safes, minibars, refrigerators, pool, bar, lounge, dry cleaning, laundry service, business services, airport shuttle, travel services; no room TVs* ⊟ *AE, DC, MC, V* ⦿*FAP.*

★ **$$$$** 🏨 **Lost Camel.** Blocks and splashes of lime, purple, and orange in contemporary, boxy white rooms make this the funkiest hotel for a thousand miles. Central to each room is the bed, which backs onto an open hand-basin area. The only windows are in the divided bathroom—so remember to draw the curtains. Grouped around courtyard gardens, the rooms have sound systems and CDs, as well as irons, ironing boards, and tea- and coffee-making equipment. A café, wine bar, and plasma screen with cable channels encourage socializing in the lobby lounge. ⊠ *Yulara Dr., Yulara 0872* ☎ *08/8957–5650* 🖶 *08/8957–7657* ⊕ *www.voyages.com.au* ⟱ *99 rooms* ⟱ *Café, room service, in-room safes,* *minibars, refrigerators, pool, lobby lounge, wine bar, free parking; no room TVs* ☲ *AE, DC, MC, V.*

$$$$ ⊡ **Sails in the Desert.** Architectural shade sails, ghost-gum-fringed lawns, Aboriginal art, and numerous facilities distinguish the resort's best traditional option. Step out of your richly colored gold, green, and midnight-blue room onto a private balcony overlooking either the huge, lawn-surrounded pool area or the garden. Six deluxe rooms have outside whirlpool baths on the balcony. Climb a lookout tower for views of Uluṟu in the distance. ⊠ *Yulara Dr., Yulara 0872* ☎ *08/8957–7417* 🖷 *08/8957–7474* ⊕ *www.voyages.com.au* ↦ *230 rooms, 2 suites* ⟂ *3 restaurants, room service, in-room data ports, some in-room hot tubs, minibars, refrigerators, room TVs with movies, 2 tennis courts, pool, massage, bar, shops, babysitting, dry cleaning, laundry service, Internet, business services, meeting rooms, airport shuttle, travel services, free parking; no smoking* ☲ *AE, DC, MC, V.*

★ $$–$$$$ ⊡ **Outback Pioneer Hotel & Lodge.** The theme of this property is the 1860s Outback, complete with corrugated iron, timber beams, and camel saddles, but you won't be roughing it here—not with a pool and two restaurants. Guests at the adjoining lodge, a budget accommodation with large and small dorms, and a communal kitchen, share the hotel's facilities. The Bough House serves a set-price dinner buffet of traditional roasts and bush specialties like kangaroo, and the Pioneer BBQ self-cook restaurant opens at 6:30 PM. A shuttle bus connects the lodge to the other properties every 15 minutes. ⊠ *Yulara Dr., Yulara 0872* ☎ *08/8957–7606* 🖷 *08/8957–7615* ⊕ *www.voyages.com.au* ↦ *167 hotel rooms, 125 without bath; 168 lodge bunk beds* ⟂ *2 restaurants, snack bar, some kitchenettes, some minibars, some microwaves, some refrigerators, some room TVs with movies, pool, bar, shop, laundry facilities, Internet, car rental, travel services, free parking; no phones in some rooms, no TV in some rooms, no smoking* ☲ *AE, DC, MC, V.*

△ **Ayers Rock Resort Campground.** Sand goannas wander around this large campground amid the red dunes, where 220 tent sites are scattered around 29 green lawns. Powered sites and air-conditioned cabins are also available; cabins come with linens, full kitchens, and TVs—but no bathrooms. It's a 50-yard walk to the nearest amenities block. There's also a well-equipped camper's kitchen, a grocery, an Outback-style shelter with free gas barbecues, and bicycle rentals. Leashed dogs are allowed. ⊠ *Yulara Dr., Ayers Rock Resort, Yulara 0872* ☎ *08/8956–2055* 🖷 *08/8956–2260* ✉ *A$13–A$150* ↦ *418 sites without bath, 14 cabins without bath* ⟂ *Flush toilets, partial hookups (electric and water), drinking water, laundry facilities, showers, fire grates, grills, picnic tables, electricity, public telephone, general store, playground, pool* ☲ *AE, DC, MC, V.*

Uluṟu & Kata Tjuṯa A to Z

AIR TRAVEL

Qantas operates daily direct flights from Sydney and Cairns to Ayers Rock Airport, which is 5 km (3 mi) north of the resort complex. Passengers from other capital cities fly to Alice Springs to connect with flights to Ayers Rock Airport.

All other air services are charter flights. AAT Kings runs a complimentary shuttle bus between the airport and Yulara, which meets every flight. If you have reservations at the resort, there's no need to call ahead to reserve a spot on one of these shuttles; you'll find resort representatives waiting outside the baggage claim area of the airport to whisk you and other guests away on the 10-minute drive.

✈ Airline Qantas ☎ 13-1313 ⊕ www.qantas.com.

✈ Airport & Shuttles AAT Kings ☎ 08/8952-1700 or 1800/334009. **Ayers Rock Airport** ☎ 08/8956-2020.

BUS TRAVEL

Bus companies traveling to Ayers Rock Resort from Alice Springs include AAT Kings and Greyhound Australia. AAT Kings also conducts daily tours of the area.

✈ AAT Kings ☎ 08/8952-1700 or 1800/334009 ⊕ www.aatkings.com. **Greyhound Australia** ☎ 08/8952-7888 or 08/8956-2171 ⊕ www.greyhound.com.au.

CAR RENTAL

Renting your own car is a very good idea if you prefer to explore the national park on your own schedule; the only other ways to get to Uluṟu & Kata Tjuṯa are on group bus tours, or by renting a chauffered taxi or coach. Avis, Hertz, and Thrifty–Territory Rent-a-Car all rent cars at the resort. Be sure you arrange for your rental early; there are a limited number of cars available.

✈ Avis ☎ 13-6333 ⊕ www.avis.com.au. **Hertz** ☎ 1300/132105 ⊕ www.hertznt.com. **Thrifty-Territory Rent-a-Car** ☎ 08/8956-2030 ⊕ www.rentacar.com.au.

CAR TRAVEL

The 440-km (273-mi) trip from Alice Springs to Ayers Rock Resort takes about five hours. The paved Lasseter Highway is in fine condition.

From the resort it's 19 km (12 mi) to Uluṟu or 53 km (33 mi) to Kata Tjuṯa. The road to Kata Tjuṯa is paved. Routes between hotels and sights are clearly marked, and since car-rental costs are competitive with bus tours, renting a car may be best for larger parties.

EMERGENCIES

In an emergency, dial **000** to reach an ambulance, the police, or the fire department. The medical clinic at the Royal Flying Doctor Base is open weekdays 9–noon and 2–5 and weekends 10 AM–11 PM.

✈ Police ☎ 08/8956-2166. **Royal Flying Doctor Base Medical Clinic** ✉ Yulara Dr., near police station ☎ No direct phone, dial 000 ⊕ www.rfds.org.au/central/yulara.htm.

MAIL, THE INTERNET & SHIPPING

Australia Post has a shop in the Ayers Rock Resort Shopping Centre. It's open daily, with reduced hours on weekends and public holidays. Internet facilities are in the shopping center information and tour office, and at all hotels.

✈ Australia Post ✉ Resort Shopping Centre, Yulara Dr. ☎ 08/8956-2288.

MONEY MATTERS

ANZ Bank has a branch and ATM in the Resort Shopping Centre. Foreign exchange and banking services are available weekdays. The Commonwealth Bank has an agency within the Australia Post office.

🚺 **ANZ** ✉ Resort Shopping Centre, Yulara Dr. ☎ 08/8956-2070. **Commonwealth Bank** ✉ Resort Shopping Centre, Yulara Dr. ☎ 08/8956-2288

TAXIS

For a chauffeur-driven limousine, contact V.I.P. Chauffeur Cars. Uluṟu Express minibuses can whisk you from the resorts to the sights for much less than the cost of a guided bus tour—plus, you can go at your own convenience.

🚺 **Uluṟu Express** ☎ 08/8956-2152 ⊕ www.uluruexpress.com.au. **V.I.P. Chauffeur Cars** ☎ 08/8956-2283.

TELEPHONES

The area code for Ayers Rock Resort (and all the Northern Territory, Western Australia, and South Australia) is 08. Mobile–cell phones work within a 10-km (6-mi) radius of Ayers Rock Resort, but not within Uluṟu-Kata Tjuṯa National Park; you can ring friends back at the resort from public phones at the Cultural Centre inside the park. There's a bank of public pay phones in the Ayers Rock Resort Shopping Centre and at all hotels.

TOURS

Anangu Tours, owned and operated by local Aboriginal people, organizes several trips through the region. Included are the Aboriginal Uluṟu Tour (A$119 with breakfast), led by an Aboriginal guide; the Kuniya Sunset Tour (A$89); and the Anangu Culture Pass, which combines the first two tours over one or two days (A$189). You can drive to the trailhead of the Liru Walk (A$58) and the Kuniya Walk (A$58). Guides are Aborigines who work with interpreters. New tours include Dot Painting workshops (A$79) and the Aboriginal Camp Fire (A$49) where participants gather around a fire at the base of Uluṟu and listen to stories told by Aboriginal elders.

Central Australia has some of the clearest and cleanest air in the world—just look up into the night sky. A Night Sky Show takes place each night in a small observatory (which has telescope) on the resort grounds. Viewing times vary with the seasons; sessions last for an hour, and can be booked through Discovery Ecotours for A$32.

🚺 **Anangu Tours** ☎ 08/8956-2123 ⊕ www.anangutours.com.au. **Discovery Ecotours** ☎ 08/8956-2563 ⊕ www.ecotours.com.au.

AIR TOURS The best views of Uluṟu and Kata Tjuṯa are from the air. Lightplane tours, with courtesy hotel pickup, include 40-minute flights over Ayers Rock and the Olgas, and day tours to Kings Canyon. Prices run from A$135 to A$510 per person; for options, contact Ayers Rock Scenic Flights. Helicopter flights are A$100 per person for 15 minutes over Ayers Rock, or A$180 for 30 minutes over the Olgas and the rock. You can book the three-seater helicopter for a Kings Canyon tour, which includes Lake Amadeus, for A$1,680.

🔢 **Ayers Rock Helicopters** ☎ 08/8956-2077 ⊕ www.helicoptergroup.com/ayers_rock. htm. **Ayers Rock Scenic Flights** ☎ 08/8956-2345 🖷 08/8956-2472 ⊕ www. ayersrockflights.com.au.

MOTORCYCLE TOURS
The balmy desert climate makes Uluru Motorcycle Tours enjoyable (and popular), and provides the chance for unique vacation photographs. Guides communicate with their passengers by helmet intercoms. Prices run from A$85 for a half-hour, 30-km (19-mi) "Pat Special" ride, to A$155 for the Ayers Rock Sunset tour. The 4½-hour sunset trip to Ayers Rock and the Olgas is A$345, including champagne.

🔢 **Uluru Motorcycle Tours** ☎ 08/8956-2019 🖷 08/8956-2196.

WALKING TOURS
The free Mala Walk is led by Aboriginal rangers who show you the land from their perspective. The walk starts from the base of the Uluru climbing trail at 8 AM daily from October to April and at 10 AM the rest of the year. Discovery Ecotours specializes in small-group tours of Uluru with guides who have extensive local knowledge. The Uluru Walk, a 10-km (6-mi) hike around the base, gives fascinating insight into the area's significance to the Aboriginal people. It departs daily, includes breakfast and hotel transfers, and costs A$110. Book at least a day in advance.

🔢 **Discovery Ecotours** ☎ 08/8956-2563 or 1800/803174. **Mala Walk** ☎ 08/8956-3138.

VISITOR INFORMATION

The Uluru–Kata Tjuta Cultural Centre is on the park road just before you reach the rock. It also contains the park's ranger station. The Cultural Centre is open daily 7 AM–6 PM year-round. The visitor center next to the Desert Gardens Hotel on Yulara Drive is open daily 8:30–5.

🔢 **Uluru–Kata Tjuta Cultural Centre** ☎ 08/8956-3138. **Visitor Center** ☎ 08/8957-7377.

Darwin, the Top End & the Kimberley

WORD OF MOUTH

"There is nowhere in the world like Darwin. It is an ancient land that is part American 'wild west' with a touch of Asia thrown in."

—lizF

Updated by
Graham
Hodgson and
Shamara
Williams

THE TOP END IS A GEOGRAPHIC DESCRIPTION—but it's also a state of mind. Isolated from the rest of Australia by thousands of miles of desert and lonely scrubland, Top Enders are different and proud of it. From the remote wetlands and stone country of Arnhem Land—home to thousands of Aborigines—to the lush tropical city of Darwin, the Top End is a gateway to a region where people from 50 different national and cultural backgrounds live in what they regard as the real Australia. It's an isolation that contributes to strong feelings of independence from the rest of the country—Southerners are regarded with a mixture of pity and ridicule.

For thousands of years, this area of northern Australia has been home to Aboriginal communities. Stunning examples of ancient Aboriginal rock art remain—on cliffs, in hidden valleys, and in Darwin art galleries. Today, however, the region is a melting pot of cultures and traditions. Darwin and Broome—closer geographically to the cities of Southeast Asia than to any Australian counterparts—host the nation's most racially diverse populations: Aborigines, Anglos, and Asians sharing a tropical lifestyle.

The starkness of the isolation of the Top End and Western Australia's Kimberley is reflected in its tiny population. Although the Northern Territory occupies one-sixth of Australia's landmass, its population of 192,000 makes up just more than 1% of the continent's citizenry—an average density of around one person per 8 square km (3 square mi). In many areas kangaroos and cattle vastly outnumber the locals. The Kimberley, an area larger than the state of Kansas, is home to only 30,000 people. Traveling by road from Darwin to Broome is the best way to see the Kimberley, but you pass through only nine communities in 2,016 km (1,250 mi).

The Kimberley possesses some of the most dramatic landscapes in Australia. A land of rugged ranges, tropical wetlands, and desert, of vast cattle stations and wonderful national parks, including the bizarre, beautiful, red-and-black-striped sandstone domes and towers of Purnululu National Park, the Kimberley is still the frontier. Like Top Enders, the people of the Kimberley region see themselves as living in a land apart from the rest of the nation, and it's easy to see why: landscape and distance combine to make the Kimberley one of the world's few uniquely open spaces.

See Chapter 13 for more information on four-wheel-driving in the Top End and the Kimberley's great outdoors.

Exploring Darwin, the Top End & the Kimberley

The telltale recurring phrase "tyranny of distance" was first used to describe Australia's relationship to the rest of the world. In many ways it still describes the Top End and the Kimberley, with vast distances setting this region apart from the rest of the nation. Especially if you plan to get out to the Kimberley, you should consider seeing it over a couple of weeks and combining it with another week visiting the Red Centre for full effect.

11

If you have
3 days

Start from **Darwin** just after dawn and head east on the Arnhem Highway to Fogg Dam to view the birdlife. Continue into **Kakadu National Park,** and picnic at the rock-art site at Ubirr. Take a scenic flight in the afternoon, then a trip to the Bowali Visitors Centre, and you can overnight in **Jabiru.** On the second day, head to Nourlangie Rock; then continue to the Yellow Water cruise at **Cooinda** and stay there for the night. The next day, drive to **Litchfield National Park** and visit Florence, Tjaynera, or Wangi Falls for a late picnic lunch, followed by a stop at Tolmer Falls before returning to Darwin.

If you have
5 days

From **Darwin,** drive to **Litchfield National Park,** entering through Batchelor. A swim at the Florence Falls plunge pool and a picnic in the rain forest will help you sleep well here. After an early start on the second day, head toward **Kakadu National Park** via the Arnhem Highway. Pause en route at the Bark Hut Inn for morning tea. You should reach the rock-art site and magnificent floodplain vistas at Ubirr in time for a late lunch. After Ubirr, stop at Bowali Visitors Centre before continuing to the art sites at Nourlangie Rock. In the afternoon visit the Warradjan Aboriginal Cultural Centre at Cooinda, then take the evening Yellow Water cruise. On the third day head down to the southern half of Kakadu National Park. After lunch continue to Edith Falls to camp in **Nitmiluk (Katherine Gorge) National Park** or head into **Katherine** for the night. Next morning cruise up Katherine Gorge in Nitmiluk National Park. After lunch head south to **Cutta Cutta Caves** and the thermal pools, and spend the night in **Mataranka.** On Day 5 meander back toward Darwin, exploring the sights around the townships of Pine Creek and Adelaide River along the way.

If you have
10 days

Take the five-day tour above, then from Mataranka head back through **Katherine** and take the Victoria Highway, passing through mesa formations and Timber Creek to **Kununurra** for the night. On the sixth day, take in the spectacular landscapes of **Purnululu National Park** by four-wheel drive or with a guided tour, and spend the night in **Halls Creek.** It'll be a long haul west the seventh day on the Great Northern Highway, but you can make it to **Geikie Gorge National Park** for an afternoon boat tour, a welcome and interesting respite before heading off to camp the night at **Windjana Gorge National Park.** Another early start on Day 8 will get you to **Broome,** the fascinating old pearling town. Spend the night, then take a fishing charter the ninth day or just amble around this attractive and historic town for a while. Spend a second night and then fly back to Darwin.

Here the year is divided into two seasons: the Wet (December–April) and the Dry (May–November). The Dry is a period of idyllic weather with warm days and cool nights, while the Wet brings monsoonal storms that dump an average of 52 inches of rain in a few short months. However, the sights are much less crowded during the Wet, plus the rain paints the landscape vivid green. You can also catch spectacular electrical storms, particularly over the ocean.

About the Restaurants

As well as restaurants and cafés serving up local seafood and Aussie tucker (including buffalo, crocodile, and kangaroo), Darwin and Broome have establishments specializing in European and Asian fare. Reservations are advisable at all but the most casual of places, and tipping is welcomed but not expected. On the road, wayside inns and roadhouses supply basic burgers, steaks, pies, and refreshments. If you're driving long distances, it's a good idea to stock up on snacks and drinks in Darwin, Katherine, or Broome.

	WHAT IT COSTS In Australian Dollars				
	$$$$	**$$$**	**$$**	**$**	**¢**
AT DINNER	over $50	$36–$50	$21–$35	$10–$20	under $10

Prices are for a main course at dinner.

About the Hotels

Apart from Darwin hotels and Top End resorts, accommodations fall into the more basic category. Roadhouse accommodations can be anything from rudimentary rooms in prefabricated huts with sagging mattresses, wheezing air-conditioners, and doors without locks to clean, comfortable, no-frills lodgings. Places without air-conditioning are rare. Homestays and working cattle stations provide a true bush experience that often includes trail rides, fishing, and participation in station activities.

	WHAT IT COSTS In Australian Dollars				
	$$$$	**$$$**	**$$**	**$**	**¢**
FOR 2 PEOPLE	over $300	$201–$300	$151–$200	$100–$150	under $100

Prices are for two people in a standard double room in high season, including tax and service, based on the European Plan (with no meals) unless otherwise noted.

Timing

Unless you're used to heat and humidity, the best time to tour is between May and August, during the peak months of the Dry. May and June are when the waterfalls of Kakadu and the Kimberley are at their most dramatic. When you're on the road, early starts beat the heat and get you to swimming holes in the middle of the day—the crucial time for cooling off. Morning and evening cruises are best to avoid the heat, to see animals, and to take advantage of the ideal light for photography (by noon the light is often harsh and flat).

DARWIN

There's no other city in Australia that dates its history by a single cataclysmic event. For the people of Darwin—including the vast majority who weren't here at the time—everything is dated as before or after 1974's Cyclone Tracy, which hit on Christmas Eve. It wasn't just the death toll (65 people) that left a lasting scar in the area; it was the immensity of

11

Bushwalking

The national parks of the Top End and the Kimberley are ideal for hiking—Australians call it bushwalking—and suit all fitness levels. Major rock-art sites in Kakadu, for example, incorporate bushwalks from an hour or so to a half day in length. Park rangers supply maps and route information for walks that last overnight and longer. The rugged adventures require care and planning, but the rewards are unforgettable memories of trekking through some of the most remote places on Earth. Bring a net to wrap around your face and head to combat blackflies, which are plentiful in the Outback, and have the annoying habit of swarming around your eyes, ears, and mouth. Always wear a hat and carry ample supplies of water.

Gourmet Game

The menus in Darwin seem to indicate that there is little the average Territorian won't eat—buffalo, crocodile, camel, and kangaroo are all frequently featured. Another local favorite, barramundi, is one of the tastiest fish in the world. Buffalo can be tough, but a tender piece is like a gamey piece of beef. Opinion is divided about crocodile; it, too, can be tough, but (like every other reptile, it seems) a good piece tastes like chicken. The newest eating precinct of Cullen Bay, only five minutes from the city and overlooking the marina near where Darwin Harbour cruises embark, has chic indoor and outdoor eating venues with great views of the harbor or marina.

Homestays & Homesteads

A number of pastoral properties in the region provide accommodations ranging from basic tent sites to homestays and luxurious suites. On many you'll have the chance to experience—and even participate in—life on a working cattle station. If you're keen on fishing, isolated coastal resorts can cater to your every whim, with vessels, guides, and delightful lodgings provided.

National Parks

Along with the iconic Kakadu, the Top End and Kimberley regions are adorned with rugged national parks rich in spectacular terrain, flora and fauna, and ancient art. Between Katherine and Broome, the highway passes among such natural wonders as the Bungle Bungle, Geikie Gorge, Tunnel Creek, and Windjana Gorge national parks in the Kimberley.

Stargazing

From Darwin to Broome, camping out under the stars is one of the real pleasures of traveling through the Outback. It can be a bit of a trial in the Wet—if you don't get rained on, you still have to contend with the mosquitoes—but camping in the Dry is perfect. Depending on personal taste, you may not even need a tent. Most locals just take a swag—a heavy canvas wrapped around a rolled mattress. The region abounds in out-of-the-way spots to pull up and sleep in the open. Wherever you go, ask a local to tell you the best place to throw down your swag, brew a billy (pot) of tea, and contemplate the glories of the southern night sky.

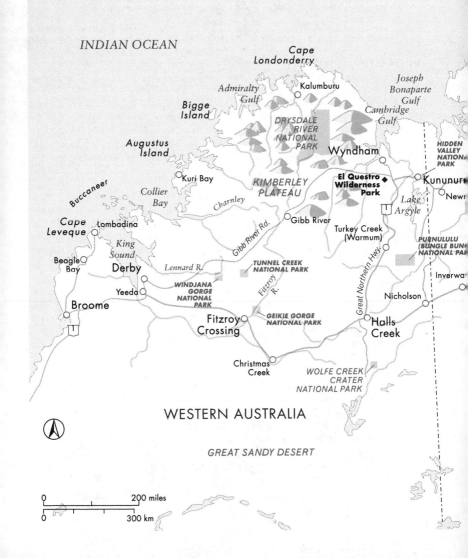

The Top End & the Kimberley

Timor Sea

INDIAN OCEAN

Cape Londonderry

Admiralty Gulf

Kalumburu

Joseph Bonaparte Gulf

Bigge Island

Cambridge Gulf

DRYSDALE RIVER NATIONAL PARK

Augustus Island

Wyndham

HIDDEN VALLEY NATIONAL PARK

Kuri Bay

KIMBERLEY PLATEAU

El Questro Wilderness Park

Kununurra

Buccaneer

Collier Bay

Charnley

Newr

Cape Leveque

Lombadina

Gibb River

Lake Argyle

Gibb River Rd.

Turkey Creek (Warmum)

PURNULULU (BUNGLE BUN NATIONAL PAR

King Sound

Lennard R.

TUNNEL CREEK NATIONAL PARK

Beagle Bay

Great Northern Hwy.

Derby

Inverwa

WINDJANA GORGE NATIONAL PARK

Fitzroy R.

Yeeda

Nicholson

Broome

Fitzroy Crossing

GEIKIE GORGE NATIONAL PARK

Halls Creek

Christmas Creek

WOLFE CREEK CRATER NATIONAL PARK

WESTERN AUSTRALIA

GREAT SANDY DESERT

| 0 | | 200 miles |
| 0 | | 300 km |

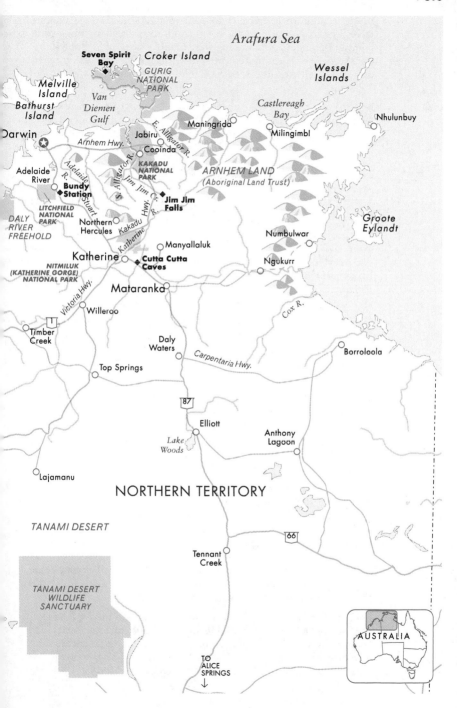

Arafura Sea

Seven Spirit Bay
Croker Island

GURIG NATIONAL PARK

Melville Island

Van Diemen Gulf

Bathurst Island

Wessel Islands

Castlereagh Bay

Nhulunbuy

Darwin

Arnhem Hwy.

Jabiru

Maningrida

Milingimbl

Adelaide River

Adelaide R.

Bundy Station

Alligator R.

Cooinda

KAKADU NATIONAL PARK

Jim Jim Cr.

ARNHEM LAND
(Aboriginal Land Trust)

E. Alligator R.

Groote Eylandt

LITCHFIELD NATIONAL PARK

Stuart

Jim Jim Falls

DALY RIVER FREEHOLD

Northern Hercules

Kakadu Hwy.

Numbulwar

Katherine R.

Manyallaluk

Katherine

Cutta Cutta Caves

Ngukurr

NITMILUK (KATHERINE GORGE) NATIONAL PARK

Victoria Hwy.

Mataranka

Willeroo

Cox R.

Timber Creek

Daly Waters

Carpentaria Hwy.

Borroloola

Top Springs

87

Elliott

Anthony Lagoon

Lake Woods

Lajamanu

NORTHERN TERRITORY

TANAMI DESERT

66

TANAMI DESERT WILDLIFE SANCTUARY

Tennant Creek

AUSTRALIA

TO ALICE SPRINGS
↓

the destruction wrought by Tracy. More than 70% of Darwin's homes were destroyed or suffered severe structural damage; all services—communications, power, and water—were cut off. The resulting food shortage, lack of water, and concerns about disease moved government officials to evacuate the city; some 25,600 were airlifted out and another 7,200 left by road.

It's a tribute to those who stayed and to those who have come to live here after Tracy that the rebuilt city now thrives as an administrative and commercial center for northern Australia. Old Darwin has been replaced by something of an edifice complex—such buildings as Parliament House and the Supreme Court all seem a bit too grand for such a small city, especially one that prides itself on its relaxed, multicultural openness.

The seductiveness of contemporary Darwin lifestyles belies a Top End history of failed attempts by Europeans dating back to 1824 to establish an enclave in a harsh, unyielding climate. The original 1869 settlement, called Palmerston, was built on a parcel of mangrove wetlands and scrub forest that had changed little in 15 million years. It was not until 1911, after it had already weathered the disastrous cyclones of 1878, 1882, and 1897, that the town was named after the scientist who had visited Australia's shores aboard the *Beagle* in 1839.

Today Darwin is the best place from which to explore the beauty and diversity of Australia's Top End, as well as the wonders of Kakadu, Nitmiluk (Katherine Gorge), and the mighty Kimberley region.

Exploring Darwin

The orientation point for visitors is the Smith Street Mall. The downtown grid of streets around the mall is at the very tip of a peninsula. Most of the suburbs and outlying attractions lie out beyond the airport.

Numbers in the text correspond to numbers in the margin and on the Darwin map.

a good
walk

From the Smith Street Mall head southwest down Knuckey Street across Mitchell Street. On the right, at the intersection with the Esplanade, is the 1925 **Lyons Cottage** ❶ ▶ museum, which focuses on local history, including early settlement, pearling, and relations with Indonesian and Chinese groups. On the other side of Knuckey Street, the **Old Admiralty House** ❷ is elevated on columns, once a common Darwin architectural feature. Across the Esplanade, in Bicentennial Park and overlooking the harbor, stand the **USS *Peary* Memorial/USAAF Memorial** ❸ and the **Cenotaph/War Memorial** ❹. Farther southeast, behind the Esplanade, stands the modern **Northern Territory Parliament House** ❺.

On a corner in front of the Parliament building, on the Esplanade, is the **Overland Telegraph Memorial** ❻, the site of Australia's first telegraph connection with the rest of the world in 1871. Facing the memorial is **Government House** ❼. Built in 1883, it has remarkably withstood the ravages of cyclones, as well as Japanese bombing in World War II.

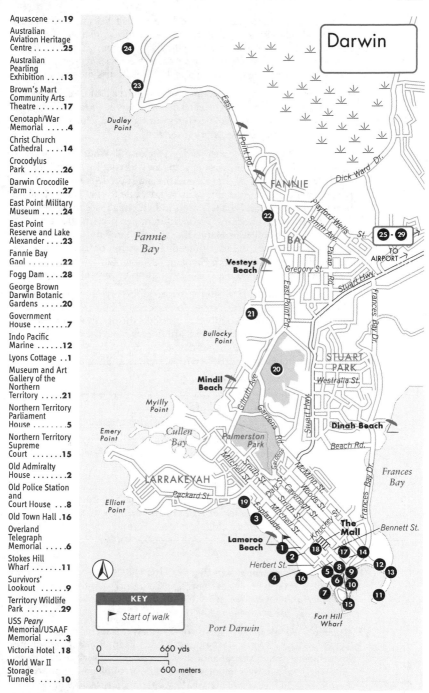

Darwin

KEY

► *Start of walk*

0   660 yds

0   600 meters

On the opposite side of the Esplanade, between Mitchell and Smith streets, are the **Old Police Station and Court House** ⑧, which date from 1884, with their long porches and old stone facades. They currently function as governmental offices. **Survivors' Lookout** ⑨, a memorial to the victims of Japan's first bombing of Australia in 1942, is across the road.

To get to the wharf area, take the stairs down the cliff face. Directly at the bottom of the stairs is the entrance to Darwin's **World War II Storage Tunnels** ⑩, which secured fuel stores during World War II. Inside there are photographs of Darwin during wartime.

A walk of 435 feet to the east leads to **Stokes Hill Wharf** ⑪. The wharf now has a dual function: serving ships and serving locals with restaurants, weekend markets, and a good fishing spot. The wharf is a great place to wind up at sunset for a drink and a bite to eat. The view of the harbor is fantastic, and chances are good you might see some local dolphins waiting for fish scraps. For a different perspective on fish, stop in at the wharf's **Indo Pacific Marine** ⑫, where a large indoor tank with a coral-reef ecosystem and its astonishing collection of fish reside. In the same building, the **Australian Pearling Exhibition** ⑬ has a lively presentation of northern Australia's history of hunting and cultivating pearls.

Returning up the cliff to Smith Street, look to your right for **Christ Church Cathedral** ⑭. A little farther down the block, on the left, the **Northern Territory Supreme Court** ⑮ has a collection of Aboriginal art and burial poles. On the same side of Smith Street stand the ruins of the **Old Town Hall** ⑯, built in 1883 and destroyed by Cyclone Tracy in 1974. **Brown's Mart Community Arts Theatre** ⑰, built in 1885, is across the road.

Stop in at the 1894 **Victoria Hotel** ⑱, across Bennett Street on the left-hand side of the Smith Street Mall. Proceed to the balcony for a drink—a fine way to conclude a walking tour of Darwin.

TIMING This scenic stroll takes just a couple of hours unless you pause to take in the exhibits. Summer temperatures can be exhausting, so dress lightly and carry an umbrella for extra shade. Museum hours may be shortened during the Wet.

What to See: City Center

⑬ **Australian Pearling Exhibition.** Since the early 19th century, fortune seekers have hunted for pearls in Australia's northern waters. Exhibits at this museum cover everything from pearl farming to pearl jewelry settings. ⊠ *Stokes Hill Wharf, Wharf Precinct* ☎ *08/8999–6573* 💲 *A$6.60* ⊙ *Daily 10–5.*

⑰ **Brown's Mart Community Arts Theatre.** This 1885 building has seen duty as an emporium, a mining exchange, and currently as a theater. ⊠ *Smith St. and Harry Chan Ave., City Center* ☎ *08/8981–5522* 💲 *Free admission, fee for performances* ⊙ *During performances.*

④ **Cenotaph/War Memorial.** The site of World War II memorial services on February 19 and Anzac Day on April 25, this monument is dedicated to members of the Australian armed forces, rescue services, and civilians who lost their lives in times of war. The monument is opposite Herbert Street. ⊠ *Bicentennial Park, Esplanade, Bicentennial Park.*

need a break?

18 The balcony of the **Victoria Hotel** (✉ 27 Smith St. Mall, City Center ☎ 08/8981–4011), overlooking the passing parade on Smith Street Mall, is a good place for a cool drink. A Darwin institution since its construction in 1894, the Vic has been hit by every cyclone and rebuilt afterward.

14 **Christ Church Cathedral.** Darwin's Anglican church was largely destroyed by Cyclone Tracy, and the remains of the original 1902 structure have been incorporated into the renovated building. ✉ *Smith St. and Esplanade S, East Esplanade* ☎ *Free* ☉ *During worship hrs.*

7 **Government House.** The oldest building in Darwin, Government House has been the home of the administrator for the area since 1870. Despite being bombed by Japanese aircraft in 1942 and damaged by the cyclones of 1897, 1937, and 1974, the building looks much as it did in 1879 when it was first completed. The house, which is not open to the public, faces the Overland Telegraph Memorial. ✉ *Esplanade S, East Esplanade.*

★ **12** **Indo Pacific Marine.** This marine interpretative center houses a large open tank with one of the few self-contained coral-reef ecosystems in the Southern Hemisphere. Other exhibits include a static display of rare, deep-water coral skeletons and an exhibit explaining the effects of global warming on the planet. Night tours, which begin at 7 on Wednesday, Friday, and Sunday and take you by flashlight to view fluorescent reef plants and animals, include a lecture, a seafood buffet dinner, and wine. Bookings are essential. The pearling exhibition tracks the history of this important local industry. ✉ *Stokes Hill Wharf, Wharf Precinct* ☎ *08/8981–1294 Indo Pacific* 🖘 *A\$18, night tours A\$80* ☉ *Apr.–Oct., daily 10–5; Nov.–Mar., daily 9–1.*

▶ **1** **Lyons Cottage.** One of several buildings dating back to the early settlement of northern Australia in downtown Darwin, Lyons Cottage was built in 1925 for executives of the British-Australian Telegraph Company (B.A.T.). The stone building is now a historical museum with exhibits on the town's history, Chinese immigrants, pearl diving, early explorers, and the Macassans, who came by boat from Indonesia, touched down in Australia, and had contact with the Aborigines centuries ago. ✉ *74 Esplanade, Bicentennial Park* ☎ *08/8981–1750* 🖘 *Free* ☉ *Daily 10–4:30.*

5 **Northern Territory Parliament House.** Australia's northernmost parliament resides in a gleaming home set on cliffs at the edge of the sea. On Saturday, 90-minute tours of the building are conducted at 9 AM and 11 AM from the foyer of Parliament House (reservations essential). Spend your spare time in the extensive library brushing up on local history, or relax with a drink at the Speaker's Corner Cafe. ✉ *Smith St. and Esplanade, State Square, East Esplanade* ☎ *08/8946–1509* 🖘 *Free* ☉ *Weekdays 8–6, weekends 9–6.*

15 **Northern Territory Supreme Court.** This impressive modern building opposite Civic Park complements the neighboring Parliament House. An impressive selection of Aboriginal and contemporary art is displayed in the Great Hall, including intricately painted burial poles from northeast Arnhem Land and Pukamani funeral poles from the Tiwi Islands. ⊠ *Smith St., State Square, East Esplanade* ☎ *08/8999–7953* ☒ *Free* ⊙ *Weekdays 8–5:30.*

❷ Old Admiralty House. Built in 1937 to provide lodging for the naval officer commanding northern Australia, this house is one of the few of its kind that survived Cyclone Tracy. Although you can't go inside, the exterior is definitely worth a look; it's a great example of the old style of architecture—where homes were elevated on columns to beat the heat—that was once common in Darwin. ⊠ *Knuckey St. and Esplanade, Bicentennial Park.*

❽ Old Police Station and Court House. These side-by-side 1884 buildings were reconstructed after Cyclone Tracy to serve as offices for the Northern Territory administrator. The buildings now house government offices, so you can't go past the reception area—but their long verandas and stone facades are lovely examples of period architecture. ⊠ *Esplanade S between Mitchell and Smith Sts., East Esplanade* ☎ *08/8999–7103.*

⑯ Old Town Hall. Built of stone in 1883 during the first mining boom, the building was a naval administration center during World War II; later it was a library and art gallery. It was destroyed by Cyclone Tracy in 1974. The ruins are now used for outdoor theater performances and concerts during the Dry. ⊠ *Smith St. opposite Brown's Mart, City Center* ☎ *No phone* ☒ *Free.*

❻ Overland Telegraph Memorial. On the harbor side of the Esplanade—near the front of Parliament House—is a cairn that marks the place where the first international telegraph cable came ashore from Java in 1871. This monumental event in Australia's history provided the first direct link with the mother country, England. Before that, information and orders from "home" took months to arrive by ship. ⊠ *Esplanade, East Esplanade.*

⑪ Stokes Hill Wharf. The best views of Darwin Harbour are from this working pier, which receives cargo ships, trawlers, defense vessels, and, occasionally, huge cruise liners. It's also a favorite spot for Darwinites to fish, and when the mackerel are running you can join scores of locals over a few beers. The cluster of cafés and restaurants gets busy on weekends and when cruise ships arrive. ⊠ *McMinn St., Darwin Harbour* ☎ *08/8981–4268.*

❾ Survivors' Lookout. On the site of World War II's first Japanese bombing raid on Australia, this memorial commemorates those who died, including sailors of the USS *Peary.* The shaded viewing platform holds a panoramic illustrated map describing the events of that fateful day. The lookout is also the gateway, via stairs down the cliff face, to the wharf precinct. ⊠ *Esplanade S, East Esplanade.*

❸ USS *Peary* Memorial/USAAF Memorial. Although this ship was sunk in Darwin Harbour by Japanese bombers on February 19, 1942, a 4-inch gun salvaged from its deck is now the centerpiece of a memorial to the officers and crew who lost their lives. Also overlooking the harbor is a memorial to USAAF fighter pilot Lieutenant Robert Buel, who was shot down in a P-40 Kittyhawk on February 15, 1942, while defending an Allied convoy in the Timor Sea. His was one of only two serviceable fighters in the Top End at the time. ☒ *Bicentennial Park, Esplanade, opposite Holiday Inn, Bicentennial Park.*

⑩ World War II Storage Tunnels. Darwin's storage tunnels were built during World War II to protect fuel from Japanese bombing raids on the city. Carved into solid rock, the main tunnel is 22 feet high and 210 feet deep. There is a self-guided tour of the atmospheric tunnels, which now house photographic records of the war period. The entrance is at the bottom of the stairs below Survivors' Lookout. ☒ *Esplanade S, Darwin Harbour* ☎ *08/8985–6333* ☜ *A$4.50* ☉ *May–Sept., daily 9–5; Oct.–Apr., Tues.–Fri. 10–2, weekends 10–4.*

Around Darwin

⑲ Aquascene. You can hand-feed hundreds of fish at this beach on the northwestern end of the Esplanade. At high tide, people wade into the water with buckets of bread to feed the schools of batfish, bream, catfish, milkfish, and mullet that come inshore in a feeding frenzy. ☒ *28 Doctor's Gully Rd., Doctor's Gully* ☎ *08/8981–7837* ⊕ *www.aquascene.com. au* ☜ *A$6* ☉ *Daily at high tide.*

㉕ Australian Aviation Heritage Centre. Due to its isolation and sparse population, the Northern Territory played an important role in the expansion of aviation in Australia, and this impressive museum traces the history of flight Down Under. Planes on exhibition include a massive B-52 bomber on permanent loan from the United States—one of very few not on U.S. soil—as well as a Japanese Zero shot down on the first day of bombing raids in 1942. ☒ *557 Stuart Hwy., 8 km (5 mi) northeast of city center, Winnellie* ☎ *08/8947–2145* ⊕ *www.pacificwrecks.com/ restore/darwin.html* ☜ *A$11* ☉ *Daily 9–5.*

★ ㉖ Crocodylus Park. This world-renowned research facility has an excellent air-conditioned crocodile museum and education center. The saurian section of the zoo includes the croc-infested Bellairs Lagoon and pens for breeding and raising. The park also has enclosures with lions, tigers, cassowaries, primates, and turtles. Tours and feedings are at 10, noon, and 2. ☒ *Lot 3439, McMillans Rd. opposite Berrimah Police Centre, Berrimah* ☎ *08/8922–4500* ☜ *A$25* ☉ *Daily 9–5.*

㉗ Darwin Crocodile Farm. With more than 15,000 fresh- and saltwater crocodiles, this farm supplies much of the meat on menus around the Northern Territory. Guided tours are offered at noon. Since the crocs are fed at 2 PM, this is also an ideal time to visit. The café serves crocodile delicacies such as Croc Burger and Crocodile Drumsticks. ☒ *Stuart Hwy., past Arnhem Hwy. turnoff 40 km (25 mi) south of Darwin, Berry Springs* ☎ *08/8988–1450* ⊕ *www.crocfarm.com.au* ☜ *A$10* ☉ *Daily 9–4.*

㉔ East Point Military Museum. This hub of local military history is attractively framed by tropical gardens at the edge of Fannie Bay. Exhibits detail the city's role as a major military base in World War II and include some of the actual weapons and vehicles, observation towers, and bunkers used to defend the city against frequent Japanese air attacks.

⊠ *E. Point Rd., Fannie Bay* ☎ *08/8981–9702* ⊕ *www.epmm.com.au* ☜ *A$10* ⊙ *Daily 9:30–5.*

☺ ㉓ **East Point Reserve and Lake Alexander.** East Point Road leads past the beaches of Fannie Bay onto the headland occupied by the reserve. This is a pleasant expanse of small beaches, cliffs, lawns, and forest, where wallabies can be seen grazing at dawn and dusk. There's also a saltwater lake safe for swimming, a children's playground, and barbecue facilities. ⊠ *E. Point Rd., Fannie Bay* ☜ *Free* ⊙ *Daily 5 AM–11 PM.*

㉒ **Fannie Bay Gaol.** If the sordid stuff of prison life stirs your blood, take a trip out to the gaol (pronounced "jail"), which served as a prison from 1883 to 1979. When it was hit during Japanese raids in World War II, all prisoners were pardoned and released. The grounds, which are now a museum, include even the gallows where the last executions in the Northern Territory took place in 1952. The gaol also houses a Cyclone Tracy display with an excellent photographic collection and a 30-minute video of the devastation. ⊠ *E. Point Rd., Fannie Bay* ☎ *08/8999–8290* ☜ *Free* ⊙ *Daily 10–4:30.*

㉘ **Fogg Dam.** Built as a water supply for the ill-fated rice-growing project of Humpty Doo in the late 1950s, Fogg Dam remains untouched by commercialism. The project failed largely because the birds of the region regarded the rice crop as a rather tasty smorgasbord. The birds—some 230 species, including orange-footed scrubfowl, magpie geese, green pygmy geese, egrets, and royal spoonbills—have remained, and they provide an unforgettable sight at sunrise and sunset during the Dry. Also, look for snakes in the trees along the causeway. Be careful not to get stuck driving through this swampland, and wear clothes that you don't mind getting dirty. ✛ *From Darwin take Stuart Hwy. to Arnhem Hwy. After 24 km (15 mi) turn left and go another 6 km (4 mi); then turn left and drive the last ¾ km (½ mi) to the dam* ⊕ *www.foggdam.com.au/nature.htm.*

☺ ⑳ **George Brown Darwin Botanic Gardens.** First planted in 1879 and previously destroyed by Cyclone Tracy, the grounds today display rain-forest, coastal fore dunes, mangroves, and open woodland environments. There are more than 400 species of palms growing in the gardens. A popular walk takes visitors on a self-guided tour of plants Aborigines used for medicinal purposes. There's also a waterfall and a children's playground. The greenhouse displays ferns and orchids. ⊠ *Gardens Rd. and Geranium St., Mindil Beach* ☎ *08/8981–1958* ☜ *Free* ⊙ *Geranium St. gates daily 24 hrs, Gardens Rd. gates daily 7 AM–7 PM.*

★ ㉑ **Museum and Art Gallery of the Northern Territory.** Natural history, Pacific Island cultures, and visual-arts exhibits fill this regional museum. One room is devoted to Cyclone Tracy, and the Gallery of Aboriginal Man has displays of Aboriginal art and culture that provide solid insight into the lives of the most ancient inhabitants of the Top End. You can also see "Sweetheart," a 16-foot stuffed saltwater crocodile that attacked fishing boats on the Finniss River in the 1970s. Explore the collection of Macassan praus, luggers (wooden boats with large open decks for collecting heaps of oyster shells), and refugee boats in the adjoining **Maritime Museum,** then retire to the Cornucopia Museum Cafe overlooking tropical gardens and the waters of Fannie Bay for a meal. ✉ *Conacher St., Bullocky Point, Fannie Bay* ☎ *08/8999–8201* 💳 *Free* ☉ *Weekdays 9–5, weekends 10–5.*

★ ㉙ **Territory Wildlife Park.** In 1,000 acres of natural bushland, this impressive park is dedicated to the Northern Territory's native fauna and flora. In addition to saltwater crocodiles, water buffalo, dingoes, and waterbirds, it also has an underwater viewing area from which to observe freshwater fish and a nocturnal house kept dark for viewing animals. The treetop-level walkway through the huge aviary provides an opportunity to watch native birds from the swamps and forests at close range. ✉ *Cox Peninsula Rd., 47 km (29 mi) south of Darwin, Berry Springs* ☎ *08/8988–7200* ⊕ *www.territorywildlifepark.com.au* 💳 *A$18* ☉ *Daily 8:30–4; exit open until 6.*

> off the beaten path

LITCHFIELD NATIONAL PARK – This beautiful, relatively new park lies just 122 km (76 mi) south of Darwin off the Stuart Highway. The 1,340 square km (515 square mi) here are covered by an untouched wilderness of monsoonal rain forests, rivers, and striking rock formations. The highlights are four separate, spectacular waterfalls—**Florence, Tjaynera, Wangi, and Tolmer Falls**—all of which have secluded plunge pools (there are crocs here, though; swim at your own risk). There is also a dramatic group of large, freestanding sandstone pillars known as the **Lost City**; and the **Magnetic Termite Mounds**, which have an eerie resemblance to eroded grave markers, dot the black-soiled plains of the park's northern area. You'll need to camp if you want to stay in the park; campgrounds and RV sites are located near several of the major sights (call the Parks and Wildlife Commission of the Northern Territory at ☎ 08/8999–5511 for information). There are also a few restaurants and a modest hotel (the Batchelor Resort, which also has RV and camping facilities available in the nearby town of Batchelor ☎ 08/8976–0123).

Where to Eat

$$–$$$$ ✕ **Crustaceans on the Wharf.** In a corrugated-iron storage shed at the end of a commercial pier, this large restaurant is dominated by a traditional Macassan fishing prau. Open to sea breezes, it's an ideal place to escape the city's summer heat. Seafood takes center stage here; standout choices include the Moreton Bay bugs (which are like small lobsters), calamari, and chili mud crabs, a specialty of the house. ✉ *Stokes Hill Wharf, Wharf Precinct* ☎ *08/8981–8658* 🍽 *AE, DC, MC, V* ☉ *Closed Sun. Oct.–Apr. No lunch.*

★ **$$** ✕ **Pee Wee's at the Point.** Uninterrupted views of Darwin Harbour at East Point Reserve make this restaurant a favorite with locals and visitors. Dine inside with views of the harbor through large glass doors, or out on the tiered timber decks beneath the stars. The cooking is modern Australian with a touch of creole spice, and the carefully considered wine list has good values. Highlights include pan-roasted kangaroo fillet on baked sweet potato, char-grilled local jumbo tiger-prawn kebabs, and

CloseUp

ABORIGINAL ART & MUSIC

ABORIGINES CAN LAY CLAIM to one of the oldest art and music traditions in the world. Traditionally a hunter-gatherer society with an oral lore, Aborigines used these modes to impart knowledge and express beliefs.

The underlying sacred and ritual themes were based primarily upon the Dreaming (an oral history that established the pattern of life for each clan). Pictures were drawn in sand, painted on trees or implements, and carved or painted onto rock surfaces. Similarly, songs and music were used to portray events such as sacred rituals, bushfires, or successful hunts. Traditionally, only men created works of art—painted or carved—while women expressed themselves through body decoration and by making artifacts such as bags or necklaces. Today, however, there are many female Aboriginal artists, some of whom follow the traditional styles and others who have adapted their own style of art.

There are several different and easily recognizable types of Aboriginal art. X-ray art reveals the exterior of creatures, as well as their internal organs and skeleton. Mimi art is myriad small matchlike figures of men, women, and animals engaged in some obvious activity, such as a hunt. Another type is stenciling, especially of the hands, which are sprayed with an outline of paint to leave an impression on a particular surface or object. Symbolic art uses diagonal, parallel, or concentric lines painted or carved onto surfaces of the body art.

The oldest form of Aboriginal art is painting or engraving on rocks. Archaeologists have evidence that the marks made in Koonalda cave, beneath the Nullarbor Plain in South Australia, are up to 20,000 years old. Rock art is predominately magical-cum-religious expression in ghostly red or white figures.

Like visual art, music also had a purpose and followed regional or song lines. For example, a clan might sing about the bushfire in different ways according to their song line—how and where the fire started, how it spread, and how it eventually died down. Music was also used to recount stories of travels made by animal or human ancestors, often in minute detail describing each place and event, to define tribal lands and boundaries.

The didgeridoo, made from tree trunks hollowed out by termites, is possibly the world's oldest musical instrument. Originally found in northern Australia, it's played by sealing your mouth at one end and vibrating your lips so the tube acts as an amplifier to produce a haunting, hollow sound.

Today there is not only a resurgence of Aboriginal art and music, but also an acceptance of it in contemporary mainstream Australian art. At the Tjapukai Aboriginal Cultural Park near Cairns, local Aborigines have resurrected their tribal language and culture, presenting it to the public through music and art. They can also exhibit contemporary artworks that are connected with their Dreaming, and keep their ancestral connection alive to pass on to future generations.

chili-basil scallops over coconut rice. ⊠ *Alec Fong Ling Dr., East Point Reserve, Fannie Bay* ☎ *08/8981–6868* ⚄ *Reservations essential* ⊟ *AE, DC, MC, V* ⊗ *No lunch.*

$–$$ ✕ **Buzz Café.** This is just one of many thriving waterfront eateries on the finger peninsula northwest of downtown, where Darwinites come to socialize. You can mingle at the bar with neighborhood millionaires, visiting boaties, and locals relaxing by the water, then dine on fresh seafood presented in a contemporary Australian style. There's air-conditioned comfort in the glass-walled dining room, or you can head out to the umbrella-shaded decks overlooking yachts and cruisers moored in the marina. One of the more curious panoramas is from the men's glass-sheeted urinal, which has one-way views over the restaurant. ⊠ *The Slipway, 48 Marina Blvd., Cullen Bay* ☎ *08/8941–1141* ⊟ *AE, DC, MC, V* ⊗ *Closed Sun., and Christmas Eve–New Year's Day.*

$–$$ ✕ **EVOO.** Set atop the MGM Grand Hotel Casino, this intimate restaurant (whose name stands for Extra Virgin Olive Oil) serves modern Australian cuisine with Asian and Mediterranean undertones. Bland pastel walls and blue carpets are tempered by extensive views across Fannie Bay and a very good Australian wine list. ⊠ *Gilruth Ave., Mindil Beach* ☎ *08/8943–8888* ⚄ *Reservations essential* ⊟ *AE, DC, MC, V* ⊗ *Closed Sun. and Mon. No lunch Tues.–Thurs. and Sat.*

$–$$ ✕ **Hanuman Thai and Nonya Restaurant.** Dark furniture and warm colors make the perfect backdrop for fine food and a wine list that includes the best from every grape-growing region in Australia. By drawing on Thai, Nonya (Malaysian), and Indian tandoori culinary traditions, Hanuman's chefs turn local herbs, vegetables, and seafood into sumptuous and innovative dishes. Of special note are Hanuman oysters, lightly cooked in a spicy coriander-and-lemongrass sauce; barramundi baked with ginger flower; and any of the curries. ⊠ *28 Mitchell St., City Center* ☎ *08/8941–3500* ⊟ *AE, DC, MC, V* ⊗ *No lunch weekends.*

FodorsChoice ★

★ $–$$ ✕ **Twilight On Lindsay.** Tropical gardens surround this air-conditioned restaurant in an old-style, elevated house. The menu is regularly updated, but the theme is modern Australian with Mediterranean and French influences. Popular choices include the prawn ravioli with pink peppercorns, and the macadamia-crusted barramundi with baba ghanoush, sage, and lemon vinaigrette. ⊠ *2 Lindsay St., City Center* ☎ *08/8981–8631* ⊟ *AE, DC, MC, V* ⊗ *Closed Sun. and Mon.*

¢–$ ✕ **Ten Litchfield.** Tropical gardens and a seashell waterfall grace this stylish, indoor-outdoor courtyard restaurant, on a backstreet next to a Chinese temple. The surf-and-turf menu focuses on tasty steaks, seafood, chicken, and pasta. Weekdays the restaurant is closed from 2:30 to 5:30. ⊠ *10 Litchfield St., City Center* ☎ *08/8981–1024* 🖶 *08/8981–0932* ⊟ *AE, V* ⊗ *No lunch weekends.*

Where to Stay

City Center

$$$ 🏨 **Crowne Plaza Hotel.** The city's tallest hotel stands 12 stories above the business district. Rooms have pleasant, cool pastel furnishings, and some have harbor views. With its piano bar and elegant armchairs, the high-ceiling lobby can seem a bit formal if you're coming straight from

a fishing trip, but it's a popular spot for an evening drink. ☒ *32 Mitchell St., City Center, 0800* ☎ *08/8982–0000 or 1800/891107* 🖷 *08/ 8981–1765* ⊕ *www.crowneplaza.com.au* ⬦ *233 rooms, 12 suites* ⚇ *Restaurant, in-room data ports, minibars, room TVs with movies, pool, hot tub, health club, hair salon, 2 bars, piano bar, shops, laundry service, business services, meeting rooms, travel services, free parking* 🗩 *AE, DC, MC, V.*

$$$ 🖬 **Darwin Central Hotel.** The city's architectural obsession with corrugated iron is vividly illustrated in this unusual-looking modern hotel. As the name implies, it's the city's most central accommodation, overlooking the Smith Street Mall. All rooms have city views and cool color schemes, and they surround a delightful eight-story atrium. ☒ *Smith and Knuckey Sts., City Center, 0800* ☎ *08/8944–9000 or 1300/364263* 🖷 *08/8944–9100* ⊕ *www.darwincentral.com.au* ⬦ *102 rooms, 30 suites* ⚇ *2 restaurants, minibars, in-room data ports, room TVs with movies, pool, bar, laundry service, free parking, no-smoking rooms* 🗩 *AE, DC, MC, V.*

$$$ 🖬 **Holiday Inn Esplanade Darwin.** With its colorful, round exterior, this five-story hotel is one of the city's most architecturally striking. Rooms, arranged around a central foyer, are decorated in subtle greens and pinks and accented by natural wood. Most have city or harbor views. ☒ *Esplanade, Bicentennial Park, 0800* ☎ *08/8980–0800 or 1800/891119* 🖷 *08/8980–0888* ⊕ *www.holiday-inn.com.au* ⬦ *164 rooms, 33 suites* ⚇ *Restaurant, in-room data ports, in-room safes, minibars, cable TV, room TVs with movies, pool, exercise equipment, gym, hair salon, 2 saunas, 3 bars, shops, laundry service, Internet, business services, travel services, free parking, no-smoking rooms* 🗩 *AE, DC, MC, V.*

★ $$$ 🖬 **Novotel Atrium.** Vying for the title of Darwin's prettiest hotel, the Atrium has seven floors served by glass elevators opening onto a central, vine-hung atrium. The bar and restaurant are set around a tiny artificial stream amid palm trees and ferns. Pastel-blue guest rooms are attractive and airy. ☒ *100 Esplanade, Lameroo Beach, 0800* ☎ *08/8941–0755* 🖷 *08/ 8981–9025* ⊕ *www.noveldarwin.com.au* ⬦ *138 rooms, 17 suites* ⚇ *Restaurant, in-room data ports, minibars, room TVs with movies, pool, wading pool, bar, laundry service, Internet, business services, meeting rooms, travel services, free parking, no-smoking rooms* 🗩 *AE, DC, MC, V.*

★ $$$ 🖬 **Saville Park Suites.** Spectacular views of the harbor and city are highlights of this eight-story hotel. Rooms are light, open, and equipped with kitchen facilities. Washers, dryers, and flexible room configurations make the apartment-style suites ideal for larger groups. ☒ *88 Esplanade, Bicentennial Park, 0800* ☎ *08/8943–4333 or 1800/681686* 🖷 *08/8943–4388* ⊕ *www.savillesuites.com.au/darwin.html* ⬦ *64 rooms, 140 suites* ⚇ *Restaurant, in-room data ports, kitchenettes, minibars, room TVs with movies and video games, pool, hair salon, hot tub, bicycles, bar, babysitting, laundry facilities, laundry service, business services, car rental, travel services, free parking, no-smoking floors* 🗩 *AE, DC, MC, V.*

$$–$$$ 🖬 **Sky City Darwin.** Shaped like pyramids with square tops, this casino and the smaller adjoining hotel are two of the most distinctive structures in the city. The three-story hotel has beachfront accommodations

set amid lush lawns and gardens. Dark marble, cherrywood furniture, and Italian-designer lighting fixtures fill the rooms, some of which have Jacuzzi tubs. ⊠ *Gilruth Ave., Mindil Beach, 0800* ☎ *08/8943–8888 or 1800/891118* 🖷 *08/8943–8999* ⊕ *www.skycitydarwin.com.au* 🖙 *96 rooms, 16 suites* ♨ *3 restaurants, coffee shop, in-room data ports, some in-room safes, minibars, refrigerators, room TVs with movies, some in-room VCRs, 9-hole golf course, tennis court, 2 pools, wading pool, health club, hot tub, sauna, beach, 8 bars, casino, nightclub, shops, babysitting, laundry service, concierge, business services, convention center, meeting rooms, car rental, travel services, free parking, no-smoking rooms* ▤ *AE, DC, MC, V.*

$$ ▦ **Mount Bundy Station.** This farm near Adelaide River, 115 km (72 mi) south of Darwin, provides myriad outdoor activities amid country hospitality. Rooms in the homestead have king-size beds and private baths; some have a balcony. Older children are often given their own room. A cooked breakfast and afternoon tea are provided; bring your own barbecue supplies and beverages. There's a communal kitchen, a camp kitchen, and a TV lounge. Wild creatures ranging from egrets to buffalo roam the property, and you can even fish (bring your own tackle) during the Wet. ⊠ *Haynes Rd., Adelaide River 0846* ☎ *08/8976–7009* 🖷 *08/8976–7113* ⊕ *www.bed-and-breakfast.au.com/Bundy/ MountBundyStation.htm* 🖙 *6 rooms* ♨ *Pool, fishing, hiking, horseback riding, library, laundry facilities; no room phones, no room TVs, no smoking* ▤ *AE, DC, MC, V* ¶❙ *BP.*

¢ ▦ **Chilli's Backpackers.** In the center of the tourist precinct, this popular budget choice has a great location and lots of on-site perks. Drop your bags in a dorm, twin, or double room, then head up the rooftop deck, barbecue area, and hot tubs. There's also a large, modern communal kitchen, a TV room, Internet access, lockers, and a travel desk. Continental breakfast is included. ⊠ *69A Mitchell St., City Center, 0800* ☎ *08/8941–9722 or 1800/351313* ⊕ *www.chillis.com.au* 🖙 *162 beds in 6 twins, 6 doubles, and 48 dorms* ♨ *Dining room, 2 outdoor hot tubs, laundry facilities, Internet, travel services; no room phones, no room TVs* ▤ *AE, DC, MC, V* ¶❙ *CP.*

¢ ▦ **Frogshollow Backpackers.** Opposite the Frogs Hollow parklands, this modern establishment sits in peaceful, shady surroundings. Dormitories sleep 3, 6, 8, 10, or 12 people, and some of the private rooms have bathrooms. There's a plunge pool and two hot tubs, plus a common room with TV, a good communal kitchen, and an open-air dining and common area. A Continental breakfast is included in the rates. ⊠ *27 Lindsay St., City Center, 0800* ☎ *08/8941–2600* 🖷 *08/8941–0758* ⊕ *www. frogs-hollow.com.au* 🖙 *3 dorms, 22 rooms, some with shared bath* ♨ *Dining room, pool, 2 outdoor hot tubs, laundry facilities, Internet; no room phones, no TV in some rooms, no smoking* ▤ *MC, V* ¶❙ *CP.*

¢ ▦ **Value Inn.** A step up from the youth hostel, this is a one-of-a-kind, self-service hotel where you check in using a credit card that doubles as your room key. This large hotel bills itself as having the best rates for double rooms in town, and doesn't disappoint. Although front-desk service is nonexistent (follow directions on the automated check-in outside), the small double rooms are comfortable and clean. Best of all, you're right in the heart of downtown. ✉ *50 Mitchell St., City Center, 0800* ☎ *08/8981–4733* 🖷 *08/8981–4730* ⊕ *www.valueinn.com.au* 🛏 *93 rooms ⚓ Pool, dry cleaning* 🗖 *AE, DC, MC, V.*

¢ 🖳 **YHA Hostel.** In the heart of the tourist precinct by the bus station, this hostel has sleeping areas that are basic but clean and spacious. You'll need to bring your own sheets—or rent them on-site—but there's a fully equipped kitchen, a TV room, and a quiet room for reading or writing letters. Most rooms sleep three or four and are suitable for families, and there are also twin and double rooms (two of the latter have private bathrooms). Nonmembers pay an extra A$3.50 nightly charge. A tour desk in the hostel reception is open seven days and staff can book domestic air travel, bus and rail tickets, or car hire. ✉ *69A Mitchell St., City Center, 0800* ☎ *08/8981–3995* 🖷 *08/8981–6674* ⊕ *www.yha.com.au* 🛏 *93 rooms, 2 with bath ⚓ Pool, recreation room, laundry facilities, travel services, free parking; no room phones, no room TVs* 🗖 *MC, V.*

Gurig National Park

$$$$ 🖳 **Seven Spirit Bay Wilderness Lodge.** This remote resort on the pristine
Fodor'sChoice   Cobourg Peninsula in Arnhem Land is accessible only by a 45-minute
★   flight from Darwin. Hexagonal huts with private outdoor bathrooms are linked by winding paths to the main complex, lagoon-style pool, and ocean beyond. Guided nature walks and four-wheel-drive safaris are available to the wildlife sanctuary, where dingoes, wallabies, crocodiles, buffalo, and Timorese ponies make their home. Meals, which are included, emphasize light, Mod-Oz cuisine using local seafood, meats, and produce. 🖅 *PMB 261, Winnellie, NT 0822* ☎ *08/8979–0281* 🖷 *08/ 8979–0284* ⊕ *www.sevenspiritbay.com* 🛏 *23 huts ⚓ Restaurant, minibars, pool, bar, lounge, library, laundry service, meeting room, airstrip, travel services; no a/c, no room TVs, no kids under 12* 🗖 *AE, MC, V* ❍ *FAP.*

Nightlife & the Arts

Bars & Lounges

The atmospheric **Blue Heeler Bar** (✉ Mitchell and Herbert Sts., City Center ☎ 08/8941–7945) is a typically laid-back watering hole with good dancing and Australian Outback decor. Irish flavor and pub food are available at **Kitty O'Shea's** (✉ Mitchell and Herbert Sts., City Center ☎ 08/ 8941–7947). **Rorke's Drift** (✉ 46 Mitchell St., City Center ☎ 08/ 8941–7171) resembles an English pub with 10 beers on tap. There's a large menu available until 10 PM with kids' meals and premium steaks. **Shenannigans Irish Pub** (✉ 69 Mitchell St., City Center ☎ 08/8981–2100) has Guinness on tap, along with those other two famous Irish beers, Kilkenny and Harp. Traditional Irish pub food is also available, with meat roasts on Sunday. **Throb** (✉ 64 Smith St., City Center ☎ 08/ 8942–3435) is a wild and wicked nightclub renowned for its floor shows and drag acts. The fun starts around 11 PM and doesn't end until 4 AM. Cover charge is A$10. The young and hip frequent **Time Nightclub** (✉ 3 Edmunds St., City Center ☎ 08/8981–9761), next door to Squire's tavern, where you can dance the night away to techno and funk. For a beer and live contemporary music, visit the **Top End Hotel** (✉ Daly and Mitchell Sts., Bicentennial Park ☎ 08/8981–6511), a Darwin landmark, which has the city's biggest beer garden, a sports bar, nightclub, and band room.

Casino

MGM Grand Hotel Casino (✉ Gilruth Ave., Mindil Beach ☎ 08/8943–8888 📠 08/8946–9777 ⊕ www.skycitydarwin.com.au) is one of Darwin's most popular evening entertainment spots. Gaming machines are open 24 hours, while gaming tables are open noon–6 AM Friday and Saturday, noon–4 AM Sunday–Thursday.

Cinema

Deckchair Cinema. At this outdoor, 350-seat movie theater you can catch a flick beneath the stars against a backdrop of harbor lights. On show are Australian and high-profile foreign films, screened April–November, Wednesday–Monday. Gates open at 6:30 for the sunset, and picnic baskets are permitted, although there's a snack kiosk and bar. ✉ *Mavie St. off Kitchener Dr., Wharf Precinct* ☎ *08/8981-0700* ⊕ *www. deckchaircinema.com* 🎫 *A$12* ⊙ *Apr.–Nov., Wed.–Mon. 6:30 PM.*

Theaters & Concerts

The **Darwin Entertainment Centre** (✉ 93 Mitchell St., City Center ☎ 08/8980–3333), behind the Carlton Hotel, has a large theater that regularly stages concerts, dance, and drama. It also doubles as booking office for other touring concerts in town—especially those at the Amphitheatre, Australia's best outdoor concert venue (entrance next to Botanic Gardens on Gardens Road). Check the *Northern Territory News* or the *Sunday Territorian* for current shows.

Sports & the Outdoors

Bicycling

Darwin is fairly flat and has a good network of bike paths, so cycling is a good way to get around—although you might need something waterproof during the Wet. Rentals are available at some hotels.

Boating

The mangrove-fringed arms of Darwin Harbour have a tidal rise and fall of up to 24 feet. While there have been no crocodile-related fatalities in Darwin Harbour in recent decades, it's worth noting that up to 180 crocs are removed from the harbor and its immediate surroundings each year. Due to the seasonal influx of deadly box jellyfish, these waters are unsafe for swimming between October and May. Sailing races on the harbor are conducted year-round. Dry season competition is conducted by **Darwin Sailing Club** (✉ Aitkins Dr., Vesteys Beach ☎ 08/8981–1700 ⊕ www.dwnsail.com.au). Wet season races are run by the **Dinah Beach Cruising Yacht Association** (✉ Frances Bay Dr., Tipperary Waters ☎ 08/8981–7816 ⊕ www.dinahbeachcya.com.au).

Canoes can be rented at Nitmiluk (Katherine Gorge) and on the upper reaches of the Roper River at Mataranka.

Fishing

Barramundi, the best-known fish of the Top End, can weigh up to 110 pounds and are excellent fighting fish that taste great on the barbecue afterward. The **Northern Territory Fisheries Division's Recreational Fishing Office** (✉ Berrimah Research Farm, Makagon Rd., Berrimah ☎ 08/8999–2372 ⊕ www.fishingtheterritory.com) has information on licenses and catch limits.

Cullen Bay Dive (✉ 66 Marina Blvd., Cullen Bay ☎ 08/8981–3049 ⊕ www.divedarwin.com) charters fishing vessels for A$185 per person for a full day.

Equinox Fishing Charters has day and extended fishing trips on *Equinox,* a 33-foot aluminum vessel, and the 38-foot *Tsar.* Both are licensed to carry 12 passengers and two crew. Full-day cruises with all meals and tackle provided are A$220 per person. ✉ *Shop 8, 56 Marina Blvd., Cullen Bay* ☎ *08/8942–2199* ⊕ *www.equinoxcharters.com.au.*

Scuba Diving

Coral Divers (✉ 42 Stuart Hwy., Stuart Park ☎ 08/8981–2686 ⊕ www.coraldivers.com.au) conducts day and night dives on reefs and wrecks in Darwin Harbour on neap tides (low tides at the first and third moon quarters), as well as freshwater dives at sites as far south as Mataranka.

Cullen Bay Dive (✉ 66 Marina Blvd., Cullen Bay ☎ 08/8981–3049 ⊕ www.divedarwin.com) runs reef trips and dives on wrecks from World War II and Cyclone Tracy. Training and classes are available, including PADI and technical diving certification courses. Prices are A$80 for two dives with your own gear, and A$160 for two dives with all gear.

Shopping

Markets

The **Mindil Beach Sunset Market** (✉ Beach Rd., Mindil Beach ☎ 08/8981–3454) is an extravaganza that takes place April–October, Thursday 5 PM–10 PM, as well as May–October, Sunday 4 PM–9 PM. Come in the late afternoon to snack at a choice of 60 stalls offering food from more than 30 different countries, shop at more than 200 artisans' booths, and watch singers, dancers, and musicians. Or join the other Darwinites with a bottle of wine to watch the sun plunge into the harbor.

The **Darwin Night Markets** (✉ 52 Mitchell St., City Center ☎ 0418/600830) are open daily 5 PM–11 PM and include arts, crafts, souvenirs, and Aboriginal artifacts. **Nightcliff Market** (✉ Progress Dr., Nightcliff) takes place Sunday 8 AM–2 PM in Nightcliff Village, with craft and food stalls and entertainers. North of downtown, the **Parap Markets** (✉ Parap Sq., Parap) are open Saturday 8 AM–2 PM and have a great selection of ethnic Asian food. The **Rapid Creek Markets** (✉ Rapid Creek Shopping Centre, Trower Rd., Rapid Creek), open Sunday 8 AM–1 PM, is a trash-and-treasure-style flea market.

Specialty Shops

The best buys in Darwin are Aboriginal paintings and artifacts. Among the top Aboriginal-art sellers is the **Raintree Aboriginal Fine Art Gallery** (✉ Shop 5, 20 Knuckey St., City Center ☎ 08/8941–9933). At **Framed**

(⊠ 55 Stuart Hwy., The Gardens ☎ 08/8981–2994 ⊕ www.framed.com.
au), a gallery near the Botanic Gardens, you can find expensive but
exquisite art pieces. It's open Monday to Saturday 9–5:30, Sundays and
holidays 11–4.

Darwin A to Z

AIR TRAVEL

Darwin's International Airport is serviced from overseas by Qantas, Australian Airlines, Garuda, Virgin Blue, and Royal Brunei. Qantas and
Garuda fly from Darwin to Bali several times a week. Malaysia Airlines
flies twice weekly nonstop to Kuala Lumpur.

Qantas, Air North, and Virgin Blue Airlines fly into Darwin regularly
from other parts of Australia and also operate regional flights within
the Top End. Air North flies west to Kununurra and Broome, south to
Katherine and Alice Springs, and east to Cairns and Brisbane. Check
the Qantas Web site for last-minute regional air specials.

The airport is 15 km (9 mi) northeast of the city by car. After leaving
the terminal, turn left onto McMillans Road and left again onto Bagot
Road. Continue until you cross the overpass that merges onto the Stuart Highway, which later becomes Daly Street. Turn left onto Smith Street
to reach the Smith Street Mall in the heart of the city.

The Darwin Airport Shuttle has regular service between the airport and
the city's hotels. The cost is A$8.50 one-way, A$15 round-trip; be sure
to book a day in advance. Taxis are available from the taxi rank at the
airport. The journey downtown costs about A$15.

🛪 Airlines **Air North** ☎ 08/8920-4000 or 1800/627474 ⊕ www.airnorth.com.au. **Australian Airlines** ☎ 1300/799798 ⊕ www.australianairlines.com.au. **Garuda Indonesia** ☎ 1300/365330 ⊕ www.garuda-indonesia.com. **Malaysia Airlines** ☎ 13-2627
⊕ www.malaysiaairlines.com.au. **Qantas** ☎ 13-1313 ⊕ www.qantas.com. **Royal Brunei**
☎ 08/8941-0966 ⊕ www.bruneiair.com. **Virgin Blue Airlines** ☎ 13-6789 ⊕ www.
virginblue.com.au.

🛪 Airport & Shuttle **Darwin International Airport** ☎ 08/8920-1811 ⊕ www.
darwinairport.com.au. **Darwin Airport Shuttle** ☎ 08/8981-5066.

BUS TRAVEL

Greyhound Australia operates from the Darwin Transit Centre in the
Mitchell Street tourist precinct. There are daily services to and from Alice
Springs, Tennant Creek (connections to Queensland), Katherine, Broome,
and Perth.

🛪 Bus Station **Darwin Transit Centre** ⊠ 67-69 Mitchell St., City Center.
🛪 Bus Line **Greyhound Australia** ☎ 08/8981-8700, 13-1499 central reservations
⊕ www.greyhound.com.au.

BUS TRAVEL
WITHIN DARWIN
The bus network in Darwin links the city with its far-flung suburbs, and
24-hour Arafura minibuses run all over town for fixed prices starting
at A$3. The main bus terminal (Darwin Bus) is on Harry Chan Avenue,
near the Bennett Street end of Smith Street Mall.

🛪 **Arafura Shuttle** ☎ 08/8981-3300. **Darwin Bus** ☎ 08/8924-7666.

CAR RENTAL

Avis, Budget, Hertz, Thrifty, and Europcar are the major agencies, with branches at the airport. Locally, you can depend on Britz-Rentals and Advance Car Rental. Four-wheel-drive vehicles are available.

Advance Car Rental ⊠ 86 Mitchell St., City Center ☎ 1800/002227 ⊕ www.advancecar.com.au. **Avis** ⊠ Airport ⊠ 91 Smith St., City Center ☎ 08/8981–9922 ⊕ www.avis.com.au. **Britz-Rentals** ⊠ 44–46 Stuart Hwy., Stuart Park ☎ 08/8981–2081. **Budget** ⊠ Airport ⊠ 108 Mitchell St., City Center ☎ 08/8981–9800 ⊕ www.budget.com. **Europcar** ⊠ Airport ⊠ 77 Cavenagh St., City Center ☎ 08/8941–0300 ⊕ www.europcar.com. **Hertz** ⊠ Airport ⊠ Smith and Daly Sts., City Center ☎ 08/8945–0999 ⊕ www.hertz.com.au. **Thrifty** ⊠ 64 Stuart Hwy., Stuart Park ☎ 08/8924–0000 ⊕ www.thrifty.com.au.

CAR TRAVEL

The best way to get around Darwin is by car. The Stuart Highway is Darwin's land connection with the rest of Australia, and anyone arriving by car will enter the city on this road. By road Darwin is 15 hours from Alice Springs (1,491 km [926 mi]), 2½ days from Broome via the Great Northern Highway (1,875 km [1,165 mi]), 4–5 days from Brisbane (3,387 km [2,105]), and 5–6 days from Perth (3,981 km [2,474 mi]). Driving times include rest breaks and are approximations only.

For drivers headed outside the Northern Territory, one-way drop-off fees can be prohibitive, often twice as much as twice a weekly rental. Also, very few travelers, even Australians, drive the highways after dark, due to the dangers presented by buffalo, cattle, horses, donkeys, wallabies, and potoroos on the road.

EMERGENCIES

In an emergency, dial **000** to reach an ambulance, the police, or the fire department.

Doctors & Dentists Night & Day Medical & Dental Surgery ⊠ Shop 31, Casuarina Shopping Centre, Trower Rd., Casuarina ☎ 08/8927–1899.

Hospital Royal Darwin Hospital ⊠ Rocklands Dr. and Floreyr Ave., Tiwi ☎ 08/8922–8888.

MAIL, THE INTERNET & SHIPPING

Australia Post provides reliable service. Darwin Post Office is open weekdays 8:30 to 5. Suburban post offices are in Parap, Winnellie, Nightcliff, Casuarina, Sanderson, and Palmerston. Internet cafés are concentrated in the Mitchell Street tourist precinct. Photocopies can be made at the state library in Parliament House. Faxes can be sent from the Darwin Post Office, major hotels, and Didjworld Internet Shop, which is open Monday–Saturday 9–8 and Sunday 10–8.

Postal Services Darwin Post Office ⊠ 48 Cavenagh St., City Center ☎ 13–1318.

Internet Cafés Computer Info ⊠ Shop 5, 21 Cavenagh St., City Center ☎ 08/8941–3800. **Didjworld Internet Shop** ⊠ Shops 6 and 10, 60 Smith St., Harry Chan Arcade, City Center ☎ 08/8981–3510 ⊕ www.didjworld.com. **Global Gossip** ⊠ 44 Mitchell St., City Center ☎ 08/8942–3044 ⊕ www.globalgossip.com.au. **Internet Out Post** ⊠ Shop 5, 69 Mitchell St., City Center ☎ 08/8981–0720 ⊕ www.internet-outpost.com.

MONEY MATTERS

The main banks with tourist services are Westpac and Commonwealth, both on the corners of Smith Street and Bennet Street. Banking hours are Monday–Thursday 9:30–4 and Friday 9:30–5. Currency exchange facilities are available on Smith Street Mall and Mitchell Street.

TAXIS

In town look for Yellow Cab Co. and Darwin Radio Taxis for local transport.

Darwin Radio Taxis ☎ 13-1008. **Yellow Cab Co.** ☎ 13-1924.

TOURS

Every day but Sunday, Darwin Day Tours conducts afternoon trips for A$52, and for A$89 (May–September) you can take a sunset harbor cruise with a glass of champagne. Tours include historic buildings, the main harbor, the Botanic Gardens, the Northern Territory Museum of Arts and Sciences, East Point Reserve, and Stokes Hill Wharf. Alternatively, for A$25 you can hop on and off the Tour Tub "City Sights" bus, which takes in most of Darwin's attractions. It picks up at Knuckey Street, at the end of Smith Street Mall, and runs daily 9–4. The YHA on Mitchell Street also organizes tours across the Top End and the Kimberley.

Daytime and sunset cruises allow you to cool off and explore a beautiful harbor five times the size of Sydney's. A 2½ hour cruise on the *Spirit of Darwin* begins at A$39, while a sunset cruise with dinner costs A$49. Trips depart daily from Cullen Bay Marina between April and October.

Darwin Day Tours ☎ 1800/811633 ⊕ www.aussieadventure.com.au. *Spirit of Darwin* ☎ 08/8981-3711. **Tour Tub** ☎ 08/8985-6322 ⊕ www.tourtub.com. **YHA** ☎ 08/8981-3995.

TRAIN TRAVEL

The *Ghan* train connects Darwin with Adelaide via Alice Springs. The two-night 2,979-km (1,861-mi) journey departs from Adelaide for Alice Springs on Sunday and Friday at 5:15 PM, and from Alice for Darwin on Monday at 4:10 PM. Heading south, the *Ghan* departs from Darwin on Wednesday at 10 AM and from Alice at 12:45 PM Thursday and 2 PM Saturday. The transcontinental trip costs A$1,740 for Gold Kangaroo Service, including all meals; A$1,390 for a sleeper; and A$440 for a reclining seat. Book two Gold Kangaroo seats and you can take your car on the Motorail vehicle carrier for just A$99.

The *Ghan* ☎ 13-2147 bookings, 1300/132147 holiday packages ⊕ www.gsr.com.au.

VISITOR INFORMATION

Darwin City Council operates a tourist information booth toward the Bennett Street end of Smith Street Mall. The most extensive selection of information and tour bookings can be found at Top End Tourism. Tours can also be booked through hostel travel desks and hotels.

Darwin City Council ✉ Civic Centre, Harry Chan Ave., City Center ☎ 08/8930-0300 **Top End Tourism** ✉ Beagle House, Mitchell and Knuckey Sts., City Center ☎ 08/8936-2499 ⊕ www.tourismtopend.com.au.

KAKADU NATIONAL PARK

Begins 166 km (104 mi) east of Darwin.

Fodor's Choice   Kakadu National Park is a jewel among the many Top End parks, and
★   many come to the region just to experience this tropical wilderness. Beginning east of Darwin, and covering some 19,800 square km (7,645
square mi), the park protects a large system of unspoiled rivers and creeks,
as well as a rich Aboriginal heritage that extends back to the earliest
days of humankind.

The superb gathering of Aboriginal rock art is one of Kakadu's major
highlights. Two main types of Aboriginal artwork can be seen here. The
Mimi style, which is the oldest, is believed to be up to 20,000 years old.
Aborigines believe that Mimi spirits created the red-ocher stick figures
to depict hunting scenes and other pictures of life at the time. The more
recent artwork, known as X-ray painting, dates back fewer than 9,000
years and depicts freshwater animals—especially fish, turtles, and geese—
living in floodplains created after the last ice age.

Most of the region is virtually inaccessible during the Wet. As the dry
season progresses, billabongs (water holes) become increasingly important to the more than 280 species of birds that inhabit the park. Huge
flocks often gather at Yellow Water, South Alligator River, and Magela
Creek. Scenic flights over the wetlands and Arnhem Land escarpment
provide unforgettable moments in any season.

Bowali Visitors Centre has state-of-the-art audiovisual displays and traditional exhibits that give an introduction to the park's ecosystems and
its bird population, the world's most diverse. ⊠ *Arnhem and Kakadu
Hwys.* ☎ *08/8938–1120* ⊠ *Free* ⊙ *Daily 8–5.*

Warradjan Aboriginal Cultural Centre, named after the pig-nose turtle unique
to the Top End, provides an excellent experience of local Bininj (pronounced *bin*-ing) tribal culture. Displays take you through the Aboriginal Creation period, following the path of the creation ancestor Rainbow
Serpent through the ancient landscape of Kakadu. ⊕ *5 km (3 mi) off
Kakadu Hwy. on road to Gagudju Lodge, Cooinda* ☎ *08/8979–0051*
⊠ *Free* ⊙ *Daily 9–5.*

Exploring Kakadu National Park

Like the main Kakadu escarpment, **Nourlangie Rock** is a remnant of an
ancient plateau that is slowly eroding, leaving sheer cliffs rising high above
the floodplains. The main attraction is the **Anbangbang Gallery,** an excellent frieze of Aboriginal rock paintings. ⊕ *19 km (12 mi) from park
headquarters on Kakadu Hwy.; turn left toward Nourlangie Rock, then
follow paved road, accessible year-round, 11 km (7 mi) to parking area*
⊠ *Free* ⊙ *Daily 7 AM–sunset.*

Ubirr has an impressive display of Aboriginal paintings scattered through
six shelters in the rock. The main gallery contains a 49-foot frieze of X-
ray paintings depicting animals, birds, and fish. A 1-km (½-mi) path
around the rock leads to all the galleries. It's just a short clamber to the

top for wonderful views over the surrounding wetlands, particularly at sunset. ✢ *43 km (27 mi) north of park headquarters along paved road* ⬚ *Free* ☉ *Apr.–Nov., daily 8:30–sunset; Dec.–Mar., daily 2–sunset.*

The best way to gain a true appreciation of the natural beauty of Kakadu is to visit the waterfalls running off the escarpment. Some 39 km (24 mi) south of the park headquarters along the Kakadu Highway, a track leads off to the left toward **Jim Jim Falls,** 60 km (37 mi) away (about a two-hour drive). The track is unpaved, and you'll need a four-wheel-drive vehicle to navigate it. From the parking lot you have to walk 1 km (½ mi) over boulders to reach the falls and the plunge pools they have created at the base of the escarpment. After May, the water flow over the falls may cease, and the unpaved road is closed in the Wet.

As you approach the **Twin Falls,** the ravine opens up dramatically to reveal a beautiful sandy beach scattered with palm trees, as well as the crystal waters of the falls spilling onto the end of the beach. This spot is a bit difficult to reach, but the trip is rewarding. After a short walk from the parking lot, you must swim along a small creek for a few hundred yards to reach the falls—many people use inflatable air beds as rafts to transport their lunch and towels. The parking lot is 10 km (6 mi) farther on the dirt road from Jim Jim Falls.

Where to Stay

There are several lodges in the park, and campgrounds at Merl, Muirella Park, Mardugal, and Gunlom have toilets, showers, and water. Sites are A$5 per night. Alcohol is not available in Jabiru, so stock up in Darwin.

$$ ▦ **Gagudju Crocodile Holiday Inn.** Shaped like a crocodile, this unusual hotel with spacious rooms is the best of the area's accommodation options. The reception area, a de facto art gallery, is through the mouth, and the swimming pool is in the open courtyard in the belly. ✉ *Flinders St., Jabiru 0886* ☎ *08/8979–2800 or 1300/666747* 🖷 *08/ 8979–2707* ⊕ *www.gagudju-crocodile.holiday-inn.com* 🛏 *110 rooms* ⚷ *Restaurant, pool, bar, shop, travel services, free parking* ▤ *AE, DC, MC, V.*

$ ▦ **Gagudju Lodge Cooinda.** Near Yellow Water, this facility has light, airy lodgings looking out over tropical gardens. Rooms, which sleep four, have TVs, refrigerators, and plug-in hot-water kettles. Budget quarters— with bunks and shared baths but no phone or TV—are also available. ✉ *Kakadu Hwy., 2 km (1¼ mi) toward Yellow Water Wetlands, Cooinda 0886* ☎ *08/8979–0145 or 1800/500401* 🖷 *08/8979–0148* ⊕ *www. gagudjulodgecooinda.com.au* 🛏 *82 rooms* ⚷ *Restaurant, pool, bar, free parking* ▤ *AE, MC, V.*

¢–$ ▦ **Aurora Kakadu.** This comfortable hotel has doubles, dorms that sleep four, and family rooms. Spread through lush tropical gardens, the rooms, bare cabins, and campgrounds are clean and provide good value for the money. Rates are significantly lower during the Wet. Gas and diesel fuel are available. ✢ *On Arnhem Hwy., 2½ km (1½ mi) before the highway crosses the S. Alligator River* ⬚ *Box 221, Winnellie 0822* ☎ *08/ 8979–0166 or 1800/818845* 🖷 *08/8979–0147* ⊕ *www.auroraresorts. com.au* 🛏 *138 rooms, 20 powered sites, 250 tent sites* ⚷ *Restaurant,* *tennis court, pool, shops, playground, laundry facilities, free parking* ⊟ *AE, DC, MC, V.*

⚠ **Aurora Kakadu Lodge and Caravan Park.** Lush grounds surround this privately operated campground with budget accommodation, cabins, power-equipped sites for motor homes, and basic tent sites. Lodge rooms have queen-size beds or bunks, and the cabins come in studio and one- and two-bedroom sizes. The caravan park is within walking distance of trailheads, the Jabiru recreational lake, and shops. A camp kitchen, bar-cum-bistro, and lagoon-style pool are also on the property. ⊠ *Jabiru Dr., Jabiru 0886* ☎ *08/8979–2422 or 1800/811154* ⊕ *www. auroraresorts.com.au* ⊠ *Campsites A$18–$25, rooms A$127* ⤳ *200 tent sites, 190 powered RV sites, 15 cabins, 32 lodge rooms* ♨ *Flush toilets, full hookups, drinking water, showers, general store, pool* ⊟ *AE, DC, MC, V.*

⚠ **Gagudju Lodge Cooinda Campground.** Campsites are in the tropical forest near the resort. Some are supplied with power for motor homes, but basic, bare-bones tent sites with shared bath facilities are also available. ⊠ *Kakadu Hwy., Cooinda 0886* ☎ *08/8979–0145 or 1800/500401* 🖷 *08/8979–0148* ⊠ *A$12–A$16* ⤳ *80 powered sites, 300 unpowered sites* ♨ *Pit toilets, full hookups, showers, fire pits* ⊟ *No credit cards.*

Kakadu National Park A to Z

AIR TRAVEL

Light aircraft charters from Darwin to Kakadu can be arranged through local operators like Air North, Hardy Aviation, Northern Air Charter, and Vincent Aviation.

🚩 **Air North** ☎ 08/8920–4000 ⊕ www.airnorth.com.au. **Hardy Aviation** ☎ 08/ 8927–8111. **Northern Air Charter** ☎ 08/8945–5444. **Vincent Aviation** ☎ 08/8928–1366 ⊕ www.vincentair.co.nz.

CAR TRAVEL

From Darwin take the Arnhem Highway east to Jabiru. Although four-wheel-drive vehicles are not necessary to travel to the park, they are required for many of the unpaved roads within, including the track to Jim Jim Falls. Entry is free.

TOURS

During the Dry, park rangers conduct free walks and tours at several popular locations. You can pick up a program at the entry station or at either of the visitor centers.

Kakadu Air makes scenic hour- and half-hour flights out of Jabiru. In the Dry, the flight encompasses the northern region, including floodplains, East Alligator River, and Jabiru Township. During the Wet only, a one-hour flight takes in Jim Jim and Twin Falls.

Northern Air Charter has scenic flights from Darwin over Kakadu National Park and Katherine Gorge. Albatross Helicopters has scenic flights from Darwin Wharf Helipad for a Darwin City tour, from Litchfield over Litchfield National Park, and from Jabiru over Kakadu National Park.

The Gagudju Lodge Cooinda arranges boat tours of Yellow Water, the major water hole where innumerable birds and crocodiles gather. There are six tours throughout the day; the first (6:45 AM) is the coolest. Tours, which run most of the year, cost A$33 for 90 minutes and A$40 for two hours.

Billy Can Tours provides two-, three-, and four-day camping and accommodation tours in Kakadu. Far Out Adventures runs customized tours of Kakadu, as well as other regions of the Top End, for small groups. Odyssey Tours and Safaris offers two- to seven-day deluxe four-wheel-drive safaris into Kakadu, Litchfield, and Nitmiluk national parks, as well as a two-day Arnhem Land Aboriginal Tour to Nipbamjen.

Air Tours Albatross Helicopters ☎ 08/8988–5081 🖷 08/8988–5083. **Kakadu Air** ☎ 1800/089113. **Northern Air Charter** ☎ 08/8945–5444 🖷 08/8945–5977 ⊕ www. flynac.com.au.

Boat Tours Gagudju Lodge Cooinda ☎ 08/8979–0111 or 08/8979–0145 ⊕ yellowwatercruises.com.

Vehicle Tours Billy Can Tours 🖃 Box 1206, Darwin 0801 ☎ 08/8981–9813 or 1800/813484 🖷 08/8941–0803 ⊕ www.billycan.com.au. **Far Out Adventures** ⊠ 5 Rutt Ct., Katherine 0850 ☎ 08/8972–2552 🖷 08/8972–2228 ⊕ www.farout.com.au. **Odyssey Tours and Safaris** 🖃 Box 3012, Darwin 0801 ☎ 08/8948–0091 or 1800/891190 🖷 08/8948–0646 ⊕ www.odysaf.com.au.

VISITOR INFORMATION
You can contact the Kakadu National Park directly for information, or Top End Tourism.

Kakadu National Park 🖃 Box 71, Jabiru 0886 ☎ 08/8938–1120 ⊕ www.ea.gov.au/parks/kakadu. **Top End Tourism** ⊠ Beagle House, Mitchell and Knuckey Sts., Darwin 0800 ☎ 08/8936–2499 ⊕ www.tourismtopend.com.au.

KATHERINE

317 km (196 mi) southeast of Darwin.

If you're heading south to the Red Centre, the Katherine River is the last permanently flowing water you'll find until you reach Adelaide—2,741 km (1,700 mi) to the south! A veritable oasis, Katherine is the crossroads of the region, making it the second-largest town in the Top End with a booming population of more than 11,000. The town was first established to service the Overland Telegraph that linked the south with Asia and Europe, and it had the first cattle and sheep stations in the Top End. The Springvale Homestead 8 km (5 mi) west of town is the oldest still standing in the Northern Territory.

Katherine is now a regional administrative and supply center for the cattle industry, as well as being the site for the largest military air base in northern Australia. The Katherine River is popular for fishing, swimming, and canoeing. The town is also a good base for exploring the spectacular gorges of Nitmiluk National Park, the Cutta Cutta Caves, and Mataranka.

Among other things, Katherine is home to the world's largest school "classroom," the **Katherine School of the Air** (✉ Giles St. ☎ 08/8972–1833 ⊕ www.schools.nt.edu.au/ksa), which broadcasts to about 250 students over 800,000 square km (308,880 square mi) of isolated cattle country. Tours (A$5) are available on weekdays from mid-March to mid-December at 9, 10, 11, 1, and 2, and other times by appointment.

off the beaten path

CUTTA CUTTA CAVES – This 3,704-acre nature park, located just 29 km (18 mi) south of Katherine, is a series of limestone caverns 45 feet underground. Rare Ghost and Orange horseshoe bats congregate there. Daily 45-minute, ranger-led tours into the system take place at 9, 10, 11, 1, 2, and 3, weather permitting. ✉ *Stuart Hwy.* ☎ *08/ 8972–1940* ✆ *Tours A$12.50.*

MANYALLALUK–THE DREAMING PLACE – The community of Manyallaluk is on Aboriginal-owned land 100 km (62 mi) southeast of Katherine by road. Aboriginal residents here lead informative guided walks, and workshops in traditional arts, crafts, and spear-throwing. Bookings are essential. ⊹ *51 km (32 mi) south along Stuart Hwy., 16 km (10 mi) along Mainoru Rd., 35 km (22 mi) up Eva Valley Rd. (dirt)* ☎ *08/8975–4727 or 1800/644727* ✆ *08/ 8975–4724* ⊕ *www.manyallaluk.com* ✆ *Self-drive A$110, pickup from Katherine A$143* ☉ *Apr.–Sept., weekdays; Oct. and Nov., Mon., Wed., and Fri.*

MATARANKA – On the Stuart Highway just a few kilometers farther south of Manyallaluk is this tiny township, made famous by Jeannie Gunn's book about turn-of-the-20th-century life on a cattle station, *We of the Never Never.* The main draw here is the palm-shrouded Mataranka Thermal Pool, which maintains a constant temperature of 34°C (92°F). The modest **Mataranka Homestead Tourist Resort** (☎ 08/8975–4544 or 1800/754544) offers a clean, comfy place to stay, with all the amenities.

Where to Stay

$–$$$ ▦ **St. Andrews Serviced Apartments.** One block from the main street, these clean, spacious, and fully self-contained two-bedroom units look out over the swimming pool and barbecue area. Cots, tour bookings, and video rentals are available. ✉ *27 1st St., 0850* ☎ *08/8971–2288 or 1800/686106* ✆ *08/8971–2277* ⊕ *www.standrewsapts.com.au* ✍ *14 apartments* △ *Fans, kitchens, microwaves, refrigerators, in-room VCRs, laundry facilities, travel services* ▤ *MC, V.*

¢–$ ▦ **Knotts Crossing Resort.** Nestled on the bank of the Katherine River, this resort is a mix of well-designed motel rooms and low-slung cabins. Two pools and an outside bar are favorite hangouts after a hot day. Katie's bistro serves local fish. Self-catering rooms and caravan and camping sites are also available. ✉ *Cameron and Giles Sts., 0850* ☎ *08/8972–2511 or 1800/222511* ✆ *08/8972–2628* ⊕ *www.knottscrossing.com.au* ✍ *123 rooms, 36 cabins, 35 powered van sites, 40 tent sites* △ *Restau-*

rant, some kitchens, 2 pools, bar, laundry facilities, free parking ▤ *AE, DC, MC, V.*

Nitmiluk (Katherine Gorge) National Park

31 km (19 mi) north of Katherine.

One of the Northern Territory's most famous parks, Nitmiluk—named after a site at the first of 13 gorges—is owned by the local Jawoyn Aboriginal tribe and leased back to the Parks and Wildlife Commission. Katherine Gorge, the park's European name, is derived from the Katherine River, which connects the gorges. Rapids separate the chasms, much to the delight of canoeists. Flat-bottom tour boats make two-hour to full-day safaris to the fifth gorge, a trip that requires hiking to circumnavigate each rapid. During the Wet, jet boats provide access into the flooded gorges. In general, the best time to visit is May through early November.

For adventurous travelers, the park has more than 100 km (62 mi) of the best bushwalking trails in the Top End. Ten well-marked walking tracks, ranging from one hour to five days, lead hikers on trails parallel to the Katherine River and north toward Edith Falls at the edge of the park. Some of the longer, overnight walks lead past Aboriginal paintings and through swamps, heath, cascades, waterfalls, and rain forest. The best is the four-day, 66-km (41-mi) **Jatbula Trail,** which passes a number of Edenesque pools and spectacular waterfalls on its route from **Katherine Gorge** to **Edith Falls.** Before departure, register with the Nitmiluk Visitor Centre. Located in a beautiful ocher-color building near the mouth of the gorge, **Nitmiluk Visitor Centre** (☎ 08/8972–1253 ⊜ 08/8971–0715) houses an interpretive center, an open-air children's playground, and souvenir and restaurant facilities.

Where to Stay

Campgrounds, near the Katherine River and opposite the Nitmiluk Visitor Centre, cost A$8 per person per night. The **Nitmiluk National Park station** (☎ 08/8972–1886) has information on camping in the park. The designated campsites are well marked at every crossroads. Camping is only allowed in the fourth, fifth, and eighth gorges. The cost is A$3.30 per person per night.

Sports & the Outdoors

Canoes can be rented from Nitmiluk Visitor Centre or at the gorge boat ramp. Single-seater canoes rent for A$13 per hour, A$32.50 for a half day, and A$44.50 for a full day; double-seaters cost A$15 per hour, and A$49 for a half day or full day. A deposit is required at the time of hire. Overnight rentals can also be arranged.

Exciting multiday trips down less-frequented parts of the Katherine and other river systems in this area are run by an excellent local tour company, **Gecko Canoeing** (☎ 08/8972–2224 ⊕ www.geckocanoeing. com.au).

Katherine A to Z

AIR TRAVEL
Air North serves Katherine to and from Darwin at least once daily. The flight time is one hour, and the airport is 10 minutes south of town.

Air North ☎ 08/8920-4000 or 1800/627474 ⊕ www.airnorth.com.au.

BUS TRAVEL
Greyhound Australia runs between Darwin and Alice Springs with a stop at Katherine. It's about 16 hours from Alice Springs to Katherine and 4 hours from Katherine to Darwin.

Greyhound Australia ☎ 13-1499 ⊕ www.greyhound.com.au.

CAR RENTAL
Europcar ✉ Katherine Airport ☎ 13-1390. **Hertz** ✉ Katherine Airport ☎ 08/8971-1111.

CAR TRAVEL
Katherine is 317 km (196 mi) southeast of Darwin via the Stuart Highway. Driving to Katherine will allow you to stop along the way at Litchfield National Park and get around easily to Nitmiluk National Park and other sights nearby. You can also continue to Kununurra, 516 km (322 mi) west, or to Alice Springs, 1,145 km (710 mi) to the south.

EMERGENCIES
In an emergency, dial **000** to reach an ambulance, the police or the fire department.

Katherine Hospital ☎ 08/8973-9211. **Police** ☎ 08/8973-8000.

TOURS
Manyallaluk Tours hosts a series of one- to three-day tours with Aboriginal guides that focus on bush tucker (food), arts, interaction with Aboriginal people, and visits to rock-art sites.

Billy Can Tours combines excursions to Nitmiluk with Litchfield and Kakadu national parks. Based in Katherine, Far Out Adventures runs fully catered four-wheel-drive tours of Nitmiluk, Kakadu, and other less-explored parts of the region.

Gecko Canoeing, also based in Katherine, explores the Katherine River and other tropical savannah river systems on escorted canoe and camping safaris. Nitmiluk Tours has two- (A$40), four- (A$60), and eight-hour (A$98) trips up the Katherine Gorge aboard a flat-bottom boat. Two-person canoes can be hired from A$49 for a half day and A$67 for a full day. Guided canoe trips cost A$47 per person.

Billy Can Tours ☎ 08/8981-9813 or 1800/813484 🖷 08/8941-0803 ⊕ www.billycan.com.au. **Far Out Adventures** ☎ 08/8972-2552 🖷 08/8972-2228 ⊕ www.farout.com.au. **Gecko Canoeing** ☎ 08/8972-2224 🖷 08/8972-2294 ⊕ www.geckocanoeing.com.au. **Manyallaluk Tours** ☎ 08/8975-4727 or 1800/644727 🖷 08/8975-4724. **Nitmiluk Tours** ☎ 08/8971-9999 or 1800/089103.

VISITOR INFORMATION

Katherine Visitors Information Centre is open weekdays 8:30–5, weekends and holidays 10–3. The Parks and Wildlife Commission of the Northern Territory can provide information on Nitmiluk National Park.

🇮🇹 **Katherine Visitors Information Centre** ⊠ Lindsay St. and Katherine Terr. ☎ 08/8972-2650 or 1800/653142 ⊕ www.krta.com.au. **Parks and Wildlife Commission of the Northern Territory** ✑ Box 344, Katherine 0851 ☎ 08/8973-8888 🖶 08/8973-8899 ⊕ www.nt.gov.au/ipe/pwcnt.

THE KIMBERLEY

Perched on the northwestern hump of the loneliest Australian state, only half as far from Indonesia as it is from Sydney, the Kimberley remains a frontier of sorts. The first European explorers, dubbed by one of their descendants as "cattle kings in grass castles," ventured into the heart of the region in 1879 to establish cattle stations. They subsequently became embroiled in one of the country's longest-lasting conflicts between white settlers and Aborigines, who were led by Jandamarra of the Bunuba people.

The Kimberley remains sparsely populated, with only 30,000 people living in an area of 351,200 square km (135,600 square mi). That's 12 square km (4½ square mi) per person. The region is dotted with cattle stations and raked with desert ranges, rivers, tropical forests, and towering cliffs. Several of the country's most spectacular national parks are here, including Purnululu (Bungle Bungle) National Park, a vast area of bizarrely shaped and colored rock formations that became widely known to white Australians only in 1983. Facilities in this remote region are few, but if you're looking for a genuine bush experience, the Kimberley represents the opportunity of a lifetime.

This section begins in Kununurra, just over the northwestern border of the Northern Territory, in Western Australia.

Kununurra

516 km (322 mi) west of Katherine, 840 km (525 mi) southwest of Darwin.

Kununurra is the eastern gateway to the Kimberley. With a population of 6,000, it's a modern, planned town developed in the 1960s for the nearby Lake Argyle and Ord River irrigation scheme. It's a convenient base from which to explore local attractions such as Mirima National Park (a mini–Bungle Bungle on the edge of town), Lake Argyle, and the River Ord. The town is also the starting point for adventure tours of the Kimberley.

Where to Stay & Eat

$–$$ ✕ **Chopsticks Chinese Restaurant.** As its name suggests, this restaurant in the Country Club Hotel serves fresh and tasty Aussie-style Chinese cuisine. The dining room is simple but stylish, and brightly lighted by the floor-to-ceiling windows looking out to the veranda and tropical gardens. The menu features local dishes like barramundi, and Szechuan specialties like honey-chili king prawns. ⊠ *47 Coolibah Dr.* ☎ *08/9168–1024* ▤ *AE, DC, MC, V.*

¢–$ ✕ **George Room in Gulliver's Tavern.** Lots of dark jarrah timber gives this restaurant an Old English atmosphere. Although the tavern alongside it has simple counter meals, the George aims higher with steaks and seafood. ⊠ *196 Cottontree Ave.* ☎ *08/9168–1435* ▵ *Reservations essential* ▤ *AE, DC, MC, V* ⊙ *Closed Sun. No lunch.*

$$ ▥ **Kununurra Lakeside Resort.** On the shores of Lake Kununurra, at the edge of town, sits this understated, tranquil resort. Views of the sun setting over the lake—especially toward the end of the Dry—are worth the stay. The resort also has a small campground. ⌖ *Box 1129, Casuarina Way, Kununurra 6743* ⊠ *Casuarina Way off Victoria Hwy.* ☎ *08/9169–1092 or 1800/786692* 🖷 *08/9168–2741* ⊕ *www.lakeside.com. au* ↪ *50 rooms* ♨ *2 restaurants, pool, lake, 2 bars, laundry facilities* ▤ *AE, DC, MC, V.*

$$ ▥ **Mercure Inn Kununurra.** Set in tropical gardens, the brightly furnished rooms here provide a comfortable base from which to explore the eastern Kimberley. The hotel is at the edge of town, just 4 km (2½ mi) from the airport; its swimming pool, which is surrounded by shady palm trees, is the place to be on a hot day. ⊠ *Victoria Hwy. and Messmate Way, 6743* ☎ *08/9168–1455 or 1800/656565* 🖷 *08/9168–2622* ⊕ *www. accorhotel.com* ↪ *60 rooms* ♨ *Restaurant, pool, bar, laundry facilities, free parking* ▤ *AE, DC, MC, V.*

$–$$ ▥ **Country Club Hotel.** In the center of town, this hotel is encircled by its own little rain forest of tropical gardens. Standard, ground-floor rooms are basic but clean; there are also two-story units, as well as a budget section. The hotel has a cocktail bar and several spots for dining, including one beside the pool. ⊠ *47 Coolibah Dr., 6743* ☎ *08/9168–1024* 🖷 *08/9168–1189* ⊕ *www.countryclubhotel.com.au* ↪ *90 rooms* ♨ *3 restaurants, pool, 2 bars, laundry facilities, free parking* ▤ *AE, DC, MC, V.*

Gibb River Road, El Questro & Beyond

Gibb River Road is the cattle-carrying route through the heart of the Kimberley. It also provides an alternative—albeit a rough one—to the Great Northern Highway between Kununurra–Wyndham and the coastal town of Derby.

FodorśChoice The 1-million-acre **El Questro Wilderness Park** is a working ranch in some
★ of the most rugged country in Australia. Besides providing an opportunity to see Outback station life, the award-winning El Questro has a full complement of such recreational activities as fishing and swimming, and horse, camel, and helicopter rides. Individually tailored walking and four-wheel-drive tours let you bird-watch or examine ancient spirit figures depicted in the unique *wandjina* style of Kimberley Aboriginal rock painting—one of the world's most striking forms of spiritual art. ⊹ *Turnoff for El Questro 27 km (17 mi) west of Kununurra on Gibb River Rd.* ☎ *08/9169–1777* 🖾 *Wilderness permits required, A$15 for 7 days. Emma Gorge permit A$7.50 for 7 days* ⊙ *Daily, year-round.*

Branching off toward the coast from Gibb River Road, 241 km (149 mi) from where it begins in the east, is the turnoff for the extraordinary **Mitchell Plateau and Falls.** The natural attraction is a slow-going 162 km (100 mi) north on Kalumburu Road.

The small, historic port of **Wyndham,** the most northerly town in Western Australia, was established in 1886 to service the Halls Creek gold-fields, and it looks as if nothing much has happened here in the century since. The wharf is the best location in the Kimberley for spotting salt-water crocodiles as they bask on the mudflats below. There are also excellent bird-watching possibilities at the nearby Parry Lagoons Reserve, a short drive from the town. Wyndham is located 105 km (65 mi) northwest of Kununurra, at the northernmost end of the Great Northern Highway.

Adcock Gorge, 380 km (236 mi) from Kununurra on Gibb River Road, conjures up images of Eden with its large swimming hole, lush vegetation, and flocks of tropical parrots. **Bell Gorge,** 433 km (268 mi) from Kununurra, is a series of small falls that are framed by ancient rock and drop into a deep pool. The gorge is reached by a 29-km (18-mi) four-wheel-drive track from the Gibb River Road. There are campsites at nearby Silent Grove and Bell Creek.

Lennard Gorge, 456 km (283 mi) from Kununurra, is a half-hour drive down a rough four-wheel-drive track. But the discomfort is worth it: Lennard is one of the Kimberley's most spectacular gorges. Here a thin section of the Lennard River is surrounded by high cliffs that bubble with several breathtaking waterfalls.

Where to Stay

Just off Kalumburu Road there are campsites at Mitchell Plateau (at King Edward River on the early part of the Mitchell Plateau Track) and at Mitchell Falls Car Park; the latter grounds have toilets. The atmospheric Silent Grove campsite (close to Bell Gorge), has showers, toilets, firewood, and secluded sites (with no facilities) beside Bell Creek. Access is restricted from December to April. Camping information can be obtained from the **Department of Conservation and Land Management** (⌂ Box 942, Kununurra, WA 6743 ⊠ Konkerry Dr., Kununurra ☎ 08/9168-4200 ⊕ www.calm.wa.gov.au).

$$$$ ⊞ **Bush Camp Faraway Bay.** Far away both in name and in nature, this
Fodor'sChoice idyllic hideaway is perched upon a cliff along the remote Kimberley coast
★ 280 km (173 mi) northwest of Kununurra. Accessible only by light aircraft from Kununurra and catering to a maximum of 12 guests, the camp epitomizes tranquillity. You can explore the nearby untouched coastline by boat and on foot, or simply sit back and enjoy the scenery. Accommodations are simple, bush-style cabins overlooking the bay; sea breezes float through on even the hottest days. The room rate includes all meals, beverages, transfers, and activities. ⌂ *Box 901, Kununurra 6743* ☎ *08/9169-1214* ☐ *08/9168-2224* ⊕ *www.farawaybay.com.au* ⇨ *8 cabins* ⚸ *Restaurant, pool, boating, bar, laundry service; no a/c, no room phones, no room TVs* ⊟ *AE, MC, V* ⎮⊙⎮ *AI.*

★ **$–$$$$** 🏨 **El Questro.** The location of this property, at the top of a cliff face above the Chamberlain River, is one of the most spectacular in Australia. Five independent accommodation facilities are on-site, each different in style and budget: the luxury Homestead; the safari-style tented cabins at Emma Gorge Resort; air-conditioned Riverside Bungalows and Riverside Campgrounds at the Station Township; and Mt Cockburn Lodge, which runs two-day adventure safaris around Cockburn Range. Each has a restaurant, and rates at the Homestead include drinks and food, laundry, activities, and round-trip transportation from Kununurra. If you want to get away from telephones and television, this is the place. ✛ *100 km (60 mi) west of Kununurra, via Great Northern Hwy.; take Gibb River Rd. for 42 km (14 mi) from the highway exit* 📮 *Box 909, Kununurra 6743* 📞 *08/9169–1777, 08/9161–4388 Emma Gorge Resort* 📠 *08/9169–1383* 🌐 *www.elquestro.com.au* 🛏 *6 suites, 55 cabins, 12 bungalows, 31 campsites, 6 lodge cabins* ♿ *4 restaurants, tennis court, 2 pools, hot tub, fishing, horseback riding, 2 bars, shops, laundry facilities, travel services, 2 airstrips, helipad, free parking; no a/c in some rooms, no room phones, no room TVs* 🛏 *AE, DC, MC, V* ☺ *Closed Nov.–Mar.*

Purnululu (Bungle Bungle) National Park

Fodor's Choice *252 km (156 mi) southwest of Wyndham and Kununurra.*
★

Purnululu (Bungle Bungle) National Park covers nearly 3,120 square km (1,200 square mi) in the southeast corner of the Kimberley. Australians of European descent first "discovered" its great beehive-shape domes—their English name is the Bungle Bungle—in 1983, proving how much about this vast continent remains outside of "white" experience. The local Kidja Aboriginal tribe, who knew about these scenic wonders long ago, called the area Purnululu.

The striking, black-and-orange-stripe mounds seem to bubble up from the landscape. Climbing on them is not permitted because the sandstone layer beneath their thin crust of lichen and silica is fragile, and would quickly erode without protection. Walking tracks follow rocky, dry creek beds. One popular walk leads hikers along the **Piccaninny Creek** to **Piccaninny Gorge,** passing through gorges with towering 328-foot cliffs to which slender fan palms cling.

Although there are two designated campsites in the area, neither has facilities. Both the Bellburn Creek and Walardi campgrounds have simple pit toilets; fresh drinking water is available only at Bellburn Creek. Kununurra Visitor Centre (📞 08/9168–1177) has information about the campsites. The nearest accommodations are in Kununurra. Tour operators often fly clients in from Kununurra, Broome, and Halls Creek and drive them around in four-wheel-drive vehicles. April through December, the most popular tours include a night of camping. The mounds are closed from January through March.

Halls Creek

352 km (218 mi) southwest of Kununurra.

Old Halls Creek is the site of the short-lived Kimberley gold rush of 1885. Set on the edge of the Great Sandy Desert, the town has been a crumbling shell since its citizens decided in 1948 to move 15 km (9 mi) away to the site of the present Halls Creek, which has a better water supply. The old town is a fascinating place to explore, however, and small gold nuggets are still found in the surrounding gullies.

Halls Creek is the closest town to the **Wolfe Creek Meteorite Crater,** the world's second largest after the Coon Butte Crater in Arizona. The crater is 1 km (½ mi) wide and was formed as a result of a meteor that weighed tens of thousands of tons colliding with the Earth about 300,000 years ago. **Oasis Air** (☎ 1800/501462) operates scenic flights over the crater. **Northern Air Charter** (☎ 08/9168–5100) also has trips which take you to view the crater from above.

Where to Stay & Eat

★ **$$** ✕🖭 **Kimberley Hotel.** Originally a simple Outback pub with a few rooms, this hotel at the end of the airstrip now has green lawns, airy quarters with pine furnishings and tile floors, and a swimming pool. The high-ceilinged restaurant, which overlooks the lawns and pool, has an excellent wine list and serves mostly meat and seafood dishes. ✉ *Roberta Ave. adjacent to the airport, 6770* ☎ *08/9168–6101 or 1800/355228* 🖷 *08/9168–6071* ⊕ *www.kh.kimberley-accom.com.au* ⇝ *60 rooms* ♨ *Restaurant, pool, bar, free parking* ▤ *AE, DC, MC, V.*

Geikie Gorge National Park

16 km (10 mi) northeast of Fitzroy crossing, 400 km (250 mi) east of Broome.

Geikie Gorge is part of a 350-million-year-old reef system formed from fossilized layers of algae—evolutionary precursors of coral reefs—when this area was still part of the Indian Ocean. The limestone walls you see today were cut and shaped by the mighty Fitzroy River; during the Wet, the normally placid waters roar through the region. The walls of the gorge are stained red from iron oxide, except where they have been leached of the mineral and turned white by the floods, which have washed as high as 52 feet from the bottom of the gorge.

When the Indian Ocean receded, it stranded a number of sea creatures, which managed to adapt to their altered conditions. Geikie is one of the few places in the world where freshwater barramundi, mussels, stingrays, and prawns swim. The park is also home to the freshwater archerfish, which can spit water as far as a yard to knock insects out of the air. Aborigines call this place Kangu, meaning "big fishing hole."

Although there's a 5-km (3-mi) walking trail along the west side of the gorge, the opposite side is off-limits because it's a wildlife sanctuary.

The best way to see the gorge is aboard one of the several daily one-hour boat tours led by a ranger from the **National Park Ranger Station** (✆ Box 37, Fitzroy Crossing, WA 6765 ☎ 08/9191–5121 or 08/9191–5112 ⊕ www.calm.wa.gov.au). The rangers are extremely knowledgeable and helpful in pointing out the vegetation, strange limestone formations, and the many freshwater crocodiles along the way. You may also see part of the noisy fruit bat colony that inhabits the region. The park is open for day visits from 6:30 AM to 6:30 PM between April and November. Entry is restricted during the Wet, from December to March when the Fitzroy River floods.

The closest accommodations to the park are in the nearby town of Fitzroy Crossing, which is 16 km (10 mi) southwest on the Great Northern Highway. There are a few basic restaurants and hotels here, including the **Crossing Inn** (✉ Skulthorpe Rd. ☎ 08/9191–5080), established in 1897 and the oldest hotel in the Kimberley region, where some of the Kimberley's more colorful characters gather on weekend afternoons, and **Fitzroy River Lodge** (✉ Great Northern Hwy. ☎ 08/9191–5141), with campsites, safari-style lodges, and motel rooms.

off the
beaten
path

TUNNEL CREEK & WINDJANA GORGE NATIONAL PARKS – North of Fitzroy Crossing are these two geological oddities. **Tunnel Creek** (111 km [69 mi] north of Fitzroy Crossing) was created when a stream cut an underground course through a fault line in a formation of limestone. You can follow the tunnel's path on foot for 1 km (½ mi), with the only natural light coming from those areas where the tunnel roof has collapsed. Flying foxes and other types of bats inhabit the tunnel. About 100 years ago, a band of outlaws and their Aboriginal leader Jandamarra—nicknamed "Pigeon"—used the caves as a hideout. **Windjana Gorge** (145 km [90 mi] northwest of Fitzroy Crossing) has cliffs nearly 325 feet high, which were carved out by the flooding of the Lennard River. During the Wet, the Lennard is a roaring torrent, but it dwindles to just a few still pools in the Dry.

Broome

1,032 km (640 mi) southwest of Kununurra via Halls Creek, 1,544 km (957 mi) southwest of Katherine, 1,859 km (1,152 mi) southwest of Darwin.

Broome is the holiday capital of the Kimberley. It's the only town in the region with sandy beaches, and is the base from which most strike out to see more of the region. In some ways, with its wooden sidewalks and charming Chinatown, it still retains the air of its past as a boisterous shantytown. However, with tourism increasing every year it is becoming more upscale all the time.

Long ago Broome depended on pearling for its livelihood, and by the early 20th century 300 to 400 sailing boats employing 3,000 men provided most of the world's mother-of-pearl shell. Many of the pearlers were Japanese, Malay, and Filipino, and the town is still a wonderful multicultural center today. Each August during the famous Shinju Matsuri (Festival of the Pearl), Broome commemorates its early pearling years and heritage. The 10-day festival features many traditional Japanese ceremonies. Because of the popularity of the festival, advance bookings for accommodations are highly recommended. Several tour operators have multiday cruises out of Broome along the magnificent Kimberley coast. The myriad deserted islands and beaches, with 35-foot tides that create horizontal waterfalls and whirlpools, make it an adventurer's delight.

Broome marks the end of the Kimberley. From here it's another 2,250 km (1,395 mi) south to Perth, or 1,859 km (1,152 mi) back to Darwin.

City Center

At **Broome Crocodile Park** there are more than 1,500 saltwater (estuarine) crocodiles, as well as many of the less fearsome freshwater variety. The park is also home to a collection of South American caimans and some grinning alligators from the United States. Feeding time is 3 PM during the Dry and 3:45 PM during the Wet. ☒ *Cable Beach Rd.* ☎ *08/9193–7824* ☜ *A$18.50* ☼ *Apr.–Oct., weekdays 10–5, weekends 3:30–5; Nov.–Mar., daily 3:30–5.*

The life-size bronze statues of the **Cultured Pearling Monument** are near Chinatown. The monument depicts three pioneers of the cultured pearling industry that is so intertwined with the city's development and history. ☒ *Carnarvon St.*

More than 900 pearl divers are buried in the **Japanese Cemetery,** on the road out to Broome's deep-water port. The graves are a testimony to the contribution of the Japanese to the development of the industry in Broome, as well as to the perils of gathering the pearls in the early days. ☒ *Port Dr.*

★ The **Pearl Luggers** historical display sheds light on the difficulties and immense skill involved in pearl harvesting. It has two restored luggers along with other such pearling equipment as diving suits. Informative videos run all day. Pearl divers, who spent years living aboard pearling luggers and diving for pearl shells, also offer tours (allow 1½ hours). Tours run at 9 AM, 11 AM, 2 PM, and 4 PM weekdays from April to October; 11 AM and 2 PM weekdays from November to March; and weekends at 11 AM only. This is a must-see for those interested in Broome's history. ☒*31 Dampier Terr.* ☎*08/9192–2059* ☜*A$18.50* ☼ *May–Dec., daily 9:30–5; Jan.–Apr., weekdays 10–4, weekends 10–1.*

Opened in 1916, **Sun Pictures** is the world's oldest operating outdoor movie theater. Here silent movies—accompanied by a pianist—were once shown to the public. These days current releases are shown in the undeniably pleasant outdoors. Historical tours of the theater are also available weekdays for A$2.20 per person. ☒ *8 Carnarvon St.* ☎ *08/9192–3738* ⊕ *www.sunpictures.com.au* ☜ *A$14* ☼ *Daily 6:30 PM–11 PM.*

Around Broome

The **Broome Bird Observatory,** a nonprofit research and education facility, provides the perfect opportunity to see many of the Kimberley's 310 bird species, some of which migrate annually from Siberia. On the

CloseUp

BROOME BY CAMELBACK

THOUGH NOT NATIVE TO AUSTRALIA, camels played a big part in exploring and opening up the country's big, dry, and empty interior. In the 1800s, around 20,000 camels were imported from the Middle East to use for cross-country travel—along with handlers (many from Afghanistan) who cared for them.

When railways and roads became the prime methods of transport in the early 20th century, many camels were simply set free in the desert. A steady wild population of wild camels—some 400,000 of them—now roams across the Australian Outback.

Broome has for many years been a place where people enjoy camel rides—especially along the broad, desertlike sands of Cable Beach. Two tour companies in town now offer camel "adventures" on a daily basis; they're a great way to see the coast and get a taste of history.

Red Sun Camels (☎ 08/9193–7423 🖷 08/9193–7423 ⊕ www.redsuncamels.com.au) runs both morning and sunset rides every day on Cable Beach. The outfit's 18-camel train can accommodate up to 36 riders. The morning rides last for 40 minutes and cost A$30; the sunset rides take an hour and cost A$45.

Broome Camel Safaris (☎ 0419–916101 🖷 08/9192-3617 ⊕ www.bushwalks.com/broomecamels) operates Monday to Saturday, and offers 30-minute afternoon rides (A$25) and one-hour sunset rides (A$40).

shores of Roebuck Bay, 25 km (15 mi) east of Broome, the observatory has a prolific number of migratory waders. ⊠ *Crab Creek Rd., 15 km (9 mi) from Broome Hwy.* ☎ *08/9193–5600* 🖃 *A$5 for day visitors* ⊗ *By appointment.*

You can watch demonstrations of the cultured pearling process, including the seeding of a live oyster, at **Willie Creek Pearl Farm**, 38 km (23½ mi) north of Broome. Drive out to the farm yourself (you must make reservations first), or join a tour bus leaving from town. ⊹ *Drive 9 km (51//2 mi) east from Broome on Broome Hwy., turn left into Cape Leveque Rd., for 15 (9 mi), turn left into Manari Rd. for 5 km (3 mi), turn left and follow signs for 2½ km (1½ mi)* ☎ *08/9193–6000* ⊕ *www.williecreekpearls.com.au* 🖃 *Self-drive A$27.50, coach tour A$59* ⊗ *Guided tours daily 9 AM and 2 PM.*

Where to Stay & Eat

★ **$–$$** ✕ **Matso's Café, Art Gallery, and Broome Brewery.** There's a bit of everything at this convivial eatery: good food, beer brewed on site, and Kimberley artwork adorning the walls. A great place to meet locals, the café and brewery are both open for breakfast and until late at night. ⊠ *60 Hammersley St.* ☎ *08/9193–5811* 🖃 *AE, DC, MC, V.*

★ $$$$ 🏨 **Cable Beach Club Resort Broome.** Just a few minutes out of town opposite the broad, beautiful Cable Beach, this resort is the area's most luxurious accommodation. Single and double bungalows are spread through tropical gardens; studio rooms and suites are also available. The decor is colonial with a hint of Asian influence. Some rooms and facilities are closed during the Wet. ⊠ *Cable Beach Rd., 6725* 📞 *08/9192–0400 or 1800/199099* 🖷 *08/9192–2249* ⊕ *www.cablebeachclub. com* 🛏 *263 rooms, 34 bungalows, 2 villas, 3 suites* 🍴 *4 restaurants, coffee shop, some kitchens, minibars, room TVs with movies, 12 tennis courts, 2 pools, gym, massage, beach, 4 bars, shops, laundry service, concierge, Internet, business services, meeting rooms, travel services, free parking* 🖃 *AE, DC, MC, V.*

★ $$$–$$$$ 🏨 **McAlpine House.** Originally built for a pearling master, this atmospheric luxury guesthouse in tropical gardens is full of exquisite Javanese teak furniture. With an inviting pool, an airy library, and a personalized approach to service, this is a good place to recover from the rigors of a regional tour, as well as a great place to simply hang out for a day or two. Breakfast can be either light and tropical in style (with fruits and pastries) or a substantial affair. Dinner is also available on request. ⊠ *84 Herbert St., 6725* 📞 *08/9192–3886* 🖷 *08/9192–3887* ⊕ *www. mcalpinehouse.com* 🛏 *6 rooms* 🍴 *Dining room, pool, bar, library, laundry facilities, free parking* 🖃 *AE, DC, MC, V* 🍴 *BP.*

$$$ 🏨 **Mangrove Hotel.** Overlooking Roebuck Bay, this highly regarded hotel has one of the best locations of any accommodation in Broome. All the spacious rooms have private balconies or patios, many with bay views, and several dining and drinking spots are on site. Plus, it's a five-minute walk to Chinatown. ⊠ *47 Carnarvon St., 6725* 📞 *08/9192–1303 or 1800/094818* 🖷 *08/9193–5169* ⊕ *www.mangrovehotel.com.au* 🛏 *68 rooms* 🍴 *2 restaurants, refrigerators, 2 pools, outdoor hot tub, 2 bars, laundry facilities, business services, meeting rooms, travel services, free parking* 🖃 *AE, DC, MC, V.*

★ $$$ 🏨 **Moonlight Bay Quality Suites.** Rooms with bay views and a five-minute stroll from Chinatown add luxury and convenience to this complex of posh, self-contained apartments. It's great place to recuperate by the pool after a rugged Kimberley tour. ⊠ *51 Carnarvon St., 6725* 📭 *Box 198, Broome 6725* 📞 *08/9193–7888 or 1800/818878* 🖷 *08/9193–7999* ⊕ *www.broomeaccommodation.com.au* 🛏 *59 apartments* 🍴 *Restaurant, kitchens, pool, gym, hot tub, laundry facilities, free parking* 🖃 *AE, DC, MC, V.*

$ 🏨 **Ocean Lodge.** Rates plummet during the Wet at this budget-price motel, which sits amid shady gardens between Chinatown and Cable Beach. Lodgings are in self-contained double and twin motel-style rooms and two-room family suites. Children can splash in the wading pool. The Broome Recreation & Aquatic Centre and Café is across the road. The center is open year-round and has swimming pools, tennis courts, netball and basketball courts, and a skate park. ⊠ *1 Cable Beach Rd., 6725* 📞 *08/9193–7700 or 1800/600603* 🖷 *08/9193–7496* ⊕ *www.oceanlodge. com.au* 🛏 *44 rooms, 14 suites* 🍴 *Pool, wading pool, shop, laundry facilities, free parking* 🖃 *AE, DC, MC, V.*

Shopping

Prices for Aboriginal art in the Kimberley are generally well below those in Darwin or Alice Springs. **Matso's Café, Art Gallery, and Broome Brewery** (✉ 60 Hammersley St. ☎ 08/9193–5811) specializes in Kimberley arts and crafts, displaying works by the region's most talented Aboriginal artists.

Broome has an abundance of jewelry stores. **Kailis Australian Pearls** (✉ 27 Dampier Terr. ☎ 08/9192–2061 ⊕ www.kailis australianpearls.com.au) specializes in high-quality expensive pearls and jewelry.

Linneys (✉ Dampier Terr. ☎ 08/9192–2430 ⊕ www.linneys.com) sells high-end jewelry.

Family-owned **Paspaley Pearling** (✉ 2 Short St. ☎ 08/9192–2203 ⊕ www.paspaleypearling.com), in Chinatown, sells pearls and stylish local jewelry.

The Kimberley A to Z

AIR TRAVEL

Distances in this part of the continent are colossal. Flying is the fastest and easiest way to get to the Kimberley.

Qantas and its subsidiaries fly to Broome from Brisbane, Sydney, Melbourne, and Adelaide via Perth. On Saturday there are faster flights from Sydney and Melbourne via Alice Springs (with connections from Brisbane and Adelaide). Air North has an extensive air network throughout the Top End, linking Broome and Kununurra with Darwin, Alice Springs, and Perth. Virgin Blue also services Broome from Perth and Adelaide. Skywest flies to Broome from Perth. Broome's airport is right next to the center of town, on the northern side. Though it's called Broome International Airport, there are no scheduled overseas flights, but charter flights and private flights arrive there. Approvals are in place for international flights in the future.

🛪 **Airlines Air North** ☎ 08/8920–4000 or 1800/627474 ⊕ www.airnorth.com.au. **Qantas** ☎ 13–1313 ⊕ www.qantas.com. **Skywest** ☎ 1300/660088 ⊕ www.skywest.com.au. **Virgin Blue** ☎ 13–6789 ⊕ www.virginblue.com.au.

🛪 **Airports Broome International Airport** ☎ 08/9193–5455 ⊕ www.broomeair.com.au. **Darwin International Airport** ☎ 08/8920–1811 ⊕ www.darwinairport.com.au.

BUS TRAVEL

Greyhound Australia traverses the 1,859 km (1,152 mi) between Darwin and Broome in just under 24 hours. Greyhound also operates the 32-hour regular route and a 27-hour express daily between Perth and Broome. The Broome bus station is handily next door to the visitor center, at the corner of Broome Highway and Bagot Road.

🛪 **Greyhound Australia** ☎ 13–1499 ⊕ www.greyhound.com.au.

CAR TRAVEL

The unpaved, 700-km (434-mi) Gibb River Road runs through a remote area between Derby and Kununurra. If you like views, it's considered best to start the drive at Kununurra, and the trip should be done only with a great deal of caution. The road is passable by conventional vehicles only after it has been recently graded (smoothed). At other times you need a four-wheel-drive vehicle, and in the Wet it's mostly impassable.

The Bungle Bungle are 252 km (156 mi) south of Kununurra along the Great Northern Highway. A rough, 55-km (34-mi) unpaved road, negotiable only in a four-wheel-drive vehicle, is the last stretch of road leading to the park from the turnoff near the Turkey Creek–Warmum Community. That part of the drive takes about 2½ hours.

From Broome to Geikie Gorge National Park, follow the Great Northern Highway east 391 km (242 mi) to Fitzroy Crossing, then 16 km (10 mi) north on a paved side road to the park. Camping is not permitted at the gorge, so you must stay in Fitzroy Crossing.

From Darwin to Kununurra and the eastern extent of the Kimberley it's 827 km (513 mi). From Darwin to Broome on the far side of the Kimberley it's 1,859 km (1,152 mi), a long, two-day drive. The route runs from Darwin to Katherine along the Stuart Highway, and then along the Victoria Highway to Kununurra. The entire road is paved but quite narrow in parts—especially so, it may seem, when a road train (an extremely long truck convoy) is coming the other way. Drive with care. Fuel and supplies can be bought at small settlements along the way, but you should always keep supplies in abundance.

The West Australian Main Roads Information Service provides information on road conditions, including the Gibb River Road.
🛈 **West Australian Main Roads Information Service** ☎ 1800/013314 ⊕ www.mrwa. wa.gov.au/realtime/kimberley.htm.

EMERGENCIES

In an emergency dial **000** to reach an ambulance, the police, or the fire department.
🛈 **Doctors Royal Flying Doctor Service** ⊠ Derby ☎ 08/9191-1211.
🛈 **Hospitals Broome District Hospital** ⊠ Robinson St., Broome ☎ 08/9192-9222. **Derby Regional Hospital** ⊠ Clarendon St., Derby ☎ 08/9193-3333. **Kununurra District Hospital** ⊠ 96 Coolibah Dr., Kununurra ☎ 08/9166-4222.

TOURS

Kimberley Wilderness Adventures conducts tours from Broome and Kununurra, which include excursions along Gibb River Road and into Purnululu National Park. East Kimberley Tours also runs multiday adventures along Gibb River Road, and fly-drive packages into Purnululu.

Broome Day Tours conducts several tours via air-conditioned coach with informative commentary in the western Kimberley region—including a three-hour Broome Explorer tour of the town's major sights, and day trips farther afield to Windjana Gorge and Geikie Gorge. Another company that can show the Kimberley is Flak Track Tours.

Alligator Airways operates both fixed-wing floatplanes from Lake Kununurra and land-based flights from Kununurra airport. A two-hour scenic flight costs A$220. Belray Diamond Tours has a daily air tour (for a minimum of four passengers) from Kununurra to the Argyle Diamond

Mine, the world's largest, which produces about 8 tons of diamonds a year. Slingair Tours conducts two-hour flights over the Bungle Bungle for A$198.

A 30-minute helicopter flight with Slingair Heliwork costs A$200 from their helipad in the Purnululu National Park. An alternative two-hour tour of the Bungle Bungle and Lake Argyle is A$215.

Lake Argyle Cruises operates excellent trips on Australia's largest expanse of freshwater, the man-made Lake Argyle. Tours run daily March to October, and it's A$40 for the two-hour morning cruise, A$125 for the six-hour cruise, and A$50 for the sunset cruise (which starts around 2:45 PM).

Pearl Sea Coastal Cruises has multiday Kimberley adventures along the region's magnificent coastline in their luxury *Kimberley Quest* cruiser. All meals and excursions (including fishing trips) are included in the cost. Cruising season runs from March to October.

Astro Tours organizes entertaining, informative night sky tours of the Broome area, as well as four-wheel-drive Outback stargazing adventures farther afield. Discover the Kimberley Tours operates four-wheel-drive adventures into the Bungle Bungle massif.

🔢 Adventure Tours **Broome Day Tours** ☎ 1800/801068 🖶 08/9193-5575 ⊕ www.broomedaytours.com. **East Kimberley Tours** ☎08/9168-2213 ⊕www.eastkimberleytours.com.au. **Flak Track Tours** ☎ 08/8894-2228 🖶 08/9192-1275. **Kimberley Wilderness Adventures** ☎ 08/9168-1711 or 1800/804005 ⊕ www.kimberleywilderness.com.au.
🔢 Air Tours **Alligator Airways** ☎08/9168-1333 or 1800/632533 ⊕www.alligatorairways.com.au. **Belray Diamond Tours** ⊂Box 10, Kununurra 6743 ☎ 08/9168-1014 or 1800/632533 🖶 08/9168-2704 ⊕ www.alligatorairways.com.au. **Slingair Heliwork** ☎08/9168-1811 ⊕ www.slingair.com.au.
🔢 Boat Tours **Lake Argyle Cruises** ⊂Box 1310, Kununurra 6743 ☎08/9168-7687 🖶08/9168-7461 ⊕ www.lakeargyle.com. **Pearl Sea Coastal Cruises** ⊂ Box 2838, Broome 6725 ☎ 08/9193-6131 🖶 08/9193-6303 ⊕ www.pearlseacruises.com.
🔢 Four-Wheel-Drive Tours **Astro Tours** ⊂ Box 2537, Broome 6725 ☎ 08/9193-5362 🖶 08/9193-5362 ⊕ www.astrotours.net. **Discover the Kimberley Tours** ⊂ Box 2615, Broome 6725 ☎ 08/9193-7267 or 1800/636802 ⊕ www.bunglebungle.com.au.

VISITOR INFORMATION

🔢 **Broome Visitor Centre** ⊠ Great Northern Hwy. and Bagot St., Broome ☎ 08/9192-2222 🖶08/9192-2063 ⊕www.broomevisitorcentre.com.au. **Kununurra Visitor Centre** ⊠75 Coolibah Dr., Kununurra ☎08/9168-1177 🖶08/9168-2598 ⊕www.eastkimberley.com. **Western Australian Tourism Commission** ⊠ Wellington St. and Forrest Pl., Perth ☎ 08/9483-1111 or 1300/361351 🖶 08/9481-0190 ⊕ www.westernaustralia.com.

Perth & Western Australia

WORD OF MOUTH

"Just back from 3 weeks in Perth . . . as a native put it, 'the best things in Perth cost nothing.' The beaches are wonderful . . . the ocean is like bath water. Rottnest [Island] is great for kids and families; low-key, back-to-nature, comfortable—we just loved it. I felt like I was transported back about 40 years ago, to a time when you could leave your doors unlocked, and let your kids go out to play without fear."

—KathyM

Updated by
Graham
Hodgson and
Shamara
Williams

WESTERN AUSTRALIA IS ENORMOUS; twice the size of Texas, it sprawls across more than 1 million square mi. It's also a stunningly diverse place, with rugged interior deserts, a tropical coast of white-sand beaches, and a temperate, forested south. A growing number of excellent wineries, restaurants, seaside parks, and hiking trails mean that Australia's "undiscovered state" likely won't stay undiscovered for much longer.

Although the existence of a southern continent—*terra australis*—was known long before Dutch seafarer Dirk Hartog first landed on the coast of "New Holland" in 1616 in today's Shark Bay, the landscape he encountered was so bleak he didn't even bother to plant his flag and claim it for the Dutch crown. It took an intrepid English seaman, William Dampier, to see past the daunting prospect of endless sands, rugged cliffs, heat, flies, and sparse, scrubby plains to claim the land for Britain, 20,000 km (12,400 mi) away.

Such isolation would ordinarily doom a community to life as a backwater, but the discovery of natural resources here eventually helped the region become vibrant. A gold rush around Kalgoorlie and Coolgardie in the 1890s brought people and wealth, especially to the fledgling city of Perth; much later, in the 1970s, the discovery of massive mineral deposits throughout the state attracted international interest and began an economic upswing that still continues.

Today Western Australia produces much of Australia's mineral, energy, and agricultural wealth. Perth, the capital city and home to nearly 75% of the state's 1.9 million residents, is a modern, pleasant metropolis with an easygoing, welcoming attitude. However, at 3,200 km (2,000 mi) from any other major city in the world, it has fondly been dubbed "the most isolated city on earth." In fact, since it is closer to Indonesia than to its overland Australian cousins, many West Australians choose to take their vacations in Bali rather than in, say, Sydney or Melbourne.

The remoteness, though, is part of what makes Western Australia so awe-inspiring. The scenery here is magnificent; whether you travel through the rugged gorges and rock formations of the north; the green pastures, vineyards, and hardwood forests of the south; or the coastline's vast, pristine beaches, you'll be struck by how much space there is here. If the crowds and crush of big-city life aren't your thing, this is the part of Australia you may never want to leave.

The Kimberley region in Western Australia's tropical north is closer geographically and in character to the Northern Territory city of Darwin than it is to Perth. For this reason, information about Broome and the Kimberley is included in Chapter 11.

Exploring Perth & Western Australia

Most trips to Western Australia begin in Perth. Apart from its own points of interest, there are a few great day trips to take from the city: to Rottnest Island, for example, or north to the coastal Nambung National

12

Planning your time out west requires focus on a couple of areas. It's unlikely you'll cover the whole state, even if you decide to permanently relocate. To narrow down your choices, consider whether you have a few days to spend in and around Perth and Fremantle. Does the thought of cooler air and the coastal scenery of the South West appeal to you, or would you rather get in a car and drive to far reaches east or north? Or, do you want to trek north along the coast to Monkey Mia or Ningaloo Reef Marine Park to frolic in and under the waves with amazing sea creatures?

**If you have
3 days**

Spend most of the first day knocking around **Perth**'s city center. Take the train to pleasantly restored **Fremantle** and stroll through the streets, stopping for breaks at sidewalk cafés. In the evening in either city, have dinner overlooking the water. Over the next two days, take a ferry to **Rottnest Island** and cycle around, walk on the beach, fish, or try to spot the small local marsupials called quokkas. For a longer excursion, take a coach tour to **Nambung National Park** Pinnacles, the captivating coastal rock formations, or south to the Treetop Walk.

**If you have
5 days**

Now you can take on some of the larger distances in Western Australia. Fly north to **Monkey Mia** to learn about and interact with dolphins, or to **Ningaloo Reef Marine Park** to dive with whale sharks and watch the annual coral spawning. Or drive a couple of hours to the **South West** coastal area to see spring wildflowers, wineries, orchards, forests, grazing dairy and beef herds, and national parks, and to generally enjoy the good life. You'll have enough time for a day or two around **Perth** before flying to the old goldfields towns of **Kalgoorlie** and **Coolgardie**. They may remind you of America's Wild West—except that camel teams rather than stagecoaches used to pull into town—but this is pure Oz all the way.

**If you have
7 days
or more**

With seven days you can consider all options, mixing parts of the three- and five-day itineraries. Of course, you could opt to spend the entire week leisurely making your way along the coast of the **South West,** tasting the top-quality regional wines and locally grown foods. Or, you could head for the caves and rough shorelines that define **Leeuwin–Naturaliste National Park. Stirling Range National Park** is a great place for hiking, especially in spring amid the vast wildflowers. If you plan to go north to view **Karijini National Park** and its stunning gorges and rockscapes, taking a plane will give you more time to explore. Alternatively, you could drive northwest to **Nambung National Park,** then take the coastal road north. You may want to continue to the Western Australian city of Broome and the Kimberley region, or even beyond them to Darwin.

Park. The port city of Fremantle is a good place to unwind, and, if you have the time, a tour of the South West—with its seashore, parks, hardwood forests, wildflowers, and first-rate wineries and restaurants—is highly recommended. The old goldfield towns east of Perth are a slice of the dust-blown Australia of yore.

About the Restaurants

Perth's restaurants and cafés reflect Western Australia's energetic outdoor lifestyle, with menus strongly influenced by the state's continual influx of European, Asian, and African immigrants. First-class food is matched by wines and beers from some of Australia's most innovative vineyards and breweries. A jacket and tie are rarely needed, and most places are either licensed (able to serve wine and beers with food) or BYO (bring your own wine or beer). Tips aren't expected, but leaving 10% extra for exceptional service is welcome.

WHAT IT COSTS In Australian Dollars				
	$$$$	$$$	$$	$	¢
AT DINNER	over $50	$36–$50	$21–$35	$10–$20	under $10

Prices are for a main course at dinner.

About the Hotels

Most first-class properties and international names are in Perth's city center, and all have many modern facilities. Apartment-style accommodations have two or three bedrooms, a kitchen, and a larger living space, although these lack the hotel advantages of room service and 24-hour restaurants. Outside the city, bed-and-breakfasts provide comfort, charm, and a glimpse of local life. In farther-flung parts of the state—and there are plenty of these—much of the lodging is motel style.

WHAT IT COSTS In Australian Dollars				
	$$$$	$$$	$$	$	¢
FOR 2 PEOPLE	over $300	$201–$300	$151–$200	$100–$150	under $100

Prices are for two people in a standard double room in high season, including tax and service, based on the European Plan (with no meals) unless otherwise noted.

When to Visit

There's no wrong time to visit Western Australia. In Perth and south, you can view wildflowers in spring (September through November) and watch whales along the coast in fall (February through May). Although winter (May through August) is the wettest season, it's also when the orchards and forests are lush and green. North of Perth, winter is the dry season, and it can get chilly inland throughout the state. Summer (December through February) is *hot*, when temperatures can rise to 40°C (100°F).

PERTH

Buoyed by mineral wealth and foreign investment, high-rise buildings dot the skyline of Perth, and an influx of immigrants gives the city a healthy diversity. Some of Australia's finest sands, sailing, and fishing

Beaches Some of Australia's finest beaches are in Western Australia, stretching from the snow-white salt beaches of Frenchman's Bay in the south to beyond Port Hedland in the north. In a day's drive from Perth you can enjoy a sojourn just about anywhere along the coast in the South West, or explore the emerald waters of the Batavia Coast, north of where the Pinnacles keep watch over the turbulent Indian Ocean.

Local Cuisine Although Perth's cuisine has been shaped by such external influences as the postwar European immigration and an influx of Asian and African cultures, an indigenous west-coast style is emerging. Like much of the innovative cooking in Australia, this style fuses Asian, European, African, and native Australian herbs and spices with French, Mediterranean, and Asian techniques to bring out the best in what is grown locally. In Western Australia's case, this means some of the country's finest seafood, as well as beef, lamb, kangaroo, venison, and emu.

12

Fine Wines Western Australia is a relative newcomer on the global wine scene, though wine grapes have been grown since early European settlement. Nevertheless, it now has regions of premier vineyards, on a par with those of the Bordeaux region of France. Although many of the winemakers produce relatively tiny quantities from small acreages of grapes, they still are renowned on the international market. Wineries and wine trails abound from Perth to the Swan Valley, as well as south to the Geographe, Margaret River, Warren-Blackwood, and Great Southern regions.

The Outdoors Western Australia's national parks are full of natural wonders, including fascinating rock formations, exotic birdlife, jarrah and karri hardwood forests, and, in spring, great expanses of wildflowers. These parks rank among the best in Australia, in many cases because they are remote and uncrowded. Plan for long journeys to reach some, but others are easily accessible, being close to Perth and in the South West. In the marine parks and locations such as Ningaloo, Monkey Mia, and Bunbury, expect to see dolphins and whales (in season). On land, kangaroos are fairly prolific, and quokkas are easily spotted on Rottnest Island.

Water Sports Wind-in-your-hair types can get their fill of jet skiing and parasailing in Perth. Divers should seriously consider going all the way north to Exmouth to take the scuba trip of a lifetime with whale sharks at Ningaloo Reef Marine Park. And in the South West, particularly near Margaret River, surfing is a way of life, with major international surf festivals each year.

---

are on the city's doorstep, and seaside villages and great beaches lie just north of Fremantle. The main business thoroughfare is St. George's Terrace, an elegant street with many of the city's most intriguing sights. Perth's literal highlight is King's Park, 1,000 acres of greenery atop Mt. Eliza, which affords panoramic views of the city.

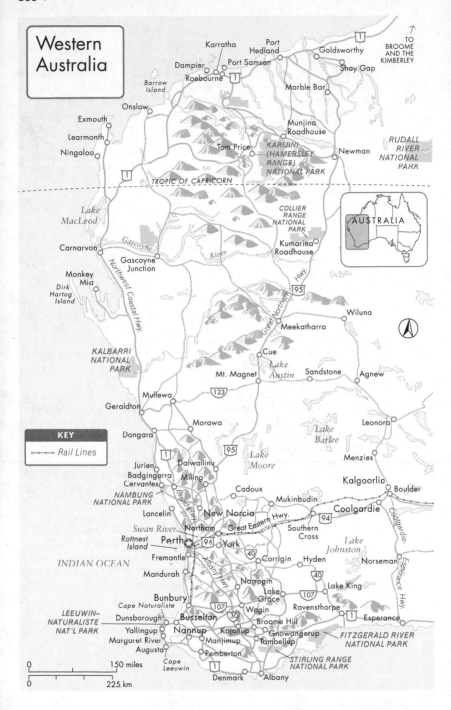

Western Australia

TO
BROOME
AND THE
KIMBERLEY

Karratha
Port
Hedland
Goldsworthy
Dampier
Port Samson
Shay Gap
Roebourne
Barrow
Island
Marble Bar

Onslow
Munjina
Roadhouse
RUDALL
RIVER
NATIONAL
PARK
Exmouth
Learmonth
Tom Price
KARIJINI
(HAMERSLEY
RANGE)
NATIONAL PARK
Newman
Ningaloo

TROPIC OF CAPRICORN

Lake
MacLeod
COLLIER
RANGE
NATIONAL
PARK
AUSTRALIA

Gascoyne
Carnarvon
Kumarina
Roadhouse
Gascoyne
Junction
River
Monkey
Mia
Dirk
Hartog
Island
Northwest Coastal Hwy.
95
Wiluna
Great Northern Hwy.
Meekatharra
KALBARRI
NATIONAL
PARK
Cue
Lake
Austin
Sandstone
Agnew
Mt. Magnet
Geraldton
Mullewa
Lake
Barlee
Leonora
123
Morawa
Dongara
Lake
Moore
Menzies
Jurien
Dalwallinu
95
Badgingarra
Cervantes
Miling
Cadoux
Kalgoorlie
Boulder
NAMBUNG
NATIONAL PARK
Mukinbudin
Coolgardie
Lancelin
New Norcia
94
Swan River
Northam
Great Eastern Hwy.
Southern
Cross
Coolgardie-Esperance Hwy.
Rottnest
Island
Perth
91
York
Lake
Johnston
INDIAN OCEAN
Fremantle
40
Corrigin
Hyden
Norseman
Mandurah
Brand Hwy.
Narrogin
40
Lake King
Lake
Grace
Bunbury
107
Cape Naturaliste
Ravensthorpe
Albany Hwy.
Wagin
1
Esperance
Dunsborough
Busselton
30
Broome Hill
Yallingup
Nannup
Kojonup
Gnowangerup
FITZGERALD RIVER
NATIONAL PARK
Margaret River
Manjimup
Tambellup
Augusta
Pemberton
STIRLING RANGE
NATIONAL PARK
Cape
Leeuwin
1
LEEUWIN-
NATURALISTE
NAT'L PARK
Denmark
Albany

KEY
⊢→→ Rail Lines

0   150 miles
0   225 km

Exploring Perth

Because of its relative colonial youth, Perth has an advantage over most other capital cities in that it was laid out with foresight and elegance. Streets were planned so that pedestrian traffic could flow smoothly from one avenue to the next, and this compact city remains easy to negotiate on foot. Most of the points of interest are in the downtown area close to the banks of the Swan River. Although the East End of the city has long been the fashionable part of town, the West End is fast becoming the chic shopping precinct.

Central Business District

The city center, a pleasant blend of old and new, runs along Perth's major business thoroughfare, St. George's Terrace, as well as on parallel Hay and Murray streets.

Numbers in the text correspond to numbers in the margin and on the Perth map.

a good walk

Start at the **General Post Office** ❶ ►, a solid sandstone edifice facing Forrest Place, one of the city's bustling pedestrian malls and a venue for regular free concerts and street theater. Head east along Murray Street, passing the Forrest Chase Shopping Plaza. Beyond this, near the corner at Irwin Street, three blocks away, is the **Fire Safety Education Centre and Museum** ❷, which displays historic firefighting artifacts.

Continue east on Murray Street to Victoria Square, one of Perth's finest plazas, which is dominated by **St. Mary's Cathedral** ❸. Turn right onto Victoria Avenue for a block, then right again on Hay Street, passing two of Perth's newer buildings—the Central Fire Station on your right and the **Law Courts** ❹ on your left. Turn left onto Pier Street and head toward St. George's Terrace. On the corner, adjacent to the simple, Gothic-style **St. George's Cathedral** ❺, is the Deanery, one of Perth's oldest houses.

Look across St. George's Terrace for the Gothic Revival turrets and English-style gardens of **Government House** ❻, then stroll south to **Supreme Court Gardens** ❼, with its stately Moreton Bay fig trees, some of the finest in Perth. At the western end of the gardens is the charming Georgian **Francis Burt Law Museum** ❽. Turn left down Barrack Street toward the Swan River to view the **Swan Bells Tower** ❾.

Return to St. George's Terrace and walk west for a look at many of Perth's newest and most impressive office buildings, including the notable **Bankwest Tower** ❿. Continuing on St. George's Terrace, look right to see **the Cloisters** ⓫, built as a boys' high school in 1858. At the top of the terrace is the lone remnant of the first military barracks, the **Barracks Arch** ⓬, which stands in front of **Parliament House** ⓭.

For a detour into the greener reaches of Perth, head up Malcolm Street, then left at the roundabout to **King's Park** ⓮. The huge botanic garden within its bounds is a great place for an introduction to Western Australia's flora and natural bushland. In spring the native wildflowers alone are worth the trip. You can return to the city on the Number 33 bus if you'd like to end the tour here.

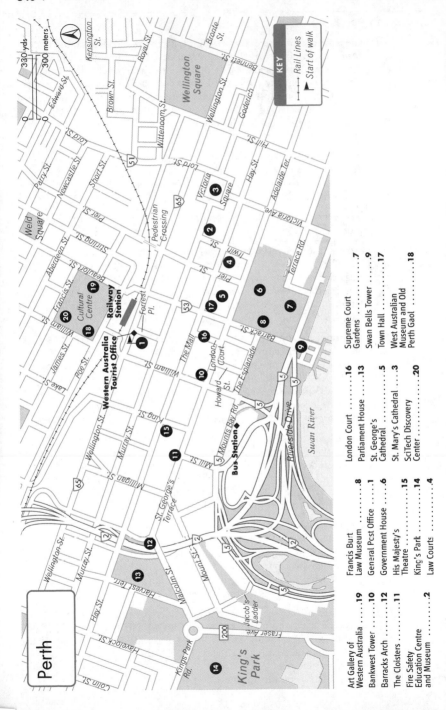

Perth

KEY

→← *Rail Lines*
▲ *Start of walk*

Art Gallery of
Western Australia **19**
Bankwest Tower **10**
Barracks Arch **12**
The Cloisters **11**
Fire Safety
Education Centre
and Museum **2**

Francis Burt
Law Museum **8**
General Post Office **1**
Government House **6**
His Majesty's
Theatre **15**
King's Park **14**
Law Courts **4**

London Court **16**
Parliament House **13**
St. George's
Cathedral **5**
St. Mary's Cathedral **3**
SciTech Discovery
Center **20**

Supreme Court
Gardens **7**
Swan Bells Tower **9**
Town Hall **17**
West Australian
Museum and Old
Perth Gaol **18**

From Barracks Arch, turn around and walk back along St. George's Terrace to Milligan Street and turn left. When you reach Hay Street, turn right and walk toward the opulent Edwardian exterior of **His Majesty's Theatre** ⑮ at the corner of King and Hay streets. Continue to the Hay Street Mall, one of many city streets closed to traffic, where the **London Court** ⑯ shopping arcade runs north to south between Hay Street and St. George's Terrace. The mechanical clock with three-dimensional animated figures chimes every quarter hour. Pause at the intersection of Hay and Barrack streets, at **Town Hall** ⑰, one of Perth's handsome, convict-built structures. From here you can take a break, or continue four blocks northeast on Barrack Street toward the James Street Mall, where you can wander through the **Western Australian Museum and Old Perth Gaol** ⑱, or the **Art Gallery of Western Australia** ⑲.

TIMING It will take about two hours just to pace off the above route, without the Western Australian Museum or the Art Gallery of Western Australia, and you can lengthen this by stopping in shops and gardens. The heat from December through February can make all but early-morning or evening strolls uncomfortable.

What to See

⑲ **Art Gallery of Western Australia.** More than 1,000 treasures from the state's art collection are on display, including one of the best exhibits of Aboriginal art in Australia. Other works include Australian and international paintings, sculpture, prints, crafts, and decorative arts. Free guided tours run at 1 PM Tuesday, Friday, and Sunday. On Friday the 12:30 PM Friday's Focus tour examines one particular painting, and guest speakers are scheduled at 2 PM the first Sunday of every month. ⊠ *47 James St. Mall, CBD* ☎ *08/9492–6600* ⊕ *www.artgallery.wa.gov.au* ⊠ *Free* ⊗ *Daily 10–5.*

⑩ **Bankwest Tower.** This 1988 tower wraps around the facade of the historic 1895 **Palace Hotel,** now used for bank offices. The hotel typified the ornate architecture that dominated the city in the late 19th century. ⊠ *108 St. George's Terr., at William St., CBD.*

⑫ **Barracks Arch.** Perth's oddest architectural curiosity, this freestanding brick arch in the middle of the city center stands more or less in front of the seat of government—the highway actually comes between them. All that remains of the former headquarters of the Pensioner Forces (demolished in 1966) is this Tudor-style edifice, built in the 1860s with Flemish bond brickwork, a memorial to the earliest settlers. ⊠ *St. George's Terr. and Malcolm St., CBD.*

⑪ **The Cloisters.** Originally built as a school for boys, this 1858 brick building now houses mining company offices. ⊠ *200 St. George's Terr., at Mill St., CBD.*

② **Fire Safety Education Centre and Museum.** Also known as the Old Fire Station, the building is now a museum housing an exhibit on the history of the fire brigade. Photos trace its beginnings, when horses and carts were used, to the present day. There's also a splendid display of old vehicles and equipment. The old limestone building is a fine example of colonial architecture. ⊠ *25 Murray St., at Irwin St., CBD* ☎ *08/ 9323–9353* ✉ *Free* ☉ *Weekdays 10–3.*

⑧ Francis Burt Law Museum. A former courthouse and Perth's oldest public building, this charming 1836 Georgian structure sits amid the ⇨ **Supreme Court Gardens.** ⊠ *5/33 Barrack St., CBD* ☎ *08/9325–4787* ✉ *Donation suggested* ☉ *Feb.–Dec., Mon., Tues., Wed., and Fri. 10–2:30.*

⚑ **❶ General Post Office.** A handsome, colonnaded sandstone building, the post office forms an impressive backdrop to the city's major public square, Forrest Place. ⊠ *Forrest Pl. between Murray and Wellington Sts., CBD.*

⑥ Government House. This is the official residence of the governor and home to members of the royal family during visits to Perth. It was constructed between 1859 and 1864 in Gothic Revival style, with arches and turrets reminiscent of the Tower of London. You can't tour the house, but the gardens are open to the public Tuesday noon–2. ⊠ *Supreme Court Gardens, CBD.*

⑮ His Majesty's Theatre. Restoration has transformed this Edwardian 1904 building, one of Perth's most gracious, into a handsome home for the Western Australian opera and ballet companies. The busiest month for performances is February, during the Perth International Arts Festival. Auditorium and backstage tours, which run weekdays 10–4, must be booked in advance. The Grand Historical Tour (two hours) takes you on a gossipy and anecdotal wander through nine decades of colorful show-business history. You will view theater foyers, the auditorium, dressing rooms, backstage, and the Museum of Performing Arts. Available weekdays 10–4 for groups of 10–30; the cost is A$20 per person. The Behind the Scenes Tour (one hour) commences in the Stalls foyer and includes a view of the auditorium and backstage areas of the theater as well as a visit to the Museum of Performing Arts. It's conducted Thursday mornings 10:30–noon; the cost is A$12. Visitors may then choose to attend the weekly Lunchtime Concert in the Dress Circle Bar, from 12:30 to 1:10 PM (A$7). Both tours can include refreshments for an extra charge. Downstairs, the **Museum of Performing Arts** has rotating exhibitions of costumes and memorabilia. ⊠ *825 Hay St., CBD* ☎ *08/9265–0900* ⊕ *www. hismajestystheatre.com.au* ✉ *Theater tours free, backstage tours A$12, museum donations suggested* ☉ *Box office weekdays 9–5:30, museum weekdays 10–4.*

★ ☼ **⑭ King's Park.** Once a gathering place for Aboriginal people and established as a public space in 1890, this 1,000-acre park overlooking downtown Perth is one of the city's most-visited attractions. Both tourists and locals enjoy picnics, parties, and weddings in the gardens, as well as walks in the bushland. In springtime the gardens blaze with orchids, kangaroo paw, banksias, and other wildflowers. The steel-and-timber **Lotteries Federation Walkway** takes you into the treetops and the 17-acre botanic garden of Australian flora. The **Western Power Parkland** details Western Australia's fossil and energy history. The **Lotteries Family Area** has a playground for youngsters. Free walking tours take place daily, and details on seasonal and themed tours are available from the information kiosk near Fraser's Restaurant. ⊠ *Fraser Ave. and King's Park Rd., West Perth* ☎ *08/9480–3600* 🎟 *Free* ⊙ *Daily 24 hrs.*

❹ Law Courts. The 1903 building is surrounded by lively gardens, and inside it can be almost as colorful. Many cases tried here are high profile—and guests can be part of the viewing gallery. ⊠ *30 St. George's Terr., CBD* ☎ *08/9425–2222* 🎟 *Free* ⊙ *During trials.*

⑯ London Court. Gold-mining entrepreneur Claude de Bernales built this outdoor shopping arcade in 1937. Today it's a magnet for buskers (street performers) and anyone with a camera. Along its length are statues of Sir Walter Raleigh and Dick Whittington, the legendary lord mayor of London. Above the arcade, costumed mechanical knights joust with one another when the clock strikes the quarter hour. ⊠ *Between St. George's Terr. and Hay St., CBD.*

⑬ Parliament House. From its position on the hill at the top of St. George's Terrace, this building dominates Perth's skyline and serves as a respectable backdrop for the Barracks Arch. Shady old Moreton Bay fig trees and landscaped gardens make the hub of Western Australian government one of the most pleasant spots in the city. Drop in for a free one-hour tour Monday or Thursday at 10:30; groups are accommodated by appointment. You can visit the Public Galleries whenever Parliament is sitting. ⊠ *Harvest Terr., West Perth* ☎ *08/9222–7429* ⊕ *www.parliament.wa.gov.au* 🎟 *Free* ⊙ *Tours Mon. and Thurs. 10:30.*

Perth Concert Hall. When it was built, this small rectangular 1960s concert hall was considered both elegant and impressive. Although its architectural merit may now seem questionable to some, its acoustics are still clean and clear. The hall serves as the city's main music performance venue. ⊠ *5 St. George's Terr., CBD* ☎ *08/9321–9900* ⊕ *www.perthconcerthall.com.au* 🎟 *Ticket prices vary* ⊙ *During performances.*

❺ St. George's Cathedral. The church and its **Deanery** form one of the city's most distinctive European-style complexes. Built during the late 1850s as a home for the first dean of Perth, the Deanery is one of the few remaining houses in Western Australia from this period. It's now used as offices for the Anglican Church and is not open to the public. ⊠ *Pier St. and St. George's Terr., CBD* ☎ *08/9325–5766* 🎟 *Free* ⊙ *Weekdays 7:30–5, Sun. services at 8, 10, and 5.*

❸ St. Mary's Cathedral. One of Perth's most appealing plazas, **Victoria Square** is the home of the Gothic Revival St. Mary's. Its environs house the headquarters for the Roman Catholic Church. ⊠ *Victoria Sq., CBD* ☎ *08/9325–9177* 🎟 *Free* ⊙ *Mass weekdays 7 AM and 12:10 PM; Sat. 7 AM and 6:30 PM; Sun. 7:30, 9, 10, 11:30, and 5.*

♻ ⑳ Scitech Discovery Centre. The interactive displays of science and technology here educate and entertain children of all ages. There are more than 100 hands-on exhibits, including a stand where you can freeze your own shadow, and another where you can play the Mystical Laser Harp. Scitech was inducted into the Western Australian Tourism Commission's Hall of Fame as an outstanding Major Tourist Attraction. ⊠ *City West*

Railway Parade, Sutherland St., West Perth ☎ *08/9481–6295* ⊕ *www. scitech.org.au* ✉ *A$12* ⊙ *Daily 10–5.*

❼ Supreme Court Gardens. This favorite lunch spot for hundreds of office workers is also home to some of the finest Moreton Bay fig trees in the state. A band shell in the rear of the gardens hosts summer concerts, which take place in the evenings December through February and twice weekly as part of the Perth International Arts Festival. ✉ *Barrack St. and Adelaide Terr., CBD* ☎ *08/9461–3333* ✉ *Free; some concerts require prepaid tickets* ⊙ *Daily 9–5.*

❾ Swan Bells Tower. Comprising one of the world's largest musical instruments, the 12 ancient bells installed in the tower are originally from St. Martin-in-the-Fields Church of London, England. The same bells rang to celebrate the destruction of the Spanish Armada in 1588, the homecoming of Captain James Cook in 1771, and the coronation of every British monarch. The tower contains fascinating displays on the history of the bells and bell ringing, and provides stunning views of the Perth skyline. ✉ *Barrack Sq., Barrack St. and Riverside Dr., CBD* ☎ *08/ 9218–8183* ⊕ *www.swanbells.com.au* ✉ *A$6* ⊙ *Daily 10–4:30.*

⓱ Town Hall. In the 1860s convicts built this hall in the style of a Jacobean English market. Today the building is used for public events. ✉ *Hay and Barrack Sts., CBD* ☎ *08/9229–2960.*

☾⓲ West Australian Museum and Old Perth Gaol. The state's largest and most comprehensive museum includes some of Perth's oldest structures, such as the Old Perth Gaol. Built of stone in 1856, this was Perth's first prison until 1888. Today, it has been reconstructed in the museum courtyard, and you can go inside the cells for a taste of life in Perth's criminal past. Exhibitions include Diamonds to Dinosaurs, which uses fossils, rocks, and gemstones to take you back 3.5 billion years into Western Australia's past; and Katta Djinoong: First Peoples of Western Australia, which has a fascinating collection of primitive tools and lifestyle items used thousands of years ago by Australia's Aborigines. In the Marine Gallery there's an 80-foot-long skeleton of a blue whale that washed ashore in the South West. ✉ *James and Beaufort Sts., CBD* ☎ *08/9427–2700* ⊕ *www. museum.wa.gov.au* ✉ *Free* ⊙ *Daily 9:30–5.*

Around Perth

☾ AQWA: Aquarium of Western Australia. Huge tanks filled with all sorts of local sea creatures let you view what's beneath the waves. Sharks, stingrays, octopus, cuttlefish, lobsters, turtles, and thousands of fish swim overhead as you take the moving walkway beneath a clear acrylic tunnel. You can even snorkel or scuba dive with the sharks at 1 PM and 3 PM daily. Mammals like Australian sea lions and New Zealand fur seals are also part of the show. ✉ *Hillarys Boat Harbour, 91 Southside Dr., Hillarys* ☎ *08/9447–7500* ⊕ *www.aqwa.com.au* ✉ *A$25; shark experience A$90, plus A$15 snorkel or A$30 scuba equipment rental* ⊙ *Daily 10–5.*

☾ Cohunu Koala Park. The 40-acre Cohunu (pronounced co-*hu*-na) lets you cuddle with a koala. But the other native animals, such as emus and wombats in their natural surroundings, are worth visiting too. The walk-through aviary is the largest in the Southern Hemisphere, and there's also a kid-friendly miniature railway and a revolving restaurant that over-looks the city. ⊠ *Mill Rd. E, Gosnells* ☎ *08/9390–6090* 🖷 *08/9495–1341* ⊕ *www.cohunu.com.au* 🖃 *A$20* ⊘ *Daily 10–5, koala cuddle with photo souvenir daily 10–4.*

⊙ **Museum of Childhood.** A pioneer in the conservation of childhood her-itage in Australia, this museum is an enchanting hands-on journey for both children and parents. Its 18,000 items constitute the largest and most diverse children's collection the country. Among the most prized exhibits are an original alphabet manuscript written, illustrated, and bound by William Makepeace Thackeray in 1833 and dolls from around the world. ⊠ *Thomas Sten Bldg., Edith Cowan University Campus, Bay Rd., Claremont* ☎ *08/9442–1398* ⊕ *www.cowan.edu.au/ses/museum* 🖃 *A$4* ⊘ *Weekdays 10–4, Sun. 10–4.*

⊙ **Perth Zoo.** Some 2,000 creatures—from 280 different species—are housed in this gathering of spacious natural habitats. Popular attractions include the Australian Walkabout, the Penguin Plunge, and the Australian Bush-walk. You can also wander down a dry riverbed in the African Savannah, or delve through the thick foliage in the Asian Rainforest. To reach the zoo, it's a 5-minute walk across the Narrows Bridge, or a ferry ride across the Swan River from the bottom of Barrack Street and then a 10-minute walk following the signs. ⊠ *20 Labouchere Rd., South Perth* ☎ *08/ 9474–0444 or 08/9474–3551* ⊕ *www.perthzoo.wa.gov.au* 🖃 *A$16* ⊘ *Daily 9–5.*

⊙ **Whiteman Park.** Barbecue facilities, picnic spots, bike trails, vintage trains and electric trams, and historic wagons and tractors fill this enor-mous recreation area linked by more than 30 km (19 mi) of bushwalk-ing trails and bike paths. You can watch potters, blacksmiths, leather workers, toy makers, printers, and stained-glass artists at work here in their shops. Naturally, the wildlife includes free-ranging (or, more ac-curately, free-lazing) kangaroos. **Caversham Wildlife Park** (☎ 08/ 9248–1984 ⊕ www.cavershamwildlife.com.au), in Whiteman Park, has more than 200 wildlife species, and you can greet birds, feed ani-mals, and cuddle koalas or wombats. ⊠ *Lord St. and Gnangara Rd., West Swan* ☎ *08/9249–2446* ⊕ *www.whitemanpark.com.au* 🖃 *Free* ⊘ *Daily 8:30–6.*

off the beaten path | **NAMBUNG NATIONAL PARK –** Set on the Swan coastal plain 245 km (152 mi) north of Perth, Nambung National Park surrounds its most famous attraction: the **Pinnacles Desert.** Over the years, wind and drifting sand have sculpted eerie limestone forms that loom as high as 15 feet. These "pinnacles" are actually the fossilized roots of ancient coastal plants fused with sand, and you can walk among them along a 1,650-foot-long trail that starts at the parking area. There's also a 3-km (2-mi), one-way Pinnacles Desert Loop scenic drive (not suitable for large RVs or buses). August through October the heath blazes with wildflowers. Entrance fees are A$8 per car or A$3 per bus passenger. Call ☎ 08/9652–7043 for more information.

BATAVIA COAST – A drive along this part of the coast, which starts at Greenhead 285 km (178 mi) north of Perth, and runs up to Kalbarri, takes you past white sands and emerald seas, and some lovely small towns. Among them are the fig-shaded, seaside village of **Dongara;** and the more northerly **Greenough Historical Hamlet,** whose restored colonial buildings—including a jail with original leg irons— date from 1858. A few miles north is **Geraldton,** whose skyline is dominated by the beautiful Byzantine St. Francis Xavier Cathedral. The huge Batavia Coast Marina has a pedestrian plaza, shopping arcades, and the Western Australian Museum.

Beaches

Perth's beaches and waterways are among the city's greatest attractions. Traveling north from Fremantle, the first beach you come to is **Leighton,** where windsurfers and astonishing wave-jumpers ride boards against the surf and hurl themselves airborne. **Cottesloe** and **North Cottesloe** attract families. **Trigg,** a top surf site and arguably Perth's best beach, overlooks an emerald-green bay. **Scarborough** is favored by teenagers and young adults. **Swanbourne** (between North Cottesloe and City Beach) is a "clothing-optional" beach.

Where to Eat

Northbridge, northwest of the railway station, is *the* dining and night-clubbing center of Perth, and reasonably priced restaurants are everywhere. Elsewhere around Perth are seafood and international restaurants, many with stunning views over the Swan River or city, and cantilevered windows that make for a seamless transition between indoor and alfresco dining.

For those on a budget, the noisy fun of a dim sum lunch at one of Perth's many traditional Asian teahouses (especially in Northbridge) is cheap and delicious. Along with a refreshing cup of green tea, you can enjoy steamed pork buns, fried chicken feet, and egg tarts served at your table from the trolley. Food halls in Perth, Northbridge, and Fremantle are other budget options. These one-stop eateries cater to diverse tastes; not all are the same, but you can usually take your pick from stalls selling vegetarian items, roast meats, fresh fruits and juices, Aussie burgers, and fried chicken. Some also serve Southeast Asian, Indian, Japanese, Korean, and Thai cuisine, usually for less than A$10.

Chinese

$–$$$$ ✕ **Genting Palace.** Some of the best Chinese food in the city is served at this elegant casino restaurant. Cantonese flavors predominate, but several Szechuan, Shanghai, and Chiu Chow dishes stand out as well. Highlights include sautéed scallops with seasonal vegetables, Spicy Kung Po King Prawns with dried chili peppers, and deep-fried crispy almond chicken. Dim sum lunch is served weekends 10:30–2:30. ⊠ *InterContinental Burswood Resort Perth, Great Eastern Hwy. and Bolton Ave., Burswood* ☎ *08/9362–7551* ▭ *AE, DC, MC, V.*

$$–$$$ ✕ **Shun Fung on the River.** Right on the waterfront next to the Swan Bells Tower, this Chinese restaurant has rapidly gained accolades as one of

Perth's classiest. There's a huge selection of fresh seafood here, including abalone in oyster sauce, steamed Sydney rock oysters with black bean sauce, and crispy king prawns with spiced salt and chili. Banquet menus (8–10 courses) are a specialty, and an extensive collection of rare vintage wines complements the menu. ⊠ *Barrack Sq. Jetty, CBD* ☎ *08/9221–1868* ⊟ *AE, DC, MC, V.*

Contemporary

$$–$$$ ✕ **CBD.** The trendiest place in Perth's West End, this spot has an unusual leaf-shape bar where both diners and drinkers congregate. The steamed chicken breast, marinated in red bean curd and served with coriander pesto, is one of the most popular dishes, and 24 varieties of table wine and "stickies" (dessert wines) are available by the glass. Late hours bring in the nightcap crowd after shows at the adjacent His Majesty's Theatre. ⊠ *Hay and King Sts., CBD* ☎ *08/9263–1859* ⊟ *AE, DC, MC, V.*

Eclectic

$–$$ ✕ **Oriel Café-Brasserie.** At this quintessential 24-hour Perth brasserie just outside the city center, both the dimly lighted interior and the outdoor areas are packed with tables, people, and noise. Crowds come for the breakfasts of pancakes with fresh strawberries and clotted cream and maple syrup, or smoked salmon scrambled eggs with crème fraîche. The lunch and dinner menus—which include prawn and pesto risotto, and shredded Peking duck with fried rice and spring onion salad—are equally popular. ⊠ *483 Hay St., Subiaco* ☎ *08/9382–1886* ⚇ *Reservations not accepted* ⊟ *AE, DC, MC, V.*

French

$$$$ ✕ **Loose Box.** Perth's finest French restaurant is run by owner-chef Alain
Fodor's Choice Fabregues, who has received France's highest culinary honor, the Meilleur
★ Ouvrier de France, as well as a French knighthood—Chevalier Dans L'Ordre National du Merite—for his contribution to French culture and cuisine. His degustation menu applies classical French culinary principles to Australia's best seasonal bounty: there's La Couronne d'Escargots Façon Loose Box—a crown made of profiteroles, filled with mushrooms and snails braised in Pernod; and Le Canard á L'Orange—a half duck marinated in orange zest and Cointreau, slow-cooked until tender and served with orange sauce. Each of the rooms here (the restaurant used to be a house) is cozy, intimate, and warm. Accommodations are also available, if you just can't bring yourself to leave. ⊠ *6825 Great Eastern Hwy., Mundaring* ☎ *08/9295–1787* ⚇ *Reservations essential* ⊟ *AE, DC, MC, V* ⊘ *Closed Mon., Tues., and last 2 wks July. No lunch Sat., Wed., and Thurs.*

Italian

★ **$$–$$$** ✕ **Perugino.** Chef Giuseppe Pagliaricci takes an imaginative yet simple approach to the cuisine of his native Umbria here. Only the freshest produce is used for such creations as *saltimbocca alla Romana* (scallops of veal topped with Parma ham, panfried with sage and white wine); or *congilio in salmi* (rabbit stew with capers, white wine, and lemon juice). The A$60 five-course degustation menu highlights the best of the house. ⊠ *77 Outram St., West Perth* ☎ *08/9321–5420* ⚇ *Reservations essential* ⊟ *AE, DC, MC, V* ⊘ *Closed Sun. No lunch Sat.*

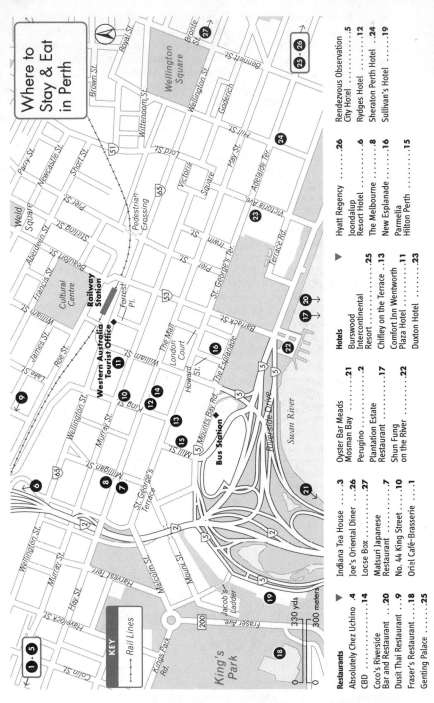

Where to Stay & Eat in Perth

KEY
— Rail Lines

330 yds
300 meters

Restaurants ▶

Absolutely Chez Uchino .**4**
CBD **14**
Coco's Riverside
Bar and Restaurant ...**20**
Dusit Thai Restaurant ...**9**
Fraser's Restaurant **18**
Genting Palace **25**

Indiana Tea House **3**
Joe's Oriental Diner ..**26**
Locse Box **27**
Matsuri Japanese
Restaurant **7**
No. 44 King Street.....**10**
Oriel Café-Brasserie **1**

Oyster Bar Meads **21**
Mosman Bay **2**
Perugino **2**
Plantation Estate
Restaurant **17**
Shun Fung
on the River **22**

Hotels ▶

Burswood
Intercontinental
Resort **25**
Chifley on the Terrace .**13**
Comfort Inn Wentworth
Plaza Hotel **11**
Duxton Hotel **23**

Hyatt Regency **26**
Joondalup
Resort Hotel **6**
The Melbourne **8**
New Esplanade **16**
Parmelia
Hilton Perth **15**

Rendezvous Observation
City Hotel **5**
Rydges Hotel **12**
Sheraton Perth Hotel ...**24**
Sullivan's Hotel **19**

Japanese

$–$$ ✕ **Matsuri Japanese Restaurant.** Discerning diners fill every table most nights at this palatial glass-and-steel restaurant. Set at the base of an office tower, Perth's most popular casual Japanese dining spot is famous for its fresh, flavorful, and authentic cuisine. Served with steamed rice, miso soup, salad, and green tea, the sushi and sashimi sets start at A$12 and are an excellent value. House specialties include delicately light tempura vegetables and *una don* (grilled eel in teriyaki sauce). ✉ *Lower level 1, QV1 Bldg., 250 St. George's Terr., CBD* ☎ *08/9322–7737* ⊟ *AE, DC, MC, V* ☺ *No lunch weekends.*

Modern Australian

$$–$$$$ ✕ **Indiana Tea House.** Overlooking the beach at Cottesloe, this opulent restaurant serves food that's as spectacular as the ocean views. The menu emphasizes seafood, but there are choices for landlubbers, too. Highlights are herbed Parmesan lamb cutlets; beef Rendang (simmered in a spicy Indonesian curry sauce with coconut milk and ginger, with fresh chili and jasmine rice); and panfried lambs brain with pumpkin mash and lime caper sauce. Despite the revamped colonial exterior, you're more likely to find Indiana Jones than Somerset Maugham among the wicker chairs and cool Indian decor. ✉ *99 Marine Parade, Cottesloe* ☎ *08/9385–5005* ⚱ *Reservations essential* ⊟ *AE, DC, MC, V.*

$$$ ✕ **Absolutely Chez Uchino.** Japanese and French cuisine are skillfully fused here by Osamu Uchino, one of Perth's most innovative chefs. The results—panfried sea scallops in bouillabaisse, beef teriyaki topped with freshwater lobster—are delicious. The minimalist, no-smoking dining room is elegant and just a 15-minute cab ride from downtown. ✉ *622 Stirling Hwy., Mosman Park* ☎ *08/9385–2202* ⚱ *Reservations essential* ⊟ *AE, DC, MC, V* ☺ *Closed Sun.–Tues. No lunch.*

$$$ ✕ **Plantation Estate Restaurant.** Reminiscent of a tropical colonial plantation, this mansion with its wood-paneled dining room attracts crowds of dining cognoscenti. Chef Craig Young creates sumptuous breakfasts that include *nasi goreng* (Indonesian fried rice) and vanilla flapjacks with berry compote; dinner choices include local freshwater lobsters and seafood stir-fry with organic noodles, lemongrass, and coconut cream. ✉ *79 Esplanade, at Mends St., South Perth* ☎ *08/9474–5566* ⊟ *AE, DC, MC, V.*

$$–$$$ ✕ **Fraser's Restaurant.** In fair weather the large outdoor area at this Kings Park restaurant fills with people enjoying food and views of the city and Swan River. The ever-changing menu highlights daily seafood specials, depending on what's at the local markets, and the wine list is 100% Australian. Look for spiced beef fillet with dal and palak paneer (spinach and cubes of soft cheese); cucumber raita and tomato chutney; panfried king snapper with sautéed potatoes, green beans, and mini capers; or roast kangaroo loin with celeriac and onion crumble. ✉ *Fraser Ave., King's Park, West Perth* ☎ *08/9481–7100* ⚱ *Reservations essential* ⊟ *AE, DC, MC, V.*

$–$$ ✕ **Coco's Riverside Bar and Restaurant.** Overlooking the Swan River in South Perth, this restaurant has a menu that changes daily depending on fresh produce. Most items are available in both appetizer and main-course portions. The fresh sautée of prawns, scallops, and snapper in a roasted roma tomato–and–basil sauce is especially noteworthy; the wine list is extensive. ⊠ *Southshore Centre, 85 Esplanade, South Perth* ☎ *08/9474–3030* ⚐ *Reservations essential* ☱ *AE, DC, MC, V.*

$–$$ ✕ **No. 44 King Street.** Noted for its cutting-edge modern Australian cuisine, this no-smoking restaurant is popular with a see-and-be-seen lunchtime business crowd. The seasonal menu changes weekly. Winter brings savory soups, while the summer menu highlights seafood salads. The coffee, cakes, and wines are all excellent, and the service is super-efficient. ⊠ *44 King St., CBD* ☎ *08/9321–4476* ☱ *AE, DC, MC, V.*

Pan-Asian

$–$$ ✕ **Joe's Oriental Diner.** On the street level of the Hyatt Regency Hotel on Adelaide Terrace, Joe's features a wide range of dishes from Indonesia, Thailand, Malaysia, and Singapore. The rattan-and-bamboo decor is reminiscent of the many noodle houses one finds throughout Southeast Asia, and you can watch as meals are prepared in the spectacular open kitchen. Hearty soups and delicious noodle dishes, like *laksa* (rice noodles in a spicy coconut-milk broth with chicken, bean curd, and prawns) are the standouts here. Each dish carries a chili coding indicating its relative spiciness—so you won't breathe fire unless you want to. ⊠ *Hyatt Regency, 99 Adelaide Terr., CBD* ☎ *08/9225–1268* ☱ *AE, DC, MC, V* ☻ *Closed Sun. No lunch Sat.*

Seafood

$–$$ ✕ **Oyster Bar Meads Mosman Bay.** Visitors to this spot can never seem to
FodorsChoice decide what's more spectacular: the delicious seafood or the gorgeous
★ setting on the Swan River, overlooking yachts and mansions. The hip bar and oyster bar are popular, but the reliably excellent daily menu is the real draw here. While gazing at a squadron of pelicans lazily gliding over the river, you can feast on whole baby barramundi, crispy-fried with vegetables; or red emperor wings (the sweetest parts of a locally caught fish) lightly fried, and served on mashed potatoes with lemon sauce. Reservations are essential. The restaurant is a 15-minute cab ride from town. ⊠ *15 Johnson Parade, Mosman Park* ☎ *08/9383–3388* ☱ *AE, DC, MC, V.*

Thai

$$–$$$ ✕ **Dusit Thai Restaurant.** Authentic Thai food, lovingly prepared and served among traditional sculptures and artwork, is the order of the day here. Starters include *kra thong tong* (stir-fried diced prawns, minced chicken, and sweet corn on deep-fried tarlets); or *nuea dad-diew* (deep-fried marinated beef with chili sauce). Main-course specialties include *gang keo-wan jai* (green curry chicken) and *pard ki-mow moo* (stir-fried spicy pork with runner beans and basil). Complete the experience with sticky rice and ice cream for dessert. ⊠ *249 James St., Northbridge* ☎ *08/9328–7647* ☱ *AE, DC, MC, V* ☻ *No lunch Sat.–Wed. No dinner Mon.*

Where to Stay

$$$ ▥ **Burswood Intercontinental Resort.** From the 10-story glass atrium atop
FodorsChoice its pyramid-shape exterior to its 18-hole golf course, everything about
★ Burswood says "luxury." Spacious rooms have Japanese shoji screens

between the bedrooms and bathrooms, as well as views of either the river or the city. Suites have spa baths. The adjoining casino is one of the largest in the Southern Hemisphere, open around-the-clock for roulette, blackjack, baccarat, keno, and video games. Nine restaurants within the complex include upscale and buffet-style dining. *⌂ Box 500, Victoria Park 6979 ✉ Great Eastern Hwy. and Bolton Ave., Burswood 6100 ☎ 08/9362–7777 or 1800/999667 🖷 08/9470–2553 ⊕ www.burswood. com.au ↘ 413 rooms, 16 suites ♨ 9 restaurants, room service, inroom data ports, 18-hole golf course, 4 tennis courts, 2 pools (1 indoor), health club, sauna, spa, 6 bars, casino, dance club, video game room, shops, babysitting, playground, laundry service, concierge, business services, free parking, no-smoking rooms ⊟ AE, DC, MC, V.*

$$$ ▥ **Sheraton Perth Hotel.** Towering above the Swan River, this hotel is one of Perth's best-known five-star hotels. The lobby glitters with glass chandeliers, while the well-appointed rooms are furnished in Tasmanian oak and have sweeping river views. One of the two restaurants, Montereys Brasserie, has lavish breakfasts, and the Lobby Lounge is popular with locals for predinner and preshow drinks: Perth Concert Hall is just a short walk away. *✉ 207 Adelaide Terr., CBD, 6000 ☎ 08/9224–7777 🖷 08/9224–7788 ⊕ www.sheraton.com/perth ↘ 368 rooms, 18 suites ♨ 2 restaurants, room service, in-room data ports, inroom safes, cable TV, pool, health club, steam room, bicycles, 2 bars, dry cleaning, laundry service, concierge, business services, parking (fee) ⊟ AE, DC, MC, V.*

★ $$–$$$ ▥ **Joondalup Resort Hotel.** Although it's 30 km (19 mi) from Perth's business district, this palm-shaded building—which resembles a southern plantation owner's mansion—is a comfortable place to relax for a few days, especially if you like golf. Spacious rooms, decorated in subdued pastels and warm tones, all have views over the lagoon or the 27-hole, Robert Trent Jones Jr.–designed golf course. A free shuttle runs daily to the Joondalup train station and Lakeside Shopping Centre. *✉ Country Club Blvd., Connolly 6027 ☎ 08/9400–8888 or 1800/803488 🖷 08/9400–8889 ⊕ www.joondalupresort.com.au ↘ 69 rooms, 4 suites, 6 villas ♨ 2 restaurants, in-room data ports, in-room safes, inroom VCRs, 3 9-hole golf courses, 3 tennis courts, pool, gym, hot tub, sauna, 2 bars, laundry service, business services, meeting rooms, free parking ⊟ AE, DC, MC, V.*

$$–$$$ ▥ **Parmelia Hilton Perth.** The opulence of this hotel is evident from the moment you enter the foyer; rich wood paneling, parquet floors, and many antiques—including Chinese silk tapestries and Mussolini's mirror (near the elevator)—immediately surround you. Many of the rooms have private balconies. All suites enjoy river views, and 10 have crystal chandeliers, gilt mirrors, deep-pile carpeting, and luxurious marble bathrooms. There's personal service around the clock, with a valet and seamstress on call, and a 24-hour business center. *✉ 14 Mill St., CBD, 6000 ☎ 08/9215–2000 🖷 08/9215–2001 ⊕ www.perth.hilton.com ↘ 218 rooms, 55 suites ♨ 2 restaurants, room service, in-room data ports, pool, gym, sauna, bicycles, 3 bars, nightclub, dry cleaning, laundry service, concierge, business services, car rental, parking (fee) ⊟ AE, DC, MC, V.*

$$ ⊞ **Chifley on the Terrace.** Amenities at this bright, breezy business hotel—such as in-room Internet connections and spacious baths with aromatherapy oils—are equal to those found at much pricier establishments. Rooms are furnished in earth tones, and executive suites have open-plan bathrooms with hot tubs. Casual alfresco dining is available at the Chifley Bar and Café, right off the lobby. ☒ *185 St. George's Terr., CBD, 6000* ☎ *08/9226–3355* ⊟ *08/9226–1055* ⊕ *www. constellationhotels.com* ☞ *58 rooms, 27 suites* ⚬ *Restaurant, in-room data ports, cable TV, bar, laundry service, business services, free parking* ⊟ *AE, DC, MC, V.*

★ **$$** ⊞ **Hyatt Regency.** Within walking distance of Perth's central business district, this hotel on the Swan River is both comfortable and convenient. Standard rooms are spacious, while the higher-priced Regency Club rooms and suites (reached by a private elevator) have stunning views, complimentary Continental breakfast, and evening drinks and canapés. The Conservatory, a sitting area with tasteful cane furniture and a fountain under a large domed atrium, is a civilized spot for relaxing. ☒ *99 Adelaide Terr., CBD, 6000* ☎ *08/9225–1234* ⊟ *08/9325–8899* ⊕ *www. perth.hyatt.com* ☞ *367 rooms, 32 suites* ⚬ *3 restaurants, room service, in-room safes, tennis court, pool, health club, 2 bars, shops, babysitting, dry cleaning, laundry service, concierge, Internet, business services, meeting room, free parking* ⊟ *AE, DC, MC, V* ⊗ *CP.*

$$ ⊞ **Rendezvous Observation City Hotel.** Watching the sun sink into the Indian Ocean from this beachside resort is a memorable experience. Elegant blues, golds, and mauves decorate the stylish rooms, all of which have superb ocean views, and marble bathrooms and mirrored wardrobes add just the right touch of luxury. You can dine at the epicurean Savannahs Restaurant, enjoy alfresco beachside fare at Café Estrada, or hit the extensive breakfast buffet at Pines. The hotel is just 15 minutes from the city center by free shuttle. ☒ *Esplanade, Scarborough Beach 6019* ☎ *08/9245–1000 or 1800/067680* ⊟ *08/9245–1345* ⊕ *www. rendezvoushotels.com* ☞ *327 rooms, 6 suites* ⚬ *3 restaurants, cable TV, 2 tennis courts, pool, gym, hot tub, sauna, 4 bars, playground, concierge, free parking* ⊟ *AE, DC, MC, V.*

$$ ⊞ **Rydges Hotel.** Ultramodern furnishings in chrome, glass, and black leather fill the rooms at this 16-story hotel. Rooms above the 12th floor afford commanding views of the river and city. King executive suites have floor-to-ceiling windows and goldfish tanks, and Executive Club floors include security-key access and oversize desks with printer, scanner, and fax capabilities. Complimentary membership passes are provided for a private fitness center nearby. ☒ *Hay and King Sts., Northbridge, 6000* ☎ *1800/ 063283* ⊟ *08/9263–1801* ⊕ *www.rydges.com/perth* ☞ *245 rooms, 6 suites* ⚬ *Restaurant, room service, in-room data ports, cable TV, pool, gym, bar, laundry service, business services, parking (fee)* ⊟ *AE, DC, MC, V.*

★ **$** ⊞ **Duxton Hotel.** Adjacent to the Perth Concert Hall, this elegant hotel is within easy walking distance of the city center. Soothing autumn colors, paintings by local artists, and furniture crafted from Australian timber fill the comfortable rooms, some of which have views of the Swan River. The Brasserie provides casual dining, and breakfasts are substantial. ☒ *1 St. George's Terr., CBD, 6000* ☎ *08/9261–8000 or 1800/681118*

⌂08/9261–8020 ⊕www.duxton.com ⤺291 rooms, 15 suites ⌂Restaurant, room service, pool, gym, hot tub, sauna, steam room, bar, laundry service, business services, free parking ▭ AE, DC, MC, V.

$ ▦ **The Melbourne.** A restored 1890s building listed on the National Heritage Register houses this stylish boutique hotel. The Perth landmark retains all the original design elements of the era, including a grand staircase and elevator. The elegant Louisiana's Restaurant serves excellent Australian cuisine and you can have a drink in the Orleans Bar or the Mississippi Bar, with its atmospheric period photographs of river paddle steamers. ⊠ *Hay and Milligan Sts., CBD, 6000* ☎ *08/9320–3333 or 1800/685671* ⌂ *08/9320–3344* ⊕ *www.melbournehotel.com.au* ⤺ *32 rooms, 3 suites* ⌂ *Restaurant, room service, cable TV, 2 bars, dry cleaning, laundry service, convention center, meeting rooms, free parking* ▭ *AE, DC, MC, V.*

$ ▦ **Sullivan's Hotel.** "The guest reigns supreme" seems to be the rule at this innovative, family-run hotel opposite waterfront parkland. Poolside barbecues, free movies, and drinks served to your room (at bar prices) are all part of the fun. The airport shuttle bus stops at the hotel; there are guest showers for those arriving early or departing late. The spacious open foyer complements the design of the light airy rooms. ⊠ *166 Mounts Bay Rd., CBD, 6000* ☎ *08/9321–8022* ⌂ *08/9481–6762* ⊕ *www.sullivans.com.au* ⤺ *70 rooms* ⌂ *Restaurant, picnic area, pool, bicycles, bar, laundry service, free parking* ▭ *AE, DC, MC, V.*

¢–$ ▦ **Comfort Inn Wentworth Plaza Hotel.** This Federation-era inn is one of
Fodor'sChoice Perth's most centrally located hotels; it's a block away from the Perth
 ★ Railway Station in one direction and a block from the Hay Street Mall in the other. The rooms here (there are also some two-room apartments) have period decor; downstairs, the Garage Bar, Horsefeathers, Bobby Dazzler, and Moon and Sixpence are popular watering holes where you can rub shoulders with locals. ⊠ *300 Murray St., CBD, 6000* ☎ *08/9481–1000 or 1800/355109* ⊕ *www.wentworthplazahotel.com. au* ⤺ *96 rooms* ⌂ *Restaurant, room service, 4 bars, laundry facilities, free parking* ▭ *AE, DC, MC, V.*

¢–$ ▦ **New Esplanade.** This hotel on the Esplanade enjoys the same million-dollar view of the Swan River for which flamboyant mining tycoons have forked over fortunes. And it's just a chopstick's toss from the Grand Palace, one of the more popular Chinese restaurants in town. Shades of green and cream contrast nicely with the teak woodwork in the comfortable, spacious rooms. ⊠ *18 Esplanade, CBD, 6000* ☎*08/9325–2000* ⌂ *08/9221–2190* ⊕*www.newesplanade.com.au* ⤺ *65 rooms* ⌂ *Restaurant, bar, free parking* ▭ *AE, DC, MC, V.*

Nightlife & the Arts

Details on cultural events in Perth are published in the comprehensive Saturday edition of the *West Australian*. A free weekly, *X-Press Magazine,* lists music, concerts, movies, entertainment reviews, and who's playing at pubs, clubs, and hotels. *Scoop* magazine (⊕ www.scoop.com.au), published quarterly, is an excellent guide to the essential Western Australian lifestyle.

The Arts

BOCS Ticketing (☎ 08/9484–1133) is the main booking hotline in Perth for the performing arts.

Local talent dominates the arts scene in Perth, although the acclaimed **Perth International Arts Festival (PIAF)** (✉ University of Western Australia, 3 Crawley Ave., Crawley 6009 ☎ 08/6488–2000 ⊕ www.perthfestival.com.au), held January and February in venues throughout the city, attracts international music, dance, and theater stars. This is Australia's oldest and biggest annual arts festival, and it's been running for more than 50 years. As part of the festival, the PIAF Sunset Cinema Season, adjacent to Winthrop Hall on Mounts Bay Road at the University of Western Australia, screens films outdoors December–March.

BALLET The **West Australian Ballet Company** (✉ 825 Hay St., CBD ☎ 08/9481–0707 ⊕ www.waballet.com.au), one of just three ballet companies in Australia, focuses on classical ballet but also has contemporary ballet and dance in its diverse repertoire. Performances are at His Majesty's Theatre, although you can also see the 17-person troupe at such outdoor venues as the Quarry Amphitheatre (at City Beach) and on country tours.

CONCERTS The **Perth Concert Hall** (✉ 5 St. George's Terr., CBD ☎ 08/9231–9900 ⊕ www.perthconcerthall.com.au), a modern building overlooking the Swan River, stages regular recitals by the excellent West Australian Symphony Orchestra, as well as Australian and international performers. Adding to the appeal of the fine auditorium is the 3,000-pipe organ surrounded by a 160-person choir gallery.

OPERA The **West Australian Opera Company** (✉ 825 Hay St., CBD ☎ 08/9321–5869 ⊕ www.waopera.asn.au) presents three seasons annually—in April, August, and November—at His Majesty's Theatre. The company's repertoire includes classic opera, Gilbert and Sullivan operettas, and occasional musicals.

THEATER The opulent Edwardian **His Majesty's Theatre** (✉ 825 Hay St., CBD ☎ 08/9265–0900 ⊕ www.hismajestystheatre.com.au), opened in 1904, is loved by all who step inside. Home to the West Australian Opera Company and the West Australian Ballet Company, it hosts most theatrical productions in Perth. The **Playhouse Theatre** (✉ 3 Pier St., CBD ☎ 08/9323–3400 ⊕ www.playhousetheatre.com.au) stages local productions. For outdoor performances, the **Quarry Amphitheatre** (✉ Ocean Dr., City Beach ☎ 08/9385–7144) is popular, particularly during the Perth International Arts Festival. The **Regal Theatre** (✉ 474 Hay St., at Rokeby Rd., Subiaco ☎ 08/9484–1133) hosts local performances. The **Burswood Theatre** (✉ Great Eastern Hwy., Burswood ☎ 08/9362–7777 ⊕ www.burswood.com.au) has regular theatrical and musical productions from around Australia.

Nightlife

Most luxury hotels in Perth have upscale nightclubs that appeal to the over-30 crowd. Apart from these, however, nightlife in the city center is virtually nonexistent. Twentysomethings most often head to Northbridge, Subiaco, or Fremantle. Pubs and bars generally close by 11 PM, which is when the crowds start arriving at the nightclubs; these tend to stay open until around 5 AM.

BARS The **Brass Monkey** (✉ 209 William St., Northbridge ☎ 08/9227–9596 🌐 www.brassmonkey.com.au) is in a huge, old, crimson-painted building with potted plants flowing over the antique verandas. A jazz quartet plays on Wednesday nights, with an acoustic group on Thursday. On Saturday nights a DJ keeps the music flowing. There's no cover charge. **Carnegie's** (✉ 356 Murray St., at King St., CBD ☎ 08/9481–3222), a relaxed, upscale café by day, turns into an attractive pub in the afternoon and then a disco late at night. With rock-and-roll decor, a raised dance floor, and DJs playing music from the 1960s to today's Top 40, the bar attracts an older clientele from the business and tourist sectors. On Wednesday night, cocktails are half price until 1 AM. The **Grosvenor Hotel** (✉ 339 Hay St., CBD ☎ 08/9325–3799) has DJs who spin alternative music; it's popular with the younger crowd. **Lava Lounge** (✉ 1 Rokeby Rd., Subiaco ☎ 08/9382–8889) has excellent Mediterranean food and wine, with an alfresco courtyard in summer and a big fireplace for winter. **Queen's Tavern** (✉ 520 Beaufort St., Highgate ☎ 08/9328–7267) has an excellent outdoor beer garden. The upstairs bar has a relaxed lounge vibe, with DJs on Thursday and Sunday. The bar at the **Subiaco Hotel** (✉ 465 Hay St., Subiaco ☎ 08/9381–3069) attracts a lively after-work crowd during the week, with live rock bands on Thursday and Saturday and live jazz on Wednesday.

JAZZ & BLUES On Tuesday nights try the **Charles Hotel** (✉ 509 Charles St., North Perth ☎ 08/9444–1051) for live blues performances. The **Hyde Park Hotel** (✉ 331 Bulwer St., North Perth ☎ 08/9328–6166), a no-nonsense Aussie pub, hosts contemporary jazz Monday night and Dixieland Tuesday night. The **Universal Bar** (✉ 221 William St., Northbridge ☎ 08/9227–6771) has live jazz and blues nightly.

NIGHTCLUBS **Club A** (✉ Esplanade, next to the lookout, Scarborough ☎ 08/9340–5735) is one of the city's top dance spots, attracting 18- to 35-year-olds. The **Hip-e Club** (✉ 663 Newcastle St., Leederville ☎ 08/9227–8899), a Perth legend, capitalizes on its hippy-era image with a neon kaleidoscope, 3-D color explosions, murals, and 1960s paraphernalia decorating the walls. Regular surf parties and backpacker nights take place monthly. **Margeaux's** (✉ Parmelia Hilton Perth, 14 Mill St., CBD ☎ 08/9322–3622) is an upmarket, late-night drinking and dancing venue that's open Wednesday, Friday, and Saturday nights. The **Ruby Room** (✉ Burswood Interconti-nental Resort, Great Eastern Hwy. and Bolton Ave., Burswood ☎ 08/9362–7777) is a glitzy, two-story venue done up with stainless steel and retro fittings. Thursday through Sunday, the four bars, cozy lounge areas, stage, and dance floor with sound-and-light show are packed with merrymakers. **Varga Lounge** (✉ 161 James St., Northbridge ☎ 08/9328–7200) mixes it up New York–style, with DJs who spin techno, rap, and hip-hop.

Sports & the Outdoors

Participant Sports

BICYCLING Perth and Fremantle have an extensive and expanding network of bike paths, which means you can ride along the rivers and coast without having to worry about traffic. Most freeways also have separate parallel cycle paths. Bicycle helmets are compulsory. Details on trails and free brochures are available from the **Western Australia Visitor Centre** (⊠ Forrest Pl. and Wellington St., CBD ☎ 08/9483–1111, 1300/361351, or 61/ 89483–1111 from outside Australia). Maps are also available from **BikeWest** (⊠ 441 Murray St., CBD ☎ 08/9216–8000).

GOLF Perth has numerous public golf courses, all of which rent out clubs. The **Western Australia Golf Association** (☎ 08/9367–2490) can provide details on golf courses in the state.

The 18-hole, par-70 course at **Burswood Park Public Golf Course** (⊠ Great Eastern Hwy. and Bolton Ave., Burswood ☎ 08/9362–7576 ⊕ www.burswoodparkgolfcourse.com) is closest to the city. The finest golfing venue is the **Joondalup Country Club** (⊠ Country Club Blvd. and Spyglass Dr., Connolly ☎ 08/9400–8888 ⊕ www.joondalupresort.com.au), 25 minutes north of Perth, which offers three challenging 9-hole, par-36 courses. The **Vines Resort** (⊠ Verdelho Dr. and Vines Ave., Upper Swan ☎ 08/ 9297–0777 ⊕ www.vines.com.au) is Western Australia's only 36-hole championship course. The layout comprises two 18-hole courses, Lakes and Ellenbrook, which provide plenty of variety for golfers of any ability. The resort is in the Swan Valley, 35 minutes from Perth.

MOTORCYCLING **Deluxe Trike Tours** (☎ 08/9405–4949 ⊕ www.holiday-wa.net/trikehire. htm) runs one- to eight-hour excursions on trikes (three-wheeled motorcycles that seat three people apiece) or aboard the more familiar Harley-Davidson motorcycles.

RUNNING Jogging tracks lead along the Swan River and through King's Park.

SKYDIVING The **Western Australian Skydiving Academy** (⊠ Shop 9–10, 199 William St., Northbridge ☎ 08/9227–6066 ⊕ www.waskydiving.com.au) conducts everything from tandem jumps to accelerated free-fall courses. A tandem jump starts from A$220 for 6,000 feet up to A$380 for the maximum jump—14,000 feet. Tandem jumps don't require training, just 20 minutes of instruction. The accelerated free-fall course, which takes nine hours, costs A$650.

SWIMMING Aside from Perth's glorious beaches, there are three Olympic-size pools at **Challenge Stadium** (⊠ Stephenson Ave., Mt. Claremont ☎ 08/ 9441–8222). Admission costs A$4.40, and the pools are open weekdays 5:30 AM–9:30 PM, Saturday 5:30 AM–6 PM, and Sunday 8–6.

TENNIS **Tennis West** (☎ 08/9361–1112 ⊕ www.tenniswest.com.au) provides details on tennis courts in the metropolitan area.

WATER SPORTS Parasailing is available from the Narrows Bridge on the South Perth shore every weekend from November to May, weather and winds permitting. It's A$75 for a single for 15 minutes and A$120 tandem. Contact **South**

Perth Parasailing (✉ Narrows Bridge, South Perth ☎ 08/9447–7450). If you want to enjoy the Swan River at a leisurely pace, hire a catamaran or a sailboard from **Funcats Surfcat Hire** (✉ Coode St. Jetty, South Perth ☎ 0408/926003). It costs A$27 per hour; reservations are essential on weekends.

Spectator Sports

CRICKET   The national summer game is played professionally at the **Western Australia Cricket Association** (WACA; ☎ 08/9265–7222 ⊕ www.waca.com.au) grounds in Nelson Crescent, East Perth. The **WACA Museum** (☎ 08/9265–7318), at the same address, has a display of cricketing and sporting memorabilia from the 1800s to the present. Tours of the grounds and museum take place every Tuesday and Thursday at 10 AM and 1 PM. Admission is A$10.

FOOTBALL   The Australian Football League (AFL) plays weekends March through September at Subiaco Oval and at the Western Australia Cricket Association (WACA) grounds. The local league plays every Saturday. For details contact the **West Australian Football Commission** (☎ 08/9381–5599 ⊕ www.wafl.com.au).

SURFING   Western Australians take to the surf from a young age—and with world-famous surfing beaches right on the city's doorstep, it's no wonder. The most popular year-round beaches for body and board surfing are Scarborough and Trigg; at Scarborough the WA Masters Series takes place each year, usually in August. The World Masters Surf Circuit championships in November take place at Surfers Point, 8 km (5 mi) from Margaret River.

Shopping

Shopping in Perth, with its pedestrian-friendly central business district, vehicle-free malls, and many covered arcades, is a delight. Hay Street Mall and Murray Street Mall are the main city shopping areas, linked by numerous arcades with small shops. In the suburbs, top retail strips include Napoleon Street in Cottesloe (for clothing and cooking items), Hampden Road in Nedlands (for crafts), and Beaufort Street in Mount Lawley (for antiques).

Malls & Arcades

Forrest Place, flanked by the post office and the Forrest Chase Shopping Plaza, is the largest mall area in the city. **David Jones** (☎ 08/9210–4000) department store opens onto the Murray Street pedestrian mall. **Myer** (✉ Murray St. Mall and Forrest Pl. ☎ 08/9221–3444) is a popular department store that carries goods and sundries. The **Hay Street Mall,** running parallel to Murray Street and linked by numerous arcades, is another extensive shopping area. Make sure you wander through the arcades that connect Hay and Murray streets, such as **Carillion Arcade,** which have many more shops.

Australiana

Australian souvenirs and knickknacks are on sale at small shops throughout the city and suburbs. **Looking East** (✉ Unit 3, 160 Hampden Rd.,

Nedlands ☎ 08/9389–5569) sells contemporary, minimalist Aussie clothing, furnishings, and pottery. **Purely Australian Clothing Company** (✉ 731 Hay St., CBD ☎ 08/9321–4697 ✉ 38 London Ct., CBD ☎ 08/9325–4328 ⊕ www.purelyaustralian.com) carries the most comprehensive selection of Oz-abilia in Perth, with stores in London Court and Hay Street Mall. **R. M. Williams** (✉ Carillon Arcade, Hay St. Mall, CBD ☎ 08/9321–7786 ⊕ www.rmwilliams.com.au) sells everything for the Australian bushman, including moleskin pants, hand-tooled leather boots, and Akubra hats.

Crafts

Craftwest (✉ King St. Arts Centre, 357 365 Murray St., CBD ☎ 08/9226–2799) carries a large selection of Western Australian crafts and giftware, including some Aboriginal art, jewelry, cards, and accessories. You can find authentic Aboriginal artifacts at **Creative Native** (✉ 32 King St., CBD ☎ 08/9322–3398 ⊕ www.creativenative.com.au); the Dreamtime Gallery, upstairs, is one of Australia's finest. Each piece of original artwork comes with a certificate of authenticity. A former car dealer's workshop has been transformed into the Outback at **Indigenart** (✉ 115 Hay St., Subiaco ☎ 08/9388–2899 ⊕ www.indigenart.com.au), an art gallery–cum–Aboriginal culture center where you can view works and talk with the Aboriginal creators. **Maalia Mia** (✉ 8991 W. Swan Rd., Henley Brook ☎ 08/9296–0704 ⊕ www.maalimia.com.au), an Aboriginal-owned and -operated cultural center, art gallery, and gift shop, sells art and artifacts purchased only from Aboriginal artists. Boomerangs, didgeridoos, and clapping sticks are made on-site.

Gems

Opals from South Australia's Coober Pedy are available at **Costello's** (✉ 5–6 London Ct., CBD ☎ 08/9325–8588 ⊕ www.costellos.com.au). **Linneys** (✉ 37 Rokeby Rd., Subiaco ☎ 08/9382–4077 ⊕ www.linneys.com.au), whose designers and craftspeople have won national awards, carries an excellent selection of Broome pearls, Argyle diamonds, and Kalgoorlie gold, and will set the gems and pearls in the design of your choice. **Rosendorf's** (✉ 673 Hay St. Mall, CBD ☎ 08/9321–4015), regarded as Perth's premier diamond jeweler, specializes in white and colored diamonds. They also have outlets in Karrinyup and Graden City shopping centers in the suburbs.

Perth A to Z

AIR TRAVEL

Perth International Airport has two separate terminals. The domestic terminal is about 11 km (7 mi) from Perth, and the international terminal is about 16 km (10 mi) from the city. International airlines serving Perth International Airport include: Air New Zealand, Qantas, Singapore Airlines, Cathay Pacific, Emirates, and South African Airlines. Qantas and Virgin Blue connect Perth to other Australian capital cities. Qantas Airlink and Skywest connect Perth with other towns in the state.

Taxis are available at the airport 24 hours a day. Trips to the city cost about A$30 and take around a half hour. Shuttle buses run between terminals (A$9), as well as to hotels in Perth and Fremantle. Transperth bus services are cheaper, but may not drop you off near your hotel.

⚡ Airlines Air New Zealand ☎ 13-2476 ⊕ www.airnz.com.au. **Cathay Pacific** ☎ 13-1747 ⊕ www.cathaypacific.com/au. **Emirates** ☎ 1300/303777 ⊕ www.emirates. com.au. **Qantas/Qantaslink** ☎ 13-1313 ⊕ www.qantas.com.au. **Singapore Airlines** ☎ 13-1011 ⊕ www.singaporeair.com.au. **Skywest** ☎ 13-1300 ⊕ www.skywest.com.au. **South African Airways** ☎ 08/9216-2200. **Virgin Blue** ☎ 13-6789 ⊕ www.virginblue. com.au.

⚡ Airport & Shuttles Airport City Shuttles ☎ 08/9277-7958 operates frequent coach services from both terminals to Perth city hotels, as well as between the airport terminals. The cost between terminals is A$9 unless prepaid with your air ticket.

BIKE TRAVEL

Perth's climate and its network of excellent trails make cycling a safe and enjoyable way to discover the city. But beware: summer temperatures can exceed 40°C (100°F) in the shade. A bicycle helmet is required by law, and carrying water is prudent. About Bike Hire, which rents bikes for A$27 a day or A$60 a week, is open Monday through Saturday 10–6 and Sunday 9–6. Free brochures detailing trails, including stops at historical spots, are available from the Western Australia Visitor Centre.

⚡ About Bike Hire ⊠ Behind Causeway Car Park, Riverside Dr. ☎ 08/9221-2665 ⊕ www. aboutbikehire.com.au.

BOAT & FERRY TRAVEL

Transperth ferries make daily runs from 6:50 AM to 7:15 PM between Barrack Street Jetty in Perth to Mends Street, across the Swan River in South Perth. Reduced service runs on weekends and holidays.

⚡ Transperth ☎ 08/9428-1900 or 13-6213 ⊕ www.transperth.wa.gov.au.

BUS TRAVEL

Greyhound Australia buses are routed through the Public Transport Authority terminal in East Perth. It's 60 hours to Darwin, 36 hours to Adelaide, 48 hours to Melbourne, and 60 hours to Sydney. TransWA has interstate train and bus services.

⚡ Greyhound Australia ☎ 13-1499 ⊕ www.greyhound.com.au. **Public Transport Authority** ⊠ W. Parade, East Perth ☎ 13-6213 ⊕ www.pta.wa.gov.au. **TransWA** ⊠ E. Perth Terminal, W. Parade, East Perth ☎ 08/9326-2600.

BUS TRAVEL
WITHIN PERTH
The Perth central business district and suburban areas are well connected by the Transperth line. The main terminals are at Perth Central Bus Station on Mounts Bay Road and at Wellington Street Bus Station.

Transperth tickets are valid for two hours and can be used on Transperth trains and ferries. Buses run daily 6 AM–11:30 PM, with reduced service on weekends and holidays. Rides within the city center are free. CAT (Central Area Transit) buses circle the city center, running approximately every 10 minutes weekdays 7–6 and Saturday 9–5. Routes and timetables are available from Transperth.

⚡ Transperth ☎ 13-6213 ⊕ www.transperth.wa.gov.au.

CAR RENTAL

All major car-rental companies have branches at the international and domestic airport terminals. A good budget alternative is Network Car Rentals, which can arrange airport pickup and drop-off.

☎ **Avis** ☎ 08/9325-7677 or 13-6333 ⊕ www.avis.com.au. **Budget Rent A Car** ☎ 1300/ 362848 ⊕ www.budgetwa.com.au. **Hertz** ☎ 1800/550067 ⊕ www.hertz.com.au. **Network Car Rentals** ☎ 1800/736825 ⊕ www.1800rentals.com.au.

CAR TRAVEL

The Eyre Highway crosses the continent from Port Augusta in South Australia to Western Australia's transportation gateway, Norseman. From there, take the Coolgardie–Esperance Highway north to Coolgardie, and the Great Eastern Highway on to Perth. Driving to Perth—2,580 km (1,600 mi) and 30 hours from Adelaide, and 4,032 km (2,500 mi) and 56 hours from Sydney—is an arduous journey, which should be undertaken only with a car (and mental faculties) in top condition. Spare tires and drinking water are essential. Service stations and motels are spaced at regular intervals along the route.

Driving in Perth is relatively easy; just remember to stay on the left-hand side of the road. Peak traffic hours are 7:30–9 AM heading into Perth and 4:30–6 PM heading away from the city center. Country roads are generally well maintained and have little traffic. There are no freeways and few two-lane highways outside the Perth metropolitan area. "Self-Drive Tours within WA," a free 72-page booklet that suggests itineraries around Perth, Fremantle, and the state, is available from the Western Australia Visitor Centre and major car-rental companies.

EMERGENCIES

In an emergency, dial **000** to reach an ambulance, the police, or the fire department.

Perth Dental Emergencies recommends private practitioners for emergency service. Royal Perth Hospital has a 24-hour emergency room.

☎ **Perth Dental Emergencies** ✉ 425 Wellington St., upper walkway level, Forrest Chase opposite Perth Railway Station, CBD ☎ 08/9221-4749. **Police** ☎ 08/9222-1111. **Royal Perth Hospital** ✉ Victoria Sq., East Perth ☎ 08/9224-2244.

MAIL, THE INTERNET & SHIPPING

There are many places where you can access the Internet in Perth. Coin-operated terminals can be found both around the city and at the airport. In Perth and Northbridge these are often found along Williams and Wellington streets. Most Internet cafés charge in blocks of 5–20 minutes; you'll pay A$5–A$10 for an hour's connection. Prices do vary, though, so you may want to shop around. The main post office, on Forrest Place, is open weekdays 9–5:30, Saturday 9–noon, and Sunday noon–4. Fedex and DHL can provide overnight mail services.

All major hotels provide fax, photocopy, and computer services for guests, although there may be a fee. Serviced Office Specialists has round-the-clock services, including data entry, word processing, e-mailing, and faxing.

DHL ☎ 13-1406. **Fedex** ☎ 13-2610. **Main Post Office** ☎ 08/9237-5000. **Serviced Office Specialists** ✉ Level 21, 197 St. George's Terr., CBD ☎ 08/9214-3838 ⊕ www.servicedoffices.com.au.

MONEY MATTERS

Banks with dependable check-cashing and money-changing services include ANZ, Westpac, Commonwealth, and National Australia Bank. ATMs—which accept Cirrus, Plus, Visa, and MasterCard—are ubiquitous and nearly always reliable.

ANZ ☎ 13-1314 ⊕ www.anz.com. **Commonwealth** ☎ 13-2221 ⊕ www.commbank.com.au. **National Australia Bank** ☎ 13-2265 ⊕ www.national.com.au. **Westpac** ☎ 13-1862 ⊕ www.westpac.com.au.

TAXIS

Cab fare between 6 AM and 6 PM weekdays is an initial A$3 plus A$1.50 every 1 km (½ mi). From 6 PM to 6 AM and on weekends the rate rises to A$4.50 plus A$1.50 per 1 km (½ mi).

Black & White ☎ 13-1008. **Swan Taxis** ☎ 13-1330.

TOURS

Australian Pacific Touring, Australian Pinnacle Tours, and Feature Tours conduct day tours of Perth and its major attractions. You can also take a day tour of outer sights like Nambung National Park and the Pinnacles, Wave Rock near Hyden, and the Treetop Walk near Walpole.

Boat Torque runs excursions to Rottnest Island three times daily from Perth and five times daily from Fremantle; they also have wine cruises, and whale-watching trips between September and late November. For a trip upriver to the famous Swan River wineries, the ferry *Mystique,* another craft in the fleet of Boat Torque, makes daily trips from Barrack Street Jetty, serving wine coming and going and lunch at one of the wineries.

Captain Cook Cruises has trips on the Swan River, traveling from Perth to the Indian Ocean at Fremantle. Cruises cost A$17–A$125 and may include meals and wine. Oceanic Cruises runs several boat cruises, including tours of the Swan River with stops at wineries. Golden Sun Cruises also has tours upriver to the vineyards, as well as trips to Fremantle.

West Coast Rail and Coach uses trains and buses in conjunction with local operators to provide tours to such popular destinations as Margaret River, Bunbury, Busselton, Esperance, Walpole, Kalbarri, Albany, and Kalgoorlie.

Springtime in Western Australia (Sept.–November) is synonymous with wildflowers, as 8,000 species blanket an area that stretches 645 km (400 mi) north and 403 km (250 mi) south of Perth. Tours of these areas, by companies such as Feature Tours, are popular, and early reservations are essential.

Orientation & Wildflower Tours **Australian Pacific Touring** ☎ 1300/655965 ⊕ www.aptouring.com.au. **Australian Pinnacle Tours** ☎ 08/9471-5555 ⊕ www.pinnacletours.com.au. **Feature Tours** ☎ 08/9475-2900.

⬛ Boat Tours Boat Torque ✉ Barrack St. Ferry Terminal, CBD ☎ 08/9430-5844 ⊕ www.boattorque.com.au. **Captain Cook Cruises** ✉ Pier 3, Barrack Sq. Jetty, CBD ☎ 08/9325-3341 ⊕ www.captaincookcruises.com.au. **Golden Sun Cruises** ✉ Pier 5, Barrack Sq. Jetty, CBD ☎ 08/9325-9916 ⊕ www.goldensuncruises.com.au. **Oceanic Cruises** ✉ Pier 2A, Barrack Sq. Jetty, CBD ☎ 08/9325-1911 ⊕ www.oceaniccruises.com.au. **⬛ Bus Tour West Coast Rail and Coach** ☎ 08/9221-9522.

TRAINS

Crossing the Nullarbor Plain from the eastern states is one of the great rail journeys of the world. The *Indian Pacific* makes three-day runs from Sydney on Monday and Thursday and two-day runs from Adelaide on Tuesday and Friday.

TransWA trains cover routes in Western Australia, including the *Prospector* to Kalgoorlie, the *Australind* to Bunbury, and the *Avonlink* to Northam. Transperth trains provide a quick, easy way to get around the city. The east–west line runs to Midland and Fremantle, while the north line runs to Joondalup, and the southeast line runs to Armadale. Perth to Fremantle takes about 30 minutes. Tickets must be purchased at vending machines before boarding.

⬛ Transperth ✉ E. Perth terminal, W. Parade, East Perth ☎ 13-6213 ⊕ www.transperth. wa.gov.au. **TransWA** ✉ E. Perth Terminal, W. Parade, East Perth ☎ 08/9326-2600 ⊕ www. transwa.wa.gov.au.

VISITOR INFORMATION

⬛ City of Perth Information Kiosk ✉ Murray St. Mall and Forrest Pl., CBD. **Western Australia Visitor Centre** ✉ Forrest Pl. and Wellington St., CBD, 6000 ☎ 08/9483-1111, 1300/361351, or 61/89483-1111 from outside Australia ⊕ www.westernaustralia.com.

FREMANTLE & ROTTNEST ISLAND

The second-largest city on the west coast, Fremantle is also the jewel in Western Australia's crown. The major state port since Europeans first settled here in the early 1800s, the town basks in its maritime heritage. This is a city where locals know each other, and everyone smiles and says "hello" as they pass in the street. It's also a good jumping-off point for a day trip to Rottnest Island, where lovely beaches, rocky coves, and unique wallaby-like inhabitants called quokkas are among the charms.

Fremantle

About 19 km (12 mi) southwest of Perth.

Modern Fremantle is a far cry from the barren, sandy plain that greeted the first wave of English settlers back in 1829, at the newly constituted Swan River Colony. Most were city dwellers, and after five months at sea in sailing ships, they landed on salt-marsh flats that sorely tested their fortitude. Living in tents, with packing cases for chairs, they found no edible crops, and the nearest fresh water was a distant 51 km (32 mi)— and a tortuous trip up the salty waters of the Swan. As a result they soon moved the settlement upriver to the vicinity of present-day Perth.

Fremantle remained the location of the seaport, however, and it is to this day Western Australia's premier port. Local architects have brought about a stunning transformation of the town without defacing the colonial streetscape or its fine limestone buildings. In the leafy suburbs nearly every other house is a restored 19th-century gem.

Like all great port cities, Freo (as the locals call it) is cosmopolitan, with mariners from all parts of the world strolling the streets—including 20,000 U.S. Navy personnel on rest and recreation throughout the year. There are plenty of interesting (and sometimes eccentric) residents, who find the mood of Freo much more interesting than the coastal suburbs north and south of the city.

An ideal place to start a leisurely stroll around town is South Terrace, known as the Fremantle cappuccino strip. Soak up the ambience as you wander alongside locals through sidewalk cafés or browse in bookstores, art galleries, and souvenir shops. No matter how aimlessly you meander, you'll invariably end up where you began.

Between Phillimore Street and Marine Terrace in the West End is a collection of some of the best-preserved heritage buildings in the state. The Fremantle Railway Station on Elder Place is a good place to start a walk.

Outside the port gates on the western end of town is **Arthur's Head,** a limestone cliff with cottages built to house employees of the Customs Department. Nearby **J-Shed** contains the workshop of perhaps the nation's foremost exponent of public art, the sculptor Greg James. His extraordinarily lifelike figures grace a number of Perth and metropolitan sites, including King's Square.

Seagulls squawk overhead, boat horns blare in the distance, and the tangy scent of the sea permeates the air along **Marine Terrace,** which skirts the water's edge. You can visit the **Kidogo Arthouse,** a gallery and arts center, or linger over fresh fish-and-chips as you watch the tide roll in from the old seawall. Or you can just dangle your feet from the wooden jetty that was rebuilt on the spot where it stood in the days of tall ships.

Like most of Fremantle, the fine, Gothic Revival **Fremantle Museum and Arts Centre** was built by convicts in the 19th century. First used as a lunatic asylum, by 1900 it was overcrowded and nearly shut down. It became a home for elderly women until 1942, when the U.S. Navy made it into its local headquarters. Artifacts trace the early days of Fremantle's settlement in one wing, while another wing houses the **Arts Centre.** The complex contains a restaurant and gift shop, and Sunday-afternoon courtyard concerts are a regular feature. ✉ *Ord and Finnerty Sts.* ☎ *08/9430–7966* 💻 *Donation suggested* ⊘ *Sun.–Fri. 10:30–4:30, Sat. 1–5.*

The former **Fremantle Prison,** built in 1855, is where 44 inmates met their fate on the prison gallows between 1888 and 1964. Tours include the classic-art cell, where a superb collection of drawings by convict James Walsh decorates his quarters. Reservations are essential for the Torchlight Tours (evening tours by flashlight). ✉ *1 The Terr.* ☎ *08/9336–9200* ⊕ *www. fremantleprison.com.au* 💻 *A$14.90, including tour every 30 mins. Torch-*

light Tour A$18.90 ⊙ *Daily 10–6; last tour at 5. Torchlight Tours Wed. and Fri., every 20 mins from 7 PM on demand; last tour usually 9 PM.*

The **Fremantle Market,** housed in a classic Victorian building, sells everything from potatoes to paintings, incense to antiques, and sausages to Chinese takeout from around 150 stalls. On weekends and public holidays the market can get crowded, but a small café and bar make it a wonderful place to refresh yourself while buskers and street musicians entertain. ⊠ *South Terr. and Henderson St.* ☎ *08/9335–2515* ⊕ *www.fremantlemarkets.com.au* ⊙ *Fri. 9–9, Sat. 9–5, Sun. and public holidays 10–5.*

For a glimpse of local color, wander through **High Street Mall**, in the center of the business district. This pedestrian mall is the haunt of people from all walks of Fremantle life, including retired Italian fishermen who now while away their days in conversation. ⊠ *High, Market, William, and Adelaide Sts.*

One of the oldest commercial heritage–listed structures in Western Australia is **Moores' Building,** an exhibition and performance space run by the Artists' Performance Centre. ⊠ *46 Henry St.* ☎ *08/9335–8366* ▨ *Donation suggested* ⊙ *Exhibitions daily 10–5.*

A landmark of early Fremantle atop the limestone cliff known as Arthur's Head, the **Round House** was built in 1831 by convicts to house other convicts. This curious, 12-sided building is the state's oldest surviving structure. From its ramparts there are great vistas of High Street out to the Indian Ocean. Underneath, a tunnel was carved through the cliffs in the mid-1800s to give ships lying at anchor offshore easy access from town. Volunteer guides are on duty during opening hours. ⊠ *West end of High St.* ☎ *08/9336–6897* ▨ *Donation suggested* ⊙ *Daily 10:30–3:30.*

Bounded by High, Queen, and William streets, **King's Square** is at the heart of the central business district. Shaded by 100-year-old Moreton Bay fig trees, it makes a perfect place for a rest. Medieval-style benches complete the picture of European elegance. Bordering the square are **St. John's Anglican Church** and the **town hall.**

Ⓒ The **Spare Parts Puppet Theatre,** which stages imaginative productions for children several times a year, has an international reputation and regularly tours abroad. The foyer is a showplace for its puppetry. ⊠ *1 Short St., opposite railway station* ☎ *08/9335–5044* ⊕ *www.sppt.asn.au* ▨ *Free* ⊙ *Daily 9–5.*

Ⓒ The **Western Australian Maritime Museum,** which resembles an upside-down **Fodor'sChoice** boat, sits at the edge of Fremantle Harbour. It houses *Australia 11,* win- ★ ner of the 1983 America's Cup, and the hands-on exhibits are great fun for children. You can also take one-hour guided tours of the adjacent submarine *Ovens,* a former Royal Australian Navy World War II submarine. The Shipwreck Gallery houses the recovered remains of the Dutch East Indiaman *Batavia* (wrecked offshore in 1629), and the 1872 SS *Xantho* steamer. ⊠ *Maritime Museum: west end of Victoria Quay; Shipwreck Gallery: Cliff St.* ☎ *08/9335–8921 museum, 08/9431–8444 gallery* ⊕ *www.mm.wa.gov.au* ▨ *Museum A$10 day pass, museum and*

Ovens A$15, gallery free ☉ *Museum and gallery daily 9:30–5, Ovens Fri.–Sun. and school holidays 10–4:30.*

off the beaten path

MANDURAH – Just 94 km (59 mi) south of Fremantle is this charming city set along the horseshoe-shape Peel Inlet. Strolling along the scenic boardwalk, dining at stylish restaurants, and cruising the more than 150 square km (60 square mi) of inland waterways are among the attractions here. See **www.peeltour.net.au** for information about Mandurah and the surrounding area.

Where to Eat

★ **$-$$$** ✕ **The Essex.** This 1886 cottage is one of the top places for upscale dining in Western Australia. Its elegant dining room has flickering candlelight, plush carpets, and antiques, and the fresh local seafood is top-notch. Head chef Mark Spencer offers an extensive menu, including grilled fillet of beef with local scallops, topped with garlic cream sauce; and panfried chicken breast stuffed with macadamia nuts and finished with lemon-myrtle beurre blanc. The extensive wine list includes some of Australia's best vintages. ⊠ *20 Essex St.* ☎ *08/9335–5725* ⊟ *AE, DC, MC, V.*

$$ ✕ **Gino's Café.** There are 21 different ways to take your coffee at this hot, cappuccino-strip property with its alfresco terrace. Among the most popular drinks are the house coffee (Gino's Blend), and the Baby Chino—a froth of milk dusted with chocolate powder that young children love. Gino's opens at 6 AM to serve coffee, then cooked breakfasts from 7. Later in the day more than two dozen different pasta dishes are also available, including a superb Penne alla Vodka with chicken. ⊠ *South Terr. and Collie St.* ☎ *08/9336–1464* ⊟ *MC, V.*

$-$$ ✕ **Capri Restaurant.** You may need to wait for a table, but the complimentary minestrone and crusty bread will tide you over at this Fremantle institution. You'll likely get a warm welcome from the Pizzale family, who have owned and run the restaurant for more than 50 years, before you sit down to fried calamari, panfried scaloppine in white wine, rich spaghetti Bolognese, and fresh salads. Simple white-linen tablecloths, carafes of chilled water, and the sounds of laughter and clinking glasses round out the experience. This is old-style Fremantle at its best. ⊠ *21 South Terr.* ☎ *08/9335–1399* ⊟ *MC, V.*

$-$$ ✕ **Cicerello's.** No visit to Fremantle is complete without a stop at this locally famous and widely beloved fish-and-chip shop. Housed in a boathouse-style building fronting the famous Fishing Boat Harbour, this place serves the real thing: freshly caught oysters, mussels, crabs, fish, lobsters, and chips, all wrapped up in butcher paper (no cardboard boxes or plastic plates here). While you eat, you can check out the huge aquarium, where more than 50 species of Fremantle marine life are on display. ⊠ *Fisherman's Wharf, 44 Mews Rd.* ☎ *08/9335–1911* ⊟ *No credit cards.*

$-$$ ✕ **Joe's Fish Shack.** Fremantle's quirkiest restaurant looks like everyone's vision of a run-down, weather-beaten Maine diner. With uninterrupted harbor views, authentic nautical bric-a-brac, and great food, you can't go wrong. Recommendations include the salt-and-pepper squid, stuffed tiger prawns, and chili mussels. An outdoor dining area provides restaurant food at take-away prices. ⊠ *42 Mews Rd.* ☎ *08/9336–7161* ☰ *AE, DC, MC, V.*

$ ✕ **Istanbul Cuisine.** This bright, breezy street-front venue serves specialties from the Turkish cities of Samsun, Adana, and Iskendar. A secret of this restaurant's success is the fresh-baked Turkish flat bread that accompanies every meal. Start with one of the traditional dips—hummus, eggplant, or potato—then move on to delicacies like grilled lamb and *burek* (meat- or vegetable-stuffed pastries). Kavuma chicken, a house specialty, is grilled with peppers and served with tabbouleh and steamed rice. Save room for sweet, sticky baklava. Traditional music and belly dancing are performed Friday and Saturday nights. ⊠ *19B Essex St.* ☎ *08/9335–6068* ☰ *MC, V* ⌂ *BYOB* ☉ *Closed Mon.*

Where to Stay

¢–$ ✕ **Rosie O'Grady's Fremantle.** The restored heritage rooms of this Irish-theme, landmark Australian pub offer comfy lodging right in the middle of town. The deluxe rooms are spacious, and furnished with heavy pine furniture and floral print upholstery and bedspreads. Bars and a restaurant are right downstairs. ⊠ *23 William St., 6160* ☎ *08/9335–1645* ⊕ *www.roseiogradys.com.au* ➫ *17 rooms* ⌂ *Restaurant, 2 bars, meeting rooms* ☰ *AE, DC, MC, V.*

$$$–$$$$ ▦ **Esplanade Hotel.** Part of a colonial-era hotel, this establishment has provided seafront accommodation and waterfront views for more than a century. The property is geared toward business travelers, and the stylish, bright pastel rooms have desks and in-room data ports. Studio rooms and complimentary valet parking are available. Café Panache, right on the Esplanade, draws crowds all day. ⊠ *Marine Terr. and Essex St., 6160* ☎ *08/9432–4000 or 1800/998201* 🖷 *08/9430–4539* ⊕ *www.esplanadehotelfremantle.com.au* ➫ *259 rooms, 7 suites* ⌂ *2 restaurants, café, in-room data ports, 2 pools, dry cleaning, laundry service, business services, meeting rooms, free parking* ☰ *AE, DC, MC, V.*

¢–$$ ▦ **Fothergills of Fremantle.** Antiques and Italian pottery furnish this two-story, 1892 limestone terrace house opposite the old Fremantle prison. Food and service are excellent here, and although the house is some distance from the waterfront, the balconies afford harbor and sunset views. Breakfast in the elegant Provençal-style dining room is included. ⊠ *20–22 Ord St., 6160* ☎ *08/9335–6784* 🖷 *08/9430–7789* ⊕ *www.babs.com.au/fothergills* ➫ *4 rooms* ⌂ *Dining room, refrigerators, laundry service* ☰ *AE, DC, MC, V* ⦿ *BP.*

¢–$ ▦ **Fremantle Prison Cottages.** These restored colonial-style cottages are conveniently next to the old Fremantle prison, just a few minutes' walk from town. Rooms here are cozy, furnished in colonial style with lace curtains at the windows, eiderdown quilts on the antique wrought-iron beds, and Victorian-era lamp shades. Each has a kitchen and laundry facilities, with modern touches including TVs and microwave ovens. ⊠ *215 High St., 6160* ☎ *08/9430–6568* 🖷 *08/9430–6405* ⊕ *www.fremantlecolonialaccommodation.com.au* ➫ *4 cottages* ⌂ *Kitchens, laundry facilities, laundry service, free parking* ☰ *AE, DC, MC, V.*

Nightlife

There's nothing more pleasant than relaxing in the evening at one of the sidewalk tables on the cappuccino strip. This area, along South Terrace, opens at 6 AM and closes around 3 AM.

The Dome (⊠ 13 South Terr. ☎ 08/9336–3040) is a big, airy space that gets a little frantic at busy periods. **Little Creatures** (⊠ 40 Mews Rd. ☎ 08/9430–5555) is a funky bar and restaurant surrounded by a gleaming state-of-the-art microbrewery. The industrial-style warehouse building, which overlooks Fremantle's busy harbor, spills into a courtyard. The Pale Ale was voted as Australia's best craft beer (microbrewery beer) in 2003 by members of Australia's liquor industry. It's open Monday–Saturday 10 AM–midnight and Sunday 10–10.

Many great pubs and nightlife venues have sprung up along the boardwalk of Fremantle's Fishing Boat Harbour. Describing itself as "Friends of the Guinness," **National Hotel** (⊠ 98 High St. ☎ 08/9335–1786) hosts live Irish music Friday and Sunday. Away from the waterfront, **Rosie O'-Grady's** (⊠ 23 William St. ☎ 08/9335–1645 ⊕ www.rosieogradys.com.au) is as Irish as it gets in the heart of Fremantle. Locals come for the numerous draft beers and filling food, as well as nightly live music. Thanks to its selection of home-brewed beers, the **Sail and Anchor Pub–Brewery** (⊠ 64 South Terr. ☎ 08/9335–8433) is a popular watering hole. A shady courtyard beer garden makes a fair-weather gathering place.

Fremantle's classiest nightclub, the **Clink** (⊠ 14–16 South Terr. ☎ 08/9336–1919), caters to a well-dressed, sophisticated clientele Thursday–Sunday. The industrial-style decor reflects the building's heritage—it used to be the police station with prison cells. Many local bands and soloists owe their big breaks to **Fly By Night Musicians Club** (⊠ 1 Holdsworth St. ☎ 08/9430–5976), a smoke-free venue.

In the heart of Fremantle's cappuccino strip, **Metropolis Concert Club Fremantle** (⊠ 58 South Terr. ☎ 08/9336–1880), a nonstop techno and funk dance venue, is a great place to go on Saturday night. **Zanzibar** (⊠ 42 Mews Rd. ☎ 08/9433–3999) is an ultracool multilevel bar and club on Fishermen's Wharf, with resident DJs playing the latest hits and classics from the 1980s and '90s.

Shopping

At **Bannister Street Craftworks** (⊠ 8–12 Bannister St. ☎ 08/9336–2035), a restored 19th-century warehouse, craftspeople have gathered in their own workshops to turn out everything from screen printing to woodwork, handblown glass, leather goods, and souvenirs. The artists, working as a cooperative, invite you to come in and watch as they demonstrate their skills, or just to browse among the exhibits. All of the crafts on display are for sale.

Into Camelot (⊠ Shop 9, South Terr. Piazza ☎ 08/9335–4698), a medieval-style dress shop, sells romantic wedding gowns and cloaks, street and evening wear, and peasant smocks for all occasions. Period boots, classic Saxon and Celtic jewelry, and masks (feathered and plain) are all available at affordable prices.

Kakulas Sisters (✉ 29–31 Market St. ☎ 08/9430–4445), a unique produce shop, overflows with fragrances and sacks of goodies from across the globe, including Costa Rican coffee beans, Colorado black-eyed beans, Brazilian quince and guava pastries, and Japanese teas.

A fairy theme pervades the **Pickled Fairy & Other Myths** (✉ Shop 7B, South Terr. Piazza ☎ 08/9430–5827), making it a delight for children (and children at heart). Celtic jewelry is sold here, along with books on magic and mythology.

Rottnest Island

19 km (12 mi) west of Fremantle.

An easy cruise from Fremantle, or down the Swan River from Perth, sunny, quirky Rottnest Island makes an ideal day trip. The island has an interesting past. Though records of human occupation date back 6,500 years, when Aboriginal people inhabited the area, European settlement only dates back to 1829. Since then the island has been used for a variety of purposes, including attempts at agriculture, as a location to reform young boys who were in conflict with the law, and for military purposes in both the Great War and the Second World War. The Rottnest Museum is a great place to get the history of the place, and you can take a train trip and tour to the Oliver Hill fort to see gun emplacements from the Second World War.

Of course, most West Australians go to the island for the beaches, the swimming, and the laid-back atmosphere on Perth's doorstep.

The most convenient way to get around Rottnest is by bicycle, as cars are not allowed on the island and bus service is infrequent. A bicycle tour of the island covers 26 km (16 mi) and can take as little as three hours, although you really need an entire day to enjoy the beautiful surroundings. It's impossible to get lost, since the one main road circles the island and will always bring you back to your starting point.

Heading south from Thomson Bay, between Government House and Herschell lakes, is a quokka colony. Quokkas are marsupials, small wallabies that were mistaken for rats by the first discoverers. In fact, the island's name means "rats' nest" in Dutch. Another colony lies down the road to the east, near the amphitheater at the civic center in sparkling Geordie Bay. Here tame quokkas eat right out of your hand.

Past the quokka colony are gun emplacements from World War II. As you continue south to Bickley Bay, you can spot the wreckage of ships—the oldest dates from 1842—that came to rest on Rottnest's rocky coastline.

Follow the main road past Porpoise, Salmon, Strickland, and Wilson bays to West End, the westernmost point on the island and another graveyard for unfortunate vessels. Heading back to Thomson Bay, the road passes a dozen rocky inlets and bays. Parakeet Bay, the prettiest, is at the northernmost tip of the island.

At the Thomson Bay settlement, visit the **Rottnest Museum** (✉ Digby Ave., Thomson Bay ☎ 08/9372–9752 ⌨ Donation suggested), which includes memorabilia recalling the island's long and turbulent past. Displays show local geology, natural history, and maritime lore; there's also a convict building and an Aboriginal prison. It's open daily 11–4.

The **Rottnest Island Railway Train** (✉ Thomson Bay ☎ 08/9372–9752), known as the Captain Hussey, is an ideal way to see the island. The route from the Main Settlement to Oliver Hill is run daily at 10:30, 11:30, 12:30, and 1:30 and connects with a guided tour of the historic Oliver Hill gun battery. The fare is A$15.40 and includes the guided tour. The train also runs at 2:30 without the guided tours for A$11. Tickets are available at the visitor information center.

The **Bayseeker Bus** (✉ Thomson Bay ☎ 08/9372–9752), which runs a continuous "hop-on, hop-off" island circuit, picks up and drops off passengers at the most beautiful bays and beaches. Day tickets are A$7 and can be purchased from the driver.

You can also rent bikes at **Rottnest Bike Hire** (✉ Thomson Bay ☎ 08/9292–5105) for A$15 per day, with a returnable deposit of A$25 per bike. It's open daily 8:30–5.

Where to Stay & Eat

Accommodation on the island ranges from basic camping sites to self-contained holiday villas and upscale hotels. Advance bookings are essential in summer and on school holidays.

$$ ✕ ⊡ **Rottnest Hotel.** Affectionately known as the Quokka Arms, this hotel was once the official summer residence for the governors of Western Australia. Comfortable rooms, which overlook Thompson Bay or a grassy courtyard area, are motel-style, with cane furniture and neutral decor. As well as a popular beer garden, there are two restaurants: Vlamingh's is open daily for breakfast, lunch, and dinner, with seafood dishes a specialty; Hampton's Sportsmen's Bar and Chargrill is open every day for lunch and dinner, and features a charcoal grill with buffet salad bar. ✉ *Bedford Ave., Thomson Bay* ☎ *08/9292–5011* ⊕ *www. rottnestisland.com* ⇝ *18 rooms* ⌂ *2 restaurants, pool, bar* ⊟ *AE, MC, V.*

$–$$ ✕ ⊡ **Rottnest Lodge.** Rooms at the island's largest hotel range from premium to budget. After a day of walking or biking around the island, you can take a dip in the pool or relax at the bar. The Marlin Restaurant serves up Thai seafood salad, chowder, and bruschetta with prawns and mango, and there's a buffet lunch from 11 to 2. ✉ *Kitson St.* ☎ *08/ 9292–5161* ⊕ *www.rottnestlodge.com.au* ⇝ *80 rooms* ⌂ *Restaurant, pool, 3 bars* ⊟ *AE, DC, MC, V.*

⚠ **Allison Camping Area,** a major site for more than 50 years, has fresh water and washrooms, but no electricity. Bookings can be made up to 12 months in advance. ✉ *Thomson Bay* ☎ *08/9432–9111* ⊕ *www. rottnest.wa.gov.au* ⌨ *A$16* ⇝ *50 sites* ⌂ *Flush toilets, pit toilets, drinking water* ⊟ *AE, MC, V.*

Fremantle & Rottnest Island A to Z

AIR TRAVEL

Speedy air service to Rottnest Island is available from Perth's domestic airport with Rottnest Air Taxi. Round-trip fare is from A$60 per person, and the service operates daily, weather permitting. Telephone for flight times.

Rottnest Air Taxi ☎ 08/9292-5027 or 1800/500006 ⊕ www.rottnest.de.

BOAT & FERRY TRAVEL

Oceanic Cruises and Boat Torque Cruises/Rottnest Express run ferries to Rottnest Island from Fremantle, as well as from Perth; Boat Torque Cruises/Rottnest Express also runs ferries from Perth, and Hillarys Fast Ferries runs boats from Hillarys Boat Harbour. The ferries take approximately 25 minutes from Fremantle, 45 minutes from Hillarys, or an hour-plus from Perth—though the latter trip also includes a scenic cruise on the Swan River. Round-trip prices, including entry to Rottnest, are from A$48 per person from Fremantle and from A$63 per person from Perth and Hillarys.

Boat Torque Cruises/Rottnest Express ☎ 08/9430-5844 in Fremantle, 08/9421-5888 in Perth ⊕ www.boattorque.com.au. **Hillarys Fast Ferries** ☎ 08/9246-1039 ⊕ www. hillarysfastferries.com.au. **Oceanic Cruises** ☎ 08/9335-2666 in Fremantle, 08/9325-1191 in Perth ⊕ www.oceaniccruises.com.au.

BUS TRAVEL

Bus information for service from Perth is available from Transperth. Their Central Area Bus Service (CAT) provides free transportation around Fremantle in distinctive orange buses. The route begins and ends outside the Fremantle Bus/Train terminus, and stops include the Fremantle Museum and Arts Centre, the cappuccino strip, and the Fremantle Market. CAT buses run every 10 minutes weekdays 7:30–6:30, and 10–6:30 on weekends and public holidays.

Transperth ☎ 13-6213 ⊕ www.transperth.wa.gov.au.

EMERGENCIES

In an emergency, dial **000** to reach an ambulance, the police, or the fire department. The Rottnest Nursing Post, operated by qualified nurses, is open daily 8:30 to 5.

Fremantle Hospital ✉ Alma St. ☎ 08/9431-3333. **Rottnest Nursing Post** ✉ Thomson Bay ☎ 08/9292-5030.

TOURS

In Fremantle, Trams West has five trams and runs several tours, including sightseeing trips around all four harbors, a trip to the shipping signal station (the tallest building in Fremantle, with views all the way to Rottnest), a history trail, and a Fremantle tour combined with a river cruise to Perth. A tour around Fremantle is a great way to orient yourself and get to know each area of the port city. Trips leave every hour on the hour from the Fremantle Town Hall (Williams and Adelaide streets) 10–4 daily. On Friday nights, "ghostly tours" take in suspected haunted premises, with dinner of fish-and-chips served on board. The cost is A$35 per person.

The Rottnest Island Authority runs a daily two-hour coach tour of the island's highlights, including convict-built cottages, World War II gun emplacements, and salt lakes. The Oliver Hill Railway made its debut in the mid-1990s, utilizing 6 km (4 mi) of reconstructed railway line to reach the island's gun batteries. Information is available from the Rottnest Island Visitor Information Centre.

⚡ Rottnest Island Visitor information Center ✉ Adjacent to Dome Café, Thomson Bay beachfront ☎ 08/9372-9752 ⊕ www.rottnest.wa.gov.au. **Trams West** ✉ 39A Malsbury St., Bicton 6157 ☎ 08/9339-8719 ⊕ www.tramswest.com.au.

TRAIN TRAVEL

Trains bound for Fremantle depart from Perth approximately every 20–30 minutes from the Perth Central Station on Wellington Street. You can travel from Perth to Fremantle (or vice versa) in about 30 minutes. Tickets must be purchased prior to travel at the ticket vending machines. It is illegal to travel without a ticket.

⚡ Transperth ☎ 13-6213 ⊕ www.transperth.wa.gov.au.

VISITOR INFORMATION

The Fremantle Tourist Bureau on Kings Square is open weekdays 9–5, Saturday 10–3, and Sunday 11:30–2:30. The Rottnest Island Visitor Information Centre is open Saturday–Thursday 7:30–5:30, and Friday 7:30–8 PM.

⚡ Fremantle Tourist Bureau ✉ Kings Square, High St., Fremantle ☎ 08/9431-7878 🖶 08/9431-7755 ⊕ www.fremantlewesternaustralia.com. **Rottnest Island Visitor Information Centre** ✉ Adjacent to Dome Café, Thomson Bay beachfront ☎ 08/9372-9752 ⊕ www.rottnest.wa.gov.au.

THE SOUTH WEST

With a balmy Mediterranean climate, world-class wines, and pristine, white, sandy beaches, it's easy to see why the South West is Western Australia's most popular visitor destination. But it's not all coastal beauty—inland, rare hardwood forests make excellent hiking terrain. Add easy road and rail access from Perth and plenty of affordable, comfortable accommodations, and you have an ideal break from the city.

Bunbury

184 km (114 mi) south of Perth, 109 km (68 mi) south of Mandurah.

As Western Australia's second-largest city and the major seaport of the South West, Bunbury provides a comfortable introduction to the region. The cappuccino strip stretches down Victoria Street, and Marlston Waterfront, which overlooks the Outer Harbor and Koombana Bay, is a bustling area for cafés, restaurants, and bars.

Around 100 bottlenose dolphins make their home in Koombana Bay, and a half dozen of them regularly visit the sandy beach in front of the excellent **Dolphin Discovery Centre.** Visitors here are permitted to wade into the water while the dolphins swim around them. There are some restrictions on actually swimming with the dolphins, but the helpful center vol-

CloseUp

AUSTRALIA'S ANIMALS

AUSTRALIA'S ANIMALS ARE *among nature's oddest creations. So weird are the creatures that hop, burrow, slither, and amble across the Australian landmass that, until the 20th century it was believed that the continent's fauna had a different evolutionary starting point from the rest of the Earth's species.*

Australia's animal life was shaped by its plants, and they, in turn, were determined by the climate, which dramatically changed around 15 million years ago. Moist, rain-bearing winds that once irrigated the heart of the continent died, the great inland sea dried up, and the inland rain forests vanished—flamingos and freshwater dolphins along with them.

In times of drought, the water-holding frog locks itself away in an underground chamber, where it remains in a state of suspended animation waiting for rain for up to seven years. Despite its ferocious appearance, the heavy armor of another desert dweller, the thorny devil, also serves as a water-conservation measure. Its exaggerated spikes and spines give the creature an enormous surface area on which dew condenses and is then channeled into its mouth.

The kangaroo is a superb example of adaptation. In the parched semidesert that covers most of central Australia, kangaroos must forage for food over a wide area. Their powerful hind legs act as springs, enabling them to travel long distances while using relatively little energy. Young kangaroos are born underdeveloped, when they are barely an inch long. The mother then enters estrus again within days of giving birth. The second embryo develops for just a week and stays dormant until its older sibling leaves the pouch, at which time it enters a 30-day gestation period before being born.

Kangaroos, wallabies, and their midsize relations vary enormously in size, habitat, and location. Australia has everything from rat-size specimens to 6-foot, 200-pound red kangaroos from the cool, misty forests of Tasmania to the northern tip of Cape York.

One of the most fascinating groups of Australian animals is the monotremes, who lay eggs, as reptiles do, but are warm-blooded and suckle their young with milk. Only three species of monotremes survive: the platypus, a reclusive crustacean-eater found in freshwater streams in eastern Australia, and two species of echidna, a small, spiny termite-eater.

Best loved of all Australia's animals is the koala. A tree-dwelling herbivore, the koala eats a diet entirely of eucalyptus leaves, which are low in nutrients and high in toxins. As a result, koalas must restrict their energy level. Typically, a koala will spend about 20 hours of each day dozing in a tree fork. Even the koala's brain has adapted to its harsh regimen. A human brain uses about 17% of the body's energy, but the koala saves on the wasteful expenditure by starting out with a brain the size of a small walnut.

However deficient in the cerebellum it may be, though, one thing that the koala will not tolerate is being called a bear. Cute and cuddly as it is—and despite its resemblance to every child's favorite bedmate—the koala is a marsupial, not a bear.

— Michael Gebicki

unteers explain all the rules, which are aimed at ensuring the dolphins aren't harmed by the human interaction. The center also conducts "Swim on the Wild Side" tours which allow you to swim with wild dolphins in their natural environment. The tour is led by the center's own marine biologists and the cost of A$115 per person includes entry to the interpretive center, instruction, equipment (mask, snorkel, fins, and wet suit), and light refreshments. Tours depart (weather permitting) at midday in November and April; from December to March there are two tours daily at 8 AM and 11 AM. ⊠ *Koombana Dr.* ☎ *08/9791–3088* ⊕ *www.dolphindiscovery. com.au* ⊡ *A$4* ⏰ *June–Aug., daily 9–3; Sept.–May, daily 8–5.*

Naturaliste Charters (☎ 08/9755–2276 ⊕ www.whales-australia.com) operates dolphin cruises on the bay year-round. From November to April the cruises depart from in front of the Dolphin Discovery Centre, while from May to October departures are from the Yellow Jetty at the Marlston Waterfront. Departures times are 11 AM and 2 PM, with additional cruises during the busy summer months. The cruise costs A$33.

Dardanup (⊕ www.dardanup.wa.gov.au) is a small gathering of historic 19th-century buildings nestled at the entry point to the Ferguson Valley. If you take the winding Ferguson Valley Road up into the Darling Scarp, you'll discover wineries, art and crafts galleries, and farm-stay lodgings. The best time to come is between April and November, when the pastures are green from seasonal rains. **Willow Bridge Estate** (⊠ Lot 4, Gardincourt Dr. ☎ 08/9728–0055) is open daily 11–5. **Ferguson Falls Wines** (⊹ Pile Rd., 2 km [1 mi] from Ferguson Valley Rd. ☎ 08/9728–1083) is open weekends 10–5. Dardanup is 20 km (12 mi) inland from Bunbury.

Where to Stay & Eat

★ **$$** ✕ **Vat 2.** A waterfront spot overlooking the Outer Harbour and marina is the setting for this local favorite. Grown-ups can while away a lazy Sunday afternoon dining and wining alfresco to a live band while children frolic at the adjacent playground. Chef Danny Angove's menu includes herb-crusted rack of lamb with pumpkin rosti, and char-grilled veal steaks on a bed of soft polenta. The extensive wine list taps the best of the region. If you love oysters, they're the Tuesday-night special. ⊠ *2 Jetty Rd.* ☎ *08/9791–8833* ⊟ *AE, DC, MC, V.*

¢–$$ ✕⊡ **Clifton Best Western.** With 42 tourism and restaurant awards since 1990,
Fodor'sChoice this small hotel is the most awarded lodging in the region. In addition to
★ the typical motel-style rooms, you can upgrade to one of four tastefully appointed suites furnished with antiques in the adjacent 1885 Grittleton Lodge. Louisa's, regarded as one of the best country restaurants in Western Australia, serves casual, brasserie-style fare paired with a strong local wine list. Starters include char-grilled scallops with risotto fritte, or house-smoked lemon chicken with fresh mango; main courses include homemade fettuccine with prawns, octopus, and mussels, or fresh local dhufish with steamed baby potato and asparagus verjus. ⊠ *15 Clifton St., 6230* ☎ *08/ 9721–4300 hotel, 08/9721–9959 Louisa's Restaurant* ⊕ *www.theclifton. com.au* ⤳ *48 rooms, 4 suites* ⚬ *Restaurant, pool, hot tub, sauna, laundry facilities, free parking* ⊟ *AE, DC, MC, V.*

$ ⊞ **Lord Forrest Hotel.** This central hotel is within walking distance of the cappuccino strip, cinemas, shops, and restaurants. Greenery dangles from garden beds around the eight-story atrium, where sunlight streams through clerestory windows. Rooms are pleasantly furnished and decorated in pastels; upper floors have city views. Spa at the Forrest offers massages and reflexology treatments, facials, and salt scrubs. ⊠ *20 Symmons St., 6230* ☎ *08/9721–9966 or 1800/097811* ⊕ *www.lordforresthotel.com.au* ➳ *102 rooms, 13 suites* ⚫ *2 restaurants, indoor pool, hot tub, 2 saunas, 2 bars, nightclub, free parking* ⊟ *AE, DC, MC, V.*

Nightlife

Barbados (⊠ 15 Bonnefoi Blvd., Marlston Waterfront ☎ 08/9791–6555 ⊕ www.barbados.com.au), a second-story venue on the Marlston Waterfront, has views over Koombana Bay. Monday nights bring live Latin and jazz music, and the Mod-Oz food served in two dining areas is complemented by an extensive selection of regional wines. The energetic can migrate to the dance floor, while conversationalists can head to the quieter lounge area. It's open daily, Monday–Saturday 11 AM–midnight and Sunday until 10.

Fitzgerald's (⊠ 22 Victoria St. ☎ 08/9791–2295) is Bunbury's authentic Irish bar, housed in the historic Customs House Bond Store.

The lively **Reef Hotel** (⊠ 12 Victoria St. ☎ 08/9791–6677) bar bustles from 8 PM into the wee hours. DJs spin rock, hip-hop, rhythm and blues, and heavy metal Sunday through Thursday, and there's live music Friday and Saturday nights. Admission is free.

> **en route** From Bunbury to Busselton, take the scenic route through **Ludlow Forest,** the only natural tuart forest in the world. These magnificent tuart trees, a type of eucalyptus or gum tree that thrives in arid conditions, have been standing on this land for 400 years. Just south of Ludlow Forest is Wonnerup House, first settled by the Layman family in 1834. Wonnerup House is an important surviving example of early farm pioneering. The homestead (1859) and dairy (1837) are managed by the National Trust.

Busselton

53 km (33 mi) south of Bunbury.

Settled by the Bussell family in 1834, and among the state's oldest towns, seaside Busselton was once largely pastureland for dairy cows. Now, however, it's a popular weekend getaway spot with many choices for dining and lodging. The small **Busselton Historic Museum,** housed in the Old Butter Factory, records Busselton's history and that of the South West dairy industry's early years. ⊠ *Peel Terr. and Brown St.* ☎ *08/9754–2166* ⚑ *A$4* ☉ *Wed.–Mon. 2–5.*

Fodor'sChoice **Busselton Jetty,** at 1.9 km (1.2 mi), is the longest timber jetty in the South-
★ ern Hemisphere. An hourly jetty train takes you almost to the end, where the **Busselton Underwater Observatory** allows you to walk down more than 25 feet below the surface into a marine forest. The warmth of the

Leeuwin Current coming down Western Australia's west coast, combined with the depth of Geographe Bay and the width of the jetty timbers (which protect the corals), creates the perfect environment for colorful soft corals, other resident marine life, and passing schools of fish. ⊠ *Main Beachfront* ☎ *08/9754–0900* ⊕ *www.busseltonjetty.com.au* ⊠ *Jetty A$2.50; train A$7.50; interpretive center free; underwater observatory A$20, includes return train ride and jetty entrance fee* ☉ *Jetty daily 24 hrs. Trains leave daily on the hr. Dec.–Apr., 8–5; May–Sept., 10–4; Oct.–Nov., 9–5, weather permitting. Observatory Dec.–Apr., daily 8–5; May–Nov., daily 9–4; tours on the hr. Interpretive center Dec.–Apr. daily 8–6; May–Sept. daily 9–5.*

Where to Stay

$ 🏨 **Abbey Beach Resort.** One of Western Australia's largest and most highly regarded resorts is on the beachfront 8 km (5 mi) west of Busselton. Its horseshoe shape houses an impressive lobby, as well as a combination of accommodations. All apartments have kitchens and can sleep up to eight people; there are also 16 beachfront units. A restaurant, bar, two sizable outdoor pools, and a heated indoor pool are also in the complex. ⊠ *595 Bussell Hwy., 6280* ☎ *08/9755–4600 or 1800/017097* 🖷 *08/ 9755–4610* ⊕ *www.abbeybeach.com.au* ⊠ *86 suites, 100 apartments* ♨ *Restaurant, café, in-room hot tubs, some kitchens, some kitchenettes, room TVs with movies, in-room VCRs, 2 tennis courts, 3 pools (1 indoor), gym, hot tub, sauna, bicycles, squash, 2 bars, free parking* ☰ *AE, DC, MC, V.*

¢ 🏨 **Geographe Bayview Resort.** The bright, cheerful rooms at this stylish resort are just a two-minute walk from the beach, and surrounded by 28 acres of beautiful gardens. Self-contained villas that sleep eight are also available. On-site dining includes Spinnakers Café and the more elegant Tuart Restaurant. ⊠ *555 Bussell Hwy., 6280, 6 km (4 mi) west of Busselton* ☎ *08/9755–4166 or 1800/674147* 🖷 *08/9755–4075* ⊕ *www.geographebayview.com.au* ⊠ *27 rooms, 70 villas* ♨ *Restaurant, café, picnic area, refrigerators, miniature golf, putting green, 3 tennis courts, 2 pools, 2 hot tubs, beach, windsurfing, squash, bar, free parking* ☰ *AE, DC, MC, V.*

¢ 🏨 **Prospect Villa.** Laura Ashley fabrics decorate the rooms, and Victorian bric-a-brac provides an atmospheric backdrop for this comfortable 1850s B&B. The historic two-story house stands 100 yards or so from town but a half mile from the Geographe Bay beaches. An adjacent cottage that sleeps two, with a claw-foot bathtub, a woodstove, and antique furnishings, is also available. ⊠ *1 Pries Ave., 6280* ☎ *0417/ 099307 or 08/9752–2273 after 7 PM* ⊕ *www.members.optusnet.com. au/~prospect villa* ⊠ *4 rooms, 1 cottage* ♨ *Dining room, laundry service, free parking* ☰ *AE, MC, V* ⧖| *CP.*

Dunsborough

21 km (13 mi) west of Busselton.

The attractive seaside town of Dunsborough is perfect for a few days of swimming, sunning, and fishing—which is why it's become a popular holiday destination for many Perth families. Onshore attractions include Meelup Beach, a protected cove with calm swimming water, and the nearby wineries of Margaret River. Offshore, you can dive on the wreck of the HMAS *Swan,* the former Royal Australian Navy ship deliberately sunk in Geographe Bay at the end of its useful life, or take a cruise to see migrating humpback and southern right whales September–December.

Where to Stay & Eat

$$ ✕ **Wise Vineyard Restaurant.** Verdant bushland and a carefully manicured vineyard surround Heath Townsend's restaurant at the Wise winery. Simple ingredients are transformed here into such culinary delights as spiced chicken with tabbouleh and preserved lemon salad, duck and eggplant curry with steamed rice, or sea-salt crusted veal cutlet with new potatoes and mint butter. Views of Eagle Bay complete the dining experience. Five homey chalets with names such as the Barn, Teahouse, Potter's Cottage, and Doll House are also available for accommodation. ✉ *80 Eagle Bay Rd.* ☎ *08/9755–3331 restaurant, 08/9756–8627 winery, 08/9756–8098 accommodations* ▤ *AE, DC, MC, V* ☉ *No dinner Mon.–Thurs.*

$–$$ ⊞ **Dunsborough Beach Resort.** Sunny public areas and extensive sports facilities make this one of the best accommodation choices on the Geographe Bay beach strip. Romantic king rooms, done in pastel colors, have deluxe facilities, while the two- and three-bedroom apartments each have a lounge, dining room, and kitchen. Many rooms have superb ocean views. The casual, airy restaurant serves fusion cuisine using fresh local produce, cheeses, and olive oils. A selection of Margaret River wines is on hand to complement the meal. The resort has its own chapel in an attractive garden setting, which is often used for weddings. ✉ *Caves and Holgate Rds., Marybrook 6281* ☎ *08/9756–9777* ▤ *08/9756–8788* ⊕ *www.broadwaters.com.au* ⏎ *50 rooms, 50 apartments* ⌖ *Restaurant, café, picnic area, room service, putting green, 2 tennis courts, pool, gym, hot tub, beach, volleyball, bar, playground, concierge, business services, meeting rooms, travel services, free parking* ▤ *AE, DC, MC, V.*

¢   ⊞ **Dunsborough Motel.** This motel for the dollar-conscious provides comfortable accommodations and proximity to town and the beach. Rooms are equipped with basic amenities, including electric kettles and supplies for making coffee and tea, while the property includes a restaurant, swimming pool, and barbecue area. ✉ *Caves Rd. and Seymour Blvd., 6281* ☎ *08/9756–7711* ▤ *08/9756–7722* ⏎ *48 rooms* ⌖ *Restaurant, cable TV, pool, lounge* ▤ *AE, DC, MC, V.*

Leeuwin–Naturaliste National Park

Fodor'sChoice
★ *The northernmost part of the park is 266 km (165 mi) south of Perth, 25 km (16 mi) northwest of Dunsborough.*

This 150-km (93-mi) stretch of coastline on the southwest tip of the continent is one of Australia's most fascinating areas. The limestone Leeuwin–Naturaliste Ridge directly below the park contains more than 360 known caves. Evidence dates both human and animal habitation here to more than 40,000 years ago.

At the northern end of the park stands **Cape Naturaliste Lighthouse,** open daily 9:30–5 December to February, closing at 4 the rest of the year. Fully guided tours of the lighthouse cost A$8, with the last tour at 3:30. A 1½-km- (1-mi-) long trail leads from Cape Naturaliste to Canal Rocks, passing rugged cliffs, quiet bays, and curving beaches. This is also the start of the 120-km (75-mi) Cape to Cape Walk.

Four major cave systems are easily accessible. **Jewel** (☎ 08/9757–7411), the southernmost of the system, has one of the longest straw stalactites to be found in any tourist cave in the world. It's open daily with tours every hour 9:30 AM–3:30 PM. **Lake** (☎ 08/9757–7411), centered around a tranquil, eerie-looking underground lake, is also open daily with tours every hour 9:30–3:30. Tour cost at both Jewel and Lake Caves is A$16.50. **Mammoth** (☎ 08/9757–7411), which has ancient fossil remains of extinct animals, is open daily 9–5, with the last entry at 4. Self-guided tours cost A$16.50.

Ngilgi (☎ 08/9755–2152), near Yallingup, is a main site for adventure caving. It's open daily 9:30–4:30, staying open to 6 PM during summer school holidays. Cave tours cost A$15 and run every half hour. Flashlight tours, where all the cave lights are turned off and the only light is from the flashlights, cost A$18, and adventure tours are A$70. The **Cave-Works** (☎ 08/9757–7411) display center at Lake Cave presents a good introduction to the whole cave system.

The view from the top of the **Cape Leeuwin Lighthouse** (☎ 08/9757–7411 ⊕ www.margaretriver.com), a 10-minute drive south of Augusta and the third-highest working lighthouse in Australia, allows you to witness the meeting of the Southern and the Indian oceans. In some places this alliance results in giant swells that crash against the rocks. In others, small coves are blessed with calm waters ideal for swimming. The lighthouse precinct is open daily 8:45–5. Guided tours to the top of the lighthouse cost A$8 and run every 45 minutes between May 1 and September 15, and every 30 minutes between September 16 and April 30. The last tour is at 4:30 PM.

If you don't plan to camp, consider staying at Dunsborough or Margaret River. Campgrounds with toilets, showers, and an information center are north in Injidup. Campsites (including firewood) cost A$6 per adult per night. Facilities include toilets and barbecue facilities. For more information on camping in the state, visit ⊕ www.calm.wa.gov.au/tourism/camping.html.

Margaret River

★ *181 km (112 mi) south of Perth, 38 km (24 mi) south of Cape Naturaliste.*

The town of Margaret River is considered the center of the South West's wine region, though vineyards and wineries stretch from well north of Bunbury to the south coast. Nevertheless, close to Margaret River are some 80 wineries offering tastings and sales of some of the best wines in the world. The region, which is often compared to France's Bordeaux for its similar climate and soils, produces only around 1% of Australia's total wine grape crush, but this is spread into around 25% of the country's premium and ultrapremium wines. Both red and white vintages here are exceptional, the most notable labels toting chardonnay, sauvignon blanc, or sauvignon blanc–semillon and cabernet-merlot blends.

The **Margaret River Visitor Center** (✉ 100 Bussell Hwy. ☎ 08/9757–2911 ⊕ www.margaretriver.com), open daily 9–5, has detailed brochures for individual cellars. You can also get information here on the World Masters Surf Circuit championships, which take place each November at Surfers Point, just 8 km (5 mi) outside Margaret River.

★ **Clairault Wines** (✉ Henry Rd., Willyabrup ☎ 08/9755–6225 ⊕ www.clairault.com.au) is one of the region's best wineries, known for its cabernet/merlot, cabernet sauvignon, and semillon. The property's manicured lawns and charming gardens are floodlighted after dark. The spacious restaurant has glass doors that swing back for expansive views in warm weather, while two huge stone fireplaces warm the tables in winter. Chef Andrea Ilott's menus are innovative, and include steamed Pemberton marron (freshwater crayfish) with hot and sour salad, and an aromatic curry of free-range chicken, sweet potato, basil, shallots, and pickled cucumber.

Cape Mentelle (✉ Wallcliffe Rd., 3 km [2 mi] west of Margaret River ☎ 08/9757–0888) was one of the first wineries in the area, and it's still one of the most notable. The adobe-style rammed-earth building and tasting rooms, so typical of the buildings in the Margaret River district, are as handsome and memorable as the wine. The winery produces chardonnay, sauvignon blanc, cabernet/merlot, cabernet sauvignon, shiraz, and zinfandel wines. Winemaker Vanya Cullen produces one of Australia's best chardonnays and an outstanding cabernet/merlot at **Cullen Wines** (✉ Caves and Harmans S Rds., Willyabrup ☎ 08/9755–5277), a family-run business.

★ **Leeuwin Estate** (✉ Stevens Rd. off Gnaraway Rd. ☎ 08/9759–0000 ⊕ www.leeuwinestate.com.au) is one of Australia's leading wineries. Their Art Series wines—especially the chardonnay and cabernet sauvignon—have a deserved reputation as some of the best in the country. Tastings and guided tours (A$9.90) are conducted on the property, and the restaurant has daily lunch and Saturday dinner. In February the estate holds a series of concerts, and many international superstars—including Tom Jones, Diana Ross, and Sting—have performed there against a backdrop of floodlighted karri trees. **Vasse Felix** (✉ Harmans S and Caves Rds., Cowaramup ☎ 08/9756–5000) has an excellent upstairs restaurant, a basement cellar, and photogenic grounds.

Eagle's Heritage has the largest collection of birds of prey in Australia, all living in a natural bush environment. It is also a rehabilitation center for sick and injured birds of prey. The ancient art of falconry is shown in the free-flight display, with tours at 11 and 1:30. ✛ *Boodjidup Rd., 5 km (3 mi) south west of Margaret River* ☎ *08/9757–2960* ⊕ *www.eaglesheritage.com.au* 🎫 *A$10* ☉ *Daily 10–5.*

Where to Stay & Eat

★ **$$–$$$** ✕ **Flutes Restaurant.** The pastoral setting here—over the dammed waters of the Willyabrup Brook and encircled by olive groves in the midst of the Brookland Valley Vineyard—is almost as compelling as the food. The modern Australian cooking makes use of prime local produce. Margaret River venison, Capel marron, and water buffalo are all excellent, prepared simply yet with flair. ⊹ *Caves Rd., 5 km (3 mi) south of Metricup Rd.,* ☎ *08/9755–6250* ⌂ *Reservations essential* ▤ *AE, DC, MC, V.*

$$–$$$ ✕ **Vat 107.** Biodynamic and organic ingredients are the draws at this open, airy, and friendly restaurant. Menu offerings include Malaysian-style *laksa lemak* (spicy, coconut-based curry with tiger prawns, tofu, and hokkien noodles), and seared sea scallops with asparagus, Cloverdene pecorino, and Parmesan oil. There are plenty of vegetarian choices. Luxury studio apartments upstairs are available for overnight stays from A$180. ✉ *107 Bussell Hwy.* ☎ *08/9758–8877* ▤ *AE, DC, MC, V* ☾ *Closed Mon.*

$$ ✕ **Lamont's.** The signature dish at this lovely lakefront restaurant is the local marron—served grilled with fresh tomato and basil, or poached with a lime-and-chive beurre blanc. Another sure bet is the prosciutto-wrapped chicken breast, served with grilled Gorgonzola polenta, arugula, Ligurian olives, and cherry tomatoes. ✉ *Lot 1, Gunyulgup Valley Dr., Yallingup* ☎ *08/9755–2434* ▤ *AE, DC, MC, V* ☾ *No dinner Sun.–Fri.*

$$$$ ▦ **Cape Lodge.** The Cape Dutch architecture perfectly suits this elegant **FodorsChoice** lodge in the midst of Margaret River wine country. Since undergoing a ★ A$3 million refurbishment in 2004, the property now offers 10 new luxury suites, a lakeside restaurant with over-water alfresco dining, and a 14,000 bottle, temperature-controlled wine cellar stocked with premium vintage Margaret River wines. Several of the opulent, airy suites have their own balconies or terraces overlooking a private lake; others look out over woodlands or landscaped gardens. ✉ *Caves Rd., Yallingup 6282* ☎ *08/9755–6311* ⎙ *08/9755–6322* ⊕ *www.capelodge.com.au* ⌸ *22 suites* ⌂ *Restaurant, room service, tennis court, pool, free parking; no kids under 15* ▤ *AE, DC, MC, V* ⦿ *CP.*

$$$ ▦ **Basildene Manor.** Each of the rooms in this grand, circa-1912 house has been lovingly refurbished. Rich lilac, gold, and red colors decorate the guest rooms. Breakfast—included in the rates—is served in the conservatory, where you can look out over the property's 14 beautifully landscaped acres. Special wedding packages are available. ✉ *100 Wallcliffe Rd., 6285* ☎ *08/9757–3140* ⎙ *08/9757–3383* ⊕ *www.basildene.com.au* ⌸ *17 rooms* ⌂ *Dining room, pool, library, laundry facilities, Internet, free parking* ▤ *AE, DC, MC, V* ⦿ *BP.*

$$$ ▦ **Gilgara Homestead.** This stunning property, a replica of an 1870 station homestead, sits amid 23 gently rolling, bucolic acres. Antiques and lace furnish the romantic rooms, so it's no surprise that honeymooners frequently choose to stay here. A rose-covered veranda, open fireplaces, and a cozy lounge add to the charm. You might breakfast surrounded by spectacular blue wrens and sacred ibises, or catch a few kangaroos lounging near the front door. Rates include a Mediterranean-style breakfast. ✉ *Caves and Carter Rds., 6285* ☎ *08/9757–2705* ⎙ *08/9757–3259* ⊕ *www.gilgara.com.au* ⌸ *14 rooms* ⌂ *Dining room, some in-room hot tubs, horseback riding, library, laundry facilities, free parking; no* *room phones, no TV in some rooms, no kids under 15* 🛏 *AE, DC, MC, V* ⊗ *BP.*

$$–$$$ 🏨 **Heritage Trail Lodge.** Nestled among the trees, this luxury retreat is only about ½-km (¼-mi) from Margaret River township. Spacious suites have spa baths, king-size beds, and private balconies overlooking the forest. Walk the trails early, then enjoy a complimentary Continental breakfast of local produce in the conservatory. ⊠ *31 Bussell Hwy., 6285* ☎ *08/9757–9595* 📠 *08/9757–9596* ⊕ *www.heritage-trail-lodge. com.au* 🛏 *10 suites* ⚒ *Dining room, hiking, free parking* 🛏 *AE, DC, MC, V* ⊗ *CP.*

---

en route

Rustic timber cottages and historic buildings characterize the small, lovely town of **Nannup,** 100 km (62 mi) east of Margaret River. Several scenic drives wind through the area, including the Blackwood River Tourist Drive, a 10-km (6-mi) ride along a section of river surrounded by hills with karri and jarrah forests. You can also canoe on the Blackwood River and wander through the Blythe Gardens. If you'd like to spend the night, **Holberry House** (☎ 08/9756–1276 ⊕ www.holberryhouse.com), a charming colonial B&B with exposed beams and stone fireplaces, sits amid timbered acres overlooking the Blackwood Valley.

Pemberton

280 km (150 mi) southeast of Perth.

Pemberton is the heartland of the magnificent karri forest of Western Australia. These timber giants—said to be the third-tallest tree in the world behind mountain ash and Californian redwood—grow in their natural state only in this southern region of Western Australia.

The town was settled in 1913, and has relied on harvesting the karri trees since. If you take a walk through pristine forest in Warren National Park, you can climb to the top of the Dave Evans Bicentennial Tree, one of the tall karri trees used in summer by fire spotters on the lookout for bushfires. Just outside Pemberton is Gloucester Tree, another fire spotters' tree, which also allows you to climb to the top 200 feet above the ground. Beedelup National Park has a gathering of 400-year-old karri trees.

Pemberton is the home of numerous woodworking artisans. A must-see is the **Fine Woodcraft Gallery,** which offers outstanding examples of wood as art, as well as more practical pieces such as fine furniture. ⊠ *Dickinson St.; follow signs from center of town* ☎ 08/9776–1399 ⊗ *Daily 9–5.*

Pemberton is also expanding its reputation as the center of a premium wine region. **Gloucester Ridge Winery** was one of the first wineries in the area, and is now recognized for its excellent pinot noir. Sample a vintage or two with a meal at the excellent restaurant. ⊠ *Burma Rd.* ☎ 08/9776–1035 🎟 *Free* ⊗ *Daily 10–5, later on Sat.*

Where to Stay

$$ 🏨 **Karri Valley Resort.** Built on the edge of a huge man-made lake, the resort has 32 rooms in a two-story timber building. The lakeside rooms, with private balconies overlooking the lake, are comfortably furnished in muted pastel tones; two- and three-bedroom chalets, with brightly colored cane and pine furniture, fireplaces, and kitchen facilities, are also scattered along the forested slopes surrounding the lake. The resort is about 20 minutes' drive from Pemberton. *Vasse Hwy. south from Pemberton at 17-km (10-mi) mark* ☎ *08/9776–2020 or 1800/245757* ⊕ *www.karrivalleyresort.com.au* ➮ *32 rooms, 10 chalets* ⟁ *Restaurant, miniature golf, boating, shop, laundry facilities, free parking; no a/c* ▤ *AE, DC, MC, V.*

---

en route

Valley of the Giants. Giant tingle trees, which grow only along the south coast near Walpole, are protected in this fascinating park. You can experience the environment of these trees from up in the canopy ★ ☾ by talking the **Treetop Walk,** a 1,000-foot-long steel walkway that slopes gently upward and is suitable for children and wheelchairs. At 132 feet above the ground you have prime views of the forest, as well as of birdlife and flowers that most people never see. The ground-level **Ancient Empire Boardwalk** meanders through the park, occasionally winding through groves of veteran tingle trees. *Valley of the Giants Rd., 13 km (8 mi) east on South Coast Hwy.* ☎ *08/ 9840–8263* ⊕ *www.naturebase.net/tourism/valley_of_the_giants.html* ☒ *A$6* ☉ *Daily 9–4:15, mid-Dec.–mid-Jan. until 5:15.*

Albany

410 km (254 mi) southeast of Perth via Rte. 30, 377 km (234 mi) east of Margaret River.

Lying on the southernmost tip of Western Australia's rugged coastline, this sophisticated port city is a surprising find. The earliest settlement in Western Australia, it was founded in 1826 as a penal outpost—three years earlier than northern Swan River, which later became Perth. Originally named Frederickstown after Frederick, Duke of York and Albany, the town was renamed Albany in 1831 by Governor James Stirling. Its 1840s whaling fleet turned it into a boomtown, and though the whaling heyday ended in 1978, the town's heritage is still very much evident. Solid stone buildings clustered around the beautiful waterways of Princess Royal Harbour spread out around King George Sound.

Whalers brought huge numbers of sperm whales into Albany's harbor every season—the greatest number being 1,174, in 1975—until the practice was stopped in 1978. Today whales are found in King George Sound between May and October. The old whaling station has been con- ☾ verted to the **Whaleworld** museum, which has memorable displays of cetaceans (whales and dolphins) and pinnipeds (seals and sea lions), as well as the restored whaling brig *Cheyne IV*. The museum lies 20 km (12 mi) from Albany along the shore of Frenchman's Bay. ☒ *Frenchmans Bay Rd.* ☎ *08/9844–4021* ⊕ *www.whaleworld.org* ☒ *A$18* ☉ *Daily 9–5, hourly guided tours 10–4.*

Built in 1851, the **Old Gaol** on Stirling Terrace served as the district jail from 1872 until it was closed in the 1930s. Restored by the Albany Historical Society in 1968, it now contains a collection of social and historical artifacts. A ticket also grants you access to **Patrick Taylor Cottage,** a wattle-and-daub (twig-and-mud) dwelling built on Duke Street in 1832 and believed to be the oldest in the district. It contains more than 2,000 objects, including period costumes, old clocks, silverware, and kitchenware. ⊠ *Stirling Terr. and Parade St.* ☎ *08/9841–1401* ⊡ *A$4* ⊙ *Old Gaol, daily 10–4:15; Patrick Taylor Cottage, daily 1–4:15.*

The 1850 Residency building once accommodated government officials and later became offices. Since 1985 it has housed the **Western Australian Museum Albany,** one of the finest small museums in Australia and a focal point for both the social and natural history of the Albany region. Exhibits explore the local Noongar Aboriginal culture, as well as local geology, flora, and fauna. Also worth visiting are the adjoining saddlery and artisans' gallery. The lovely sandstone building affords sweeping views of the harbor. ⊠ *Residency Rd. and Princess Royal Dr.* ☎ *08/9841–4844* ⊡ *Donation suggested* ⊙ *Daily 10–5.*

Adjacent to the Residency Museum is a faithful replica of the brig **Amity,** on which Albany's original settlers arrived. Local artisans used timber from the surrounding forest to build the replica. If you board the ship, climb below deck and try to imagine how 45 men, plus livestock, could fit into such a small craft. ⊠ *Parade Rd. off Princess Royal Dr.* ☎ *08/ 9841–6885* ⊡ *A$5* ⊙ *Daily 9–5.*

Created for snorkelers and divers, the **Albany Artificial Reef** is set on the former Royal Australian Navy ship HMAS *Perth.* Most of the original ship is intact, including the mast, forward gun, and the main radar dishes. It was scuttled in 100 feet of water in King George Sound; a scuba permit is required to dive at the site. ⊠ *Frenchman's Bay Rd.* ☎ *08/ 9841–9333* ⊡ *A$7.50* ⊙ *Daily, daylight hrs.*

The 963-km (597-mi) **Bibbulmun Walking Trail** (☎ 08/9481–0551 ⊕ www. bibbulmuntrack.org.au) meanders through scenic forest country all the way from Perth to Albany, the southern trailhead. The motif of the rainbow serpent Waugal marks the trail.

off the beaten path

DENMARK – This charming old town 53 km (33 mi) west from Albany is nestled on a riverside—"where forest meets the sea," as the town motto goes. It's an ideal place to stop for a swim in the sparkling clear waters at Ocean Beach, or to browse through artisans' wares at the Old Butter Factory. If you want to stay a while, the **Chimes Spa Retreat** (☎ 08/9848–2255, www.chimes.com.au) offers luxury accommodations and spa services on a secluded 60-acre property, while the **Cove** (☎ 08/9848–1770 ⊕ www.thecovechalets. com) has five craftsman-built chalets set in the forest with expansive views of the inlet.

Where to Stay & Eat

$$–$$$ ✕ **Genevieve's.** The restaurant takes its name from a veteran English motorcar made famous by a witty British movie of 1953. Delicious bistro-style breakfasts and à la carte dinners are created from local produce—the seafood is caught daily in King George Sound. The Thai-style chili squid makes an excellent starter; standout main courses include seared salmon, kangaroo fillet, and oven-baked lamb shank. ⊠ *Esplanade Hotel, Esplanade, Middleton Beach* ☎ *08/9842–1711 or 1800/678757* ▭ *AE, DC, MC, V* ⊘ *No lunch.*

$$–$$$ ✕ **Kooka's.** Kookaburras of every description frequent this timeless colonial cottage—on lamp shades, trays, saltshakers, teapots, and ornaments. The Australian menu changes every two to three months. Highlights might include fillet of steak stuffed with blue Castello cheese or Moroccan-spiced quail. ⊠ *204 Stirling Terr.* ☎ *08/9841–5889* ▭ *AE, DC, MC, V* ☖ *BYOB* ⊘ *Closed Sun. and Mon. No lunch Sat.*

$$ ✕ **Gosyu-Ya.** When Perth restaurateur Jun Fujiki, proprietor of no fewer than five popular Japanese restaurants, wanted a change of pace, Albany seemed a logical choice. The town's first Japanese restaurant has quickly become one of its most popular eating venues. Specialties include grilled fish, Japanese steaks, the *amimoto-no-sara* (seafood platter), and green-tea ice cream for dessert. ⊠ *1 Mermaid Ave., Emu Point* ☎ *08/9844–1111* ▭ *AE, DC, MC, V* ⊘ *Closed Sun.*

$–$$ ✕ **Shamrock Café.** This Irish-theme café has become one of the most popular such establishments in the state. The walls positively groan with Irish memorabilia. Specialties include soda bread, potato bread, and huge Irish breakfasts for just A$7. ⊠ *184 York St.* ☎ *08/9841–4201* ⚫ *Reservations not accepted* ▭ *MC, V.*

★ **$$–$$$** ⊞ **Esplanade Hotel.** The elegant, colonial-style hotel is renowned for its high-quality accommodations and views over Middleton Beach. The rooms are spacious, decorated in subdued tones, with timber and cane furniture in keeping with the colonial-style public areas. Doubles and executive rooms have king-size beds, while twin rooms have two queen-size beds apiece. Recreational facilities include a tennis court, pool, indoor hot tub, sauna, and minigym. Open wood fires blaze in the bars and restaurant in winter. ⊠ *Adelaide and Flinders Sts., 6330* ☎ *08/9842–1711 or 1800/678757* 🖶 *08/9841–7527* ⊕ *www.albanyesplanade.com.au* ⇨ *40 rooms, 8 suites* ⚭ *Restaurant, tennis court, pool, health club, sauna, 2 bars, library, laundry facilities, free parking* ▭ *AE, DC, MC, V.*

$ ⊞ **Balneaire Seaside Resort.** This property brings a bit of the south of France to the south of the state, just a short stroll from a prime stretch of Middleton Beach. Two- and three-bedroom villa-style apartments overlook lush gardens and a central courtyard designed to resemble a Provençal village square. Soft aquas, blues, and yellows decorate each fully equipped villa. ⊠ *27 Adelaide Crescent, Middleton Beach, 6330* ☎ *08/9842–2877* 🖶 *08/9842–2899* ⊕ *www.balneaire.com.au* ⇨ *28 apartments* ⚭ *Café, kitchens, beach, playground, laundry facilities, free parking* ▭ *AE, DC, MC, V.*

Stirling Range National Park

403 km (250 mi) south of Perth, 71 km (44 mi) north of Albany.

During the height of the wildflower season (September and October), the Stirling Ranges, north of Albany, rival any botanical park in the world. Rising from the flat countryside, the ranges fill the horizon with a kaleidoscope of color. More than 1,000 wildflower species have been identified here, including 69 species of orchid. This profusion of flowers attracts equal numbers of insects, reptiles, and birds, as well as a host of nocturnal honey possums. Emus and kangaroos are frequent visitors.

The Stirlings, together with the ranges of the adjacent Porongurup National Park, are considered the only true mountain range in the South West. They were formed by the uplifting and buckling of sediments laid down by a now-dry ancient sea. An extensive road system, including the superscenic Stirling Range Drive, makes travel from peak to peak easy. Treks begin at designated parking areas. Don't be fooled by apparently short distances—a 3-km (2-mi) walk up 3,541-foot Bluff Knoll takes about three hours round-trip. Take plenty of water and wet-weather gear—the park's location near the south coast makes Stirling subject to sudden storms. Before attempting longer hikes, register your intended routes in the ranger's log book, and log out upon return. ✉ *Stirling Range Dr., Amelup via Borden* ☎ *08/9827–9230.*

Where to Stay & Eat

Albany is close enough to serve as a good base for exploring the park, but there are also dining and lodging options in the nearby town of Borden.

¢–$ ✕▥ **The Lily.** Inside the restored 1924 Gnowangerup Railway Station, this captivating little restaurant serves lunch and candlelight dinners. You can't miss the place—right next door owners Hennie and Pleun Hitzert have constructed an authentic Dutch windmill based on a 16th-century design. The five-story-high windmill has a 22-ton cap, and a sail length of about 80 feet. It's the only fully operational windmill in Australia, and it still produces stone-ground flour for local bakers, shops, and individuals. You can also buy the Lily's own premium wines—chardonnay, cabernet sauvignon, and chenin blanc. Accommodation is available in self-catering double rooms. ⚑ *Chester Pass Rd., 94 km (59 mi) north of Albany, 11 km (7 mi) past Bluff Knoll turnoff* ☎ *08/9827–9205* ⊕ *www.thelily.com.au* ⇌ *3 rooms* ⚒ *Laundry facilities; no a/c* ▤ *MC, V* ⊙| *CP.*
The ⚠ **Stirling Range Retreat** (✉ Chester Pass Rd. directly opposite Bluff Knoll turnoff, Borden ☎ 08/9827–9229 ⊕ www.stirlingrange.com.au) lies just north of the park's boundary, opposite Bluff Knoll. Hot and cold showers, laundry facilities, swimming pool, powered and unpowered sites, chalets, and cabins are available. Campfires are permitted. Camping fees are A$20 for two adults; other accommodations start at A$20 per night. The only camping within the park is at ⚠ **Moingup Springs** (✉ Chester Pass Rd. ☎ 08/9827–9230), which has toilets, water, and barbecues. Campfires are prohibited. Fees are A$8 per night for two adults, A$4 for additional adults.

South West A to Z

AIR TRAVEL
Skywest provides daily service to the southern coastal town of Albany.
🛪 **Skywest** ☎ 13–2300 ⊕ www.skywest.com.au.

CAR TRAVEL

A comprehensive network of highways makes exploring the South West practical and easy. Take Highway 1 down the coast from Perth to Bunbury, switch to Route 10 through Busselton and Margaret River, Karridale, and finally Bridgetown, where you rejoin Highway 1 south to Albany via Manjimup.

From Perth you can reach Stirling Range National Park by traveling along the Albany Highway to Kojonup, proceeding east via Broome Hill and Gnowangerup, and then veering south through Borden onto the Albany Road. For a more scenic route, head south from Kojonup and then proceed east along the Stirling Range Drive.

EMERGENCIES

In case of an emergency, dial **000** to reach an ambulance, the police, or the fire department.

Albany Regional Hospital ⊠ Warden Ave. and Hardie Rd., Albany ☎ 08/9841-2955. **Peel Health Campus** ⊠ 110 Lakes Rd., Mandurah ☎ 08/9531-8000. **South West Health Campus** ⊠ Bussell Hwy. and Robertson Dr., Bunbury ☎ 08/9722-1000.

MAIL, INTERNET & SHIPPING

Australia Post has licensed agencies in virtually every town in the region. Internet and e-mail access are available in most public libraries. Some towns have an Internet café. Cyber Corner Café in Margaret River is open daily 10–8. Log on in Busselton at Novatech 2000 and in Bunbury at Bunbury Internet Café.

Australia Post ☎ 13-1318 ⊕ www.austpost.com.au. **Bunbury Internet Café** ⊠ Carmody Pl., Bunbury ☎ 08/9791-1254. **Cyber Corner Café** ⊠ Shop 2/70, Wilmot St., Margaret River ☎ 08/9757-9388. **Novatech 2000** ⊠ Shop 10, Boulevarde Shopping Centre, Price St., Busselton ☎ 08/9754-2838.

MONEY MATTERS

Bunbury, Busselton, Margaret River, and Albany have banks where you can exchange money and cash travelers checks. ANZ, Westpac, National Australia, Bankwest and the Commonwealth Bank branches are open weekdays, generally 9:30–4. In smaller towns expect to find only one or two banks with full-service branches. However, ATMs (which accept Cirrus, Plus, Visa, and MasterCard) are in almost every town and village. All major credit cards are widely accepted at restaurants, lodgings, and shops.

ANZ ☎ 13-1314 ⊕ www.anz.com. **Bankwest** ☎ 13-1718 ⊕ www.bankwest.com.au. **Commonwealth Bank** ☎ 13-2221 ⊕ www.commbank.com.au. **National Australia** ☎ 13-2265 ⊕ www.national.com.au. **Westpac** ☎ 13-1862 ⊕ www.westpac.com.au.

TOURS

Skywest provides three- to five-day packages throughout the South West that incorporate either coaches (buses) and hotels or four-wheel-driving and camping. Westcoast Rail and Coach runs regular tours of the South West, with departures from Perth Central Station. You can go whale-watching with Naturaliste Charters, take four-wheel-drive tours into wilderness areas with Pemberton Discovery Tours, and take a cruise on Walpole's inlets with WOW Wilderness Cruises.

🚣 Naturaliste Charters ☎ 08/9755-2276 ⊕ www.whales-australia.com. **Pemberton Discovery Tours** ☎ 08/9776-0484. **Skywest** ☎ 1300/368168 ⊕ www.skywestholidays. com.au. **Westcoast Rail and Coach** ☎ 08/9221-9522. **WOW Wilderness Cruises** ☎ 08/9840-1036 ⊕ www.wowwilderness.com.au.

VISITOR INFORMATION

The Western Australia Visitor Centre maintains an excellent library of free information for visitors, including B&B and farm-stay accommodations throughout the region.

Farm and Country Holidays Association of Western Australia has extensive details of farm-stay accommodations throughout the state, from small holdings with rustic cottages to sheep stations of more than 654,000 acres where guests stay in sheep shearers' quarters and participate in station activities.

All major South West towns have visitor information centers that can arrange tours, book accommodations, and provide free information.

🚣 Albany Visitor Centre ⊠ Old Railway Station, Proudlove Parade, Albany ☎ 08/ 9841-1088 or 1800/644088 ⊕ www.albanytourist.com.au. **Bunbury Visitor Information Centre** ⊠ Old Railway Station, Carmody Pl., Bunbury ☎ 08/9791-7922 ⊕ www. bunburybreaks.com.au. **Busselton Visitor Centre** ⊠ 38 Peel Terr., Busselton ☎ 08/ 9752-1288 ⊕ www.downsouth.com.au. **Denmark Tourist Bureau** ⊠ 60 Strickland St., Denmark ☎ 08/9848-2055. **Farm and Country Holidays Association of Western Australia** ⊕ www.farmstaywa.com. **Mandurah Visitor Centre** ⊠ 75 Mandurah Terr., Mandurah ☎ 08/9550-3999 ⊕ www.peeltour.net.au. **Margaret River Visitor Centre** ⊠ 100 Bussell Hwy., Margaret River ☎ 08/9757-2911 ⊕ www.margaretriver.com. **Pemberton Visitor Centre** ⊠ Brockman St., Pemberton ☎ 08/9776-1133 ⊕ www. pembertontourist.com.au. **Western Australia Visitor Centre** ⊠ 469 Wellington St., Perth ☎ 1300/361351 ⊕ www.westernaustralia.com.

THE GOLDFIELDS

Since the day in 1893 when Paddy Hannan stumbled over a sizable gold nugget on the site of what is now Kalgoorlie, Western Australia's goldfields have ranked among the richest in the world. In fact, this "Golden Mile" is said to have had the world's highest concentration of gold. In the area's heyday, more than 100,000 men and women scattered throughout the area, all hoping to make their fortunes. It's still an astonishingly productive area, and the population of Kalgoorlie-Boulder is now increasing rapidly after falling to below 25,000 in the 1980s. Many nearby communities, however, are now nothing more than ghost towns.

Kalgoorlie-Boulder

602 km (373 mi) east of Perth.

"Kal," comprising the twin cities of Kalgoorlie and Boulder, retains the rough-and-ready air of a frontier town, with streets wide enough to accommodate the camel teams that were once a common sight here. Open-cut mines gouge the earth everywhere. Most obvious is the Super Pit,

1,090 feet deep, 3 km (2 mi) long, and 1½ km (1 mi) wide, which is expected to nearly double its depth by 2010.

The center of Kalgoorlie-Boulder is compact enough to explore on foot. Hannan Street, named after the man who discovered gold here, is the main thoroughfare and contains the bulk of the hotels and places of interest.

The miners in Kalgoorlie favored slaking their thirst at the **Exchange Hotel** before filling their bellies, but now you can do both at once. A superb example of a goldfields pub, the redecorated Exchange is replete with exquisite stained glass and pressed-tin ceilings. From here you can stumble into the hotel's Wild West Saloon or its Irish-theme Paddy's Alehouse. ✉ *Hannan and Maritana Sts.* ☎ *08/9021–2833* ⊕ *www. exchangehotelkalgoorlie.com.au.*

Hannan's North Tourist Mine provides a comprehensive look at the century-old goldfields, with audiovisual displays, a reconstructed prospector's camp, historic buildings, and opportunities to go underground or to witness a real gold-pour. The **Mining Hall of Fame** explores the history of mining in the region with exhibits and films. ✛ *Goldfields Hwy., 3 km (2 mi) from Kalgoorlie toward Menzies* ☎ *08/9026–2700* ⊕ *www.mininghall. com* 🎫 *Full tour A$20, surface tour A$15* ⊙ *Daily 9–4:30.*

The 1908 **Kalgoorlie Town Hall,** with its stamped-tin ceiling, serves as an excellent example of a common building style used around the goldfields. The cast-iron Edwardian seats in the balcony were imported from England at the turn of the 20th century. An art collection also graces the walls. ✉ *Hannan and Wilson Sts.* ☎ *08/9021–9809* 🎫 *Free* ⊙ *Weekdays 9–4:30.*

☾ The **Western Australian Museum Kalgoorlie-Boulder** is housed partly within the historic British Arms—once the narrowest pub in the Southern Hemisphere. Exhibits here include a re-created sandalwood cutter's camp, a replica of the first bank in Western Australia, and a massive red Ivanhoe headframe—once used to haul ore out from the mines—for 360-degree views of the city. ✉ *Goldfields Hwy., 3 km (2 mi) from center of Kalgoorlie toward Menzies* ☎ *08/9021–8533* ⊕ *www.museum. wa.gov.au* 🎫 *Donation suggested* ⊙ *Daily 10–4:30.*

Outside Kalgoorlie Town Hall stands **Paddy Hannan,** arguably the most photographed statue in the nation. This life-size bronze replica of the town's founder replaced the weathered original, which now stands inside the town hall.

Built from local pink stone, Kalgoorlie's **post office** has dominated Hannan Street since it was constructed in 1899.

The **York Hotel,** opposite the post office, is one of the few hotels in Kalgoorlie to remain untouched by time. Take a look at its fine staircase and intricate cupola.

The **Golden Pipeline Heritage Trail** celebrates the century since water came to the goldfields via a pipeline from Mundaring Weir (near Perth). You can follow this engineering feat from its origins all the way to Kalgoorlie. The trail is a fascinating story of gold, water, and the development of a remote and harsh land. A guidebook is available from the Kalgoorlie Goldfields Visitor Centre. ✉ *250 Hannan St., Kalgoorlie* ☏ *08/9021–1966* ⊕ *www.goldenpipeline.com.au.*

The history of Kalgoorlie would not be complete without the infamous **Hay Street** "red light" district. Today only three brothels remain. The million-dollar complex at **Langtrees 181** (✉ Hay St. ☏ 08/9026–2181) even offers tours at A$35 per person.

Where to Stay & Eat

$$–$$$ ✕ **Amalfi.** This alfresco, à la carte dining spot serves up Asian dishes, pasta, Cajun chicken, fillet of beef, char-grilled squid, and other Australian brasserie foods. Snapper crevette, lamb cutlets with sweet date couscous, and steaks bigger than the plates they're served on are house specialties. ✉ *Midas Motel, 409 Hannan St.* ☏ *08/9021–3088* ⌆ *Reservations essential* ⊟ *AE, DC, MC, V.*

$–$$ ⛳ **Quest Yelverton Kalgoorlie.** This comfortable Kalgoorlie hotel is named for Charles Yelverton O'Connor, the engineer who masterminded the 350-mi pipeline that brought a regular water supply from Mundaring Weir to Kalgoorlie in 1903. Roomy one- and two-bedroom apartments have full kitchens and modern furnishings. Spa suites have king-size beds, and two-bedroom apartments can accommodate six. ✉ *210 Egan St., 6430* ☏ *08/9022–8181* ⊟ *08/9022–8191* ⊕ *www.theyelverton.com.au* ⟿ *50 apartments* ⌂ *Room service, in-room safes, cable TV, pool, dry cleaning, laundry facilities, Internet, meeting rooms, free parking* ⊟ *AE, DC, MC, V* ⏐⊘⏐ *BP.*

$ ⛳ **Mercure Hotel Plaza.** Though just a stone's throw from busy Hannan Street, this modern hotel complex has a quiet location on a tree-lined lane. In the morning you can open your windows to the sound of kookaburras and the heady smell of eucalyptus. Rooms in the refurbished four-story building have balconies. The higher floors enjoy views over town. ✉ *45 Egan St., 6430* ☏ *08/9021–4544* ⊟ *08/9091–2195* ⊕ *www.accorhotels.com.au* ⟿ *100 rooms* ⌂ *Restaurant, room service, refrigerators, pool, hot tub, bar, free parking* ⊟ *AE, DC, MC, V.*

¢ ⛳ **York Hotel.** The historic York, dating from 1901, has retained its lovely stained-glass windows and pressed-tin ceilings. Its staircase and dining room are a historian's dream. Rooms are small but functional, and rates include breakfast. ✉ *259 Hannan St., 6430* ☏ *08/9021–2337* ⊕ *www.yorkhotelkalgoorlie.com* ⟿ *16 rooms without bath* ⌂ *Restaurant* ⊟ *AE, MC, V* ⏐⊘⏐ *BP.*

Coolgardie

561 km (348 mi) east of Perth, 39 km (24 mi) west of Kalgoorlie.

Tiny Coolgardie is probably the best-maintained ghost town in Australia. A great deal of effort has gone into preserving this historic community, where some 150 markers placed around town indicate important historic sights.

The Coolgardie Railway Station operated until 1971 and now houses the **Railway Station Museum.** The history of rail transport is explained at this museum through exhibits, photographs, books, and artifacts. Together the displays paint a gripping portrayal of a famous mining rescue that was once carried out in these goldfields. ✉ *75–87 Woodward St.* ☎ *08/9026–6388* ✆ *Donation suggested* ⊙ *Sat.–Thurs. 10–4.*

Ben Prior's Open Air Museum displays the machinery, boilers, and other equipment used to mine the region at the turn of the 20th century. If you didn't know it was a museum, you would think this was a private junkyard. Relics from Coolgardie's boom years include covered wagons, old cars, and statues of explorers. ✉ *55–59 Bayley St.* ☎ *08/9021–1966* ✆ *Free* ⊙ *Daily 24 hrs.*

Coolgardie Cemetery, with its stark, weathered headstones, recalls stories of tragedy and the grim struggle for survival in a harsh, unrelenting environment. Many of the graves remain unmarked because the identities of their occupants were lost during the wild rush to the eastern goldfields. Look for the graves of several Afghan camel drivers at the rear of the cemetery. ✉ *Great Eastern Hwy., 1 km (½ mi) east of Coolgardie* ☎ *No phone* ✆ *Free* ⊙ *Daily 24 hrs.*

Coolgardie Camel Farm lets you take a look at the animals that played a vital role in the exploration of inland Australia. Camel rides are available, including trips around the yard and one-hour, daylong, or overnight treks. Longer trips allow the chance to hunt for gems and gold. Prior booking is necessary. Reservations are essential for multiday excursions. The popular 30-minute treks cost A$18, while an hour-long trek is A$30. The A$3.50 admission fee includes entry into the camel farm, where you can meet the camels and look through the little museum that features the history of these creatures in the goldfields. Overnight camel treks are available by appointment. ✉ *Great Eastern Hwy., 4 km (2½ mi) west of Coolgardie* ☎ *08/9026–6159* ✆ *A$3.50* ⊙ *Public and school holidays.*

Goldfields A to Z

AIR TRAVEL
Qantas and Qantaslink operate daily services from Perth to Kalgoorlie and twice weekly from Adelaide to Kalgoorlie. Skywest operates services between Perth and Kalgoorlie daily except Saturday.

🛪 **Qantas/Qantaslink** ☎ 13-1313 ⊕ www.qantas.com.au. **Skywest** ☎ 1300/660088 ⊕ www.skywest.com.au.

BUS TRAVEL
Greyhound Australia operates a Friday service from Perth to Adelaide, with stops at Coolgardie, Kalgoorlie, and Norseman. Perth–Goldfields Express operates a regular luxury coach service linking Perth to Kalgoorlie, Menzies, Leonora, and Laverton.

🛪 **Greyhound Australia** ☎ 13-1499 ⊕ www.greyhound.com.au. **Perth–Goldfields Express** ✉ 16 Lane St., Kalgoorlie ☎ 08/9021-2954 or 1800/620440.

EMERGENCIES
In an emergency, dial **000** to reach an ambulance, the police, or the fire department.

🛪 **Kalgoorlie Regional Hospital** ✉ Piccadilly St., Kalgoorlie ☎ 08/9080-5888.

MAIL, INTERNET & SHIPPING

The Netzone Internet Lounge in Kalgoorlie is open weekdays 10–7 and weekends 10–5. Kalgoorlie's main post office is on Hannan Street.

ℹ Australia Post Kalgoorlie ✉ 204 Hannan St., Kalgoorlie ☎ 08/9021-3313. **Netzone Internet Lounge** ✉ Shop 6, St. Barbara's Sq., Kalgoorlie ☎ 08/9091-4178.

TAXIS

Kalgoorlie taxis are available around the clock.

ℹ Kalgoorlie-Boulder Taxis ☎ 08/9091-5233. **Twin City Cabs** ☎ 08/9021-2177 or 131-008.

TOURS

Goldfields Air Services has an air tour that gives you a bird's-eye view of the open-cut mining technique now used instead of more traditional shaft mining. Goldrush Tours runs excellent tours on the goldfields' history and ghost towns, the profusion of wildflowers in the area, and the ghost town of Coolgardie. Yamatji Bitja runs individually tailored experiences with an Aboriginal guide.

ℹ Goldfields Air Services ☎ 08/9093-2116 or 1800/620440. **Goldrush Tours** ✉ 16 Lane St., Kalgoorlie ☎ 08/9021-2954 ⊕ www.goldrushtours.info. **Yamatji Bitja** ✉ 16 Richardson St., Boulder ☎ 08/9093-3745 or 0407/387602.

TRAIN TRAVEL

The clean and efficient *Prospector* is an appropriate name for the train that runs a daily service between Perth and Kalgoorlie. A new train, which came into service in June 2004, is capable of attaining speeds up to 160 km (100 mi) per hour—which cuts the travel time to just under six hours. It departs from the East Perth Railway Terminal. The *Indian Pacific* stops at Kalgoorlie four times a week as its journeys across the continent from Perth to Sydney via Adelaide.

ℹ East Perth Railway Terminal ✉ W. Parade, East Perth. *Indian Pacific* ☎ 13-2147 ⊕ www.trainways.com.au. *Prospector* ☎ 1300/662205 ⊕ www.transwa.wa.gov.au.

VISITOR INFORMATION

The Coolgardie Visitor Centre is open weekdays 9–5. Staff members at the Kalgoorlie Goldfields Visitor Centre are as enthusiastic and welcoming as they are knowledgeable. The office is open weekdays 8:30–5, weekends and holidays 9–3.

ℹ Coolgardie Visitor Centre ✉ 62 Bayley St., Coolgardie ☎ 08/9026-6090. **Kalgoorlie Goldfields Visitor Centre** ✉ 250 Hannan St., Kalgoorlie ☎ 08/9021-1966 or 1800/004653 🖷 08/9021-2180 ⊕ www.kalgoorlie.com/tourism.

Karijini National Park

★ *1,411 km (875 mi) northeast of Perth, 285 km (178 mi) south of Port Hedland.*

The huge rocks, crags, and gorges that make up the Hamersley Range, in the Pilbara region of the northwestern corner of the state, are among the most ancient land surfaces in the world. Sediments deposited by an inland sea more than 2.5 billion years ago were forced up by movements in the earth's crust and slowly weathered by natural elements through succeeding eons. Much of the 320-km (200-mi) range is today being mined for its rich iron deposits, but a small section is incorporated into the national park. Towering cliffs, lush fern-filled gullies, and richly colored rock formations make this one of the most beautiful parks in Australia.

Karijini has trails for hikers of every level. The one-hour Dales Gorge Trail is the most popular and easily accessible, with the Fortescue Falls and Ferns pool (a leisurely 20 minutes from the parking lot) as a highlight. Other trails are far more challenging and should be undertaken only by experienced hikers, who must brave freezing water, cling to rock ledges, and scramble over boulders through the Joffre, Knox, and Hancock gorges. You should notify a ranger before hiking into any of these gorges.

Because summer temperatures often top 43°C (110°F) in this area, it's best to visit in the cooler months, between May and August.

Where to Stay

There are a couple of basic motels in the fast-growing mining town of Tom Price, about 50 km (31 mi) west of the park. Food and supplies can be purchased there as well. Drinking water is available at Yampire and Joffre roads and at Mujina Roadhouse.

Camping is permitted only in designated sites at Circular Pool and Savannah Campground. Camping is no longer permitted at Weano and Joffre. Campsites have no facilities except toilets, but gas barbecues are free. Burning wood is prohibited. Entry fees are A$9 per car, plus a A$10 camping fee (for two people). You can pay by self-registration at either of two entrances near Ranger Station and Mount Bruce Road.

¢ ⚑ **Tom Price Tourist Park.** It's nice to find a few comforts in this remote area, and this place has them: simple one- and two-bedroom chalets, caravan and camping sites, and dorm-style backpackers facilities, including a shared kitchen and small shop for buying necessities. ⊠ *Nameless Valley Rd., Tom Price 6751* ☎ *08/9189–1515* 🖷 *08/9189–1515* ⌖ *14 rooms* ⚒ *BBQs, pool, playground, laundry facilities* ⊟ *MC, V.*

Karijini National Park A to Z

AIR TRAVEL

Northwest Regional Airlines provides a link between four of Australia's tourism icons: Ningaloo Reef, Karijini National Park, Broome's Cable Beach, and the Bungle Bungle Ranges. The airline has several holiday packages to locations on the route network. Qantaslink flies from Perth to Port Hedland and Tom Price.

⚑ **Northwest Regional Airlines** ☎ 1300/136629 ⊕ www.northwestregional.com.au. **Qantas/Qantaslink** ☎ 13–1313 ⊕ www.qantas.com.au.

CAR TRAVEL

You can best reach this remote park by flying from Perth to Port Hedland and renting a car from there, or by flying to Broome (⇨ The Kimberley *in* Chapter 11) and driving 551 km (342 mi) on the Great Northern Highway to Port Hedland. From the west, leave the North West Coastal Highway near Nanutarra and head toward Tom Price. Enter the park via Marandoo Road. From the east, leave the Great Northern

Highway 35 km (22 mi) south of Munjina Roadhouse and travel west along Karijini Drive to the Banjima Drive intersection. Turn right and travel 8 km (5 mi) to the Dales Gorge turnoff, or continue west along Banjima Drive to Kalamina, Joffre, Weano, and Hancock gorges and Oxers Lookout. From Roebourne, head south to Millstream Chichester National Park, then continue east along the Roebourne–Munjina Road. Finally, turn southwest along Nanutarra–Wittenoom Road through Rio Tinto Gorge, past Hamersley Gorge turnoff, and southeast onto the Hamersley–Mount Bruce Road. All roads within the park are unpaved. Yampire Gorge Road is closed and there's no access.

TELEPHONES

There's a public telephone at the visitor center in the parking lot, and another at the Savannah campgrounds. There is no cell phone reception in the park.

TOURS

Dingo's Treks has weekly adventure tours of Karijini National Park for groups of 10 or fewer. Your meals, drinks, and *swag* (a soft bedroll backpack) are included. Lestok Tours has full-day trips to Karijini National Park Gorges, departing from Tom Price, with swimming and guided walks.
🔲 **Dingo's Treks** ✉ 59 Kingsmill St., Port Hedland 6721 ☎ 08/9172-5666 ⊕ www. dingotrek.com.au. **Lestok Tours** ✉ Tom Price 6751 ☎ 08/9189-2032 ⊕ www.lestoktours. com.au.

VISITOR INFORMATION

The Karijini Visitor Centre (managed by the Department of Conservation and Land Management in partnership with the traditional landowners) interprets the natural and cultural history of the area. The Karratha Visitor Center is open April–November, weekdays 8:30–5, and weekends and public holidays 9–4. Hours December–March are weekdays 9–5 and Saturday 9–noon; closed Sunday and holidays. The Tom Price Visitor Centre is open April–September, weekdays 8:30–5:30, weekends and holidays 9–noon. October to March it's open weekdays 8:30–2:30, Saturday 9–noon; closed Sunday and holidays.
🔲 **Australia's North West Tourism** ✉ Shop 3, Karratha Village Shopping Centre, Sharpe Ave., Karratha 6714 ☎ 08/9185-5455 ⊕ www.pilbara.com. **Karratha Visitor Centre** ✉ 4548 Karratha Rd. Karratha 6741 ☎ 08/9144-4620 ⊕ www.thecentralpilbaracoast. com. **Karijini Visitor Centre** ✉ Banyjima Dr., Karijini National Park ☎ 08/9189-8121 🖨 08/9189-8113. **Tom Price Visitor Centre** ✉ Central Ave. and Tamarind St., Tom Price 6751 ☎ 08/9188-1112.

MONKEY MIA & NINGALOO REEF

Two marine wonders await in the northwestern corner of the state. At Monkey Mia, a World Heritage Site, dolphins interact freely with human beings. Ningaloo Reef Marine Park is a great spot to dive or snorkel among coral reefs, whale sharks, manta rays, and a wealth of other fabulous sea creatures.

Monkey Mia

Fodor's Choice   *985 km (611 mi) north of Perth, 450 km (280 mi) from Karijini Na-*
★   *tional Park.*

Monkey Mia is a World Heritage Site and the setting for one of the world's
most extraordinary natural wonders; nowhere else do wild dolphins interact so freely with human beings. In 1964 a woman from one of the
makeshift fishing camps in the area hand-fed one of the dolphins that
regularly followed the fishing boats home. Other dolphins followed that
lead, and an extensive family of wild dolphins now comes of its own
accord to be fed.

For many, standing in the shallow waters of Shark Bay to hand-feed a
dolphin is the experience of a lifetime. There are no set feeding times.
Dolphins show up at any hour of the day at the public beach, where
park rangers feed them. Rangers share their food with people who want
to get close to the sea creatures. The Monkey Mia Visitor Centre has
videos and information. ⚐ *Follow Hwy. 1 north from Perth for 806
km (500 mi) to Denham–Hamelin Rd., then follow signs* ☎ *08/
9948–1366* ☒ *Free* ☉ *Information center daily 7–4:30.*

Where to Stay

¢–$$ ⊡ **Monkey Mia Dolphin Resort.** This resort has everything from un-
powered tent sites to shared rooms and houses. Budget travelers sack
out in the five- and seven-bed dorms, while groups can rent a private
home or share one with other guests. Eight villas open straight onto
Dolphin Beach, while other accommodations are surrounded by trop-
ical gardens. Dolphin-watch cruises leave the resort's jetty daily at 10:30
AM. Several ecotours and cruises are escorted by a resident naturalist.
⚐ *Box 119, Denham 6537* ☎ *08/9948–1320 or 1800/653611* ⎙ *08/
9948–1034* ⊕ *www.monkeymia.com.au* ⊷ *8 villas, 26 homes, 11
dorms with 78 beds, 200 campsites* ⚲ *Restaurant, café, grocery, ten-
nis court, pool, hot tub, beach, dock, volleyball, bar, laundry facili-
ties, free parking; no phones in some rooms, no room TVs* ▭ *AE, DC,
MC, V.*

⌜ en route ⌟   Between Monkey Mia, 354 km (220 mi) south, and Ningaloo Reef
Marine Park, 370 km (230 mi) north, the town of **Carnarvon** is a
popular stopover. Stroll the Fascine, a palm-lined harborside
boardwalk, where the Gascoyne River flows into the Indian Ocean.
One Mile Jetty, built in 1899, is the longest jetty in the north of
Western Australia, and you can walk to the end or take the Coffee
Pot Ocean Tramway. It's a top local fishing spot, with mulloway,
tailor, mackerel, trevally, and bream below year-round. From March
to July you can watch locals catch blue manna crabs in drop nets.
Drive 70 km (44 mi) north of Carnarvon to view the **Blow Holes,**
where ocean swells force trapped air and streams of water up to 66
feet in the air.

Ningaloo Reef Marine Park

Fodor's Choice   *1,512 km (937 mi) north of Perth, 550 km (341 mi) from Monkey Mia.*
★

Some of Australia's most pristine coral reef runs 251 km (156 mi) along the coast of the Exmouth Peninsula, very far north of Perth. A happy conjunction of migratory routes and accessibility makes it one of the best places on Earth to see huge manta rays, giant whale sharks, humpback whales, nesting turtles, and the annual coral spawning. Exmouth makes a good overnight base for exploring the marine park.

Also worth seeing near Exmouth is the **Cape Range National Park**, including the Yardie Creek Gorge. ✛ *Follow N.W. Coastal Hwy. north 1,170 km (725 mi) to Minilya turnoff; Exmouth is 374 km (232 mi) farther north.*

Where to Stay

The town of Exmouth, close to the tip of North West Cape at the northernmost edge of Ningaloo Reef Marine Park, is the biggest center for lodging, dining, shopping, and tours. Coral Bay, the park's southern gateway, has a laid-back setting that's ideal for getting close to nature.

¢–$$ 🏨 **Bayview Coral Bay.** The beachfront overlooking Coral Bay makes this property especially appealing. Two-bedroom holiday units here sleep up to six, while cabins sleep four. Most of the RV and camp sites have electricity. This is an ideal spot for families and those seeking a relaxing environment near the water. The on-site café serves basic pizza, pasta, steak, and fish-and-chips. ⊠ *Robinson St., 6701* ☎ *08/9942–5932 or 08/ 9385–6655* 🖷 *08/9385–7413* ⊕ *www.coralbaywa.com* ⇋ *8 holiday units, 12 cabins, 250 powered sites* ♨ *Café, BBQs, 2 tennis courts, pool, volleyball, playground, laundry facilities, free parking* ⊟ *MC, V.*

$ 🏨 **Sea Breeze Resort.** This Best Western hotel 5 km (3 mi) north of Exmouth occupies the converted officers' quarters of the town's former U.S. Naval Base. The small "cyclone-proof" property has an à la carte restaurant and a bar. All rooms have queen-size beds (if you're tall and sleeping alone, you can also order an extra-long single bed). Daily dive trips and whale-shark tours are scheduled. ⊠ *Harold E. Holt Naval Base, 116 North C St., 6707* ☎ *08/9949–1800* 🖷 *08/9949–1300* ⊕ *www. seabreezeresort.com.au* ⇋ *27 rooms* ♨ *Restaurant, room service, IDD phones, in-room data ports, tennis court, pool, wading pool, gym, squash, bar, laundry facilities* ⊟ *MC, V.*

Monkey Mia & Ningaloo Reef A to Z

AIR TRAVEL

Skywest has daily flights from Perth to Learmonth Airport, 37 km (23 mi) from Exmouth and 120 km (75 mi) from Coral Bay. A shuttle bus meets every flight and for a fee you can catch a ride to Exmouth. Skywest also connects Learmonth with Karratha to the north.

🖪 Skywest ☎ 1300/660088 ⊕ www.skywest.com.au.

BUS TRAVEL

Greyhound Australia and Integrity Coach Lines service Monkey Mia, Carnarvon, Coral Bay, and Exmouth. The Exmouth Visitor Centre on Murat Road is the booking agent and bus terminal for these companies. Ningaloo Reef Bus has a daily bus service from Exmouth to Ningaloo Reef, departing at 8:30 AM and returning at 4:30 PM.

Greyhound Australia ☎ 13-1499 ⊕ www.greyhound.com.au. **Integrity Coach Lines** ☎ 08/9226-1339 or 1800/226339 ⊕ www.intregitycoachlines.com.au. **Ningaloo Reef Bus** ☎ 1800/999941.

TOURS

Ningaloo Reef Marine National Park, accessible from both Exmouth and Coral Bay, has opportunities to mix with the local wildlife. Coral Bay Adventures takes small groups out to the reef to swim with the whale sharks from March to June. Their glass-bottom boat also allows you to view the coral and tropical fish life without getting wet. Monkey Mia Yacht Charters has daily cruises ranging from one to eight hours on board the *Aristocat 2* catamaran; passengers get to see dolphins, dugongs, turtles, sea snakes, and sharks in the wild. Wildsight Tours also offers daily cruises on board their 60-foot catamaran, including a Dugong Cruise to see these elusive sea creatures.

Exmouth Diving Centre and Ningaloo Reef Dive both offer dive tours to various sites on Ningaloo Reef, including diving with whale sharks. For anglers—both expert and neophyte—Sportfishing Safaris operates daily fishing trips from Monkey Mia. Black snapper, pink snapper, cobia, mack tuna, mackerel, bluebone groper, coral trout, trevally, tailor, sharks, and mulloway are among the species seasonally available here; the best time of the year to fish is between March and August. Half-day fishing trips around Monkey Mia cost A$90 per person. Coral Bay Ocean Game Fishing also offers half-day or full-day fishing tours.

Coral Bay Adventures ☎ 08/9942-5955 ⊕ www.coralbayadventures.com.au. **Coral Bay Ocean Game Fishing** ☎ 08/9942-5874. **Exmouth Diving Centre** ☎ 08/9949-1201 ⊕ www.exmouthdiving.com.au. **Monkey Mia Yacht Charters** ☎ 08/9948-1446 ⊕ www.monkey-mia.net. **Ningaloo Reef Dive** ☎ 08/9942-5824 ⊕ www.ningalooreefdive.com. **Sportfishing Safaris** ☎ 08/9948-1846 ⊕ www.sportfish.com.au. **Wildsight Tours** ☎ 1800/241481 ⊕ www.monkeymiawildsights.com.au.

VISITOR INFORMATION

Carnarvon Tourist Bureau ✉ 11 Robinson St., Carnarvon 6701 ☎ 08/9942-1146 ⊕ www.coralbayonline.com. **Exmouth Visitor Centre** ✉ Murat Rd., Exmouth ☎ 08/9949-1176 or 1800/287328 ⊕ www.exmouthwa.com.au. **Monkey Mia Visitor Centre** ✛ 23 km (14 mi.) east of Denham on the eastern shore of Peron Peninsula. ☎ 08/9948-1366 ⊕ www.sharkbay.asn.au. **Shark Bay Tourist Bureau** ✉ 71 Knight St., Denham ☎ 08/9948-1253 ⊕ www.ozpal.com/tourist.

Adventure Vacations

13

Antarctica

Bicycling

Bushwalking (Hiking)

Camel Trekking

Cross-Country Skiing

Diving

Downhill Skiing

Four-Wheel-Drive Tours

Horseback Riding

Rafting

Sailing

Updated by
Liza Power

YOU'LL MISS AN IMPORTANT ELEMENT of Australia if you don't get away from the cities to explore "the bush" that is so deeply ingrained in the Australian character. Many of the adventure vacations today were journeys of exploration only a generation ago.

Adventure vacations are commonly split into soft and hard adventures. A hard adventure requires a substantial degree of physical participation; in soft adventures the destination rather than the means of travel is often what makes it an adventure. With most companies, the adventure guides' knowledge of flora and fauna—and love of the bush—is matched by a level of competence that ensures your safety even in dangerous situations.

Tour Operators

There are far more adventure-tour operators in Australia than it's possible to include in this chapter. Most are small and receive little publicity outside their local areas, so contact the relevant state tourist office if you have a specific interest.

Adventure Associates. ✆ *Box 612, Bondi Junction, NSW 2022* ☎ *02/9389–7466* 🖷 *02/9369–1853* ⊕ *www.adventureassociates.com.*
Adventure Center. ✉ *1311 63rd St., Suite 200, Emeryville, CA 94608 U.S.* ☎ *510/654–1879 or 800/228–8747* 🖷 *510/654–4200* ⊕ *www.adventure-center.com.*
Adventure Charters of Kangaroo Island. ✆ *Box 169, Kingscote, Kangaroo Island, SA 5223* ☎ *08/8553–9119* 🖷 *08/8553–9122* ⊕ *www.adventurecharters.com.au.*
Adventure Company. ✆ *Box 1938, Cairns, QLD 4870* ☎ *07/4051–4777* 🖷 *07/4051–4888* ⊕ *www.adventures.com.au.*
Adventure Guides Australia. ✆ *Box 230, Beechworth, VIC 3747* ☎ *03/5728–1804* ⊕ *www.adventureguidesaustralia.com.au.*
Aurora Expeditions. ✆ *182A Cumberland St., The Rocks, NSW 2000* ☎ *02/9252–1033* ⊕ *www.auroraexpeditions.com.au.*
Australian Wild Escapes. ✆ *Box 172, West Pennant Hills, NSW 2125* ☎ *02/9980–8788* 🖷 *02/9980–9616* ⊕ *www.australianwildescapes.com.*
Beyond Tours. ✉ *1 Pony Ridge, Belair, SA 5052* ☎ *08/8374–3580* 🖷 *08/8374–3091* ⊕ *www4.tpgi.com.au/users/andreacc/beyondtours.*
Bicheno Dive Centre. ✉ *2 Scuba Ct., Bicheno, TAS 7215* ☎ *03/6375–1138* 🖷 *03/6375–1504* ⊕ *www.bichenodive.com.*
Blue Mountains Adventure Company. ✉ *84a Main St., Katoomba, NSW 2780* ☎ *02/4782–1271* 🖷 *02/4782–1277* ⊕ *bmac.com.au.*
Bogong Horseback Adventures. ✆ *Box 230, Mt. Beauty, VIC 3699* ☎ *03/5754–4849* 🖷 *03/5754–4181* ⊕ *www.bogonghorse.com.au.*
Boomerang Bicycle Tours. ✆ *Box 5054, Kingsdene, NSW 2118* ☎ *02/9890–1996* 🖷 *02/9630–3436* ⊕ *members.ozemail.com.au/~ozbike.*
Camels Australia. ✆ *PMB 74 Stuarts Well, Alice Springs, NT 0872* ☎ *08/8956–0925* 🖷 *08/8956–0909* ⊕ *www.camels-australia.com.au.*
Cradle Mountain Huts. ✆ *Box 1879, Launceston, TAS 7250* ☎ *03/6331–9339* 🖷 *03/6331–9338* ⊕ *www.cradlehuts.com.au.*

Croydon Travel. ✉ *34 Main St., Croydon, VIC 3136* ☎ *03/9725–8555* 📠 *03/9723–6700* ⊕ *www.croydontravel.com.au.*

Discover West Holidays. 🖃 *Box 7355, Perth, WA 6850* ☎ *08/6263–6475* ⊕ *www.discoverwest.com.au.*

Dive Adventures. ✉ *32 York St., 9th level, Sydney, NSW 2000* ☎ *02/ 9299–4633* 📠 *02/9299–4644* ⊕ *www.diveadventures.com.*

Ecotrek Bogong Jack Adventures. 🖃 *Box 4, Kangarilla, SA 5157* ☎ *08/ 8383–7198* 📠 *08/8383–7377* ⊕ *www.ecotrek.com.au.*

Equitrek Australia. ✉ *5 King Rd., Ingleside, NSW 2101* ☎ *02/9913–9408* 📠 *02/9970–6303* ⊕ *www.equitrek.com.au.*

Exmouth Diving Centre. ✉ *Payne St., Exmouth, WA 6707* ☎ *08/9949–1201* 📠 *08/9949–1680* ⊕ *www.exmouthdiving.com.au.*

Freycinet Experience. 🖃 *Box 43, Battery Point, TAS 7004* ☎ *03/ 6223–7565* 📠 *03/6224–1315* ⊕ *www.freycinet.com.au.*

Frontier Camel Tours. 🖃 *Box 2836, Alice Springs, NT 0871* ☎ *08/ 8953–0444* 📠 *08/8955–5015* ⊕ *www.cameltours.com.au.*

Kangaroo Island Odysseys. ✉ *34 Addison St., Kingscote, Kangaroo Island, SA 5223* ☎ *08/8553–0386* 📠 *08/8553–0387* ⊕ *www.kiodysseys. com.au.*

Kangaroo Island Wilderness Tours. ✉ *42 Cook St., Parndana, Kangaroo Island, SA 5220* ☎ *08/8559–5033* ⊕ *www.wildernesstours.com.au.*

Kimberley Wilderness Adventures. ✉ *475 Hampton St., Hampton, VIC 3188* ☎ *03/9277–8444* 📠 *03/9251–0721* ⊕ *www.kimberleywilderness. com.au.*

King Island Dive Charter. 🖃 *Box 1, Currie, TAS 7256* ☎ *03/6461–1133* 📠 *03/6461–1293* ⊕ *www.kingislanddivecharter.com.au.*

Live Adrenalin. 🖃 *80 McDougall St., Kirribilli, NSW 2061* ☎ *02/ 8456–7777* 📠 *02/9923–1562* ⊕ *www.adrenalin.com.au.*

Megalong Australian Heritage Centre. ✉ *Megalong Rd., Megalong Valley, NSW 2785* ☎ *02/4787–8188* 📠 *02/4787–9116* ⊕ *www.megalong.cc.*

Mike Ball Dive Adventures. ✉ *143 Lake St., Cairns, QLD 4870* ☎ *07/ 4031–5484 in Australia, 800/952–4319 in U.S.* ⊕ *www.mikeball.com.*

Morrell Adventure Travel. ✉ *64 Jindabyne Rd., Berridale, NSW 2628* ☎ *02/ 6456–3681* 📠 *02/6465–3679* ⊕ *www.morrell.com.au.*

Paddy Pallin Jindabyne. ✉ *5 Kosciuszko Rd, Jindabyne, NSW 2627* ☎ *02/6456–2922* 📠 *02/6456–2836* ⊕ *www.adventurepro.com.au/ paljin.*

Peregrine Adventures. ✉ *258 Lonsdale St., Melbourne, VIC 3000* ☎ *03/ 9663–8611* 📠 *03/9663–8618* ⊕ *www.peregrineadventures.com/ antarctica.*

Pro Dive Travel. ✉ *330 Wattle St., Suite 34, Level 2, Ultimo, NSW 2007* ☎ *02/9281–6166* 📠 *02/9281–0660* ⊕ *www.prodive.com.au.*

ProSail. 🖃 *Box 973, Airlie Beach, QLD 4802* ☎ *07/4946–5433* 📠 *07/ 4948–8609* ⊕ *www.prosail.com.au.*

Reynella Kosciuszko Rides. ✉ *Bolaro Rd., Adaminaby, NSW 2630* ☎ *02/ 6454–2386* 📠 *02/6454–2530* ⊕ *www.reynellarides.com.au.*

Sail Australia. 🖃 *Box 417, Cremorne, NSW 2090* ☎ *02/4322–8227* 📠 *02/ 4322–8199* ⊕ *www.sailaustralia.com.au.*

Stoneys High Country. 🖃 *Box 287, Mansfield, VIC 3722* ☎ *03/5775–2212* 📠 *03/5775–2598* ⊕ *www.stoneys.com.au.*

Sydney by Sail. ✉ *National Maritime Museum, 2 Murray St., Darling Harbour, NSW 2000* ☎ *02/9280–1110* 📠 *02/9280–1119* ⊕ *sydneybysail.com.*
Tasmanian Expeditions. ✉ *23 Earl St., Launceston, TAS 7250* ☎ *03/6334–3477* 📠 *03/6334–3463* ⊕ *www.tas-ex.com/tas-ex.*
Tasmanian Wild River Adventures. ✆ *Box 90, Sandy Bay, TAS 7006* ☎ *0409/977506* 📠 *03/6227–9141* ⊕ *www.wildrivers.com.au.*
Walkabout Gourmet Adventures. ✆ *Box 52, Dinner Plain, VIC 3898* ☎ *03/5159–6556* 📠 *03/5159–6508* ⊕ *www.walkaboutgourmet.com.*
Wilderness Challenge. ✆ *Box 254, Cairns, QLD 4870* ☎ *07/4035–4488* 📠 *07/4035–4188* ⊕ *www.wilderness-challenge.com.au.*
Wildwater Adventures. ✉ *754 Pacific Hwy., Boambee South, NSW 2450* ☎ *02/6653–3500* 📠 *02/6653–3900* ⊕ *www.wildwateradventures.com.au.*
World Expeditions. ✉ *71 York St., 5th fl., Sydney, NSW 2000* ☎ *02/9279–0188* 📠 *02/9279–0566* ⊕ *www.worldexpeditions.com.au.*

Antarctica

Australia competes with Argentina, Chile, and New Zealand as one of the major stepping-off points for trips to Antarctica. Indeed, Australia claims the largest share of Antarctica for administrative purposes, with the Australian Antarctic Territory comprising 42% of the continent. Passenger ships specially adapted for the frozen continent depart for the Ross Sea from the Tasmanian port of Hobart between December and February.

A faster and cheaper option is to take a one-day Qantas overflight of Antarctica organized by Croydon Travel. Taking off from Sydney, Melbourne, or Perth, you fly directly to the ice continent. You'll have good views of the mountains and ice, although you'll still be too high to see animals. It's worthwhile paying extra for a window seat not over the wing.

Season: December–February.
Locations: Cruises from Hobart; flights from Sydney, Melbourne, and Perth, with connections from other Australian cities.
Cost: From A$1,299 for one day to A$15,000 for three weeks.
Tour Operators: Adventure Associates, Croydon Travel, Peregrine Adventures, World Expeditions.

Bicycling

Cycling is an excellent way to explore a small region, allowing you to cover more ground than on foot and to observe far more than you could from the window of a car or bus. Riding down quiet country lanes is a great way to relax and get fit at the same time. Cycling rates as a hard adventure because of the amount of exercise involved.

New South Wales

Against the backdrop of Australia's highest peaks, Blue Mountains Adventure Company has several one-day rides on mountain bikes through the plunging walled valleys that border Sydney, including a spectacular ride along Narrow Neck and through a glowworm tunnel. Boomerang

Bicycle Tours offers one- to six-day tours of the Hunter Valley (including the region's boutique wineries), Snowy Mountains, Southern Highlands, and Sydney. High-quality front-suspension mountain bikes, helmets, wind jackets, camping gear, and meals are all supplied. An air-conditioned support vehicle, and all accommodation (from guesthouses and wilderness resorts to hotels).

Season: Year-round.
Locations: Blue Mountains, Snowy Mountains, Southern Highlands.
Cost: From A$90 for a half day and A$160 for one day to about A$900 for seven days.
Tour Operators: Blue Mountains Adventure Company, Boomerang Bicycle Tours, Morrell Adventure Travel.

Queensland

Spreading inland from the coastal city of Cairns, the Atherton Tableland is a mixture of tropical rain forests and sleepy towns—an area to be savored rather than rushed. The Adventure Company operates a two-day trip that takes in some of the natural wonders of the region, with one night in a historic country pub.

Season: Year-round.
Location: Atherton Tableland.
Cost: A$400.
Tour Operator: Adventure Company.

South Australia

South Australia affords gentle cycling on quiet country roads, particularly on Kangaroo Island and around the famous wine regions of the Barossa and Clare valleys, as well as more challenging mountain-bike expeditions into the rugged Flinders Ranges, far to the north of Adelaide. Ecotrek Bogong Jack Adventures has several such cycling trips, varying from weekends in the wine areas to one-week rides on Kangaroo Island and through the Flinders Ranges.

Season: April–October.
Locations: Barossa and Clare valleys, Flinders Ranges, Kangaroo Island.
Cost: From A$525 for a weekend to around A$2,750 for a 10-day Flinders Ranges safari.
Tour Operator: Ecotrek Bogong Jack Adventures.

Tasmania

The relatively small size of Tasmania makes cycling a great option for exploring. The classic tour is Tasmanian Expeditions' Cycle Tasmania, a 6-day trip from Launceston that leads through pastoral lands down to the fishing villages of the east coast. The 13-day tour, Tasmanian Panorama, includes cycling, bushwalking, and rafting. All of these tours are also sold by World Expeditions.

Season: November–March.
Locations: Central Tasmania and the north and east coasts.
Cost: From A$490 for 2 days, to A$1,980 for 6 days or A$2,490 for 13 days, including camping equipment, support vehicle, bicycles, and all meals.
Tour Operators: Tasmanian Expeditions, World Expeditions.

Victoria

The two main areas of interest in the state are the Great Ocean Road and the northeast. However, although it's a spectacular ride, the Great Ocean Road is fairly narrow and heavily used, and therefore best avoided during the peak December and January summer holidays. The northeast is a more varied experience, combining sights of contemporary wineries, country towns that thrived during the gold boom, and the forests and hills of the Australian Alps.

Season: October–April.
Locations: Great Ocean Road, northeast Victoria.
Cost: From A$550 for a two-day tour of the northeast wineries to around A$1,490 for a six-day tour of the Alpine region.
Tour Operator: Ecotrek Bogong Jack Adventures.

Bushwalking (Hiking)

The Australian bush is unique. The olive-green foliage of the eucalyptus may seem drab at first, but when you walk into a clearing carpeted with thick grass and surrounded by stately blue gums, the appeal (and wonderful fragrance) of these trees becomes evident. Chances are good that you'll cross paths with kangaroos, wallabies, goannas, and even echidnas (spiny anteaters)—but your success rate will be much higher if you travel with an expert guide. Depending on the type of trail, bushwalking can be a soft or hard adventure. Associated high-adrenaline hard adventures are abseiling (rappelling) and canyoning, forms of vertical bushwalking well suited to the Blue Mountains of New South Wales.

New South Wales

The scope for casual bushwalking in New South Wales is extensive. One of the finest one-day walks in the Blue Mountains begins in Blackheath and winds through Grand Canyon. The National Pass to Wentworth Falls is also stunning. The Snowy Mountains beyond Perisher are excellent for walking, as are the national parks to the north—especially Barrington Tops, a basalt-capped plateau with rushing streams that have carved deep chasms in the extensive rain forest. The same areas are ideal for longer treks, too.

Paddy Pallin Jindabyne operates three- to nine-day camping and lodge-based walking tours in the Snowy Mountains between November and April. Australian Wild Escapes specializes in small-group tours (two-person minimum).

The deeply eroded sandstone canyons of the Blue Mountains provide exhilarating terrain for abseiling as well as bushwalking. There's intense competition among tour operators in this area, so a full day of canyoning in the spectacular Grand Canyon or the sublime Claustral Canyon costs less than A$100, including lunch. Blue Mountains Adventure Company has more than a dozen different canyoning, climbing, and abseiling programs around this area.

Season: Year-round.
Locations: Barrington Tops, Blue Mountains, Snowy Mountains.

Cost: Rates start at A$75 for a half day. Longer trips cost on average about A$135 per day, including packs, equipment, guide, and food.
Tour Operators: Australian Wild Escapes, Blue Mountains Adventure Company, Morrell Adventure Travel, Paddy Pallin Jindabyne.

South Australia

The Flinders Ranges is Australia's most sensational Outback park. The arid sandstone hills are actually the stumps of eroded mountains, and they're a first-rate site for bushwalking, wildlife-watching, and photography. In several places the hills are dissected by creeks lined with towering river red gums, making fine spots for camping. The Gammon Ranges, the northern extremity of the Flinders Ranges, are even more rugged and severe, and highly recommended for hikers who enjoy challenging terrain. In addition to those in the Flinders and Gammon ranges, Ecotrek Bogong Jack Adventures also operates walks on Kangaroo Island.

Season: April–October.
Locations: Flinders Ranges, Gammon Ranges, Kangaroo Island.
Cost: From A$535 for three days to A$1,299 for seven days.
Tour Operator: Ecotrek Bogong Jack Adventures.

Tasmania

At one time some of the best overnight walks in Tasmania were major expeditions suitable only for the highly experienced and very fit. Plenty of these treks are still available, including the nine-day South Coast Track Expedition operated by Tasmanian Expeditions. The trail includes some easy stretches along pristine, secluded beaches, as well as difficult legs through rugged coastal mountains. You must fly into this remote area. It's the combination of difficult trails, extreme isolation, and the likelihood of foul weather that gives this walk spice.

Much easier hiking terrain can be found on the Freycinet Peninsula, on the east coast about a three-hour drive north of Hobart. Much of the peninsula can be explored only on foot. The road ends at the pink granite domes of the Hazards, which form a rampart across the middle of the peninsula. Beyond lies a pristine seascape of white-sand coves and sparkling water, edged with granite knuckles. The only guided hike is the four-day walk conducted by Freycinet Experience. The optional 18-km (11-mi) hike over Mt. Graham on the second day is just for experienced trekkers. Hikers carry light day packs and spend the first two nights in comfortable camps, complete with wooden platforms, beds, and pillows. The final night is in a Tasmanian hardwood lodge situated to take advantage of the best views.

The best-known walk in Tasmania is the trail from Cradle Mountain to Lake St. Clair. It's so popular that boardwalks have been placed along some sections to prevent the path from turning into a quagmire. The walk starts and finishes in dense forest, but much of it runs along exposed highland ridges. The construction of the Cradle Mountain Huts has made this trail far more accessible. However, these huts are available only to hikers on one of Cradle Mountain Huts' escorted walks. Huts are well heated and extensively supplied; there are even warm showers. Other operators continue to conduct camping tours along the trail as well as elsewhere in Tasmania.

Season: November–May.
Locations: Central highlands; south, east, and west coasts.
Cost: From about A$130 per day, including camping equipment and meals, to A$1,895 for the 6-day Cradle Mountain Huts walk, or about A$2,490 for a comprehensive 13-day tour of the island.
Tour Operators: Cradle Mountain Huts, Freycinet Experience, Peregrine Adventures, Tasmanian Expeditions, World Expeditions.

Victoria

Victoria's alpine region affords bushwalking vacations to suit every taste. Ecotrek Bogong Jack Adventures has several five- to eight-day guided walks, many of which focus on the region's abundant wildflowers. Tours are based in a comfortable lodge in the alpine village of Dinner Plain. Optional activities include trout fishing and nocturnal tours. Walkabout Gourmet Adventures has an epicurean five-day bushwalking experience, where travelers stay in a country resort and eat good food and drink fine wine while seeing wildlife and relaxing.

Season: October–May.
Locations: Alpine National Park and the Victorian Alps.
Cost: From about A$85 for a day walk to about A$1,630 for eight days.
Tour Operators: Ecotrek Bogong Jack Adventures, Walkabout Gourmet Adventures.

Camel Trekking

Strange as it may seem, a camel trek is an extremely pleasant way to spend a week or two in Australia; the experience beautifully recaptures desert travel as it was in the past. Camels were imported to Australia in the 19th century when they formed the backbone of the heavy-duty transport industry of the Outback. The Indian cameleers who drove them were known as "Afghans" (hence the name of the *Ghan* train, which follows the old desert route of the Afghan camel trains from Adelaide to Alice Springs). Many camels now roam wild in the Outback.

Northern Territory–The Red Centre

From their camel farm 100 km (60 mi) south of Alice Springs, Neil and Jayne Waters of Camels Australia arrange several camel-riding experiences, from short yard rides to five-day camel camping safaris through Rainbow Valley National Park, remote gorge country that includes the oldest watercourse in the world and an ancient stand of palms. Safaris take place in the cooler months between March and October.

Frontier Camel Tours conducts popular "Take A Camel Out To Dinner" and "Take A Camel Out To Breakfast" tours from their headquarters near Alice Springs, as well as one-hour camel rides that operate every morning and afternoon. The company also runs the Camel Depot near Uluru (Ayers Rock) that arranges sunrise and sunset camel rides away from the tourist crowds.

Season: April–September (weekly departures), October–March (every two weeks).
Locations: Alice Springs, Uluru (Ayers Rock).
Cost: From A$50 for a one-hour ride to about A$500 for three days or A$1,000 for a week.
Tour Operators: Camels Australia, Frontier Camel Tours.

Cross-Country Skiing

Unlike the jagged peaks of alpine regions elsewhere in the world, the rounded summits of the Australian Alps are ideal for cross-country skiing. In stark contrast to downhill skiers on crowded slopes, cross-country skiers have a chance to get away from the hordes and experience the unforgettable sensation of skiing through forests of eucalyptus trees, with their spreading branches, pale leaves, and impressionistic bark patterns.

New South Wales
Some 450 km (279 mi) south of Sydney, Jindabyne is the major gateway to the Snowy Mountains. Paddy Pallin Jindabyne is an offshoot of Australia's most respected outdoor-equipment retail store. It has a complete selection of ski tours and cross-country instructional programs, from half-day trips to two-, five-, or seven-day lodge-based trips and five-day snow-camping tours across the trails of the main range.

Season: July–September.
Location: Snowy Mountains.
Cost: From A$65 for a full day of instruction to A$1,100 for a five-day snow-camping tour.
Tour Operator: Paddy Pallin Jindabyne.

Diving

Australia is one of the world's premier diving destinations. Much of the attention centers on Queensland's Great Barrier Reef, but there's very good diving elsewhere as well—including Tasmania, Western Australia, and Lord Howe Island. Australian diving operations are generally well run and regulated, and equipment is modern and well maintained. Since this is a competitive industry, prices are fairly low by world standards, and the warm waters off the Queensland coast are an ideal location to practice basic dive skills. Still, if you're planning on learning to dive in Australia you should closely examine each operator's dive package (especially equipment rental and the number of open-water dives) rather than basing a decision solely on cost.

Queensland
The main diving centers in Queensland are the island resorts: Cairns and the Whitsunday Islands and Port Douglas.

Season: Year-round.
Locations: All along the coast and Great Barrier Reef islands.
Cost: From A$75 for a single dive and A$160 for a day trip that includes a boat cruise and two dives. Five-day certification courses start at around A$645.

Tour Operators: Dive Adventures, Mike Ball Dive Adventures, Pro Dive Travel.

Tasmania

Australia's southernmost state is not the obvious place to go diving. However, Tasmania's east coast has a remarkably sunny climate and some exceptional kelp forests, magnificent sponge gardens, and exquisite sea life that includes anemones, basket stars, squid, octopus, and butterfly perch. In winter there's a chance to dive with dolphins and whales that visit here on annual migration from Antarctica. And King Island in Bass Strait, off the north coast, has some very good wreck diving. Overall, Tasmania has one of Australia's most wreck-strewn coastlines. There are more than 20 sites, including the 1845 wreck of the *Cataraqui*, the country's worst maritime disaster.

Season: Mainly summer, but the best east-coast conditions are in winter.
Locations: Bicheno, King Island.
Cost: From A$140 per boat dive, including equipment.
Tour Operators: Bicheno Dive Centre, King Island Dive Charter.

Western Australia

Whale sharks are the world's largest fish—they can weigh up to 40 tons and measure 50 feet from nose to tail. However, although whale sharks *are* members of the shark family, they're also completely harmless. Like many whales, these creatures live on tiny krill—not fish, seals, or people. From about March through May each year, more than 100 whale sharks can be found along the Western Australian coast near Exmouth. The exact season varies, depending on the time of the spawning of the coral of Ningaloo Reef. Exmouth is one of the few places in the world where you can be fairly certain of encountering whale sharks.

If you decide to swim with them, it's as if you have adopted a puppy the size of a truck—or have your own pet submarine. Government regulations prohibit touching them or swimming closer to them than a yard or so. It's an expensive day of diving because you need a large boat to take you out to the sharks, a spotter plane to find them, and a runabout to drop you in their path. Although most of the day is spent with whale sharks, it begins with a dive on Ningaloo Reef. The diversity of coral and marine life here isn't as remarkable as at the Great Barrier Reef, but there is a spectacular juxtaposition of large open-water fish and huge schools of bait fish. Outside of whale-shark season you can encounter a passing parade of humpback whales (from July through September) and nesting turtles (from November through February). Nondivers who wish to go snorkeling may join the expedition for a slightly reduced fee.

Season: Diving year-round; with whale sharks March–May.
Location: Exmouth.
Cost: From A$360, including all equipment, transfer to the boat, an optional dive on Ningaloo Reef, a salad lunch, and soft drinks. The cost also includes the spotter aircraft, the runabout to keep you in contact with the whale shark, and the whale shark interaction license fee.
Tour Operator: Exmouth Diving Centre.

Downhill Skiing

Despite Australia's lack of high mountains, downhill skiing remains a popular winter sport with thousands of well-heeled urbanites from Melbourne, Canberra, and Sydney. To cater to the demand, Australia's alpine region has a well-developed infrastructure of ski resorts and lift facilities. The alpine skiing region is concentrated in the undulating hills that form the eastern border between Victoria and New South Wales. Tasmania has some skiing; however, facilities and accommodations are far less developed than on the mainland.

New South Wales

The state's downhill ski areas are Thredbo and Perisher Blue, both within the borders of Kosciuszko National Park. With a total of 50 lifts giving access to an area of more than 4,000 acres, Perisher Blue is the largest ski area in the country, incorporating the adjacent resorts of Perisher, Smiggins, and Blue Cow. Vertical drop measures about 1,160 feet, and the resort has on-snow accommodation from luxurious to basic, as well as feisty nightlife. Access to Perisher Blue is via the Skitube from the parking area at Bullocks Flat, which is conveniently accessible by car from the subalpine town of Jindabyne. This allows skiers to take advantage of the less-expensive accommodation options in Jindabyne. Thredbo has the greatest vertical drop of any ski resort in the country: a total of 2,240 feet. However, the low base elevation means that artificial snow must often be made to ensure top-to-bottom cover. The village at Thredbo has a European flavor, with ski-in ski-out accommodation available.

Season: July–September.
Location: Snowy Mountains.
Cost: Lift passes cost around A$87 per day.

Victoria

Mt. Buller is the largest ski resort in the state and the closest to Melbourne; accordingly, the slopes are especially crowded on weekends. It has the second-largest lifting capacity in Australia after Perisher Blue, and the resort contains extensive snowmaking facilities as well as ski-in ski-out accommodations. Set at the foot of a bowl surrounded by mountains, Falls Creek is the prettiest of the Victorian ski resorts. The vertical drop measures only 600 feet, yet the 1,000-acre resort combines vastly different types of terrain. Serious skiers who like a challenge can head to Mt. Hotham, where more than 40% of the runs are rated "advanced."

Season: July–September.
Locations: Falls Creek, Mt. Buller, Mt. Hotham.
Cost: Lift passes cost around A$85 per day.

Four-Wheel-Drive Tours

Australia is a vast land with a small population, so many Outback roads are little more than desert tracks. Black soil that turns muddy and slick after rain, the ubiquitous red dust of the center, and the continent's great sandy deserts make a four-wheel-drive vehicle a necessity for exploring the more remote areas. Outback motoring has a real element of adventure—on some roads it's standard practice to call in at the few homesteads along the way so they can initiate search procedures if you fail to turn up at the next farm down the track. The laconic Aussies you meet in such places are a different breed from urban Australians, and time spent with them is often memorable.

Northern Territory

Although the number of tourists at Kakadu National Park has risen dramatically each year, some sites can still be reached only by a four-wheel-drive vehicle, including Jim Jim Falls and Twin Falls—two of Australia's most scenic attractions. At both of these falls, the water plunges over the escarpment to the floodplains beneath. Below the falls are deep, cool pools and beautiful palm-shaded beaches. The Adventure Center has comprehensive tours of this remarkable area. World Expeditions conducts a one-week adventure safari into the wilderness of Kakadu that concludes with a canoe safari along the Katherine River. If you have a particular interest in Aboriginal culture, the eight-day Coburg and Kakadu trip organized by World Expeditions is particularly recommended.

The **Northern Territory Tourist Commission** (✉ 43 Mitchell St., Darwin, NT 0800 ☎ 13–6110 📠 08/8951–8550) can provide more information about the numerous tour operators based in Darwin.

Season: April–October.
Locations: Throughout the Northern Territory, but mainly in Kakadu.
Cost: From about A$550 for three days to A$1,600 for seven days.
Tour Operators: Adventure Center, World Expeditions.

Queensland

Every four-wheel-drive enthusiast in Australia seeks out Cape York, the most northerly point of the Australian mainland. After passing through the rain forest north of Port Douglas, the track travels through relatively dry vegetation the rest of the way. Several galleries of spectacular Aboriginal rock paintings are here, as are a historic telegraph station and the notorious Jardine River, whose shifting bottom made fording very tricky in the past. Until a few years ago, reaching the Cape was a major achievement; now a ferry service across the Jardine makes it easier, but Cape York is still frontier territory—a land of mining camps, Aboriginal settlements, and enormous cattle stations. For all intents and purposes, civilization stops at Cooktown, some 700 km (434 mi) from the tip of Cape York. From their base in Cairns, Wilderness Challenge arranges several four-wheel-drive experiences in the region, including a 1-day fly-drive trip to Cooktown and the 14-day Cape York Complete Camping Safari: a four-wheel-drive trip to the tip of Cape York, including a fishing trip into the Torres Strait islands.

Season: Cooktown year-round; Cape York June–December.
Location: North of Cairns.
Cost: From A$275 for a 1-day fly-drive Cooktown safari to A$2,295 for the 14-day Cape York Complete Camping Safari.
Tour Operator: Wilderness Challenge.

South Australia

Unless you have the time to walk, the rugged areas of South Australia are best explored by four-wheel-drive vehicle. Kangaroo Island is home to many Australian animals, including kangaroos, koalas, fur seals, fairy penguins, and sea lions, as well as such bizarre natural features as huge limestone arches and weatherworn rocks that resemble Henry Moore sculptures. Adventure Charters of Kangaroo Island operates a series of tours, the most comprehensive being a three-day, two-night package. Kangaroo Island Odysseys has a similar program of tours lasting from one to four days, with short optional wildlife-based extension tours.

To the north of Adelaide, the rugged gorges, hills, and creeks of the Flinders Ranges provide an ideal backdrop for four-wheel-drive adventures. Beyond Tours operates two-, three-, and four-day trips from Adelaide to the Flinders Ranges, but be aware that the round-trip journey from Adelaide—485 km (300 mi) in each direction—absorbs much of the itinerary on the shorter trips.

Season: Year-round.
Locations: Flinders Ranges, Kangaroo Island.
Cost: Kangaroo Island from about A$230 for a one-day tour to A$1,400 for a four-day nature retreat tour; Flinders Ranges from about A$170 for a one-day tour to A$900 for a four-day tour.
Tour Operators: Adventure Charters of Kangaroo Island, Beyond Tours, Kangaroo Island Odysseys, Kangaroo Island Wilderness Tours.

Western Australia—The Kimberley

Most of the four-wheel-drive adventures in Western Australia take place in the Kimberley region in the far north. The only practical time to visit the Kimberley is during the Dry, May through November, because roads are very often flooded during the Wet.

Tour operators in the region are based either in Kununurra, at the eastern end of the Kimberley, or Broome, in the western end. Broome is also a resort center, a multicultural town with a wonderful beach and a number of hotel options—an ideal place to recover from the rigors of the Kimberley. Reaching Windjana Gorge, at the western end of the Kimberley, takes two days from Broome, while an absolute minimum of five days is required to experience some of the more remote parts of the region. Kununurra is the starting point for trips to the Bungle Bungle, spectacular beehive-stripe domes. A fly-drive safari to the Bungle Bungle takes a minimum of two days.

Kimberley Wilderness Adventures operates several tours from both Broome and Kununurra. Many of these tours use permanent campsites, which provide a reasonable level of comfort. Discover West Holidays has a one-day fly-in tour from Kununurra, with a combined four-wheel-drive and hiking tour of the highlights. The company also operates four-wheel-drive trips to the Bungle Bungle from Turkey Creek.

Season: May–November.
Location: The Kimberley.

Cost: About A$800 for a 4-day safari; about A$1,000 for a 2-day fly-drive Bungle Bungle tour, or A$750 for a 1-day fly-in tour; about A$3,000 for a 13-day camping safari.

Tour Operators: Discover West Holidays, Kimberley Wilderness Adventures.

Horseback Riding

Trail bikes and four-wheel-drive vehicles have slowly been replacing horses on Australian farms and stations for the past two decades. On the plains and coastal lowlands the transformation is complete, but horses still remain a part of rural life in the highlands, and it's here that the best horseback adventures can be found. On a horse trek you come closer to the life of the pioneer Australian bushmen than in any other adventure pursuit. Indeed, the majority of treks are led by Australians with close links to the traditions of bush life.

Riding through alpine meadows, following mountain trails, and sleeping under the stars are excellent ways to see the Australian bush. A typical horseback vacation lasts several days, and the food and equipment for each night's camp is brought in by packhorse or four-wheel-drive vehicle. Although a cook, a guide, and all specialist equipment are provided, participants are expected to help look after the horses. An Australian saddle is a cross between the high Western saddle and the almost flat English one.

New South Wales

The Great Dividing Range, which extends right through New South Wales, has some excellent trails for horseback riding. Almost every country town has a riding school with horses for hire, but a few long rides are particularly outstanding. In the Snowy Mountains high country, a six-day summer ride from Reynella homestead through Kosciuszko National Park covers terrain ranging from open plains to alpine forests. Riders camp out in some of the most beautiful valleys in the park—valleys not easily accessible except by horse. A hundred years ago this was the stuff of pioneer legend. From its base at the foot of the Blue Mountains just outside Sydney, Megalong Australian Heritage Centre conducts guided horse rides along forest trails. Paddy Pallin Jindabyne organizes trail rides through the ranges of Kosciuszko National Park, from two hours to overnight camping treks.

In addition to its several New South Wales riding trips, Equitrek Australia arranges riding in South Australia, Queensland, Western Australia, and the Northern Territory.

Season: Year-round, but mainly November–April.

Locations: Blue Mountains, New England Highlands, Snowy Mountains.

Cost: From A$225 for a day ride to A$600 for a weekend and A$1,200 for five days.

Tour Operators: Equitrek Australia, Megalong Australian Heritage Centre, Paddy Pallin Jindabyne, Reynella Kosciuszko Rides.

Victoria

An important part of the Australian rural mythology is an A. B. (Banjo) Paterson 1895 poem entitled "The Man from Snowy River, " based on the equestrian feats of riders in the Victorian high plains who rounded up stock and horses from seemingly inaccessible valleys. For those who wish to emulate the hero of that work, several operators, such as Bogong Horseback Adventures, have rides of 2 to 12 days in the area. Part of the journey is spent above the tree line, where, as Banjo Paterson said, "the horses' hooves strike firelight from the flintstones every stride." Accommodations are either in tents or in the original bushmen's huts that dot the high country.

In addition to weekend rides, Stoneys High Country arranges cattle drives, in which riders accompany the herd on the long journey to or from their high-country summer pastures.

Season: October–May.
Location: Victorian high plains.
Cost: From about A$550 for two days to A$1,375 for five days.
Tour Operators: Bogong Horseback Adventures, Stoneys High Country.

Rafting

The exhilaration of sweeping down into the foam-filled jaws of a rapid is always tinged with fear—white-water rafting is, after all, much like being tossed into a supersize washing machine. Although this sort of excitement appeals to many people, the attraction of rafting in Australia involves much more. As you drift downriver during the lulls between the white water, it's wonderful to sit back and watch the wilderness unfold, whether it's stately river gums overhanging the stream, towering cliffs, or forests of eucalyptus on the surrounding slopes. Rafting means camping by the river at night, drinking billy tea brewed over the campfire, letting the sound of the stream lull you to sleep at night, or spying an elusive platypus at dawn. Rivers here are smaller and trickier than the ones used for commercial rafting in North America, and rafts usually hold only four to six people. Rafting companies provide all rafting and camping equipment—you only need clothing that won't be damaged by water (cameras are carried in waterproof barrels), a sleeping bag (in some cases), and sunscreen.

New South Wales

The upper reaches of Australia's longest waterway, the Murray River, are open for rafting between September and November, when melting snow feeds the stream. The river is cold, but the rapids are challenging, and the Australian Alps are dressed in all their spring glory.

The Gwydir River is fed by a large dam, and the scenery downriver is mainly pastoral, but the river has a series of challenging rapids.

The Nymboida River is the premier white-water river in the state and also the warmest, flowing through beautiful subtropical rain forest near Coffs Harbour.

Season: Generally September–May.
Locations: The Murray River in the southern part of New South Wales, the Gwydir River in the center, and the Nymboida River in the north.
Cost: From about A$153 for a one-day Nymboida trip to about A$560 for four days, including all camping and rafting equipment.
Tour Operator: Wildwater Adventures.

Tasmania

With deep rocky chasms, grand forested valleys, beautiful sandy beaches, and miles of untouched wilderness, the Franklin River has the most spectacular and rewarding rafting in Australia. The river leads through a truly remote area of Tasmania—there are few places where you can join or leave the river. You have the choice of exploring either the lower or upper parts of the Franklin, or the entire navigable length. By far the most rewarding option is covering the entire river. The combination of isolation, beauty, difficult rapids, and strenuous portages ensures that rafters finish the trip with a real feeling of achievement. It's a difficult and challenging journey that should be tackled only by travelers who are reasonably fit and comfortable in the bush.

Season: November–March.
Locations: Franklin River, west coast.
Cost: From about A$1,400 for 6 days to A$1,900 for 11 days.
Tour Operators: Peregrine Adventures, Tasmanian Wild River Adventures, World Expeditions.

Sailing

Australia has wonderful conditions for sailing, a population addicted to the water, and a climate that allows comfortable boating year-round. Take a cruise on Sydney Harbour to see just how eagerly Australians embrace their maritime tradition, in boats from sea kayaks to sailing yachts to vast luxury cruisers and the amazing 16-footers, the Formula 1 craft of the Australian sailing world.

New South Wales

Sydney Harbour is the finest single sailing destination in the country, both in terms of its natural credentials and the selection of sailing options. Choices include small catamarans that can be hired by the hour, yachts that can be chartered by day, and sailboats that let you gain hands-on experience as a crew member. Summer weekends are the busiest time; however, the harbor is sufficiently large and diversified to offer quiet anchorages even in peak season.

Season: Year-round.
Location: Sydney Harbour.
Cost: Catamarans start at about A$35 per hour; a Beneteau yacht runs about A$1,200 per day.
Tour Operators: Sail Australia, Sydney by Sail.

Queensland

The state's premier sailing area is the Whitsunday Islands. Stretching off the mid-Queensland coast, these rugged, jigsaw-shape islands are encircled by bays that make marvelous natural marinas. Of the 100 islands in the group, at least half have comfortable anchorages.

There are several yacht charter specialists in the region with craft to suit most budgets and levels of nautical know-how. For experienced sailors, bareboat charters are the best option; despite the name, a bareboat generally comes complete with such creature comforts as a barbecue, stereo system, hot showers, a well-equipped kitchen, and complete safety gear. You provide the crew and supplies for the cruise—you can even hire a skipper (for about A$200 a day) who can do the sailing for you. For solo travelers or couples looking to share a boat, several sailing vessels offer scheduled cruises through the Whitsundays, usually on a five- or seven-day itinerary. Passengers can either sleep in multiberth cabins or camp on the beach.

The most convenient starting points for Whitsunday cruising are the jet airports at Hamilton Island and Proserpine. Hamilton is linked to both Sydney and Melbourne via direct flights, but the choice of charter operators here is more restricted. Proserpine is about 25 km (15 ½ mi) inland from the marinas at Airlie Beach. Although sailing is possible year-round, the wettest months are January to March and the windiest are March to May.

ProSail operates crewed yachts exclusively, while Sail Australia operates both crewed yachts and bareboat charters.

Season: Year-round.
Location: Whitsunday Islands.
Cost: From about A$300 to A$1,000 per day for a bareboat charter, about A$200 per person per day on a crewed vessel.
Tour Operators: ProSail, Sail Australia.

INDEX